1996

BROOKMAN

UNITED STATES, UNITED NATIONS & CANADA STAMPS & POSTAL COLLECTIBLES

FEATURING

SPECIALIZED LISTINGS

OF

STATE DUCK STAMPS

PLATE NO. COILS & UNEXPLODED BOOKLETS

U.S. SOUVENIR PAGES • PANELS • CEREMONY PROGRAMS

U.S. & U.N. FIRST DAY COVERS AND SOUVENIR CARDS

Plus

Confederate States

U.S. Possessions

U.S. Trust Territories

Canadian Provinces

ILLUSTRATEDGRADING GUIDE

SUBJECT INDEX, IDENTIFIER & BIBLIOGRAPHY

EDITOR

David S. Macdonald

1996
BROOKMAN

TERMS AND INFORMATION

CONDITION - We price United States stamps issued prior to 1890 in two grades - Average and Fine. From 1890 to present we list a price for F-VF and VF quality. **FOR INFORMATION ON GRADING SEE PAGE vii.**

GUM AND HINGING

Unused, Original Gum (O.G.)
Prior to 1882, Unused stamps may have partial or no gum. If you require o.g., add the percentage indicated in ( ). **Example** (OG + 25%). From 1882 to present, o.g. can be expected, but stamps may have been hinged or have hinge remnants.

Mint, Never Hinged
Most issues are priced in F-VF, Never Hinged condition. Premiums for Average, NH usually run about half the F-VF premium. Prices for Never Hinged stamps on issues prior to1882 will be quoted upon request.

SPECIAL PRICING INSTRUCTIONS

Average - From 1890-1934 **Average hinged perforated** stamps, when available, will be priced at 60-70% of the F-VF Hinged price depending upon the general quality of the issue.

Average hinged imperforate stamps, when available, will be priced at 70-75% of the F-VF Hinged price depending upon the general quality of the issue.

From 1935 to present, average quality, when available, will be priced at 20% below the F-VF price.

Very Fine NH, 1935-Date
VF NH singles, plate blocks, line pairs, etc. are available (unless specifically priced at the following premiums:
Add 10¢ to any item priced under 50¢. Add 20% to any item priced at 50¢ and up. Unless priced as Very Fine, sets are not available Very Fine and stamps should be listed individually with appropriate premium.

Very Fine Unused O.G. Plate Blocks & Line Pairs
Very Fine Unused Plate Blocks and Line Pairs prior to #749 & 723 (and selected Back-of-the-Book Issues) are generally available at the respective F-VF NH price.

Very Fine Used
From 1847-1934, Very Fine Used stamps, when available, are priced by adding the % indicated to the appropriate Fine or F-VF price. **Example** (VF + 50%).
From 1935 to date, the premiums are the same as for VF NH copies.

MINIMUM ORDER OF $20 - Present day costs force us to require that mail orders total a minimum of $20.00. Send payment with order.

PRICES - Every effort will be made to maintain these prices throughout the life of this edition. However, prices are subject to change if market conditions require. We are not responsible for typographical errors.

BROOKMAN STAMP COMPANY
10 Chestnut Drive
Bedford, NH 03110
Phone (603) 472-5575
Fax (603) 472-8795
PRINTED IN USA

TABLE OF CONTENTS

STAMPS

INDEX TO ADVERTISERS

We wish to thank the advertisers who through their patronage help to keep the Brookman Price Guide available at the lowest possible price. We urge you to support our advertisers and let them know their ads were helpful to you in your philatelic pursuits.

BROOKMAN GRADING GUIDE

The following guide is a simplified approach to stamp grading designed to help you better understand the quality you can expect to receive when you order a specific grade. All grades listed below are for undamaged stamps free of faults such as tears, thin spots, creases, straight edges, scrapes, etc. Stamps with those defects are considered "seconds" and sell for prices below those listed. The stamps you receive may not always match the criteria given since each stamp must be judged on its own special merits such as freshness, color, cancellation, etc. For example: a well centered stamp may be graded only as "Average" because of a very heavy cancellation. Grading stamps is an art, not a science, and frequently the cliche "beauty is in the eye of the beholder" applies. Stamps offered throughout this price list fall into the "Group A" category unless the heading contains a (B) or (C).

GROUP A - WELL CENTERED ISSUES

Average Average Average Average

F-VF F-VF F-VF F-VF

Very Fine Very Fine Very Fine Very Fine

GROUP A	AVERAGE	F-VF	VERY FINE
PERFORATED STAMPS	Perforations touch or barely clear of design on one or two sides.	Perforations well clear of design on all sides.	Design very well centered within perforations.
IMPERFORATE STAMPS	One edge may touch design.	All four edges are clear of design.	Four edges are well clear of and well centered around design.
COILS AND BOOKLET PANES	Perforated and imperforate edge may touch design on one or two edges.	Perforated and imperforate edges are clear of the design.	Design very well centered within perforated and imperf. edges.

NOTE: Stamps of poorer centering than "Average" grade are considered seconds.

"EXTREMELY FINE" is a grading term used to descibe stamps that are almost "Perfect" in centering, color, freshness, cancellations, etc. This grade, when available, is priced substantially higher than Very Fine quality.

GROUP B - MEDIAN CENTERED ISSUES

Average Average Average Average Average

F-VF F-VF Very Fine Very Fine Very Fine

GROUP B	AVERAGE	F-VF	VERY FINE
PERFORATED STAMPS	Perforations touch or barely cut into design on one or two sides.	Perforations clear of design on all four sides.	Design well centered within perforations.
IMPERFORATE STAMPS	One or two edges may touch or barely cut into design.	All four edges are clear of design as in "A".	Four edges are well clear of and well centered around design as in "A".
COILS AND BOOKLET PANES	Perforated and imperforate edge may touch or barely cut into design.	Perforated and imperforate edges are clear of design as in "A".	Design well centered within perforated and imperforated edges.

GROUP C - POORLY CENTERED ISSUES

Average Average Average Average Average

Fine Fine Very Fine Very Fine Very Fine

GROUP C	AVERAGE	FINE	VERY FINE
PERFORATED STAMPS	Perforations may cut into design on one or more sides.	Perforations touch or just clear of design on or more sides.	Perforations will clear design on all four sides.
IMPERFORATE STAMPS	One or more edges may cut into design.	One or more edges touch the design.	All four edges clear of the design.
COILS AND BOOKLET PANES	Perforated and imp. edge may cut into design on one or more sides.	Perforated and imperforate edges may touch or just clear design.	Perforated & imperforated edges well clear of design on all four sides.

WELCOME TO STAMP COLLECTING

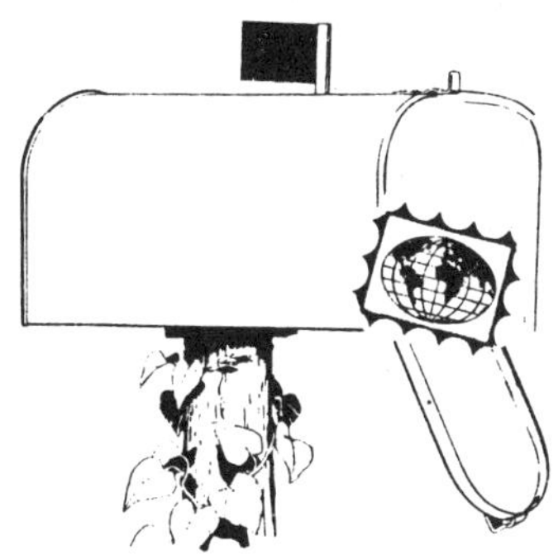

The world in your mailbox? It's an everyday happening for the millions of people who ave made collecting stamps their favorite hobby! Friendships, information, challenge, nd just plain fun can perk up anyone's daily routine through the "World's Most Popular door Hobby."

In the early days of the hobby - the late nineteenth century - most stamp collectors erally "saved the world," mostly because it was still a reasonable goal. Then the idea using gummed bits of paper to show that postal charges had been paid really caught n, and the trickle of new stamps became a flood.

So people started "specialty collecting": saving stamps that focus on a specific ountry, or a topical area (an idea, or thing, or activity, such as sports, art, animals, utomobiles, aviation, space, medicine, etc.) or even narrower than that - maybe a rtain time period in just one country's stamp-issuing history, or one color of a series stamps that came in several colors.

For more than 130 years, stamp collecting has been a chosen leisure activity of yalty, heads of state, movie stars, sports celebrities, and hundreds of thousands of her men, women, and children. With so many people eager to devote time and effort stamps, the hobby must have some powerfully attractive qualities, right?... herwise, all those people would be out golfing, or square dancing, or climbing ountains! Well, stamp collectors do golf and climb mountains, and work at careers, well as save stamps, and this hobby goes well with almost any life style. It is very daptable, and it is very personal.

You can do it in a very simple way, using ready-made albums that require little effort: st getting hold of the right stamps and placing them in the marked spaces. A "want t" given to a stamp dealer will yield the stamps needed in as much time as it takes e dealer to pull the stamps from stock and the collector to hand over payment.

Or, you can choose to spend hours at stamp shows or in dealers' shops burrowing rough boxes of materials, searching for a particular stamp in a certain condition, or a ecial postmark to illustrate a point in an exhibit for philatelic competition.

Stamp collecting is a special combination of the structured and the unstructured, so u can get involved in a way unlike any other hobby in the world. No two collectors ather material in the same way, even if they collect the same kinds of stamps! From hat to collect, to how to arrange it, to deciding whether to be a "closet collector" or get to the world of organized philately: you can express yourself freely and put your own amp on the way you collect!

TAMP COLLECTOR" OR "PHILATELIST"?

Some people differentiate between "stamp collector" and "philatelist," believing that me level of seriousness or expertise has to be reached in order to qualify as a ilatelist. There's no truth to this idea! But one advantage of the word philately is that allows for all the collecting areas, such as postal markings and postal history, and all e postal items from the centuries before there were stamps - folded letters from the teenth century, etc.

NDING MATERIAL

It's only fitting that a hobby based on postal communications can be enjoyed easily mail! Stamps and other philatelic material, as well as needed accesories such as talogues, books, albums, etc., can be mail-ordered from all over the world. These urces advertise widely in the philatelic press (which will be mentioned further on), d also sell sometimes at stamp shows and stamp stores.

Stamp shows are a superb source of materials. There are literally "thousands" of stamp-show events held in the course of a year in the United States alone, ranging from very small, one-day community efforts, to very large exhibitions with hundreds of dealers, thousands of frames of exhibits, and lasting for several days. The largest international-level shows can last more than a week.

In addition to mail order and shows, your local dealer can provide the kind of personal service which may not be available elsewhere. Check your yellow pages for the dealer(s) in your vicinity.

LEARN THE LANGUAGE

Any hobby has its own unique terminology, which any newcomer should learn in order to fully participate. The language of philately is not difficult, and it does make sense. It will make collecting easier and more enjoyable if you learn it, and you can then understand catalogues, price lists, and other written materials in the hobby, and be able to talk easily to fellow collectors.

Many of the hobby's words and phrases can be translated from their context, but it is faster and easier to do a sort of "crash course" at the local library, using some of the many basic books about collecting. The "hobbies and recreational activities" section of the library should have at least one or two of the beginning philately books, and they make easy and interesting reading. Very often there will be a little dictionary as part of the book, or the text itself will give words and phrases and then explain them.

If your local library lets you down, you can purchase your own copies of catalogues (most of the major ones have new editions each year), or you can borrow them. Major philatelic libraries with large collections of catalogues and books are located in several places in the United States. Foremost among these is the American Philatelic Research Library (P.O. Box 8338, State College, PA 16803), the educational arm of the American Philatelic Society.

The APRL has the largest public-access philatelic collection in the United States. Members of the APS and APRL can borrow directly (in person or by mail) from the library, and the general public can borrow books by means of the nationwide inter-library loan system.

In addition to catalogues, the stamp hobby also is well supplied with journals, books, and newspapers. Introductory books on the hobby usually have lists of other sources of information, so that you can keep expanding your reading list. There are many weekly and monthly stamp publications, worth reading regularly for up-to-date information on happenings in the hobby (stamp show calendars, advertisements, notices of new stamp issues) and useful instructional articles. There are several columns strictly to help beginners in some of these periodicals.

Linn's Stamp News, a weekly, appears on large newsstands and in many hobby shops. Stamp Collector, Stamps, and Mekeels, also newspapers, and Scott's Stamp Monthly magazine are among the U.S. publications available by subscription. The American Philatelist, the largest U.S. monthly stamp magazine, is free with membership in the American Philatelic Society, or can be purchased by subscription.

So there is plenty to read, and it is a good idea to have a reference book collection at home, so that your evenings-and-weekends hobby doesn't run into problems with questions when the "regular library" isn't open!

CARE AND FEEDING OF YOUR COLLECTIBLE PAPER

It should be mentioned that there are some basic things to learn about physically handling stamps and other philatelic material.

For starters, keep in mind that paper is among the most fragile of all man-made materials. There are tools and methods to help preserve the items in a collection, and the sooner a new collector can get into the habit of using them, the better!

Stamp tongs, which are similar to cosmetic tweezers, keep oily, dirty fingers away from stamps, so the stamp stays clean with all its perforations intact. Tongs are very inexpensive and come in a choice of lengths and styles. Do not substitute drugstore tweezers for stamp tongs! The stamp tongs preferred by most collectors have flat, blunt, wedge-shaped "business ends," so the stamp is not punctured or torn when picked up.

Other habits a new collector should learn include skill at soaking cancelled stamps from paper, and drying them properly so they stay in good condition. Knowing how to find the watermark in the paper of some stamps is another "talent" to develop, using either a commercial watermarking fluid or special lighting.

Perforation gauges are items unique to philately: small rulers sized to measure the different perforations (holes cut into the stamps so they separate easily). Knowing the "perf" count of a stamp can help to identify, for example, a different printing of what otherwise looks like the same stamp. Magnifying glasses are helps in identifying stamps as well as aids to appreciating the fine points of the designs.

When it comes to storing stamps, it is wise to avoid some of the "great traditions" of the hobby and think in terms of long-term safekeeping. Shoeboxes for storage, and glassine envelopes (see-through envelopes made of a kind of waxed paper) are not good at all, but there probably isn't a collector anywhere who does not have quantities of both!

Shoeboxes, or cheap paper boxes like them, are made of paper with very high acid content, and so are glassines. They may be okay for short-term storage, but no important philatelic items should be kept in them for long. There are boxes made of acid-free cardboard, and there are small envelopes made of safe plastic: both cost more than their better known counterparts, but they could be worth it in the long run.

It's safer and also easier to work with stamps kept in albums or "stockbooks," which are like scrapbooks but with pages that have pockets, so that part of the stamp is exposed and the items can be quickly and easily moved around with tongs.

Albums can be purchased or made by hand, and beginners may want to make their own albums just to get a feel for arranging a collection, or, maybe you will want to arrange your material in a certain way for which no standard album exists. You can buy blank album pages (or not), and just use an ordinary ringed binder to make a very nice, personalized album.

Stamps can be fastened into albums either with small squares of gummed glassine adhesives called "hinges," or by using special stamp mounts: little plastic envelopes of various sizes that have self-adhesive backing to attach to pages. Using mounts keeps the stamp in the same condition in which you acquired it, with no extra glue from a stamp hinge. Mounts come in a variety of sizes to fit stamps and covers both large and small.

Never use cellophane tapes on or around your stamps - not even the so-called "magic" tapes that do not seem as sticky as some of the other kinds. Both the plastic part of the tape and, especially, the sticky part, can cause great damage over time to stamps and covers. Do not use cheap papers such as colored construction paper to make albums - this pulpy paper with large quantities of coloring is a true hazard to have around stamps.

Don't take chances with items that you have spent time and money acquiring! It seems very foolish to spend a considerable amount of money to buy some stamps, and then to store them in a cheap and unsafe way.

Plastic can be the worst offender - especially in page protectors that have leached their softeners and other additives onto the pages and the stamps they contain. The adhesive parts of plastic mounts may have migrated onto the faces or backs of the stamps they hold, and some kinds of hinges signal their presence on the back of the stamp by making rectangular stains on the front. Damage is almost always irreversible; "prevention is the best cure"!

Buying something new on the market is no guarantee of safety, however. There are modern items that are even worse than old ones. Try to choose materials that are known to be safe because they have been tested and are used by libraries and museums and similar places where long-term safekeeping is the most important matter. Acid-free papers and cardboards and plastics such as Mylar and polypropylene perform well in archival uses, and can be found in philatelic products.

JUST LITTLE PICTURES ... HA!

On the face of it, a stamp may appear to be just a bit of paper with a picture on it, but a stamp is really a complicated animal ... complicated in that there are many different ways to consider it.

Literally on the face of it, you can be content with just feasting your eyes on the stamp's design: enjoying the colors, thinking about what idea the artist was trying to convey. Many collectors are perfectly happy to accumulate material solely because of what they see. And this is as good a reason as any to have a stamp collection! Each person's collection is a thing of beauty to him or her.

However, admiring the design can lead to curiosity about its meaning, and many collectors enjoy researching what is known as the "story behind the stamp" - what led the postal agency to honor this person, or that event. Other hobbyists become interested in the technical aspects of the stamps, studying printing methods and stamp manufacturing, and learning about printing presses, inks, perforating, and other production aspects.

From that stage it's just a short hop to wondering about what happens when things go wrong in stamp production, and stamp varieties, errors, feaks, and oddities result.

A stamp's paper forms another interesting area, leading to specialty studies such as finding watermarks in the papers of certain stamps of certain countries (not all countries use watermarked paper, and even then not consistently). "Reading" these marks put into tho paper when it was made involves using special fluids or lighting equipment so that the marks can be made visible without damage to the stamp.

Face down, stamps challenge some hobbyists interested in "gum," as the jargon refers to stamp glue. Gum is an area of some squabbling in the stamp hobby, with many collectors who insist that the "only way" to save a stamp is if it's mint, never hinged (MNH for short): that is, in the same condition as when it came from the post office. The MNH collector will always use plastic stamp mounts in albums, never permitting a hinge to disturb the gum.

However, many other collectors are of the strong opinion that the stamps are intended for postal use, and if they are not actually attached to a piece of mail and sent through the postal system, and then saved either on the piece or soaked off with the cancel visible, they are not really stamps but rather just pretty labels!

As in any argument, both sides can be very persuasive, and also neither side will ever be swayed to the other's viewpoint! If you collect your stamps mainly because you like the way they look, you probably always will prefer to have a MNH copy, simply because it is in the best condition to fully display its prettiness. However, if you are trying to complete a collection, and a stamp you need is available only in used condition, then that one is probably enough...at least until a better one comes along!

Beyond the stamp itself lies the whole world of postal history, which involve geography, history, politics, foreign languages, and sociology, where a collect studies how mail traveled. Clues in this detective process are the stamps, the post markings, and other marks appearing on the stamp or cover, plus knowledge of th period of history involved.

Some examples of popular postal history areas are military mail, including prisone of-war and censored letters, and air mail, such as items from the early days of airpo when zeppelins were used.

Postal historians want the entire piece of mail - the stamps still "on cover." This something to consider if you come across a batch of old letters and your first thoug is to soak off all the stamps. Think again, and then get some advice, as even som very common stamps are of great interest (and perhaps monetary value) if they are o their original cover, with all the markings intact.

Other branches of philately also involve more than just stamps, such as first da cover collecting. FDC's are envelopes carrying a new stamp that has been cancelle with a postmark of the day and place where the new stamp was issued (put on publ sale by the government postal agency). FDC's usually have a special artistic desig known as a "cachet," related to the design of the stamp. Collecting first day covers a popular specialty especially in the United States, and there are organizations an catalogues devoted entirely to these collectibles.

SPEAKING OF CLUBS

It is possible to be an avid stamp collector without becoming involved in "organize philately" - the clubs and societies attached to the hobby. But collecting can be easie more fun, and take on a whole new outlook when you have a relationship with a stam organization. Local clubs can provide immediate, convenient opportunities f learning and for socializing with collectors in the community, while also offerin chances to become involved in stamp shows and exhibitions.

Philatelic exhibiting (showing parts of one's collection in a structured format c album pages, for fun or for awards) can start - and finish! - on the local level, but als can lead to competition on a national or international level.

Local clubs tend to focus on general collecting interests, suited to their ow members. Organizations that concentrate on a more narrow range of interests - single country, or even a single stamp issue - have most of their activities by ma Members participate through newsletters and journals and correspondence, an sometimes have meetings at stamp shows.

Membership in a national "general interest" stamp organization provides a speci kind of boost to a collector, who then has the chance to get a larger view of the hobb plus add to a collection and personal knowledge.

The major example is the American Philatelic Society, formed in 1886 and the olde and largest stamp organization in the United States. APS services include a larg monthly magazine, lending library, "sales circuits" where members can buy and se stamps with one another by mail, publications for sale, slide programs for use at clu meetings, plus stamp insurance and expertizing of philatelic material (expert opinions on whether an item is authentic).

So, while it is possible to have a lot of fun with the hobby without ever leaving hom except to go to the post office or the mailbox, joining a club can result proportionately greater rewards. "Talking stamps" with others of similar enthusiasm an experience most collectors wouldn't trade for anything!

AND THE MORAL OF THE STORY IS ...

Stamp collecting...philately...a great hobby by whatever name you call it! And w hope that you will find it to be as much fun yourself as millions of others have all ov the world, over the past century. Happy collecting!

This introduction was prepared by the American Philatelic Society, the olde and largest national stamp organization in the United States. Information c membership benefits and services is available from the APS, P.O. Box 800 State College, PA 16803; telephone (814) 237-3803.

COMMEMORATIVE, SPECIAL ISSUE & AIR MAIL IDENTIFIER

COMMEMORATIVE, SPECIAL ISSUE & AIR MAIL IDENTIFIER

W

Wildlife 1921-24,2286-2335,2709a
Wildlife Conservation 1077-79,1098, 1392,1427,1430,1464-67
Wiley, Harvey W 1080
Wilkes, Lt. Charles 2387
Willard, Frances E 872
Williams, Hank 2723
Wilson, Woodrow 2218i
Win the War 905
Wisconsin 739,755,957
Wolf, "Howlin" 2861
Wolf Trap Farm Park 1452,2018
Wolverine 2327
Woman Suffrage 1406
Women 1152
Women, Armed Services 1013
Women, Progress of 959
Women's Clubs 1316
Wood Carvings 2240-2243
Woodchuck 2307
Woodson, Carter G 2073
Wool Industry 1423
Workman's Compensation 1186
World Columbian Expo 2586
World Peace Through Law 1576
World Peace / World Trade 1129
World Refugee Year 1149
World Columb. Stamp Expo 2586
World Stamp Expo '89 2410,2433
World's Fair 323-327,853, 1196,1244,2006-2009,2086
World University Games 2748
World War II 2559,2697,2765,2838
Wright Brothers C45,C91-C92
Wyoming Statehood 897,2444

XYZ

YMCA Youth Camping 2160
Yorktown, Battle of 703,1686,1937
Young, Whitney Moore 1875
Youth Month 963
Youth, Support Our 1342
Yugoslavia Flag 917
Zaharias, Mildred Didrikson 1932
Zeppelin, Graf C13-C15,C18

DEFINITIVE ISSUE IDENTIFIER

The purpose of these listings is to aid the novice and intermediate collector in identifying U.S. definitive issues.

The first step in identification should be to note the stamp's denomination, color, and subject and then locate it on the list below. If that tep does not provide you with a definitive Scott No., you will have to do some additional work.

If the identification can only be made by determining the stamp's "type", grill size or press from which the stamp was printed, it will e necessary to check the appropriate pages of the Brookman or Scott catalogs for this information.

If the identification can only be made by determining the stamp's perf measurements or watermark, you will then have to use your perf gauge nd/or watermark detector. If you do not own these "tools," contact your favorite dealer.

* With few exceptions, this list features major Scott Nos. and omits Reprints, Re-issues and Special Printings.
* Watermark and Press notations are not listed when they do not contribute to the stamp's identification.
* Scott nos. followed by a "*" were issued both Untagged and Tagged.
* All bklt. singles are perforated on two or three sides only.

803 Prexie Issue — 1030 Liberty Issue — 5/40 — 63/92 — 134/206

en.	Color	Subject	Type / Comment	Press	Perf.	Wmk.	Scott #
¢	olive brn	N. Hale		F	11		551
¢	olive brn	N. Hale		R	11x10.5		653
¢	dp orng	B. Franklin	1938 Prexie Issue		11x10.5		803
¢	rd orng	B. Franklin	1954 Liberty Issue		11x10.5		1030
¢	blue	B. Franklin	Ty I		Imperf		5
¢	blue	B. Franklin	Ty Ib		Imperf		5A
¢	blue	B. Franklin	Ty Ia		Imperf		6
¢	blue	B. Franklin	Ty II		Imperf		7
¢	blue	B. Franklin	Ty III		Imperf		8
¢	blue	B. Franklin	Ty IIIa		Imperf		8A
¢	blue	B. Franklin	Ty IV		Imperf		9
¢	blue	B. Franklin	Ty I		15		18
¢	brt. bl	B. Franklin	Ty I, reprint, w/o gum		12		40
¢	blue	B. Franklin	Ty Ia		15		19
¢	blue	B. Franklin	Ty II		15		20
¢	blue	B. Franklin	Ty III		15		21
¢	blue	B. Franklin	Ty IIIa		15		22
¢	blue	B. Franklin	Ty IV		15		23
¢	blue	B. Franklin	Ty V		15		24
¢	blue	B. Franklin			12		63
¢	blue	B. Franklin	"Z" Grill		12		85A
¢	blue	B. Franklin	"E" Grill		12		86
¢	blue	B. Franklin	"F" Grill		12		92
¢	buff	B. Franklin	Issue of 1869 "G grill"		12		112
¢	buff	B. Franklin	w/o grill, original gum		12		112b
¢	buff	B. Franklin	Re-iss/wht crackly gum		12		123
¢	buff	B. Franklin	Same, soft porous paper		12		133
¢	brn. orng.	B. Franklin	Same, w/o gum		12		133a
¢	ultra	B. Franklin	hard paper, w/grill		12		134
¢	ultra	B. Franklin	Same, w/o grill		12		145
¢	ultra	B. Franklin	Same, w/Secret mark		12		156
¢	dk. ultra	B. Franklin	Soft porous paper		12		182
¢	gray bl.	B. Franklin	Same, re-engraved		12		206
¢	ultra	B. Franklin			12		212
¢	dull bl.	B. Franklin	w/o Triangles		12		219
¢	ultra	B. Franklin	w/ Tri. in Top corners		12	NW	246
¢	blue	B. Franklin	w/ Tri. in Top corners		12	NW	247
¢	blue	B. Franklin	w/ Tri. in Top corners		12	DL	264
¢	dp. grn	B. Franklin	w/ Tri. in Top corners		12	DL	279
¢	blue grn	B. Franklin	"Series 1902"		12	DL	300
¢	blue grn	B. Franklin	"Series 1902"		Imperf	DL	314
¢	blue grn	B. Franklin	"Series 1902" B. Pn./6		12	DL	300b
¢	blue grn	B. Franklin	"Series 1902" Coil		12 Hz	DL	316
¢	blue grn	B. Franklin	"Series 1902" Coil		12 Vert	DL	318
¢	green	B. Franklin			12	DL	331
¢	green	B. Franklin	Blue Paper		12	DL	357
¢	green	B. Franklin			12	SL	374
¢	green	B. Franklin			Imperf	DL	343
¢	green	B. Franklin			Imperf	SL	383
¢	green	B. Franklin	Bklt. Pn. of 6		12	DL	331a
¢	green	B. Franklin	Bklt. Pn. of 6		12	SL	374a
¢	green	B. Franklin	Coil		12 Hz	DL	348
¢	green	B. Franklin	Coil		12 Hz	SL	385
¢	green	B. Franklin	Coil		12 Vert	DL	352
¢	green	B. Franklin	Coil		12 Vert	SL	387
¢	green	B. Franklin	Coil		8.5 Hz	SL	390
¢	green	B. Franklin	Coil		8.5 Vert	SL	392
¢	green	Washington			12	SL	405
¢	green	Washington			10	SL	424
¢	green	Washington		F	10	NW	462
¢	green	Washington		R	10	NW	543
¢	green	Washington		F	11	NW	498
¢	gray grn	Washington	Offset	F	11	NW	525
¢	green	Washington	19mm x 22.5mm	R	11	NW	544
¢	green	Washington	19.5-20mm x 22mm	R	11	NW	545
¢	gray grn	Washington	Rossbach Press		12.5	NW	536
¢	green	Washington		R	11x10	NW	538
¢	green	Washington		R	10x11	NW	542
¢	green	Washington			Imperf	SL	408
¢	green	Washington			Imperf	NW	481
¢	green	Washington	Offset		Imperf	NW	531
¢	green	Washington	Bklt. Pn. of 6		12	SL	405b

Den.	Color	Subject	Type / Comment	Press	Perf.	Wmk.	Scott #
1¢	green	Washington	Bklt. Pn. of 6		10	SL	424d
1¢	green	Washington	Bklt. Pn. of 6		10	NW	462a
1¢	green	Washington	Bklt. Pn. of 6		11	NW	498e
1¢	green	Washington	Bklt. Pn. of 30		11	NW	498f
1¢	green	Washington	Coil		8.5 Hz	SL	410
1¢	green	Washington	Coil		8.5 Vert	SL	412
1¢	green	Washington	Coil	F	10 Hz	SL	441
1¢	green	Washington	Coil	R	10 Hz	SL	448
1¢	green	Washington	Coil	R	10 Hz	SL	441
1¢	green	Washington	Coil	R	10 Hz	NW	486
1¢	green	Washington	Coil	F	10 Vert	SL	443
1¢	green	Washington	Coil	R	10 Vert	SL	452
1¢	green	Washington	Coil	R	10 Vert	NW	490
1¢	deep grn	B. Franklin		F	11		552
1¢	green	B. Franklin	19¾ x 22¼mm	R	11		594
1¢	green	B. Franklin	19¼ x 22¾mm	R	11		596
1¢	green	B. Franklin		R	11x10		578
1¢	green	B. Franklin		R	10		581
1¢	green	B. Franklin		R	11x10.5		632
1¢	green	B. Franklin		F	Imperf		575
1¢	deep grn	B. Franklin	Bklt. Pn. of 6	F	11		552a
1¢	green	B. Franklin	Bklt. Pn. of 6	R	11x10.5		632a
1¢	green	B. Franklin	Coil	R	10 Vert		597
1¢	yel. grn.	B. Franklin	Coil	R	10 Hz		604
1¢	green	B. Franklin	Kansas Ovpt.		11x10.5		658
1¢	green	B. Franklin	Nebraska Ovpt.		11x10.5		669
1¢	green	Washington	1938 Prexie Issue		11x10.5		804
1¢	green	Washington	Bklt. Pn. of 6		11x10.5		804b
1¢	green	Washington	Coil		10 Vert		839
1¢	green	Washington	Coil		10 Hz		848
1¢	dk green	Washington	1954 Liberty Issue		11x10.5		1031
1¢	dk green	Washington	Coil		10 Vert		1054
1¢	green	A. Jackson			11x10.5		1209*
1¢	green	A. Jackson	Coil		10 Vert		1225*
1¢	green	T. Jefferson			11x10.5		1278
1¢	green	T. Jefferson	Bklt. Pn. of 8		11x10.5		1278a
1¢	green	T. Jefferson	B.Pn./4 + 2 labels		11x10.5		1278b
1¢	green	T. Jefferson	Coil		10 Vert		1299
1¢	dk blue	Inkwell & Quill			11x10.5		1581
1¢	dk blue	Inkwell & Quill	Coil		10 Vert		1811
1¢	black	Dorothea Dix			11		1844
1¢	violet	Omnibus	Coil		10 Vert		1897
1¢	violet	Omnibus	Coil, re-engraved		10 Vert	B	2225
1¢	brnish verm	Margaret Mitchell			11		2168
1¢	multi	Kestrel			11		2481
1¼¢	turquoise	Palace of Governors			10.5x11		1031A
1¼¢	turquoise	Palace of Governors	Coil		10 Hz		1054A
1¼¢	lt. grn	Albert Gallatin			11x10.5		1279
1½¢	yel brn	W.G. Harding		F	11		553
1½¢	yel brn	W.G. Harding		R	10		582
1½¢	yel brn	W.G. Harding		R	11x10.5		633
1½¢	brown	W.G. Harding	"Full Face"	R	11x10.5		684
1½¢	yel brn	W.G. Harding		F	Imperf		576
1½¢	yel brn	W.G. Harding		R	Imperf		631
1½¢	brown	W.G. Harding	Coil		10 Vert		598
1½¢	yel brn	W.G. Harding	Coil		10 Hz		605
1½¢	brown	W.G. Harding	"Full Face," Coil		10 Vert		686
1½¢	brown	W.G. Harding	Kansas Ovpt.		11x10.5		659
1½¢	brown	W.G. Harding	Nebraska Ovpt.		11x10.5		670
1½¢	bstr brn	M. Washington			11x10.5		805
1½¢	bstr brn	M. Washington	Coil		10 Vert		840
1½¢	bstr brn	M. Washington	Coil		10 Hz		849
1½¢	brn carm	Mount Vernon			10.5x11		1032
2¢	**black**	**A. Jackson**			**12**		**73**
2¢	black	A. Jackson	"D" Grill		12		84
2¢	black	A. Jackson	"Z" Grill		12		85B
2¢	black	A. Jackson	"E" Grill		12		87
2¢	black	A. Jackson	"F" Grill		12		93
2¢	brown	Horse & Rider	Issue of 1869 "G grill"		12		113
2¢	brown	Horse & Rider	w/o grill, original gum		12		113b
2¢	brown	Horse & Rider	Re-iss/wht crackly gum		12		124
2¢	red brown	A. Jackson	Hard paper, w/grill		12		135
2¢	red brown	A. Jackson	Hard paper,w/o grill		12		146
2¢	brown	A. Jackson	Same, w/secret mark		12		157
2¢	vermillion	A. Jackson	Yellowish wove (hard)		12		178
2¢	vermillion	A. Jackson	Soft porous paper		12		183
2¢	red brown	Washington			12		210
2¢	pl rd brn	Washington	Special Printing		12		211B
2¢	green	Washington			12		213
2¢	lake	Washington	w/o Triangles		12		219D
2¢	carmine	Washington	w/o Tri.		12		220
2¢	pink	Washington	Ty I Tri. in Top corners		12	NW	248
2¢	carm. lake	Washington	Ty I Tri. "		12	NW	249
2¢	carmine	Washington	Ty I Tri. "		12	NW	250

DEFINITIVE ISSUE IDENTIFIER

Den.	Color	Subject	Type / Comment	Press	Perf.	Wmk.	Scott #
2¢	carmine	Washington	Ty I Tri. "		12	DL	265
2¢	carmine	Washington	Ty II Tri. "		12	NW	251
2¢	carmine	Washington	Ty II Tri. "		12	DL	266
2¢	carmine	Washington	Ty III Tri. "		12	NW	252
2¢	carmine	Washington	Ty III Tri. "		12	DL	267
2¢	red	Washington	Ty III Tri. "		12	DL	279B
2¢	carm rose	Washington	Ty III Tri. "		12	DL	279Bc
2¢	red	Washington	Bklt. Pn. of 6		12	DL	279Be
2¢	carmine	Washington	"Series 1902"		12	DL	301
2¢	carmine	Washington	"Series 1902" B.Pn./6		12	DL	301c

319/322 "Shield" | 332/393 "TWO" Cents | 406/546 "2" Cents | 554/671

Den.	Color	Subject	Type / Comment	Press	Perf.	Wmk.	Scott #
2¢	carmine	Washington	"Shield" Design, Die I		12	DL	319
2¢	carmine	Washington	"Shield", Die II		12	DL	319i
2¢	carmine	Washington	"Shield", B.Pn./6, Die I		12	DL	319g
2¢	carmine	Washington	"Shield", B.Pn./6, Die II		12	DL	319h
2¢	lake	Washington	"Shield", B.Pn./6, Die II		12	DL	319q
2¢	carmine	Washington	"Shield" Design		Imperf	DL	320
2¢	lake	Washington	"Shield" Design		Imperf	DL	320a
2¢	carmine	Washington	"Shield" Coil		12 Hz	DL	321
2¢	carmine	Washington	"Shield" Coil		12 Vert	DL	322
2¢	carmine	Washington	"TWO CENTS" Design		12	DL	332
2¢	carmine	Washington	"TWO..." Blue Paper		12	DL	358
2¢	carmine	Washington	"TWO..."		12	SL	375
2¢	lake	Washington	"TWO..."		12	SL	375v
2¢	carmine	Washington	"TWO..."	F	11	DL	519
2¢	carmine	Washington	"TWO..."		Imperf	DL	344
2¢	carmine	Washington	"TWO..."		Imperf	SL	384
2¢	dark carm	Washington	"TWO..."		Imperf	SL	384v
2¢	carmine	Washington	"TWO..." Bklt. Pn. of 6		12	DL	332a
2¢	carmine	Washington	"TWO..." Bklt. Pn. of 6		12	SL	375a
2¢	carmine	Washington	"TWO..." Coil		12 Hz	DL	349
2¢	carmine	Washington	"TWO..." Coil		12 Hz	SL	386
2¢	carmine	Washington	"TWO..." Coil		12 Vert	DL	353
2¢	carmine	Washington	"TWO..." Coil		12 Vert	SL	388
2¢	carmine	Washington	"TWO..." Coil		8.5 Hz	SL	391
2¢	carmine	Washington	"TWO..." Coil		8.5 Vert	SL	393
2¢	carmine	Washington	"2 CENTS" Design		12	SL	406
2¢	lake	Washington	"2..."		12	SL	406v
2¢	carmine	Washington	"2..."		10	SL	425
2¢	carmine	Washington	"2..."		10	NW	463
2¢	pf carm rd	Washington	"2..."		11	SL	461
2¢	carmine	Washington	"2..." Ty I	F	11	NW	499
2¢	carmine	Washington	"2..." Ty Ia	F	11	NW	500
2¢	carmine	Washington	"2..." Offset Ty. IV		11	NW	526
2¢	carmine	Washington	"2..." Offset Ty. V		11	NW	527
2¢	carmine	Washington	"2..." Offset Ty. Va		11	NW	528
2¢	carmine	Washington	"2..." Offset Ty. VI		11	NW	528A
2¢	carmine	Washington	"2..." Offset Ty. VII		11	NW	528B
2¢	carm rose	Washington	"2..." Coil Waste:				
2¢	carm rose	Washington	Ty III	R	11	NW	546
2¢	carm rose	Washington	Ty II	R	11x10	NW	539
2¢	carm rose	Washington	Ty III	R	11x10	NW	540
2¢	carmine	Washington	"2 CENTS"	F	Imperf	SL	409
2¢	carmine	Washington	"2..."	F	Imperf	NW	482
2¢	carm rose	Washington	"2..." Offset Ty IV		Imperf	NW	532
2¢	carmine	Washington	"2..." Offset Ty V		Imperf	NW	533
2¢	carmine	Washington	"2..." Offset Ty Va		Imperf	NW	534
2¢	carmine	Washington	"2..." Offset Ty VI		Imperf	NW	534A
2¢	carmine	Washington	"2..." Offset Ty VII		Imperf	NW	534B
2¢	carmine	Washington	"2..." Bklt. Pn. of 6		12	SL	406a
2¢	carmine	Washington	"2..." Bklt. Pn. of 6		10	SL	425e
2¢	carmine	Washington	"2..." Bklt. Pn. of 6		10	NW	463a
2¢	carmine	Washington	"2..." Bklt. Pn. of 6	F	11	NW	499e
2¢	carmine	Washington	"2..." Bklt. Pn. of 30	F	11	NW	499f
2¢	carmine	Washington	"2 CENTS" Coil		8.5 Hz	SL	411
2¢	carmine	Washington	"2..." Coil		8.5 Vert	SL	413
2¢	carmine	Washington	"2..." Coil Ty I	F	10 Hz	SL	442
2¢	red	Washington	"2..." Coil Ty I	R	10 Hz	SL	449
2¢	carmine	Washington	"2..." Coil Ty II	R	10 Hz	NW	487
2¢	carmine	Washington	"2..." Coil Ty III	R	10 Hz	SL	450
2¢	carmine	Washington	"2..." Coil Ty III	R	10 Hz	NW	488
2¢	carmine	Washington	"2..." Coil Ty I	F	10 Vert	SL	444
2¢	carm red	Washington	"2..." Coil Ty I	R	10 Vert	SL	453
2¢	red	Washington	"2..." Coil Ty II	R	10 Vert	SL	454
2¢	carmine	Washington	"2..." Coil Ty II	R	10 Vert	NW	491
2¢	carmine	Washington	"2..." Coil Ty III	R	10 Vert	SL	455
2¢	carmine	Washington	"2..." Coil Ty III	R	10 Vert	NW	492
2¢	carmine	Washington	"2..." Hz Coil Ty I	R	Imperf	SL	459
2¢	deep rose	Washington	"2..." Hz Coil Ty Ia/ Shermack Ty III Perfs	F	*	NW	482A
2¢	carmine	Washington		F	11		554
2¢	carmine	Washington	19¾ x 22¼ mm	R	11		595
2¢	carmine	Washington	19¾ x 22¼ mm	R	11x10		579
2¢	carmine	Washington	Die I	R	11x10.5		634
2¢	carmine	Washington	Die II	R	11x10.5		634A

Den.	Color	Subject	Type / Comment	Press	Perf.	Wmk.	Scott
2¢	carmine	Washington		R	10		583
2¢	carmine	Washington		F	Imperf		577
2¢	carmine	Washington	Bklt. Pn. of 6	F	11		554c
2¢	carmine	Washington	Bklt. Pn. of 6	R	10		583a
2¢	carmine	Washington	Bklt. Pn. of 6	R	11x10.5		634d
2¢	carmine	Washington	Coil		10 Vert		599
2¢	carmine	Washington	Coil Die II		10 Vert		599A
2¢	carmine	Washington	Coil		10 Hz		606
2¢	carmine	Washington	Kansas Ovpt.		11x10.5		660
2¢	carmine	Washington	Nebraska Ovpt.		11x10.5		671
2¢	rose carm	J. Adams			11x10.5		806
2¢	rose carm	J. Adams	Bklt. Pn. of 6		11x10.5		806b
2¢	rose carm	J. Adams	Coil		10 Vert		841
2¢	rose carm	J. Adams	Coil		10 Hz		850
2¢	carm rose	T. Jefferson			11x10.5		1033
2¢	carm rose	T. Jefferson	Coil		10 Vert		1055*
2¢	dk bl gray	Frank Lloyd Wright			11x10.5		1280
2¢	dk bl gray	Frank Lloyd Wright	B. Pn. of 5 + Label		11x10.5		1280a
2¢	dk bl gray	Frank Lloyd Wright	Booklet Pn. of 6		11x10.5		1280c
2¢	red brn	Speaker's Stand			11x10.5		1582
2¢	brn black	Igor Stravinsky			10.5x11		1845
2¢	black	Locomotive	Coil		10 Vert		1897A
2¢	black	Locomotive	Coil, "Re-engraved"		10 Vert	B	2226
2¢	brt blue	Mary Lyon			11		2169
2.5¢	gray bl	Bunker Hill			11x10.5		1034
2.5¢	gray bl	Bunker Hill	Coil		10 Vert		1056

10/26a | 64/94 | 136/214 | 221 | 253/268

Den.	Color	Subject	Type / Comment	Press	Perf.	Wmk.	Scott
3¢	orng brn	Washington	Ty I		Imperf		10
3¢	dull red	Washington	Ty I		Imperf		11
3¢	rose	Washington	Ty I		15		25
3¢	dull red	Washington	Ty II		15		26
3¢	dull red	Washington	Ty IIa		15		26a
3¢	pink	Washington			12		64
3¢	pgn bld pink	Washington			12		64a
3¢	rose pink	Washington			12		64b
3¢	rose	Washington			12		65
3¢	lake	Washington			12		66
3¢	scarlet	Washington			12		74
3¢	rose	Washington	"A" Grill		12		79
3¢	rose	Washington	"B" Grill		12		82
3¢	rose	Washington	"C" Grill		12		83
3¢	rose	Washington	"D" Grill		12		85
3¢	rose	Washington	"Z" Grill		12		85C
3¢	rose	Washington	"E" Grill		12		88
3¢	rose	Washington	"F" Grill		12		94
3¢	ultra	Locomotive	"G grill"		12		114
3¢	ultra	Locomotive	w/o grill, Original gum		12		114a
3¢	green	Washington	Hard paper, w/grill		12		136
3¢	green	Washington	Same, w/o grill		12		147
3¢	green	Washington	Same, w/secret mark		12		158
3¢	green	Washington	Same, Soft porous paper		12		184
3¢	blue grn	Washington	Same, re-engraved		12		207
3¢	vermillion	Washington			12		214
3¢	purple	A. Jackson	w/o Triangles		12		221
3¢	purple	A. Jackson	w/ Tri. in Top corners		12	NW	253
3¢	purple	A Jackson	w/ Tri. in Top corners		12	DL	268

302 | 333/541 | 720/722 | 12/30A | 67/95

Den.	Color	Subject	Type / Comment	Press	Perf.	Wmk.	Scott
3¢	violet	A. Jackson	"Series 1902"		12	DL	302
3¢	dp violet	Washington		F	12	DL	333
3¢	dp violet	Washington	Blue paper	F	12	DL	359
3¢	dp violet	Washington		F	12	SL	376
3¢	dp violet	Washington		F	10	SL	426
3¢	violet	Washington		F	10	NW	464
3¢	lt violet	Washington	Ty I	F	11	NW	501
3¢	dk violet	Washington	Ty II	F	11	NW	502
3¢	violet	Washington	Ty III Offset		11	NW	529
3¢	purple	Washington	Ty IV Offset		11	NW	530
3¢	violet	Washington	Ty II Coil Waste	R	11x10	NW	541
3¢	dp violet	Washington		F	Imperf	DL	345
3¢	violet	Washington	Ty I	F	Imperf	NW	483
3¢	violet	Washington	Ty II	F	Imperf	NW	484
3¢	violet	Washington	Ty IV Offset		Imperf	NW	535
3¢	lt violet	Washington	B. Pn. of 6, Ty I	F	11	NW	501b

DEFINITIVE ISSUE IDENTIFIER

Den.	Color	Subject	Type / Comment	Press	Perf.	Wmk.	Scott #
¢	dk violet	Washington	B. Pn. of 6, Ty II	F	11	NW	502b
¢	dp violet	Washington	Coil "Orangeburg"	F	12 Vert	SL	389
¢	dp violet	Washington	Coil	F	8.5 Vert	SL	394
¢	violet	Washington	Coil, Ty I	F	10 Vert	SL	445
¢	violet	Washington	Coil, Ty I	R	10 Vert	SL	456
¢	violet	Washington	Coil, Ty I	R	10 Hz	NW	489
¢	dp violet	Washington	Coil, Ty I	R	10 Vert	NW	493
¢	dull violet	Washington	Coil, Ty II	R	10 Vert	NW	494
¢	violet	A. Lincoln		F	11		555
¢	violet	A. Lincoln		R	10		584
¢	violet	A. Lincoln		R	11x10.5		635
¢	violet	A. Lincoln	Coil		10 Vert		600
¢	violet	A. Lincoln	Kansas Ovpt.		11x10.5		661
¢	violet	A. Lincoln	Nebraska Ovpt.		11x10.5		672
¢	dp violet	Washington	Stuart Portrait		11x10.5		720
¢	dp violet	Washington	Stuart B. Pn. of 6		11x10.5		720b
¢	dp violet	Washington	Stuart Coil		10 Vert		721
¢	dp violet	Washington	Stuart Coil		10 Hz		722
¢	dp violet	T. Jefferson			11x10.5		807
¢	dp violet	T. Jefferson	Bklt. Pn. of 6		11x10.5		807a
¢	dp violet	T. Jefferson	Coil		10 Vert		842
¢	dp violet	T. Jefferson	Coil		10 Hz		851
¢	dp violet	Statue of Liberty			11x10.5		1035*
¢	dp violet	Liberty	Bklt. Pn. of 6		11x10.5		1035a
¢	dp violet	Liberty	Coil		10 Vert		1057*
¢	violet	F. Parkman			10.5x11		1281
¢	violet	F. Parkman	Coil		10 Vert		1297
¢	olive	Early Ballot Box			11x10.5		1583
¢	olive grn	Henry Clay			11x10.5		1846
¢	dark grn	Handcar	Coil		10 Vert		1898
¢	brt blue	Paul D. White MD			11		2170
¢	claret	Conestoga Wagon	Coil		10 Vert		2252
¢	multi	Bluebird			11		2482
3¢)	multi	Dove	ABN		11x10.8		2877
3¢)	multi	Dove	SVS		10.8x10.9		2878
.1¢	brn (yel)	Guitar	Coil		10 Vert		1613
.4¢	dk blsh grn	School Bus	Coil		10 Vert		2123
.5¢	prpl (yel)	Weaver Violins	Coil		10 Vert		1813
¢	**blue grn**	**A. Jackson**			**12**		**211**
¢	carmine	A. Jackson			12		215
¢	dk brn	A. Lincoln	w/ Triangles		12		222
¢	dk brn	A. Lincoln	w/ Tri. in Top corners		12	NW	254
¢	dk brn	A. Lincoln	w/ Tri. in Top corners		12	DL	269
¢	rose brn	A. Lincoln	w/ Tri. in Top corners		12	DL	280
¢	brown	U.S. Grant	"Series 1902"		12	DL	303
¢	brown	U.S. Grant	Coil, Shermack Ty III		*	DL	314A
¢	orng brn	Washington		F	12	DL	334
¢	orng brn	Washington	Blue Paper	F	12	DL	360
¢	brown	Washington		F	12	SL	377
¢	brown	Washington		F	10	SL	427
¢	orng brn	Washington		F	10	NW	465
¢	brown	Washington		F	11	NW	503
¢	orng brn	Washington		F	Imperf	DL	346
¢	orng brn	Washington	Coil	F	12 Hz	DL	350
¢	orng brn	Washington	Coil	F	12 Vert	DL	354
¢	brown	Washington	Coil	F	8.5 Vert	SL	395
¢	brown	Washington	Coil	F	10 Vert	SL	446
¢	brown	Washington	Coil	R	10 Vert	SL	457
¢	orng brn	Washington	Coil	R	10 Vert	NW	495
4¢	yel brn	M. Washington		F	11		556
4¢	yel brn	M. Washington		R	10		585
4¢	yel brn	M. Washington		R	11x10.5		636
4¢	yel brn	M. Washington	Coil		10 Vert		601
4¢	yel brn	M. Washington	Kansas Ovpt.		11x10.5		662
4¢	yel brn	M. Washington	Nebraska Ovpt.		11x10.5		673
4¢	brown	W.H. Taft			11x10.5		685
4¢	brown	W.H. Taft	Coil		10 Vert		687
4¢	red violet	J. Madison			11x10.5		808
4¢	red violet	J. Madison	Coil		10 Vert		843
4¢	red violet	A. Lincoln			11x10.5		1036*
4¢	red violet	A. Lincoln	Bklt. Pn. of 6		11x10.5		1036a
4¢	red violet	A. Lincoln	Coil		10 Vert		1058
4¢	black	A. Lincoln			11x10.5		1282*
4¢	black	A. Lincoln	Coil		10 Vert		1303
4¢	rose mag	"Books, etc."			11x10.5		1584
4¢	violet	Carl Schurz			10.5x11		1847
4¢	rdsh brn	Stagecocach	Coil		10 Vert		1898A
4¢	rdsh brn	Stagecoach	Coil, re-engr.	B	10 Vert		2228
4¢	bl violet	Father Flanagan			11		2171
4¢	claret	Steam Carriage	Coil		10		2451
4½¢	**dark gray**	**White House**			**11x10.5**		**809**
4½¢	dark gray	White House	Coil		10 Vert		844
4½¢	blue grn	The Hermitage			10.5x11		1037
4½¢	blue grn	The Hermitage	Coil		10 Hz		1059
4.9¢	brn blk	Buckboard	Coil		10 Vert		2124
5¢	**rd brn**	**B. Franklin**			**Imperf**		**1**
5¢	rd brn	B. Franklin	Bluish paper (reprint)		Imperf		3
5¢	rd brn	T. Jefferson	Ty I		Imperf		12
5¢	brick red	T. Jefferson	Ty I		15		27
5¢	rd brn	T. Jefferson	Ty I		15		28
5¢	brt rd brn	T. Jefferson	Ty I		15		28b
5¢	Indian red	T. Jefferson	Ty I		15		28A
5¢	brown	T. Jefferson	Ty I		15		29
5¢	orng brn	T. Jefferson	Ty II		15		30
5¢	brown	T. Jefferson	Ty II		15		30A
5¢	buff	T. Jefferson			12		67
5¢	red brn	T. Jefferson			12		75

Den.	Color	Subject	Type / Comment	Press	Perf.	Wmk.	Scott #
5¢	brown	T. Jefferson			12		76
5¢	brown	T. Jefferson	"A" Grill		12		80
5¢	brown	T. Jefferson	"F" Grill		12		95
5¢	blue	Z. Taylor	Yellowish wove (hard)		12		179
5¢	blue	Z. Taylor	Soft Porous Paper		12		185
5¢	yel brn	J. Garfield			12		205
5¢	indigo	J. Garfield			12		216
5¢	choc	U.S. Grant	w/o Triangles		12		223
5¢	choc	U.S. Grant	w/ Tri. in Top corners		12	NW	255
5¢	choc	U.S. Grant	w/ Tri. in Top corners		12	DL	270
5¢	dk blue	U.S. Grant	w/ Tri. in Top corners		12	DL	281
5¢	blue	A. Lincoln	"Series 1902"		12	DL	304
5¢	blue	A. Lincoln	"Series 1902"		Imperf	DL	315
5¢	blue	Washington			12	DL	335
5¢	blue	Washington	Blue Paper		12	DL	361
5¢	blue	Washington			12	SL	378
5¢	blue	Washington			10	SL	428
5¢	blue	Washington			10	NW	466
5¢	blue	Washington			11	NW	504
5¢	blue	Washington			Imperf	DL	347
5¢	blue	Washington	Coil		12 Hz	DL	351
5¢	blue	Washington	Coil		12 Vert	DL	355
5¢	blue	Washington	Coil		8.5 Vert	SL	396
5¢	blue	Washington	Coil	F	10 Vert	SL	447
5¢	blue	Washington	Coil	R	10 Vert	SL	458
5¢	blue	Washington	Coil	R	10 Vert	NW	496
5¢	carmine	Washington	Error of Color		10	NW	467
5¢	rose	Washington	Error of Color		11	NW	505
5¢	carmine	Washington	Error of Color		Imperf	NW	485
5¢	dk blue	T. Roosevelt		F	11		557
5¢	blue	T. Roosevelt		R	10		586
5¢	dk blue	T. Roosevelt	Coil	R	10 Vert		602
5¢	dk blue	T. Roosevelt		R	11x10.5		637
5¢	dp blue	T. Roosevelt	Kansas Ovpt.		11x10.5		663
5¢	dp blue	T. Roosevelt	Nebraska Ovpt.		11x10.5		674
5¢	brt blue	J. Monroe			11x10.5		810
5¢	brt blue	J. Monroe	Coil		10 Vert		845
5¢	blue	J. Monroe			11x10.5		1038
5¢	dk bl gray	Washington			11x10.5		1213*
5¢	dk bl gray	Washington	Bklt. Pn. of 5 +				
			"Mailman" Label		11x10.5		1213a
			"Use Zone Nos." Label		11x10.5		1213a*
			"Use Zip Code" Label		11x10.5		1213a*
5¢	dk bl gray	Washington	Coil		10 Vert		1229*
5¢	blue	Washington			11x10.5		1283*
5¢	blue	Washington	Re-engr. (clean face)		11x10.5		1283B
5¢	blue	Washington	Coil		10 Vert		1304
5¢	henna brn	Pearl Buck			10.5x11		1848
5¢	gray grn	Motorcycle	Coil		10 Vert		1899
5¢	dk olv grn	Hugo Black			11		2172
5¢	carmine	Luis Munoz Marin			11		2173*
5¢	black	Milk Wagon	Coil		10 Vert		2253
5¢	red	Circus Wagon	Coil Engraved		10 Vert		2452
5¢	carmine	Circus Wagon	Coil Gravure		10 Vert		2452B
5¢	brown	Canoe	Coil Engraved		10 Vert		2453
5¢	red	Canoe	Coil Gravure		10 Vert		2454
5.2¢	carmine	Sleigh	Coil		10 Vert		1900
5.3¢	black	Elevator	Coil		10 Vert		2254
5.5¢	dp mag	Star Rt Truck	Coil		10 Vert		2125
5.9¢	blue	Bicycle	Coil		10 Vert		1901
6¢	**ultra**	**Washington**	**"G" Grill**		**12**		**115**
6¢	carmine	A. Lincoln	hard wh paper, w/grill		12		137
6¢	carmine	A. Lincoln	Same, w/o grill		12		148
6¢	dull pink	A. Lincoln	Same, secret mark		12		159
6¢	pink	A. Lincoln	Same, sft porous pap		12		186
6¢	rose	A. Lincoln	Same, re-engraved		12		208
6¢	brn red	A. Lincoln	Same, re-engraved		12		208a
6¢	brn red	J. Garfield	w/o Triangles		12		224
6¢	dull brn	J. Garfield	w/ Tri. in Top corners		12	NW	256
6¢	dull brn	J. Garfield	w/ Tri. in Top corners		12	DL	271
6¢	dull brn	J. Garfield	w/ Tri. in Top corners		12	USIR	271a
6¢	lake	J. Garfield	w/ Tri. in Top corners		12	DL	282
6¢	claret	J. Garfield	"Series 1902"		12	DL	305
6¢	rd orng	Washington			12	DL	336
6¢	rd orng	Washington	Blue paper		12	DL	362
6¢	rd orng	Washington			12	SL	379
6¢	rd orng	Washington			10	SL	429
6¢	rd orng	Washington			10	NW	468
6¢	rd orng	Washington			11	NW	506
6¢	rd orng	J. Garfield		F	11		558
6¢	rd orng	J. Garfield		R	10		587
6¢	rd orng	J. Garfield		R	11x10.5		638
6¢	rd orng	J. Garfield	Kansas Ovpt.		11x10.5		664
6¢	rd orng	J. Garfield	Nebraska Ovpt.		11x10.5		675
6¢	dp orng	J. Garfield	Coil		10 Vert		723
6¢	red orng	J.Q. Adams			11x10.5		811
6¢	red orng	J.Q. Adams	Coil		10 Vert		846
6¢	carmine	T. Roosevelt			11x10.5		1039
6¢	gray brn	F.D. Roosevelt			10.5x11		1284*
6¢	gray brn	F.D. Roosevelt	Bklt. Pn. of 8		11x10.5		1284b
6¢	gray brn	F.D. Roosevelt	Bklt. Pn. of 5 + Label		11x10.5		1284c
6¢	gray brn	F.D. Roosevelt	Coil		10 Hz		1298
6¢	gray brn	F.D. Roosevelt	Coil		10 Vert		1305
6¢	dk bl,rd & grn	Flag & White House			11		1338
6¢	dk bl,rd & grn	Flag & White House			11x10.5		1338D
6¢	dk bl,rd & grn	Flag & White House	Coil		10 Vert		1338A
6¢	dk bl gray	D.D. Eisenhower			11x10.5		1393

DEFINITIVE ISSUE IDENTIFIER

Den.	Color	Subject	Type / Comment	Press	Perf.	Wmk.	Scott #
6¢	dk bl gray	Eisenhower	Bklt. Pn of 8		11x10.5		1393a
6¢	dk bl gray	Eisenhower	Bklt. Pn of 5 + Label		11x10.5		1393b
6¢	dk bl gray	Eisenhower	Coil		10 Vert		1401
6¢	orng verm	Walter Lippmann			11		1849
6¢	multi	Circle of Stars	Bklt. Single		11		1892
6¢	red brn	Tricycle	Coil		10 Vert		2126
6.3¢	brick red	Liberty Bell	Coil		10 Vert		1518
7¢	**vermilion**	**E.M. Stanton**	**Hard wh paper, w/grill**		**12**		**138**
7¢	vermilion	E.M. Stanton	Same, w/o grill		12		149
7¢	orng verm	E.M. Stanton	Same, w/secret mark		12		160
7¢	black	Washington			12	SL	407
7¢	black	Washington			10	SL	430
7¢	black	Washington			10	NW	469
7¢	black	Washington			11	NW	507
7¢	black	Wm. McKinley		F	11		559
7¢	black	Wm. McKinley		R	10		588
7¢	black	Wm. McKinley		R	11x10.5		639
7¢	black	Wm. McKinley	Kansas Ovpt.		11x10.5		665
7¢	black	Wm. McKinley	Nebraska Ovpt.		11x10.5		676
7¢	sepia	A. Jackson			11x10.5		812
7¢	rose carm	W. Wilson			11x10.5		1040
7¢	brt blue	B. Franklin			10.5x11		1393D
7¢	brt carm	Abraham Baldwin			10.5x11		1850
7.1¢	lake	Tractor	Coil		10 Vert		2127
7.4¢	brown	Baby Buggy	Coil		10 Vert		1902
7.6¢	brown	Carreta	Coil		10 Vert		2255
7.7¢	brn (brt yl)	Saxhorns	Coil		10 Vert		1614
7.9¢	carm (yl)	Drum	Coil		10 Vert		1615
8¢	**lilac**	**W.T. Sherman**	**w/o Triangles**		**12**		**225**
8¢	violet brn	W.T. Sherman	w/ Tri. in Top corners		12	NW	257
8¢	violet brn	W.T. Sherman	w/ Tri. in Top corners		12	DL	272
8¢	violet brn	W.T. Sherman	w/ Tri. in Top corners		12	USIR	272a
8¢	violet blk	M. Washington	"Series 1902"		12	DL	306
8¢	olive grn	Washington			12	DL	337
8¢	olive grn	Washington	Blue Paper		12	DL	363
8¢	olive grn	Washington			12	SL	380
8¢	pl olv grn	B. Franklin			12	SL	414
8¢	pl olv grn	B. Franklin			10	SL	431
8¢	olv grn	B. Franklin			10	NW	470
8¢	olv grn	B. Franklin			11	NW	508
8¢	olv grn	U.S. Grant		F	11		560
8¢	olv grn	U.S. Grant		R	10		589
8¢	olv grn	U.S. Grant		R	11x10.5		640
8¢	olv grn	U.S. Grant	Kansas Ovpt.		11x10.5		666
8¢	olv grn	U.S. Grant	Nebraska Ovpt.		11x10.5		677
8¢	olv grn	M. Van Buren			11x10.5		813
8¢	dk viol bl & carm	Statue of Liberty		F/R	11		1041
		Statue of Liberty Redrawn		Giori	11		1042
8¢	brown	Gen. J.J. Pershing		R	11x10.5		1042A
8¢	violet	Albert Einstein			11x10.5		1285*
8¢	multi	Flag & Wh House			11x10.5		1338F
8¢	multi	Flag & Wh House	Coil		10 Vert		1338G
8¢	blk,rd & bl gry	Eisenhower			11		1394
8¢	dp claret	Eisenhower	Bklt. sgl./B.Pn. of 8		11x10.5		1395a
8¢	dp claret	Eisenhower	Bklt. Pn. of 6		11x10.5		1395b
8¢	dp claret	Eisenhower	Bklt. Pn. of 4 + 2 Labels		11x10.5		1395c
8¢	dp claret	Eisenhower	Bklt. Pn. of 7 + Label		11x10.5		1395d
8¢	multi	Postal Service Emblem			11x10.5		1396
8¢	dp claret	Eisenhower	Coil		10 Vert		1402
8¢	olive blk	Henry Knox			10.5x11		1851
8.3¢	green	Ambulance	Coil		10 Vert		2128
8.3¢	green	Ambulance	Coil Precan.	B	10 Vert		2231
8.4¢	dk bl (yel)	Grand Piano	Coil		10 Vert		1615C
8.4¢	dp claret	Wheel Chair	Coil		10 Vert		2256
8.5¢	dk pris grn	Tow Truck	Coil		10 Vert		2129
9¢	**salmn rd**	**B. Franklin**			**12**	**SL**	**415**
9¢	salmn rd	B. Franklin			10	SL	432
9¢	salmn rd	B. Franklin			10	NW	471
9¢	salmn rd	B. Franklin			11	NW	509
9¢	rose	T. Jefferson		F	11		561
9¢	rose	T. Jefferson		R	10		590
9¢	orng red	T. Jefferson		R	11x10.5		641
9¢	lt rose	T. Jefferson	Kansas Ovpt.		11x10.5		667
9¢	lt rose	T. Jefferson	Nebraska Ovpt.		11x10.5		678
9¢	rose pink	W.H. Harrison			11x10.5		814
9¢	rose lilac	Alamo			10.5x11		1043
9¢	slate grn	Capitol Dome			11x10.5		1591
9¢	slate grn	Capitol Dome	Bklt. Single		11x10.5		1590
9¢	slate grn	Capitol Dome	Bklt. Single		10		1590a
9¢	slate grn	Capitol Dome	Coil		10 Vert		1616
9¢	dark grn	Sylvanus Thayer			10.5x11		1852
9.3¢	carm rose	Mail Wagon	Coil		10 Vert		1903
10¢	**black**	**Washington**			**Imperf**		**2**
10¢	black	Washington	Bluish paper (reprint)		Imperf		4
10¢	green	Washington	Ty I		Imperf		13
10¢	green	Washington	Ty II		Imperf		14
10¢	green	Washington	Ty III		Imperf		15
10¢	green	Washington	Ty IV		Imperf		16
10¢	green	Washington	Ty I		15		31

13/35 62B/96 17/36b 69/97

Den.	Color	Subject	Type / Comment	Press	Perf.	Wmk.	Scott #
10¢	green	Washington	Ty II		15		32
10¢	green	Washington	Ty III		15		33
10¢	green	Washington	Ty IV		15		34
10¢	green	Washington	Ty V		15		35
10¢	dark grn	Washington	Premier Gravure, Ty I		12		62B
10¢	yel grn	Washington	Ty II		12		68
10¢	green	Washington	"Z" Grill		12		85D
10¢	green	Washington	"E" Grill		12		89
10¢	yel grn	Washington	"F" Grill		12		96
10¢	yellow	Eagle & Shield	"G" Grill		12		116
10¢	brown	T. Jefferson	w/grill, Hard wh paper		12		139
10¢	brown	T. Jefferson	Same, w/o grill		12		150
10¢	brown	T. Jefferson	Same, w/secret mark		12		161
10¢	brown	T. Jefferson	Soft porous paper:				
		w/o secret mark			12		187
		w/secret mark			12		188
10¢	brown	T. Jefferson	Soft paper, re-engr.		12		209
10¢	green	D. Webster	w/o Triangles		12		226
10¢	dark grn	D. Webster	w/ Tri. in Top corners		12	NW	258
10¢	dark grn	D. Webster	w/ Tri. in Top corners		12	DL	273
10¢	brown	D. Webster	Ty I "		12	DL	282C
10¢	orng brn/brn	D. Webster	Ty II "		12	DL	283
10¢	pl rd brn	D. Webster	"Series 1902"		12	DL	307
10¢	yellow	Washington			12	DL	338
10¢	yellow	Washington	Blue Paper		12	DL	364
10¢	yellow	Washington			12	SL	381
10¢	yellow	Washington	Coil		12 Vert	DL	356
10¢	orng yel	B. Franklin			12	SL	416
10¢	orng yel	B. Franklin			10	SL	433
10¢	orng yel	B. Franklin			10	NW	472
10¢	orng yel	B. Franklin			11	NW	510
10¢	orng yel	B. Franklin	Coil	R	10 Vert	NW	497
10¢	yel orng	J. Monroe		F	11	NW	562
10¢	yel orng	J. Monroe		R	10	NW	591
10¢	orange	J. Monroe		R	11x10.5	NW	642
10¢	orange	J. Monroe	Coil	R	10 Vert	NW	603
10¢	orng yel	J. Monroe	Kansas Ovpt.		11x10.5	NW	668
10¢	orng yel	J. Monroe	Nebraska Ovpt.		11x10.5	NW	679
10¢	brn red	J. Tyler			11x10.5		815
10¢	brn red	J. Tyler	Coil		10 Vert		847
10¢	rose lake	Indep. Hall			10.5x11		1044*
10¢	lilac	A. Jackson			11x10.5		1286*
10¢	red & bl	Crossed Flags			11x10.5		1509
10¢	red & bl	Crossed Flags	Coil		10 Vert		1519
10¢	blue	Jefferson Mem.			11x10.5		1510
10¢	blue	Jefferson Mem.	Bklt. Pn. of 5 + Label		11x10.5		1510b
10¢	blue	Jefferson Mem.	Bklt. Pn. of 8		11x10.5		1510c
10¢	blue	Jefferson Mem.	Bklt. Pn. of 6		11x10.5		1510d
10¢	blue	Jefferson Mem.	Coil		10 Vert		1520
10¢	multi	"Zip Code"			11x10.5		1511
10¢	violet	Justice			11x10.5		1592
10¢	violet	Justice	Coil		10 Vert		1617
10¢	prus bl	Richard Russell			10.5x11		1853
10¢	lake	Red Cloud			11		2176
10¢	sky blue	Canal Boat	Coil		10 Vert		2257
10¢	green	Tractor Trailer	Coil Intaglio		10 Vert		2457
10¢	green	Tractor Trailer	Coil Gravure		10 Vert		2458
10¢	multi	Eagle & Shield	Coil "Bulk Rate, USA"		10 Vert		2602
10¢	multi	Eagle & Shield	Coil "USA Bulk Rate"		10 Vert	BEP	2603
10¢	multi	Eagle & Shield	Coil "USA Bulk Rate"		10 Vert	SVS	2604
10.1¢	slate blue	Oil Wagon	Coil		10 Vert		2130
10.9¢	purple	Hansom Cab	Coil		10 Vert		1904
11	**dark grn**	**B. Franklin**			**10**	**SL**	**434**
11¢	dark grn	B. Franklin			10	NW	473
11¢	light grn	B. Franklin			11	NW	511
11¢	lt bl/bl grn	R.B. Hayes		F	11		563
11¢	light blue	R.B. Hayes		R	11x10.5		692
11¢	ultra	J.K. Polk			11x10.5		816
11¢	carm & dk viol bl	Statue of Liberty			11		1044A*
11¢	orange	Printing Press			11x10.5		1593
11¢	dk blue	Alden Partridge			11		1854
11¢	red	RR Caboose	Coil		10 Vert		1905
11¢	dk green	Stutz Bearcat	Coil		10 Vert		2131
12¢	**black**	**Washington**			**Imperf**		**17**
12¢	black	Washington	Plate 1		15		36
12¢	black	Washington	Plate 3		15		36b
12¢	black	Washington			12		69
12¢	black	Washington	"Z" Grill		12		85E
12¢	black	Washington	"E" Grill		12		90
12¢	black	Washington	"F" Grill		12		97
12¢	green	S.S. Adriatic	"G grill"		12		117
12¢	dull violet	H. Clay	Hard wh paper, w/grill		12		140
12¢	dull violet	H. Clay	Same, w/o grill		12		151
12¢	blksh viol	H. Clay	Same, w/secret mark		12		162
12¢	claret brn	B. Franklin			12	SL	417
12¢	claret brn	B. Franklin			10	SL	435

DEFINITIVE ISSUE IDENTIFIER

Den.	Color	Subject	Type / Comment	Press	Perf.	Wmk.	Scott #
12¢	copper rd	B. Franklin			10	SL	435a
12¢	claret brn	B. Franklin			10	NW	474
12¢	claret brn	B. Franklin			11	NW	512
12¢	brn carm	B. Franklin			11	NW	512a
12¢	brn violet	G. Cleveland		F	11		564
12¢	brn violet	G. Cleveland		R	11x10.5		693
12¢	bright viol	Z. Taylor			11x10.5		817
12¢	red	B. Harrison			11x10.5		1045*
12¢	black	Henry Ford			10.5x11		1286A*
12¢	rd brn (bge)	Liberty Torch	Coil		10 Vert		1816
12¢	dk blue	Stanley Stmr	Ty I Coil		10 Vert		2132
12¢	dk blue	Stanley Stmr	Ty II Coil, precanc.		10 Vert		2132b
12.5¢	olive grn	Pushcart	Coil		10 Vert		2133
13¢	**purp blk**	**B. Harrison**	**"Series 1902"**		**12**	**DL**	**308**
13¢	blue grn	Washington			12	DL	339
13¢	blue grn	Washington	Blue Paper		12	DL	365
13¢	apple grn	B. Franklin			11	NW	513
13¢	green	B. Harrison		F	11		622
13¢	yel grn	B. Harrison		R	11x10.5		694
13¢	bue grn	M. Fillmore			11x10.5		818
13¢	brown	J.F. Kennedy			11x10.5		1287*
13¢	brown	Liberty Bell			11x10.5		1595
13¢	brown	Liberty Bell	Bklt. Pn. of 6		11x10.5		1595a
13¢	brown	Liberty Brll	Bklt. Pn. of 7 + Label		11x10.5		1595b
13¢	brown	Liberty Bell	Bklt. Pn of 8		11x10.5		1595c
13¢	brown	Liberty Bell	Bklt. Pn of 5 + Label		11x10.5		1595d
13¢	brown	Liberty Bell	Coil		10 Vert		1618
13¢	multi	Eagle & Shield	Bullseye Perfs		11x10.5		1596
13¢	multi	Eagle & Shield	Line Perfs		11		1596d
13¢	dk bl & rd	Flag Over Indep. Hall			11x10.5		1622
13¢	dk. bl & rd	Flag Over Indep. Hall			11		1622c
13¢	dk bl & rd	Flag Over Indep. Hall	Coil		10 Vert		1625
13¢	bl & rd	Flag Over Captl	Bklt. Single		11x10.5		1623
13¢	bl & rd	Flag Over Captl	Bklt. Single		10		1623b
13¢	bl & rd	Flag Over Captl	B. Pn. of 8 (7 #1623 (13¢) + 1 # 1590 (9¢))		11X10.5		1623a
13¢	bl & rd	Flag Over Capt	B. Pn. of 8 (7 #1623b (13¢) + 1 #1590a (9¢))		10		1623c
13¢	brn & bl (grn bistr)	Indian Head Penny			11		1734
13¢	lt maroon	Crazy Horse			10.5x11		1855
13¢	black	Patrol Wagon	Coil		10 Vert		2258
13.2¢	slate grn	Coal Car	Coil		10 Vert		2259
14¢	**blue**	**American Indian**		**F**	**11**		**565**
14¢	dk blue	American Indian		R	11x10.5		695
14¢	blue	F. Pierce			11x10.5		819
14¢	gray brn	Fiorello LaGuardia			11x10.5		1397
14¢	slate grn	Sinclair Lewis			11		1856
14¢	sky blue	Iceboat	Coil, overall tag		10 Vert		2134
14¢	sky blue	Iceboat, Ty II	Coil, block tag	B	10 Vert		2134b
14¢	crimson	Julia Ward Howe			11		2177
15¢	**black**	**A. Lincoln**			**12**		**77**
15¢	black	A. Lincoln	"Z" Grill		12		85F
15¢	black	A. Lincoln	"E" Grill		12		91
15¢	black	A. Lincoln	"F" Gril		12		98
15¢	brn & bl	Landing of Columbus:					
			Ty I Frame, "G grill"		12		118
			Same, w/o grill, o.g.		12		118a
			Ty II Frame, "G grill"		12		119
			Ty III, wh crackly gum		12		129
15¢	orange	D. Webster	Hard wh paper, w/grill		12		141
15¢	brt orng	D. Webster	Same, w/o grill		12		152
15¢	yel orng	D. Webster	Same, w/secret mark		12		163
15¢	red orng	D. Webster	Soft porous paper		12		189
15¢	indigo	H. Clay	w/o Triangles		12		227
15¢	dk blue	H. Clay	w/ Tri. in Top corners		12	NW	259
15¢	dk blue	H. Clay	w/ Tri. in Top corners		12	DL	274
15¢	olive grn	H. Clay	w/ Tri. in Top corners		12	DL	284
15¢	olive grn	H. Clay	"Series 1902"		12	DL	309
15¢	pl ultra	Washington			12	DL	340
15¢	pl ultra	Washington	Blue Paper		12	DL	366
15¢	pl ultra	Washington			12	SL	382
15¢	gray	B. Franklin			12	SL	418
15¢	gray	B. Franklin			10	SL	437
15¢	gray	B. Franklin			10	NW	475
15¢	gray	B. Franklin			11	NW	514
15¢	gray	Statue of Liberty		F	11		566
15¢	gray	Statue of Liberty		R	11x10.5		696
15¢	blue gray	J. Buchanan			11x10.5		820
15¢	rose lake	John Jay			11x10.5		1046*
15¢	maroon	O.W. Holmes			11x10.5		1288
15¢	dk rse clrt	O.W. Holmes	Type II		11x10.5		1288d
15¢	dk rse clrt	O.W. Holmes	Bklt. sgl./B.Pn. of 8		10		1288Bc
15¢	gray, dk bl & red	Ft McHenry Flag			11		1597
15¢		Ft McHenry Flag	Bklt. sgl./B. Pn. of 8		11x10.5		1598a
15¢		Ft McHenry Flag	Coil		10 Vert		1618C
15¢	multi	Roses	Bklt. sgl./B. Pn. of 8		10		1737a
15¢	sepia (yel)	Windmills	Bklt. Pn. of 10		11		1742a
15¢	rd brn & sepia	Dolley Madison			11		1822
15¢	claret	Buffalo Bill Cody			11		2178
15¢	violet	Tugboat	Coil		10 Vert		2260
15¢	multi	Beach Umbrella	Bklt. sgl./B. Pn. of 10		11.5x11		2443a
16¢	**black**	**A. Lincoln**			**11x10.5**		**821**
16¢	brown	Ernie Pyle			11x10.5		1398
16¢	blue	Statue of Liberty			11x10.5		1599
16¢	blue	Statue of Liberty	Coil		10 Vert		1619
16.7¢	rose	Popcorn Wagon	Coil		10 Vert		2261
17¢	**black**	**W. Wilson**		**F**	**11**		**623**
17¢	black	W. Wilson		R	10.5x11		697
17¢	rose red	A. Johnson			11x10.5		822
17¢	green	Rachel Carson			10.5x11		1857
17¢	ultra	Electric Auto	Coil		10 Vert		1906
17¢	sky blue	Dog Sled	Coil		10 Vert		2135
17¢	dk bl grn	Belva Ann Lockwood			11		2179
17.5¢	dk violet	Racing Car	Coil		10 Vert		2262
18¢	**brn carm**	**U.S. Grant**			**11x10.5**		**823**
18¢	violet	Dr. Elizabeth Blackwell			11x10.5		1399
18¢	dark bl	George Mason			10.5x11		1858
18¢	dark brn	Wildlife Animals	Bklt. Pn. of 10		11		1889a
18¢	multi	Flag/Amber Waves...			11		1890
18¢	multi	Flag/Sea to...Sea	Coil		10 Vert		1891
18¢	multi	Flag/Purple Mtns...	Bklt. Single		11		1893
18¢	multi	Flag/Purple Mnts...	Bklt. Pn. of 8 (7 #1893 (18¢) + 1 #1892 (6¢))		11		1893a
18¢	dk brn	Surrey	Coil		10 Vert		1907
18¢	multi	Washington & Monument	Coil		10 Vert		2149
19¢	**brt violet**	**R.B. Hayes**			**11x10.5**		**824**
19¢	brown	Sequoyah			10.5x11		1859
19¢	multi	Fawn			11.5x11		2487
19¢	multi	Fishing Boat	Coil Type I		10 Vert		2529
19¢	multi	Fishing Boat	Coil Type III		9.8 Vert		2529C
19¢	multi	Balloon	Bklt. sgl./B. Pn. of 10		10		2530,a
20¢	**ultra**	**B. Franklin**			**12**	**SL**	**419**
20¢	ultra	B. Franklin			10	SL	438
20¢	lt. ultra	B. Franklin			10	NW	476
20¢	lt. ultra	B. Franklin			11	NW	515
20¢	carm rse	Golden Rose		F	11		567
20¢	carm rse	Golden Gate		R	10.5x11		698
20¢	brt bl grn	J. Garfield			11x10.5		825
20¢	ultra	Monticello			10.5x11		1047
20¢	dp olive	George C. Marshall			11x10.5		1289*
20¢	claret	Ralph Bunche			10.5x11		1860
20¢	green	Thomas H. Gallaudet			10.5x11		1861
20¢	black	Harry S. Truman			11		1862
20¢	blk, dk bl & red	Flag/Supreme Court			11		1894
20¢		Flag/Sup. Ct.	Coil		10 Vert		1895
20¢		Flag/Sup. Ct.	Bklt. sgl./Pns. of 6 & 10		11x10.5		1896,a,b
20¢	vermilion	Fire Pumper	Coil		10 Vert		1908
20¢	dk blue	Rocky Mtn. Bighorn	Bklt. sgl./Pn. of 10		11		1949a
20¢	sky blue	Consumer Ed.	Coil		10 Vert		2005
20¢	bl violet	Cable Car	Coil		10 Vert		2263
20¢	red brown	Virginia Agpar			11.1x11		2179B
20.5¢	rose	Fire Engine	Coil		10 Vert		2264
21¢	**dull blue**	**Chester A. Arthur**			**11x10.5**		**826**
21¢	green	Amadeo Giannini			11x10.5		1400
21¢	bl violet	Chester Carlson			11		2180
21¢	olive grn	RR Mail Car	Coil		10 Vert		2265
21.1¢	multi	Envelopes	Coil		10 Vert		2150
22¢	**vermilion**	**G. Cleveland**			**11x10.5**		**827**
22¢	dk chlky bl	John J. Audubon			11		1863
22¢	bl rd blk	Flag/Capitol			11		2114
22¢	bl rd blk	Flag/Capitol	Coil		10 Vert		2115
22¢	bl rd blk	Flag/Capitol/"of the People"	Bklt. Sgl.		10 Hz		2116
22¢	bl rd blk	Flag/Capitol/"of the People"	B. Pn. of 5		10 Hz		2116a
22¢	blk & brn	Seashells	Bklt. Pn. of 10		10		2121a
22¢	multi	Fish	Bklt. Pn. of 5		10 Hz		2209a
22¢	multi	Flag & Fireworks			11		2276
22¢	multi	Flag & Fireworks	Bklt. Pn. of 20		11		2276a
23¢	**purple**	**Mary Cassatt**			**11**		**2182**
23¢	dk blue	Lunch Wagon	Coil		10 Vert		2464
23¢	multi	Flag & Presorted First Class	Coil		10 Vert		2605
23¢	multi	USA & Flag Presort First Cl	Coil		10 Vert	ABNC	2606
23¢	multi	USA & Flag Presort First Cl	Coil		10 Vert	BEP	2607
23¢	multi	USA & Flag Presort First Cl	Coil		10 Vert	SVS	2608
24¢	**gray lilac**	**Washington**	**"Twenty Four Cents"**		**15**		**37**
24¢	red lilac	Washington	"24 Cents"		12		70
24¢	brn lilac	Washington			12		70a
24¢	steel blue	Washington			12		70b
24¢	violet	Washington			12		70c
24¢	grayish lil	Washington			12		70d
24¢	lilac	Washington			12		78
24¢	grayish lil	Washington			12		78a
24¢	gray	Washington			12		78b
24¢	blkish viol	Washington			12		78c
24¢	gray lilac	Washington	"F" Grill		12		99
24¢	grn & viol	Decl. of Indep.	"G grill"		12		120
24¢	grn & viol	Decl. of Indep.	w/o grill, original gum		12		120a
24¢	purple	Gen'l. W. Scott	Hard wh paper, w/grill		12		142
24¢	purple	Gen'l. W. Scott	Same, w/o grill		12		153
24¢	gray blk	B. Harrison			11x10.5		828
24¢	red (blue)	Old North Church			11x10.5		1603
24.1¢	dp ultra	Tandem Bicycle	Coil		10 Vert		2266
25¢	**yel grn**	**Niagara Falls**		**F**	**11**		**568**
25¢	blue grn	Niagara Falls		R	10.5x11		699
25¢	dp rd lil	Wm. McKinley			11x10.5		829
25¢	green	Paul Revere			11x10.5		1048
25¢	green	Paul Revere	Coil		10 Vert		1059A*
25¢	rose	Frederick Douglass			11x10.5		1290*
25¢	orng brn	Bread Wagon	Coil		10 Vert		2136
25¢	blue	Jack London			11		2183
25¢	blue	Jack London	Bklt. Pn. of 10		11		2183a
25¢	blue	Jack London	Bklt. Sgl./B. Pn. of 6		10		2197,a
25¢	multi	Flag & Clouds			11		2278
25¢	multi	Flag & Clouds	Bklt. Sgl./B. Pn. of 6		10		2285Ac
25¢	multi	Flag/Yosemite	Coil		10 Vert		2280

DEFINITIVE ISSUE IDENTIFIER

Den.	Color	Subject	Type / Comment	Press	Perf.	Wmk.	Scott #
25¢	multi	Honeybee	Coil		10 Vert		2281
25¢	multi	Pheasant	Bklt. Sgl./B. Pn. of 10		11		2283,a
25¢	multi	Pheasant	Same, w/o red in sky		11		2283b,c
25¢	multi	Grossbeak	Bklt. Single		10		2284
25¢	multi	Owl	Bklt. Single		10		2285
25¢	multi	Grossbk & Owl	Bklt. Pn. of 10 (5 ea.)		10		2285b
25¢	multi	Eagle & Shield	Self-adhesive		Die cut		2431
25¢	dk rd & bl	Flag	Self-adhesive		Die cut		2475
28¢	**brn (bl)**	**Ft. Nisqually**			**11x10.5**		**1604**
28¢	myrtle grn	Sitting Bull			11		2184
29¢	**blue (bl)**	**Sandy Hook Lighthouse**			**11x10.5**		**1605**
29¢	blue	Earl Warren			11		2184A
29¢	dk violet	T. Jefferson			11		2184B
29¢	multi	Red Squirrel	Self-adhesive		Die cut		2478
29¢	multi	Rose	Self-adhesive		Die cut		2479
29¢	multi	Pine Cone	Self-adhesive		Die cut		2480
29¢	blk & multi	Wood Duck	Bklt. sgl./B. Pn. of 10		10		2493,a
29¢	red & multi	Wood Duck	Bklt. sgl./B. Pn. of 10		11		2493B,c
29¢	multi	African Violet	Bklt. sgl./B. Pn. of 10		10x11		2495,95a
29¢	bl,rd,clar	Flag/Rushmore	Coil, Engraved		10		2523
29¢	bl,rd,brn	Flag/Rushmore	Coil, Gravure		10		2523A
29¢	multi	Tulip			11		2524
29¢	multi	Tulip			12.5x13		2524a
29¢	multi	Tulip	Coil	Roulette	10 Vert		2525
29¢	multi	Tulip	Coil		10 Vert		2526
29¢	multi	Tulip	Bklt. sgl./B. Pn. of 10		11		2527,a
29¢	multi	Flag/Rings	Bklt. sgl./B. Pn. of 10		11		2528
29¢	multi	Flags on Parade			11		2531
29¢	blk,gld,grn	Liberty/Torch	Self-adhesive		Die cut		2531A
29¢	multi	Flag & Pledge	blk. denom Bklt. sgl., Bklt. Pn. of 10		10		2593,a
29¢	multi	Flag & Pledge	red denom., Bklt. sgl., Bklt. Pn. of 10		10		2594,a
29¢	brn,multi	Eagle & Shield	Self-adhesive		Die cut		2595
29¢	grn,multi	Eagle & Shield	Self-adhesive		Die cut		2596
29¢	red,multi	Eagle & Shield	Self-adhesive		Die cut		2597
29¢	multi	Eagle	Self-adhesive		Die cut		2598
29¢	blue,red	Flag/White House	Coil		10 Vert		2609
29¢	multi	Liberty	Self-adhesive		Die cut		2599
30¢	**orange**	**B. Franklin**	**Numeral at bottom**		**15**		**38**
30¢	orange	B. Franklin	Numerals at Top		12		71
30¢	orange	B. Franklin	"A" Grill		12		81
30¢	orange	B. Franklin	"F" Grill		12		100
30¢	bl & carm	Eagle, Shield & Flags, "G" Grill			12		121
			w/o grill, original gum		12		121a
30¢	black	A. Hamilton	Hard wh paper, w/grill		12		143
30¢	black	A. Hamilton	Same, w/o grill		12		154
30¢	gray blk	A. Hamilton	Same		12		165
30¢	full blk./grnish blk	A. Hamilton	Soft porous paper		12		190
30¢	orng brn	A. Hamilton			12		217
30¢	black	T. Jefferson			12		228
30¢	orng red	B. Franklin			12	SL	420
30¢	orng red	B. Franklin			10	SL	439
30¢	orng red	B. Franklin			10	NW	476A
30¢	orng red	B. Franklin			11	NW	516
30¢	olive brn	Buffalo		F	11		569
30¢	brown	Buffalo		R	10.5x11		700
30¢	dp ultra	T. Roosevelt			11x10.5		830
30¢	blue	T. Roosevelt			11x10.5		830 var
30¢	dp blue	T. Roosevelt			11x10.5		830 var
30¢	black	R.E. Lee			11x10.5		1049
30¢	red lilac	John Dewey			10.5x11		1291*
30¢	green	Morris School			11x10.5		1606
30¢	olv gray	Frank C. Laubach			11		1864
30¢	multi	Cardinal			11		2189
35¢	**gray**	**Charles R. Drew M.D.**			**10.5x11**		**1865**
35¢	black	Dennis Chavez			11		2185
37¢	**blue**	**Robert Millikan**			**10.5x11**		**1866**
39¢	**rose lilac**	**Grenville Clark**			**11**		**1867**
40¢	**brn red**	**J. Marshall**			**11x10.5**		**1050**
40¢	bl black	Thomas Paine			11x10.5		1292*
40¢	dk grn	Lillian M. Gilbreth			11		1868
40¢	dk blue	Claire Chennault			11		2186
45¢	**brt blue**	**Harvey Cushing, MD**			**11**		**2188**
45¢	multi	Pumpkinseed Fish			11		2491
50¢	**orange**	**T. Jefferson**	**w/ Tri. in Top corners**		**12**	**NW**	**260**
50¢	orange	T. Jefferson	w/ Tri. in Top corners		12	DL	275
50¢	orange	T. Jefferson	"Series 1902"		12	DL	310
50¢	violet	Washington			12	DL	341
50¢	violet	B. Franklin			12	SL	421
50¢	violet	B. Franklin			12	DL	422
50¢	violet	B. Franklin			10	SL	440
50¢	lt violet	B. Franklin			10	NW	477
50¢	rd violet	B. Franklin			11	NW	517
50¢	lilac	Arlington Amph		F	11		570
50¢	lilac	Arlington Amph		R	10.5x11		701
50¢	lt rd viol	W.H. Taft			11x10.5		831
50¢	brt prpl	S.B. Anthony			11x10.5		1051
50¢	rose mag	Lucy Stone			11x10.5		1293*
50¢	blk & orng	Iron "Betty" Lamp			11		1608
50¢	brown	Chester W. Nimitz			11		1869
52¢	**purple**	**Hubert Humphrey**			**11**		**2190**
56¢	**scarlet**	**John Harvard**			**11**		**2191**
65¢	**dk blue**	**"Hap" Arnold**			**11**		**2192**
75¢	dp mag	Wendell Wilkie			11		2193
90¢	**blue**	**Washington**	**"Ninety Cents"**		**15**		**39**
90¢	blue	Washington	"90 Cents"		12		72
90¢	blue	Washington	Same, "F" Grill		12		101

Den.	Color	Subject	Type / Comment	Press	Perf.	Wmk.	Scott #
90¢	carm & blk	A. Lincoln	"G grill"		12		122
90¢	carm & blk	A. Lincoln	w/o grill, o.g.		12		122a
90¢	carmine	Com. Perry	Hard wh paper, w/grill		12		144
90¢	carmine	Com. Perry	Same, w/o grill		12		155
90¢	rose carm	Com. Perry	Same		12		166
90¢	carmine	Com. Perry	Soft porous paper		12		191
90¢	purple	Com. Perry	Soft porous paper		12		218
90¢	orange	Com. Perry			12		229
$1.00	**black**	**Com. Perry**	**Ty I**		**12**	**NW**	**261**
$1.00	black	Com. Perry	Ty I		12	DL	276
$1.00	black	Com. Perry	Ty II		12	NW	261A
$1.00	black	Com. Perry	Ty II		12	DL	276A
$1.00	black	D.G. Farragut			12	DL	311
$1.00	violet brn	Washington			12	DL	342
$1.00	violet brn	B. Franklin			12	DL	423
$1.00	violet blk	B. Franklin			10	DL	460
$1.00	violet blk	B. Franklin			10	NW	478
$1.00	violet brn	B. Franklin			11	NW	518
$1.00	deep brn	B. Franklin			11	NW	518b
$1.00	violet blk	Lincoln Memorial			11		571
$1.00	prpl & blk	W. Wilson			11		832
$1.00	prpl & blk	W. Wilson			11	USIR	832b
$1.00	rd viol & blk	W. Wilson	Dry Print, smooth gum		11		832c
$1.00	purple	P. Henry			11x10.5		1052
$1.00	dl purple	Eugene O'Neill			11x10.5		1294*
$1.00	dl purple	Eugene O'Neill	Coil		10 Vert		1305
$1.00	brn,orng&yel (tan)	Rush Lamp & Candle Holder			11		1610
$1.00	dk prus grn	Bernard Revel			11		2194
$1.00	dk blue	Johns Hopkins			11		2194A
$1.00	bl & scar	Seaplane	Coil		10 Vert		2468
$1.00	gold,multi	Eagle & Olympic Rings			11		2539
$1.00	blue	Burgoyne			11.5		2590
$2.00	**brt blue**	**J. Madison**	**w/ Tri. in Top corners**		**12**	**NW**	**262**
$2.00	brt blue	J. Madison	w/ Tri. in Top corners		12	DL	277
$2.00	dk blue	J. Madison	"Series 1902"		12	DL	312
$2.00	dk blue	J. Madison	"Series 1902"		10	NW	479
$2.00	orng rd & blk	B. Franklin			11		523
$2.00	carm & blk	B. Franklin			11		547
$2.00	dp blue	U.S. Capitol			11		572
$2.00	yel grn&blk	W.G. Harding			11		833
$2.00	dk grn&rd (tan)	Kerosene Table Lamp			11		1611
$2.00	brt viol	William Jennings Bryan			11		2195
$2.00	multi	Bobcat			11		2476
$2.90	multi	Eagle			11		2540
$2.90	multi	Space Shuttle	Self-adhesive		11x10½		2543
$5.00	**dk green**	**J. Marshall**	**w/ Tri. in Top corners**		**12**	**NW**	**263**
$5.00	dk green	J. Marshall	w/ Tri. in Top corners		12	DL	278
$5.00	dk green	J. Marshall	"Series 1902"		12	DL	313
$5.00	lt green	J. Marshall	"Series 1902"		10	NW	480
$5.00	dp grn & blk	B. Franklin			11		524
$5.00	carm & bl	Freedom Statue/Capitol			11		573
$5.00	carm & blk	C. Coolidge			11		834
$5.00	rd brn & blk	C. Coolidge			11		834a
$5.00	black	A. Hamilton			11		1053
$5.00	gray blk	John Bassett Moore			11x10.5		1295*
$5.00	rd brn,yel&orng (tan)	RR Conductors Lantern			11		1612
$5.00	copper rd	Bret Harte			11		2196
$5.00	slate grn	Washington & Jackson			11.5		2592
$8.75	**multi**	**Eagle & Moon**			**11**		**2394**
$9.35	multi	Eagle & Moon	Bklt. sgl./B. Pn. of 3		10 Vert		1909,a
$9.95	**multi**	**Eagle**			**11**		**2541**
$10.75	multi	Eagle & Moon	Bklt. sgl./B. Pn. of 3		10 Vert		2122,a
$14.00	**multi**	**Spread winged Eagle**			**11**		**2542**
* (4¢)	gold,carm	Text only	Make-up rate		11		2521
A (15¢)	**orange**	**Eagle**			**11**		**1735**
A	orange	Eagle	Bklt. Sgl./Pn. of 8		11x10.5		1736,a
A	orange	Eagle	Coil		10 Vert		1743
B (18¢)	**violet**	**Eagle**			**11x10.5**		**1818**
B	violet	Eagle	Bklt. sgl./Pn of 8		10		1819,a
B	violet	Eagle	Coil		10 Vert		1820
C (20¢)	**brown**	**Eagle**			**11x10.5**		**1946**
C	brown	Eagle	Coil		10 Vert		1947
C	brown	Eagle	Bklt. sgl./Pn. of 10		11x10.5		1948,a
D (22¢)	**green**	**Eagle**			**11**		**2111**
D	green	Eagle	Coil		10 Vert		2112
D	green	Eagle	Bklt. sgl./Pn. of 10		11		2113,a
E (25¢)	**multi**	**Earth**			**11**		**2277**
E	multi	Earth	Coil		10 Vert		2279
E	multi	Earth	Bklt. sgl./Pn. of 10		10		2282a
F (29¢)	**multi**	**Tulip**			**13**		**2517**
F	multi	Tulip	Coil		10		2518
F	multi	Tulip	Bklt. Stamp	BEP	11 bullseye		2519
F	multi	Tulip	Bkt. Stamp	KCS	11		2520
F	blk,dk bl,red	Flag	Self-adhesive		Die cut		2522
G (20¢)	**multi**	**FlagBlack "G"**		**BEP**	**11.2x11.1**		**2879**
G (20¢)	multi	Flag Red "G"		SVS	11x10.9		2880
G (25¢)	multi	Flag, Black "G"	Coil	SVS	9.8 vert.		2888
G (32¢)	multi	Flag, Black "G"		BEP	11.2x11.1		2881
G (32¢)	multi	Flag, Red "G"		SVS	11x10.9		2882
G (32¢)	multi	Flag, Black "G"	Bklt. Stamp	BEP	10x9.9		2883
G (32¢)	multi	Flag, Blue "G"	Bklt. Stamp	ABN	10.9		2884
G (32¢)	multi	Flag, Red "G"	Bklt. Stamp	SVS	11x10.9		2885
G (32¢)	multi	Flag	Self-adhesive		Die cut		2886,87
G (32¢)	multi	Flag, Black "G"	Coil	BEP	9.8 vert.		2889
G (32¢)	multi	Flag, Blue "G"	Coil	ABN	9.8 vert.		2890
G (32¢)	multi	Flag, Red "G"	Coil	SVS	9.8 vert.		2891
G (32¢)	multi	Flag, Red "G"	Coil	Roulette	9.8 vert.		2892

SELECTED and ANNOTATED BIBLIOGRAPHY

The volumes listed below are recommended for the library of any collector who ishes to gain more knowledge in the areas covered by the *1996 Brookman*. While ie main emphasis is on stamps, many of these volumes contain good postal history formation. Check with your favorite dealer for availability and price. (To conserve pace, some bibliographic notations have been abbreviated).

19th & 20th Century

Cummings, William W., ed., *Scott 1995 Specialized Catalogue of U.S. Stamps*
This annual publication offers a treasure trove of information on virtually every area of the ostage and revenue stamps of the US, UN & US Possesstions. A "must have."

Sloane, George B., *Sloane's Column*, arr. by George Turner, 1961, (BIA 1980)
A subject by subject arrangement of Sloane's 1350 columns which appeared in "STAMPS" agazine from1932-1958 covering virtually every facet of U.S. philately.

White, Roy, *Encyclopedia of the Colors of U.S. Postage Stamps*, Vol 1-5, 1981, 86.
The first four volumes cover US stamps from 1847-1918 plus a few selected issues. olume five covers the US Postage Dues from1879-1916. They are the finest available orks for classifying the colors of U.S. postage stamps.

19th Century

General

Brookman, Lester G., *The United States Postage Stamps of the 19th Century*, 3 vol., 1966. (Reprinted in 1989 by D.G.Phillipps Co.)
This is the finest and most informative work on 19th Century issues. Each stamp, from the ¢ Franklin of 1847 thru the $2 Trans-Mississippi of 1898, is given separate, and often in-epth treatment. This is a must for any collector.

Luff, John N., *The Postage Stamps of the United States*, 1902.
While much of Luff's information has been superseded by Brookman, his treatment of ostmaster Provisionals and several Back-of-the-book sections make this a worthwhile olume. (The "Gossip Reprint", 1937, is more useful and recommended.)

Perry, Elliot, *Pat Paragraphs*, arr by George Turner & Thomas Stanton, BIA, 1981.
A subject by subject arrangement of Perry's 58 pamphlets which were published from 931-1958. The emphasis is on the 19th century classics as well as carriers & locals.

Baker, Hugh J. and J. David, *Bakers' U.S. Classics*, 1985
An annotated compilation of the Bakers' columns from "STAMPS" magazine which ppeared from 1962-1969. This major work provides extensive coverage of nearly all spects of U.S. and Confederate philately.

By Issue or Subject

Ashbrook, Stanley B., *The United States One Cent Stamp of 1851-57*, 2 vol, 1938.
Although most of stamp and plating information in Volume 1 has been superseded by Aortimer Neinken's great work, Vol. 2 features an indispensible amount of information on he postal history of the period.

Neinken, Mortimer L., *The United States One Cent Stamp of 1851 to 1861*, 1972.
United States, The 1851-57 Twelve Cent Stamp, 1964.
The One cent book supplements and updates, but does not replace, Ashbrook's study. The Twelve cent booklet deals almost exclusively with the plating of this issue. Both are undamental works.

Chase, Dr. Carroll, *The 3¢ Stamp of the U.S. 1851-57 Issue*, Rev. ed., 1942.
This outstanding work provides the most comprehensive information available in one lace on this popular issue. (The Quarterman reprint, 1975, contains a new forward, corrections, additions and a selected bibliography of articles.

Hill, Henry W., *The United States Five Cent Stamps of 1856-1861*, 1955.
This extensively illustrated volume is the only work dealing exclusively with this issue. It ncludes studies on stamps, plating, cancels, and postal history.

Neinken, Mortimer L., *The United States Ten Cent Stamps of 1855-1859*, 1960.
This work not only provides an indispensable amount of stamp and plating information, but t also reprints Chapters 50-53 from Ashbrook Vol. 2 dealing with California, Ocean and Western Mails.

Cole, Maurice F., *The Black Jacks of 1863-1867*, 1950.
A superb study of the issue with major emphasis on postal history.

Lane, Maryette B., *The Harry F. Allen Collection of Black Jacks, A Study of the Stamp and it's Use*, 1969
The title says it all. This book beautifully complements, but does not replace, Cole.

Ashbrook, Stanley B., *The U.S. Issues of 1869, Preceded by Some Additional Notes on "The premieres Gravures of 1861"*, 1943
This work concentrates on the design sources and production of the 1869 issue. Ashbrook concludes with his "Addendum" attacking Scott for listing the Premieres.

Willard, Edward L., *The U.S. Two Cent Red Brown of 1883-1887*, 2 vol., 1970.
Volume I deals with the background, production and varieties of the stamp. Vol. II deals exclusively with the cancellations found on the stamp. A good Banknote intro.

20th Century

General

King, Beverly S. and Johl, Max G. *The United States Postages Stamps of the Twentieth Century*, Vol. 1 revised, Vol. 2-4, 1934-38.
These volumes are still the standard work on 20th Century U.S. postage stamps from 1901 to 1937. (The 1976 Quarterman reprint contains only the regular issue, air mail and Parcel Post sections from the original volumes. It is highly recommended.

By Issue or Subject

Armstrong, Martin A., *Washington-Franklins, 1908-1921*, 2nd Edition, 1979.
Armstrong, Martin A., *US Definitive Series, 1922-1938*, 2nd Edition, 1980.
Armstrong, Martin A., *United States Coil Issues, 1906-38*, 1977
Each of these volumes not only supplements the information found in Johl, but expands each area to include studies of essays, proofs, booklet panes, private perfs, Offices in China and the Canal Zone. One major plus is the wealth of illustrations, many of rare and unusual items, which were not included in Johl's work due to laws restricting the publication of stamp pictures prior to 1938.

20th Century

By Issue or Subject (cont.)

Schoen, DeVoss & Harvey, *Counterfeit Kansas-Nebraska Overprints on 1922-34 Issue plus First Day Covers of the Kansas-Nebraska Overprints*, 1973.
A fine pamphlet covering K-N varieties, errors and First Day covers, plus important information pointing out the differences between genuine and fake overprints.

Datz, Stephen, *U.S. Errors: Inverts, Imperforates, Colors Omitted*, 1992 Ed., 1991.
This volume does a superb job covering the subjects listed in its title, It is extensively illustrated and provides price, quantity and historical information.

Air Mail & Back-of-the-Book

Amercian Air Mail Society, *American Air Mail Catalog, Fifth Ed.*, 5 vols + 1990 Pricing Supplement, 1974-1990.
Virtually everything there is to know about air mail stamps and postal history.

Arfken, George B., *Postage Due, The United States Large Numeral Postage Due Stamps, 1879-1894*, 1991.
A Comprehensive study of virtually every aspect of these interesting stamps. Additionally, about half the book is devoted to their extensive usage which helps to clarify some of the more complex markings and routings found on "Due" covers.

Gobie, Henry M. *The Speedy, A History of the U.S. Special Delivery Service*, 1976
Gobie, Henry M., *U.S. Parcel Post, A Postal History*, 1979.
Each of these volumes includes information on the stamps, but their main thrust is on the postal history of the respective services. Official documents and Postal Laws & Regulations have been extensively reproduced and numerous covers illustrating the various aspects of the services are pictured.

Markovits, Robert L., *United States, The 10¢ Registry Stamp of 1911*, 1973.
This pamphlet provides a superb blueprint for the formation of specialized collection around a single stamp. It is extensively illustrated and concludes with an extensive bibliography which touches upon a multitude of additional subjects.

McGovern, Edmund C., ed, *Catalog of the 19th Century Stamped Envelopes and Wrappers of the United States*, USPSS 1984

Haller, Austin P., ed., *Catalog of the 20th Century Stamped Envelopes and Wrappers of the United States*, USPSS 1990

Beachboard, John H., ed., *United States Postal Card Catalog*, USPSS 1990
Each of the three previous volumes contains the finest available information in their respective fields. They are indispensable to the postal stationery collector.

First Day Covers & Related Collectibles

Planty, Dr. Earl & Mellone, Michael, *Planty's Photo Encyclopedia of Cacheted FDCs*, 1923-1939, Vol. 1-10, 1976-1984

Mellone, Mike, *Specialized Catalog of First Day Covers of the 1940's (2nd ed.), 1950's and 1960's*, 2 vol., 2 vol., 3 vol. respectively, 1983-1985.

Pelcyger, Dr. Scott, *Mellone's Specialized Catalog of First Day Ceremony Programs & Events*, 1989
Each of these volumes illustrates virtually every known cachet and ceremony program for the stamps listed within. They each provide an invaluable resource.

Radford, Dr. Curtis D., *The Souvenir Card Collectors Society Numbering System for Forerunner and Modern Day Souvenir Card*, 1989.
The most informative work on this popular collecting area.

Revenues

Toppan, Deats and Holland, *'An Historical Reference List of the Revenue Stamps of the United States...'*, 1899.
The information in this volume, while almost 100 years old, still provides the collector with much of the basic knowledge available today on US Revenues and "Match and Medicines" from 1862-1898. (The "Gossip" reprint is recommended.)

Confederate States

Dietz, August, *The Postal Service of the Confederate States of America*, 1929
This monumental work has been the "Bible" for Confederate collectors. Covering virtually every aspect of Confederate philately, its content remains useful, even after 60+ years. (A 1989 reprint makes this work more affordable for the average collector.)

Skinner, Gunter and Sanders, *The New Dietz Confederate States Catalog and Handbook*, 1986.
This volume makes an effort to cover every phase of Confederate philately and postal history. Despite the presence of some flaws, it is highly recommended.

Possessions

Plass, Brewster and Salz, *Canal Zone Stamps*, 1986.
Published by the Canal Zone Study Group, this outstanding well written and extensively illustrated volume, is now the "bible" for these fascinating issues.

Meyer, Harris, et. at, *Hawaii, Its Stamps and Postal History*, 1948.
After 45 years, this volume, which deals with virtually every facet of Hawaiian stamps and postal history, remains the finest work written on the subject.

Palmer, Maj. F.L., *The Postal Issues of the Philippines*, 1912
An ancient, but still useful study, with interesting information on the U.S. overprints.

British North America

Boggs, Winthrop S., *The Postage Stamps and Postal History of Canada*, 2 vol., 1945. (Quarterman reprint, One vol., 1975)
For almost 50 years the standard work on Canadian stamps and postal history. One of the "must have" books. (The reprint omits most of the Vol. 2 appendices.)

Lowe, Robson, *The Encyclopedia of British Empire Postage Stamps, Vol. 5, North America*, 1973
This work continues the fine tradition of Robson Lowe's earlier volumes dealing with the British Empire. Covering all of BNA, it is an essential tool for the collector.

SCOTT CATALOG NUMBERS ARE USED WITH THE EXPRESS PERMISSION OF SCOTT PUBLISHING CO.

PLEASE READ INFORMATION ABOUT CONDITION ON PAGES II AND IV

1847 General Issue, Imperforate VF + 50% (C)

1,3,948a 2,4,948b

Scott's No.		Unused Fine	Unused Ave.	Used Fine	Used Ave.
1	5¢ Franklin, Red Brown	...	2250.00	525.00	350.00
1	5¢ Red Brown, Pen Cancel	...	...	250.00	175.00
2	10¢ Washington, Black	...	9000.00	1250.00	750.00
2	10¢ Black, Pen Cancel	...	...	600.00	425.00
3	5¢ Red Brown, 1875 Repro	825.00	600.00	...	...
4	10¢ Black, 1875 Reproduction	1000.00	750.00	...	...

NOTE: SEE #948 FOR 5¢ BLUE AND 10¢ BROWN ORANGE.

1851-1856 Issue, Imperf "U.S. Postage" at Top (VF+50% OG+50%) (C)

5A-9 10-11 12 13-16 17

Scott's No.		Unused Fine	Unused Ave.	Used Fine	Used Ave.
5A	1¢ Franklin, Blue, Type Ib	...	...	3500.00	2000.00
6	1¢ Blue, Type Ia	...		5500.00	3250.00
7	1¢ Blue, Type II	500.00	300.00	95.00	55.00
8	1¢ Blue, Type III	...	...	1400.00	850.00
8A	1¢ Blue, Type IIIa	2150.00	1200.00	575.00	350.00
9	1¢ Blue, Type IV	350.00	210.00	82.50	50.00
10	3¢ Wash., Orange Brown, Ty. I	995.00	625.00	40.00	25.00
11	3¢ Dull Red, Type I	110.00	65.00	6.50	4.00
12	5¢ Jefferson, Red Brown, Ty. I	...	...	925.00	550.00
13	10¢ Wash., Green, Type I	...	...	595.00	350.00
14	10¢ Green, Type II	1650.00	975.00	210.00	150.00
15	10¢ Green, Type III	1650.00	975.00	210.00	150.00
16	10¢ Green, Type IV	...	...	1175.00	695.00
17	12¢ Washington, Black	...	1200.00	225.00	135.00

1857-61 Same Design as Above but Perf. 15 (VF+150% OG+50%) (C)

18-24 25-26 37 38 39

Scott's No.		Unused Fine	Unused Ave.	Used Fine	Used Ave.
18	1¢ Franklin, Blue, Type I	700.00	425.00	335.00	190.00
19	1¢ Blue, Type Ia	...	...	...	1450.00
20	1¢ Blue, Type II	450.00	250.00	135.00	80.00
21	1¢ Blue, Type III (Plate 4)	...	2150.00	1125.00	625.00
22	1¢ Blue, Type IIIa	750.00	450.00	260.00	150.00
23	1¢ Blue, Type IV	2500.00	1500.00	295.00	165.00
24	1¢ Blue, Type V	100.00	55.00	22.50	13.50
25	3¢ Washington, Rose, Type I	875.00	500.00	28.00	16.00
26	3¢ Dull Red, Type II	40.00	21.50	3.00	1.75
27	5¢ Jefferson, Brick Red, Type I	...	4250.00	700.00	450.00
28	5¢ Red Brown, Type I	1175.00	700.00	250.00	140.00
28A	5¢ Indian Red, Type I	...	...	1650.00	1050.00
29	5¢ Brown, Type I	825.00	450.00	175.00	100.00
30	5¢ Orange Brown, Type II	675.00	360.00	850.00	450.00
30A	5¢ Brown, Type II	475.00	250.00	160.00	95.00
31	10¢ Wash., Green, Type I	...	3500.00	450.00	260.00
32	10¢ Green, Type II	2275.00	1300.00	160.00	95.00
33	10¢ Green, Type III	2275.00	1300.00	160.00	95.00
34	10¢ Green, Type IV	...	...	1475.00	795.00
35	10¢ Green, Type V	165.00	85.00	47.50	30.00
36	12¢ Wash., Black, Plate I	365.00	190.00	90.00	53.50
36b	12¢ Black, Plate III	300.00	160.00	95.00	60.00
37	24¢ Washington, Gray Lilac	575.00	315.00	190.00	110.00
38	30¢ Franklin, Orange	750.00	435.00	250.00	140.00
39	90¢ Washington, Blue	1050.00	650.00	...	...

NOTE: #5A THROUGH 38 WITH PEN CANCELS USUALLY SELL FOR 50-60% OF LISTED USED PRICES. USED EXAMPLES OF #39 SHOULD ONLY BE PURCHASED WITH, OR SUBJECT TO, A CERTIFICATE OF AUTHENTICITY.

IMPORTANT NOTICE

PRIOR TO 1882 `UNUSED' PRICES ARE FOR STAMPS THAT MAY HAVE NO GUM OR PART GUM. FOR ORIGINAL GUM ADD % INDICATED !

1861 New Designs, Perforated 12, Thin Paper (VF+75% OG+50%) (C)

Scott's No.		Unused Fine	Unused Ave.	Used Fine	Used Ave.
62B	10¢ Wash., Dark Green	...	...	450.00	250.00

1861-62 Modified Designs, Perforated 12 (VF+125% OG+50%) (C)

63 73 65 67,75-76 68

69 77 70,78 71 72

Scott's No.		Unused Fine	Unused Ave.	Used Fine	Used Ave.
63	1¢ Franklin, Blue	120.00	70.00	16.50	10.00
64	3¢ Washington, Pink	...	1850.00	295.00	175.00
64b	3¢ Rose Pink	250.00	145.00	80.00	45.00
65	3¢ Rose	72.50	39.50	1.50	.85
67	5¢ Jefferson, Buff	...	3750.00	350.00	195.00
68	10¢ Wash., Yellow Green	275.00	150.00	26.00	15.00
69	12¢ Washington, Black	465.00	265.00	47.50	26.50
70	24¢ Wash., Red Lilac	700.00	395.00	70.00	39.50
70b	24¢ Steel Blue	...	3000.00	250.00	130.00
70c	24¢ Violet, Thin Paper	...	2750.00	475.00	265.00
71	30¢ Franklin, Orange	550.00	290.00	65.00	36.50
72	90¢ Washington, Blue	1195.00	625.00	225.00	125.00

1861-66 New Vals. or Designs, Perforated 12 (VF+125% OG+50%) (C)

Scott's No.		Unused Fine	Unused Ave.	Used Fine	Used Ave.
73	2¢ Jackson, Black	150.00	75.00	25.00	12.50
75	5¢ Jefferson, Red Brn.	1875.00	1050.00	200.00	115.00
76	5¢ Brown	425.00	250.00	57.50	33.50
77	15¢ Lincoln, Black	575.00	325.00	57.50	33.50
78	24¢ Washington, Lilac/Gray Lilac	325.00	180.00	43.50	25.00

1867 Designs of 1861-66 with Grills of Var. Sizes (VF+150% OG+50%)

Grills consist of small pyramids impressed on the stamp and are classified by area, shape of points and number of rows of points. On Grilled-All-Over and "C" Grills, points thrust upward on FACE of stamp; on all other grills points thrust upward on BACK of stamp. Points of "Z" grill show horizontal ridges (-); other grills from "D" through "I" show vertical (I) ridges or come to a point. It is important to see a Scott catalog for details of these interesting stamps.

Scott's No.		Unused Fine	Unused Ave.	Used Fine	Used Ave.
	1867 "A" Grill (Grill All Over)				
79	3¢ Washington, Rose	...	1100.00	475.00	265.00
	1867 "C" Grill 13 x 16mm Points Up				
83	3¢ Washington, Rose	3250.00	1500.00	475.00	265.00
	1867 "D" Grill 12 x 14mm Points Down				
84	2¢ Jackson, Black	...	5500.00	1250.00	725.00
85	3¢ Washington, Rose	2750.00	1550.00	385.00	225.00
	1867 "Z" Grill 11 x 14mm				
85B	2¢ Jackson, Black	2600.00	1575.00	340.00	175.00
85C	3¢ Washington, Rose	...	2100.00	950.00	550.00
85E	12¢ Washington, Black	3250.00	1850.00	485.00	275.00
	1867 "E" Grill 11 x 13mm				
86	1¢ Franklin, Blue	900.00	515.00	240.00	140.00
87	2¢ Jackson, Black	425.00	240.00	60.00	32.50
88	3¢ Washington, Rose	300.00	165.00	9.50	5.25
89	10¢ Washington, Green	1595.00	925.00	175.00	100.00
90	12¢ Washington, Black	1800.00	1050.00	175.00	100.00
91	15¢ Lincoln, Black	3950.00	2100.00	395.00	225.00
	1867 "F" Grill 9 x 13mm				
92	1¢ Franklin, Blue	425.00	260.00	90.00	50.00
93	2¢ Jackson, Black	175.00	95.00	25.00	12.50
94	3¢ Washington, Red	140.00	80.00	3.50	1.95
95	5¢ Jefferson, Brown	1200.00	650.00	225.00	135.00
96	10¢ Wash., Yellow Green	975.00	525.00	95.00	55.00
97	12¢ Washington, Black	1175.00	650.00	100.00	60.00
98	15¢ Lincoln, Black	1175.00	650.00	150.00	85.00
99	24¢ Washington, Gray Lilac	1600.00	875.00	415.00	235.00
100	30¢ Franklin, Orange	2300.00	1275.00	325.00	175.00
101	90¢ Washington, Blue	4000.00	2250.00	835.00	475.00

1869 Pictorial Issues - "G" Grill 9½ mm. (VF+125% OG+40%) (C)

112,123,133 113,124 114 115 116

117 119 120 121 122

Scott's No.		Unused Fine	Unused Ave.	Used Fine	Used Ave.
12	1¢ Franklin, Buff	225.00	125.00	55.00	31.50
13	2¢ Horse & Rider, Brown	180.00	110.00	22.50	12.50
14	3¢ Locomotive, Ultramarine	150.00	85.00	6.25	3.50
15	6¢ Washington, Ultramarine	825.00	475.00	85.00	50.00
16	10¢ Shield & Eagle, Yellow	875.00	495.00	85.00	50.00
17	12¢ "S.S. Adriatic", Green	775.00	425.00	85.00	50.00
18	15¢ Columbus, Brn & Blue,Ty.I	2250.00	1300.00	325.00	195.00
19	15¢ Brown & Blue, Type II	900.00	525.00	135.00	75.00
20	24¢ Decl. of Indep., Grn & Vio	2800.00	1600.00	425.00	240.00
21	30¢ Shield, Eagle & Flags	2350.00	1350.00	250.00	145.00
22	90¢ Lincoln, Carm. & Black	4500.00	2500.00	1000.00	650.00

1875 and 1880 Re-issues, without Grill (VF+125% OG+30%) (C)

Scott's No.		Unused Fine	Unused Ave.	Used Fine	Used Ave.
23	1¢ Buff, Hard White Paper	290.00	165.00	200.00	115.00
24	2¢ Brown, Hard White Paper	325.00	175.00	295.00	165.00
33	1¢ Buff, Soft Porous Paper (1880)	175.00	100.00	140.00	77.50
33a	1¢ Brown Orange, w/o gum	160.00	110.00	125.00	70.00

1870-71 Nat'l Print-Grilled-Hard Paper (VF+150% OG+40%) (C)

134/206 135/183 136/214 179,185 137/208

138,149,160 139/209 141/189 143/217 144/218

Scott's No.		Unused Fine	Unused Ave.	Used Fine	Used Ave.
134	1¢ Franklin, Ultramarine	695.00	425.00	50.00	27.50
135	2¢ Jackson, Red Brown	425.00	225.00	30.00	17.50
136	3¢ Washington, Green	325.00	180.00	9.00	5.00
137	6¢ Lincoln, Carmine	1650.00	900.00	245.00	150.00
138	7¢ Stanton, Vermilion	1200.00	700.00	225.00	135.00
139	10¢ Jefferson, Brown	1500.00	850.00	375.00	225.00
140	12¢ Clay, Dull Violet		...	...	1100.00
141	15¢ Webster, Orange		1500.00	650.00	375.00
143	30¢ Hamilton, Black		3000.00	775.00	450.00
144	90¢ Perry, Carmine		4000.00	650.00	360.00

1870-71 Same as above but Without Grill (VF + 150% OG + 40%) (C)

Scott's No.		Unused Fine	Unused Ave.	Used Fine	Used Ave.
145	1¢ Franklin, Ultramarine	165.00	95.00	7.00	4.00
146	2¢ Jackson, Red Brown	95.00	52.50	4.50	2.75
147	3¢ Washington, Green	130.00	75.00	.65	.35
148	6¢ Lincoln, Carmine	235.00	130.00	10.50	6.00
149	7¢ Stanton, Vermilion	300.00	165.00	45.00	25.00
150	10¢ Jefferson, Brown	235.00	125.00	11.00	6.50
151	12¢ Clay, Dull Violet	575.00	325.00	65.00	38.50
152	15¢ Webster, Bright Orange	550.00	310.00	70.00	40.00
153	24¢ Scott, Purple	575.00	325.00	70.00	40.00
154	30¢ Hamilton, Black	1100.00	625.00	82.50	47.50
155	90¢ Perry, Carmine	1400.00	790.00	165.00	95.00

PRIOR TO 1882, UNUSED PRICES ARE FOR STAMS WITH PARTIAL OR NO GUM, FOR ORIGINAL GUM, ADD % PREMIUM INDICATED IN ( ).

1870-71 National Print - Without Secret Marks

1¢ 2¢ 3¢ 6¢ 7¢ 10¢ 12¢

Arrows point to distinguishing characteristics: 1¢ ball is clear; 2¢ no spot of color; 3¢ light shading; 6¢ normal vertical lines; 7¢ no arcs of color cut around lines; 10¢ ball is clear; 12¢ normal 2.

1873 Continental Print-White Hard Paper (VF+150% OG+30%) (C)

Same designs as preceding issue but with secret marks as shown below.

Arrows point to distinguishing characteristics: 1¢ dash in ball; 2¢ spot of color where lines join in scroll ornaments; 3¢ under part of ribbon heavily shaded; 6¢ first four vertical lines strengthened; 7¢ arcs of color cut around lines; 10¢ a crescent in the ball; 12¢ ball of 2 is crescent shaped.

Scott's No.		Unused Fine	Unused Ave.	Used Fine	Used Ave.
156	1¢ Franklin, Ultramarine	90.00	57.50	2.00	1.10
157	2¢ Jackson, Brown	185.00	105.00	8.50	4.75
158	3¢ Washington, Green	57.50	30.00	.25	.18
159	6¢ Lincoln, Dull Pink	210.00	115.00	8.50	5.00
160	7¢ Stanton, Org. Vermilion	450.00	250.00	50.00	27.50
161	10¢ Jefferson, Brown	275.00	160.00	10.00	6.00
162	12¢ Clay, Blackish Violet	725.00	400.00	57.50	32.50
163	15¢ Webster, Yellow Orange	700.00	385.00	52.50	30.00
165	30¢ Hamilton, Gray Black	700.00	385.00	57.50	32.50
166	90¢ Perry, Rose Carmine	1350.00	775.00	160.00	95.00

1875-Continental Print-Yellowish Hard Paper(VF+150% OG+30%) (C)

Scott's No.		Unused Fine	Unused Ave.	Used Fine	Used Ave.
178	2¢ Jackson, Vermilion	180.00	105.00	4.25	2.50
179	5¢ Taylor, Blue	210.00	120.00	8.00	4.50

1879 American Prtg. - Continental Design, Soft Porous Paper (VF + 125% OG + 30%) (C)

Soft porous paper is less transparent than hard paper. When held to the light it usually appears mottled, somewhat like newsprint.

Scott's No.		Unused Fine	Unused Ave.	Used Fine	Used Ave.
182	1¢ Franklin, Dark Ultramarine	135.00	75.00	1.35	.75
183	2¢ Jackson, Vermilion	62.50	35.00	1.35	.75
184	3¢ Washington, Green	47.50	28.50	.25	.18
185	5¢ Taylor, Blue	275.00	135.00	7.75	4.25
186	6¢ Lincoln, Pink	465.00	265.00	10.50	6.00
187	10¢ Brown (no secret mark)	725.00	385.00	12.75	7.50
188	10¢ Brown (secret mark)	535.00	300.00	14.50	8.00
189	15¢ Webster, Red Orange	170.00	95.00	15.00	8.25
190	30¢ Hamilton, Full Black	500.00	260.00	32.50	18.75
191	90¢ Perry, Carmine	1150.00	675.00	130.00	75.00

212 210,213 211,215 205,216

1882 New Design (VF NH+100%, VF OG & Used+50% OG) (C)

Scott's No.		NH Fine	Unused,OG Fine	Unused,OG Ave.	Used Fine	Used Ave.
205	5¢ Garfield, Yel. Brn.	160.00	115.00	65.00	4.25	2.35
	1881-82 Re-engraved Designs (VF NH+100%, VF OG & Used+75%) (C)					
206	1¢ Franklin, Gray Blue	47.50	32.50	18.00	.65	.35
207	3¢ Washington, Blue Grn	55.00	37.50	21.50	.25	.18
208	6¢ Lincoln, Rose	295.00	210.00	110.00	45.00	25.00
208a	6¢ Brown Red	265.00	185.00	100.00	52.50	30.00
209	10¢ Jefferson, Brown	110.00	75.00	42.50	2.50	1.40
209b	10¢ Black Brown	175.00	115.00	60.00	9.75	5.75
	1883-88 New Designs or Colors (VF NH+100%, VF OG & Used+75%) (C)					
210	2¢ Washington Red Brn	40.00	30.00	17.50	.25	.18
211	4¢ Jackson, Blue Green	185.00	135.00	75.00	7.00	4.00
212	1¢ Franklin, Ultramarine	80.00	57.50	30.00	.75	.40
213	2¢ Washington, Green	30.00	21.50	12.00	.25	.18
214	3¢ Wash., Vermilion	60.00	42.50	25.00	30.00	18.50
215	4¢ Jackson, Carmine	185.00	135.00	70.00	10.50	6.25
216	5¢ Garfield, Indigo	185.00	135.00	70.00	6.00	3.35
217	30¢ Hamilton, Orange Brn	425.00	300.00	180.00	75.00	40.00
218	90¢ Perry, Purple	975.00	725.00	425.00	140.00	80.00

1890-1893 No Triangles (VF Used + 50%) (C)

219 219D,220 221 222 223

224 225 226 227 228

Scott's No.		NH VF	NH F-VF	Unused VF	Unused F-VF	Used F-VF
219	1¢ Franklin, Dull Blue	37.50	21.50	22.50	15.00	.20
219D	2¢ Washington, Lake	315.00	185.00	190.00	125.00	.50
220	2¢ Carmine	30.00	17.50	19.50	13.00	.15
220a	2¢ Cap on left "2"	90.00	50.00	57.50	37.50	1.00
220c	2¢ Cap on both "2's"	235.00	135.00	150.00	100.00	6.50
221	3¢ Jackson, Purple	115.00	65.00	67.50	45.00	4.00
222	4¢ Lincoln, Dark Brn	115.00	65.00	67.50	45.00	1.65
223	5¢ Grant, Chocolate	115.00	65.00	67.50	45.00	1.65
224	6¢ Garfield, Brn Red	125.00	67.50	72.50	47.50	13.50
225	8¢ Sherman, Lilac (1893)	85.00	47.50	55.00	35.00	7.00
226	10¢ Webster, Green	215.00	125.00	140.00	90.00	1.85
227	15¢ Clay, Indigo	310.00	175.00	200.00	130.00	13.50
228	30¢ Jefferson, Black	515.00	300.00	315.00	200.00	17.00
229	90¢ Perry, Orange	715.00	400.00	450.00	300.00	80.00

1893 Columbian Issue (VF Used + 50%) (B)

230 231 232

237 239 245

Scott's No.		NH VF	NH F-VF	Unused VF	Unused F-VF	Used F-VF
230	1¢ Blue	48.50	27.50	31.50	19.50	.35
231	2¢ Violet	45.00	25.00	29.50	18.50	.15
231v	2¢ Violet, "Broken Hat" 3rd person to left of Columbus has a triangular "cut" in his hat	145.00	82.50	90.00	57.50	.50
232	3¢ Green	100.00	60.00	65.00	40.00	13.00
233	4¢ Ultramarine	150.00	90.00	95.00	57.50	5.00
234	5¢ Chocolate	160.00	100.00	110.00	65.00	6.00
235	6¢ Purple	150.00	90.00	100.00	57.50	17.00
236	8¢ Magenta	120.00	72.50	75.00	50.00	7.00
237	10¢ Black Brown	235.00	140.00	150.00	92.50	6.00
238	15¢ Dark Green	425.00	240.00	250.00	160.00	52.50
239	30¢ Orange Brown	550.00	325.00	350.00	215.00	72.50
240	50¢ Slate Blue	950.00	575.00	575.00	375.00	120.00
241	$1 Salmon	2750.00	1600.00	1750.00	1100.00	475.00
242	$2 Brown Red	2750.00	1650.00	1750.00	1125.00	425.00
243	$3 Yellow Green	4500.00	2750.00	2800.00	1875.00	875.00
244	$4 Crimson Lake	6000.00	3500.00	3750.00	2450.00	1100.00
245	$5 Black	7250.00	4250.00	4500.00	2950.00	1350.00

1894 Issue - Triangles - No Watermark (VF Used + 75%) (C)

246/279 252/279B 253,268 254,269,280 255,270,281

256,271,282 258/283 259,274,284 261,276 262,277

Scott's No.		NH VF	NH F-VF	Unused VF	Unused F-VF	Used F-VF
246	1¢ Franklin, Ultramarine	45.00	25.00	27.50	18.00	3.00
247	1¢ Blue	100.00	57.50	67.50	42.50	1.50
248	2¢ Wash., Pink, Tri. I	35.00	19.00	21.00	14.00	1.75
249	2¢ Carmine Lake, Tri. I	235.00	135.00	135.00	90.00	1.40
250	2¢ Carmine, Triangle I	40.00	23.00	25.00	17.00	.25
251	2¢ Carmine, Triangle II	325.00	190.00	210.00	140.00	2.50
252	2¢ Carmine, Triangle III	200.00	110.00	125.00	80.00	2.75
253	3¢ Jackson, Purple	175.00	87.50	90.00	60.00	6.00
254	4¢ Lincoln, Dark Brown	195.00	97.50	110.00	72.50	2.50
255	5¢ Grant, Chocolate	175.00	87.50	90.00	60.00	3.35
256	6¢ Garfield, Dull Brown	275.00	160.00	165.00	110.00	13.50
257	8¢ Sherman, Violet Brn	215.00	125.00	130.00	87.50	9.75
258	10¢ Webster, Dark Grn	340.00	195.00	210.00	140.00	6.00
259	15¢ Clay, Dark Blue	475.00	275.00	300.00	200.00	35.00
260	50¢ Jefferson, Orange	650.00	375.00	400.00	260.00	60.00
261	$1 Perry, Black, Type I	1350.00	795.00	825.00	550.00	200.00
261A	$1 Black, Type II	3850.00	2250.00	2400.00	1600.00	400.00
262	$2 Madison, Bright Blue	4750.00	2800.00	3000.00	2000.00	525.00
263	$5 Marshall, Dark Green	7000.00	4250.00	4500.00	3000.00	950.00

Triangle Varieties on the 2¢ Stamps

Triangle I Triangle II Triangle III

TRIANGLE I - The horizontal background lines run across the triangle and are of the same thickness within the triangle as the background lines.
TRIANGLE II - Horizontal lines cross the triangle but are thinner within the triangle than the background lines.
TRIANGLE III - The horizontal lines do not cross the triangle and the lines within the triangle are as thin as in Triangle II.

Circle Varieties on the $1 Stamps

Type I Type II

Types of $1.00 stamps. Type I, the circles enclosing "$1" are broken where they meet the curved lines below "One Dollar." Type II, the circles are complete.

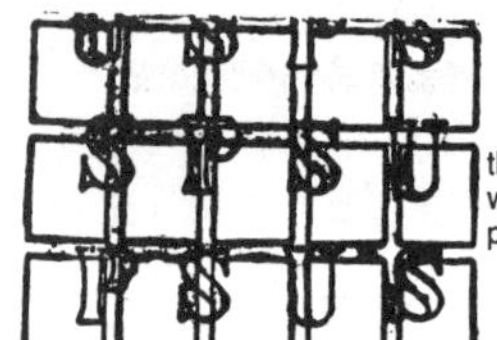

This illustration shows a block of 15 with the Double Line watermark. Since only 90 letters were used per 100 stamps, they appear in various positions on the stamps.

1895 Same Designs - Double Line Wmk. (VF Used + 50%) (C)

Scott's No.		NH VF	NH F-VF	Unused VF	Unused F-VF	Used F-VF
264	1¢ Franklin, Blue	9.50	6.00	6.00	4.00	.15
265	2¢ Wash., Carmine, Tri. I	45.00	27.50	27.50	18.50	.70
266	2¢ Carmine, Triangle II	40.00	25.00	75.00	16.50	2.75
267	2¢ Carmine, Triangle III	8.00	5.00	5.50	3.75	.15
268	3¢ Jackson, Purple	65.00	40.00	42.50	27.50	1.00
269	4¢ Lincoln, Dark Brown	67.50	42.50	42.50	27.50	1.65
270	5¢ Grant, Chocolate	65.00	40.00	42.50	27.50	1.65
271	6¢ Garfield, Dull Brown	115.00	72.50	72.50	47.50	3.50
272	8¢ Sherman, Violet Brn	90.00	55.00	57.50	37.50	1.00
273	10¢ Webster, Dark Green	110.00	67.50	72.50	47.50	1.10
274	15¢ Clay, Dark Blue	295.00	185.00	190.00	125.00	7.50
275	50¢ Jefferson, Orange	425.00	265.00	275.00	185.00	16.50
276	$1 Perry, Black, Type I	950.00	600.00	635.00	425.00	57.50
276A	$1 Black, Type II	2000.00	1275.00	1400.00	950.00	110.00
277	$2 Madison, Bright Blue	1500.00	950.00	1125.00	750.00	235.00
278	$5 Marshall, Dark Green	3350.00	2150.00	2250.00	1500.00	350.00

1898 New Colors - Double Line Wmk. (VF Used + 50%) (C)

Scott's No.		NH VF	NH F-VF	Unused VF	Unused F-VF	Used F-VF
279	1¢ Franklin, Green	16.50	10.50	11.50	7.50	.15
279B	2¢ Wash., Red, Tri.III	15.00	9.50	10.50	7.00	.15
279Bc	2¢ Rose Carmine, Tri. III	300.00	200.00	225.00	150.00	32.50
279Bd	2¢ Orange Red, Tri. III	19.50	12.00	13.50	9.00	.18
279Be	Bklt. Pane of 6, Tri. III	595.00	400.00	425.00	285.00	..
280	4¢ Lincoln, Rose Brown	54.50	32.50	37.50	24.00	.80
281	5¢ Grant, Dark Blue	57.50	35.00	40.00	26.00	.80
282	6¢ Garfield, Lake	90.00	57.50	55.00	37.50	2.00
282a	6¢ Purplish Lake	95.00	60.00	67.50	45.00	2.65
282C	10¢ Webster, Brn., Type I	280.00	175.00	185.00	125.00	2.15
283	10¢ Orange Brn., Type II	175.00	110.00	115.00	75.00	1.75
284	15¢ Clay, Olive Green	250.00	150.00	165.00	110.00	6.50

1898 Trans-Mississippi Issue (VF Used + 50%) (B)

285 286 288

290 292 293

Scott's No.		NH VF	NH F-VF	Unused VF	Unused F-VF	Used F-VF
285	1¢ Marquette, Green	47.50	30.00	33.50	22.50	5.25
286	2¢ Farming, Copper Red	45.00	27.50	30.00	20.00	1.30
287	4¢ Indian, Orange	260.00	160.00	165.00	110.00	20.00
288	5¢ Fremont, Dull Blue	250.00	150.00	150.00	100.00	18.50
289	8¢ Wagon Train, Vio. Brn.	335.00	210.00	210.00	140.00	35.00
290	10¢ Emigration, Gray Vio.	300.00	225.00	225.00	150.00	17.00
291	50¢ Mining, Sage Green	1250.00	775.00	785.00	525.00	145.00
292	$1 Cattle in Storm, Black	2400.00	1550.00	1500.00	1025.00	450.00
293	$2 Bridge, Orange Brn.	4250.00	2650.00	2550.00	1750.00	725.00

1901 Pan-American Issue VF Used + 50% (B)

294 295 297 299

Scott's No.		NH VF	NH F-VF	Unused VF	Unused F-VF	Used F-VF
294-99	**Set of 6**	**925.00**	**640.00**	**650.00**	**445.00**	**115.00**
294	1¢ Steamship, Grn. & Blk.	31.50	21.00	22.50	15.00	3.50
295	2¢ Train, Carmine & Blk.	31.50	21.00	22.50	15.00	1.00
296	4¢ Auto, Choc. & Blk.	150.00	100.00	100.00	70.00	15.00
297	5¢ Bridge, Ultra & Black	195.00	130.00	135.00	87.50	15.00
298	8¢ Canal, Brn. Vio & Blk.	240.00	165.00	165.00	110.00	57.50
299	10¢ Steamship, Brn. & Blk.	325.00	225.00	240.00	160.00	27.50

1902-03 Issue Perf. 12 VF Used + 50% (C)

300 301 302 304 306

308 310 312,479 313,480 319

Scott's No.		NH VF	NH F-VF	Unused VF	Unused F-VF	Used F-VF
300	1¢ Franklin, Blue Green	16.50	11.00	11.50	7.50	.15
300b	Booklet Pane of 6	900.00	600.00	625.00	425.00	...
301	2¢ Washington, Carmine	20.00	13.50	13.50	9.00	.15
301c	Booklet Pane of 6	695.00	475.00	500.00	340.00	...
302	3¢ Jackson, Bright Violet	82.50	55.00	57.50	37.50	3.00
303	4¢ Grant, Brown	82.50	55.00	57.50	37.50	1.00
304	5¢ Lincoln, Blue	100.00	65.00	62.50	42.50	1.00
305	6¢ Garfield, Claret	105.00	70.00	67.50	45.00	2.25
306	8¢ M. Wash., Violet Black	65.00	42.50	42.50	28.50	1.85
307	10¢ Webster, Red Brown	110.00	72.50	72.50	47.50	1.35
308	13¢ B. Harrison, Purp. Black	65.00	42.50	42.50	28.50	8.00
309	15¢ Clay, Olive Green	225.00	150.00	150.00	100.00	5.75
310	50¢ Jefferson, Orange	675.00	450.00	450.00	300.00	22.50
311	$1 Farragut, Black	950.00	750.00	750.00	500.00	45.00
312	$2 Madison, Dark Blue	1450.00	975.00	950.00	700.00	160.00
313	$5 Marshall, Dark Green	3950.00	2800.00	2800.00	1850.00	525.00

1906-08 Same Designs, Imperforate VF Used + 30% (B)

Scott's No.		NH VF	NH F-VF	Unused VF	Unused F-VF	Used F-VF
314	1¢ Franklin, Blue Green	35.00	27.50	27.50	18.50	17.50
315	5¢ Lincoln, Blue	650.00	525.00	500.00	350.00	...

*** Genuinely used examples of #315 are rare. Copies should have contemporary cancels and be purchased with, or subject to, a certificate of authenticity.**

1903 Shield Issue, Perforated 12 VF Used + 50% (C)

Scott's No.		NH VF	NH F-VF	Unused VF	Unused F-VF	Used F-VF
319	2¢ Carmine, Die I	10.00	6.75	6.75	4.50	.15
319f	2¢ Lake, Die II	11.50	7.50	7.50	5.00	.25

1906 Shield Issue, Imperforate VF Used + 30% (B)

Scott's No.		NH VF	NH F-VF	Unused VF	Unused F-VF	Used F-VF
320	2¢ Carmine, Die I	36.50	28.50	28.50	19.50	15.00
320a	2¢ Lake, Die II	125.00	90.00	85.00	60.00	35.00

1904 Louisiana Purchase Issue VF Used + 50% (B)

323 325 327

Scott's No.		NH VF	NH F-VF	Unused VF	Unused F-VF	Used F-VF
323-27	**Set of 5**	**595.00**	**395.00**	**425.00**	**280.00**	**72.50**
323	1¢ Livingston, Green	46.50	30.00	32.50	21.50	4.50
324	2¢ Jefferson, Carmine	37.50	25.00	27.50	18.50	1.50
325	3¢ Monroe, Violet	125.00	85.00	90.00	60.00	27.50
326	5¢ McKinley, Blue	150.00	100.00	110.00	70.00	17.50
327	10¢ Map, Brown	275.00	175.00	185.00	125.00	25.00

1907 Jamestown Issue VF Used + 100% (C)

328 329 330

Scott's No.		NH VF	NH F-VF	Unused VF	Unused F-VF	Used F-VF
328-30	**Set of 3**	**335.00**	**170.00**	**200.00**	**125.00**	**32.50**
328	1¢ John Smith, Green	45.00	22.50	30.00	16.00	3.50
329	2¢ Jamestown, Carmine	57.50	28.50	35.00	20.00	5.50
330	5¢ Pocahontas, Blue	250.00	125.00	150.00	95.00	25.50

PLATE BLOCKS

Scott #	NH VF	NH F-VF	Unused F-VF	Scott #	NH VF	NH F-VF	Unused F-VF
294 (6)	375.00	275.00	200.00	319 (6)	110.00	85.00	65.00
295 (6)	375.00	275.00	200.00	320 (6)	325.00	250.00	185.00
300 (6)	250.00	175.00	125.00	323	275.00	180.00	135.00
301 (6)	260.00	185.00	130.00	324	275.00	180.00	135.00
314 (6)	295.00	225.00	140.00	328 (6)	475.00	285.00	225.00
				329 (6)	650.00	395.00	315.00

1908-09 Wash-Franklins Double Line Wmk. - Perf. 12 VF Used + 50% (B)

331,357,374 332/519 333/541 338/381 342

Scott's No.		NH VF	NH F-VF	Unused VF	Unused F-VF	Used F-VF
331	1¢ Franklin, Green	13.50	8.75	8.50	5.50	.15
331a	1¢ Booklet Pane of 6	250.00	175.00	195.00	130.00	...
332	2¢ Washington, Carmine	13.50	8.75	8.50	5.50	.15
332a	2¢ Booklet Pane of 6	240.00	150.00	170.00	115.00	...
333	3¢ Deep Violet	60.00	38.50	38.50	25.50	2.85
334	4¢ Orange Brown	65.00	42.50	42.50	27.50	.95
335	5¢ Blue	80.00	52.50	55.00	37.50	2.00
336	6¢ Red Orange	95.00	65.00	62.50	42.50	4.50
337	8¢ Olive Green	75.00	47.50	48.50	32.50	2.50
338	10¢ Yellow	110.00	75.00	80.00	52.50	1.35
339	13¢ Blue Green	77.50	48.50	48.50	32.50	20.00
340	15¢ Ultramarine	120.00	77.50	75.00	50.00	5.50
341	50¢ Violet	475.00	300.00	325.00	225.00	15.00
342	$1 Violet Brown	795.00	495.00	525.00	350.00	75.00

1908-09 Series, Double Line Wmk. - Imperf. VF Used + 30% (B)

Scott's No.		NH VF	NH F-VF	Unused VF	Unused F-VF	Used F-VF
343	1¢ Franklin, Green	9.75	7.50	7.50	5.50	3.50
344	2¢ Washington, Carmine	12.00	9.50	9.50	7.00	3.50
345	3¢ Deep Violet	23.50	17.50	17.50	13.00	14.00
346	4¢ Orange Brown	37.50	28.75	28.75	22.50	17.50
347	5¢ Blue	66.50	51.50	51.50	38.50	28.75

PLATE BLOCKS

Scott #	NH VF	NH F-VF	Unused F-VF	Scott #	NH VF	NH F-VF	Unused F-VF
331 (6)	125.00	80.00	60.00	343 (6)	85.00	65.00	45.00
332 (6)	125.00	80.00	60.00	344 (6)	165.00	125.00	85.00
				345 (6)	295.00	225.00	175.00

1908-10 Coils, Double Line Wmk. - Perf. 12 Horiz. VF Used + 50% (C)

Scott's No.		NH VF	NH F-VF	Unused VF	Unused F-VF	Used F-VF
348	1¢ Franklin, Green	40.00	28.50	30.00	20.00	10.50
349	2¢ Washington, Carmine	75.00	52.50	52.50	35.00	7.00
350	4¢ Orange Brown	180.00	120.00	125.00	80.00	65.00
351	5¢ Blue	200.00	135.00	135.00	90.00	80.00

(#348-351 Pairs are valued at 2.3 x the single price.)

1909 Coils, Double Line Wmk. - Perf. 12 Vert. VF Used + 50% (C)

Scott's No.		NH VF	NH F-VF	Unused VF	Unused F-VF	Used F-VF
352	1¢ Franklin, Green	90.00	60.00	60.00	40.00	25.00
353	2¢ Washington, Carmine	85.00	57.50	55.00	37.50	7.00
354	4¢ Orange Brown	185.00	125.00	125.00	85.00	42.50
355	5¢ Blue	210.00	140.00	140.00	95.00	60.00
356	10¢ Yellow	...	1800.00	2000.00	1350.00	P.O.R.

(#352-356 Pairs are valued at 2.4 x the single price.)
(#348-56, 385-89 should be purchased with, or subject to, a certificate of authenticity.)

LINE PAIRS

Scott #	NH VF	NH F-VF	Unused F-VF	Scott #	NH VF	NH F-VF	Unused F-VF
348	295.00	200.00	135.00	352	515.00	350.00	250.00
349	485.00	335.00	240.00	353	515.00	350.00	250.00

1909 "Blue Papers", Double Line Wmk., Perf. 12 VF Used + 75% (B)

Scott's No.		NH VF	NH F-VF	Unused VF	Unused F-VF	Used F-VF
357	1¢ Franklin, Green	225.00	130.00	135.00	85.00	85.00
358	2¢ Washington, Carmine	210.00	125.00	130.00	80.00	65.00
359	3¢ Deep Violet	...	...	2250.00	1275.00	...
361	5¢ Blue	...	...	...	3350.00	...
362	6¢ Red Orange	...	...	1850.00	1075.00	...
364	10¢ Yellow	...	...	2150.00	1250.00	...
365	13¢ Blue Green	...	...	...	1850.00	1150.00
366	15¢ Pale Ultramarine	...	...	1700.00	1000.00	...

*** Blue Papers, which were printed on experimental paper with approximately 35% rag content, actually have a grayish appearance which can best be observed by looking at the stamps from the gum side. Additionally, the watermark is more clearly visible than on the stamps printed on regular paper (#331-340). The stamps are also noted for having carbon specks imbedded in the texture of the paper.**

*** Blue Papers should be purchased with, or subject to, a certificate of authenticity. Genuinely used Blue Papers, other than the 1¢, 2¢ & 13¢ values, are extremely rare. Examples should have contemporary cancels.**

NOTE: PLATE BLOCKS, AND OTHER BLOCKS, ARE ALL BLOCKS OF 4 UNLESS OTHERWISE INDICATED IN ( ).
NOTE: VF UNUSED PLATE BLOCKS AND LINE PAIRS ARE GENERALLY AVAILABLE AT THE RESPECTIVE F-VF NH PRICE.

1909 Commems. (Used) Perf. VF + 40% - Imperf. VF + 30% (B)

367 370 372

Scott's No.		NH VF	NH F-VF	Unused VF	Unused F-VF	Used F-VF
367	2¢ Lincoln, Perf. 12	13.75	9.75	8.50	6.25	2.00
368	2¢ Lincoln, Imperf.	40.00	30.00	30.00	22.50	19.50
369	2¢ Bluish Paper, Perf. 12	375.00	260.00	265.00	175.00	175.00
370	2¢ Alaska-Yukon, Perf. 12	15.00	10.75	10.75	7.00	1.75
371	2¢ Alaska-Yukon, Imperf.	55.00	41.50	36.50	27.50	21.50
372	2¢ Hudson-Fulton, Perf. 12	20.00	14.50	13.50	10.00	4.00
373	2¢ Hudson-Fulton, Imperf.	57.50	43.50	43.50	32.50	24.50

1910-11 Single Line Wmk. Perf 12 VF Used + 75% (B)

(Same designs as 1908-1909 Series)

This illustration shows a block of 15 stamps with the Single Line Watermark. The watermark appears in various positions on the stamps.

Scott's No.		NH VF	NH F-VF	Unused VF	Unused F-VF	Used F-VF
374	1¢ Franklin, Green	13.50	7.50	8.25	5.50	.18
374a	1¢ Booklet Pane of 6	235.00	150.00	165.00	110.00	...
375	2¢ Washington, Carmine	12.50	7.00	7.50	5.25	.18
375a	2¢ Booklet Pane of 6	200.00	130.00	140.00	95.00	...
376	3¢ Deep Violet	37.50	22.50	22.50	15.00	1.65
377	4¢ Brown	52.50	33.50	33.50	22.50	.50
378	5¢ Blue	52.50	33.50	33.50	22.50	.50
379	6¢ Red Orange	67.50	42.50	42.50	28.50	.80
380	8¢ Olive Green	200.00	125.00	130.00	85.00	12.00
381	10¢ Yellow	200.00	120.00	130.00	80.00	3.50
382	15¢ Pale Ultramarine	425.00	280.00	300.00	200.00	12.50

1911 Single Line Wmk., Imperf. VF Used + 30% (B)

Scott's No.		NH VF	NH F-VF	Unused VF	Unused F-VF	Used F-VF
383	1¢ Franklin, Green	4.50	3.25	3.00	2.25	2.25
384	2¢ Washington, Carmine	7.75	5.75	5.00	3.75	1.75

PLATE BLOCKS

Scott #	NH VF	NH F-VF	Unused F-VF	Scott #	NH VF	NH F-VF	Unused F-VF
367 (6)	200.00	160.00	110.00	374 (6)	125.00	85.00	60.00
368 (6)	300.00	235.00	175.00	375 (6)	135.00	90.00	65.00
370(6)	325.00	250.00	165.00	376 (6)	250.00	175.00	120.00
371 (6)	325.00	265.00	195.00	377 (6)	325.00	225.00	150.00
372 (6)	425.00	335.00	225.00	378 (6)	375.00	260.00	175.00
373 (6)	385.00	300.00	215.00	383 (6)	60.00	45.00	35.00
				384 (6)	200.00	160.00	115.00

1910 Coils S. Line Wmk. - Perf. 12 Horiz. VF Used + 50% (C)

Scott's No.		NH VF	NH F-VF	Unused VF	Unused F-VF	Used F-VF
385	1¢ Franklin, Green	42.50	28.50	29.50	19.50	12.00
386	2¢ Washington, Carmine	70.00	47.50	48.50	32.50	12.50

1910-11 Coils S. Line Wmk. - Perf. 12 Vert. VF Used + 50% (C)

Scott's No.		NH VF	NH F-VF	Unused VF	Unused F-VF	Used F-VF
387	1¢ Franklin, Green	165.00	110.00	105.00	70.00	29.50
388	2¢ Washington, Carmine	1000.00	675.00	725.00	450.00	...
389	3¢ Washington, Deep Violet	...	...	**USED FINE**		**6750.00**

(Examples of #388 and 389 must be purchased with, or subject to, a certificate.)

1910 Coils S. Line Wmk. - Perf. 8½ Horizontally VF Used + 50% (B)

Scott's No.		NH VF	NH F-VF	Unused VF	Unused F-VF	Used F-VF
390	1¢ Franklin, Green	7.50	5.00	5.00	3.25	3.75
391	2¢ Washington, Carmine	48.50	32.50	33.50	22.50	8.00

1910-13 Coils S. Line Wmk. - Perf. 8½ Vertically VF Used + 50% (B)

Scott's No.		NH VF	NH F-VF	Unused VF	Unused F-VF	Used F-VF
392	1¢ Franklin, Green	33.50	22.50	21.50	14.50	15.00
393	2¢ Washington, Carmine	67.50	45.00	45.00	30.00	5.50
394	3¢ Deep Violet	75.00	52.50	55.00	37.50	37.50
395	4¢ Brown	75.00	52.50	55.00	37.50	35.00
396	5¢ Blue	75.00	52.50	55.00	37.50	35.00

Coil Pairs are valued as follows:
#385, 387 @ 2.5 x a single, #386, 388 @ 3 x a single, #390-396 @ 2.3 x a single.

LINE PAIRS

Scott #	NH VF	NH F-VF	Unused F-VF	Scott #	NH VF	NH F-VF	Unused F-VF
385	425.00	275.00	195.00	392	195.00	130.00	90.00
386	895.00	575.00	395.00	393	295.00	210.00	140.00
387	575.00	375.00	250.00	394	425.00	325.00	225.00
390	47.50	32.00	22.50	395	425.00	325.00	225.00
391	275.00	185.00	125.00	396	425.00	325.00	225.00

1913 Panama-Pacific, Perf. 12 VF Used + 50% (B)

397,401 398,402 399,403 400,400A,404

Scott's No.		NH VF	NH F-VF	Unused VF	Unused F-VF	Used F-VF
397-400A	**Set of 5**	**775.00**	**525.00**	**515.00**	**360.00**	**47.50**
397	1¢ Balboa, Green	30.00	20.00	20.00	13.50	1.50
398	2¢ Panama Canal, Carmine	30.00	20.00	21.00	14.00	.50
399	5¢ Golden Gate, Blue	135.00	90.00	90.00	60.00	9.25
400	10¢ San Fran., Orange Yel	240.00	160.00	165.00	110.00	20.00
400A	10¢ Orange	385.00	260.00	250.00	180.00	17.50

1914-15 Panama-Pacific, Perf. 10 VF Used + 50% (B)

Scott's No.		NH VF	NH F-VF	Unused VF	Unused F-VF	Used F-VF
401-04	**Set of 4**	**1950.00**	**1375.00**	**1350.00**	**1050.00**	**77.50**
401	1¢ Balboa, Green	42.50	27.50	27.50	18.50	6.00
402	2¢ Panama, Carmine	150.00	100.00	95.00	65.00	1.50
403	5¢ Golden Gate, Blue	295.00	195.00	200.00	135.00	15.00
404	10¢ San Fran., Orange	1500.00	1100.00	1075.00	850.00	60.00

1912-14 Single Line Wmk. - Perf. 12 VF Used + 50% (B)

405/545 406/546 337/380 419/515 423/518

NOTE: THE 1¢ TO 7¢ STAMPS FROM 1912-21 PICTURE WASHINGTON. THE 8¢ TO $5 STAMPS PICTURE FRANKLIN.

Scott's No.		NH VF	NH F-VF	Unused VF	Unused F-VF	Used F-VF
405	1¢ Washington, Green	11.75	7.75	7.50	5.00	.15
405b	1¢ Booklet Pane of 6	110.00	80.00	80.00	55.00	...
406	2¢ Carmine	10.50	7.00	6.75	4.50	.15
406a	2¢ Booklet Pane of 6	130.00	87.50	90.00	60.00	...
407	7¢ Black	150.00	95.00	100.00	67.50	7.50

1912 Single Line Wmk. - Imperf. VF Used + 20% (B)

Scott's No.		NH VF	NH F-VF	Unused VF	Unused F-VF	Used F-VF
408	1¢ Washington, Green	2.00	1.65	1.50	1.15	.55
409	2¢ Carmine	2.25	1.85	1.65	1.30	.65

PLATE BLOCKS

Scott #	NH VF	NH F-VF	Unused F-VF	Scott #	NH VF	NH F-VF	Unused F-VF
397 (6)	225.00	150.00	100.00	405 (6)	135.00	90.00	65.00
398 (6)	395.00	265.00	190.00	406 (6)	165.00	110.00	75.00
401 (6)	450.00	295.00	210.00	408 (6)	33.50	26.50	18.50
				409 (6)	57.50	46.50	32.50

1912 Coils Single Line Wmk. - Perf. 8½ Horiz. VF Used + 50% (B)

Scott's No.		NH VF	NH F-VF	Unused VF	Unused F-VF	Used F-VF
410	1¢ Washington, Green	10.00	6.75	6.75	4.50	3.50
411	2¢ Carmine	13.50	9.00	9.00	6.00	3.25

1912 Coils Single Line Wmk. - Perf. 8½ Vert. VF Used + 50% (B)

Scott's No.		NH VF	NH F-VF	Unused VF	Unused F-VF	Used F-VF
412	1¢ Washington, Green	39.50	26.50	26.50	17.50	6.00
413	2¢ Carmine	67.50	45.00	45.00	30.00	.90

(#410-413 Pairs are valued at 2.3 x the single price.)

LINE PAIRS

Scott #	NH VF	NH F-VF	Unused F-VF	Scott #	NH VF	NH F-VF	Unused F-VF
410	60.00	40.00	27.50	412	160.00	110.00	75.00
411	75.00	50.00	33.50	413	325.00	210.00	150.00

1912-14 Franklin Design. Single Line Wmk. - Perf. 12 VF Used + 50% (B)

Scott's No.		NH VF	NH F-VF	Unused VF	Unused F-VF	Used F-VF
414	8¢ Franklin, Olive Green	70.00	45.00	45.00	30.00	1.50
415	9¢ Salmon Red	90.00	57.50	60.00	40.00	13.50
416	10¢ Orange Yellow	75.00	46.50	47.50	31.50	.40
417	12¢ Claret Brown	85.00	53.50	55.00	36.50	4.00
418	15¢ Gray	135.00	90.00	90.00	60.00	3.50
419	20¢ Ultramarine	315.00	200.00	200.00	135.00	15.00
420	30¢ Orange Red	230.00	150.00	150.00	100.00	16.00
421	50¢ Violet	815.00	540.00	565.00	375.00	19.50

*** #421 usually shows an offset on the back; #422 usually does not.**

1912 Franklin Design. Double Line Wmk. - Perf. 12 VF Used + 50% (B)

Scott's No.		NH VF	NH F-VF	Unused VF	Unused F-VF	Used F-VF
422	50¢ Franklin, Violet	500.00	325.00	315.00	210.00	19.50
423	$1 Violet Brown	1000.00	650.00	700.00	435.00	60.00

1914-15 Flat Press Single Line Wmk., Perf. 10 VF Used + 50% (B)

Scott's No.		NH VF	NH F-VF	Unused VF	Unused F-VF	Used F-VF
424	1¢ Washington, Green	6.00	3.75	3.75	2.50	.15
424d	1¢ Booklet Pane of 6	7.75	5.25	5.25	3.50	...
425	2¢ Rose Red	5.00	3.00	3.00	2.00	.15
425e	2¢ Booklet Pane of 6	38.50	25.00	26.50	17.50	...
426	3¢ Deep Violet	27.50	17.50	17.50	11.50	1.75
427	4¢ Brown	70.00	43.50	43.50	29.50	.65
428	5¢ Blue	50.00	32.50	35.00	22.50	.65
429	6¢ Red Orange	70.00	45.00	45.00	30.00	1.80
430	7¢ Black	160.00	100.00	100.00	67.50	5.00
431	8¢ Franklin, Olive Green	70.00	42.50	42.50	28.50	1.75
432	9¢ Salmon Red	95.00	57.50	57.50	38.50	10.00
433	10¢ Orange Yellow	90.00	56.50	56.50	37.50	.40
434	11¢ Dark Green	45.00	28.50	30.00	20.00	7.50
435	12¢ Claret Brown	52.50	32.50	32.50	21.50	4.00
435a	12¢ Copper Red	57.50	37.50	37.50	25.00	4.25
437	15¢ Gray	200.00	125.00	130.00	87.50	7.50
438	20¢ Ultramarine	375.00	240.00	250.00	165.00	4.50
439	30¢ Orange Red	475.00	295.00	325.00	210.00	18.50
440	50¢ Violet	1050.00	750.00	700.00	495.00	17.50

PLATE BLOCKS

Scott #	NH VF	NH F-VF	Unused F-VF	Scott #	NH VF	NH F-VF	Unused F-VF
424 (6)	80.00	52.50	35.00	428 (6)	550.00	365.00	275.00
425 (6)	57.50	37.50	25.00	429 (6)	575.00	400.00	300.00
"COIL STAMPS" Impt. & Pl.# Blk. / 10				431 (6)	750.00	525.00	375.00
424 CS (10)	250.00	175.00	125.00	434 (6)	385.00	260.00	180.00
425 CS (10)	285.00	200.00	140.00	435 (6)	435.00	290.00	215.00
426 (6)	285.00	200.00	140.00	435a (6)	500.00	350.00	250.00
427 (6)	800.00	550.00	400.00				

1914 Coils Flat Press S.L Wmk. - Perf. 10 Horiz. VF Used + 50% (B)

Scott's No.		NH VF	NH F-VF	Unused VF	Unused F-VF	Used F-VF
441	1¢ Washington, Green	2.15	1.50	1.60	1.10	.90
442	2¢ Carmine	16.50	11.00	10.50	7.50	6.50

1914 Coils Flat Press S.L. Wmk. - Perf. 10 Vert. VF Used + 50% (B)

Scott's No.		NH VF	NH F-VF	Unused VF	Unused F-VF	Used F-VF
443	1¢ Washington, Green	37.50	25.00	25.00	16.50	5.25
444	2¢ Carmine	55.00	37.00	37.50	25.00	1.40
445	3¢ Violet	375.00	250.00	275.00	180.00	95.00
446	4¢ Brown	250.00	170.00	160.00	110.00	35.00
447	5¢ Blue	85.00	58.50	60.00	39.50	18.50

(#441-447 Pairs are valued at 2.3 x the single price.)

The two top stamps are Rotary Press while the underneath stamps are Flat Press. Note that the designs of the Rotary Press stamps are a little longer or wider than Flat Press stamps. Flat Press stamps usually show spots of color on back.

Perf. Horizontally **Perf. Vertically**

1915-16 Coils Rotary S.L. Wmk. - Perf. 10 Horiz. VF Used + 50% (B)

Scott's No.		NH VF	NH F-VF	Unused VF	Unused F-VF	Used F-VF
448	1¢ Washington, Green	14.00	9.00	9.00	6.00	3.00
449	2¢ Red, Type I	...	...	2850.00	1650.00	250.00
450	2¢ Carmine, Type III	22.00	14.00	14.00	9.50	2.75

1914-16 Coils Rotary S.L. Wmk. - Perf. 10 Vert. VF Used + 50% (B)

Scott's No.		NH VF	NH F-VF	Unused VF	Unused F-VF	Used F-VF
452	1¢ Washington, Green	21.50	13.50	13.50	9.00	1.90
453	2¢ Carm. Rose, Type I	210.00	140.00	140.00	95.00	3.75
454	2¢ Red, Type II	175.00	120.00	120.00	80.00	11.00
455	2¢ Carmine, Type III	18.50	12.00	12.00	8.00	.95
456	3¢ Violet	450.00	300.00	325.00	210.00	85.00
457	4¢ Brown	52.50	35.00	37.50	25.00	18.50
458	5¢ Blue	52.50	35.00	37.50	25.00	18.50

LINE PAIRS

Scott #	NH VF	NH F-VF	Unused F-VF	Scott #	NH VF	NH F-VF	Unused F-VF
441	12.50	8.50	5.50	452	125.00	85.00	57.50
442	90.00	60.00	40.00	453	925.00	625.00	425.00
443	185.00	125.00	85.00	454	850.00	575.00	375.00
444	350.00	210.00	140.00	455	100.00	67.50	45.00
447	375.00	250.00	165.00	457	265.00	175.00	120.00
448	75.00	52.50	35.00	458	275.00	185.00	125.00
450	110.00	75.00	50.00				

NOTE: VF UNUSED PLATE BLOCKS AND LINE PAIRS ARE GENERALLY AVAILABLE AT THE RESPECTIVE F-VF NH PRICE.

1914 Imperf. Coil Rotary Press S.L. Wmk. - VF Used + 30% (B)

Scott's		NH		Unused		Used
No.		VF	F-VF	VF	F-VF	F-VF
459	2¢ Washington, Carmine	650.00	500.00	450.00	350.00	...

*** Genuinely used examples of #459 are rare. Copies should have contemporary cancels and be purchased with, or subject to, a certificate of authenticity.**

1915 Flat Press Double Line Wmk. - Perf. 10 VF Used + 75% (B)

460	$1 Franklin, Violet Black	1350.00	975.00	975.00	675.00	82.50

1915 Flat Press S. Line Wmk. - Perf. 11 VF Used + 100% (B)

461	2¢ Pale Carmine Red	250.00	135.00	165.00	90.00	165.00

(Counterfeits of #461 are common. Purchase with, or subject to, a certificate.)

1916-17 Flat Press, No Wmk. - Perf. 10
(#462-478 VF Used + 50%) (#479-480 VF Used + 35%) (B)

462	1¢ Washington, Green	15.00	9.00	9.00	6.00	.35
462a	1¢ Booklet Pane of 6	20.00	12.50	13.50	9.00	...
463	2¢ Carmine	9.00	5.50	5.00	3.75	.20
463a	2¢ Booklet Pane of 6	160.00	110.00	100.00	75.00	...
464	3¢ Violet	150.00	90.00	90.00	60.00	13.50
465	4¢ Orange Brown	85.00	52.50	55.00	37.50	1.80
466	5¢ Blue	140.00	87.50	90.00	60.00	1.80
467	5¢ Carmine ERROR	1050.00	750.00	750.00	500.00	...
	5¢ Single in Block of 9	1350.00	950.00	950.00	700.00	...
	5¢ Pair in Block of 12	2250.00	1750.00	1200.00	1175.00	...
468	6¢ Red Orange	175.00	110.00	110.00	72.50	7.50
469	7¢ Black	215.00	135.00	135.00	90.00	12.00
470	8¢ Franklin, Olive Green	100.00	67.50	72.50	47.50	6.00
471	9¢ Salmon Red	110.00	65.00	67.50	45.00	13.50
472	10¢ Orange Yellow	200.00	125.00	125.00	82.50	1.25
473	11¢ Dark Green	60.00	36.50	37.50	25.00	17.50
474	12¢ Claret Brown	90.00	55.00	57.50	38.50	5.00
475	15¢ Gray	315.00	200.00	200.00	135.00	12.50
476	20¢ Ultramarine	440.00	275.00	275.00	190.00	12.50
477	50¢ Light Violet	1825.00	1295.00	1250.00	895.00	65.00
478	$1 Violet Black	1175.00	850.00	850.00	575.00	19.50
479	$2 Madison, Dark Blue	650.00	495.00	500.00	350.00	42.50
480	$5 Marshall, Light Green	525.00	450.00	400.00	300.00	45.00

NOTE: #479 & 480 have the same designs as #312 & 313

1916-17 Flat Press, No Wmk. - Imperforate VF Used + 20% (B)

481	1¢ Washington, Green	1.50	1.20	1.10	.90	.80
482	2¢ Carmine, Type I	2.15	1.70	1.50	1.20	1.20
483	3¢ Violet, Type I	18.50	15.00	14.50	11.50	7.50
484	3¢ Violet, Type II	17.00	14.00	12.00	10.00	4.50

***3¢ Type I, the 5th line from the left of the toga rope is broken or missing; 3¢ Type II, the 5th line is complete. See Scott for more details.**

PLATE BLOCKS

	NH		Unused		NH		Unused
Scott #	VF	F-VF	F-VF	Scott #	VF	F-VF	F-VF
462 (6)	250.00	165.00	110.00	481 (6)	16.00	13.00	9.50
463 (6)	225.00	150.00	100.00	482 (6)	32.50	26.50	20.00
473 (6)	525.00	365.00	250.00	483 (6)	165.00	135.00	100.00
474 (6)	1025.00	700.00	475.00	484 (6)	150.00	125.00	90.00

1916-19 Coils Rotary, No Wmk. - Perf. 10 Horiz. VF Used + 40% (B)

486	1¢ Washingto, Green	1.40	1.00	.90	.65	.20
487	2¢ Carmine, Type II	27.50	18.50	17.50	12.50	4.00
488	2¢ Carmine, Type III	5.50	3.75	3.50	2.50	1.50
489	3¢ Violet, Type I	9.00	6.00	5.50	4.00	1.35

1916-22 Coils, Rotary, No Wmk. - Perf. 10 Vert. VF Used + 40% (B)

490	1¢ Washington, Green	1.20	.80	.75	.55	.20
491	2¢ Carmine, Type II		...	1950.00	1250.00	400.00
492	2¢ Carmine, Type III	18.00	12.00	11.50	8.00	.20
493	3¢ Violet, Type I	32.50	24.00	22.50	16.00	2.75
494	3¢ Violet, Type II	20.00	14.00	14.00	10.00	.75
495	4¢ Orange Brown	20.75	14.50	13.75	9.75	3.50
496	5¢ Blue	6.50	4.50	4.50	3.25	.75
497	10¢ Franklin, Orng. Yel.	35.00	25.00	24.50	17.50	9.50

LINE PAIRS

	NH		Unused		NH		Unused
Scott #	VF	F-VF	F-VF	Scott #	VF	F-VF	F-VF
486	7.50	5.25	3.75	493	200.00	150.00	110.00
487	235.00	160.00	110.00	494	105.00	75.00	55.00
488	46.50	28.50	19.50	495	120.00	90.00	65.00
489	60.00	40.00	27.50	496	40.00	28.00	20.00
490	8.25	5.50	3.75	497	195.00	140.00	100.00
492	100.00	70.00	45.00				

NOTE: PRIOR TO 1935, TO DETERMINE VERY FINE USED PRICE, ADD VF% AT BEGINNING OF EACH SET TO THE APPROPRIATE FINE PRICE. MINIMUM 10¢ PER STAMP.

FOR INFORMATION CONCERNING VERY FINE SEE PAGE II

1917-19 Flat Press, No Watermark - Perf. 11 VF Used + 50% (B)

Scott's		NH		Unused		Used
No.		VF	F-VF	VF	F-VF	F-V
498	1¢ Washington, Green	.80	.55	.60	.42	.1
498e	1¢ Booklet Pane of 6	5.25	3.50	3.75	2.50	...
499	2¢ Carmine, Ty. I	.65	.45	.45	.30	.4
499e	2¢ Booklet Pane of 6	8.25	5.50	5.50	3.65	...
500	2¢ Deep Rose, Ty. Ia	375.00	285.00	275.00	190.00	135.0
501	3¢ Light Violet, Type I	27.00	18.00	18.00	11.50	.2
501b	3¢ Booklet Pane of 6	95.00	65.00	70.00	47.50	...
502	3¢ Dark Violet, Type II	33.75	22.50	22.50	15.00	.3
502b	3¢ Booklet Pane of 6	85.00	57.50	62.50	45.00	...
503	4¢ Brown	22.50	15.00	15.00	10.00	.2
504	5¢ Blue	17.50	12.00	12.00	8.00	.2
505	5¢ Rose ERROR	725.00	525.00	525.00	375.00	...
	5¢ ERROR in Block of 9	950.00	700.00	750.00	550.00	...
	5¢ Pair in Block of 12	1650.00	1200.00	1250.00	900.00	...
506	6¢ Red Orange	26.50	17.00	16.50	11.50	.3
507	7¢ Black	52.50	35.00	35.00	23.50	1.1
508	8¢ Franklin, Olive Bistre	24.00	16.00	16.00	11.00	.7
509	9¢ Salmon Red	27.50	18.00	18.50	12.50	2.2
510	10¢ Orange Yellow	35.00	23.00	24.00	15.75	.1
511	11¢ Light Green	18.00	12.00	11.00	8.25	3.5
512	12¢ Claret Brown	18.00	12.00	11.00	8.25	.5
513	13¢ Apple Green (1919)	21.50	14.50	14.75	9.75	6.7
514	15¢ Gray	80.00	50.00	52.50	35.00	1.0
515	20¢ Light Ultramarine	95.00	62.50	65.00	42.50	.3
516	30¢ Orange Red	85.00	55.00	55.00	37.50	.9
517	50¢ Red Violet	150.00	100.00	100.00	70.00	.7
518	$1 Violet Brown	130.00	87.50	87.50	60.00	1.7
518b	$1 Deep Brown		1350.00	1200.00	800.00	475.0

PLATE BLOCKS

	NH		Unused		NH		Unused
Scott #	VF	F-VF	F-VF	Scott #	VF	F-VF	F-VF
498 (6)	27.50	18.50	13.50	509 (6)	250.00	185.00	135.00
499 (6)	25.00	16.50	12.00	510 (6)	325.00	240.00	175.00
501 (6)	225.00	150.00	100.00	511 (6)	195.00	135.00	100.00
502 (6)	275.00	190.00	135.00	512 (6)	195.00	135.00	100.00
503 (6)	250.00	175.00	125.00	513 (6)	215.00	150.00	110.00
504 (6)	225.00	150.00	110.00	514 (6)	775.00	550.00	400.00
506 (6)	295.00	210.00	150.00	515 (6)	850.00	625.00	450.00
507 (6)	425.00	300.00	210.00	516 (6)	850.00	625.00	450.00
508 (6)	265.00	200.00	140.00				

1917 Same Design as #332, D.L. Wmk. - Perf. 11 VF Used + 100% (C)

519	2¢ Washington, Carmine	525.00	295.00	350.00	210.00	...

(* Mint and used copies of #519 have been extensively counterfeited. Examples of either should be purchased with, or subject to, a certificate of authenticity.)

523,547 524 537

1918 Flat Press, No Watermark, Perf. 11 VF Used + 40% (B)

523	$2 Franklin, Orng. Red & Blk.	1200.00	950.00	950.00	700.00	190.0
524	$5 Deep Green & Black	525.00	400.00	375.00	265.00	27.5

1918-20 Offset Printing, Perforated 11 VF Used + 40% (B)

525	1¢ Washington, Gray Grn.	3.00	2.25	2.00	1.50	.6
526	2¢ Carmine, Type IV (1920)	45.00	32.50	30.00	22.50	4.2
527	2¢ Carmine, Type V (1920)	28.00	20.00	18.00	13.50	1.1
528	2¢ Carmine, Type Va (1920)	16.50	12.00	12.00	8.50	.2
528A	2¢ Carmine, Type VI (1920)	80.00	60.00	57.50	40.00	1.4
528B	2¢ Carmine, Type VII (1920)	33.75	25.00	22.50	16.00	.3
529	3¢ Violet, Type III	5.50	3.75	3.35	2.50	.1
530	3¢ Purple, Type IV	2.10	1.50	1.35	1.00	.1

1918-20 Offset Printing, Imperforate VF Used + 20% (B)

531	1¢ Washington, Green (1919)	17.00	14.00	12.00	10.00	10.0
532	2¢ Carmine Rose, Type IV (20)	50.00	42.50	38.50	32.50	27.5
533	2¢ Camine, Type V (1920)	290.00	240.00	210.00	175.00	65.0
534	2¢ Carmine, Type Va (1920)	19.50	16.00	14.50	12.00	8.5
534A	2¢ Carmine, Type VI (1920)	50.00	42.50	36.50	30.00	26.5
534B	2¢ Carmine, Type VII (1920)		1850.00	1650.00	1350.00	525.0
535	3¢ Violet, Type IV	16.00	13.00	11.00	9.00	6.2

1919 Offset Printing, Perforated 12½ VF Used + 75% (B)

536	1¢ Washington, Gray Grn	27.50	17.50	18.75	12.50	12.5

PLATE BLOCKS

	NH		Unused		NH		Unused
Scott #	VF	F-VF	F-VF	Scott #	VF	F-VF	F-VF
525 (6)	33.75	25.00	16.50	530 (6)	19.50	14.00	10.00
526 (6)	275.00	200.00	150.00	531 (6)	120.00	95.00	70.00
527 (6)	195.00	140.00	100.00	532 (6)	385.00	325.00	235.00
528 (6)	115.00	85.00	60.00	534 (6)	140.00	110.00	85.00
528A (6)	495.00	375.00	250.00	534A (6)	425.00	350.00	250.00
528B (6)	210.00	160.00	110.00	535 (6)	110.00	90.00	65.00
529 (6)	90.00	65.00	45.00	536 (6)	260.00	175.00	125.00

1919 Victory Issue VF Used + 50% (B)

Scott's No.		NH VF	NH F-VF	Unused VF	Unused F-VF	Used F-VF
537	3¢ Violet	20.00	12.50	11.50	7.50	3.95
537a	3¢ Deep Red Violet	625.00	425.00	465.00	300.00	50.00
537c	3¢ Red Violet	80.00	52.50	55.00	37.50	12.75

1919-21 Rotary Press Printing - Various Perfs. VF Used + 75% (C)

Scott's No.		NH VF	NH F-VF	Unused VF	Unused F-VF	Used F-VF
538	1¢ Wash. Perf. 11x10	19.50	11.00	11.50	7.50	8.50
538a	1¢ Vert. Pr. Imperf. Horiz.	85.00	57.50	67.50	45.00	...
539	2¢ Car. Rose, Ty. II, Pf. 11x10	...	...	...	2500.00	...
540	2¢ Car. Rose,T.III, Pf.11x10	23.50	13.50	13.50	9.00	9.50
540a	2¢ Vert. Pr., Imperf. Horiz.	85.00	57.50	67.50	45.00	...
541	3¢ Violet, Perf. 11x10	65.00	38.50	37.50	25.00	29.50
542	1¢ Green, Perf. 10x11 (1920)	25.00	13.50	13.50	8.50	.95
543	1¢ Green, Perf. 10 (1921)	1.35	.75	.85	.50	.20
544	1¢ Perf. 11 (19x22½ mm) (1922)	...	...	...	...	2400.00
545	1¢ Pf.11 (19½x22 mm) (21)	295.00	165.00	175.00	110.00	115.00
546	2¢ Carmine Rose, Pf.11 (21)	195.00	115.00	125.00	75.00	85.00

1920 Flat Press, No Watermark, Perf. 11 VF Used + 4-% (B)

Scott's No.		NH VF	NH F-VF	Unused VF	Unused F-VF	Used F-VF
547	$2 Franklin, Carm. & Blk.	375.00	280.00	265.00	195.00	35.00

1920 Pilgrim Issue VF Used + 40% (B)

548 549 550

Scott's No.		NH VF	NH F-VF	Unused VF	Unused F-VF	Used F-VF
548-50	**Set of 3**	**83.50**	**60.00**	**61.50**	**43.50**	**17.50**
548	1¢ Mayflower, Green	7.00	5.00	4.85	3.50	2.40
549	2¢ Landing, Car. Rose	11.50	8.25	8.00	5.75	1.85
550	5¢ Compact, Deep Blue	67.50	48.50	50.00	35.00	13.50

PLATE BLOCKS

Scott #	NH VF	NH F-VF	Unused F-VF	Scott #	NH VF	NH F-VF	Unused F-VF
537 (6)	195.00	130.00	90.00	542 (6)	250.00	175.00	120.00
538	150.00	95.00	67.50	543 (4)	25.00	18.50	12.50
538a	950.00	750.00	600.00	543 (6)	55.00	40.00	27.50
540	160.00	100.00	70.00	548 (6)	80.00	57.50	42.50
540a	950.00	750.00	600.00	549 (6)	100.00	72.50	55.00
541	600.00	415.00	285.00	550 (6)	775.00	600.00	425.00

1922-25 Regular Issue, Flat Press, Perf. 11 VF Used + 40% (B)

551,653 553/633 556/636 562/642 566,696

567,698 570,701 572 573

Scott's No.		NH VF	NH F-VF	Unused VF	Unused F-VF	Used F-VF
551	½¢ Hale, Olive Brn ('25)	.30	.25	.25	.20	.15
552	1¢ Franklin, Green ('23)	3.00	2.25	2.10	1.50	.15
552a	1¢ Booklet Pane of 6	10.50	7.50	7.50	5.50	...
553	1½¢ Harding, Yel. Brn. ('25)	5.50	3.85	3.50	2.50	.35
554	2¢ Wash. Carmine ('23)	3.35	2.50	2.35	1.75	.15
554c	2¢ Booklet Pane of 6	14.50	10.50	9.50	6.75	...
555	3¢ Lincoln, Violet ('23)	33.50	24.75	22.75	16.50	1.10
556	4¢ M. Wash., Yel. Brn. ('23)	37.00	27.00	26.00	18.00	.25
557	5¢ T. Roosevelt, Dk. Blue	33.50	24.75	22.75	16.50	.15
558	6¢ Garfield, Red Orange	56.50	42.50	41.50	30.00	.90
559	7¢ McKinley, Black ('23)	15.00	11.00	10.50	7.50	.75
560	8¢ Grant, Ol.Grn. ('23)	75.00	55.00	50.00	37.50	.80
561	9¢ Jefferson, Rose ('23)	27.50	20.00	19.00	13.50	1.30
562	10¢ Monroe, Orange ('23)	46.75	32.50	30.00	21.50	.20
563	11¢ Hayes, Greenish Blue	3.00	2.25	2.10	1.50	.30
564	12¢ Cleveland, Br. Vio. ('23)	16.75	12.00	11.00	8.00	.25
565	14¢ Indian, Blue ('23)	10.00	7.25	7.00	5.00	.90
566	15¢ Liberty, Gray	45.00	31.50	31.50	22.50	.20
567	20¢ Golden Gate,C.Rose ('23)	45.00	31.50	31.50	22.50	.20
568	25¢ Niagara Falls, Yel. Grn.	37.50	28.50	27.50	19.50	.65
569	30¢ Buffalo, Ol Brown ('23)	69.50	51.50	48.00	33.50	.50
570	50¢ Amphitheater, Lilac	120.00	85.00	80.00	57.50	.20
571	$1 Lincoln, Vio. Blk. (1923)	80.00	58.50	56.50	42.50	.50
572	$2 Capitol, Blue (1923)	200.00	155.00	150.00	110.00	10.00
573	$5 Carmine & Blue (1923)	385.00	280.00	270.00	215.00	13.50

1922-25 Regular Issue, Flat Press, Perf. 11

PLATE BLOCKS

Scott #	NH VF	NH F-VF	Unused F-VF	Scott #	NH VF	NH F-VF	Unused F-VF
551 (6)	8.50	6.50	5.25	561 (6)	265.00	195.00	130.00
552 (6)	32.50	25.00	20.00	562 (6)	375.00	295.00	195.00
553 (6)	52.50	40.00	27.50	563 (6)	45.00	35.00	25.00
554 (6)	32.50	25.00	20.00	564 (6)	130.00	100.00	75.00
555 (6)	325.00	235.00	165.00	565 (6)	80.00	60.00	45.00
556 (6)	350.00	250.00	180.00	566 (6)	375.00	295.00	220.00
557 (6)	300.00	225.00	165.00	567 (6)	350.00	275.00	200.00
558 (6)	595.00	425.00	325.00	568 (6)	300.00	240.00	185.00
559 (6)	125.00	90.00	60.00	569 (6)	575.00	435.00	295.00
560 (6)	895.00	675.00	475.00	571 (6)	625.00	475.00	375.00

1923-25 Flat Press - Imperforate VF Used + 25% (B)

Scott's No.		NH VF	NH F-VF	Unused VF	Unused F-VF	Used F-VF
575	1¢ Franklin, Green	12.00	9.00	9.00	7.00	3.5
576	1½¢ Harding, Yel. Brn. (1925)	2.50	1.95	1.95	1.25	1.1
577	2¢ Washington, Carmine	2.60	2.00	2.00	1.50	1.3

1923 Rotary Press, Perforated 11 x 10 VF Used + 75% (C)

Scott's No.		NH VF	NH F-VF	Unused VF	Unused F-VF	Used F-VF
578	1¢ Franklin, Green	185.00	95.00	125.00	65.00	80.0
579	2¢ Washington, Carmine	150.00	65.00	95.00	50.00	70.0

1923-26 Rotary Press, Perforated 10 VF Used + 50% (B)

Scott's No.		NH VF	NH F-VF	Unused VF	Unused F-VF	Used F-VF
581-91	**Set of 11**	**300.00**	**200.00**	**210.00**	**145.00**	**16.5**
581	1¢ Franklin, Green	15.00	10.00	10.00	7.50	.9
582	1½¢ Harding, Brown (1925)	6.50	4.50	4.50	3.00	.9
583	2¢ Wash., Carmine (1924)	3.75	2.50	2.50	1.75	.2
583a	2¢ Booklet Pane of 6	125.00	87.50	85.00	57.50	...
584	3¢ Lincoln, Violet (1925)	40.00	25.50	28.50	20.00	2.1
585	4¢ M. Wash., Yel Brn (1925)	30.00	20.00	21.00	13.50	.6
586	5¢ T. Roos., Blue (1925)	30.00	20.00	21.00	13.50	.3
587	6¢ Garfield, Red Or. (1925)	14.75	8.75	8.50	5.75	.6
588	7¢ McKinley, Blk. (1926)	19.00	13.50	12.75	8.50	5.5
589	8¢ Grant, Ol. Grn. (1926)	47.50	31.50	32.50	21.50	3.5
590	9¢ Jefferson, Rose (1926)	8.50	5.75	5.95	4.00	2.2
591	10¢ Monroe, Orange (1925)	100.00	70.00	72.50	50.00	.2

PLATE BLOCKS

Scott #	NH VF	NH F-VF	Unused F-VF	Scott #	NH VF	NH F-VF	Unused F-VF
575 (6)	110.00	90.00	65.00	584	350.00	250.00	175.00
576 (6)	30.00	25.00	17.50	585	250.00	175.00	135.00
577 (6)	37.50	30.00	22.50	586	225.00	165.00	125.00
579	850.00	500.00	350.00	587	115.00	80.00	60.00
581	175.00	125.00	85.00	588	140.00	100.00	75.00
582	60.00	43.50	30.00	589	350.00	250.00	175.00
583	40.00	29.00	20.00	590	65.00	45.00	35.00
				591	950.00	650.00	450.00

1923 Rotary Press, Perforated 11 VF Used + 100% (C)

Scott's No.		NH VF	NH F-VF	Unused VF	Unused F-VF	Used F-VF
594	1¢ Franklin, Green	...	...	FINE	USED	3850.0
595	2¢ Washington, Carmine	450.00	250.00	300.00	175.00	185.0

1923-29 Rotary Press Coils, VF Used + 30% (B), (599A VF Used + 75%)

Scott's No.		NH VF	NH F-VF	Unused VF	Unused F-VF	Used F-VF
597-99,600-06	**Set of 10**	**27.50**	**19.75**	**19.50**	**14.50**	**1.9**
	Perforated 10 Vertically					
597	1¢ Franklin, Green	.55	.40	.40	.30	.1
598	1½¢ Harding, Brown (1925)	1.30	1.00	1.00	.75	.2
599	2¢ Washington, Car. Type I	.65	.50	.45	.35	.1
599A	2¢ Carmine, Type II (1929)	225.00	135.00	150.00	100.00	11.0
600	3¢ Lincoln, Violet (1924)	10.75	8.00	7.25	5.50	.2
601	4¢ M. Washington, Yel. Brn	6.50	4.75	4.75	3.50	.5
602	5¢ T. Roos., Dk. Blue (1924)	2.50	1.90	1.75	1.35	.2
603	10¢ Monroe, Orange (1924)	6.50	4.75	4.75	3.50	.2
	Perforated 10 Horizontally					
604	1¢ Franklin, Green (1924)	.40	.30	.28	.22	.1
605	1½¢ Harding, Yel. Brn. (1925)	.45	.35	.32	.25	.2
606	2¢ Washington, Carmine	.45	.35	.32	.25	.1

NOTE: Type I, #599, 634 - No heavy hair lines at top center of head.
Type II, #599A, 634A - Three heavy hair lines at top center of head.

LINE PAIRS

Scott #	NH VF	NH F-VF	Unused F-VF	Scott #	NH VF	NH F-VF	Unused F-VF
597	3.50	2.65	2.00	602	17.75	12.95	9.75
598	10.00	7.50	5.75	603	39.50	29.50	23.50
599	3.15	2.25	1.75	604	5.25	4.00	3.00
599A	975.00	650.00	500.00	605	4.25	3.25	2.50
600	50.00	36.50	27.50	606	3.50	2.65	2.00
601	53.50	40.00	30.00				

NOTE: STAMP ILLUSTRATIONS INDICATE DESIGNS. PERFORATIONS AND TYPES MAY VARY.

1923 Harding Memorial (#610 VF Used + 30%, #612 VF Used + 50%) Imperf. VF Used + 20% (B)

610-612 614 616

Scott's No.		NH VF	NH F-VF	Unused VF	Unused F-VF	Used F-VF
610-12	Set of 3	45.00	31.50	32.75	22.50	7.00
610	2¢ Black, Flat Press, Perf. 11	.95	.75	.70	.55	.15
611	2¢ Black, Flat Press Imperf.	11.50	9.00	8.75	6.50	5.25
612	2¢ Black, Rotary, Perf. 10	35.00	22.50	24.00	16.50	2.00

1924 Huguenot - Walloon Issue VF Used + 30% (B)

614-16	Set of 3	66.50	50.75	48.50	35.00	21.00
614	1¢ "New Netherlands"	5.25	4.00	4.00	3.00	2.75
615	2¢ Fort Orange	10.00	7.50	7.00	5.50	2.50
616	5¢ Ribault Monument	55.00	41.75	39.50	29.50	16.50

617 618 619

1925 Lexington - Concord Issue VF Used + 30% (B)

617-19	Set of 3	57.50	44.50	42.50	33.50	21.00
617	1¢ Cambridge	5.75	4.50	4.00	3.00	2.75
618	2¢ "Birth of Liberty"	10.00	7.50	7.00	5.50	2.75
619	5¢ "Minute Man"	45.00	35.00	33.50	26.50	16.50

PLATE BLOCKS

Scott #	NH VF	NH F-VF	Unused F-VF	Scott #	NH VF	NH F-VF	Unused F-VF
610 (6)	35.00	27.50	20.00	616 (6)	525.00	400.00	325.00
611 (6)	150.00	125.00	90.00	617 (6)	65.00	50.00	40.00
612	500.00	335.00	250.00	618 (6)	110.00	85.00	65.00
614 (6)	65.00	50.00	40.00	619 (6)	465.00	360.00	285.00
615 (6)	100.00	80.00	65.00				

620 621 622,694 623,697

1925 Norse American VF Used + 30% (B)

20	2¢ Sloop, Carmine & Blk.	8.50	6.50	6.00	4.50	3.50
21	5¢ Viking Ship, Blue & Black	35.00	27.50	25.00	19.50	13.75

1925-26 Designs of 1922-25, Flat Press, Perf. 11 VF Used + 40% (B)

22	13¢ Harrison, Green (1926)	24.00	17.50	18.50	13.50	.65
23	17¢ Wilson, Black	35.00	26.50	25.75	18.00	.40

627 628 629,630

1926 Commemoratives VF Used + 30% (B)

27	2¢ Sesquicentennial	5.00	3.75	3.75	2.75	.60
28	5¢ Ericsson Memorial	10.50	8.00	8.00	5.75	3.50
29	2¢ Battle of White Plains	4.25	3.00	2.80	2.00	1.75
30	2¢ White Plains, Phil. Exhib. Souvenir Sheet of 25	700.00	575.00	575.00	450.00	475.00
30v	2¢ "Dot over S" Var. Sheet	725.00	595.00	595.00	465.00	495.00

1926 Rotary Press, Imperforate VF Used + 20% (B)

31	1½¢ Harding, Brown	3.75	3.00	2.85	2.25	1.85
31v	1½¢ Vert. Pair, Horiz. Gutter	8.50	7.00	6.50	5.50	...
31h	1½¢ Horiz. Pair, Vert. Gutter	8.50	7.00	6.50	5.50	...

FOR INFORMATION CONCERNING VERY FINE SEE PAGE II

1925-1926 Commemorative & Regular Issues

PLATE BLOCKS

Scott #	NH VF	NH F-VF	Unused F-VF	Scott #	NH VF	NH F-VF	Unused F-VF
620 (8)	300.00	230.00	180.00	627 (6)	77.50	60.00	45.00
621 (8)	900.00	700.00	550.00	628 (6)	150.00	115.00	85.00
622 (6)	280.00	200.00	140.00	629 (6)	60.00	47.50	37.50
623 (6)	300.00	225.00	175.00	631	85.00	72.50	52.50

1926-1928 Rotary. Pf. 11x10½, Same as 1922-25 VF Used +30% (634A VF Used +75%)

Scott's No.		NH VF	NH F-VF	Unused VF	Unused F-VF	Used F-VF
632-34,635-42	Set of 11	30.00	23.50	23.50	18.75	1.60
632	1¢ Franklin, Green (1927)	.30	.25	.25	.20	.15
632a	1¢ Booklet Pane of 6	7.50	5.75	6.00	4.75	...
633	1½¢ Harding, Yel. Brn. (1927)	3.25	2.50	2.25	1.75	.20
634	2¢ Wash., Carmine, Ty. I	.30	.25	.25	.20	.15
634d	2¢ Booklet Pane of 6 (1927)	2.75	2.10	2.15	1.65	...
634A	2¢ Carmine, Type II (1928)	550.00	300.00	260.00	160.00	15.00
635	3¢ Lincoln, Violet (1927)	.70	.55	.55	.45	.18
636	4¢ M. Wash., Yel. Brn. (1927)	4.25	3.25	3.25	2.50	.18
637	5¢ T. Roos., Dk. Blue (1927)	3.25	2.50	2.50	2.00	.18
638	6¢ Garfield, Red Or. (1927)	3.50	2.70	2.70	2.15	.18
639	7¢ McKinley, Black (1927)	3.50	2.70	2.70	2.15	.18
640	8¢ Grant, Ol. Grn. (1927)	3.50	2.70	2.70	2.15	.18
641	9¢ Jefferson, Or. Red (1927)	3.50	2.70	2.70	2.15	.18
642	10¢ Monroe, Or. (1927)	6.50	5.00	5.25	4.00	.20

PLATE BLOCKS

Scott #	NH VF	NH F-VF	Unused F-VF	Scott #	NH VF	NH F-VF	Unused F-VF
632	3.50	2.60	2.10	637	33.50	25.00	18.00
633	140.00	105.00	75.00	638	33.50	25.00	18.00
634 (4)	2.75	2.25	1.75	639	33.50	25.00	18.00
634 EE (10)	7.50	5.75	4.50	640	33.50	25.00	18.00
635	16.00	12.00	8.75	641	33.50	25.00	18.00
636	150.00	110.00	80.00	642	47.50	35.00	27.50

1927-28 Commemoratives VF Used + 30% (B) (#646-648 VF Used + 50%)

643 644 645 649

643	2¢ Vermont Sesqui	2.25	1.75	1.65	1.30	1.20
644	2¢ Burgoyne Campaign	6.75	5.00	4.50	3.50	2.75
645	2¢ Valley Forge (1928)	1.65	1.30	1.25	1.00	.50
646	2¢ "Molly Pitcher" ovpt (on #634)	2.00	1.35	1.50	1.00	1.00
647	2¢ "Hawaii" ovpt. (on #634)	9.00	6.25	6.75	4.50	4.25
648	5¢ "Hawaii" ovpt. (on #637)	27.00	18.00	20.00	13.50	13.50
649	2¢ Aeronautics (1928)	1.95	1.50	1.45	1.10	1.00
650	5¢ Aeronautics (1928)	8.50	6.50	6.50	5.00	3.50

651 654-656 657 663

1929 Commemorative VF Used + 30% (B)

651	2¢ George Rogers Clark	1.00	.80	.75	.60	.60

1929 Rotary, Perf. 11x10½, Design of #551 VF Used + 30% (B)

653	½¢ Hale, Olive Brown	.30	.25	.25	.20	.15

1929 Commemoratives VF Used + 30% (B)

654	2¢ Edison, Flat, Perf. 11	1.35	1.00	.95	.75	.80
655	2¢ Edison, Rtry, Perf. 11x10½	1.40	.95	.95	.70	.25
656	2¢ Edison Coil, Perf. 10 Vert	22.50	16.50	16.50	12.50	1.90
657	2¢ Sullivan Expedition	1.20	.90	.90	.70	.60

NOTE: VF UNUSED PLATE BLOCKS AND LINE PAIRS ARE GENERALLY AVAILABLE AT THE RESPECTIVE F-VF NH PRICE.

1927-1929 Commemorative & Regular Issues

PLATE BLOCKS & LINE PAIRS

	NH		Unused		NH		Unused
Scott #	VF	F-VF	F-VF	Scott #	VF	F-VF	F-VF
643 (6)	58.50	45.00	37.50	650 (6)	115.00	87.50	62.50
644 (6)	82.50	63.50	47.50	651 (6)	23.50	18.00	13.50
645 (6)	53.50	41.50	28.50	653	2.10	1.60	1.20
646	60.00	40.00	30.00	654 (6)	45.00	35.00	28.50
647	280.00	200.00	135.00	655	85.00	65.00	47.50
648	460.00	310.00	250.00	656 Ln. Pr.	110.00	85.00	65.00
649 (6)	24.00	19.50	14.50	657 (6)	42.50	32.50	27.50

KANSAS - NEBRASKA ISSUES

1929 "Kans." Overprints on Stamps #632-42 VF Used + 60% (C)

Scott's No.		NH VF	NH Fine	Unused VF	Unused Fine	Used Fine
658-68	**Set of 11**	**385.00**	**250.00**	**265.00**	**175.00**	**130.00**
658	1¢ Franklin, Green	3.85	2.50	2.95	1.90	1.75
659	1½¢ Harding, Brown	5.25	3.50	4.00	2.75	3.00
660	2¢ Washington, Carmine	5.25	3.50	4.00	2.75	.70
661	3¢ Lincoln, Violet	30.00	21.00	21.50	14.50	10.00
662	4¢ M. Washington, Yel. Brn	30.00	21.00	21.50	14.50	7.00
663	5¢ T. Roosevelt, Deep Blue	26.50	17.50	18.00	12.00	8.25
664	6¢ Garfield, Red Orange	50.00	32.50	33.50	22.50	13.50
665	7¢ McKinley, Black	50.00	32.50	33.50	22.50	18.00
666	8¢ Grant, Olive Green	145.00	95.00	97.50	65.00	55.00
667	9¢ Jefferson, Light Rose	24.00	16.00	16.50	11.00	9.50
668	10¢ Monroe, Orng. Yel	40.00	26.50	27.00	18.00	10.00

1929 "Nebr." Overprints on Stamps #632-42 VF Used + 60% (C)

Scott's No.		NH VF	NH Fine	Unused VF	Unused Fine	Used Fine
669-79	**Set of 11**	**475.00**	**315.00**	**335.00**	**220.00**	**110.00**
669	1¢ Franklin, Green	4.75	3.25	3.25	2.25	1.85
670	1½¢ Harding, Brown	4.75	3.25	3.25	2.25	2.00
671	2¢ Washington, Carmine	3.75	2.50	2.50	1.75	.95
672	3¢ Lincoln, Violet	21.00	14.00	15.00	10.00	7.75
673	4¢ M. Washington, Yel. Brn	29.50	20.00	23.00	15.00	9.50
674	5¢ T. Roosevelt, Deep Blue	25.00	17.00	18.50	12.50	11.50
675	6¢ Garfield, Red Orange	75.00	49.50	50.00	33.50	16.50
676	7¢ McKinley, Black	40.00	27.00	28.50	18.50	12.50
677	8¢ Grant, Olive Green	56.50	37.50	37.50	25.00	17.00
678	9¢ Jefferson, Light Rose	67.50	45.00	45.00	29.50	20.00
679	10¢ Monroe, Orng. Yel	175.00	115.00	125.00	80.00	16.50

NOTE: IN 1929, SOME 1¢-10¢ STAMPS WERE OVERPRINTED "Kans." AND "Nebr." AS A MEASURE OF PREVENTION AGAINST POST OFFICE ROBBERIES IN THOSE STATES, THEY WERE USED ABOUT ONE YEAR, THEN DISCONTINUED.
Genuine unused, o.g. K-N's have either a single horiz. gum breaker ridge or two widely spaced horiz. ridges (21 mm apart). Unused, o.g. stamps with two horiz. ridges spaced 10 mm apart have counterfeit ovpts. Unused stamps without ridges are regummed and/or have a fake ovpt.

PLATE BLOCKS

Kansas				Nebraska			
	NH		Unused		NH		Unused
Scott #	VF	Fine	Fine	Scott #	VF	Fine	Fine
658	57.50	40.00	30.00	669	57.50	40.00	30.00
659	100.00	67.50	50.00	670	100.00	67.50	50.00
660	80.00	53.50	40.00	671	50.00	35.00	25.00
661	295.00	200.00	135.00	672	250.00	165.00	110.00
662	295.00	200.00	135.00	673	360.00	240.00	165.00
663	270.00	180.00	120.00	674	370.00	245.00	170.00
664	700.00	500.00	350.00	675	850.00	575.00	400.00
665	700.00	500.00	350.00	676	475.00	315.00	225.00
666	1250.00	850.00	650.00	677	650.00	435.00	325.00
667	315.00	210.00	140.00	678	715.00	475.00	350.00
668	585.00	400.00	275.00	679	1450.00	1000.00	750.00

1929-1930 Commemoratives VF Used + 30% (B)

680 681 682 683

Scott's No.		NH VF	NH F-VF	Unused VF	Unused F-VF	Used F-VF
680	2¢ Battle of Fallen Timbers	1.25	.95	1.00	.75	.70
681	2¢ Ohio River Canal	.85	.65	.65	.50	.60
682	2¢ Mass. Bay (1930)	1.10	.85	.75	.60	.55
683	2¢ Carolina-Charleston ('30)	2.00	1.50	1.40	1.10	1.10

1930 Regular Issues, Rotary Press VF Used + 30% (B)

684,686 685,687 688 689 690

Scott's No.		NH VF	NH F-VF	Unused VF	Unused F-VF	Used F-VF
684	1½¢ Harding, Brn., Pf. 11x10½	.40	.30	.30	.25	.15
685	4¢ Taft, Brn., Pf. 11x10½	1.40	1.10	1.15	.90	.15
686	1½¢ Brown, Coil, Pf. 10 Vert	3.00	2.30	2.25	1.70	.20
687	4¢ Brown, Coil, Pf. 10 Vert.	6.25	4.35	3.85	3.00	.65

1930-31 Commemoratives VF Used + 30% (B)

Scott's No.		NH VF	NH F-VF	Unused VF	Unused F-VF	Used F-VF
688	2¢ Braddock's Field	1.80	1.40	1.35	1.00	.85
689	2¢ Baron Von Steuben	.90	.65	.65	.50	.50
690	2¢ General Pulaski (1931)	.35	.30	.30	.25	.20

PLATE BLOCKS & LINE PAIRS

	NH		Unused		NH		Unused
Scott #	VF	F-VF	F-VF	Scott #	VF	F-VF	F-VF
680 (6)	50.00	39.50	29.50	688 (6)	70.00	53.50	37.50
681 (6)	32.50	25.00	20.00	689 (6)	37.50	28.50	22.50
682 (6)	62.50	46.50	32.50	690 (6)	25.00	20.00	15.00
683 (6)	90.00	70.00	50.00	**Line Pairs**			
684	3.95	2.95	2.10	686	13.50	9.50	7.00
685	17.50	12.50	10.00	687	28.75	21.00	15.00

1931 Rotary Press, Pf. 11x10½ or 10½x11 VF Used + 30% (B)
Designs of #563-70, 622-23

Scott's No.		NH VF	NH F-VF	Unused VF	Unused F-VF	Used F-VF
692-701	**Set of 10**	**200.00**	**145.00**	**140.00**	**99.50**	**2.50**
692	11¢ Hayes, Light Blue	5.50	3.75	3.35	2.50	.18
693	12¢ Cleveland, Brown Violet	11.50	8.75	8.25	6.00	.18
694	13¢ Harrison, Yel. Grn	4.50	2.95	3.00	2.00	.25
695	14¢ Indian, Dark Blue	7.75	5.75	5.50	4.00	.65
696	15¢ Liberty, Gray	16.50	12.00	11.75	8.25	.20
697	17¢ Wilson, Black	9.75	7.00	6.75	5.00	.40
698	20¢ Golden Gate, Car. Rose	21.50	14.50	14.00	10.00	.20
699	25¢ Niagara Falls, Blue Green	21.50	14.50	14.00	10.00	.23
700	30¢ Buffalo, Brown	31.50	23.00	22.50	16.00	.25
701	50¢ Amphitheater, Lilac	80.00	60.00	60.00	41.50	.23

PLATE BLOCKS

	NH		Unused		NH		Unused
Scott #	VF	F-VF	F-VF	Scott #	VF	F-VF	F-VF
692	24.50	18.50	14.00	697	47.50	34.00	24.00
693	49.50	39.50	26.50	698	82.50	60.00	45.00
694	24.50	18.50	14.00	699	82.50	60.00	45.00
695	38.50	28.75	20.00	700	150.00	115.00	80.00
696	70.00	52.50	39.50	701	395.00	295.00	210.00

702 703 704 715

1931 Commemoratives VF Used + 30% (B)

Scott's No.		NH VF	NH F-VF	Unused VF	Unused F-VF	Used F-VF
702	2¢ Red Cross	.30	.25	.25	.20	.18
703	2¢ Battle of Yorktown	.65	.50	.50	.40	.40

1932 Washington Bicentennial VF Used + 40% (B)

Scott's No.		NH VF	NH F-VF	Unused VF	Unused F-VF	Used F-VF
704-15	**Set of 12**	**41.50**	**29.85**	**29.95**	**24.50**	**2.50**
704	½¢ Olive Brown	.35	.25	.25	.20	.15
705	1¢ Green	.35	.25	.25	.20	.15
706	1½¢ Brown	.80	.55	.55	.45	.18
707	2¢ Carmine Rose	.35	.25	.25	.20	.15
708	3¢ Deep Violet	1.10	.75	.80	.60	.15
709	4¢ Light Brown	.50	.40	.38	.30	.18
710	5¢ Blue	2.65	2.00	2.10	1.60	.20
711	6¢ Red Orange	6.50	4.65	4.65	3.50	.20
712	7¢ Black	.50	.40	.38	.30	.20
713	8¢ Olive Bistre	5.75	4.25	4.35	3.25	.85
714	9¢ Pale Red	5.00	3.65	3.65	2.75	.28
715	10¢ Orange Yellow	20.00	14.00	14.00	12.50	.15

★ FLASH - SPECIAL NEWS BULLETIN ★

BROOKMAN'S "SIGNATURES" IS HERE!

YOUR NEW HEADQUARTERS FOR PHILATELIC AUTOGRAPHS

AMELIA EARHART

CHARLES A. LINDBERGH

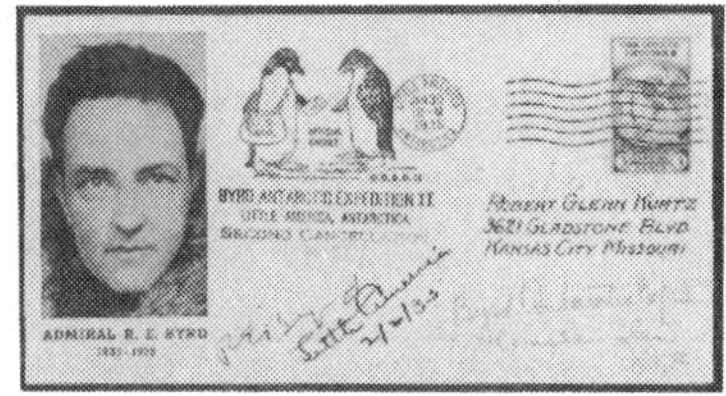

ADM. RICHARD E. BYRD

ELEANOR ROOSEVELT

HENRY WALLACE

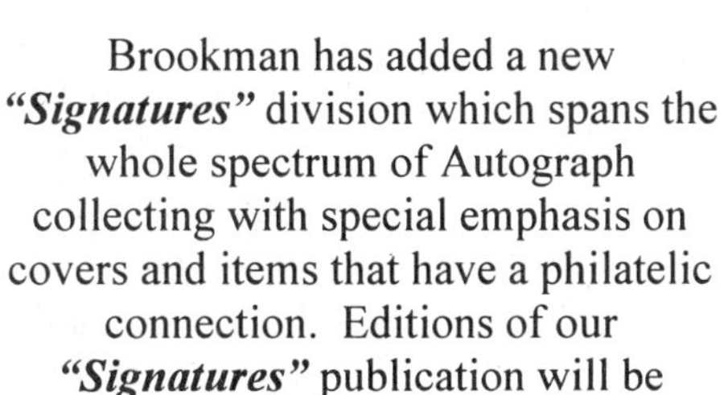

Brookman has added a new *"Signatures"* division which spans the whole spectrum of Autograph collecting with special emphasis on covers and items that have a philatelic connection. Editions of our *"Signatures"* publication will be issued several times a year.

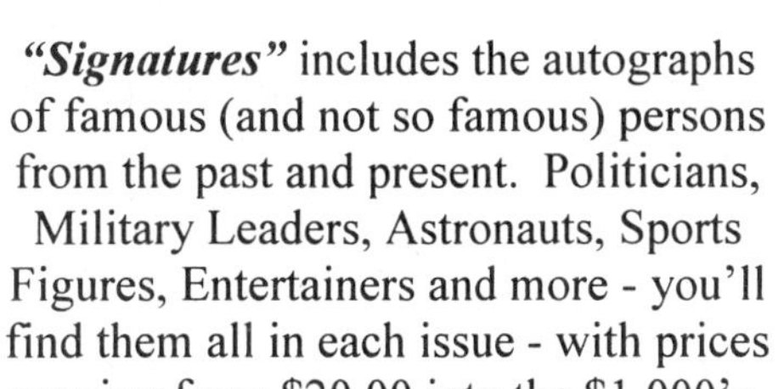

"Signatures" includes the autographs of famous (and not so famous) persons from the past and present. Politicians, Military Leaders, Astronauts, Sports Figures, Entertainers and more - you'll find them all in each issue - with prices ranging from $20.00 into the $1,000's. Even if you haven't considered collecting Autographs before, you'll find something of interest in every issue of ***Brookman's "Signatures."*** It's **FREE**, so call or write for the latest edition.

CHAING KAI-SHEK

JOHN PHILIP SOUSA

J.H. DOOLITTLE

GEORGE MARSHALL

1939 DETROIT TIGERS

BABE RUTH

ORIGINAL 6 ASTRONAUTS

SEND FOR YOUR FREE COPY TODAY OR, BETTER YET, CALL ANYTIME DAY OR NIGHT

TOLL-FREE 1-800-332-3383

AND WE'LL RUSH A COPY TO YOU

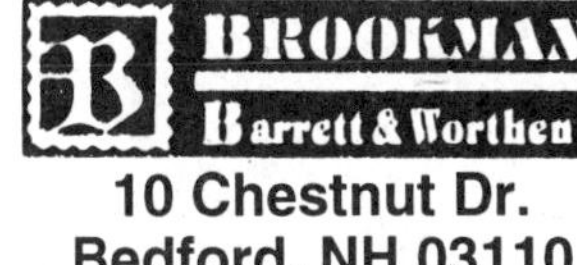

10 Chestnut Dr.
Bedford, NH 03110
Fax 603-472-8795

1931-1932 Commemoratives

PLATE BLOCKS

Scott #	NH VF	NH F-VF	Unused F-VF	Scott #	NH VF	NH F-VF	Unused F-VF
702	4.00	3.25	2.50	708	29.50	22.00	16.50
703 (4)	4.75	3.75	3.00	709	11.00	8.25	6.50
703 (6)	5.75	4.50	3.50	710	31.50	23.00	18.50
704-15	**700.00**	**515.00**	**385.00**	711	135.00	97.50	72.50
704	6.50	4.75	3.75	712	14.50	10.75	8.00
705	7.00	5.00	4.00	713	130.00	95.00	70.00
706	36.50	26.50	19.50	714	95.00	67.50	50.00
707	3.50	2.60	2.00	715	250.00	185.00	135.00

1932 Commemoratives VF Used + 30% (B)

716 717 718 720-22 723

Scott's No.		NH VF	NH F-VF	Unused VF	Unused F-VF	Used F-VF
716	2¢ Winter Olym., Lake Placid	.70	.55	.50	.40	.28
717	2¢ Arbor Day	.30	.25	.25	.20	.15
718	3¢ Summer Olympics	2.75	2.15	2.15	1.65	.20
719	5¢ Summer Olympics	3.75	3.00	2.75	2.25	.27

1932 Regular Issues, Rotary Press VF Used + 30% (B)

Scott's No.		NH VF	NH F-VF	Unused VF	Unused F-VF	Used F-VF
720	3¢ Washington, D. Violet	.30	.25	.25	.20	.15
720b	3¢ Booklet Pane of 6	72.50	52.50	47.50	35.00	...
721	3¢ D. Violet, Coil, Pf. 10 Vert.	3.75	3.00	3.00	2.50	.20
722	3¢ D. Violet, Coil, Pf. 10 Hor.	2.00	1.60	1.60	1.25	.65
723	6¢ Garfield, Orange, Coil, Perf. 10 Vertically	15.00	12.00	11.75	9.00	.30

1932 Commemoratives VF Used + 30% (B)

724 725 726 727,752

Scott's No.		NH VF	NH F-VF	Unused VF	Unused F-VF	Used F-VF
724	3¢ William Penn	.50	.40	.35	.28	.20
725	3¢ Daniel Webster	.60	.45	.45	.35	.33

1933 Commemoratives VF Used + 30% (B)

Scott's No.		NH VF	NH F-VF	Unused VF	Unused F-VF	Used F-VF
726	3¢ Georgia, Oglethorpe	.50	.40	.40	.32	.25
727	3¢ Peace, Newburgh	.30	.25	.25	.20	.15

PLATE BLOCKS & LINE PAIRS

Scott #	NH VF	NH F-VF	Unused F-VF	Scott #	NH VF	NH F-VF	Unused F-VF
716 (6)	22.50	17.00	12.50	726 (6)	22.50	18.00	13.50
717	12.00	9.50	7.50	726 (10)	27.50	22.50	17.50
718	36.50	27.50	20.00	727	9.50	7.50	6.00
719	47.50	37.50	30.00	**Line Pairs**			
720	2.85	2.25	1.65	721	9.75	7.50	6.00
724 (6)	20.00	16.00	11.50	722	8.00	6.00	4.50
725 (6)	37.50	30.00	22.50	723	85.00	65.00	48.50

1933 Commemoratives VF Used + 30% (B)

728,730a,766a 729,731a,767a 732 733,735a,753 734

Scott's No.		NH VF	NH F-VF	Unused VF	Unused F-VF	Used F-VF
728	1¢ Chicago, Ft. Dearborn	.30	.25	.25	.20	.15
729	3¢ Chicago, Fed. Bldg.	.30	.25	.25	.20	.15
730	1¢ Chicago, Imperf S/S of 25	...	...	...	40.00	32.50
730a	1¢ Single Stamp from sheet	...	...	.75	.65	.55
731	3¢ Chicago, Imperf. S/S of 25	...	...	...	32.50	27.50
731a	3¢ Single Stamp from Sheet	...	...	.65	.55	.50
732	3¢ Natl. Recovery Act	.30	.25	.25	.20	.15
733	3¢ Byrd. Antarctic Exp	.80	.65	.65	.55	.65
734	5¢ Gen. Kosciuszko	.95	.75	.70	.60	.35
735	3¢ Byrd, Imperf S/S of 6	...	...	...	17.50	16.50
735a	3¢ Single Stamp from sheet	...	...	3.00	2.75	2.65

NOTE: #730, 731 AND 735 WERE ISSUED WITHOUT GUM.

FOR INFORMATION CONCERNING VERY FINE SEE PAGE II

1934 Commemoratives VF Used + 30% (B)

736 737,738,754 739,755

Scott's No.		NH VF	NH F-VF	Unused VF	Unused F-VF	Used F-VF
736	3¢ Maryland Tercentary	.30	.25	.25	.20	.18
737	3¢ Mother's Day, Rotary, Perf. 11x10½	.30	.25	.25	.20	.15
738	3¢ Mother's Day, Flat Press, Perf. 11	.35	.30	.30	.25	.20
739	3¢ Wisconsin Tercentenary	.35	.30	.30	.25	.15

PLATE BLOCKS

Scott #	NH VF	NH F-VF	Unused F-VF	Scott #	NH VF	NH F-VF	Unused F-VF
728	4.75	3.35	2.65	734 (6)	60.00	47.50	35.00
729	7.25	5.65	4.25	736 (6)	17.50	13.00	10.00
732	3.00	2.40	2.00	737	2.50	2.00	1.65
733 (6)	27.50	21.50	16.50	738 (6)	8.00	6.25	5.00
				739 (6)	7.25	5.50	4.50

1934 National Parks Issue - Perf. 11 VF Used + 30% (B)

740,756 744,760 747,763 749,765

741,757 742,758 743,759

745,761 746,762 748,764

Scott's No.		NH VF	NH F-VF	Unused VF	Unused F-VF	Used F-VF
740-49	**Set of 10**	**16.50**	**13.50**	**13.50**	**10.75**	**6.75**
740	1¢ Yosemite, Green	.30	.25	.25	.20	.15
741	2¢ Grand Canyon, Red	.30	.25	.25	.20	.15
742	3¢ Mt. Rainier, Violet	.35	.28	.28	.22	.15
743	4¢ Mesa Verde, Brown	.70	.55	.55	.45	.45
744	5¢ Yellowstone, Blue	1.50	1.25	1.25	1.00	.80
745	6¢ Crater Lake, Dk. Blue	1.85	1.50	1.50	1.25	1.15
746	7¢ Acadia, Black	1.25	1.00	1.00	.80	.80
747	8¢ Zion, Sage Green	3.15	2.50	2.50	2.00	1.90
748	9¢ Glacier, Red Orange	3.25	2.60	2.60	2.10	.75
749	10¢ Great Smoky, Gray Blk	5.50	4.35	4.35	3.50	1.25

NATIONAL PARKS PLATE BLOCKS

Scott #	NH VF	NH F-VF	Unused F-VF	Scott #	NH VF	NH F-VF	Unused F-VF
740-49	**200.00**	**160.00**	**125.00**	745 (6)	33.00	26.00	20.00
740 (6)	2.35	1.85	1.50	746 (6)	21.00	17.00	13.50
741 (6)	2.65	2.10	1.65	747 (6)	31.50	25.00	20.00
742 (6)	3.50	2.90	2.40	748 (6)	33.50	26.50	21.50
743 (6)	15.75	12.50	10.00	749 (6)	53.75	42.50	32.50
744 (6)	16.75	13.50	10.75				

1934 National Parks Souvenir Sheets

Scott's No.		NH VF	NH F-VF	Unused VF	Unused F-VF	Used F-VF
750	3¢ Parks, Imperf. Sheet of 6	...	55.00	...	45.00	30.00
750a	3¢ Single Stamp from Sheet	5.75	5.25	5.00	4.50	3.75
751	1¢ Parks, Imperf. Sheet of 6	...	16.50	...	13.50	11.50
751a	1¢ Single Stamp from Sheet	2.25	1.95	1.85	1.65	1.75

NOTE: PRICES THROUGHOUT THIS LIST ARE SUBJECT TO CHANGE WITHOUT NOTICE IF MARKET CONDITIONS REQUIRE. MINIMUM MAIL ORDER MUST TOTAL AT LEAST $20.00.

1933-1934 Souvenir Sheets

730,766

731,767

735,768

750,770

751,769

OTE: PRICES THROUGHOUT THIS LIST ARE SUBJECT TO CHANGE WITHOUT NOTICE IF ARKET CONDITIONS REQUIRE. MINIMUM MAIL ORDER MUST TOTAL AT LEAST $20.00.

VERY FINE COPIES OF #752-DATE ARE AVAILABLE FOR THE FOLLOWING PREMIUMS: ADD 10¢ TO ANY ITEM PRICED UNDER 50¢. ADD 20% TO ANY ITEM PRICED AT 50¢ & UP. UNLESS PRICED AS VERY FINE, SETS ARE NOT AVAILABLE VERY FINE AND STAMPS SHOULD BE LISTED INDIVIDUALLY WITH APPROPRIATE PREMIUM.

1935 Farley Special Printing Issue

These stamps were issued imperforate (except #752 & 753) and without gum. For average quality on #752 and 753, deduct 20%. Horiz. and Vert. Gutter or Line Blocks are available at double the pair price.

NOTE: #752, 766A-70A HAVE GUTTERS INSTEAD OF LINES.

Horizontal Pairs Vertical Gutters — **Vertical Pair Horizontal Line**

Cross Gutter Block — **Arrow Block**

Scott's No.		F-VF Plate Blocks	Hz. Pair Vert.Line	Vert. Pr. Hz.Line	Singles Unused	Singles Used
752-71	**Set of 20......................................**		**132.50**	**92.50**	**28.75**	**22.50**
752	3¢ Newburgh, Pf.10½x11........	18.00	7.00	4.00	.20	.15
753	3¢ Byrd, Perf. 11............ (6)	18.50	43.50	1.75	.55	.55
754	3¢ Mother's Day, Imperf (6)	18.50	2.00	2.25	.60	.55
755	3¢ Wisconsin, Imperf..... (6)	18.50	2.00	2.25	.60	.55
	National Parks, Imperforate					
756-65	**Set of 10........................ (6)**	**315.00**	**41.50**	**41.50**	**15.75**	**14.75**
756	1¢ Yosemite.................. (6)	7.50	.55	.45	.20	.18
757	2¢ Grand Canyon .... (6)	8.25	.60	.75	.24	.20
758	3¢ Mt. Rainier .... (6)	17.50	1.40	1.60	.55	.50
759	4¢ Mesa Verde .... (6)	25.00	2.50	3.00	1.10	1.10
760	5¢ Yellowstone .... (6)	31.50	5.25	4.25	2.00	1.85
761	6¢ Crater Lake............... (6)	43.50	6.00	6.75	2.50	2.25
762	7¢ Acadia....................... (6)	41.50	4.50	5.00	1.90	1.75
763	8¢ Zion........................... (6)	45.00	6.50	4.85	2.00	1.90
764	9¢ Glacier .... (6)	51.50	5.75	6.00	2.10	2.00
765	10¢ Great Smoky........... (6)	60.00	12.00	11.00	4.00	3.85
	Singles And Pairs From Souvenir Sheets, Imperforate					
766a-70a	**Set of 5.........................**	...	**39.50**	**36.50**	**9.50**	**8.25**
766a	1¢ Chicago.......................	...	8.00	7.00	.90	.55
767a	3¢ Chicago.......................	...	8.00	7.00	.90	.55
768a	3¢ Byrd	...	9.00	7.50	3.00	2.75
769a	1¢ Park	...	5.25	4.75	1.65	1.50
770a	3¢ Park	...	11.00	12.00	3.50	3.25
	Airmail Special Delivery, Imperforate (Design of CE1)					
771	16¢ Dark Blue............. (6)	77.50	7.00	9.00	3.00	2.50

FARLEY SPECIAL PRINTING POSITION BLOCKS
All stamps are F-VF and without gum as issued

Scott's No.	Center Line Block	T or B Arrow Block	L or R Arrow Block	Scott's No.	Center Line Block	T or B Arrow Block	L or R Arrow Block
752-71	**465.00**	**...**	**...**	762	18.50	10.00	11.25
752	50.00	15.00	8.50	763	20.00	14.00	11.00
753	95.00	90.00	3.75	764	20.00	12.50	13.50
754	9.50	4.25	4.75	765	35.00	25.00	23.00
755	9.50	4.25	4.75	**766a-70a**	**81.50**	**...**	**...**
756-65	**160.00**	**92.50**	**91.50**	766a	15.00	...	...
756	4.50	1.25	1.00	767a	16.50	...	...
757	5.00	1.40	1.75	768a	17.50	...	...
758	7.50	3.25	3.60	769a	10.75	...	...
759	13.50	5.50	6.50	770a	23.50	...	...
760	18.50	11.50	9.50	771	80.00	15.00	19.50
761	25.00	13.50	15.00				

1935 Commemoratives

772 773 775

774 784 777

778

776 782 783

Scott's No.		Mint Sheet	Plate Block	F-VF NH	F-VF Used
772-75	**Set of 4**	...	...	**.70**	**.55**
772	3¢ Connecticut	11.00	1.90	.20	.15
773	3¢ California-Pacific	7.00	1.65	.20	.15
774	3¢ Boulder Dam	8.50	(6)2.25	.20	.15
775	3¢ Mich. Centenary	7.50	1.65	.20	.15

1936 Commemoratives

Scott's No.		Mint Sheet	Plate Block	F-VF NH	F-VF Used
776-78,782-84	**Set of 6**	...	...	**3.70**	**3.40**
776	3¢ Texas Centennial	8.00	1.75	.20	.15
777	3¢ Rhode Island	9.00	1.75	.20	.15
778	3¢ TIPEX Souv. Sht. of 4	...	...	2.85	2.85
778a	3¢ Conn., Imperf	...	...	.70	.60
778b	3¢ Calif., Imperf	...	...	.70	.60
778c	3¢ Mich., Imperf	...	...	.70	.60
778d	3¢ Texas, Imperf	...	...	.70	.60
782	3¢ Arkansas Cent	8.00	1.65	.20	.15
783	3¢ Oregon Territory	8.00	1.65	.20	.15
784	3¢ Susan B. Anthony (100)	14.50	1.10	.20	.15

1936-1937 Army - Navy Series

785 786 787

788 789

1936-1937 Army - Navy Series

790 791 792

793 794

Scott's No.		Mint Sheet	Plate Block	F-VF NH	F-VF Used
785-94	**Set of 10**	**210.00**	**53.50**	**3.65**	**1.95**
785-94	**Very Fine Set of 10**	...	**67.50**	**4.65**	**2.85**
785	1¢ Army-Wash. & Greene	5.75	1.20	.20	.15
786	2¢ Army-Jackson & Scott	7.00	1.20	.20	.15
787	3¢ Army-Sherman, Grant. Sheridan	29.00	2.50	.50	.15
788	4¢ Army-Lee & Jackson	32.50	12.00	.45	.35
789	5¢ Army-West Point	47.50	13.00	.80	.35
790	1¢ Navy-Jones & Barry	5.75	1.20	.20	.15
791	2¢ Navy-Decatur & MacDonough	7.00	1.20	.20	.15
792	3¢ Navy-Farragut & Porter	12.00	1.50	.25	.15
793	4¢ Navy-Sampson, Dewey, Schley	30.00	13.50	.40	.35
794	5¢ Navy-U.S. Naval Acad	45.00	13.50	.80	.35

1937 Commemoratives

795 796 798 799

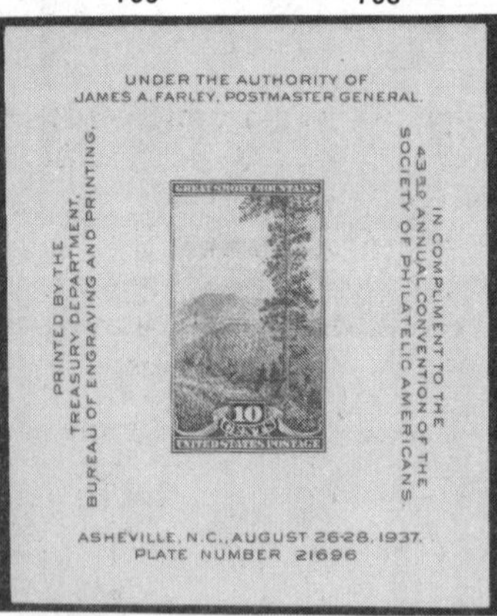

797

800 801 802

Scott's No.		Mint Sheet	Plate Block	F-VF NH	F-VF Used
795-802	**Set of 8**	...	...	**2.10**	**1.50**
795	3¢ Ordinance of 1787	7.50	1.60	.20	.15
796	5¢ Virginia Dare (48)	19.00	(6) 9.00	.25	.20
797	10¢ SPA Souvenir Sheet	...	...	.85	.65
798	3¢ Constitution	11.75	1.70	.25	.15
799	3¢ Hawaii Territory	8.75	1.65	.20	.15
800	3¢ Alaska Territory	9.75	1.65	.20	.15
801	3¢ Puerto Rico Territory	8.75	1.65	.20	.15
802	3¢ Virgin Is. Territory	8.75	1.65	.20	.15

NOTE: FROM 1935 TO DATE, WITH FEW LISTED EXCEPTIONS, UNUSED PRICES ARE FOR NEVER HINGED STAMPS. HINGED STAMPS, WHEN AVAILABLE, ARE PRICED AT APPROXIMATELY 15% BELOW THE NEVER HINGED PRICE.

1938 Presidential Series

803 | 804,839,848 | 805,840,849 | 806,841,850 | 807,842,851

808,843 | 809,844 | 810,845 | 811,846 | 812

813 | 814 | 815,847 | 816 | 817

818 | 819 | 820 | 821 | 822

823 | 824 | 825 | 826 | 827

828 | 829 | 830 | 831

832 | 833 | 834

cott's No.		Mint Sheet	Plate Block	F-VF NH	F-VF Used
03-34	**Set of 32**	...	**875.00**	**190.00**	**16.50**
03-34	**Very Fine Set of 32**	...	**1050.00**	**230.00**	**21.50**
03-31	**Set of 29 (½¢-50¢)**	...	**185.00**	**37.50**	**5.25**
03-31	**Very Fine Set of 29**	...	**225.00**	**45.00**	**7.75**
03	½¢ Franklin (100)	8.50	.50	.20	.15
04	1¢ Washington (100)	10.00	.45	.20	.15
04b	1¢ Booklet Pane of 6	...	...	2.25	...
05	1½¢ Martha Washington (100)	10.00	.45	.20	.15
06	2¢ John Adams (100)	14.50	.50	.20	.15
06	Electric Eye Plate	...	(10) 6.50	...	...
06b	2¢ Booklet Pane of 6	...	...	4.75	...
07	3¢ Jefferson (100)	12.00	.65	.20	.15
07	Electric Eye Plate	...	(10) 25.00	...	...
07a	3¢ Booklet Pane of 6	...	...	8.25	...
08	4¢ Madison (100)	125.00	5.25	1.15	.15
09	4½¢ White House (100)	35.00	1.60	.30	.15
10	5¢ Monroe (100)	28.00	1.20	.25	.15
11	6¢ John Quincy Adams (100)	35.00	1.50	.30	.15
12	7¢ Jackson (100)	45.00	1.90	.40	.15
13	8¢ Van Buren (100)	50.00	2.25	.45	.15

Scott's No.		Mint Sheet	Plate Block	F-VF NH	F-VF Used
814	9¢ William H. Harrison (100)	65.00	2.50	.50	.15
815	10¢ Tyler (100)	60.00	1.65	.45	.15
816	11¢ Polk (100)	67.50	4.50	.70	.15
817	12¢ Taylor (100)	125.00	6.00	1.35	.18
818	13¢ Fillmore (100)	210.00	9.50	2.25	.18
819	14¢ Pierce (100)	105.00	6.25	1.10	.18
820	15¢ Buchanan (100)	90.00	2.50	.75	.15
821	16¢ Lincoln (100)	110.00	6.00	1.10	.55
822	17¢ Andrew Johnson (100)	115.00	6.00	1.20	.18
823	18¢ Grant (100)	225.00	10.00	2.30	.22
824	19¢ Hayes (100)	190.00	9.25	2.00	.70
825	20¢ Garfield (100)	130.00	5.00	1.25	.15
826	21¢ Arthur (100)	215.00	10.75	2.25	.20
827	22¢ Cleveland (100)	135.00	13.00	1.40	.75
828	24¢ Benjamin Harrison (100)	425.00	19.50	4.25	.30
829	25¢ McKinley (100)	100.00	4.75	1.10	.15
830	30¢ Theodore Roosevelt (100)	485.00	22.50	5.00	.18
831	50¢ Taft	...	38.50	8.50	.18
832	$1 Wilson, Purple. & Black	...	45.00	10.00	.20
832b	$1 Wtmk. "USIR"	...	...	300.00	65.00
832c	$1 Dry Printing,Red Vlt/Blk(1954)	...	40.00	9.00	.20
833	$2 Harding	...	135.00	27.50	6.00
834	$5 Coolidge	...	550.00	125.00	5.50

1938 Commemoratives

835 | 836 | 837 | 838

835-38	**Set of 4**	...	...	**1.00**	**.50**
835	3¢ Const. Ratification	21.00	5.00	.45	.15
836	3¢ Swedish-Finnish Terr (48)	9.50	(6) 3.50	.20	.15
837	3¢ Northwest Territory (100)	26.50	12.50	.20	.15
838	3¢ Iowa Territory	19.50	8.50	.25	.15

1939 Presidential Coils

Scott's No.		Line Pairs NH	F-VF NH	F-VF Used
839-51	**Set of 13**	**135.00**	**33.50**	**5.25**
839-51	**Very Fine Set of 13**	**165.00**	**40.00**	**6.50**
	Perforated 10 Vertically			
839	1¢ Washington	1.20	.30	.15
840	1½¢ M. Washington	1.35	.30	.15
841	2¢ John Adams	1.65	.35	.15
842	3¢ Jefferson	1.75	.50	.15
843	4¢ Madison	30.00	8.00	.60
844	4½¢ White House	5.00	.65	.55
845	5¢ Monroe	27.50	5.50	.40
846	6¢ John Q. Adams	7.00	1.10	.30
847	10¢ Tyler	46.50	11.00	.90
	Perforated 10 Horizontally			
848	1¢ Washington	2.50	.85	.20
849	1½¢ M. Washington	4.50	1.40	.60
850	2¢ John Adams	6.75	2.65	.70
851	3¢ Jefferson	6.25	2.50	.70

1939 Commemoratives

852 | 853 | 854 | 857

855 | 856 | 858

Scott's No.		Mint Sheet	Plate Block	F-VF NH	F-VF Used
852-58	**Set of 7**	...	...	**4.15**	**.95**
852	3¢ Golden Gate Expo	10.00	1.80	.20	.15
853	3¢ N.Y. World's Fair	10.50	2.40	.20	.15
854	3¢ Washington Inaugural	45.00	(6) 5.75	.95	.18
855	3¢ Baseball Centennial	110.00	11.00	2.30	.20
856	3¢ Panama Canal	24.50	(6) 4.50	.40	.18
857	3¢ Printing	10.00	1.50	.20	.15
858	3¢ 4 States to Statehood	10.00	1.75	.20	.15

1940 Famous Americans Series

863 868 873 878

883 888 893

Scott's No.		Mint Sheet	Plate Block	F-VF NH	F-VF Used
859-93	**Set of 35**	**2575.00**	**475.00**	**37.50**	**18.50**
859-93	**Very Fine Set of 35**	**...**	**575.00**	**45.00**	**22.50**
859/91	1¢,2¢,3¢ Values (21)	...	36.50	3.95	2.50
	Authors				
859	1¢ Washington Irving (70)	8.75	1.50	.20	.15
860	2¢ James F. Cooper (70)	15.00	1.50	.25	.15
861	3¢ Ralph W. Emerson (70)	9.50	1.70	.20	.15
862	5¢ Louisa M. Alcott (70)	37.50	13.50	.40	.30
863	10¢ Samuel L. Clemens (70)	175.00	49.50	2.10	2.00
	Poets				
864	1¢ Henry W. Longfellow (70)	8.75	2.50	.20	.15
865	2¢ John G. Whittier (70)	10.75	2.35	.20	.15
866	3¢ James R. Lowell (70)	12.50	3.00	.20	.15
867	5¢ Walt Whitman (70)	50.00	13.50	.60	.30
868	10¢ James W. Riley (70)	185.00	49.50	2.25	2.15
	Educators				
869	1¢ Horace Mann (70)	25.00	3.00	.30	.15
870	2¢ Mark Hopkins (70)	8.75	1.60	.20	.15
871	3¢ Charles W. Eliot (70)	16.50	3.00	.24	.15
872	5¢ Frances E. Willard (70)	42.50	14.50	.40	.30
873	10¢ Booker T. Washington (70)	200.00	45.00	3.00	2.00
	Scientists				
874	1¢ John James Audubon (70)	8.75	1.40	.20	.15
875	2¢ Dr. Crawford W. Long (70)	15.00	1.25	.25	.15
876	3¢ Luther Burbank (70)	9.50	1.40	.20	.15
877	5¢ Dr. Walter Reed (70)	27.50	8.50	.60	.25
878	10¢ Jane Addams (70)	115.00	33.50	1.65	1.60
	Composers				
879	1¢ Stephen C. Foster (70)	6.50	1.25	.20	.15
880	2¢ John Philip Sousa (70)	15.00	1.50	.25	.15
881	3¢ Victor Herbert (70)	10.75	1.50	.20	.15
882	5¢ Edward A. MacDowell (70)	47.50	12.50	.60	.30
883	10¢ Ethelbert Nevin (70)	365.00	52.50	4.75	2.00
	Artists				
884	1¢ Gilbert C. Stuart (70)	6.00	1.30	.20	.15
885	2¢ James A. Whistler (70)	7.00	1.15	.20	.15
886	3¢ Augustus Saint-Gaudens (70)	7.50	1.25	.20	.15
887	5¢ Daniel Chester French (70)	60.00	12.75	.90	.30
888	10¢ Frederic Remington (70)	185.00	42.50	2.15	1.85
	Inventors				
889	1¢ Eli Whitney (70)	15.00	2.75	.25	.15
890	2¢ Samuel F.B. Morse (70)	10.00	1.40	.20	.15
891	3¢ Cyrus H. McCormick (70)	32.50	2.50	.40	.15
892	5¢ Elias Howe (70)	95.00	19.50	1.25	.40
893	10¢ Alexander Graham Bell (70)	975.00	100.00	15.75	3.25

1940 Commemoratives

894 895 896 897

Scott's No.		Mint Sheet	Plate Block	F-VF NH	F-VF Used
894-902	**Set of 9**	**...**	**...**	**2.10**	**1.30**
894	3¢ Pony Express	25.00	4.50	.40	.20
895	3¢ Pan American Union	18.75	4.75	.28	.18
896	3¢ Idaho Statehood	12.50	2.50	.22	.15
897	3¢ Wyoming Statehood	12.50	2.35	.22	.15

NOTE: FROM #752 TO DATE, AVERAGE QUALITY STAMPS, WHEN AVAILABLE, WILL BE PRICED AT APPROXIMATELY 20% BELOW THE APPROPRIATE FINE QUALITY PRICE.

VERY FINE COPIES OF #752 - DATE ARE AVAILABLE FOR THE FOLLOWING PREMIUMS: ADD 10¢ TO ANY ITEM PRICED UNDER 50¢. ADD 20% TO ANY ITEM PRICED AT 50¢ & UP. UNLESS PRICED AS VERY FINE, SETS ARE NOT AVAILABLE VERY FINE AND STAMPS SHOULD BE LISTED INDIVIDUALLY WITH APPROPRIATE PREMIUM.

1940 Commemoratives (cont.)

898 899 900 901 902

Scott's No.		Mint Sheet	Plate Block	F-VF NH	F-V Use
898	3¢ Coronado Expedition	12.50	2.35	.22	.1
899	1¢ Defense, Liberty (100)	12.50	.65	.20	.1
900	2¢ Defense, Anti-Aircraft (100)	12.50	.65	.20	.1
901	3¢ Defense, Torch (100)	15.00	.90	.20	.1
902	3¢ Thirteenth Amendment	25.00	4.95	.35	.2

1941-1943 Commemoratives

903 904 905

906 907 908

Scott's No.		Mint Sheet	Plate Block	F-VF NH	F-V Use
903-08	**Set of 6**	**...**	**...**	**1.40**	**.9**
903	3¢ Vermont	17.50	2.50	.30	.1
904	3¢ Kentucky (1942)	10.00	1.75	.20	.1
905	3¢ Win the War (1942) (100)	18.00	.80	.20	.1
906	5¢ China (1942)	30.00	12.00	.50	.2
907	2¢ United Nations (1943) (100)	10.00	.45	.20	.1
908	1¢ Four Freedoms (1943) (100)	10.00	.75	.20	.1

1943-44 Overrun Nations (Flags)

909 910 911

912 913 914

Scott's No.		Mint Sheet	Plate Block	F-VF NH	F-V Use
909-21	**Set of 13**	**200.00**	**67.50**	**3.25**	**2.6**
909-21	**Very Fine Set of 13**	**...**	**79.50**	**4.25**	**3.5**
909	5¢ Poland	12.00	7.95	.20	.2
910	5¢ Czechoslovakia	13.50	4.00	.22	.1
911	5¢ Norway	12.00	1.95	.20	.1
912	5¢ Luxembourg	12.00	1.75	.20	.1
913	5¢ Netherlands	12.00	1.75	.20	.1
914	5¢ Belgium	12.00	1.75	.20	.1
915	5¢ France	12.00	1.75	.20	.1
916	5¢ Greece	35.00	16.50	.60	.4
917	5¢ Yugoslavia	24.50	9.00	.35	.3
918	5¢ Albania	22.50	8.50	.40	.2
919	5¢ Austria	18.00	5.75	.30	.2
920	5¢ Denmark	19.50	7.00	.30	.2
921	5¢ Korea (1944)	13.00	6.00	.25	.2
921v	5¢ "KORPA" Variety	45.00	...	25.00	...

(On #909-21, the country name rather than a plate number appears in the margin.)

1944 Commemoratives

922

923

924

925

926

cott's lo.		Mint Sheet	Plate Block	F-VF NH	F-VF Used
:2-26	Set of 5	...	...	1.10	.70
:2	3¢ Transcontinental RR	25.00	2.00	.40	.20
:3	3¢ Steamship "Savannah"	8.50	1.90	.20	.15
:4	3¢ Telegraph	6.50	1.15	.20	.15
:5	3¢ Corregidor	8.00	1.40	.20	.15
:6	3¢ Motion Pictures	8.00	1.25	.20	.15

1945 Commemoratives

927

928

929

930

931

932

933

934

935

936

937

938

		Mint Sheet	Plate Block	F-VF NH	F-VF Used
27-38	Set of 12	...	...	2.20	1.50
27	3¢ Florida Statehood	6.00	.75	.20	.15
28	5¢ United Nations Conf	8.00	.70	.20	.15
29	3¢ Iwo Jima (Marines)	10.00	.65	.30	.15
30-33	Set of 4	17.50	1.80	.70	.50
30	1¢ Roosevelt	2.25	.30	.20	.15
31	2¢ Roosevelt	3.50	.40	.20	.15
32	3¢ Roosevelt	6.00	.65	.20	.15
33	5¢ Roosevelt (1946)	7.25	.65	.20	.15
34	3¢ Army	7.00	.65	.20	.15
35	3¢ Navy	7.00	.65	.20	.15
36	3¢ Coast Guard	5.50	.65	.20	.15
37	3¢ Alfred E. Smith (100)	10.00	.65	.20	.15
38	3¢ Texas Statehood	7.00	.65	.20	.15

1946 Commemoratives

939

940

941

942

943

944

Scott's No.		Mint Sheet	Plate Block	F-VF NH	F-VF Used
939-44	**Set of 6**	...	...	**1.10**	**.80**
939	3¢ Merchant Marine	5.50	.65	.20	.15
940	3¢ Honorable Discharge (100)	10.00	.65	.20	.15
941	3¢ Tennessee	5.00	.65	.20	.15
942	3¢ Iowa Centennial	5.00	.65	.20	.15
943	3¢ Smithsonian	5.00	.65	.20	.15
944	3¢ Santa Fe	5.50	.65	.20	.15

1947 Commemoratives

945

946

947

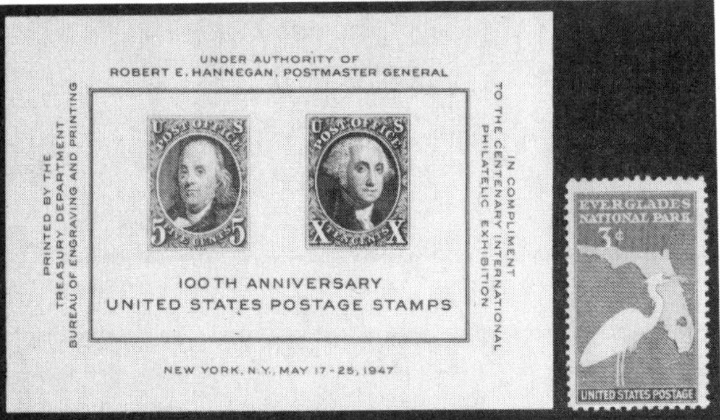

948

952

949

950

951

		Mint Sheet	Plate Block	F-VF NH	F-VF Used
945-52	**Set of 8**	...	...	**2.00**	**1.55**
945	3¢ Thomas A. Edison (70)	7.00	.65	.20	.15
946	3¢ Pulitzer	5.50	.65	.20	.15
947	3¢ Postage Centenary	5.00	.65	.20	.15
948	5¢ & 10¢ CIPEX Souv. Sheet	...	...	.85	.65
948a	5¢ Franklin, Blue	...	...	.30	.25
948b	10¢ Wash., Brown Orange	...	...	.55	.30
949	3¢ Doctors	5.00	.65	.20	.15
950	3¢ Utah Centennial	5.00	.65	.20	.15
951	3¢ Frigate Constitution	6.00	.65	.20	.15
952	3¢ Everglades Park	5.50	.65	.20	.15

NOTE: FROM 1935 TO DATE, WITH FEW LISTED EXCEPTIONS, UNUSED PRICES ARE FOR NEVER HINGED STAMPS. HINGED STAMPS, WHEN AVAILABLE, ARE PRICED AT APPROXIMATELY 15% BELOW THE NEVER HINGED PRICE.

1948 Commemoratives

953 954 955

956 957 958

959 960 961

962 963 964

965 966 967 969

968 970 971

972 973 974

975 976 977

1948 Commemoratives

978 979 980

Scott's No.		Mint Sheet	Plate Block	F-VF NH	F-VF Used
953-80	**Set of 28**	...	...	**5.25**	**3.75**
953	3¢ George W. Carver (70)	7.00	.65	.20	.15
954	3¢ California Gold Rush	5.00	.65	.20	.15
955	3¢ Mississippi Territory	5.00	.65	.20	.15
956	3¢ Four Chaplains	5.00	.65	.20	.15
957	3¢ Wisconsin Centennial	5.00	.65	.20	.15
958	5¢ Swedish Pioneers	7.50	.70	.20	.15
959	3¢ American Woman	5.00	.65	.20	.15
960	3¢ William A. White (70)	7.00	.70	.20	.15
961	3¢ U.S. - Canada Friendship	5.50	.65	.20	.15
962	3¢ Francis Scott Key	5.50	.65	.20	.15
963	3¢ American Youth	5.00	.65	.20	.15
964	3¢ Oregon Territory	5.50	.65	.20	.15
965	3¢ Harlan F. Stone (70)	7.50	.90	.20	.15
966	3¢ Palomar Observatory (70)	7.50	1.50	.20	.15
967	3¢ Clara Barton	7.50	.85	.25	.15
968	3¢ Poultry Industry	5.50	.65	.20	.15
969	3¢ Gold Star Mothers	5.50	.65	.20	.15
970	3¢ Fort Kearney, Nebraska	5.00	.65	.20	.15
971	3¢ Volunteer Firemen	7.50	.85	.25	.15
972	3¢ Indian Centennial	5.50	.65	.20	.15
973	3¢ Rough Riders	5.50	.65	.20	.15
974	3¢ Juliette Low, Girl Scouts	5.50	.65	.20	.15
975	3¢ Will Rogers, Humorist (70)	9.50	.75	.20	.15
976	3¢ Fort Bliss (70)	8.25	1.65	.20	.15
977	3¢ Moina Michael, Educator	5.50	.65	.20	.15
978	3¢ Gettysburg Address	10.00	1.10	.30	.15
979	3¢ Turners Society	5.50	.65	.20	.15
980	3¢ Joel Chandler Harris (70)	7.00	.70	.20	.15

1949 Commemoratives

981 982 983

984 985 986

Scott's No.		Mint Sheet	Plate Block	F-VF NH	F-VF Used
981-86	**Set of 6**	...	...	**1.10**	**.80**
981	3¢ Minnesota Territory	5.00	.65	.20	.15
982	3¢ Washington & Lee Univ	5.00	.65	.20	.15
983	3¢ Puerto Rico Election	5.00	.65	.20	.15
984	3¢ Annapolis Tercentenary	5.00	.65	.20	.15
985	3¢ Grand Army of the Rep	5.00	.65	.20	.15
986	3¢ Edgar Allan Poe, Writer (70)	7.00	.65	.20	.15

NOTE: PRICES THROUGHOUT THIS LIST ARE SUBJECT TO CHANGE WITHOUT NOTICE IF MARKET CONDITIONS REQUIRE. MINIMUM MAIL ORDER MUST TOTAL AT LEAST $20.00.

1950 Commemoratives

987 988 990

991 989 992

993 994 995

996 997

cott's No.		Mint Sheet	Plate Block	F-VF NH	F-VF Used
87-97	**Set of 11**	...	...	**1.95**	**1.50**
87	3¢ Bankers Association	5.00	.65	.20	.15
88	3¢ Samuel Gompers, Labor ..... (70)	7.00	.65	.20	.15
89	3¢ Freedom Statue	5.50	.65	.20	.15
90	3¢ Executive Mansion	7.50	.85	.25	.15
91	3¢ Supreme Court	6.00	.65	.20	.15
92	3¢ U.S. Capitol	5.75	.75	.20	.15
93	3¢ Railroad Engineers	7.50	.85	.25	.15
94	3¢ Kansas City Centenary	5.00	.65	.20	.15
95	3¢ Boy Scouts	6.50	.65	.20	.15
96	3¢ Indiana Territory	5.00	.65	.20	.15
97	3¢ California Statehood	5.75	.65	.20	.15

1951 Commemoratives

998 999 1000

1001 1002 1003

98-1003	**Set of 6**	...	...	**1.10**	**.80**
98	3¢ Confederate Veterans	7.50	.85	.25	.15
99	3¢ Nevada Centennial	5.00	.65	.20	.15
000	3¢ Landing of Cadillac	5.50	.65	.20	.15
001	3¢ Colorado Statehood	5.50	.65	.20	.15
002	3¢ Chemical Society	5.00	.65	.20	.15
003	3¢ Battle of Brooklyn	6.00	.65	.20	.15

VERY FINE COPIES OF #752-DATE ARE AVAILABLE FOR THE FOLLOWING PREMIUMS: ADD 10¢ TO ANY ITEM PRICED UNDER 50¢. ADD 20% TO ANY ITEM PRICED AT 50¢ & UP. UNLESS PRICED AS VERY FINE, SETS ARE NOT AVAILABLE VERY FINE AND STAMPS SHOULD BE LISTED INDIVIDUALLY WITH APPROPRIATE PREMIUM.

1952 Commemoratives

1004

1005

1006

1007

1008

1009

1011

1010

1012

1013

1014

1015

1016

Scott's No.		Mint Sheet	Plate Block	F-VF NH	F-VF Used
1004-16	**Set of 13**	...	...	**2.30**	**1.75**
1004	3¢ Betsy Ross	7.50	.85	.25	.15
1005	3¢ 4H Clubs	5.50	.65	.20	.15
1006	3¢ B & O Railroad	6.00	.65	.20	.15
1007	3¢ Amer. Auto Assoc	5.00	.65	.20	.15
1008	3¢ N.A.T.O. ..... (100)	10.00	.65	.20	.15
1009	3¢ Grand Coulee Dam	5.00	.65	.20	.15
1010	3¢ Marquis de Lafayette	5.75	.65	.20	.15
1011	3¢ Mt. Rushmore	6.00	.65	.20	.15
1012	3¢ Civil Engineers Society	5.50	.65	.20	.15
1013	3¢ Service Women	5.50	.65	.20	.15
1014	3¢ Gutenberg Bible	5.00	.65	.20	.15
1015	3¢ Newspaper Boys	5.50	.65	.20	.15
1016	3¢ Int'l. Red Cross	5.00	.65	.20	.15

1953 Commemoratives

1017

1018

1019

1020

1021

1022

1017-28	**Set of 12**	...	...	**2.25**	**1.60**
1017	3¢ National Guard	6.50	.65	.20	.15
1018	3¢ Ohio Statehood ..... (70)	7.25	.65	.20	.15
1019	3¢ Washington Territory	5.00	.65	.20	.15
1020	3¢ Louisiana Purchase	5.00	.65	.20	.15
1021	5¢ Opening of Japan, Perry	8.75	1.10	.25	.15
1022	3¢ American Bar Association	7.50	.85	.25	.15

1953 Commemoratives (cont.)

1023 1024 1025

1026 1027 1028

Scott's No.		Mint Sheet	Plate Block	F-VF NH	F-VF Used
1023	3¢ Sagamore Hill	5.00	.65	.20	.15
1024	3¢ Future Farmers	5.50	.65	.20	.15
1025	3¢ Trucking Industry	5.00	.65	.20	.15
1026	3¢ General Patton	7.50	.75	.25	.15
1027	3¢ New York City	6.00	.65	.20	.15
1028	3¢ Gadsden Purchase	5.50	.65	.20	.15

1954 Commemoratives

1029 1060 1061

1062 1063

1029,1060-63	**Set of 5**	...	...	.90	.65
1029	3¢ Columbia University	5.00	.65	.20	.15

1954-61 Liberty Series (B)

(Sheets of 100)

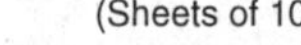

1030 1031,1054 1031A,1054A 1032 1033,1055

1034,1056 1035,1057 1036,1058 1037,1059 1038

1039 1040 1041 1042 1042A

1030-53	**Set of 27**	...	**560.00**	**125.00**	**11.00**
1030-53	**Very Fine Set of 27**	...	**675.00**	**150.00**	**13.50**
1030-51	½¢-50¢ Values only (25)	...	62.50	13.50	2.75
1030	½¢ Franklin ('55)	5.00	.60	.20	.15
1030a	½¢ Dry Printing	5.25	.60	.20	...
1031	1¢ Washington	5.00	.60	.20	.15

1954-1961 Liberty Series (B)

(Sheets of 100)

Scott's No.		Mint Sheet	Plate Block	F-VF NH	F-VF Used
1031b	1¢ Wet Printing	5.25	.60	.20	...
1031A	1¼¢ Palace of Gov. ('60)	5.00	.65	.20	.15
1032	1½¢ Mount Vernon (1956)	6.50	1.95	.20	.15
1033	2¢ Jefferson	6.00	.60	.20	.15
1034	2½¢ Bunker Hill ('59)	8.50	.65	.20	.15
1035	3¢ Statue of Liberty	9.00	.60	.20	.15
1035a	Booklet Pane of 6	...	...	4.75	2.50
1035b	Tagged (1966)	...	9.75	.28	...
1035e	3¢ Wet Printing	...	.75	.22	...
1035f	Booklet Pane of 6, Wet Printing	...	...	5.50	...
1036	4¢ Abraham Lincoln	9.75	.65	.20	.15
1036a	Booklet Pane of 6	...	...	2.85	2.25
1036b	Tagged (1963)	...	12.95	.70	...
1036c	4¢ Wet Printing	14.75	1.00	.25	...
1037	4½¢ The Hermitage ('59)	11.50	.75	.20	.15
1038	5¢ James Monroe	12.50	.65	.20	.15
1039	6¢ T. Roosevelt (1955)	44.75	2.10	.50	.15
1039a	6¢ Wet Printing	...	2.95	.70	...
1040	7¢ Woodrow Wilson ('56)	32.50	1.50	.35	.15
1041	8¢ St. of Liberty, Orig	34.50	2.75	.35	.15
1042	8¢ St. Lib., Redrawn ('58)	31.50	1.35	.32	.15

#1041: Torch Flame between "U.S." and "POSTAGE".
#1042: Torch Flame goes under "P" of "POSTAGE".

1042A	8¢ J.J. Pershing ('61)	32.50	1.30	.30	.15

1043 1044 1044A 1045 1046

1047 1048,1059A 1049 1050 1051

1052 1053

1043	9¢ The Alamo ('56)	65.00	2.50	.60	.15
1044	10¢ Indep. Hall ('56)	37.50	1.50	.35	.15
1044b	Tagged (1966)	...	55.00	3.50	...
1044A	11¢ St. of Liberty ('61)	35.00	1.75	.40	.18
1044Ac	Tagged (1967)	...	50.00	2.50	...
1045	12¢ Ben. Harrison ('59)	50.00	2.50	.55	.15
1045a	Tagged (1968)	...	5.00	.70	...
1046	15¢ John Jay ('58)	120.00	5.25	1.20	.15
1046a	Tagged (1966)	...	12.50	1.95	...
1047	20¢ Monticello ('56)	80.00	3.75	.80	.15
1048	25¢ Paul Revere ('58)	150.00	6.75	1.50	.15
1049	30¢ Robert E. Lee ('55)	165.00	7.50	1.75	.15
1049a	Wet Printing	...	7.95	1.85	...
1050	40¢ John Marshall ('55)	315.00	14.00	3.25	.15
1050a	Wet Printing	...	16.00	3.75	...
1051	50¢ S.B. Anthony ('55)	195.00	8.25	1.80	.15
1051a	Wet Printing	...	10.75	2.25	...
1052	$1 Patrick Henry ('55)	...	28.50	6.75	.15
1052a	Wet Printing	...	36.50	8.50	...
1053	$5 Alex Hamilton ('56)	...	475.00	110.00	8.50

NOTE: USED STAMPS ARE OUR CHOICE OF WET OR DRY, TAGGED OR UNTAGGED.

1954-65 Liberty Series Coil Stamps, Perf. 10 (B)

1054-59A	**Set of 8**	**Line Pr**	**27.50**	**3.50**	**2.15**
1054-59A	**Very Fine Set of 8**	**Line Pr.**	**32.75**	**4.15**	**2.95**
1054	1¢ Washington, Perf. Vert.	Line Pr.	1.10	.25	.15
1054c	1¢ Wet Printing	Line Pr.	3.00	.60	...
1054A	1¼¢ Pal., Pf. Horiz. (1960)	Line Pr.	3.00	.20	.15
1055	2¢ Jefferson, Perf. Vert.	Line Pr.	.70	.20	.15
1055a	Tagged (1968)	Line Pr	.45	.20	...
1055d	2¢ Wet Printing	Line Pr.	3.00	.45	...
1056	2½¢ Bunker Hill, Perf. Vert. (1959)	Line Pr.	4.00	.30	.25
1057	3¢ Liberty, Perf. Vertically	Line Pr.	.70	.20	.15
1057b	Tagged (1967)	Line Pr.	32.50	2.10	...
1057c	3¢ Wet Printing	Line Pr.	4.50	.70	...
1058	4¢ Lincoln, Pf. Vert. (1958)	Line Pr.	.75	.20	.15
1059	4½¢ Hermitage, Perf. Horiz. (1959)	Line Pr.	16.50	1.50	1.10
1059A	25¢ Revere, Pf. Vert. (1965)	Line Pr.	2.95	.90	.25
1059Ab	Tagged (1973)	Line Pr.	2.25	.75	...

1954 Commemoratives (See also No. 1029)

Scott's No.		Mint Sheet	Plate Block	F-VF NH	F-VF Used
1060	3¢ Nebraska Territory	5.50	.65	.20	.15
1061	3¢ Kansas Territory	5.50	.65	.20	.15
1062	3¢ George Eastman .... (70)	7.50	.65	.20	.15
1063	3¢ Lewis & Clark.........................	6.00	.65	.20	.15

1955 Commemoratives

1064 1065 1068

1066 1067 1069

1070 1071 1072

		Mint Sheet	Plate Block	F-VF NH	F-VF Used
1064-72	**Set of 9......................................**	...	...	**1.75**	**1.20**
1064	3¢ Penn. Academy of Arts...........	5.50	.65	.20	.15
1065	3¢ Land Grant Colleges..............	5.00	.65	.20	.15
1066	8¢ Rotary International	18.50	1.95	.40	.15
1067	3¢ Armed Forces Reserves.........	5.50	.65	.20	.15
1068	3¢ Old Man of the Mtns	6.50	.65	.20	.15
1069	3¢ Soo Locks Centennial............	5.00	.65	.20	.15
1070	3¢ Atoms for Peace	5.75	.65	.20	.15
1071	3¢ Fort Ticonderoga	5.75	.65	.20	.15
1072	3¢ Andrew Mellon..................... (70)	7.25	.65	.20	.15

1956 Commemoratives

1073 1074 1076

1075

		Mint Sheet	Plate Block	F-VF NH	F-VF Used
1073-85	**Set of 13......................................**	...	...	**4.75**	**3.95**
1073	3¢ Franklin 250th Anniv..............	5.75	.65	.20	.15
1074	3¢ Booker T. Washington	5.50	.65	.20	.15
1075	3¢ & 8¢ FIPEX Souv. Sheet........	...	...	2.75	2.50
1075a	3¢ Liberty Single.........................	...	...	1.25	1.10
1075b	8¢ Liberty Single.........................	...	...	1.50	1.35
1076	3¢ FIPEX Stamp..........................	5.00	.65	.20	.15

1956 Commemoratives (cont.)

1077 1078 1079

1080 1081 1082

1083 1084 1085

Scott's No.		Mint Sheet	Plate Block	F-VF NH	F-VF Used
1077	3¢ Wildlife - Wild Turkey.............	5.50	.65	.20	.15
1078	3¢ Wildlife - Antelope..................	5.50	.65	.20	.15
1079	3¢ Wildlife - King Salmon	5.50	.65	.20	.15
1080	3¢ Pure Food & Drug Act	5.00	.65	.20	.15
1081	3¢ Wheatland..............................	5.00	.65	.20	.15
1082	3¢ Labor Day	5.00	.65	.20	.15
1083	3¢ Nassau Hall, Princeton	5.00	.65	.20	.15
1084	3¢ Devils Tower...........................	5.00	.65	.20	.15
1085	3¢ Children's Issue	5.00	.65	.20	.15

1957 Commemoratives

1086 1087 1088

1089 1090 1091

		Mint Sheet	Plate Block	F-VF NH	F-VF Used
1086-99	**Set of 14......................................**	...	...	**2.60**	**1.85**
1086	3¢ Alexander Hamilton	5.50	.65	.20	.15
1087	3¢ Polio, March of Dimes	5.00	.65	.20	.15
1088	3¢ Coast & Geodetic Soc	5.00	.65	.20	.15
1089	3¢ Architects Institute	5.00	.65	.20	.15
1090	3¢ Steel Industry...........................	5.00	.65	.20	.15
1091	3¢ Int'l. Naval Review	5.75	.65	.20	.15

NOTE: FROM 1935 TO DATE, WITH FEW LISTED EXCEPTIONS, UNUSED PRICES ARE FOR NEVER HINGED STAMPS. HINGED STAMPS, WHEN AVAILABLE, ARE PRICED AT APPROXIMATELY 15% BELOW THE NEVER HINGED PRICE.

1957 Commemoratives (Cont.)

1092 1093 1094

1095 1096 1097

1098 1099

Scott's No.		Mint Sheet	Plate Block	F-VF NH	F-VF Used
1092	3¢ Oklahoma Statehood	5.50	.65	.20	.15
1093	3¢ School Teachers	7.50	.85	.25	.15
1094	4¢ U.S. Flag	6.00	.65	.20	.15
1095	3¢ Shipbuilding Anniv (70)	7.00	.65	.20	.15
1096	8¢ Magsaysay (48)	10.75	1.10	.24	.15
1097	3¢ Birth Lafayette	6.00	.65	.20	.15
1098	3¢ Wildlife - Whooping Crane	5.00	.65	.20	.15
1099	3¢ Religious Freedom	5.50	.65	.20	.15

1958 Commemoratives

1100 1104 1105

1106 1107 1108

Scott's No.		Mint Sheet	Plate Block	F-VF NH	F-VF Used
1100,1104-1123	Set of 21	...	...	3.95	2.75
1100	3¢ Gardening-Horticulture	5.00	.65	.20	.15
1104	3¢ Brussels World Fair	5.00	.65	.20	.15
1105	3¢ James Monroe (70)	7.50	.65	.20	.15
1106	3¢ Minnesota Centennial	5.50	.65	.20	.15
1107	3¢ Geophysical Year	5.50	.65	.20	.15
1108	3¢ Gunston Hall	5.00	.65	.20	.15

1958 Commemoratives (cont.)

1109 1110 1112

Scott's No.		Mint Sheet	Plate Block	F-VF NH	F-VF Used
1109	3¢ Mackinac Bridge	5.00	.65	.20	.15
1110	4¢ Simon Bolivar (70)	8.50	.65	.20	.15
1111	8¢ Simon Bolivar (72)	17.50	1.85	.25	.15
1112	4¢ Atlantic Cable Cent.	6.25	.65	.20	.15

1113 1114 1115

1116 1118 1119

1120 1121

1122 1123

1958-59 Lincoln Commemoratives

Scott's No.		Mint Sheet	Plate Block	F-VF NH	F-VF Used
1113	1¢ Beardless Lincoln ('59)	2.50	.45	.20	.15
1114	3¢ Bust of Lincoln ('59)	5.75	.65	.20	.15
1115	4¢ Lincoln-Douglas	9.00	.85	.25	.15
1116	4¢ Statue of Lincoln ('59)	10.00	1.10	.30	.15

1958 Commemoratives (continued)

Scott's No.		Mint Sheet	Plate Block	F-VF NH	F-VF Used
1117	4¢ Lajos Kossuth (70)	8.00	.65	.20	.15
1118	8¢ Lajos Kossuth (72)	17.50	1.65	.25	.15
1119	4¢ Freedom of Press	6.75	.65	.20	.15
1120	4¢ Overland Mail	6.50	.65	.20	.15
1121	4¢ Noah Webster (70)	8.00	.65	.20	.15
1122	4¢ Forest Conservation	6.25	.65	.20	.15
1123	4¢ Fort Duquesne	6.25	.65	.20	.15

1959 Commemoratives

1124 1126 1127 1134

1128 1129 1130

1131 1132 1133

1135 1136 1137 1138

Scott's No.		Mint Sheet	Plate Block	F-VF NH	F-VF Used
1124-38	**Set of 15**	...	...	**2.85**	**1.95**
1124	4¢ Oregon Statehood	6.25	.65	.20	.15
1125	4¢ Jose San Martin (70)	8.25	.65	.20	.15
1126	8¢ Jose San Martin (72)	16.50	1.25	.25	.15
1127	4¢ 10th Anniv. N.A.T.O. (70)	8.25	.65	.20	.15
1128	4¢ Arctic Explorations	6.00	.65	.20	.15
1129	8¢ World Peace & Trade	10.00	1.10	.25	.15
1130	4¢ Silver Discovery	6.25	.65	.20	.15
1131	4¢ St. Lawrence Seaway	6.25	.65	.20	.15
1132	4¢ 49-Star Flag	6.25	.65	.20	.15
1133	4¢ Soil Conservation	6.25	.65	.20	.15
1134	4¢ Petroleum Industry	6.25	.65	.20	.15
1135	4¢ Dental Health	11.50	1.10	.25	.15
1136	4¢ Ernst Reuter (70)	8.50	.65	.20	.15
1137	8¢ Ernst Reuter (72)	16.50	1.25	.25	.15
1138	4¢ Dr. Ephraim McDowell (70)	8.00	.65	.20	.15

1960 Commemoratives

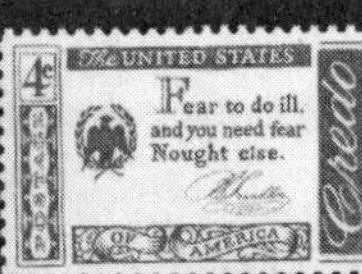

1139 1140 1141

1142 1143 1144

		Mint Sheet	Plate Block	F-VF NH	F-VF Used
1139-73	**Set of 35**	...	...	**6.75**	**4.65**
1139	4¢ Washington Credo	6.50	.65	.20	.15
1140	4¢ Franklin Credo	6.50	.65	.20	.15
1141	4¢ Jefferson Credo	7.00	.70	.20	.15
1142	4¢ F.S. Key Credo	7.00	.70	.20	.15
1143	4¢ Lincoln Credo	12.50	1.10	.30	.15
1144	4¢ Henry Credo (1961)	12.50	1.10	.30	.15

1960 Commemoratives (cont.)

1145 1146 1147 1151

1149 1150 1152

1153 1154 1155

Scott's No.		Mint Sheet	Plate Block	F-VF NH	F-VF Used
1145	4¢ Boy Scout Jubilee	7.95	.90	.23	.15
1146	4¢ Winter Olympics	7.50	.90	.25	.15
1147	4¢ Thomas G. Masaryk (70)	8.00	.65	.20	.15
1148	8¢ Thomas G. Masaryk (72)	16.50	1.50	.25	.15
1149	4¢ World Refugee Year	6.25	.65	.20	.15
1150	4¢ Water Conservation	6.25	.65	.20	.15
1151	4¢ Southeast Asia Treaty (70)	8.00	.65	.20	.15
1152	4¢ American Woman	6.25	.65	.20	.15
1153	4¢ 50-Star Flag	6.25	.65	.20	.15
1154	4¢ Pony Express Cent.	7.50	.90	.25	.15
1155	4¢ Employ Handicapped	6.25	.65	.20	.15

1156 1157 1158 1159

1161 1162 1163 1167

		Mint Sheet	Plate Block	F-VF NH	F-VF Used
1156	4¢ World Forestry Congress	6.25	.65	.20	.15
1157	4¢ Mexican Independence	6.25	.65	.20	.15
1158	4¢ U.S. - Japan Treaty	6.50	.65	.20	.15
1159	4¢ Ignacy J. Paderewski (70)	8.00	.65	.20	.15
1160	8¢ Ignacy J. Paderewski (72)	16.50	1.50	.25	.15
1161	4¢ Robert A. Taft (70)	8.00	.65	.20	.15
1162	4¢ Wheels of Freedom	6.25	.65	.20	.15
1163	4¢ Boys' Club of America	6.25	.65	.20	.15
1164	4¢ Automated Post Office	6.25	.65	.20	.15

1960 Commemoratives (continued)

1164 1165 1169

1170 1171 1172 1173

Scott's No.		Mint Sheet	Plate Block	F-VF NH	F-VF Used
1165	4¢ Gustaf Mannerheim............(70)	8.00	.65	.20	.15
1166	8¢ Gustaf Mannerheim............(72)	16.50	1.25	.25	.15
1167	4¢ Camp Fire Girls......................	6.25	.65	.20	.15
1168	4¢ Guiseppe Garibaldi.............(70)	8.00	.65	.20	.15
1169	8¢ Guiseppe Garibaldi.............(72)	16.50	1.25	.25	.15
1170	4¢ Walter F. George................(70)	8.00	.65	.20	.15
1171	4¢ Andrew Carnegie.................(70)	8.00	.65	.20	.15
1172	4¢ John Foster Dulles..............(70)	8.00	.65	.20	.15
1173	4¢"Echo I" Satellite......................	10.50	1.00	.24	.15

1961 Commemoratives

1174 1175 1176 1177

1178 1179 1180

1181 1182 1183

1174-1190	**Set of 17**................................	...	...	**4.50**	**2.25**
1174	4¢ Mahatma Gandhi.................(70)	8.00	.65	.20	.15
1175	8¢ Mahatma Gandhi.................(72)	16.50	1.50	.25	.15
1176	4¢ Range Conservation..............	7.00	.65	.20	.15
1177	4¢ Horace Greeley...................(70)	8.00	.65	.20	.15

1961-1965 Civil War Centennial

1178	4¢ Fort Sumter (1961).................	15.00	1.75	.40	.15
1179	4¢ Battle of Shiloh (1962)...........	15.00	1.75	.40	.15
1180	5¢ Gettysburg (1963)..................	20.00	2.00	.50	.15
1181	5¢ Wilderness (1964)..................	20.00	2.00	.50	.15
1182	5¢ Appomattox (1965).................	33.75	3.00	.70	.15

1961 Commemoratives (cont.)

1184 1185 1186

1187 1188 1189 1190

Scott's No.		Mint Sheet	Plate Block	F-VF NH	F-VF Used
1183	4¢ Kansas Statehood.................	6.50	.65	.20	.15
1184	4¢ George W. Norris...................	6.25	.65	.20	.15
1185	4¢ Naval Aviation........................	6.75	.65	.20	.15
1186	4¢ Workmen's Compensation......	6.25	.65	.20	.15
1187	4¢ Frederic Remington...............	6.50	.65	.20	.15
1188	4¢ Republic of China..................	7.00	.75	.20	.15
1189	4¢ Basketball - Naismith.............	9.50	1.00	.25	.15
1190	4¢ Nursing..................................	13.75	1.30	.30	.15

1962 Commemoratives (See also 1179)

1191 1192 1193

1195 1194 1196

1197 1198 1199

1191-1207	**Set of 17**................................	...	...	**3.00**	**2.25**
1191	4¢ New Mexico Statehood..........	6.25	.65	.20	.15
1192	4¢ Arizona Statehood.................	7.00	.65	.20	.15
1193	4¢ Project Mercury......................	7.00	.65	.20	.15
1194	4¢ Malaria Eradication................	6.25	.65	.20	.15
1195	4¢ Charles Evans Hughes...........	6.25	.65	.20	.15
1196	4¢ Seattle World's Fair...............	6.25	.65	.20	.15
1197	4¢ Louisiana Statehood..............	6.25	.65	.20	.15
1198	4¢ Homestead Act.......................	6.25	.65	.20	.15
1199	4¢ Girl Scouts.............................	6.50	.65	.20	.15

1962 Commemoratives (cont.)

1200 1201

1202 1203 1205

1206 1207

Scott's No.		Mint Sheet	Plate Block	F-VF NH	F-VF Used
1200	4¢ Brien McMahon	6.25	.65	.20	.15
1201	4¢ Apprenticeship Act	6.25	.65	.20	.15
1202	4¢ Sam Rayburn	6.25	.65	.20	.15
1203	4¢ Dag Hammarskjold................	6.25	.65	.20	.15
1204	4¢ Hammarskjold "Error"	7.00	1.50	.20	.15
1205	4¢ Christmas .... (100)	11.50	.65	.20	.15
1206	4¢ Higher Education...................	6.50	.65	.20	.15
1207	4¢ Homer Seascape...................	6.50	.65	.20	.15

1962-1963 Regular Issues

1208 1209,1225 1213,1229

1208	5¢ Flag & Wh. Hse. ('63) .... (100)	13.50	.65	.20	.15
1208a	5¢ Flag Tagged (1966)	...	2.50	.35	...
1209	1¢ Jackson (1963).................... (100)	5.50	.45	.20	.15
1209a	1¢ Tagged (1966).........................	...	.50	.20	...
1213	5¢ Washington .... (100)	11.50	.65	.20	.15
1213a	5¢ Pane of 5 "Mailman", Slog. I...	...	...	6.50	2.25
1213a	5¢ Pane of 5 "Use Zone", Slog. II	...	...	23.50	9.50
1213a	5¢ Pane of 5 "Use Zip Code", Slog. III	...	...	3.00	2.25
1213b	5¢ Tagged (1963)	...	7.00	.75	...
1213c	5¢ Pane of 5 "Zone" Tagged, Slog. II	...	...	80.00	...
1213c	5¢ Pane of 5 "Zip" Tagged, Slog. III	...	...	1.50	...
1225	1¢ Jackson Coil	Line Pr.	3.00	.25	.15
1225a	1¢ Coil, Tagged (1966)...............	Line Pr.	.85	.20	...
1229	5¢ Washington Coil	Line Pr.	3.50	1.25	.15
1229a	5¢ Coil, Tagged (1963)...............	Line Pr.	8.95	1.75	...

NOTE: USED STAMPS ARE OUR CHOICE OF TAGGED OR UNTAGGED.

1963 Commemoratives (See also 1180)

1230 1231 1232

1230-41	**Set of 12**	...	...	**2.15**	**1.60**
1230	5¢ Carolina Charter	7.00	.65	.20	.15
1231	5¢ Food for Peace	7.00	.65	.20	.15
1232	5¢ West Virgina Statehood..........	7.00	.65	.20	.15

1963 Commemoratives (cont.)

1233 1234 1235

1236 1237 1238

1239 1240 1241

Scott's No.		Mint Sheet	Plate Block	F-VF NH	F-VF Used
1233	5¢ Emancipation Proc	7.50	.95	.25	.15
1234	5¢ Alliance for Progress	7.00	.65	.20	.15
1235	5¢ Cordell Hull............................	7.00	.65	.20	.15
1236	5¢ Eleanor Roosevelt	8.00	.75	.22	.15
1237	5¢ The Sciences..........................	7.00	.65	.20	.15
1238	5¢ City Mail Delivery....................	7.00	.65	.20	.15
1239	5¢ Int'l. Red Cross Centenary	7.00	.65	.20	.15
1240	5¢ Christmas Tree.................. (100)	13.00	.65	.20	.15
1240a	5¢ Tagged	...	8.95	.70	...
1241	5¢ Audubon-Columbia Jays	8.00	.75	.22	.15

1964 Commemoratives (See also 1181)

1243 1242 1244

1245 1246 1247

1242-60	**Set of 19**	...	...	**4.35**	**2.50**
1242	5¢ Sam Houston..........................	8.00	.75	.22	.15
1243	5¢ Charles M. Russell	8.00	.75	.22	.15
1244	5¢ N.Y. World's Fair	7.00	.65	.20	.15
1245	5¢ John Muir, Naturalist................	7.00	.65	.20	.15
1246	5¢ John F. Kennedy Mem	20.00	2.00	.40	.15
1247	5¢ New Jersey Tercentenary.......	8.00	.75	.25	.15

FOR INFORMATION CONCERNING VERY FINE SEE PAGE II

1964 Commemoratives (cont.)

1248 1249 1250 1251

1252 1254-57 1253

1258 1259 1260

Scott's No.		Mint Sheet	Plate Block	F-VF NH	F-VF Used
1248	5¢ Nevada Statehood	7.00	.65	.20	.15
1249	5¢ Register and Vote	7.00	.65	.20	.15
1250	5¢ William Shakespeare	7.00	.65	.20	.15
1251	5¢ Doctors Mayo	14.50	1.25	.30	.15
1252	5¢ American Music	7.00	.65	.20	.15
1253	5¢ Homemakers	7.00	.65	.20	.15
1254-7	5¢ Christmas, attached ....(100)	32.50	1.75	1.40	1.25
1254-7	5¢ Set of 4 Singles	...	...	1.25	.60
1254-7a	5¢ Christmas Tagged, attd	...	8.75	3.50	...
1254-7a	5¢ Set of 4 Singles	...	...	3.00	...
1258	5¢ Verrazano-Narrows Bdg	7.00	.65	.20	.15
1259	5¢ Fine Arts - S. Davis	7.00	.65	.20	.15
1260	5¢ Amateur Radio	10.00	1.20	.30	.15

1965 Commemoratives

1262 1261 1263

1265 1264 1266

1261-76	**Set of 16**	...	...	**3.35**	**2.25**
1261	5¢ Battle of New Orleans	7.00	.65	.20	.15
1262	5¢ Physical Fitness - Sokol	7.00	.65	.20	.15
1263	5¢ Crusade Against Cancer	7.00	.65	.20	.15
1264	5¢ Churchill Memorial	7.50	.90	.25	.15
1265	5¢ Magna Carta	7.00	.65	.20	.15
1266	5¢ Int'l. Cooperation Year	7.00	.65	.20	.15

1965 Commemoratives (cont.)

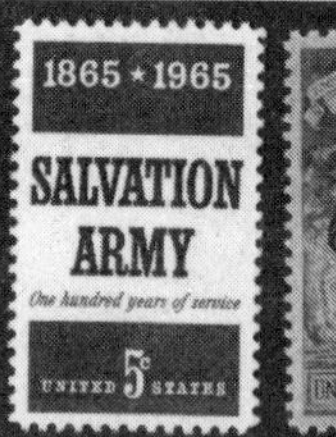

1267 1268 1269 1270

1271 1272 1273

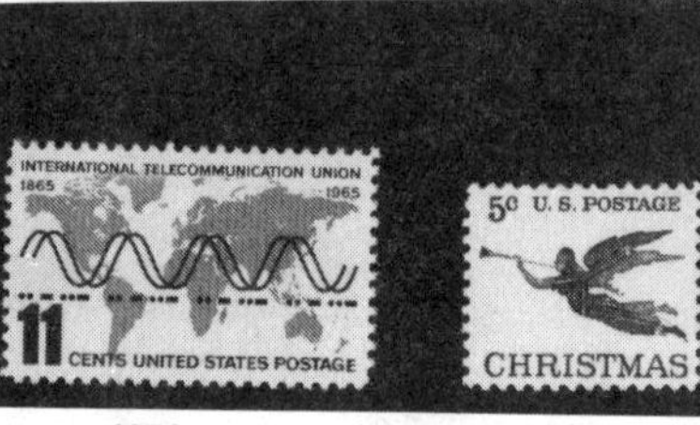

1274 1276 1275

Scott's No.		Mint Sheet	Plate Block	F-VF NH	F-VF Used
1267	5¢ Salvation Army	7.00	.65	.20	.15
1268	5¢ Dante Alighieri	7.00	.65	.20	.15
1269	5¢ Herbert Hoover	7.00	.65	.20	.15
1270	5¢ Robert Fulton	7.00	.65	.20	.15
1271	5¢ 400th Anniv. of Florida	7.00	.65	.20	.15
1272	5¢ Traffic Safety	7.00	.65	.20	.15
1273	5¢ John S. Copley Painting	8.00	.75	.22	.15
1274	11¢ Telecommun. Union	27.50	7.50	.50	.30
1275	5¢ Adlai Stevenson	7.00	.65	.20	.15
1276	5¢ Christmas Angel................ (100)	13.50	.65	.20	.15
1276a	5¢ Christmas, Tagged	...	10.75	.75	...

1965-79 Prominent Americans Series

(Sheets of 100)

1278,1299 1279 1280 1281,1297 1282,1303

1278-88,1289-95	**Set of 20**	...	**99.50**	**21.50**	**4.95**
1278-88, 1289-95	**Very Fine Set of 20....**	...	**119.50**	**25.75**	**6.95**

NOTE: OUR SETS WILL CONTAIN OUR CHOICE OF TAGGED OR UNTAGGED. ALSO, USED STAMPS MAY OR MAY NOT BE TAGGED.

1278	1¢ Thomas Jefferson ('68)	5.00	.45	.20	.15
1278a	Booklet Pane of 8	...	...	1.10	.95
1278ae	Pane of 8, Dull Exp. Gum	...	...	1.75	...
1278b	Booklet Pane of 4 ('71)	...	...	.90	.75
1279	1¼¢ Albert Gallatin ('67)	15.00	9.00	.20	.15
1280	2¢ Frank Lloyd Wright ('66)	6.00	.50	.20	.15
1280a	Booklet Pane of 5 (S4 or S5) ('68)	...	...	1.30	1.10
S4 is "Mail Early", S5 is "Use Zip Code"					
1280c	2¢ Booklet Pane of 6 ('71)	...	...	1.15	.95
1280ce	Pane of 6, Dull Exp. Gum	...	...	1.00	...
1281	3¢ Francis Parkman ('67)	7.50	.60	.20	.15
1282	4¢ Abraham Lincoln	14.00	.75	.22	.15
1282a	4¢ Lincoln, Tagged	11.00	.65	.20	...

NOTE: PRICES THROUGHOUT THIS LIST ARE SUBJECT TO CHANGE WITHOUT NOTICE IF MARKET CONDITIONS REQUIRE. MINIMUM MAIL ORDER MUST TOTAL AT LEAST $20.00.

1965-79 Prominent Americans Series (Cont.)
(Sheets of 100)

1283,1304 1283B,1304C 1284,1298 1285 1286

1286A 1287 1288/1305E 1289 1290

1291 1292 1293 1294,1305C 1295

cott's No.		Mint Sheet	Plate Block	F-VF NH	F-VF Used
283	5¢ Washington, Dirty Face ('66)...	18.75	.75	.22	.15
283a	5¢ Washington, Tagged..............	15.00	.65	.20	...
283B	5¢ Washington,Clean Face ('67)..	13.50	.80	.20	.15
284	6¢ F.D. Roosevelt ('66)...............	25.00	1.30	.27	.15
284a	6¢ F.D.R., Tagged......................	20.00	.95	.22	...
284b	Booklet Pane of 8 ('67).............	...	...	1.60	1.50
284c	Pane of 5 (S4 or S5) ('68)............	...	...	1.60	1.35
285	8¢ Albert Einstein ('66)................	28.50	1.40	.30	.15
285a	8¢ Einstein, Tagged....................	22.50	1.15	.25	...
286	10¢ Andrew Jackson ('67)...........	28.50	1.35	.30	.15
286A	12¢ Henry Ford ('68)..................	34.50	1.50	.35	.15
287	13¢ John F. Kennedy ('67)..........	55.00	2.25	.60	.15
288	15¢ O.W. Holmes, Die I ('68).......	42.50	1.95	.45	.15
288d	15¢ Holmes, Die II ('79).............	95.00	13.50	1.00	.20
288B	15¢ Bklt. Single, Pf. 10 Die III......	...	...	.45	.15
288Bc	Bk. Pane of 8, Die III ('78)..........	...	...	3.50	3.00
289	20¢ George C. Marshall ('67).......	72.50	3.25	.75	.15
289a	20¢ Marshall, Tagged ('73)..........	57.50	2.50	.60	...
290	25¢ Frederick Douglass ('67).......	97.50	4.25	1.10	.15
290a	25¢ Douglass, Tagged ('73).........	90.00	3.50	1.00	...
291	30¢ John Dewey ('68)..................	100.00	4.65	1.05	.15
291a	30¢ Dewey, Tagged('73)..............	80.00	3.75	.85	...
292	40¢ Thomas Paine ('68)...............	125.00	5.95	1.35	.15
292a	40¢ Paine, Tagged ('73).............	100.00	4.75	1.10	...
293	50¢ Lucy Stone ('68)....................	165.00	7.50	1.75	.15
293a	50¢ Stone, Tagged ('73).............	130.00	5.75	1.75	...
294	$1 Eugene O'Neill ('67)...............	325.00	14.50	3.50	.15
294a	$1 O'Neill, Tagged ('73)..............	250.00	11.50	2.75	...
295	$5 John B. Moore ('66).................	...	67.50	15.00	2.75
295a	$5 Moore, Tagged ('73)................	...	52.50	12.00	...

1288 and 1305E: Die I top bar of "5" is horiz., tie touches lapel.
1288d and 1305Ei: Die II top bar of "5" slopes down to right, tie does not touch lapel.
1288B and 1288Bc: Die III booklets only, design shorter than Die I or II.

1305 1306 1307

1966-81 Prominent Americans, Coils, Perf. 10

297-1305C	**Prominent Am. Coils (9) ...**		**13.75**	**4.50**	**1.95**
297-1305C	**Very Fine Set of 9............**		**16.50**	**5.40**	**2.75**
297	3¢ Parkman ('75)..........................	Line Pr.	.70	.20	.15
298	6¢ F.D. Roosevelt, Pf. Hz. ('67) ...	Line Pr.	1.65	.22	.15
299	1¢ Jefferson ('68)........................	Line Pr.	.40	.20	.15
303	4¢ Lincoln....................................	Line Pr.	.80	.20	.15
304	5¢ Wash., Orig.............................	Line Pr.	.60	.20	.15
304C	5¢ Redrawn ('81)..........................	Line Pr.	2.00	.35	.15
305	6¢ F.D.R., Pf. Vert. ('68)...............	Line Pr.	.75	.25	.15
1305E	15¢ Holmes, Die I ('78)...............	Line Pr.	1.25	.45	.15
1305Ei	15¢ Holmes, Die II ('79)..............	Line Pr.	2.00	.60	.25
1305C	$1 O'Neill ('73)...........................	Line Pr.	6.50	2.75	1.00

1966 Commemoratives

1306-22	**Set of 17...................................**	...	...	**3.35**	**2.35**
1306	5¢ Migratory Bird Treaty	8.50	.90	.25	.15
1307	5¢ Humane Trtmnt. Animals........	7.00	.65	.20	.15

NOTE: UNUSED YEAR SETS HAVE SE-TENANTS ATTACHED, USED SETS HAVE SINGLES.

1966 Commemoratives (cont.)

1308 1309 1310 1312

1313 1314 1315

1316 1317 1318

1319 1320 1321 1322

Scott's No.		Mint Sheet	Plate Block	F-VF NH	F-VF Used
1308	5¢ Indiana Statehood...................	7.00	.65	.20	.15
1309	5¢ American Circus (Clown)........	8.50	.90	.25	.15
1310	5¢ Sipex Stamp	7.00	.65	.20	.15
1311	5¢ Sipex Souvenir Sheet.............	...	...	.20	.20
1312	5¢ Bill of Rights...........................	8.50	.90	.25	.15
1313	5¢ Polish Millenium......................	7.00	.65	.20	.15
1314	5¢ National Park Service	8.50	.90	.25	.15
1315	5¢ Marine Corps Reserve...........	7.00	.65	.20	.15
1316	5¢ Fed. of Women's Clubs	7.00	.65	.20	.15
1317	5¢ Johnny Appleseed..................	7.00	.65	.20	.15
1318	5¢ Beautification of America........	8.00	.75	.22	.15
1319	5¢ Great River Road....................	7.50	.65	.20	.15
1320	5¢ Sav. Bond - Servicemen.........	8.00	.75	.22	.15
1321	5¢ Xmas - Madonna & Child....(100)	13.50	.65	.20	.15
1322	5¢ M. Cassatt Painting	8.50	.80	.22	.15
1314a-22a	**Tagged Issues, each.............**	...	**2.50**	**.35**	...

1967 Commemoratives

1323 1324 1325

1323-37	**Set of 15...................................**	...	...	**4.50**	**2.15**
1323	5¢ National Grange......................	8.00	.75	.22	.15
1324	5¢ Canada Centenary..................	7.00	.65	.20	.15
1325	5¢ Erie Canal...............................	7.00	.65	.20	.15

1967 Commemoratives (cont.)

1326 1327 1328

VOICE OF AMERICA · Davy Crockett · plan for better cities · Finland Independence 1917-67

1329 1330 1333 1334

1331-32 1338/1338D

1335 1336 1337

Scott's No.		Mint Sheet	Plate Block	F-VF NH	F-VF Used
1326	5¢ Search for Peace - Lions	8.00	.75	.22	.15
1327	5¢ Henry David Thoreau	8.25	.75	.22	.15
1328	5¢ Nebraska Statehood	8.00	.75	.22	.15
1329	5¢ Voice of America	7.00	.65	.20	.15
1330	5¢ Davy Crockett	8.00	.75	.22	.15
1331-2	5¢ Space Twins, Attached	47.50	4.50	2.10	1.75
1331-2	Set of 2 Singles	...	...	1.40	.45
1333	5¢ Urban Planning	7.50	.75	.22	.15
1334	5¢ Finnish Independence	7.50	.75	.22	.15
1335	5¢ Thomas Eakins Painting	7.50	.75	.22	.15
1336	5¢ Xmas - Madonna & Child	7.00	.65	.20	.15
1337	5¢ Mississippi Statehood	8.75	.85	.24	.15

1968-71 Regular Issues

Scott's No.		Mint Sheet	Plate Block	F-VF NH	F-VF Used
1338	6¢ Flag & White House (100)	16.50	.75	.22	.15
1338D	6¢ Same, Huck Press ('70) (100)	16.00	(20)3.50	.22	.15
1338F	8¢ Flag & White House ('71) (100)	21.50	(20)4.50	.24	.15
1338A	6¢ Flag & W.H.-Huck Coil ('69)	Full Line Pr.	2.75	.22	.15
1338G	8¢ Flag & W.H.-Huck Coil ('71)	...	...	.25	.15

NOTE: #1338 is 19mm x 22mm, #1338D is 18¼mm x 21 mm.

1968 Commemoratives

1339 1341 1340

Scott's No.		Mint Sheet	Plate Block	F-VF NH	F-VF Used
1339-40,42-64	**Set of 25**	...	...	**6.95**	**4.15**
1339	6¢ Illinois Statehood	8.25	.75	.22	.15
1340	6¢ Hemis Fair '68	8.25	.75	.22	.15

1968 Airlift to Servicemen

Scott's No.		Mint Sheet	Plate Block	F-VF NH	F-VF Used
1341	$1 Eagle Holding Pennant	150.00	13.75	3.25	2.10

1968 Commemoratives (cont.)

1342 1343 1344

1345 1346 1347

1348 1349 1350

1351 1352 1353

1354 1355 1356

Scott's No.		Mint Sheet	Plate Block	F-VF NH	F-VF Used
1342	6¢ Support Our Youth - Elks	8.25	.75	.22	.15
1343	6¢ Law and Order	15.75	1.50	.35	.15
1344	6¢ Register and Vote	8.25	.75	.22	.15

1968 Historic American Flags

Scott's No.		Mint Sheet	Plate Block	F-VF NH	F-VF Used
1345-54	Hist. Flag, Strip/10	17.75	(20)8.50	3.75	3.50
1345-46	Plate Blk. of 4	...	1.50	...	...
1345-54	Set of Singles	...	...	3.00	2.35
1345	6¢ Fort Moultrie	...	...	.45	.30
1346	6¢ Fort McHenry	...	...	.45	.30
1347	6¢ Washington Cruisers	...	...	.25	.24
1348	6¢ Bennington	...	...	.25	.24
1349	6¢ Rhode Island	...	...	.35	.24
1350	6¢ First Stars & Stripes	...	...	.35	.24
1351	6¢ Bunker Hill	...	...	.25	.24
1352	6¢ Grand Union	...	...	.25	.24
1353	6¢ Philadelphia Light Horse	...	...	.25	.24
1354	6¢ First Navy Jack	...	...	.30	.24

1968 Commemoratives (continued)

Scott's No.		Mint Sheet	Plate Block	F-VF NH	F-VF Used
1355	6¢ Walt Disney	22.50	2.25	.50	.15
1356	6¢ Father Marquette	9.50	.90	.22	.15

NOTE: UNUSED YEAR SETS HAVE SE-TENANTS ATTACHED, USED SETS HAVE SINGLES.

1968 Commemoratives (cont.)

1357 1358 1359

1360 1361 1362

CHRISTMAS 6c UNITED STATES

United States Postage 6c

1363 1364

Scott's No.		Mint Sheet	Plate Block	F-VF NH	F-VF Used
1357	6¢ Daniel Boone	8.25	.75	.22	.15
1358	6¢ Arkansas River Navigation	8.25	.75	.22	.15
1359	6¢ Leif Erikson	8.25	.75	.22	.15
1360	6¢ Cherokee Strip	10.75	1.00	.25	.15
1361	6¢ John Trumbull Painting	9.50	1.00	.25	.15
1362	6¢ Waterfowl Conservation	12.75	1.10	.25	.15
1363	6¢ Christmas, Gabriel	8.25	(10)1.95	.22	.15
1363a	6¢ Christmas, Untagged	...	(10)3.25	.30	...
1364	6¢ American Indian - Joseph	12.75	1.25	.30	.15

1969 Commemoratives

1365-68

1369 1370 1371 1373

		Mint Sheet	Plate Block	F-VF NH	F-VF Used
1365-86	**Set of 22 (no precancels)**	...	...	**8.65**	**3.15**
1365-8	6¢ Beautification, attached	30.00	2.50	2.25	1.90
1365-8	Set of 4 Singles	...	...	1.85	.70
1369	6¢ American Legion	8.25	.75	.22	.15
1370	6¢ Grandma Moses Painting	8.50	.85	.22	.15
1371	6¢ Apollo 8	12.00	1.10	.27	.15
1372	6¢ W.C. Handy	9.50	.90	.22	.15
1373	6¢ California Settlement	8.25	.75	.22	.15

1969 Commemoratives (cont.)

1372 1374 1375

1376-79

1381 1380 1382

1383 1385 1386

1384 1384 Precancel

Scott's No.		Mint Sheet	Plate Block	F-VF NH	F-VF Used
1374	6¢ John Wesley Powell	8.25	.75	.22	.15
1375	6¢ Alabama Statehood	8.25	.75	.22	.15
1376-9	6¢ Botanical Congress, att'd.	35.00	3.50	3.00	2.70
1376-9	Set of Singles	...	...	2.50	.70
1380	6¢ Dartmouth College	9.50	.95	.25	.15
1381	6¢ Professional Baseball	50.00	4.95	1.10	.15
1382	6¢ College Football	22.50	2.00	.50	.15
1383	6¢ D.D. Eisenhower Memorial..(32)	5.75	.90	.22	.15
1384	6¢ Christmas, Winter Sunday	8.25	(10)1.95	.22	.15
1384a	6¢ Precancelled (Set of 4 Cities)	175.00	(10)85.00	2.75	...
1385	6¢ Crippled Children	8.25	.85	.22	.15
1386	6¢ William M. Harnett Painting.(32)	5.75	.85	.22	.15

NOTE: UNUSED YEAR SETS HAVE SE-TENANTS ATTACHED, USED SETS HAVE SINGLES.

NOTE: PRICES THROUGHOUT THIS LIST ARE SUBJECT TO CHANGE WITHOUT NOTICE IF MARKET CONDITIONS REQUIRE. MINIMUM MAIL ORDER MUST TOTAL AT LEAST $20.00.

1970 Commemoratives

1387-90

1391 1392

Scott's No.		Mint Sheet	Plate Block	F-VF NH	F-VF Used
1387-92,1405-22	**Set of 24 (no prec.)....**	**...**	**...**	**7.00**	**3.75**
1387-90	6¢ Natural History, attached...(32)	7.75	1.10	1.00	.80
1387-90	Set of 4 Singles	...	...	.95	.70
1391	6¢ Maine Statehood	8.25	.85	.22	.15
1392	6¢ Wildlife Conserv. - Buffalo	8.25	.95	.25	.15

1970-74 Regular Issue

1393,1401 1393D 1394/1402 1396

1397 1398 1399 1400

Scott's No.		Mint Sheet	Plate Block	F-VF NH	F-VF Used
1393-94,1396-1400	**Set of 8**	**...**	**...**	**2.90**	**1.00**
1393	6¢ Eisenhower (100)	18.50	.80	.22	.15
1393a	Booklet Pane of 8	...	...	1.40	1.35
1393ae	Pane of 8, Dull Exper. Gum	...	...	1.60	...
1393b	Bklt. Pane of 5, (S4 or S5) ('71)...	...	...	1.40	1.25
1393D	7¢ Benjamin Franklin ('72) (100)	18.50	.95	.24	.15
1394	8¢ Ike, Multicolored ('71) (100)	21.50	1.00	.24	.15
1395	8¢ Ike, Deep Claret, Bklt. Single..	...	...	.28	.15
1395a	Booklet Pane of 8 ('71)	...	...	2.25	2.10
1395b	Booklet Pane of 6 ('71)	...	...	1.75	1.65
1395c	Booklet Pane of 4 ('72)	...	...	1.70	1.60
1395d	Booklet Pane of 7, (S4) (1972)....	...	...	2.95	2.75
1395d	Booklet Pane of 7, (S5) (1972)....	...	...	1.95	1.80
S4 is "Mail Early", S5 is "Use Zip Code"					
1396	8¢ U.S. Postal Service ('71) (100)	21.50	(12)3.00	.24	.15
1396	8¢ U.S. Postal Service	...	(20) 4.75	...	...
1397	14¢ Fiorello La Guardia ('72) (100)	35.00	1.65	.40	.15
1398	16¢ Ernie Pyle ('71) (100)	42.50	1.85	.45	.15
1399	18¢ Dr. Eliz. Blackwell ('74) (100)	57.50	2.65	.60	.15
1400	21¢ Amadeo P. Giannini ('73)..(100)	60.00	2.75	.65	.15
1401	6¢ Eisenhower Coil, Perf. Vert. ...	Line Pr.	.55	.22	.15
1402	8¢ Ike Coil, Perf. Vert. ('71)	Line Pr.	.60	.25	.15

NOTE: #1395 ONLY EXISTS WITH ONE OR MORE STRAIGHT EDGES SINCE IT COMES FROM BOOKLET PANES.

1970 Commemoratives (continued)

1405 1406 1407

1408 1409 1419

1410-13

1414 1414a 1420

1415-18 1421-22

Scott's No.		Mint Sheet	Plate Block	F-VF NH	F-VF Used
1405	6¢ Edgar Lee Masters - Poet	8.25	.85	.22	.15
1406	6¢ Women Suffrage	8.25	.85	.22	.15
1407	6¢ South Carolina Founding	8.25	.85	.22	.15
1408	6¢ Stone Mountain Memorial	11.00	1.00	.25	.15
1409	6¢ Fort Snelling	8.25	.85	.22	.15
1410-13	6¢ Anti-Pollution, Attached	14.50	(10)3.50	1.35	1.25
1410-13	Set of 4 Singles	...	...	1.10	.80
1414	6¢ Christmas, Nativity, Ty. I	8.25	(8) 1.50	.22	.15
1414a	6¢ Christmas, Nativity, Precncl....	9.50	(8) 2.50	.22	.15
1414d	6¢ Type II, Horiz. Gum Breakers .	...	(8) 8.50	.85	.30
1414e	6¢ Type II, Precancelled	...	(8)12.50	1.00	.35
1415-18	6¢ Christmas Toys, attd	25.00	(8) 6.00	2.35	2.00
1415-18	Set of 4 Singles	...	...	2.10	.70
1415a-18a	6¢ Toys, Precan., attached	37.50	(8) 8.25	3.50	3.50
1415a-18a	Set of 4 Singles	...	...	3.25	.85
1419	6¢ United Nations 25th Anniv	8.25	.85	.22	.15
1420	6¢ Landing of the Pilgrims	8.25	.85	.22	.15
1421-22	6¢ DAV - Servicemen, attd	10.00	1.95	.50	.40
1421-22	Set of 2 Singles	...	...	.44	.30

1971 Commemoratives

1423 1425 1424

1427-30

1426 1432 1431

1433 1434-35

1436 1437 1438 1439

1440-43

1971 Commemoratives (cont.)

1444 1445 1446 1447

Scott's No.		Mint Sheet	Plate Block	F-VF NH	F-VF Used
1423-45	**Set of 23**	...	...	**5.35**	**3.35**
1423	6¢ American Wool Industry	8.25	.85	.22	.15
1424	6¢ Gen. Douglas MacArthur	8.25	.85	.22	.15
1425	6¢ Blood Donor	8.25	.85	.22	.15
1426	8¢ Missouri Sesquicentennial	11.75	(12)3.25	.26	.15
1427-30	8¢ Wildlife, attached (32)	8.75	1.20	1.10	1.00
1427-30	Set of 4 Singles	...	...	1.00	.70
1431	8¢ Antarctic Treaty	10.75	1.00	.24	.15
1432	8¢ Bicentennnial Emblem	11.00	1.10	.24	.15
1433	8¢ John Sloan Painting	10.75	1.00	.24	.15
1434-5	8¢ Space Achievement, attd	11.50	1.10	.50	.45
1434-5	Set of 2 Singles	...	...	.45	.30
1436	8¢ Emily Dickinson	10.75	1.00	.24	.15
1437	8¢ San Juan, Puerto Rico	10.75	1.00	.24	.15
1438	8¢ Prevent Drug Abuse	10.75	(6) 1.50	.24	.15
1439	8¢ Care	10.75	(8) 1.95	.24	.15
1440-3	8¢ Historic Preservation, attd (32)	8.75	1.10	1.00	.95
1440-3	Set of 4 Singles	...	...	.95	.70
1444	8¢ Christmas, Adoration	10.75	(12)2.95	.24	.15
1445	8¢ Christmas, Partridge	10.75	(12)2.95	.24	.15

1972 Commemoratives

1448-51 1454 1452 1453

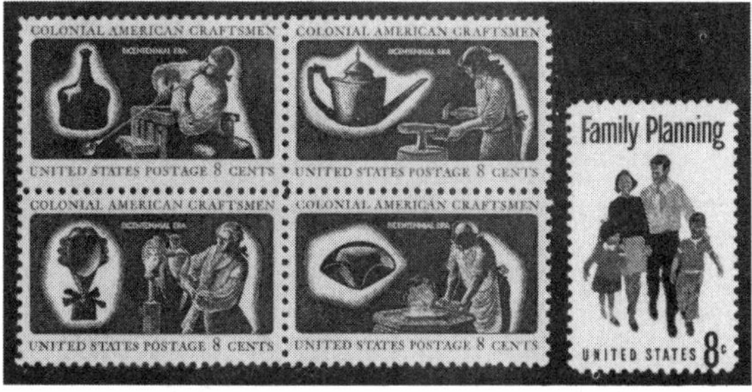

1456-59 1455

Scott's No.		Mint Sheet	Plate Block	F-VF NH	F-VF Used
1446-74	**Set of 29**	...	...	**6.85**	**4.35**
1446	8¢ Sidney Lanier	10.75	1.00	.24	.15
1447	8¢ Peace Corps	12.75	(6) 1.70	.28	.15
1448-51	2¢ Cape Hatteras, attached (100)	8.50	.75	.60	.60
1448-51	Set of 4 Singles	...	...	.60	.50
1452	6¢ Wolf Trap Farm	8.25	.85	.22	.15
1453	8¢ Old Faithful (32)	7.50	1.00	.24	.15
1454	15¢ Mt. McKinley	19.50	1.90	.45	.25
	See #C84 for 11¢ City of Refuge National Park Issue				
1455	8¢ Family Planning	10.75	1.10	.24	.15
1456-9	8¢ Colonial Craftsmen, attd	11.50	1.60	1.00	1.00
1456-9	Set of 4 Singles	...	...	.90	.70

1972 Commemoratives (cont.)

1460 1461 1462

1463 1464-67

1469 1468 1470

1471 1472 1473 1474

Scott's No.		Mint Sheet	Plate Block	F-VF NH	F-VF Used
1460	6¢ Olympics - Bicycling	9.50 (10)	1.95	.22	.15
1461	8¢ Olympics - Bobsledding	10.75 (10)	2.50	.24	.15
1462	15¢ Olympics - Running	21.50 (10)	4.75	.45	.25
See #C85 for 11¢ Olympics					
1463	8¢ Parent Teacher Assn	10.75	1.00	.24	.15
1463	8¢ P.T.A. Error Plate #	11.00	1.10	...	...
1464-7	8¢ Wildlife Conserv., attd (32)	7.50	1.10	1.00	.90
1464-7	Set of 4 Singles	...	...	.90	.70
1468	8¢ Mail Order	10.75 (12)	3.00	.24	.15
1469	8¢ Osteopathic Medicine	10.75 (6)	1.60	.25	.15
1470	8¢ Tom Sawyer	10.75	1.10	.25	.15
1471	8¢ Christmas Angel	10.75 (12)	3.00	.24	.15
1472	8¢ Christmas, Santa Claus	10.75 (12)	3.00	.24	.15
1473	8¢ Pharmacy	20.00	2.00	.50	.15
1474	8¢ Stamp Collecting (40)	8.50	1.00	.24	.15

1973 Commemoratives

1475 1476 1477

1475-1508	**Set of 34**	...	...	**8.25**	**4.75**
1475	8¢ Love	10.75 (6)	1.50	.24	.15
1476-79	Communications in Colonial America				
1476	8¢ Printers and Patriots	10.75	1.00	.24	.15
1477	8¢ Posting a Broadside	10.75	1.00	.24	.15

1973 Commemoratives (cont.)

1478 1479 1488

1480-83 1484

1485 1486 1487

1489-98

Scott's No.		Mint Sheet	Plate Block	F-VF NH	F-VF Used
1478	8¢ Postrider	10.75	1.00	.24	.15
1479	8¢ Drummer	10.75	1.00	.24	.15
1480-83	8¢ Boston Tea Party, attd	12.00	1.25	1.00	.90
1480-83	Set of Singles	...	...	.90	.60
1484	8¢ Arts - George Gershwin (40)	9.00 (12)	3.25	.25	.15
1485	8¢ Arts - Robinson Jeffers (40)	8.50 (12)	3.00	.24	.15
1486	8¢ Arts - Henry Tanner (40)	8.50 (12)	3.00	.24	.15
1487	8¢ Arts - Willa Cather (40)	8.50 (12)	3.00	.24	.15
1488	8¢ Nicolaus Copernicus	11.50	1.10	.25	.15

1973 Postal People

1489-98	8¢ Postal Employees, attd	13.00 (20)	5.50	2.50	2.50
1489-98	8¢ Set of Singles	...	...	2.40	1.80

VERY FINE COPIES OF #752-DATE ARE AVAILABLE FOR THE FOLLOWING PREMIUMS: ADD 10¢ TO ANY ITEM PRICED UNDER 50¢. ADD 20% TO ANY ITEM PRICED AT 50¢ & UP.

1973 Commemoratives (cont.)

1500 1499 1501

1502 1503 1504

1505 1506 1507 1508

Scott's No.		Mint Sheet	Plate Block	F-VF NH	F-VF Used
1499	8¢ Harry S. Truman .... (32)	7.00	1.00	.24	.15
1500	6¢ Electronics - Marconi	8.25	.90	.22	.15
1501	8¢ Electronics - Transistors	10.75	1.00	.24	.15
1502	15¢ Electronics - Inventions	19.50	1.85	.45	.25
1503	8¢ Lyndon B. Johnson .... (32)	8.25 (12)	3.50	.28	.15
1504	8¢ Rural America - Cattle	10.75	1.00	.24	.15
1505	10¢ Rural America - Tent ('74)	12.50	1.20	.28	.15
1506	10¢ Rural America - Wheat ('74)	12.50	1.20	.28	.15
1507	8¢ Christmas, Madonna	10.75 (12)	3.00	.24	.15
1508	8¢ Christmas, Needlepoint	10.75 (12)	3.00	.24	.15

1509,1519 1510,1520 1511 1518

1973-1974 Regular Issues

Scott's No.		Mint Sheet	Plate Block	F-VF NH	F-VF Used
1509	10¢ Crossed Flags .... (100)	28.50 (20)	6.50	.30	.15
1510	10¢ Jefferson Memorial .... (100)	26.50	1.20	.28	.15
1510b	Booklet Pane of 5	...	...	2.25	1.75
1510c	Booklet Pane of 8	...	...	2.50	2.00
1510d	Booklet Pane of 6	...	...	8.50	5.00
1511	10¢ Zip Code ('74) .... (100)	26.00	(8) 2.35	.28	.15
1518	6.3¢ Liberty Bell Coil ('74) ....Line Pr.		.65	.22	.15
1519	10¢ Crossed Flags Coil Line Prs./Full	4.75	Part 1.50	.35	.15
1520	10¢ Jeff. Memorial Coil ....Line Pr.		.75	.30	.15

1974 Commemoratives (See also 1505-06)

1525 1526 1527

1528 1529

1530-37

1538-41 1542

Scott's No.		Mint Sheet	Plate Block	F-VF NH	F-VF Used
1525-52	**Set of 28**	...	...	**8.20**	**3.95**
1525	10¢ Veterans of Foreign Wars	12.50	1.20	.28	.15
1526	10¢ Robert Frost	12.50	1.20	.28	.15
1527	10¢ Expo '74 .... (40)	14.00 (12)	4.75	.40	.15
1528	10¢ Horse Racing	12.50 (12)	3.50	.28	.15
1529	10¢ Skylab	12.50	1.20	.28	.15
1530-37	10¢ U.P.U. Centenary Set, attd. (32)	11.50 (10)	3.75	2.75	2.50
1530-37	Same, Plate Block of 16	... (16)	5.95	...	...
1530-37	Set of Singles	...	...	2.50	1.60
1538-41	10¢ Mineral Heritage, attd .... (48)	14.00	1.30	1.20	1.10
1538-41	Set of Singles	...	...	1.10	.60
1542	10¢ Kentucky Settlement	12.50	1.20	.28	.15

1974 Commemoratives (cont.)

1543-46

1547 1548 1549

1551 1550 1552

Scott's No.		Mint Sheet	Plate Block	F-VF NH	F-VF Used
1543-46	10¢ Cont. Congress, attd	14.00	1.30	1.20	1.10
1543-46	Set of 4 Singles	...	...	1.10	.60
1547	10¢ Energy Conservation	12.50	1.20	.28	.15
1548	10¢ Sleepy Hollow	12.50	1.20	.28	.15
1549	10¢ Retarded Children	12.50	1.20	.28	.15
1550	10¢ Christmas, Angel	12.50	(10) 3.00	.28	.15
1551	10¢ Christmas, Currier & Ives	12.50	(12) 3.50	.28	.15
1552	10¢ Xmas, Peace, Self-Sticking	12.50	(20) 5.75	.28	.15
1552	10¢ Same - Plate Block of 12	...	(12) 3.50	...	...

1975 Commemoratives

1553 1555 1554

1556 1557 1558

Scott's No.		Mint Sheet	Plate Block	F-VF NH	F-VF Used
1553-80	**Set of 28**	...	...	**8.15**	**3.75**
1553-55	American Arts Issue				
1553	10¢ Benjamin West Portrait	12.50	(10) 3.00	.28	.15
1554	10¢ Paul Laurence Dunbar - Poet	12.50	(10) 3.00	.28	.15
1555	10¢ D.W. Griffith	15.00	1.50	.35	.15
1556	10¢ Space Pioneer - Jupiter	14.00	1.40	.33	.15
1557	10¢ Space Mariner 10	14.00	1.40	.33	.15
1558	10¢ Collective Bargaining	12.50	(8) 2.40	.28	.15

NOTE: UNUSED YEAR SETS HAVE SE-TENANTS ATTACHED, USED YEAR SETS HAVE SINGLES.

VERY FINE COPIES OF #752-DATE ARE AVAILABLE FOR THE FOLLOWING PREMIUMS: ADD 10¢ TO ANY ITEM PRICED UNDER 50¢. ADD 20% TO ANY ITEM PRICED AT 50¢ & UP. UNLESS PRICED AS VERY FINE, SETS ARE NOT AVAILABLE VERY FINE AND STAMPS SHOULD BE LISTED INDIVIDUALLY WITH APPROPRIATE PREMIUM.

1975 Commemoratives (cont.)

1559 1560 1561

1562 1563 1564

1565-68 1569-70

Scott's No.		Mint Sheet	Plate Block	F-VF NH	F-VF Use
1559-62	Contributors to the Cause				
1559	8¢ Sybil Ludington	10.75	(10) 2.50	.24	.15
1560	10¢ Salem Poor	12.50	(10) 3.25	.30	.15
1561	10¢ Haym Salomon	12.50	(10) 3.00	.28	.15
1562	18¢ Peter Francisco	22.50	(10) 6.25	.50	.15
1563	10¢ Lexington-Concord (40)	10.00	(12) 3.50	.28	.15
1564	10¢ Battle of Bunker Hill (40)	10.00	(12) 3.50	.28	.15
1565-68	10¢ Military Uniforms, attd	13.50	(12) 4.00	1.20	1.10
1565-68	Set of 4 Singles	...	...	1.10	.60
1569-70	10¢ Apollo Soyuz, attd (24)	7.25	(12) 4.00	.65	.65
1569-70	Set of 2 Singles	...	...	.60	.35

1571 1572-75

Scott's No.		Mint Sheet	Plate Block	F-VF NH	F-VF Used
1571	10¢ Int'l. Women's Year	12.50	(6) 1.75	.28	.15
1572-75	10¢ Postal Service Bicent., attd	14.00	(12) 4.00	1.20	1.10
1572-75	Set of Singles	...	...	1.10	.60

1975 Commemoratives (cont.)

1576 1577-78

1579 1580

cott's No.		Mint Sheet	Plate Block	F-VF NH	F-VF Used
576	10¢ World Peace through Law	16.00	1.45	.35	.15
577-78	10¢ Banking Commerce, attd.... (40)	12.00	1.85	.65	.65
577-78	Set of 2 Singles	...	...	.60	.30
579	10¢ Xmas, Madonna & Child	12.50	(12) 3.50	.28	.15
580	10¢ Christmas Card	12.50	(12) 3.50	.28	.15
580b	10¢ Christmas (P. 10½ x 11)	...	(12)17.50	.75	...

1975-1981 Americana Issue (Perf. 11 x 10½)

1581,1811 1582 1584 1585

1590/1616 1592,1617 1593 1594,1816

1595,1618 1596 1597/1618C 1599,1619

1603 1604 1605 1606

1608 1610 1611 1612

1975-1981 Americana Issue (continued)

(Sheets of 100)

Scott's No.		Mint Sheet	Plate Block	F-VF NH	F-VF Used
1581-85,91-94,96-97,99-1612	**Set of 19....**	**...**	**125.00**	**26.50**	**5.25**
1581	1¢ Ability to Write ('77)	7.50	.60	.20	.15
1581v	Dry Gum	...	.60	.20	...
1582	2¢ Frdm/Speak Out ('77)	7.50	.60	.20	.15
1582v	Dry Gum, white paper	...	1.75	.30	...
1582b	Dry Gum, cream paper	...	.60	.20	...
1584	3¢ Cast a Free Ballot ('77)	9.50	.65	.20	.15
1584v	Dry Gum	...	.90	.20	.15
1585	4¢ Public That Reads ('77)	12.50	.65	.20	.15
1585v	Dry Gum	...	1.50	.25	...
1590	9¢ Assem., Bklt. Single ('77)	...	...	.40	.30
1590 & 1623	attached Pair (from 1623a)	...	...	.75	.75
1590a	9¢ Booklet Single, Perf. 10	...	...	35.00	14.50
1590a & 1623b	attd. Pair (from 1623c)	...	...	36.50	...
1591	9¢ Assemble, Large Size	25.00	1.25	.27	.15
1591v	Dry Gum	...	7.50	1.20	...
1592	10¢ Right to Petition ('77)	28.50	1.40	.30	.15
1592v	Dry Gum	...	1.60	.35	...
1593	11¢ Freedom of Press	29.00	1.35	.30	.15
1594	12¢ Freedom of Conscience ('81)	31.50	1.85	.33	.15
1595	13¢ Liberty Bell, Bklt. Single	...	...	.38	.15
1595a	Booklet Pane of 6	...	...	2.50	2.00
1595b	Booklet Pane of 7	...	...	2.65	2.25
1595c	Booklet Pane of 8	...	...	2.75	2.40
1595d	Booklet Pane of 5 (1976)	...	...	2.50	1.80
1596	13¢ Eagle & Shield, Bullseye Pf. 11	36.50	(12) 4.75	.38	.15
1596d	Line Perfs *	...	(12) 595.00	37.50	...
1597	15¢ McHenry Flag, Pf. 11 ('78)	37.50	(20) 9.50	.45	.15
1598	15¢ McHenry Flag, Bklt. Sgl. ('78)	...	...	.60	.15
1598a	Booklet Pane of 8	...	...	5.00	2.50
1599	16¢ Statue of Liberty ('78)	47.50	2.25	.50	.18
1603	24¢ Old North Church	60.00	2.75	.65	.15
1604	28¢ Fort Nisqually ('78)	67.50	3.50	.75	.15
1604v	Dry Gum	...	13.50	1.50	...
1605	29¢ Lighthouse ('78)	72.50	3.75	.80	.50
1605v	Dry Gum	...	14.50	2.00	...
1606	30¢ Schoolhouse ('79)	72.50	3.75	.80	.15
1608	50¢ Iron "Betty" ('79)	120.00	6.50	1.35	.15
1610	$1 Rush Lamp ('79)	225.00	11.00	2.65	.20
1611	$2 Kerosene Table Lamp ('78)	...	22.50	5.25	.50
1612	$5 Railroad Lantern ('79)	...	53.50	12.50	2.25

* #1596 Bullseye Perforations line up perfectly where horizontal and vertical rows meet. #1596d Line Perfs. do not meet evenly.

1975-79 Americana Coil Issues - Perf. 10 Vert.

1613 1614 1615 1615C

Scott's No.		Line Pair	F-VF NH	F-VF Used
1613-19,1811-16	**Americana Coils (12)....... (11)**	**11.50**	**3.15**	**1.65**
1613	3.1¢ Guitar ('79)	.90	.20	.15
1614	7.7¢ Saxhorns ('76)	1.10	.25	.15
1615	7.9¢ Drum ('76)	1.00	.25	.15
1615v	Dry Gum	2.50	.35	...
1615C	8.4¢ Steinway Grand Piano ('78)	2.50	.28	.15
1616	9¢ Right to Assemble ('76)	1.20	.28	.15
1617	10¢ Right to Petition ('77)	1.10	.28	.15
1617v	Dry Gum	1.65	.33	...
1618	13¢ Liberty Bell	.95	.35	.15
1618v	Dry Gum	1.75	.50	...
1618C	15¢ Fort McHenry Flag ('78)	...	.45	.15
1619	16¢ Statue of Liberty ('78)	1.50	.50	.25

1975-77 Regular Issue

1622,1625 1623

Scott's No.		Mint Sheet	Plate Block	F-VF NH	F-VF Used
1622	13¢ Flag/Ind. Hall, Pf. 11x10½ (100)	35.00	(20) 8.25	.38	.15
1622c	Same, Perf. 11 (1981) .... (100)	175.00	(20)90.00	1.10	.95
*** Plate Blocks of #1622 have Pl. #'s at Top or Bottom.**					
*** Plate Blocks of #1622c have Pl. #'s at Left or Right.**					
1623	13¢ Flag over Capitol, Bklt. Sgl. Pf. 11 x 10½ ('77)	...	...	.38	.15
1623a	13¢ & 9¢ Bklt. Pn./8 (7#1623,1#1590)	...	...	3.00	2.50
1623b	13¢ B. Sgl., Pf. 10 ('77)	...	...	.70	.65
1623c	13¢ & 9¢ B.P./8 (7#1623b,1#1590a)	...	...	38.75	18.50
1625	13¢ Flag over Ind. Hall, Coil ....(Partial Line)		2.50	.40	.15

1976 Commemoratives

1629-31

1632

Scott's No.		Mint Sheet	Plate Block	F-VF NH	F-VF Used
1629-32,83-85,90-1703	**Set of 21**	**...**	**...**	**9.50**	**2.85**
1629-31	13¢ Spirit of '76, attd	18.50 (12)	5.00	1.20	1.10
1629-31	Set of Singles	...	...	1.10	.45
1632	13¢ Interphil '76	17.50	1.60	.38	.15

1633

1635

1654

1976 State Flags Issue

1633-82	13¢ States, attd	26.50 (12)	6.50	...	...
1633-82	13¢ Set of Singles	...	...	...	13.50

1633	DE	1646	VT	1659	FL	1671	ND
1634	PA	1647	KY	1660	TX	1672	SD
1635	NJ	1648	TN	1661	IA	1673	MT
1636	GA	1649	OH	1662	WI	1674	WA
1637	CT	1650	LA	1663	CA	1675	ID
1638	MA	1651	IN	1664	MN	1676	WY
1639	MD	1652	MS	1665	OR	1677	UT
1640	SC	1653	IL	1666	KS	1678	OK
1641	NH	1654	AL	1667	WV	1679	NM
1642	VA	1655	ME	1668	NV	1680	AZ
1643	NY	1656	MO	1669	NE	1681	AK
1644	NC	1657	AR	1670	CO	1682	HI
1645	RI	1658	MI				

1976 Commemoratives (continued)

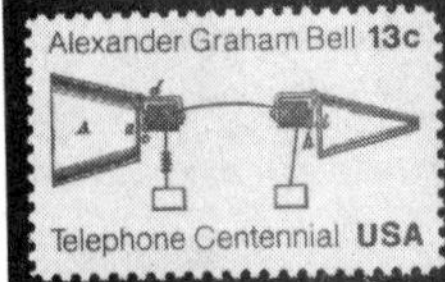

1683

1684

1685

1686-89

1683	13¢ Telephone Centennial	17.50	1.60	.38	.15
1684	13¢ Commercial Aviation	17.50 (10)	4.00	.38	.15
1685	13¢ Chemistry	17.50 (12)	4.70	.38	.15

1976 American Bicentennial Souvenir Sheets

Scott's No.		Mint Sheet	Plate Block	F-VF NH	F-VF Used
1686-89	**Set of Four Souvenir Sheets**	**...**	**...**	**26.50**	**25.00**
1686	13¢ Surrender of Cornwallis	...	...	4.25	4.00
1686a-e	Any Single	...	...	.95	.90
1687	18¢ Decl. of Independence	...	...	6.00	5.75
1687a-e	Any Single	...	...	1.35	1.30
1688	24¢ Washington Crossing Del	...	...	8.25	8.00
1688a-e	Any Single	...	...	1.80	1.70
1689	31¢ Washington at Valley Forge	...	...	10.75	10.50
1689a-e	Any Single	...	...	2.25	2.15

1976 Commemoratives (continued)

1691-94

1699 1690 1700

1695-98

1701

1702

1690	13¢ Ben Franklin and Map	17.50	1.60	.38	.15
1691-94	13¢ Dec. of Independence, attd	30.00 (16)	12.00	3.00	1.75
1691-94	Set of 4 Singles	...	...	2.90	.60
1695-98	13¢ Winter Olym. Games, attd	24.50 (12)	7.50	2.00	1.70
1695-98	Set of 4 Singles	...	...	1.90	.60
1699	13¢ Clara Mass (40)	15.75 (12)	5.25	.42	.15
1700	13¢ Adolph S. Ochs (32)	11.00	1.60	.38	.15
1701	13¢ Christmas, Nativity	17.50 (12)	4.75	.38	.15
1702	13¢ Xmas Winter Pastime, Andriotti Press	17.50 (10)	3.95	.38	.15
1703	13¢ Same, Gravure-Intaglio	17.50 (20)	7.75	.38	.15

#1702: Andriotti Press, lettering at Base is Black, No Snowflakes in Sky.
#1703: Intaglio-Gravure, lettering at Base is Gray Black, Snowflakes in Sky.

NOTE: PRICES THROUGHOUT THIS LIST ARE SUBJECT TO CHANGE WITHOUT NOTICE IF MARKET CONDITIONS REQUIRE. MINIMUM MAIL ORDER MUST TOTAL AT LEAST $20.00.

1977 Commemoratives

1704 1706-09

1705 1710 1711

1712-15 1716

1717-20 1721

ott's o.		Mint Sheet	Plate Block	F-VF NH	F-VF Used
)4-1730	**Set of 27**	...	...	**10.00**	**3.60**
)4	13¢ Battle of Princeton (40)	14.00 (10)	3.95	.38	.15
)5	13¢ Sound Recording	17.50	1.60	.38	.15
)6-09	13¢ Pueblo Art, attd (40)	15.75 (10)	4.50	1.65	1.60
)6-09	Set of 4 Singles	...	...	1.50	.60
0	13¢ Lindbergh's Flight	17.50 (12)	4.75	.38	.15
1	13¢ Colorado Sthd., Line Perfs	17.50 (12)	4.75	.38	.15
1c	Bullseye Perfs	49.50 (12)	24.50	1.35	...
2-15	13¢ American Butterflies, attd	18.50 (12)	5.50	1.65	1.60
2-15	Set of 4 Singles	...	...	1.50	.60
6	13¢ Lafayette's Landing (40)	14.00	1.60	.38	.15
7-20	13¢ Revolutionary War Civilian Skills, attd	18.50 (12)	5.50	1.65	1.60
7-20	Set of 4 Singles	...	...	1.50	.60
21	13¢ Peace Bridge 10th Ann	17.50	1.60	.38	.15

1977 Commemoratives (continued)

1725

1722 1723-24 1726

1727 1728 1729 1730

Scott's No.		Mint Sheet	Plate Block	F-VF NH	F-VF Used
1722	13¢ Herkimer at Oriskany (40)	14.00 (10)	3.95	.38	.15
1723-24	13¢ Energy Conservation, attd. (40)	15.00 (12)	5.00	.80	.75
1723-24	Set of 2 Singles	...	...	.75	.30
1725	13¢ California Settlement	17.50	1.60	.38	.15
1726	13¢ Articles of Confederation	17.50	1.60	.38	.15
1727	13¢ Talking Pictures	17.50	1.60	.38	.15
1728	13¢ Surrender at Saratoga (40)	14.00 (10)	4.00	.38	.15
1729	13¢ Xmas - Wash. at Prayer (100)	34.50 (20)	8.00	.38	.15
1730	13¢ Xmas - Mailbox (100)	33.50 (10)	4.00	.38	.15

1731 1732-33 1734 1735

1737 1738-42

1978 Commemoratives

Scott's No.		Mint Sheet	Plate Block	F-VF NH	F-VF Used
1731-33,44-69	**Set of 29**	...	...	**14.75**	**5.75**
1731	13¢ Carl Sandburg, Poet	17.50	1.60	.38	.15
1732-33	Captain Cook, attached	17.50 (20)	8.00	1.25	.75
1732	13¢ Captain Cook Portrait	...	1.60	.38	.15
1733	13¢ Hawaii Seascape	...	1.60	.38	.15

1978-80 Regular Issues

Scott's No.		Mint Sheet	Plate Block	F-VF NH	F-VF Used
1734	13¢ Indian Head Penny (150)	50.00	1.70	.38	.15
1735	(15¢) "A" & Eagle, Perf. 11 (100)	37.50	1.70	.40	.15
1735c	(15¢) Bullseye Perf. 11.2	...	2.95	.60	...
1736	(15¢) "A" & Eagle, Perf. 11x10½ Booklet Single	...	...	.42	.15
1736a	Booklet Pane of 8	...	...	3.00	2.75
1737	15¢ Roses, Perf. 10, Bklt. Single	...	...	.45	.15
1737a	Booklet Pane of 8	...	...	3.50	3.00
1738-42	15¢ Windmills, Strip of 5 (1980)	...	...	2.50	...
1742a	Booklet Pane of 10 (2 ea. #1738-42) (1980)	...	...	4.95	4.50
1743	(15¢) "A" & Eagle, Coil, Pf. Vert. ....Line Pr.		1.10	.42	.15

NOTE: Modern booklet panes are glued into booklets and prices listed are for panes without selvedge and, usually, folded. Limited quantities exist unfolded with full selvedge—these are usually priced anywhere from 1½ to 4 times these prices when available.

1978 Commemoratives (continued)

1744 1745-48

1749-52 1753

1754 1755 1756

1757

Scott's No.		Mint Sheet	Plate Block	F-VF NH	F-VF Used
1744	13¢ Harriet Tubman	23.50	(12) 6.50	.50	.15
1745-48	13¢ Quilts, attd (48)	20.00	(12) 5.75	1.75	1.60
1745-48	Set of 4 Singles	...	...	1.60	.60
1749-52	13¢ American Dance, attd (48)	19.00	(12) 5.50	1.65	1.50
1749-52	Set of 4 Singles	...	...	1.50	.60
1753	13¢ French Alliance (40)	14.00	1.60	.38	.15
1754	13¢ Cancer Detection	19.50	1.90	.45	.15
1755	13¢ Jimmie Rodgers	17.50	(12) 5.00	.38	.15
1756	15¢ George M. Cohan	20.00	(12) 5.75	.45	.15

1978 CAPEX Souvenir Sheet

Scott's No.		Mint Sheet	Plate Block	F-VF NH	F-V Use
1757	13¢x8 ($1.04) CAPEX Souvenir Sheet (6)	15.00	...	2.75	2.2
1757	S.Sh. with Plate No	...	3.75	...	...
1757a-h	Set of 8 Singles	...	...	2.65	1.5
	Strip of Four (a-d)	...	...	1.40	1.1
	Strip of Four (e-h)	...	...	1.40	1.1
	Block of 8, attached	...	...	3.95	3.7

1978 Commemoratives (continued)

1758 1759 1760-63

1764-67 1768 1769

		Mint Sheet	Plate Block	F-VF NH	F-V Used
1758	15¢ Photography (40)	15.00	(12) 6.25	.50	.1
1759	15¢ Viking Space Mission	20.00	2.25	.50	.1
1760-63	15¢ American Owls, attd	22.50	2.25	2.00	2.0
1760-63	Set of 4 Singles	...	...	1.80	.6
1764-67	15¢ American Trees, attd (40)	17.50	(12) 6.00	1.80	1.8
1764-67	Set of 4 Singles	...	...	1.70	.6
1768	15¢ Xmas Madonna (100)	39.50	(12) 5.50	.42	.1
1769	15¢ Xmas Hobbyhorse (100)	39.50	(12) 5.50	.42	.1

1979 Commemoratives

1770 1771 1772

		Mint Sheet	Plate Block	F-VF NH	F-V Used
1770-1802	**Set of 33**	...	...	**14.85**	**4.5**
1770	15¢ R.F. Kennedy (48)	18.50	1.80	.42	.1
1771	15¢ Martin Luther King	20.00	(12) 6.25	.50	.1
1772	15¢ Int'l. Year of Child	19.50	1.80	.42	.1

NOTE: PRICES THROUGHOUT THIS LIST ARE SUBJECT TO CHANGE WITHOUT NOTICE IF MARKET CONDITIONS REQUIRE. MINIMUM ORDER MUST TOTAL AT LEAST $20.00.

1774 1775-78 1773

1779-82 1783-86

ott's o.		Mint Sheet	Plate Block	F-VF NH	F-VF Used
73	15¢ John Steinbeck	19.00	1.80	.42	.15
74	15¢ Albert Einstein	19.00	1.80	.42	.15
75-78	15¢ Toleware, attd (40)	20.00 (10)	5.00	1.90	1.75
75-78	Set of 4 Singles	...	...	1.80	.60
79-82	15¢ Am. Architecture, attd (48)	25.00	3.00	2.00	1.75
79-82	Set of 4 Singles	...	...	1.90	.60
83-86	15¢ Endangered Flowers, attd	22.75 (12)	7.75	1.90	1.75
83-86	Set of 4 Singles	...	...	1.80	.60

1787 1788 1789

1790 1791-94

1979 Commemoratives (cont.)

1799

1795-98 1800

1801 1802

Scott's No.		Mint Sheet	Plate Block	F-VF NH	F-VF Used
1787	15¢ Seeing Eye Dog	19.50 (20)	9.00	.42	.15
1788	15¢ Special Olympics	19.50 (10)	4.50	.42	.15
1789	15¢ John P. Jones, Perf. 11x12	19.50 (10)	4.50	.42	.15
1789a	Same, Perf. 11	32.50 (10	8.25	.70	.25
1790	10¢ Olympics - Decathalon	14.50 (12)	4.50	.30	.15
1791-94	15¢ Summer Olympics, attd	22.50 (12)	6.50	2.10	1.75
1791-94	Set of 4 Singles	...	...	1.95	.60
1795-98	15¢ Winter Olym., attd. (1980)	22.50 (12)	6.50	2.10	1.75
1795-98	Set of 4 Singles	...	...	1.95	.60
1798-98a	Perf. 11 attd	...	(12)14.00	4.00	...
1799	15¢ Xmas Madonna (100)	39.50 (12)	5.50	.42	.15
1800	15¢ Xmas Ornament (100)	39.50 (12)	5.50	.42	.15
1801	15¢ Will Rogers	21.00 (12)	6.00	.45	.15
1802	15¢ Vietnam Veterans	26.50 (10)	5.95	.55	.15

1980 Commemoratives (See also 1795-98)

1803 1804

1805-10

		Mint Sheet	Plate Block	F-VF NH	F-VF Used
1803-10,21-43	**Set of 31**	**...**	**...**	**14.95**	**4.15**
1803	15¢ W.C. Fields	21.00 (12)	6.00	.45	.15
1804	15¢ Benjamin Banneker	19.50 (12)	5.50	.42	.15
1805-10	15¢ Letter Writing, attd (60)	31.50 (36)	23.50	2.95	2.50
1805-10	Set of 6 Singles	...	...	2.75	.90

1980-81 Regular Issues

1813 1816 1818/1820

Scott's No.		Mint Sheet	Plate Block	F-VF NH	F-VF Used
1811	1¢ Inkwell & Quill, Coil	Line Pr.	.50	.20	.15
1811v	Dry Gum	Line Pr.	.75	.20	...
1813	3.5¢ Two Violins, Coil	Line Pr.	1.10	.20	.15
1816	12¢ Conscience, Coil ('81).............	Line Pr.	1.95	.35	.15
1818	(18¢) "B" & Eagle, Perf. 11x10½ (1981) .... (100)	47.50	2.25	.50	.15
1819	(18¢) "B" & Eagle, Perf. 10, Booklet Single................................	...	...	.55	.15
1819a	Booklet Pane of 8 ('81)	...	...	5.25	3.50
1820	(18¢) "B" & Eagle Coil ('81)	Line Pr.	1.80	.55	.15

1980 Commemoratives (continued)

1821 1822 1823

1824 1825 1826

1827-30 1834-37

1980 Commemoratives (continued)

1831 1832 1833 1842

1838-41 1843

Scott's No.		Mint Sheet	Plate Block	F-VF NH	F-VF Used
1821	15¢ Frances Perkins	21.00	1.95	.45	[illegible]
1822	15¢ Dolley Madison .... (150)	57.50	1.80	.42	[illegible]
1823	15¢ Emily Bissell	19.50	1.80	.42	[illegible]
1824	15¢ H. Keller/A. Sullivan	19.50	1.80	.42	[illegible]
1825	15¢ Veterans Administration	19.50	1.80	.42	[illegible]
1826	15¢ Gen. Bernardo de Galvez	19.50	1.80	.42	[illegible]
1827-30	15¢ Coral Reefs, attd	20.50	(12) 6.00	1.85	[illegible]
1827-30	Set of 4 Singles	...	...	1.70	[illegible]
1831	15¢ Organized Labor	19.50	(12) 5.50	.42	[illegible]
1832	15¢ Edith Wharton	37.50	3.75	.80	[illegible]
1833	15¢ Education in America	45.00	(6) 6.50	.95	[illegible]
1834-37	15¢ Indian Masks, attd .... (40)	24.50	(10) 6.75	2.25	[illegible]
1834-37	Set of 4 Singles	...	...	2.10	[illegible]
1838-41	15¢ Am. Architecture, attd .... (40)	22.50	2.75	2.25	[illegible]
1838-41	Set of 4 Singles	...	...	2.00	[illegible]
1842	15¢ Xmas Madonna	19.50	(12) 5.50	.42	[illegible]
1843	15¢ Xmas Toys	19.50	(20) 9.50	.42	[illegible]

ZIP, MAIL EARLY & COPYRIGHT BLOCKS

Due to space limitations, we do not list prices for zip code, mail early, copyright and other Inscription Blocks. With a few exceptions, these are usually priced at the total price of the single stamps plus one additional stamp. For example, if the stamp retailed for 45¢, a zip block of 4 would be priced at $2.25 (5 x .45).

THE BROOKMAN TIMES

"The Brookman Times" is published 6 times a year and has ads from leading stamp dealers and articles from leading Philatelic writers. There are bargains galore and of particular notes that only dealer's who advertise in the Brookman Price Guide can advertise in "The Brookman Times." We feel these dealers are the "cream of the crop" and heartely endorse them.

The Brookman Times

Serving Collectors for Over 60 Years

May-June 1995 **4th Edition**

Instead of my usual commentary, I thought I'd lead off with an excerpt from a recent letter to the editor. I think it sums up what we're trying to achieve with this publication. ***. . . Arlene Dunn, President***

Gentlemen,

I have known and used your company since you were located in the Loeb Arcade, in Minneapolis, and have followed your growth with interest. It looks like you've a chance to become the top dealer in the land. Keep up the honest prices and dealing.

Having read the March-April edition of "The Brookman Times," I feel I have to comment on the article on collecting for youngsters, by Jeffrey Ryan. They should paste stamps in the books? They should want wallpaper instead of decent stamps? I'm sure that he would advocate using stamp hinges to mount stamps, instead of buying stamp mounts. ***Heresy! Nothing but hereshy! And I just have to say, it's the most sensible thing I have ever read on the subject.*** *I hope to read more of this sort of thing in your journal. I know for a fact, I'll never be reading it in "Linn's Stamp News," or other journals. They have lost all touch with the real fun of collecting. I guess it comes with growing up and becoming "Mature." I hope your company never suffers from that affliction.* ***Sherwood J. Syverson***

U.S. STAMP SALE
Dale Enterprises
Page 2

COVER BARGAINS
John McDonald
Pages 3

CANADA PLATE BLOCK SPECIAL
Gary J. Lyon
Pages 5

SOUVENIR CARDS, PAGES & PANELS SALE
Brookman
Pages 15-19

MARSHALL ISLANDS OFFER
Unicover
Page 9

ZEPP COVER SALE
Brookman
Page 30

Index to Advertisers **Page #**

Published by Brookman / Barrett & Worthen 10 Chestnut Drive, Bedford, N.H. 03110

SOME OF THE LEADING DEALERS YOU WILL FIND IN "THE BROOKMAN TIMES:"

Artmaster
Kenmore Stamp Co.
RKA Cachets
Colorano Covers
Alan Miller Stamps
Brooklyn Gallery
Dale Enterprises, Inc.
Gary Lyons Ltd.
Cover Connection

University Stamp Co.
Plate Block Stamp Co.
Henry Gitner Philatelists, Inc.
Michael Jaffe Stamps
James McCusker
Stamps 'n Stuff
Unicover
H.E. Harris
Gary Posner, Inc.

Subscribe for Only $7.95

You can get the next six issues of "The Brookman Times (a full year's subscription) for only $7.95. For less than $1.00 an issue, you will have an opportunity to purchase a wide range of philatelic merchandise from North America's leading stamp dealers.

FREE SAMPLE COPY ON REQUEST OR USE THE HANDY ORDER FORM

TOLL-FREE 1-800-332-3383
FAX (603) 472-8795
10 CHESTNUT DRIVE • BEDFORD, NH 03110

1980-85 Great Americans Series,
Perforated II (Sheets of 100)

1844 1845 1846 1847

1848 1849 1850 1851

1852 1853 1854 1855

1856 1857 1858 1859

1860 1861 1862 1863

1864 1865 1866 1867

1868 1869

Scott's No.		Mint Sheet	Plate Block	F-VF NH	F-VF Used
844-69	**Set of 26**	...	**155.00**	**12.50**	**3.50**
844	1¢ Dix, Bullseye Perfs., Pf 11.2 ('83)	11.50 (20)	2.75	.20	...
844c	1¢ Dorothea Dix, Line Pfs. ('83)	7.50 (20)	1.75	.20	.15
845	2¢ Igor Stravinsky ('82)	7.50	.60	.20	.15
846	3¢ Henry Clay ('83)	11.50	.65	.20	.15
847	4¢ Carl Schurz ('83)	11.00	.65	.20	.15
848	5¢ Pearl Buck ('83)	13.50	.80	.20	.15
849	6¢ Walter Lippmann ('85)	18.00 (20)	3.85	.20	.15
850	7¢ Abraham Baldwin ('85)	20.00 (20)	4.50	.22	.15
851	8¢ Gen. Henry Knox ('85)	21.50	1.25	.24	.15
852	9¢ Sylvanus Thayer ('85)	23.50 (20)	5.50	.25	.15
853	10¢ R. Russell ('84)	28.50 (20)	7.25	.30	.15
854	11¢ Alden Partridge ('85)	30.00	1.60	.32	.15
855	13¢ Crazy Horse ('82)	42.00	2.10	.50	.15
856	14¢ Sinclair Lewis ('85)	39.50 (20)	9.75	.42	.15
857	17¢ Rachel Carson ('81)	42.50	2.15	.45	.15
858	18¢ George Mason ('81)	47.50	3.25	.50	.15
859	19¢ Sequoyah	52.50	3.00	.60	.15
860	20¢ Dr. Ralph Bunche ('82)	62.50	4.00	.65	.15
861	20¢ Thomas Galladet ('83)	62.50	4.00	.65	.15
862	20¢ Harry Truman, Line Pfs. ('84)	57.50 (20)	13.00	.60	.15
862v	Truman, Bullseye Perfs, Perf 11.2	...	(4) 4.00	.70	...

1980-85 Great Americans Series, (cont.)
Perforated II (Sheets of 100)

Scott's No.		Mint Sheet	Plate Block	F-VF NH	F-VF Used
1863	22¢ Audubon, Line Pfs. ('85)	77.50 (20)	17.50	.80	.15
1863v	Audubon, Bullseye Perfs, Perf 11.2	...	(4) 5.25	.85	...
1864	30¢ F.C. Laubach, Line Pfs. ('84)	77.50 (20)	18.75	.80	.15
1864v	Laubach, Bullseye Perfs, Perf 11.2	...	(4) 5.25	.80	...
1865	35¢ Dr. Charles Drew ('81)	100.00	5.00	1.10	.15
1866	37¢ R. Millikan ('82)	92.50	4.50	1.00	.15
1867	39¢ Grenville Clark, Line Pfs. ('85)	100.00 (20)	22.50	1.10	.15
1867v	Clark, Bullseye Perfs, Perf 11.2	...	(4) 5.50	1.10	...
1868	40¢ L. Gilbreth, Line Pfs. ('84)	100.00 (20)	22.50	1.10	.15
1868v	Gilbreth, Bullseye Perfs, Perf 11.2	...	5.75	1.10	.15
1869	50¢ Admiral Nimitz, Line Pfs. ('85)	135.00 (4)	7.50	1.40	.15
1869v	Nimitz, Bullseye Perfs, Perf 11.2	...	(4) 9.50	1.60	...

1981 Commemoratives

1874 1875 1876-79

		Mint Sheet	Plate Block	F-VF NH	F-VF Used
1874-79,1910-45	**Set of 42**	...	...	**26.50**	**5.50**
1874	15¢ Everett Dirksen	19.50	1.80	.42	.15
1875	15¢ Whitney Young	19.50	1.80	.42	.15
1876-79	18¢ Flowers, attd (48)	31.50	3.00	2.75	2.40
1876-79	Set of 4 Singles	...	...	2.50	.60

1981-82 Regular Issues

1889a

1890 1891 1892 1893 1894-96

		Mint Sheet	Plate Block	F-VF NH	F-VF Used
1880-89	18¢ Wildlife Bklt. Singles	...	...	8.50	1.50
1889a	Wildlife Bklt., Pane of 10	...	...	9.00	5.00
1890	18¢ Flag & "Amber Waves" (100)	52.50 (20)	11.50	.55	.15
1891	18¢ Flag "Sea", Coil (Pl. # Strip)	6.75 (5)	5.00 (3)	.55	.15
1892	6¢ Circle of Stars, Bklt. Sgl	...	...	.75	.20
1893	18¢ Flag & "For Purple" Bklt. Sgl.	...	...	.50	.15
1892-93	6¢ & 18¢, Vertical Pair	...	...	1.35	...
1893a	Bklt Pn of 8 (2 #1892, 6 #1893)	...	...	4.25	3.95
1894	20¢ Flag over Supreme Court, Line Pf. 11, Dry Gum	...	(20) 19.50	.90	.15
1894e	Same, Bullseye Pf. 11.2 (100)	57.50 (20)	12.50	.60	...
1895	20¢ Flag over S.C., Coil Pl. # Strip	6.50 (5)	4.75 (3)	.55	.15
1895e	20¢ Flag, Precancelled Pl. # Strip	80.00 (5)	75.00 (3)	1.15	...
1896	20¢ Flag over S.C., Bk. Sgl	...	...	.60	.15
1896a	Booklet Pane of 6	...	...	3.25	2.75
1896b	Booklet Pane of 10 ('82)	...	...	5.50	4.75

NOTE: Modern booklet panes are glued into booklets and prices listed are for panes without selvedge and, usually, folded. Limited quantities exist unfolded with full selvedge—these are usually priced anywhere from 1½ to 4 times these prices when available.

1981-91 Transportation Coil Series

11¢ RR Untagged Issue not included in Set.
<u>Pl. #s must appear on center stamp</u>

1897 1897A 1898 1898A

1899 1900 1901 1902

1903 1904 1905 1906

1907 1908

Scott's No.		Pl# Strip of 5	Pl# Strip of 3	F-VF NH	F-VF Used
1897-1908	**Mint (14 values)....................**	**120.00**	**65.75**	**3.95**	**1.75**
1897	1¢ Omnibus ('83)............................	.75	.60	.20	.15
1897A	2¢ Locomotive ('82)........................	.85	.70	.20	.15
1898	3¢ Handcar ('83)............................	1.10	.90	.20	.15
1898A	4¢ Stagecoach ('82)........................	2.25	1.80	.20	.15
1899	5¢ Motorcycle ('83).........................	1.50	1.10	.20	.15
1900	5.2¢ Sleigh ('83)............................	13.00	7.50	.25	.15
1901	5.9¢ Bicycle ('82)...........................	19.00	9.75	.25	.15
1902	7.4¢ Baby Buggy ('84).....................	12.75	8.75	.28	.15
1903	9.3¢ Mail Wagon..............................	17.50	8.25	.30	.15
1904	10.9¢ Hansom Cab ('82).................	38.50	16.50	.50	.15
1905	11¢ RR Caboose ('84).....................	6.25	3.50	.35	.15
1905b	11¢ Untagged, not precanc. ('91)...	2.95	2.25	.35	...
1906	17¢ Electric Car..............................	4.00	3.25	.45	.15
1907	18¢ Surrey......................................	4.50	3.50	.50	.15
1908	20¢ Fire Pumper.............................	4.00	3.25	.55	.15
	#1898A: See #2228 for "B" Press				

1981-91 Transportation Coil Series
Precancelled Stamps

Scott's No.		Pl# Strip of 5	Pl# Strip of 3	F-VF NH	F-VF Used
1898Ab/1906a	**Precancelled (8 values).**	**120.00**	**110.00**	**2.50**	**1.40**
1898Ab	4¢ Stagecoach ('82).....................	9.50	8.50	.20	.15
1900a	5.2¢ Sleigh ('83)...........................	15.00	13.50	.25	.15
1901a	5.9¢ Bicycle ('82)..........................	37.50	35.00	.25	.18
1902a	7.4¢ Baby Buggy ('84)..................	6.50	5.95	.30	.18
1903a	9.3¢ Mail Wagon............................	4.50	3.75	.30	.20
1904a	10.9¢ Hansom Cab ('82).............	42.50	40.00	.50	.20
1905a	11¢ RR Caboose ('84).................	4.50	3.75	.40	.22
1906a	17¢ Electric Car...........................	5.25	4.50	.50	.30

NOTE: FROM 1935 TO DATE, AVERAGE QUALITY STAMPS, WHEN AVAILABLE, WILL BE PRICED AT APPROXIMATELY 20% BELOW THE APPROPRIATE F-VF QUALITY PRICE.

1983 Express Mail Issue

1909

Scott's No.		Mint Sheet	Plate Block	F-VF NH	F-V Use
1909	$9.35 Eagle, Booklet Single.........	...	...	30.00	22.50
1909a	$9.35 Booklet Pane of 3...............	...	...	90.00	...

1981 Commemoratives (continued)

1910 1911 1920

1912-19

1921-24

1910	18¢ American Red Cross...............	27.50	2.75	.60	.1
1911	18¢ Savings & Loan.......................	25.00	2.50	.55	.1
1912-19	18¢ Space Achievement, attd....(48)	35.00 (8)	6.00	5.50	4.5
1912-19	Set of Singles..............................	...	...	4.85	1.5
1920	18¢ Professional Mgmnt................	23.00	2.25	.50	.1
1921-24	18¢ Wildlife Habitats, attd	26.50	3.00	2.75	2.5
1921-24	Set of 4 Singles...........................	...	...	2.50	.6

1981 Commemoratives (continued)

1925 1926 1927

1928-31

1932 1934 1933

1935 1936 1939

1937-38 1940

cott's No.		Mint Sheet	Plate Block	F-VF NH	F-VF Used
925	18¢ Disabled Persons	23.50	2.25	.50	.15
926	18¢ Edna St. Vincent Millay	28.50	2.65	.60	.15
927	18¢ Alchoholism	67.50	(20)50.00	.70	.15
928-31	18¢ Architecture, attd (40)	31.50	3.50	3.00	2.50
928-31	Set of 4 Singles	...	...	2.80	.60
932	18¢ Babe Didrikson Zaharias	45.00	4.00	1.00	.15
933	18¢ Bobby Jones	67.50	6.50	1.40	.15
934	18¢ Remington Sculpture	23.50	2.25	.50	.15
935	18¢ James Hoban	23.50	2.25	.50	.15
936	20¢ James Hoban	26.00	2.50	.55	.15
937-38	18¢ Yorktown - Capes, attd	27.50	3.00	1.40	1.25
937-38	Set of Singles	...	...	1.30	.30
939	(20¢) Xmas Madonna (100)	50.00	2.50	.55	.15
940	(20¢) Xmas Child Art	26.00	2.50	.55	.15

1981 Commemoratives (continued)

1941 1942-45

Scott's No.		Mint Sheet	Plate Block	F-VF NH	F-VF Used
1941	20¢ John Hanson	26.50	2.50	.55	.15
1942-45	20¢ Desert Plants, attached (40)	26.00	3.25	2.75	2.50
1942-45	Set of 4 Singles	...	...	2.50	.60

1981-82 Regular Issues

1946-1948 1949

No.		Mint Sheet	Plate Block	F-VF NH	F-VF Used
1946	(20¢) "C" & Eagle, Pf. 11x10½ .. (100)	52.50	2.50	.55	.15
1947	(20¢) "C" & Eagle, Coil	Line Pr.	2.35	.90	.15
1948	(20¢) "C" & Eagle,Perf.10,Bklt. Sgl.	...	...	.60	.15
1948a	Booklet Pane of 10	...	...	5.95	5.00
1949	20¢ Ty. I,Bighorn Sheep,Bklt. Sgl.	...	...	.75	.15
1949a	Ty. I, Booklet Pane of 10	...	...	7.25	5.50
1949c	Type II, Bklt Single	...	...	1.50	...
1949d	Ty. II, Booklet Pane of 10	...	...	14.50	...

*** Ty. I is 18¾ mm wide and has overall tagging. Ty. II is 18½ mm wide and has block tagging.**

1982 Commemoratives

1950 1951 1952

No.		Mint Sheet	Plate Block	F-VF NH	F-VF Used
1950-52,2003-4,2006-30	**Set of 30**	**...**	**...**	**22.50**	**3.95**
1950	20¢ Franklin D. Roosevelt (48)	26.50	2.50	.55	.15
1951	20¢ "LOVE", Perf. 11 x 10½	45.00	5.50	.95	.25
1951a	Perf. 11	36.50	3.25	.75	.15
1952	20¢ George Washington	28.50	2.75	.60	.15

1982 State Birds & Flowers Issue

1953	Alabama	1969	Kentucky	1986	North Dakota
1954	Alaska	1970	Louisiana	1987	Ohio
1955	Arizona	1971	Maine	1988	Oklahoma
1956	Arkansas	1972	Maryland	1989	Oregon
1957	California	1973	Massachusetts	1990	Pennsylvania
1958	Colorado	1974	Michigan	1991	Rhode Island
1959	Connecticut	1975	Minnesota	1992	South Carolina
1960	Delaware	1976	Mississippi	1993	South Dakota
1961	Florida	1977	Missouri	1994	Tennessee
1962	Georgia	1978	Montana	1995	Texas
1963	Hawaii	1979	Nebraska	1996	Utah
1964	Idaho	1980	Nevada	1997	Vermont
1965	Illinois	1981	New Hampshire	1998	Virginia
1966	Indiana	1982	New Jersey	1999	Washington
1967	Iowa	1983	New Mexico	2000	West Virginia
1968	Kansas	1984	New York	2001	Wisconsin
		1985	North Carolina	2002	Wyoming

1982 State Birds & Flowers Issue

1957

1961

1966

1972

Scott's No.		Mint Sheet	Plate Block	F-VF NH	F-VF Used
1953-2002	20¢ 50 States, attd, Pf. 10½ x 11	49.50	...	...	...
1953a-2002a	20¢ 50 States, attd., Pf. 11	51.50	...	...	...
1953-2002	Set of Singles, Mixed Perf. Sizes...........	...	...	...	28.50

1982 Commemoratives (continued)

2003

2004

2005

Scott's No.		Mint Sheet	Plate Block	F-VF NH	F-VF Used
2003	20¢ U.S. & Netherlands............	35.00	(20)17.95	.60	.15
2004	20¢ Library of Congress...........	26.50	2.50	.55	.15

1982 Consumer Education Coil

2005	20¢ Clothing Label .... (Pl# Strip)	135.00(5)	39.50(3)	1.15	.15

1982 Commemoratives (continued)

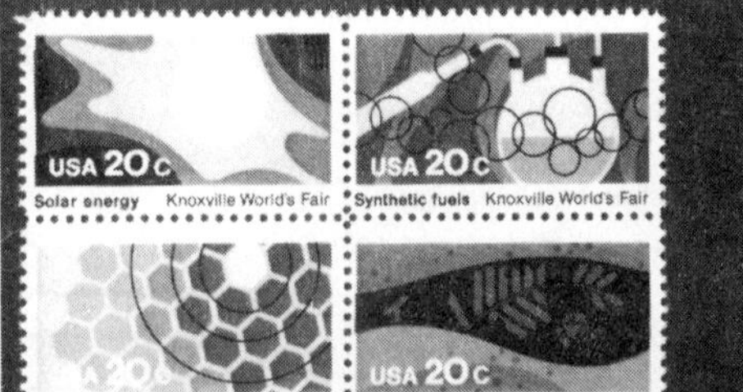

2006-09

2010

2012 2011 2013

Scott's No.		Mint Sheet	Plate Block	F-VF NH	F-VF Used
2006-09	20¢ Knoxville Fair, attd	38.50	3.95	3.25	2.50
2006-09	Set of 4 Singles.........................	...	...	3.10	.60
2010	20¢ Horatio Alger......................	26.50	2.50	.55	.15
2011	20¢ "Aging Together"..................	26.50	2.50	.55	.15
2012	20¢ Arts - The Barrymores........	26.50	2.50	.55	.15
2013	20¢ Mary Walker, Surgeon	36.50	3.50	.75	.15

1982 Commemoratives (continued)

2015 2014 2016

2019-22

2017

2018

2023

2024

2025

2026

2027-30

Scott's No.		Mint Sheet		Plate Block	F-VF NH	F-V Use
2014	20¢ Peace Garden....................	26.50		2.50	.55	.1
2015	20¢ Libraries of America	26.50		2.50	.55	.1
2016	20¢ Jackie Robinson.................	95.00		9.50	1.95	.1
2017	20¢ Touro Synagogue...............	39.50	(20)	18.50	.85	.1
2018	20¢ Wolf Trap Farm Park..........	26.50		2.50	.55	.1
2019-22	20¢ Architecture, attached ..... (40)	35.00		5.00	3.50	3.0
2019-22	Set of 4 Singles.........................	...		...	3.25	.6
2023	20¢ St. Francis of Assisi	28.50		2.75	.60	.1
2024	20¢ Ponce de Leon...................	39.50	(20)	18.50	.85	.1
2025	13¢ Xmas, Kitten & Puppy........	20.00		2.10	.45	.1
2026	20¢ Xmas, Tiepolo Madonna....	29.50	(20)	16.50	.60	.1
2027-30	20¢ Xmas Scenes, attd............	47.50		5.50	3.75	2.7
2027-30	Set of 4 Singles.........................	...		...	3.50	.6

NOTE: FROM 1935 TO DATE, WITH FEW LISTED EXCEPTIONS, UNUSED PRICES ARE FOR NEVER HINGED STAMPS. HINGED STAMPS, WHEN AVAILABLE, ARE PRICED AT APPROXIMATELY 20% BELOW THE NEVER HINGED PRICE.

1983 Commemoratives

2032-35

2036 2031 2037

2039 2038 2040

2041 2042 2043

2044 2045 2046 2047

Scott's No.		Mint Sheet	Plate Block	F-VF NH	F-VF Used
031-65	**Set of 35**	...	...	**25.00**	**4.65**
031	20¢ Sciences & Industry	26.50	2.50	.55	.15
032-35	20¢ Ballooning, attached.......... (40)	26.00	3.00	2.75	2.50
032-35	Set of 4 Singles	...	...	2.50	.60
036	20¢ Sweden	26.50	2.50	.55	.15
037	20¢ Civilian Conserv. Corp	26.50	2.50	.55	.15
038	20¢ Joseph Priestley....................	29.50	3.00	.65	.15
039	20¢ Volunteerism	39.50	(20) 18.50	.85	.15
040	20¢ German Immigration..............	26.50	2.50	.55	.15
041	20¢ Brooklyn Bridge.....................	26.50	2.50	.55	.15
042	20¢ Tennessee Valley Auth	39.50	(20) 18.50	.85	.15
043	20¢ Physical Fitness	39.50	(20) 18.50	.85	.15
044	20¢ Scott Joplin............................	29.50	3.00	.65	.15
045	20¢ Medal of Honor.................. (40)	25.50	3.00	.65	.15
046	20¢ Babe Ruth	100.00	10.50	2.25	.15
047	20¢ Nathaniel Hawthorne.............	26.50	2.50	.55	.15

1983 Commemoratives (cont.)

2048-51

2052 2053 2054

2055-58

2059-62

2063 2064 2065

Scott's No.		Mint Sheet	Plate Block	F-VF NH	F-VF Used
2048-51	13¢ Summer Olympics, attd	35.50	4.50	3.50	2.50
2048-51	Set of 4 Singles	...	...	3.25	.60
2052	20¢ Treaty of Paris.................. (40)	23.50	2.75	.60	.15
2053	20¢ Civil Service..........................	38.75	(20) 18.50	.85	.15
2054	20¢ Metropolitan Opera................	33.50	3.25	.70	.15
2055-58	20¢ Inventors, attd........................	35.00	4.50	3.75	2.75
2055-58	Set of 4 Singles	...	...	3.50	.60
2059-62	20¢ Streetcars, attd	32.00	3.75	3.25	2.75
2059-62	Set of 4 Singles	...	...	3.00	.60
2063	20¢ Xmas, Raphael Madonna......	26.50	2.50	.55	.15
2064	20¢ Xmas, Santa Claus................	33.50	(20) 17.75	.60	.15
2065	20¢ Martin Luther	26.50	2.50	.55	.15

1984 Commemoratives

2066 2067-70 2071

SOIL AND WATER CONSERVATION USA 20c — CREDIT UNION ACT OF 1934 USA 20c

2072 2073 2074 2075

2076-79

2080 2081 2086

Scott's No.		Mint Sheet	Plate Block	F-VF NH	F-VF Used
2066-2109	**Set of 44**	...	...	**33.75**	**5.75**
2066	20¢ Alaska Statehood	26.50	2.50	.55	.15
2067-70	20¢ Winter Olympics, attd	42.50	4.75	3.50	2.75
2067-70	Set of 4 Singles	...	...	3.25	.60
2071	20¢ Fed. Deposit Insurance	26.50	2.50	.55	.15
2072	20¢ Love, Hearts	35.00	(20) 16.95	.65	.15
2073	20¢ Carter G. Woodson	29.50	2.75	.60	.15
2074	20¢ Soil & Water Conserv	26.50	2.50	.55	.15
2075	20¢ Credit Union Act	26.50	2.50	.55	.15
2076-79	20¢ Orchids, attached (48)	33.00	3.50	3.25	2.75
2076-79	Set of 4 Singles	...	...	3.00	.60
2080	20¢ Hawaii Statehood	31.50	3.00	.65	.15
2081	20¢ Nat'l. Archives	33.75	3.50	.75	.15

1984 Commemoratives (cont.)

2082-85

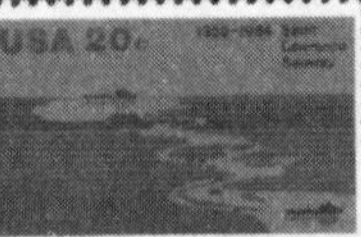

2087 2091 2092

2088 2089 2090 2093

2094 2095 2096 2097

Scott's No.		Mint Sheet	Plate Block	F-VF NH	F-V Use
2082-85	20¢ Summer Olympics, attd	47.50	5.50	4.65	2.7
2082-85	Set of 4 Singles	...	...	4.50	.6
2086	20¢ Louisiana World's Fair (40)	23.50	2.75	.60	.1
2087	20¢ Health Research	31.50	3.00	.65	.1
2088	20¢ Douglas Fairbanks	36.50	(20) 19.75	.65	.1
2089	20¢ Jim Thorpe	31.50	3.00	.65	.1
2090	20¢ John McCormack	26.50	2.50	.55	.1
2091	20¢ St. Lawrence Seaway	26.50	2.50	.55	.1
2092	20¢ Waterfowl Preservation	43.50	4.00	.90	.1
2093	20¢ Roanoke Voyages	29.50	2.75	.60	.1
2094	20¢ Herman Melville	26.50	2.50	.55	.1
2095	20¢ Horace Moses	50.00	(20) 23.50	1.00	.1
2096	20¢ Smokey Bear	35.00	3.25	.80	.1
2097	20¢ Roberto Clemente	130.00	12.75	3.00	.1

NOTE: PRICES THROUGHOUT THIS LIST ARE SUBJECT TO CHANGE WITHOUT NOTICE IF MARKET CONDITIONS REQUIRE. MINIMUM ORDER MUST TOTAL AT LEAST $20.00.

1984 Commemoratives (cont.)

2098-2101 2102

2103 2104 2105

2106 2107 2108 2110

2109

cott's lo.		Mint Sheet	Plate Block	F-VF NH	F-VF Used
98-2101	20¢ Dogs, attd........................(40)	27.50	4.25	3.50	3.00
98-2101	Set of 4 Singles........................	...	...	3.25	.60
02	20¢ Crime Prevention..................	26.50	2.50	.55	.15
03	20¢ Hispanic Americans...........(40)	21.50	2.50	.55	.15
04	20¢ Family Unity..........................	45.00	(20) 22.50	1.00	.15
05	20¢ Eleanor Roosevelt ....(48)	25.00	2.50	.55	.15
06	20¢ Nation of Readers................	29.50	2.95	.65	.15
07	20¢ Madonna & Child..................	26.50	2.50	.55	.15
08	20¢ Santa Claus..........................	26.50	2.50	.55	.15
09	20¢ Vietnam Memorial.............(40)	33.75	4.25	.90	.15

1985 Commemoratives

10,2137-47,52-66	**Set of 27....................**	**...**	**...**	**37.50**	**3.85**
10	22¢ Jerome Kern.........................	31.50	3.00	.65	.15

1985-87 Regulars

2111-2113 2114-2115 2115b 2116

11	(22¢) "D" Stamp.......................(100)	100.00	(20) 37.50	.85	.15
12	(22¢) "D" Coil.................. (Pl# Strip)	8.75 (5)	6.50 (3)	.65	.15
13	(22¢) "D" Booklet Sgl...............	...	...	1.20	.15
13a	"D" Bklt. Pane of 10.................	...	...	11.75	5.00
14	22¢ Flag over Capitol.......... (100)	60.00	3.00	.65	.15
15	22¢ Flag over Cap. Coil.. (Pl# Strip)	4.75 (5)	3.75 (3)	.60	.15
15b	Flag "T" Test Coil........... (Pl# Strip)	6.25 (5)	5.00 (3)	.60	.15

#2115b has a tiny "T" below capitol building

16	22¢ Flag over Cap. Bklt. Sgl....	...	...	1.00	.15
16a	Booklet Pane of 5....................	...	...	4.95	2.50

1985 Regulars

2117-21

2122

Scott's No.		Mint Sheet	Plate Block	F-VF NH	F-VF Used
2117-21	22¢ Seashells Bklt. Sgls...............	...	...	3.25	.75
2121a	Bklt. Pane of 10............................	...	...	5.95	5.00
2122	$10.75 Exp. Mail B. Sgl., Type I...	...	...	27.50	9.95
2122a	Bklt. Pane of 3 (Pl. #11111).........	...	...	80.00	...
2122b	$10.75 Ty. II, Bklt. Sgl..................	...	...	35.00	11.95
2122c	Ty. II Bklt. Pane of 3 (Pl. #22222)	...	...	97.50	...

*** Ty. I: washed out appearance; "$10.75" is grainy.**
*** Ty. II: brighter colors; "$10.75" is smoother and less grainy.**

1985-89 TRANSPORTATION COIL SERIES II

2123 2124 2125 2126

2127 2128 2129 2130

2131 2132 2133 2134

2135 2136

1985-89 TRANSPORTATION COIL SERIES II

*** Pl. #s must appear on center stamp. Sets do not include "B" press issue.**

Scott's No.		Pl.# Strip of 5	Pl.# Strip of 3	F-VF NH	Used
2123-36	**Mint (14 values)....................**	**37.75**	**29.50**	**4.25**	**1.85**
2123	3.4¢ School Bus	1.50	1.25	.20	.15
2124	4.9¢ Buckboard	1.65	1.00	.20	.15
2125	5.5¢ Star Route Truck ('86)	2.65	2.25	.20	.15
2126	6¢ Tricycle	2.10	1.75	.20	.15
2127	7.1¢ Tractor ('87)	3.35	2.95	.22	.15
2128	8.3¢ Ambulance	2.50	1.50	.25	.15
2129	8.5¢ Tow Truck ('87)..................	4.00	3.50	.25	.15
2130	10.1¢ Oil Wagon.........................	3.75	2.25	.28	.15
2131	11¢ Stutz Bearcat......................	2.10	1.50	.32	.15
2132	12¢ Stanley Steamer.................	2.50	2.15	.35	.15
2133	12.5¢ Pushcart	3.75	2.75	.35	.15
2134	14¢ Iceboat................................	2.75	2.25	.42	.15
2134b	"B" Press (no line) ('86)	5.00	4.25	.45	.15
2135	17¢ Dog Sled ('86)	3.75	3.00	.55	.15
2136	25¢ Bread Wagon ('86)	4.75	3.50	.70	.15

PRECANCELLED COILS

Scott's No.		Pl.# Strip of 5	Pl.# Strip of 3	F-VF NH	Used
2123a/33a	**Precanc. (12 values) ....**	**44.50**	**37.75**	**2.85**	**1.80**
2123a	3.4¢ School Bus	8.75	7.95	.20	.15
2124a	4.9¢ Buckboard	2.50	2.25	.20	.15
2125a	5.5¢ Star Route Truck ('86)	2.65	2.25	.20	.15
2126a	6¢ Tricycle	2.65	2.25	.20	.15
2127a	7.1¢ Tractor ('87)	5.50	4.75	.22	.15
2127av	Zip + 4 Precancel ('89)	3.50	3.00	.22	.15
2128a	8.3¢ Ambulance	2.40	1.50	.25	.15
2129a	8.5¢ Tow Truck ('87)..................	4.25	3.75	.27	.15
2130a	10.1¢ Oil Wagon.........................	3.75	2.75	.28	.20
2130av	Oil Wag., Red Prec ('88)	3.75	3.25	.28	.20
2132a	12¢ Stanley Steamer.................	3.25	2.75	.37	.20
2132b	"B" Press, Prec. (no line) ('87)...	28.75	27.50	.70	.20
2133a	12.5¢ Pushcart	4.25	3.75	.35	.20

1985 Commemoratives (cont.)

2137 2138-41

2142 2143 2144

2145 2146 2147

Scott's No.		Mint Sheet	Plate Block	F-VF NH	F-VF Used
2137	22¢ Mary Mcleod Bethune	33.50	3.25	.70	.15
2138-41	22¢ Duck Decoys, attached	95.00	12.00	9.00	3.00
2138-41	Set of 4 Singles	...	...	8.50	.60
2142	22¢ Winter Spec. Olympics...... (40)	25.00	2.95	.65	.15
2143	22¢ Love......................................	31.50	2.95	.65	.15
2144	22¢ Rural Electrification Ad.	65.00	(20) 32.50	.85	.15
2145	22¢ Ameripex .... (48)	27.50	2.75	.60	.15

1985 Regulars and Commemoratives (cont.)

2149 2150 2152

2153 2159 2154

2155-58

2160-63 2165

2164 2166 2167

Scott's No.		Mint Sheet	Plate Block	F-VF NH	F-V Us
2146	22¢ Abigail Adams.......................	28.50	2.75	.60	.1
2147	22¢ Frederic A. Bartholdi............	28.50	2.75	.60	.1
2149	18¢ Wash. Pre-Sort Coil.. (Pl#Strip)	4.50 (5)	3.50 (3)	.65	.1
2149a	Same, Precancelled ....(Pl# Strip)	5.25 (5)	4.25 (3)	.65	.3
2149b	Same, Precan., Dry Gum (Pl# Strip)	5.50 (5)	4.75	.60	...
2150	21.1¢ Envelope Coil ....(Pl# Strip)	5.50 (5)	3.50 (3)	.60	.1
2150a	Zip + 4 Precancel ....(Pl# Strip)	5.50 (5)	4.50 (3)	.60	.3
2152	22¢ Korean War Vets	36.50	3.50	.75	.1
2153	22¢ Social Security Act	28.50	2.75	.60	.1
2154	22¢ World War I Vets	36.50	3.50	.75	.1
2155-58	22¢ Horses, attached .... (40)	130.00	19.50	14.00	3.5
2155-58	Set of 4 Singles	...	...	13.00	.8
2159	22¢ Public Education..................	67.50	6.50	1.40	.1
2160-63	22¢ Int'l. Youth Year, attd	59.50	9.75	5.25	3.0
2160-63	Set of 4 Singles	...	...	4.75	.7
2164	22¢ Help End Hunger..................	31.50	3.00	.65	.1
2165	22¢ Madonna and Child	28.50	2.75	.60	.1
2166	22¢ Christmas, contemp.............	28.50	2.75	.60	.1

1986 Commemoratives

cott's No.		Mint Sheet	Plate Block	F-VF NH	F-VF Used
167,2202-04,2210-11, 220-24,2235-45	**Set of 22 (1986)**	...	...	**19.00**	**3.15**
167	22¢ Arkansas Statehood	31.50	3.00	.65	.15

2168 2169 2170 2171

2172 2173 2176 2177

2178 2179 2179B 2180 2182

2183,2197 2184 2184A 2184B 2185

2186 2188 2190 2191 2192

2193 2194 2194A 2195 2196

1986-94 Great Americans
(Sheets of 100)

Scott's No.		Mint Sheet	Plate Block	F-VF NH	F-VF Used
2168/96	**Set of 28**	...	**153.50**	**33.50**	**5.50**
2168	1¢ Margarte Mitchell	6.00	.60	.20	.15
2169	2¢ Mary Lyon ('87)	6.50	.60	.20	.15
2170	3¢ Dr. Paul Dudley White	9.00	.60	.20	.15
2171	4¢ Father Flanagan	9.75	.65	.20	.15
2171a	Untagged	...	.75	.20	...
2172	5¢ Hugo Black	14.50	.85	.20	.15
2173	5¢ Luis Munoz Marin ('90)	10.00	.85	.20	.15
2173v	5¢ Marin, Pl No &Zip Blk of 4 Combo,LL or LR		1.00	...	...
2173a	Marin, Untagged	10.00	.85	.20	...
2176	10¢ Red Cloud ('87)	30.00	1.75	.35	.15
2176b	Untagged	19.75	1.25	.20	...
2177	14¢ Julia Ward Howe ('87)	35.00	1.85	.38	.15
2178	15¢ Buffalo Bill Cody ('88)	37.50	2.10	.40	.15
2179	17¢ Belva Ann Lockwood	55.00	2.75	.60	.15
2179B	20¢ Virginia Agpar ('94)	38.50	2.10	.40	.15

1986-93 Great Americans
(Sheets of 100)

Scott's No.		Mint Sheet	Plate Block	F-VF NH	F-VF Used
2180	21¢ Chester Carlson ('88)	52.50	2.95	.55	.15
2182	23¢ Maryy Cassatt ('88)	47.50	3.00	.50	.15
2183	25¢ Jack London	60.00	3.00	.65	.15
2183a	Bklt. Pn/10, Perf. 11 ('88)	...	...	6.75	6.00
2184	28¢ Sitting Bull ('89)	65.00	4.00	.80	.15
2184A	29¢ Earl Warren ('92)	57.50	3.35	.60	.15
2184B	29¢ Thomas Jefferson ('93)	57.50	6.25	.60	.15
	Jefferson, Plate Block of 8	...	4.25	...	...
2185	35¢ Dennis Chavez ('91)	65.00	4.75	.70	.15
2186	40¢ Gen'l. Claire Chennault ('90)	75.00	4.25	.80	.15
2188	45¢ Dr. H. Cushing ('88)	125.00	6.00	1.30	.15
2190	52¢ Hubert H. Humphrey ('91)	105.00	5.95	1.10	.15
2191	56¢ John Harvard	150.00	7.50	1.60	.15
2192	65¢ Gen. "Hap" Arnold ('88)	125.00	7.25	1.35	.15
2193	75¢ Wendell Willkie ('92)	135.00	7.75	1.50	.15
2194	$1 Dr. Bernard Revel	...	16.75	4.00	.25
2194A	$1 Johns Hopkins ('89) (20)	37.50	9.50	2.00	.30
2195	$2 William Jennings Bryan	...	20.00	4.75	.45
2196	$5 Bret Harte ('87)	...	39.50	9.75	1.65
2197	25¢ J. London Bklt. Sgl., Pf. 10 ('88)	...	...	.70	.15
2197a	Bklt. Pane of 6 ('88)	...	...	4.25	3.00

1986 Commemoratives (cont.)

2201a

2202 2203 2204 2211

2205-09 2210

Scott's No.		Mint Sheet	Plate Block	F-VF NH	F-VF Used
2198-2201	22¢ Stamp Coll. Bklt. Set of 4 Singles	...	...	2.80	.75
2201a	Booklet Pane of 4	...	...	3.00	2.75
2202	22¢ Love	31.50	2.75	.65	.15
2203	22¢ Sojourner Truth	40.00	3.75	.85	.15
2204	22¢ Texas, 150th Anniv	35.00	3.50	.75	.15
2205-09	22¢ Fish Bklt., Set of 5 Sgls	...	...	9.75	.75
2209a	Booklet Pane of 5	...	...	10.00	3.75
2210	22¢ Public Hospitals	37.50	3.50	.80	.15
2211	22¢ Duke Ellington	31.50	3.00	.65	.15

NOTE: Modern booklet panes are glued into booklets and prices listed are for panes without selvedge and, usually, folded. Limited quantities exist unfolded with full selvedge—these are usually priced anywhere from 1½ to 4 times these prices when available.

1986 Commemoratives (cont.)

2216a 2216d 2217g

2220-23

2225 2224 2226

Scott's No.		Mint Sheet	Plate Block	F-VF NH	F-VF Used
2216-19	22¢ Presidents, Set of 4 S/S	...	...	23.50	22.50
2216a-19i	Pres., Set of 36 Sgls	...	...	...	12.50
2220-23	22¢ Polar Explorers, attd	60.00	9.50	5.50	3.75
2220-23	Set of 4 Singles	...	...	5.25	.80
2224	22¢ Statue of Liberty	28.50	2.75	.60	.15

1986-94 Transportation "B" Press Coils

Scott's No.		Pl.# Strip of 5	Pl.# Strip of 3	F-VF NH	F-VF Used
2225	1¢ Omnibus ("B" Press)	1.00	.80	.20	.15
2225a	Untagged ('91)	1.20	.95	.20	...
2225 var	1¢ "C" Press (1994)	1.00	.80	.20	.15
2226	2¢ Locomotive ('87)	1.00	.80	.20	.15
2226a	Untagged ('94)	1.20	.95	.20	...
2228	4¢ Stagecoach	1.75	1.50	.20	.15
2228a	Overall Tagging ('90)	21.50	19.50	.80	...
2231	8.3¢ Ambulance, Precancel	4.75	4.25	.40	.15

4¢ Stagecoach:

1898A: "Stagecoach 1890s" is 19½ mm. long
2228: "Stagecoach 1890s" is 17 mm. long

8.3¢ Ambulance:

2128: "Ambulance 1860s" is 18½ mm. long
2231: "Ambulance 1860s" is 18 mm. long

1986 Commemoratives (continued)

2235-38

1986 Commemoratives (continued)

2240-43

2239 2244 2245

Scott's No.		Mint Sheet	Plate Block	F-VF NH	F-VF Used
2235-38	22¢ Navajo Art, attd	45.00	4.00	4.00	2.50
2235-38	Set of 4 Singles	...	...	3.75	.60
2239	22¢ T.S. Eliot	28.50	2.75	.60	.15
2240-43	22¢ Woodcarved Fig., attd	36.50	6.75	3.75	3.00
2240-43	Set of 4 Singles	...	...	3.50	.60
2244	22¢ Christmas Madonna (100)	55.00	2.75	.60	.15
2245	22¢ Xmas Village Scene (100)	55.00	2.75	.60	.15

1987 Commemoratives

2246 2247 2248

2249 2250 2251

2246-51,75,2336-38,2349-54,2360-61,2367-68	Set of 20			15.60	2.65
2246	22¢ Michigan Statehood	28.50	2.75	.60	.15
2247	22¢ Pan American Games	28.50	2.75	.60	.15
2248	22¢ Love (100)	55.00	2.75	.60	.15
2249	22¢ Jean Baptiste, Pointe du Sable	28.50	2.75	.60	.15
2250	22¢ Enrico Caruso	28.50	2.75	.60	.15
2251	22¢ Girl Scouts	32.50	3.25	.70	.15

2252 2253 2254 2255

2256 2257 2258 2259

2260 2261 2262 2263

2264 2265 2266

Scott's No.		Pl.# Strip of 5	Pl.# Strip of 3	F-VF NH	F-VF Used
2252-66	**Set of 15 Different Values**	**52.50**	**43.50**	**5.75**	**2.50**
2252	3¢ Conestoga Wagon ('88)	1.15	.95	.20	.15
2252a	Untagged ('92)	1.75	1.50	.20	...
2253	5¢ Milk Wagon	1.65	1.35	.20	.15
2254	5.3¢ Elevator, Prec. ('88)	2.25	1.95	.20	.15
2255	7.6¢ Carretta, Prec. ('88)	3.25	2.75	.25	.15
2256	8.4¢ Wheelchair, Prec. ('86)	3.25	2.75	.25	.15
2257	10¢ Canal Boat	2.00	1.50	.25	.15
2257v	Overall Tagged ('92)	4.25	3.75	.35	...
2257vd	Overall Tagged, dull gum ('91)	5.50	4.75	.35	...
2257g	Gravure Reissue ('93)	2.00	1.50	.25	.15
2257g has deeper, sharper color and whiter paper than #2257					
2258	13¢ Police Wagon, Prec. ('88)	3.85	3.25	.38	.20
2259	13.2¢ R.R. Coat Car, Prec. ('88)	3.65	3.00	.38	.20
2260	15¢ Tugboat ('88)	3.50	3.00	.35	.15
2260a	Overall Tagging, shiny gum ('90)	5.00	4.25	.40	...
2261	16.7¢ Popcorn Wagon, Prec. ('88)	4.25	3.75	.45	.22
2262	17.5¢ Marmon Wasp	5.00	4.25	.50	.20
2262a	Precancelled	5.50	4.75	.50	.25
2263	20¢ Cable Car ('88)	4.75	3.95	.55	.20
2263b	Overall Tagged ('90)	7.00	6.00	.70	...
2264	20.5¢ Fire Engine, Prec. ('88)	5.00	4.25	.60	.25
2265	21¢ R.R. Mail Car, Prec	5.00	4.25	.60	.20
2266	24.1¢ Tandem Bic., Prec. ('88)	5.75	4.75	.65	.25

1987-89 Regular & Commemorative Issues

2267-74

1987-89 Regulars & Commemoratives

2275 2276 2277/82

2278,2285A 2280 2281 2283

2284 2285

2286-2335 Examples

Scott's No.		Mint Sheet	Plate Block	F-VF NH	F-VF Used
2267-74	22¢ Spec. Occ. Bklt. Sgls. (8)	...	...	14.00	1.50
2274a	Bklt. Pane of 10	...	...	18.00	10.00
2275	22¢ United Way	28.50	2.75	.60	.15
2276	22¢ Flag & Fireworks (100)	57.50	3.00	.60	.15
2276a	22¢ Fireworks B. Pane of 20	...	...	10.00	10.00
2277	(25¢) "E" Earth Issue ('88) (100)	70.00	3.50	.75	.15
2278	25¢ Flag & Clouds ('88) (100)	67.50	3.25	.70	.15
2279	(25¢) "E" Earth Coil ('88) .... Pl# Strip	4.50 (5)	3.50 (3)	.65	.15
2280	25¢ Flag/Yosem Coil ('88).. Pl# Strip	4.75 (5)	3.75 (3)	.65	.15
2280v	Phosphor Paper ('89) .... Pl# Strip	4.75 (5)	3.75 (3)	.65	.15
2281	25¢ Honeybee Coil............ Pl# Strip	4.50 (5)	3.00 (3)	.70	.15
2282	(25¢) "E" Bklt. Sgl. ('88)	...	...	.95	.15
2282a	Bklt. Pane of 10	...	...	9.50	7.00
2283	25¢ Pheas. Bk. Sgl., **red & blue sky** ('88)		...	.85	.15
2283a	Bklt. Pane of 10	...	...	8.50	7.50
2283b	25¢ Blue Sky, **(red omitted)**, bklt. sgl. ('89)		...	9.50	...
2283c	Bklt. Pn. 10 **(Pl# A3111,A3222)**	...	...	95.00	...
2284	25¢ Grosbeak Bklt, Sgl. ('88)	...	...	.70	.15
2285	25¢ Owl Bklt. Sgl. ('88)	...	...	.70	.15
2284-85	Attached Pair	...	...	1.40	.95
2285b	Bklt. Pn. (5 ea. #2284,2285)	...	...	6.75	5.75
2285A	25¢ Flag/Cloud Bk. Sgl. ('88)	...	...	.75	.15
2285Ac	Bklt. Pn. 6	...	...	4.25	4.00
2286-2335	22¢ American Wildlife	87.50	...	...	...
2286-2335	Set of 50 Singles	...	...	...	19.95

NOTE: Modern booklet panes are glued into booklets and prices listed are for panes without selvedge and, usually folded. Limited quantities exist unfolded with full selvedge—these are usually priced anywhere from 1½ to 4 times these prices when available.

1987-90 Bicentennial Issues

2336 2337 2338 2339

2340 2341 2342 2343

2344 2345 2346 2347

2348 2349 2350

Scott's No.		Mint Sheet	Plate Block	F-VF NH	F-VF Used
2336	22¢ DE Statehood Bicent.	31.50	3.00	.65	.15
2337	22¢ PA Bicentennial	40.00	3.95	.85	.15
2338	22¢ NJ Bicentennial..................	35.75	3.50	.75	.15
2339	22¢ GA Bicent. ('88)	35.75	3.50	.75	.15
2340	22¢ CT Bicent. ('88)..................	33.75	3.25	.70	.15
2341	22¢ MA Bicent. ('88)	33.75	3.25	.70	.15
2342	22¢ MD Bicent. ('88)	33.75	3.25	.70	.15
2343	25¢ SC Bicent. ('88)	45.00	4.50	.95	.15
2344	25¢ NH Bicent. ('88)	33.50	3.25	.70	.15
2345	25¢ VA Bicent. ('88)..................	45.00	4.50	.95	.15
2346	25¢ NY Bicent. ('88)	33.50	3.25	.70	.15
2347	25¢ NC Bicent. ('89)	33.50	3.25	.70	.15
2348	25¢ RI Bicent. ('90)....................	33.50	3.25	.70	.15

2351-54

1987 Commemoratives (cont'd.)

2355-59 2360 2361

2362-66 2367 2368

Scott's No.		Mint Sheet	Plate Block	F-VF NH	F-VF Used
2349	22¢ U.S.-Morocco Relations	28.50	2.75	.60	.15
2350	22¢ William Faulkner.................	28.50	2.75	.60	.15
2351-54	22¢ Lacemaking, attd............. (40)	37.50	7.00	3.50	2.50
2351-54	Set of 4 Sgls.............................	...	...	3.25	.60
2355-59	22¢ Drafting of Const., Bklt. Sgls. (5)............................	...	...	3.95	.75
2359a	Bklt. Pane of 5..........................	...	...	4.25	3.00
2360	22¢ Signing the Const.	31.50	3.00	.65	.15
2361	22¢ Cert. Pub. Accounting	175.00	15.00	3.50	.15
2362-66	22¢ Loco. Bklt. Sgls. (5)	...	...	3.75	.75
2366a	Bklt. Pane of 5..........................	...	...	3.95	3.00
2367	22¢ Xmas Mor. Mad. .... (100)	55.00	2.75	.60	.15
2368	22¢ Xmas Orn .... (100)	55.00	2.75	.60	.15

1988 Commemoratives

2369 2370 2371

2372-75 2376

		Mint Sheet	Plate Block	F-VF NH	F-VF Used
2339-46,69-80,86-93,99-2400	**Set of 30.**	**...**	**...**	**26.75**	**4.00**
2369	22¢ 1988 Winter Olympics	36.00	3.50	.80	.15
2370	22¢ Australia Bicent .... (40)	24.00	2.75	.60	.15
2371	22¢ J.W. Johnson	28.50	2.75	.60	.15
2372-75	22¢ Cats, attd......................... (40)	36.50	8.00	3.75	3.25
2372-75	Set of 4 Sgls............................	...	...	3.50	.60
2376	22¢ Knute Rockne.....................	38.50	3.95	.80	.15

1988 Issues (cont.)

2377 2378 2379 2380

2381-85

2386-89

2390-93

1988 Issues (cont.)

Scott's No.		Mint Sheet	Plate Block	F-VF NH	F-VF Used
2377	25¢ Francis Ouimet..................	50.00	5.00	1.10	.15
2378	25¢ Love..............................(100)	67.50	3.25	.70	.15
2379	45¢ Love..................................	65.00	5.75	1.35	.15
2380	25¢ Summer Olympics.............	36.00	3.50	.80	.15
2381-85	25¢ Classic Cars, Bklt. Sgls.....	...	...	9.50	.75
2385a	Bk. Pn. 5..................................	...	...	10.00	3.75
2386-89	25¢ Antarctic Exp., attd	58.75	10.75	5.25	3.00
2386-89	Set of 4 Sgls.............................	...	...	4.75	.75
2390-93	25¢ Carousel, attd....................	57.50	6.00	5.50	3.00
2390-93	Set of 4 Sgls.............................	...	...	5.00	.75

2394

2395-98

2399 2400

2394	$8.75 Express Mail....................	...	105.00	23.75	8.75
2395-98	25¢ Special Occasions, Bklt. Sgls.	...	...	3.50	.60
2396a	Happy Birthday & Best Wishes				
	B. Pn. of 6 (3&3) w/gutter..........	...	...	5.50	4.00
2398a	Thinking of You & Love You				
	B. Pn. of 6 (3&3) w/gutter..........	...	...	5.50	4.00
2399	25¢ Xmas (Madonna)................	31.50	3.00	.65	.15
2400	25¢ Xmas (Horse & Sleigh).......	31.50	3.00	.65	.15

1989 Issues

2401 2402 2403

2404 2405-09 Examples

2410 2411 2412 2413

2417 2416 2418

2419 2420 2421

2422-25 2426

Scott's No.		Mint Sheet	Plate Block	F-VF NH	F-VF Used
2347,2401-04,10-18,20-28,34-37	**Set of 27**	**...**	**...**	**24.00**	**3.95**
2401	25¢ Montana Sthd. Cent	42.50	4.00	.90	.15
2402	25¢ A. Philip Randolph	31.50	3.00	.65	.15
2403	25¢ North Dakota Sthd. Cent	31.50	3.00	.65	.15
2404	25¢ Washington Sthd. Cent	35.00	3.50	.75	.15
2405-09	25¢ Steamboats, Bklt. Sgls	...	...	3.70	.75
2409a	Bklt. Pane of 5	...	...	3.95	3.50
2410	25¢ World Stamp Expo	31.50	3.00	.65	.15
2411	25¢ Arturo Toscanini	35.00	3.50	.75	.15
2412	25¢ House of Representatives	35.00	3.50	.75	.15
2413	25¢ U.S. Senate	35.00	3.50	.75	.15
2414	25¢ Exec. Branch/G.W. Inaug	40.00	4.25	.90	.15
2415	25¢ U.S. Supreme Court (1990)	38.50	4.00	.85	.15
2416	25¢ South Dakota Sthd. Cent	31.50	3.00	.65	.15
2417	25¢ Lou Gehrig	38.50	4.00	.85	.15
2418	25¢ Ernest Hemingway	31.50	3.00	.65	.15
2419	$2.40 Moon Landing	...	26.50	6.25	3.50
2420	25¢ Letter Carriers (40)	25.00	3.00	.65	.15
2421	25¢ Drafting Bill of Rights	60.00	6.00	1.30	.15
2422-25	25¢ Prehistoric Animals, attd. (40)	62.50	7.50	6.50	3.00
2422-25	Set of 4 Singles	...	...	6.00	.80
2426	25¢ Pre-Columbian Customs	31.50	3.00	.65	.15
2427	25¢ Christmas Madonna	31.50	3.00	.65	.15
2427a	Bklt. Pane of 10	...	...	7.50	6.50

1989 Issues (cont.)

2427 2428,2429 2431

Scott's No.		Mint Sheet	Plate Block	F-VF NH	F-VF Used
2428	25¢ Christmas Sleigh	31.50	3.00	.65	.15
2429	25¢ Christmas Sleigh, Bklt. Sgl.	...	...	.90	.15
2429a	Bklt. Pane of 10	...	...	8.95	7.50
2431	25¢ Eagle & Shield, self adhes.	...	...	.85	.20
2431a	Booklet Pane of 18	...	...	14.95	12.50
2431v	25¢ Eagle & Shield, Coil	Strip of 3	2.50	.85	...

2433

2434-37

2438

Scott's No.		Mint Sheet	Plate Block	F-VF NH	F-VF Used
2433	90¢ World Stamp Expo S/S of 4	...	...	19.50	15.00
2434-37	25¢ Traditional Mail Deliv., attd (40)	45.00	6.00	5.00	3.75
2434-37	Set of 4 Singles	...	...	4.70	.75
2438	25¢ Traditional Mail S/S of 4	...	...	7.00	4.00

1990 Issues

2439 2440,2441 2442 2443

2444

2449

2445-48

Scott's No.		Mint Sheet	Plate Block	F-VF NH	F-VF Used
2348,2439-40,2442,44-49,96-2500,2506-15		**Set of 25**	**...**	**24.95**	**3.50**
2439	25¢ Idaho Sthd. Centenary........	31.50	3.00	.65	.15
2440	25¢ Love....................................	31.50	3.00	.65	.15
2441	25¢ Love, Bklt. Sgl.....................	...	...	.90	.15
2441a	Booklet Pane of 10	...	...	8.95	6.50
2442	25¢ Ida B. Wells	31.50	3.00	.65	.15
2443	15¢ Beach Umbrella, Bklt. Sgl...	...	...	.45	.15
2443a	Booklet Pane of 10	...	...	4.35	3.95
2444	25¢ Wyoming Sthd. Centenary..	40.00	4.00	.85	.15
2445-48	25¢ Classic Films, attd ....(40)	95.00	10.00	9.00	5.00
2445-48	Set of 4 Singles	...	...	8.75	.80
2449	25¢ Marianne Moore	31.50	3.00	.65	.15

1990-95 Transportation Coils IV

2451 2452 2452B 2452D 2453,2454

2457 2458 2464 2468

Scott's No.		Pl# Strip of 5	Pl# Strip of 3	F-VF NH	Used
2451/2468	**Set of 10 values.................. ...**	**32.00**	**24.75**	**3.75**	**1.75**
2451	4¢ Steam Carriage ('91)	1.60	1.35	.20	.15
2451b	Untagged.................................	2.65	2.25	.20	...
2452	5¢ Circus Wagon, Engraved......	1.75	1.50	.20	.15
2452a	Untagged.................................	2.40	2.00	.20	...
2452B	5¢ Circus Wagon, Gravure ('92)	2.10	1.75	.20	.15
2452D	5¢ Circus Wagon(¢ sign) ('95)...	2.10	1.75	.20	.15
2453	5¢ Canoe, Brown ('91)..............	2.00	1.75	.20	.15
2454	5¢ Canoe, Red ('91)	2.00	1.75	.20	.15
2454 var	5¢ Canoe, Red, Low gloss gum ('93)	2.35	2.00	.20	...
2457	10¢ Tractor Trailer, Intaglio ('91)	2.25	1.75	.20	.15
	#2457"Additional Presort Postage Paid" In Gray.				
2458	10¢ Gravure (1994)	2.25	1.75	.20	.15
	#2458 "Additional, etc." in black. Whiter paper.				
2464	23¢ Lunch Wagon ('91)	4.95	3.95	.60	.15
2468	$1.00 Seaplane	12.95	9.00	1.95	.50

Circus Wagon: #2452 Short letters and date, #2452B Taller, thinner letters and date

1990-93 Issues (cont.)

2470-74

2475 2476 2478 2479

2480 2481 2481v 2482 2487

2489 2491 2493,2494 2495

2496-2500

Scott's No.		Mint Sheet	Plate Block	F-VF NH	F-VF Used
2470-74	25¢ Lighthouse Bklt. Singles	...	...	4.75	.75
2474a	Booklet Pane of 5	...	...	4.95	2.75
2475	25¢ ATM Self Adhes., Plastic Stamp	...	...	1.00	.40
2475a	Pane of 12	...	...	10.95	...
2476	$2.00 Bobcat............................(20)	75.00	17.00	3.95	.50
2478	29¢ Red Squirrel, self adhesv	...	...	.90	.30
2478a	Pane of 18 ('93)	...	...	14.00	11.75
2478v	Squirrel Coil, self adhesive.......... **Strip of 3**		2.70	.90	...
2479	29¢ Rose, self-adhesive	...	...	.80	.30
2479a	Pane of 18 ('93)	...	...	10.75	8.75
2479v	Rose coil, self-adhesive.............. **Strip of 3**		2.40	.80	...
2480	29¢ Pine Cone, self-adhesive......	...	...	.80	.30
2480a	Pane of 18 ('93)	...	...	10.75	8.75
2480v	Pine Cone coil, self-adhesive ...... **Pl. #Strip of 3**		7.50	.80	...
2481	1¢ Kestrel ('91) ....(100)	5.00	.60	.20	.15
2481v	Redesign with "¢" sign ('95).....(100)	5.00	.60	.20	.15
2482	3¢ Bluebird ('91) ....(100)	7.50	.65	.20	.15
2487	19¢ Fawn ('91)...........................(100)	37.50	2.50	.40	.15
2489	30¢ Cardinal ('91) ....(100)	55.00	4.00	.60	.15
2491	45¢ Pumpkinseed Sunfish ('92)(100)	85.00	5.25	.90	.15
2493	29¢ Wood Duck,BEP bklt sgl Pf 10	...	...	.90	.15
2493a	BEP Booklet Pane of 10 ('91)......	...	...	8.95	7.75
2494	29¢ Wood Duck, KCS bklt sgl Pf 11	...	...	1.10	.15
2494a	KCS Booklet Pane of 10 ('91)......	...	...	10.95	8.95
2495	29¢ African Violet	...	...	.70	.15
2495a	Booklet Pane of 10 ('93)	...	...	6.95	4.95
2496-2500	25¢ Olympians, attd...............(35)	39.50	(10)11.50	5.25	4.35
2496-2500	Set of 5 Singles...........................	...	...	5.00	.75
2496-2500	Tab singles, attd, Top or Bot....	...	...	6.25	5.75

1990 Commemoratives

2501-05

2506-07

2508-11

2512 2513

2514 2515,2516

Scott's No.		Mint Sheet	Plate Block	F-VF NH	F-VF Used
2501-05	25¢ Indian Headdresses bklt. sgls.	...	...	4.00	.75
2505a	Booklet Pane of 10 (2 ea.)...........	...	...	7.95	7.50
2506-07	25¢ Micronesia/Marshall Isl., attd	39.50	3.85	1.75	1.50
2506-07	Set of 2 Singles	...	...	1.60	.30
2508-11	25¢ Sea Creatures, attd. .... (40)	33.50	3.95	3.50	3.25
2508-11	Set of 4 Singles	...	...	3.25	.60
2512	25¢ America, Grand Canyon.......	31.50	3.00	.65	.15
2513	25¢ Dwight Eisenhower............ (40)	37.50	4.50	.95	.15
2514	25¢ Chistmas Madonna & Child..	31.50	3.00	.65	.15
2514a	Booklet Pane of 10	...	...	6.95	5.95
2515	25¢ Christmas Tree, Perf. 11	31.50	3.00	.65	.15
2516	25¢ Same, Bklt. Sgl., Perf. 11½x11	...	...	.70	.15
2516a	Booklet Pane of 10	...	...	6.95	5.95

1991-94 Issues

2517-2520 2521 2522

2523 2523A 2524 2526

2528 2529 2530 2531 2531A

2533 2532 2534

Scott's No.		Mint Sheet	Plate Block	F-VF NH	F-VF Used
2517	(29¢) "F" Flower Stamp .... (100)	70.00	3.75	.75	.15
2518	(29¢) "F" Flower Coil .... Pl# Strip	5.50 (5)	4.25 (3)	.75	.15
2519	(29¢) "F" Flower, BEP bklt. sgl. ...	...	...	.80	.15
2519a	Bklt. Pane of 10, BEP, bullseye perfs	...	...	7.95	6.95
2520	(29¢) "F" Flower, KCS bklt. sgl....	...	...	1.90	.15
2520a	Bklt. Pane of 10, KCS..................	...	...	18.95	14.95

#2519: Bullseye perforations (11.2). Horizontal and vertical perforations meet exactly in stamp corners
#2520: Normal (line) perforations, Perf. 11

Scott's No.		Mint Sheet	Plate Block	F-VF NH	F-VF Used
2521	(4¢) Non-Denom. "make-up" ... (100)	9.50	.70	.20	.15
2522	(29¢) "F" Flag Stamp, ATM self adhes.	...	...	.85	.35
2522a	Pane of 12	...	...	9.95	9.50
2523	29¢ Flag/Mt. Rushmore Intaglio Coil .... Pl# Strip	7.25 (5)	6.00 (3)	.70	.15
2523A	29¢ Same, Gravure, ... Pl# Strip	7.50 (5)	6.25 (3)	.70	.15

* On #2523A, "USA" & "29" are not outlined in white.

Scott's No.		Mint Sheet	Plate Block	F-VF NH	F-VF Used
2524	29¢ Flower, Perf. 11 .... (100)	70.00	3.75	.75	.15
2524a	29¢ Flower, Perf. 12½x13 .... (100)	70.00	3.75	.75	.15
2525	29¢ Flower Coil, rouletted, Pl# Strip	6.50 (5)	5.50 (3)	.60	.15
2526	29¢ Flower Coil, perf ('92) Pl# Strip	7.50 (5)	6.50 (3)	.60	.15
2527	29¢ Flower Bklt. Sgl.....................	...	...	.75	.15
2527a	Booklet Pane of 10	...	...	7.50	6.95
2528	29¢ Flag with Olympic Rings, bklt. sgl.	...	...	.75	.15
2528a	Booklet Pane of 10	...	...	7.50	6.95
2529	19¢ Fishing Boat Coil, **Ty. I** Pl# Strip	5.75 (5)	5.00 (3)	.45	.15
2529a	19¢ Boat Coil, **Ty. II** ('93) Pl# Strip	5.75 (5)	5.00 (3)	.45	.15
2529b	Type II, Untagged .... Pl# Strip	12.50 (5)	10.00 (3)	1.20	...
2529C	19¢ Boat Coil, **Ty. III** (94) .. Pl# Strip	6.00 (5)	5.25 (3)	.45	.15

***Type I: Darker color & large color cells, Perf. 10**
Type II: Lighter color & small color cells, Perf. 10
Type III: Numerals and U.S.A. taller and thinner, only one loop of rope around piling, Perf. 9.8

Scott's No.		Mint Sheet	Plate Block	F-VF NH	F-VF Used
2530	19¢ Hot-Air Balloons, bklt. sgl	...	...	.50	.15
2530a	Booklet Pane of 10	...	...	4.75	4.50
2531	29¢ Flags/Mem. Day Anniv ..... (100)	55.00	2.75	.70	.15
2531A	29¢ Liberty & Torch, ATM self adh	...	...	.75	.30
2531Ab	Pane of 18	...	...	12.50	11.50

1991 Commemoratives

Scott's No.		Mint Sheet	Plate Block	F-VF NH	F-VF Used
2532-35,37-38,50-51,53-61,67,78-79	**Set of 29**	**...**	**...**	**23.00**	**4.95**
2532	50¢ Switzerland joint issue .... (40)	47.50	5.75	1.25	.25
2533	29¢ Vermont Bicent	36.50	3.50	.75	.15
2534	29¢ Savings Bond, 50th Anniv	36.50	3.50	.75	.15

NOTE: Modern booklet panes are glued into booklets and prices listed are for panes without selvedge and, usually, folded. Limited quantities exist unfolded with full selvedge—these are usually priced anywhere from 1½ to 4 times these prices when available.

2535,2536 2537 2538

2539 2540 2541

2542 2543

2545-49

2550 2551 2552

cott's No.		Mint Sheet	Plate Block	F-VF NH	F-VF Used
535	29¢ Love Stamp, Pf. 12½x13	35.00	3.75	.75	.15
535a	Same, Perf. 11	...	5.00	.95	...
536	29¢ Booklet Sgl., Pf. 11 on 2-3 sides	...	...	.85	.15
536a	Booklet Pane of 10	...	...	8.50	6.75
OTE: "29" is further from edge of design on #2536 than on #2535.					
537	52¢ Love Stamp, two ounces	62.50	5.95	1.30	.20
538	29¢ William Saroyan	35.00	3.50	.75	.15
539	$1.00 USPS Logo&Olym. Rings (20)	52.50	12.50	2.75	.50
540	$2.90 Priority Mail, Eagle (20)	140.00	31.50	7.25	2.50
541	$9.95 Express Mail, Domestic Rate	...	95.00	22.50	8.50
542	$14.00 Express Mail, Internat'l. Rate	...	110.00	26.50	23.50
543	$2.90 Priority Mail, Space ('93) (40)	240.00	26.50	6.25	2.50
545-49	29¢ Fishing Flies, bklt. sgls.	...	...	5.25	.75
549a	Booklet Pane of 5	...	...	5.50	3.50
550	29¢ Cole Porter	40.00	4.00	.90	.15
551	29¢ Desert Shield/Desert Storm	35.00	3.50	.75	.15
552	29¢ Desert Storm, Bklt. Sgl., ABNCo	...	...	.85	.15
552a	Booklet Pane of 5	...	...	4.25	4.00

1991 Issues (cont.)

2553-57

2558 2561 2560

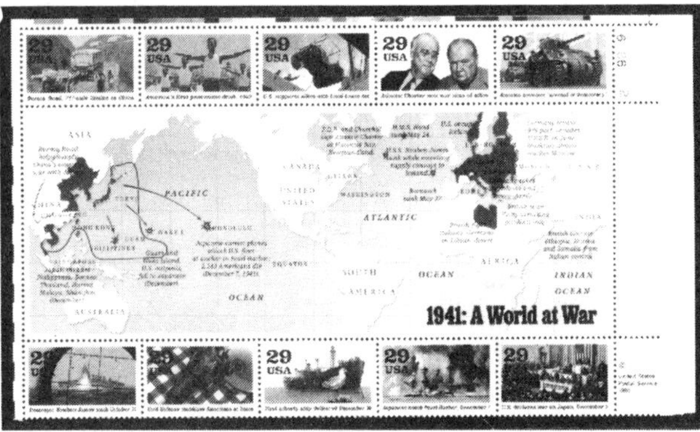

2559

2562-66

Scott's No.		Mint Sheet	Plate Block	F-VF NH	F-VF Used
2553-57	29¢ Summer Olympics, attd (40)	35.00	(10) 10.00	4.75	2.00
2553-57	Set of 5 Singles	...	...	4.50	.75
2558	29¢ Numismatics	42.50	4.50	.90	.15
2559	29¢ World War II S/S of 10 (20)	14.95	...	7.50	7.50
2559a-j	Set of 10 Singles	...	...	...	2.50
2560	29¢ Basketball, 100th Anniversary	45.00	4.75	1.00	.15
2561	29¢ District of Columbia Bicent	35.00	3.50	.75	.15
2562-66	29¢ Comedians, bklt. sgls	...	...	4.25	.75
2566a	Booklet Pane of 10 (2 each)	...	...	8.50	6.95

1991 Issues (cont.)

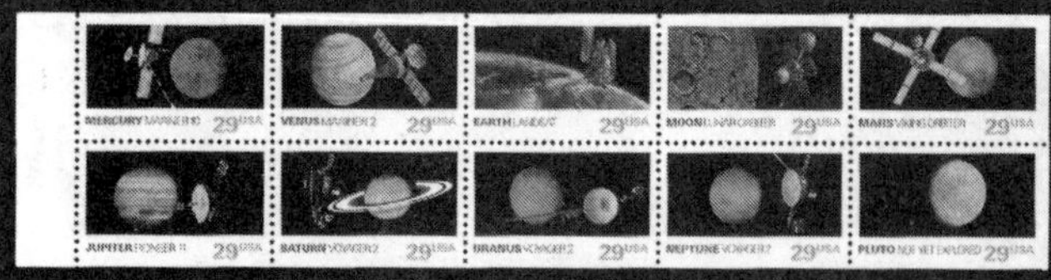

2568-77

2567 2578 2579 2580-81

2582-85

Scott's No.		Mint Sheet	Plate Block	F-VF NH	F-VF Used
2567	29¢ Jan Matzeliger......................	35.00	3.50	.75	.15
2568-77	29¢ Space Exploration bklt. sgls .	...	...	8.50	2.00
2577a	Booklet Pane of 10......................	...	...	8.75	6.95
2578	(29¢) Christmas, Madonna & Child	35.00	3.50	.75	.15
2578a	Booklet Pane of 10......................	...	...	8.00	6.50
2579	(29¢) Christmas, Santa & Chimney	35.00	3.50	.75	.15
2580-81	(29¢) Bklt. Singles, Ty. I & II, attd	...	...	9.50	...
* Ty. II, the far left brick from the top row of the chimney is missing from #2581					
2580-85	Bklt. Singles, Set of 6.................	...	...	12.50	1.75
2581b-2585a	Bklt. Panes of 4, Set of 5......	...	...	27.50	17.50

2590 2592

2593,2594 2595-97 2598 2599

		Mint Sheet	Plate Block	F-VF NH	F-VF Used
	1994 Definitives Designs of 1869 Essays				
2590	$1 Surrender of Burgoyne (20)....	38.75	9.00	1.95	.75
2592	$5 Washington & Jackson (20) ...	190.00	45.00	9.75	3.75
	1992-93 Regular Issues				
2593	29¢ "Pledge", **black** denom., bklt. sgl.	...	...	.70	.15
2593a	Booklet Pane of 10......................	...	...	6.95	5.95
2594	29¢ "Pledge",**red** denom,bklt.sgl.('93)	...	...	.70	.15
2594a	Booklet Pane of 10......................	...	...	6.95	5.95
	1992 Eagle & Shield Self-Adhesive Stamps				
2595	29¢ **"Brown"** denomination	...	...	1.00	.25
2595a	29¢ "Brown" denomination, Pane of 17 ...	...	...	12.75	12.75
2596	29¢ **"Green"** denomination	...	...	1.00	.25
2596a	29¢ "Green" denomination, Pane of 17 ...	...	...	12.75	12.75
2597	29¢ **"Red"** denomination.............	...	...	1.00	.25
2597a	29¢ "Red" denomination, Pane of 17	...	...	12.75	12.75
	1992 Eagle & Shield Self-Adhesive Coils				
2595v	29¢ "Brown" denomination .... Strip of 3		2.95	1.00	...
2596v	29¢ "Green" denomination .... Strip of 3		2.95	1.00	...
2597v	29¢ "Red" denomination............. Strip of 3		2.95	1.00	...

Scott's No.		Mint Sheet	Plate Block	F-VF NH	F-VF Used
	1994 Eagle Self-Adhesive Issue				
2598	29¢ Eagle, self-adhesive............	...	...	.75	.25
2598a	Pane of 18..................................	...	...	10.75	10.75
2598v	29¢ Eagle Coil, self-adhesive...... Pl# Strip of 3		7.50	.85	...
	1994 Statue of Liberty Self-Adhesive Issue				
2599	29¢ Statue of Liberty, self-adhesive		...	.75	.25
2599a	Pane of 18..................................		...	10.75	10.75
2599v	29¢ Liberty Coil, Self-adhesive Pl# Strip of 3		7.50	.85	...

1991-93 Coils

2602 2603,2604 2605

2606 2607 2608 2609

Scott's No.		Pl# Strip of 5	Pl# Strip of 3	F-VF NH	F-VF Used
2602	(10¢) Eagle, Bulk rate....................	4.25	3.75	.25	.15
2603	(10¢) Eagle,Bulk rate, **BEP** (1993)	4.75	4.00	.25	.15
2603v	Dull Gum..	5.00	4.25	.25	...
2604	(10¢) Eagle, Blk rate, **Stamp Venturers**	5.25	4.75	.25	.15
#2603 Orange yellow & multicolored, #2604 Gold & multicolored.					
2605	23¢ Flag, Pre-sort First Class........	6.50	5.50	.60	.15
2606	23¢ USA, Pre-sort 1st Cl., **ABNCo**('92)	6.50	5.50	.60	.15
2607	23¢ USA, Pre-sort 1st Cl., **BEP**..('92)	6.50	5.50	.60	.15
2607a	Dull Gum..	6.75	5.75	.70	...
2608	23¢ USA, Pre-sort 1st Cl., **S.V.**...('93)	6.50	5.50	.60	.15
#2606 Light blue at bottom, "23" 6 mm wide, "First Class" 9½ mm wide.					
#2607 Dark blue at bottom, "23" 7 mm wide, "First Class" 9½ mm wide.					
#2608 Violet blue, "23" 6 mm wide, "First Class" 8½ mm wide.					
2609	29¢ Flag/Wh. House ('92).............	6.75	5.75	.70	.15

1992 Issues

2611-15

2616 2617 2618 2619

Scott's No.		Mint Sheet	Plate Block	F-VF NH	F-VF Used
2611-23,2630-41,2697-2704,2710-14,2720	**Set of 48**		**...**	**38.50**	**7.50**
2611-15	29¢ Winter Olympics, attd ....(35)	29.50 (10)	9.50	4.50	3.95
2611-15	Set of 5 Singles	...		4.25	.75
2616	29¢ World Columbian Expo.........	35.00	3.50	.75	.15
2617	29¢ W.E.B. DuBois, Black Heritage	35.00	3.50	.75	.15
2618	29¢ Love......................................	35.00	3.50	.75	.15
2619	29¢ Olympic Baseball...................	60.00	5.25	1.20	.15

2620-23

1992
Columbian Issues

2624-29

Scott's No.		Mint Sheet	Plate Block	F-VF NH	F-VF Used
2620-23	29¢ Voyage of Columbus, attd. (40)	36.00	4.50	3.75	3.25
2620-23	Set of 4 Singles............................	...	...	3.50	.60
2624-29	1¢-$5 Columbian Expo S/S, Set of 6	...	...	50.00	45.00

1992 Issues (cont.)

2631-34

2630 2635 2636

2637-41

2642-46

Scott's No.		Mint Sheet	Plate Block	F-VF NH	F-VF Used
2630	29¢ New York Stock Exchange (40)	28.00	3.50	.75	.15
2631-34	29¢ Space Joint Issue, attd	42.50	3.95	3.50	2.50
2631-34	Set of 4 Singles............................	...	...	3.25	.60
2635	29¢ Alaska Highway	35.00	3.50	.75	.15
2636	29¢ Kentucky Statehood..............	35.00	3.50	.75	.15
2637-41	29¢ Summer Olympics, attd ..... (35)	31.50	(10) 10.00	4.75	3.95
2637-41	Set of 5 Singles............................	...	...	4.35	.75
2642-46	29¢ Hummingbirds, Set of 5 bklt. sgls.	...	...	4.75	.75
2646a	Booklet Pane of 5	...	...	5.00	3.50

1992 Issues (cont.)

2647-96

2697

2698 2699 2704

2700-03

Scott's No.		Mint Sheet	Plate Block	F-VF NH	F-VF Used
2647-96	29¢ Wildflowers, Pane of 50 diff ..	45.00	...	...	...
2647-96	Set of 50 Singles..........................	...	...	...	18.50
2697	29¢ World War II S/S of 10 ....(20)	13.95	...	7.00	7.00
2697a-j	Set of 10 Singles..........................	...	...	...	2.50
2698	29¢ Dorothy Parker, Literary Arts	35.00	3.50	.75	.15
2699	29¢ Dr. Theodore von Karman	35.00	3.50	.75	.15
2700-03	29¢ Minerals, attd ....(40)	37.50	4.50	4.00	3.50
2700-03	Set of 4 Singles............................	...	...	3.75	.60
2704	29¢ Juan Rodriguez Cabrillo	35.00	3.50	.75	.15

1992 Issues (cont.)

2705-09

2719

2710 2711-14,15-18 2720

Scott's No.		Mint Sheet	Plate Block	F-VF NH	F-VF Used
2705-09	29¢ Wild Animals, bklt. sgls.........	...	...	4.00	.75
2709a	Booklet Pane of 5	...	...	4.25	3.50
2710	29¢ Christmas, Madonna & Child	35.00	3.50	.75	.15
2710a	Booklet Pane of 10	...	...	7.95	7.50
2711-14	29¢ Christmas Toys, **offset**, attd.	41.50	4.25	3.75	3.75
2711-14	Set of 4 Singles	...	...	3.50	.60
2715-18	29¢ Christmas Toys, **gravure**, 4 bklt. sgls		...	3.50	.60
2718a	Booklet Pane of 4	...	...	3.75	3.50
2719	29¢ Locomotive, ATM, self adhes. sgl.	...	...	.80	.30
2719a	29¢ Locomotive, ATM, pane of 18	...	...	14.50	14.50
2720	29¢ Happy New Year .... (20)	16.00	3.50	.90	.15

1993 Issues

2721 2722 2723

Scott's No.		Mint Sheet	Plate Block	F-VF NH	F-VF Used
2721-30,2746-59,2765-66,2771-74,2779-89,2791-94, 2804-06	**Set of 57**	...	...	**44.75**	**8.95**
2721	29¢ Elvis Presley ....(40)	28.00	3.50	.75	.15
2722	29¢ "Oklahoma!" ....(40)	28.00	3.50	.75	.15
2723	29¢ Hank Williams, Perf. 10......(40)	28.00	3.50	.75	.15
2723a	Same, Perf. 11.2 x 11.4	...		23.95	...

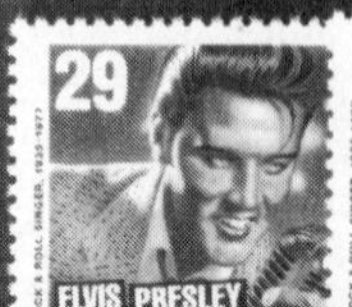

2724-30,31-37

Scott's No.		Mint Sheet	Plate Block	F-VF NH	F-VF Used
2724-30	29¢ Rock 'n Roll, R & B attd .....(35)	39.50	(8)7.50	5.95	5.95
2724-30	Top Horiz. Plate Block of 10	...	9.50	...	...
2724-30	Rock 'n Roll, R & B, set of 7 sgls .	...	...	...	1.75
2731-37	29¢ Rock 'n Roll, R & B, 7 bklt. sgls.	...	...	5.95	1.75

1993 Issues (cont.)

2745a

2747 2746 2748

2749 2754 2755

2750-53

Scott's No.		Mint Sheet	Plate Block	F-VF NH	F-VF Used
2737a	Booklet Pane of 8.........................	...	...	6.75	7.50
2737b	Booklet Pane of 4.........................	...	...	3.75	3.85
2741-45	29¢ Space Fantasy, bklt. sgls......	...	...	4.35	.75
2745a	Booklet Pane of 5	...	...	4.50	4.50
2746	29¢ Percy Lavon Julian	35.00	3.50	.75	.15
2747	29¢ Oregon Trail..........................	35.00	3.50	.75	.15
2748	29¢ World Univ. Games	35.00	3.50	.75	.15
2749	29¢ Grace Kelly...........................	35.00	3.50	.75	.15
2750-53	29¢ Circus, attd .... (40)	35.00	(6) 5.95	3.75	3.75
2750-53	Set of 4 Singles	...		3.60	.60
2754	29¢ Cherokee Strip.................. (20)	14.50	3.50	.75	.15
2755	29¢ Dean Acheson	35.00	3.50	.75	.15

2756-59

2760-64

2765

2766

2783-84

2806

Scott's No.		Mint Sheet	Plate Block	F-VF NH	F-VF Used
2756-59	29¢ Sporting Horses, blk. of 4.....(40)	42.50	4.75	4.25	3.75
2756-59	Set of 4 Singles	...	...	3.60	.60
2760-64	29¢ Garden Flowers, 5 bklt. sgls....	...	...	4.35	.75
2764a	Booklet Pane of 5	...	...	4.50	4.35
2765	29¢ World War II S/S of 10 ....(20)	13.75	...	6.95	6.95
2765a-j	Set of 10 Singles	...	...	...	2.50
2766	29¢ Joe Louis	39.50	3.95	.85	.15
2767-70	29¢ Broadway Musicals, 4 bklt. sgls.	...	...	3.35	.60
2770a	Booklet Pane of 4	...	...	3.50	3.35
2771-74	29¢ Country Music, attd .... (20)	16.50	3.95	3.50	3.50
2771-74	Set of 4 Singles	...	...	3.35	.60
2775-78	29¢ Country Music, 4 bklt. sgls.	...	...	3.35	.60
2778a	Booklet Pane of 4	...	...	3.50	3.50
2779-82	29¢ Nat'l. Postal Museum .... (20)	18.00	4.25	3.75	3.75
2779-82	Set of 4 Singles	...	...	3.60	.60
2783-84	29¢ Deaf Communication, pair...... (20)	14.75	3.50	1.60	1.60
2783-84	Set of 2 Singles	...	...	1.55	.30
2785-88	29¢ Children's Classics, blk. of 4 .. (20)	18.50	4.50	4.00	4.00
2785-88	Set of 4 Singles	...	...	3.90	.60

1993 Issues (cont.)

2767-70

2771-74,2775-78

2779-82

2785-88

2791-94,2795-98,2799-2802

2789,2790 2803 2804 2805

Scott's No.		Mint Sheet	Plate Block	F-VF NH	F-VF Used
2789	29¢ Christmas Madonna	32.50	3.25	.70	.15
2790	29¢ Madonna, Booklet Single	...	...	.75	.15
2790a	Booklet Pane of 4	...	...	3.00	3.00
2791-94	29¢ Christmas Designs, block of 4...	39.50	3.95	3.50	3.50
2791-94	Set of 4 Singles	...	...	3.35	.60
2795-98	29¢ Christmas Designs, set of 4 bklt. sgls.		...	3.00	.60
2798a	Booklet Pane of 10 (3 Snowmen).....	...	...	7.50	7.50
2798b	Booklet Pane of 10 (2 Snowmen).....	...	...	7.50	7.50
2799-2802	29¢ Christmas Designs, self adhes.,4 sgls		...	3.25	1.40
2799-2802 var.	Coil, self-adhesive	Strip of 4	...	3.75	...
2802a	Pane of 12, self-adhesive	...	...	8.75	8.75
2803	29¢ Christmas Snowman, self adhes.	...	...	.75	.30
2803a	Pane of 18, self adhesive	...	...	13.50	13.50
2804	29¢ No. Mariana Is. Comm'nwlth. . (20)	13.50	3.25	.70	.15
2805	29¢ Columbus at Puerto Rico	32.50	3.25	.70	.15
2806	29¢ AIDS Awareness	32.50	3.25	.70	.15
2806a	29¢ AIDS Booklet Single	...	...	.75	.15
2806b	Booklet Pane of 5	...	...	3.75	3.75

1994 Commemoratives

2807-11

2812 2813 2814 2815

Scott's No.		Mint Sheet	Plate Block	F-VF NH	F-VF Used
2807-12,2814C-28,2834-38,2839-41, 2848-68,2871-72,2875,2876	**Set of 53...........**	...	...	**69.50**	...
2807-11	29¢ Winter Olympics, attd..............(20)	14.50	(10)7.95	3.75	3.75
2807-11	Set of 5 Singles..................................	...	...	3.65	.75
2812	29¢ Edward R. Murrow..................(50)	32.50	3.25	.70	.15
2813	29¢ Love & Sunrise, self adhesive ...	...	...	.75	.30
2813a	Pane of 18	...	...	12.75	12.75
2813v	Love Coil, self adhesive.........**Pl# Strip of 3**		7.50	.85	...
2814	29¢ Love & Dove, Booklet Single.....	...	...	.70	.15
2814a	Booklet Pane of 10	...	...	6.95	6.95
2814C	29¢ Love & Dove, sheet stamp.........	32.50	3.25	.70	.15
2815	52¢ Love & Doves ....(50)	53.50	5.50	1.15	.20

2816 2817 2818

2828a

Scott's No.		Mint Sheet	Plate Block	F-VF NH	F-VF Used
2816	29¢ Dr. Allison Davis ....(20)	13.50	3.25	.70	.15
2817	29¢ Chinese New Year, Dog.........(20)	15.00	3.65	.80	.15
2818	29¢ Buffalo Soldiers.......................(20)	13.50	3.25	.70	.15
2819-28	29¢ Silent Screen Stars, attd.........(40)	27.50	(10)7.95	7.25	7.25
2819-28	Half-Pane of 20 with selvedge..........	...	...	13.95	...
2819-28	Set of 10 singles	...	...	7.15	1.50

1994 Commemoratives (continued)

2833a

2834 2835 2836

2837

Scott's No.		Mint Sheet	Plate Block	F-VF NH	F-VF Used
2829-33	29¢ Garden Flowers, set of 5 bklt. sgls.	...	...	3.35	.75
2833a	Booklet Pane of 5	...	...	3.50	3.50
2834	29¢ World Cup Soccer...................(20)	13.50	3.25	.70	.15
2835	40¢ World Cup Soccer...................(20)	17.50	4.85	.95	.18
2836	50¢ World Cup Soccer...................(20)	21.75	5.95	1.15	.22
2837	29¢,40¢,50¢ World Cup Soccer, Souvenir Sheet of 3	...	...	3.00	3.00

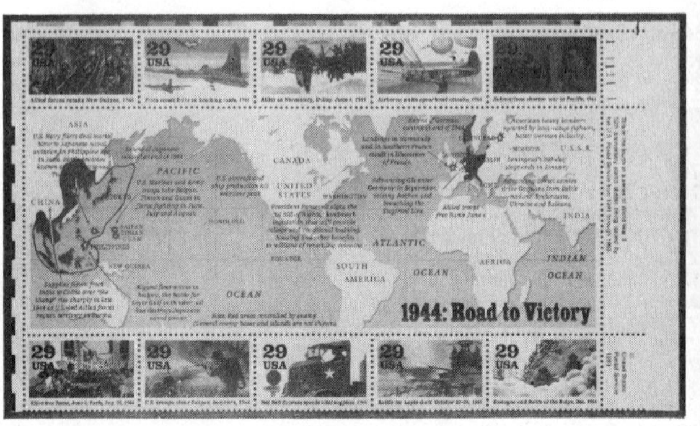

2838

Scott's No.		Mint Sheet	Plate Block	F-VF NH	F-VF Used
2838	29¢ World War II S/S of 10 ....(20)	13.75	...	6.95	6.95
2838a-j	Set of 10 Singles..............................	...	...	...	2.50

1994 Commemoratives (continued)

2840

2839 2841a 2842 2848

2843-47

Scott's No.		Mint Sheet	Plate Block	F-VF NH	F-VF Used
2839	29¢ Norman Rockwell	32.50	3.25	.70	.15
2840	50¢ N. Rockwell, s/s of 4	...	...	4.95	4.95
	1994 Moon Landing, 25th Anniversary				
2841	29¢ Moon Landing s/s of 12	...	...	7.95	7.95
2841a	29¢ Single Stamp from sheet	...	...	.70	.25
2842	$9.95 Moon Landing Express Mail ... (20)	365.00	80.00	18.50	8.50
	1994 Commemoratives (continued)				
2843-47	29¢ Locomotive, set of 5 bklt. sgles	...	...	3.35	.75
2847a	Booklet Pane of 5	...	...	3.50	3.50
2848	29¢ George Meany	32.50	3.25	.70	.15

2849-53

1994 Commemoratives (continued)

Scott's No.		Mint Sheet	Plate Block	F-VF NH	F-VF Used
2849-53	29¢ Popular Singers, attd ... (20)	13.50	(6)4.75	3.50	3.25
2849-53	Top Plate Block of 12	...	8.95	...	...
2849-53	Set of 5 Singles	...	...	3.35	.90

2854-61

2854-61	29¢ Blues & Jazz Artists, attd. ... (35)	22.75	(10)7.75	(10)6.95	6.95
2854-61	Top Plate Block of 10	...	8.75	...	...
2854-61	Set of 8 Singles	...	...	5.75	1.60

2862 2867-68

2863-66

2862	29¢ James Thurber	31.00	3.25	.65	.15
2863-66	29¢ Wonders of the Sea, attd. ... (24)	14.95	3.50	2.65	2.65
2863-66	Set of 4 Singles	...	...	2.60	.60
2867-68	29¢ Cranes, attd. ... (20)	12.95	3.50	1.35	1.35
2867-68	Set of 2 Singles	...	...	1.30	.30

SE-TENANT NOTE: Many modern se-tenants are issued in "staggered" form. Stamp designs in blocks and plate block will not always follow "Scott Order" but will vary depending upon their location in sheet.

2869

2870

1994 Legends of the West Miniature Sheet

Scott's No.		Mint Sheet	Plate Block	F-VF NH	F-VF Used
2869	29¢ Revised Sheet of 20 ....(6)	89.95	...	13.95	13.95
2869a-t	Set of 20 Singles	...	...	13.75	6.95
2869a/t	Horiz. Gutter Block of 10	...	...	13.95	...
2869a/t	Vert. Gutter Block of 8	...	...	11.95	...
2869a/t	Set of 4 Vert.Gutter Pairs	...	...	10.95	...
2869a/t	Set of 5 Horiz. Gutter Pairs	...	...	12.95	...
2869a/t	Center Gutter Block of 4	...	...	14.95	...
2870	29¢ Original (recalled) sheet of 20	...	...	325.00	...

2871 2872 2873 2874

1994 Commemoratives (continued)

Scott's No.		Mint Sheet	Plate Block	F-VF NH	F-VF Used
2871	29¢ Madonna & Child	31.00	3.15	.65	.15
2871a	29¢ Madonna & Child, Bklt. Single	...	...	.65	.15
2871b	Booklet Pane of 10	...	...	6.35	6.35
2872	29¢ Christmas Stocking	31.00	3.15	.65	.15
2872a	Booklet Pane of 20	...	...	12.50	12.50
2873	29¢ Santa Claus, self-adhesive	...	...	.65	.30
2873a	Pane of 12, self-adhesive	...	...	7.50	7.50
2873v	29¢ Santa Claus Coil, self-adh. Pl# Strip of 3		6.50	.65	...
2874	29¢ Cardinal in Snow, self-adhesive	...	...	.65	.30
2874a	Pane of 18, self-adhesive	...	...	11.00	11.00

2875

2876

2875	$2 Bureau of Engraving Centennial Souvenir Sheet of 4	...	...	15.75	15.75
2875a	$2 Madison, Single Stamp from S/S	...	...	3.95	2.25
2876	29¢ Year of the Boar, New Year ....(20)	14.00	3.50	.75	.15

2877,2878 2879,2880 2881-87,2889-92 2888

1994 Interim Regular Issues

2877	(3¢) Dove, ABN, Light Blue ....(100)	8.50	.90	.20	.15
2878	(3¢) Dove, SVS, Darker Blue ....(100)	8.50	.90	.20	.15
	#2877 Thin, taller letters. #2878 Heavy, shorter letters.				
2879	(20¢)"G",Postcard Rate, BEP,Black "G: ....(100)	38.50	2.00	.40	.15
2880	(20¢) "G",Postcard Rate, SVS,Red "G" ....(100)	38.50	2.00	.40	.15
2881	(32¢) "G",BEP, Black "G" ....(100)	62.50	3.25	.65	.15
2881a	Booklet Pane of 10, Perf. 11	...	...	6.35	5.95
2882	(32¢) "G", SVS, Red "G" ....(100)	62.50	3.25	.65	.15
2883	(32¢) "G", BEP, Black "G", bklt. sgl.	...	...	.65	.15
2883a	Booklet Pane of 10, BEP, Perf. 10	...	...	6.35	5.95
2884	(32¢) "G", ABN, Blue "G", bklt. sgl.	...	...	.65	.15
2884a	Booklet Pane of 10, ABN	...	...	6.35	5.95
2885	(32¢) "G", KCS, Red "G", bklt. sgl.	...	...	.65	.15
2885a	Booklet Pane of 10, KCS	...	...	6.35	5.95
2886	(32¢) "G", Surface Tagged, self-adhesive	...	...	.70	.30
2886a	Pane of 18, self-adhesive	...	...	11.50	...
2886v	(32¢) "G", Coil, self-adhesive . ...Plt. Strip of 3		7.50	.70	...
2887	(32¢) "G", Overall Tagging, self-adhesive	...	...	.70	.30
2887a	Pane of 18, self-adhesive	...	...	11.50	...
	#2886 Limited amount of blue shading in the white stripes below field of stars. #2887 Stronger blue shading in the white stripes.				
2888	(25¢) "G" Presort, Coil ....Pl.# Strip	7.50(5)	6.75(3)	.60	.15
2889	(32¢) "G" Coil, BEP, Black "G" ....Pl.# Strip	7.50(5)	6.75(3)	.70	.15
2890	(32¢) "G" Coil, ABN, Blue "G" ....Pl.# Strip	7.50(5)	6.75(3)	.70	.15
2891	(32¢) "G" Coil, SVS, Red "G" ....Pl.# Strip	7.75(5)	7.00(3)	.65	.15
2892	(32¢) "G" Coil, SVS, Rouletted ......Pl.# Strip	8.50(5)	7.50(3)	.70	.1

BEP=Bureau of Engraving and Printing ABN=American Bank-Note Co.
SVS=Stamp Venturers KCS=KCS Industries

1995 Interim Rate Coil Stamps

2893 2902 2905 2908,9 2911,12

Scott's No.		Pl. Strip of 5	Pl. Strip of 3	F-VF NH	F-VF Used
2893	(5¢) "G" Non-Profit, green	3.15	2.75	.20	.15
2902	(5¢) Butte	2.25	2.00	.20	.15
2905	(10¢) Automobile	2.75	2.25	.20	.15
2908	(15¢) Auto Tail Fin, BEP	3.50	3.00	.30	.15
2909	(15¢) Auto Tail Fin, SVS	3.50	3.00	.30	.15
2911	(25¢) Juke Box, BEP	4.50	3.50	.50	.15
2912	(25¢) Juke Box, SVS	4.50	3.50	.50	.15

NOTE: The SVS varieties of the above 15¢ & 25¢ coils are fainter than the BEP varieties which are sharp and darker.

1995 Transportation Coils

Cog Railway Car Ferry Boat

Scott's No.		Pl. Strip of 5	Pl. Strip of 3	F-VF NH	F-VF Used
...	20¢ Cog Railway Car	5.00	4.25	.40	.15
...	32¢ Ferry Boat	7.75	6.75	.65	.15

1995 Regular Issues

Flag over Field Flag over Porch Pink Rose Blue Jay

Scott's No.		Mint Sheet	Plate Block	F-VF NH	F-VF Used
2919	32¢ Flag over Field, self-adhesive sgl...	...	...	.70	.30
2919a	Pane of 18, Self-adhesive	...	...	11.50	...
2920	32¢ Flag over Porch, self-adhesive single small date	...	...	.70	.30
2920a	Pane of 20, Self-adhesive, small date...	...	...	13.75	...
2920b	32¢ Flag over Porch, self adhesive single, large date	...	...	.70	.30
2920c	Pane of 20, self-adhesive, large date....	...	...	13.75	...
...	32¢ Flag over Porch (100)	62.50	3.25	.65	.15
...	32¢ Flag over Porch, BEP, Coil Pl# Strip	6.75(5)	5.75(3)	.65	.15
...	32¢ Flag over Porch, SVS, Coil Pl# Strip	6.75(5)	5.75(3)	.65	.15
	NOTE: The SVS variety is fainter/duller than the BEP variety.				
...	32¢ Flag over Porch, booklet single......	...	...	.65	.15
...	Booklet Pane of 10	...	...	6.35	5.95
...	32¢ Flag over Porch, Coil,Self-adhesive,	Pl. Strip 3	7.50	.70	...
...	32¢ Pink Rose, self-adhesive single.....	...	...	.70	.30
...	Pane of 20, self-adhesive	...	...	13.75	...
...	32¢ Pink Rose, Coil, Self-adhesive	Pl. Strip 3	7.50	.70	...
...	20¢ Blue Jay, booklet single	...	...	.40	.15
...	Booklet Pane of 10	...	...	3.95	3.75

Challenger Shuttle

1995 Regular Issues (continued)

Scott's No.		Mint Sheet	Plate Block	F-VF NH	F-V Use
...	$3 Challenger Shuttle, Priority Mail....(20)	115.00	25.00	5.95	2.75
...	$10.75 Endeavor Shuttle, Express Mail	...	92.50	21.00	9.95
...	32¢ Peach, booklet single	...	...	.65	.15
...	32¢ Pear, booklet single	...	...	.65	.15
...	32¢ Peach & Pear, Attached Pair	...	...	1.30	.95
...	Booklet Pane of 10	...	...	6.35	5.95
...	32¢ Peach, Self-adhesive single	...	...	.70	.30
...	32¢ Pear, Self-adhesive single	...	...	.70	.30
...	32¢ Peach & Pear, Attached Pair	...	...	1.40	...
...	Pane of 20, Self-adhesive	...	...	13.75	...
...	32¢ Peach, Coil, Self-adhesive	...	...	.70	...
...	32¢ Pear, Coil, Self-adhesive	...	...	.70	...
...	32¢ Peach & Pear, Coil Pair	Pl. Strip of 3	7.50	1.40	...
	1995 Great Americans Series				
...	32¢ Milton S. Hershey (100)	62.50	3.25	.65	.15
...	55¢ Alice Hamilton, MD (100)	105.00	5.50	1.10	.15
...	78¢ Alice Paul (100)	155.00	7.95	1.60	.20

1995 Commemoratives

2948 2949 2950 2955

2951-54 2956

Scott's No.		Mint Sheet	Plate Block	F-VF NH	F-V Use
2948	(32¢) Love & Cherub	33.50	2.95	.65	.15
2949	(32¢) Love & Cherub, Self-adhesive....	...	...	.65	.25
2949a	Pane of 20, Self-adhesive	...	...	12.75	...
2950	32¢ Florida Statehood (20)	12.75	2.95	.65	.15
2951-54	32¢ Earth Day/Kids Care, attd. (16)	10.00	2.95	2.60	2.00
2951-54	Set of 4 Singles	...	...	2.50	.60
2955	32¢ Richard Nixon	31.50	3.15	.65	.15
2956	32¢ Bessie Coleman, Black Heritage Series	31.50	3.15	.65	.15

32¢ Love-Cherub 55¢ Love-Cherub 55¢ Love-Cherub

Scott's No.		Mint Sheet	Plate Block	F-VF NH	F-V Use
...	32¢ Love Cherub	31.50	3.15	.65	.15
...	32¢ Love Cherub, booklet single	...	...	.65	.15
...	Booklet Pane of 10	...	...	6.35	5.95
...	55¢ Love Cherub	52.50	4.95	1.10	.15
...	Self-Adhesive single	...	...	1.20	.35
...	Pane of 20, Self-Adhesive	...	...	21.95	...

Recreational Sports

Scott's No.		Mint Sheet	Plate Block	F-VF NH	F-VF Used
...	32¢ Recreational Sports attd..............(20)	12.75	(10)6.95	3.20	2.95
...	Set of 5 Singles	...	...	3.15	.75

POW & MIA Marilyn Monroe Texas

Great Lakes Lighthouses

Scott's No.		Mint Sheet	Plate Block	F-VF NH	F-VF Used
...	32¢ POW & MIA................................(20)	12.75	2.95	.65	.15
...	32¢ Marilyn Monroe	...	2.95	.65	.15
...	M. Monroe Miniature Sheet of 20	...	...	12.75	12.75
...	32¢ Texas Statehood........................(20)	12.75	2.95	.65	.15
...	32¢ Great Lakes Lighthouses 5 booklet singles	...	...	3.20	.75
...	Booklet Pane of 5	...	...	3.25	2.95

1995 Commemoratives (continued)

United Nations

Civil War

Scott's No.		Mint Sheet	Plate Block	F-VF NH	F-VF Used
...	32¢ United Nations............................(20)	12.75	2.95	.65	.15
...	32¢ Civil War, Miniature Sheet of 20.....	...	...	12.95	12.95
...	Set of 20 Singles	...	...	12.85	6.95
...	32¢ Carousel Horses, attd..................(20)	12.75	2.95	2.60	2.00
...	Set of 4 Singles	...	...	2.50	.60
...	32¢ Fall Garden Flowers, 5 bklt. Sgls. ..	...	...	3.20	.75
...	Booklet Pane of 5	...	...	3.25	2.95
...	32¢ Prehistoric Animals, attd.............(20)	12.75	2.95	2.60	2.00
...	Set of 4 Singles	...	...	2.50	.60
...	32¢ Women's Suffrage	...	2.95	.65	.15
...	32¢ Louis Armstrong..........................(20)	12.75	2.95	.65	.15
...	32¢ Jazz Musicians, attd.....................(20)	12.75	(10)6.95	6.50	5.95
...	Set of 10 Singles	...	...	6.25	2.00
...	32¢ World War II S/S of 10.................(20)	12.75	...	6.50	6.50
...	Set of 10 Singles	...	...	6.25	2.25

EARLY U.S. MINT SHEETS

All F-VF Never Hinged Sheets of 50 unless otherwise indicated in brackets ( ).

Scott's No.		NH F-VF
	1926-1929	
632	1¢ Franklin....................(100)	19.50
634	2¢ Washington..............(100)	17.50
645	2¢ Valley Forge.............(100)	180.00
646	2¢ M. Pitcher.................(100)	165.00
649	2¢ Aeronautics	82.50
651	2¢ G.R. Clark	45.00
653	½¢ N. Hale....................(100)	11.00
654	2¢ Edison, Flat..............(100)	125.00
655	2¢ Edis., Rot..................(100)	140.00
657	2¢ Sullivan.....................(100)	120.00
680	2¢ Fall. Timbers............(100)	140.00
681	2¢ Ohio Canal...............(100)	110.00
	1930-1932	
682	2¢ Mass. Bay.................(100)	145.00
683	2¢ Carolina.....................(100)	185.00
684	1½¢ Harding..................(100)	30.00
685	4¢ Taft............................(100)	135.00
688	2¢ Braddock...................(100)	160.00
689	2¢ Von Stueben.............(100)	80.00
690	2¢ Pulaski......................(100)	40.00
702	2¢ Red Cross...............(100)	22.50
703	2¢ Yorktown	25.00
704	½¢ Bicent......................(100)	15.00
705	1¢ Bicent.......................(100)	19.50
706	1½¢ Bicent....................(100)	75.00
707	2¢ Bicent.......................(100)	13.50
708	3¢ Bicent.......................(100)	90.00
709	4¢ Bicent.......................(100)	40.00
712	7¢ Bicent.......................(100)	37.50
	1932-1934	
716	2¢ Winter Olym.............(100)	65.00
717	2¢ Arbor Day.................(100)	26.50
718	3¢ Olympics...................(100)	215.00
719	5¢ Olympics...................(100)	295.00
720	3¢ Washington..............(100)	25.00
724	3¢ Penn..........................(100)	50.00
725	3¢ Webster....................(100)	75.00
726	3¢ Georgia.....................(100)	50.00
727	3¢ Newburgh.................(100)	22.50
728	1¢ Chicago....................(100)	16.50
729	3¢ Chicago....................(100)	21.00
732	3¢ N.R.A.........................(100)	18.50
733	3¢ Byrd	50.00
734	5¢ Kosciuszko...............(100)	100.00
736	3¢ Maryland..................(100)	30.00
737	3¢ Mother's, Rot	10.00
738	3¢ Mother's, Flat	15.00
739	3¢ Wisconsin	15.00
	1934 National Parks	
740-49	1¢-10¢ Set	625.00
740	1¢ Yosemite	7.50
741	2¢ Grand Canyon	9.00
742	3¢ Mt. Rainier	12.50
743	4¢ Mesa Verde	32.50
744	5¢ Yellowstone	57.50
745	6¢ Crater Lake	77.50
746	7¢ Acadia	50.00
747	8¢ Zion	120.00
748	9¢ Glacier	115.00
749	10¢ Great Smoky	210.00

MINT SETS

COMMEMORATIVE YEAR SETS

Year	Scott's No.	Qty.	F-VF NH
1935	772-75	4	.70
1936	776-84	6	3.70
1937	795-802	8	2.10
1938	835-38	4	1.00
1939	852-58	7	4.15
1940	894-902	9	2.10
1941-3	903-08	6	1.40
1944	922-26	5	1.10
1945	927-38	12	2.20
1946	939-44	6	1.10
1947	945-52	8	2.00
1948	953-80	28	5.25
1949	981-86	6	1.10
1950	987-97	11	1.95
1951	998-1003	6	1.10
1952	1004-16	13	2.30
1953	1017-28	12	2.25
1954	1029,60-63	5	.90

Year	Scott's No.	Qty.	F-VF NH
1955	1064-72	9	1.75
1956	1073-85	13	4.75
1957	1086-99	14	2.60
1958	1100,04-23	21	3.95
1959	1124-38	15	2.85
1960	1139-73	35	6.75
1961	1174-90	17	4.50
1962	1191-1207	17	3.00
1963	1230-41	12	2.15
1964	1242-60	19	4.35
1965	1261-76	16	3.35
1966	1306-22	17	3.35
1967	1323-37	15	4.50
1968	1339-40,42-64	25	6.95
1969	1365-86	22	8.65
1970	1387-92,1405-22	24	7.00
1971	1423-45	23	5.35
1972	1446-74	29	6.85

Year	Scott's No.	Qty.	F-VF NH
1973	1475-1508	34	8.25
1974	1525-52	28	8.20
1975	1553-80	28	8.15
1976	1629-32,83-85 1690-1703	21	9.50
1977	1704-30	27	10.00
1978	1731-33,44-69	29	14.75
1979	1770-1802	33	14.85
1980	1803-10,21-43	31	14.95
1981	1874-79,1910-45	42	26.50
1982	1950-52,2003-4, 2006-30	30	22.50
1983	2031-65	35	25.00
1984	2066-2109	44	33.75
1985	2110,37-47,52-66	27	37.50
1986	2167,2202-4,10-11, 2220-24,2235-2245		19.00

Year	Scott's No.	Qty.	F-VF NH
1987	2246-51,75, 2336-38,2349-54, 2360-61,2367-68	20	15.60
1988	2239-46,69-80, 86-93,2399-2400	30	26.75
1989	2347,2401-04, 10-18,20-28,34-37	27	24.00
1990	2348,2349-40,2442, 44-49,96-2500, 2506-15	25	24.95
1991	2532-35,37-38,50-51, 2553-61,67,78-79	29	23.00
1992	2611-23,30-41,97-99, 2700-04,10-14,20	48	38.50
1993	2721-30,46-59,65-66, 2771-74,79-89,91-94, 2804-06	57	44.75
1994	2807-12,14C-28,2834-38, 39-41,48-68,2871-72, 75,76	53	69.50

USPS MINT SETS

Commemoratives and Definitives

These are complete with folder or hard cover albums as produced by the U.S. Postal Service

Year	Scott's Nos.	# Stamps	Price
	Commemoratives		
1968 (1)	"Cover #334-890", #1339-40, 1342-64,C74	26	175.00
1968 (2)	"Cover #369-245", Contents same as (1)		150.00
1969	#1365-86,C76	23	120.00
1970	#1387-92,1405-22	24	175.00
1971 (1)	"Mini Album" #1396,1423-45	24	40.00
1971 (2)	With black strips, Contents same as (1)		120.00
1972	#1446-74,C84-85	31	18.00
1973	#1475-1504,1507-08,C86	33	18.00
1974	#1505-06,1525-51	29	13.50
1975	#1553-80	28	17.50
1976	#1629-32,1633/82 (1 single), 1683-85,1690-1702	21	27.50
1977	#1704-30	27	15.00
1978	#1731-33,44-56,58-69	28	17.50
1979	#1770-94,1799-1802,C97	30	18.50
1980	#1795-98,1803-04,21,23-43	28	23.50
1981	#1874-79,1910-26,28-45	41	30.00
1982	#1950,52,1953/2002 (1 single), 2003-04,06-24,26-30	29	26.50
1983	#2031-65,C101-12	47	45.00
1984	#2066-71,73-2109	43	36.75

Year	Scott's Nos.	# Stamps	Price
1985	#2110,37-47,52-66	27	35.00
1986	#2167,2201a,2202-04,2209a, 2210-11,2216a-9i (1 single), 2220-24,35-45	25	29.50
1987	Soft Cover, #2246-51,2274a,75, 2286/2335 (1 single), 2336-38, 2349-54,59a,60-61,66a,67-68	24	42.50
1987	Hard Cover, Same contents		52.50
1988	Soft Cover, #2339-46,69-80,85a, 86-93,95-99,2400,C117	37	42.50
1988	Hard Cover, Same contents		57.50
1989	#2347,2401-04,09a,10-14, 16-18,20-28	22	45.00
1990	#2348,2415,39-40,42,44-49,74a, 2496-2515	32	50.00
1991	#2532-35,37-38,49a,50-51,53-67,2577a, 78,80 or 81,82-85,C130-31	33	57.50
1992	Hard Cover, #2611-23,30-41,46a, 2647/96 (1 single), 2697-99,2700-04, 2709a,10-14	41	49.75
1993	Hard Cover, #2721-23,31-37,45a, 2746-59,64a,65-66,70a,78a,79-89, 2791-94,2804-05	47	59.50
1994	Hard Cover, #2807-12,2814-28, 2833a,34-36,38-40,2841a,2847a, 2848-69,71-72	52	69.50

Year	Scott's Nos.	# Stamps	Price
	Definitives & Stationery		
1980	#1738-42,1805-11,13,22,59,C98-100, U590,U597-99,UC53,UX82-86	27	55.00
1981	#1582b,1818,1819-20 PRS,57-58,65,89a, 90,91 PR,93a,94,95 PR,96a,1903 PR, 1906-08 PRS,1927,46,47-48 PRS	22	37.50
1982	#1615v PR,1845,55,60,66,97A PR, 1698A PR,1901 PR,1904 PR,49a, 1951,2005 PR,2025,U591,U602-03, UC55,UX94-97,UXC20	22	25.00
1983	#1844,46-48,61,97 PR,98 PR,99 PR, 1900 PR,O127-29,O130,32,35 PR, U604-05,UC56-57,UO73,UX98-100, UXC21,UZ2	25	17.50
1984	#1853,62,64,68,1902 PR,1905 PR, 2072,U606,UX101-04	12	12.50
1987-88	#2115b,2127,29,30av,69,76-78,80, 2182,83,88,92,2226,52-66,C118-19, O138A-B,40-41	35	50.00
1989-90	#2127av,73,84,86,94A,2280v,2419, 2431 (6),43a,52,75a,76,O143,U611, U614-18,UC62,UO79-80,UX127-38, UX143-48,UX150-52	44	62.50

or a free sample magazine and information about membership America's national philatelic society send the attached card or contact:

American Philatelic Society
P.O. Box 8000, Dept. TB
State College, PA 16803
Phone: (814) 237-3803
FAX: (814) 237-6128

SEND FOR YOUR FREE COPY!

TO REALLY ENJOY STAMP COLLECTING!

YES! Please send a **FREE** sample copy of *The American Philatelist* and an illustrated membership brochure describing APS member services. The sample is yours absolutely free - nothing to cancel! You may apply for membership, including a magazine subscription, only by completing the membership application. **PLEASE PRINT:**

Name ____________________

Address ____________________

____

ALE Enterprises, Inc.
P.O. Box 539-BG
maus, PA 18049-0539
U.S.A.

Offers you 'lots' to choose from.

r monthly Price List & l Sales Send this card or call (610) 433-3303 or FAX (610) 965-6089

DALE Enterprises Inc. Offers You "LOTS" To Choose From!

MONTHLY MAIL BID SALES

"*SOMETHING FOR EVERYONE*"

That's our goal for our monthly Mail Bid Sale. Each sale offers 1,500 to 3,500 lots to choose from! (U.S. and Foreign!) Return this postcard today for for your . . . . . .

FREE LISTS

!! FREE !! U. S. PRICE LIST

If you are a U.S. collector who likes a wide selection, competitive prices and efficient 24-hour service, you should be receiving our price list!

Our 16-page list features 400-600 "Pictured One-Of-A-Kinds", & contains a comprehensive offering of mint and used U.S. singles, mint plt blks and strips, bklt panes and a smattering of unusual items to dress up your collection or get you started collecting stamps.

We're ready and able to help you build the kind of collection you want! ***Simply send in this postcard and we'll fire off a copy of our current list.***

*** SATISFACTION GUARANTEED * ALWAYS BUYING ***

VISA *Over 25 Years of Quality Service to Collectors Everywhere* MasterCard

Phone: (610) 433-3303 Fax : (610) 965-6089

Est. 1914

DA...

Your Symbol Of Integrity

For information please write us at:
ASDA
3 School Street
Suite 205
en Cove, N.Y. 11542-2548

❑ Please send me information on all "Mega-Events."
❑ Please send me information on "stamp dealers in my area"
❑ Please send me information on "expertizing" my stamps.
❑ Please send me information on "How to sell my collection."

NAME: ____________________

ADDRESS: ____________________

____

CITY: ____________________

STATE: __________ ZIP: __________

PHONE: ____________________

AIR MAIL STAMPS

C1

C4

C5

C6

1918 First Issue VF Used + 35% (B)

:ott's lo.		NH VF	F-VF	Unused VF	F-VF	Used F-VF
1-3	**Set of 3**	**435.00**	**325.00**	**320.00**	**240.00**	**105.00**
1	6¢ Curtiss Jenny, Orange	130.00	95.00	93.50	70.00	32.50
2	16¢ Green	165.00	125.00	120.00	90.00	35.00
3	24¢ Carmine Rose & Blue	165.00	125.00	120.00	90.00	40.00

1923 Second Issue VF Used + 35% (B)

4-6	**Set of 3**	**400.00**	**300.00**	**290.00**	**215.00**	**70.00**
4	8¢ Propeller, Dark Green	50.00	37.50	35.00	26.50	13.50
5	16¢ Emblem, Dark Blue	165.00	125.00	120.00	90.00	35.00
6	24¢ Biplane, Carmine	200.00	150.00	145.00	105.00	27.50

C7

C10

C11

C12,C16

1926-27 Map & Mail Planes VF Used + 30% (B)

7-9	**Set of 3**	**28.50**	**20.75**	**20.75**	**15.75**	**4.15**
7	10¢ Map, Dark Blue	5.50	4.00	4.00	3.00	.35
8	15¢ Map, Brown	6.50	4.75	4.75	3.50	2.25
9	20¢ Map, Green (1927)	17.50	13.00	13.00	9.75	1.75

1927 Lindbergh Tribute VF + 30% (B)

Scott's No.		NH VF	F-VF	Unused VF	F-VF	Used F-VF
C10	10¢ Lindbergh, Dark Blue	15.00	11.50	11.00	8.50	2.25
C10a	Booklet Pane of 3	150.00	115.00	115.00	90.00	...

1928 Beacon VF Used + 30% (B)

C11	5¢ Carmine & Blue	7.75	5.75	5.75	4.25	.55

1930 Winged Globe, Flat Press, Perf. 11 VF Used + 30% (B)

C12	5¢ Violet	16.50	12.50	12.75	9.50	.40

1918-30 PLATE BLOCKS

	NH VF	F-VF	Unused F-VF		NH VF	F-VF	Unused F-VF
C1 (6)	1150.00	850.00	650.00	C10 (6)	275.00	210.00	160.00
C2 (6)	2100.00	1550.00	1150.00	C11 (6)	85.00	65.00	50.00
C3 (12)	2350.00	1850.00	1350.00	C11 Double "TOP"			
C4 (6)	550.00	400.00	285.00	**Plate of 6**	160.00	125.00	90.00
C5 (6)	3250.00	2500.00	1850.00				
C6 (6)	3750.00	2850.00	2100.00	C11 No "TOP"			
C7 (6)	80.00	60.00	45.00	**Plate of 8**	295.00	225.00	175.00
C8 (6)	95.00	70.00	52.50				
C9 (6)	210.00	160.00	125.00	C12 (6)	295.00	225.00	170.00

1930 GRAF ZEPPELIN ISSUE VF Used + 20% (B)

C13 C15 C14

C13-15	**Set of 3**	**3000.00**	**2500.00**	**2325.00**	**1950.00**	**1350.00**
C13	65¢ Zeppelin, Green	515.00	425.00	395.00	325.00	250.00
C14	$1.30 Zeppelin, Brown	1050.00	885.00	825.00	675.00	450.00
C15	$2.60 Zeppelin, Blue	1550.00	1275.00	1200.00	975.00	700.00

1931-32 Rotary Press, Perf. 10½x11, Designs of #C12 VF Used + 30% (B)

Scott's No.		NH VF	NH F-VF	Unused VF	Unused F-VF	Used F-VF
C16	5¢ Winged Globe, Violet..........	10.50	7.75	7.50	5.75	.50
C17	8¢ Winged Globe (1932)	3.75	2.85	2.85	2.25	.25

C18 C20

1933 Century of Progress VF Used + 20% (B)

C18	50¢ Graf Zeppelin, Green......	165.00	135.00	115.00	95.00	80.00

1934 Winged Globe, Design of #C12 VF Used + 30% (B)

C19	6¢ Orange.................................	3.75	3.00	3.15	2.50	.15

ZEPPELIN & WINGED GLOBE PLATE BLOCKS

	NH VF	NH F-VF	Unused F-VF		NH VF	NH F-VF	Unused F-VF
C13 (6)	3950.00	3250.00	2800.00	C17	60.00	45.00	35.00
C14 (6)	8000.00	6700.00	5650.00	C18 (6)	1075.00	900.00	750.00
C15 (6)	13000.00	10750.00	8650.00	C19	42.50	32.50	24.50
C16	175.00	130.00	100.00				

1935-37 Trans-Pacific Issue (VF + 25%)

Scott's No.		Plate Blocks NH	Plate Blocks Unused	F-VF NH	F-VF Unused	F-VF Used
C20-22	**Clipper Set of 3 ....**	**315.00**	**265.00**	**24.50**	**19.50**	**6.95**
C20	25¢ China Clipper.......... (6)	32.50	27.50	1.60	1.25	1.00
C21	20¢ China Cliiper (1937) (6)	150.00	125.00	12.00	9.50	1.65
C22	50¢ China Clipper ('37).. (6)	150.00	125.00	12.00	9.50	4.50

C23 C24

1938 Eagle (VF + 30%)

C23	6¢ Dark Blue & Carmine..........	10.00	7.50	.55	.45	.15

1939 Trans-Atlantic Issue (VF + 30%)

C24	30¢ Winged Globe, Blue (6)	200.00	165.00	10.75	8.25	1.50

C25 C32 C33

1941-44 Transport Plane

Scott's No.		Mint Sheet	Plate Block	F-VF NH	F-VF Used
C25-31	**Set of 7 ....**	**...**	**130.00**	**22.50**	**5.00**
C25	6¢ Carmine..................................	9.50	1.10	.20	.15
C25a	Booklet Pane of 3.........................	...	...	4.00	3.00
C26	8¢ Olive Green (1944).................	11.50	2.00	.24	.15
C27	10¢ Violet	67.50	10.00	1.30	.20
C28	15¢ Brown Carmine	135.00	12.50	2.75	.40
C29	20¢ Bright Green..........................	115.00	12.50	2.25	.35
C30	30¢ Blue	130.00	13.50	2.65	.45
C31	50¢ Orange	...	85.00	13.00	3.75

1946-1948 Issues

C32	5¢ DC-4 Skymaster......................	7.50	.65	.20	.15
C33	5¢ Small Plane (1947)............. (100)	15.00	.65	.20	.15

C34 C38 C40

C34	10¢ Pan-Am Building (1947)	13.75	1.35	.30	.15
C35	15¢ New York Skyline (1947)......	22.50	2.00	.45	.15
C36	25¢ Oakland Bay Bridge (1947) ..	52.50	4.75	1.10	.15

1948-49 Issues

		Mint Sheet	Plate Block	F-VF NH	F-VF Used
			Line Pair		
C37	5¢ Small Plane, Coil.....................		9.50	.95	.90
			Plate Blocks		
C38	5¢ New York City Jubilee .... (100)	18.75	5.50	.20	.15
C39	6¢ Plane (Design of C33) ('49) (100)	16.75	.70	.20	.15
C39a	6¢ Booklet Pane of 6....................	...	...	11.00	7.50
C40	6¢ Alexandria Bicentennial ('49) ..	8.50	.75	.20	.15
			Line Pair		
C41	6¢ Small Plane, Coil (1949)	...	13.75	3.50	.15

C43 C45 C46

C42-44	**Univ. Postal Un., Set of 3 (1949)**	**...**	**10.50**	**1.35**	**1.20**
C42	10¢ Post Office Building..............	14.50	1.65	.30	.25
C43	15¢ Globe & Doves	21.75	2.00	.45	.40
C44	25¢ Stratocruiser & Globe............	35.00	7.50	.70	.65
C45	6¢ Wright Brothers Flight (1949)..	11.00	1.25	.30	.15

1952 Hawaii Issue

C46	80¢ Diamond Head	335.00	32.50	7.00	1.25

1953-58 Issues

C47 C48 C49 C51,C52,C60,C61

C47	6¢ Anniv. of Powered Flight.........	8.50	.85	.20	.15
C48	4¢ Eagle in Flight (1954) ....(100)	13.50	2.00	.20	.15
C49	6¢ Air Force 50th (1957)..............	10.75	.95	.23	.15
C50	5¢ Eagle (as C48) (1958) ....(100)	16.00	1.85	.20	.15
C51	7¢ Jet Silhouette, Blue (1958) . (100)	18.50	.85	.22	.15
C51a	7¢ Booklet Pane of 6	...	...	11.75	5.25
			Line Pair		
C52	7¢ Jet Blue Coil (1958)................	...	17.50	2.25	.15

1959-60 Issues

C53 C54 C55

C57 C56 C58

C53	7¢ Alaska Statehood	12.50	1.25	.30	.15
C54	7¢ Balloon Jupiter........................	12.50	1.25	.30	.15
C55	7¢ Hawaii Statehood	12.50	1.25	.30	.15
C56	10¢ Pan-Am Games.....................	13.50	1.50	.30	.30
C57	10¢ Liberty Bell (1960)	75.00	7.50	1.50	.90
C58	15¢ Stat. of Lib. (1959)	25.00	2.25	.50	.15

1960-67 Issues

C59 C63 C64,C65

cott's No.		Mint Sheet	Plate Block	F-VF NH	F-VF Used
59	25¢ Abraham Lincoln	35.00	3.25	.70	.15
59a	Lincoln Tagged (1966)	...	4.00	.90	...
60	7¢ Jet Silh., Carmine (100)	19.00	.85	.22	.15
60a	7¢ Bk. Pane of 6	...	...	16.50	6.50
61	7¢ Jet, Carmine Coil	Line Pair	40.00	5.00	.30
62	13¢ Liberty Bell (1961)	24.50	2.25	.50	.15
62a	Lib. Bell Tagged (1967)	...	14.00	1.25	...
63	15¢ Liberty, Re-engraved (1961).	22.50	1.95	.45	.15
63a	Lib. Tagged (1967)	...	2.30	.50	...

C58 has wide border around statue, #C63 is divided in center.

64	8¢ Jet over Capitol (1962) (100)	22.50	1.00	.24	.15
64a	Jet Tagged (1963)	...	1.15	.27	...
64b	8¢ B. Pane of 5, Sl. 1, "Your Mailman"	...	...	6.50	1.75
64b	8¢ B. Pane of 5, Sl. 2, "Use Zone Numbers"		...	75.00	...
64b	8¢ B. Pane of 5, Sl. 3, "Always Use Zip"	...	...	13.75	...
64c	8¢ Pane/5, Tagged, Slogan 3	...	...	1.65	...
65	8¢ Capitol & Jet Coil (1962)	Line Pair	6.50	.50	.15
65a	Capitol & Jet Coil, Tagged	Line Pair	3.50	.40	...

1963-68 Issues

C66 C67 C68

C70 C69 C71

C72,C73 C74 C75

66	15¢ Montgomery Blair	35.00	3.50	.75	.70
67	6¢ Bald Eagle (100)	19.50	2.25	.22	.15
67a	Eagle Tagged (1967)	...	87.50	3.85	...
68	8¢ Amelia Earhart	15.00	1.95	.40	.15
69	8¢ R.H. Goddard (1964)	24.50	2.25	.50	.20
70	8¢ Alaska Purchase (1967)	13.50	2.00	.30	.20
71	20¢ Columbia Jays (1967)	50.00	4.75	1.10	.20
72	10¢ 50-Star Runway (1968) (100)	28.50	1.35	.30	.15
72b	10¢ Booklet Pane of 8	...	...	2.75	2.50
72c	10¢ B. Pane of 5 with Sl. 4 or Sl. 5		...	4.00	...
72v	10¢ Congressional Precancel	...	110.00	1.75	...
73	10¢ 50-Star Runway Coil (1968)	Line Pair	2.40	.40	.15
74	10¢ Air Mail Service 50th Anniv ('68)	18.50	3.00	.35	.15
75	20¢ "USA" and Jet (1968)	29.50	2.75	.60	.20

1969-76 Issues

C76 C77 C78,C82

C79,C83 C80 C81

C85 C84 C86

C87 C88 C89

Scott's No.		Mint Sheet	Plate Block	F-VF NH	F-VF Used
C76	10¢ Moon Landing (32)	14.50	2.25	.50	.20
C77	9¢ Delta Wing Plane Silh. ('71) (100)	24.75	1.20	.27	.20
C78	11¢ Jet Airliner Silhouette ('71) (100)	32.50	1.50	.35	.15
C78a	11¢ Booklet Pane of 4	...	...	1.35	1.25
C78v	11¢ Congressional Precancel	...	23.75	.50	...
C79	13¢ Winged Envelope (1973) (100)	35.00	1.70	.38	.15
C79a	13¢ Booklet Pane of 5	...	...	1.75	1.50
C79v	13¢ Congressional Precancel	...	10.50	.40	...
C80	17¢ Statue of Lib. Head (1971)	26.50	2.50	.55	.15
C81	21¢ "USA" and Jet (1971)	25.00	2.50	.55	.15
C82	11¢ Jet Silhouette Coil (1971)	Line Pair	1.00	.35	.15
C83	13¢ Winged Env. Coil (1973)	Line Pair	1.25	.40	.15
C84	11¢ City of Refuge Park ('72)	16.75	1.50	.35	.15
C85	11¢ Olympic Games - Skiing ('72).	14.50	(10) 3.50	.32	.15
C86	11¢ Electronics (1973)	13.50	1.35	.30	.15
C87	18¢ Statue of Liberty (1974)	27.50	2.40	.55	.50
C88	26¢ Mt. Rushmore Memorial (1974)	35.00	3.25	.75	.15
C89	25¢ Plane & Globes (1976)	33.50	3.25	.70	.20
C90	31¢ Plane, Globe and Flag (1976).	37.50	3.75	.80	.20

1978-79 Issues

C91-92 C93-94 C95-96 C97

C91-92	31¢ Wright Bros., attd (100)	95.00	4.75	2.00	1.50
C91-92	Set of 2 Singles		...	1.90	.50
C93-94	21¢ Octave Chanute, attd. ('79). (100)	95.00	5.00	2.00	1.50
C93-94	Set of 2 Singles	...	...	1.90	.50
C95-96	25¢ Wiley Post, attd. ('79) (100)	185.00	10.00	3.50	1.50
C95-96	Set of 2 Singles	...	...	3.35	.50
C97	31¢ Olympics - High Jump ('79)	45.00	(12)13.50	1.00	.30

C99 C98 C100

Scott's No.		Mint Sheet	Plate Block	F-VF NH	F-VF Used
C98	40¢ Ph. Mazzei, Perf. 11	52.50	(12) 13.50	1.10	.25
C98a	Mazzei, Perf. 10½x11	...	(12) 97.50	5.50	3.75
C99	28¢ Blanche Scott	37.50	(12) 10.50	.80	.20
C100	35¢ Glenn Curtiss	46.50	(12) 12.50	.95	.22

1983 Los Angeles Olympic Issues

C101-04

C105-08

C109-12

C101-4	28¢ Summer Olympics, attd	65.00	6.50	6.00	3.00
C101-4	Set of 4 Singles	...	...	5.75	1.00
C105-8	40¢ Summer Olympics, Bullseye Perfs, attd	70.00	6.50	6.00	3.50
C105-8	Set of 4 Singles	...	...	5.75	1.20
C105-108a	40¢ Same, Line Perfs, attd	...	13.50	8.75	...
C109-12	35¢ Summer Olympics, attd	75.00	10.00	7.00	3.50
C109-12	Set of 4 Singles	...	...	6.50	1.40

1985-1989 Issues

C113 C114 C115

C116 C117 C118

C119 C120 C121

Scott's No.		Mint Sheet	Plate Block	F-VF NH	F-V Use
C113	33¢ Alfred Verville	45.00	4.75	.95	.2
C114	39¢ Sperry Brothers	50.00	5.50	1.10	.2
C115	44¢ Transpacific Airmail	57.50	5.75	1.20	.2
C116	44¢ Father Junipero Serra	75.00	10.00	1.50	.2
C117	44¢ New Sweden (1988)	65.00	8.75	1.35	.2
C118	45¢ Samuel Langley (1988)	60.00	5.75	1.30	.2
C119	36¢ Igor Sikorsky (1988)	48.50	4.75	1.00	.3
C120	45¢ French Revolution ('89)... (30)	35.00	5.75	1.25	.2
C121	45¢ Pre-Columbian Customs ('89)	57.50	5.95	1.25	.2

1989 Universal Postal Congress Issues

C122-125

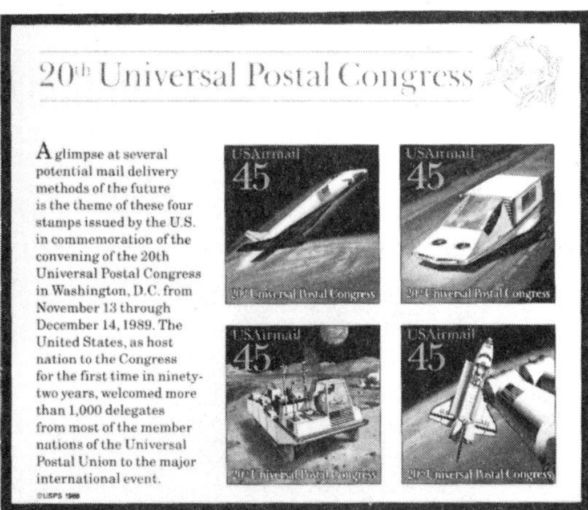

C126

cott's No.		Mint Sheet	Plate Block	F-VF NH	F-VF Used
122-25	45¢ Futuristic Mail Deliv., Attd ..(40)	70.00	7.50	7.00	4.50
122-25	Set of 4 Singles...........................	...	...	6.50	1.00
126	$1.80 Future Mail Del., S/S, Imp..	...	...	6.75	6.00

1990-93 Issues

C127 C128 C129

C130 C131 C132

Scott's No.		Mint Sheet	Plate Block	F-VF NH	F-VF Used
C127	45¢ America, Caribbean Coast....	62.50	6.75	1.30	.20
C128	50¢ Harriet Quimby, Pf. 11 (1991)	65.00	7.00	1.35	.22
C128b	H. Quimby, Perf. 11.2 ('93)..........	60.00	6.50	1.25	.22
C129	40¢ William T. Piper (1991)	51.00	5.50	1.15	.25
C130	50¢ Antarctic Treaty (1991)	65.00	6.50	1.35	.25
C131	50¢ America (1991)	65.00	6.50	1.35	.25
C132	40¢ W.T. Piper, new design ('93).	48.50	5.25	1.10	.25

#C19: Blue sky clear along top of design, Perf. 11
#C132: Piper's hair is touching top of design, Bullseye Perf. 11.2

1934-36 AIR MAIL SPECIAL DELIVERY VF + 20%

CE1,CE2

Scott's No.		Mint Sheet	Plate Block NH	F-VF NH	F-VF Used
CE1	16¢ Great Seal, Dark Blue..........	57.50 (6)	23.50	.80	.70
CE2	16¢ Seal, Red & Blue	32.50	9.50	.55	.25

SPECIAL DELIVERY STAMPS

E1 E2,E3 E4,E5

1885 "At A Special Delivery Office", Unwmkd., Perf. 12 (VF Used+60%)(C)

Scott's No.		NH Fine	Unused Fine	Unused Ave.	Used Fine	Used Ave.
E1	10¢ Messenger, Blue............	300.00	215.00	125.00	35.00	20.75

1888-93 "At Any Post Office", No Line Under "TEN CENTS" Unwatermarked, Perf. 12 VF + 60% (C)

E2	10¢ Blue................................	295.00	210.00	120.00	9.00	5.50
E3	10¢ Orange (1893)	200.00	125.00	80.00	15.00	9.50

1894 Line Under "TEN CENTS", Unwmkd., Perf. 12 VF + 60% (C)

E4	10¢ Blue................................	750.00	550.00	350.00	18.50	10.50

1895 Line Under "TEN CENTS, Double Line Wmk. Perf. 12 VF + 50% (C)

E5	10¢ Blue................................	150.00	100.00	65.00	2.50	1.60

E6,E8-11 E7

Scott's No.		NH VF	NH F-VF	Unused VF	Unused F-VF	Used F-VF
	1902-08 Double Line Watermark VF Used + 50% (B)					
E6	10¢ Ultramarine, Perf. 12.......	160.00	110.00	105.00	70.00	2.95
E7	10¢ Mercury, Green (1908) ...	110.00	75.00	72.50	50.00	30.00
	1911-14 Single Line Watermark VF Used + 50% (B)					
E8	10¢ Ultramarine, Perf. 12.......	170.00	115.00	110.00	75.00	4.00
E9	10¢ Ultra., Perf. 10 (1914)	300.00	200.00	200.00	135.00	5.50
	1916-17 Unwatermarked VF Used + 50% (B)					
E10	10¢ Pale Ultra., Perf. 10	450.00	325.00	335.00	225.00	19.50
E11	10¢ Ultra., Perf. 11 (1917)	30.00	20.00	19.50	13.75	.45

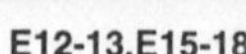

E12-13,E15-18 E14,E19

1922-1925 Flat Press Printings, Perf. 11 VF Used + 30% (B)

E12	10¢ Motorcycle, Gray Violet.....	39.50	28.00	27.50	21.50	.22
E13	15¢ Deep Orange (1925).........	35.00	25.00	24.00	18.50	1.00
E14	20¢ P.O. Truck, Black (1925)	4.50	3.50	3.50	2.75	1.50

PLATE BLOCKS

Plate Blocks	NH VF	NH F-VF	Unused F-VF	Plate Blocks	NH VF	NH F-VF	Unused F-VF
E11 (6)	295.00	200.00	150.00	E13 (6)	350.00	250.00	175.00
E12 (6)	450.00	350.00	250.00	E14 (6)	60.00	47.50	32.50

1927-1951 Rotary Press Printings, Perf. 11x10½ VF Used + 20%

Scott's No.		Pl# Blk. NH VF	Pl# Blk. NH F-VF	NH VF	NH F-VF	F-V Use
E15	10¢ Motorcycle, Gray Violet.......	8.50	6.75	1.10	.85	.1
E16	15¢ Orange (1931)......................	5.75	4.75	1.15	.90	.1
E17	13¢ Blue (1944)	5.00	4.00	.90	.75	.1
E18	17¢ Orange Yellow (1944).......	33.50	26.50	4.35	3.50	2.5
E19	20¢ P.O. Truck, Black (1951) ..	10.00	8.25	2.40	2.00	.1

E20,E21 E22,E23

1954-1971

Scott's No.		Mint Sheet	Plate Block NH	F-VF NH	F-VF Us
E20	20¢ Letter & Hands......................	32.50	3.00	.70	.1
E21	30¢ Letter & Hands......................	35.00	3.50	.75	.1
E22	45¢ Arrows (1969)	65.00	6.50	1.40	.3
E23	60¢ Arrows (1971)	70.00	6.75	1.50	.2

F1 FA1

1911 REGISTRATION VF Used + 40% (B)

Scott's No.		NH VF	NH F-VF	Unused VF	Unused F-VF	Used F-V
F1	10¢ Eagle, Ultramarine..........	120.00	85.00	85.00	60.00	4.5

1955 CERTIFIED MAIL

Scott's No.		Sheet F-VF NH	Pl.Block NH	F-VF NH	F-VF Used
FA1	15¢ Postman, Red	22.50	5.00	.45	.3

NOTE: PRICES THROUGHOUT THIS LIST ARE SUBJECT TO CHANGE WITHOUT NOTICE IF MARKET CONDITIONS REQUIRE. MINIMUM MAIL ORDER MUST TOTAL AT LEAST $20.00.

BROOKMAN PRESENTS THE

Disney

© Disney

Brookman's carries a comprehensive stock of Disney stamps. Ask for our latest price list!

WORLD OF POSTAGE STAMPS ALBUM

The Finest Disney Stamp Album on the Market Today!

This handsome, three-volume album features full-color, 2-post binders with original Disney Stamp Artwork and fully-illustrated, lavishly printed album pages. The pages are printed on one side only and will be amply protected in sturdy Kivar binders. This album includes spaces for Disney stamps, sheetlets and souvenir sheets. Supplements are published annually to keep the album up to date at all times.

VOLUME I ONLY $59.95
(Pages thru 1988 and a binder)
or
VOLUME II ONLY $59.95
(Pages 1989 through 1991 and a binder)
or
VOLUME III ONLY $59.95
(Pages 1992 through 1993 and a binder)
or
THE THREE VOLUME SET ONLY $179.85

1994 Supplement $16.95
Binder Only $19.95

THE BROOKMAN WORLD OF BASEBALL STAMPS ALBUM

The most complete Album on the market today! This two-volume album features a full-color, 2-post binder and fully illustrated album pages, printed on one side only with spaces for stamps issued in honor of our national pastime, and is complete through 1994. This album is supplemented annually to keep your collection up to date at all times!

Complete through 1994 ONLY $79.90

"THAT'S ENTERTAINMENT" ON STAMPS ALBUM

This multi-colored Brookman Album makes the collecting of World Wide Entertainment Topicals fun and easy. A rugged, 2-post binder holds fully-illustrated pages printed on one side only: the only comprehensive album available for this topic. Relive memories of the past Great Stars or thrill to the glitter of today's Stars, and enjoy the World's greatest hobby at the same time. The album is supplemented annually to keep your collection up to date at all times!

Complete through 1994 ONLY $72.95

PLEASE SEND FOR OUR DISNEY, BASEBALL AND ENTERTAINMENT PRICE LISTS.

AVAILABLE FROM YOUR FAVORITE DEALER OR DIRECT FROM BROOKMAN
TOLL-FREE 1-800-332-3383

10 CHESTNUT DRIVE
BEDFORD, N.H. 03110

POSTAGE DUE STAMPS

J1/J22 J29/61 J35/65

1879 Perforated 12 (NH + 50%, VF OG & Used + 75%, VF NH + 125%) (C)

Scott's No.		Unused Fine	Unused Ave.	Used Fine	Used Ave.
J1	1¢ Brown	33.50	20.00	6.50	3.75
J2	2¢ Brown	185.00	110.00	4.50	2.50
J3	3¢ Brown	23.50	14.50	3.00	1.75
J4	5¢ Brown	285.00	175.00	30.00	17.50
J5	10¢ Brown	335.00	200.00	15.00	9.00
J6	30¢ Brown	175.00	110.00	32.50	19.50
J7	50¢ Brown	215.00	130.00	37.50	22.50
1884-1889, Same Design Perf. 12 (NH + 50%, VF OG & Used + 75%, VF NH + 125%)					
J15	1¢ Red Brown	32.50	19.50	3.25	1.95
J16	2¢ Red Brown	39.50	23.50	3.25	1.95
J17	3¢ Red Brown	475.00	285.00	100.00	60.00
J18	5¢ Red Brown	235.00	140.00	15.00	9.00
J19	10¢ Red Brown	235.00	140.00	12.00	7.50
J20	30¢ Red Brown	115.00	70.00	32.50	19.50
J21	50¢ Red Brown	950.00	575.00	125.00	75.00

*** Red Brown issues can be distinguished from Bright Claret issues by placing the stamps under long wave UV light. Bright Clarets give off a warm orange glow, Red Browns do not.**

1891-1893 Same Design Perf. 12 (NH + 50%, VF OG & Used + 75%, VF NH + 125%)

Scott's No.		Unused Fine	Unused Ave.	Used Fine	Used Ave.
J22	1¢ Bright Claret	13.00	7.75	.65	.40
J23	2¢ Bright Claret	14.00	8.50	.60	.35
J24	3¢ Bright Claret	30.00	18.00	4.75	2.85
J25	5¢ Bright Claret	37.50	22.50	4.75	2.85
J26	10¢ Bright Claret	67.50	40.00	11.50	7.00
J27	30¢ Bright Claret	225.00	135.00	85.00	50.00
J28	50¢ Bright Claret	250.00	150.00	85.00	50.00

1894-95 Unwatermarked, Perf. 12 VF Used + 60% (C)

Scott's No.		NH VF	NH F-VF	Unused VF	Unused F-VF	Used F-VF
J29	1¢ Vermilion	1750.00	1050.00	1175.00	700.00	185.00
J30	2¢ Vermilion	750.00	450.00	500.00	300.00	65.00
J31	1¢ Claret	55.00	32.50	36.50	21.50	3.75
J32	2¢ Claret	52.50	29.50	32.50	19.50	2.50
J33	3¢ Claret	185.00	110.00	120.00	72.50	18.50
J34	5¢ Claret	295.00	170.00	190.00	115.00	22.50
J35	10¢ Claret	295.00	170.00	190.00	115.00	16.50
J36	30¢ Claret	500.00	295.00	350.00	200.00	65.00
J36b	Pale Rose	485.00	285.00	325.00	190.00	55.00
J37	50¢ Claret	1350.00	675.00	795.00	450.00	175.00
J37a	Pale Rose	1250.00	625.00	750.00	425.00	150.00
1895-97, Double Line Watermark, Perf. 12 VF Used + 60% (C)						
J38	1¢ Claret	12.50	7.00	7.50	4.50	.35
J39	2¢ Claret	12.50	7.00	7.50	4.50	.25
J40	3¢ Claret	85.00	50.00	55.00	32.50	1.25
J41	5¢ Claret	90.00	55.00	60.00	35.00	1.25
J42	10¢ Claret	95.00	57.50	62.50	37.50	2.50
J43	30¢ Claret	825.00	500.00	550.00	325.00	30.00
J44	50¢ Claret	475.00	275.00	300.00	180.00	24.00
1910-12, Single Line Watermark, Perf. 12 VF Used + 60% (C)						
J45	1¢ Claret	45.00	28.50	31.50	18.50	2.25
J46	2¢ Claret	45.00	28.50	31.50	18.50	.30
J47	3¢ Claret	875.00	550.00	575.00	350.00	20.00
J48	5¢ Claret	135.00	85.00	90.00	55.00	4.50
J49	10¢ Claret	175.00	110.00	115.00	70.00	8.50
J60	50¢ Claret	1375.00	900.00	975.00	575.00	75.00
1914-16, Single Line Watermark, Perf. 10 VF Used + 50% (C)						
J52	1¢ Carmine	90.00	56.50	57.50	37.50	7.35
J53	2¢ Carmine	70.00	45.00	46.50	30.00	.22
J54	3¢ Carmine	975.00	550.00	675.00	395.00	22.50
J55	5¢ Carmine	56.50	36.50	36.00	23.50	1.65
J56	10¢ Carmine	90.00	56.50	57.50	37.50	1.00
J57	30¢ Carmine	315.00	210.00	210.00	140.00	13.50
J58	50¢ Carmine	...	...	...	5500.00	395.00
J59	1¢ Rose (No Watermark)	...	...	1850.00	1100.00	195.00
J60	2¢ Rose (No Watermark)	225.00	135.00	140.00	90.00	12.50
1917-25 Unwatermarked, Perf. 11 VF Used + 50% (B)						
J61	1¢ Carmine Rose	4.00	2.65	2.50	1.70	.15
J62	2¢ Carmine Rose	3.50	2.25	2.10	1.40	.15
J63	3¢ Carmine Rose	19.00	12.00	11.50	7.75	.15
J64	5¢ Carmine Rose	19.00	12.00	11.50	7.75	.17
J65	10¢ Carmine Rose	27.50	17.50	17.00	11.50	.17
J66	30¢ Carmine Rose	140.00	92.50	90.00	60.00	.50
J67	50¢ Carmine Rose	180.00	115.00	120.00	75.00	.17
J68	½¢ Dull Red ('25)	1.30	.90	.90	.65	.15

J69,J79 J77,J87 J88 J101

1930-31 Flat Press, Perf. 11 VF Used + 40% (B)

Scott's No.		NH VF	NH F-VF	Unused VF	Unused F-VF	Used F-V
J69	½¢ Carmine	6.75	5.00	5.25	3.75	.9
J70	1¢ Carmine	4.75	3.35	3.50	2.50	.2
J71	2¢ Carmine	5.50	4.00	4.00	3.00	.2
J72	3¢ Carmine	42.50	28.50	28.50	20.00	1.1
J73	5¢ Carmine	32.50	22.50	22.50	16.00	1.6
J74	10¢ Carmine	90.00	52.50	50.00	35.00	.6
J75	30¢ Carmine	185.00	125.00	120.00	85.00	1.2
J76	50¢ Carmine	265.00	150.00	145.00	105.00	.3
J77	$1 Carmine or Scarlet	42.50	30.00	27.50	20.00	.1
J78	$5 Carmine or Scarlet	60.00	42.50	38.50	27.50	.2

1931-56 Rotary Press, Perf. 11x10½ or 10½x11

Scott's No.		Mint Sheet	Pl.Blk NH	F-VF NH	F-VF Use
J79	½¢ Carmine (100)	125.00	27.50	1.00	.1
J80	1¢ Carmine (100)	12.75	2.00	.20	.1
J81	2¢ Carmine (100)	13.75	2.00	.20	.1
J82	3¢ Carmine (100)	22.50	3.00	.23	.1
J83	5¢ Carmine (100)	38.50	4.50	.40	.1
J84	10¢ Carmine (100)	100.00	8.50	1.10	.1
J85	30¢ Carmine	...	55.00	7.50	.1
J86	50¢ Carmine	...	60.00	9.50	.1
J87	$1 Red ('56)	...	235.00	35.00	.2
1959-85 Rotary Press, Perf. 11x10½					
J88	½¢ Carmine Rose & Black	...	235.00	1.65	1.2
J89	1¢ Carmine Rose & Black (100)	4.00	.50	.20	.1
J90	2¢ Carmine Rose & Black (100)	5.50	.50	.20	.1
J91	3¢ Carmine Rose & Black (100)	8.00	.55	.20	.1
J92	4¢ Carmine Rose & Black (100)	10.00	1.00	.20	.1
J93	5¢ Carmine Rose & Black (100)	12.50	.85	.20	.1
J94	6¢ Carmine Rose & Black (100)	15.00	1.25	.20	.1
J95	7¢ Carmine Rose & Black (100)	22.50	2.25	.25	.1
J96	8¢ Carmine Rose & Black (100)	22.50	1.50	.25	.1
J97	10¢ Carmine Rose & Black (100)	22.50	1.50	.25	.1
J98	30¢ Carmine Rose & Black (100)	70.00	4.50	.75	.1
J99	50¢ Carmine Rose & Black (100)	120.00	5.75	1.25	.1
J100	$1 Carmine Rose & Black	...	11.75	2.40	.1
J101	$5 Carmine Rose & Black	...	50.00	11.50	.1
J102	11¢ Carmine Rose & Blk. ('78) (100)	27.50	3.85	.30	.2
J103	13¢ Carmine Rose & Blk. ('78) (100)	32.50	3.00	.35	.2
J104	17¢ Carmine Rose & Blk. ('85) (100)	79.50	42.50	.45	.4

U.S. OFFICES IN CHINA

K1 K2 K13 K17

1919 U.S. Postal Agency in China
VF Used + 50% (B)

Scott's No.		NH VF	NH F-VF	Unused VF	Unused F-VF	Used F-V
K1	2¢ on 1¢ Green (on #498)	35.00	24.50	23.50	16.00	20.0
K2	4¢ on 2¢ Rose (on #499)	35.00	24.50	23.50	16.00	20.0
K3	6¢ on 3¢ Violet (#502)	75.00	47.50	45.00	32.50	45.0
K4	8¢ on 4¢ Brown (#503)	90.00	57.50	52.50	37.50	45.0
K5	10¢ on 5¢ Blue (#504)	100.00	62.50	60.00	42.50	50.0
K6	12¢ on 6¢ Red Orange(#506)	125.00	77.50	75.00	52.50	65.0
K7	14¢ on 7¢ Black (#507)	130.00	80.00	77.50	55.00	75.0
K8	16¢ on 8¢ Olive Bister (#508)	100.00	62.50	60.00	42.50	50.0
K8a	16¢ on 8¢ Olive Green	95.00	60.00	57.50	40.00	45.0
K9	18¢ on 9¢ Salmon Red (#509)	100.00	62.50	60.00	42.50	55.0
K10	20¢ on 10¢ Or. Yellow (#510)	95.00	60.00	57.50	40.00	50.0
K11	24¢ on 12¢ Brn. Carm. (#512)	110.00	67.50	62.50	45.00	57.5
K11a	24¢ on 12¢ Claret Brown	160.00	97.50	92.50	65.00	80.0
K12	30¢ on 15¢ Gray (#514)	135.00	82.50	77.50	55.00	75.0
K13	40¢ on 20¢ Deep Ultra (#515)	195.00	120.00	115.00	80.00	110.0
K14	60¢ on 30¢ Or. Red (#516)	175.00	110.00	105.00	75.00	100.0
K15	$1 on 50¢ Lt. Violet (#517)	750.00	475.00	450.00	325.00	400.0
K16	$2 on $1 Vlt. Brown (#518)	600.00	375.00	375.00	275.00	300.0
1922 Surcharged in Shanghai, China						
K17	2¢ on 1¢ Green (#498)	190.00	110.00	115.00	80.00	80.0
K18	4¢ on 2¢ Carmine (#528B)	175.00	97.50	105.00	70.00	70.0

DEPARTMENTAL STAMPS

O3,O95 O12 O16,O97 O27,O106 O40

1873 Continental Bank Note Co. - Thin Hard Paper
(NH + 75%, VF OG & Used + 50%, VF NH + 150%) (C)

AGRICULTURE

cott's No.		Unused Fine	Unused Ave.	Used Fine	Used Ave.
1	1¢ Yellow	82.50	48.50	65.00	38.75
2	2¢	65.00	38.50	22.50	15.00
3	3¢	60.00	35.00	4.75	3.00
4	6¢	70.00	42.50	18.50	11.50
5	10¢	135.00	80.00	85.00	52.50
6	12¢	185.00	110.00	90.00	55.00
7	15¢	140.00	82.50	87.50	52.50
8	24¢	160.00	95.00	75.00	45.00
9	30¢	200.00	115.00	115.00	70.00

EXECUTIVE

10	1¢ Carmine	335.00	195.00	175.00	110.00
11	2¢	210.00	125.00	95.00	60.00
12	3¢	260.00	155.00	90.00	52.50
13	6¢	350.00	210.00	275.00	165.00
14	10¢	350.00	210.00	225.00	135.00

INTERIOR

15	1¢ Vermilion	18.75	11.00	4.75	2.85
16	2¢	16.50	10.00	2.85	1.60
17	3¢	26.00	15.00	2.85	1.60
18	6¢	19.00	11.00	2.85	1.60
19	10¢	17.50	10.00	6.25	3.75
20	12¢	28.75	16.75	4.50	2.50
21	15¢	47.50	27.50	9.75	5.75
22	24¢	36.50	20.00	7.00	4.25
23	30¢	47.50	27.50	8.25	5.00
24	90¢	100.00	57.50	19.50	11.50

JUSTICE

25	1¢ Purple	57.50	33.50	42.50	25.00
26	2¢	90.00	52.50	40.00	24.00
27	3¢	90.00	52.50	8.50	5.15
28	6¢	85.00	48.50	14.00	8.50
29	10¢	90.00	52.50	35.00	18.00
30	12¢	72.50	45.00	18.50	11.00
31	15¢	160.00	90.00	65.00	40.00
32	24¢	425.00	250.00	150.00	90.00
33	30¢	375.00	225.00	95.00	55.00
34	90¢	550.00	325.00	210.00	125.00

NAVY

35	1¢ Ultramarine	42.50	25.00	14.00	8.50
36	2¢	32.50	19.50	10.00	6.00
37	3¢	35.00	20.00	4.50	2.50
38	6¢	30.00	16.50	6.75	3.75
39	7¢	210.00	125.00	75.00	43.50
40	10¢	42.50	25.00	14.00	8.50
41	12¢	55.00	32.50	12.00	7.25
42	15¢	90.00	52.50	27.50	16.50
43	24¢	90.00	52.50	31.50	19.00
44	30¢	80.00	47.50	15.50	9.50
45	90¢	425.00	250.00	87.50	55.00

O49,O108 O60 O74,O109 O83,O114

POST OFFICE

O47	1¢ Black	7.00	4.25	3.25	1.85
O48	2¢	8.50	5.00	2.75	1.55
O49	3¢	2.50	1.50	.90	.50
O50	6¢	7.75	4.50	1.85	1.10
O51	10¢	37.50	22.50	18.50	11.50
O52	12¢	20.00	11.50	5.50	3.00
O53	15¢	22.50	13.50	8.50	5.00
O54	24¢	30.00	17.50	10.50	6.00
O55	30¢	30.00	17.50	10.00	5.50
O56	90¢	45.00	26.50	13.00	7.50

STATE

Scott's No.		Unused Fine	Unused Ave.	Used Fine	Used Ave.
O57	1¢ Green	57.50	32.50	18.75	11.00
O58	2¢	120.00	70.00	27.50	15.75
O59	3¢	47.50	27.50	9.50	5.25
O60	6¢	45.00	25.00	10.50	5.85
O61	7¢	82.50	47.50	21.50	11.75
O62	10¢	70.00	37.50	16.00	9.00
O63	12¢	100.00	57.50	42.50	24.50
O64	15¢	115.00	70.00	30.00	18.00
O65	24¢	225.00	130.00	70.00	42.50
O66	30¢	225.00	130.00	55.00	30.00
O67	90¢	450.00	270.00	140.00	85.00
O68	$2 Green & Black	525.00	300.00	375.00	225.00
O69	$5 Green & Black	4250.00	2600.00	1800.00	1250.00
O70	$10 Green & Black	2800.00	1575.00	1400.00	950.00
O71	$20 Green & Black	1950.00	1100.00	950.00	525.00

TREASURY

O72	1¢ Brown	21.50	12.75	2.15	1.25
O73	2¢	22.50	13.50	2.15	1.25
O74	3¢	15.00	8.75	1.25	.75
O75	6¢	21.50	12.75	1.85	1.10
O76	7¢	52.50	30.00	12.00	6.75
O77	10¢	55.00	32.50	5.25	3.00
O78	12¢	55.00	32.50	3.50	2.00
O79	15¢	47.50	27.50	5.00	2.75
O80	24¢	225.00	130.00	42.50	23.50
O81	30¢	77.50	45.00	5.50	3.00
O82	90¢	80.00	47.50	5.50	3.00

WAR

O83	1¢ Rose	80.00	47.50	4.25	2.50
O84	2¢	70.00	41.50	6.25	3.50
O85	3¢	67.50	38.50	1.75	1.00
O86	6¢	225.00	135.00	4.00	2.25
O87	7¢	70.00	41.50	37.50	21.00
O88	10¢	21.50	12.75	4.75	2.75
O89	12¢	70.00	41.50	4.50	2.50
O90	15¢	19.00	11.00	3.50	1.95
O91	24¢	19.00	11.00	3.50	1.95
O92	30¢	21.50	13.00	3.25	1.75
O93	90¢	47.50	27.50	12.50	7.00

1879 American Bank Note Co. - Soft Porous Paper
(NH + 60%, VF OG & Used + 50%, VF NH + 135%) (C)

O94	1¢ Agric. Dept. (Issued w/o gum)	1400.00	800.00	...	...
O95	3¢	175.00	100.00	37.50	21.50
O96	1¢ Interior Department	125.00	70.00	85.00	47.50
O97	2¢	2.25	1.20	.90	.50
O98	3¢	1.95	1.10	.75	.40
O99	6¢	2.75	1.60	2.25	1.30
O100	10¢	35.00	21.50	28.50	17.50
O101	12¢	65.00	35.00	40.00	25.00
O102	15¢	150.00	85.00	70.00	38.50
O103	24¢	1795.00	1100.00	...	...
O106	3¢ Justice Department	47.50	25.00	25.00	15.00
O107	6¢	100.00	55.00	85.00	52.50
O108	3¢ Post Office Department	8.50	4.50	2.35	1.40
O109	3¢ Treasury Department	25.00	13.50	4.00	2.25
O110	6¢	47.50	25.00	16.50	9.25
O111	10¢	67.50	38.50	19.00	11.50
O112	30¢	750.00	435.00	130.00	72.50
O113	90¢	750.00	435.00	130.00	72.50
O114	1¢ War Department	2.00	1.20	1.35	.85
O115	2¢	3.00	1.80	1.35	.85
O116	3¢	3.00	1.75	.85	.50
O117	6¢	3.00	1.65	.80	.45
O118	10¢	20.00	12.50	16.50	9.50
O119	12¢	15.00	8.50	4.75	2.75
O120	30¢	45.00	26.50	33.50	19.75

1910-11 Official Postal Savings VF Used + 50% (B)

O122 O123 O124

Scott's No.		NH VF	NH F-VF	Unused VF	Unused F-VF	Used F-VF
O121	2¢ Black, D.L. Wmk	21.50	13.50	12.50	8.00	1.25
O122	50¢ Dark Green, D.L. Wmk	235.00	140.00	145.00	95.00	30.00
O123	$1 Ultramarine, D.L. Wmk	225.00	135.00	135.00	90.00	9.00
O124	1¢ Dark Violet, S.L. Wmk	12.50	7.75	7.50	5.00	1.15
O125	2¢ Black, S.L. Wmk	65.00	40.00	42.50	27.50	3.75
O126	10¢ Carmine, S.L. Wmk	22.50	15.00	14.00	9.50	1.10

MODERN OFFICIAL ISSUES

O127 O133 O138 O143 O148

1983-85 Offical Stamps

Scott's No.		Mint Sheet	Pl# Blk. F-VF NH	F-VF NH	F-VF Used
O127	1¢ Eagle .... (100)	7.50	.50	.20	.15
O128	4¢ Eagle .... (100)	11.00	.70	.20	.22
O129	13¢ Eagle .... (100)	37.50	1.95	.40	.75
O129A	14¢ Eagle (No Pl.#) ('85) .... (100)	37.50	...	.40	.55
O130	17¢ Eagle .... (100)	45.00	2.35	.50	.35
O132	$1 Eagle	...	12.50	2.75	1.50
O133	$5 Eagle	...	40.00	9.75	5.50
O135	20¢ Eagle, Coil .... **(Pl.# Strip)**	75.00(5)	17.50(3)	.85	1.10
O136	22¢ Eagle, Coil (No Pl.#) ('85).....	...	...	1.35	.95
O138	(14¢) "D" Postcard rate ('85).... (100)	...	37.50	3.50	1.75
O139	(22¢) "D" Coil ('85).............. **(Pl.# Strip)**	90.00(5)	55.00(3)	3.50	1.75

1988-95 Official Stamps

(Sheets and Coils have no Pl. #s)

Scott's No.		Mint Sheet	Pl# Blk. F-VF NH	F-VF NH	F-VF Used
O138A	15¢ Coil ('88)	...	...	.55	.60
O138B	20¢ Coil (No ¢ sign) ('88)............	...	...	.75	.80
O140	(25¢) "E" Coil ('88)	...	...	1.20	1.70
O141	25¢ Coil ('88)	...	...	.95	.30
O143	1¢ Offset (No ¢ sign) ('89) .... (100)	7.50	...	.20	.25
O144	(29¢) "F" Coil ('91)	...	...	1.65	.50
O145	29¢ Coil ('91)	...	...	.90	.40
O146	4¢ Make-up rate ('91) .... (100)	8.75	...	.20	.30
O146A	10¢ Eagle (1993) .... (100)	20.00	...	.22	.50
O147	19¢ Postcard rate ('91) .... (100)	37.50	...	.40	.45
O148	23¢ 2nd Ounce rate ('91)......... (100)	45.00	...	.50	.40
O151	$1 Eagle (1993)	...	...	1.95	1.75
O152	(32¢) "G" Coil (94)	...	...	.65	...
...	1¢ "¢" Sign added,No "USA"('95)(100)	7.50	...	.20	...
...	20¢ Sheet Stamp (1995) .... (100)	39.50	...	.42	...
...	23¢ Reprint, Line above "23"('95)(100)	45.00	...	.50	...
...	32¢ Eagle, Coil (1995)................	...	...	.65	...

U.S. AUTOPOST ISSUES
Computer Vended Postage

Type I

Type II

Washington, D.C., Machine 82
CV1a 25¢ First Class, Ty. 1 ....
CV2a $1.00 3rd Class, Ty. 1 ....
CV3a $1.69 Parcel Post, Ty. 1....
CV4a $2.40 Priority Mail, Ty. 1....
CV5a $8.75 Express Mail, Ty. 1..
Set of 5 .... $95.00

Washington, D.C., Machine 83
CV6a 25¢ First Class, Ty. 1 ....
CV7a $1.00 3rd Class, Ty. 1 ....
CV8a $1.69 Parcel Post, Ty. 2....
CV9a $2.40 Priority Mail, Ty. 1....
CV10a $8.75 Express Mail, Ty. 1..
Set of 5 .... $67.50

Kensington, MD, Machine 82
CV11a 25¢ First Class, Ty. 1 ...
CV12a $1.00 3rd Class, Ty. 1 ....
CV13a $1.69 Parcel Post, Ty. 2.
CV14a $2.40 Priority Mail, Ty. 1.
CV15a $8.75 Express Mail, Ty. 1
Set of 5 .... $67.50

Kensington, MD, Machine 83
CV16a 25¢ First Class, Ty. 1 .....
CV17a $1.00 3rd Class, Ty. 1
CV18a $1.69 Parcel Post, Ty. 2.
CV19a $2.40 Priority Mail, Ty. 1.
CV20a $8.75 Express Mail, Ty. 1
Set of 5 .... $67.50

CV31 CV31b CV32

1992-94 Variable Rate Coils

Scott's No.		Pl# Strip of 5	Pl# Strip of 3	F-VF NH	F-VF Used
CV31	29¢ Shield, horizontal design	10.75	9.75	.75	.50
CV31b	32¢ new denomination style (1994)	10.75	9.75	.75	...
CV32	29¢ Shield, vertical design (1994)	9.75	8.75	.60	.50

NOTE: #CV31 and CV32 come in a number different denominations but the first class rate of 29¢ is the only rate regularly available.

Q1 QE1 JQ1

1912-13 PARCEL POST STAMPS VF Used + 40% (B)

Scott's No.		NH VF	NH F-VF	Unused VF	Unused F-VF	Used F-VF
Q1	1¢ Post Office Clerk..................	6.50	4.50	4.00	2.75	1.10
Q2	2¢ City Carrier...........................	7.50	5.25	4.50	3.25	.85
Q3	3¢ Railway Clerk (1913)	13.75	9.50	8.75	6.00	4.50
Q4	4¢ Rural Carrier	42.50	26.50	25.00	16.50	2.25
Q5	5¢ Mail Train	42.50	26.50	25.00	16.50	1.50
Q6	10¢ Steamship & Tender.........	67.50	45.00	40.00	27.50	2.00
Q7	15¢ Automobile Service.........	100.00	65.00	60.00	42.50	8.50
Q8	20¢ Airplane Carrying Mail	200.00	125.00	115.00	82.50	16.50
Q9	25¢ Manufactured..................	100.00	65.00	57.50	40.00	4.50
Q10	50¢ Dairying (1913)	350.00	235.00	230.00	165.00	32.50
Q11	75¢ Harvesting.......................	115.00	75.00	70.00	50.00	23.50
Q12	$1 Fruit Growing (1913).........	525.00	375.00	350.00	250.00	18.00

1925-1929 SPECIAL HANDLING STAMPS VF + 30% (B)

Scott's No.		NH VF	NH F-VF	Unused VF	Unused F-VF	Used F-VF
QE1	10¢ Yellow Green (1928)...........	2.25	1.65	1.60	1.25	.90
QE2	15¢ Yellow Green (1928)...........	2.25	1.75	1.65	1.25	.90
QE3	20¢ Yellow Green (1928)...........	3.65	2.65	2.50	1.90	1.80
QE4	25¢ Yellow Green (1929).........	25.00	20.00	19.50	15.00	7.50
QE4a	25¢ Deep Green (1925)...........	42.50	31.50	29.50	22.50	5.25

1912 PARCEL POST DUE VF + 40% (B)

Scott's No.		NH VF	NH F-VF	Unused VF	Unused F-VF	Used F-VF
JQ1	1¢ Dark Green	15.00	10.00	9.50	6.50	3.00
JQ2	2¢ Dark Green	125.00	85.00	80.00	55.00	14.50
JQ3	5¢ Dark Green	22.50	15.00	14.00	9.50	3.75
JQ4	10¢ Dark Green	275.00	175.00	175.00	125.00	35.00
JQ5	25¢ Dark Green	175.00	100.00	100.00	70.00	3.50

PLATE BLOCKS

	NH VF	NH F-VF	Unused F-VF		NH VF	NH F-VF	Unused F-VF
Q1 (6)	170.00	115.00	85.00	QE1 (6)	29.50	22.50	17.50
Q2 (6)	175.00	115.00	85.00	QE2 (6)	42.50	32.50	25.00
Q3 (6)	340.00	230.00	175.00	QE3 (6)	47.50	37.50	30.00

SAVINGS STAMPS (B) PS & WS (NH + 20%) VF + 30%, S (NH + 10%) VF + 20%

PS8 PS14 S2 S7 WS8

Scott's No.	F-VF Unused
1911-41 Postal Savings	
PS1 10¢ Orange.....................	8.00
PS2 10¢ Orange, Card.......	140.00
PS4 10¢ D. Blue, Pf. 12	4.00
PS5 10¢ Dp, Blue, Card	85.00
PS6 10¢ Blue, Perf. 11 ('36)...	4.00
PS7 10¢ Ultramarine (1940).	12.50
PS8 25¢ Carmine Rose ('40)	15.00
PS9 50¢ Blue Green ('40)	40.00
PS10 $1 Gray Black (1940)..	110.00
PS11 10¢ Rose Red (1941)	.50
PS11 Plate Block of 4...............	7.00
PS11b Bklt. Pane of 10	45.00
PS12 25¢ Blue Green ('41)......	2.00
PS12 Plate Block of 4............	17.50
PS12b Bklt. Pane of 10	55.00
PS13 50¢ Ultramarine ('41)......	5.50
PS13 Plate Block of 4............	45.00
PS14 $1 Gray Black ('41).......	11.00
PS15 $5 Sepia (1941)	35.00
1954-61 Savings	
S1 10¢ Rose Red...................	.45
S1 Plate Block of 4..............	3.00
S1a Bklt. Pane of 10	140.00
S2 25¢ Blue Green	6.00
S2 Plate Block of 4............	30.00
S2a Bklt. Pane of 10	775.00
S3 50¢ Ultramarine ('56)......	7.00

Scott's No.	F-VF Unused
S3 50¢ Plate Block of 4	47.50
S4 $1 Gray Black (1957) ...	19.50
S5 $5 Sepia (1956)............	75.00
S6 25¢ 48 Star Flag (1958) .	1.75
S6 Plate Block of 4	9.00
S6a Bklt. Pane of 10............	67.50
S7 25¢ 50 Star Flag (1961) .	1.10
S7 Plate Block of 4	8.50
S7a Bklt. Pane of 10..........	275.00
1917-45 War Savings	
WS1 25¢ Thrift Stamp...........	10.00
WS2 $5 Washington	75.00
WS4 $5 Franklin ('19)	225.00
WS7 10¢ Rose Red (1942)	.45
WS7 Plate Block of 4	4.75
WS7b Bklt. Pane of 10............	45.00
WS8 25¢ Blue Green (1942)...	1.00
WS8 Plate Block of 4	10.00
WS8b Bklt. Pane of 10	45.00
WS9 50¢ Ultramarine (1942) ..	3.75
WS9 Plate Block of 4	27.50
WS10 $1 Gray Black (1942)	9.50
WS10 Plate Block of 4	60.00
WS11 $5 Violet Brown (1945).	45.00
WS12 10¢ Rose Red, Coil ('43)	2.25
WS12 Line Pair	9.50
WS13 25¢ Blue Green,Coil '43)	4.00
WS13 Line Pair	18.50

Prices are for Pl# Strips of 3

1897

2127

ott No.		F-VF NH
97	1¢ Omnibus	
	Pl# 1,2,5,6	.60
	Pl# 3,4	1.10
25	1¢ Omnibus "B" Press	
	Pl# 1,2	.80
25a	Pl# 2,3 untagged	.95
97A	2¢ Locomotive	
	Pl# 2,6	.80
	Pl# 3,4,8,10	.70
26	2¢ Loco. "B" Press	
	Pl# 1	.80
26a	Pl# 2 untagged	.95
98	3¢ Handcar	
	Pl# 1-4	.90
52	3¢ Conestoga Wagon	
	Pl# 1	.95
52a	Pl# 2,3 untagged	1.50
23	3.4¢ School Bus	
	Pl# 1,2	1.25
23a	Pl# 1,2	7.95
98A	4¢ Stagecoach	
	Pl# 1,2,3,4	1.80
	Pl# 5,6	3.00
98Ab	Pl# 3,4,5,6	8.50
28	4¢ Stagecoach "B"	
	Pl# 1	1.50
28a	Pl# 1, overall tag	19.50
51	4¢ Steam Carriage	
	Pl# 1	1.35
51b	Pl# 1, untagged	2.25
24	4.9¢ Buckboard	
	Pl# 3,4	1.00
24a	Pl# 1-6	2.25
99	5¢ Motorcycle	
	Pl# 1-4	1.10

Scott No.		F-VF NH
2253	5¢ Milk Wagon	
	Pl# 1	1.35
2452	5¢ Circus Wagon, Engr.	
	Pl# 1	1.50
2452a	Pl# 1, untagged	2.00
2452B	5¢ Circus Wagon, Gravure	
	Pl# A1,A2,A3	1.75
2453	5¢ Canoe, Brown, Engr.	
	Pl# 1,2,3	1.75
2454	5¢ Canoe, Red, Gravure	
	Pl# S11	1.75
2893	(5¢) "G" Non-Profit	
	Pl# A11111,A21111	2.75
1900	5.2¢ Sleigh	
	Pl# 1,2	7.50
	Pl# 3,5	165.00
1900a	Pl# 1-6	13.50
2254	5.3¢ Elevator, Prec.	
	Pl# 1	1.95
2125	5.5¢ Star Route Truck	
	Pl# 1	2.25
2125a	Pl# 1,2	2.25
1901	5.9¢ Bicycle	
	Pl# 3,4	9.75
1901a	Pl# 3,4	35.00
	Pl# 5,6	85.00
2126	6¢ Tricycle	
	Pl# 1	1.75
2126a	Pl# 1	2.25
	Pl# 2	8.00
2127	7.1¢ Tractor	
	Pl# 1	2.95
2127a	Pl# 1	4.75
2127av	Zip + 4	
	Pl# 1	3.00

Scott No.		F-VF NH
1902	7.4¢ Baby Buggy	
	Pl# 2	8.75
1902a	Pl# 2	5.95
2255	7.5¢ Carreta, Prec.	
	Pl# 1,2	2.75
	Pl# 3	6.50
2128	8.3¢ Ambulance	
	Pl# 1,2	1.50
2128a	Pl# 1,2	1.50
	Pl# 3,4	5.25
2231	8.3¢ Ambul."B" Press,Prec.	
	Pl# 1	4.25
	Pl# 2	7.00
2256	8.4¢ Wheel Chair, Prec.	
	Pl# 1,2	2.75
	Pl# 3	22.50
2129	8.5¢ Tow Truck	
	Pl# 1	3.50
2129a	Pl# 1	3.75
	Pl# 2	12.50
1903	9.3¢ Mail Wagon	
	Pl# 1,2	8.25
	Pl# 3,4	23.50
	Pl# 5,6	285.00
1903a	Pl# 1,2	16.50
	Pl# 3,4	27.50
	Pl# 5,6	3.75
	Pl# 8	180.00
2257	10¢ Canal Boat	
	Pl# 1	1.50
2257v	Pl# 1,2 overall tag.	3.75
2257vd	Pl# 1, o.t., dull gum	4.75
2257g	Pl# 2, Gravure	1.50
2457	10¢ Tractor Trailer,intaglio	
	Pl# 1	1.75

Scott No.		F-VF NH
2458	(10¢) Tractor Trailer, Gravure	
	Pl#11,22	1.75
2602	(10¢) Eagle &Shield	
	A11111,A11112,A21112, A22112,A22113,A43334, A43335,A53335	3.75
	A21113,A33333,A33335, A43324,A43325,A43326, A43426,A54444,A54445	7.50
	A34424,A34426,A77777, A88888,A89999,A99999, A88889,A99998	5.00
	A12213	25.00
	A32333	P.O.R.
	A33334	67.50
	A1010101010,A1110101010, A1011101011,etc.	4.75
2603	(10¢) Eagle & Shield (BEP)	
	Pl# 11111,22221, 22222	4.00
2603v	(10¢) Dull Gum,	
	Pl# 22222,33333	4.25
2604	(10¢) Eagle & Shield (SV)	
	Pl# S11111,S22222	4.75
2130	10.1¢ Oil Wagon	
	Pl# 1	2.25
2130a	Pl# 1,2	2.75
2130av	Pl# 2,3 **Red Prec.**	3.25
1904	10.9¢ Hansom Cab	
	Pl# 1,2	16.50
1904a	Pl# 1,2	40.00
	Pl# 3,4	325.00

PLATE NO. COILS
Prices are for Pl# Strips of 3

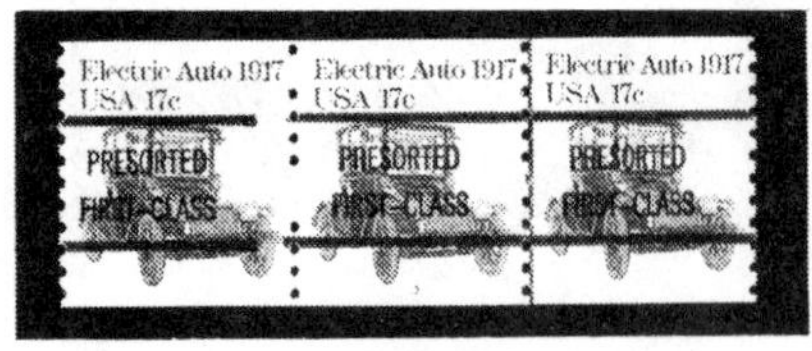

1906a

O135

Scott No.		F-VF NH
1905	**11¢ Caboose**	
	Pl# 1	3.50
1905b	Pl# 2, untagged	2.25
1905a	Pl# 1	3.75
2131	**11¢ Stutz Bearcat**	
	Pl# 1-4	1.50
2132	**12¢ Stanley Steamer**	
	Pl# 1,2	2.15
2132a	Pl# 1,2	2.75
2132b	12¢ "B" Press, Prec.	
	Pl# 1	27.50
2133	**12.5¢ Pushcart**	
	Pl# 1,2	2.75
2133a	Pl# 1,2	3.75
2258	**13¢ Patrol Wagon, Prec.**	
	Pl# 1	3.25
2259	**13.2¢ Coal Car, Prec.**	
	Pl# 1,2	3.00
2134	**14¢ Iceboat**	
	Pl# 1-4	2.25
2134b	"B" Press	
	Pl# 2	4.25
2260	**15¢ Tugboat**	
	Pl# 1,2	3.00
2260a	Pl# 2, overall tag	4.25
2261	**16.7¢ Popcorn Wagon, Prec.**	
	Pl# 1,2	3.75
1906	**17¢ Electric Car**	
	Pl# 1-5	3.25
	Pl# 6	17.50
	Pl# 7	4.75
1906a	Pl# 3A-5A	4.50
	Pl# 6A,7A	15.00
	Pl# 3B,4B	17.50
	Pl# 5B,6B	22.50
	Pl# 1C,2C,3C,4C	10.00
	Pl# 5C,7C	21.50
2135	**17¢ Dog Sled**	
	Pl# 2	3.00
2262	**17.5¢ Marmon Wasp**	
	Pl# 1	4.25
2262a	Pl# 1	4.75
1891	**18¢ Flag**	
	Pl# 1	130.00
	Pl# 2	23.50
	Pl# 3	350.00
	Pl# 4	6.00
	Pl# 5	5.00

Scott No.		F-VF NH
	Pl# 6	P.O.R.
	Pl# 7	30.00
1907	**18¢ Surrey**	
	Pl# 1	80.00
	Pl# 2,5,6,8	3.50
	Pl# 3,4	65.00
	Pl# 7	35.00
	Pl# 9,10	7.50
	Pl# 11,12,15,16	14.50
	Pl# 13-14,17-18	6.50
2149	**18¢ GW Monument**	
	Pl# 1112,3333	3.50
2149a	Pl# 11121,33333	4.25
	Pl# 33333 Dry Gum	6.75
	Pl# 43444 Dry Gum	12.00
2529	**19¢ Fishing Boat, Ty. I**	
	Pl# A1111,A1212, A2424	5.00
	Pl# A1112	13.50
2529a	**Ty. II**, Andreotti Gravure Pl# A5555,A5556, A6667,A7667,A7679 A7766,A7779	5.00
2529b	Type II,untagged A5555	10.00
2529C	Type III, S111	5.25
1895	**20¢ Flag**	
	Pl# 1,2	7.50
	Pl# 3,5,9-10,13-14	4.75
	Pl# 4	55.00
	Pl# 6	90.00
	Pl# 8	7.50
	Pl# 11,12	7.00
1895e	Pl# 14	75.00
1908	**20¢ Fire Pumper**	
	Pl# 1	32.50
	Pl# 2	225.00
	Pl# 3,4,13,15,16	3.75
	Pl# 5,9,10	3.25
	Pl# 6	19.50
	Pl# 7,8	100.00
	Pl# 11	40.00
	Pl# 12,14	5.50
2005	**20¢ Consumer**	
	Pl# 1,2	52.50
	Pl# 3,4	39.50
2263	**20¢ Cable Car**	
	Pl# 1,2	3.95
2263b	Pl# 2, overall tag	6.00

Scott No.		F-VF NH
2264	**20.5¢ Fire Engine, Prec.**	
	Pl# 1	4.25
2265	**20.5¢ RR Mail Car, Prec.**	
	Pl# 1,2	4.25
2150	**21.1¢ Pre-Sort**	
	Pl# 111111	3.50
	Pl# 111121	4.25
2150a	Pl# 111111	4.50
	Pl# 111121	5.00
2112	**(22¢) "D" Eagle Coil**	
	Pl# 1,2	6.50
2115	**22¢ Flag/Capitol**	
	Pl# 1,7	9.75
	Pl# 2,4,8,12	3.75
	Pl# 3	13.00
	Pl# 5,6,10	6.00
	Pl# 7,13	12.50
	Pl# 11,17,18,20	7.50
	Pl# 14	27.50
	Pl# 15-16,19,21,22	3.75
2115b	22¢ Flag Test Coil	
	Pl# T1	5.00
2464	**23¢ Lunch Wagon**	
	Pl# 2,3	3.95
2605	**23¢ Flag, Bulk Rate**	
	Pl# A111,A212, A222	5.50
	Pl# A112,A122,A333	6.50
2606	**23¢ USA Pre-sort, ABNCo.**	
	Pl# A1111,A2222,A2232, A2233,A3333,A4443, A4444,A4453, A4364	5.50
2607	**23¢ USA Pre-sort, BEP**	
	Pl# 1111	5.50
2607a	23¢ Dull Gum #1111	5.75
2608	**23¢ USA Pre-sort, S.V.**	
	Pl# S1111	5.50
2266	**24.1¢ Tandem Bike, Prec.**	
	Pl# 1	4.75
2136	**25¢ Bread Wagon**	
	Pl# 1-5	3.50
2279	**(25¢) "E" Series**	
	Pl# 1111,1222	3.50
	Pl# 1211,2222	5.00
2280	**25¢ Yosemite Block tagged**	
	Pl# 1,7	7.50
	Pl# 2-5,8	3.75
	Pl# 9	12.50

Scott No.		F-VF NH
2280v	**25¢ Yosemite Phos. tag.**	
	Pl# 1	45.00
	Pl# 2-3,7-11,13-14	3.75
	Pl# 5,15	7.50
	Pl# 6	14.00
2281	**25¢ Honeybee**	
	Pl# 1,2	3.00
2888	**(25¢) "G"**	
	Pl# S11111	6.75
2518	**(29¢) "F" Flower**	
	Pl# 1111,1222,2222	4.25
	Pl# 1211	35.00
	Pl# 2211	7.75
2523	**29¢ Flag/Mt. Rushmore**	
	Pl# 1-9	6.00
2523A	**29¢ Rushmore/Gravure**	
	Pl# A11111,A22211	6.25
2525	**29¢ Flower, rouletted**	
	Pl# S1111,S2222	5.50
2526	**29¢ Flower, perforated**	
	Pl# S2222	6.50
2609	**29¢ Flag/White House**	
	Pl# 1-16,18	5.75
2889	**(32¢) Black "G"**	
	Pl# 1111, 2222	6.75
2890	**(32¢) Blue "G"**	
	Pl# A1111,A1112,A1113, A1211,A1212,A1311, A1313,A1314,A1324, A1417,A1433,A2211, A2212,A2213,A2214, A2223,A3113,A3314, A3315,A3323,A3324, A3423,A3433,A3435, A3436,A4426,A4427, A5327,A5417,A5427, A5437	6.75
	Pl# A1222,A3114, A3426	9.75
	Pl# A4435	165.00
2891	**(32¢) Red "G"**	
	Pl# S1111	7.00
2892	(32¢) "G" Rouletted	
	Pl# S1111,S2222	7.50
2468	**$1 Seaplane**	
	Pl# 1,3	9.00
O135	**20¢ Official**	
	Pl# 1	17.50
O139	**(22¢) "D" Official**	
	Pl# 1	55.00

MODERN ERRORS

Due to the increasing popularity of modern errors, listings of this nature, formerly scattered throughout the catalogue, have been consolidated in an effort to provide a more useful format. Several new listings have been included as well.

While the listing is not intended to be complete, additions will be considered for subsequent editions of this catalogue.

1519a 1895a

IMPERFORATE MAJOR ERRORS

Scott's No.		F-VF NH
25c	1¢ Washington, horiz. pair, Imperf. Between	95.00
54a	2¢ Washington, horiz. pair, Imperf. Vert	225.00
44a	5¢ Yellowstone, horiz. pair, imperf. vert	550.00
05b	1.5¢ M. Washington, horiz. pair, imperf. between	150.00
05b	1.5¢ M. Washington, horiz. pair, imperf. between, precancelled	25.00
99b	1¢ Defense, Horizontal Pair, Imperf. Between	45.00
00a	2¢ Defense, Horizontal Pair, Imperf. Between	47.50
01a	3¢ Defense, Horizontal Pair, Imperf. Between	32.50
66a	3¢ Palomar, vert. pair, imperf. between	625.00
055b	2¢ Jefferson, coil pair, imperf., precancelled	500.00
055c	2¢ Jefferson, coil pair, imperf.	600.00
058a	4¢ Linncoln, Coil Pair, Imperf	125.00
058a	4¢ Same, Line Pair	225.00
059Ac	25¢ Revere, Coil Pair, Imperf., VG-Fine	35.00
059Ac	Same, F-VF	55.00
059Ac	Same, Line Pair, VG-Fine	85.00
138a	4¢ McDowell, Vert. Pair, Imperf. between	450.00
138b	4¢ McDowell, vert. pair, imperf. horizontal	325.00
151a	4¢ SEATO, vertical pair, imperf. between	175.00
229b	5¢ Washington, Coil Pair, Imperf	350.00
297a	3¢ Parkman, Coil Pair, Imperf	30.00
297a	Same, Line Pair	55.00
297c	Same, Precancelled	8.75
297c	Same, Precancelled, Line Pair	25.00
299b	1¢ Jefferson, Coil Pair, Imperf	35.00
299b	Same, Line Pair	75.00
303b	4¢ Lincoln, Coil Pair, Imperf	895.00
304b	5¢ Washington, Coil Pair Imperf	225.00
1304e	Same, Precancelled	375.00
1305a	6¢ FDR, Coil Pair, Imperf	80.00
1305a	Same, Line Pair	125.00
1305Eg	15¢ Holmes, Coil Pair, Imperf	37.50
1305Eg	Same, Line Pair	100.00
1305Ej	Holmes, Type II, Dry Gum, Coil Pair, Imperf	85.00
1305Ej	Same, Line Pair	300.00
1338k	6¢ Flag, vert. pair, imperf. between	550.00
1338Ab	6¢ Flag, Coil Pair, Imperf	500.00
1338De	6¢ Flag, horiz. pair, imperf. between	150.00
1338Fi	8¢ Flag, Vert. Pair, Imperf	50.00
1338Fj	8¢ Flag, horiz. pair, imperf. between	45.00
1338Gh	8¢ Flag, Coil Pair	70.00
1355b	6¢ Disney, Vert. Pair, imperf. horiz	875.00
1355c	6¢ Disney, Imperf. Pair	1000.00
1362a	6¢ Waterfowl, vertical pair, imperf. between	600.00
1363b	6¢ Christmas, imperf. pair	250.00
1370a	6¢ Grandma Moses, horiz. pair, imperf. between	265.00
1402a	8¢ Eisenhower, Coil Pair, Imperf	52.50
1402a	Same, Line Pair	95.00
1484a	8¢ Gershwin, vert. pair, imperf. horiz	265.00
1485a	8¢ Jefferson, vert. pair, imperf. horiz	300.00
1487a	8¢ Cathers, vert. pair, imperf. horiz	350.00
1503a	8¢ Johnson, horiz. pair, imperf. vert	325.00
1508a	8¢ Christmas, vert. pair, imperf. between	500.00
1509a	10¢ Flags, Horiz. Pair, Imperf. Between	55.00
1510e	10¢ Jefferson Memorial, Vert. Pair, imperf. horiz	350.00
1518b	6.3¢ Bell Coil Pair, Imperf	275.00
1518b	Same, Line Pair	385.00
1518c	Same, Precancelled Pair	150.00
1518c	Same, Line Pair	300.00
1519a	10¢ Flag Coil Pair, Imperf	42.50
1520b	10¢ Jefferson Memorial, Coil Pair, Imperf	50.00
1520b	Same, Line Pair	70.00
1563a	10¢ Lexington-Concord, vert. pair, imperf. horiz	500.00
1579a	10¢ Madonna, Imperf. Pair	125.00
1580a	10¢ Prang, Imperf. Pair	125.00
1596a	13¢ Eagle & Shield, Imperf. Pair	50.00
1597a	15¢ Flag (from Sheet), Imperf. Pair	20.00
1615b	7.9¢ Drum, Coil, Pair, Imperf	550.00
1615Ce	8.4¢ Piano, Coil, Precancelled Pr., Imperf. Between	55.00
1615Cf	8.4¢ Piano, Coil, Precancelled Pair, Imperf	17.50
1615Cf	Same, Line Pair	35.00
1616a	9¢ Capitol, Coil Pair, Imperf. (VG)	75.00
1616a	Same, Line Pair (VG)	175.00
1616a	Same, Pair F-VF	180.00
1616a	Same, Line Pair F-VF	475.00

IMPERFORATE MAJOR ERRORS (cont.)

Scott's No.		F-VF NH
1617b	10¢ Petition, Coil Pair, Imperf	65.00
1617b	Same, Line Pair	150.00
1617bv	Same, Pair, dull finish gum	65.00
1618b	13¢ Liberty Bell, Coil Pair, Imperf	30.00
1618b	Same, Line Pair	60.00
1618Cd	15¢ Flag, Coil Pair, Imperf	25.00
1618Ce	Same, Strip of 4, middle pair imperf. between	175.00
1622a	13¢ Flag, Horiz. Pair, Imperf. Between	50.00
1622d	Same, Imperf. Pair	175.00
1625a	13¢ Flag, Coil Pair, Imperf	25.00
1699a	13¢ Maas, horiz. pair, imperf. vert	425.00
1701a	13¢ Nativity, Imperf. Pair	125.00
1702a	13¢ Currier & Ives, Imperf. Pair	135.00
1703a	13¢ Currier & Ives, Imperf. Pair	150.00
1704a	13¢ Princeton, Horiz. Pair, Imperf. Vert	550.00
1711a	13¢ Colorado, Horiz. Pair, Imperf. between	535.00
1729a	13¢ G.W. at Valley Forge, Imperf. Pair	100.00
1730a	13¢ Christmas Mailbox, Imperf. Pair	295.00
1734a	13¢ Indian Head Penny, Horiz. Pair, Imperf. Vert	350.00
1735a	(15¢) "A" Eagle, Vert. Pair, Imperf	75.00
1735b	(15¢) "A" Eagle, Vert. Pair, Imperf. horiz.	325.00
1743a	(15¢) "A" Eagle, Coil Pair, Imperf	125.00
1768a	15¢ Christmas Madonna, Imperf. Pair	100.00
1769a	15¢ Hobby Horse, Imperf. Pair	125.00
1783-86b	15¢ Flora, Block of 4, Imperf	675.00
1787a	15¢ Seeing Eye Dog, Imperf. Pair	475.00
1789c	Same, Perf. 12, vert. pair, imperf. horiz	210.00
1789d	Same, Perf. 11, vert. pair, imperf. horiz	165.00
1799a	15¢ 1979 Madonna & Child, Imperf. Pair	110.00
1801a	15¢ Will Rogers, Imperf. Pair	275.00
1811a	1¢ Quill Pen, Coil Pair, Imperf	225.00
1811a	Same, Line Pair	350.00
1813b	3.5¢ Violin, Coil Pair, Imperf. (VG)	120.00
1813b	Same, F-VF	265.00
1816b	12¢ Torch, Coil Pair, Imperf	225.00
1816b	Same, Line Pair	450.00
1820a	(18¢) "B" Eagle, Coil Pair, Imperf	120.00
1823a	15¢ Bissel, vert. pair, imperf. horiz	400.00
1825a	15¢ Veterans, horiz. pair, imperf. vert	525.00
1831a	15¢ Organized Labor, Imperf. Pair	390.00
1833a	15¢ Learning, horiz. pair, imperf. vert	265.00
1842a	15¢ 1980 Madonna, Imperf. Pair	100.00
1843a	15¢ Toy Drum, Imperf. Pair	100.00
1844a	1¢ Dorothea Dix, Imperf. Pair	400.00
1856a	14¢ S. Lewis, Vert. Pair, Imperf. Horiz	175.00
1856b	14¢ S. Lewis, Horizontal Pair, Imperf. Between	12.50
1867a	39¢ Clark, vert. pair, imperf. horiz	675.00
1890a	18¢ "Amber" Flag, Imperf. Pair	120.00
1891a	18¢ "Shining Sea", Coil Pair, Imperf	22.50
1893b	6¢/18¢ Booklet, Imperf. Vertical Between, Perfs at Left	95.00
1894a	20¢ Flag, Vert. Pair, Imperf	50.00
1895a	20¢ Flag, Coil Pair, Imperf	10.00
1897Ae	2¢ Locomotive, Coil Pair, Imperf	65.00
1901b	5.9¢ Bicycle, Precancelled Coil Pair, Imperf	225.00
1903b	9.3¢ Mail Wagon, Precancelled Coil Pair, Imperf	150.00
1904b	10.9¢ Hansom Cab, Prec. Coil Pair, Imperf	225.00
1906b	17¢ Electric Car, Coil Pair, Imperf	210.00
1906c	Same, Precancelled Pair, Imperf	675.00
1907a	18¢ Surrey, Coil Pair, Imperf	135.00
1908a	20¢ Firepumper, Coil Pair, Imperf	150.00
1908a	Same, Line Pair	325.00
1927a	18¢ Alcoholism, Imperf. Pair	400.00
1934a	18¢ Remington, vert. pair, imperf. between	265.00
1939a	20¢ 1981 Madonna, Imperf. Pair	115.00
1940a	20¢ Teddy Bear, Imperf. Pair	250.00
1949b	20¢ Ram Bklt. (2 Panes) Vert. Imperf. Btwn., Perfs. at Left	175.00
1951b	20¢ Love, Imperf. Pair	325.00
2003a	20¢ Netherlands, Imperf. Pair	450.00
2005a	20¢ Consumer, Coil Pair, Imperf	120.00
2015a	20¢ Libraries, vert. pair, imperf. horiz	350.00
2026a	20¢ Madonna & Child, Imperf. Pair	160.00
2044a	20¢ Joplin, Imperf. Pair	500.00
2064a	20¢ 1983 Santa Claus, Imperf. Pair	185.00
2072a	20¢ Love, horiz. pair, imperf. vert	235.00
2092a	20¢ Waterfowl, horiz. pair, imperf. vert	475.00
2096a	20¢ Smokey the Bear, horiz. pair, imperf. between	350.00
2096b	Same, vert. pair, imperf. between	250.00
2104a	20¢ Family Unity, horiz. pair, imperf. vert	600.00
2111a	(22¢) "D" Eagle, Vert. Pair, Imperf	75.00
2112a	(22¢) "D" Eage, Coil Pair, Imperf	57.50
2115a	22¢ Flag, Coil Pair, Imperf	12.50
2126b	6¢ Tricycle, Precancelled Coil Pair, Imperf	250.00
2130b	10.1¢ Oil Wagon, Black Precancel, Coil Pair, Imperf	135.00
2130b var	10.1¢ Oil Wagon, Red Precancel, Coil Pair, Imperf	22.50
2133b	12.5¢ Pushcart, Precancelled Coil Pair, Imperf	65.00
2134a	14¢ Iceboat, Coil Pair, Imperf	110.00
2135a	17¢ Dogsled, Coil Pair, Imperf. Miscut	650.00
2136a	25¢ Bread Wagon, Coil Pair, Imperf	18.50
2142a	22¢ Winter Olympics, vert. pair, imperf. horiz	700.00
2146a	22¢ A. Adams, Imperf. Pair	325.00
2165a	22¢ 1985 Madonna, Imperf. Pair	135.00
2166a	22¢ Poinsettia, Imperf. Pair	150.00
2210a	22¢ Public Hospitals, vert. pair, imperf. horiz	375.00
2228b	4¢ Stagecoach "B" Press, Coil Pair, Imperf	450.00
2259a	13.2¢ Coal Car, Coil Pair, Imperf	125.00

IMPERFORATE MAJOR ERRORS (cont.)

Scott's No.		F-VF NH
2261a	16.7¢ Popcorn Wagon Pair, Imperf	250.00
2263a	20¢ Cable Car, Coil Pair, Imperf	110.00
2265a	21¢ Railway Car, Coil Pair, Imperf	80.00
2279a	(25¢) "E" Earth, Coil Pair, Imperf	115.00
2280a	25¢ Flag Over Yosemite, Coil Pair, Block Tagged, Imperf	25.00
2280a var	25¢ Flag Over Yosemite, Coil Pair, Prephosphor paper, Impf	12.50
2281a	25¢ Honeybee Coil, Imperf. Pair	60.00
2453a	5¢ Canoe, Coil Pair, Imperf	575.00
2457a	10¢ Tractor Trailer, Coil Pair, Imperf	650.00
2464a	23¢ Lunch Wagon, Coil Pair, Imperf	300.00
2518a	(29¢) "F" Coil, Imperf. Pair	45.00
2521a	4¢ Non-denominated, vert. pair, imperf. horiz	225.00
2523b	29¢ Mt. Rushmore, Coil Pair, Imperf	25.00
2550a	29¢ Cole Porter, vert. pair, imperf. horiz	675.00
2579a	(29¢) Santa in Chimney, horiz. pair, imperf. vertically	500.00
2579b	(29¢) Santa in Chimney, Vert. Pair, Imperf. Horiz	600.00
2603a	(10¢) Eagle & Shield, Coil Pair, Imperf	45.00
2607a	23¢ USA Pre-sort, Coil Pair, Imperf	150.00
2609a	29¢ Flag over White House, Coil Pair, Imperf	32.50
2609b	Same, Pair, Imperf. Between	95.00

AIRMAILS & SPECIAL DELIVERY

Scott's No.		F-VF NH
C23a	6¢ Vertical Pair, Imperf. Horizontal	325.00
C73a	10¢ Stars, Coil Pair, Imperf	590.00
C82a	11¢ Jet, Coil Pair, Imperf	250.00
C82a	Same, Line Pair	350.00
C83a	13¢ Winged Env., Coil Pair, Imperf	90.00
C83a	Same, Line Pair	165.00
E15c	10¢ Motorcycle, horiz. pair, imperf. between	325.00

COLOR ERRORS & VARIETIES

Scott's No.		F-VF NH
499 var.	2¢ Washington, "Boston Lake", with PFC	175.00
1895 var.	20¢ Flag, Blue "Supreme Court" color var	175.00
2115 var.	22¢ Flag, Blue "Capitol Bldg." color var	12.00
C23c	6¢ Ultramarine & Carmine	200.00

COLOR OMITTED - MAJOR ERRORS

Scott's No.		F-VF NH
1271a	5¢ Florida, ochre omitted	500.00
1331-32 var.	5¢ Space Twins, red stripes of capsule flag omitted, single in block of 9	195.00
1355a	6¢ Disney, ochre omitted	750.00
1363c	6¢ Christmas, 1968, light yellow omitted	110.00
1384c	6¢ Christmas, 1969, light green omitted	20.00
1414b	6¢ Christmas, 1970, black omitted	700.00
1444a	8¢ Christmas, gold omitted	575.00
1471a	8¢ Christmas, 1972, pink omitted	260.00
1501a	8¢ Electronics, black omitted	700.00
1509b	10¢ Crossed Flags, blue omitted	175.00
1511a	10¢ Zip, yellow omitted	60.00
1547a	10¢ Energy Conservation, blue & orange omitted	800.00
1547b	10¢ Energy Conservation, orange & green omitted	800.00
1547c	10¢ Energy Conservation, green omitted	950.00

COLOR OMITTED - MAJOR ERRORS (cont.)

Scott's No.		F-VF NH
1557a	10¢ Mariner, red omitted	600.00
1559a	8¢ Ludington, green inscription on gum omitted	325.00
1560a	10¢ Salem Poor, green inscription on gum omitted	325.00
1561a	10¢ Salomon, green inscription on gum omitted	325.00
1561b	10¢ Salomon, red color omitted	275.00
1596b	13¢ Eagle & Shield, yellow omitted	225.00
1597b	15¢ McHenry Flag, gray omitted	475.00
1608a	50¢ Lamp, black color omitted	400.00
1610a	$1.00 Lamp, brown color omitted	325.00
1610b	$1.00 Lamp, tan, yellow & orange omitted	375.00
1618Cf	15¢ Flag Coil, grey omitted	55.00
1690a	13¢ Franklin, light blue omitted	425.00
1800b	15¢ Christmas, yellow, green & tan omitted	775.00
1894c	20¢ Flag, dark blue omitted	100.00
1894d	20¢ Flag, black omitted	350.00
1895b	20¢ Flag Coil, black omitted	65.00
1926a	18¢ Millay, black omitted	525.00
1934b	18¢ Remington, brown omitted	600.00
1937-38b	18¢ Yorktown, se-tenant pair, black omitted	575.00
1951c	20¢ Love, blue omitted	225.00
2014a	20¢ Peace Garden, black, green & brown omitted	285.00
2045a	20¢ Medal of Honor, red omitted	325.00
2055-58b	20¢ Inventors, Block of 4, black omitted	490.00
2059-62b	20¢ Streetcars, Block of 4, black omitted	550.00
2145a	22¢ Ameripex, black, blue & red omitted	250.00
2201b	22¢ Stamp Collecting, cplt. bklt. of 2 panes, black omitted	140.00
2235-38b	22¢ Navajo Art, black omitted	375.00
2281b	25¢ Honeybee, black (engraved) omitted	85.00
2281c	25¢ Honeybee, Black (litho) omitted	550.00
2349a	22¢ U.S./Morocco, black omitted	350.00
2399a	25¢ Christmas, 1988, gold omitted	35.00
2421a	25¢ Bill of Rights, black (engraved) omitted	325.00
2443b	15¢ Beach Umbrella, sgl. from bklt., dark blue omitted	250.00
2474b	25¢ Lighthouse bklt., white omitted, cplt. bklt. of 4 panes	350.00
	Same, Individual Pane	90.00
2476a	$2 Bobcat, black omitted	350.00
2491a	45¢ Sunfish, black omitted	550.00
2561a	29¢ Washington, DC Bicentennial, black "USA 29¢" omitted	250.00
C76a	10¢ Man on the Moon, red omitted	450.00
C76 var.	10¢ Man on the Moon, patch only omitted	250.00
J89a	1¢ Postage Due, Black Numeral omitted	350.00

POSTAL STATIONERY ENTIRES

Scott's No.		F-VF NH
U583b	13¢ Golf, black & blue omitted	550.00
U586a	15¢ Star, black surcharge omitted	450.00
U587a	15¢ Auto Racing, black omitted	150.00
U595 var.	15¢ Veterinarians, brown & grey omitted	125.00
U597a	15¢ Bicycle, blue omitted	95.00
U599a	15¢ Honeybee, brown omitted	165.00
U612 var.	8.4¢ Constellation, black omitted	625.00
U615 var.	25¢ Stars, dark red omitted	175.00
U623 var.	29¢ Stars & Bars, red omitted	450.00
UX50a	4¢ Customs, blue omitted	450.00

U.S. ARROW AND CENTER LINE BLOCKS

NOTE: VF HINGED (#285/329) ARE AVAILABLE AT A DISCOUNT OF 35%
NOTE: VF HINGED (#314/CE2) ARE AVAILABLE AT A DISCOUNT OF 25%

Scott's No.		ARROW BLOCKS NH VF	ARROW BLOCKS NH F-VF	ARROW BLOCKS Unused F-VF	CENTER LINE BLKS. NH VF	CENTER LINE BLKS. NH F-VF	CENTER LINE BLKS. Unused F-VF
	1898-1907 Commemoratives, Perf. 12						
285	1¢ Trans-Miss.	200.00	125.00	95.00	...	...	...
286	2¢ Trans-Miss	185.00	115.00	85.00	...	...	...
294	1¢ Pan-American	140.00	95.00	67.50	...	...	...
295	2¢ Pan-American	140.00	95.00	67.50	...	...	...
323	1¢ Louisiana	200.00	125.00	90.00	...	...	...
324	2¢ Louisiana	160.00	105.00	80.00	...	...	...
328	1¢ Jamestown	165.00	95.00	67.50	...	...	...
329	2¢ Jamestown	210.00	120.0	85.00	...	...	...
	1906-09 Imperforates, D.L. Wmk.						
314	1¢ Franklin	155.00	120.00	85.00	225.00	175.00	140.00
320	2¢ Washington	155.00	120.00	85.00	215.00	165.00	135.00
343	1¢ Franklin	45.00	35.00	27.50	72.50	55.00	45.00
344	2¢ Washington	55.00	42.50	32.50	85.00	65.00	55.00
345	3¢ Washington	110.00	85.00	62.50	160.00	120.00	100.00
346	4¢ Washington	185.00	140.00	105.00	275.00	210.00	185.00
347	5¢ Washington	300.00	235.00	175.00	425.00	325.00	295.00
368	2¢ Lincoln Mem.	170.00	125.00	95.00	220.00	170.00	135.00
371	2¢ Alaska-Yukon	240.00	185.00	125.00	300.00	230.00	180.00
373	2¢ Hudson-Fulton	260.00	200.00	150.00	360.00	275.00	200.00
	1911-12 Imperforate, S.L. Wmk.						
383	1¢ Franklin	22.50	16.50	13.50	42.50	32.50	24.00
384	2¢ Wash. "Two"	37.50	27.50	20.00	75.00	55.00	40.00
408	1¢ Washington	10.00	7.50	5.50	17.50	13.50	10.00
409	2¢ Wash. "2"	11.50	9.00	6.50	21.50	16.50	12.50
	1916-20 Imperforates, Unwatermarked						
481	1¢ Washington	7.50	6.00	4.25	12.50	10.00	7.00
482	2¢ Washington	9.75	8.00	5.75	12.00	9.50	7.00
483	3¢ Wash., Type I	95.00	75.00	55.00	110.00	87.50	65.00
484	3¢ Wash., Type II	80.00	65.00	45.00	95.00	77.50	55.00
531	1¢ Offset	80.00	65.00	45.00	95.00	75.00	55.00
532	2¢ Offset, Type IV	250.00	200.00	140.00	300.00	240.00	190.00
533	2¢ Offset, Type V	1250.00	1000.00	750.00	1375.00	1100.00	850.00
534	2¢ Offset, Type Va	90.00	70.00	55.00	110.00	85.00	65.00
534A	2¢ Offset, Type VI	235.00	185.00	135.00	275.00	225.00	175.00
535	3¢ Offset	75.00	60.00	42.50	85.00	67.50	47.50
	1923-31 Perforated Issues						
571	$1 Lincoln Mem.	350.00	250.00	185.00	...	...	...
572	$2 Capitol	850.00	675.00	475.00	...	...	...
573	$5 Freedom	1600.00	1200.00	900.00	1750.00	1300.00	975.00
620	2¢ Norse	35.00	26.50	20.00	40.00	32.50	26.00
621	5¢ Norse	150.00	120.00	85.00	165.00	135.00	100.00
651	2¢ G.R. Clark	4.75	3.60	3.00	...	...	...
702	2¢ Red Cross	1.35	1.10	.85	...	...	...
703	2¢ Yorktown	2.95	2.25	1.75	3.25	2.50	1.95
	1923-26 Imperforate Issues						
575	1¢ Franklin	55.00	40.00	30.00	65.00	47.50	35.00
576	1½¢ Harding, Flat	11.00	8.50	5.50	17.50	13.50	10.00
577	2¢ Washington	14.00	11.00	8.00	25.00	20.00	16.00
611	2¢ Harding Mem	47.50	37.50	27.50	95.00	75.00	55.00
631	1½¢ Harding, Rotary	17.50	13.50	10.00	32.50	25.00	18.00
	1938 Presidential Series						
832	$1 Wilson	52.50	45.00	...	57.50	50.00	...
833	$2 Harding	150.00	125.00	...	160.00	120.00	...
834	$5 Coolidge	650.00	550.00	...	685.00	575.00	...
	1918-38 Airmail Issues						
C1	6¢ Curtiss Jenny	550.00	400.00	300.00	600.00	435.00	335.00
C2	16¢ Curtiss Jenny	700.00	525.00	395.00	775.00	575.00	425.00
C3	24¢ Curtiss Jenny	700.00	525.00	395.00	775.00	575.00	425.00
C11	5¢ Beacon	33.50	25.00	18.00	...	...	...
C23	6¢ Eagle	3.00	2.50	2.00	3.35	2.75	2.25
CE2	16¢ Air Special	3.00	2.50	2.00	3.35	2.75	2.25

UNEXPLODED BOOKLETS

Complete booklets from BK104 to date will have fresh, uncreased covers. Prior to BK104, covers may show some evidence of handling such as minor creases, wear & pencil marks. Numbers in "( )" indicate the number of panes in each booklet. The absence of ( ) indicates that the booklet contains only one pane. Many of the booklets exist with a variety of different covers. Those interested in more complete information should refer to the latest edition of the Scott U.S. Specialized Catalog or contact: The Bureau Issues Assn., P.O. Box 1047, Belleville, IL 62223.

BK 58

BK 105

Scott #	Cvr. Value/Panes	F-VF NH
424d		
BK 41	25¢ (4)	32.50
BK 42	97¢ (16)	100.00
498e		
BK 53	25¢ (4) "POD" cvr	35.00
BK 54	97¢ (16)	55.00
BK55	25¢ (4)	67.50
498e, 499e		
BK 56	73¢ Combo (4+4)	65.00
498e, 554c		
BK 57	73¢ Combo (4+4)	75.00
499e		
BK 58	25¢ (2)	45.00
501b		
BK 62	37¢ (2)	150.00
502b		
BK 63	37¢ (2)	135.00

Scott #	Cvr. Value/Panes	F-VF NH
552a		
BK 66	25¢ (4)	35.00
552a, 554c		
BK 68	73¢ Combo (4+4)	85.00
554c		
BK 69	25¢ (2)	25.00
583a		
BK 72	25¢ (2)	225.00
632a		
BK 75	25¢ (4)	60.00
632a, 634d		
BK 79	73¢ Combo (4+4) "Postrider" cvr	70.00
634d		
BK 80	25¢ (2)	7.50
BK 81	49¢ (4)	14.50
BK 82	97¢ "Postrider" (8)	30.00

Scott #	Cvr. Value/Panes	F-VF NH
720b		
BK 84	37¢ (2)	115.00
804b **3 mm gutters**		
BK 86	25¢ (4)	45.00
804b, 806a		
BK 89	73¢ Combo (4+4)	165.00
804b **2.5 mm gutters**		
BK 90	25¢ (4)	10.00
BK 91	97¢ "POD" cvr. (16)	60.00
804b, 806a		
BK 92	73¢ Combo (4+4), "Postrider"	32.50
BK 93	73¢ Combo (4+4), "P.O. Seal"	40.00
806b **2.5 mm gutters**		
BK 96	25¢ "Postrider" (2)	18.50
BK 97	25¢ "P.O. Seal" (2)	75.00
BK 98	49¢ "Postrider" (4)	40.00
BK 99	49¢ "P.O. Seal" (4)	45.00
807a **3 mm gutters**		
BK 100	37¢ (2)	90.00
807a **2.5 mm gutters**		
BK 102	37¢ (2)	18.50
BK 103	73¢ (4)	45.00
1035a **"Wet Printing"**		
BK 104	37¢ (2)	20.00
BK 105	73¢ (4)	35.00

Scott #	Cvr. Value/Panes	F-VF NH
1035f **"Dry Printing"**		
BK 104	37¢ (2)	15.00
BK 105	73¢ (4)	25.00
1036a		
BK 106	97¢ on 37¢ (4)	50.00
BK 107	97¢ on 73¢ (4)	37.50
BK 108	97¢ blue, *yellow* (4)	50.00
BK 109	97¢ blue, *pink* (4)	14.50
1213a		
BK 110	$1.00 Slogan 1 (4)	32.50
BK 111	$1.00 Slogan 2 (4) "Postrider" cvr.	115.00
BK 112	$1.00 Slogan 2 (4) "Mr. Zip" cvr	97.50
BK 113	$1.00 Slogan 3 (4)	12.50
1213c **"Tagged"**		
BK 114	$1.00 Slogan 2 (4) "Mr. Zip"	325.00
BK 115	$1.00 Slogan 3 (4) "Mr. Zip"	6.50
1278a, 1284b		
BK 116	$2 Combo (1+4)	8.00
1280c, 1284c		
BK 117	$1 Combo (1+3)	6.25
1288Bc		
BK 117A	$3.60 (3)	11.00

UNEXPLODED BOOKLETS

Scott # Cvr. Value/Panes F-VF NH

1393a, 1278a
BK117B $2 Combo (4+1), "P.O. Seal" cvr .. 10.75
BK118 $2 Combo (4+1), "Ike" cvr 7.00
1393ae,1278ae
BK119 $2 Combo (4+1), Dull gum............. 8.75
1393b, 1280a
BK120 $1 Combo (3+1) 5.95
1395a
BK121 $1.92 (3).................... 7.00
1395b, 1278b
BK122 $1 Combo (2+1) 4.75
1395d, 1395c
BK123 $2 Combo (3+1)...... 10.95
1510b
BK124 $1 (2)......................... 4.75
1510c
BK125 $4 (5)....................... 13.00
1510d, C79a
BK126 $1.25 Combo (1+1). 10.75
1595a, 1280c
BK127 90¢ Combo (1+2)...... 5.00
1595c, 1595b
BK128 $2.99 Combo (2+1)... 8.25
1595d BK129 $1.30 (2)....... 5.00
1598a BK130 $1.20 .... 5.25
1623a BK131 $1 .... 3.25
1623c BK132 $1 .... 39.75
1736a BK133 $3.60 (3)....... 8.95
1737a BK134 $2.40 (2)....... 6.95
1742a BK135 $3 (2)........... 9.95
1819a BK136 $4.32 (3)..... 15.75
1889a BK137 $3.60 (2)..... 18.50
1893a BK138 $1.20 .... 4.25
1896a BK139 $1.20 .... 3.50
1896b BK140 $2 .... 5.75
1896b BK140A $4 (2) 11.50
1909a BK140B $28.05 (3) 83.50
1948a BK141 $4 (2).......... 11.95
1949a BK142 $4 (2).......... 14.50
1949d BK142a $4 Type II(2)... 29.50
2113a BK143 $4.40 (2).......... 23.50
2116a BK144 $1.10................. 5.00

Scott # Cvr. Value/Panes F-VF NH

2116a BK145 $2.20 (2).......... 10.00
2121a BK146 $4.40 (2) Multi-Seashells cvr....... 12.75
*** 7 diff. cvrs. needed for all 25 shells.**
2121a BK147 $4.40 (2) "Beach" cvr 11.95
2122a BK148 $32.25 (3)........ 82.50
2122c BK149 $32.25 (3)...... 100.00
2183a BK150 $5.00 (2).......... 13.50
2197a BK151 $1.50................. 4.50
2197a BK152 $3.00 (2)............ 8.95
2201a BK153 $1.76 (2)............ 6.00
2201b BK153 $1.76 (2) **Missing Black**........... 140.00
2209a BK154 $2.20 (2).......... 19.50
2274a BK155 $2.20............... 18.00
2276a BK156 $4.40............... 12.00
2282a BK157 $5.00 (2).......... 19.50
2283a BK158 $5.00 (2).......... 17.50
2283c BK159 $5.00 (2) "Blue Sky" 190.00
2285b BK160 $5.00 (2).......... 13.50
2285Ac BK161 $3.00 (2)............ 8.50
2359a BK162 $4.40 (4).......... 16.95
2366a BK163 $4.40 (4).......... 15.95
2385a BK164 $5.00 (4).......... 39.95
2396a, 2398a
BK 165 $3.00 Combo (1+1).... 11.00
2409a BK166 $5.00 (4).......... 15.95
2427a BK167 $5.00 (2).......... 14.95
2429a BK168 $5.00 (2).......... 17.95
2441a BK169 $5.00 (2).......... 17.95
2443a BK170 $3.00 (2)............ 8.75
2474a BK171 $5.00 (4).......... 19.75
2493a BK172 $5.80 BEP(2) .. 17.95
2493a BK174 $2.90 (1)............ 9.95
2494a BK173 $5.80 KCS(2)... 21.95
2495a BK175A $2.90............... 5.95
2495a BK175 $5.80 (2).......... 13.95
2505a BK179 $5.00 (2).......... 15.95
2514a BK180 $5.00 (2).......... 13.95
2516a BK181 $5.00 (2).......... 13.95
2519a BK182 ($2.90) BEP 8.00
2519a BK183 ($5.80) BEP(2). 16.00
2520a BK184 ($2.90) KCS.... 19.00

Scott # Cvr. Value/Panes F-VF NH

2527a BK185 $5.80 (2) 14.95
2528a BK186 $2.90 (1) 7.50
2528a BK186A WCSE Ticket Cvr 19.95
2530a BK187 $3.80 (2) 9.50
2536a BK188 $5.80 (2) 16.95
2549a BK189 $5.80 (4) 21.95
2552a BK190 $5.80 (4) 16.95
2566a BK191 $5.80 (2) 16.95
2577a BK192 $5.80 (2) 17.50
2578a BK193 ($5.80) (2)........15.95
2585a BK194 ($5.80) (5)........27.50
2593a BK196 $2.90 (1) 7.95
2593a BK197 $5.80 (2) 13.95
2594a BK197A $2.90 (1)..........6.95
2646a BK195 $5.80 (4) 19.95
2709a BK202 $5.80 (4) 16.95
2710a BK202A $5.80 (2)........15.95
2718a BK203 $5.80 (5) 18.75
2737a,2737b
BK204 $5.80 Combo (2 + 1) 17.50
2745a BK207 $5.80 (4) 17.95
2764a BK208 $5.80 (4) 17.95
2770a BK209 $5.80 (5) 17.50
2778a BK210 $5.80 (5) 17.50
2790a BK211 $5.80 (5) 14.95
2798a,b BK212 $5.80 (2) 14.95
2806b BK213 $2.90 (2) 7.50
2814a BK214 $5.80 (2) 13.95
2833a BK215 $5.80 (4) 13.95
2847a BK216 $5.80 (4) 13.95
2871b BK217 $5.80 (2) 12.60
2872a BK218 $5.80 (1) 12.50
2881a BK219 ($3.20) (1)..........6.35
2883a BK220 ($3.20) (1)..........6.35
2883a BK221 ($6.40) (2)........12.60
2884a BK222 ($6.40) (2)........12.60
2885a BK223 ($6.40) (2)........12.60

Scott # Cvr. Value/Panes F-VF NH

AIRMAIL BOOKLETS

C10a BKC1 61¢ (2) 235.00
C25a
BKC2 37¢ (2) 9.00
BKC3 73¢ (4) 17.50
C39a
BKC4 73¢ (2) 24.50
C51a
BKC5 85¢ on 73¢ (2) 45.00
BKC6 85¢ (2) 27.50
C60a
BKC7 85¢ (2) Blue covers.... 37.50
BKC8 85¢ (2)Red covers 40.00
C64b
BKC9 80¢ Slogan 1 (2) 14.50
BKC10 $2.00 Slogan 1 (5) 39.50
BKC11 80¢ Slogan 3 (2) 29.50
BKC12 $2.00 Slog. 2 (5), "Wings" cvr.............. 385.00
BKC13 $2.00 Slog. 2 (5), "Mr. Zip" cvr 375.00
BKC15 $2.00 Slog. 3 (5) 100.00
C64c **Slogan 3, Tagged**
BKC16 80¢ black (2).............. 33.75
BKC19 $2.00 red (5), "Mr. Zip" cvr 8.75
C72b BKC20 $4.00 (5)....... 13.75
C72c BKC21 $1.00 (2)......... 8.50
C78a, 1280c
BKC22 $1 Combo (2+1)4.00
C79a, 1510d
BKC23 $1.25 Combo (1+1).............. 10.75

POSTAL INSURANCE BOOKLETS

QI1 (10¢) "Insured P.O.D. V" ... 125.00
QI2 (20¢) "Insured U.S. Mail" White cover........ 6.00
Black cover........ 5.00
QI3 (40¢) "Insured U.S. Mail" (black)................ 4.50
QI4 (50¢) "Insured U.S. Mail" (green) 2.50
QI5 (45¢) "Insured U.S. Mail" (red) 4.50

BK 173

BK 196

Ten-10¢ Airmail Stamps
UNITED STATES POSTAGE STAMPS
PRICE $1.00
For Vending Machine Sale Only

BKC 21

MINT POSTAL STATIONERY ENTIRES

U 362

U546

Scott's No.		Mint Entire
	1893 Columbian Issue	
U348	1¢ Deep Blue	2.75
U349	2¢ Violet	2.50
U350	5¢ Chocolate	15.00
U351	10¢ Slate Brown	60.00
	1899 Issues	
U352	1¢ Green	1.50
U353	1¢ Green, amber	7.75
U354	1¢ Green, or. buff	13.50
U355	1¢ Green, blue	12.75
U356	1¢ Green, manila	6.50
W357	1¢ Wrapper	8.75
U358	2¢ Carmine	8.50
U359	2¢ Carmine, amber	26.75
U360	2¢ Carmine, or. buff	29.75
U361	2¢ Carmine, blue	67.50
U362	2¢ Carmine	.65
U363	2¢ Carmine, amber	3.25
U364	2¢ Carmine, or. buff	2.75
U365	2¢ Carmine, blue	3.50
W366	2¢ Wrapper	12.50
U367	2¢ Carmine	9.50
U368	2¢ Carmine, amber	22.50
U369	2¢ Carmine, or. buff	33.50
U370	2¢ Carmine, blue	22.50
U371	4¢ Brown	28.75
U372	4¢ Brown, amber	29.50
U374	4¢ Brown	25.00
U375	4¢ Brown, amber	50.00
W376	4¢ Wrapper	23.75
U377	5¢ Blue	13.75
U378	5¢ Blue, amber	20.75
	1903-04 Issues	
U379	1¢ Green	1.10
U380	1¢ Green, amber	18.75
U381	1¢ Green, or. buff	16.50
U382	1¢ Green, blue	19.50
U383	1¢ Green, manila	4.35
W384	1¢ Wrapper	2.00
U385	2¢ Carmine	.85
U386	2¢ Carmine, amber	3.65
U387	2¢ Carmine, or. buff	2.50
U388	2¢ Carmine, blue	3.25
W389	2¢ Wrapper	21.50
U390	4¢ Chocolate	26.50
U391	4¢ Chocolate, amber	26.50
W392	4¢ Wrapper	25.00
U393	5¢ Blue	25.00
U394	5¢ Blue, amber	25.00
U395	2¢ Carmine (1904)	1.00
U396	2¢ Carmine, amber	11.75

Scott's No.		Mint Entire
U397	2¢ Carmine, or. buff	7.50
U398	2¢ Carmine, blue	5.75
W399	2¢ Wrapper	20.00
	1907-16 Issues	
U400	1¢ Green	.50
U401	1¢ Green, amber	1.10
U402	1¢ Green, or. buff	5.95
U403	1¢ Green, blue	5.95
U404	1¢ Green, manila	4.50
W405	1¢ Wrapper	.75
U406	2¢ Brown red	1.75
U407	2¢ Brown red, amber	7.75
U408	2¢ Brown red, or. buff	10.75
U409	2¢ Brown red, blue	6.75
W410	2¢ Wrapper	52.50
U411	2¢ Carmine	.60
U412	2¢ Carmine, amber	1.10
U413	2¢ Carmine, or. buff	.65
U414	2¢ Carmine, blue	1.10
W415	2¢ Wrapper	9.50
U416	4¢ Black	10.00
U417	4¢ Black, amber	12.50
U418	5¢ Blue	12.50
U419	5¢ Blue, amber	18.50
	1916-32 Issues	
U420	1¢ Green	.30
U421	1¢ Green, amber	.60
U422	1¢ Green, or. buff	2.75
U423	1¢ Green, blue	.85
U424	1¢ Green, manila	9.50
W425	1¢ Wrapper	.60
U428	1¢ Green, brown	12.50
U429	2¢ Carmine	.35
U430	2¢ Carmine, amber	.45
U431	2¢ Carmine, or. buff	4.50
U432	2¢ Carmine, blue	.60
W433	2¢ Wrapper	.50
U436	3¢ Dark violet	.70
U436f	3¢ Purple (1932)	.50
U437	3¢ Dark violet, amber	6.75
U437a	3¢ Purple, amber (1932)	.75
U438	3¢ Dark violet, buff	32.50
U439	3¢ Dark violet, blue	10.75
U439a	3¢ Purple, blue (1932)	.70
U440	4¢ Black	3.25
U441	4¢ Black, amber	5.50
U442	4¢ Black, blue	5.50
U443	5¢ Blue	6.50
U444	5¢ Blue, amber	6.00
U445	5¢ Blue, blue	8.75

Scott's No.		Mint Entire
	1920-21 Surcharge Issues	
U446	2¢ on 3¢ (U436)	18.50
U447	2¢ on 3¢ (U436)	9.50
U448	2¢ on 3¢ (U436)	3.25
U449	2¢ on 3¢ (U437)	7.75
U450	2¢ on 3¢ (U438)	19.50
U451	2¢ on 3¢ (U439)	14.75
U458	2¢ on 3¢ (U436)	.70
U459	2¢ on 3¢ (U437)	4.25
U460	2¢ on 3¢ (U438)	5.00
U461	2¢ on 3¢ (U439)	6.00
U468	2¢ on 3¢ (U436)	1.00
U469	2¢ on 3¢ (U437)	5.50
U470	2¢ on 3¢ (U438)	7.75
U471	2¢ on 3¢ (U439)	11.00
U472	2¢ on 4¢ (U390)	30.00
U473	2¢ on 4¢ (U391)	27.50
	1925 Issues	
U481	1½¢ Brown	.65
U482	1½¢ Brown, amber	1.80
U483	1½¢ Brown, blue	2.25
U484	1½¢ Brown, manila	12.50
W485	1½¢ Wrapper	1.20
U490	1½¢ on 1¢ (U400)	7.00
U491	1½¢ on 1¢ (U401)	14.50
U495	1½¢ on 1¢ (U420)	.75
U496	1½¢ on 1¢ (U421)	25.00
U497	1½¢ on 1¢ (U422)	6.25
U498	1½¢ on 1¢ (U423)	2.25
U499	1½¢ on 1¢ (U424)	22.50
U500	1½¢ on 1¢ (U428)	70.00
U501	1½¢ on 1¢ (U426)	70.00
U508	1½¢ on 1¢ (U353)	70.00
U509	1½¢ on 1¢ (U380)	27.50
U509B	1½¢ on 1¢ (U381)	70.00
U510	1½¢ on 1¢ (U400)	4.00
U512	1½¢ on 1¢ (U402)	12.50
U513	1½¢ on 1¢ (U403)	8.50
U514	1½¢ on 1¢ (U404)	32.50
U515	1½¢ on 1¢ (U420)	.70
U516	1½¢ on 1¢ (U421)	55.00
U517	1½¢ on 1¢ (U422)	5.50
U518	1½¢ on 1¢ (U423)	5.50
U519	1½¢ on 1¢ (U424)	32.50
U521	1½¢ on 1¢ (U420)	5.75
	1926-58 Issues	
U522	2¢ Sesquicent	2.50
U522a	Same, Die 2	13.50
U523	1¢ Wash. Bicent. ('32)	2.50
U524	1½¢ Wash. Bicent	3.75

Scott's No.		Mint Entire
U525	2¢ Wash. Bicent	.70
U526	3¢ Wash. Bicent	4.00
U527	4¢ Wash. Bicent	30.00
U528	5¢ Wash. Bicent	6.50
U529	6¢ Orange	8.75
U530	6¢ Orange, amber	16.00
U531	6¢ Orange, blue	15.75
U532	1¢ Franklin (1950)	8.00
U533	2¢ Washington	1.35
U534	3¢ Washington	.55
U535	1½¢ Washington (1952)	6.50
U536	2¢ Franklin (1958)	1.10
U537	2¢ + 2¢ Sur., Circle	4.75
U538	2¢ + 2¢ Sur., Oval	.90
U539	3¢ + 1¢ Sur., Circle	18.00
U540	3¢ + 1¢ Sur., Oval	.65
	1960-74 Issues	
U541	1¼¢ Franklin	.90
U542	2½¢ Washington	1.10
U543	4¢ Pony Express	.70
U544	5¢ Lincoln (1962)	1.00
U545	4¢ + 1¢ Sur., Frank	1.65
U546	5¢ NY World's Fair ('64)	.80
U547	1¼¢ Liberty Bell (1965)	1.00
U548	1-4/10¢ Liberty Bell ('68)	1.10
U548A	1-6/10¢ Liberty Bell ('69)	1.00
U549	4¢ Old Ironsides ('65)	1.10
U550	5¢ Eagle	1.00
U551	6¢ Liberty Head (1968)	.90
U552	4¢ + 2¢ Surcharge	4.50
U553	5¢ + 1¢ Surcharge	4.25
U554	6¢ Moby Dick (1970)	.65
U555	6¢ Brotherhood (1971)	.95
U556	1-7/10¢ Liberty Bell	.45
U557	8¢ Eagle	.55
U561	6¢ + 2¢ Liberty	1.15
U562	6¢ + 2¢ Brotherhood	2.75
U563	8¢ Bowling	.65
U564	8¢ Aging	.65
U565	8¢ Transpo. '72 (1972)	.80
U566	8¢ + 2¢ Sur., Eagle ('73)	.50
U567	10¢ Liberty Bell	.50
U568	1-8/10¢ Volunteer ('74)	.35
U569	10¢ Tennis	.50
	1975-82 Issues	
U571	10¢ Seafaring	.50
U572	13¢ Homemaker (1976)	.60
U573	13¢ Farmer (1976)	.60
U574	13¢ Doctor (1976)	.60
U575	13¢ Craftsman (1976)	.60

MINT POSTAL STATIONERY ENTIRES

U597

UC17

Scott's No.		Mint Entire
U576	13¢ Liberty Tree (1975)..	.45
U577	2¢ Star & Pinwheel ('76)	.30
U578	2.1¢ Hexagon (1977).....	.30
U579	2.7¢ U.S.A (1978).........	.35
U580	(15¢) "A" & Eagle..........	.55
U581	15¢ Uncle Sam.............	.55
U582	13¢ Bicentennial (1976).	.50
U583	13¢ Golf (1977).............	.70
U584	13¢ Conservation..........	.55
U585	13¢ Development..........	.55
U586	15¢ on 16¢ Surch ('78) ..	.55
U587	15¢ Auto Racing...........	.55
U588	15¢ on 13¢ Tree............	.55
U589	3.1¢ Non Profit..............	.30
U590	3.5¢ Violins....................	.30
U591	5.9¢ Circle (1982)..........	.30
U592	(18¢) "B" & Eagle (1981)	.55
U593	18¢ Star........................	.55
U594	(20¢) "C" & Eagle..........	.55
U595	15¢ Veterinary (1979)....	.55
U596	15¢ Soccer.....................	.90
U597	15¢ Bicycle (1980).........	.60
U598	15¢ America's Cup.........	.60
U599	15¢ Honeybee...............	.55
U600	18¢ Blinded Veteran......	.60
U601	20¢ Capitol Dome..........	.55
U602	20¢ Great Seal (1982) ...	.55
U603	20¢ Purple Heart...........	.55
	1983-89 Issues	
U604	5.2¢ Non Profit..............	.50
U605	20¢ Paralyzed Vets........	.55
U606	20¢ Small Business ('84)	.70
U607	(22¢) "D" & Eagle (1985)	.60
U608	22¢ Bison......................	.60
U609	6¢ Old Ironsides............	.35
U610	8.5¢ Mayflower (1986)...	.45
U611	25¢ Stars (1988)...........	.60
U612	8.4¢ USS Const............	.40
U613	25¢ Snowflake..............	.70
U614	25¢ Philatelic Env. ('89).	.55
U615	25¢ Stars Security Env ..	.55
U616	25¢ Love........................	.55
U617	25¢ WSE Space Sta......	.65
	1990-94 Issues	
U618	25¢ Football...................	.60
U619	29¢ Star (1991).............	.65
U620	11.1¢ Non Profit............	.40
U621	29¢ Love........................	.65
U622	29¢ Magazine Industry...	.65
U623	29¢ Stars & Bars............	.65
U624	29¢ Country Geese........	.65
U625	29¢ Space Station ('92)	.65
U626	29¢ Western Americana	.65
U627	29¢ Environment.........	.65
U628	19.8¢ Bulk Rate..........	.55
U629	29¢ Disabled Americans	.65
U630	29¢ Kitten (1993)........	.65

Scott's No.		Mint Entire
U631	29¢ Football (1994).....	.65
	1995 Issues	
U632	32¢ Liberty Bell...........	.75
U633	(32¢) "G"......................	.75
U634	(32¢) "G", Security Envelope.......	.75
U635	(5¢) Sheep..................	.22
U636	(10¢) Eagle.................	.32
...	(32¢) Spiral Heart........	.75
	AIR MAIL ENTIRES	
	1929-44 Issues	
UC1	5¢ Blue, Die 1.............	4.50
UC2	5¢ Blue, Die 2.............	16.50
UC3	6¢ Orange, Die 2a (1934).........	1.50
UC3v	6¢ No Border..............	2.10
UC4	6¢ Orange, Die 2b (1942).........	52.50
UC4v	6¢ No Border..............	4.95
UC5	6¢ No Border, Die 2c (1944).........	1.10
UC6	6¢ Orange, Die 3 ('42)	1.65
UC6v	6¢ No Border..............	2.75
UC7	8¢ Olive Green ('32)....	16.50
	1945-47 Issues	
UC8	6¢ on 2¢ Sur., Wash...	1.65
UC9	6¢ on 2¢ Wash. Bic...	100.00
UC10	5¢ on 6¢ Orange Die 2a (1946).........	3.75
UC11	5¢ on 6¢ Or. Die 2b.....	10.00
UC12	5¢ on 6¢ Or. Die 2c......	1.25
UC13	5¢ on 6¢ Or. Die 3......	1.00
UC14	5¢ Plane, Die 1...........	1.15
UC15	5¢ Plane, Die 2...........	1.15
UC17	5¢ CIPEX (1947)..........	.55
	1950-58 Issues	
UC18	6¢ Skymaster..............	.55
UC19	6¢ on 5¢, Die 1 ('51)...	1.25
UC20	6¢ on 5¢, Die 2...........	1.15
UC21	6¢ on 5¢, Die 1 ('52)...	35.00
UC22	6¢ on 5¢, Die 2...........	5.00
UC25	6¢ FIPEX (1956).........	1.00
UC26	7¢ Skymaster (1958)...	1.00
UC27	6¢ + 1¢ Or., Die 2a....	280.00
UC28	6¢ + 1¢ Or., Die 2b......	90.00
UC29	6¢ + 1¢ Or., Die 2c......	50.00
UC30	6¢ + 1¢ Skymaster......	1.25
UC31	6¢ + 1¢ FIPEX...........	1.35
UC33	7¢ Jet, Blue................	.70
	1960-73 Issues	
UC34	7¢ Jet, Carmine..........	.70
UC36	8¢ Jet Airliner (1962)...	.80
UC37	8¢ Jet, Triangle (1965)	.55
UC37a	Same, Tagged (1967)..	1.60
UC40	10¢ Jet, Triangle ('68)..	.80
UC41	8¢ + 2¢ Surcharge.......	.90

Scott's No.		Mint Entire
UC43	1¢ Three Circles ('71)..	.65
UC45	10¢ + 1¢ Triangle........	1.85
UC47	13¢ Bird in Flight ('73).	.55
	AIRLETTER SHEETS	
	1947-71 Issues	
UC16	10¢ DC3, 2 Lines........	7.50
UC16a	10¢ 4 Lines Letter (1951)....................	17.50
UC16c	10¢ Aero., 4 Lines (1953)....................	52.50
UC16d	10¢ Aero., 3 Lines (1955)....................	8.00
UC32	10¢ Jet, 2 Lines ('59)...	6.50
UC32a	10¢ Jet, 3 Lines ('58)...	10.75
UC35	11¢ Jet & Globe ('61)..	3.25
UC38	11¢ J.F. Kennedy (1965)....................	3.50
UC39	13¢ J.F. Kennedy (1967)....................	3.00
UC42	13¢ Human Rights (1968)..........................	9.00
UC44	15¢ Birds,Letter ('71)...	1.50
UC44a	15¢ w/"Aerogramme" ..	1.50
	1973-81 Issues	
UC46	15¢ Ballooning...........	.75
UC48	18¢ "USA" (1974)........	.85
UC49	18¢ NATO..................	.85
UC50	22¢ "USA" (1976)........	.85
UC51	22¢ "USA" (1978)........	.85
UC52	22¢ Moscow Olym. ('79)	1.50
UC53	30¢ "USA", Blue, Red & Brown (1980)	.75
UC54	30¢ "USA", Yel., Bl.&Blk (1981)........	.75
	1982-91 Issues	
UC55	30¢ World Trade.........	.75
UC56	30¢ Comm. Year (1983)	.75
UC57	30¢ Olympics.............	.75
UC58	36¢ Landsat Satellite (85)	.85
UC59	36¢ Travel.................	.85
UC60	36¢ Mark Twain/ Halley's Comet.......	.85
UC61	39¢ Styl. Aero (1988)..	.90
UC62	39¢ Mont. Blair (1989).	.90
UC63	45¢ Eagle,blue paper(91)	.95
UC63a	Eagle, white paper	.95

Scott's No.		Mint Entire
	OFFICIAL MAIL ENTIRES	
UO73	20¢ Eagle ('83)...........	1.25
UO74	22¢ Eagle ('85)...........	.80
UO75	22¢ Bond Env. ('87).....	.80
UO76	(25¢) "E" Bond Env ('88)	.80
UO77	25¢ Eagle......................	.75
UO78	25¢ Bond Env..............	.75
UO79	45¢ Passport 2 oz ('90)	1.30
UO80	65¢ Passport env.3 oz.	1.80
UO81	45¢ Self-sealing 2 oz...	1.30
UO82	65¢ Self-sealing 3 oz...	1.80
UO83	(29¢) "F" Sav. Bond (91)	1.10
UO84	29¢ Official Mail..........	.75
UO85	29¢ Sav. Bond Env......	.75
UO86	52¢ Consular Service ..	4.50
UO86a	52¢ Reprint (1994).......	1.20
UO87	75¢ Consular Service (1992)....................	9.95
UO87a	75¢ Reprint (1994).......	2.75
UO88	32¢ Official Mail..........	.80

Note: Reprints have copyright date.

MINT POSTAL CARDS

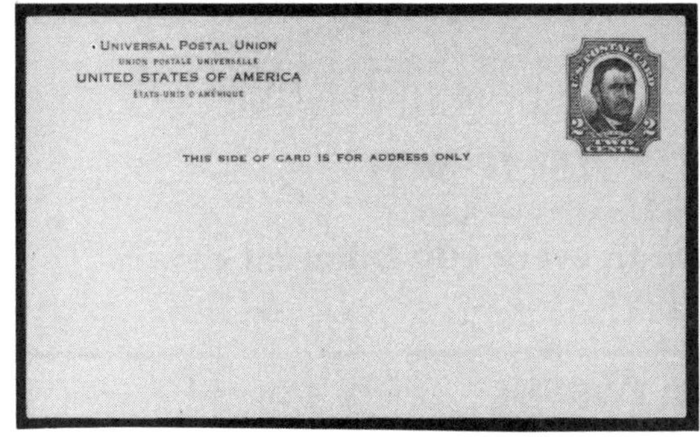

UX 25

UXC 24

cott's No.		Mint Card
	1873-98 Issues	
X1	1¢ Liberty, brown, large watermark	300.00
X3	Same, small watermark	65.00
X5	1¢ Liberty, black, "Write" (1875)	50.00
X6	2¢ Liberty, blue on buff (1879)	20.00
X7	1¢ Liberty, black, "Nothing" (1881)	50.00
X8	1¢ Jefferson,brown (85)	37.50
X9	1¢ Jeff., black (1886)...	16.50
X10	1¢ Grant, black (1891)	32.50
X11	Same, blue	12.00
X12	1¢ Jeff., black, small wreath (1894)	30.00
X13	2¢ Liberty, blue on cream (1897)	140.00
X14	1¢ Jeff., black, large wreath	24.50
X15	1¢ Adams, black (1898)	32.50
X16	2¢ Liberty, black, "No Frame" (1898)	10.00
	1902-18 Issues	
X18	1¢ McKinley, oval........	10.50
X19	1¢ McKinley ('07)	30.00
X20	1¢ Correspond Space at L (1908)........	45.00
UX21	1¢ McKnly,shaded ('10)	90.00
UX22	Same, White backgrd..	13.00
UX23	1¢ Lincoln, red ('11)	7.50
UX24	1¢ McKinley, red	9.50
UX25	2¢ Grant, red..............	1.35
UX26	1¢ Lincoln, green ('13)	8.50
UX27	1¢ Jeff, Die 1 (1914)....	.30
UX28	1¢ Lincoln, green ('17)	.75
UX29	2¢ Jeff, Die 1	37.50
UX30	2¢ Jeff, Die 2 (1918).....	21.50
	1920-64 Issues	
UX32	1¢ on 2¢ red, die 1	42.50
UX33	1¢ on 2¢ red, die 2	9.50
UX37	3¢ McKinley (1926)......	4.50
UX38	2¢ Franklin (1951).......	.35
UX39	2¢ on 1¢ Jeff, green ('52)	.55
UX40	2¢ on 1¢ Linc., grn	.65
UX41	2¢ on 1¢ Jeff, dk grn ...	3.50
UX42	2¢ on 1¢ Linc, dk grn...	5.00
UX43	2¢ Lincoln, carmine.....	.25
UX44	2¢ FIPEX (1956)	.30
UX45	4¢ Liberty	1.60
UX46	3¢ Liberty (1958).........	.45
UX46c	Precancelled ('61)..	3.75
UX48	4¢ Linc., precan ('62) ..	.25
UX48a	Same, Tagged ('66)	.55
UX49	7¢ "USA" (1963)..........	4.50
UX50	4¢ Customs (1964)......	.45
UX51	4¢ Social Security	.45
	1965-73 Issues	
UX52	4¢ Coast Guard...........	.40
UX53	4¢ Census..................	.40
UX54	8¢ "USA" (1967)..........	4.25
UX55	5¢ Lincoln (1968)	.32
UX56	5¢ Women Marines.....	.35
UX57	5¢ Weather (1970)	.30
UX58	6¢ Paul Revere (1971)	.30
UX59	10¢ "USA"	4.00
UX60	6¢ Hospitals	.30
UX61	6¢ Constellation ('72)..	.60
UX62	6¢ Monument Valley ...	.50
UX63	6¢ Gloucester.............	.50
UX64	6¢ John Hanson..........	.30
UX65	6¢ Liberty (1973).........	.30

Scott's No.		Mint Card
UX66	8¢ Samuel Adams	.30
	1974-79 Issues	
UX67	12¢ Visit USA...............	.40
UX68	7¢ Thomson (1975)......	.30
UX69	9¢ Witherspoon............	.30
UX70	9¢ Rodney (1976)	.30
UX71	9¢ Galveston (1977)	.45
UX72	9¢ Nathan Hale	.40
UX73	10¢ Music Hall (1978)..	.30
UX74	(10¢) John Hancock.....	.30
UX75	10¢ John Hancock	.30
UX76	14¢ Cutter "Eagle"	.40
UX77	10¢ Molly Pitcher	.40
UX78	10¢ G.R. Clark (1979)..	.30
UX79	10¢ Pulaski	.30
UX80	10¢ Olympics	.65
UX81	10¢ Iolani Palace	.30
	1980-83 Issues	
UX82	14¢ Winter Olympics....	.70
UX83	10¢ Salt Lake Temple..	.30
UX84	10¢ Rochambeau.........	.30
UX85	10¢ King's Mt	.30
UX86	19¢ Golden Hinde	.80
UX87	10¢ Cowpens (1981)....	.30
UX88	(12¢) Eagle	.35
UX89	12¢ Isaiah Thomas	.35
UX90	12¢ N. Greene	.30
UX91	12¢ Lewis & Clark........	.30
UX92	(13¢) Morris..................	.33
UX93	13¢ Morris	.33
UX94	13¢ F. Marion (1982) ...	.33
UX95	13¢ LaSalle..................	.33
UX96	13¢ Music Academy	.33
UX97	13¢ St. Louis P.O.........	.33
UX98	13¢ Georgia (1983)......	.33
UX99	13¢ Old P. Office	.33
UX100	13¢ Yachting	.33
	1984-88 Issues	
UX101	13¢ Maryland	.33
UX102	13¢ Olympics	.33
UX103	13¢ Baraga	.33
UX104	13¢ Rancho S.Pedro ...	.33
UX105	(14¢) Charles Carroll(85)	.35
UX106	14¢ Charles Carroll......	.35
UX107	25¢ Flying Cloud..........	.75
UX108	14¢ George Wythe.......	.35
UX109	14¢ Conn. Anniv	.35
UX110	14¢ Stamp Coll (1986).	.35
UX111	14¢ Francis Vigo..........	.35
UX112	14¢ Rhode Island.........	.35
UX113	14¢ Wisconsin Ty	.35
UX114	14¢ Nat'l. Guard...........	.35
UX115	14¢ Steel Plow (1987) .	.35
UX116	14¢ Const. Conv	.35
UX117	14¢ U.S. Flag...............	.35
UX118	14¢ Pride in America ...	.35
UX119	14¢ Timberline Ldg	.35
UX120	15¢ Am. the Beaut ('88)	.35
UX121	15¢ Blair House	.35
UX122	28¢ Yorkshire...............	.70
UX123	15¢ Iowa Terr...............	.35
UX124	15¢ NW/Ohio Terr........	.35
UX125	15¢ Hearst Castle........	.35
UX126	15¢ Fed. Papers	.35
	1989-92 Issues	
UX127	15¢ The Desert	.35
UX128	15¢ Healy Hall	.35
UX129	15¢ Wetlands...............	.35
UX130	15¢ Oklahoma..............	.35
UX131	21¢ Can. Geese/Mtns.	.50
UX132	15¢ Seashore..............	.35
UX133	15¢ Woodlands	.35

Scott's No.		Mint Card
UX134	15¢ Hull House..........	.35
UX135	15¢ Independence Hall	.35
UX136	15¢ Balt. Inner Harbor	.35
UX137	15¢ 59th St.Bridge,NY	.35
UX138	15¢ Capitol Bldg........	.35
UX139-42	15¢ Cityscape sheet of 4 postcards............	6.95
UX143	15¢ The White House	1.10
UX144	15¢ Jefferson Memorial	1.10
UX145	15¢ Papermaking ('90)	.35
UX146	15¢ World Literacy Yr.	.35
UX147	15¢ Geo. Bingham Art	1.10
UX148	15¢ Isaac Royall House	.35
UX150	15¢ Stanford Univ	.35
UX151	15¢ DAR/Const. Hall.	1.10
UX152	15¢ Chicago Orch.Hall	.35
UX153	19¢ Flag (1991).........	.45
UX154	19¢ Carnegie Hall	.45
UX155	19¢ "Old Red", U of TX	.45
UX156	19¢ Bill of Rights Bicent	.45
UX157	19¢ Notre Dame........	.45
UX158	30¢ Niagara Falls......	.70
UX159	19¢ Old Mill, U of VT.	.45
UX160	19¢ Wadsw'th Athen (92)	.45
UX161	19¢ Cobb Hall, U of Chi	.45
UX162	19¢ Waller Hall..........	.45
UX163	19¢ America's Cup....	1.10
UX164	19¢ Columbia River...	.45
UX165	19¢ Grt. Hall, Ellis Island	.45
	1993-94 Issues	
UX166	19¢ National Cathedral	.45
UX167	19¢ Wren Building.....	.45
UX168	19¢ Holocaust Mem'l.	1.10
UX169.	19¢ Ft. Recovery.......	.45
UX170	19¢ Playmaker's Theater	.45
UX171	19¢ O'Kane Hall	.45
UX172	19¢ Beecher Hall........	.45
UX173	19¢ Massachusetts Hall	.45
UX174	19¢ Lincoln Home ('94)	.40
UX175	19¢ Myers Hall	.40
UX176	19¢ Canyon de Chelly	.40
UX177	19¢ St. Louis Station.	.40
UX178-97	19¢ Legends of the West (20)..................	8.75
	1995 Issues	
UX198	20¢ Red Barn	.40
UX199	(20¢) "G"....................	.40
...	20¢ Clipper Ship........	.40
	AIRMAIL POSTAL CARDS	
UXC1	4¢ Eagle	.60
UXC2	5¢ Eagle (1958).........	1.75
UXC3	5¢ Eagle, redrawn (60)	6.50
UXC4	6¢ Bald Eagle ('63)....	.50
UXC5	11¢ SIPEX, Travel (66)	.55
UXC6	6¢ Virgin Islands ('67)	.45
UXC7	6¢ Boy Scouts	.45
UXC8	13¢ Travel USA..........	1.60
UXC9	8¢ Eagle, Precan ('68)	.70
UXC9a	Same, Tagged ('69)...	2.65
UXC10	9¢ Eagle, Precan ('71)	.50
UXC11	15¢ Travel USA..........	1.65
UXC12	9¢ Grand Canyon ('72)	.55
UXC13	15¢ Niagara Falls	.70
UXC14	11¢ Mail Early (1974)	.75
UXC15	18¢ Visit USA............	.90
UXC16	21¢ Visit USA (1975).	.85
UXC17	21¢ Curtiss Jenny ('78)	.80
UXC18	21¢ Olympics (1979).	1.10
UXC19	28¢ Trans-Pacific ('81)	.90
UXC20	28¢ Soaring (1982)....	.90
UXC21	28¢ Speedskating ('83)	.80
UXC22	33¢ China Clipper ('85)	.85

Scott's No.		Mint Card
UXC23	33¢ Ameripex (1986)	.85
UXC24	36¢ DC-3 (1988).......	.85
UXC25	40¢ Yankee Clipper (91)	.90
	OFFICIAL POSTAL CARDS	
UZ2	13¢ Emblem (1983)..	.65
UZ3	14¢ Emblem ('85)	.65
UZ4	15¢ Emblem ('88)	.65
UZ5	19¢ Emblem ('91)	.50
UZ6	20¢ Emblem ('95)	.45
	POSTAL REPLY CARDS	
	1892-1920 Issues	
	Unsevered Cards-Folded	
UY1	1¢ Grant, black	37.50
UY2	2¢ Liberty, blue ('93).	18.50
UY3	1¢ Grant, no frame(98)	70.00
UY4	1¢ + 1¢ Sherman and Sheridan (1904).	48.50
UY5	1¢ + 1¢ M&G Wash., Blue (1910)	150.00
UY6	Same, Green (1911).	150.00
UY7	Same,sgl.frm. line ('15)	1.35
UY8	2¢ + 2¢ M&G Wash., red (1918)	80.00
UY9	1¢ on 2¢ + 1¢ on 2¢, red (1920)	20.00
	1924-68	
	Unsevered cards-Unfolded	
UY11	2¢ + 2¢ Liberty, red...	3.00
UY12	3¢ + 3¢ McKinley ('26)	15.00
UY13	2¢ + 2¢ M&G Wash.(51)	1.50
UY14	2¢ on 1¢ + 2¢ on 1¢ M&G Wash (1952)....	1.75
UY15	2¢ on 1¢ + 2¢ on 1¢, green.........................	135.00
UY16	4¢ + 4¢ Liberty ('56)..	1.75
UY17	3¢ + 3¢ Liberty ('58)..	4.50
UY18	4¢ + 4¢ Lincoln ('62).	4.50
UY19	7¢ + 7¢ "USA" (1963)	3.00
UY20	8¢ + 8¢ "USA" (1967)	3.00
UY21	5¢ + 5¢ Lincoln (1968)	1.50
	1971-95	
	Unsevered Cards-Unfolded	
UY22	6¢ + 6¢ Revere	1.50
UY23	6¢ + 6¢ Hanson (1972)	1.35
UY24	8¢ + S. Adams (1973)..	1.10
UY25	7¢ + 7¢ Thomson ('75)	1.10
UY26	9¢ + 9¢ Witherson	1.10
UY27	9¢ + 9¢ Rodney (1976)	1.10
UY28	9¢ + 9¢ Hale (1977).....	1.10
UY29	(10¢+10¢) Hancock (78)	9.50
UY30	10¢ + 10¢ Hancock......	1.10
UY31	(12¢ + 12¢) Eagle ('81)	1.10
UY32	12¢ + 12¢ Thomas.......	1.10
UY33	(13¢ + 13¢) Morris	2.25
UY34	13¢ + 13¢ Morris..........	1.10
UY35	(14¢ + 14¢) Carroll ('85)	3.00
UY36	14¢ + 14¢ Carroll	1.10
UY37	14¢ + 14¢ Wythe	1.10
UY38	14¢ + 14¢ U.S. Flag ('87)	1.10
UY39	15¢+15¢ Am./Beaut ('88)	1.10
UY40	19¢ + 19¢ Flag (1991).	1.25
UY41	20¢ + 20¢ Red Barn ('95)	1.00
	"POSTAL BUDDY" CARDS	
1	15¢ (1990)	8.00
	Sheet of 4	32.50
2	19¢ (1991)	3.75
	Sheet of 4	15.00
3	19¢ (1992) Plain	7.50
	(1992) With Logo ..	11.00
	Sheet of 4	32.50
4	19¢ New Back	75.00
	Sheet of 4	300.00

BARGAIN PRICED UNITED STATES SPACE AND FIRST DAY COVER COLLECTIONS

★ *WITH FREE FIRST DAY COVER ALBUMS* ★

ALL COVERS ARE CACHETED AND UNADDRESSED

Receive a FREE cover album ($15.95 value) with every 100 Different covers ordered in the collections offered below.

500 DIFFERENT SPACE COVERS

OUR LARGEST COLLECTION EVER!!

All with Rank Cachets & Unaddressed at a 70% Discount from Normal Retail Fantastic collection of 500 different multi-colored Space Covers at a tremendous savings of over 70% off the retail value of at least $1,160.00

SPECIAL BROOKMAN PRICE ONLY $349.95

REMEMBER WHEN YOU'RE THINKING COVERS, THINK BROOKMAN - YOUR COVER HEADQUARTERS

1000 DIFFERENT U.S. FIRST DAY COVERS

SAVE ALMOST 70% OFF OF NORMAL RETAIL PRICES

Our collection of 1,000 different Cacheted and Unaddressed U.S. First Day Covers includes many better varieties with a retail value over $1950.00

ONLY $599.00

500 DIFFERENT U.S. FIRST DAY COVERS

SAVE 70% OFF OF NORMAL RETAIL PRICES

For the more budget-minded, we offer a collection of 500 different Cacheted and Unaddressed U.S. First Day Covers. Retail Value over $875.00

ONLY $275.00

200 DIFFERENT U.S. FIRST DAY COVERS

ALL CACHETED & UNADDRESSED

Great Starter Collection.
Over $350.00
Retail Value
for a
LOW, LOW PRICE OF $110.00

1-800-332-3383
FAX 1-603-472-8795

10 CHESTNUT DRIVE
BEDFORD, NH 03110

UNITED STATES REVENUES

R15 R24c R36c R44c R60c

1862-71 (All Used) (C)

cott's No.		Imperforate(a) Fine	Ave.	Part Perforate(b) Fine	Ave.	Perforated(c) Fine	Ave.
1	1¢ Express	47.50	25.00	32.50	17.50	1.00	.60
2	1¢ Play Cards	795.00	450.00	475.00	295.00	90.00	52.50
3	1¢ Proprietary	525.00	285.00	95.00	52.50	.45	.25
4	1¢ Telegraph	375.00	200.00	...	...	7.50	4.50
5	2¢ Bank Ck.,Blue	1.10	.70	1.10	.70	.20	.15
6	2¢ Bank Ck.,Orange	...	...	65.00	37.50	.20	.15
7	2¢ Certif.,Blue	9.50	5.00	...	...	25.00	13.50
8	2¢ Certif.,Orange	...	...	...	...	22.50	13.00
9	2¢ Express,Blue	9.50	5.00	15.00	8.50	.25	.15
10	2¢ Express,Orange	...	...	...	...	5.50	3.25
11	2¢ Ply.Cds.,Blue	...	...	110.00	65.00	3.00	1.50
12	2¢ Ply.Cds.,Orange	...	...	...	...	25.00	14.00
13	2¢ Propriet.,Blue	275.00	200.00	90.00	52.50	.35	.20
14	2¢ Propriet.,Orange	...	...	...	...	30.00	16.00
15	2¢ U.S.I.R.	...	...	...	...	.20	.15
16	3¢ Foreign Exchange	...	...	150.00	85.00	2.75	1.50
17	3¢ Playing Cards	...	...	...	...	90.00	52.50
18	3¢ Proprietary	...	...	175.00	110.00	1.85	1.00
19	3¢ Telegraph	47.50	25.00	16.50	9.50	2.35	1.25
20	4¢ Inland Exchange	...	...	...	...	1.50	1.00
21	4¢ Playing Cards	...	...	...	...	350.00	175.00
22	4¢ Proprietary	...	...	165.00	95.00	5.00	3.00
23	5¢ Agreement	...	...	...	...	.25	.15
24	5¢ Certificate	2.25	1.25	8.00	4.50	.20	.15
25	5¢ Express	3.75	2.25	4.25	2.60	.30	.17
26	5¢ Foreign Exch	...	...	...	...	.30	.17
27	5¢ Inland Exch	3.85	2.35	3.25	1.95	.20	.15
28	5¢ Playing Cards	...	...	...	...	11.00	6.75
29	5¢ Proprietary	...	...	...	...	17.00	9.50
30	6¢ Inland Exch	...	...	...	...	1.35	.80
32	10¢ Bill of Lading	42.50	25.00	130.00	70.00	.85	.50
33	10¢ Certificate	82.50	45.00	130.00	70.00	.30	.17
34	10¢ Contract,Blue	...	...	100.00	55.00	.30	.17
35	10¢ For.Exch.,Blue	...	...	...	...	6.00	4.00
36	10¢ Inland Exch	110.00	60.00	3.25	1.95	.22	.15
37	10¢ Power of Atty	350.00	200.00	18.50	11.00	.35	.20
38	10¢ Proprietary	...	...	...	...	12.50	7.50
39	15¢ Foreign Exch	...	...	...	...	12.00	7.00
R40	15¢ Inland Exch	22.50	12.50	10.00	5.50	1.10	.65
R41	20¢ Foreign Exch	38.50	21.50	...	...	26.50	15.00
R42	20¢ Inland Exch	11.50	6.50	15.00	8.50	.35	.20
R43	25¢ Bond	87.50	47.50	5.25	3.15	1.90	1.10
R44	25¢ Certificate	7.50	4.25	5.00	2.75	.20	.15
R45	25¢ Entry Goods	15.00	8.50	37.50	21.00	.55	.28
R46	25¢ Insurance	8.00	5.00	9.00	5.00	.25	.15
R47	25¢ Life Insurance	28.50	16.00	115.00	65.00	6.00	4.00
R48	25¢ Power of Atty	5.00	3.00	19.00	11.50	.25	.15
R49	25¢ Protest	20.00	11.00	150.00	85.00	6.50	4.00
R50	25¢ Wareh'se. Rct	32.50	18.00	125.00	70.00	19.50	10.50
R51	30¢ Foreign Exch	55.00	32.50	550.00	315.00	33.50	18.50
R52	30¢ Inland Exch	37.50	20.00	47.50	26.50	2.50	1.50
R53	40¢ Inland Exch	350.00	200.00	5.00	3.00	2.50	1.50
R54	50¢ Convey,Blue	9.00	5.00	1.10	.65	.20	.15
R55	50¢ Entry of Goods	...	...	10.00	5.50	.25	.15
R56	50¢ Foreign Exch	33.50	18.50	28.50	16.00	4.75	3.00
R57	50¢ Lease	19.50	11.00	50.00	27.50	6.25	4.00
R58	50¢ Life Insurance	25.00	14.00	47.50	26.00	.75	.42
R59	50¢ Mortgage	9.50	5.25	2.10	1.20	.35	.20
R60	50¢ Orig.Process	2.25	1.25	400.00	300.00	.30	.17
R61	50¢ Passage Ticket	60.00	32.50	95.00	50.00	.50	.30
R62	50¢ Probate of Will	28.50	16.00	40.00	22.00	15.00	8.50
R63	50¢ Sty. Bond,Blue	110.00	60.00	2.35	1.30	.25	.15
R64	60¢ Inland Exch	70.00	38.50	40.00	22.00	5.25	3.00
R65	70¢ Foreign Exch	265.00	150.00	75.00	42.50	5.25	3.00
R66	$1 Conveyance	9.50	5.25	260.00	140.00	3.25	1.85
R67	$1 Entry of Goods	22.50	12.50	...	...	1.40	.80
R68	$1 Foreign Exch	45.00	24.50	...	...	.65	.37
R69	$1 Inland Exch	9.50	5.25	200.00	110.00	.50	.28
R70	$1 Lease	29.50	16.00	...	...	1.65	1.00
R71	$1 Life Insurance	125.00	72.50	...	...	5.00	3.00
R72	$1 Manifest	40.00	22.50	...	...	19.00	11.00
R73	$1 Mortgage	16.50	9.75	...	...	115.00	60.00
R74	$1 Passage Ticket	165.00	95.00	...	...	140.00	70.00
R75	$1 Power of Atty	55.00	30.00	...	...	1.60	.90
R76	$1 Probate of Will	50.00	27.50	...	...	30.00	16.50

1862-71 Issue (continued) (All Used) (C)

R71c R82c R85c

Scott's No.		Imperforate(a) Fine	Ave.	Part Perforate(b) Fine	Ave.	Perforated(c) Fine	Ave.
R77	$1.30 Foreign Exch	...	...	...	...	40.00	22.50
R78	$1.50 Inland Exch	19.00	10.50	...	...	2.85	1.75
R79	$1.60 Foreign Exch	675.00	375.00	...	...	80.00	42.50
R80	$1.90 Foreign Exch	...	1650.00	...	...	55.00	30.00
R81	$2 Conveyance	80.00	45.00	675.00	400.00	2.50	1.50
R82	$2 Mortgage	70.00	38.50	...	...	2.50	1.50
R83	$2 Probate of Will	...	1500.00	...	...	42.50	22.50
R84	$2.50 Inland Exch	900.00	500.00	...	...	3.25	2.00
R85	$3 Charter Party	82.50	47.50	...	...	4.75	2.75
R86	$3 Manifest	80.00	45.00	...	...	19.00	10.50
R87	$3.50 Inland Exch	...	850.00	...	...	40.00	22.50
R88	$5 Charter Party	200.00	115.00	...	...	5.75	3.50
R89	$5 Conveyance	27.50	15.00	...	...	5.75	3.50
R90	$5 Manifest	80.00	45.00	...	...	75.00	41.50
R91	$5 Mortgage	72.50	40.00	...	...	15.00	8.25
R92	$5 Probate of Will	350.00	200.00	...	...	15.00	8.25
R93	$10 Charter Party	400.00	225.00	...	...	19.00	10.50
R94	$10 Conveyance	70.00	39.50	...	...	50.00	27.50
R95	$10 Mortgage	275.00	150.00	...	...	19.00	10.50
R96	$10 Probate of Will	850.00	465.00	...	...	19.00	10.50
R97	$15 Mortgage,Blue	800.00	435.00	...	...	90.00	57.50
R98	$20 Conveyance	70.00	42.50	...	...	42.50	30.00
R99	$20 Probate of Will	775.00	435.00	...	...	750.00	500.00
R100	$25 Mortgage	775.00	435.00	...	...	75.00	42.50
R101	$50 U.S.I.R	140.00	80.00	...	...	70.00	40.00
R102	$200 U.S.I.R.	1000.00	550.00	...	...	475.00	275.00

1ST ISSUE HANDSTAMPED CANCELLATIONS ARE GENERALLY AVAILABLE FOR A 20% PREMIUM.

1871 SECOND ISSUE (C)

R104,R135 R107,R137 R113,R140 R118,R144

R103 through R131 have blue frames and a black center.

Scott's No.		Used Fine	Ave.
R103	1¢	32.50	16.50
R104	2¢	1.10	.55
R105	3¢	11.50	7.00
R106	4¢	42.50	25.00
R107	5¢	1.10	.55
R108	6¢	70.00	37.50
R109	10¢	.80	.45
R110	15¢	18.00	10.00
R111	20¢	5.00	2.75
R112	25¢	.60	.33
R113	30¢	45.00	25.00
R114	40¢	26.50	15.00
R115	50¢	.50	.33
R116	60¢	67.50	38.50
R117	70¢	23.50	15.00

Scott's No.		Used Fine	Ave.
R118	$1	2.75	1.50
R119	$1.30	200.00	110.00
R120	$1.50	10.00	5.50
R121	$1.60	250.00	140.00
R122	$1.90	110.00	60.00
R123	$2	9.50	5.25
R124	$2.50	17.50	9.75
R125	$3	25.00	14.00
R126	$3.50	100.00	50.00
R127	$5	15.00	8.50
R128	$10	75.00	45.00
R129	$20	265.00	165.00
R130	$25	265.00	165.00
R131	$50	285.00	175.00

1871-72 Third Issue - Same Designs as Second Issue (C)
R134 through R150 have black centers.

Scott's No.		Used Fine	Ave.
R134	1¢ Claret	25.00	14.00
R135	2¢ Orange	.20	.15
R136	4¢ Brown	25.00	13.75
R137	5¢ Orange	.25	.15
R138	6¢ Orange	28.50	16.00
R139	15¢ Brown	10.50	6.50
R140	30¢ Orange	11.50	7.50
R141	40¢ Brown	23.50	13.50
R142	60¢ Orange	42.50	23.75
R143	70¢ Green	27.50	15.00
R144	$1 Green	1.35	.75
R145	$2 Vermillion	18.00	9.50
R146	$2.50 Claret	28.50	16.00
R147	$3 Green	28.50	16.00
R148	$5 Vermillion	16.00	9.50
R149	$10 Green	60.00	35.00
R150	$20 Orange	425.00	235.00

1874 Fourth Issue (C)

Scott's No.		Uncancelled Fine	Ave.	Used Fine	Ave.
R151	2¢ Orange and Black, Green Paper	...	...	.20	.15

1875-78 Fifth Issue (C)

R152a	2¢ Liberty, Blue, Silk Paper	1.50	.90	.20	.15
R152b	2¢ Blue, Watermarked	1.50	.90	.20	.15
R152c	2¢ Blue, Rouletted, Watermarked	...	...	28.50	14.50

* 1898 Postage Stamps Overprinted "I.R." (C)
* 1898 Newspaper Stamps Surcharged "INT. REV./$5/DOCUMENTARY" (C)

R153	1¢ Green, Small I.R. (#279)	2.25	1.35	2.75	1.65
R154	1¢ Green, Large I.R. (#279)	.25	.20	.20	.15
R154a	1¢ Green, Inverted Surcharge	9.75	5.25	6.75	3.75
R155	2¢ Carmine, Large I.R. (#267)	.25	.20	.55	.30
R159	$5 Blue, Surcharge down (#PR121)	180.00	110.00	140.00	85.00
R160	$5 Blue, Surcharge up (#PR121)	90.00	50.00	60.00	35.00

*** Used prices are for stamps with contemporary cancels.**

R163 R174 R197,R208 R219

1898 Documentary "Battleship" Designs (C) (Rouletted 5½)

1874 Fourth Issue (C)

R161	½¢ Orange	3.00	1.80	5.50	3.50
R162	½¢ Dark Gray	.30	.20	.20	.15
R163	1¢ Pale Blue	.25	.20	.20	.15
R164	2¢ Carmine	.25	.20	.20	.15
R165	3¢ Dark Blue	1.10	.60	.20	.15
R166	4¢ Pale Rose	.55	.30	.20	.15
R167	5¢ Lilac	.25	.20	.20	.15
R168	10¢ Dark Brown	.85	.50	.20	.15
R169	25¢ Purple Brown	1.10	.60	.20	.15
R170	40¢ Blue Lilac (cut .25)	62.50	32.50	2.00	1.00
R171	50¢ Slate Violet	8.00	4.75	.20	.15
R172	80¢ Bistre (cut .15)	28.50	17.50	.35	.20

Commerce Design (C) (Rouletted 5½)

R173	$1 Commerce, Dark Green	5.50	3.25	.20	.15
R174	$3 Dark Brown (cut .18)	10.00	5.50	.75	.45
R175	$5 Orange Red (cut .20)	14.50	9.50	1.35	.80
R176	$10 Black (cut .60)	42.50	27.50	2.50	1.50
R177	$30 Red (cut 35.00)	125.00	75.00	80.00	50.00
R178	$50 Gray Brown (cut 1.60)	65.00	36.50	5.50	3.50

NOTE: SOME VALUES EXIST WITH HYPHEN HOLE PERF. 7.

1899-1900 Documentary Stamps (C)

R179	$100 Marshall, Brn. & Blk.(cut 15.00)	75.00	47.50	25.00	14.00
R180	$500 Hamilton,Car.Lk/Blk(cut 210.00)	500.00	325.00	400.00	250.00
R181	$1000 Madison,Grn&Blk (cut 95.00)	500.00	325.00	300.00	240.00
R182	$1 Commerce, Carmine (cut .15)	8.50	5.00	.50	.30
R183	$3 Lake (cut 7.50)	65.00	38.50	37.50	22.50

1900 Surcharged Large Black Numerals (C)

Scott's No.		Uncancelled Fine	Ave.	Used Fine	Ave.
R184	$1 Gray (cut .06)	7.50	4.25	.20	.15
R185	$2 Gray (cut .06)	7.50	4.25	.20	.15
R186	$3 Gray (cut $2.00)	42.50	22.50	10.50	6.00
R187	$5 Gray (cut $1.00)	25.00	15.00	6.50	3.95
R188	$10 Gray (cut 3.35)	42.50	25.00	13.00	7.50
R189	$50 Gray (cut 70.00)	500.00	275.00	325.00	185.00

1902 Surcharged Ornamental Numerals (C)

R190	$1 Green (cut .25)	11.50	5.75	3.25	1.95
R191	$2 Green (cut .20)	9.25	5.00	1.30	.80
R192	$5 Green (cut $4.00)	75.00	45.00	26.50	16.50
R193	$10 Green (cut 45.00)	225.00	125.00	130.00	70.00
R194	$50 Green (cut 210.00)	875.00	495.00	725.00	400.00

1914 Documentary Single Line Watermark "USPS" (40%) (B)

R195	½¢ Rose	6.25	3.85	2.50	1.50
R196	1¢ Rose	1.00	.55	.20	.15
R197	2¢ Rose	1.65	.95	.20	.15
R198	3¢ Rose	35.00	18.50	21.50	12.50
R199	4¢ Rose	9.50	5.75	1.50	.80
R200	5¢ Rose	3.00	1.65	.20	.15
R201	10¢ Rose	3.00	1.65	.20	.15
R202	25¢ Rose	21.75	13.50	.60	.35
R203	40¢ Rose	10.00	6.00	.50	.30
R204	50¢ Rose	4.00	2.50	.20	.15
R205	80¢ Rose	65.00	39.50	8.00	5.00

1914 Documentary Double Line Watermark "USIR" (40%) (B)

R206	½¢ Rose	1.00	.50	.50	.30
R207	1¢ Rose	.25	.20	.20	.15
R208	2¢ Rose	.25	.20	.20	.15
R209	3¢ Rose	1.35	.70	.20	.15
R210	4¢ Rose	2.75	1.50	.35	.22
R211	5¢ Rose	1.30	.70	.20	.15
R212	10¢ Rose	1.00	.65	.20	.15
R213	25¢ Rose	4.00	2.40	1.10	.65
R214	40¢ Rose (cut .50)	50.00	28.50	9.50	5.75
R215	50¢ Rose	8.00	5.00	.25	.15
R216	80¢ Rose (cut .90)	70.00	37.50	12.00	6.25
R217	$1 Liberty, Green (cut .15)	19.50	11.50	.25	.18
R218	$2 Carmine (cut .15)	27.50	16.50	.25	.18
R219	$3 Purple (cut .20)	38.50	20.00	2.00	1.10
R220	$5 Blue (cut .60)	32.50	17.50	2.10	1.20
R221	$10 Orange (cut .90)	75.00	42.50	4.00	2.40
R222	$30 Vermillion (cut 2.00)	150.00	87.50	9.75	6.00
R223	$50 Violet (cut 230.00)	850.00	485.00	600.00	325.00
R224	$60 Lincoln, Brown (cut 42.50)	...	...	100.00	60.00
R225	$100 Wash., Green (cut 16.50)	...	...	37.50	20.00
R226	$500 Hamilton, Blue (cut 185.00)	...	...	450.00	250.00
R227	$1000 Madison, Orange (cut 185.00)	...	...	450.00	250.00

R224-27 were issued without gum.

R228,R251 R240 R733

1917-33 Documentary Stamps - Perf. 11 (20%) (B)

R228	1¢ Rose	.25	.20	.20	.15
R229	2¢ Rose	.25	.20	.20	.15
R230	3¢ Rose	1.00	.60	.20	.15
R231	4¢ Rose	.40	.25	.20	.15
R232	5¢ Rose	.25	.20	.20	.15
R233	8¢ Rose	1.65	1.00	.20	.15
R234	10¢ Rose	.28	.20	.20	.15
R235	20¢ Rose	1.00	.60	.20	.15
R236	25¢ Rose	1.00	.60	.20	.15
R237	40¢ Rose	1.00	.60	.20	.15
R238	50¢ Rose	1.25	.75	.20	.15
R239	80¢ Rose	3.50	1.75	.20	.15
R240	$1 Green, Without Date	5.00	3.00	.20	.15
R241	$2 Rose	8.00	5.00	.20	.15
R242	$3 Violet (cut .15)	26.50	16.00	.65	.35
R243	$4 Brown (cut .15)	17.50	10.00	1.35	.80
R244	$5 Blue (cut .15)	11.00	6.00	.25	.18
R245	$10 Orange (cut .15)	25.00	15.00	.85	.50

1917 Documentary Stamps - Perforated 12, Without Gum (B)

R246	$30 Grant, Orange (cut 1.25)	35.00	21.50	7.50	4.50
R247	$60 Lincoln, Brown (cut .85)	40.00	25.00	6.50	4.00
R248	$100 Wash., Green (cut .40)	25.00	15.00	1.10	.65
R249	$500 Hamilton, Blue (cut 9.00)	...	...	30.00	17.50
R250	$1000 Madison, Orange (cut 4.25)	95.00	52.50	13.00	7.50

1928-29 Documentary Stamps - Perf. 10 (20%) (B)

Scott's No.		Unused Fine	Unused Ave.	Used Fine	Used Ave.
251	1¢ Carmine Rose	1.90	1.15	.90	.55
252	2¢ Carmine Rose	.50	.30	.20	.15
253	4¢ Carmine Rose	5.50	3.00	3.75	2.25
254	5¢ Carmine Rose	1.00	.45	.55	.35
255	10¢ Carmine Rose	1.50	.90	1.10	.70
256	20¢ Carmine Rose	5.75	3.25	5.00	3.00
257	$1 Green (cut 3.75)	60.00	35.00	25.00	15.00
258	$2 Rose	21.50	11.50	2.25	1.30
259	$10 Orange (cut 20.00)	85.00	52.50	37.50	22.50

1929-30 Documentary Stamps - Perf. 11x10 (20%) (B)

260	2¢ Carmine Rose	2.75	1.50	2.50	1.40
261	5¢ Carmine Rose	1.75	1.10	1.75	1.10
262	10¢ Carmine Rose	7.50	4.00	6.50	4.00
263	20¢ Carmine Rose	16.50	10.00	8.50	5.00

1940-1958 Documentary Stamps (Dated)

We will be glad to quote prices on any of these items we have in stock.

1962-1963 Documentary Stamps

Scott's No.		Plate Block	Fine NH	Fine Used
733	10¢ Internal Revenue Bldg	12.75	1.00	.40
734	10¢ Bldg., Without Date (1963)	23.50	3.25	.40

RB1 RB12 RB33,RB45 RB66

1871-74 Proprietary (All Used) (C)

Scott's No.		Violet Paper(a) Fine	Violet Paper(a) Ave.	Green Paper(b) Fine	Green Paper(b) Ave.
RB1	1¢ Green and Black	3.25	1.95	5.00	3.00
RB2	2¢ Green and Black	4.25	2.50	11.00	6.50
RB3	3¢ Green and Black	10.00	6.00	32.50	17.50
RB4	4¢ Green and Black	6.25	3.50	10.00	6.00
RB5	5¢ Green and Black	100.00	60.00	105.00	65.00
RB6	6¢ Green and Black	25.00	15.00	75.00	41.50
RB7	10¢ Green and Black	375.00	225.00	32.50	17.50
RB8	50¢ Green and Black	525.00	300.00	825.00	450.00

1875-81 Proprietary (All Used) (C)

Scott's No.		Silk Paper(s) Fine	Silk Paper(s) Ave.	Watermarked(b) Fine	Watermarked(b) Ave.	Rouletted(c) Fine	Rouletted(c) Ave.
RB11	1¢ Green	1.65	1.00	.40	.25	42.50	22.50
RB12	2¢ Brown	1.75	1.00	1.35	.75	60.00	37.50
RB13	3¢ Orange	9.50	5.00	4.00	2.50	50.00	30.00
RB14	4¢ Red Brown	4.00	2.25	5.25	2.95	...	...
RB15	4¢ Red	...	...	3.50	1.95	70.00	42.50
RB16	5¢ Black	87.50	50.00	75.00	37.50	...	...
RB17	6¢ Violet Blue	18.50	11.00	14.00	8.00	170.00	100.00
RB18	6¢ Violet	...	...	20.00	12.50	165.00	92.50
RB19	10¢ Blue	...	...	210.00	125.00	...	...

1898 Proprietary Stamps (Battleship) (C)
(Rouletted 5½)

Scott's No.		Uncancelled Fine	Uncancelled Ave.	Used Fine	Used Ave.
RB20	1/8¢ Yellow Green	.25	.20	.20	.15
RB21	¼¢ Pale Brown	.25	.20	.20	.15
RB22	3/8¢ Deep Orange	.25	.20	.20	.15
RB23	5/8¢ Deep Ultramarine	.25	.20	.20	.15
RB24	1¢ Dark Green	.50	.30	.30	.20
RB25	1¼¢ Violet	.25	.20	.20	.15
RB26	1 1/8¢ Dull Blue	3.50	2.25	1.10	.70
RB27	2¢ Violet Brown	.35	.20	.20	.15
RB28	2½¢ Lake	1.65	1.00	.20	.15
RB29	3¾¢ Olive Gray	15.00	10.00	6.50	4.50
RB30	4¢ Purple	4.00	2.50	.85	.50
RB31	5¢ Brown Orange	5.00	3.00	.75	.45

NOTE: THESE ALSO EXIST WITH HYPHEN HOLE PERF. 7.

1914 Black Proprietary Stamps - S.L. Wmk. "USPS" (40%) (B)

Scott's No.		Unused Fine	Unused Ave.	Used Fine	Used Ave.
RB32	1/8¢ Black	.25	.20	.20	.15
RB33	¼¢ Black	1.25	.75	1.10	.65
RB34	3/8¢ Black	.25	.20	.20	.15
RB35	5/8¢ Black	2.50	1.50	2.25	1.35
RB36	1¼¢ Black	1.80	1.20	1.10	.70
RB37	1 7/8¢ Black	25.00	15.00	15.00	9.50

1914 Black Proprietary Stamps - S.L. Wmk. "USPS" (40%) (continued)

Scott's No.		Unused Fine	Unused Ave.	Used Fine	Used Ave.
RB38	2½¢ Black	4.50	2.75	2.35	1.50
RB39	3 1/8¢ Black	60.00	35.00	42.50	25.00
RB40	3¼¢ Black	25.00	15.00	20.00	12.50
RB41	4¢ Black	37.50	22.50	23.50	14.00
RB42	4 3/8¢ Black	...	695.00	...	...
RB43	5¢ Black	85.00	52.50	60.00	35.00

1914 Black Proprietary Stamps - D.L. Wmk. "USIR" (40%) (B)

RB44	1/8¢ Black	.25	.20	.20	.15
RB45	¼¢ Black	.25	.20	.20	.15
RB46	3/8¢ Black	.55	.33	.30	.18
RB47	½¢ Black	3.25	1.95	2.25	1.40
RB48	5/8¢ Black	.25	.20	.20	.15
RB49	1¢ Black	4.50	2.50	3.25	1.90
RB50	1¼¢ Black	.40	.25	.35	.22
RB51	1½¢ Black	3.25	1.90	2.00	1.10
RB52	1 7/8¢ Black	1.10	.65	.65	.40
RB53	2¢ Black	5.50	3.50	3.25	1.95
RB54	2½¢ Black	1.10	.65	1.10	.65
RB55	3¢ Black	3.75	2.10	2.25	1.35
RB56	3 1/8¢ Black	5.00	3.00	2.50	1.50
RB57	3¾¢ Black	9.00	5.50	8.00	4.75
RB58	4¢ Black	.50	.30	.20	.15
RB59	4 3/8¢ Black	10.00	6.00	6.25	3.75
RB60	5¢ Black	2.65	1.50	2.50	1.40
RB61	6¢ Black	47.50	29.50	36.50	21.75
RB62	8¢ Black	15.00	9.00	11.00	6.75
RB63	10¢ Black	9.00	5.50	7.50	4.50
RB64	20¢ Black	16.50	10.00	14.00	8.50

1919 Proprietary Stamps (30%) (B)

RB65	1¢ Dark Blue	.25	.20	.20	.15
RB66	2¢ Dark Blue	.25	.20	.20	.15
RB67	3¢ Dark Blue	1.10	.65	.65	.40
RB68	4¢ Dark Blue	1.10	.65	.55	.30
RB69	5¢ Dark Blue	1.35	.80	.65	.40
RB70	8¢ Dark Blue	9.00	5.50	9.00	5.50
RB71	10¢ Dark Blue	3.25	2.10	2.10	1.30
RB72	20¢ Dark Blue	5.25	3.50	3.25	1.95
RB73	40¢ Dark Blue	25.00	15.00	10.50	6.50

1918-34 Future Delivery Stamps (20%) (B)

RC1	2¢ Carmine Rose	1.80	1.20	.20	.15
RC2	3¢ Carmine Rose (cut 8.75)	25.00	15.00	18.00	11.00
RC3	4¢ Carmine Rose	3.25	1.90	.20	.15
RC3A	5¢ Carmine Rose	35.00	21.50	6.50	3.75
RC4	10¢ Carmine Rose	5.75	3.50	.20	.15
RC5	20¢ Carmine Rose	5.75	3.50	.20	.15
RC6	25¢ Carmine Rose (cut .15)	16.50	11.50	.75	.45
RC7	40¢ Carmine Rose (cut .15)	16.50	11.50	.85	.50
RC8	50¢ Carmine Rose	4.00	2.50	.35	.20
RC9	80¢ Carmine Rose (cut .85)	35.00	22.50	8.00	5.00
RC10	$1 Green (cut .15)	10.00	6.00	.25	.18
RC11	$2 Rose (cut .15)	16.50	10.00	.25	.18
RC12	$3 Violet (cut .20)	35.00	20.00	2.25	1.30
RC13	$5 Dark Blue (cut .15)	18.50	10.00	.50	.25
RC14	$10 Orange (cut .20)	37.50	25.00	1.00	.60
RC15	$20 Olive Bistre (cut .50)	77.50	45.00	5.00	3.00
RC16	$30 Vermillion (cut 1.50)	65.00	40.00	3.25	1.95
RC17	$50 Olive Green (cut .55)	50.00	28.50	1.10	.65
RC18	$60 Brown (cut .80)	55.00	30.00	2.10	1.30
RC19	$100 Yellow Green (cut 5.75)	65.00	35.00	22.50	13.50
RC20	$500 Blue (cut 4.50)	55.00	32.50	10.50	6.25
RC21	$1000 Orange (cut 1.65)	55.00	35.00	5.25	3.25
RC22	1¢ Carm. Rose, Narrow Overprt.	1.10	.70	.20	.15
RC23	80¢ Narrow Overprint (cut .18)	50.00	35.00	3.00	1.80
RC25	$1 Self Overprint (cut .15)	8.00	5.00	.75	.45
RC26	$10 Self Overprint (cut 7.50)	...	...	15.00	10.00

1918-29 Stock Transfer Stamps, Perf. 11 or 12 (20%) (B)

RD1	1¢ Carmine Rose	.80	.45	.20	.15
RD2	2¢ Carmine Rose	.25	.20	.20	.15
RD3	4¢ Carmine Rose	.25	.20	.20	.15
RD4	5¢ Carmine Rose	.25	.20	.20	.15
RD5	10¢ Carmine Rose	.25	.20	.20	.15
RD6	20¢ Carmine Rose	.50	.30	.20	.15
RD7	25¢ Carmine Rose (cut .15)	1.25	.70	.25	.20
RD8	40¢ Carmine Rose	1.25	.70	.20	.15
RD9	50¢ Carmine Rose	.55	.35	.20	.15
RD10	80¢ Carmine Rose (cut .15)	2.15	1.25	.25	.18
RD11	$1 Green, Red Overprint (cut 4.00)	35.00	20.00	10.75	6.75
RD12	$1 Green, Black Overprint	1.60	.90	.20	.15
RD13	$2 Rose	1.60	.90	.20	.15
RD14	$3 Violet (cut .22)	11.00	5.75	3.25	2.00
RD15	$4 Brown (cut .15)	5.50	3.00	.25	.18
RD16	$5 Blue (cut .15)	3.50	2.00	.25	.18
RD17	$10 Orange (cut .15)	9.00	5.50	.25	.18
RD18	$20 Bistre (cut 3.00)	55.00	33.50	16.00	9.50
RD19	$30 Vermillion (cut 2.00)	14.00	8.50	4.25	2.50
RD20	$50 Olive Green (cut 13.50)	82.50	45.00	52.50	28.75
RD21	$60 Brown (cut 6.75)	82.50	45.00	20.00	13.00
RD22	$100 Green (cut 1.75)	21.50	13.00	5.25	3.00
RD23	$500 Blue (cut 50.00)	...	...	100.00	60.00
RD24	$1000 Orange (cut 26.75)	...	...	65.00	40.00

1928-32 Transfer Stamps, Pf. 10 (20%)

Scott's No.		Fine Unused	Used
RD25	1¢ Carm rose	2.10	.25
RD26	4¢ Carm rose	1.60	.25
RD27	10¢ Carm rose	1.50	.25
RD28	20¢ Carm rose	1.50	.25
RD29	50¢ Carm rose	1.65	.25
RD30	$1 Green	15.00	.20
RD31	$2 Carm rose	15.00	.20
RD32	$10 Orng (cut .15)	15.00	.20

1920-28 Transfers, Serif Ovpts. (20%)
RD33-38, Pf. 11; RD39-41, Pf. 10

RD33	2¢ Carm rose	4.00	.50
RD34	10¢ Carm rose	1.00	.25
RD35	20¢ Carm rose	1.00	.25
RD36	50¢ Carm rose	2.00	.25
RD37	$1 Green (cut .20)	16.50	8.50
RD38	$2 Rose (cut .20)	15.00	8.50
RD39	2¢ Carm rose	3.75	.45
RD40	10¢ Carm rose	1.10	.40
RD41	20¢ Carm rose	1.30	.25

We will be glad to quote on any of the following Revenue categories:
1940-58 Dated Documentaries
Wine Stamps & Playing Card Stamps

SILVER TAX STAMPS

The Silver Purchase Act of 1934 imposed a 50% tax on the net profit resulting from the transfer of silver bullion. The Silver Tax Stamps, authorized by Congress on Feb. 20, 1934, were to be affixed to the transfer documents as payment of the tax.

RG 1

RG 111

1934 Documentary Stamps of 1917 Overprinted, D.L. Wmk., Perf. 11

Scott's No.		F-VF Unused	Used
RG1	1¢ Carm rose	1.00	.75
RG2	2¢ Carm rose	1.50	.25
RG3	3¢ Carm rose	1.50	.75
RG4	4¢ Carm rose	2.00	1.50
RG5	5¢ Carm rose	3.25	1.50
RG6	8¢ Carm rose	4.25	2.50
RG7	10¢ Carm rose	4.50	1.75
RG8	20¢ Carm rose	6.50	3.00
RG9	25¢ Carm rose	6.75	3.50
RG10	40¢ Carm rose	7.25	5.00
RG11	50¢ Carm rose	6.50	6.00
RG12	80¢ Carm rose	12.50	8.50
RG13	$1 Green	16.50	10.00
RG14	$2 Rose	17.50	13.50
RG15	$3 Violet	32.50	23.50
RG16	$4 Yellow brn	30.00	16.00
RG17	$5 Dark blue	32.50	16.00
RG18	$10 Orange	45.00	16.00

Without Gum, Perf. 12

RG19	$30 Vermillion	80.00	40.00
	Cut cncl	...	17.50
RG20	$60 Brown	100.00	62.50
	Cut cncl	...	25.00
RG21	$100 Green	90.00	25.00
RG22	$500 Blue	275.00	195.00
	Cut cncl	...	85.00
RG23	$1000 Orange	...	90.00
	Cut cncl	...	52.50

1936 Same Ovpt., 11 mm between words "SILVER TAX"

RG26	$100 Green	125.00	60.00
RG27	$1000 Orange	...	395.00

1940 Documentary Stamps of 1917 D.L. Wmk., Perf. 11, Overprinted
SERIES 1940

SILVER TAX

RG37	1¢ Rose pink	14.00	...
RG38	2¢ Rose pink	14.00	...
RG39	3¢ Rose pink	14.00	...
RG40	4¢ Rose pink	15.00	...
RG41	5¢ Rose pink	8.00	...

Silver Tax (cont.)

Scott No.		F-VF Unused	Used
RG42	8¢ Rose pink	15.00	...
RG43	10¢ Rose pink	14.00	...
RG44	20¢ Rose pink	15.00	...
RG45	25¢ Rose pink	15.00	...
RG46	40¢ Rose pink	22.50	...
RG47	50¢ Rose pink	22.50	...
RG48	80¢ Rose pink	22.50	...
RG49	$1 Green	75.00	...
RG50	$2 Rose	125.00	...
RG51	$3 Violet	175.00	...
RG52	$4 Yellow brn	375.00	...
RG53	$5 Dark blue	425.00	...
RG54	$10 Orange	475.00	...

Ovpt in Blk. SERIES OF 1941 pf.11 (Gray)

RG58	1¢ Hamilton	3.00	...
RG59	2¢ Wolcott, Jr	3.00	...
RG60	3¢ Dexter	3.00	...
RG61	4¢ Gallatin	4.50	...
RG62	5¢ Campbell	4.50	...
RG63	8¢ Dallas	6.50	...
RG64	10¢ Crawford	7.50	...
RG65	20¢ Rush	9.00	...
RG66	25¢ Ingham	13.00	...
RG67	40¢ McLane	23.00	...
RG68	50¢ Duane	27.50	...
RG69	80¢ Taney	47.50	...
RG70	$1 Woodbury	60.00	25.00
RG71	$2 Ewing	125.00	45.00
RG72	$3 Forward	100.00	50.00
RG73	$4 Spencer	135.00	65.00
RG74	$5 Bibb	135.00	65.00
RG75	$10 Walker	215.00	85.00
RG76	$20 Meredith	425.00	265.00

Without Gum, Perf. 12

RG77	$30 Corwin	225.00	125.00
	Cut cncl	...	65.00
RG79	$60 Cobb	...	175.00
	Cut cncl	...	85.00
RG80	$100 Thomas	...	275.00
	Cut cncl	...	90.00

#RG58-82 Overprinted SERIES OF 1942

RG83	1¢ Hamilton	2.00	...
RG84	2¢ Wolcott, Jr	2.00	...
RG85	3¢ Dexter	2.00	...
RG86	4¢ Gallatin	2.00	...
RG87	5¢ Campbell	2.00	...
RG88	8¢ Dallas	4.50	...
RG89	10¢ Crawford	5.00	...
RG90	20¢ Rush	7.50	...
RG91	25¢ Ingham	15.00	...
RG92	40¢ McLane	17.50	...
RG93	50¢ Duane	17.50	...
RG94	80¢ Taney	50.00	...
RG95	$1 Woodbury	40.00	...
RG96	$2 Ewing	40.00	...
RG97	$3 Forward	85.00	...
RG98	$4 Spencer	85.00	...
RG99	$5 Bibb	100.00	...
RG100	$10 Walker	265.00	...
RG101	$20 Meredith	425.00	...

1944 Silver Stamps of 1941 w/o ovpt.

RG108	1¢ Hamilton	1.00	...
RG109	2¢ Wolcott, Jr	1.00	...
RG110	3¢ Dexter	1.00	...
RG111	4¢ Gallatin	1.00	...
RG112	5¢ Campbell	2.10	...
RG113	8¢ Dallas	3.15	...
RG114	10¢ Crawford	3.15	...
RG115	20¢ Rush	6.50	...
RG116	25¢ Ingham	8.25	...
RG117	40¢ McLane	12.75	...
RG118	50¢ Duane	12.75	...
RG119	80¢ Taney	18.50	...
RG120	$1 Woodbury	25.00	12.50
RG121	$2 Ewing	42.50	27.50
RG122	$3 Forward	45.00	20.00
RG123	$4 Spencer	65.00	45.00
RG124	$5 Bibb	65.00	25.00
RG125	$10 Walker	85.00	37.50
	Cut cncl		13.50
RG126	$20 Meredith	350.00	250.00

Without Gum, Perf. 12

RG127	$30 Corwin	165.00	90.00
	Cut cncl	...	50.00
RG128	$50 Gutherie	525.00	500.00
	Cut cncl	...	285.00
RG129	$60 Cobb	...	235.00
	Cut cncl	...	110.00
RG130	$100 Thomas	...	32.50
	Cut cncl	...	12.50
RG131	$500 Dix	...	400.00
	Cut cncl	...	225.00
RG132	$1000 Chase	...	135.00
	Cut cncl	...	65.00

CIGARETTE TUBE STAMPS

On Feb. 26, 1926, a law was enacted placing a tax on Cigarette Tubes at the rate of 1¢ per 50, or fraction thereof. The tax on tubes, which a smoker would use to make his own cigarettes, was collected by means of 1¢ & 2¢ stamps, which were affixed to the packages.

RH 1

Doc. Stamp of 1917 ovpt., D.L. Wmk.

Scott No.		F-VF Unused	Used
RH1	1¢ Carm rose ('19)	.50	.25

Perf. 11

RH2	1¢ Carm rose ('29)	23.50	9.50

RH4

RH3	1¢ Rose (1933)	2.00	.75
RH4	2¢ Rose (1933)	6.00	1.75

POTATO TAX STAMPS

Potato Tax Stamps were issued to comply with the Agricultural Adjustment Act of Dec. 1, 1935. The tax of ¾¢ per pound was to be paid by potato growers who grew more than their official allotments. The Supreme Court declared the Act unconstitutional.

RI 1

Issue of 1935

Scott's No.		F-VF Unused
RI1	¾¢ Carm rose	.25
RI2	1¼¢ Black brn	.50
RI3	2¼¢ Yellow grn	.50
RI4	3¢ Light Violet	.50
RI5	3¾¢ Olive Bistre	.50
RI6	7½¢ Orange brn	1.35
RI7	11¼¢ Deep orange	1.65
RI8	18¾¢ Violet brn	4.00
RI9	37½¢ Red orange	4.00
RI10	75¢ Blue	4.00
RI11	93¾¢ Rose lake	6.50
RI12	$1.12½¢ Green	11.50
RI13	$1.50 Yellow brn	10.50

TOBACCO SALE TAX STAMPS

The Kerr-Smith Tobacco Control Act, effective June 29, 1934, created the need for these tax stamps. The tax was to apply to the sale of tobacco in excess of officially established quotas and was to be paid in stamps. The Supreme Court declared the Act unconstitutional.

TOBACCO SALE TAX STAMPS
1934 Doc. Issue of 1917, Ovpt. D.L. Wmk., pf. 11

RJ 1

RJ 7

Scott's No.		F-VF Unused	Used
RJ1	1¢ Carm rose	.35	.1
RJ2	2¢ Carm rose	.35	.2
RJ3	5¢ Carm rose	1.25	.3
RJ4	10¢ Carm rose	1.50	.3
RJ5	25¢ Carm rose	4.00	1.5
RJ6	50¢ Carm rose	4.00	1.5
RJ7	$1 Green	8.50	1.7
RJ8	$2 Rose	13.50	1.7
RJ9	$5 Dark blue	22.50	3.7
RJ10	$10 Orange	32.50	10.0
RJ11	$20 Olive bistre	72.50	12.5

NARCOTIC TAX STAMPS

Narcotic Tax Stamps were issued as result of the Revenue Act of 1918 whic imposed a tax on narcotics and narcot derivatives. Narcotic Tax Stamps we affixed to the drug containers to indica payment of the 1¢ per ounce tax.

It is interesting to note that around 192 the Federal Government discouraged the collecting by forbidding dealers to trade the stamps. Listings in the Scott catalo which were dropped after 1929, we restored after the use of the stamps wa discontinued in 1971.

1919 Doc. Issue of 1914, D.L. Wmk., pf. 10, Handstamped "NARCOTIC" in Magenta, Blue or Black

Scott's No.		Fine Unused	Used
RJA1	1¢ Rose	75.00	50.0

1919 Doc. Issue of 1917, D.L. Wmk.,
perf. 11, Handstamped "NARCOTIC," "Narcotic," "NARCOTICS," or "ACT/NARCOTIC/1918"
in Magenta, Blue, Black, Violet or Red

Scott's No.		F-VF Unused	Used
RJA9	1¢ Carm rose	1.75	1.0
RJA10	2¢ Carm rose	4.50	2.75
RJA11	3¢ Carm rose	25.00	20.0
RJA12	4¢ Carm rose	7.50	5.0
RJA13	5¢ Carm rose	11.50	9.5
RJA14	8¢ Carm rose	10.50	8.0
RJA15	10¢ Carm rose	45.00	8.5
RJA16	20¢ Carm rose	50.00	35.0
RJA17	25¢ Carm rose	32.50	26.5
RJA18	40¢ Carm rose	80.00	62.5
RJA19	50¢ Carm rose	17.50	15.0
RJA20	80¢ Carm rose	95.00	65.0
RJA21	$1 Green	65.00	35.0

RJA 33

1919 Doc. Issue of 1917, D.L. Wmk., perf. 11, Overprinted
NARCOTIC
17½ mm wide

RJA33	1¢ Carm rose	1.00	.50
RJA34	2¢ Carm rose	1.50	1.00
RJA35	3¢ Carm rose	32.50	22.50
RJA36	4¢ Carm rose	5.00	3.00
RJA37	5¢ Carm rose	12.00	9.00
RJA38	8¢ Carm rose	21.50	16.50
RJA39	10¢ Carm rose	3.00	3.00
RJA40	25¢ Carm rose	24.00	16.50

Overprint Reading Up

RJA41	$1 Green	35.00	17.50

arcotic Issues of 1919-1970,D.L. Wmk.

RJA44b

ott's o.		F-VF Used a.Impf.	b.roult.
A42	1¢ Violet	4.25	.25
A43	1¢ Violet	.50	.25
A44	2¢ Violet	1.00	.50
A45	3¢ Violet	...	90.00
A46	1¢ Violet	2.25	.75
A47	2¢ Violet	1.75	.75
A49	4¢ Violet	...	7.00
A50	5¢ Violet	38.50	6.50
A51	6¢ Violet	...	1.50
A52	8¢ Violet	6.00	3.00
A53	9¢ Violet	75.00	8.50
A54	10¢ Violet	1.00	.50
A55	16¢ Violet	52.50	4.00
A56	18¢ Violet	100.00	8.50
A57	19¢ Violet	135.00	15.00
A58	20¢ Violet	350.00	175.00
	"Cents" below value		
A59	1¢ Violet	50.00	10.00
A60	2¢ Violet	...	18.50
A61	4¢ Violet	42.50	32.50
A62	5¢ Violet	...	25.00
A63	6¢ Violet	65.00	22.50
A64	8¢ Violet	...	40.00
A65	9¢ Violet	12.00	9.50
A66	10¢ Violet	12.50	14.00
A67	16¢ Violet	15.00	12.50
A68	18¢ Violet	350.00	400.00
A69	19¢ Violet	10.00	...
A70	20¢ Violet	350.00	195.00
A71	25¢ Violet	...	23.50
A72	40¢ Violet	425.00	...
A73	$1 Green	...	1.00
A74	$1.28 Green	25.00	10.50

Imperf.

1963 Denom. added in blk. by rubber plate (similar to 1959 Postage Dues)

		Unused	Used
A76	1¢ Violet	75.00	75.00

1964 Denomination on Stamp Plate

A77	1¢ Violet	...	5.50

CONSULAR SERVICE FEE STAMPS

S. Consular Service Fee Stamps went into e on June 1, 1906 at U.S. consulates oughout the world. The stamps were ixed to documents to show that a fee for rvices had been paid. The revenue was to used to defray the expense of maintaining consular services.

RK 5 RK 36

1906 "Consular Service" Pf. 12

ott No.		Fine Used
1	25¢ Dark green	25.00
2	50¢ Carmine	35.00
3	$1 Dark violet	5.00
4	$2 Brown	4.25
5	$2.50 Dark blue	1.00
6	$5 Brown red	10.50
7	$10 Orange	32.50

Perf. 10

8	25¢ Dark green	25.00
9	50¢ Carmine	28.50
10	$1 Dark violet	200.00
11	$2 Brown	40.00
12	$2.50 Dark blue	10.75
13	$5 Brown red	52.50

Consular Service, Pf. 11

Scott No.		Fine Used
RK14	25¢ Dark green	32.50
RK15	50¢ Carmine	50.00
RK16	$1 Dark violet	1.50
RK17	$2 Brown	2.25
RK18	$2.50 Dark blue	.50
RK19	$5 Brown red	3.25
RK20	$9 Gray	8.50
RK21	$10 Orange	15.00

1924 "Foreign Service" Pf. 11

RK22	$1 Dark violet	32.50
RK23	$2 Brown	37.50
RK24	$2.50 Dark blue	7.50
RK25	$5 Brown red	25.00
RK26	$9 Gray	100.00

Issue of 1925-52 Perf. 10

RK27	$1 Violet	12.50
RK28	$2 Brown	32.50
RK29	$2.50 Ultramarine	1.35
RK30	$5 Carmine	8.00
RK31	$9 Gray	23.50

Perf. 11

RK32	25¢ Green	25.00
RK33	50¢ Orange	23.50
RK34	$1 Violet	2.50
RK35	$2 Brown	2.50
RK36	$2.50 Blue	.50
RK37	$5 Carmine	3.25
RK38	$9 Gray	10.50
RK39	$10 Blue gray	42.50
RK40	$20 Violet	50.00

CUSTOMS FEES

Customs Fees Stamps were issued in 1887 to indicate payment of fees to the U.S. Customs House, N.Y. They were affixed to documents and cancelled with a "PAID" handstamp.

RL 5

		F-VF Used
RL1	20¢ Dull Rose	1.00
RL2	30¢ Orange	1.75
RL3	40¢ Green	2.00
RL4	50¢ Dark blue	3.75
RL5	60¢ Red violet	1.75
RL6	70¢ Brown violet	23.50
RL7	80¢ Brown	57.50
RL8	90¢ Black	80.00

MOTOR VEHICLE USE STAMPS

Motor Vehicle Use Stamps were authorized by the Revenue Act of 1941. The annual tax amounted to $5.00, extending from July 1 to June 30, the government's fiscal year. Since the tax was to be reduced 1/12 of $5.00 each month after July, it was necessary to produce 12 stamps, each with a different dennomination and each decreasing in face value by 1/12 of the annual fee.

MOTOR VEHICLE USE STAMPS

RV 6 RV 42

1942 Gum on Back

		F-VF Unused
RV1	$2.09 Light green	1.00

Gum on Face, Inscription on Back

RV2	$1.67 Light green	12.00
RV3	$1.25 Light green	10.00
RV4	84¢ Light green	12.00
RV5	42¢ Light green	10.00

1942 Gum and Control # on Face

RV6	$5.00 Rose red	2.50
RV7	$4.59 Rose red	20.00
RV8	$4.17 Rose red	25.00
RV9	$3.75 Rose red	25.00
RV10	$3.34 Rose red	25.00
RV11	$2.92 Rose red	25.00

1943

RV12	$2.50 Rose red	25.00
RV13	$2.09 Rose red	20.00
RV14	$1.67 Rose red	15.00
RV15	$1.25 Rose red	15.00
RV16	84¢ Rose red	15.00
RV17	42¢ Rose red	15.00
RV18	$5.00 Yellow	2.50
RV19	$4.59 Yellow	25.00
RV20	$4.17 Yellow	35.00
RV21	$3.75 Yellow	35.00
RV22	$3.34 Yellow	42.50
RV23	$2.92 Yellow	50.00

1944

RV24	$2.50 Yellow	52.50
RV25	$2.09 Yellow	36.50
RV26	$1.67 Yellow	25.00
RV27	$1.25 Yellow	25.00
RV28	84¢ Yellow	21.00
RV29	42¢ Yellow	21.00

Gum on Face
Control # and Inscription on Back

RV30	$5.00 Violet	2.50
RV31	$4.59 Violet	41.50
RV32	$4.17 Violet	30.00
RV33	$3.75 Violet	30.00
RV34	$3.34 Violet	25.00
RV35	$2.92 Violet	25.00

1945

RV36	$2.50 Violet	25.00
RV37	$2.09 Violet	20.00
RV38	$1.67 Violet	20.00
RV39	$1.25 Violet	20.00
RV40	84¢ Violet	15.00
RV41	42¢ Violet	12.50

1945
Bright blue green & Yellow green

RV42	$5.00	2.50
RV43	$4.59	30.00
RV44	$4.17	30.00
RV45	$3.75	26.50
RV46	$3.34	25.00
RV47	$2.92	20.00

1946
Bright blue green & Yellow green

RV48	$2.50	20.00
RV49	$2.09	20.00
RV50	$1.67	14.50
RV51	$1.25	12.50
RV52	84¢	12.50
RV53	42¢	9.50

BOATING STAMPS

The Federal Boating Stamps, issued in 1960, covered boats of more than 10 horsepower. The $3 stamp indicated payment of the fee for a Coast Guard certificate. The $1 stamp covered the replacement of lost or destroyed certificates.

RVB 2

	1960 Rouletted	F-VF NH
RVB1	$1.00 Rose red,blk.#	32.50
	Plate Blk. of 4	140.00
RVB2	$3.00 Blue, red #	35.00
	Plate Blk. of 4	160.00

DISTILLED SPIRITS

Distilled Spirits Stamps were used to indicate payment of a tax on all whiskey held in bonded warehouses that had been on hand for four years or longer. Upon payment of the tax, the stamps were **stapled** to documents.

RX 18

Inscribed "STAMP FOR SERIES 1950" Yellow, Green & Black

Scott's No.		F-VF Unused	Used
RX1	1¢	27.50	22.50
RX2	3¢	90.00	85.00
RX3	5¢	18.50	15.00
RX4	10¢	16.50	13.50
RX5	25¢	9.50	7.50
RX6	50¢	9.50	7.50
RX7	$1	2.50	2.00
RX8	$3	20.00	16.50
RX9	$5	6.50	5.00
RX10	$10	3.00	2.50
RX11	$25	13.50	11.50
RX12	$50	7.50	6.50
RX13	$100	5.50	4.00
RX14	$300	25.00	22.50
RX15	$500	16.50	12.50
RX16	$1000	9.50	7.50
RX17	$1500	52.50	42.50
RX18	$2000	5.50	4.50
RX19	$3000	23.50	17.50
RX20	$5000	23.50	17.50
RX21	$10,000	27.50	22.50
RX22	$20,000	35.00	28.50
RX23	$30,000	75.00	55.00
RX24	$40,000	75.00	55.00
RX25	$50,000	85.00	75.00

DISTILLED SPIRITS
Inscription
"STAMP FOR SERIES 1950"
omitted

Yellow, Green & Black

		F-VF Punch Cancel
RX28	5¢	35.00
RX29	10¢	4.00
RX30	25¢	15.00
RX31	50¢	11.50
RX32	$1	1.75
RX33	$3	21.50
RX34	$5	23.50
RX35	$10	1.75
RX36	$25	9.50
RX37	$50	23.50
RX38	$100	2.25
RX39	$300	7.50
RX40	$500	32.50
RX41	$1000	6.50
RX42	$1500	57.50
RX43	$2000	57.50
RX44	$3000	...
RX45	$5000	38.50
RX46	$10,000	65.00

FIREARMS TRANSFER TAX STAMPS

Firearms Transfer Tax Stamps are applied to licenses issued by the Bureay of Alcohol, Tobacco and Firearms to indicate the registration of special classes of firearms. The $200 stamp is usually used with machine guns and is often referred to as the "Tommy Gun" stamp.

Documentary Stamp of 1917
Overprinted Vertically in Black

NATIONAL
FIREARMS
ACT

Without Gum		F-VF Unused
RY1	$1 Green	300.00

RY 2
Without Gum
$200 Face Value

		Unused
RY2	Dull blue & red Serial #3001 & up	225.00
RY2a	Dark blue & red Serial #1-1500	1250.00
RY2b	Dull blue & red Serial #1501-3000	450.00

FIREARMS TRANSFER TAX STAMPS

RY 3

With Gum

		F-VF Unused
RY3	$1 Green	75.00
RY4	$5 Red	10.00

RECTIFICATION TAX STAMPS

Rectification Tax Stamps were for the use of rectifiers in paying tax on liquor in bottling tanks. **Used stamps have staple holes.**

RZ12

		F-VF Unused	Used
RZ1	1¢	7.50	3.00
RZ2	3¢	25.00	8.50
RZ3	5¢	16.50	2.50
RZ4	10¢	16.50	2.50
RZ5	25¢	16.50	3.00
RZ6	50¢	20.00	5.00
RZ7	$1	20.00	5.00
RZ8	$3	...	17.50
RZ9	$5	37.50	10.00
RZ10	$10	30.00	3.25
RZ11	$25	...	10.50
RZ12	$50	...	8.00
RZ13	$100	...	9.50
RZ14	$300	...	9.50
RZ15	$500	...	9.50
RZ16	$1000	...	15.00
RZ17	$1500	...	40.00
RZ18	$2000	...	75.00

HUNTING PERMIT STAMPS

RW 1

RW 26

On each stamp the words "Void After ..." show a date 1 year later than the actual date of issue. Even though RW1 has on it "Void After June 30, 1935," the stamp was issued in 1934.
RW1-RW25, RW31 Plate Blocks of 6 Must Have Margins on Two Sides

RW1-RW10 VF Used + 50% (B)

Scott's No.		NH VF	NH F-VF	Unused VF	Unused F-VF	Used F-VF
RW1	1934, $1 Mallards	750.00	500.00	475.00	350.00	100.00
RW2	1935, $1 Canvasbacks	700.00	450.00	400.00	300.00	125.00
RW3	1936, $1 Canada Geese	395.00	250.00	225.00	150.00	65.00
RW4	1937, $1 Scaup Duck	325.00	200.00	160.00	120.00	40.00
RW5	1938, $1 Pintails	350.00	200.00	175.00	130.00	45.00
RW6	1939, $1 Teal	210.00	135.00	120.00	85.00	30.00
RW7	1940, $1 Mallards	210.00	135.00	120.00	85.00	30.00
RW8	1941, $1 Ruddy Ducks	210.00	135.00	120.00	85.00	30.00
RW9	1942, $1 Baldplates	210.00	135.00	125.00	90.00	25.00
RW10	1943, $1 Ducks	85.00	55.00	50.00	35.00	25.00

RW10-RW12 VF Used + 50% RW13-RW15 VF Used + 40%

RW11	1944, $1 Geese	95.00	55.00	50.00	35.00	25.00
RW12	1945, $1 Shovellers	70.00	45.00	42.50	30.00	16.50
RW13	1946, $1 Redheads	70.00	45.00	42.50	30.00	13.50
RW14	1947, $1 Snow Geese	70.00	45.00	42.50	30.00	13.50
RW15	1948, $1 Buffleheads	55.00	37.50	35.00	25.00	13.50

Plate Blocks	NH VF	NH F-VF	Unused F-VF
RW10 (6)	600.00	395.00	250.00
RW11 (6)	675.00	375.00	250.00
RW12 (6)	450.00	300.00	210.00

Plate Blocks	NH VF	NH F-VF	Unused F-VF
RW13 (6)	450.00	300.00	210.00
RW14 (6)	450.00	300.00	210.00
RW15 (6)	350.00	250.00	175.00

1949-58 Issues VF Used + 40%

Scott's No.		Pl# Blocks F-VF NH	VF NH	F-VF NH	F-VF Unus.	F-VF Used
RW16	1949, $2 Goldeneyes (6)	350.00	72.50	52.50	35.00	10.00
RW17	1950, $2 Swans (6)	400.00	82.50	60.00	40.00	10.00
RW18	1951, $2 Gadwalls (6)	400.00	82.50	60.00	40.00	10.00
RW19	1952, $2 Harlequins (6)	400.00	82.50	60.00	40.00	7.50
RW20	1953, $2 Teal (6)	400.00	82.50	60.00	40.00	7.50
RW21	1954, $2 Ring-neckeds (6)	400.00	82.50	60.00	40.00	7.50
RW22	1955, $2 Blue Geese (6)	400.00	82.50	60.00	40.00	7.50
RW23	1956, $2 Merganser (6)	400.00	82.50	60.00	40.00	7.50
RW24	1957, $2 Eider (6)	400.00	82.50	60.00	40.00	7.50
RW25	1958, $2 Canada Geese (6)	400.00	82.50	60.00	40.00	7.50

1959-71 Issues VF Used + 30%

RW26	1959, $3 Retriever	350.00	105.00	77.50	50.00	7.50
RW27	1960, $3 Redhead Ducks	350.00	100.00	75.00	50.00	7.50
RW28	1961, $3 Mallard	375.00	110.00	80.00	52.50	7.50
RW29	1962, $3 Pintail Ducks	400.00	120.00	85.00	60.00	9.00
RW30	1963, $3 Brant Landing	400.00	120.00	85.00	60.00	9.00
RW31	1964, $3 Hawaiian Nene (6)	1800.00	120.00	85.00	60.00	9.00
RW32	1965, $3 Canvasback Ducks	400.00	120.00	85.00	60.00	9.00
RW33	1966, $3 Whistling Swans	400.00	120.00	85.00	60.00	9.00
RW34	1967, $3 Old Squaw Ducks	400.00	120.00	85.00	60.00	9.00
RW35	1968, $3 Hooded Mergansers	240.00	70.00	55.00	37.50	9.00
RW36	1969, $3 White-winged Scooters	240.00	70.00	55.00	37.50	7.00
RW37	1970, $3 Ross's Geese	225.00	65.00	50.00	33.50	7.00
RW38	1971, $3 Cinnamon Teals	155.00	47.50	35.00	25.00	7.00

1972-95 Issues VF Used + 25%

Scott's No.		F-VF Pl# Blk	NH VF	NH F-VF	Used F-VF
RW39	1972, $5 Emperor Geese	110.00	30.00	22.50	7.00
RW40	1973, $5 Steller's Eiders	100.00	26.50	20.00	7.00
RW41	1974, $5 Wood Ducks	90.00	23.75	18.00	7.00
RW42	1975, $5 Decoy & Canvasbacks	62.50	18.75	14.00	7.00
RW43	1976, $5 Canada Geese	62.50	18.75	14.00	7.00
RW44	1977, $5 Pair of Ross's Geese	75.00	22.50	17.50	7.00
RW45	1978, $5 Hooded Merganser Drake	62.50	18.75	14.00	7.00
RW46	1979, $7.50 Green-winged Teal	75.00	22.50	17.50	7.00
RW47	1980, $7.50 Mallards	75.00	22.50	17.50	7.00
RW48	1981, $7.50 Ruddy Ducks	75.00	22.50	17.50	7.00
RW49	1982, $7.50 Canvasbacks	75.00	22.50	17.50	7.00
RW50	1983, $7.50 Pintails	75.00	22.50	17.50	7.00
RW51	1984, $7.50 Wigeon	75.00	22.50	17.50	7.00
RW52	1985, $7.50 Cinnamon Teal	75.00	22.50	17.50	7.00
RW53	1986, $7.50 Fulvous Whistling Duck	75.00	22.50	17.50	7.00
RW54	1987, $10 Red Head Ducks	90.00	25.00	20.00	10.00
RW55	1988, $10 Snow Goose	90.00	25.00	20.00	10.00
RW56	1989, $12.50 Lesser Scaups	100.00	28.00	22.50	10.00
RW57	1990, $12.50 Blk-Bellied Whistl. Duck	100.00	28.00	22.50	10.00
RW58	1991, $15.00 King Eiders	135.00	32.50	27.50	12.50
RW59	1992, $15.00 Spectacled Eider	135.00	32.50	27.50	12.50
RW60	1993, $15.00 Canvasbacks	135.00	32.50	27.50	12.50
RW61	1994, $15.00 Redbreasted Merganser	135.00	32.50	27.50	12.50
RW62	1995,*$15.00	135.00	32.50	27.50	12.50

MICHAEL JAFFE IS YOUR *TOTAL* DUCK DEALER.

Lists today for 825 times the original price.

Michael Jaffe introduced these super-rare Indian Ducks.

Michael knows Dogs - - and Fish and Birds and a lot more.

Why shop around when you can find 99% of all pictorial Duck stamps ever issued (including foreigns) in stock at Michael Jaffe at very competitive prices?

Michael Jaffe is also your best source for Duck Prints...albums...first day covers...and just about everything else related to Ducks. And Michael Jaffe guarantees 100% satisfaction on every purchase.

TOLL FREE 1-800-782-6770 (U.S. and Canada)
P.O. Box 61484, Vancouver, WA 98666 • fax (360) 695-1616
Dealer inquires welcome.

Michael Jaffe's New Issue Service is #1 for price, flexibility And now it's better than ever with the inclusion of Fish and Indian Reservation Fish & Game new issues.

Fax or call for your FREE copy of Michael Jaffe's complete price list, normally $2. It includes all Federal and State Ducks and because Michael Jaffe is the #1 dealer in the country in this exciting new area of specialized collection, it also includes 15 illustrated pages of Indian Reservation issues.

STATE DUCK STAMPS

State Duck Stamps provide a natural area for the person who wishes to expand his or her field interest beyond the collecting of Federal Ducks. In 1971, California became the first state to issue a picto duck stamp. Other states followed with the sales providing a much needed source of revenue for wetlan By 1994, all 50 states will have issued duck stamps.

Similar to Federal policy, many states hold an art competition to determine the winning design. Ot states commission an artist. Beginning in 1987, some states started to issue a "Governor's" stamp. The stamps with high face values were designed to garner additional wetland funds. In 1989, the Crow Cre Sioux Tribe of South Dakota became the first Indian Reservation to issue a pictorial duck stamp.

Hunter or Agent stamps generally come in booklets with a tab attached to the stamp, or specific se numbers on the stamp issued in sheet format that allows collectors' orders to be filled more easily. Many these stamps exist with plate numbers in the margin. The items illustrated below represent just a sampling the interesting varieties which have been produced by the various states.

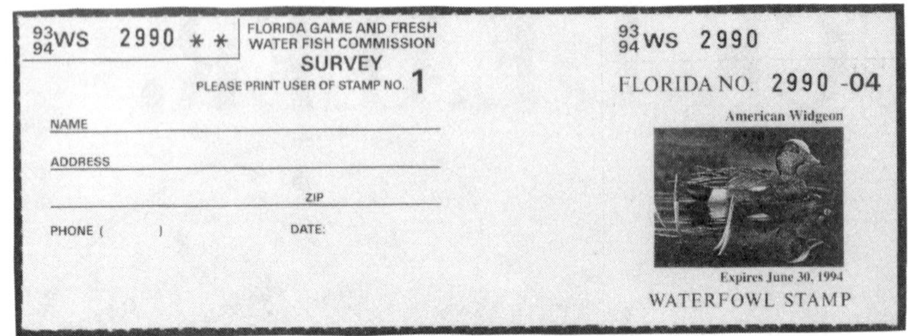

FL 15T SURVEY TAB

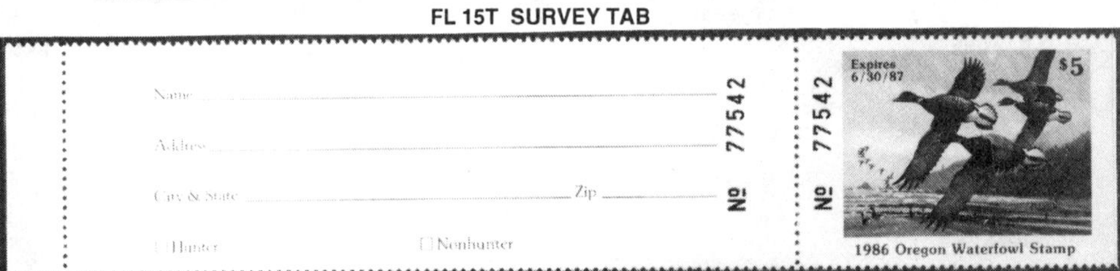

OR 3A HUNTER TYPE WITH TAB

WA 6AN MINI SHEET

MT 4A HZ. PAIR WITH SIDE MARGINS

AR 12 PROOF PAIR, IMPERF.

TN 1A NON-RES. LICENSE

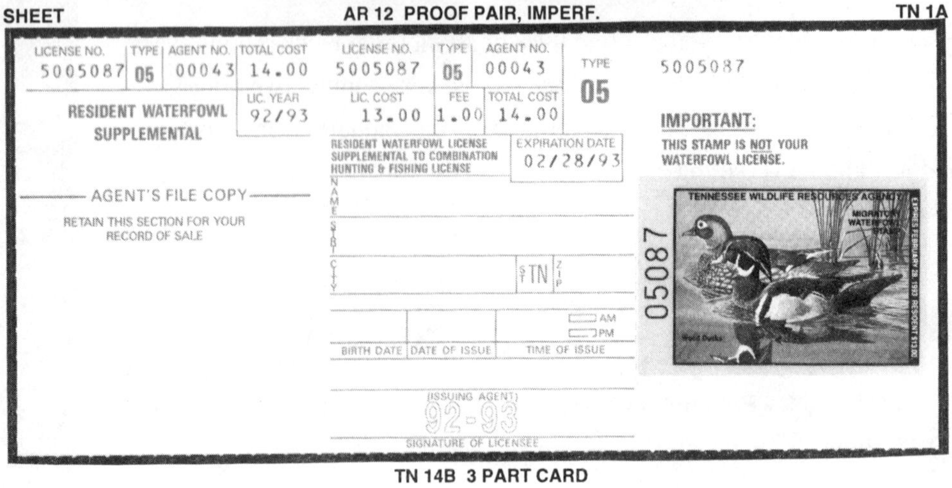

LICENSE NO. 5005087 | TYPE 05 | AGENT NO. 00043 | TOTAL COST 14.00 | LIC. YEAR 92/93

RESIDENT WATERFOWL SUPPLEMENTAL

AGENT'S FILE COPY

RETAIN THIS SECTION FOR YOUR RECORD OF SALE

LICENSE NO. 5005087 | TYPE 05 | AGENT NO. 00043 | LIC. COST 13.00 | FEE 1.00 | TOTAL COST 14.00 | TYPE 05

RESIDENT WATERFOWL LICENSE SUPPLEMENTAL TO COMBINATION HUNTING & FISHING LICENSE

EXPIRATION DATE 02/28/93

NAME / STREET / CITY / ST TN / ZIP

AM / PM

BIRTH DATE | DATE OF ISSUE | TIME OF ISSUE

(ISSUING AGENT)

92-93

SIGNATURE OF LICENSEE

5005087

IMPORTANT: THIS STAMP IS NOT YOUR WATERFOWL LICENSE.

TENNESSEE WILDLIFE RESOURCES AGENCY

MIGRATORY WATERFOWL STAMP

05087

TN 14B 3 PART CARD

STATE DUCK STAMPS

AL 1

AR 1

CA 8

CO 1

No.	Description	F-VF NH
	ALABAMA	
1	'79 $5 Wood Ducks	10.00
2	'80 $5 Mallards	10.00
3	'81 $5 Canada Geese	10.00
4	'82 $5 Grn Winged Teal	10.00
5	'83 $5 Widgeon	12.00
6	'84 $5 Buffleheads	12.00
7	'85 $5 Wood Ducks	17.00
8	'86 $5 Canada Geese	14.50
9	'87 $5 Pintails	17.00
10	'88 $5 Canvasbacks	12.00
11	'89 $5 Hooded Mergan	11.00
12	'90 $5 Wood Ducks	11.00
13	'91 $5 Redheads	11.00
14	'92 $5 Cinnamon Teal	10.00
15	'93 $5 Grn Winged Teal	10.00
16	'94 $5 Canvasbacks	10.00
17	'95 $5 Canda Geese	10.00
	Alabama Set 1979-94 (16)	**165.00**
	ALASKA	
1	'85 $5 Emperor Geese	17.00
2	'86 $5 Steller's Elders	12.00
3	'87 $5 Spectacled Elders	12.00
3A	'87 $5 Hunted Full Tab	16.00
4	'88 $5 Trumpeter Swan	11.50
4A	'88 $5 Hunter/Full Tab	14.00
5	'89 $5 Goldeneyes	9.00
5A	'89 $5 Hunter/Full Tab	10.00
5G	'89 $5 Governor's Ed	155.00
5GH	Same, Hand signed	250.00
6	'90 $5 Oldsquaw	9.00
6A	'90 $5 Hunter/Full Tab	9.50
7	'91 $5 Snowgeese	9.00
7A	'91 $5 Hunter/Full Tab	9.50
8	'92 $5 Canvasbacks	9.00
8A	'92 $5 Hunter/Full Tab	9.50
9	'93 $5 Wh. Fronted Geese	9.00
9A	'93 $5 Hunter/Full Tab	9.50
10	'94 $5 Harlequin	9.00
10A	'94 $5 Hunter/Full Tab	9.50
11	'95 $5 Pacific Brant	9.00
	Alaska Set 1985-94 (10)	**94.50**
	Alaska Hunter type, cplt. set (8)	**81.00**
	ARIZONA	
1	'87 $5.50 Pintails	11.00
1A	'87 $5.50 Hunter w/tab	17.00
2	'88 $5.50 Grn. Winged Teal	11.00
2A	'88 $5.50 Hunter w/tab	12.00
3	'89 $5.50 Cinnamon Teal	11.00
3A	'89 $5.50 Hunter w/tab	12.00
3G	'89 $5.50 Gov. Ed	72.50
3GH	Same, Hand signed	150.00
4	'90 $5.50 Canada Geese	11.00
4A	'90 $5.50 Hunter w/tab	12.00
4G	'90 $55.50 Gov. Ed	77.50
4GH	Same, Hand signed	170.00
5	'91 $5.50 Bl. Winged Teal	9.50
5A	'91 $5.50 Hunter w/tab	12.00
5G	'91 $55.50 Gov. Ed	83.50
5GH	Same, Hand signed	170.00
6	'92 $5.50 Buffleheads	9.50
6A	'92 $5.50 Hunter w/tab	12.00
6G	'92 $55.50 Gov. Ed	72.50
6GH	Same, Hand signed	155.00
7	'93 $5.50 Mexican Duck	9.50

No.	Desscription	F-VF NH
	ARIZONA	
AZ 7A	'93 $5.50 Hunter w/tab	9.50
AZ 7G	'93 $55.50 Gov. Ed	72.50
AZ 7GH	Same, Hand signed	140.00
AZ 8	'94 $5.50 Mallards	9.50
AZ 8A	'94 $5.50 Hunter w/tab	9.50
AZ 8G	'94 $55.50 Gov. Ed	72.50
AZ 8GH	Same, Hand signed	140.00
AZ 9	'95 $5.50 Wigeon	9.50
AZ 9A	'95 $5.50 Hunter w/tab	9.50
	Arizona Set 1987-94 (8)	**69.50**
	Arizona Hunter type, cplt. set	**83.50**
	ARKANSAS	
AR 1	'81 $5.50 Mallards	50.00
AR 1B	'81 Hunter (S# 110,001-200,000)	56.00
AR 1P	'81 Imperf Proof Pair	40.00
AR 2	'82 $5.50 Wood Ducks	50.00
AR 2B	'82 Hunter (S# 110,001-200,000)	50.00
AR 2P	'82 Imperf Proof Pair	34.00
AR 3	'83 $5.50 Grn.Wngd Teal	55.00
AR 3B	'83 Hunter (S# 70,001-160,000)	1000.00
AR 3P	'83 Imperf Proof Sgl	67.50
AR 4	'84 $5.50 Pintails	28.00
AR 4B	'84 Hunter (S# 25,001-100,000)	34.00
AR 4P	'84 Imperf Proof Pair	40.00
AR 5	'85 $5.50 Mallards	14.00
AR 5B	'85 Hunter (S# 25,001-100,000)	28.00
AR 5P	'85 Imperf Proof Pair	34.00
AR 6	'86 $5.50 Blk. Swamp Mallards	12.00
AR 6B	'86 Hunter (S# 25,001-100,000)	17.00
AR 6P	'86 Imperf Proof Pair	34.00
AR 7	'87 $7 Wood Ducks	12.00
AR 7A	'87 $5.50 Wood Ducks	13.00
AR 7B	'87 Hunter (S# 25,001-100,000)	14.00
AR 7P	'87 Imperf Proof Pair	23.00
AR 8	'88 $7 Pintails	11.00
AR 8A	'88 $5.50 Pintails	13.00
AR 8B	'88 Hunter (S# 25,001-100,000)	14.00
AR 8P	'88 Imperf Proof Pair	23.00
AR 9	'89 $7 Mallards	11.00
AR 9B	'89 Hunter (S# 30,001-100,000)	12.00
AR 9P	'89 Imperf Proof Pair	23.00
AR 10	'90 $7 Blk Duck/Mallards	11.00
AR 10B	'90 Hunter (S# 30,001-100,000)	12.00
AR 10P	'90 Imperf Proof Pair	23.00
AR 11	'91 $7 Widgeons	11.00
AR 11B	'91 Hunter (S# 30,001-100,000)	11.00
AR 11P	'91 Imperf Proof Pair	17.00
AR 12	'92 $7 Shovelers	11.00
AR 12B	'92 Hunter (S# 30,001-100,000)	11.00
AR 12P	'92 Imperf Proof Pair	17.00
AR 13	'93 $7 Mallards	11.00
AR 13B	'93 Hunter (S# 30,001-100,000)	11.00
AR 13P	'93 Imperf Proof Pair	17.00
AR 14	'94 $7 Canada Geese	11.00

No.	Description	F-VF NH
	ARKANSAS	
AR 14B	'94 Hunter (S# 25,001-100,000)	11.00
AR 14P	'94 Imperf. Proof Pair	16.00
AR 15	'95 $7 Mallard	11.00
AR 15B	'95 Hunter (S# 25,001-100,000)	11.00
	Arkansas Set 1981-94 (16)	**300.00**
	Arkansas Hunter, cplt (14)	**1225.00**
	Arkansas Imperfs, cplt (14)	**385.00**
	CALIFORNIA	
CA 1	'71 $1 Pintails Original Backing	825.00
CA 1	'71 $1 Unsigned w/o Orig. Backing	165.00
CA 2	'72 $1 Canvasback Original Backing	3500.00
CA 2	'72 $1 Unsigned w/o Orig. Backing	375.00
CA 3	'73 $1 Mallards	17.00
CA 4	'74 $1 Wh. Fronted Geese	5.00
CA 5	'75 $1 Grn. Winged Teal Clear Wax Back	165.00
CA 5R	'75 $1 Same, Ribbed Back	40.00
CA 6	'76 $1 Widgeon	17.00
CA 7	'77 $1 Cinnamon Teal	55.00
CA 7A	'78 $5 Cinnamon Teal	10.00
CA 8	'78 $5 Hooded Mergans	165.00
CA 9	'79 $5 Wood Ducks	9.00
CA 9P	'79 Imperf Proof Pair	55.00
CA 10	'80 $5 Pintails	9.00
CA 10P	'80 Imperf Proof Pair	55.00
CA 11	'81 $5 Canvasbacks	9.50
CA 12	'82 $5 Widgeon	9.50
CA 13	'83 $5 Grn.Winged Teal	9.50
CA 14	'84 $7.50 Mallard Decoy	12.00
CA 15	'85 $7.50 Ring Neck Duck	12.00
CA 16	'86 $7.50 Canada Goose	12.00
CA 17	'87 $7.50 Redheads	12.00
CA 18	'88 $7.50 Mallards	12.00
CA 19	'89 $7.50 Cinnamon Teal	12.00
CA 20	'90 $7.50 Canada Goose	12.00
CA 21	'91 $7.90 Gadwalls	12.00
CA 22	'92 $7.90 Wh.Frntd Goose	12.00
CA 23	'93 $10.50 Pintails	14.50
CA 24	'94 $10.50 Wood Ducks	14.50
CA 25	'95 $10.50 Snow Geese	14.50
	California Set 1973-94 (23)	**575.00**
	COLORADO	
CO 1	'90 $5 Canada Geese	17.00
CO 1A	'90 $5 Hunter w/tab	17.00
CO 1G	'90 $55 Governor's Ed	67.50
CO 1GH	'90 $55 Gov. Ed., Hand Signed	155.00
CO 1P	'90 Imperf. Proof perf.	395.00
CO 2	'91 $5 Mallards	14.00
CO 2A	'91 $5 Hunter w/tab	12.00
CO 2G	'91 $55 Governor's Ed	67.50
CO 2GH	'91 $55 Gov. Ed., Hand Signed	140.00
CO 3	'92 $5 Pintails	9.00
CO 3A	'92 $5 Hunter w/tab	11.00
CO 3G	'92 $55 Governor's Ed	67.50
CO 3GH	'92 $55 Gov. Ed., Hand Signed	135.00
CO 4	'93 $5 Grn. Winged Teal	9.00

No.	Description	F-VF NH
	COLORADO	
CO 4A	'93 $5 Hunter w/tab	9.50
CO 4G	'93 $55 Governor's Ed	62.50
CO 4GH	'93 $55 Gov. Ed., Hand Signed	135.00
CO 5	'94 $5 Wood Ducks	9.00
CO 5A	'94 $5 Hunter w/tab	9.50
CO 6	'95 $5 Buffleheads	9.00
CO 6A	'95 $5 Hunter w/tab	9.50
	Colorado Set 1990-94 (5)	**52.50**
	Colorado Hunter Set 1990-94 (5)	**52.50**
	CONNECTICUT	
CT 1	'93 $5 Black Ducks	9.00
CT 1A	'93 $5 Hunter Hz. Pair	18.00
CT 1G	'93 $55 Governor's Ed	85.00
CT 1GH	'93 $55 Gov. Ed. Hand Signed	175.00
CT 1M	'93 Commem. Sht. of 4	75.00
CT 2	'94 $5 Canvasbacks	8.50
CT 2A	'94 $5 Hunter Horiz. Pair	17.00
CT 2M	'94 Commem Sheet of 4	39.00
CT 3	'95 $5 Mallards	8.50
CT 3A	'95 $5 Hunter Horiz. Pair	17.00
	DELAWARE	
DE 1	'80 $5 Black Ducks	105.00
DE 2	'81 $5 Snow Geese	95.00
DE 3	'82 $5 Canada Geese	90.00
DE 4	'83 $5 Canvasbacks	62.50
DE 5	'84 $5 Mallards	28.00
DE 6	'85 $5 Pintail	16.00
DE 7	'86 $5 Widgeon	13.00
DE 8	'87 $5 Redheads	12.00
DE 9	'88 $5 Wood Ducks	10.00
DE 10	'89 $5 Buffleheads	9.50
DE 11	'90 $5 Grn. Winged Teal	9.50
DE 11G	'90 $5 Governor's Ed	95.00
DE 11GH	'90 $55 Gov. Ed., Hand Signed	245.00
DE 12	'91 $5 Hooded Mergans	9.50
DE 12A	'91 Hunter-S# on Back	11.00
DE 13	'92 $5 Bl. Wngd. Teal	9.50
DE 13A	'92 Hunter-S# on Back	9.50
DE 14	'93 $5 Goldeneyes	9.50
DE 14A	'93 Hunter-S# on Back	9.50
DE 15	'94 $5 Blue Geese	9.50
DE 15A	'94 Hunter-Serial Number on back	9.50
DE 16	'95 $5 Scaup	9.00
DE 16A	'95 Hunter-Serial Number on back	9.50
	Delaware Set 1980-94 (15)	**509.00**

STATE DUCK STAMPS

FL 5

IL 1

KS 1AS

KY 7

FLORIDA

No.	Description	F-VF NH
FL 1	'79 $3.25 Grn Wngd Teal	175.00
FL 1T	'79 $3.25 Full Tab Attd	215.00
FL 2	'80 $3.25 Pintails	28.00
FL 2T	'80 $3.25 Full Tab Attd	40.00
FL 3	'81 $3.25 Widgeon	28.00
FL 3T	'81 $3.25 Full Tab Attd	40.00
FL 4	'82 $3.25 Ring-Neck Duck	40.00
FL 4T	'82 $3.25Full Tab Attd	50.00
FL 5	'83 $3.25 Buffleheads	67.00
FL 5T	'83 $3.25Full Tab Attd	77.50
FL 6	'84 $3.25 Hooded Merg	23.00
FL 6T	'84 $3.25 Full Tab Attd	28.00
FL 7	'85 $3.25 Wood Ducks	23.00
FL 7T	'85 $3.25 Full Tab Attd	28.00
FL 8	'86 $3.00 Canvasbacks	11.00
FL 8T	'86 $3.00 Survey Tab Attd	28.00
FL 9	'87 $3.50 Mallards	9.50
FL 9T	'87 $3.50 Survey Tab Attd	25.00
FL 10	'88 $3.50 Redheads	9.50
FL 10T	'88 $3.50 Survey Tab Attd	23.00
FL 11	'89 $3.50 Bl. Winged Teal	7.50
FL 11T	'89 $3.50 Survey Tab Attd	23.00
FL 12	'90 $3.50 Wood Ducks	7.50
FL 12T	'90 $3.50 Survey Tab Attd	23.00
FL 13	'91 $3.50 Northern Pintail	7.50
FL 13T	'91 $3.50 Survey Tab Attd	17.00
FL 14	'92 $3.50 Ruddy Duck	7.50
FL 14T	'92 $3.50 Survey Tab Attd	14.00
FL 15	'93 $3.50 Amer. Widgeon	7.00
FL 15T	'93 $3.50 Survey Tab Attd	14.00
FL 16	'94 $3.50 Mottled Duck	6.50
FL 16T	'94 $3.50 Survey Tab Attd.	14.00
FL 17	'95 $3.50 Fulvous Whistling Duck	6.50
FL 17T	'95 Survey Tab Attd.	12.00

Florida Set 1979-94 (16) 425.00
Florida Tabs Set 1979-94 (16) 625.00

GEORGIA

No.	Description	F-VF NH
GA 1	'85 $5.50 Wood Ducks	14.00
GA 2	'86 $5.50 Mallards	12.00
GA 3	'87 $5.50 Canada Geese	8.50
GA 4	'88 $5.50 Ring Neck Ducks	8.50
GA 5	'89 $5.50 Duckling/Puppy	8.50
GA 6	'90 $5.50 Wood Ducks	8.50
GA 7	'91 $5.50 Grn. Winged Teal	8.50
GA 8	'92 $5.50 Buffleheads	8.50
GA 9	'93 $5.50 Mallards	8.50
GA 10	'94 $5.50 Ringnecks	8.50
GA 11	'95 $5.50 Widgeons/Black Lab	8.50

Georgia Set 1985-93 (10) 85.00

IDAHO

No.	Description	F-VF NH
ID 1	'87 $5.50 Cinnamon Teals	23.00
ID 1A	'87 $5.50 Bklt. sgl. w/Tab	17.00
ID 2	'88 $5.50 Grn. Winged Teal	13.00
ID 2A	'88 $5.50 Bklt. sgl. w/Tab	13.00
ID 3	'89 $6.00 Bl. Winged Teal	11.00
ID 3A	'89 $6.00 Bklt. sgl. w/Tab	11.00
ID 4	'90 $6.00 Trumpeter Swan	14.00
ID 4A	'90 $6.00 Bklt. sgl. w/Tab	11.00
ID 5	'91 $6.00 Amer. Widgeons	9.50
ID 5A	'91 $6.00 Bklt. sgl. w/Tab	11.00
ID 5X	'91 $6.00 Provisional	110.00
ID 6	'92 $6.00 Canada Geese	9.50
ID 6A	'92 $6.00 Bklt. sgl. w/Tab	9.50
ID 7	'93 $6.00 Com'n Goldeneye	10.00
ID 7A	'93 $6.00 Bklt. sgl. w/Tab	9.50
ID 8	'94 $6.00 Harlequin	9.50
ID 8A	'94 $6.00 Bklt. sgl. w/Tab	9.50
ID 9	'95 $6	9.50
ID 9A	'95 $6 Bklt. Sgl. w/tab	9.50

IDAHO

Idaho Set 1987-94 (8) 90.00
Idaho Bklt. Set 1987-94 (8) 82.50

ILLINOIS

No.	Desscription	F-VF NH
IL 1	'75 $5 Mallard	750.00
IL 2	'76 $5 Wood Ducks	390.00
IL 3	'77 $5 Canada Goose	250.00
IL 4	'78 $5 Canvasbacks	135.00
IL 5	'79 $5 Pintail	135.00
IL 6	'80 $5 Grn. Winged Teal	135.00
IL 7	'81 $5 Widgeon	145.00
IL 7A	'81 $5 G.W. Teal Error	585.00
IL 8	'82 $5 Black Ducks	72.50
IL 9	'83 $5 Lesser Scaup	67.50
IL 10	'84 $5 Bl. Winged Teal	67.50
IL 11	'85 $5 Red Head	27.00
IL 11T	'85 $5 Full Tab Attd	33.00
IL 12	'86 $5 Gadwalls	15.00
IL 12T	'86 $5 Full Tab Attd	17.00
IL 13	'87 $5 Buffleheads	12.00
IL 13T	'87 $5 Full Tab Attd	14.00
IL 14	'88 $5 Com'n Goldeneye	12.00
IL 14T	'88 $5 Full Tab Attd	14.00
IL 15	'89 $5 Ring Neck Duck	10.00
IL 15T	'89 $5 Full Tab Attd	11.00
IL 16	'90 $10 Lesser Snow Gs	16.00
IL 16T	'90 $10 Full Tab Attd	17.00
IL 17	'91 $10 Blk. Lab/Can. Gs.	15.00
IL 17G	'91 $10 Gov. Edition	95.00
IL 17GH	'91 $10 Gov. Ed., Hand Signed	185.00
IL 17T	'91 $10 Full Tab Attd	17.00
IL 18	'92 $10 Retvr./Mallards	15.00
IL 18T	"92 $10 Full Tab Attd	17.00
IL 19	'93 $10 Puppy/Decoy	15.00
IL 19T	'93 $10 Full Tab Attd	17.00
IL 20	'94 $10 Chessies & Canvasbacks	15.00
IL 20T	'94 $10 Full Tab Attd	16.00
IL 21	'95 *Green Winged Teal/C. Lab	14.50
IL 21T	'95 Full Tab Attd.	16.00

Illinois Set 1975-94 Without Error (20) 2175.00

INDIANA

No.	Description	F-VF NH
IN 1	'76 $5 Grn. Winged Teal	9.00
IN 2	'77 $5 Pintail	9.00
IN 3	'78 $5 Canada Geese	9.00
IN 4	'79 $5 Canvasbacks	9.00
IN 5	'80 $5 Mallard Ducklings	9.00
IN 6	'81 $5 Hooded Mergans	9.00
IN 7	'82 $5 Bl. Winged Teal	9.00
IN 8	'83 $5 Snow Geese	9.00
IN 9	'84 $5 Redheads	9.00
IN 10	'85 $5 Pintail	9.00
IN 10T	'85 $5 Full Tab Attd	12.00
IN 11	'86 $5 Wood Duck	9.00
IN 11T	'86 $5 Full Tab Attd	12.00
IN 12	'87 $5 Canvasbacks	9.00
IN 12T	'87 $5 Full Tab Attd	12.00
IN 13	'88 $6.75 Redheads	11.00
IN 13T	'88 $6.75 Full Tab Attd	12.00
IN 14	'89 $6.75 Canada Goose.	11.00
IN 14T	'89 $6.75 Full Tab Attd	12.00
IN 15	'90 $6.75 Bl. Winged Teal	11.00
IN 15T	'90 $6.75 Full Tab Attd	12.00
IN 16	'91 $6.75 Mallards	11.00
IN 16T	'91 $6.75 Full Tab Attd	12.00
IN 17	'92 $6.75 Grn. Winged Tl.	11.00
IN 17T	'92 $6.75 Full Tab Attd	12.00
IN 18	'93 $6.75 Wood Ducks	11.00
IN 18T	'93 $6.75 Full Tab Attd	12.00
IN 19	'94 $6.75 Pintail	11.00
IN 19T	'94 $6.75 Full Tab Attd	12.00
IN 20	'95 $6.75 Goldeneyes	11.00
IN 20T	'95 $6.75 Full Tab Attd.	12.00

Indiana Set 1976-94 (19) 161.00

IOWA

No.	Description	F-VF NH
IA 1	'72 $1 Mallards	195.00
IA 2	'73 $1 Pintails	45.00
IA 3	'74 $1 Gadwalls	85.00
IA 4	'75 $1 Canada Geese	125.00
IA 5	'76 $1 Canvasbacks	21.00
IA 6	'77 $1 Lesser Scaup	21.00
IA 7	'78 $1 Wood Ducks	67.50
IA 8	'79 $5 Buffleheads	420.00
IA 9	'80 $5 Redheads	35.00
IA 10	'81 $5 Grn. Winged Teal	40.00
IA 11	'82 $5 Snow Geese	18.00
IA 12	'83 $5 Widgeon	17.00
IA 13	'84 $5 Wood Ducks	45.00
IA 14	'85 $5 Mallard & Decoy	23.00
IA 15	'86 $5 Bl. Wngd. Teal	16.00
IA 16	'87 $5 Canada Goose	14.00
IA 17	'88 $5 Pintails	12.00
IA 18	'89 $5 Bl. Winged Teal	12.00
IA 19	'90 $5 Canvasback	8.00
IA 19A	'90 Serial #26001-80000	12.00
IA 20	'91 $5 Mallards	8.00
IA 21	'92 $5 Blk. Lab/Ducks	9.50
IA 22	'93 $5 Mallards	9.50
IA 23	'94 $5 Grn. Winged Teal	9.00
IA 24	'95 $5 Canada Geese	9.00

Iowa Set 1972-94 (23) 1175.00

KANSAS

No.	Description	F-VF NH
KS 1	'87 $3 Grn. Winged Teal	8.50
KS 1	'87 $3 Horiz. Pair	17.00
KS 1AD	'87 Hunter sgl. with DD in Serial Number	8.50
KS 1AD	'87 Horiz. Pair with DD in Serial Number	17.00
KS 1AS	'87 Hunter sgl. with SS in Serial Number	8.50
KS 1AS	'87 Horiz. Pair with SS in Serial Number	17.00
KS 2	'88 $3 Canada Geese	6.50
KS 2A	'88 Hunter sgl.	8.50
KS 2A	'88 $3 Horiz. Pair	17.00
KS 3	'89 $3 Mallards	6.50
KS 3A	'89 Hunter sgl.	7.00
KS 3A	'89 $3 Horiz. Pair	14.00
KS 4	'90 $3 Wood Ducks	6.50
KS 4A	'90 Hunter sgl.	7.00
KS 4A	'90 $3 Horiz. Pair	12.50
KS 5	'91 $3 Pintail	6.00
KS 5A	'91 Hunter sgl.	7.00
KS 5A	'91 $3 Horiz. Pair	12.50
KS 6	'92 $3 Canvasbacks	6.00
KS 7	'93 $3 Mallards	6.00
KS 8	'94 $3 Blue Winged Teal.	6.00
KS 9	'95 $3 Barrow's Goldeneyes	6.00

Kansas Set 1987-94 (8) 47.00
Kansas Hunters Pairs Set 1987-91 (5) 85.00

KENTUCKY

No.	Description	F-VF NH
KY 1	'85 $5.25 Mallards	14.00
KY 1T	'85 $5.25 Full Tab Attd	15.00
KY 2	'86 $5.25 Wood Ducks	9.50
KY 2T	'86 $5.25 Full Tab Attd	12.00
KY 3	'87 $5.25 Black Ducks	9.50
KY 3T	'87 $5.25 Full Tab Attd	12.00
KY 4	'88 $5.25 Canada Goose	9.50
KY 4T	'88 $5.25 Full Tab Attd	12.00
KY 5	'89 $5.25 Cnvsbk/Retrvr.	9.50
KY 5T	'89 $5.25 Full Tab Attd	12.00
KY 6	'90 $5.25 Widgeons	9.50
KY 6T	'90 $5.25 Full Tab Attd	12.00
KY 7	'91 $5.25 Pintails	9.50
KY 7T	'91 $5.25 Full Tab Attd	12.00
KY 8	'92 $5.25 Grn. Winged Teal	12.00
KY 8T	'92 $5.25 Full Tab Attd	12.00
KY 9	'93 $5.25 Canvasbk/Decoy	12.00
KY 9T	'93 $5.25 Full Tab Attd	12.00
KY 10	'94 $5.25 Canada Goose	9.50
KY 10T	'94 $5.25 Full Tab Attd	9.50
KY 11	'95 $7.50 Ringnecks/ Black Lab	11.50
KY 11T	'95 $7.50 Full tab attd	12.00

Kentucky Set 1985-94 (10) 95.63

LOUISIANA

No.	Description	F-VF NH
LA 1	'89 $5 Bl. Winged Teal	12.00
LA 1A	'89 $7.50 Non-Resident	15.00
LA 1G & 1AG	Gov. Resident & Non-Resident	275.00
LA 1GH & 1AGH	Governor Ed., Hand Signed	585.00
LA 2	'90 $5 Grn. Winged Teal	9.00
LA 2A	'90 $7.50 Non-Resident	13.00
LA 3	'91 $5 Wood Ducks	9.50
LA 3A	'91 $7.50 Non-Resident	13.00
LA 4	'92 $5 Pintails	8.50
LA 4A	'92 $7.50 Non-Resident	11.75
LA 5	'93 $5 Amer. Widgeons	8.50
LA 5A	'93 $7.50 Non-Resident	11.75
LA 6	'94 $5 Mottled Duck	8.50
LA 6A	'94 $7.50 Non-Resident	11.50
LA 7	'95 $5 Speckled Belly Goose	8.50
LA 7A	'95 $7.50 Non-Resident	11.50

Louisiana Set Resident & Non-Res. 1989-94 (12) 117.00

MAINE

No.	Description	F-VF NH
ME 1	'84 $2.50 Black Ducks	34.00
ME 2	'85 $2.50 Common Eiders	55.00
ME 3	'86 $2.50 Wood Ducks	11.00
ME 4	'87 $2.50 Buffleheads	8.50
ME 5	'88 $2.50 Grn. Winged Teal	8.50
ME 6	'89 $2.50 Goldeneyes	6.00
ME 7	'90 $2.50 Canada Geese	6.00
ME 8	'91 $2.50 Ring Neck Duck	6.00
ME 9	'92 $2.50 Old Squaw	6.00
ME 10	'93 $2.50 Hooded Mergans	6.00
ME 11	'94 $2.50 Mallards	6.00
ME 12	'95 $2.50 White Winged Scoter	6.00

Maine Set 1984-94 (11) 139.00

STATE DUCK STAMPS

MA 18

MI 6

MT 1

NE 2

Description	F-VF NH
MARYLAND	
1 '74 $1.10 Mallards	14.50
2 '75 $1.10 Canada Geese	12.00
3 '76 $1.10 Canvasbacks	12.00
4 '77 $1.10 Greater Scaup	12.00
5 '78 $1.10 Redheads	12.00
6 '79 $1.10 Wood Ducks	11.00
7 '80 $1.10 Pintail Decoy	11.00
8 '81 $3.00 Widgeon	7.00
9 '82 $3.00 Canvasbacks	10.00
10 '83 $3.00 Wood Duck	14.00
11 '84 $6.00 Black Duck	12.00
12 '85 $6.00 Canada Geese	11.00
13 '86 $6.00 Hooded Mergan	11.00
14 '87 $6.00 Redheads	11.00
15 '88 $6.00 Ruddy Duck	11.00
16 '89 $6.00 Bl. Wngd. Teal	12.00
17 '90 $6.00 Lesser Scaup	10.00
18 '91 $6.00 Shovelers	10.00
19 '92 $6.00 Bufflehead	10.00
20 '93 $6.00 Canvasbacks	10.00
21 '94 $6.00 Redheads	10.00
yland Set 1974-94 (21)	**205.00**
MASSACHUSETTS	
1 '74 $1.25 Wood Duck	16.00
2 '75 $1.25 Pintail	12.00
3 '76 $1.25 Canada Goose	12.00
4 '77 $1.25 Goldeneye	12.00
5 '78 $1.25 Black Duck	12.00
6 '79 $1.25 Ruddy Turnstone	12.00
7 '80 $1.25 Old Squaw	12.00
8 '81 $1.25 Rd Brstd Mrgnsr	10.00
9 '82 $1.25 Grtr. Yellowlegs	10.00
10 '83 $1.25 Redhead	9.50
11 '84 $1.25 Wh. Ringed Scooter	9.50
12 '85 $1.25 Ruddy Duck	9.50
13 '86 $1.25 Preening Bluebill	9.50
14 '87 $1.25 Amer. Widgeon	9.50
15 '88 $1.25 Mallard Drake	9.00
16 '89 $1.25 Brant	6.00
17 '90 $1.25 Whistler Hen	6.00
18 '91 $5 Canvasback	8.50
19 '92 $5 Blk-Bellied Plover	8.50
20 '93 $5 Rd Breasted Merg	8.50
21 '94 $5 Wh. Winged Scoter	8.50
22 '95 $5 Hooded Merganser	8.50
sachusetts Set 1974-94 (21)	**178.00**
MICHIGAN	
'76 $2.10 Wood Duck	5.00
'77 $2.10 Canvasbacks	330.00
'78 $2.10 Mallards	28.00
T '78 $2.10 Full Tab	50.00
'79 $2.10 Canada Geese	50.00
T '79 $2.10 Full Tab	67.50
'80 $3.75 Lesser Scaup	23.00
T '80 $3.75 Full Tab	34.00
'81 $3.75 Buffleheads	28.00
'82 $3.75 Redheads	28.00
'83 $3.75 Wood Ducks	28.00
'84 $3.75 Pintails	28.00
0 '85 $3.75 Ring Neck Duck	28.00
1 '86 $3.75 Com'n Goldeneyes	21.00
2 '87 $3.85 Grn. Winged Teal	12.00
3 '88 $3.85 Canada Goose	10.00

No.	Desscription	F-VF NH
	MICHIGAN	
MI 14	'89 $3.85 Widgeon	8.00
MI 15	'90 $3.85 Wood Ducks	8.00
MI 16	'91 $3.85 Bl. Wngd. Teal	7.00
MI 17	'92 $3.85 Rd Breasted Merg	7.00
MI 18	'93 $3.85 Hooded Mergan	7.00
MI 19	'94 $3.85 Black Duck	7.00
MI 20	'95 $4.35 Blue Winged Teal	8.00
Michigan Set 1976-94 (19)		**630.00**
	MINNESOTA	
MN 1	'77 $3 Mallards	17.00
MN 2	'78 $3 Lesser Scaup	11.00
MN 3	'79 $3 Pintails	11.00
MN 4	'80 $3 Canvasbacks	11.00
MN 5	'81 $3 Canada Geese	10.00
MN 6	'82 $3 Redheads	11.00
MN 7	'83 $3 Bl & Snow Geese	11.00
MN 8	'84 $3 Wood Ducks	11.00
MN 9	'85 $3 Wh. Front Geese	9.00
MN 10	'86 $5 Lesser Scaup	10.00
MN 11	'87 $5 Goldeneyes	12.00
MN 11T	'87 $5 Full Tab	14.50
MN 12	'88 $5 Buffleheads	11.00
MN 12T	'88 $5 Full Tab	14.50
MN 13	'89 $5 Amer. Widgeons	11.00
MN 13T	'89 $5 Full Tab	14.50
MN 14	'90 $5 Hooded Mergan	17.00
MN 14T	'90 $5 Full Tab	21.50
MN 15	'91 $5 Ross' Goose	9.00
MN 15T	'91 $5 Full Tab	9.50
MN 16	'92 $5 Barrow's Gold'eye	9.00
MN 16T	'92 $5 Full Tab	9.50
MN 17	'93 $5 Bl. Winged Teal	9.00
MN 17T	'93 $5 Full Tab	9.50
MN 18	'94 $5 Ring Necked Duck	9.00
MN 18T	'94 $5 Full Tab	9.50
MN 19	'95 $5 Gadwalls	9.00
MN 19T	'95 $5 Full Tab	9.50
Minnesota Set 1977-94 (18)		**175.00**
	MISSISSIPPI	
MS 1	'76 $2 Wood Duck	23.00
MS 1B	'76 $2 Full Comput. Card	28.00
MS 2	'77 $2 Mallards	9.00
MS 3	'78 $2 Grn. Winged Teal	9.00
MS 4	'79 $2 Canvasbacks	9.00
MS 5	'80 $2 Pintails	9.00
MS 5	'81 $2 Redheads	9.00
MS 6	'82 $2 Canada Geese	8.00
MS 7	'82 $2 Canada Geese	9.00
MS 8	'83 $2 Lesser Scaup	9.00
MS 9	'84 $2 Black Ducks	9.00
MS 10	'85 $2 Mallards	9.00
MS 10A	'85 Serial # Error-No Hz#	165.00
MS 10B	'85 Serial # Var.- No Silver Bar	500.00
MS 11	'86 $2 Widgeon	9.00
MS 12	'87 $2 Ring Neck Ducks	9.00
MS 13	'88 $2 Snow Geese	9.00
MS 14	'89 $2 Wood Ducks	6.50
MS 15	'90 $2 Snow Geese	14.00
MS 15GH	'90 Governor's Ed., Hand Signed	1000.00
MS 16	'91 $2 Blk. Lab/ Canvasbk Decoy	5.50
MS 17	'92 $2 Grn. Winged Teal	5.00
MS 17GH	'92 $2 Governor's Ed., Hand Signed	650.00
MS 18	'93 $5 Mallards	8.00
MS 18GH	'93 $5 Governor's Ed., Hand Signed	450.00
MS 19	'94 $5 Canvasbacks	8.00

No.	Description	F-VF NH
	MISSISSIPPI	
MS 19GH	'94 $5 Governor's Ed., Hand signed	295.00
MS 20	'95 $5 Blue Winged Teal	8.00
Mississippi Set 1976-94 (19)		**162.00**
	MISSOURI	
MO 1	'79 $3.40 Canada Geese	835.00
MO 1T	'79 $3.40 Full Tab Attd	1050.00
MO 2	'80 $3.40 Wood Ducks	139.00
MO 2T	'80 $3.40 Full Tab Attd	195.00
MO 3	'81 $3 Lesser Scaup	85.00
MO 3T	'81 $3 Full Tab Attd	105.00
MO 4	'82 $3 Buffleheads	55.00
MO 4T	'82 $3 Full Tab Attd	85.00
MO 5	'83 $3 Bl. Wngd. Teal	50.00
MO 5T	'83 $3 Full Tab Attd	85.00
MO 6	'84 $3 Mallards	45.00
MO 6T	'84 $3 Full Tab Attd	72.50
MO 7	'85 $3 Widgeon	28.00
MO 7T	'85 $3 Full Tab Attd	40.00
MO 8	'86 $3 Hooded Mergans	17.00
MO 8T	'86 $3 Full Tab Attd	28.00
MO 9	'87 $3 Pintails	12.00
MO 9T	'87 $3 Full Tab Attd	21.00
MO 10	'88 $3 Canvasbacks	11.00
MO 10T	'88 $3 Full Tab Attd	12.00
MO 11	'89 $3 Ring Neck Ducks	8.50
MO 11T	'89 $3 Full Tab Attd	9.50
MO 12	'90 $3 Redheads	8.00
MO 12T	'90 $3 Full Tab Attd	10.00
MO 12G	'90 $50 Governor's Ed	85.00
MO 12GH	'90 $100 Governor's Ed., Hand Signed	1500.00
MO 13	'91 $5 Snow Geese	8.00
MO 13T	'91 $5 Full Tab Attd	11.00
MO 13G	'91 $50 Governor's Ed	85.00
MO 13GH	"91 $100 Governor's Ed., Hand Signed	1000.00
MO 14	'92 $5 Gadwalls	8.00
MO 14G	'92 $50 Governor's Ed	80.00
MO 14GH	'92 $100 Governor's Ed., Hand Signed	950.00
MO 15	'93 $5 Grn. Winged Teal	8.00
MO 15T	'93 $5 Full Tab Attd	10.00
MO 15G	'93 $50 Governor's Ed	80.00
MO 15GH	'93 $100 Governor's Ed., Hand Signed	950.00
MO 16	'94 $5 Wh Fronted Geese	8.00
MO 16T	'94 $5 Full Tab Attd	9.00
MO 16G	'94 $50 Governor's Ed	80.00
MO 16GH	'94 $100 Governor's Ed., Hand Signed	750.00
Missouri Set 1979-94 (16)		**1250.00**
Missouri Tab Set 1979-94 (16)		**1655.00**
	MONTANA	
MT 1	'86 $5 Canada Geese	17.00
MT 1A	'86 $5 Horiz. Pair w/ Side Margins	2800.00
MT 2	'87 $5 Redheads	17.00
MT 2A	'87 $5 Hz.Pr./side mgns	55.00
MT 3	'88 $5 Mallards	14.00
MT 3A	'88 $5 Hz.Pr./side mgns	34.00
MT 4	'89 $5 Blk. Lab & Pintail	9.00
MT 4A	'89 $5 Hz.Pr./side mgns	34.00
MT 4G	'89 $5 Governor's Edit'n	145.00
MT 4GH	'89 Same, Hand Signed	275.00
MT 5	'90 $5 Cinn & Bl.Wng.Teal	8.50
MT 5A	'90 $5 Hz.Pr./side mgns	22.00
MT 6	'91 $5 Snow Geese	8.50
MT 6A	'91 $5 Hz.Pr./side mgns	23.00
MT 7	'92 $5 Wood Ducks	8.50
MT 7A	'92 $5 Hz.Pr./side mgns	23.00

No.	Description	F-VF NH
	MONTANA	
MT 8	'93 $5 Harlequin	8.50
MT 8A	'93 $5 Hz.Pr./side mgns	23.00
MT 9	'94 $5 Widgeon	8.50
MT 9A	'94 $5 Hz.Pr./side mgns.	23.00
MT 10	'95 $5 Tundra Swans	8.50
MT 10A	'95 Horz. Pr/side magns.	23.00
Montana Set 1986-94 (9)		**91.00**
	NEBRASKA	
NE 1	'91 $6 Canada Goose	11.00
NE 1GH	'91 Gov. Ed. Hand Sig	139.00
NE 2	'92 $6 Pintails	9.00
NE 3	'93 $6 Canvasbacks	9.00
NE 4	'94 $6 Mallard	9.00
NE 5	'95 $6 Wood Ducks	9.00
Nebraska Set 1991-94 (4)		**36.00**
	NEVADA	
NV1	'79 $2 Canvasbks/Decoy	55.00
NV 1T	'79 $2 Serial # Tab Attd.	72.50
NV 2	'80 $2 Cinnamon Teal	11.00
NV 2T	'80 $2 Serial # Tab Attd.	13.00
NV 3	'81 $2 Whistling Swans	12.00
NV 3T	'81 $2 Serial # Tab Attd.	14.00
NV 4	'82 $2 Shovelers	12.00
NV 4T	'82 $2 Serial # Tab Attd.	14.00
NV 5	'83 $2 Gadwalls	12.00
NV 5T	'83 $2 Serial # Tab Attd.	14.00
NV 6	'84 $2 Pintails	12.00
NV 6T	'84 $2 Serial # Tab Attd.	14.00
NV 7	'85 $2 Canada Geese	12.00
NV 7T	'85 $2 Serial # Tab Attd.	14.00
NV 8	'86 $2 Redheads	12.00
NV 8T	'86 $2 Serial # Tab Attd.	15.00
NV 9	'87 $2 Buffleheads	12.00
NV 9T	'87 $2 Serial # Tab Attd.	14.00
NV 10	'88 $2 Canvasback	12.00
NV 10T	'88 $2 Serial # Tab Attd.	14.00
NV 11	'89 $2 Ross' Geese	8.00
NV 11T	'89 $2 Serial # Tab Attd.	11.00
NV 11A	'89 Hunter Tab #50,001-75,000	21.00
NV 12	'90 $5 Grn. Winged Teal	9.00
NV 12T	'90 $5 Serial # Tab Attd.	12.00
NV 12A	'90 Hunter Tab #50,001-75,000	16.00
NV 13	'91 $5 Wh. Faced Ibis	19.00
NV 13T	'91 $5 Serial # Tab Attd.	12.00
NV 13A	'91 Hunter Tab #50,001-75,000	13.00
NV 14	'92 $5 Amer. Widgeon	8.50
NV 14T	'92 $5 Serial # Tab Attd.	9.00
NV 14A	'92 Hunter Tab #50,001-75,000	12.00
NV 15	'93 $5 Com'n Goldeneye	8.50
NV 15T	'93 $5 Serial # Tab Attd.	9.00
NV 15A	'93 Hunter Tab #50,001-75,000	9.00
NV 16	'94 $5 Mallard	8.50
NV 16T	'94 $5 Serial # Tab Attd.	9.00
NV 16A	'94 Hunter Tab #50,001-75,000	9.00
NV 17	'95 $5 Wood Ducks	8.50
NV 17T	'95 $5 Serial # Tab Attd.	9.00
NV17A	'95 Hunter Tab #50,001-75,000	9.00
Nevada Set 1979-94 (16)		**195.00**
Nevada Tab Set 1979-94 (16)		**235.00**

STATE DUCK STAMPS

NJ 6

NM 1

OH 4

OR 2

No.	Description	F-VF NH
	NEW HAMPSHIRE	
NH 1	'83 $4 Wood Ducks	170.00
NH 1A	'83 3 Part Bklt. Type	190.00
NH 2	'84 $4 Mallards	155.00
NH 2A	'84 3 Part Bklt. Type	280.00
NH 3	'85 $4 Bl. Wngd. Teal	139.00
NH 3A	'85 3 Part Bklt. Type	165.00
NH 4	'86 $4 Mergansers	34.00
NH 4A	'86 3 Part Bklt. Type	45.00
NH 5	'87 $4 Canada Geese	18.00
NH 5A	'87 3 Part Bklt. Type	23.00
NH 5G	'87 $50 Governor's Ed.	500.00
NH 5GH	'87 Same, Hand Sig	1000.00
NH 6	'88 $4 Buffleheads	8.50
NH 6A	'88 3 Part Bklt. Type	17.00
NH 6G	'88 $50 Governor's Ed.	70.00
NH 6GH	'88 Same, Hand Sig	390.00
NH 7	'89 $4 Black Ducks	8.50
NH 7A	'89 3 Part Bklt. Type	12.00
NH 7G	'89 $54 Governor's Ed.	72.50
NH 7GH	'89 Same, Hand Sig	250.00
NH 8	'90 $4 Grn. Winged Teal	8.00
NH 8A	'90 3 Part Bklt. Type	9.00
NH 8G	'90 $54 Governor's Ed.	70.00
NH 8GH	'90 Same, Hand Sig	165.00
NH 9	'91 $4 Gldn Retr/Mallard	8.00
NH 9A	'91 3 Part Bklt. Type	10.00
NH 9G	'91 $54 Governor's Ed.	70.00
NH 9GH	'91 Same, Hand Sig	135.00
NH 10	'92 $4 Ring Neck Ducks	8.00
NH 10A	'92 3 Part Bklt. Type	9.00
NH 10GH	'92 Governor's Ed., Hand Signed	650.00
NH 11	'93 $4 Hooded Mergans	8.00
NH 11A	'93 3 Part Bklt. Type	8.00
NH 11GH	'93 Governor's Ed., Hand Signed	700.00
NH 12	'94 $4 Common Goldeneyes	8.00
NH 12A	'94 3 Part Bklt. Type	8.00
NH 12GH	'94 Governor's Ed., Hand signed	175.00
NH 13	'95 $4 Pintails	8.00
NH 13A	'95 3 Part Bklt. Type	8.00
New Hampshire Set '83-'94 (12)		**530.00**
NH Bklt. Type Set '83-'94 (12)		**730.00**
	NEW JERSEY	
NJ 1	'84 $2.50 Canvasbacks	57.50
NJ 1A	'84 $5.00 Non-Resident	72.50
NJ 1B	'84 $2.50 Hunter Bklt. Sgl	83.00
NJ 2	'85 $2.50 Mallards	23.00
NJ 2A	'85 $5.00 Non-Resident	28.00
NJ 2B	'85 $2.50 Hunter Bklt. Sgl	45.00
NJ 3	'86 $2.50 Pintails	14.00
NJ 3A	'86 $5.00 Non-Resident	17.00
NJ 3B	'86 $2.50 Hunter Bklt. Sgl	23.00
NJ 4	'87 $2.50 Canada Geese	12.00
NJ 4A	'87 $5.00 Non-Resident	17.00
NJ 4B	'87 $2.50 Hunter Bklt. Sgl	17.00
NJ 4AB	'87 $5.00 Hunter Bklt. Sgl	17.00
NJ 5	'88 $2.50 Grn. Winged Teal	8.50
NJ 5A	'88 $5.00 Non-Resident	14.00
NJ 5B	'88 $2.50 Hunter Bklt. Sgl	12.00
NJ 5AB	'88 $5.00 Hunter Bklt. Sgl	18.00
NJ 6	'89 $2.50 Snow Geese	6.00
NJ 6A	'89 $5.00 Non-Resident	12.00
NJ 6B	'89 $2.50 Hunter Bklt. Sgl	7.00
NJ 6AB	'89 $5.00 Hunter Bklt. Sgl	12.00
NJ 6G & 6AG	'89 Gov. Edition, Res. & Non-Res.	225.00
NJ 6GH & 6AGH	Gov. Eds., Hand Signed	450.00
NJ 7	'90 $2.50 Wood Ducks	6.00
NJ 7A	'90 $5.00 Non-Resident	9.50
NJ 7B	'90 $2.50 Hunter Bklt. Sgl	6.00
NJ 7AB	'90 $5.00 Hunter Bklt. Sgl	12.00
NJ 8	'91 $2.50 Atlantic Brant	6.00
NJ 8A	'91 $5.00 Non-Resident	9.50

No.	Desscription	F-VF NH
	NEW JERSEY	
NJ 8B	'91 $2.50 Hunter Bklt. Sgl	6.00
NJ 8AB	'91 $5.00 Hunter Bklt. Sgl	12.00
NJ 8AV	'91 $5.00 Atlantic "Brandt"	25.00
NJ 8V	'91 $2.50 Atlantic "Brandt"	16.00
NJ 9	'92 $2.50 Bluebills	6.00
NJ 9A	'92 $5.00 Non-Resident	8.50
NJ 9B	'92 $2.50 Hunter Bklt. Sgl	6.00
NJ 9AB	'92 $5.00 Hunter Bklt. Sgl	12.00
NJ 10	'93 $2.50 Buffleheads	6.00
NJ 10A	'93 $5.00 Non-Resident	8.50
NJ 10B	'93 $2.50 Hunter Bklt. Sgl	6.00
NJ 10AB	'93 $5.00 Hunter Bklt. Sgl	12.00
NJ 10G-10AG	Resident & Non-Res. Gov. Editions	135.00
NJ 10GH-10AGH	Governor's Ed, Hand Signed	230.00
NJ 10M-NJ 10AM	Commem. Sheets of 4	57.50
NJ 10GM-NJ 10AGM	Gov. Signed Commem.Sheets of 4 (4)	525.00
NJ 11	'94 $2.50 Black Ducks	6.00
NJ 11A	'94 $5.00 Black Ducks	8.00
NJ 11B	'94 $2.50 Hunter Bklt. Sgl	6.00
NJ 11AB	'94 $5.00 Hunter Bklt. Sgl	12.00
NJ 12	'95 $2.50 Widgeon	6.00
NJ 12A	'95 $5 Widgeon	8.00
NJ 12B	'95 $2.50 Hunter Bklt. Sgl.	6.00
NJ 12AB	'95 $5 Hunter Bklt. Sgl.	12.00
New Jersey Set 1984-94 (24)		**365.00**
NJ Bklt. Type Set '84-'94 (19)		**289.00**
	NEW MEXICO	
NM 1	'91 $7.50 Pintails	11.00
NM 1A	'91 $7.50 Booklet sgl	12.00
NM 1G	'91 $57.50 Gov. Edition	80.00
NM 1GH	'91 $57.50 Gov. Edition, Hand Signed	150.00
NM 2	'92 $7.50 Amer. Widgeon	11.00
NNM 2A	'92 $7.50 Booklet sgl	12.00
NM 2G	'92 $57.50 Gov. Edition	72.50
NM 2GH	'92 $57.50 Gov. Edition, Hand Signed	135.00
NM 3	'93 $7.50 Mallards	11.00
NM 3A	'93 $7.50 Booklet sgl	12.00
NM 3G	'93 $57.50 Gov. Edition	67.50
NM 3GH	'93 $57.50 Gov. Edition, Hand Signed	135.00
NM 3M	'93 Commem. Sheet of 4	55.00
NM 3MI	'93 Imperf. Commem. Sheet of 4	100.00
NM 4	'94 $7.50 Grn.Wngd.Teal	11.00
NM 4A	'94 $7.50 Booklet sgl	12.00
NM 4A	'94 Strip of 4 different attd	48.00
NM 4M	'94 Commem. Sheet of 4	50.00
NM 4MI	'94 Imperf. Commem. Sheet of 4	100.00
NM 5	'95 $7.50 White Fronted Geese	11.00
NM 5A	'95 $7.50 Hunter	12.00
New Mexico Set 1991-94 (7)		**73.00**
N.M. Hunter Set 1991-94 (7)		**75.00**
	NEW YORK	
NY 1	'85 $5.50 Canada Geese	18.00
NY 2	'86 $5.50 Mallards	12.00
NY 3	'87 $5.50 Wood Ducks	12.00
NY 4	'88 $5.50 Pintails	12.00
NY 5	'89 $5.50 Greater Scaup	9.00
NY 6	'90 $5.50 Canvasbacks	9.00
NY 7	'91 $5.50 Redheads	8.50
NY 8	'92 $5.50 Wood Duck	8.50
NY 9	'93 $5.50 Bl. Wngd. Teal	8.50
NY 10	'94 $5.50 Canada Geese	8.50
NY 11	'95 $5.50 Canada Geese	8.50
New York Set 1985-94 (10)		**97.00**

No.	Description	F-VF NH
	NORTH CAROLINA	
NC 1	'83 $5.50 Mallards	89.00
NC 2	'84 $5.50 Wood Ducks	62.50
NC 3	'85 $5.50 Canvasbacks	36.50
NC 4	'86 $5.50 Canada Geese	23.00
NC 5	'87 $5.50 Pintails	17.00
NC 6	'88 $5.00 Grn. Winged Teal	14.00
NC 7	'89 $5.00 Snow Geese	12.00
NC 8	'90 $5.00 Redheads	11.00
NC 9	'91 $5.00 Bl. Wngd. Teal.	8.50
NC 10	'92 $5.00 Amer. Widgeon	8.50
NC 11	'93 $5.00 Tundra Swan	8.50
NC 12	'94 $5.00 Buffleheads	8.50
NC 13	'95 $5.00 Brant	8.50
North Carolina Set '83-'94 (12).		**278.00**
	NORTH DAKOTA	
	North Dakota Hunter Stamps have the following serial #'s: 1982-86 #20,001-150,000; 1987-95 #20,0011-140,000	
ND 1	'82 $9 Canada Geese Serial #>150K	175.00
ND 1A	'82 $9 Hunter Type with Selvedge	2250.00
ND 2	'83 $9 Mallards	105.00
ND 2A	'83 $9 Hunter Type with Selvedge	3900.00
ND 3	'84 $9 Camvasbacks	45.00
ND 3A	'84 $9 Hunter Type	3500.00
ND 4	'85 $9 Blue Bills	34.00
ND 4A	'85 $9 Hunter Type	5000.00
ND 5	'86 $9 Pintails	28.00
ND 5A	'86 $9 Hunter Type	1000.00
ND 6	'87 $9 Snow Geese	23.00
ND 6A	'87 $9 Hunter Type	85.00
ND 7	'88 $9 Wh.Wngd.Scooter	17.00
ND 7A	'88 $9 Hunter Type	34.00
ND 8	'89 $6 Redheads	12.00
ND 8A	'89 $6 Hunter Type	17.00
ND 9	'90 $6 Blk Labs/Mallards	12.00
ND 9A	'90 $6 Hunter Type	17.00
ND 10	'91 $6 Grn. Winged Teal	11.00
ND 10A	'91 $6 Hunter Type	14.50
ND 11	'92 $6 Bl. Winged Teal	9.00
ND 11A	'92 $6 Hunter Type	14.00
ND 12	'93 $6 Wood Ducks	9.00
ND 12A	'93 $6 Hunter Type	11.00
ND 13	'94 $6 Canada Geese	9.00
ND 13A	'94 $6 Hunter Type	12.00
ND 14	'95 $6 Widgeon	9.00
ND 14A	'95 $6 Hunter Type	12.00
North Dakota Set 1982-94 (13)		**461.00**
North Dakota Standing Rock Sioux Tribe:	1992 Waterfowl	18.00
	1993 Waterfowl	10.00
	1994 Waterfowl	10.00
	OHIO	
OH 1	'82 $5.75 Wood Ducks	95.00
OH 2	'83 $5.75 Mallards	95.00
OH 3	'84 $5.75 Grn.Winged Teal	90.00
OH 4	'85 $5.75 Redheads	55.00
OH 5	'86 $5.75 Canvasbacks	34.00
OH 6	'87 $5.75 Bl.Winged Teal	16.00
OH 7	'88 $5.75 Goldeneyes	12.00
OH 8	'89 $5.75 Canada Geese	12.00
OH 9	'90 $9.00 Black Ducks	14.00
OH 10	'91 $9.00 Lesser Scaup.	14.00
OH 11	'92 $9.00 Wood Ducks	13.00
OH 12	'93 $9.00 Buffleheads	13.00
OH 13	'94 $11.00 Mallard	16.00
OH 14	'95 $11.00 Pintails	16.00
Ohio Set 1982-94 (13)		**444.00**

No.	Description	F-VF NH
	OKLAHOMA	
OK 1	'80 $4 Pintails	50.0
OK 2	'81 $4 Canada Goose	40.0
OK 3	'82 $4 Grn.Wngd.Teal	12.0
OK 4	'83 $4 Wood Ducks	12.0
OK 5	'84 $4 Ring Neck Ducks	9.0
OK 5T	'84 $4 Same, with Tab	12.0
OK 6	'85 $4 Mallards	7.5
OK 6T	'85 $4 Full Tab Attd	9.0
OK 7	'86 $4 Snow Geese	7.5
OK 7T	'86 $4 Full Tab Attd	9.0
OK 8	'87 $4 Canvasbacks	7.5
OK 8T	'87 $4 Full Tab Attd	9.0
OK 9	'88 $4 Widgeons	7.5
OK 9T	'88 $4 Full Tab Attd	9.0
OK 9TV	'88 $4 Full Tab Attd. Serial #>30,000	28.0
OK 10	'89 $4 Redheads	7.5
OK 10A	'89 $4 Hunter Ty., w/Tab	9.0
OK 10G	'89 $4 Governor's Ed	155.0
OK 10GH	'89 $4 Governor's Ed., Hand Signed	280.0
OK 11	'90 $4 Hood'd Mergans'r	7.5
OK 11A	'90 $4 Hunter Ty., w/Tab	9.0
OK 12	'91 $4 Gadwalls	7.5
OK 12A	'91 $4 Hunter Ty., w/Tab	9.0
OK 13	'92 $4 Lesser Scaup	7.0
OK 13A	'92 $4 Hunter Ty., w/Tab	9.0
OK 14	'93 $4 Wh. Frnt'd Geese	7.0
OK 14A	'93 $4 Hunter Ty., w/Tab	8.0
OK 15	'94 $4 Widgeon	7.0
OK 15A	'94 $4 Hunter Ty., w/Tab	7.0
OK 16	'95 $4 Ruddy Ducks	7.0
OK 16A	'95 $4 Hunter Ty., w/Tab	7.0
Oklahoma Set 1980-94 (15)		**178.0**
	OREGON	
OR 1	'84 $5 Canada Geese	40.0
OR 2	'85 $5 Snow Geese	50.0
OR 2A	'85 $5 Hunter Ty. w/Tab	660.0
OR 2A	'85 $5 Same, w/o Tab	150.0
OR 3	'86 $5 Pacific Brant	18.0
OR 3A	'86 $5 Hunter Ty. w/Tab	34.0
OR 3A	'86 $5 Same, w/o Tab	14.0
OR 4	'87 $5 Wh. Frnt'd Geese	14.0
OR 4A	'87 $5 Hunter Ty. w/Tab	23.0
OR 4A	'87 $5 Same, w/o Tab	10.0
OR 5	'88 $5 Grt. Basin Geese	12.0
OR 5A	'88 Hunter Ty (89X197mm)	17.
OR 6	'89 $5 Blk. Lab/Pintail	9.0
OR 6A	'89 Hunter Ty (89X197mm)	14.
OR 6YB	'89 $5 Provisional Issue, Black Serial #	28.0
OR 6VR	'89 $5 Provisional Issue, Red Serial #	12.5
OR 7	'90 $5 Gldn. Retr/Mallard	12.0
OR 7A	'90 Hunter Ty (89X197mm)	12.
OR 8	'91 $5 Ch'pk Bay Retrvr	8.5
OR 8A	'91 $5 Hunter Ty. w/Tab	12.
OR 9	'92 $5 Grn. Winged Teal	8.5
OR 9A	'92 Hunter Ty (216X152mm)	11.0
OR 10	'93 $5 Mallards	8.5
OR 10A	'93 $5 Hunter Type	12.
OR 10G	'93 $50 Governor's Ed	85.0
OR 10GH	'93 $50 Governor's Ed., Hand Signed	125.0
OR 10GI	'93 Imperf. Gov. Stamp.	395.0
OR 10M	'93 Mini. Sheet of 2	25.
OR 10MI	'93 Same, Imperf.	170.
OR 11	'94 $5 Pintails	10.0
OR 11A	'94 Hunter Ty (216X152mm)	12
OR 11AN	'94 $25 Hunter Type	37.
OR 12	'95 $5 Wood Ducks	10.
OR 12A	'95 Hunter Type	12.
Oregon Set 1984-94 (11)		**175.**

STATE DUCK STAMPS

RI 1

1989 CROW CREEK SIOUX TRIBE

UT 6

VT 2

PENNSYLVANIA

o.	Description	F-VF NH
A 1	'83 $5.50 Wood Ducks..	28.00
A 2	'84 $5.50 Canada Geese	28.00
A 3	'85 $5.50 Mallards.........	17.00
A 4	'86 $5.50 Bl. Winged Teal	13.00
A 5	'87 $5.50 Pintails...........	12.00
A 6	'88 $5.50 Wood Ducks..	11.00
A 7	'89 $5.50 Hood'd Mergans'r	9.00
A 8	'90 $5.50 Canvasbacks.	9.00
A 9	'91 $5.50 Widgeon........	9.00
A 10	'92 $5.50 Canada Geese	8.50
A 11	'93 $5.50 North'n Shovelers	8.50
A 12	'94 $5.50 Pintails...........	8.50
A 13	'95 $5.50 Buffleheads ...	8.50

ennsylvania Set '83-'94 (12)... 150.00

RHODE ISLAND

No.	Description	F-VF NH
1	'89 $7.50 Canvasbacks	12.00
1A	'89 $7.50 Hunter Type........	17.00
1G	'89 $57.50 Gov. Edition	105.00
1GH	'89 $57.50 Gov. Edition, Hand Signed........................	250.00
2	'90 $7.50 Canada Geese....	12.00
2A	'90 $7.50 Hunter Type........	15.00
2G	'90 $57.50 Gov. Edition	80.00
2GH	'90 $57.50 Gov. Edition, Hand Signed........................	135.00
3	'91 $7.50 Blk. Lab/Wd Dks .	13.00
3A	'91 $7.50 Hunter Type........	14.50
3G	'91 $57.50 Gov. Edition	67.50
3GH	'91 $57.50 Gov. Edition, Hand Signed........................	135.00
4	'92 $7.50 Bl. Winged Teal ..	12.00
4A	'92 $7.50 Hunter Type........	12.00
4G	'92 $57.50 Gov. Edition	67.50
4GH	'92 $57.50 Gov. Edition, Hand Signed........................	135.00
5	'93 $7.50 Pintails	11.00
5A	'93 $7.50 Hunter Type........	12.00
5GH	'93 $57.50 Gov. Edition Hand signed	100.00
5M	'93 Commem. Sheet of 4....	55.00
5MI	'93 Same, Imperf.	100.00
6	'94 $7.50 Wood Duck	11.00
6A	'94 $7.50 Hunter Type........	12.00
7	'95 $7.50 Hooded Mergansers	11.00
7A	'95 $7.50 Hunter Type........	12.00

hode Island Set 1989-94 (6)...... 70.00
Hunter Type Set 1989-94 (6)... 74.00

SOUTH CAROLINA

No.	Description	F-VF NH
C 1	'81 $5.50 Wood Ducks	85.00
C 2	'82 $5.50 Mallards	125.00
C 2A	'82 Hunter-Ser'l # on Rev ...	550.00
C 3	'83 $5.50 Pintails	125.00
C 3A	'83 Hunter-Ser'l # on Rev ...	500.00
C 4	'84 $5.50 Canada Geese....	80.00
C 4A	'84 Hunter-Ser'l # on Rev ...	220.00
C 5	'85 $5.50 Grn. Winged Teal	80.00
C 5A	'85 Hunter Ser'l # on Rev....	115.00
C 6	'86 $5.50 Canvasbacks	34.00
C 6A	'86 Hunter-Ser'l # on Rev ...	55.00
C 7	'87 $5.50 Black Ducks	28.00
C 7A	'87 Hunter-Ser'l # on Rev ...	34.00
C 8	'88 $5.50 Spaniel/Widg'n....	28.00
C 8A	'88 Hunter-Ser'l # on Rev ...	40.00
C 9	'89 $5.50 Bl. Wingd. Teal ...	17.00
C 9A	'89 Hunter-Ser'l # on Rev ...	19.00
C 10	'90 $5.50 Wood Ducks	13.00
C 10A	'90 Hunter-Ser'l # on Rev ...	14.00
C 10G	'90 $50 Governor's Ed...........	95.00
C 10GH	'90 $100 Gov. Edition, Hand Signed	245.00
SC 11	'91 $5.50 Blk. Lab/Pintails ..	...9.00
SC 11A	'91 Hunter-Ser'l # on Rev ...	...9.00
SC 12	'92 $5.50 Buffleheads.........	...9.00
SC 12A	'92 Hunter-Ser'l # on Front .	...9.00
SC 13	'93 $5.50 Lesser Scaup......	...8.50
SC 13A	'93 Hunter-Ser'l # on Front .	...9.00
SC 14	'94 $5.50 Canvasbacks......	...8.50
SC 14A	'94 Hunter-Ser'l # on Front	...9.00
SC 15	'95 $5.50 Shovelers	...8.50
SC 15A	'95 Hunter, Ser'l # on Front	...9.00

South Carolina Set 1981-94 (14) 595.00
SC Hunter Type Set '81-'94 (13) 1495.00

SOUTH DAKOTA

No.	Description	F-VF NH
SD 1	'76 $1 Mallards	34.00
SD 1V	'76 Small Serial # Variety	67.50
SD 2	'77 $1 Pintails	23.00
SD 3	'78 $1 Canvasbacks	14.00
SD 4	'86 $2 Canada Geese	14.00
SD 5	'87 $2 Blue Geese...........	8.00
SD 6	'88 $2 Wh. Fronted Geese	6.00
SD 7	'89 $2 Mallards	6.00
SD 8	'90 $2 Bl. Winged Teal	5.00
SD 9	'91 $2 Pintails	5.00
SD 10	'92 $2 Canvasbacks	5.00
SD 11	'93 $2 Lesser Scaup........	5.00
SD 12	'94 $2 Redhead...............	5.00
SD 13	'95 $2 Wood Ducks	5.00

South Dakota Set 1976-94 (12) 117.00

SOUTH DAKOTA CROW CREEK SIOUX TRIBE

No.	Description	F-VF NH
1989	$10 Canada Geese Reservation	600.00
1989	$30 SD Resident	...
1989	$65 Non-Resident	1400.00
1990	$10 Canada Geese Reservation	400.00
1990	$30 SD Resident	350.00
1990	$65 Non-Resident	1300.00

1989-1990 Sportsman Set (8 stamps) ($770 Face Val.) 3900.00

No.	Description	F-VF NH
1994	$5 Tribal Member	25.00
1994	$15 Resident	40.00
1994	$30 Non-Resident Daily .	70.00
1994	$75 Non-Resident	115.00

SOUTH DAKOTA SISSETON-WAHPETON TRIBE

Sisseton-Wahpeton
1992 $10 Wood Duck...... 20.00

TENNESSEE

No.	Description	F-VF NH
TN 1	'79 $2.30 Mallards	195.00
TN 1A	'79 $5.30 Non-Resident.	1400.00
TN 2	'80 $2.30 Canvasbacks ...	85.00
TN 2A	'80 $5.30 Non-Resident...	530.00
TN 2B	'80 $2.30 3 Part Card	895.00
TN 3	'81 $2.30 Wood Ducks	60.00
TN 3B	'81 $2.30 3 Part Card	...
TN 4	'82 $6.50 Canada Geese	85.00
TN 5	'83 $6.50 Pintails	80.00
TN 5B	'83 $6.50 3 Part Card	105.00
TN 6	'84 $6.50 Black Ducks	80.00
TN 6B	'84 $6.50 3 Part Card	115.00
TN 7	'85 $6.50 Bl. Winged Teal	40.00
TN 7B	'85 $6.50 3 Part Card	72.50
TN 8	'86 $6.50 Mallards	23.00
TN 8B	'86 $6.50 3 Part Card......	72.50
TN 9	'87 $6.50 Canada Geese	17.00
TN 9B	'87 $6.50 3 Part Card	28.00
TN 10	'88 $6.50 Canvasbacks	14.00
TN 10B	'88 $6.50 3 Part Card....	23.00
TN 11	'89 $6.50 Grn Wngd Teal	12.00
TN 11B	'89 $6.50 3 Part Card......	14.00
TN 12	'90 $13 Redheads.........	18.00
TN 12B	'90 $13 3 Part Card.......	22.00
TN 13	'91 $13 Mergansers......	18.00
TN 13B	'91 $13 3 Part Card.......	22.00
TN 14	'92 $14 Wood Ducks.....	18.50
TN 14B	'92 $14 3 Part Card.......	22.00
TN 15	'93 $14 Pintail/Decoy	18.50
TN 15B	'93 $14 3 Part Card.......	22.00
TN 16	'94 $16 Mallard	21.00
TN 16B	'94 $16 3 Part Card	22.50
TN 17	'95 $16 Ring Necked Ducks............................	22.00
TN 17B	'95 $16 3 Part Card	22.50

Tennessee Set 1979-94 (18)... 2550.00
Tennessee Set 1979-94 (16) w/o Non-Res.............. 735.00

TEXAS

No.	Description	F-VF NH
TX 1	'81 $5 Mallards...............	67.00
TX 2	'82 $5 Pintails.................	55.00
TX 3	'83 $5 Widgeon	215.00
TX 4	'84 $5 Wood Ducks	40.00
TX 5	'85 $5 Snow Geese.........	17.00
TX 6	'86 $5 Grn. Winged Teal .	14.00
TX 7	'87 $5 Wh. Frnt'd Geese .	12.00
TX 8	'88 $5 Pintails.................	12.00
TX 9	'89 $5 Mallards...............	12.00
TX 10	'90 $5 Widgeons	8.50
TX 11	'91 $7 Wood Duck	10.00
TX 12	'92 $7 Canada Geese	10.00
TX 13	'93 $7 Bl. Wngd. Teal......	10.00
TX 14	'94 $7 Shovelers	10.00
TX 15	'95 $7 Buffleheads	10.00

Texas Set 1981-94 (14) 465.00

UTAH

No.	Description	F-VF NH
UT 1	'86 $3.30 Whistling Swans	14.00
UT 2	'87 $3.30 Pintails............	10.00
UT 3	'88 $3.30 Mallards	8.00
UT 4	'89 $3.30 Canada Geese	7.00
UT 5	'90 $3.30 Canvasbacks...	7.00
UT 5A	'90 $3.30 Bklt, sgl. w/Tab	8.00
UT 6	'91 $3.30 Tundra Swans .	6.50
UT 6A	'91 $3.30 Bklt. sgl w/Tab .	7.00
UT 6GH	'91 $3.30 Gov. Edition, Hand Signed	175.00
UT 7	'92 $3.30 Pintails	6.50
UT 7A	'92 $3.30 Bklt. sgl w/Tab .	7.00
UT 7GH	'92 $3.30 Gov. Edition, Hand Signed	139.00
UT 8	'93 $3.30 Canvasbacks...	6.50
UT 8A	'93 $3.30 Bklt. sgl w/Tab .	7.00
UT 8GH	'93 $3.30 Gov. Edition, Hand Signed	139.00
UT 9	'94 $3.30 Chesepeake	6.50
UT 9A	'94 $3.30 Bklt. sgl. w/Tab	7.00
UT 9GH	'94 $3.30 Gov. Edition Hand Signed	115.00
UT10	'95 $3.30 Green Winged Teal	6.50
UT 10A	'95 $3.30 Bklt. Sgl. w/Tab	7.00

Utah Set 1986-94 (9) 64.50
Utah Set Bklt. Sgl. 1990-94 (5) 32.50

VERMONT

No.	Description	F-VF NH
VT 1	'86 $5 Aut'mn Wd Ducks..	17.00
VT 2	'87 $5 Wintr Goldeneyes..	10.00
VT 3	'88 $5 Spring Blk. Ducks..	10.00
VT 4	'89 $5 Summer Canada Geese	10.00
VT 5	'90 $5 Grn Wngd Teal......	10.00
VT 6	'91 $5 H'ded Mergans'r	8.00
VT 7	'92 $5 Snow Geese..........	8.00
VT 8	'93 $5 Mallards.................	8.00
VT 9	'94 $5 Ring Necked Duck	8.00
VT 10	'95 $5 Bufflehead	8.00

Vermont Set 1986-94 (9)........... 83.50

VIRGINIA

No.	Description	F-VF NH
VA 1	'88 $5 Mallards................	17.00
VA 1A	'88 $5 Bklt. Single	15.00
VA 1A	'88 $5 Hz. pr./side mgns ..	34.00
VA 2	'89 $5 Canada Geese	17.00
VA 2A	'89 $5 Bklt. Single	14.50
VA 2A	'89 $5 Hz. pr./side mgns ..	28.00
VA 3	'90 $5 Wood Ducks	9.00
VA 3A	'90 $5 Bklt. Single	12.00
VA 3A	'90 $5 Hz. pr./side mgns ..	23.00
VA 4	'91 $5 Canvasbacks.........	9.00
VA 4A	'91 $5 Bklt. Single	12.00
VA 4A	'91 $5 Hz. pr./side mgns ..	23.00
VA 5	'92 $5 Buffleheads	9.00
VA 5A	'92 $5 Bklt. Single	12.00
VA 5A	'92 $5 Hz. pr./side mgns ..	23.00
VA 6	'93 $5 Black Ducks	8.50
VA 6A	'93 $5 Bklt. Single	8.50
VA 6A	'93 $5 Hz. pr./side mgns ..	17.00
VA 7	'94 $5 Lesser Scaup	8.00
VA 7A	'94 $5 Hz. pr./side mgns. .	17.00
VA 8	'95 $5 Snow Geese..........	8.00
VA 8A	'95 $5 hz. pr./side Mgns...	17.00

Virginia Set 1988-94 (7)............ 71.00
VA Hunter Pairs Set 1988-94 (7) 150.00

WASHINGTON

No.	Description	F-VF NH
WA 1	'86 $5 Mallards................	12.00
WA 1A	'86 $5 Hunter Type (77X82MM)	28.00
WA 2	'87 $5 Canvasbacks.........	15.00
WA 2A	'87 $5 Hunter Type (77X82MM)	17.00
WA 3	'88 $5 Harlequin..............	9.00
WA 3A	'88 $5 Hunter Type (77X82MM)	15.00
WA 4	'89 $5 Amer. Widgeon	9.00
WA 4A	'89 $5 Hunter Type (77X82MM)	14.00
WA 5	'90 $5 Pintails/Sour Duck.	9.00
WA 5A	'90 $5 Hunter Type (77X82MM)	13.00
WA 6	'91 $5 Wood Duck............	9.00
WA 6A	'91 $5 Hunter Type (77X82MM)	12.00
WA 6V	'91 $6 Wood Duck............	12.00
WA 6AN	'91 $6 Mini Sheet/ No Staple Holes..............	40.00
WA 6AV	'91 $6 Hunter Type (77X82MM)	12.00
WA 7	'92 $6 Puppy/Can. Geese	10.00
WA 7N	'92 $6 Mini Sheet/ No Staple Holes..............	40.00
WA 7A	'92 $6 Hunter Type (77X82MM)	12.00

STATE DUCK STAMPS

WA 1

WI 2

WV 2B

WY 2

No.	Description	F-VF NH
	WASHINGTON	
WA 8	'93 $6 Snow Geese	9.00
WA 8N	'93 $6 Mini Sheet/ No Staple Holes	17.00
WA 8A	'93 $6 Hunter Type (77X82MM)	10.00
WA 9	'94 $6 Black Brent	9.00
WA 9A	'94 $6 Hunter Type (77X82MM)	10.00
WA 9N	'94 $6 Mini Sheet, No staple holes	17.00
WA 10	'95 $6 Mallards	9.00
WA 10A	'95 $6 Hunter Type (77 x 82 mm)	10.00
WA 10N	'95 $6 Mini Sheet No staple holes	17.00
Washington Set 1986-94 (10)		**92.00**
WA Hunter Set 1986-94 (10)		**145.00**
	WEST VIRGINIA	
WV 1	'87 $5 Can. Geese/Res	17.00
WV 1A	'87 $5 Non-Resident	17.00
WV 1B	'87 $5 Bklt. sgl-Resident	45.00
WV 1AB	'87 Same, Non-Res	45.00
WV 2	'88 $5 Wood Ducks/Res	14.00
WV 2A	'88 $5 Non-Resident	17.00
WV 2B	'88 $5 Bklt. sgl-Resident	28.00
WV 2AB	'88 Same, Non-Res	28.00
WV 3	'89 $5 Decoys/Res	13.00
WV 3A	'89 $5 Non-Resident	13.00

No.	Desscription	F-VF NH
	WEST VIRGINIA	
WV 3B	'89 $5 Bklt. sgl-Resident	13.00
WV 3AB	'89 Same, Non-Res	13.00
WV 3G & 3AG	'89 Govs. Res./ Non-Res	170.00
WV 3GH & 3AGH	'89 Same, Hand Signed	390.00
WV 4	'90 Lab/Decoys/Res	12.00
WV 4A	'90 $5 Non-Resident	12.00
WV 4B	'90 $5 Bklt. sgl-Resident	12.00
WV 4AB	'90 Same, Non-Res	12.00
WV 5	'91 $5 Mallards/Res	8.50
WV 5A	'91 $5 Non-Resident	8.50
WV 5B	'91 $5 Bklt. sgl-Resident	12.00
WV 5AB	'91 Same, Non-Res	12.00
WV 5S	'91 WV Ohio Riv. Sht of 6	55.00
WV 6	'92 $5 Can. Geese/Res.	9.50
WV 6A	'92 $5 Non-Resident	9.50
WV 6B	'92 $5 Bklt. sgl-Resident	9.50
WV 6AB	'92 Same, Non-Res	9.50
WV 7	'93 $5 Pintails/Res	9.00
WV 7A	'93 $5 Non-Resident	9.00
WV 7B	'93 $5 Bklt. sgl-Resident	9.00
WV 7AB	'93 Same, Non-Res	9.00
WV 8	'94 $5 Grn. Winged Teal	8.50
WV 8A	'94 Same, Non-Res	8.50
WV 8B	'94 $5 Pintails-Hunter	9.00
WV 8AB	'94 Same, Non-Res	9.00
WV 9	'95 $5 Wood Duck	8.50
WV 9A	'95 Same, Non-Resident	8.50
WV 9B	'95 $5 Hunter Type	9.00
WV 9AB	'95 Same, Non-Resident	9.00

No.	Description	F-VF NH
	WEST VIRGINIA	
West Virginia Set 1987-94 (16)		**172.50**
WV Hunter Ty. Set 1987-94 (16)		**256.00**
	WISCONSIN	
WI 1	'78 $3.25 Wood Ducks	135.00
WI 2	'79 $3.25 Buffleheads	35.00
WI 3	'80 $3.25 Widgeon	17.00
WI 4	'81 $3.25 Lesser Scaup	14.00
WI 5	'82 $3.25 Pintails	8.00
WI 5T	'82 $3.25 Full Tab Attd	12.00
WI 6	'83 $3.25 Bl. Winged Teal	8.50
WI 6T	'83 $3.25 Full Tab Attd	12.00
WI 7	'84 $3.25 Hd'd Mergans'r.	8.50
WI 7T	'84 $3.25 Full Tab Attd	12.00
WI 8	'85 $3.25 Lesser Scaup	12.00
WI 8T	'85 $3.25 Full Tab Attd	12.00
WI 9	'86 $3.25 Canvasbacks	12.00
WI 9T	'86 $3.25 Full Tab Attd	14.00
WI 10	'87 $3.25 Canada Geese	6.50
WI 10T	'87 $3.25 Full Tab Attd	8.00
WI 11	'88 $3.25 Hd'd Mergans'r.	6.50
WI 11T	'88 $3.25 Full Tab Attd	8.00
WI 12	'89 $3.25 Cm'n Gldneye	6.50
WI 12T	'89 $3.25 Full Tab Attd	8.00
WI 13	'90 $3.25 Redheads	6.50
WI 13T	'90 $3.25 Full Tab Attd	8.00
WI 14	'91 $5.25 Grn. Wngd. Teal	8.50
WI 14T	'91 $5.25 Full Tab Attd	9.50
WI 15	'92 $5.25 Tundra Swans	8.50

No.	Description	F-VF NH
	WISCONSIN	
WI 15T	'92 $5.25 Full Tab Attd	9.50
WI 16	'93 $5.25 Wood Ducks	8.50
WI 16T	'93 $5.25 Full Tab Attd	9.50
WI 17	'94 $5.25 Pintails	8.50
WI 17A	'94 $5.25 Full Tab Attd	9.50
WI 18	'95 $5.25 Mallards	8.50
WI 18A	'95 $5.25 Full Tab Attd	9.50
Wisconsin Set 1978-94 (17)		**283.00**
	WYOMING	
WY 1	'84 $5 Meadowlark	28.00
WY 2	'85 $5 Canada Geese	27.50
WY 3	'86 $5 Prnghrn Antelope	27.50
WY 4	'87 $5 Sage Grouse	27.50
WY 5	'88 $5 Cut-Throat Trout	27.50
WY 6	'89 $5 Mule Deer	27.50
WY 7	'90 $5 Grizzly Bear	27.50
WY 8	'91 $5 Big Horn Sheep	27.50
WY 9	'92 $5 Bald Eagle	23.00
WY 10	'93 $5 Elk	10.00
WY 11	'94 $5 Bobcat	10.00
WY 12	'95 $5 Moose	10.00
Wyoming Set 1984-94 (11)		**240.00**

NOTE: SEE PAGE 223 FOR CANADA FEDERAL AND PROVINCIAL DUCK STAMPS.

WELCOME TO FIRST DAY COVER COLLECTING !

/HAT IS A FIRST DAY COVER?

A First Day Cover (FDC) is an envelope or card bearing a :amp cancelled on the day the stamp was initially placed on ale by the postal authorities of a particular country or the nited Nations.

/HERE ARE STAMPS FIRST SOLD?

In the United States the U.S. Postal Service (USPS), epending upon circumstance, designates one or more cities s "official" - the location where the stamp is first released to e public. This location is usually appropriate to the subject of e stamp. For example, the 1985 Christmas stamp was leased in Nazareth, MI, a city whose name is associated with e holiday. Most foreign countries follow similar procedures.

OW ARE STAMPS FIRST RELEASED?

Generally, a stamp is officially released at a First Day of Issue FDOI) ceremony which is sponsored by the Postal Service or ı organization associated with the stamp. The dedication is oth colorful and entertaining, not only providing speaking pportunities for dignitaries from both the public and private ectors, but also enabling collectors to obtain an official ogram with the new stamp affixed and cancelled FDOI. nese programs are usually distributed to the attendees free of ıarge.

'HERE ARE FDC's PREPARED?

Cancellations of the new U.S. stamp or postal stationery can e obtained at the FDOI site. These will be serviced with the fficial" slogan cancellation containing the words "FIRST DAY F ISSUE" and a postmark showing the date of issue. lternatively, cancellations may be obtained by sending covers the Postmaster of the "official" city within 30 days of the sue's release.

OW DOES ONE FIND OUT WHERE AND WHEN TAMPS ARE TO BE ISSUED?

The best way to obtain advance information is to subscribe to eekly philatelic publications such as "STAMPS" magazine, Stamp Collector" or "Linn's Stamp News". These periodicals ovide all the details for impending issues and provide structions on how to obtain FDOI cancellations by mail. formation is also available in U.S. Post Offices. On the other and, for those who do not wish to "do it themselves", ıbscriptions to new issue services are available from many ealers.

WHAT IS AN UNOFFICIAL FDC?

The most widely accepted interpretation defines an "unofficial" (UO) FDC as a cover cancelled anywhere on the first day of issue with any cancel other than the official FDOI slogan cancel. UO's can only be obtained in person and on the FDOI. This is in direct contrast to the "official" FDOI cancel which can be acquired by mail, and up to 30 days after the official first day of issue. The American First Day Cover Society (AFDCS) publishes a regular column on this popular aspect of the hobby in its magazine "FIRST DAYS".

WHAT IS A CACHET?

A cachet (pronounced ka-shay) is defined by the AFDCS as a design that is printed, stamped, or drawn, usually on the left side, but possibly covering the entire face, of the envelope bearing the stamp with the FDOI cancel. Unless it is identified as a general purpose cachet, the design is most likely to bear a direct relationship to the stamp, the event, or the postmark.

WHAT IS THE SIGNIFICANCE OF THE CACHET?

The cachet enhances the cover by complementing the stamp and is usually attractive, educational, humorous, or in many instances, a combination of all three. There are many different cachets for each new stamp and a list of people currently preparing and selling cachets is published annually by the AFDCS.

HOW DO I CHOOSE A CACHET?

Cachet designs are produced in all sizes, shapes and colors. They may be printed, thermographed, handpainted, or produced by a wide variety of other methods. One collecting challenge is to see how many different cachets one can find for a particular issue. Another challenge is to obtain one each of all the cachets made by a particular individual or company.

WHAT IS A FIRST CACHET?

A first cachet is quite simply the first in a series produced by an individual, company or organization for use as a commercial product or for trade with others. For example, the First Cachet from the House of Farnam was issued for the TIPEX souvenir sheet in 1936. First Cachet collecting is a popular facet of the hobby and these cachets often command a premium price in years subsequent to their issue. The AFDCS journal, "FIRST DAYS", regularly features articles on First Cachets.

WHAT IS A SCOTT NUMBER?

Each stamp issued is assigned a catalog number by the Scott Publishing Company, whose catalog is advertised elsewhere in this volume. These numbers are commonly used by hobbyists to identify stamps and covers. Scott numbers appear in the left hand column on the pages that follow.

This introduction was prepared by the American First Day Cover Society. They will be pleased to provide additional information if you write them in c/o Monte Elserman, 14359 Chadbourne, Houston, TX 77079.

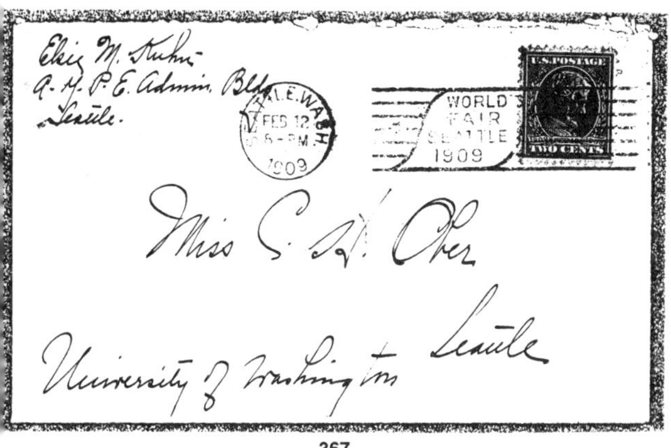

367

FDC's will be addressed from #10-952 and unaddressed from 953 to date
Cacheted prices are for FDC's with common printed cachets.
From #704 all FDC's will be cacheted.
ultiples are generally priced @ 1.25x for blocks & 2x for plate blks. or line pairs

ott #	Description	Uncacheted
	1851-1890	
	3¢ Washington, Orange Brown 7/1/1851 Any City	7000.00
	3¢ Washington "A" Grill 8/13/67 Any City	7500.00
0	2¢ Washington, Red Brown 10/1/1883 Any City	1750.00
0-211	2¢ Wash., 4¢ Jackson on one cvr, 10/1/83	*12,500.00*
9D	2¢ Washington, Lake 2/22/1890 Any City	*13,500.00*
	1893 COLUMBIAN ISSUE	
0	1¢ Columbian 1/2/1893 Any City	3750.00
	Salem, MA 12/31/1892	*10,000.00*
1	2¢ Columbian 1/2/1893 Any City	2750.00
	New York, NY or Boston, MA 1/1/93	3250.00
	Salem, MA 12/31/1892	*10,000.00*
2	3¢ Columbian 1/2/93 Any City	*6000.00*
3	4¢ Columbian 1/2/93 Any City	*6000.00*
4	5¢ Columbian 1/2/93 Any City	*6250.00*
5	6¢ Columbian 1/2/93 Any City	*6750.00*
7	10¢ Columbian 1/2/93 Any City	*7500.00*
	East Lexington, MA 12/31/92 bkstp	*12,000.00*

*** Since Jan. 1, 1893 was a Sunday and few post offices were open, both Jan. 1 and Jan. 2 covers are considered FDC's by collectors.**

ott #	Description	Uncacheted
	1898 TRANS-MISSISSIPPI ISSUE	
5	1¢ Trans-Mississippi 6/17/1898 Any City	*7000.00*
6	2¢ Trans-Mississippi 6/17/1898 DC	*7000.00*
	6/17/1898 Pittsburgh, PA	*7000.00*
8	5¢ Trans-Mississippi 6/17/1898 DC	*8000.00*
9	8¢ Trans-Mississippi 6/17/1898 DC	*8500.00*
1	50¢ Trans-Mississippi 6/17/1898 DC	*15,000.00*
2	$1 Trans-Mississippi 6/17/1898 DC	*25,000.00*
	1901 PAN AMERICAN ISSUE	
4	1¢ Pan-American 5/1/01 Any City	*5000.00*
5	2¢ Pan-American 5/1/01 Any City	*2750.00*
6	4¢ Pan-American 5/1/01 Any City	*7000.00*
7	5¢ Pan-American 5/1/01 Any City	*7000.00*
8	8¢ Pan-American 5/1/01 Any City	*8500.00*
8,296	4¢ & 8¢ on one FDC Boston, MA	*8500.00*
4-299	1¢-10¢ Pan-American, cplt. set on one FDC, Any City	*15,000.00*
	1904-1907 LOUISIANA PURCHASE & JAMESTOWN ISSUES	
3	1¢ Louisiana Purchase 4/30/04 Any City	5000.00
4	2¢ Louisiana Purchase 4/30/04 Any City	4500.00
5	3¢ Louisiana Purchase 4/30/04 Any City	*7000.00*
6	5¢ Louisiana Purchase 4/30/04 Any City	*8000.00*
7	10¢ Louisiana Purchase 4/30/04 Any City	*12,000.00*
3-327	1¢-10¢ Louisiana Purchase, complete set on one FDC	*30,000.00*
8	1¢ Jamestown Expedition 4/26/07 Any City	*6000.00*
9	2¢ Jamestown Expedition 4/26/07 Any City	*9000.00*
0	5¢ Jamestown Expedition 5/10/07 Norfolk, VA **(eku)**	*12,500.00*
1a	1¢ Franklin, bklt. sgl. 12/2/08 DC	*18,000.00*
2a	2¢ Washington, bklt. sgl. 11/16/08 DC	*32,500.00*
	1909 COMMEMORATIVES	
7	2¢ Lincoln 2-12-09 Any City	*350.00*
8	2¢ Lincoln Imperf. 2/12/09 Canton, OH	*7000.00*
0	2¢ Alaska-Yukon 6/1/09 Any City	3000.00
2	2¢ Hudson-Fulton 9/25/09 Any City	*900.00*
3	2¢ Hudson-Fulton Imperf. 9/25/09 Any City	*4500.00*
	1913 PAN-PACIFIC ISSUE	
7	1¢ Pan-Pacific Expo 1/1/13 Any City	3500.00
9	5¢ Pan-Pacific Expo 1/1/13 Any City	*7500.00*
0	10¢ Pan-Pacific Expo 1/1/13 Any City	*8000.00*
7,399,400	1¢,5¢ & 10¢ Pan-Pacific on one FDC, SF, CA	*17,500.00*

'DC's priced in *italics* are unique or extremely rare. Prices are tentative e to the lack of recent sales.

564

Scott #	Description	Uncacheted
497	10¢ Franklin Coil 1/31/22 DC (all are Hammelman cvrs)	4000.00
526	2¢ Offset Ty. IV 3/15/20 Any City **(eku)**	825.00
537	3¢ Victory 3/3/19 Any City	750.00
542	1¢ Rotary Perf. 10 x 11 5/26/20 Any City	1200.00
	1920 PILGRIM TERCENTENARY	
548	1¢ "Mayflower" Pair 12/21/20 DC	1000.00
549	2¢ "Landing of the Pilgrims" 12/21/20 DC	750.00
	12/21/20 Philadelphia, PA	2000.00
	12/21/20 Plymouth, MA	2500.00
548-50	1¢-5¢ Complete set on one cover, Phila., PA	2350.00
	Complete set on one cover, DC	2850.00
	1922-25 FLAT PLATE PERF. 11	
551	½¢ Hale (Block of 4) 4/4/25 DC	15.00
	New Haven, CT	20.00
	551 & 576 on one FDC 4/4/25 DC	75.00
552	1¢ Franklin 1/17/23 DC	22.50
	Philadelphia, PA	45.00
553	1½¢ Harding 3/19/25 DC	25.00
554	2¢ Washington 1/15/23 DC	35.00
555	3¢ Lincoln 2/12/23 DC	30.00
	Hodgenville, KY	200.00
556	4¢ Martha Washington 1/15/23 DC	70.00
557	5¢ Teddy Roosevelt 10/27/22 DC	115.00
	New York, NY	175.00
	Oyster Bay, NY	1200.00
558	6¢ Garfield 11/20/22 DC	200.00
559	7¢ McKinley 5/1/23 DC	125.00
	Niles, OH	175.00
560	8¢ Grant 5/1/23 DC	150.00
561	9¢ Jefferson 1/15/23 DC	150.00
562	10¢ Monroe 11/15/23 DC	160.00
	562,554,556 & 561 on one FDC	2000.00
563	11¢ Hayes 10/4/22 DC	650.00
	Fremont, OH	1250.00
564	12¢ Cleveland 3/20/23 DC	175.00
	Boston, MA	175.00
	Caldwell, NJ	175.00
565	14¢ Indian 5/1/23 DC	325.00
	Muskogee, OK	1800.00
	565 & 560 on one FDC, DC	1500.00
566	15¢ Statue of Liberty 11/11/22 DC	425.00
567	20¢ Golden Gate 5/1/23 DC	500.00
	San Francisco, CA	1500.00
568	25¢ Niagara Falls 11/11/22 DC	600.00
569	30¢ Bison 3/20/23 DC	725.00
	569 & 564 on one FDC, DC	2500.00
570	50¢ Arlington 11/11/22 DC	1100.00
	570,566 & 568 on one FDC	3500.00
571	$1 Lincoln Memorial 2/12/23 DC	5000.00
	Springfield, IL	5500.00
	571 & 555 on one FDC, DC	7000.00
572	$2 U.S. Capitol 3/20/23 DC	12,000.00
573	$5 Freedom Statue 3/20/23 DC	17,500.00
576	1½¢ Harding Imperf. 4/4/25 DC	50.00
	1925-26 ROTARY PRESS PERF. 10	
581	1¢ Franklin, unprecancelled 10/17/23 DC	2500.00
582	1½¢ Harding 3/19/25 DC	40.00
583a	2¢ Washington bklt pane of 6, 8/27/26 DC	1400.00
584	3¢ Lincoln 8/1/25 DC	50.00
585	4¢ Martha Washington 4/4/25 DC	50.00
586	5¢ T. Roosevelt 4/4/25 DC	50.00
587	6¢ Garfield 4/4/25 DC	55.00
588	7¢ McKinley 5/29/26 DC	65.00
589	8¢ Grant 5/29/26 DC	65.00
590	9¢ Jefferson 5/29/26 DC	70.00
	590, 588 & 589 on one FDC	275.00
591	10¢ Monroe 6/8/25 DC	90.00

*** eku: earliest known use**

598

Scott #	Description	Uncacheted	Cacheted
	1923-25 COIL ISSUES		
597	1¢ Franklin 7/18/23 DC	500.00	...
598	1½¢ Harding 3/19/25 DC	45.00	...
*599	2¢ Washington 1/15/23 DC (37 known)	1500.00	...
	* These are the eku from DC and prepared by Phil Ward. Other covers are known date 1/10, 1/11 & 1/13.		
600	3¢ Lincoln 5/10/24 DC	80.00	...
602	5¢ T. Roosevelt 3/5/24 DC	85.00	...
603	10¢ Monroe 12/1/24 DC	110.00	...
604	1¢ Franklin 7/19/24 DC	80.00	...
605	1½¢ Harding 5/9/25 DC	60.00	...
606	2¢ Washington 12/31/23 DC	125.00	...
610	2¢ Harding 9/1/23 DC	25.00	...
	Marlon, OH	20.00	...
	George W. Linn cachet (1st modern cachet)	**...**	**750.00**
611	2¢ Harding Imperf. 11/15/23 DC	85.00	...
612	2¢ Harding Perf. 10 9/12/23 DC	100.00	...
	1924 HUGENOT-WALLOON ISSUE		
614	1¢ Hugenot-Walloon 5/1/24 DC	40.00	...
	Albany, NY	40.00	...
	Allentown, PA	40.00	...
	Charleston, SC	40.00	...
	Jacksonville, FL	40.00	...
	Lancaster, PA	40.00	...
	Mayport, FL	40.00	...
	New Rochelle, NY	40.00	...
	New York, NY	40.00	...
	Philadelphia, PA	40.00	...
	Reading, PA	40.00	...
615	2¢ Hugenot-Walloon 5/1/24	60.00	...
	Albany, NY	60.00	...
	Allentown, PA	60.00	...
	Charleston, SC	60.00	...
	Jacksonville, FL	60.00	...
	Lancaster, PA	60.00	...
	Mayport, FL	60.00	...
	New Rochelle, NY	60.00	...
	New York, NY	60.00	...
	Philadelphia, PA	60.00	...
	Reading, PA	60.00	...
616	5¢ Hugenot-Walloon 5/1/24 DC	85.00	...
	Albany, NY	85.00	...
	Allentown, PA	85.00	...
	Charleston, SC	85.00	...
	Jacksonville, FL	85.00	...
	Lancaster, PA	85.00	...
	Mayport, FL	85.00	...
	New Rochelle, NY	85.00	...
	New York, NY	85.00	...
	Philadelphia, PA	85.00	...
	Reading, PA	85.00	...
614-16	1¢-5¢ Complete set on one cover, any official city	175.00	...
614-16	Same, Any Unofficial City	300.00	...
	1925 LEXINGTON-CONCORD ISSUE		
617	1¢ Lexington-Concord 4/4/25 DC	30.00	125.00
	Boston, MA	30.00	125.00
	Cambridge, MA	30.00	125.00
	Concord, MA	30.00	125.00
	Concord Junction, MA	35.00	...
	Lexington, MA	35.00	125.00
618	2¢ Lexington-Concord 4/4/25 DC	35.00	125.00
	Boston, MA	35.00	125.00
	Cambridge, MA	35.00	125.00
	Concord, MA	35.00	125.00
	Concord Junction, MA	40.00	...
	Lexington, MA	40.00	125.00
619	5¢ Lexington-Concord 4/4/25 DC	80.00	175.00
	Boston, MA	80.00	175.00
	Cambridge, MA	80.00	175.00
	Concord, MA	80.00	175.00
	Concord Junction, MA	90.00	...
	Lexington, MA	90.00	175.00
617-19	1¢-5¢ **1st Jackson cachet** (see above listings for prices)		
617-19	1¢-5¢ Lexington-Concord, cplt. set on one cover	150.00	...
	Same, Concord-Junction or Lexington	175.00	...
	Same, Any Unofficial City	250.00	...

Scott #	Description	Uncacheted	Cacheted
	1925 NORSE-AMERICAN ISSUE		
620	2¢ Norse-American 5/18/25 DC	20.00	...
	Algona, IN	20.00	...
	Benson, MN	20.00	...
	Decorah, IA	20.00	...
	Minneapolis, MN	20.00	...
	Northfield, MN	20.00	...
	St. Paul, MN	20.00	...
621	5¢ Norse-American 5/18/25 DC	30.00	...
	Algona, IN	30.00	...
	Benson, MN	30.00	...
	Decorah, IA	30.00	...
	Minneapolis, MN	30.00	...
	Northfield, MN	30.00	...
	St. Paul, MN	30.00	...
620-21	2¢-5¢ Norse-Amer., one cover 5/18/25 DC	50.00	275.00
	2¢-5¢ Algona, IN	50.00	275.00
	2¢-5¢ Benson, MN	50.00	275.00
	2¢-5¢ Decorah, IA	50.00	275.00
	2¢-5¢ Minneapolis, MN	50.00	275.00
	2¢-5¢ Northfield, MN	50.00	275.00
	2¢-5¢ St. Paul, MN	50.00	275.00
	1st Ernest J. Weschcke cachet	**...**	**275.00**
	1st A.C. Roessler cachet	**...**	**300.00**
622	13¢ Harrison 1/11/26 DC	15.00	...
	Indianapolis, IN	25.00	...
	North Bend, OH	140.00	...
623	17¢ Wilson 12/28/25	20.00	275.00
	New York, NY	20.00	275.00
	Princeton, NJ	30.00	275.00
	Staunton, VA	25.00	275.00
	1st Nickles cachet	**...**	**275.00**
627	2¢ Sesquicentennial 5/10/26 DC	8.00	65.00
	Boston, MA	8.00	65.00
	Philadelphia, PA	8.00	65.00
628	5¢ Ericsson Memorial 5/29/26 DC	25.00	450.00
	Chicago, IL	25.00	450.00
	Minneapolis, MN	25.00	450.00
	New York, NY	25.00	450.00
629	2¢ White Plains 10/18/26 New York, NY	6.00	50.00
	New York, NY Int. Phil. Ex. Agency	6.00	50.00
	White Plains, NY	6.00	50.00
630a	2¢ White Plains S/S, sgl. 10/18/26 NY, NY	10.00	55.00
	New York, NY Int. Phil. Ex. Agency	10.00	55.00
	White Plains, NY	10.00	55.00
630	Complete Sheet 10/18/26	1700.00	...
630	10/28/26	1000.00	...
631	1½¢ Harding Rotary Imperf. 8/27/26 DC	45.00	...
	1926-27 ROTARY PRESS PERF. 11 X 10½		
632	1¢ Franklin 6/10/27 DC	42.50	...
632a	Bklt. Pane of 6 11/27	3500.00	...
633	1½¢ Harding 5/17/27 DC	42.50	...
634	2¢ Washington 12/10/26 DC	45.00	...
634EE	Experimental Electric Eye 3/28/35	750.00	...
635	3¢ Lincoln 2/3/27 DC	40.00	...
635a	3¢ Lincoln Re-issue 2/7/34 DC	25.00	45.00
636	4¢ Martha Washington 5/17/27 DC	45.00	...
637	5¢ T. Roosevelt 3/24/27 DC	45.00	...
638	6¢ Garfield 7/27/27 DC	55.00	...
639	7¢ McKinley 3/24/27 DC	55.00	...
	639, 637 on one FDC	300.00	...
640	8¢ Grant 6/10/27 DC	60.00	...
	640, 632 on one FDC	300.00	...
641	9¢ Jefferson 5/17/27 DC	70.00	...
	641, 633, & 636 on one FDC	350.00	...
642	10¢ Monroe 3/3/27 DC	85.00	...
	1927		
643	2¢ Vermont 8/3/27 DC	5.00	50.00
	Bennington, VT	5.00	50.00
644	2¢ Burgoyne 8/3/27 DC	11.00	55.00
	Albany, NY	11.00	55.00
	Rome, NY	11.00	55.00
	Syracuse, NY	11.00	55.00
	Utica, NY	11.00	55.00

620-21

650

Scott #	Description	Uncacheted	Cacheted
	1928		
645	2¢ Valley Forge 5/26/28 DC	4.00	45.00
	Cleveland, OH	60.00	140.00
	Lancaster, PA	4.00	45.00
	Norristown, PA	4.00	45.00
	Philadelphia, PA	4.00	45.00
	Valley Forge, PA	4.00	45.00
	West Chester, PA	4.00	45.00
	Cleveland Midwestern Phil. Sta	4.00	45.00
	1st J.W. Stoutzenberg cachet	...	**250.00**
	1st Adam K. Bert cachet	...	**75.00**
646	2¢ Molly Pitcher 10/20/28 DC	12.50	85.00
	Freehold, NJ	12.50	85.00
	Red Bank, NJ	12.50	85.00
647	2¢ Hawaii 8/13/28 DC	15.00	65.00
	Honolulu, HI	17.50	65.00
648	5¢ Hawaii 8/13/28 DC	20.00	70.00
	Honolulu, HI	22.50	70.00
647-48	Hawaii on one cover	40.00	140.00
	1st F.W. Reid Cachet	...	**250.00**
649	2¢ Aeronautics Conf., green pmk. 12/12/28 DC	6.00	40.00
	Black pmk.	10.00	40.00
650	5¢ Aeronautics Conf., green pmk. 12/12/28 DC	10.00	45.00
	Black pmk	12.50	50.00
649-50	Aero. Conf., one cover, green pmk	15.00	65.00
	One cover, black pmk	17.50	70.00
	1929		
651	2¢ Clark 2/25/29 Vinncennes, in	5.00	30.00
	1st Floyd Shockley cachet	...	**30.00**
	1st Harry loor cachet	...	**175.00**
653	½¢ Hale (block of 4) 5/25/29 DC	30.00	...
654	2¢ Electric Lt., flat press 6/5/29 Menlo Park, NJ	8.00	35.00
655	2¢ Electric Light, rotary press 6/11/29 DC	75.00	175.00
656	2¢ Electric Light, coil 6/11/29 DC	85.00	200.00
656	Coil Line Pair	150.00	275.00
655-56	Rotary & Coil sgls. on one FDC	150.00	375.00
657	2¢ Sullivan 6/17/29 Auburn, NY	4.00	27.50
	Binghamton, NY	4.00	27.50
	Canajoharie, NY	4.00	27.50
	Canandaigua, NY	4.00	27.50
	Elmira, NY	4.00	27.50
	Geneva, NY	4.00	27.50
	Geneseo, NY	4.00	27.50
	Horseheads, NY	4.00	27.50
	Owego, NY	4.00	27.50
	Penn Yan, NY	4.00	27.50
	Perry, NY	4.00	27.50
	Seneca Falls, NY	4.00	27.50
	Waterloo, NY	4.00	27.50
	Watkins Glen, NY	4.00	27.50
	Waverly, NY	4.00	27.50
	1st Robert Beazell cachet	...	**400.00**
	1st A.C. Elliot cachet	...	**75.00**
	KANSAS OVERPRINTS		
658-68	Kansas Set of11 covers	750.00	...
658	1¢ Franklin 5/1/29 DC	35.00	...
	4/15/29 Newton, KS	300.00	...
659	1½¢ Harding 5/1/29 DC	40.00	...
660	2¢ Washington 5/1/29 DC	40.00	...
661	3¢ Lincoln 5/1/29 DC	50.00	...
662	4¢ Martha Washington 5/1/29 DC	55.00	...
663	5¢ T. Roosevelt 5/1/29 DC	55.00	...
664	6¢ Garfield 5/1/29 DC	75.00	...
	4/15/29 Newton, KS	400.00	...
665	7¢ McKinley 5/1/29 DC	90.00	...
666	8¢ Grant 5/1/29 DC	90.00	...
	4/15/29 Newton, KS	400.00	...
667	9¢ Jefferson 5/1/29 DC	100.00	...
668	10¢ Monroe 5/1/29 DC	125.00	...
658-68	1¢-10¢ Kansas cplt. set on one FDC 5/1/29 DC	1100.00	...

U.S. FIRST DAY COVERS

Scott #	Description	Uncacheted	Cacheted
	NEBRASKA OVERPRINTS		
669-79	Nebraska Set of 11 Covers	750.00	...
669	1¢ Franklin 5/1/29 DC	35.00	...
	4/15/29 Beatrice, NE	POR	...
670	1½¢ Harding 5/1/29 DC	40.00	...
	4/15/29 Hartington, NE	250.00	...
671	2¢ Washington 5/1/29 DC	40.00	...
	4/15/29 Auburn, NE	POR	...
	4/15/29 Beatrice, NE	POR	...
	4/15/29 Hartington, NE	250.00	...
672	3¢ Lincoln 5/1/29 DC	50.00	...
	4/15/29 Beatrice, NE	300.00	...
	4/15/29 Hartington, NE	300.00	...
673	4¢ Martha Washington 5/1/29 DC	50.00	...
	4/15/29 Beatrice, NE	300.00	...
	4/15/29 Hartington, NE	300.00	...
674	5¢ T. Roosevelt 5/1/29 DC	55.00	...
	4/15/29 Beatrice, NE	300.00	...
	4/15/29 Hartington, NE	300.00	...
675	6¢ Garfield 5/1/29 DC	75.00	...
676	7¢ McKinley 5/1/29 DC	90.00	...
677	8¢ Grant 5/1/29 DC	90.00	...
678	9¢ Jefferson 5/1/29 DC	100.00	...
679	10¢ Monroe 5/1/29 DC	125.00	...
669-79	1¢-10¢ Nebraska cplt. set on one FDC 5/1/29 DC	1100.00	...
680	2¢ Fallen Timbers 9/14/29 Erie, PA	3.00	30.00
	Maumee, OH	3.00	30.00
	Perrysburgh, OH	3.00	30.00
	Toledo, OH	3.00	30.00
	Waterville, OH	3.00	30.00
681	2¢ Ohio River 10/19/29 Cairo, IL	3.00	30.00
	Cincinnati, OH	3.00	30.00
	Evansville, IN	3.00	30.00
	Homestead, PA	3.00	30.00
	Louisville, KY	3.00	30.00
	Pittsburgh, PA	3.00	30.00
	Wheeling, WV	3.00	30.00
	1930-31		
682	2¢ Mass. Bay Colony 4/8/30 Boston, MA	3.00	30.00
	Salem, MA	3.00	30.00
683	2¢ Carolina-Charleston 4/10/30 Charleston, SC	3.00	30.00
684	1½¢ Harding 12/1/30 Marion, OH	4.00	40.00
685	4¢ Taft 6/4/30 Cincinnati, OH	6.00	50.00
686	1½¢ Harding, coil 12/1/30 Marion, OH	5.00	50.00
687	4¢ Taft, coil 9/18/30 DC	25.00	90.00
688	2¢ Braddock 7/9/30 Braddock, PA	4.00	30.00
689	2¢ Von Steuben 9/17/30 New York, NY	4.00	30.00
690	2¢ Pulaski 1/16/31 Brooklyn, NY	4.00	30.00
	Buffalo, NY	4.00	30.00
	Chicago, IL	4.00	30.00
	Cleveland, OH	4.00	30.00
	Detroit, MI	4.00	30.00
	Gary, IN	4.00	30.00
	Milwaukee, WI	4.00	30.00
	New York, NY	4.00	30.00
	Pittsburgh, PA	4.00	30.00
	Savannah, GA	4.00	30.00
	South Bend, IN	4.00	30.00
	Toledo, OH	4.00	30.00
	1931 ROTARY PRESS HI-VALUES		
692	11¢ Hayes 9/4/31 DC	100.00	...
693	12¢ Cleveland 8/25/31 DC	100.00	...
694	13¢ Harrison 9/4/31 DC	100.00	...
695	14¢ Indian 9/8/31 DC	100.00	...
696	15¢ Statue of Liberty 8/27/31 DC	110.00	...
697	17¢ Wilson 7/27/31 DC	350.00	...
	7/25/31 Brooklyn, NY	1500.00	...
698	20¢ Golden Gate 9/8/31 DC	300.00	...
699	25¢ Niagara Falls 7/27/31 DC	350.00	...
	7/25/31 Brooklyn, NY	1500.00	...
	697, 699 on one FDC, Brooklyn, NY	2000.00	...
700	30¢ Bison 9/8/31 DC	300.00	...
701	50¢ Arlington 9/4/31 DC	400.00	...

680

707

ott #	Description	Uncacheted	Cacheted
	1931		
2	2¢ Red Cross 5/21/31 DC	3.00	30.00
	Dansville, NY	3.00	30.00
	1st Edward Hacker cachet	...	**150.00**
3	2¢ Yorktown 10/19/31 Wethersfield, CT	3.00	45.00
	Yorktown, VA	3.00	45.00
	1st Crosby cachet	...	**400.00**
	1932 WASHINGTON BICENTENNIAL ISSUE		
4-15	Bicentennial Set of 12 Covers		185.00
4	½¢ olive brown 1/1/32 DC		15.00
5	1¢ green 1/1/32 DC		15.00
6	1½¢ brown 1/1/32 DC		15.00
7	2¢ carmine rose 1/1/32 DC		15.00
8	3¢ deep violet 1/1/32 DC		15.00
9	4¢ light brown 1/1/32 DC		15.00
0	5¢ blue 1/1/32 DC		15.00
1	6¢ red orange 1/1/32 DC		15.00
2	7¢ black 1/1/32 DC		17.50
3	8¢ olive bistre 1/1/32 DC		17.50
4	9¢ pale red 1/1/32 DC		17.50
5	10¢ orange yellow 1/1/32 DC		17.50
4-15	Wash. Bicent. on one cover		200.00
	1932		
6	2¢ Winter Olympic Games 1/25/32 Lake Placid, NY		20.00
7	2¢ Arbor Day 4/22/32 Nebraska City, NE		15.00
	1st Linnprint cachet		**15.00**
8	3¢ Summer Olympics 6/15/32 Los Angeles, CA		22.50
9	5¢ Summer Olympics 6/15/32 Los Angeles, CA		22.50
8-19	Summer Olympics cplt. set on one FDC		30.00
0	3¢ Washington 6/16/32 DC		35.00
0b	3¢ Booklet Pane 7/25/32 DC		175.00
1	3¢ Washington, coil, vert. 6/24/32 DC		50.00
2	3¢ Washington, coil, horiz. 6/24/32 DC		50.00
3	6¢ Garfield, coil 8/18/32 Los Angeles, CA		50.00
4	3¢ William Penn 10/24/32 New Castle, DE		15.00
	Chester, PA		15.00
	Philadelphia, PA		15.00
5	3¢ Daniel Webster 10/24/32 Franklin, NH		15.00
	Exeter, NH		15.00
	Hanover, NH		15.00
	1933-34		
6	3¢ Gen'l Oglethorpe 2/12/33 Savannah, GA		15.00
	1st Anderson cachet		**150.00**
7	3¢ Peace Proclamation 4/19/33 Newburgh, NY		15.00
	1st Grimsland cachet		**350.00**
8	1¢ Century of Progress 5/25/33 Chicago, IL		15.00
9	3¢ Century of Progress 5/25/33 Chicago, IL		15.00
8-29	Progress on one cover		20.00
0	1¢ Amer. Phil. Soc., sht. of 25 8/25/33 Chicago, IL		175.00
0a	1¢ Amer. Phil. Soc., single 8/25/33 Chicago, IL		15.00
1	3¢ Amer. Phil. Soc., sht. of 25 8/25/33 Chicago, IL		175.00
1a	3¢ Amer. Phil. Soc., single 8/25/33 Chicago, IL		15.00
0a-31a	Amer. Phil. Soc. on one cover		22.50
2	3¢ National Recovery Act 8/15/33 DC		15.00
	Nira, IA 8/17/33, unofficial		20.00
3	3¢ Byrd Antarctic 10/9/33 DC		25.00
4	5¢ Kosciuszko 10/13/33 Boston, MA		17.50
	Buffalo, NY		17.50
	Chicago, NY		17.50
	Detroit, MI		17.50
	Pittsburgh, PA		40.00
	Kosciuszko, MS		17.50
	St. Louis, MO		17.50
5	3¢ Nat'l Exhibition, sht. of 6 2/10/34 New York, NY		65.00
5a	3¢ National Exhibition, single 2/10/34 New York NY		15.00
6	3¢ Maryland 3/23/34 St. Mary's City, MD		15.00
	1st Torkel Gundel cachet		**300.00**
	1st Don Kapner cachet		**25.00**
	1st Louis Nix cachet		**250.00**
	1st Top Notch cachet		**25.00**
7	3¢ Mothers of Am., rotary 5/2/34 any city		10.00
8	3¢ Mothers of Am., flat 5/2/34 any city		10.00
7-38	Mothers of Am. on one cover		35.00
9	3¢ Wisconsin 7/7/34 Green Bay, WI		12.00

U.S. FIRST DAY COVERS

Scott #	Description	Cacheted
	1934 NATIONAL PARKS ISSUE	
740-49	National Parks set of 10 covers	100.00
740-49	On 1 Cover 10/8/34	125.00
740	1¢ Yosemite 7/16/34 Yosemite, CA	10.00
	DC	10.00
741	2¢ Grand Canyon 7/24 34 Grand Canyon, AZ	10.00
	DC	10.00
742	3¢ Mt. Rainier 8/3/34 Longmire, WA	10.00
	DC	10.00
743	4¢ Mesa Verde 9/25/34 Mesa Verde, CO	10.00
	DC	10.00
744	5¢ Yellowstone 7/30/34 Yellowstone, WY	10.00
	DC	10.00
745	6¢ Crater Lake 9/5/34 Crater Lake, OR	10.00
	DC	10.00
746	7¢ Acadia 10/2/34 Bar Harbor, ME	10.00
	DC	10.00
747	8¢ Zion 9/18/34 Zion, UT	10.00
	DC	10.00
748	9¢ Glacier Park 8/27/34 Glacier Park, MT	10.00
	DC	10.00
749	10¢ Smoky Mts. 10/8/34 Sevierville, TN	10.00
	DC	10.00
750	3¢ Amer. Phil. Soc., sheet of 6 8/28/34 Atlantic City, NJ..	60.00
750a	3¢ Amer. Phil. Soc., single 8/28/34 Atlantic City, NJ	15.00
751	1¢ Trans-Miss. Phil. Expo., sht. of 6 10/10/34 Omaha, NE	60.00
751a	1¢ Trans-Miss. Phil. Expo., single 10/10/34 Omaha, NE..	15.00

Scott #	Description	Cacheted Gutter or Line Pair	Singles
	1935 FARLEY SPECIAL PRINTING		
752-71	Set of 20 covers	...	500.00
752-71	Set on 1 cover 3/15/35	...	450.00
752-55,766a-71	10 varieties on 1 cover 3/15/35	...	250.00
752	3¢ Peace Proclamation 3/15/35 DC	50.00	35.00
753	3¢ Byrd 3/15/35 DC	50.00	35.00
754	3¢ Mothers of America 3/15/35 DC	45.00	35.00
755	3¢ Wisconsin 3/15/35 DC	45.00	35.00
756-65	Parks set of 10 covers	400.00	300.00
756-65	Set on 1 cover 3/15/35	...	175.00
756	1¢ Yosemite 3/15/35 DC	40.00	30.00
757	2¢ Grand Canyon 3/15/35 DC	40.00	30.00
758	3¢ Mount Rainier 3/15/35	40.00	30.00
759	4¢ Mesa Verde 3/15/35 DC	40.00	30.00
760	5¢ Yellowstone 3/15/35 DC	40.00	30.00
761	6¢ Crater Lake 3/15/35 DC	40.00	30.00
762	7¢ Acadia 3/15/35 DC	40.00	30.00
763	8¢ Zion 3/15/35 DC	40.00	30.00
764	9¢ Glacier Park 3/15/35 DC	40.00	30.00
765	10¢ Smoky Mountains 3/15/35 DC	40.00	30.00
766a	1¢ Century of Progress 3/15/35 DC	50.00	40.00
767a	3¢ Century of Progress 3/15/35 DC	50.00	40.00
768a	3¢ Byrd 3/15/35 DC	55.00	40.00
769a	1¢ Yosemite 3/15/35 DC	55.00	40.00
770a	3¢ Mount Rainier 3/15/35	55.00	40.00
771	16¢ Air Mail-Spec. Del. 3/15/35 DC	60.00	40.00

Scott #	Description	Cacheted
	1935-36	
772	3¢ Connecticut 4/26/35 Hartford, CT	8.00
	1st Winfred Grandy cachet	**30.00**
773	3¢ Calif. Exposition 5/29/35 San Diego, CA	10.00
	1st W. Espenshade cachet	**30.00**
774	3¢ Boulder Dam 9/30/35 Boulder City, NV	10.00
775	3¢ Michigan 11/1/35 Lansing, MI	8.00
	1st Risko Art Studio cachet	**200.00**
776	3¢ Texas 3/2/36 Gonzales, TX	15.00
	1st John Sidenius cachet	**60.00**
	1st Walter Czubay cachet	**75.00**
777	3¢ Rhode Island 5/4/36 Providence, RI	8.00
	1st J.W. Clifford cachet	**30.00**
778	3¢ TIPEX sheet 5/9/36 New York, NY	15.00
	1st House of Farnam cachet	**500.00**
778a-78d	Single from sheet	5.00
782	3¢ Arkansas 6/15/36 Little Rock, AK	8.00
783	3¢ Oregon 7/14/36 Astoria, OR	8.00
	Daniel, WY	8.00
	Lewiston, ID	8.00
	Missoula, MT	8.00
	Walla Walla, WA	8.00
784	3¢ Susan B. Anthony 8/26/36 DC	8.00
	1st Historic Arts cachet	**25.00**

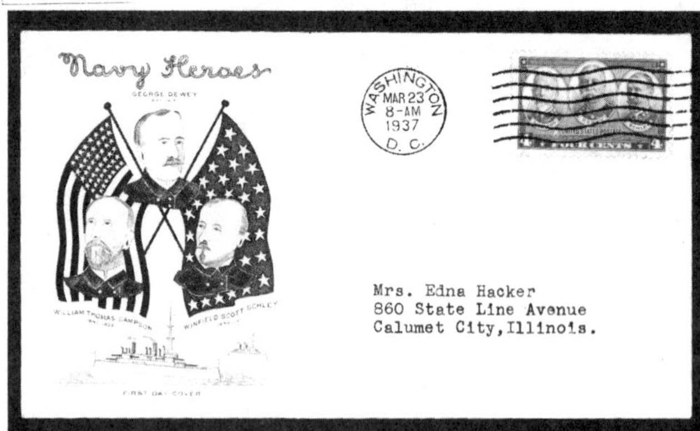

Scott #	Description	Price
	1936-37 ARMY - NAVY	
785-94	Army-Navy set of 10 covers	50.00
785	1¢ Army 12/15/36 DC	5.00
786	2¢ Army 1/15/37 DC	5.00
787	3¢ Army 2/18/37 DC	5.00
788	4¢ Army 3/23/37 DC	5.00
789	5¢ Army 5/26/37 West Point, NY	5.00
	#785-89, Army set on one cover, 5/26/37	35.00
790	1¢ Navy 12/15/36 DC	5.00
791	2¢ Navy 1/15/37 DC	5.00
792	3¢ Navy 2/18/37 DC	5.00
793	4¢ Navy 3/23/37 DC	5.00
794	5¢ Navy 5/26/37 Annapolis, MD	5.00
	#790-94, Navy set on one cover, 5/26/37	35.00
	#785-94, Army-Navy set on one cover, 5/26/37	75.00
	1937	
795	3¢ Ordinance of 1787 7/13/37 Marietta, OH	7.00
	New York, NY	7.00
	1st Cachet Craft cachet	**60.00**
796	5¢ Virginia Dare 8/18/37 Manteo, NC	7.00
797	10¢ S.P.A. sheet 8/26/37 Asheville, NC	7.00
798	3¢ Constitution 9/17/37 Philadelphia, PA	7.00
	1st Pilgrim cachet	**90.00**
	1st Fidelity Stamp Co. cachet	**12.00**
799-802	Territory set of 4 covers	50.00
799-802	On 1 Cover 12/15/37	40.00
799	3¢ Hawaii 10/18/37 Honolulu, HI	15.00
800	3¢ Alaska 11/12/37 Juneau, AK	12.00
801	3¢ Puerto Rico 11/25/37 San Juan, PR	12.00
802	3¢ Virgin Islands 12/15/37 Charlotte Amalie, VI	12.00
	1938-1954 PRESIDENTIAL SERIES	
803-34	Presidents set of 32 covers	525.00
803-31	Presidents set of 29 covers	135.00
803-31	Pres. Electric Eyes set of 29 covers	550.00
803	½¢ Franklin 5/19/38 Philadelphia, PA	3.00
804	1¢ Washington 4/25/38 DC	3.00
804b	booklet pane 1/27/39 DC	12.50
805	1½¢ Martha Washington 5/5/38 DC	3.00
806	2¢ J. Adams 6/3/38 DC	3.00
806b	booklet pane 1/27/39 DC	12.50
807	3¢ Jefferson 6/16/38 DC	3.00
807a	booklet pane 1/27/39 DC	12.50
	#804b, 806b, 807a Bklt. set on one cover, 1/27/38 DC	60.00
808	4¢ Madison 7/1/38 DC	3.00
809	4½¢ White House 7/11/38 DC	3.00
810	5¢ Monroe 7/21/38 DC	3.00
811	6¢ J.Q. Adams 7/28/38 DC	3.00
812	7¢ Jackson 8/4/38 DC	3.00
813	8¢ Van Buren 8/11/38 DC	3.00
814	9¢ Harrison 8/18/38 DC	3.00
815	10¢ Tyler 9/2/38 DC	3.00
816	11¢ Polk 9/8/38 DC	5.00
817	12¢ Taylor 9/14/38 DC	5.00
818	13¢ Fillmore 9/22/38 DC	5.00
819	14¢ Pierce 10/6/38 DC	5.00
820	15¢ Buchanan 10/13/38 DC	5.00
821	16¢ Lincoln 10/20/38 DC	6.00
822	17¢ Johnson 10/27/38 DC	6.00
823	18¢ Grant 11/3/38 DC	6.00
824	19¢ Hayes 11/10/38 DC	6.00
825	20¢ Garfield 11/10/38 DC	6.00
	#824-825 on one FDC	40.00
826	21¢ Arthur 11/22/38 DC	7.00
827	22¢ Cleveland 11/22/38 DC	7.00
	#826-827 on one FDC	40.00
828	24¢ Harrison 12/2/38 DC	8.00
829	25¢ McKinley 12/2/38 DC	8.00
	#828-829 on one FDC	40.00
830	30¢ Roosevelt 12/8/38 DC	10.00
831	50¢ Taft 12/8/38 DC	15.00
	#830-831 on one FDC	40.00
832	$1 Wilson 8/29/38 DC	65.00
832c	$1 Wilson, dry print 8/31/54 DC	30.00
833	$2 Harding 9/29/38 DC	125.00

U.S. FIRST DAY COVERS

Scott #	Description	Price
834	$5 Coolidge 11/17/38 DC	210.00
	PRESIDENTIAL ELECTRIC EYE FDC's	
803EE	½¢ Electric Eye 9/8/41 DC	10.00
804EE	1¢ Electric Eye 9/8/41 DC	10.00
	#803, 804, E15 on one FDC	30.00
805EE	1½¢ Electric Eye 1/16/41 DC	10.00
806EE	2¢ Electric Eye (Type I) 6/3/38 DC	15.00
806EE	2¢ Electric Eye (Type II) 4/5/39 DC	8.00
807EE	3¢ Electric Eye 4/5/39 DC	8.00
	#806-807 on one FDC 4/5/39	15.00
807EE	3¢ Electric Eye convertible 1/18/40	12.50
808EE	4¢ Electric Eye 10/28/41 DC	17.50
809EE	4½¢ Electric Eye 10/28/41 DC	17.50
810EE	5¢ Electric Eye 10/28/41 DC	17.50
811EE	6¢ Electric Eye 9/25/41 DC	15.00
812EE	7¢ Electric Eye 10/28/41 DC	17.50
813EE	8¢ Electric Eye 10/28/41 DC	17.50
814EE	9¢ Electric Eye 10/28/41 DC	17.50
815EE	10¢ Electric Eye 9/25/41 DC	15.00
	#811, 815 on one FDC	25.00
816EE	11¢ Electric Eye 10/8/41 DC	20.00
817EE	12¢ Electric Eye 10/8/41 DC	20.00
818EE	13¢ Electric Eye 10/8/41 DC	20.00
819EE	14¢ Electric Eye 10/8/41 DC	20.00
820EE	15¢ Electric Eye 10/8/41 DC	20.00
	#816-820 on one FDC	30.00
821EE	16¢ Electric Eye 1/7/42 DC	25.00
822EE	17¢ Electric Eye 10/28/41 DC	25.00
	#808-10, 812-14, 822 on one FDC	60.00
823EE	18¢ Electric Eye 1/7/42 DC	25.00
824EE	19¢ Electric Eye 1/7/42 DC	25.00
825EE	20¢ Electric Eye 1/7/42 DC	25.00
	#824-825 on one FDC	30.00
826EE	21¢ Electric Eye 1/7/42 DC	25.00
	#821, 823-26 on one FDC	60.00
827EE	22¢ Electric Eye 1/28/42 DC	25.00
828EE	24¢ Electric Eye 1/28/42 DC	25.00
829EE	25¢ Electric Eye 1/28/42 DC	25.00
830EE	30¢ Electric Eye 1/28/42 DC	30.00
831EE	50¢ Electric Eye 1/28/42 DC	40.00
	#827-831 on one FDC	60.00
	1938	
835	3¢ Ratification 6/21/38 Philadelphia, PA	7.50
836	3¢ Swedes and Finns 6/27/38 Wilmington, DE	7.50
837	3¢ NW Territory 7/15/38 Marietta, OH	7.50
838	3¢ Iowa Territory 8/24/38 Des Moines, IA	7.50
	1939 PRESIDENTIAL COILS	
839-51	Presidents set of 13 covers	55.00
839	1¢ Washington, pair 1/20/39 DC	4.00
840	1½¢ M. Wash., pair 1/20/39 DC	4.00
841	2¢ J. Adams, pair 1/20/39 DC	4.00
842	3¢ Jefferson 1/20/39 DC	4.00
842	Same, pair	5.00
843	4¢ Madison 1/20/39 DC	5.00
843	Same, pair	6.00
844	4½¢ White House 1/20/39 DC	4.00
844	Same, pair	5.00
845	5¢ Monroe 1/20/39 DC	5.00
845	Same, pair	6.00
846	6¢ J.Q. Adams, vert. 1/20/39 DC	5.00
846	Same, pair	6.00
847	10¢ Tyler 1/20/39 DC	7.50
847	Same, pair	10.00
839-847	On 1 Cover	50.00
848	1¢ Washington, pair, vert. coil 1/27/39 DC	4.00
849	1½¢ M. Wash., pair, vert. coil 1/27/39 DC	4.00
850	2¢ J. Adams, pair, vert. coil 1/27/39 DC	4.00
851	3¢ Jefferson 1/27/39 DC	4.00
851	Same, pair, vert. coil	5.00
848-51	On 1 Cover	30.00
839-51	On 1 cover	110.00

832

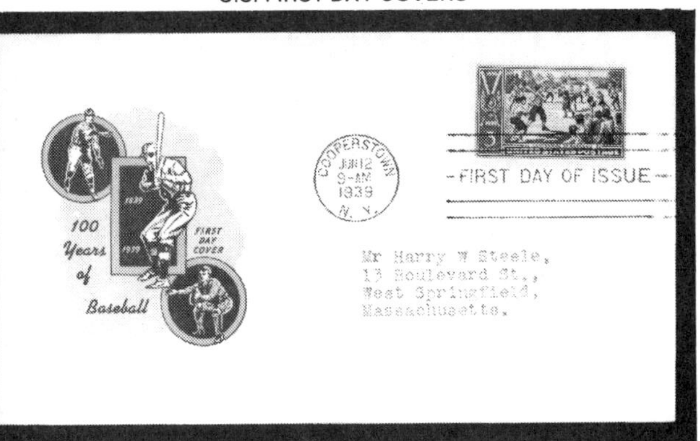

855

cott #	Description	Price
	1939	
52	3¢ Golden Gate 2/18/39 San Francisco, CA	8.00
53	3¢ World's Fair 4/1/39 New York, NY	10.00
	1st Artcraft cachet	**200.00**
54	3¢ Wash. Inauguration 4/30/39 NY, NY	8.00
55	3¢ Baseball 6/12/39 Cooperstown, NY	40.00
56	3¢ Panama Canal 8/15/39 USS Charleston	8.00
57	3¢ Printing Tercent. 9/25/39 NY, NY	6.00
58	3¢ 50th Anniv. 4 States 11/2/39 Bismarck, ND	5.00
	11/2/39 Pierre, SD	5.00
	11/8/39 Helena, MT	5.00
	11/11/39 Olympia, WA	5.00
	1940 FAMOUS AMERICANS	
59-93	**Famous Americans set of 35 covers**	**125.00**
59	1¢ Washington Irving 1/29/40 Terrytown, NY	3.00
60	2¢ James Fenimore Cooper 1/29/40 Cooperstown, NY	3.00
61	3¢ Ralph Waldo Emerson 2/5/40 Boston, MA	3.00
62	5¢ Louisa May Alcott 2/5/40 Concord, MA	4.00
63	10¢ Samuel Clemens 2/13/40 Hannibal, MO	6.00
59-63	Authors on one cover 2/13/40	40.00
64	1¢ Henry W. Longfellow 2/16/40 Portland, ME	3.00
65	2¢ John Greenleaf Whittier 2/16/40 Haverhill, MA	3.00
66	3¢ James Russell Lowell 2/20/40 Cambridge, MA	3.00
67	5¢ Walt Whitman 2/20/40 Camden, NJ	4.00
68	10¢ James Whitcomb Riley 2/24/40 Greenfield, IN	5.00
64-68	Poets on one cover 2/24/40	40.00
69	1¢ Horace Mann 3/14/40 Boston, MA	3.00
70	2¢ Mark Hopkins 3/14/40 Williamstown, MA	3.00
71	3¢ Charles W. Eliot 3/28/40 Cambridge, MA	3.00
72	5¢ Frances E. Willard 3/28/40 Evanston, IL	4.00
73	10¢ Booker T. Washington 4/7/40 Tuskegee Inst., AL	10.00
69-73	Educators on one cover 4/7/40	45.00
74	1¢ John James Audubon 4/8/40 St. Francesville, LA	4.00
75	2¢ Dr. Crawford W. Long 4/8/40 Jefferson, GA	4.00
76	3¢ Luther Burbank 4/17/40 Santa Rosa, CA	3.00
77	5¢ Dr. Walter Reed 4/17/40 DC	4.00
78	10¢ Jane Addams 4/26/40 Chicago, IL	5.00
74-78	Scientists on one cover 4/26/40	40.00
79	1¢ Stephen Collins Foster 5/3/40 Bardstown, KY	3.00
80	2¢ John Philip Sousa 5/3/40 DC	3.00
81	3¢ Victor Herbert 5/13/40 New York, NY	3.00
82	5¢ Edward A. MacDowell 5/13/40 Peterborough, NH	4.00
83	10¢ Ethelbert Nevin 6/10/40 Pittsburgh, PA	5.00
79-83	Composers on one cover 6/10/40	40.00
84	1¢ Gilbert Charles Stuart 9/5/40 Narragansett, RI	3.00
85	2¢ James A. McNeill Whistler 9/5/40 Lowell, MA	3.00
86	3¢ Augustus Saint-Gaudens 9/16/40 New York, NY	3.00
87	5¢ Daniel Chester French 9/16/40 Stockbridge, MA	4.00
88	10¢ Frederic Remington 9/30/40 Canton, NY	5.00
84-88	Artists on one cover 9/30/40	40.00
89	1¢ Eli Whitney 10/7/40 Savannah, GA	3.00
90	2¢ Samuel F.B. Morse 10/7/40 NY, NY	3.00
91	3¢ Cyrus Hall McCormick 10/14/40 Lexington, VA	3.00
92	5¢ Elias Howe 10/14/40 Spencer, MA	4.00
93	10¢ Alexander Graham Bell 10/28/40 Boston, MA	6.00
89-93	Inventors on one cover 10/28/40	40.00
59-93	Famous American set on one cover 10/28/40	175.00
	1940-43	
94	3¢ Pony Exxpress 4/3/40 St. Joseph, MO	6.00
	Sacramento, CA	6.00
	1st Aristocrats cachet	**15.00**
95	3¢ Pan American Union 4/14/40 DC	4.00
96	3¢ Idaho Statehood 7/3/40 Boise, ID	4.00
97	3¢ Wyoming Statehood 7/10/40 Cheyenne, WY	4.00
98	3¢ Coronado Expedition 9/7/40 Albuquerque, NM	4.00
99	1¢ National Defense 10/16/40 DC	4.00
00	2¢ National Defense 10/16/40 DC	4.00
01	3¢ National Defense 10/16/40 DC	4.00
99-901	National Defense on one cover	10.00
02	3¢ 13th Amend. 10/20/40 World's Fair, NY	8.00
03	3¢ Vermont Statehood 3/4/41 Montpelier, VT	7.00
	1st Fleetwood cachet	**60.00**
	1st Dorothy Knapp hand painted cachet	**800.00**

U.S. FIRST DAY COVERS

Scott #	Description	Name Blks.	Price / Singles
904	3¢ Kentucky Statehood 6/1/42 Frankfort, KY		4.00
905	3¢ Win the War 7/4/42 DC		3.50
906	5¢ China Resistance 7/7/42 Denver, CO		10.00
907	2¢ United Nations 1/14/43 DC		4.00
908	1¢ Four Freedoms 2/12/43 DC		4.00
	1943-44 OVERRUN NATIONS (FLAGS)	**Name Blks.**	**Singles**
909-21	**Flags set of 13 covers**	**130.00**	**50.00**
909	5¢ Poland 3/22/43 Chicago, IL	10.00	5.00
	DC	10.00	5.00
	1st Penn Arts cachet	...	**20.00**
	1st Smartcraft cachet	...	**15.00**
910	5¢ Czechoslovakia 7/12/43 DC	10.00	4.00
911	5¢ Norway 7/27/43 DC	10.00	4.00
912	5¢ Luxembourg 8/10/43 DC	10.00	4.00
913	5¢ Netherlands 8/24/43 DC	10.00	4.00
914	5¢ Belgium 9/14/43 DC	10.00	4.00
915	5¢ France 9/28/43 DC	10.00	4.00
916	5¢ Greece 10/12/43 DC	10.00	4.00
917	5¢ Yugoslavia 10/26/43 DC	10.00	4.00
918	5¢ Albania 11/9/43 DC	10.00	4.00
919	5¢ Austria 11/23/43 DC	10.00	4.00
920	5¢ Denmark 12/7/43 DC	10.00	4.00
	#909-920 on one cover, 12/7/43	...	70.00
921	5¢ Korea 11/2/44 DC	10.00	5.00
	#909-921 on one cover, 11/2/44	...	85.00
	1944		
922	3¢ Railroad 5/10/44 Ogden, UT		6.00
	Omaha, NE		6.00
923	3¢ Steamship 5/22/44 Kings Point, NY		5.00
	Savannah, GA		5.00
924	3¢ Telegraph 5/24/44 DC		5.00
	Baltimore, MD		5.00
925	3¢ Corregidor 9/27/44 DC		6.00
926	3¢ Motion Picture 10/31/44 Hollywood, CA		6.00
	1945		
927	3¢ Florida 3/3/45 Tallahassee, FL		4.00
928	5¢ UN Conference 4/25/45 San Francisco, CA		6.00
929	3¢ Iwo Jima 7/11/45 DC		14.00
930	1¢ Roosevelt 7/26/45 Hyde Park, NY		3.00
931	2¢ Roosevelt 8/24/45 Warm Springs, GA		3.00
932	3¢ Roosevelt 6/27/45 DC		3.00
	1st Fluegel cachet		**60.00**
933	5¢ Roosevelt 1/30/46 DC		3.00
	#930-933 on one cover 1/30/46 DC		10.00
934	3¢ Army 9/28/45 DC		6.00
935	3¢ Navy 10/27/45 Annapolis, MD		7.00
936	3¢ Coast Guard 11/10/45 New York, NY		6.00
937	3¢ Alfred E. Smith 11/26/45 New York, NY		3.00
938	3¢ Texas Centennial 12/29/45 Austin, TX		5.00
	1946		
939	3¢ Merchant Marine 2/26/46 DC		6.00
	#929, 934-36, 939 on one cover 2/26/46		25.00
940	3¢ Honorable Discharge 5/9/46 DC		6.00
	1st Artmaster cachet		**20.00**
	#929, 934-36, 939-940 on one cover 5/9/46		30.00
941	3¢ Tennessee Sthd. 6/1/46 Nashville, TN		2.50
942	3¢ Iowa Statehood 8/3/46 Iowa City, IA		2.50
943	3¢ Smithsonian 8/10/46 DC		2.50
944	3¢ New Mexico 10/16/46 Santa Fe, NM		2.50
	1947		
945	3¢ Thomas A. Edison 2/11/47 Milan, OH		4.00
946	3¢ Joseph Pulitzer 4/10/47 New York, NY		2.50
947	3¢ Stamp Centenary Sheet 5/17/47 New York, NY		2.50
	1st Fulton cachet		**30.00**
948	5¢-10¢ Stamp Centenary Sheet 5/19/47 New York, NY		3.00
949	3¢ Doctors 6/9/47 Atlantic City, NJ		6.00
950	3¢ Utah Cent. 7/24/47 Salt Lake City, UT		2.50
951	3¢ Constitution 10/21/47 Boston, MA		3.50
	1st C.W. George cachet		**75.00**
952	3¢ Everglades 12/5/47 Florida City, FL		2.50

921

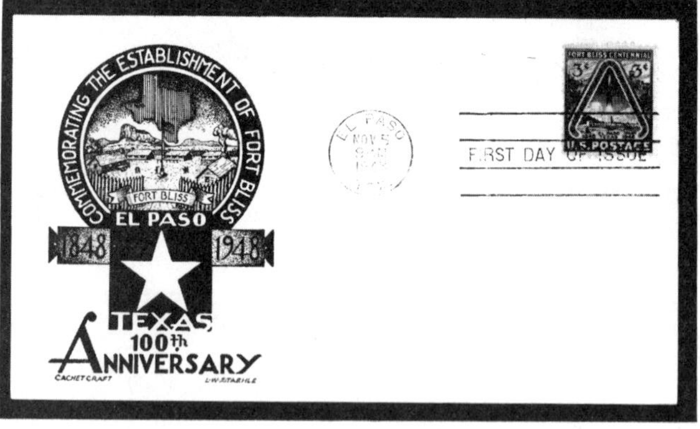

976

Scott #	Description	Price
	1948	
953	3¢ G. Washington Carver 1/5/48 Tuskegee Inst., AL	4.50
	1st Jackson cachet	**30.00**
954	3¢ Discovery of Gold 1/24/48 Coloma, CA	2.00
955	3¢ Mississippi 4/7/48 Natchez, MS	2.00
956	3¢ Four Chaplains 5/28/48 DC	2.00
957	3¢ Wisconsin Cent. 5/29/48 Madison, WI	2.00
958	5¢ Swedish Pioneers 6/4/48 Chicago, IL	2.00
959	3¢ Women's Prog. 7/19/48 Seneca Falls, NY	2.00
960	3¢ William A. White 7/31/48 Emporia, KS	2.00
961	3¢ US-Canada 8/2/48 Niagara Falls, NY	2.00
962	3¢ Francis Scott Key 8/9/48 Frederick, MD	2.25
963	3¢ Youth of America 8/11/48 DC	2.00
964	3¢ Oregon Terr. 8/14/48 Oregon City, OR	2.00
965	3¢ Harlan Fisk Stone 8/25/48 Chesterfield, NH	2.00
966	3¢ Palomar Observatory 8/30/48 Palomar Mt., CA	2.25
967	3¢ Clara Barton 9/7/48 Oxford, MA	3.00
968	3¢ Poultry Industry 9/9/48 New Haven, CT	2.00
969	3¢ Gold Star Mothers 9/21/48 DC	2.00
970	3¢ Fort Kearny 9/22/48 Minden, NE	2.00
971	3¢ Fireman 10/4/48 Dover, DE	4.00
972	3¢ Indian Centennial 10/15/48 Muskogee, OK	2.00
973	3¢ Rough Riders 10/27/48 Prescott, AZ	2.00
974	3¢ Juliette Low 10/29/48 Savannah, GA	3.50
975	3¢ Will Rogers 11/4/48 Claremore, OK	2.00
	1st Kolor Kover cachet	**100.00**
976	3¢ Fort Bliss 11/5/48 El Paso, TX	2.50
977	3¢ Moina Michael 11/9/48 Athens, GA	2.00
978	3¢ Gettysburgh Address 11/19/48 Gettysburg, PA	2.50
979	3¢ Amer. Turners 11/20/48 Cincinnati, OH	2.00
980	3¢ Joel Chandler Harris 12/9/48 Eatonton, GA	2.00
	1949	
981	3¢ Minnesota Terr. 3/3/49 St. Paul, MN	2.00
982	3¢ Washington & Lee Univ. 4/12/49 Lexington, VA	2.00
983	3¢ Puerto Rico 4/27/49 San Juan, PR	2.00
984	3¢ Annapolis 5/23/49 Annapolis, MD	2.00
985	3¢ G.A.R. 8/29/49 Indianapolis, IN	2.00
986	3¢ Edgar Allan Poe 10/7/49 Richmond, VA	2.00
	1950	
987	3¢ Bankers 1/3/50 Saratoga Springs, NY	2.00
988	3¢ Samuel Gompers 1/27/50 DC	2.00
989	3¢ Statue of Freedom 4/20/50 DC	2.00
990	3¢ White House 6/12/50 DC	2.00
991	3¢ Supreme Court 8/2/50 DC	2.00
992	3¢ Capitol 11/22/50 DC	2.00
	#989-992 on one cover 11/22/50	7.50
993	3¢ Railroad Engineers 4/29/50 Jackson, TN	4.00
994	3¢ Kansas City 6/3/50 Kansas City, MO	2.00
995	3¢ Boy Scouts 6/30/50 Valley Forge, PA	4.00
996	3¢ Indiana Terr. 7/4/50 Vincennes, IN	2.00
997	3¢ California Sthd. 9/9/50 Sacramento, CA	2.00
	1951	
998	3¢ Confederate Vets. 5/30/51 Norfolk, VA	2.00
999	3¢ Nevada Territory 7/14/51 Genoa, NY	2.00
1000	3¢ Landing of Cadillac 7/24/51 Detroit, MI	2.00
1001	3¢ Colorado Statehood 8/1/51 Minturn, CO	2.00
1002	3¢ Amer. Chem. Soc. 9/4/51 New York, NY	2.00
1003	3¢ Battle of Brooklyn 12/10/51 Brooklyn, NY	2.00
	1952	
1004	3¢ Betsy Ross 1/2/52 Philadelphia, PA	2.50
1005	3¢ 4-H Clubs 1/15/52 Springfield, OH	2.00
1006	3¢ B. & O. Railroad 2/28/52 Baltimore, MD	5.00
1007	3¢ Am. Automobile Assoc. 3/4/52 Chicago, IL	2.00
1008	3¢ NATO 4/4/52 DC	2.00
1009	3¢ Grand Coulee Dam 5/15/52 Grand Coulee, WA	2.00
1010	3¢ Lafayette 6/13/52 Georgetown, SC	2.00
1011	3¢ Mount Rushmore 8/11/52 Keystone, SD	2.00
1012	3¢ Civil Engineers 9/6/52 Chicago, IL	2.00
1013	3¢ Service Women 9/11/52 DC	2.00
1014	3¢ Gutenberg Bible 9/30/52 DC	2.00
1015	3¢ Newspaper Boys 10/4/52 Phila., PA	2.00
1016	3¢ Red Cross 11/21/52 New York, NY	3.00

Scott #	Description	Price
	1953	
1017	3¢ National Guard 2/23/53 DC	2.00
1018	3¢ Ohio Statehood 3/2/53 Chillicothe, OH	2.00
1019	3¢ Washington Terr. 3/2/53 Olympia, WA	2.00
1020	3¢ Louisiana Pur. 4/30/53 St. Louis, MO	2.00
1021	3¢ Opening of Japan 7/14/53 DC	2.00
	1st Overseas Mailers cachet	**60.00**
1022	3¢ Amer. Bar Assoc. 8/24/53 Boston, MA	3.00
1023	3¢ Sagamore Hill 9/14/53 Oyster Bay, NY	2.00
1024	3¢ Future Farmers 10/13/53 KS City, MO	2.00
1025	3¢ Trucking Ind. 10/27/53 Los Angeles, CA	2.00
1026	3¢ General Patton 11/11/53 Fort Knox, NY	2.00
1027	3¢ Founding of NYC 11/20/53 New York, NY	2.00
1028	3¢ Gadsden Purchase 12/30/53 Tucson, AZ	2.00
	1954	
1029	3¢ Columbia Univ. 1/4/54 New York, NY	2.00
	1954-61 LIBERTY SERIES	
1030-53	Liberty set of 27	110.00
1030	½¢ Franklin 10/20/55 DC	1.75
1031	1¢ Washington 8/26/54 Chicago, IL	1.75
1031A	1¼¢ Palace 6/17/60 Santa Fe, NM	1.75
1032	1½¢ Mt. Vernon 2/22/56 Mt. Vernon, VA	1.75
1033	2¢ Jefferson 9/15/54 San Francisco, CA	1.75
1034	2½¢ Bunker Hill 6/17/59 Boston, MA	1.75
1035	3¢ Statue of Liberty 6/24/54 Albany, NY	1.75
1035a	booklet pane 6/30/54 DC	4.00
1035b	Luminescent 7/6/66 DC	30.00
1036	4¢ Lincoln 11/19/54 New York, NY	1.75
1036a	booklet pane 7/31/58 Wheeling, WV	3.00
1036b	Luminescent 11/2/63 DC	100.00
1037	4½¢ Hermitage 3/16/59 Hermitage, TN	1.75
1038	5¢ Monroe 12/3/54 Fredericksburg, VA	1.75
1039	6¢ Roosevelt 11/18/55 New York, NY	1.75
1040	7¢ Wilson 1/110/56 Staunton, VA	1.75
1041	8¢ Statue of Liberty 4/9/54 DC	1.75
1042	8¢ Stat. of Lib. (Giori Press) 3/22/58 Cleveland, OH	1.75
1042A	8¢ Pershing 11/17/61 New York, NY	2.25
1043	9¢ The Alamo 6/14/56 San Antonio, TX	2.00
1044	10¢ Independence Hall 7/4/56 Phila., PA	2.00
1044b	Luminescent 7/6/66	30.00
1044A	11¢ Statue of Liberty 6/15/61 DC	2.50
1044Ac	Luminescent 1/11/67	30.00
1045	12¢ Harrison 6/6/59 Oxford, OH	2.00
1045a	Luminescent 5/6/68	30.00
1046	15¢ John Jay 12/12/58 DC	2.50
1046a	Luminescent 5/6/68	35.00
1047	20¢ Monticello 4/13/56 Charlottesville, VA	2.50
1048	25¢ Paul Revere 4/118/58 Boston, MA	2.50
1049	30¢ Robert E. Lee 9/21/55 Norfolk, VA	3.00
1050	40¢ John Marshall 9/24/55 Richmond, VA	4.00
1051	50¢ Susan Anthony 8/25/55 Louisville, KY	6.00
1052	$1 Patrick Henry 10/7/55 Joplin, MO	10.00
1053	$5 Alex Hamilton 3/19/56 Patterson, NJ	50.00
	1954-65 LIBERTY SERIES COILS	
1054	1¢ Washington 10/8/54 Baltimore, MD	1.75
1054A	1¼¢ Palace 6/17/60 Santa Fe, NM	1.75
1055	2¢ Jefferson 10/22/54 St. Louis, MO	1.75
1055a	Luminescent 5/6/68 DC	20.00
1056	2½¢ Bunker Hill 9/9/59 Los Angeles, CA	1.75
1057	3¢ Statue of Liberty 7/20/54 DC	1.75
1057b	Luminescent 5/12/67 DC	50.00
1058	4¢ Lincoln 7/31/58 Mandan, ND	1.75
1059	4½¢ Hermitage 5/1/59 Denver, CO	1.75
1059A	25¢ Paul Revere 2/25/65 Wheaton, MD	2.50
1059b	Luminescent 4/3/73 NY, NY	25.00

1048

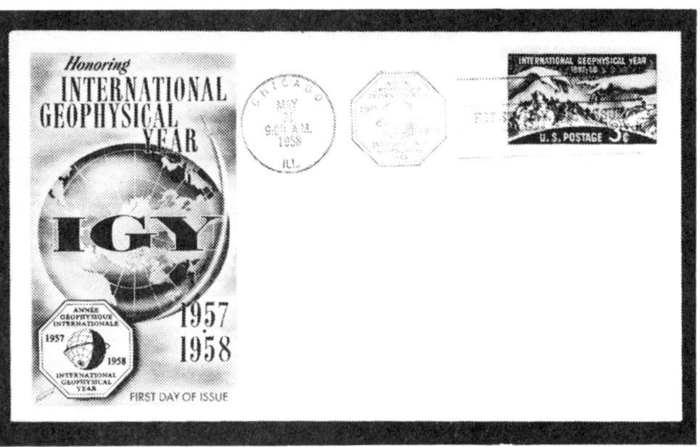

1107

cott #	Description	Price
	1954 (cont.)	
060	3¢ Nebraska Ter. 5/7/54 Nebraska City, NE	1.75
061	3¢ Kansas Terr. 5/31/54 Fort Leavenworth, KS	1.75
062	3¢ George Eastman 7/12/54 Rochester, NY	1.75
063	3¢ Lewis & Clark 7/28/54 Sioux City, IA	1.75
	1955	
064	3¢ Fine Arts 1/15/55 Philadelphia, PA	1.75
065	3¢ Land Grant Colleges 2/12/55 East Lansing, MI	2.50
066	3¢ Rotary Int. 2/23/55 Chicago, IL	2.75
067	3¢ Armed Forces Reserve 5/21/55 DC	2.00
068	3¢ New Hampshire 6/21/55 Franconia, NH	1.75
069	3¢ Soo Locks 6/28/55 Sault St. Marie, MI	1.75
070	3¢ Atoms for Peace 7/28/55 DC	1.75
071	3¢ Fort Ticonderoga 9/18/55 Ticonderoga, NY	1.75
072	3¢ Andrew W. Mellon 12/20/55 DC	1.75
	1956	
073	3¢ Benjamin Franklin 1/17/56 Phila., PA	1.75
	Poor Richard Station	1.75
074	3¢ Booker T. Washington 4/5/56	
	Booker T. Washington Birthplace, VA	2.50
075	11¢ FIPEX Sheet 4/28/56 New York, NY	5.00
076	3¢ FIPEX 4/30/56 New York, NY	1.75
077	3¢ Wild Turkey 5/5/56 Fond du Lac, WI	2.50
078	3¢ Antelope 6/22/56 Gunnison, CO	2.00
079	3¢ King Salmon 11/9/56 Seattle, WA	2.00
080	3¢ Pure Food and Drug Laws 6/27/56 DC	1.75
081	3¢ Wheatland 8/5/56 Lancaster, PA	1.75
082	3¢ Labor Day 9/3/56 Camden, NJ	1.75
083	3¢ Nassau Hall 9/22/56 Princeton, NJ	1.75
084	3¢ Devils Tower 9/24/56 Devils Tower, NY	1.75
085	3¢ Children 12/15/56 DC	1.75
	1957	
086	3¢ Alex Hamilton 1/11/57 New York, NY	1.75
087	3¢ Polio 1/15/57 DC	2.00
088	3¢ Coast & Geodetic Survey 2/11/57 Seattle, WA	1.75
089	3¢ Architects 2/23/57 New York, NY	1.75
090	3¢ Steel Industry 5/22/57 New York, NY	1.75
091	3¢ Naval Review 6/10/57 USS Saratoga, Norfolk, VA	1.75
092	3¢ Oklahoma Statehood 6/14/57 Oklahoma City, OK	1.75
093	3¢ School Teachers 7/1/57 Phila., PA	1.75
	"Philadelpia" error cancel	7.50
094	4¢ American Flag 7/4/57 DC	1.75
095	3¢ Shipbuilding 8/15/57 Bath, ME	1.75
096	8¢ Ramon Magsaysay 8/31/57 DC	1.75
097	3¢ Lafayette 9/6/57 Easton, PA	1.75
	Fayetteville, NC	1.75
	Louisville, KY	1.75
098	3¢ Whooping Crane 11/22/57 New York, NY	1.75
	New Orleans, LA	1.75
	Corpus Christi, TX	1.75
099	3¢ Religious Freedom 12/27/57 Flushing, NY	1.75
	1958-59	
100	3¢ Horticulture 3/15/58 Ithaca, NY	1.75
104	3¢ Brussels Exhibit. 4/17/58 Detroit, MI	1.75
105	3¢ James Monroe 4/28/58 Montross, VA	1.75
106	3¢ Minnesota Sthd. 5/11/58 St. Paul, MN	1.75
107	3¢ Int'l. Geo. Year 5/31/58 Chicago, IL	1.75
108	3¢ Gunston Hall 6/12/58 Lorton, VA	1.75
109	3¢ Mackinaw Bridge 6/25/58 Mackinaw Bridge, MI	1.75
110	4¢ Simon Bolivar 7/24/58 DC	1.75
111	8¢ Simon Bolivar 7/24/58 DC	1.75
110-11	Bolivar on one cover	2.50
112	4¢ Atlantic Cable 8/15/58 New York, NY	1.75
113	1¢ Lincoln 2/12/59 Hodgenville, NY	1.75
114	3¢ Lincoln 2/27/59 New York, NY	1.75
115	4¢ Lincoln & Douglas 8/27/58 Freeport, IL	1.75
116	4¢ Lincoln Statue 5/30/59 DC	1.75
113-16	On 1 Cover	8.00
117	4¢ Lajos Kossuth 9/19/58 DC	1.75
118	8¢ Lajos Kossuth 9/19/58 DC	1.75
117-18	Kossuth on one cover	2.50
119	4¢ Freedom of Press 9/22/58 Columbia, MO	1.75
120	4¢ Overland Mail 10/10/58 San Fran., CA	1.75

U.S. FIRST DAY COVERS

Scott #	Description	Price
	1958 (cont.)	
1121	4¢ Noah Webster 10/16/58 W. Hartford, CT	1.75
1122	4¢ Forest Conserv. 10/27/58 Tucson, AZ	1.75
1123	4¢ Fort Duquesne 11/25/58 Pittsburgh, PA	1.75
	1959	
1124	4¢ Oregon Sthd. 2/14/59 Astoria, OR	1.75
1125	4¢ Jose de San Martin 2/25/59 DC	1.75
1126	8¢ Jose de San Martin 2/25/59 DC	1.75
1125-26	San Martin on one cover	2.50
1127	4¢ NATO 4/1/59 DC	1.75
1128	4¢ Arctic Explorers 4/6/59 Cresson, PA	1.75
1129	8¢ World Trade 4/20/59 DC	1.75
1130	4¢ Silver Cent. 6/8/59 Virginia City, NV	1.75
1131	4¢ St. Lawrence Seaway 6/26/59 Massena, NY	2.00
1132	4¢ 49-Star Flag 7/4/59 Auburn, NY	1.75
1133	4¢ Soil Conserv. 8/26/59 Rapid City, SD	1.75
1134	4¢ Petroleum Ind. 8/27/59 Titusville, PA	2.00
1135	4¢ Dental Health 9/14/59 New York, NY	5.00
1136	4¢ Ernst Reuter 9/29/59 DC	1.75
1137	8¢ Ernst Reuter 9/29/59 DC	1.75
1136-37	Reuter on one cover	2.50
1138	4¢ Dr. McDowell 12/3/59 Danville, KY	1.75
	1960	
1139	4¢ Washington Credo 1/20/60 Mt. Vernon, VA	1.75
1140	4¢ Franklin Credo 3/31/60 Phila., PA	1.75
1141	4¢ Jefferson Credo 5/18/60 Charlottesville, VA	1.75
1142	4¢ Francis Scott Key Credo 9/14/60 Baltimore, MD	1.75
1143	4¢ Lincoln Credo 11/19/60 New York, NY	1.75
1144	4¢ Patrick Henry Credo 1/11/61 Richmond, VA	1.75
	#1139-1144 on one cover, 1/11/61	6.00
1145	4¢ Boy Scouts 2/8/60 DC	3.50
1146	4¢ Winter Olympics 2/18/60 Olympic Valley, CA	1.75
1147	4¢ Thomas G. Masaryk 3/7/60 DC	1.75
1148	8¢ Thomas G. Masaryk 3/7/60 DC	1.75
1147-48	Masaryk on one cover	2.50
1149	4¢ World Refugee Year 4/7/60 DC	1.75
1150	4¢ Water Conservation 4/18/60 DC	1.75
1151	4¢ SEATO 5/31/60 DC	1.75
1152	4¢ American Women 6/2/60 DC	2.00
1153	4¢ 50-Star Flag 7/4/60 Honolulu, HI	1.75
1154	4¢ Pony Express Centennial 7/19/60 Sacramento, CA	2.00
1155	4¢ Employ the Handicapped 8/28/60 New York, NY	1.75
1156	4¢ World Forestry Co. 8/29/60 Seattle, WA	1.75
1157	4¢ Mexican Indep. 9/16/60 Los Angeles, CA	1.75
1158	4¢ US-Japan Treaty 9/28/60 DC	1.75
1159	4¢ Paderewski 10/8/60 DC	1.75
1160	8¢ Paderewski 10/8/60 DC	1.75
1159-60	Paderewski on one cover	2.50
1161	4¢ Robert A. Taft 10/10/60 Cincinnati, OH	1.75
1162	4¢ Wheels of Freedom 10/15/60 Detroit, MI	1.75
1163	4¢ Boys Clubs 10/18/60 New York, NY	1.75
1164	4¢ Automated P.O. 10/20/60 Providence, RI	1.75
1165	4¢ Gustav Mannerheim 10/26/60 DC	1.75
1166	8¢ Gustav Mannerheim 10/26/60 DC	1.75
1165-66	Mannerheim on one cover	2.50
1167	4¢ Camp Fire Girls 11/1/60 New York, NY	2.50
1168	4¢ Giuseppe Garibaldi 11/2/60 DC	1.75
1169	8¢ Guiseppe Garibaldi 11/2/60 DC	1.75
1168-69	Garibaldi on one cover	2.50
1170	4¢ Walter F. George 11/5/60 Vienna, GA	1.75
1171	4¢ Andrew Carnegie 11/25/60 New York, NY	1.75
1172	4¢ John Foster Dulles 12/6/60 DC	1.75
1173	4¢ Echo 1 12/15/60 DC	3.00
	1961-65	
1174	4¢ Mahatma Gandhi 1/26/61 DC	1.75
1175	8¢ Mahatma Gandhi 1/26/61 DC	1.75
1174-75	Gandhi on one cover	2.50
1176	4¢ Range Cons. 2/2/61 Salt Lake City, UT	1.75
1177	4¢ Horace Greeley 2/3/61 Chappaqua, NY	1.75
1178	4¢ Fort Sumter 4/12/61 Charleston, SC	3.00
1179	4¢ Battle of Shiloh 4/7/62 Shiloh, TN	3.00
1180	5¢ Battle of Gettysburg 7/1/63 Gettysburg, PA	3.00
1181	5¢ Battle of Wilderness 5/5/64 Fredericksburg, VA	3.00
1182	5¢ Appomattox 4/9/65 Appomattox, VA	3.00
1178-82	Civil War on 1 cover 4/9/65	10.00

1152

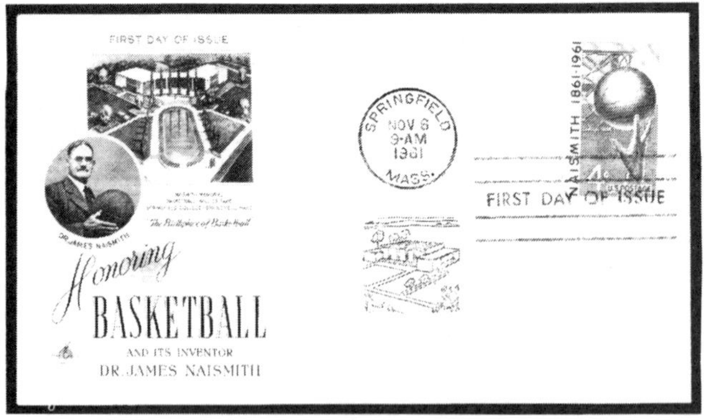

1189

Scott #	Description	Price
	1961 (cont.)	
1183	4¢ Kansas Statehood 5/10/61 Council Grove, KS	1.75
1184	4¢ George Norris 7/11/611 DC	1.75
1185	4¢ Naval Aviation 8/20/61 San Diego, CA	2.00
1186	4¢ Workmen's Comp. 9/4/61 Milwaukee, WI	1.75
1187	4¢ Frederic Remington 10/4/61 DC	2.00
1188	4¢ Sun Yat-Sen 10/10/61 DC	5.00
1189	4¢ Basketball 11/6/61 Springfield, MA	8.00
1190	4¢ Nursing 12/28/61 DC	12.00
	1962	
1191	4¢ New Mexico Sthd. 1/6/62 Santa Fe, NM	2.25
1192	4¢ Arizona Sthd. 2/14/62 Phoenix, AZ	2.25
	1st Glory cachet	**35.00**
1193	4¢ Project Mercury 2/20/62 Cape Canaveral, FL	3.00
	1st Marg cachet	**25.00**
1194	4¢ Malaria Eradication 3/30/62 DC	1.75
1195	4¢ Charles Evans Hughes 4/11/62 DC	1.75
1196	4¢ Seattle Fair 4/25/62 Seattle, WA	1.75
1197	4¢ Louisiana 4/30/62 New Orleans, LA	1.75
1198	4¢ Homestead Act 5/20/62 Beatrice, NE	1.75
1199	4¢ Girl Scouts 7/24/62 Burlington, VT	3.50
1200	4¢ Brien McMahon 7/28/62 Norwalk, CT	1.75
1201	4¢ Apprenticeship 8/31/62 DC	1.75
1202	4¢ Sam Rayburn 9/16/62 Bonham, TX	1.75
1203	4¢ Dag Hammarskjold 10/23/62 NY, NY	1.75
1204	4¢ Hammarskjold Invert. 11/16/62 DC	5.00
1205	4¢ Christmas 11/1/62 Pittsburgh, PA	2.00
1206	4¢ Higher Education 11/14/62 DC	2.00
1207	4¢ Winslow Homer 12/15/62 Gloucester, MA	2.25
	1962-63 REGULAR ISSUES	
1208	5¢ 50-Star Flag 1/9/63 DC	1.75
1208a	5¢ Luminescent 8/25/66 DC	25.00
1209	1¢ Andrew Jackson 3/22/63 New York, NY	1.75
1209a	Luminescent 7/6/66 DC	25.00
1213	5¢ Washington 11/23/62 New York, NY	1.75
1213a	Booklet Pane 11/23/62 New York, NY	3.00
1213b	Luminescent 10/28/63 Dayton, OH	25.00
1213c	Luminescent bklt. pair 10/28/63 Dayton, OH	40.00
1213c	Luminescent bklt. pane 10/28/63 Dayton, OH	100.00
	DC	125.00
1225	1¢ Jackson, coil 5/31/63 Chicago, IL	1.75
1225a	Luminescent 7/6/66 DC	20.00
1229	5¢ Washington, coil 11/23/62 New York, NY	1.75
1229a	Luminescent 10/28/63 Dayton, OH	30.00
	DC	30.00
	#1213b, 1213c, & 1229a (singles of ea.) on one FDC 10/28/63 Dayton, OH	60.00
	1963	
1230	5¢ Carolina Charter 4/6/63 Edenton, NC	1.75
1231	5¢ Food for Peace 6/4/63 DC	1.75
1232	5¢ W. Virginia Sthd. 6/20/63 Wheeling, WV	1.75
1233	5¢ Emancipation Proc. 8/16/63 Chicago, IL	2.50
1234	5¢ Alliance for Progress 8/17/63 DC	1.75
1235	5¢ Cordell Hull 10/5/63 Carthage, TN	1.75
1236	5¢ Eleanor Roosevelt 10/11/63 DC	1.75
1237	5¢ Science 10/14/63 DC	1.75
1238	5¢ City Mail Delivery 10/26/63 DC	2.00
1239	5¢ Red Cross 10/29/63 DC	2.50
1240	5¢ Christmas 11/1/63 Santa Claus, IN	2.00
1240a	5¢ Luminescent 11/2/63 DC	60.00
1241	5¢ Audobon 12/7/63 Henderson, KY	2.00
	1964	
1242	5¢ Sam Houston 1/10/64 Houston, TX	2.00
1243	5¢ Charle Russell 3/19/64 Great Falls, MT	2.50
1244	5¢ NY World's Fair 4/22/64 World's Fair, NY	2.00
	1st Sarzin Metallic cachet	**20.00**
1245	5¢ John Muir 4/29/64 Martinez, CA	1.75
1246	5¢ John F. Kennedy 5/29/64 Boston, MA	2.50
	1st Cover Craft cachet	**30.00**
1247	5¢ New Jersey Terc. 6/15/64 Elizabeth, NJ	1.75
1248	5¢ Nevada Sthd. 7/22/64 Carson City, NV	1.75
1249	5¢ Register & Vote 8/1/64 DC	1.75

U.S. FIRST DAY COVERS

Scott #	Description	Price
	1964 (cont.)	
1250	5¢ Shakespeare 8/14/64 Stratford, CT	2.00
1251	5¢ Doctors Mayo 9/11/64 Rochester, MN	5.00
1252	5¢ American Music 10/15/64 New York, NY	2.50
1253	5¢ Homemakers 10/26/64 Honolulu, HI	1.75
1254-57	5¢ Christmas attd. 11/9/64 Bethlehem, PA	4.00
1254-57	Christmas set of 4 singles	10.00
1254-57a	Luminescent Christmas attd 11/10/64 Dayton, OH	60.00
1254-57a	Luminescent Christmas set of 4 singles	80.00
1258	5¢ Verrazano-Narrows Bridge 11/21/64 Stat. Is., NY	1.75
1259	5¢ Fine Arts 12/2/64 DC	1.75
1260	5¢ Amateur Radio 12/15/64 Anchorage, AK	2.50
	1965	
1261	5¢ Battle of New Orleans 1/8/65 New Orleans, LA	1.75
1262	5¢ Physical Fitness 2/15/65 DC	2.00
1263	5¢ Cancer Crusade 4/1/65 DC	3.50
1264	5¢ Winston Churchill 5/13/65 Fulton, MO	2.00
1265	5¢ Magna Carta 6/15/65 Jamestown, VA	1.75
1266	5¢ Int'l. Cooperation Year 6/26/65 San Francisco, CA	1.75
1267	5¢ Salvation Army 7/2/65 New York, NY	1.75
1268	5¢ Dante 7/17/65 San Francisco, CA	1.75
1269	5¢ Herbert Hoover 8/10/65 West Branch, IA	1.75
1270	5¢ Robert Fulton 8/19/65 Clermont, NY	1.75
1271	5¢ 400th Anniv. of FL 8/28/65 St. Augustine, FL	1.75
1272	5¢ Traffic Safety 9/3/65 Baltimore, MD	1.75
1273	5¢ John Copley 9/17/65 DC	1.75
1274	11¢ Int'l. Telecomm. Union 10/6/65 DC	1.75
1275	5¢ A. Stevenson 10/23/65 Bloominton, IL	1.75
1276	5¢ Christmas 11/2/65 Silver Bell, AZ	1.75
1276a	Luminescent 11/16/65 DC	50.00
	1965-68 PROMINENT AMERICANS SERIES	
1278	1¢ Jefferson 1/12/68 Jeffersonville, IN	1.75
1278a	bklt. pane of 8 1/12/68 Jeffersonville, IN	2.00
1278a	bklt. pane of 8, dull gum 3/1/71 DC	90.00
1278b	booklet pane of 4 5/10/71 DC	15.00
1279	1¼¢ Gallatin 1/30/67 Gallatin, MO	1.75
1280	2¢ Wright 6/8/66 Spring Green, WI	1.75
1280a	booklet pane of 5 1/8/68 Buffalo, NY	3.00
1280c	booklet pane of 6 5/7/71 Spokane, WA	15.00
1280c var.	bklt. pane of 6, dull gum 10/31/75 Cleveland, OH	100.00
1281	3¢ Parkman 9/16/67 Boston, MA	1.75
1282	4¢ Lincoln 11/19/65 New York, NY	1.75
1282a	Luminescent 12/1/65 Dayton, OH	40.00
	DC	45.00
1283	5¢ Washington 2/22/66 DC	1.75
1283a	Luminescent 2/23/66 Dayton, OH	100.00
	DC	27.50
1283B	5¢ Washington, redrawn 11/17/67 New York, NY	1.75
1284	6¢ Roosevelt 1/29/66 Hyde Park, NY	1.75
1284a	Luminescent 12/29/66	20.00
1284b	booklet pane of 8 12/28/67 DC	2.50
1284c	booklet pane of 5 1/9/68 DC	125.00
1285	8¢ Einstein 3/14/66 Princeton, NJ	2.00
1285a	Luminescent 7/6/66 DC	20.00
1286	10¢ Jackson 3/15/67 Hermitage, TN	1.75
1286A	12¢ Ford 7/30/68 Greenfield Village, MI	2.50
1287	13¢ Kennedy 5/29/67 Brookline, MA	2.50
1288	15¢ Holmes 3/8/68 DC	1.75
1288B	booklet single 6/14/78 Boston, MA	1.75
1288Bc	15¢ bklt. pane of 8 6/14/78 Boston, MA	3.50
1289	20¢ Marshall 10/24/67 Lexington, VA	2.00
1289a	Luminescent 4/3/73 New York, NY	25.00
1290	25¢ Douglass 2/14/67 DC	3.50
1290a	Luminescent 4/3/73 DC	25.00
1291	30¢ Dewey 10/21/68 Burlington, VT	2.50
1291a	Luminescent 4/3/73 New York, NY	25.00
1292	40¢ Paine 1/29/68 Philadelphia, PA	3.00
1292a	Luminescent 4/3/73 New York, NY	25.00
1293	50¢ Stone 8/13/68 Dorchester, MA	4.00
1293a	Luminescent 4/3/73 New York, NY	30.00
1294	$1 O'Neill 10/16/67 New London, CT	7.00
1294a	Luminescent 4/3/73 New York, NY	40.00
1295	$5 Moore 12/3/66 Smyrna, DE	40.00
1295a	Luminescent 4/3/73 New York NY	100.00
	#1295 & 1295a on one cover 4/3/73	225.00

1285

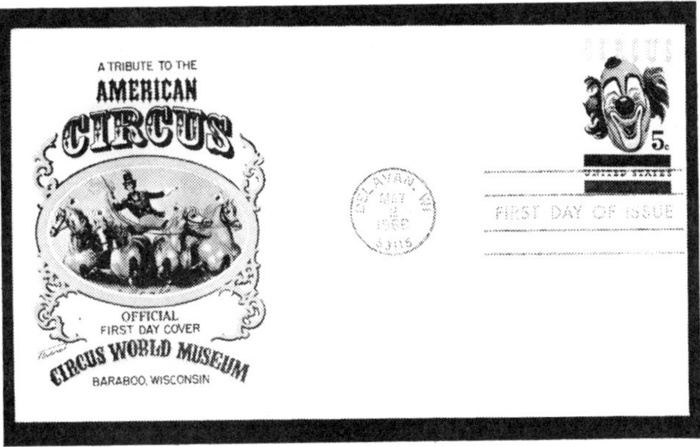

1309

Scott #	Description	Price
	1966-81 PROMINENT AMERICAN COILS	
1297	3¢ Parkman 11/4/75 Pendleton, OR	1.75
1298	6¢ Roosevelt, vert. coil 12/28/67 DC	1.75
1299	1¢ Jefferson 1/12/68 Jeffersonville, IN	1.75
1303	4¢ Lincoln 5/28/66 Springfield, IL	1.75
1304	5¢ Washington 9/8/66 Cinncinnati, OH	1.75
1304C	5¢ Washington re-engraved 3/31/81 DC	25.00
1305	6¢ Roosevelt, horiz. coil 2/28/68 DC	1.75
1305E	15¢ Holmes 6/14/78 Boston, MA	1.75
1305C	$1 O-Neill 1/12/73 Hampstead, NY	4.00
	1966	
1306	5¢ Migratory Bird 3/16/66 Pittsburgh, PA	2.50
1307	5¢ Humane Treatment 4/9/66 New York, NY	2.00
1308	5¢ Indiana Sthd. 4/16/66 Corydon, IN	1.75
1309	5¢ Circus 5/2/66 Delevan, WI	2.50
1310	5¢ SIPEX 5/21/66 DC	1.75
1311	5¢ SIPEX sheet 5/23/66 DC	2.00
1312	5¢ Bill of Rights 7/1/66 Miami Beach, FL	1.75
1313	5¢ Polish Millenium 7/30/66 DC	1.75
1314	5¢ Nat'l. Park Service 8/25/66 Yellowstone Nat'l. Park	2.00
1314a	Luminescent 8/26/66	30.00
1315	5¢ Marine Corps Reserve 8/29/66 DC	2.50
1315a	Luminescent 8/29/66 DC	30.00
1316	5¢ Women's Clubs 9/12/66 New York, NY	2.00
1316a	Luminescent 9/13/66 DC	30.00
1317	5¢ Johnny Appleseed 9/24/66 Leominster, MA	1.75
1317a	Luminescent 9/26/66 DC	30.00
1318	5¢ Beautification 10/5/66 DC	1.75
1318a	Luminescent 10/5/66 DC	30.00
1319	5¢ Great River Road 10/21/66 Baton Rouge, LA	1.75
1319a	Luminescent 10/22/66 DC	30.00
1320	5¢ Savings Bonds 10/26/66 Sioux City, IA	1.75
1320a	Luminescent 10/27/66 DC	30.00
1321	5¢ Christmas 11/1/66 Christmas, MI	1.75
1321a	Luminescent 11/2/66	30.00
1322	5¢ Mary Cassatt 11/17/66 DC	2.00
1322a	Luminescent 11/17/66 DC	30.00
	1967	
1323	5¢ National Grange 4/17/67 DC	1.75
1324	5¢ Canada Centenary 5/25/67 Montreal, CAN	1.75
1325	5¢ Erie Canal 7/4/67 Rome, NY	1.75
1326	5¢ Search for Peace 7/5/67 Chicago, IL	1.75
1327	5¢ Henry Thoreau 7/12/67 Concord, MA	1.75
1328	5¢ Nebraska Sthd. 7/29/67 Lincoln, NE	1.75
1329	5¢ Voice of America 8/1/67	1.75
1330	5¢ Davy Crockett 8/17/67 San Antonio, TX	1.75
1331-32	5¢ Space Twins attd. 9/29/67 Kennedy Space Ctr., FL	10.00
1331-32	Space Twins set of 2 singles	10.00
1333	5¢ Urban Planning 10/2/67 DC	1.75
1334	5¢ Finland Indep. 10/6/67 Finland, MI	1.75
1335	5¢ Thomas Eakins 11/2/67 DC	2.00
1336	5¢ Christmas 11/6/67 Bethlehem, GA	2.00
1337	5¢ Mississippi Statehood 12/11/67 Natchez, MS	1.75
	1968-71 REGULAR ISSUES	
1338	6¢ Flag & White House 1/24/68 DC	1.75
1338A	6¢ Flag & W.H., coil 5/30/69 Chicago, IL	1.75
1338D	6¢ Flag & W.H. (Huck Press) 8/7/70 DC	1.75
1338F	8¢ Flag & White House 5/10/71 DC	1.75
1338G	8¢ Flag & White House, coil 5/10/71 DC	1.75
	1968	
1339	6¢ Illinois Statehood 2/12/68 Shawneetown, IL	1.75
1340	6¢ Hemis Fair '68 3/30/68 San Antonio, TX	1.75
1341	$1 Airlift 4/4/68 Seattle, WA	7.50
1342	6¢ Support Our Youth 5/1/68 Chicago, IL	1.75
1343	6¢ Law and Order 5/17/68 DC	3.00
1344	6¢ Register and Vote 6/27/68 DC	2.50
1345-54	6¢ Historic Flags attd. 7/4/68 Pittsburgh, PA	10.00
1345-54	Historic Flags set of 10 singles	50.00
1355	6¢ Walt Disney 9/11/68 Marceline, MO	20.00
1356	6¢ Marquette 9/20/68 Sault Ste. Marie, MI	1.75
1357	6¢ Daniel Boone 9/26/68 Frankfort, KY	1.75
1358	6¢ Arkansas River 10/1/68 Little Rock, AR	1.75
1359	6¢ Leif Ericson 10/9/68 Seattle, WA	1.75

U.S. FIRST DAY COVERS

Scott #	Description	Price
1360	6¢ Cherokee Strip 10/15/68 Ponca, OK	1.75
1361	6¢ John Trumbull 10/18/66 New Haven, CT	2.00
1362	6¢ Waterfowl Cons. 10/24/68 Cleveland, OH	2.00
1363	6¢ Christmas, tagged 11/1/68 DC	2.00
1363a	6¢ Not tagged 11/2/66 DC	15.00
1364	6¢ American Indian 11/4/68 DC	2.00
	1969	
1365-68	6¢ Beautification attd. 1/16/69 DC	5.00
1365-68	Beautification set of 4 singles	10.00
1369	6¢ American Legion 3/15/69 DC	1.75
1370	6¢ Grandma Moses 5/1/69 DC	2.00
1371	6¢ Apollo 8 5/5/69 Houston, TX	3.00
1372	6¢ W.C. Handy 5/17/69 Memphis, TN	2.00
1373	6¢ California 7/16/69 San Diego, CA	1.75
1374	6¢ John W. Powell 8/1/69 Page, AZ	1.75
1375	6¢ Alabama Sthd. 8/2/69 Huntsville, AL	1.75
1376-79	6¢ Botanical Congress attd. 8/23/69 Seattle, WA	6.00
1376-79	Botanical Congress set of 4 singles	10.00
1380	6¢ Dartmouth Case 9/22/69 Hanover, NH	1.75
1381	6¢ Baseball 9/24/69 Cincinnati, OH	15.00
1382	6¢ Football 9/26/69 New Brunswick, NJ	7.00
1383	6¢ Eisenhower 10/14/69 Abilene, KS	1.75
1384	6¢ Christmas 11/3/69 Christmas, FL	2.00
1384a	6¢ Christmas - Precancel 11/4/69 Atlanta, GA	150.00
	Baltimore, MD	150.00
	Memphis, TN	150.00
	New Haven, CT	150.00
1385	6¢ Hope for Crippled 11/20/69 Columbus, OH	2.00
1386	6¢ William Harnett 12/3/69 Boston, MA	1.75
	1970	
1387-90	6¢ Natural History attd. 5/6/70 NY, NY	4.00
1387-90	Natural History set of 4 singles	8.00
1391	6¢ Maine Statehood 7/9/70 Portland, ME	1.75
1392	6¢ Wildlife - Buffalo 7/20/70 Custer, SD	1.75
	1970-74 REGULAR ISSUES	
1393	6¢ Eisenhower 8/6/70 DC	1.75
1393a	booklet pane of 8 8/6/70 DC	2.50
1393a	6¢ bklt. pane of 8, dull gum 3/1/71 DC	75.00
1393b	booklet pane of 6 8/6/70 DC	3.00
1393D	7¢ Franklin 10/20/72 Philadelphia, PA	1.75
1394	8¢ Eisenhower 5/10/71 DC	1.75
1395	8¢ Eisenhower, claret 5/10/71 DC	2.00
1395a	booklet pane of 8 5/10/71 DC	2.50
1395b	booklet pane of 6 5/10/71 DC	2.50
1395c	bklt. pane of 4 1/28/72 Casa Grande, AZ	2.00
1395cs	Booklet Single 1/28/72 Casa Grande, AZ	1.75
1395d	bklt. pane of 7 1/28/72 Casa Grande, AZ	2.00
1395ds	Booklet Single 1/28/72 Casa Grande, AZ	1.75
1396	8¢ Postal Service Emblem 7/1/71 any city	1.75
1397	14¢ LaGuardia 4/24/72 New York, NY	1.75
1398	16¢ Ernie Pyle 5/7/71 DC	2.50
1399	18¢ Eliz. Blackwell 1/23/74 Geneva, NY	2.00
1400	21¢ Giannini 6/27/73 San Mateo, CA	2.25
1401	6¢ Eisenhower, coil 8/6/70 DC	1.75
1402	8¢ Eisenhower, coil 5/10/71 DC	1.75
	1970	
1405	6¢ Edgar Lee Masters 8/22/70 Petersburg, IL	1.75
1406	6¢ Woman Suffrage 8/26/70 Adams, MA	1.75
1407	6¢ South Carolina 9/12/70 Charleston, SC	1.75
1408	6¢ Stone Mountain 9/19/70 Stone Mt., GA	1.75
1409	6¢ Ft. Snelling 10/17/70 Ft. Snelling, MT	1.75
1410-13	6¢ Anti-Pollution attd. 10/28/70 San Clemente, CA	5.00
1410-13	Anti-Pollution set of 4 singles	8.00
1414	6¢ Christmas - Religious 11/5/70 DC	1.75
1414a	6¢ Christmas Precancel 11/5/70 DC	3.00
1415-18	6¢ Christmas Toys attd. 11/5/70 DC	6.00
1415-18	Christmas Toys set of 4 singles	10.00
1415a-18a	Christmas Toys-Precancel attd. 11/5/70 DC	20.00
1415a-18a	Christmas Toys-Precancel set of 4 singles	60.00
1414a-18a	Religious & Toys (5) on one FDC 11/5/70 DC	30.00
1419	6¢ UN 25th Anniv. 11/20/70 New York, NY	1.75
1420	6¢ Pilgrims' Landing 11/21/70 Plymouth, MA	1.75
1421-22	6¢ Disabled Vets - US Servicemen attd. 11/24/40 Cincinnati or Montgomery	2.00
1421-22	D.A.V. - Serv. set of 2 singles	3.50

1410-13

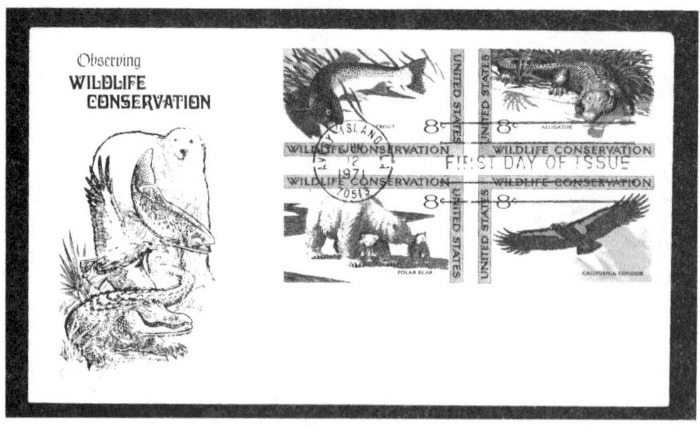

1427-30

Scott #	Description	Price
	1971	
1423	6¢ Wool Industry 1/19/71 Las Vegas, NV	1.75
	1st Bazaar cachet	**30.00**
	1st Colorano Silk cachet	**250.00**
1424	6¢ MacArthur 1/26/71 Norfolk, VA	2.00
1425	6¢ Blood Donor 3/12/71 New York, NY	1.75
1426	6¢ Missouri 5/8/71 Independence, MO	1.75
1427-30	8¢ Wildlife Conservation attd. 6/12/71 Avery Island, LA	4.00
1427-30	Wildlife set of 4 singles	8.00
1431	8¢ Antarctic Treaty 6/23/71 DC	1.75
1432	8¢ American Revolution Bic. 7/4/71 DC	1.75
1433	8¢ John Sloan 8/2/71 Lock Haven, PA	1.75
1434-35	8¢ Space Achievement Decade attd. 8/2/71	
	Kennedy Space Center, FL	2.50
	Houston, TX	2.50
	Huntsville, AL	2.50
1434-35	Space Achievement set of 2 singles	
	Kennedy Space Center, FL	3.50
	Houston, TX	3.50
	Huntsville, AL	3.50
1436	8¢ Emily Dickinson 8/28/71 Amherst, MA	1.75
1437	8¢ San Juan 9/12/71 San Juan, PR	1.75
1438	8¢ Drug Abuse 10/4/71 Dallas, TX	1.75
1439	8¢ CARE 10/27/71 New York, NY	1.75
1440-43	8¢ Historic Preservation attd. 10/29/71 San Diego, CA	4.00
1440-43	Historic Preservation set of 4 singles	8.00
1444	8¢ Christmas - Religious 11/10/71 DC	2.00
1445	8¢ Christmas - Partridge 11/10/71 DC	2.00
1444-45	Christmas on one cover	2.50
	1972	
1446	8¢ Sidney Lanier 2/3/72 Macon, GA	1.75
1447	8¢ Peace Corps 2/11/72 DC	1.75
1448-51	2¢ Cape Hatteras 4/5/72 Hatteras, NC	1.75
1452	6¢ Wolf Trap Farm 6/26/72 Vienna, VA	1.75
1453	8¢ Yellowstone 3/1/72 DC	1.50
	Yellowstone Nat'l. Park, WY	1.50
1454	15¢ Mt. McKinley 7/28/72 Mt. McKinley Nat'l. Park, AK	1.75
1448-54,C84	Parks on one cover 7/28/72	6.00
1455	8¢ Family Planning 3/18/72 New York, NY	1.75
1456-59	8¢ Colonial Craftsmen attd. 7/4/72 Williamsburg, VA	4.00
1456-59	Colonial Craftsmen set of 4 singles	8.00
1460	6¢ Olympic - Bicycling 8/17/72 DC	1.75
1461	8¢ Olympic - Bobsledding 8/17/72 DC	1.75
1462	15¢ Olympic - Runners 8/17/72 DC	1.75
1460-62,C85	Olympics on one cover	4.00
1463	8¢ P.T.A. 9/15/72 San Francisco, CA	1.75
1464-67	8¢ Wildlife attd. 9/20/72 Warm Springs, OR	4.00
1464-67	Wildlife set of 4 singles	8.00
1468	8¢ Mail Order 9/27/72 Chicago, IL	1.75
1469	8¢ Osteopathic Medicine 10/9/72 Miami, FL	2.50
1470	8¢ Tom Sawyer 10/13/72 Hannibal, MO	1.75
1471	8¢ Christmas - Religious 11/9/72 DC	1.75
1472	8¢ Christmas - Santa Claus 11/9/72 DC	1.75
1471-72	Christmas on one cover	2.50
1473	8¢ Pharmacy 11/10/72 Cincinnati, OH	10.00
1474	8¢ Stamp Collecting 11/17/72 NY, NY	2.00
	1973	
1475	8¢ Love 1/26/73 Philadelphia, PA	2.25
1476	8¢ Pamphleteer 2/16/73 Portland, OR	1.50
1477	8¢ Broadside 4/13/73 Atlantic City, NJ	1.50
1478	8¢ Post Rider 6/22/73 Rochester, NY	1.50
1479	8¢ Drummer 9/28/73 New Orleans, LA	1.50
1480-83	8¢ Boston Tea Party attd. 7/4/73 Boston, MA	4.00
1480-83	Boston Tea Party set of 4 singles	8.00
1484	8¢ Geo. Gershwin 2/28/73 Beverly Hills, CA	1.75
1485	8¢ Robinson Jeffers 8/13/73 Carmel, CA	1.75
1486	8¢ Henry O. Tanner 9/10/73 Pittsburgh, PA	2.00
1487	8¢ Willa Cather 9/20/73 Red Cloud, NE	1.75
1488	8¢ Nicolaus Copernicus 4/23/73 DC	2.00
1489-98	8¢ Postal People attd. 4/30/73 any city	7.00
1489-98	Postal People set of 10 singles	20.00
1499	8¢ Harry Truman 5/8/73 Independence, MO	2.00

U.S. FIRST DAY COVERS

Scott #	Description	Price
	1973 (cont.)	
1500	6¢ Electronics 7/10/73 New York, NY	1.75
1501	8¢ Electronics 7/10/73 New York, NY	1.75
1502	15¢ Electronics 7/10/73 New York, NY	1.75
1500-02,C86	Electronics on one cover	7.00
1503	8¢ Lyndon B. Johnson 8/27/73 Austin, TX	1.75
1504	8¢ Angus Cattle 10/5/73 St. Joseph, MO	1.75
1505	10¢ Chautauqua 8/6/74 Chautauqua, NY	1.75
1506	10¢ Wheat 8/16/74 Hillsboro, KS	1.75
1507	8¢ Christmas - Madonna 11/7/73 DC	1.75
1508	8¢ Christmas - Tree 11/7/73 DC	1.75
1507-08	Christmas on one cover	2.75
	1973-74 REGULAR ISSUES	
1509	10¢ Crossed Flags 12/8/73 San Fran., CA	1.75
1510	10¢ Jefferson Memorial 12/14/73 DC	1.75
1510b	booklet pane of 5 12/14/73 DC	2.00
1510c	booklet pane of 8 12/14/73 DC	2.25
1510d	booklet pane of 6 8/5/74 Oakland, CA	5.25
1511	10¢ Zip Code 1/4/74 DC	1.75
1518	6.3¢ Liberty Bell, coil 10/1/74 DC	1.75
1519	10¢ Crossed Flags, coil 12/8/73 San Francisco, CA	1.75
1520	10¢ Jefferson Memorial, coil 12/14/73 DC	1.75
	1974	
1525	10¢ Veterans of Foreign Wars 3/11/74 DC	1.75
1526	10¢ Robert Frost 3/26/74 Derry, NH	1.75
1527	10¢ EXPO '74 4/18/74 Spokane, WA	1.75
1528	10¢ Horse Racing 5/4/74 Louisville, KY	3.00
1529	10¢ Skylab 5/14/74 Houston, TX	2.00
1530-37	10¢ UPU Centenary attd. 6/6/74 DC	5.00
1530-37	UPU Centenary set of 8 singles	20.00
1538-41	10¢ Mineral Heritage attd. 6/13/74 Lincoln, NE	4.00
1538-41	Mineral Heritage set of 4 singles	8.00
1542	10¢ Fort Harrod 6/15/74 Harrodsburg, KY	1.75
1543-46	10¢ Continental Congr. attd. 7/4/74 Philadelphia, PA	4.00
1543-46	Continental Congress set of 4 singles	8.00
1547	10¢ Energy Conserv. 9/23/74 Detroit, MI	1.75
1548	10¢ Sleepy Hollow 10/10/74 North Tarrytown, NY	2.00
1549	10¢ Retarded Children 10/12/74 Arlington, TX	1.75
1550	10¢ Christmas - Angel 10/23/74 NY, NY	1.75
1551	10¢ Christmas - Currier & Ives 10/23/74 NY, NY	1.75
1550-51	Christmas on one cover	2.25
1552	10¢ Christmas - Weathervane 11/15/74 New York, NY	3.00
1550-52	Christmas, dual cancel	5.00
	1975	
1553	10¢ Benjamin West 2/10/75 Swarthmore, PA	1.75
1554	10¢ Paul Dunbar 5/1/75 Dayton, OH	1.75
1555	10¢ D.W. Griffith 5/27/75 Beverly, Hills, CA	1.75
1556	10¢ Pioneer - Jupiter 2/28/75 Mountain View, CA	1.75
1557	10¢ Mariner 10 4/4/75 Pasadena, CA	1.75
1558	10¢ Collective Bargaining 3/13/75 DC	1.75
1559	8¢ Sybil Ludington 3/25/75 Carmel, NY	1.75
1560	10¢ Salem Poor 3/25/75 Cambridge, MA	1.75
1561	10¢ Haym Salomon 3/25/75 Chicago, IL	1.75
1562	18¢ Peter Francisco 3/25/75 Greensboro, NC	1.75
1559-62	Contributions on one cover, any city	8.00
1563	10¢ Lexington-Concord 4/19/75 Lexington, MA	1.75
	Concord, MA	1.75
1564	10¢ Bunker Hill 6/17/75 Charlestown, MA	1.75
1565-68	10¢ Military Uniforms attd. 7/4/75 DC	4.00
1565-68	Military Uniforms set of 4 singles	8.00
1569-70	10¢ Apollo-Soyuz attd. 7/15/75 Kennedy Sp. Ctr., FL	3.00
1569-70	Apollo-Soyuz set of 2 singles	4.00
1571	10¢ Women's Year 8/26/75 Seneca Falls, NY	1.75
1572-75	10¢ Postal Serv. Bicent. attd. 9/3/75 Philadelphia, PA	4.00
1572-75	Postal Service set of 4 singles	8.00
1576	10¢ World Peace through Law 9/29/75 DC	2.00
1577-78	10¢ Banking - Commerce attd. 10/6/75 New York, NY	2.00
1577-78	Banking-Commerce set of 2 singles	3.00
1579	(10¢) Christmas - Madonna 10/14/75 DC	1.75
1580	(10¢) Christmas - Card 10/14/75 DC	1.75
1579-80	Christmas on one cover	2.50

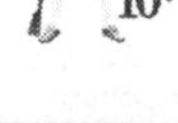

1565-68

1612

cott #	Description	Price
	1975-81 AMERICANA SERIES REGULAR ISSUES	
581	1¢ Inkwell & Quill 12/8/77 St. Louis, MO	1.75
582	2¢ Speaker's Stand 12/8/77 St. Louis, MO	1.75
584	3¢ Ballot Box 12/8/77 St. Louis, MO	1.75
585	4¢ Books & Eyeglasses 12/8/77 St. Louis, MO	1.75
581-85	4 values on one cover	3.00
590	9¢ Capitol Dome, bklt. single perf. 11 x 10½ 3/11/77 New York, NY	10.00
590a	9¢ Capitol Dome, bklt. single perf. 10 3/11/77 New York, NY	15.00
591	9¢ Capitol Dome 11/24/75 DC	1.75
592	10¢ Justice 11/17/77 New York, NY	1.75
593	11¢ Printing Press 11/13/75 Phila., PA	1.75
594	12¢ Liberty's Torch 4/8/81 Dallas, TX	1.75
595	13¢ Liberty Bell, bklt. sgl. 10/31/75 Cleveland, OH	1.75
595a	bklt. pane of 6 10/31/75 Cleveland, OH	2.25
595c	bklt. pane of 7 10/31/75 Cleveland, OH	2.50
595c	bklt. pane of 8 10/31/75 Cleveland, OH	2.75
595d	bklt. pane of 5 4/2/76 Liberty, MO	2.00
596	13¢ Eagle & Shield 12/1/75 Juneau, AK	1.75
597	15¢ Ft. McHenry Flag 6/30/78 Baltimore, MD	1.75
598	15¢ Ft. McHenry Flag,bklt. sgl. 6/30/78 Baltimore, MD	1.75
598a	booklet pane of 8 6/30/78 Baltimore, MD	2.75
599	16¢ Statue of Liberty 3/31/78 NY, NY	1.75
603	24¢ Old North Church 11/14/75 Boston, MA	1.75
604	28¢ Ft. Nisqually 8/11/78 Tacoma, WA	1.75
605	29¢ Lighthouse 4/14/78 Atlantic City, NJ	1.75
606	30¢ School House 8/27/79 Devils Lake, ND	1.75
608	50¢ Betty Lamp 9/11/79 San Jaun, PR	2.00
610	$1 Rush Lamp 7/2/79 San Francisco, CA	3.50
611	$2 Kerosene Lamp 11/16/78 New York, NY	7.00
612	$5 Railroad Lantern 8/23/79 Boston, MA	13.50
	1975-79 AMERICANA SERIES COILS	
613	3.1¢ Guitar 10/25/79 Shreveport, LA	1.75
614	7.7¢ Saxhorns 11/20/76 New York, NY	1.75
615	7.9¢ Drum 4/23/76 Miami, FL	1.75
615C	8.4¢ Grand Piano 7/13/78 Interlochen, MI	1.75
616	9¢ Capitol Dome 3/5/76 Milwaukee, WI	1.75
617	10¢ Justice 11/4/77 Tampa, FL	1.75
618	13¢ Liberty Bell 11/25/75 Allentown, PA	1.75
618C	15¢ Ft. McHenry Flag 6/30/78 Baltimore, MD	1.75
619	16¢ Statue of Liberty 3/31/78 NY, NY	1.75
	1975-77 REGULAR SERIES	
622	13¢ Flag over Ind. Hall 11/15/75 Philadelphia, PA	1.75
623	13¢ Flag over Capitol, bklt. single perf. 11 x 10½ 3/11/77 NY, NY	2.50
623a	13¢ & 9¢ booklet pane of 8 (7 #1623 & 1 #1590) perf. 11 x 10½ 3/11/77 NY, NY	25.00
623b	13¢ Flag over Capitol, bklt. single perf. 10 3/11/77 New York, NY	2.00
623c	13¢ & 9¢ booklet pane of 8 (7 #1623b & 1 #1590a) perf. 10 3/11/77 New York, NY	15.00
625	13¢ Flag over Ind. Hall, coil 11/15/75 Phila., PA	1.75
	1976	
629-31	10¢ Spirit of '76 attd. 1/1/76 Pasadena, CA	3.00
629-31	Spirit of '76 set of 3 singles	5.75
632	13¢ Interphil '76 1/17/76 Phila., PA	1.75
	1976 STATE FLAGS	
1633-82	13¢ State Flags 2/23/76 set of 50 DC	100.00
	State Capitals	110.00
	State Capital & DC cancels, set of 50 combo FDC's	150.00
1682a	Full sheet on one FDC (Uncacheted)	40.00
1683	13¢ Telephone 3/10/76 Boston, MA	1.75
1684	13¢ Aviation 3/19/76 Chicago, IL	2.00
1685	13¢ Chemistry 4/6/76 New York, NY	1.75
1686-89	13¢-31¢ Bicent. Souv. Shts. 5/29/76 Philadelphia, PA	30.00
1686a-89e	Set of 20 singles from sheets	90.00
1686a-89e	Set of 20 singles on 4 covers	40.00
1690	13¢ Franklin 6/1/76 Philadelphia, PA	1.75
1691-94	13¢ Decl. of Indep. attd. 7/4/76 Philadelphia, PA	4.00
1691-94	Decl. of Indep. set of 4 singles	8.00

Scott #	Description	Price
1695-98	13¢ Olympics attd. 7/16/76 Lake Placid, NY	4.00
1695-98	Olympics set of 4 singles	8.00
1699	13¢ Clara Maass 8/18/76 Belleville, NJ	2.00
1700	13¢ Adolph S. Ochs 9/18/76 New York, NY	1.75
1701	13¢ Nativity 10/27/76 Boston, MA	1.75
1702	13¢ "Winter Pastime" 10/27/76 Boston, MA	1.75
1701-02	Christmas on one cover	2.00
1703	13¢ "Winter Pastime", Grav.-Int. 10/27/76 Boston, MA	2.00
1701,03	Christmas on one cover	2.25
1702-03	Christmas on one cover	2.50
1701-03	Christmas on one cover	3.00
	1977	
1704	13¢ Washington 1/3/77 Princeton, NJ	1.75
	1st Carrollton cachet	**20.00**
1705	13¢ Sound Recording 3/23/77 DC	2.00
1706-09	13¢ Pueblo Pottery attd. 4/13/77 Santa Fe, NM	4.00
1706-09	Pueblo Pottery set of 4 singles	8.00
1710	13¢ Lindbergh 5/20/77 Roosevelt Field Sta., NY	2.50
	1st Doris Gold cachet	**50.00**
	1st GAMM cachet	**50.00**
	1st Spectrum cachet	**25.00**
	1st Tudor House cachet	**20.00**
	1st Z-Silk cachet	**20.00**
1711	13¢ Colorado Sthd. 5/21/77 Denver, CO	1.75
1712-15	13¢ Butterflies attd. 6/6/77 Indianapolis, IN	4.00
1712-15	Butterflies set of 4 singles	8.00
1715a	**1st Hamm cachet**	**450.00**
1716	13¢ Lafayette 6/13/77 Charleston, SC	1.75
1717-20	13¢ Skilled Hands attd. 7/4/77 Cincinnati, OH	4.00
1717-20	Skilled Hands set of 4 singles	8.00
1721	13¢ Peace Bridge 8/4/77 Buffalo, NY	1.75
	US and Canadian stamps on one cover	2.50
	Dual US & Canadian FD cancels	7.50
1722	13¢ Herkimer 8/6/77 Herkimer, NY	1.75
1723-24	13¢ Energy Conservation attd. 10/20/77 DC	2.50
1723-24	Energy Conservation set of 2 singles	3.00
1725	13¢ Alta California 9/9/77 San Jose, CA	1.75
1726	13¢ Articles of Confed. 9/30/77 York, PA	1.75
1727	13¢ Talking Pictures 10/6/77 Hollywood, CA	1.75
1728	13¢ Surrender at Saratoga 10/7/77 Schuylerville, NY	1.75
1729	13¢ Christmas - Valley Forge 10/21/77 Valley Forge, PA	1.75
1730	13¢ Christmas - Mailbox 10/21/77 Omaha, NE	1.75
1729-30	Christmas on one cover, either city	2.50
1729-30	Christmas on one cover, dual FD cancels	4.00
	1978	
1731	13¢ Carl Sandburg 1/6/78 Galesburg, IL	1.75
	1st Western Silk cachet	**35.00**
1732-33	13¢ Captain Cook attd. 1/20/78 Honolulu, HI	2.00
	Anchorage, AK	2.00
1732-33	Captain Cook set of 2 singles Honolulu, HI	3.50
	Anchorage, AK	3.50
1732-33	Set of 2 on one cover with dual FD cancels	15.00
	1st K.M.C. Venture cachet (set of 3)	**50.00**
1734	13¢ Indian Head Penny 1/11/78 Kansas City, MO	1.75
	1978-80 REGULAR ISSUES	
1735	(15¢) "A" & Eagle 5/22/78 Memphis, TN	1.75
1736	(15¢) "A", booklet single 5/22/78 Memphis, TN	1.75
1736a	(15¢) Booklet Pane of 8 5/22/78 Memphis, TN	3.00
1737	15¢ Roses, booklet single 7/11/78 Shreveport, LA	1.75
1737a	Booklet Pane of 8 7/11/78 Shreveport, LA	3.50
1738-42	15¢ Windmills set of 5 singles 2/7/80 Lubbock, TX	10.00
1742a	Windmills booklet pane of 10	5.00
1743	(15¢) "A" & Eagle, coil 5/22/78 Memphis, TN	1.75
	1st Kribbs Kover cachet	**30.00**
	1978 (cont.)	
1744	13¢ Harriet Tubman 2/1/78 DC	2.00
1745-48	13¢ American Quilts attd. 3/8/78 Charleston, WV	4.00
1745-48	American Quilts set of 4 singles	8.00
	1st Collins cachet	**450.00**

1732-33

1749-52

1978 (cont.)

Scott #	Description	Price
1749-52	13¢ American Dance attd. 4/26/78 New York, NY	4.00
1749-52	American Dance set of 4 singles	8.00
	1st Andrews cachet	**30.00**
1753	13¢ French Alliance 5/4/78 York, PA	1.75
1754	13¢ Dr. Papanicolaou 5/18/78 DC	1.75
1755	13¢ Jimmie Rodgers 5/24/78 Meridian, MS	1.75
1756	15¢ George M. Cohan 7/3/78 Providence, RI	1.75
1757	13¢ CAPEX Sheet 6/10/78 Toronto, Canada	3.50
1757a-h	CAPEX set of 8 singles	16.00
1758	15¢ Photography 6/26/78 Las Vegas, NV	1.75
1759	15¢ Viking Mission 7/20/78 Hampton, VA	1.75
1760-63	15¢ American Owls attd. 8/26/78 Fairbanks, AK	4.00
1760-63	American Owls set of 4 singles	8.00
1764-67	15¢ Amer. Trees attd. 10/9/78 Hot Springs Nat'l. Park, AR	4.00
1764-67	American Trees set of 4 singles	8.00
1768	15¢ Christmas - Madonna 10/18/78 DC	1.75
1769	15¢ Christmas - Hobby Horse 10/18/78 Holly, MI	1.75
1768-69	Christmas on one cover	2.50

1979

Scott #	Description	Price
1770	15¢ Robert F. Kennedy 1/12/79 DC	2.00
	1st DRC cachet	**50.00**
1771	15¢ Martin Luther King 1/13/79 Atlanta, GA	2.50
1772	15¢ Int'l. Yr. of the Child 2/15/79 Philadelphia, PA	1.75
1773	15¢ John Steinbeck 2/27/79 Salinas, CA	1.75
1774	15¢ Albert Einstein 3/4/79 Princeton, NJ	1.75
1775-78	15¢ Toleware attd. 4/19/79 Lancaster, PA	4.00
1775-78	Toleware set of 4 singles	8.00
1779-82	15¢ Architecture attd. 6/4/79 Kansas City, MO	4.00
1779-82	Architecture set of 4 singles	8.00
1783-86	15¢ Endangered Flora attd. 6/7/79 Milwaukee, WI	4.00
1783-86	Endangered Flora set of 4 singles	8.00
1787	15¢ Seeing Eye Dogs 6/15/79 Morristown, NJ	1.75
1788	15¢ Special Olympics 8/9/79 Brockport, NY	1.75
1789	15¢ John Paul Jones, perf. 11x12 9/23/79 Annapolis, MD	2.00
1789a	15¢ John Paul Jones, perf. 11 9/23/79 Annapolis, MD	2.00
1789,89a	Both Perfs. on 1 Cover	12.00
1790	10¢ Olympic Javelin 9/5/79 Olympia, WA	1.75
1791-94	15¢ Summer Olympics attd. 9/28/79 Los Angeles, CA	4.00
1791-94	Summer Olympics set of 4 singles	8.00
1795-98	15¢ Winter Olympics attd. 2/1/80 Lake Placid, NY	4.00
1795-98	Winter Olympics set of 4 singles	8.00
1799	15¢ Christmas - Painting 10/18/79 DC	1.75
1800	15¢ Christmas - Santa Claus 10/18/79 North Pole, AK	1.75
1799-1800	Christmas on one cover, either city	2.50
1799-1800	Christmas, dual cancel	2.50
1801	15¢ Will Rogers 11/4/79 Claremore, OK	1.75
1802	15¢ Vietnam Vets 11/11/79 Arlington, VA	2.50

1980

Scott #	Description	Price
1803	15¢ W.C. Fields 1/29/80 Beverly Hills, CA	2.50
	1st Gill Craft cachet	**25.00**
	1st Kover Kids cachet	**12.00**
1804	15¢ Benj. Banneker 2/15/80 Annapolis, MD	2.00
1805-06	15¢ Letters - Memories attd. 2/25/80 DC	2.00
1805-06	Letters - Memories set of 2 singles	3.00
1807-08	15¢ Letters - Lift Spirit attd. 2/25/80 DC	2.00
1807-08	Letters - Lift Spirit set of 2 singles	3.00
1809-10	15¢ Letters - Opinions attd. 2/25/80 DC	2.00
1809-10	Letters - Opinions set of 2 singles	3.00
1805-10	15¢ Letter Writing attd. 2/25/80 DC	4.00
1805-10	Letter Writing set of 6 singles	7.50

1980-81 REGULAR ISSUES

Scott #	Description	Price
1811	1¢ Inkwell, coil 3/6/80 New York, NY	1.75
1813	3½¢ Violins, coil 6/23/80 Williamsburg, PA	1.75
1816	12¢ Liberty's Torch, coil 4/8/81 Dallas, TX	1.75
1818	(18¢) "B" & Eagle 3/15/81 San Fran., CA	2.00
1819	(18¢) "B" & Eagle, bklt. sngl. 3/15/81 San Francisco, CA.	1.75
1819a	(18¢) Bklt. Pane of 8 3/15/81 San Francisco, CA	4.00
1820	(18¢) "B" & Eagle, coil 3/15/81 San Francisco, CA	1.75

U.S. FIRST DAY COVERS

1980

Scott #	Description	Price
1821	15¢ Frances Perkins 4/10/80 DC	1.75
1822	15¢ Dolly Madison 5/20/80 DC	1.75
	1st American Postal Arts Society cachet (Post/Art)	**35.00**
1823	15¢ Emily Bissell 5/31/80 Wilmington, DE	1.75
1824	15¢ Helen Keller 6/27/80 Tuscumbia, AL	1.75
1825	15¢ Veterans Administration 7/21/80 DC	2.00
1826	15¢ Bernardo de Galvez 7/23/80 New Orleans, LA	1.75
1827-30	15¢ Coral Reefs attd. 8/26/80 Charlotte Amalie, VI	4.00
1827-30	Coral Reefs set of 4 singles	5.00
1831	15¢ Organized Labor 9/1/80 DC	1.75
1832	15¢ Edith Wharton 9/5/80 New Haven, CT	1.75
1833	15¢ Education 9/12/80 Franklin, MA	2.00
1834-37	15¢ Indian Masks attd. 9/25/80 Spokane, WA	4.00
1834-37	Indian Masks set of 4 singles	8.00
1838-41	15¢ Architecture attd. 10/9/80 New York, NY	4.00
1838-41	Architecture set of 4 singles	8.00
1842	15¢ Christmas - Madonna 10/31/80 DC	1.75
1843	15¢ Christmas - Wreath & Toys 10/31/80 Christmas, MI..	1.75
1842-43	Christmas on one cover	2.50
1842-43	Christmas, dual cancel	3.00

1980-85 GREAT AMERICANS SERIES

Scott #	Description	Price
1844	1¢ Dorothea Dix 9/23/83 Hampden, ME	1.75
1845	2¢ Igor Stravinsky 11/18/82 New York, NY	1.75
1846	3¢ Henry Clay 7/13/83 DC	1.75
1847	4¢ Carl Shurz 6/3/83 Watertown, WI	1.75
1848	5¢ Pearl Buck 6/25/83 Hillsboro, WV	1.75
1849	6¢ Walter Lippman 9/19/85 Minneapolis, MN	1.75
1850	7¢ Abraham Baldwin 1/25/85 Athens, GA	1.75
1851	8¢ Henry Knox 7/25/85 Thomaston, ME	1.75
1852	9¢ Sylvanus Thayer 6/7/85 Braintree, MA	2.00
1853	10¢ Richard Russell 5/31/84 Winder, GA	1.75
1854	11¢ Alden Partridge 2/12/85 Norwich Un., VT	2.00
1855	13¢ Crazy Horse 1/15/82 Crazy Horse, SD	1.75
1856	14¢ Sinclair Lewis 3/21/85 Sauk Centre, MN	1.75
1857	17¢ Rachel Carson 5/28/81 Springdale, PA	1.75
1858	18¢ George Mason 5/7/81 Gunston Hall, VA	1.75
1859	19¢ Sequoyah 12/27/80 Tahlequah, OK	1.75
1860	20¢ Ralph Bunche 1/12/82 New York, NY	2.00
1861	20¢ Thomas Gallaudet 6/10/83 West Hartford, CT	2.00
1862	20¢ Harry S. Truman 1/26/84 DC	2.00
1863	22¢ John J. Audubon 4/23/85 New York, NY	2.00
1864	30¢ Frank Laubach 9/2/84 Benton, PA	1.75
1865	35¢ Charles Drew 6/3/81 DC	2.50
1866	37¢ Robert Millikan 1/26/82 Pasadena, CA	1.75
1867	39¢ Grenville Clark 3/20/85 Hanover, NH	2.00
1868	40¢ Lillian Gilbreth 2/24/84 Montclair, NJ	2.00
1869	50¢ Chester W. Nimitz 2/22/85 Fredericksburg, TX	3.00

1981

Scott #	Description	Price
1874	15¢ Everett Dirksen 1/4/81 Pekin, IL	1.75
1875	15¢ Whitney Moore Young 1/30/81 NY, NY	2.50
1876-79	15¢ Flowers attd. 4/23/81 Ft. Valley, GA	4.00
1876-79	Flowers set of 4 singles	8.00
1880-89	18¢ Wildlife set of 10 sgls. 5/14/81 Boise, ID	17.50
1889a	Wildlife booklet pane of 10	6.00

1981-82 REGULAR ISSUES

Scott #	Description	Price
1890	18¢ Flag & "Waves of Grain" 4/24/81 Portland, ME	1.75
1891	18¢ Flag & "Sea" coil 4/24/81 Portland, ME	1.75
1892	6¢ Circle of Stars, bklt. sngl. 4/24/81 Portland, ME	2.00
1893	18¢ Flag & "Mountain", bklt. sgl. 4/24/81 Portland, ME	1.75
1892-93	6¢ & 18¢ Booklet Pair 4/24/81 Portland, ME	3.75
1893a	18¢ & 6¢ B. Pane of 8 (2 #1892 & 6 #1893) 4/24/81 Portland, ME	5.00
1894	20¢ Flag over Supreme Court 12/17/81 DC	1.75
1895	20¢ Flag, coil 12/17/81 DC	1.75
1896	20¢ Flag, bklt. single 12/17/81 DC	1.75
1896a	Flag, bklt. pane of 6 12/17/81 DC	4.00
	#1894, 1895 & 1896a on one FDC	7.00
1896b	Flag, bklt. pane of 10 6/1/82 DC	6.00
1896bv	Flag, booklet single from pane of 20 11/17/83 DC	1.75

1822

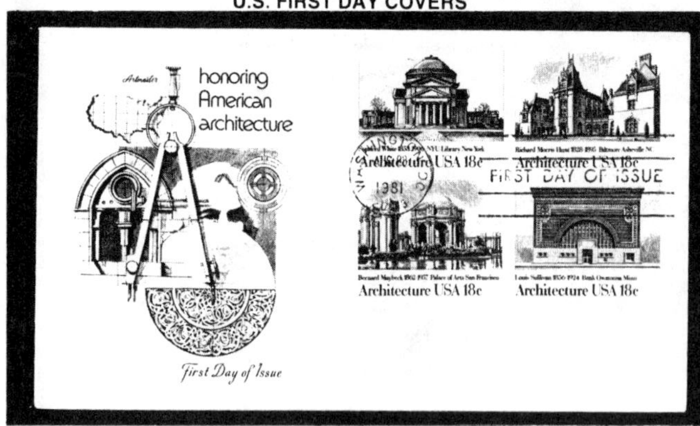

1928-31

Scott #	Description	Price
	1981-84 TRANSPORTATION COIL SERIES	
1897	1¢ Omnibus 8/19/83 Arlington, VA	2.00
1897A	2¢ Locomotive 5/20/82 Chicago, IL	2.00
1898	3¢ Handcar 3/25/83 Rochester, NY	2.00
1898A	4¢ Stagecoach 8/19/82 Milwaukee, WI	2.00
1899	5¢ Motorcycle 10/10/83 San Francisco, CA	2.00
1900	5.2¢ Sleigh 3/21/83 Memphis, TN	2.00
1900a	Precancelled	150.00
1901	5.9¢ Bicycle 2/17/82 Wheeling, WV	2.00
1901a	Precancelled	200.00
1902	7.4¢ Baby Buggy 4/7/84 San Diego, CA	2.00
1902a	Precancelled	300.00
1903	9.3¢ Mail Wagon 12/15/81 Shreveport, LA	2.00
1903a	Precancelled	300.00
1904	10.9¢ Hansom Cab 3/26/82 Chattanooga, TN	2.00
1904a	Precancelled	300.00
1905	11¢ Caboose 2/3/84 Rosemont, IL	2.50
1906	17¢ Electric Car 6/25/81 Greenfield Village, MI	2.00
1907	18¢ Surrey 5/18/81 Notch, MO	2.00
1908	20¢ Fire Pumper 12/10/81 Alexandria, VA	2.00
1909	$9.35 Express Mail, single 8/12/83 Kennedy Sp. Ctr., FL	85.00
1909a	Express Mail, booklet pane of 3	250.00
	1981 (cont.)	
1910	18¢ American Red Cross 5/1/81 DC	2.00
1911	18¢ Savings and Loans 5/8/81 Chicago, IL	1.75
1912-19	18¢ Space Ach. attd. 5/21/81 Kennedy Sp. Ctr., FL	6.00
1912-19	Space Achievement set of 8 singles	16.00
1920	18¢ Professional Management 6/18/81 Philadelphia, PA.	1.75
1921-24	18¢ Wildlife Habitats attd. 6/26/81 Reno, NV	4.00
1921-24	Wildlife Habitats set of 4 singles	8.00
1925	18¢ Disabled Persons 6/29/81 Milford, MI	1.75
1926	18¢ Edna St. Vincent Millay 7/10/81 Austeritz, NY	1.75
1927	18¢ Alcoholism 8/19/81 DC	3.00
1928-31	18¢ Architecture attd. 8/28/81 DC	4.00
1928-31	Architecture set of 4 singles	8.00
1932	18¢ Babe Zaharias 9/22/81 Pinehurst, NC	8.00
1933	18¢ Bobby Jones 9/22/81 Pinehurst, NC	12.00
1932-33	Zaharias & Jones on one cover	15.00
1934	18¢ Frederic Remington 10/9/81 Oklahoma City, OK	1.75
1935	18¢ James Hoban 10/13/81 DC	1.75
1936	20¢ James Hoban 10/13/81 DC	1.75
1935-36	Hoban on one cover	3.50
1937-38	18¢ Battle of Yorktown attd. 10/16/81 Yorktown, VA	2.00
1937-38	Battle of Yorktown set of 2 singles	3.00
1939	(20¢) Christmas - Madonna 10/28/81 Chicago, IL	1.75
1940	(20¢) Christmas - Child Art 10/28/81 Christmas Valley, OR	1.75
1939-40	Christmas on one cover	2.50
1939-40	Christmas, dual cancel	3.00
1941	20¢ John Hanson 11/5/81 Frederick, MD	1.75
1942-45	20¢ Desert Plants attd. 12/11/81 Tucson, AZ	4.00
1942-45	Desert Plants set of 4 singles	8.00
	1st Pugh cachet	**65.00**
	1981-82 REGULAR ISSUES	
1946	(20¢) "C" & Eagle 10/11/81 Memphis, TN	1.75
1947	(20¢) "C" Eagle, coil 10/11/81 Memphis, TN	1.75
1948	(20¢) "C" Eagle, bklt. single 10/11/81 Memphis, TN	1.75
1948a	(20¢) "C" Booklet Pane of 10	5.50
1949	20¢ Bighorn Sheep, bklt. single 1/8/82 Bighorn, MT	1.75
	1st New Direxions cachet	**22.50**
1949a	20¢ Booklet Pane of 10	6.00
	1982	
1950	20¢ Franklin D. Roosevelt 1/30/82 Hyde Park, NY	1.75
1951	20¢ Love 2/1/82 Boston, MA	1.75
1952	20¢ George Washington 2/22/82 Mt. Vernon, VA	2.00
	1982 STATE BIRDS AND FLOWERS	
1953-2002	20¢ Birds & Flowers 4/14/82 Set of 50 DC	80.00
	Set of 50 State Capitals	90.00
2002a	Complete pane of 50 (Uncacheted)	45.00

U.S. FIRST DAY COVERS

Scott #	Description	Price
	1982 (cont.)	
2003	20¢ US & Netherlands 4/20/82 DC	1.75
	Combo FDC with Netherland issue	7.50
2004	20¢ Library of Congress 4/21/82 DC	1.75
2005	20¢ Consumer Education, coil 4/27/82 DC	1.75
2006-09	20¢ World's Fair attd. 4/29/82 Knoxville, TN	4.00
2006-09	World's Fair set of 4 singles	8.00
2010	20¢ Horatio Alger 4/30/82 Willow Grove, PA	1.75
2011	20¢ Aging Together 5/21/82 Sun City, AZ	1.75
2012	20¢ The Barrymores 6/8/82 New York, NY	1.75
2013	20¢ Dr. Mary Walker 6/10/82 Oswego, NY	1.75
2014	20¢ Peace Garden 6/30/82 Dunseith, ND	1.75
2015	20¢ American Libraries 7/13/82 Philadelphia, PA	1.75
2016	20¢ Jackie Robinson 8/2/82 Cooperstown, NY	8.00
2017	20¢ Touro Synagogue 8/22/82 Newport, RI	2.00
2018	20¢ Wolf Trap 9/1/82 Vienna, VA	1.75
2019-22	20¢ Architecture attd. 9/30/82 DC	4.00
2019-22	Architecture set of 4 singles	8.00
2023	20¢ St. Francis of Assisi 10/7/82 San Francisco, CA	1.75
2024	20¢ Ponce de Leon 10/12/82 San Juan, PR	1.75
2025	13¢ Christmas - Kitten & Puppy 11/3/82 Danvers, MA	2.00
2026	20¢ Christmas - Religious 10/28/82 DC	1.75
2027-30	20¢ Christmas attd. 10/28/82 Snow, OK	4.00
2027-30	Christmas set of 4 singles	8.00
2026-30	Christmas on one cover either city	3.00
2026-30	Christmas, dual cancel	3.50
	1983	
2031	20¢ Science & Industry 1/19/83 Chi., IL	1.75
2032-35	20¢ Ballooning 3/31/83 DC	4.00
	Albuquerque, NM	4.00
2032-35	Ballooning set of 4 singles DC	8.00
	Albuquerque, NM	8.00
2036	20¢ US-Sweden 3/24/83 Philadelphia, PA	1.75
2036	w/Swedish issue on one cover	5.00
2037	20¢ Civilian Conservation Corps 4/5/83 Luray, VA	1.75
2038	20¢ Joseph Priestley 4/13/83 Northumberland, PA	1.75
2039	20¢ Volunteerism 4/20/83 DC	1.75
2040	20¢ German Immigration 4/29/83 Germantown, PA	1.75
2040	w/German Issue, dual cancel	8.00
2041	20¢ Brooklyn Bridge 5/17/83 Brooklyn, NY	2.00
2042	20¢ Tennessee Valley Authority 5/18/83 Knoxville, TN	1.75
2043	20¢ Physical Fitness 5/14/83 Houston, TX	2.00
2044	20¢ Scott Joplin 6/9/83 Sedalia, MO	2.00
2045	20¢ Medal of Honor 6/7/83 DC	4.00
2046	20¢ Babe Ruth 7/6/83 Chicago, IL	7.00
2047	20¢ Nathaniel Hawthorne 7/8/83 Salem, MA	1.75
2048-51	13¢ Summer Olympics attd. 7/28/83 South Bend, IN	4.00
2048-51	Summer Olympics set of 4 singles	8.00
2052	20¢ Treaty of Paris 9/2/83 DC	1.75
2053	20¢ Civil Service 9/9/83 DC	1.75
2054	20¢ Metropolitan Opera 9/14/83 NY, NY	1.75
2055-58	20¢ Inventors attd. 9/21/83 DC	4.00
2055-58	Inventors set of 4 singles	8.00
2059-62	20¢ Streetcars attd. 10/8/83 Kennebunkport, ME	4.00
2059-62	Streetcars set of 4 singles	8.00
2063	20¢ Christmas - Religious 10/28/83 DC	1.75
2064	20¢ Christmas - Traditional 10/28/83 Santa Claus, IN	1.75
2063-64	Christmas on one cover either city	2.50
2063-64	Christmas, dual cancel	3.00
2065	20¢ Martin Luther 11/11/83 DC	1.75
2065	w/German Issue, dual cancel	7.50
	1984	
2066	20¢ Alaska Sthd. 1/3/84 Fairbanks, AK	1.75
2067-70	20¢ Winter Olympics attd. 1/6/84 Lake Placid, NY	4.00
2067-70	Winter Olympics set of 4 singles	8.00
2071	20¢ Fed. Deposit Ins. Corp. 1/12/84 DC	1.75
2072	20¢ Love 1/31/84 DC	1.75
2073	20¢ Carter Woodson 2/1/84 DC	2.00
2074	20¢ Soil & Water Cons. 2/6/84 Denver, CO	1.75
2075	20¢ Credit Union Act 2/10/84 Salem, MA	1.75

2046

2123

Scott #	Description	Price
	1984 (cont.)	
2076-79	20¢ Orchids attd. 3/5/84 Miami, FL	4.00
2076-79	Orchids set of 4 singles	8.00
2080	20¢ Hawaii Sthd. 3/12/84 Honolulu, HI	2.00
2081	20¢ National Archives 4/16/84 DC	1.75
2082-85	20¢ Summer Olympics attd. 5/4/84 Los Angeles, CA	4.00
2082-85	Summer Olympics set of 4 singles	8.00
2086	20¢ Louisiana World's Fair 5/11/84 New Orleans, LA	1.75
2087	20¢ Health Research 5/17/84 New York, NY	1.75
2088	20¢ Douglas Fairbanks 5/23/84 Denver, CO	1.75
2089	20¢ Jim Thorpe 5/24/84 Shawnee, OK	5.00
2090	20¢ John McCormack 6/6/84 Boston, MA	1.75
2091	20¢ St. Lawrence Swy. 6/26/84 Massena, NY	1.75
2092	20¢ Waterfowl Preservation 7/2/84 Des Moines, IA	1.75
	1st George Van Natta cachet	**37.50**
2093	20¢ Roanoke Voyages 7/13/84 Manteo, NC	1.75
2094	20¢ Herman Melville 8/1/84 New Bedford, MA	1.75
2095	20¢ Horace Moses 8/6/84 Bloomington, IN	1.75
2096	20¢ Smokey the Bear 8/13/84 Capitan, NM	2.00
2097	20¢ Roberto Clemente 8/17/84 Carolina, PR	12.00
2098-2101	20¢ Dogs attd. 9/7/84 New York, NY	4.00
2098-2101	Dogs set of 4 singles	8.00
2102	20¢ Crime Prevention 9/26/84 DC	2.00
2103	20¢ Hispanic Americans 10/31/84 DC	1.75
2104	20¢ Family Unity 10/1/84 Shaker Heights, OH	1.75
2105	20¢ Eleanor Roosevelt 10/11/84 Hyde Park, NY	1.75
2106	20¢ Nation of Readers 10/16/84 DC	1.75
2107	20¢ Christmas - Madonna 10/30/84 DC	1.75
2108	20¢ Christmas - Santa 10/30/84 Jamaica, NY	1.75
2107-08	Christmas on one cover, either city	2.50
2107-08	Christmas, dual cancel	3.00
2109	20¢ Vietnam Memorial 11/10/84 DC	2.50
	1985 REGULARS & COMMEMS.	
2110	22¢ Jerome Kern 1/23/85 New York, NY	1.75
2111	(22¢) "D" & Eagle 2/1/85 Los Angeles, CA	1.75
2112	(22¢) "D" coil 2/1/85 Los Angeles, CA	1.75
2113	(22¢) "D" bklt. single 2/1/85 L.A., CA	1.50
2113a	(22¢) Booklet Pane of 10	7.00
2114	22¢ Flag over Capitol 3/29/85 DC	1.75
2115	22¢ Flag over Capitol, coil 3/29/85 DC	1.75
2115b	Same, Phosphor Test Coil 5/23/87 Secaucus, NJ	2.50
2116	22¢ Flag over Capitol, bklt. single 3/29/85 Waubeka, WI.	1.50
2116a	Booklet Pane of 5	3.00
2117-21	22¢ Seashells set of 5 singles 4/4/85 Boston, MA	10.00
2121a	Seashells, booklet pane of 10	7.00
2122	$10.75 Express Mail, bklt. sgl. 4/29/85 San Francisco, CA	60.00
2122a	Express Mail, booklet pane of 3	150.00
2122b	$10.75 Re-issue, bklt. sgl. 6/19/89 DC	250.00
2122c	Re-issue, booklet pane of 3	700.00
	1985-89 TRANSPORTATION COILS	
2123	3.4¢ School Bus 6/8/85 Arlington, VA	1.75
2123a	Precancelled 6/8/85 (earliest known use)	250.00
2124	4.9¢ Buckboard 6/21/85 Reno, NV	1.75
2124a	Precancelled 6/21/85 DC (earliest known use)	250.00
2125	5.5¢ Star Route Truck 11/1/86 Fort Worth, TX	1.75
2125a	Precancelled 11/1/86 DC	5.00
2126	6¢ Tricycle 5/6/85 Childs, MD	1.75
2127	7.1¢ Tractor 2/6/87 Sarasota, FL	1.75
2127a	Precancelled 2/6/87 Sarasota, FL	5.00
2127av	Zip + 4 Prec., 5/26/89 Rosemont, IL	1.75
2128	8.3¢ Ambulance 6/21/85 Reno, NV	1.75
2128a	Precancelled 6/21/85 DC (earliest known use)	250.00
2129	8.5¢ Tow Truck 1/24/87 Tucson, AZ	1.75
2129a	Precancelled 1/24/87 DC	5.00
2130	10.1¢ Oil Wagon 4/18/85 Oil Center, NM	1.75
2130a	Black Precancel 4/18/85 DC (earliest known use)	250.00
2130a	Red. Prec. 6/27/88 DC	1.75
2131	11¢ Stutz Bearcat 6/11/85 Baton Rouge, LA	1.75

U.S. FIRST DAY COVERS

Scott #	Description	Price
	1985-89 TRANSPORTATION COILS (cont.)	
2132	12¢ Stanley Steamer 4/2/85 Kingfield, ME	1.75
2132a	Precancelled 4/2/85 DC	**POR**
2132b	"B" Press cancel 9/3/87 DC	60.00
2133	12.5¢ Pushcart 4/18/85 Oil Center, NM	1.75
2133a	Precancelled 4/18/85 DC	**POR**
2134	14¢ Iceboat 3/23/85 Rochester, NY	1.75
2135	17¢ Dog Sled 8/20/86 Anchorage, AK	1.75
2136	25¢ Bread Wagon 11/22/86 Virginia Bch., VA	1.75
	1985 (cont.)	
2137	22¢ Mary McLeod Bethune 3/5/85 DC	2.00
2138-41	22¢ Duck Decoys attd. 3/22/85 Shelburne, VT	4.00
2138-41	Duck Decoys set of 4 singles	8.00
2142	22¢ Winter Special Olympics 3/25/85 Park City, UT	1.75
2143	22¢ Love 4/17/85 Hollywood, CA	1.75
2144	22¢ Rural Electrification Admin. 5/11/85 Madison, SD	1.75
2145	22¢ Ameripex '86 5/25/85 Rosemont, IL	1.75
2146	22¢ Abigail Adams 6/14/85 Quincy, MA	1.75
2147	22¢ Frederic A. Bartholdi 7/18/85 NY, NY	1.75
2149	18¢ Washington Pre-Sort, coil 11/6/85 DC	1.75
2150	21.1¢ Zip + 4, coil 10/22/85 DC	1.75
2152	22¢ Korean War Veterans 7/26/85	2.00
2153	22¢ Social Security Act 8/14/85 Baltimore, MD	1.75
2154	22¢ World War I Vets 8/26/85 Milwaukee, WI	2.00
2155-58	22¢ Horses attd. 9/25/85 Lexington, KY	4.00
2155-58	Horses set of 4 singles	8.00
2159	22¢ Public Education 10/1/85 Boston, MA	2.00
2160-63	22¢ Int'l. Youth Year attd. 10/7/85 Chicago, IL	4.00
2160-63	Set of 4 singles	8.00
2164	22¢ Help End Hunger 10/15/85 DC	1.75
2165	22¢ Christmas - Madonna 10/30/85 Detroit, MI	1.75
2166	22¢ Christmas - Poinsettia 10/30/85 Nazareth, MI	1.75
2165-66	Christmas on one cover, either city	2.50
	1986	
2167	22¢ Arkansas Sthd. 1/3/86 Little Rock, AR	1.75
	1986-94 GREAT AMERICANS SERIES	
2168	1¢ Margaret Mitchell 6/30/86 Atlanta, GA	2.50
2169	2¢ Mary Lyon 2/28/87 South Hadley, MA	1.75
2170	3¢ Dr. Paul Dudley White 9/15/86 DC	1.75
2171	4¢ Father Flanagan 7/14/86 Boys Town, NE	1.75
2172	5¢ Hugo L. Black 2/27/86 DC	1.75
2173	5¢ Luis Munoz Marin 2/18/90 San Juan, PR	1.75
2176	10¢ Red Cloud 8/15/87 Red Cloud, NE	1.75
2177	14¢ Julia Ward Howe 2/12/87 Boston, MA	1.75
2178	15¢ Buffalo Bill Cody 6/6/88 Cody, WY	1.75
2179	17¢ Belva Ann Lockwood 6/18/86 Middleport, NY	1.75
2179B	20¢ Virginia Agpar 10/24/94 Dallas, TX	1.75
2180	21¢ Chester Carlson 10/21/88 Rochester, NY	1.75
2182	23¢ Mary Cassatt 11/4/88 Phila., PA	1.75
2183	25¢ Jack London 1/11/86 Glen Ellen, CA	2.00
2183a	Bklt. Pane of 10 5/3/88 San Francisco, CA	8.00
2183as	Perf. 11 bklt. single 5/3/88 San Francisco, CA	2.00
2184	28¢ Sitting Bull 9/14/89 Rapid City, SD	2.00
2184A	29¢ Earl Warren 3/9/92 DC	2.00
2184B	29¢ Thomas Jefferson 4/13/93 Charlottesville, VA	2.00
2185	35¢ Dennis Chavez 4/3/91 Albuquerque, NM	2.00
2186	40¢ General Claire Chennault 9/6/90 Monroe, LA	2.00
2188	45¢ Dr. Harvey Cushing 6/17/88 Cleveland, OH	2.00
2190	52¢ Hubert H. Humphrey 6/3/91 Minneapolis, MN	2.00
2191	56¢ John Harvard 9/3/86 Cambridge, MA	2.00
2192	65¢ General "Hap" Arnold 11/5/88 Gladwyne, PA	2.50
2193	75¢ Wendell Wilkie 2/16/92 Bloomington, IN	3.00
2194	$1 Dr. Bernard Revel 9/23/86 NY, NY	4.00
2194A	$1 John Hopkins 6/7/89 Baltimore, MD	5.00
2195	$2 William Jennings Bryan 3/19/86 Salem, IL	7.00
2196	$5 Bret Harte 8/25/87 Twain Harte, CA	15.00
2197	25¢ Jack London, perf. 10 bklt. sgl. 5/3/88 San Fran., CA	1.75
2197a	Bklt. Pane of 6	4.00

2155-58

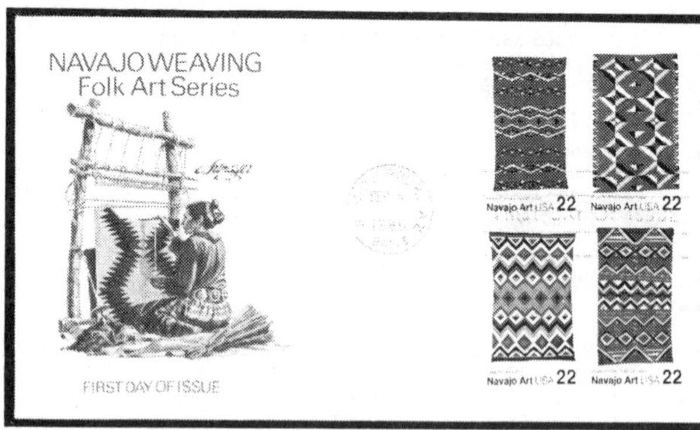

2235-38

Scott #	Description	Price
	1986 (cont.)	
2198-2201	22¢ Stamp Coll. set of 4 1/23/86 State College, PA	8.00
2201a	Stamp Collecting, bklt. pane of 4	5.00
2201b	Color error, Black omitted on #2198 & 2201	300.00
2201b	Same, set of 4 singles	300.00
2202	22¢ Love 1/30/86 New York, NY	1.75
2203	22¢ Sojourner Truth 1/4/86 New Paltz, NY	2.00
2204	22¢ Republic of Texas 3/2/86 San Antonio, TX	1.75
	Washington-on-the-Brazos, TX	1.75
2205-09	22¢ Fish set of 5 singles 3/21/86 Seattle, WA	10.00
2209a	Fish, booklet pane of 5	6.00
2210	22¢ Public Hospitals 4/11/86 NY, NY	1.75
2211	22¢ Duke Ellington 4/29/86 New York, NY	2.00
2216-19	22¢ U.S. Presidents 4 sheets of 9 5/22/86 Chicago, IL	24.00
2216a-19a	US President set of 36 singles	63.00
2220-23	22¢ Polar Explorers attd. 5/28/86 North Pole, AK	4.00
2220-23	22¢ Polar Explorers set of 4 singles	8.00
2224	22¢ Statue of Liberty 7/4/86 NY, NY	2.00
2224	w/French Issue, dual cancel	7.50
2225	1¢ Omnibus Coil Re-engraved 11/26/86 DC	1.75
2226	2¢ Locomotive Coil Re-engraved 3/6/87 Milwaukee, WI	1.75
2228	4¢ Stagecoach Coil "B" Press 8/15/86 DC (eku)	150.00
2231	8.3¢ Ambulance Coil "B" Press 8/29/86 DC (eku)	150.00
2235-38	22¢ Navajo Art attd. 9/4/86 Window Rock, AZ	4.00
2235-38	Set of 4 singles	8.00
2239	22¢ T.S. Eliot 9/26/86 St. Louis, MO	1.75
2240-43	22¢ Woodcarved Figurines attd. 10/1/86 DC	4.00
2240-43	Set of 4 singles	8.00
2244	22¢ Christmas - Madonna 10/24/86 DC	2.00
2245	22¢ Christmas Village Scene 10/24/86 Snow Hill, MD	2.00
	1987	
2246	22¢ Michigan Statehood 1/26/87 Lansing, MI	1.75
2247	22¢ Pan American Games 1/29/87 Indianapolis, IN	1.75
2248	22¢ Love 10/30/87 San Francisco, CA	1.75
2249	22¢ Jean Baptiste Point du Sable 2/20/87 Chicago, IL	1.75
2250	22¢ Enrico Caruso 2/27/87 NY, NY	1.75
2251	22¢ Girl Scouts 3/12/87 DC	3.00
	1987-88 TRANSPORTATION COILS	
2252	3¢ Conestoga Wagon 2/29/88 Conestoga, PA	1.75
2253	5¢ Milk Wagon 9/25/87 Indianapolis, IN	1.75
2254	5.3¢ Elevator, Prec. 9/16/88 New York, NY	1.75
2255	7.6¢ Carretta, Prec. 8/30/88 San Jose, CA	1.75
2256	8.4¢ Wheelchair, Prec. 8/12/88 Tucson, AZ	1.75
2257	10¢ Canal Boat 4/11/87 Buffalo, NY	1.75
2258	13¢ Police Patrol Wagon, Prec. 10/29/88 Anaheim, CA	1.75
2259	13.2¢ RR Car, Prec. 7/19/88 Pittsburgh, PA	1.75
2260	15¢ Tugboat 7/12/88 Long Beach, CA	1.75
2261	16.7¢ Popcorn Wagon, Prec. 7/7/88 Chicago, IL	1.75
2262	17.5¢ Marmon Wasp 9/25/87 Indianapolis, IN	1.75
2262a	Precancelled	5.00
2263	20¢ Cable Car 10/28/88 San Francisco, CA	1.75
2264	20.5¢ Fire Engine, Prec. 9/28/88 San Angelo, TX	1.75
2265	21¢ R.R. Mail Car, Prec. 8/16/88 Santa Fe, NM	1.75
2266	24.1¢ Tandem Bicycle, Prec. 10/26/88 Redmond, WA	1.75
	1987-88 REGULAR & SPECIAL ISSUES	
2267-74	22¢ Special Occasions, bklt. sgls. 4/20/87 Atlanta, GA	16.00
2274a	Booklet Pane of 10	7.00
2275	22¢ United Way 4/28/87 DC	1.75
2276	22¢ Flag and Fireworks 5/9/87 Denver, CO	1.75
2276a	Booklet Pane of 20 11/30/87 DC	12.00
2277	(25¢) "E" Earth Issue 3/22/88 DC	1.75
2278	25¢ Flag & Clouds 5/6/88 Boxborough, MA	1.75
2279	(25¢) "E" Earth Coil 3/22/88 DC	1.75
2280	25¢ Flag over Yosemite Coil 5/20/88 Yosemite, CA	1.75
2280 var.	Phosphor paper 2/14/89 Yosemite, CA	1.75
2281	25¢ Honeybee Coil 9/2/88 Omaha, NE	1.75
2282	(25¢) "E" Earth Bklt. Sgl. 3/22/88 DC	1.75
2282a	Bklt. Pane of 10	7.50
2283	25¢ Pheasant Bklt. Sgl. 4/29/88 Rapid City, SD	1.75
2283a	Bklt. Pane of 10	8.00

U.S. FIRST DAY COVERS

Scott #	Description	Price
	1987-88 REGULAR & SPECIAL ISSUES	
2284	25¢ Grosbeak Bklt. Sgl. 5/28/88 Arlington, VA	1.75
2285	25¢ Owl Bklt. Sgl. 5/28/88 Arlington, VA	1.75
2285b	Bklt. Pane of 10 (5 of ea.)	8.00
2285A	25¢ Flag & Clouds bklt. sgl. 7/5/88 DC	1.75
2285Ac	Bklt. Pane of 6	4.50
2286-2335	22¢ American Wildlife 6/13/87 Toronto, Canada	
	Set of 50 singles	87.50
2335a	Complete Pane of 50	40.00
	RATIFICATION OF CONSTITUTION	
	STATE BICENTENNIAL ISSUES 1987-90	
2336	22¢ Delaware Statehood Bicent. 7/4/87 Dover, DE	2.00
2337	22¢ Pennsylvania Bicent. 8/26/87 Harrisburg, PA	2.00
2338	22¢ New Jersey Bicent. 9/11/87 Trenton, NJ	2.00
2339	22¢ Georgia Bicent. 1/6/88 Atlanta, GA	2.00
2340	22¢ Connecticut Bicent. 1/9/88 Hartford, CT	2.00
2341	22¢ Massachusetts Bicent. 2/6/88 Boston, MA	2.00
2342	22¢ Maryland Bicent. 2/15/88 Annapolis, MD	2.00
2343	25¢ South Carolina Bicent. 5/23/88 Columbia, SC	2.00
2344	25¢ New Hampshire Bicent. 6/21/88 Concord, NH	2.00
2345	25¢ Virginia Bicent. 6/25/88 Williamsburg, VA	2.00
2346	25¢ New York Bicent. 7/26/88 Albany, NY	2.00
2347	25¢ North Carolina Bicent. 8/22/89 Fayetteville, NC	2.00
2348	25¢ Rhode Island Bicent. 5/29/90 Pawtucket, RI	2.00
2336-48	Set of 13 on one cover, each with a different FD cancel	100.00
2349	22¢ U.S.-Morocco Relations 7/18/87 DC	1.75
2350	22¢ William Faulkner 8/3/87 Oxford, MS	1.75
2351-54	22¢ Lacemaking attd. 8/14/87 Ypsilanti, MI	4.00
2351-54	Set of 4 singles	8.00
2355-59	22¢ Drafting of Constitution bklt. sgls. (5) 8/28/87 DC	10.00
2359a	Booklet Pane of 5	5.00
2360	22¢ Signing the Constitution 9/17/87 Philadelphia, PA	2.00
2361	22¢ Certified Public Accounting 9/21/87 NY, NY	8.00
2362-66	22¢ Locomotives, bklt. sgls. (5) 10/1/87 Baltimore, MD	10.00
2366a	Booklet Pane of 5	4.00
2367	22¢ Christmas - Moroni Madonna 10/23/87 DC	2.00
2368	22¢ Christmas Ornaments 10/23/87 Holiday, CA	2.00
	1988	
2369	22¢ 1988 Winter Olympics 1/10/88 Anchorage, AK	1.75
2370	22¢ Australia Bicent. 1/26/88 DC	1.75
2371	22¢ James Weldon Johnson 2/2/88 Nashville, TN	1.75
2372-75	22¢ Cats attd. 2/5/88 New York, NY	6.00
2372-75	Set of 4 singles	10.00
2376	22¢ Knute Rockne 3/9/88 Notre Dame, IN	4.00
2377	25¢ Francis Ouimet 6/13/88 Brookline, MA	6.50
2378	25¢ Love 7/4/88 Pasadena, CA	1.75
2379	45¢ Love 8/8/88 Shreveport, LA	2.00
2380	25¢ Summer Olympics 8/19/88 Colo. Springs, CO	1.75
2381-85	25¢ Classic Cars, Bklt. Sgls. 8/25/88 Detroit, MI	10.00
2385a	Bklt. Pane of 5	4.00
2386-89	25¢ Antarctic Explorers attd. 9/14/88 DC	4.00
2386-89	Set of 4 singles	8.00
2390-93	25¢ Carousel Animals attd. 10/1/88 Sandusky, OH	4.00
2390-93	Set of 4 singles	8.00
2394	$8.75 Express Mail 10/4/88 Terra Haute, IN	30.00
2395-98	25¢ Sp. Occasions Bklt. Sgls. 10/22/88 King of Prussia, PA	7.00
2396a	Happy Birthday & Best Wishes, Bklt. Pane of 6	5.00
2398a	Thinking of You & Love You, Bklt. Pane of 6	5.00
2399	25¢ Christmas (Traditional) 10/20/88 DC	2.00
2400	25¢ Christmas (Contemporary) 10/20/88 Berlin, NH	2.00
	1989	
2401	25¢ Montana Statehood 1/15/89 Helena, MT	2.00
2402	25¢ A. Philip Randolph 2/3/89 New York, NY	2.00
2403	25¢ North Dakota Statehood 2/21/89 Bismarck, ND	1.75
2404	25¢ Washington Statehood 2/22/89 Olympia, WA	1.75
2405-09	25¢ Steamboats, Bklt. Sgls. 3/3/89 New Orleans, LA	10.00
2409a	Bklt. Pane of 5	4.00
2410	25¢ World Stamp Expo 3/16/89 New York, NY	1.75
2411	25¢ Arturo Toscanini 3/25/89 New York, NY	1.75
2412	25¢ U.S. House of Representatives 4/4/89 DC	2.00
2413	25¢ U.S. Senate 4/6/89 DC	2.00
2414	25¢ Exec. Branch & G. Washington Inaugural	
	4/16/89 Mt. Vernon, VA	2.00
2415	25¢ U.S. Supreme Court 2/2/90 DC	2.00
2416	25¢ South Dakota Statehood 5/3/89 Pierre, SD	1.75
2417	25¢ Lou Gehrig 6/10/89 Cooperstown, NY	6.00
2418	25¢ Ernest Hemingway 7/17/89 Key West, FL	1.75
2419	$2.40 Moon Landing 7/20/89 DC	7.00
2420	25¢ Letter Carriers 8/30/89 Milwaukee, WI	2.00
2421	25¢ Drafting the Bill of Rights 9/25/89 Philadelphia, PA	1.75
2422-25	25¢ Prehistoric Animals attd. 10/1/89 Orlando, FL	4.00
2422-25	Set of 4 singles	8.00
2426	25¢ Pre-Columbian Customs 10/12/89 San Juan, PR	1.75
2427	25¢ Christmas Madonna 10/19/89 DC	1.75
2427a	Booklet Pane of 10	8.00
2428	25¢ Christmas Sleigh 10/19/89 Westport, CT	1.75
2429	25¢ Christmas Sleigh, bklt. sgl. Westport, CT	1.75
2429a	Booklet Pane of 10	8.00
2431	25¢ Eagle & Shield, self-adhes. 11/10/89 Virginia Bch., VA	1.75
2431a	Booklet Pane of 18	15.00
2433	90¢ World Stamp Expo S/S of 4 11/17/89 DC	16.50
2434-37	25¢ Classic Mail Transportation attd. 11/19/89 DC	4.00
2434-37	Set of 4 singles	8.00
2438	25¢ Classic Mail Transportation, S/S of 4 11/28/89 DC	4.50

2440

Scott #	Description	Price
	1990	
439	25¢ Idaho Statehood 1/6/90 Boise, ID	2.00
440	25¢ Love 1/18/90 Romance, AR	2.00
441	25¢ Love, bklt. sgl. 1/18/90 Romance, AR	1.75
441a	Booklet Pane of 10	8.00
442	25¢ Ida B. Wells 2/1/90 Chicago, IL	2.00
443	15¢ Beach Umbrella, bklt. sgl. 2/3/90 Sarasota, FL	1.75
443a	Booklet Pane of 10	6.00
444	25¢ Wyoming Statehood 2/23/90 Cheyenne, WY	1.75
445-48	25¢ Classic Films attd. 3/23/90 Hollywood, CA	6.00
445-48	Set of 4 singles	10.00
449	25¢ Marianne Moore 4/18/90 Brooklyn, NY	2.00
	1990-95 TRANSPORTATION COILS	
451	4¢ Steam Carriage 1/25/81 Tucson, AZ	1.75
452	5¢ Circus Wagon 8/31/90 Syracuse, NY	1.75
452B	5¢ Circus Wagon, Gravure 12/8/92 Cincinnati, OH	1.75
425D	5¢ Circus Wagon, Reissue (5¢) 3/20/95, Kansas City,MO	1.90
453	5¢ Canoe, brown 5/25/91 Secaucus, NJ	1.75
454	5¢ Canoe, red, Gravure print 10/22/91 Secaucus, NJ	1.75
457	10¢ Tractor Trailer,Intaglio 5/25/91 Secaucus, NJ	1.75
458	10¢ Tractor Trailer, Gravure 5/25/94 Secaucus, NJ	1.75
464	23¢ Lunch Wagon 4/12/91 Columbus, OH	1.75
468	$1.00 Seaplane 4/20/90 Phoenix, AZ	3.00
	1990-93	
470-74	25¢ Lighthouse bklt. sgls. 4/26/90 DC	10.00
474a	Booklet Pane of 5	4.00
475	25¢ Flag Stamp, ATM self-adhes. 5/18/90 Seattle, WA	1.75
475a	Pane of 12	10.00
476	$2.00 Bobcat 6/1/90 Arlington, VA	7.00
478	29¢ Red Squirrel, self-adhesive sgl. 6/25/93 Milwaukee, WI	1.75
478a	Pane of 18	14.00
478v	Coil Pair with paper backing	2.25
479	29¢ Rose, self-adhesive sgl. 8/19/93 Houston, TX	1.75
479a	Pane of 18	14.00
479v	Coil Pair with paper backing	2.25
480	29¢ Pine Cone, self-adhesive sgl. 11/5/93 Kansas City, MO	1.75
480a	Pane of 18	14.00
480v	Coil Pair with paper backing	2.25
481	1¢ Kestrel 6/22/91 Aurora, CO	1.75
481v	1¢ with "¢" sign 5/10/95 Aurora,CO	1.90
482	3¢ Bluebird 6/22/91 Aurora, CO	1.75
487	19¢ Fawn 3/11/91 DC	1.75
489	30¢ Cardinal 6/22/91 Aurora, CO	1.75
491	45¢ Pumpkinseed Sunfish 12/2/92 DC	2.00
493	29¢ Wood Duck, BEP bklt. single 4/12/91 Columbus, OH	1.75
493a	BEP Booklet Pane of 10	9.00
494	29¢ Wood Duck, KCS bklt. single 4/12/91 Columbus, OH	1.75
494a	KCS Booklet Pane of 10	9.00
495	29¢ African Violet, Bklt. Sgl. 10/8/93 Beaumont, TX	1.75
495a	Booklet Pane of 10	8.00
496-2500	25¢ Olympians attd. 7/6/90 Minneapolis, MN	5.00
496-2500	Set of 5 singles	10.00
496-2500	Olympians with Tab singles attd.	8.00
496-2500	Set of 5 singles with Tabs	12.00
2501-05	25¢ Indian Headdresses bklt. singles 8/17/90 Cody, WY.	10.00
2505a	Booklet Pane of 5	8.00
2506-07	25¢ Micronesia & Marshall Isles joint issue 9/28/90 DC	3.00
2506-07	Set of 2 singles	4.00
2508-11	25¢ Sea Creatures attd. 10/3/90 Baltimore, MD	5.00
2508-11	Set of 4 singles	10.00
2512	25¢ Pre-Columbian Customs 10/12/90 Grand Canyon, AZ	2.00
2513	25¢ Dwight D. Eisenhower 10/13/90 Abilene, KS	2.00
2514	25¢ Christmas Madonna 10/18/90 DC	2.00
2514a	Booklet Pane of 10 10/18/90 DC	6.50
2515	25¢ Christmas Tree 10/18/90 Evergreen, CO	2.00
2516	25¢ Christmas Tree bklt. sgl. 10/18/90 Evergreen, CO	2.00
2516a	Booklet Pane of 10 10/18/90	6.50
	1991-92	
2517	(29¢) "F" Flower stamp 1/22/91 DC	1.75
2518	(29¢) "F" Flower coil 1/22/91 DC	1.75
2519	(29¢) "F" Flower, BEP bklt. single 1/22/91 DC	1.75
2519a	Bklt. Pane of 10, BEP	7.50
2520	(29¢) "F" Flower, KCS bklt. single 1/22/91 DC	1.75

1991-92 (cont.)

2520a	Bklt. Pane of 10, KCS	9.50
2521	(4¢) Make-up rate stamp 1/22/91 DC	1.75
2522	(29¢) Flag stamp, ATM self-adhes. 1/22/91 DC	1.75
2522a	Pane of 12	10.00
2523	29¢ Flag over Mt. Rushmore Coil 3/29/91 Mt. Rushmore,SD	1.75
2523A	29¢ Same, Gravure print 7/4/91 Mt. Rushmore, SD	1.75
	* On #2523A "USA" and "29" are **not** outlined in white	
2524	29¢ Flower 4/5/91 Rochester, NY	1.75
2525	29¢ Flower coil, rouletted 8/16/91 Rochester, NY	1.75
2526	29¢ Flower coil, perforated 3/3/92 Rochester, NY	1.75
2527	29¢ Flower, bklt. single 4/5/91 Rochester, NY	1.75
2527a	Booklet Pane of 10	7.50
2528	29¢ Flag with Olympic Rings, bklt. sgl. 4/21/91 Atlanta, GA	1.75
2528a	Booklet Pane of 10	7.50
2529	19¢ Fishing Boat, coil 8/8/91 DC	1.75
2529C	19¢ Fishing Boat, coil, Type III 6/25/94 Arlington, VA	1.75
2530	19¢ Ballooning, bklt. sgl. 5/17/91 Denver, CO	1.75
2530a	Booklet Pane of 10	7.00
2531	29¢ Flags/Memorial Day, 125th Anniv. 5/30/91 Waterloo,NY	1.75
2531A	29¢ Liberty Torch, ATM self-adhes. 6/25/91 New York, NY	1.75
2531Ab	Pane of 18	14.00
2532	50¢ Switzerland joint issue	2.00
2533	29¢ Vermont Statehood 3/1/91 Bennington, VT	2.25
2534	29¢ Savings Bonds 4/30/91 DC	1.75
2535	29¢ Love 5/9/91 Honolulu, HI	1.75
2536	29¢ Love, Booklet Sgl. 5/9/91 Honolulu, HI	1.75
2536a	Booklet Pane of 10	7.50
2537	52¢ Love, 2 ounce rate 5/9/91 Honolulu, HI	2.00
2538	29¢ William Saroyan 5/22/91 Fresno, CA	2.00
2539	$1.00 USPS & Olympic Rings 9/29/91 Orlando, FL	3.00
2540	$2.90 Priority Mail 7/7/91 San Diego, CA	9.00
2541	$9.95 Express Mail,Domestic rate 6/16/91 Sacramento,CA	25.00
2542	$14.00 Express Mail,Internat'l rate 8/31/91 Indianapolis,IN	32.50
2543	$2.90 Priority Mail, Space 6/3/93 Titusville, FL	7.50
2545-49	29¢ Fishing Flies, bklt. sgls. 5/31/91 Cudlebackville, NY..	10.00
2549a	Booklet Pane of 5	5.00
2550	29¢ Cole Porter 6/8/91 Peru, IN	1.75
2551	29¢ Desert Shield / Desert Storm 7/2/91 DC	2.00
2552	29¢ Desert Shield / Desert Storm bklt. sgl. 7/2/91 DC	2.00
2552a	29¢ Booklet Pane of 5	4.50

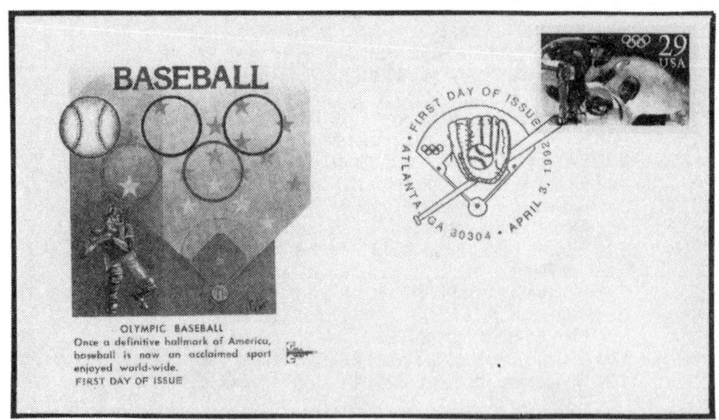

2619

Scott #	Description	Price
	1991 (cont.)	
2553-57	29¢ Summer Olympics,strip of 5 7/12/91 Los Angeles, CA	4.50
2553-57	Set of 5 singles	10.00
2558	29¢ Numismatics 8/13/91 Chicago, IL	2.00
2559	29¢ World War II S/S of 10 9/3/91 Phoenix, AZ	10.00
2559a-j	Set of 10 singles	25.00
2560	29¢ Basketball 8/28/91 Springfield, MA	3.00
2561	29¢ District of Columbia Bicent. 9/7/91 DC	1.75
2562-66	29¢ Comedians bklt. sgls. 8/29/91 Hollywood, CA	10.00
2566a	Booklet Pane of 10	7.50
2567	29¢ Jan Matzeliger 9/15/91 Lynn, MA	1.75
2568-77	29¢ Space Exploration bklt. sgls. 10/11/91 Pasadena, CA	20.00
2577a	Booklet Pane of 10	8.00
2578	(29¢) Christmas, Contemporary 10/17/91 Santa, ID	1.75
2578a	Booklet Pane of 10	8.00
2579	(29¢) Christmas, Contemporary 10/19/91 Santa, ID	1.75
2580-85	(29¢) Christmas, bklt. pane sgls. 10/17/91 Santa, ID	8.00
2581b-85a	Booklet Panes of 4, set of 5	20.00
	1992-94 REGULAR ISSUES	
2590	$1 Surrender of Burgoyne 5/5/94 New York, NY	3.00
2592	$5 Washington & Jackson 8/19/94 Pittsburgh, PA	13.50
2593	29¢ Pledge of Allegiance, bklt. sgl. 9/8/92 Rome, NY	1.75
2593a	Booklet Pane of 10	7.00
	1992 Eagle & Shield ATM Self-Adhesives (9/25/92 Dayton, OH)	
	Panes of 17	
2595	29¢ "Brown" denomination, sgl	1.75
2595a	Pane of 17 + label	12.00
2596	29¢ "Green" denomination, sgl	1.75
2596a	Pane of 17 + label	12.00
2597	29¢ "Red" denomination, sgl	1.75
2597a	Pane of 17 + label	12.00
	Coils	
2595v	29¢ "Brown" denomination, pair with paper backing	2.25
2596v	29¢ "Green" denomination, pair with paper backing	2.25
2597v	29¢ "Red" denomination, pair with paper backing	2.25
	1994 Self-Adhesive Issues	
2598	29¢ Eagle, single 2/4/94 Sarasota, FL	1.75
2598a	Pane of 18	12.50
2598v	29¢ Coil Pair with paper backing	2.25
2599	29¢ Statue of Liberty, single 6/24/94 Haines, FL	1.75
2599a	Pane of 18	12.50
2599v	29¢ Coil pair with paper backing	2.25
	1991-93 Coils	
2602	(10¢) Eagle & Shield, bulk-rate 12/13/91 Kansas City, MO	1.75
2603	(10¢) Eagle & Shield, **BEP** 5/29/93 Secaucus, NJ	1.75
2604	(10¢) Eagle & Shld., **Stamp Venturers** 5/29/93 Secaucus, NJ	1.75
2605	23¢ Flag, First Class pre-sort 9/27/91 DC	1.75
2606	23¢ USA, 1st Cl, pre-sort, **ABNCo.** 7/21/92 Kansas City, MO	1.75
2607	23¢ USA, 1st Cl, pre-sort, **BEP** 10/9/92 Kansas City, MO	1.75
2608	23¢ USA, 1st Cl, p.s., **Stamp Venturers** 5/14/93 Denver, CO	1.75
2609	29¢ Flag over White House 4/23/92 DC	1.75
	1992	
2611-15	29¢ Winter Olympics, strip of 5 1/11/92 Orlando, FL	5.00
2611-15	Set of 5 singles	10.00
2616	29¢ World Columbian Expo 1/24/92 Rosemont, IL	1.75
2617	29¢ W.E.B. DuBois 1/31/92 Atlanta, GA	2.00
2618	29¢ Love 2/6/92 Loveland. CO	1.75
2619	29¢ Olympic Baseball 4/3/92 Atlanta, GA	4.00
2620-23	29¢ First Voyage of Columbus 4/24/92 Christiansted, VI	4.00
2620-23	Set of 4 singles	8.00
2624-29	1¢-$5.00 Voyages of Columbus S/S 5/22/92 Chicago, IL	50.00
2624-29	Set of 16 singles	90.00
2630	29¢ New York Stock Exchange 5/17/92 New York, NY	2.00
2631-34	29¢ Space: U.S. & Soviet joint issue 5/29/92 Chicago, IL	4.00
2631-34	Set of 4 singles	10.00
2635	29¢ Alaska Highway 5/30/92 Fairbanks, AK	1.75

U.S. FIRST DAY COVERS

Scott #	Description	Price
	1992 (cont.)	
2636	29¢ Kentucky Statehood Bicent. 6/1/92 Danville, KY	1.75
2637-41	29¢ Summer Olympics, strip of 5 6/11/92 Baltimore, MD	5.00
2637-41	Set of 5 singles	10.00
2642-46	29¢ Hummingbirds, bklt. sgls. 6/15/92 DC	10.00
2646a	Booklet Pane of 5	5.00
2647-96	29¢ Wildflowers, set of 50 singles 7/24/92 Columbus, OH	87.50
2697	29¢ World War II S/S of 10 8/17/92 Indianapolis, IN	8.00
2697a-j	Set of 10 singles	20.00
2698	29¢ Dorothy Parker 8/22/92 West End, NJ	1.75
2699	29¢ Dr. Theodore von Karman 8/31/92 DC	1.75
2700-03	29¢ Minerals 9/17/92 DC	4.00
2700-03	Set of 4 singles	8.00
2704	29¢ Juan Rodriguez Cabrillo 9/28/92 San Diego, CA	1.75
2705-09	29¢ Wild Animals, bklt. sgls. 10/1/92 New Orleans, LA	10.00
2709a	Booklet Pane of 5	5.00
2710	29¢ Christmas, Madonna & Child 10/22/92 DC	2.00
2710a	Booklet Pane of 10 10/22/92 DC	8.00
2711-14	29¢ Christmas Toys 10/22/92 Kansas City, MO	4.00
2711-14	Set of 4 singles	10.00
2715-18	29¢ Christmas Toys, bklt. sgls. 10/22/92 Kansas City, MO	10.00
2718a	Booklet Pane of 4	4.00
2719	29¢ Christmas Train self-adhes. ATM 10/28/92 NY, NY	1.75
2719a	Pane of 18	14.00
2720	29¢ Happy New Year 12/30/92 San Francisco, CA	3.00
	1993	
2721	29¢ Elvis Presley 1/8/93 Memphis, TN	2.00
2722	29¢ Oklahoma! 3/30/93 Oklahoma City, OK	1.75
2723	29¢ Hank Williams 6/9/93 Nashville, TN	1.75
2724-30	29¢ R 'n' R/R & B 6/16/93 on one cover Cleveland, OH & Santa Monica, CA (same cancel ea. city)	7.00
2724-30	Set of 7 singles on 2 covers	9.00
2724-30	Set of 7 singles	14.00
2731-37	29¢ R 'n' R/R & B, Set/7 bklt. sgls. 6/16/93 Cleveland, OH & Santa Monica, CA (same cancel ea. city)	14.00
2731-37	Set of 7 singles of 2 covers	9.00
2737a	Booklet Pane of 8	7.00
2737b	Booklet Pane of 4	4.00
2737a,2737b	Booklet Panes on 1 cover	10.00
2741-45	29¢ Space Fantasy, bklt. sgls. 1/25/93 Huntsville, AL	10.00
2745a	Booklet Pane of 5	5.00
2746	29¢ Percy Lavon Julian 1/29/93 Chicago, IL	1.75
2747	29¢ Oregon Trail 2/12/93 Salem, OR	1.75
2748	29¢ World University Games 2/25/93 Buffalo, NY	2.00
2749	29¢ Grace Kelly 3/24/93 Hollywood, CA	1.75
2750-53	29¢ Circus 4/6/93 DC	4.00
2750-53	Set of 4 singles	10.00
2754	29¢ Cherokee Strip 4/17/93 Enid, OK	1.75
2755	29¢ Dean Acheson 4/21/93 DC	1.75
2756-59	29¢ Sport Horses 5/1/93 Louisville, KY	4.00
2756-59	Set of 4 singles	10.00
2760-64	29¢ Garden Flowers, bklt. sgls. 5/15/93 Spokane, WA	10.00
2764a	Booklet Pane of 5	5.00
2765	29¢ World War II S/S of 10 5/31/93	8.00
2765a-j	Set of 10 singles	20.00
2766	29¢ Joe Louis 6/22/93 Detroit, MI	3.00
2767-70	29¢ Broadway Musicals, bkt. sgls. 7/14/93 New York, NY	8.00
2770a	Booklet Pane of 4	4.00
2771-74	29¢ Country Music attd. 9/25/93 Nashville, TN	4.00
2771-74	Set of 4 singles	8.00
2775-78	29¢ Country Music, bklt. sgls. 9/25/93 Nashville, TN	8.00
2778a	Booklet Pane of 4	4.00
2779-82	29¢ National Postal Museum 7/30/93 DC	4.00
2779-82	Set of 4 singles	10.00
2783-84	29¢ Deaf Communication, pair 9/30/93	2.25
2783-84	Set of 2 singles	4.00
2785-88	29¢ Children's Classics, block of 4 10/1/93	4.00
2785-88	Set of 4 singles	10.00
2789	29¢ Batista's Madonna & Child 10/21/93 Raleigh, NC	1.75
2790	29¢ Madonna & Child Booklet Single	1.75
2790a	Booklet Pane of 4	4.00
2791-94	29¢ Contemp. Christmas attd. 10/21/93 New York, NY	4.00
2791-94	Set of 4 singles	10.00
2795-98	29¢ Contemp. Christmas, 4 bklt. singles	10.00
2798a	Booklet Pane of 10 (3 snowmen)	8.00
2798b	Booklet Pane of 10 (2 snowmen)	8.00
2799-2802	29¢ Contemp. Christmas, self-adhes. (4) 10/28/93 NY, NY	9.00
2802a	Pane of 12	10.00
2803	29¢ Snowman, self-adhesive	1.75
2803a	Pane of 18	14.00
2804	29¢ Northern Mariana Isles 11/4/93 DC	1.75
2805	29¢ Columbus-Puerto Rico 11/19/93 San Juan, PR	1.75
2806	29¢ AIDS Awareness 12/1/93 New York, NY	1.75
2806a	29¢ AIDS, booklet single 12/1/93 New York, NY	1.75
2806b	Booklet Pane of 5	5.00

FIRST DAY OF ISSUE

2817

Scott #	Description	Price
	1994	
2807-11	29¢ Winter Olympics, Strip of 5, 1/6/94 Salt Lake City, UT	5.00
2807-11	Set of 5 Singles	10.00
2812	29¢ Edward R. Murrow 1/21/94 Pullman, WA	1.75
2813	29¢ Love & Sunrise, self-adhesive sgl. 1/27/94 Loveland, OH	1.75
2813a	Pane of 18	14.00
2813v	Coil Pair with paper backing	2.25
2814	29¢ Love & Dove, booklet single 2/14/94 Niagara Falls, NY	1.75
2814a	Booklet Pane of 10	7.00
2814C	29¢ Love & Dove, Sheet Stamp 6/11/94 Niagara Falls, NY	1.75
2815	52¢ Love & Doves 2/14/94 Niagara Falls, NY	2.00
2816	29¢ Dr. Allison Davis 2/1/94 Williamstown, MA	1.75
2817	29¢ Chinese New Year, Dog 2/5/94 Pomona, CA	2.50
2818	29¢ Buffalo Soldiers 4/22/94 Dallas, TX	1.75
2819-28	29¢ Silent Screen Stars 4/27/94 San Francisco, CA	8.00
2819-28	Set of 10 Singles	20.00
2819-28	Set of 10 on 2 covers	9.50
2833a	29¢ Summer Garden Flowers 4/28/94 Cincinnati, OH	5.00
2829-33	Set of 5 Singles	10.00
2834	29¢ World Cup Soccer 5/26/94	1.75
2835	40¢ World Cup Soccer 5/26/94	2.00
2836	50¢ World Cup Soccer 5/26/94	2.00
2837	29¢,40¢,50¢ Soccer Souvenir Sheet of 3 5/26/94	3.50
2838	29¢ World War II Souvenir Sht of 10 6/6/94 U.S.S. Normandy	8.00
2838a-j	Set of 10 Singles	20.00
2839	29¢ Norman Rockwell 7/1/94 Stockbridge, MA	1.75
2840	50¢ Norman Rockwell, S/S of 4 7/1/94 Stockbridge, MA	5.75
2841	29¢ Moon Landing Souvenir Sheet of 12 7/20/94	10.75
2841a	Single from Souvenir Sheet	1.75
2842	$9.95 Moon Landing, Express Mail 7/20/94	25.00
2843-47	29¢ Locomotives, booklet singles 7/28/94 Chama, NM	10.00
2847a	Booklet Pane of 5	5.00
2848	29¢ George Meany 8/16/94	1.75
2849-53	29¢ Popular Singers 9/1/94 New York, NY	5.00
2849-53	Set of 5 Singles	10.00
2854-61	29¢ Blues & Jazz Artists 9/17/94 Greenville, MI	8.00
2854-61	Set of 8 on 2 covers	9.00
2854-61	Set of 8 Singles	16.00
2862	29¢ James Thurber 9/10/94 Columbus, OH	1.75
2863-66	29¢ Wonders of the Sea 10/1/94 Honolulu, HI	4.00
2863-66	Set of 4 Singles	8.00
2867-68	29¢ Cranes 10/9/94	2.25
2867-68	Set of 2 Singles	4.00
2869	29¢ Legends of the West, Pane of 20 10/8/94 Tucson, AZ, Laramie, WY and Lawton, OK	17.50
2869a-t	Set of 20 Singles	40.00
2869a-t	Set of four covers, 2 blocks of 4 and 2 blocks of 6	22.50
2871	29¢ Madonna & Child 10/20/94	1.75
2871a	Booklet single	1.75
2871b	Booklet Pane of 10	8.00
2872	29¢ Christmas Stocking 10/20/94 Harmony, MN	1.75
2872v	Booklet single	1.75
2872a	Booklet Pane of 20	14.50
2873	29¢ Santa Claus, self-adhesive 10/20/94 Harmony, MN	1.75
2873a	Pane of 12	10.00
2873v	Coil pair on paper backing	2.25
2874	29¢ Cardinal in Snow, self-adhesive 10/20/94 Harmony, MN	1.75
2874a	Pane of 18	14.00
2875	$2 Bureau of Engraving Centennial Souvenir sheet of 4 11/3/94 New York, NY	18.50
2875a	$2 Madison single from souvenir sheet	5.50
2876	29¢ Year of the Boar 12/30/94 Sacramento, CA	1.75
	1994 Interim Regular Issues	
2877	(3¢) Dove, ABN, Light blue 12/13/94	1.90
2878	(3¢) Dove, SVS, Darker blue 12/13/94	1.90
2879	(20¢) "G" Postcard Rate, BEP, Black "G" 12/13/94	1.95
2880	(20¢) "G" Postcard Rate, SVS, Red "G" 12/13/94	1.95
2881	(32¢) "G," BEP, Black "G" 12/13/94	1.90
2882	(32¢) "G," SVS, Red "G" 12/13/94	1.90
2881-82	(32¢) "G" Combo 12/13/94	2.75
2883	(32¢) "G," BEP, Black "G", Booklet Single 12/13/94	1.90
2883a	Booklet Pane of 10, BEP	8.50
2884	(32¢) "G," ABN, Blue "G", Booklet Single 12/13/94	1.90
2884a	Booklet Pane of 10, ABN	8.50
2885	(32¢) "G," KCS, Red "G", Booklet Single 12/13/94	1.90

U.S. FIRST DAY COVERS

Scott #	Description	Pric
2885a	Booklet Pane of 10, KCS	8.5
2886	(32¢) "G," Surface Tagged, self-adhesive 12/13/94	1.9
2886a	Pane of 18, Self-Adhesive	15.0
2887	(32¢) "G," Overall Tagging, self-adhesive 12/13/94	1.
2887a	Pane of 18, self-adhesive	15.0
2888	(25¢) "G" Presort, Coil 12/13/94	1.9
2888,2393	(25¢) "G" Presort and (5¢) "G" Non-profit Combo 12/13/94	2.4
2889	(32¢) "G" Coil, BEP, Black "G" 12/13/94	1.9
2890	(32¢) "G" Coil, ABN, Blue "G" 12/13/94	1.
2891	(32¢) "G" Coil, SVS, Red "G" 12/13/94	1.9
2892	(32¢) "G" Coil, Rouletted, Red "G" 12/13/94	1.9
	1995 Interim Rate Coil Stamps	
2893	(5¢) "G" Non-Profit, 12/13/94 date, available for mail order sale 1/12/95	1.9
2902	(5¢) Butte 3/10/95 State College, PA	1.9
2905	(10¢) Automobile 3/10/95 State College, PA	1.9
2908	(15¢) Auto Tail Fin, BEP 3/17/95 New York, NY	1.
2909	(15¢) Auto Tail Fin, SVS 3/17/95 New York, NY	1.9
2908-9	(15¢) Auto Tail Fin, Combo with BEP and SVS Singles	2.2
2911	(25¢) Juke Box, BEP 3/17/95 New York, NY	1.
2912	(25¢) Juke Box, SVS 3/17/95 New York, NY	1.
2911-12	(25¢) Juke Box, Combo with BEP and SVS singles	2.
	1995 Transportation Coils	
...	20¢ Cog Railway Car 6/9/95 Dallas, TX	1.9
...	32¢ Ferry Boat 6/2/95 McLean, VA	1.
	1995 Regular Issues	
2919	32¢ Flag over Field, self-adhesive 3/17/95 New York, NY	1.9
2919a	Pane of 18, Self-adhesive	14.5
2920	32¢ Flag over Porch, sheet stamp 5/19/95 Denver, CO	1.9
2920a	32¢ Flag over Porch, BEP, coil 5/19/95 Denver, CO	1.
...	32¢ Flag over Porch, SVS, coil 5/19/95 Denver, CO	1.9
...	32¢ Flag over Porch, Combo with BEP and SVS singles	2.5
...	32¢ Flag over Porch, booklet single 5/19/95 Denver, CO	1.9
...	Booklet Pane of 10	8.5
...	32¢ Flag over Porch, self-adhesive 4/18/95	1.9
...	Pane of 20, self-adhesive	15.5
...	32¢ Pink Rose, self-adhesive 6/2/95 McLean, VA	1.9
...	Pane of 20, self-adhesive	15.5
...	20¢ Blue Jay, Bklt. sgl. 6/15/95 Kansas City, MO	1.9
...	Booklet Pane of 10	8.5
...	$3 Challenger Shuttle 6/22/95 Anaheim, CA	7.7
...	$10.75 Endeavor Shuttle 8/4/95 Irvine, CA	25.0
...	32¢ Peach, Bklt. sgl. 6/17/95 Sparks, NV	1.9
...	32¢ Pear, Bklt. sgl. 6/17/95 Sparks, NV	1.9
...	32¢ Peach & Pear, Attached Pair	2.5
...	Booklet Pane of 10	8.5
...	32¢ Peach, self-adhesive 6/17/95 Sparks, NV	1.9
...	32¢ Pear, self-adhesive 6/17/95 Sparks, NV	1.9
...	32¢ Peach & Pear, Pair	2.5
...	Pane of 20, self-adhesive	15.5
	1995 Great American Series	
...	32¢ Milton S. Hershey 9/13/95 Hershey, PA	1.9
...	55¢ Alice Hamilton, M.D. 7/ /95	2.2
...	78¢ Alice Paul 8/18/95 Mount Laurel, NJ	2.7
	1995	
2948	(32¢) Love & Cherub 2/1/95 Valentines, VA	1.9
2949	(32¢) Love & Cherub, self-adhesive 2/1/95 Valentines, VA	1.9
2949a	Pane of 20, self-adhesive	15.5
2950	32¢ Florida Statehood 3/3/95 Tallahassee, FL	1.9
2951-54	32¢ Earth Day/Kids Care attd. 4/20/95 DC	4.
2951-54	Set of 4 singles	8.0
2955	32¢ Richard Nixon 4/26/95 Yorba Linda, CA	1.
2956	32¢ Bessie Coleman 4/27/95 Chicago, IL	1.9
...	32¢ Love-Cherub 5/12/95 Lakeville, PA	1.9
...	32¢ Love-Cherub, booklet single	1.
...	Booklet Pane of 10	8.5
...	55¢ Love-Cherub 5/12/95 Lakeville, PA	2.2
...	55¢ Love-Cherub, self-adhesive single	2.2
...	55¢ Pane of 20, self-adhesive	21.5
...	32¢ Recreational Sports, Strip of 5 5/20/95 Jupiter, FL	5.5
...	Set of 5 singles	10.0
...	32¢ POW & MIA 5/29/95 DC	1.9
...	32¢ Marilyn Monroe 6/1/95 Hollywood, CA	1.
...	Pane of 20 on one cover	16.5
...	32¢ Texas Statehood 6/16/95 Austin, TX	1.9
...	32¢ Great Lakes Lighthouses, bklt. sgls. 6/18/95 Cheboygan,MI	10.0
...	Booklet Pane of 5	5.5
...	32¢ United Nations 6/26/95 San Francisco, CA	1.9
...	32¢ Civil War, Miniature Sht. of 20, 6/29/95 Gettysburg, PA	16.0
...	Set of 20 singles	40.0
...	32¢ Carousel Horses attd. 7/21/95 Lahaska, PA	4.
...	Set of 4 singles	8.0
...	32¢ Fall Garden Flowers, bklt. sgles. 8/ /95	10.0
...	Booklet Pane of 5	5.
...	32¢ Prehistoric Animals attd. 8/24/95 St. Louis, MO	4.
...	Set of 4 singles	8.0
...	32¢ Women's Suffrage 8/26/95 DC	1.
...	32¢ Louis Armstrong 9/1/95 New Orleans, LA	1.
...	32¢ Jazz Musicians 9/1/95 Monterey, CA	8.
...	Set of 10 singles	20.
...	32¢ World War II s/s of 10 9/2/95 Honolulu, HI	8.
...	Set of 10 singles	20.

NOTE: Listings for late 1995 issues are tentative based on information available during editing.

JOHN F. KENNEDY

Prices are for covers with PRINTED CACHETS and Wash, D.C. cancels. Covers with cancels from other cities, except as noted, sell for somewhat less.

929	Hoover 3/4/29 **(Uncacheted)**	150.00
933	Roosevelt 3/4/33	50.00
937	Roosevelt 1/20/37	225.00
941	Roosevelt 1/20/41	225.00
945	Roosevelt 1/20/45	250.00
945	Truman 4/12/45	250.00
949	Truman 1/20/49	60.00
953	Eisenhower 1/20/53	16.00
957	Eisenhower 1/21/57	12.00
961	Kennedy 1/20/61	20.00
963	Johnson 11/22/63 Dayton, OH or New York, NY	90.00

INAUGURATION COVERS

DWIGHT D. EISENHOWER

1965	Johnson 1/20/65	8.00
1969	Nixon 1/20/69	10.00
1973	Nixon 1/20/73	8.00
1974	Ford 8/9/74	6.00
1977	Carter 1/20/77	4.00
1981	Reagan 1/20/81	3.00
1985	Reagan 1/20/85	3.00
1989	Bush 1/20/89	3.00
1993	Clinton 1/20/93	3.00

1901

The listing below omits prices on FDC's which are extremely rare or where sufficient pricing information is not available. *Due to market volatility, prices are subject to change without notice.*

Prices are for unaddressed FDC's with common cachets and cancels which do not obscure the Pl. #. Strips of 3 must have a plate # on the center stamp.

Scott #	Description	Pl# Pr.	Pl# Str of 3
1897	1¢ Omnibus 8/19/83		
	Pl # 1,2	8.50	12.50
2225	1¢ Omnibus Re-engraved 11/26/86		
	Pl# 1	6.50	12.50
1897A	2¢ Locomotive 5/20/82		
	Pl# 3,4	12.50	20.00
2226	2¢ Locomotive Re-engraved 3/6/87		
	Pl# 1	...	8.50
1898	3¢ Handcar 3/25/83		
	Pl# 1,2,3,4	10.00	20.00
2252	3¢ Conestoga Wagon 2/29/88		
	Pl# 1	...	7.50
2123	3.4¢ School Bus 6/8/85		
	Pl# 1,2	6.50	10.00
1898A	4¢ Stagecoach 8/19/82		
	Pl# 1,2,3,4	10.00	18.50
2228	4¢ Stagecoach, "B" Press 8/15/86 **(eku)**		
	Pl# 1	...	325.00
2451	4¢ Steam Carriage 1/25/91		
	Pl# 1	...	6.50
2124	4.9¢ Buckboard 6/21/85		
	Pl# 3,4	7.50	13.50
1899	5¢ Motorcycle 10/10/83		
	Pl# 1,2	10.00	15.00
	Pl# 3,4	...	...
2253	5¢ Milk Wagon 9/25/87		
	Pl# 1	...	7.50
2452	5¢ Circus Wagon 8/31/90		
	Pl# 1	...	6.50
2452B	5¢ Circus Wagon, Gravure 12/8/92		
	Pl# A1,A2	...	6.50
2453	5¢ Canoe 5/25/91		
	Pl# 1	...	6.50
2454	5¢ Canoe, Gravure Print 10/22/91		
	Pl# S11	...	6.50
1900	5.2¢ Sleigh 3/21/83		
	Pl# 1,2	15.00	30.00
1900a	Pl# 1,2	...	...
2254	5.3¢ Elevator 9/16/88		
	Pl# 1	...	7.50
2125	5.5¢ Star Route Truck 11/1/86		
	Pl# 1	7.50	12.50
2125a	Pl# 1	...	40.00
1901	5.9¢ Bicycle 2/17/82		
	Pl# 3,4	15.00	25.00
1901a	Pl# 3,4	...	...
2126	6¢ Tricycle 5/6/85		
	Pl# 1	6.50	10.00
2126a	Pl# 1	...	...
2127	7.1¢ Tractor Coil 2/6/87		
	Pl# 1	7.50	12.50
2127a	Pl# 1	...	35.00
2127a	7.1¢ Zip + 4 Pl# 1 5/26/89	...	7.50
1902	7.4¢ Baby Buggy 4/7/84		
	Pl# 2	10.00	20.00
2255	7.6¢ Carreta 8/30/88		
	Pl# 1	...	7.50
2128	8.3¢ Ambulance 6/21/86		
	Pl# 1,2	7.50	12.50
2128a	Pl# 1,2	...	...
2231	8.3¢ Ambulance, "B" Press 8/29/86 **(eku)**		
	Pl# 1	...	...
2256	8.4¢ Wheelchair 8/12/88		
	Pl# 1	...	7.50

PLATE NO. COIL FIRST DAY COVERS

Scott #	Description	Pl# Pr.	Pl# Str of
2129	8.5¢ Tow Truck 1/24/87		
	Pl# 1	6.50	10.00
2129a	Pl# 1	...	17.50
1903	9.3¢ Mail Wagon 12/15/81		
	Pl# 1,2	20.00	37.50
	Pl# 3,4	...	...
2257	10¢ Canal Boat 4/11/87		
	Pl# 1	...	8.50
2457	10¢ Tractor Trailer 5/25/91		
	Pl# 1	...	6.50
2604	10¢ Eagle & Shield, **ABNCo** 12/13/91	...	6.50
	Any Pl# **(except A12213 & A32333)**	...	6.50
	Pl# A12213	...	27.50
	Pl# A32333	...	125.00
2605	10¢ Eagle & Shield, **BEP** 5/29/93		
	Pl# 11111	...	6.50
2606	10¢ Eagle & Shield, **SV**		
	Pl# S11111	...	6.50
2130	10.1¢ Oil Wagon 4/18/85		
	Pl# 1	7.50	12.50
2130a	10.1¢ Red Prec. Pl# 2 6/27/88	...	8.50
1904	10.9¢ Hansom Cab 3/26/82		
	Pl# 1,2	17.50	35.00
1904a	Pl# 1,2	...	...
1905	11¢ Caboose 2/3/84		
	Pl# 1	15.00	35.00
2131	11¢ Stutz Bearcat 6/11/85		
	Pl# 3,4	...	12.50
2132	12¢ Stanley Steamer 4/2/85		
	Pl# 1,2	7.50	12.50
2132a	Pl# 1	...	...
2133	12.5¢ Pushcart 4/18/85		
	Pl# 1	7.50	12.50
2258	13¢ Patrol Wagon 10/29/88		
	Pl# 1	...	7.50
2259	13.2¢ Coal Car 7/19/88		
	Pl# 1	...	7.50
2134	14¢ Iceboat 3/23/85		
	Pl# 1,2	10.00	15.00
2260	15¢ Tugboat 7/12/88		
	Pl# 1	...	7.50
2261	16.7¢ Popcorn Wagon 7/7/88		
	Pl# 1	...	7.50
1906	17¢ Electric Car 6/25/82		
	Pl# 1,2	17.50	30.00
2135	17¢ Dog Sled 8/20/86		
	Pl# 2	7.50	12.50
2262	17.5¢ Racing Car 9/25/87		
	Pl# 1	...	8.50
2262a	Pl# 1	...	10.00
1891	18¢ Flag 4/24/81		
	Pl# 1	75.00	225.00
	Pl# 2	225.00	...
	Pl# 3	325.00	...
	Pl# 4	200.00	...
	Pl# 5	125.00	...
1907	18¢ Surrey 5/18/81		
	Pl# 1	30.00	...
	Pl# 2	20.00	45.00
	Pl# 3,4,7,9,10	...	...
	Pl# 5	100.00	...
	Pl# 6,8	100.00	...
2149	18¢ GW Monument 11/6/85		
	Pl# 1112,3333	20.00	35.00
2149a	Pl# 11121	45.00	...
	Pl# 33333	45.00	...
2529	19¢ Fishing Boat 8/8/91		
	Pl# 1111,1212	...	7.50
1895	20¢ Flag 12/17/81		
	Pl# 1	20.00	40.00
	Pl# 2	100.00	200.00
	Pl# 3	200.00	300.00

2259/1

2005

ott #	Description	Pl# Pr.	Pl# Str of 3
08	20¢ Fire Pumper 12/10/81		
	Pl# 1,7,8	...	...
	Pl# 2	150.00	300.00
	Pl# 3,4	15.00	40.00
	Pl# 5,6	100.00	175.00
05	20¢ Consumer 4/27/82		
	Pl# 1,2,3,4	25.00	...
63	20¢ Cable Car 10/28/88		
	Pl# 1	...	7.50
	Pl# 2	...	60.00
64	20.5¢ Fire Engine 9/28/88		
	Pl# 1	...	7.50
65	21¢ Railroad Mail Car 8/16/88		
	Pl# 1	...	7.50
	Pl# 2	...	...
50	21.1¢ Pre-Sort 10/22/85		
	Pl# 111111	15.00	25.00
50a	Pl# 111111	35.00	...
12	(22¢) "D" Coil 2/1/85		
	Pl# 1,2	10.00	17.50
15	22¢ Flag over Capitol 3/29/85		
	Pl# 1	35.00	65.00
	Pl# 2	15.00	22.50
15b	22¢ Test Coil 5/23/87		
	Pl# T1	...	12.50
64	23¢ Lunch Wagon 4/12/91		
	Pl# 2	...	8.50
	Pl# 3	...	7.50
07	23¢ Flag, First Class pre-sort 9/27/91	...	7.50
08	23¢ "USA" First Class pre-sort **ABNCo**, 7/21/92		
	Pl# A1111, A2222	...	7.50
08A	23¢ "USA" First Class pre-sort **BEP**, 10/9/92		
	Pl# 1111	...	7.50
08B	23¢ "USA" First Class pre-sort **SV**, 5/14/93		
	Pl# S111	...	7.50
66	24.1¢ Tandem Bicycle 10/26/88		
	Pl# 1	...	7.50
36	25¢ Bread Wagon 11/22/86		
	Pl# 1	7.50	12.50
79	(25¢) "E" & Earth 3/22/88		
	Pl# 1111,1222	...	7.50
	Pl# 1211	...	10.00
	Pl# 2222	...	25.00
80	25¢ Flag over Yosemite 5/20/88		
	Pl# 1,2	...	10.00
	Pl# 3,4	...	125.00
80v	Pre-Phosphor Paper 2/14/89		
	Pl# 5	...	17.50
	Pl# 6,9	...	35.00
	Pl# 7,8	...	8.50
	Pl# 10	...	...
81	25¢ Honeybee 9/2/88		
	Pl# 1	...	10.00
	Pl# 2	...	30.00
18	(29¢) "F" & Flower 1/22/91		
	Pl# 1111,1222,2222	...	10.00
	Pl# 1211	...	...
	Pl# 2211	...	25.00

2266

Scott #	Description	Pl# Pr.	Pl# Str of 3
2523	29¢ Flag over Mt. Rushmore 3/29/91		
	Pl# 1-7	7.50	...
2523A	29¢ Mt. Rushmore, Gravure Print 7/4/91		
	Pl# 11111	...	7.50
2525	29¢ Flower, rouletted 8/16/91		
	Pl# S1111	...	7.50
2526	29¢ Flower, perforated 3/3/92		
	Pl# 2222	7.50	...
2609	29¢ Flag over White House 4/23/92	...	7.50
CV31	**29¢ Variable Rate Coil 8/20/92**		
	Pl# 1	**...**	**7.50**
2468	$1.00 Seaplane 4/20/90		
	Pl# 1	...	10.00
O135	20¢ Official, Pl# 1	27.50	75.00
O139	(22¢) "D" Official, Pl# 1	32.50	75.00

C23

Cacheted prices are for FDC's with common printed cachets.
From #C4 - C31, FDC's will usually be addressed.
Prices and Dates for #C1-3 are for First Flight Covers, NOT FDC's.

Scott #	Description	Uncacheted	Cacheted
C1	6¢ Jenny 12/16/18 NYC; Phila.,PA; DC	2500.00	...
C2	16¢ Jenny 7/15/18 NYC; Phila.,PA; DC	750.00	...
C3	24¢ Jenny 5/15/18 NYC; Phila.,PA; DC	700.00	...
C4	8¢ Propeller 8/15/23 DC	350.00	...
C5	16¢ Air Service Emblem 8/17/23 DC	550.00	...
C6	24¢ DeHavilland Biplane 8/21/23 DC	700.00	...
C7	10¢ Map 2/13/26 DC	75.00	...
	Chicago, IL	90.00	...
	Detroit, MI	90.00	...
	Cleveland, OH	120.00	...
	Dearborn, MI	120.00	...
	Unofficial city	175.00	...
C8	15¢ Map 9/18/26 DC	90.00	...
C9	20¢ Map 1/25/27 DC	100.00	...
	New York, NY	110.00	...
	1st Albert E. Gorham cachet	...	**250.00**
C10	10¢ Lindbergh 6/18/27 DC	30.00	175.00
	St. Louis, MO	30.00	175.00
	Detroit, MI	40.00	175.00
	Little Falls, MN	40.00	175.00
	Air Mail Field, Chicago, unofficial	150.00	...
	Unofficial city (other than AMF Chicago)	175.00	...
	1st Milton Mauck cachet	...	**175.00**
C10a	10¢ **Booklet Single** 5/26/28 DC	100.00	...
	Booklet Sgl., Cleveland Midwest Phil. Sta.	100.00	...
	#C10a sgl. & 645 Cleveland Midwest Sta	150.00	...
C10a	10¢ **Booklet Pane of 3** 5/26/28 DC	875.00	...
	B. Pane of 3, Cleveland Midwest Sta.	825.00	...
	#C10a & 645 on one FDC, Clev. Midwst.	900.00	...
	Booklet Pane w/o tab, DC or Cleveland	425.00	...
C11	5¢ Beacon, pair 7/25/28 DC	50.00	250.00
	Single on FDC	175.00	...
	Single on FDC with postage due	250.00	...
	Unofficial city (pair)	250.00	...
C12	5¢ Winged Globe 2/10/30 DC	12.00	90.00
C13	65¢ Graf Zeppelin 4/19/30 DC	1400.00	2500.00
C13	On flight cover, any date	295.00	...
C14	$1.30 Graf Zeppelin 4/19/30 DC	1000.00	2500.00
C14	On flight cover, any date	525.00	...
C15	$2.60 Graf Zeppelin 4/19/30 DC	1150.00	2500.00
C15	On flight cover, any date	800.00	...
C13-15	Graf Zeppelin, cplt. set on one cover	15000.00	...
C16	5¢ Winged Globe, Rotary 8/19/31 DC	175.00	...
C17	8¢ Winged Globe 9/26/32 DC	16.50	45.00
C17	Combo with UC7	60.00	...
C18	50¢ Zeppelin 10/2/33 New York, NY	150.00	250.00
	Akron, OH 10/4/33	225.00	325.00
	DC 10/5/33	225.00	350.00
	Miami, FL 10/6/33	175.00	325.00
	Chicago, IL 10/7/33	225.00	325.00
C18	On flight cover, any date	95.00	...
C19	6¢ Winged Globe 6/30/34 Baltimore, MD	200.00	375.00
	New York, NY	**800.00**	**1000.00**
	First Day of Rate 7/1/34 DC	...	35.00
C19	Combo with UC3	60.00	...

1935-39

Scott #	Description	Price
C20	25¢ China Clipper 11/22/35 DC	40.00
	San Francisco, CA	40.00
C21	20¢ China Clipper 2/15/37 DC	55.00
C22	50¢ China Clipper 2/15/37 DC	60.00
C21-22	China Clipper on one cover	125.00
C23	6¢ Eagle Holding Shield 5/14/38 Dayton, OH	15.00
	St. Petersburg, FL	15.00
C24	30¢ Winged Globe 5/16/39 New York, NY	40.00

AIR MAIL FIRST DAY COVERS

Scott #	Description	Price
C25	6¢ Plane 6/25/41 DC	5.00
C25a	Booklet Pane of 3 (3/18/43) DC	30.00
	Booklet single	10.00
C26	8¢ Plane 3/21/44 DC	5.00
C27	10¢ Plane 8/15/41 Atlantic City, NJ	7.50
C28	15¢ Plane 8/19/41 Baltimore, MD	7.50
C29	20¢ Plane 8/27/41 Philadelphia, PA	10.00
C30	30¢ Plane 9/25/41 Kansas City, MO	15.00
C31	50¢ Plane 10/29/41 St. Louis, MO	30.00
C25-31,C25a	Transport Plane set of 8 covers	100.00

From #C32 - Date, prices are for unaddressed FDC's & common cachets.

1946-59

Scott #	Description	Price
C32	5¢ DC-4 Skymaster 9/25/46 DC	1.75
C33	5¢ Small Plane (DC-4) 3/26/47 DC	1.75
C34	10¢ Pan Am. Building 8/30/47 DC	1.75
C35	15¢ New York Skyline 8/20/47 NY, NY	2.00
C36	25¢ Bay Bridge 7/30/47 San Francisco, CA	2.50
C37	5¢ Small Plane, coil 1/15/48 DC	1.75
C38	5¢ NY City Jubilee 7/31/48 New York, NY	2.00
C39	6¢ DC-4 Skymaster 1/18/49 DC	1.75
C39a	Booklet Pane of 6 11/18/49 NY, NY	12.00
C40	6¢ Alexandria 5/11/49 Alexandria, VA	2.00
C41	6¢ DC-4 Skymaster, coil 8/25/49 DC	1.75
C42	10¢ Post Office Bldg. 11/18/49 New Orleans, LA	1.75
C43	15¢ Globe & Doves 10/7/49 Chicago, IL	3.00
C44	25¢ Boeing 11/30/49 Seattle, WA	4.00
C45	6¢ Wright Brothers 12/17/49 Kitty Hawk, NC	2.00
C46	80¢ Diamond Head 3/26/52 Honolulu, HI	15.00
C47	6¢ Powered Flight 5/29/53 Dayton, OH	2.00
C48	4¢ Eagle in Flight 9/3/54 Phila., PA	1.75
C49	6¢ Air Force 8/1/57 DC	2.00
C50	5¢ Eagle 7/31/58 Colorado Springs, CO	1.75
C51	7¢ Blue Jet 7/31/58 Philadelphia, PA	1.75
C51a	Booklet Pane of 6 7/31/58 San Antonio, TX	7.00
C52	7¢ Blue Jet, coil 7/31/58 Miami, FL	1.75
C53	7¢ Alaska 1/3/59 Juneau, AK	1.75
C54	7¢ Balloon 8/17/59 Lafayette, IN	1.75
C55	7¢ Hawaii Sthd. 8/21/59 Honolulu, HI	2.00
C56	10¢ Pan Am Games 8/27/59 Chicago, IL	1.75

1959-68

Scott #	Description	Price
C57	10¢ Liberty Bell 6/10/60 Miami, FL	1.75
C58	15¢ Statue of Liberty 11/20/59 NY, NY	1.75
C59	25¢ Lincoln 4/22/60 San Francisco, CA	1.75
C59a	Luminescent 12/29/66 DC	30.00
C60	7¢ Red Jet 8/12/60 Arlington, VA	1.75
C60a	Booklet Pane of 6 8/19/60 St. Louis, MO	8.00
C61	7¢ Red Jet, coil 10/22/60 Atlantic City, NJ	1.75
C62	13¢ Liberty Bell 6/28/61 New York, NY	1.75
C62a	Luminescent 2/15/67 DC	30.00
C63	15¢ Statue of Liberty 1/31/61 Buffalo, NY	1.75
C63a	Luminescent 1/11/67 DC	30.00
C64	8¢ Jet over Capitol, coil 12/5/62 DC	1.75
C64a	Luminescent 8/1/63 Dayton, OH	1.75
C64b	Booklet Pane of 5 12/5/62 DC	1.75
C65	8¢ Jet over Capitol, coil 12/5/62 DC	1.75
C65a	Luminescent 1/14/65 New Orleans, LA	30.00
C66	15¢ Montgomery Blair 5/3/63 Silver Springs, MD	2.50
C67	6¢ Bald Eagle 7/12/63 Boston, MA	1.75
C67a	Luminescent 2/15/67 DC	30.00
C68	8¢ Amelia Earhart 7/24/63 Atchinson, KS	3.00
C69	8¢ Robert Goddard 10/5/64 Roswell, NM	2.50
C70	8¢ Alaska Purchase 3/30/67 Sitka, AK	1.75
C71	20¢ Columbia Jays 4/26/67 New York, NY	2.50
C72	10¢ 50-Star Runway 1/5/68 San Fran., CA	1.75
C72b	Bklt. Pane of 8 1/5/68 San Fran., CA	3.00
C72c	Bklt. Pane of 5 1/6/68 DC	125.00
C73	10¢ 50-Star Runway, coil 1/5/68 San Francisco, CA	1.75
C74	10¢ Jenny 5/15/68 DC	2.00
C75	20¢ "USA" & Jet 11/22/68 New York, NY	1.75

C46

AIR MAIL FIRST DAY COVERS

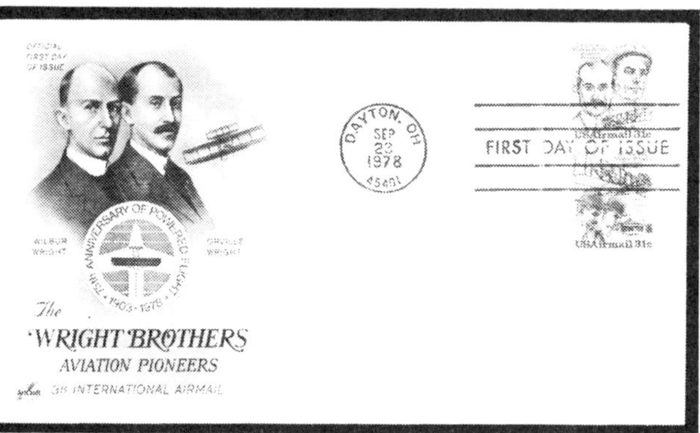

C91-92

ott #	Description	Price
	1969-91	
6	10¢ First Man on Moon 9/9/69 DC	5.00
7	9¢ Delta Plane 5/15/71 Kitty Hawk, NC	1.75
8	11¢ Jet Silhouette 5/7/71 Spokane, WA	1.75
8a	Booklet Pane of 4 5/7/71 Spokane, WA	3.00
9	13¢ Winged Envelope 11/16/73 NY, NY	1.75
9a	Bklt. Pane of 5 12/27/73 Chicago, IL	3.00
0	17¢ Statue of Liberty 7/13/71 Lakehurst, NJ	1.75
1	21¢ "USA" & Jet 5/21/71 DC	1.75
2	11¢ Jet Silhouette, coil 5/7/71 Spokane, WA	1.75
3	13¢ Winged Envelope, coil 12/27/73 Chicago, IL	1.75
4	11¢ City of Refuge 5/3/72 Honaunau, HI	1.75
5	11¢ Olympics 8/17/72 DC	1.75
6	11¢ Electronics 7/10/73 New York, NY	1.75
7	18¢ Statue of Liberty 1/11/74 Hampstead, NY	1.75
8	26¢ Mt. Rushmore 1/2/74 Rapid City, SD	1.75
9	25¢ Plane and Globe 1/2/76 Honolulu, HI	1.75
0	31¢ Plane, Globe & Flag 1/2/76 Honolulu, HI	1.75
	#C89-90 on one FDC	3.00
1-92	31¢ Wright Bros. attd. 9/23/78 Dayton, OH	2.50
1-92	Wright Bros. set of 2 singles	3.50
3-94	21¢ Octave Chanute attd. 3/29/79 Chanute, KS	2.50
3-94	Octave Chanute set of 2 singles	3.50
5-96	25¢ Wiley Post attd. 11/20/79 Oklahoma City, OK	2.50
5-96	Wiley Post set of 2 singles	3.50
7	31¢ Olympic - High Jump 11/1/79 Col. Springs, CO	1.75
8	40¢ Philip Mazzel 10/13/80 DC	1.75
9	28¢ Blanche Scott 12/30/80 Hammondsport, NY	1.75
00	35¢ Glenn Curtiss 12/30/80 Hammondsport, NY	1.75
9-100	Scott & Curtiss on one cover	3.50
01-04	28¢ Olympics attd. 6/17/83 San Antonio, TX	4.00
01-04	Olympics set of 4 singles	8.00
05-08	40¢ Olympics attd. 4/8/83 Los Angeles, CA	4.50
05-08	Olympics set of 4 singles	8.00
09-12	35¢ Olympics attd. 11/4/83 Colorado Springs, CO	4.50
09-12	Olympics set of 4 singles	8.00
3	33¢ Alfred Verville 2/13/85 Garden City, NY	1.75
4	39¢ Sperry Bros. 2/13/85 Garden City, NY	1.75
5	44¢ Transpacific Airmail 2/15/85 San Francisco, CA	2.50
6	44¢ Junipero Serra 8/22/85 San Diego, CA	2.00
7	44¢ New Sweden, 350th Anniv. 3/29/88 Wilmington, DE	2.00
8	45¢ Samuel P. Langley 5/14/88 San Diego, CA	2.00
9	36¢ Igor Sikorsky 6/23/88 Stratford, CT	2.00
20	45¢ French Revolution 7/14/89 DC	2.00
21	45¢ Pre-Columbian Customs 10/12/89 San Juan, PR	2.00
22-25	45¢ Future Mail Transportation attd. 11/27/89 DC	8.00
22-25	Set of 4 singles	10.00
26	$1.80 Future Mail Trans. S/S of 4, imperf. 11/24/89 DC	7.00
27	45¢ America, Caribbean Coast 10/12/90 Grand Canyon, AZ	2.00
28	50¢ Harriet Quimby 4/27/91 Plymouth, MI	2.00
29	40¢ William T. Piper 5/17/91 Denver, CO	2.00
30	50¢ Antarctic Treaty 6/21/91 DC	2.00
31	50¢ America 10/12/91 Anchorage, AK	2.00
	1934-36 AIRMAIL SPECIAL DELIVERY ISSUES	
1	16¢ Great Seal, blue 8/30/34 Chic., IL (AAMS Conv. Sta.)	30.00
2	16¢ Great Seal, red & blue 2/10/36 DC	25.00

tt #	Description	Uncacheted	Cacheted
	1885-1931 SPECIAL DELIVERY		
	10¢ Messenger 10/1/85 Any City	*8500.00*	...
	10¢ Motorcycle,Flat plate,perf.11 7/12/22 DC	375.00	...
	15¢ Motorcycle,Flat plate,perf.11 4/11/25 DC	225.00	...
	20¢ Truck, Flat plate, perf.11 4/25/25 DC	110.00	...
	10¢ Motorcycle, Rotary 11/29/27 DC	95.00	...
EE	Electric Eye 9/8/41 DC	...	25.00
	15¢ Motorcycle, Rotary 8/6/31 Easton, PA	*1000.00*	...
	Motorcycle, Rotary 8/13/31 DC	125.00	...

SPECIAL SERVICE FIRST DAY COVERS

Scott #	Description	Uncacheted	Cacheted
	1944-1971 SPECIAL DELIVERY		
E17	13¢ Motorcycle 10/30/44	...	8.00
E18	17¢ Motorcycle 10/30/44	...	10.00
E17-18	Motorcycles on one cover	...	15.00
E19	20¢ Post Office Truck, Rotary 11/30/51 DC	...	4.50
E20	20¢ Letter & Hands 10/13/54 Boston, MA	...	2.00
E21	30¢ Letter & Hands 9/3/57 Indpls., IN	...	2.00
E22	45¢ Arrows 11/21/69 New York, NY	...	2.25
E23	60¢ Arrows 5/10/71 Phoenix, AZ	...	2.50
	1911 REGISTERED MAIL		
F1	10¢ Eagle, blue 12/1/11 Any city	*9500.00*	...
	1955 CERTIFIED MAIL		
FA1	15¢ Postman, red 6/6/55 DC	...	2.00
	POSTAGE DUE		
	1925		
J68	½¢ P. Due (4/15/25 EKU) FDC unknown	500.00	...
	1959		
J88	½¢ Red & Black 6/19/59 Any city	75.00	...
J89	1¢ Red & Black 6/19/59 Any city	75.00	...
J90	2¢ Red & Black 6/19/59 Any city	75.00	...
J91	3¢ Red & Black 6/19/59 Any city	75.00	...
J92	4¢ Red & Black 6/19/59 Any city	75.00	...
J93	5¢ Red & Black 6/19/59 Any city	115.00	...
J94	6¢ Red & Black 6/19/59 Any city	115.00	...
J95	7¢ Red & Black 6/19/59 Any city	115.00	...
J96	8¢ Red & Black 6/19/59 Any city	115.00	...
J97	10¢ Red & Black 6/19/59 Any city	115.00	...
J98	30¢ Red & Black 6/19/59 Any city	115.00	...
J99	50¢ Red & Black 6/19/59 Any city	115.00	...
J100	$1 Red & Black 6/19/59 Any city	125.00	...
J101	$5 Red & Black 6/19/59 Any city	125.00	...
	1978-85		
J102	11¢ Red & Black 1/2/78 Any city	...	5.00
J103	13¢ Red & Black 1/2/78 Any city	...	5.00
	#J102-103 on one FDC	...	7.50
J104	17¢ Red & Black 6/10/85 Any city	...	5.00
	1983-95 OFFICIAL STAMPS		
O127	1¢ Eagle 1/12/83 DC	...	1.75
O128	4¢ Eagle 1/12/83 DC	...	1.75
O129	13¢ Eagle 1/12/83 DC	...	1.75
O129A	14¢ Eagle 5/15/85 DC	...	2.00
O130	17¢ Eagle 1/12/83 DC	...	1.75
O132	$1 Eagle 1/12/83 DC	...	5.00
O133	$5 Eagle 1/12/83 DC	...	15.00
O136	22¢ Eagle 5/15/85 DC	...	1.75
O138	(14¢) "D" Eagle 2/4/85 DC	...	1.75
O143	1¢ Eagle, Offset Printing, No ¢ sign 7/5/89 DC.	...	1.75
O146	4¢ Official Mail 4/6/91 Oklahoma City, OK	...	1.75
O146A	10¢ Official Mail 10/19/93	...	1.75
O147	19¢ Official Postcard rate 5/24/91 Seattle, WA.	...	1.75
O148	23¢ Official 2nd oz. rate 5/24/91 Seattle, WA	...	1.75
...	1¢ Eagle, with ¢ sign 5/9/95 DC	...	1.90
...	20¢ Eagle, postcard rate 5/9/95 DC	...	1.90
...	23¢ Eagle, 2nd oz. rate 5/9/95 DC	...	1.90
...	1¢, 20¢, 23¢, 32¢ Coil Combo cover 5/9/95 DC	...	2.50
	1983-95 OFFICIAL COILS		
O135	20¢ Eagle, with ¢ sign 1/12/83 DC	...	1.75
	#O127-129,O130-135 on one FDC	...	15.00
O138A	15¢ Official Mail 6/11/88 Corpus Christi, TX	...	1.75
O138B	20¢ Official Mail, No ¢ sign 5/19/88 DC	...	1.75
O139	(22¢) "D" Eagle 2/4/85 DC	...	1.75
O140	(25¢) "E" Official 3/22/88 DC	...	1.75
O141	25¢ Official Mail 6/11/88 Corpus Christi, TX	...	1.75
O144	(29¢) "F" Official 1/22/91 DC	...	1.75
O145	29¢ Official Mail 5/24/91 Seattle, WA	...	1.75
O152	(32¢) "G" Official 12/13/94	...	1.90
...	32¢ Official Mail 5/9/95 DC	...	1.90
	POSTAL NOTES		
PN1	1¢ Black 2/1/45 on cplt 3 part M.O. form, any city	45.00	...
PN1-18	1¢-90¢ Black, cplt. set on 18 forms	750.00	...
	POSTAL SAVINGS		
PS11	10¢ Minuteman, red 5/1/41 Any city	175.00	...

Scott #	Description	4th Class (1/1/13)	1st Class (7/1/13)
	PARCEL POST		
Q1	1¢ Post Office Clerk, any city	3500.00	2500.00
Q2	2¢ City Carrier, any city	*2250.00*	2500.00
Q3	3¢ Railway Postal Clerk, any city	...	*3500.00*
Q4	4¢ Rural Carrier, any city	...	*3500.00*
Q5	5¢ Mail Train, any city	*4000.00*	*3500.00*

Scott #	Description	Uncacheted	Cacheted
	1925-28 SPECIAL HANDLING		
QE1	10¢ Yellow Green 6/25/28 DC	50.00	...
QE2	15¢ Yellow Green 6/25/28 DC	50.00	...
QE3	20¢ Yellow Green 6/25/28 DC	50.00	...
QE1-3	Set of 3 on one FDC	250.00	...
QE4a	25¢ Deep Green 4/11/25 DC	225.00	...

❑ Please send me your Public Auction Catalogs/Mail Sale Catalogs
❑ I'm interested in discussing the sale of my stamps

06 Walnut Street
ıiladelphia, PA 19103
ıone: 1-800-523-4648

NAME: ____

ADDRESS: ____

____

CITY: ____

STATE: ____ ZIP: ____

PHONE: ____

YOUR SOURCE FOR
UYING OR SELLING
STAMPS

70 YEARS STRONG!

FREE ISSUE RESERVATION CARD

se this card
to get your
FREE ISSUE
of
Scott
amp Monthly

Yes, I'd like to sample the next issue of Scott Stamp Monthly absolutely FREE! If I like it, I'll get a full year's subscription (11 additional issues) for the low priceof $17.95. I'll save $18.05 off the cover price.

NAME ____

ADDRESS ____

CITY ____ ST ____ ZIP ____ 4BRK9

NO COST, NO RISK OFFER

If I choose not to subscribe, I'll simply write "cancel" on the bill, return it and owe nothing. The free issue is mine to keep.
SEND NO MONEY

publisher and editor of Linn's, I promise deliver to you each week:

HE MOST up-to-the-minute news on erything from new issues to what's happen- in your area of special interest.

HE MOST complete records on topics m trends values to under collected stamps.

HE MOST useful information in regular atures such as Stamp Market Index.... of the Week... and many more.

HE WORLD'S LARGEST stamp arketplace listing shows, auctions, buying, lling and trading. — Michael Laurence

. Box 29, Sidney, OH. 45365-9923

Get the Most Out of Your Collecting!

13 ISSUES FOR ONLY $9.95 PLUS A FREE BONUS!

☐ **Yes!** Send me the next 13 big weekly issues of the color-illustrated **Linn's Stamp News** at the introductory rate of just $9.95. And, include as my **FREE BONUS,** the 96-page Linn's *Stamp Collecting Made Easy* with my paid subscription.

NAME ____

ADDRESS ____

CITY ____ STATE ____ ZIP ____

☐ **Bill Me Later** ☐ **Payment Enclosed (use envelope)**

51BG6

FEDERAL DUCK STAMP FIRST DAY COVERS

RW49

cott #	Description	Uncacheted	Cacheted
W47	$7.50 Mallards 7/1/80 DC		150.00
W48	$7.50 Ruddy Ducks 7/1/81 DC		75.00
W49	$7.50 Canvasbacks 7/1/82 DC		55.00
W50	$7.50 Pintails 7/1/83 DC		55.00
W51	$7.50 Widgeons 7/2/84 DC		50.00
W52	$7.50 Cinnamon Teal 7/1/85		45.00
W53	$7.50 Fulvous Whistling Duck 7/1/86		45.00
W54	$10.00 Red Head Ducks 7/1/87		45.00
W55	$10.00 Snow Goose 7/1/88 Any city		45.00
W56	$12.50 Lesser Scaups 6/30/89 DC		45.00
W57	$12.50 Black-Bellied Whistling Duck 6/30/90 DC		45.00
W58	$15.00 King Elders 6/30/91 DC		45.00
W59	$15.00 Spectacled Elder 6/30/92 DC		45.00
W60	$15.00 Canvasbacks 6/30/93 DC		35.00
W60	Same, Mound, MN		35.00
W61	$15.00 Redbreasted Merganser 6/30/94 DC		35.00

POSTAL STATIONERY FIRST DAY COVERS

Prices are for standard 6¾ size envelopes, unless noted otherwise.

Scott #	Description	Uncacheted	Cacheted
	1925-32		
436a	3¢ G. Washington, white paper, extra quality		
	6/16/32 DC, size 5, die 1, wmk. 29	75.00	...
	Size 8, die 1, wmk. 29	18.00	...
436e	3¢ G. Washington, white paper, extra quality		
	6/16/32 DC, size 5, die 7, wmk. 29	12.00	30.00
436f	3¢ G. Washington, white paper, extra quality		
	6/16/32 DC, size 5, die 9, wmk. 29	12.00	50.00
	Size 12, die 9, wmk. 29	18.00	...
437a	3¢ G. Washington, amber paper, standard qual.		
	7/13/32 DC, size 5, wmk. 28	50.00	...
	7/19/32 DC, size 5, wmk. 29, extra qual.	35.00	...
439	3¢ G. Washington, blue paper, standard qual.		
	7/13/32, size 5, wmk. 28	40.00	...
	Size 13, die 9, wmk. 28	65.00	...
	9/9/32 DC, size 5, wmk. 28	85.00	...
439a	3¢ G. Washington, blue paper, extra quality		
	7/19/32 DC, size 5, die 29	40.00	...
481	1½¢ G. Wash. 3/19/25 DC, size 5, wmk. 27	35.00	...
	Size 8, wmk. 27	70.00	...
	Size 13, wmk. 26	50.00	...
	Size 5, wmk. 27 with Sc#553, 582 & 598	150.00	...
	Size 8, wmk. 27 with Sc#553, 582 & 598	125.00	...
	Size 13, wmk. 26 with Sc#553	60.00	...
495	1½¢ on 1¢ B. Franklin 6/1/25 DC, size 5	50.00	...
	6/3/25 DC, size 8	65.00	...
	6/2/25 DC, size 13	60.00	...
515	1½¢ on 1¢ B. Franklin 8/1/25 Des Moines, IA		
	size 5, die 1	50.00	
521	1½¢ on 1¢ B. Franklin 10/22/25 DC		
	size 5, die 1, watermark 25	100.00	...
522a	2¢ Liberty Bell 7/27/26 Philadelphia, PA		
	Size 5, wmk. 27	20.00	30.00
	Size 5, wmk. 27 DC	22.50	32.50
	Unofficial city, Size 5, wmk. 27	35.00	45.00
	WASHINGTON BICENTENNIAL ISSUE		
523	1¢ Mount Vernon 1/1/32 DC, size 5, wmk. 29	10.00	32.50
	Size 8, wmk. 29	12.50	37.50
	Size 13, wmk. 29	10.00	32.50
524	1½¢ Mount Vernon 1/1/32 DC, size 5, wmk.29	10.00	32.50
	Size 8, wmk. 29	12.50	37.50
	Size 13, wmk. 29	10.00	32.50
525	2¢ Mount Vernon 1/1/32 DC, size 5, wmk. 29	8.00	30.00
	Size 8, wmk. 29	10.00	30.00
	Size 13, wmk. 29	8.00	30.00
526	3¢ Mount Vernon 1/1/32 DC, size 5, wmk. 29	18.00	40.00
	Size 8, wmk. 29	25.00	80.00
	Size 13, wmk. 29	20.00	60.00
527	4¢ Mount Vernon 1/1/32 DC, size 5, wmk. 29	30.00	80.00
528	5¢ Mount Vernon 1/1/32 DC, size 5, wmk. 29	18.00	40.00
	Size 8, wmk. 29	20.00	45.00
	Size 13, wmk. 29	10.00	32.50

POSTAL STATIONERY FIRST DAY COVERS

Scott #	Description	Uncacheted	Cacheted
	1932-71		
U529	6¢ G. Washington, white paper, 8/18/32		
	Los Angeles, CA, size 8, wmk 29	15.00	...
	8/19/32 DC, size 7, wmk 29	20.00	...
	8/19/32 DC, size 9, wmk 29	20.00	...
U530	6¢ G. Washington, amber paper, 8/18/32		
	Los Angeles, CA, size 8, wmk 29	15.00	...
	8/19/32 DC, size 7, wmk 29	20.00	...
	8/19/32 DC, size 9, wmk 29	20.00	...
	size 8, wmk 29 with Sc#723 pair	40.00	...
U531	6¢ G. Washington, blue paper, 8/18/32		
	Los Angeles, CA, size 8, wmk 29	15.00	...
	8/19/32 DC, size 7, wmk 29	20.00	...
	8/19/32 DC, size 9, wmk 29	20.00	...
U532	1¢ Franklin 11/16/50 NY, NY, size 13, wmk 42.	...	1.75
U533a	2¢ Wash. 11/17/50 NY, NY, size 13, wmk 42	...	1.75
U534a	3¢ Wash.,die 1 11/18/50 NY,NY,size 13,wmk 42	...	1.75
U534b	3¢ Wash.,die 2 11/19/50 NY,NY,size 8,wmk 42	...	4.00
U536	4¢ Franklin 7/31/58 Montpelier, VT	...	1.75
	Size 8, wmk 46	60.00	...
	Size 12, wmk 46	60.00	...
	Size 13, window	25.00	...
	Wheeling, WV, size 6¾, wmk 46, w/#1036a	35.00	...
U540	3¢+1¢ G.Washington (U534c) 7/22/58 Kenvil, NJ		
	Size 8, wmk 46, die 3 (earliest known use)	50.00	...
U541	1¼¢ Franklin 6/25/60 Birmingham, AL		1.75
U542	2½¢ Washington 5/28/60 Chicago, IL		1.75
U543	4¢ Pony Express 7/19/60 St. Joseph, MO		1.75
	Sacramento, CA		3.50
U544	5¢ Lincoln 11/19/62 Springfield, IL		1.75
U546	5¢ World's Fair 4/22/64 World's Fair, NY		1.75
U547	1¼¢ Liberty Bell 1/6/65 DC		1.75
	1/8/65 DC, size 10, wmk 48		15.00
U548	1.4¢ Liberty Bell 3/26/68 Springfield, MA		1.75
	3/27/68 DC, size 10, wmk 48		8.00
U548A	1.6¢ Liberty Bell 6/16/69 DC		1.75
	Size 10, wmk 49		1.75
U549	4¢ Old Ironsides 1/6/65 DC		1.75
	1/8/65, window		15.00
	Size 10		15.00
	Size10, window		15.00
U550	5¢ Eagle 1/5/65 Williamsburg, PA		1.75
	1/8/65, window		15.00
	Size 10		15.00
	Size 10, window		15.00
U550a	5¢ Eagle, tagged 8/15/67 DC, wmk 50		1.75
	Dayton, OH		5.00
	Wmk 48		5.00
	Size 10, wmk 48		5.00
	Size 10, wmk 49, Dayton, OH only		7.50
	Size 10, wmk 49, window		5.00
U551	6¢ Liberty 1/4/68 New York, NY		1.75
	1/5/68 DC, window		3.00
	Size 10, wmk 47		3.00
	Size 10, window, wmk 49		3.00
	11/15/68 DC, shiny plastic window, wmk 48		5.00
U552	4 + 2¢ Old Ironsides, revalued 2/5/68 DC, wmk 50		7.50
	Window, wmk 48		7.50
	Size 10, wmk 47		7.50
	Size 10, window, wmk 49		7.50
U553	5 + 1¢ Eagle, revalued 2/5/68 DC		7.50
	Size 10, window		7.50
U553a	5 + 1¢ Eagle, revalued, tagged 2/5/68 DC, wmk 48		7.50
	Size 10, wmk 47 or 49		7.50
	Size 10, window, wmk 49		7.50
U554	6¢ Moby Dick 6/7/70 New Bedford, MA		1.75
U555	6¢ Youth Conf. 2/24/71 DC		1.75
U556	1.7¢ Liberty Bell 5/10/71 Balt., MD, wmk 48A		1.75
	5/10/71 DC, wmk 49 with #1394		15.00
	5/10/71 Phoenix, AZ, wmk 48A with #E23		30.00
	5/10/71 DC, with #1283		3.00
	5/11/71 DC, size 10, wmk 47 or 49		12.00
	5/11/71 DC, size 10, wmk 48A		6.00

U549

U581

Scott #	Description	Price
	1971-78	
U557	8¢ Eagle 5/6/71 Williamsburg, PA, wmk 48A	1.75
	Wmk 49	2.50
	5/7/71 DC, window, wmk 48A	3.50
	Size 10, wmk 49	3.50
	Size 10, window, wmk 47	3.50
U561	6 + 2¢ Liberty Bell, revalued 5/16/71 DC, wmk 47	3.00
	Wmk 48A	25.00
	Wmk 49	4.00
	Window, wmk 47	3.00
	Size 10, wmk 48A	3.00
	Size 10, wmk 49	6.00
	Size 10, window, wmk 47	3.00
	Size 10, window, wmk 49	5.00
U562	6 + 2¢ Youth Conf., revalued 5/16/71 DC, wmk 49	3.00
	Wmk 47	30.00
U563	8¢ Bowling 8/21/71 Milwaukee, WI	1.75
	Size 10	2.00
U564	8¢ Aging Conference 11/15/71 DC	1.75
U565	8¢ Transpo '72 5/2/72 DC, wmk 49	1.75
	Wmk 47	3.00
U566	8 + 2¢ Eagle, revalued 12/1/73 DC	2.50
	Window, wmk 48A **(uncacheted)**	7.50
	Window, wmk 49	4.50
	Size 10, wmk 47	4.50
	Size 10, window, wmk 47	4.50
U567	10¢ Liberty Bell 12/5/73 Phila., PA knife depth 58 mm	1.75
	Knife depth 51 mm	1.75
U568	1.8¢ Volunteer 8/23/74 Cincinnati, OH	1.75
	Size 10	1.75
U569	10¢ Tennis 8/31/74 Forest Hills, NY	2.00
	Size 10	3.00
	9/3/74 DC, window	4.00
	Size 10, window	4.00
U571	10¢ Seafaring 10/13/75 Minneapolis, MN	1.75
	Size 10	1.75
U572	13¢ Homemaker 2/2/76 Biloxi, MS	1.75
	Size 10	1.75
U573	13¢ Farmer 3/15/76 New Orleans, LA	1.75
	Size 10	1.75
U574	13¢ Doctor 3/30/76 Dallas, TX	2.50
	Size 10	3.00
U575	13¢ Craftsman 8/6/76 Hancock, MA	1.75
	Size 10	1.75
U576	13¢ Liberty Tree 11/8/75 Memphis, TN	1.75
	Size 10	1.75
U577	2¢ Star & Pinwheel 9/10/76 Hempstead, NY	1.75
	Size 10	1.75
U578	2.1¢ Non-Profit 6/3/77 Houston, TX	1.75
	Size 10	1.75
U579	2.7¢ Non-Profit 7/5/78 Raleigh, NC	1.75
	Size 10	1.75
U580	(15¢) "A" Eagle 5/22/78 Memphis, TN, wmk 47	2.00
	Wmk 48A	1.75
	Window, wmk 47 or 48A	2.50
	Size 10	1.75
	Size 10, window	2.50
	Size 6¾, wmk 48A with sheet, coil & bklt. pane	10.00
U581	15¢ Uncle Sam 6/3/78 Williamsburg, PA	1.75
	Window	2.50
	Size 10	1.75
	Size 10, window	2.50
U582	13¢ Bicentennial 10/15/76 Los Angeles, CA, wmk 49	1.75
	Wmk 49, dark green	7.50
	Wmk 48A	3.00
	Size 10	1.75
U583	13¢ Golf 4/7/77 Augusta, GA	7.00
	Size 10	7.50
	4/8/77 DC, Size 6¾, window	9.50
	Size 10, window	9.50

POSTAL STATIONERY FIRST DAY COVERS

Scott #	Description	Price
	1977-85	
U584	13¢ Conservation 10/20/77 Ridley Park, PA	1.75
	Window	2.50
	Size 10	1.75
	Size 10, window	2.50
U585	13¢ Development 10/20/77 Ridley Park, PA	1.75
	Window	2.50
	Size 10	1.75
	Size 10, window	2.50
U586	15¢ on 16¢ Surcharged USA 7/28/78 Williamsburg, PA	1.75
	Size 10	1.75
U587	15¢ Auto Racing 9/2/78 Ontario, CA	1.75
	Size 10	1.75
U588	13 + 2¢ Lib. Tree, revalued 11/28/78 Williamsburg, PA	1.75
	Size 10	1.75
	11/29/78 DC, size 6¾, window	2.00
	Size 10, window	2.00
U589	3.1¢ Non-Profit 5/18/79 Denver, CO	1.75
	Size 6¾, window	2.00
	Size 10	1.75
	Size 10, window	2.00
U590	3.5¢ Non-Profit 6/23/80 Williamsburg, PA	1.75
	Size 10	1.75
U591	5.9¢ Non-Profit 2/17/82 Wheeling, WV	1.75
	Size 6¾, window	2.00
	Size 10	1.75
	Size 10, window	2.00
U592	(18¢) "B" Eagle 3/15/81 Memphis, TN	1.75
	Size 6¾, window	2.00
	Size 10	1.75
	Size 10, window	2.00
U593	18¢ Star 4/2/81 Star City, IN	1.75
	Size 10	1.75
U594	(20¢) "C" Eagle 10/11/81 Memphis, TN	1.75
	Size 10	1.75
U595	15¢ Veterinary Med. 7/24/79 Seattle, WA	1.75
	Size 10	1.75
	7/25/79 Seattle, WA, size 6¾, window, **(uncacheted)**	4.00
	Size 10, window **(uncacheted)**	4.00
U596	15¢ Olympics 12/10/79 E. Rutherford, NJ	1.75
	Size 10	1.75
U597	15¢ Bicycle 5/16/80 Baltimore, MD	1.75
	Size 10	1.75
U598	15¢ America's Cup 9/15/80 Newport, RI	1.75
	Size 10	1.75
U599	15¢ Honey Bee 10/10/80 Paris, IL	1.75
	Size 10	1.75
U600	18¢ Blinded Veteran 8/13/81 Arlington, VA	1.75
	Size 10	1.75
U601	20¢ Capitol Dome 11/13/81 Los Angeles, CA	1.75
	Size 10	1.75
U602	20¢ Great Seal 6/15/82 DC	1.75
	Size 10	1.75
U603	20¢ Purple Heart 8/6/82 DC	2.00
	Size 10	2.00
U604	5.2¢ Non-Profit 3/21/83 Memphis, TN	1.75
	Size 6¾, window	1.75
	Size 10	1.75
	Size 10, window	1.75
U605	20¢ Paralyzed Vets 8/3/83 Portland, OR	1.75
	Size 10	1.75
U606	20¢ Small Business 5/7/84 DC	1.75
	Size 10	1.75
U607	(22¢) "D" Eagle 2/1/85 Los Angeles, CA	1.75
	Size 6¾, window	1.75
	Size 10	1.75
	Size 10, window	1.75
U608	22¢ Bison 2/25/85 Bison, SD	1.75
	Size 6¾, window	1.75
	Size 10	1.75
	Size 10, window	1.75

U583

U583

U619

cott #	Description	Cached
	1985-95	
609	6¢ Old Ironsides, Non-Profit 5/3/85 Boston, MA	1.75
	Size 10	2.00
610	8.5¢ Mayflower 12/4/86 Plymouth, MA	1.75
	Size 10	2.00
611	25¢ Stars 3/26/88 Star, MS	1.75
	Size 10	2.00
612	9.4¢ USS Constellation 4/12/88 Baltimore, MD	1.75
	Size 10	2.00
613	25¢ Snowflake 9/8/88 Snowflake, AZ	1.75
614	25¢ Philatelic Mail Return Env. 3/10/89 Cleveland, OH	1.75
615	25¢ Security Envelope 7/10/89 DC	1.75
616	25¢ Love 9/22/89 McLean, VA	1.75
617	25¢ Space Hologram, World Stamp Expo 12/3/89 DC	1.75
618	25¢ Football 9/9/90 Green Bay, WI	3.00
619	29¢ Star 1/24/91 DC	1.75
620	11.1¢ Non-Profit 5/3/91 Boxborough, MA	1.75
621	29¢ Love 5/9/91 Honolulu, HI	1.75
622	29¢ Magazine Industry 10/7/91 Naples, FL	1.75
623	29¢ USA & Star, Security Envelope 7/20/91 DC	1.75
624	29¢ Country Geese 11/8/91 Virginia Beach, VA	1.75
625	29¢ Space Station Hologram 1/21/92 Virginia Beach, VA	1.75
626	29¢ Western Americana 4/10/92 Dodge City, KS	1.75
627	29¢ Protect the Environment 4/22/92 Chicago, IL	1.75
628	19.8¢ Bulk-rate, third class 5/18/92 Las Vegas, NV	1.75
629	29¢ Disabled Americans 7/22/92 DC	1.75
630	29¢ Kitten 10/2/93 King of Prussia, PA	1.75
	Size 10	2.00
631	29¢ Football size 10 9/17/94 Canton, OH	2.00
632	32¢ Liberty Bell 1/3/95 Williamsburg, VA	2.00
633	(32¢) Old Glory 12/13/94 Cancel, released 1/12/95	2.00
634	(32¢) Old Glory, Security Envelope	2.00
635	(5¢) Sheep 3/10/95 State College, PA	2.00
636	(10¢) Eagle 3/10/95 State College,PA	2.00

cott #	Description	Uncacheted
	AIRMAIL POSTAL STATIONERY	
	1929-46	
C1	5¢ Blue 1/12/29 DC, size 13	40.00
	2/1/29, DC, size 5	45.00
	2/1/29, DC, size 8	65.00
C3	6¢ Orange 7/1/34, size 8	25.00
	Size 13	14.00
C3	Combo with C19	60.00
C7	8¢ Olive green 9/26/32, size 8	30.00
	Size 13	11.00
C7	Combo with C17	60.00
C10	5¢ on 6¢ Orange 10/1/46 Aiea Hts, HI, die 2a	100.00
C11	5¢ on 6¢ Orange 10/1/46 Aiea Hts, HI die 2b	150.00
C12	5¢ on 6¢ Orng. 10/1/46 Aiea Hts, HI, APO & NY, NY die 2c	75.00
C13	5¢ on 6¢ Orng. 10/1/46 Aiea Hts, HI, die 3	75.00

ott #	Description	Cacheted
	1946-67	
C14	5¢ Skymaster 9/25/46 DC	2.25
C16	10¢ Air Letter 4/29/47 DC	5.00
C17	5¢ CIPEX, Type 1 5/21/47 New York, NY	2.50
C17a	5¢ CIPEX, Type 2 5/21/47 New York, NY	2.50
C18	6¢ Skymaster 9/22/50 Philadelphia, PA	1.75
C22	6¢ on 5¢ die 2 (UC15) 8/29/52 Norfolk, VA ...**(uncacheted)**	20.00
	Cacheted	30.00
C25	6¢ FIPEX 5/2/56 New York, NY, "short clouds"	1.75
	"Long clouds"	1.75
C26	7¢ Skymaster 7/31/58 Dayton, OH, "straight left wing"	1.75
	"Crooked left wing"	3.00
	Size 8 ...**(uncacheted)**	35.00
C32a	10¢ Jet Air Letter 9/12/58 St. Louis, MO	2.00
C33	7¢ Jet, blue 11/21/58 New York, NY	1.75
C34	7¢ Jet, red 8/18/60 Portland, OR	1.75
C35	11¢ Jet Air Letter 6/16/61 Johnstown, PA	1.75
C36	8¢ Jet 11/17/62 Chantilly, VA	1.75
C37	8¢ Jet Triangle 1/7/65 Chicago, IL	1.75
	Size 10	15.00

POSTAL STATIONERY FIRST DAY COVERS

Scott #	Description	Cacheted
UC37a	8¢ Jet Triangle, tagged 8/15/67 DC	7.50
	Dayton, OH	7.50
	Size 10	7.50
	1965-91	
UC38	11¢ Kennedy Air Letter 5/29/65 Boston, MA	1.75
UC39	13¢ Kennedy Air Letter 5/29/67 Chic., IL	1.75
UC40	10¢ Jet Triangle 1/8/68 Chicago, IL	1.75
	1/9/68 DC, size 10	7.50
UC41	8 + 2¢ revalued UC37 2/5/68 DC	10.00
	Size 10	10.00
UC42	13¢ Human Rights Air Letter 12/3/68 DC	1.75
UC43	11¢ Jet & Circles 5/6/71 Williamsburg, PA	1.75
	Size 10	6.00
UC44	15¢ Birds Air Letter 5/28/71 Chicago, IL	1.75
UC44a	15¢ Birds AEROGRAMME 12/13/71 Phila., PA	1.75
UC45	10¢+1¢ revalued UC40 6/28/71 DC	5.00
	Size 10	10.00
UC46	15¢ Balloon Air Letter 2/10/73 Albuquerque, NM	1.75
UC47	13¢ Dove 12/1/73 Memphis, TN	1.75
	1/5/74, size 10, earliest known use	5.00
UC48	18¢ USA Air Letter 1/4/74 Atlanta, GA	1.75
UC49	17¢ NATO Air Letter 4/4/74 DC	1.75
UC50	22¢ USA Air Letter 1/16/76 Tempe, AZ	1.75
UC51	22¢ USA Air Letter 11/3/78 St. Petersburg, FL	1.75
UC52	22¢ Olympics 12/5/79 Bay Shore, NY	1.75
UC53	30¢ USA 12/29/80 San Francisco, CA	1.75
UC54	30¢ USA 9/21/81 Honolulu, HI	1.75
UC55	30¢ USA & Globe 9/16/82 Seattle, WA	1.75
UC56	30¢ Communications 1/7/83 Anaheim, CA	1.75
UC57	30¢ Olympics 10/14/83 Los Angeles, CA	1.75
UC58	30¢ Landsat Sat. 2/14/85 Goddard Flight Ctr., MD	1.75
UC59	36¢ Travel 5/21/85 DC	1.75
UC60	36¢ Twain / Halley's Comet 12/4/85 DC	1.75
UC61	39¢ Stylized Aerogramme 5/9/88 Miami, FL	1.75
UC62	39¢ Montgomery Blair 11/20/89 DC	1.75
UC63	45¢ Eagle 5/17/91 Denver, CO	2.00

	OFFICIAL POSTAL STATIONERY	
	1983-92	
UO73	20¢ Eagle 1/12/83 DC, size 10	2.00
	Window	3.00
UO74	22¢ Eagle 2/26/85 CD, size 10	1.75
	Window	2.00
UO75	22¢ Savings Bond Env. 3/2/87 DC	3.00
	Window	4.00
UO76	(25¢) Official "E" Savings Bond Env. 3/22/88 DC	1.75
	Window	2.00
UO77	25¢ Official Mail 4/11/88 DC	1.75
	Window	2.00
UO78	25¢ Savings Bond Env. 4/14/88 DC	1.75
	Window	2.00
UO79	45¢ Passport Envelope (2 oz.) 3/17/90 Springfield, VA	2.00
UO80	65¢ Passport Envelope (3 oz.) 3/17/90 Springfield, VA	2.50
UO81	45¢ "Stars" clear, "Official" 14.5 mm long, 8/10/90 DC	2.00
UO82	65¢ "Stars" clear, "Official" 14.5 mm long, 8/10/90 DC	2.50
UO83	(29¢) "F" Savings Bond Env. 1/22/91 DC	1.75
UO84	29¢ Official Mail 4/6/91 Oklahoma City, OK	1.75
UO85	29¢ Savings Bond Env. 4/17/91 DC	1.75
UO86	52¢ U.S. Consular Service, Passport Env. 7/10/92 DC	2.25
UO87	75¢ U.S. Consular Service, Passport Env. 7/10/92 DC	2.75

UC45

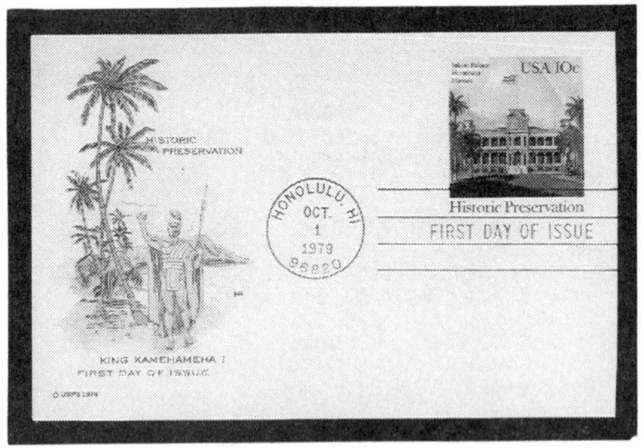

UX81

Scott #	Description	Uncacheted	Cacheted
	1873-1966		
UX1	1¢ Liberty 5/13/1873 Boston, NY, or DC	3000.00	...
UX37	3¢ McKinley 2/1/26 DC	250.00	...
UX38	2¢ Franklin 11/16/51 New York, NY	...	1.75
UX39	2¢ on 1¢ Jefferson (UX27) 1/1/52 DC	12.50	25.00
UX40	2¢ on 1¢ Lincoln (UX28) 3/22/82 DC	100.00	...
UX43	2¢ Lincoln 7/31/52 DC	...	1.75
UX44	2¢ FIPEX 5/4/56 New York, NY	...	1.75
UX45	4¢ Liberty 11/16/56 New York, NY	...	1.75
UX46	3¢ Liberty 8/1/58 Philadelphia, PA	...	1.75
UX46a	Missing "I"/"N God We Trust"	175.00	250.00
UX46c	Precancelled 9/15/61	50.00	...
UX48	4¢ Lincoln 11/19/62 Springfield, IL	...	1.75
UX48a	4¢ Lincoln, tagged 6/25/66 Bellevue, OH	25.00	30.00
	7/6/66 DC	1.50	2.50
	Bellevue, OH	7.50	12.50
	Cincinnati, OH	4.50	7.50
	Cleveland, OH	6.00	10.00
	Columbus, OH	7.50	12.50
	Dayton, OH	3.50	6.00
	Indianapolis, IN	7.50	12.50
	Louisville, KY	7.50	12.50
	Overlook, OH	4.50	7.50
	Toledo, OH	7.50	12.50

Scott #	Description	Cacheted
	1963-80	
UX49	7¢ USA 8/30/63 New York, NY	1.75
UX50	4¢ Customs 2/22/64 DC	1.75
UX51	4¢ Social Security 9/26/64 DC	1.75
	Official Gov't. Printed Cachet	12.00
	Blue hand cancel and gov't. cachet	20.00
UX52	4¢ Coast Guard 8/4/65 Newburyport, MA	1.75
UX53	4¢ Census Bureau 10/21/65 Phila, PA	1.75
UX54	8¢ USA 12/4/67 DC	1.75
UX55	5¢ Lincoln 1/4/68 Hodgenville, KY	1.75
UX56	5¢ Women Marines 7/26/68 San Fran., CA	1.75
UX57	5¢ Weathervane 9/1/70 Fort Myer, VA	1.75
UX58	6¢ Paul Revere 5/15/71 Boston, MA	1.75
UX59	10¢ USA 6/10/71 New York, NY	1.75
UX60	6¢ America's Hospitals 9/16/71 NY, NY	1.75
UX61	6¢ US Frigate Constellation 6/29/72 Any City	1.75
UX62	6¢ Monument Valley 6/29/72 Any City	1.75
UX63	6¢ Gloucester, MA 6/29/72 Any City	1.75
UX64	6¢ John Hanson 9/1/72 Baltimore, MD	1.75
UX65	6¢ Liberty Centenary 9/14/73 DC	1.75
UX66	8¢ Samuel Adams 12/16/73 Boston, MA	1.75
UX67	12¢ Ship's Figurehead 1/4/74 Miami, FL	1.75
UX68	7¢ Charles Thomson 9/14/75 Bryn Mawr, PA	1.75
UX69	9¢ J. Witherspoon 11/10/75 Princeton, NJ	1.75
UX70	9¢ Caeser Rodney 7/1/76 Dover, DE	1.75
UX71	9¢ Galveston Court House 7/20/77 Galveston, TX	1.75
UX72	9¢ Nathan Hale 10/14/77 Coventry, CT	1.75
UX73	10¢ Music Hall 5/12/78 Cincinnati, OH	1.75
UX74	(10¢) John Hancock 5/19/78 Quincy, MA	1.75
UX75	10¢ John Hancock 6/20/78 Quincy, MA	1.75
UX76	14¢ Coast Guard Eagle 8/4/78 Seattle, WA	1.75
UX77	10¢ Molly Pitcher 9/8/78 Freehold, NJ	1.75
UX78	10¢ George R. Clark 2/23/79 Vincennes, IN	1.75
UX79	10¢ Casimir Pulaski 10/11/79 Savannah, GA	1.75
UX80	10¢ Olympics 9/17/79 Eugene, OR	1.75
UX81	10¢ Iolani Palace 10/1/79 Honolulu, HI	2.00
UX82	14¢ Olympic Skater 1/15/80 Atlanta, GA	1.75
UX83	10¢ Mormon Temple 4/5/80 Salt Lake City, UT	1.75
UX84	10¢ Count Rochambeau 7/11/80 Newport, RI	1.75
UX85	10¢ King's Mountain 10/7/80 King's Mountain, NC	1.75
UX86	19¢ Golden Hinde 11/21/80 San Rafael, CA	1.75

POSTAL CARD FIRST DAY COVERS

Scott #	Description	Cacheted
	1981-87	
UX87	10¢ Battle of Cowpens 1/17/81 Cowpens, SC	1.75
UX88	(12¢) "B" Eagle 3/15/81 Memphis, TN	1.75
UX89	12¢ Isaiah Thomas 5/5/81 Worcester, MA	1.75
UX90	12¢ Nathaniel Greene 9/8/81 Eutaw Springs, SC	1.75
UX91	12¢ Lewis & Clark 9/23/81 St. Louis, MO	1.75
UX92	(13¢) Robert Morris 10/11/81 Memphis, TN	1.75
UX93	13¢ Robert Morris 11/10/81 Phila., PA	1.75
UX94	13¢ Frances Marion 4/3/82 Marion, SC	1.75
UX95	13¢ LaSalle 4/7/82 New Orleans	1.75
UX96	13¢ Philadelphia Academy 6/18/82 Philadelphia, PA	1.75
UX97	13¢ St. Louis P.O. 10/14/82 St. Louis, MO	1.75
UX98	13¢ Oglethorpe 2/12/83 Savannah, GA	1.75
UX99	13¢ Old Washington P.O. 4/19/83 DC	1.75
UX100	13¢ Olympics - Yachting 8/5/83 Long Beach, CA	1.75
UX101	13¢ Maryland 3/25/84 St. Clemente Island, MD	1.75
UX102	13¢ Olympic Torch 4/30/84 Los Angeles, CA	1.75
UX103	13¢ Frederic Baraga 6/29/84 Marquette, MI	1.75
UX104	13¢ Rancho San Pedro 9/16/84 Compton, CA	1.75
UX105	(14¢) Charles Carroll 2/1/85 New Carrollton, MD	1.75
UX106	14¢ Charles Carroll 3/6/85 Annapolis, MD	1.75
UX107	25¢ Flying Cloud 2/27/85 Salem, MA	1.75
UX108	14¢ George Wythe 6/20/85 Williamsburg, VA	1.75
UX109	14¢ Settling of CT 4/18/86 Hartford, CT	1.75
UX110	14¢ Stamp Collecting 5/23/86 Chicago, IL	1.75
UX111	14¢ Frances Vigo 5/24/86 Vincennes, IN	1.75
UX112	14¢ Rhode Island 6/26/86 Providence, RI	1.75
UX113	14¢ Wisconsin Terr. 7/3/86 Mineral Point, WI	1.75
UX114	14¢ National Guard 12/12/86 Boston, MA	1.75
UX115	14¢ Steel Plow 5/22/87 Moines, IL	1.75
UX116	14¢ Constitution Convention 5/25/87 Philadelphia, PA	1.75
UX117	14¢ Flag 6/14/87 Baltimore, MD	1.75
UX118	14¢ Pride in America 9/22/87 Jackson, WY	1.75
UX119	14¢ Historic Preservation 9/28/87 Timberline, OR	1.75
	1988-91	
UX120	15¢ America the Beautiful 3/28/88 Buffalo, NY	1.75
UX121	15¢ Blair House 5/4/88 DC	1.75
UX122	28¢ Yorkshire 6/29/88 Mystic, CT	1.75
UX123	15¢ Iowa Territory 7/2/88 Burlington, IA	1.75
UX124	15¢ Northwest/Ohio Territory 7/15/88 Marietta, OH	1.75
UX125	15¢ Hearst Castle 9/20/88 San Simeon, CA	1.75
UX126	15¢ Federalist Papers 10/27/88 New York, NY	1.75
UX127	15¢ The Desert 1/13/89 Tucson, AZ	1.75
UX128	15¢ Healy Hall 1/23/89 DC	1.75
UX129	15¢ The Wetlands 3/17/89 Waycross, GA	1.75
UX130	15¢ Oklahoma Land Run 4/22/89 Guthrie, OK	1.75
UX131	21¢ The Mountains 5/5/89 Denver, CO	1.75
UX132	15¢ The Seashore 6/19/89 Cape Hatteras, NC	1.75
UX133	15¢ The Woodlands 8/26/89 Cherokee, NC	1.75
UX134	15¢ Hull House 9/16/89 Chicago, IL	1.75
UX135	15¢ Independence Hall 9/25/89 Philadelphia, PA	1.75
UX136	15¢ Baltimore Inner Harbor 10/7/89 Baltimore, MD	1.75
UX137	15¢ Manhattan Skyline 11/8/89 New York, NY	1.75
UX138	15¢ Capitol Dome 11/26/89 DC	1.75
UX139-42	15¢ Cityscapes sheet of 4 diff.views,rouletted 12/1/89 DC	7.00
UX139-42	Cityscapes, set of 4 different, rouletted	8.00
UX143	(15¢) White House, Picture PC (cost 50¢) 11/30/89 DC	1.75
UX144	(15¢) Jefferson Mem. Pict. PC (cost 50¢) 12/2/89 DC	1.75
UX145	15¢ American Papermaking 3/13/90 New York, NY	1.75
UX146	15¢ Literacy 3/22/90 DC	1.75
UX147	(15¢)Geo. Bingham Pict.PC (cost 50¢)5/4/90 St.Louis,MO	1.75
UX148	15¢ Isaac Royall House 6/16/90 Medford, MA	1.75
UX150	15¢ Stanford University 9/30/90 Stanford, CA	1.75
UX151	15¢ DAR Mem., Continental/Constitution Hall 10/11/91 DC	1.75
UX152	15¢ Chicago Orchestra Hall 10/19/91 Chicago, IL	1.75
UX153	19¢ Flag 1/24/91 DC	1.75
UX154	19¢ Carnegie Hall 4/1/91 New York, NY	1.75
UX155	19¢ "Old Red" Bldg., U.of Texas 6/14/91 Galveston, TX	1.75
UX156	19¢ Bill of Rights Bicent. 9/25/91 Notre Dame, IN	1.75
UX157	19¢ Notre Dame Admin. Bldg. 10/15/91 Notre Dame, IN	1.75
UX158	30¢ Niagara Falls 8/21/91 Niagara Falls, NY	1.75
UX159	19¢ Old Mill, Univ. of Vermont 10/29/91 Burlington, VT	1.75

UX117

POSTAL CARD FIRST DAY COVERS

UX166

ott #	Description	Uncacheted	Cached
	1992-95		
160	19¢ Wadsworth Atheneum 1/16/92 Hartford, CT		1.75
161	19¢ Cobb Hall, Univ. of Chicago 1/23/92 Chicago, IL		1.75
162	19¢ Waller Hall 2/1/92 Salem, OR		1.75
163	19¢ America's Cup 5/6/92 San Diego, CA		1.75
164	19¢ Columbia River Gorge 5/9/92 Stevenson, WA		1.75
165	19¢ Great Hall, Ellis Island 5/11/92 Ellis Island, NY		1.75
166	19¢ National Cathedral 1/6/93 DC		1.75
167	19¢ Wren Building 2/8/93 Williamsville, VA		1.75
168	19¢ Holocaust Memorial 3/23/93 DC		2.25
169	19¢ Ft. Recovery 6/13/93 Fort Recovery, OH		1.75
170	19¢ Playmaker's Theater 9/14/93 Chapel Hill, NC		1.75
171	19¢ O'Kane Hall 9/17/93 Worcester, MA		1.75
172	19¢ Beecher Hall 10/9/93 Jacksonville, IL		1.75
173	19¢ Massachusetts Hall 10/14/93 Brunswick, ME		1.75
174	19¢ Lincoln Home 2/12/94 Springfield, IL		1.75
175	19¢ Myers Hall 3/11/94 Springfield, OH		1.75
176	19¢ Canyon de Chelly 8/11/94 Canyon de Chelly, AZ		1.75
177	19¢ St. Louis Union Station 9/1/94 St. Louis, MO		1.75
178-97	19¢ Legends of the West, set of 20 10/18/94 Tucson, AZ Lawton, OK or Laramie, WY		35.00
198	20¢ Red Barn 1/3/95 Williamsburg, PA		1.75
199	(20¢) "G" Old Glory, 12/13/94 cancel, released 1/12/95		1.75

AIRMAIL POST CARDS
1949-91

ott #	Description	Cacheted
C1	4¢ Eagle 1/10/49 DC, round "O" in January 10	2.00
	Oval "O" in January 10	5.00
C2	5¢ Eagle 7/31/58 Wichita, KS	2.00
C3	5¢ Eagle w/border 6/18/60 Minneapolis, MN	2.00
	"Thin dividing line" at top	5.00
C4	6¢ Bald Eagle 2/15/63 Maitland, FL	2.00
C5	11¢ Visit the USA 5/27/66 DC	1.75
C6	6¢ Virgin Islands 3/31/67 Charlotte Amalie, VI	1.75
C7	6¢ Boy Scouts 8/4/67 Farragut State Park, ID	1.75
C8	13¢ Visit the USA 9/8/67 Detroit, MI	1.75
C9	8¢ Eagle 3/1/68 New York, NY	1.75
C9a	8¢ Eagle, tagged 3/19/69 DC	15.00
C10	9¢ Eagle 5/15/71 Kitty Hawk, NC	1.75
C11	15¢ Visit the USA 6/10/71 New York, NY	1.75
C12	9¢ Grand Canyon 6/29/72 any city	1.75
C13	15¢ Niagara Falls 6/29/72 any city	1.75
C13a	Address side blank **(uncacheted)**	600.00
C14	11¢ Modern Eagle 1/4/74 State College, PA	1.75
C15	18¢ Eagle Weathervane 1/4/74 Miami, FL	1.75
C16	21¢ Angel Weathervane 12/17/75 Kitty Hawk, NC	1.75
C17	21¢ Jenny 9/16/78 San Diego, CA	1.75
C18	21¢ Olympic-Gymnast 12/1/79 Fort Worth, TX	1.75
C19	28¢ First Transpacific Flight 1/2/81 Wenatchee, WA	1.75
C20	28¢ Soaring 3/5/82 Houston, TX	1.75
C21	28¢ Olympic-Speedskating 12/29/83 Milwaukee, WI	1.75
C22	33¢ China Clipper 2/15/85 San Fran., CA	1.75
C23	33¢ AMERIPEX '86 2/1/86 Chicago, IL	1.75
C24	36¢ DC-3 5/14/88 San Diego, CA	2.00
C25	40¢ Yankee Clipper 6/28/91	2.00

ott #	Description	Uncacheted	Cacheted
	1892-1956 POSTAL REPLY CARDS		
1	1¢ + 1¢ U.S. Grant 10/25/1892 any city	350.00	...
12	3¢ + 3¢ McKinley 2/1/26 any city	250.00	...
13	2¢ + 2¢ Washington 12/29/51 DC	...	1.75
14	2¢ on 1¢ + 2¢ on 1¢ G. Wash. 1/1/52 any city	50.00	75.00
16	4¢ + 4¢ Liberty 11/16/56 New York, NY	...	1.75
16a	Message card printed on both halves	75.00	100.00
16b	Reply card printed on both halves	50.00	75.00

ott #	Description	Cacheted
	1958-75	
17	3¢ + 3¢ Liberty 7/31/58 Boise, ID	1.75
18	4¢ + 4¢ Lincoln 11/19/62 Springfield, IL	1.75
18a	4¢ + 4¢ Lincoln, Tagged 3/7/67 Dayton, OH	500.00
19	7¢ + 7¢ USA 8/30/63 New York, NY	1.75
20	8¢ + 8¢ USA 12/4/67 DC	1.75
21	5¢ + 5¢ Lincoln 1/4/68 Hodgenville, KY	1.75
22	6¢ + 6¢ Paul Revere 5/15/71 Boston, MA	1.75

Scott #	Description	Cacheted
	1958-75 cont.	
UY23	6¢ + 6¢ John Hanson 9/1/72 Baltimore, MD	1.75
UY24	8¢ + 8¢ Samuel Adams 12/16/73 Boston, MA	1.75
UY25	7¢ + 7¢ Charles Thomson 9/14/75 Bryn Mawr, PA	1.75
UY26	9¢ + 9¢ John Witherspoon 11/10/75 Princeton, NJ	1.75

POSTAL CARD FIRST DAY COVERS

Scott #	Description	Cacheted
	1976-91	
UY27	9¢ + 9¢ Caeser Rodney 7/1/76 Dover, DE	1.75
UY28	9¢ + 9¢ Nathan Hale 10/14/77 Coventry, CT	1.75
UY29	(10¢ + 10¢) John Hancock 5/19/78 Quincy, MA	2.50
UY30	10¢ + 10¢ John Hancock 6/20/78 Quincy, MA	1.75
UY31	(12¢ + 12¢) "B" Eagle 3/15/81 Memphis, TN	1.75
UY32	12¢ + 12¢ Isaiah Thomas 5/5/81 Worcester, MA	1.75
UY32a	"Small die"	5.00
UY33	(13¢ + 13¢) Robert Morris 10/11/81 Memphis, TN	1.75
UY34	13¢ + 13¢ Robert Morris 11/10/81 Philadelphia, PA	1.75
UY35	(14¢ + 14¢) Charles Carroll 2/1/85 New Carrollton, MD	1.75
UY36	14¢ + 14¢ Charles Carroll 3/6/85 Annapolis, MD	1.75
UY37	14¢ + 14¢ George Wythe 6/20/85 Williamsburg, PA	1.75
UY38	14¢ + 14¢ American Flag 9/1/87 Baltimore, MD	1.75
UY39	15¢ + 15¢ America the Beautiful 7/11/88 Buffalo, NY	1.75
UY40	19¢ + 19¢ American Flag 3/27/91 DC	2.00

OFFICIAL POSTAL CARDS
1983-91

Scott #	Description	Cacheted
UZ2	13¢ Eagle 1/12/83 DC	1.75
UZ3	14¢ Eagle 2/26/85 DC	1.75
UZ4	15¢ Eagle (4 colors) 6/10/88 New York, NY	1.75
UZ5	19¢ Eagle 5/24/91 Seattle, WA	1.75

"POSTAL BUDDY" REPLY CARDS

Scott #	Description	Cacheted
1	15¢ 7/5/90 Merriifield, VA	4.00
2	19¢ 2/3/91 Any city	...
3	19¢ Stylized Flag 11/13/92 Any city	...

CHRISTMAS SEAL FIRST DAY COVERS

Beginning in 1936, Santa Claus, Indiana has been used as the First Day City of U.S. National Christmas Seals. In 1936 the Postmaster would not allow the seal to be tied to the front of the cover and seals for that year are usually found on the back. Since 1937, all seals were allowed to be tied on the front of the FDC's.

All prices are for cacheted FDC's.

YEAR	PRICE	YEAR	PRICE
1936 (500 FDC's processed)	55.00	1958	9.00
1937	35.00	1959	9.00
1938	35.00	1960	9.00
1939	35.00	1961	9.00
1940	35.00	1962	9.00
1941	22.50	1963	9.00
1942	22.50	1964	30.00
1943	22.50	1965	9.00
1944	11.50	1966	9.00
1945	11.50	1967	9.00
1946	11.50	1968	9.00
1947	11.50	1969	9.00
1948	11.50	1970	5.00
1949	11.50	1971	5.00
1950	11.50	1972	5.00
1951	11.50	1973	5.00
1952	11.50	1974	5.00
1953	9.00	1975	5.00
1954	9.00	1976	5.00
1955	9.00	1977	5.00
1956	9.00	1978	5.00
1957	9.00	1979	5.00

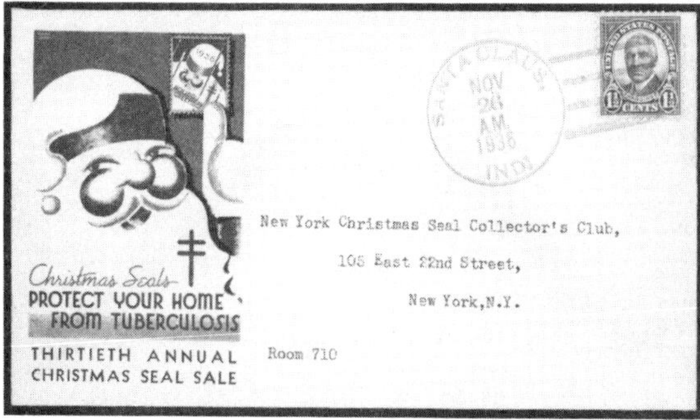

1936 WX80

WORLD WAR II PATRIOTIC EVENT COVERS

6/30/46

The listing below features the dates of significant patriotic events of World War II. The values listed are for standard size covers bearing related, printed cachets, and cancelled on the appropriate date.

Cachets produced by Minkus and others, which feature general patriotic themes such as "Win the War" are valued at 75¢ unused and $2.00 used.

Covers with Naval cancels, when available, usually sell for twice the listed prices.

From 1943 to date, prices are for unaddressed covers.

WORLD WAR II EVENT	CACHETED COVER
Pearl Harbor 12/7/41	200.00
U.S. Declares War on Japan 12/8/41	100.00
Germany and Italy Declare War on U.S. 12/11/41	100.00
U.S. Declares War on Germany and Italy 12/11/41	100.00
Churchill Arrives at the White House 12/22/41	60.00
Manila and Cavite Fall 1/2/42	60.00
Roosevelt's Diamond Jubilee Birthday 1/30/42	60.00
Singapore Surrenders 2/15/42	60.00
Japan Takes Java 3/10/42	60.00
Marshall Arrives in London 4/8/42	60.00
Dedication of MacArthur Post Office 4/15/42	60.00
Doolittle Air Raid on Tokyo 4/18/42	60.00
Fort Mills Corregidor Island Surrenders 5/6/42	60.00
Madagascar Occupied by U.S. 5/9/42	60.00
Mexico at War with Axis 5/23/42	60.00
Bombing of Cologne 6/6/42	60.00
Japan Bombs Dutch Harbor, AK 6/3/42	60.00
Six German Spies Sentenced to Death 8/7/42	60.00
Brazil at War 8/22/42	60.00
Battle of El Alamein 10/23/42	70.00
Operation Torch (Invasion of North Africa) 11/8/42	50.00
Gas Rationing in U.S. 12/1/42	50.00
The Casablanca Conference 1/14/43	50.00
The Casablanca Conference (You must remember this!) 1/22/43	40.00
Point Rationing 3/1/43	50.00
Battle of the Bismarck Sea 3/13/43	40.00
U.S. Planes Bomb Naples 4/5/43	50.00
Bizerte & Tunis Occupied 5/8/43	40.00
Invasion of Attu 5/11/43	40.00
Fall of Rome 6/4/43	40.00
Siciliy Invaded 7/14/43	35.00
The Quebec Conference 8/14/43	40.00
Sicily Encircled 8/17/43	40.00
Italy Invaded 9/3/43	40.00
Italy Surrenders 9/8/43	35.00
Mussolini Escapes 9/18/43	35.00
U.S. Drives Germans out of Naples 10/2/43	35.00
Italy Declares War on Germany 10/13/43	35.00
Hull, Eden, Stalin Conference 10/25/43	35.00
U.S. Government takes over Coal Mines 11/3/43	35.00
The Cairo Meeting 11/25/43	40.00
The Teheran Meeting 11/28/43	40.00
Roosevelt, Churchill, Kai-Shek at Cairo 12/2/43	40.00
FDR, Stalin, Churchill Agree on 3 fronts 12/4/43	40.00
Soviets Reach Polish Border 1/4/44	35.00
Marshalls Invaded 2/4/44	35.00
U.S. Captures Cassino 3/15/44	35.00
Invasion of Dutch New Guinea 4/24/44	35.00
Rome Falls 6/4/44	35.00
D-Day Single Face Eisenhower 6/6/44	100.00
D-Day: Invasion of Normandy 6/6/44	35.00
B29's Bomb Japan 6/15/44	35.00
Cherbourg Surrenders 6/27/44	40.00
Caen Falls to Allies 7/10/44	35.00
Marines Invade Guam 7/21/44	35.00
Yanks Enter Brest, etc. 8/7/44	35.00
U.S. Bombs Phillipines 8/10/44	35.00
Invasion of Southern France 8/16/44	25.00
Liberation of Paris 8/23/44	30.00
Florence Falls to Allies 8/23/44	30.00
Liberation of Brussels 9/4/44	25.00
We Invade Holland, Finland Quits 9/5/44	30.00
Soviets Invade Yugoslavia 9/6/44	30.00
Russians Enter Bulgaria 9/9/44	30.00
Liberation of Luxembourg 9/10/44	25.00

WORLD WAR II EVENT	CACHETED COVER
Albania Invaded 9/27/44	35.00
Philippines, We Will Be Back 9/27/44	25.00
Greece Invaded 10/5/44	35.00
Liberation of Athens 10/14/44	25.00
Liberation of Belgrade 10/16/44	25.00
Russia Invades Czechoslovakia 10/19/44	30.00
Invasion of the Philippines 10/20/44	25.00
The Pied Piper of Leyte-Philippine Invasion 10/21/44	35.00
Invasion of Norway 10/25/44	25.00
Liberation of Tirana 11/18/44	25.00
100,000 Yanks Land on Luzon 1/10/45	25.00
Liberation of Warsaw 1/17/45	30.00
Russians Drive to Oder River 2/2/45	25.00
Liberation of Manila 2/4/45	25.00
Yalta Conference 2/12/45	25.00
Liberation of Budapest 2/13/45	25.00
Corregidor is Ours 2/17/45	25.00
Turkey Wars Germany and Japan 2/23/45	25.00
Yanks Enter Cologne 3/5/45	25.00
Cologne is Taken 3/6/45	20.00
Historical Rhine Crossing 3/8/45	20.00
Bombing of Tokyo 3/10/45	25.00
Russia Crosses Oder River 3/13/45	25.00
Capture of Iwo Jima 3/14/45	20.00
Battle of the Inland Sea 3/20/45	20.00
Crossing of the Rhine 3/24/45	20.00
Danzig Invaded 3/27/45	25.00
Okinawa Invaded 4/1/45	20.00
Japanese Cabinet Resigns 4/7/45	20.00
Liberation of Vienna 4/10/45	20.00
We Invade Bremen, etc. 4/10/45	25.00
FDR Dies - Truman becomes President 4/12/45	65.00
Liberation of Vienna 4/13/45	25.00
Patton Invades Czechoslovakia 4/18/45	25.00
Berlin Invaded 4/21/45	25.00
Berlin Encircled 4/25/45	20.00
"GI Joe" and "Ivan" Meet at Torgau-Germany 4/26/45	20.00
Mussolini Executed 4/28/45	50.00
Hitler Dead 5/1/45	35.00
Liberation of Italy 5/2/45	20.00
Berlin Falls 5/2/45	25.00
Liberation of Rangoon 5/3/45	20.00
5th and 7th Armies Meet at Brenner Pass 5/4/45	20.00
Liberation of Copenhagen 5/5/45	20.00
Liberation of Amsterdam 5/5/45	25.00
Liberation of Oslo 5/8/45	25.00
Liberation of Prague 5/8/45	25.00
V-E Day 5/8/45	50.00
Atomic Bomb Test 5/16/45	25.00
Rome Falls 6/4/45	25.00
Invasion of Borneo 6/11/45	25.00
Eisenhower Welcomed Home 6/18/45	20.00
Okinawa Captured 6/21/45	25.00
United Nations Conference 6/25/45	25.00
American Flag Raised over Berlin 7/4/45	25.00
Big Three Meet at Potsdam 8/1/45	25.00
Atomic Bomb Dropped on Hiroshima 8/6/45	65.00
Russia Declares War on Japan 8/8/45	25.00
Japan Capitulates 8/14/45	25.00
Japan Signs Peace Treaty 9/1/45	50.00
Liberation of China 9/2/45	35.00
V-J Day 9/2/45	50.00
Liberation of Korea 9/2/45	35.00
Flag Raising over Tokyo - Gen. MacArthur Takes Over 9/8/45	25.00
Gen. Wainwright Rescued from the Japanese 9/10/45	25.00
Nimitz Post Office 9/10/45	25.00
Marines Land in Japan 9/23/45	40.00
Nimitz Day-Washington 10/5/45	25.00
War Crimes Commission 10/18/45	25.00
Premier Laval Executed as Traitor 10/15/45	25.00
Fleet Reviewed by President Truman 10/27/45	35.00
Trygue Lie Elected 1/21/46	25.00
2nd Anniversary of D-Day 6/6/46	25.00
Operation Crossroads 6/30/46	100.00
Bikini Atomic Bomb Test 7/1/46	125.00
Philippine Republic Independence 7/3/46	25.00
Atomic Age 7/10/46	25.00
Victory Day 8/14/46	25.00
Opening of UN Post Office at Lake Success 9/23/46	25.00
Goering Commits Suicide 10/16/46	40.00
Opening Day of UN in Flushing, NY 10/23/46	25.00
Marshall is Secretary of State 1/21/47	25.00
Moscow Peace Conference 3/10/47	25.00

BROOKMAN IS YOUR #1 SOURCE FOR
WORLD WAR II PATRIOTIC COVERS

Brookman carries the broadest stock of World War II Patriotic Covers available. These handsomely cacheted covers depict people, places and events that made history during those momentous days. Order from Page 146 or write/call for our latest list.

E PLURIBUS UNUM

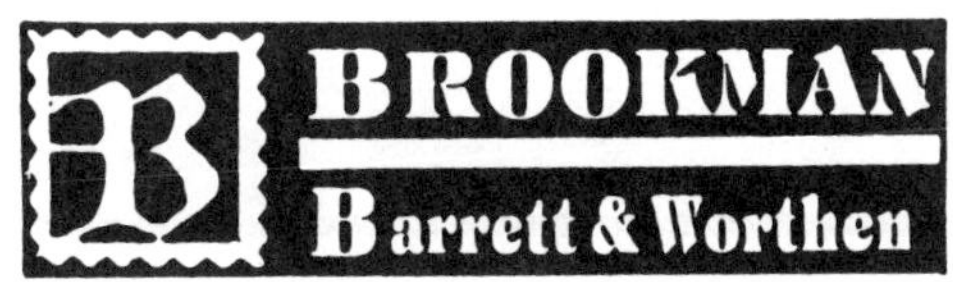

10 Chestnut Drive, Bedford, N.H. 03110
OR CALL TOLL-FREE (800) 332-3383
fAX (603) 472-8795

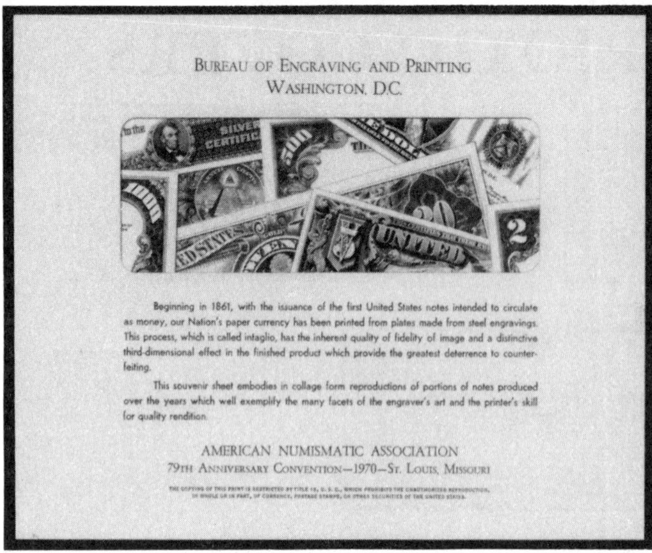

B7

SCCS#s are used with the express permission of the Souvenir Card Collectors Society. Anyone interested in additional information should write to: **Souvenir Card Collectors Society c/o Dana Marr, P.O. Box 4155, Tulsa, OK 74159-0155.**

Cancelled prices are for cards with First Day of Show or Issue postmarks applied by the USPS or BEP Visitors Center, unless designated **(SC)** or **(F)**.

(SC) Show cancel other than First Day

(F) First Day postmark applied by foreign post office.

SCCS No.	Description	Printer	FD Show/ Issue	Mint Card	Cancelled Card
	1939-1969				
FPS 1939Aa	Truck with Gum	USPS	...	77.50	...
FPS 1939Ab	Truck without Gum	USPS	...	15.00	...
F 1945A	Nat'l. Phil. Museum '54	BEP	3/13/54	1875.00	...
PS 1	Barcelona '60	USPS	3/26/60	450.00	250.00(SC)
F 1966A	SIPEX Scenes '66	BEP	5/21/66	175.00	185.00
SO 1	SIPEX Miner	USBNC	5/21/66	10.00	95.00(SC)
PS 2	EFIMEX '68	USPS	11/1/68	5.00	12.50
B 1	SANDIPEX	BEP	7/16/69	65.00	90.00
B 2	ANA '69	BEP	8/12/69	67.50	...
B 3	Fresno	BEP	10/2/69	500.00	...
B 4	ASDA '69	BEP	11/21/69	23.50	100.00
	1970				
B 5	INTERPEX '70	BEP	3/13/70	55.00	150.00
B 6	COMPEX '70	BEP	5/29/70	14.50	150.00
B 7	ANA 1970	BEP	8/18/70	95.00	...
PS 3	PHILYMPIA	USPS	9/18/70	3.00	12.00(SC)
B 8	HAPEX	BEP	11/5/70	15.00	...
	1971				
B 9	INTERPEX '71	BEP	3/12/71	2.25	50.00
B 10	WESTPEX	BEP	4/23/71	2.25	130.00
B 11	NAPEX '71	BEP	5/12/71	2.75	125.00
B 12	ANA '71	BEP	8/10/71	4.25	...
B 13	TEXANEX	BEP	8/26/71	2.75	250.00
PS 4	EXFILIMA	USPS	11/6/71	2.00	50.00
B 14	ASDA '71	BEP	11/19/71	3.00	37.50
B 15	ANPHILEX	BEP	11/26/71	2.00	...
	1972				
B 16	INTERPEX '72	BEP	3/17/72	2.00	12.50
B 17	NOPEX	BEP	4/6/72	2.00	150.00
PS 5	BELGICA	USPS	6/24/72	2.00	30.00(SC)
B 18	ANA '72	BEP	8/15/72	3.75	100.00
PS 6	Olympia Phil. Munchen	USPS	8/18/72	2.00	32.50
PS 7	EXFILBRA	USPS	8/26/72	2.00	75.00
PS 8	Postal Forum	USPS	8/28/72	2.00	32.50
B 19	SEPAD '72	BEP	10/20/72	2.00	37.50
B 20	ASDA '72	BEP	11/17/72	2.00	12.50
B 21	Stamp Expo '72	BEP	11/24/72	2.00	35.00
	1973				
B 22	INTERPEX '73	BEP	3/9/73	2.00	13.00
PS 9	Postal People (11x14") (with minor creases)	USPS	...	90.00	...
PS10	IBRA '73	USPS	5/11/73	2.25	16.00
F 1973B	Washington Statues (4)	PPU	5/21/73	15.00	70.00
B 23	COMPEX '73	BEP	5/25/73	2.00	65.00
PS 11	APEX	USPS	7/4/73	2.25	32.50
B 24	ANA '73	BEP	8/23/73	7.00	35.00
PS 12	POLSKA	USPS	8/19/73	2.25	150.00
B 25	NAPEX '73	BEP	9/14/73	2.25	50.00
B 26	ASDA '73	BEP	11/16/73	2.25	15.00
B 27	Stamp Expo '73	BEP	12/7/73	2.50	20.00
	1974				
PS 13	Hobby Show Chicago	USPS	2/3/74	3.00	20.00
B 28	MILCOPEX '74	BEP	3/8/74	2.75	15.00
PS 14	INTERNABA '74	USPS	6/6/74	2.50	32.50
B 29	ANA '74	BEP	8/13/74	11.00	47.50
PS 15	STOCKHOLMIA '74	USPS	9/21/74	3.00	18.00/22.50
PS 16	EXFILMEX '74	USPS	10/26/74	2.50	37.50(SC)
	1975				
F 1975Ba	$3 Lewiston Falls Banknote	ABNC	5/-/75	50.00	...
F 1975Bb	Declar. of Indep./Portraits	ABNC	5/-/75	29.00	...
PS 17	ESPANA '75	USPS	4/4/75	2.25	47.50/75.00/F
B 30	NAPEX '75	BEP	5/9/75	9.00	22.50
PS 18	ARPHILA '75	USPS	6/6/75	2.75	35.00
B 31	IWY (with folder)	BEP	5/2/75	22.50	...
B 32	ANA '75	BEP	8/19/75	11.00	50.00
B 33	ASDA '75 (G. Washington)	BEP	11/21/75	37.50	60.00
	1976				
PS 19	WERABA '76	USPS	4/1/76	4.00	5.50
B 34	INTERPHIL '76 (Jefferson)	BEP	5/29/76	7.50	18.50
B 35	Card from INTERPHIL Prog.	BEP	5/29/76	10.00	75.00
SO 2	INTERPHIL "America"	ABNC	5/29/76	60.00	100.00
SO 3	INTERPHIL "Lincoln"	ABNC	5/29/76	65.00	100.00
SO 4	INTERPHIL Banquet Card	ABNC	6/5/76	180.00	...
SO 5	INTERPHIL Banquet Menu	ABNC	6/5/76	315.00	...
B 36	Science BEP	BEP	5/30/76	7.95	150.00
PS 20	Science USPS	USPS	5/30/76	3.50	8.00
B 37	Stamp Expo '76	BEP	6/11/76	8.00	70.00
PS 21	Colorado Statehood	USPS	8/1/76	4.00	6.75
PS 22	HAFNIA '76	USPS	8/20/76	4.00	6.75
B 38	ANA '76	BEP	8/24/76	7.50	37.50
PS 23	ITALIA '76	USPS	10/14/76	4.00	6.75/40.00/F
PS 24	NORDPOSTA '76	USPS	10/30/76	4.00	6.75
	1977				
B 39	MILCOPEX '77	BEP	3/4/77	3.00	20.00
B 40	ROMPEX '77	BEP	5/20/77	3.00	11.00
PS 25	AMPHILEX '77	USPS	5/26/77	4.00	6.75
B 41	ANA '77	BEP	8/23/77	4.00	21.50
PS 26	San Marino '77	USPS	8/28/77	4.00	6.75
B 42	PURIPEX '77	BEP	9/2/77	3.00	10.00
B 43	ASDA '77	BEP	11/16/77	4.50	11.00
	1978-79				
PS 27	ROCPEX '78	USPS	3/20/78	5.00	100.00
PS 28	NAPOSTA '78	USPS	5/20/78	4.00	5.50/22.50/F
B 44	Money Show '78	BEP	6/2/78	5.00	12.00
B 45	CENJEX '78	BEP	6/23/78	4.00	10.00
SO 9	Int'l Paper Money Show	ABNC	6/15/79	40.00	70.00
SO 10	ANA '79	ABNC	7/28/79	15.00	40.00
PS 29	BRASILIANA '79	USPS	9/15/79	6.00	7.50
PS 30	JAPEX '79	USPS	11/2/79	6.00	7.50

B 37

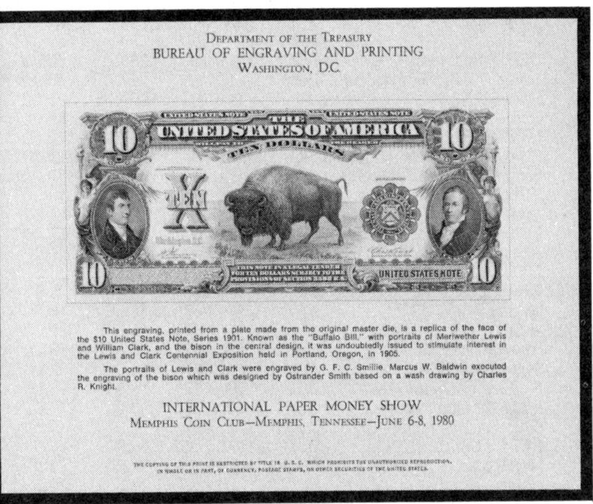

SO 11

CS No.	Description	Printer	FD Show/ Issue	Mint Card	Cancelled Card
	1980				
46	ANA '80 Albuquerque	BEP	2/15/80	20.00	50.00
S 31	London '80	USPS	5/6/80	6.00	75.00
47	Money Show '80	BEP	6/6/80	11.50	30.00
O 11	Intil. Paper Money Show	ABNC	6/6/80	30.00	40.00
S 32	NORWEX '80	USPS	6/13/80	5.00	6.50
48	NAPEX '80	BEP	7/4/80	13.50	37.50
O 12	ANA '80	ABNC	8/13/80	15.00	65.00
O 13	Bank Note Reporter	ABNC	-/-/80	12.00	...
49	Visitor Center	BEP	9/8/80	9.00	15.00
50	Stamp Festival '80	BEP	9/25/80	16.50	35.00
S 33	ESSEN '80	USPS	11/15/80	5.00	6.50
	1981				
O 14	ANA Winter '81	ABNC	2/5/81	20.00	100.00
51	Stamp Expo '81	BEP	3/20/81	18.50	47.50
52	Visitor Center '81	BEP	4/22/81	7.50	15.00
1981B	Embarkation/Pilgrims	PPU	5/17/81	45.00	...
S 34	WIPA '81	USPS	5/22/81	5.00	6.50

SCCS No.	Description	Printer	FD Show/ Issue	Mint Card	Cancelled Card
	1981 (cont.)				
B 53	Money Show '81	BEP	6/19/81	17.50	27.50
SO 15	Int'l Paper Money Show	ABNC	6/19/81	20.00	24.00
SO 16	INTERPAM	ABNC	6/15/81	12.00	...
B 54	ANA '81	BEP	7/27/81	15.00	27.50
SO 17	ANA '81	ABNC	7/28/81	16.00	28.00
SO 18	ANA Building Fund	ABNC	7/28/81	28.00	150.00
PS 35	Stamp Coll. Month '81	USPS	10/1/81	5.00	6.50
PS 36	PHILATOKYO '81	USPS	10/9/81	5.00	6.50
PS 37	NORDPOSTA '81	USPS	11/7/81	5.00	6.50
SO 20	Chester CC/Green	ABNC	12/10/81	10.00	95.00
SO 21	Chester CC/Brown	ABNC	12/10/81	10.00	95.00
	1982				
SO 22	FUN '82	ABNC	1/6/82	14.00	300.00
SO 23	ANA/Winter '82	ABNC	2/18/82	11.00	28.00
B 55	MILCOPEX '82	BEP	3/5/82	16.50	25.00
PS 38	CANADA '82	USPS	5/20/82	5.00	6.50
PS 39	PHILEXFRANCE '82	USPS	6/11/82	4.00	5.50
B 56	Money Show '82	BEP	6/18/82	13.50	25.00
SO 24	Int'l Paper Money Show	ABNC	6/18/82	23.00	25.00
F 1982A	NAPEX '82	PPU	7/2/82	14.00	28.00
SO 25	ANA '82	ABNC	8/17/82	13.00	25.00
B 57	ANA '82	BEP	8/17/82	17.50	18.50
F 1982B	BALPEX	PPU	9/4/82	14.00	40.00
PS 40	Stamp Coll. Month '82	USPS	10/1/82	5.00	6.00
B 58	ESPAMER '82	BEP	10/12/82	38.50	85.00
PS 41	ESPAMER '82 USPS	USPS	10/12/82	5.00	6.00
	1983				
B 59	FUN '83	BEP	1/5/83	25.00	42.50
SO 32	ANA Winter	ABNC	1/5/83	17.00	22.00
PS 42	US-Sweden	USPS	3/24/83	4.75	6.00
PS 43	German Settlers	USPS	4/29/83	4.75	6.00
F 1983A	North Berwick Bank	PPU	...	15.00	40.00
PS 44	TEMBAL '83	USPS	5/21/83	4.75	6.00
F 1983C	NAPEX	PPU	6/10/83	16.00	30.00
B 60	TEXANEX-TOPEX	BEP	6/17/83	26.50	35.00
SO 33	Int'l Paper Money Show	ABNC	6/17/83	19.00	20.00
PS 45	BRASILIANA '83	USPS	7/29/83	4.75	6.00
PS 46	BANGKOK '83	USPS	8/4/83	4.75	6.00
B 61	ANA '83	BEP	8/16/83	22.50	30.00
SO 34	ANA '83	ABNC	8/16/83	17.00	25.00
PS 47	Memento '83	USPS	8/19/83	3.75	4.50
F 1983F	BALPEX	PPU	9/3/83	14.00	20.00
PS 48	Stamp Collecting '83	USPS	10/4/83	4.75	6.00
B 62	Philatelic Show,Boston '83	BEP	10/21/83	15.00	42.50
B 63	ASDA '83	BEP	11/17/83	16.50	30.00

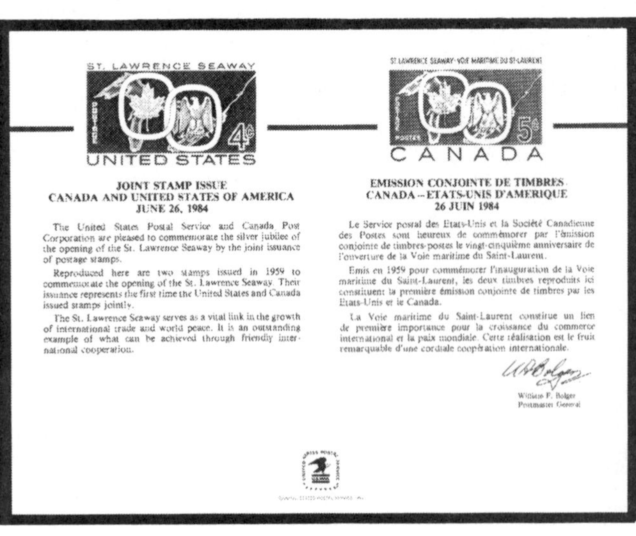

PS 51

SCCS No.	Description	Printer	FD Show/ Issue	Mint Card	Cancelled Card
		1984			
B 64	FUN '84	BEP	1/4/84	26.50	30.00
B 65	Eagle/Brown	BEP	1/4/84	300.00	425.00
SO 35	ANA Winter	ABNC	2/23/84	26.00	45.00
B 66	ESPANA '84	BEP	4/27/84	18.50	25.00
PS 49	ESPANA '84 USPS	USPS	4/27/84	4.50	6.00
B 67	Stamp Expo '84	BEP	4/27/84	22.50	27.50
B 68	COMPEX '84	BEP	5/25/84	22.50	42.50
SO 37	Int'l Paper Money Show	ABNC	6/15/84	18.00	32.00
B 69	Money Show '84,Memphis	BEP	6/15/84	42.50	45.00
B 70	Eagle/Blue	BEP	6/15/84	285.00	400.00
PS 50	Hamburg '84	USPS	6/19/84	4.50	6.00
F 1984A	NAPEX	PPU	6/24/84	11.50	25.00
PS 51	US-Canada Seaway	USPS	6/26/84	4.50	5.50
SO 38	Statue of Liberty	ABNC	7/4/84	6.00	18.00
B 71	ANA '84	BEP	7/28/84	15.00	25.00
B 72	Eagle/Green	BEP	7/28/84	280.00	425.00
SO 39	ANA '84	ABNC	7/28/84	35.00	40.00
PS 52	AUSIPEX '84	USPS	9/21/84	4.50	5.50
PS 53	Stamp Collecting '84	USPS	10/1/84	4.00	5.50
PS 54	PHILAKOREA '84	USPS	10/22/84	4.50	5.50
B 73	ASDA '84	BEP	11/15/84	16.50	42.50
B 74	Statue of Liberty/Green	BEP	11/15/84	115.00	150.00
		1985			
SO 40	FUN '85	ABNC	1/3/85	10.00	50.00
B 75	Long Beach '85	BEP	1/31/85	13.50	20.00
SO 41	ANA Winter	ABNC	2/21/85	34.00	45.00
PS 55	Memento '85	USPS	2/26/85	4.50	5.50
B 76	MILCOPEX '85	BEP	3/1/85	16.50	30.00
PS 56	OLYMPHILEX	USPS	3/18/85	4.50	5.50
SO 42	Nat'l Assn./Tobacco Distr.	ABNC	3/27/85	10.00	...
B 77	Int'l Coin Club, El Paso	BEP	4/19/85	12.50	25.00
B 78	Statue of Liberty/Maroon	BEP	4/19/85	150.00	180.00
F 1985D	Eagle/81st Convention	PPU	5/12/85	35.00	...
PS 57	ISRAPHIL	USPS	5/14/85	4.50	5.50
B 79	Pacific NW Num Assn.	BEP	5/17/85	14.00	27.50
B 80	NAPEX '85	BEP	6/7/85	13.50	27.50
B 81	Money Show, Memphis	BEP	6/14/85	13.50	17.50
PS 58	ARGENTINA '85	USPS	7/5/85	4.50	5.50
PS 61	Statue of Liberty	USPS	7/18/85	18.00	17.50
B 82	ANA '85	BEP	8/20/85	13.50	17.50
B 83	Statue of Liberty/Green	BEP	8/20/85	150.00	200.00
PS 59	MOPHILA	USPS	9/11/85	5.50	6.50
PS 60	ITALIA '85	USPS	10/25/85	4.50	5.50
B 84	Money Show '85,Cherry Hill	BEP	11/14/85	17.50	23.50
B85-6	Liberty Bell/Blue	BEP	11/14/85	160.00	200.00
		1986			
B 87	FUN '86	BEP	1/2/86	16.00	18.00
B 88	ANA, Salt Lake City	BEP	2/19/86	12.50	24.00
PS 62	Stat.of Liberty,Memento'86	USPS	2/21/86	6.50	7.00
PS 62v	Stat.of Lib.,STAMPEX Ovpt	USPS	8/4/86	15.00	25.00
B 89	Garfield-Perry '86	BEP	3/21/86	13.50	32.50
B 90	AMERIPEX	BEP	5/22/86	12.50	25.00
B 91-92	Liberty Bell/Green	BEP	5/22/86	55.00	100.00
B 93	Money Show '86	BEP	6/20/86	12.50	22.50
B 94	ANA, Milwaukee	BEP	8/5/86	12.50	22.50
B 95-96	Liberty Bell/Brown	BEP	8/5/86	55.00	100.00
PS 63	STOCKHOLMIA '86	USPS	8/28/86	6.50	6.50
B 97	HOUPEX '86	BEP	9/5/86	18.50	25.00
B 98	LOBEX '86	BEP	10/2/86	15.00	22.50
B 99	NW Paper Money Conv	BEP	11/13/86	14.00	24.00
B 100	Dallas Expo	BEP	12/11/86	14.00	22.50
SO 43	SMPC/IBNS Liberty & Holo	ABNC	...	70.00	...

SCCS No.	Description	Printer	FD Show/ Issue	Mint Card	Cancelled Card
		1987			
B 101	BEP Anniversary	BEP	1/7/87	25.00	70.00
B 101A	Same, "FUN" Embossed	BEP	1/7/87	75.00	120.00
B 101B	Same, ANA Midwinter seals	BEP	2/27/87	100.00	125.00
B 101C	Same, BEP&WMPG seals	BEP	4/9/87	95.00	165.00
B 101D	Same, BEP&IPMS seals	BEP	6/19/87	95.00	120.00
B 101E	Same, BEP&ANA '87 seals	BEP	8/26/87	85.00	125.00
B 101F	Same, BEP&GENA seals	BEP	9/18/87	60.00	120.00
B 102	FUN '87	BEP	1/7/87	14.00	18.50
B 103	ANA Mid-Winter '87	BEP	2/27/87	16.50	21.50
B 104	Ft. Worth Dedication	BEP	4/25/87	26.50	57.50
SO 56	AFL-CIO Trade Show	ABNC	6/19/87	100.00	...
...	200th Anniv. Three States	ABNC	...	15.00	...
PS 64	CAPEX '87	BEP	6/13/87	5.00	5.50
B 105	Money Show '87	BEP	6/19/87	12.50	18.00
SO 54	200th Anniv./Constitution	ABNC	6/19/87	13.00	22.00
B 106	ANA '87 Atlanta, GA	BEP	8/26/87	12.50	18.00
SO 57	$10 Hawaii/ANA	ABNC	8/26/87	16.00	25.00
B 108	Gr. Eastern Num. Assn	BEP	9/18/87	16.50	18.00
B 109	State Shields/Brown	BEP	9/18/87	90.00	170.00
PS 65	HAFNIA '87	USPS	10/16/87	5.00	5.50
B 110	SESCAL	BEP	10/16/87	16.50	25.00
SO 58	NWPMC	ABNC	10/29/87	17.00	25.00
B 111	Hawaii State Num. Assn	BEP	11/12/87	26.50	26.50
PS 66	MONTE CARLO	USPS	11/13/87	5.00	5.50
		1988			
B 112	FUN '88	BEP	1/7/88	16.50	19.50
B 113	FUN, State Shields/Green	BEP	1/7/88	100.00	140.00
SO 59	Constitution Anniv./8 states	ABNC	...	12.00	...
F 1988B	Stamporee '88	ABNC	...	40.00	...
B 114	ANA Winter, Little Rock	BEP	3/11/88	13.50	19.50
PS 67	FINLANDIA '88	USPS	6/1/88	5.00	5.50
B 115	Int'l Paper Money Show	BEP	6/24/88	11.50	18.00
SO 60	IPMS	ABNC	6/24/88	14.50	20.00
SO 66	Constitution/3 states	ABNC	...	12.00	...
B 116	ANA Cincinnati	BEP	7/20/88	14.50	18.00
B 117	ANA, State Shields/Blue	BEP	7/20/88	100.00	165.00
SO 61	ANA, $100 Hawaii note	ABNC	7/20/88	15.00	23.00
B 118	APS Detroit	BEP	8/25/88	13.00	26.50
B 119	Illinois Numis. Assn.	BEP	10/6/88	11.50	17.50
B 120	MIDAPHIL '88	BEP	11/18/88	11.50	26.50
		1989			
B 121	FUN	BEP	1/5/89	11.50	17.50
B 122	FUN/American Heritage	BEP	1/5/89	60.00	100.00
SO 62	FUN	ABNC	1/5/89	15.00	25.00
SO 63	Miami Stamp Expo	ABNC	1/27/89	24.00	35.00
B 124	ANA Mid-Winter	BEP	3/3/89	11.50	20.00
SO 64	ANA Museum(SO34 reduced)	ABNC	...	15.00	25.00
SO 65	G. Washington Inaug./Anniv.	ABNC	3/15/89	15.00	...
B 125	Int'l Coin Club of El Paso	BEP	4/28/89	13.50	18.00
B 126	IPMS	BEP	6/23/89	11.50	18.00
B 127	IPMS/Agriculture Proof	BEP	6/23/89	60.00	100.00
SO 67	IPMS	ABNC	6/23/89	15.00	20.00
PS 68	PHILEXFRANCE	USPS	7/7/89	5.50	5.50
B 129	ANA, Pittsburgh, PA	BEP	8/9/89	16.50	19.50
B 130	ANA/Decl.of Indep./Proof	BEP	8/9/89	55.00	100.00
SO 68	ANA	ABNC	8/9/89	15.00	20.00

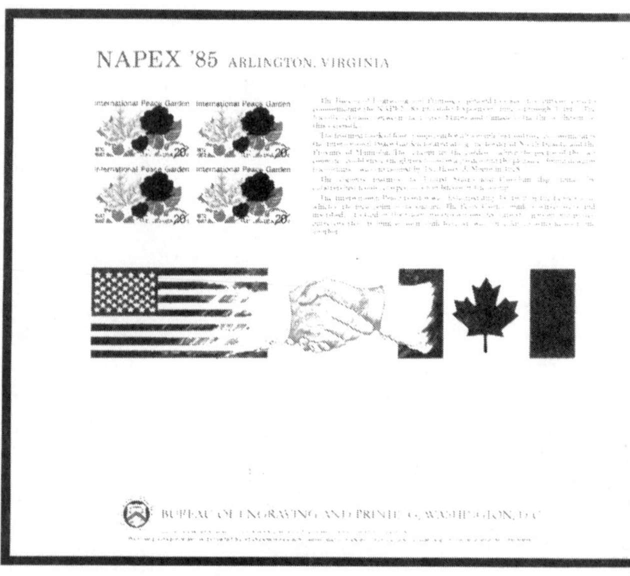

B 80

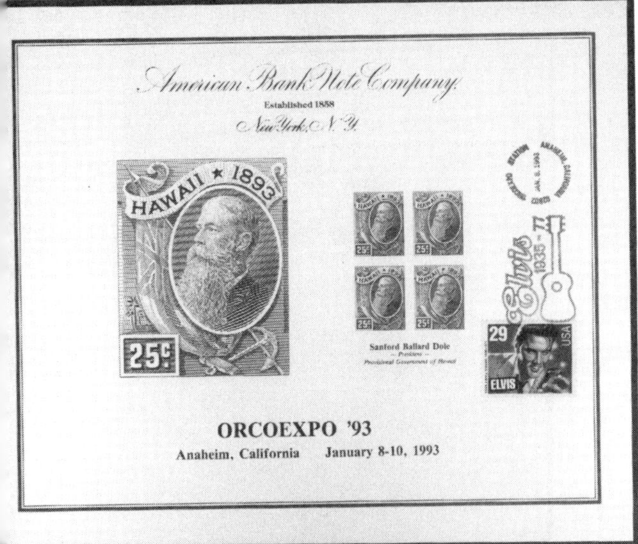

SO 109

CCS No.	Description	Printer	FD Show/ Issue	Mint Card	Cancelled Card
	1989 (cont.)				
132	APS Anaheim, CA	BEP	8/24/89	11.50	22.50
O 69	200th Anniv./North Carolina	ABNC	11/2/89	15.00	20.00
S 69	World Stamp Expo, DC	USPS	11/17/89	7.00	8.00
	1990				
133	FUN	BEP	1/4/90	11.50	18.00
134	FUN/Ships Proof	BEP	1/4/90	48.00	90.00
O 71	Miami Stamp Expo	ABNC	1/12/90	23.50	35.00
135	ANA Midwinter,San Diego,CA	BEP	3/2/90	11.50	18.00
136	CSNS '90, Milwaukee,WI	BEP	4/6/90	11.50	18.00
137	CSNS/Ships Proof	BEP	4/6/90	45.00	90.00
138	ARIPEX	BEP	4/20/90	11.50	22.50
S 70	Stamp World London	USPS	5/3/90	7.00	8.00
139	DCSE '90, Dallas, TX	BEP	6/14/90	11.50	18.00
O 72	200th Anniv./Rhode Island	ABNC	6/15/90	15.00	22.00
140	ANA National, Seattle, WA	BEP	8/22/90	14.50	18.00
141	ANA/Ships Proof	BEP	8/22/90	45.00	90.00
142	APS Stampshow	BEP	8/23/90	11.50	21.50
143	Westex Num.Exhb,Denver,CO	BEP	9/21/90	13.50	18.00
144	HSNA	BEP	11/1/90	15.00	30.00
	1991				
145	FUN	BEP	1/3/91	13.50	18.00
146	FUN/Statue of Freedom Proof	BEP	1/3/91	45.00	90.00
147	ANA, Mid-Winter	BEP	3/1/91	11.50	18.00
152	Ft. Worth Facility Dedication	BEP	4/26/91	45.00	175.00
148	IPMS, Memphis, TN	BEP	6/14/91	11.50	18.00
O 74	IPMS	ABNC	6/14/91	17.50	25.00
O 75	Flag/Hologram	ABNC	6/14/91	17.50	25.00
149	ANA, Chicago, IL	BEP	8/13/91	16.50	19.50
150	ANA, Intaglio Print	BEP	8/13/91	45.00	82.50
O 76	ANA	ABNC	8/13/91	16.50	25.00
	ANA/Capitol Proof	ABNC	8/13/91	40.00	80.00
O 77	SCCS/10th Anniv.	ABNC	8/13/91	15.00	25.00
151	APS Stampshow,Phila.,PA	BEP	8/22/91	11.50	24.00
O 78	APS	ABNC	8/22/91	15.00	25.00
O 79	APS/Limited Edition	ABNC	8/22/91	115.00	...
O 80	BALPEX	ABNC	8/31/91	15.00	25.00
O 81	ASDA	ABNC	11/7/91	15.00	25.00
O 82	ASDA/Limited Edition	ABNC	11/7/91	110.00	...
O 83	Philadelphia NSE	ABNC	11/15/91	15.00	25.00
	1992				
153	FUN '92	BEP	1/9/92	11.50	18.00
154	FUN, Limited Edition	BEP	1/9/92	45.00	85.00
O 84	FUN '92	ABNC	1/9/92	15.00	25.00
O 85	Columbus/Hologram	ABNC	1/9/92	17.00	30.00
O 86	ANA/Early Spring	ABNC	2/27/92	15.00	25.00
O 87	INTERPEX	ABNC	3/12/92	15.00	25.00
155	Central States Numis. Conv.	BEP	4/30/92	13.00	21.50
156	World Columbian Stamp Ex	BEP	5/22/92	13.00	...
157	WCSE/Intaglio Ltd. Edition	BEP	5/22/92	40.00	...
O 88	WCSE/Costa Rica	ABNC	5/22/92	15.00	25.00
O 89	WCSE/1¢ Columbian	ABNC	5/22/92	15.00	25.00
O 90	WCSE/Limited Edition	ABNC	5/22/92	70.00	95.00
O 90A	WCSE/Ltd. Edition Proof	ABNC	5/22/92	...	...
O 91-96	WCSE/1893 Ticket Reprints	ABNC	5/22/92	200.00	250.00
O 97	WCSE/Portfolio w/card	ABNC	5/22/92	...	...
O 98	WCSE/Columbus	SV	5/22/92	...	...
O 99	WCSE/Slania	SV	5/22/92	...	...
O 100	WCSE/Bonnie Blair	SV	5/22/92	...	...
O 101	WCSE/Eagle Hologram	SV	5/22/92	...	...

SCCS No.	Description	Printer	FD Show/ Issue	Mint Card	Cancelled Card
	1992 (cont.)				
B 158	Int'l Paper Money Show	BEP	6/19/92	11.50	18.00
SO 102	IPMS	ABNC	6/19/92	15.00	25.00
B 162	Savings Bonds	BEP	6/15/92	12.50	...
B 159	ANA, Orlando	BEP	8/12/92	11.50	18.00
B 160	ANA, Intaglio, Green print	BEP	8/12/92	45.00	85.00
SO 103	ANA, Orlando	ABNC	8/12/92	15.00	25.00
B 161	APS	BEP	8/27/92	11.50	22.50
SO 104	APS	ABNC	8/27/92	15.00	25.00
SO 105	APS/Limited Edition	ABNC	8/27/92	70.00	100.00
SO 105A	APS/Limited Edition Proof	ABNC	8/27/92	...	...
B 163	Columbus Fleet	BEP	10/13/92	45.00	...
SO 106	ASDA, Stamp	ABNC	10/28/92	15.00	25.00
SO 107	ASDA, Historic Event Card	ABNC	10/28/92	15.00	25.00
SO 108	ASDA/Limited Edition	ABNC	10/28/92	50.00	75.00
SO 108A	ASDA/Ltd. Ed. Proof	ABNC	10/28/92	...	...
	1993				
B 165	FUN '93	BEP	1/7/93	11.50	18.00
B 166	American Vistas, 3 views	BEP	1/7/93	45.00	75.00
SO 109	Orcoexpo	ABNC	1/8/93	16.00	25.00
SO 110	Orco Locomotive Hologram	ABNC	1/8/93	20.00	30.00
B 164	CFC,Red Cross Orlando,FL	BEP	1/13/93	11.50	18.00
SO 111	Milcopex, Milwaukee, WI	ABNC	3/5/93	16.00	25.00
F 1993A	GENA, Maple Shade, NJ	PPU	3/5/93	9.50	...
B 167	ANA Colorado Springs	BEP	3/11/93	11.50	18.00
SO 112	ANA Colorado Springs	ABNC	3/11/93	16.00	25.00
SO 113	Plymouth, MI Stamp Show	ABNC	4/24/93	16.00	25.00
B 168	ASDA Mega Event, NYC	BEP	5/5/93	11.50	17.50
SO 114	ASDA Mega Event, NYC	ABNC	5/5/93	16.00	25.00
B 169	Texas Numismatic Assn	BEP	5/6/93	11.50	17.50
B 170	Georgia Numismatic Assn	BEP	5/13/93	11.50	17.50
B 171	IPMS, Memphis, TN	BEP	6/18/93	11.50	17.50
B 172	American Vistas, 3 views	BEP	6/18/93	40.00	75.00
SO 115	IPMS Memphis, TN	ABNC	6/18/93	16.00	25.00
B 173	ANA Baltimore, MD	BEP	7/28/93	11.50	17.50
B 174	American Vistas, 3 Views	BEP	7/28/93	40.00	75.00
SO 116	ANA Baltimore, MD	BEP	7/28/93	16.00	25.00
SO 117	ANA, Limited Edition	ABNC	7/28/93	50.00	75.00
B 175	Savings Bond	BEP	8/2/93	11.50	30.00
SO 118	APS, Houston, TX	ABNC	8/19/93	16.00	25.00
SO 119	APS, Limited Edition	ABNC	8/19/93	40.00	60.00
B 176	Omaha Philatelic Society	BEP	9/3/93	11.50	23.50
SO 120	ASDA Mega Event, NYC	ABNC	10/28/93	16.50	25.00
SO 121	ASDA Mega, Money vignette	ABNC	10/28/93	16.50	25.00
SO 122	ASDA, Stamp vign., Limited	ABNC	10/28/93	40.00	60.00
SO 122A	ASDA, Stamp vign., Proof	ABNC	10/28/93	...	...
B 178	ASDA Mega Event, NYC	BEP	10/28/93	11.50	17.50
	1994				
B 179	FUN '94, Banknote	BEP	1/6/94	11.50	17.50
B 180	FUN '94, Special	BEP	1/6/94	40.00	75.00
SO 123	ARIPEX, Mesa, AZ	ABNC	1/7/94	16.00	25.00
B 181	SANDICAL, San Diego, CA	BEP	2/11/94	11.50	17.50
B 182	ANA, New Orleans	BEP	3/3/94	11.50	17.50
SO 124	ANA, New Orleans	ABNC	3/3/94	16.00	25.00
SO 125	MILCOPEX, Milwaukee, WI	ABNC	3/4/94	16.00	25.00
SO 126	Garfield-Perry, Cleveland	ABNC	3/18/94	16.00	25.00
SO 127	Central States, Indianapolis	ABNC	4/8/94	16.00	25.00
B 183	EPMB, Maastricht, NL	BEP	4/16/94	11.50	17.50
B 184	IPMS, Memphis, TN	BEP	6/17/94	11.50	17.50
B 185	IPMS, Special	BEP	6/17/94	40.00	...
SO 128	IPMS, Memphis, TN	ABNC	6/17/94	16.00	25.00
B 187	ANA, 103rd	BEP	7/27/94	12.50	18.50
B 188	ANA, Special	BEP	7/27/94	40.00	...
SO 129	ANA, 103rd	ABNC	7/27/94	16.00	25.00
SO 130	ANA, Hologram	ABNC	7/27/94	20.00	30.00
SO 131	ANA, Limited	ABNC	7/27/94	50.00	75.00
B189	BEP Savings Bond	BEP	8/1/94	12.50	...
B 190	APS - 108th, Pittsburgh, PA	BEP	8/18/94	14.50	20.00
SO 132	APS - 90¢, Pittsburgh, PA	ABNC	8/18/94	16.00	25.00
SO 133	APS, Limited	ABNC	8/18/94	40.00	60.00
SO 134	BALPEX, Baltimore, MD	ABNC	9/3/94	16.00	25.00
B 191	ASDA Mega, New York, NY	BEP	11/3/94	12.50	17.50
SO 135	ASDA Mega, 90¢ Lincoln	ABNC	11/3/94	16.00	25.00
SO 136	ASDA Mega, Limited	ABNC	11/3/94	40.00	60.00
SO 137	WPMS, Banknote	ABNC	11/11/94	16.00	25.00
	1995				
B192	FUN '95, Orlando, FL	BEP	1/5/95	13.50	...
B193	FUN '95, Special Intaglio	BEP	1/5/95	40.00	...
B194	COLOPEX', Columbus, OH	BEP	4/7/95	13.50	...
B195	NYINC, New York, NY	BEP	5/5/95	13.50	...
B196	IPMS, Memphis, TN	BEP	6/16/95	13.50	...
B197	Stamp Centennial, Intaglio Print	BEP	6/30/95	45.00	...
B198	ANA, Anaheim, CA	BEP	8/16/95	13.50	...
B199	ANA, Special Intaglio	BEP	8/16/95	45.00	...
B200	LBN/PE, Long Beach, CA	BEP	10/4/95	13.50	...
B201	ASDA, New York, NY	BEP	11/2/95	13.50	...

*** SCCS #s for 1995 are subject to revision.**

UNOFFICIAL SOUVENIR PAGES

1266

1329

Each Souvenir Page has one or more stamps affixed and cancelled with a "FD of Issue" postmark. Each page also has a picture of the issued stamp(s) and important technical data. Prior to March 1, 1972 these pages were privately distributed. The most prominent servicer was W.C. Bates, who began with Scott #1232 (West Virginia). **These pages were folded twice in order to fit into a #10 envelope.** These are known as "Unofficial" Souvenir Pages.

UNOFFICIAL

Scott No.	Subject	Price
	1962-64 Issues	
1232	West Virginia	7.00
1233	Emancipation Proc	15.00
1234	Alliance/Progress	6.00
1235	Cordell Hull	7.00
1236	Eleanor Roosevelt	6.00
1237	Science	6.00
1238	City Mail	7.00
1239	Red Cross	6.00
1240	Christmas 1963	9.00
1241	Audubon	7.00
1242	Sam Houston	12.00
1243	C.M. Russell	8.00
1244	N.Y. World's Fair	7.00
1245	Muir	12.00
1246	John F. Kennedy	12.00
1247	NJ Tercentenary	6.00
1248	Nevada Statehood	6.00
1249	Register & Vote	6.00
1250	Shakespeare	7.00
1251	Mayo Brothers	7.00
1252	Music	7.00
1253	Homemakers	6.00
1254-57	Christmas 1964	20.00
1258	Veranzano Bridge	5.00
1259	Modern Art	7.00
1260	Radio	9.00
	1965 Commemoratives	
1261	Battle/New Orleans	5.00
1262	Sokol Society	7.00
1263	Cancer	7.00
1264	Churchill	6.00
1265	Magna Carta	5.00
1266	Int'l Cooperation Year	6.00
1267	Salvation Army	6.00
1268	Dante	6.00
1269	Herbert Hoover	5.00
1270	Robert Fulton	5.00
1271	St. Augustine, FL	6.00
1272	Traffic Safety	5.00
1273	Copley	6.00
1274	ITU	7.00
1275	Adlai Stevenson	5.00
1276	Christmas 1965	6.00
	1965-81 Prominent Americans	
1278	1¢ Jefferson	6.00
1278a	Pane of 8	9.00
1279	1¼¢ Gallatin	6.00
1280	2¢ Wright	6.00

Scott No.	Subject	Price
	1965-81 Prominent Americans(cont.)	
1280a	Zip pane of 5	10.00
1280a	Mail early pn. of 5	10.00
1281	3¢ Parkman	5.00
1282	4¢ Lincoln	5.00
1283	5¢ Washington	5.00
1283B	5¢ Wash. re-engr	7.00
1284	6¢ F.D. Roosevelt	7.00
1284b	6¢ Pane of 8	15.00
1285	8¢ Einstein	10.00
1286	10¢ Jackson	6.00
1286A	12¢ Henry Ford	8.00
1287	13¢ J.F. Kennedy	20.00
1288	15¢ Holmes	8.00
1289	20¢ Marshall	9.00
1290	25¢ Douglass	12.50
1291	30¢ Dewey	30.00
1292	40¢ Paine	65.00
1293	50¢ Lucy Stone	65.00
1294	$1 O'Neill	75.00
1295	$5 Moore	150.00
1298	6¢ FDR end coil	6.00
1299	1¢ Jefferson coil	6.00
1303	4¢ Lincoln coil	6.00
1304	5¢ Wash. coil	6.00
1305	6¢ FDR side coil	10.00
	1966 Commemoratives	
1306	Migrat. Bird Treaty	7.00
1307	Hum. Treat./Animal	7.00
1308	Indiana Statehood	6.00
1309	Circus	6.00
1310	SIPEX	6.00
1311	SIPEX Souv. Sht	7.00
1312	Bill of Rights	6.00
1313	Polish Millenium	6.00
1314	Nat'l. Parks Service	6.00
1315	Marine Reserves	6.00
1316	Women's Clubs	6.00
1317	Johnny Appleseed	7.00
1318	Beautif./America	10.00
1319	Great River Road	6.00
1320	Sav. Bond/Srvcmen	8.00
1321	Christmas 1966	6.00
1322	Mary Cassatt	7.00
	1967 Commemoratives	
1323	Nat'l. Grange	6.00
1324	Canada Centenary	6.00
1325	Erie Canal	6.00
1326	Peace/Lions	6.00

Scott No.	Subject	Price
	1967 Commemoratives (cont.)	
1327	Thoreau	5.00
1328	NE Statehood	5.00
1329	Voice of America	5.00
1330	Davy Crockett	7.00
1331-32	Space Twins	20.00
1333	Urban Planning	6.00
1334	Finnish Independ	5.00
1335	Thomas Eakins	7.00
1336	Christmas 1967	7.00
1337	MS Statehood	6.00
	1968-71 Regular Issues	
1338	6¢ Flag	5.00
1338A	6¢ Flag coil	5.00
1338D	6¢ Flag huck press	6.00
1338F	8¢ Flag	6.00
1341	$1 Airlift	65.00
	1968 Commemoratives	
1339	IL Statehood	6.00
1340	Hemisfair	5.00
1342	Youth/Elks	5.00
1343	Law & Order	5.00
1344	Register and Vote	5.00
1345-54	Historic Flags	75.00
1355	Walt Disney	15.00
1356	Marquette	5.00
1357	Daniel Boone	5.00
1358	AK River Navigation	5.00
1359	Leif Erikson	10.00
1360	Cherokee Strip	9.00
1361	Trumbull Painting	5.00
1362	Waterfowl Conserv.	7.00
1363	Christmas 1968	6.00
1364	Chief Joseph	4.50
	1969 Commemoratives	
1365-68	Beautification	20.00
1369	American Legion	5.00
1370	Grandma Moses	6.00
1371	Apollo 8	8.00
1372	W.C. Handy	7.00
1373	CA Settlement	5.00
1374	John Wesley Powell	5.00
1375	AL Statehood	5.00
1376-79	Botanical Congress	20.00
1380	Daniel Webster	5.00
1381	Baseball	125.00
1382	Football	10.00
1383	Eisenhower Memor.	5.00
1384	Christmas 1969	5.00
1385	Hope/Crip. Child	5.00
1386	Harnett Painting	5.00
	1970 Commemoratives	
1387-90	Natural History	30.00
1391	Maine Statehood	6.00
1392	Wildlife Conserv.	6.00
1405	Edgar Lee Masters	5.00
1406	Women's Suffrage	5.00

Scott No.	Subject	Price
	1970 Commemoratives (cont.)	
1407	SC Founding	5.00
1408	Stone Mountain	5.00
1409	Fort Snelling	5.00
1410-13	Anti-Pollution	20.00
1414	Christmas 1970	7.00
1415-18	Christmas Toys	15.00
1415a-18a	Toys Precancelled	60.00
1419	U.N. 25th Anniv	6.00
1420	Mayflower	6.00
1421-22	D.A.V./Servicemen	27.50
	1970-74 Regular Issues	
1393	6¢ Eisenhower	6.00
1393a	Pane of 8	16.00
1393b	Zip pane of 5	20.00
1939b	Mail early p./5	20.00
1394	8¢ Eisen., multi	6.00
1395a	8¢ Eisen., claret, pane of 8	25.00
1395b	Pane of 6	25.00
1396	8¢ USPS	20.00
1398	16¢ Ernie Pyle	5.00
1401	6¢ Eisen., coil	5.00
1402	8¢ Eisen., coil	5.00
	1971 Commemoratives	
1423	American Wool Ind.	8.00
1424	Douglas MacArthur	12.50
1425	Blood Donors	6.00
1426	MO Sesquicent	6.00
	Airmails & Special Delivery	
C67	6¢ Eagle	10.00
C68	Amel. Earhart	15.00
C69	Goddard	15.00
C70	Alaska	7.50
C71	Audubon Jays	7.50
C72	10¢ Stars	8.00
C72b	Pane of 8	25.00
C72c	Pane of 5	35.00
C73	10¢ Stars coil	12.00
C74	Air Service	7.00
C75	20¢ USA	15.00
C76	Moon Landing	10.00
C77	9¢ Delta Wing	12.00
C78	11¢ Jet	9.00
C78a	Pane of 4	25.00
C80	17¢ Liberty	25.00
C81	21¢ USA	25.00
C82	11¢ Jet coil	10.00
E22	45¢ Arrows	25.00
E23	60¢ Arrows	20.00

OFFICIAL SOUVENIR PAGES

1453

OFFICIAL SOUVENIR PAGES

Since March 1, 1972 the U.S. Postal Service has offered, by subscription, ouvenir Pages with first day cancels. They are known as "Official" Souvenir ages. **These were issued flat and unfolded.**

cott No.	Subject	Price
	1972-78 Regular Issues	
297	3¢ Fran. Parkman	5.00
305C	$1 O'Neill coil	17.50
305E	15¢ O.W. Holmes	3.00
393D	7¢ B. Franklin	8.00
397	14¢ LaGuardia	110.00
399	18¢ Eliz. Blackwell	3.00
400	21¢ A. Giannini	6.00
	1972 Commemoratives	
448-51	Cape Hatteras	100.00
452	Wolf Trap Farm	40.00
453	Yellowstone Park	110.00
454	Mt. McKinley	30.00
455	Family Planning	750.00
456-59	Colonial Craftsmen	20.00
460-62	C85 Olympics	12.50
463	PTA	7.50
464-67	Wildlife	10.00
468	Mail Order	7.50
469	Osteopathic Medicine	7.50
470	Tom Sawyer	7.50
471-72	Christmas 1972	9.00
473	Pharmacy	7.50
474	Stamp Collecting	7.50
	1973 Commemoratives	
475	Love	10.00
476	Pamphleteers	6.00
477	Posting Broadside	7.50
478	Post Rider	6.00
479	Colonial Drummer	5.00
480-83	Boston Tea Party	9.00
484	George Gershwin	7.50
485	Robinson Jeffers	6.00
486	Henry O. Tanner	6.00
487	Willa Cather	5.00
488	Copernicus	7.50
489-98	Postal People	7.50
499	Harry S. Truman	6.00
500-02,C86	Electronics	10.00
503	Lyndon B. Johnson	5.00
504	Angus Cattle	5.00
505	Chautauqua	3.50
506	Kansas Wheat	3.00
507-08	Christmas 1973	7.50
	1973-74 Regular Issues	
509	10¢ Crossed Flags	4.00
510	10¢ Jeff. Memor	4.00
511	10¢ Zip Code	6.00
518	6.3¢ Bulk Rate coil	5.00
	1974 Commemoratives	
525	VFW	3.00
526	Robert Frost	3.50
527	Expo '74	3.00
528	Horse Racing	5.00

Scott No.	Subject	Price
1529	Skylab	7.50
1530-37	Univ. Postal Union	6.00
1538-41	Mineral Heritage	7.50
1542	Fort Harrod	3.00
1543-46	Cont. Congress	6.00
1547	Energy Conserv	3.00
1548	Sleepy Hollow	4.00
1549	Retarded Children	3.00
1550-52	Christmas 1974	7.50
	1975 Commemoratives	
1553	Benjamin West	3.00
1554	Paul L. Dunbar	5.00
1555	D.W. Griffith	4.50
1556	Pioneer	7.50
1557	Mariner	6.00
1558	Coll. Bargaining	3.00
1559	Sybil Ludington	4.00
1560	Salem Poor	5.00
1561	Haym Salomon	4.00
1562	Peter Francisco	4.00
1563	Lexing. & Concord	3.00
1564	Bunker Hill	3.50
1565-68	Military Services	7.50
1569-70	Apollo Soyuz	7.50
1571	Int'l Women's Year	3.00
1572-75	Postal Bicentennial	5.00
1576	Wld. Peace thru Law	3.00
1577-78	Bank & Commerce	3.00
1579-80	Christmas 1975	5.00
	1975-81 Americana Issues	
1581-82,84-85	1¢-4¢ Issues	3.50
1591	9¢ Rt. to Assemble	3.00
1592	10¢ Petit./Redress	3.50
1593	11¢ Free./Press	3.00
1594,1816	12¢ Conscience	4.00
1596	13¢ Eagle/Shield	4.00
1597,1618C	15¢ Ft. McHenry	4.00
1599,1619	16¢ Liberty	3.00
1603	24¢ Old No. Church	3.00
1604	28¢ Rem. Outpost	3.00
1605	29¢ Lighthouse	3.00
1606	30¢ Am. Schools	4.00
1608	50¢ "Betty" Lamp	6.00
1610	$1 Rush Lamp	6.00
1611	$2 Kero. Lamp	7.50
1612	$5 R.R. Lantern	15.00
1613	3.1¢ Non Prof coil	10.00
1614	7.7¢ Bulk Rate coil	3.50
1615	7.9¢ Bulk Rate coil	3.00
1615C	8.4¢ Bulk Rate coil	5.00
1616	9¢ Assembly coil	3.00
1617	10¢ Redress coil	4.00
1618	13¢ Libty. Bell coil	3.00
1622,25	13¢ Flag/Ind. Hall	3.00
1623c	$1 Vend bk. p. 10	25.00

Scott No.	Subject	Price
	1976 Commemoratives	
1629-31	Spirit of '76	5.00
1632	INTERPHIL '76	4.00
1633-82	State Flags (5 pgs.)	50.00
1683	Telephone Cent.	3.00
1684	Commer. Aviation	3.00
1685	Chemistry	3.00
1686-89	Bicentennial S/S (4)	40.00
1690	Benjamin Franklin	3.00
1691-94	Dec. of Indepen	6.00
1695-98	Olympics	6.00
1699	Clara Maass	2.50
1700	Adolph S. Ochs	2.50
1701-03	Christmas 1976	5.00
	1977 Commemoratives	
1704	Wash. at Princeton	3.00
1705	Sound Recording	3.00
1706-09	Pueblo Art	3.50
1710	Lindbergh Flight	4.00
1711	CO Centennial	3.00
1712-15	Butterflies	3.50
1716	Lafayette	3.00
1717-20	Skilled Hands (4)	3.50
1721	Peace Bridge	3.00
1722	Herkimer/Oriskany	2.50
1723-24	Energy Conserv	2.50
1725	Alta, CA	3.00
1726	Art. of Confederation	2.50
1727	Talking Pictures	3.00
1728	Surrender/Saratoga	4.00
1729-30	Christmas, Omaha	3.00
1729-30	Xmas, Valley Forge	3.00
	1978 Issues	
1731	Carl Sandburg	3.00
1732-3	Cpt. Cook, Anchor	4.00
1732-3	Cpt. Cook/Honolulu	5.00
1734	13¢ Ind. Hd. Penny	3.00
1735,43	"A" Stamp (2)	7.50
1737	15¢ Rose bklt. sgl	4.00
1742a	15¢ Windmills bklt. pane/10 (1980)	6.00
1744	Harriet Tubman	5.00
175-48	American Quilts	4.00
1749-52	American Dance	4.00
1753	French Alliance	3.00
1754	Dr. Papanicolaou	4.00
1755	Jimmie Rodgers	5.00
1756	George M. Cohan	3.00
1757	CAPEX '78	10.00
1758	Photography	3.00
1759	Viking Missions	6.00
1760-63	American Owls	4.00
1764-67	American Trees	4.00
1768	Madonna & Child	3.00
1769	Xmas Hobby Horse	3.00
	1979 Commemoratives	
1770	Robert F. Kennedy	3.00
1771	Martin L. King, Jr.	5.00
1772	Year of the Child	3.00
1773	John Steinbeck	3.00
1774	Albert Einstein	3.50
1775-78	PA Toleware	4.00
1779-82	Amer. Architecture	4.00
1783-86	Endangered Flora	4.00
1787	Seeing Eye Dogs	3.00
1788	Special Olympics	3.00
1789	John Paul Jones	4.00
1790	10¢ Olym. Games	4.00
1791-94	15¢ Summer Olym.	6.00
1795-98	15¢ Winter Olym(80)	7.50
1799	Virgin & Child	4.00
1800	Santa Claus	4.00
1801	Will Rogers	3.00
1802	Vietnam Vets	3.00
	1980-81 Issues	
1803	W.C. Fields	3.00
1804	Benjamin Banneker	5.00
1805-10	Letter Writing	3.50
1811	1¢ Quill Pen coil	2.50
1813	3.5¢ Non Profit coil	4.00
1818,20	"B" sht./coil stamps	3.50
1819a	"B" bklt. pane of 8	3.00
1821	Frances Perkins	2.50
1822	15¢ Dolly Madison	4.00
1823	Emily Bissell	3.00
1824	H. Keller/A. Sullivan	3.50
1825	Vet. Administration	2.50
1826	Gen. B. de Galvez	2.50
1827-30	Coral Reefs	3.00
1831	Organized Labor	5.00
1832	Edith Wharton	5.00
1833	Amer. Education	5.00
1834-37	NW Indian Masks	4.00
1838-41	Amer. Architecture	3.00
1842	Xmas St. Glass Win.	4.00
1843	Xmas Antique Toys	4.00

Scott No.	Subject	Price
	1980-85 Great Americans	
1844	1¢ Dorothea Dix	3.00
1845	2¢ I. Stravinsky	3.00
1846	3¢ Henry Clay	2.50
1847	4¢ Carl Shurz	2.50
1848	5¢ Pearl S. Buck	2.50
1849	6¢ W. Lippmann	3.00
1850	7¢ A. Baldwin	4.00
1851	8¢ Henry Knox	2.50
1852	9¢ S. Thayer	3.00
1853	10¢ R. Russell	2.50
1854	11¢ A. Partridge	2.50
1855	13¢ Crazy Horse	2.50
1856	14¢ S. Lewis	3.00
1857	17¢ R. Carson	2.50
1858	18¢ G. Mason	2.50
1859	19¢ Sequoyah	2.50
1860	20¢ Ralph Bunche	6.00
1861	20¢ T. Gallaudet	2.50
1862	20¢ Truman	2.50
1863	22¢ Audubon	3.00
1864	30¢ Dr. Laubach	2.50
1865	35¢ Dr. C. Drew	4.00
1866	37¢ R. Millikan	2.50
1867	39¢ G. Clark	2.50
1868	40¢ L. Gilbreth	2.50
1869	50¢ C. Nimitz	3.00
	1981-82 Issues	
1874	Everett Dirksen	2.50
1875	Whitney M. Young	5.00
1876-79	American Flowers	3.00
1889a	18¢ Animals bk/10	5.00
1890-91	18¢ Flag	4.00
1893a	6¢ & 18¢ Flag & Stars bklt. pn.	3.50
1894-95	20¢ Flag	6.00
1896a	20¢ Flag bklt. pn./6	5.00
1896b	20¢ Flag bklt. pn./10	4.00
	1981-84 Transportation Coils	
1897	1¢ Omnibus	5.00
1897A	2¢ Locomotive	5.00
1898	3¢ Handcar	5.00
1898A	4¢ Stagecoach	6.00
1899	5¢ Motorcycle	7.50
1900	5.2¢ Sleigh	7.50
1901	5.9¢ Bicycle	9.00
1902	7.4¢ Baby Buggy	5.00
1903	9.3¢ Mail Wagon	6.00
1904	10.9¢ Hansom Cab	6.00
1905	11¢ Caboose	5.00
1906	17¢ Electric Car	4.50
1907	18¢ Surrey	4.00
1908	20¢ Pumper	8.00
	1981-83 Regulars & Commem.	
1909	$9.35 Eagle bklt. sgl.	125.00
1909a	$9.35 Bklt. pane of 3	175.00
1910	Amer. Red Cross	2.50
1911	Savings & Loan	2.50
1912-19	Space Achievement	10.00
1920	Prof. Management	2.50
1921-24	Wildlife Habitats	3.00
1925	Yr. Disable Person	2.50
1926	E. St. Vincent Millay	4.00
1927	Alcoholism	4.00
1928-31	Amer. Architecture	4.00
1932	Babe Zaharias	7.50
1933	Bobby Jones	7.50
1934	Frederic Remington	2.50
1935-36	18¢ & 20¢ J. Hoban	2.50
1937-38	Btl. Yrktwn/V Capes	3.00
1939	Xmas Madonna/Ch.	5.00
1940	Xmas "Teddy Bear"	5.00
1941	John Hanson	2.50
1942-45	U.S. Desert Plants	4.00
1946-47	"C" sht./coil stamps	5.00
1948a	"C" bklt. pane/10	4.00
1949a	20¢ Sheep bk pn/10	3.50
	1982 Commemoratives	
1950	F.D. Roosevelt	2.50
1951	Love	2.50
1952	G. Washington	5.00
1953-2002	Birds&Flowers (5)	75.00
2003	Netherlands	2.50
2004	Library of Congress	2.50
2005	20¢ Consumer Coil	5.00
2006-09	World's Fair	2.50
2010	Horatio Alger	2.50
2011	Aging	2.50
2012	Barrymores	4.00
2013	Dr. Mary Walker	2.50
2014	Int'l Peace Garden	2.50
2015	America's Libraries	2.50
2016	Jackie Robinson	20.00

2202

Scott No.	Subject	Price
1982 Commemoratives (cont.)		
2017	Touro Synagogue ...	2.50
2018	Wolf Trap	2.50
2019-22	Amer. Architecture.	3.00
2023	Francis of Assisi	3.00
2024	Ponce de Leon	2.50
2025	Kitten & Puppy	4.00
2026	Xmas Tiepolo Art	4.00
2027-30	Xmas Snow Scene	4.00
1983 Commemoratives		
2031	Science & Industry .	2.50
2032-35	Balloons	3.00
2036	Sweden/US Treaty .	3.00
2037	Civ.Conserv.Corps .	2.50
2038	Joseph Priestley	2.50
2039	Volunteerism	2.50
2040	German Immigrants	2.50
2041	Brooklyn Bridge	3.00
2042	Tenn. Valley Auth ...	2.50
2043	Physical Fitness	2.50
2044	Scott Joplin	5.00
2045	Medal of Honor	4.00
2046	Babe Ruth	15.00
2047	Nath. Hawthorne	2.50
2048-51	13¢ Olympics	5.00
2052	Treaty of Paris	3.00
2053	Civil Service	2.50
2054	Metropolitan Opera .	3.00
2055-58	American Inventors	3.00
2059-62	Streetcars	3.50
2063	Xmas Traditional	3.00
2064	Xmas Contemp	3.00
2065	Martin Luther	4.00
1984 Commemoratives		
2066	Alaska Statehood ...	3.00
2067-70	Winter Olympics	4.00
2071	FDIC	2.50
2072	Love	2.50
2073	Carter G. Woodson.	5.00
2074	Soil/Water Conserv	2.50
2075	Credit Un.Act/1934 .	2.50
2076-79	Orchids	3.50
2080	Hawaii Statehood ...	2.50
2081	Nat'l. Archives	2.50
2082-85	Summer Olympics .	5.00
2086	LA World Expo	2.50
2087	Health Research	2.50
2088	Douglas Fairbanks ..	3.00
2089	Jim Thorpe	12.50
2090	John McCormack	3.00
2091	St. Lawren. Seaway	2.50
2092	Mig. Bird Stamp Act	6.00
2093	Roanoke Voyages ..	2.50
2094	Herman Melville	2.50
2095	Horace Moses	2.50
2096	Smokey the Bear	7.50
2097	Roberto Clemente ..	17.50
2098-2101	Dogs	5.00
2102	Crime Prevention	3.00
2103	Hispanic Americans	2.50

Scott No.	Subject	Price
2104	Family Unity	4.00
2105	Eleanor Roosevelt ...	4.00
2106	Nation of Readers ...	4.00
2107	Xmas Traditional	4.00
2108	Xmas Santa Claus ..	4.00
2109	Vietnam Vets Mem ..	4.00
1985-87 Issues		
2110	Jerome Kern	4.00
2111-12	"D" sht./coil stamps	3.00
2113a	"D" bklt. pane/10	5.00
2114-15	22¢ Flag	3.50
2115b	22¢ Flag "T" coil	4.00
2116a	22¢ Flag bklt. bk./5 ..	4.00
2121a	22¢ Seashells bk/10	5.00
2122	$10.75 Eagle bklt.sgl.	50.00
2122a	$10.75 Bklt. pane/3 .	100.00
1985-89 Transportation Coils		
2123	3.4¢ School Bus	6.00
2124	4.9¢ Buckboard	6.00
2125	5.5¢ Star Rt. Truck ..	5.00
2126	6¢ Tricycle	5.00
2127	7.1¢ Tractor	4.00
2127a	7.1¢ Tractor Zip+4 ...	4.00
2128	8.3¢ Ambulance	6.00
2129	8.5¢ Tow Truck	4.00
2130	10.1¢ Oil Wagon	4.00
2130a	10.1¢ Red Prec	4.00
2131	11¢ Stutz Bearcat	5.00
2132	12¢ Stanley Stmr	5.00
2133	12.5¢ Pushcart	5.00
2134	14¢ Iceboat	5.00
2135	17¢ Dog Sled	4.00
2136	25¢ Bread Wagon ...	5.00
1985 Issues (cont.)		
2137	Mary M. Bethune	5.00
2138-41	Duck Decoys	4.00
2142	Winter Spec. Olymp.	3.00
2143	Love	5.00
2144	Rural Electrification .	2.50
2145	AMERIPEX '86	2.50
2146	Abigail Adams	2.50
2147	Frederick Bartholdi ..	5.00
2149	18¢ G. Wash. coil	4.00
2150	21.1¢ Zip+4 coil	4.00
2152	Korean War Vets	3.50
2153	Social Security Act ..	3.00
2154	World War I Vets	3.00
2155-58	American Horses	5.00
2159	Public Education	3.00
2160-63	Int'l. Youth Year	4.00
2164	Help End Hunger	3.00
2165	Xmas Traditional	3.00
2166	Xmas Contemp	3.00
1986 Issues		
2167	Arkansas Statehood	2.50
1986-93 Great Americans		
2168	1¢ M. Mitchell	3.00
2169	2¢ Mary Lyon	3.00
2170	3¢ Dr. P.D. White	3.00
2171	4¢ Fr. Flanagan	2.50
2172	5¢ Hugo Black	3.00

Scott No.	Subject	Price
1986-93 Great Americans (cont.)		
2173	5¢ Munoz Marin	3.00
2176	10¢ Red Cloud	2.50
2177	14¢ Julia W. Howe ..	3.00
2178	15¢ Buffalo Bill	3.50
2179	17¢ B. Lockwood	3.50
2180	21¢ C. Carlson	2.50
2182	23¢ M. Cassatt	3.00
2183	25¢ Jack London	2.50
2183a	Bklt. pn./10	6.00
2184	28¢ Sitting Bull	2.50
2184A	29¢ Earl Warren	6.00
2184B	29¢ T. Jefferson	5.00
2185	35¢ Dennis Chavez.	4.00
2186	40¢ C.L. Chennault.	4.50
2188	45¢ Cushing	2.50
2190	52¢ H. Humphrey	4.00
2191	56¢ John Harvard ...	2.50
2192	65¢ H. Arnold	3.50
2193	75¢ Wendell Wilkie .	5.00
2194	$1 Dr. B. Revel	3.00
2194A	$1 Johns Hopkins ...	3.50
2195	$2 W.J. Bryan	5.00
2196	$5 B. Harte	12.50
2197a	25¢ London, bk/6	4.50
2201a	Stamp Col. bk./4	6.00
2202	Love	3.50
2203	Sojourner Truth	4.00
2204	Republic of Texas ...	2.50
2209a	Fish bklt. pane/5	5.00
2210	Public Hospitals	2.00
2211	Duke Ellington	5.00
2216-19	US Pres. shts.,4 pgs.	22.50
2220-23	Polar Explorers	5.00
2224	Statue of Liberty	4.00
2226	2¢ Locom. re-engr ...	4.00
2235-38	Navajo Art	4.00
2239	T.S. Elliot	2.50
2240-43	Woodcarved Figs ...	3.00
2244	Xmas Traditional	2.50
2245	Xmas Contemp	2.50
1987 Issues		
2246	MI Statehood	4.00
2247	Pan-Amer. Games ..	4.00
2248	Love	5.00
2249	J. Bap. Pnt. du Sable	7.50
2250	Enrico Caruso	3.00
2251	Girls Scouts	5.00
1987-88 Transportation Coils		
2252	3¢ Con. Wag	3.00
2253,62	5¢,17.5¢	4.00
2254	5.3¢ Elevator, Prec.	5.00
2255	7.6¢ Carretta, Prec ..	5.00
2256	8.4¢ Wheelchair, Prec.	4.00
2257	10¢ Canal Boat	5.00
2258	13¢ Police Wag,Prec.	5.00
2259	13.2¢ RR Car, Prec.	5.00
2260	15¢ Tugboat	4.00
2261	16.7¢ Pop.Wag,Prec.	5.00
2263	20¢ Cbl. Car	5.00
2264	20.5¢ Fire Eng, Prec.	5.00
2265	21¢ RR Mail Car,Prec	5.00
2266	24.1¢ Tandem Bike,Pre	5.00
1987-89 Issues		
2274a	22¢ Sp. Occ. Bk	6.00
2275	22¢ United Way	2.50
2276	22¢ Flag/Fireworks .	2.50
2276a	Bklt. pair	4.00
2277,79	(25¢) "E" sheet/coil .	5.00
2278	25¢ Flag/Clouds	2.50
2280	25¢ Flag/Yosem. coil	3.00
2280var	Pre-phos. paper	3.00
2281	25¢ Honeybee coil ..	7.50
2282a	(25¢) "E" Bklt. Pane/10	6.00
2283a	25¢ Pheasant Bk/10 ...	6.00
2284-85b	25¢ Owl/Grossbk. Bk	5.00
2285Ac	25¢ Flag/Clouds Bk.	5.00
2286-2335	Am. Wildlife (5) ..	30.00
1987-90 Bicentennial Issues		
2336	22¢ Delaware	3.00
2337	22¢ Penn	3.00
2338	22¢ New Jersey	4.00
2339	22¢ Georgia	3.00
2340	22¢ Conn	3.00
2341	22¢ Mass	3.50
2342	22¢ Maryland	3.50
2343	25¢ S. Carolina	3.00
2344	25¢ New Hamp	3.00
2345	25¢ Virginia	3.00
2346	25¢ New York	4.00
2347	25¢ North Carolina ..	3.00
2348	25¢ Rhode Island	5.00

Scott No.	Subject	Price
1987-88 Issues		
2349	22¢ U.S.-Moroc. Rel.	2.50
2350	22¢ Faulkner	2.50
2351-54	22¢ Lacemaking	5.00
2359a	22¢ Const. Bklt.	5.00
2360	22¢ Sign. Const	3.00
2361	22¢ CPA	6.00
2366a	22¢ Loco. Bklt	10.00
2367	22¢ Xmas Madon	3.00
2368	22¢ Xmas Orn	3.00
2369	22¢ '88 Wnt. Olym ..	3.00
2370	22¢ Australia Bicent.	2.50
2371	22¢ J.W. Johnson ...	5.00
2372-75	22¢ Cats	5.00
2376	22¢ Knute Rockne ..	7.50
2377	25¢ F. Ouimet	10.00
2378	25¢ Love	3.50
2379	45¢ Love	3.00
2380	25¢ Sum. Olym	3.00
2385a	25¢ Classic Cars bk	7.00
2386-89	25¢ Ant. Expl	4.00
2390-93	25¢ Carousel Anim	5.00
2394	$8.75 Express Mail .	25.00
2396a-98a	25¢ Occas.bk.(2)	30.00
2399	25¢ Xmas trad	3.00
2400	25¢ Xmas cont	3.00
1989-90 Issues		
2401	25¢ Montana Sthd ..	2.50
2402	25¢ A.P. Randolph ..	4.00
2403	25¢ N.Dakota Sthd .	3.00
2404	25¢ Washington sthd.	3.00
2409a	25¢ Steamboats bklt.	5.00
2410	25¢ Wld. Stamp Expo	3.00
2411	25¢ A. Toscanini	2.50
2412	25¢ House of Reps.	3.00
2413	25¢ U.S. Senate	3.00
2414	25¢ Exec.Branch/GW	3.00
2415	25¢U.S.Sup.Ct.('90)	3.00
2416	25¢ S.Dakota sthd. .	3.00
2417	25¢ Lou Gehrig	15.00
2418	25¢ E. Hemingway ..	2.50
2419	$2.40 Moon Landing	15.00
2420	25¢ Letter Carriers ..	2.50
2421	25¢ Bill of Rights	3.00
2422-25	25¢ Prehis. Animals	12.50
2426/C21	25¢/45¢ Pre-Columbian Customs	3.50
2427,27a	25¢ Christmas Art, Sht. & Bklt. Pn	7.50
2428,29a	25¢ Christmas Sleigh, Sht. & Bklt. Pn	7.50
2431	25¢ Eagle, self-adhes	5.00
2433	90¢ WSE S/S of 4 ...	10.00
2434-37	25¢ Classic Mail	4.00
2438	25¢ Cl.Mail S/S of 4	9.00
1990-91 Issues		
2439	25¢ Idaho Sthd	3.00
2440,41a	25¢ Love, sht. & bklt.	6.00
2442	25¢ Ida B. Wells	6.00
2443a	15¢ Bch. Umbr., bklt.	5.00
2444	25¢ Wyoming Sthd .	3.00
2445-48	25¢ Classic Films ...	7.50
2449	25¢ Marianne Moore	3.00
1990-94 Transportation Coils		
2451	4¢ Steam Carriage ..	5.00
2452	5¢ Circus Wagon	5.00
2452B	5¢ Wagon, gravure .	5.00
2453,57	5¢/10¢ Canoe/Trailer	5.00
2454	5¢ Canoe, gravure ..	5.00
2458	10¢ Tractor Trailer ..	6.00
2464	23¢ Lunch Wagon ...	4.00
2468	$1.00 Seaplane coil	9.00
1990-93		
2474a	25¢ Lighthouse bklt	7.50
2475	25¢ ATM Plastic Flag	5.00
2476	$2 Bobcat	7.50
2478	29¢ Red Squirrel	6.00
2479	29¢ Rose	5.00
2480	29¢ Pine Cone	5.00
2481,82,89	1¢/30¢ Birds	4.00
2487	19¢ Fawn	4.00
2491	45¢ Pumpkinseed ...	4.00
2493a,94a	29¢ Wood Duck bklts. BEP & KCS	15.00
2495a	29¢ African Violet, booklet pane of 10 ..	9.00
2496-2500	25¢ Olympics	8.00
2505a	25¢ Indian Headress	9.00
2506-07	25¢ Marsh Is. & Micro. Joint Issue	4.00
2508-11	25¢ Sea Creatures.	7.50
2512/C127	25¢,45¢ America	4.50

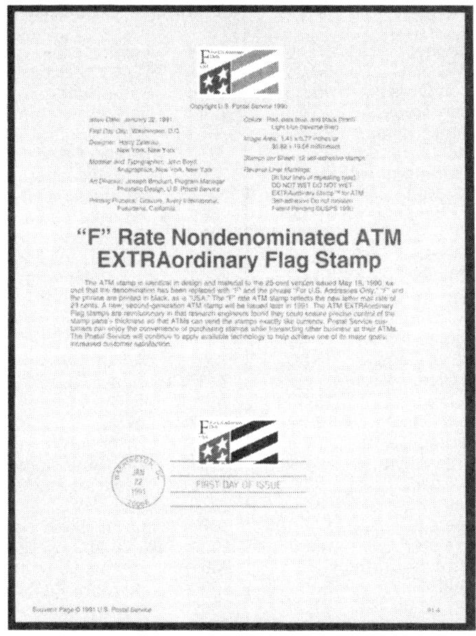

2522

C88

cott No.	Subject	Price
	1991-94 Issues	
513	25¢ D.D. Eisenhower	3.50
514,14a	25¢ Christmas sht. & Bklt. Pn./10	7.50
515,16a	25¢ Christmas Tree sht. & Bklt. Pn./10	7.50
517,18	(29¢) "F" Flower, sht. & Coil pr	5.00
519a,20a	(29¢) "F" Flower, Bklt. Pns. of 10	15.00
521	(4¢) Make-up rate	3.50
522	(29¢) "F" Self Adh	4.00
523	29¢ Flag/Rushmore	4.00
523A	29¢ Mt. Rush, grav.	4.00
524,27a	29¢ Flower,sht./bklt.	9.00
525	29¢ Flwr. coil,roulette	4.00
526	29¢ Flower coil,perf.	4.00
528a	29¢ Flag/Olympic Rings Bklt. pane	9.00
529	19¢ Fishing Boat coil	4.00
530a	19¢ Balloons, bklt	6.00
531	29¢ Flags on Parade	4.00
531A	29¢ Liberty, ATM	4.00
532	50¢ Switzerland	4.00
533	29¢ Vermont	4.00
534	29¢ Savings Bonds	3.00
535,36a,37	29¢,52¢ Love, shts. & Bklt.	10.00
538	29¢ William Saroyan	4.00
539	$1.00 USPS & Olym.	5.00
540	$2.90 Priority Mail	10.00
541	$9.95 Express Mail	30.00
542	$14.00 Express Mail	40.00
543	$2.90 Space P.M.	10.00
549a	29¢ Fishing Flies bklt.	15.00
550	29¢ Cole Porter	4.00
551	29¢ Desert Storm/Shield sht. & bklt. pane	10.00
553-57	29¢ Summer Olymp.	7.50
558	29¢ Numismatics	4.00
559	29¢ WW II S/S	10.00
560	29¢ Basketball	7.50
561	29¢ Washington, D.C.	4.00
562-66	29¢ Comedians bklt.	10.00
567	29¢ Jan Matzeliger	7.50
577a	29¢ Space bklt	10.00
578,78a	29¢ Madonna, sht./bklt	12.00
579,80, r 81,82-85	29¢ Santa Claus sht./bklt	20.00

Scott No.	Subject	Price
2590	$1.00 Burgoyne	7.50
2594a	29¢ Pledge bklt.	7.50
2595-97	29¢ Eagle & Shield/ Die Cut (3 Pgs.)	7.50
2598	29¢ Eagle S/A	5.00
2604	(10¢)Eagle&Shld. coil	4.00
2605-6	(10¢) BEP & SV	6.00
2607	23¢ Flag/Pre-sort	5.00
2608	23¢ USA/Pre-sort	5.00
2608A	23¢ Same, BEP	5.00
2608B	23¢ Same, SV	5.00
2609	29¢ Flag/W.H. Coil	4.00
	1992 Issues	
2611-15	29¢ Winter Olympics	6.00
2616	29¢ World Columbian	3.50
2617	29¢ W.E.B. DuBois	7.50
2618	29¢ Love	4.00
2619	29¢ Olympic BB	20.00
2620-23	29¢ Columb. Voyages	5.00
2624-29	1¢-$5 Columbus S/S	60.00
2630	29¢ NY Stock Exchg	4.00
2631-34	29¢ Space Accomp	6.00
2635	29¢ Alaska Hwy	4.00
2636	29¢ Kentucky Sthd	4.00
2637-41	29¢ Summer Olymp.	6.00
2646a	29¢ Hummingbird Pn.	7.50
2647-96	29¢ Wildflowers (5)	50.00
2697	29¢ WW II S/S	10.00
2698	29¢ Dorothy Parker	4.00
2699	29¢ Dr. von Karman	7.50
2700-03	29¢ Minerals	7.50
2704	29¢ Juan Cabrillo	4.00
2709a	29¢ Wild Animals Bklt.	7.50
2710a	29¢ Christmas Trad. Sheet & Bklt.	12.50
2711-14,19	29¢ Toys, sheet & Die Cut	10.00
2720	29¢ Chinese New Yr	6.00
	1993 Issues	
2721	29¢ Elvis Presley	15.00
2722	29¢ Oklahoma	5.00
2723	29¢ Hank Williams	7.50
2737b	29¢ Rock 'n Roll	15.00
2745a	29¢ Space Fantasy, Bklt. Pane of 5	10.00
2746	29¢ Perry L. Julian	5.00
2747	29¢ Oregon Trail	5.00
2748	29¢ World Games	5.00

Scott No.	Subject	Price
2749	29¢ Grace Kelly	7.50
2750-3	29¢ Circus	7.50
2754	29¢ Cherokee Strip	5.00
2755	29¢ Dean Acheson	5.00
2756-9	29¢ Sports Horses	7.50
2764a	29¢ Garden Flowers, Bklt. Pane of 5	7.50
2765	29¢ WW II S/S	10.00
2766	29¢ Joe Louis	10.00
2770a	29¢ Broadway, Booklet of 4	10.00
2775-8,2771-4	Country Music, Booklet & Single	10.00
2779-82	29¢ Postal Museum	6.00
2783-4	29¢ Deaf Commun	5.00
2785-8	29¢ Youth Classics	6.00
2789,2790a	29¢ Madonna	7.50
2791-4,2798b,2799-2802,2803	29¢ Contem. Xmas	12.50
2804	29¢ N. Marianas	5.00
2805	29¢ Columbus Landing in Puerto Rico	6.00
2806,2806b	29¢ AIDS	10.00
	1994 Issues	
2807-11	29¢ Winter Olympics	7.50
2812	29¢ Edward R.Murrow	5.00
2813	29¢ Sunrise Love	5.00
2814a,15	29¢-52¢ Love	10.00
2816	29¢ Dr. Allison Davis	5.00
2817	29¢ Chinese New Year	5.00
2818	29¢ Buffalo Soldiers	10.00
2819-28	29¢ Silent Screen Stars	12.50
2833a	29¢ Garden Flowers, Bklt. Pane of 5	7.50
	Airmails (1973-85)	
C79	13¢ Winged Env	4.00
C83	13¢ Winged Coil	4.00
C84	11¢ City of Refuge	100.00
C87	18¢ Stat. of Liberty	10.00
C88	26¢ Mt. Rushmore	7.50
C89-90	25¢ & 31¢ Airmails	4.00
C91-92	31¢ Wright Brothers	4.00
C93-94	21¢ Octave Chanute	4.00
C95-96	25¢ Wiley Post	5.00
C97	31¢ Olym. Games	6.00
C98	40¢ P. Mazzei	4.00
C99	28¢ Blanche Scott	2.50
C100	35¢ Glenn Curtiss	2.50

Scott No.	Subject	Price
C101-04	28¢ Olympics	5.00
C105-08	40¢ Olympics	4.00
C109-12	35¢ Olympics	4.50
C113	33¢ A. Verville	2.50
C114	39¢ L. & E. Sperry	3.00
C115	44¢ Transpacific Flt.	3.00
C116	44¢ Fr. J. Serra	3.00
	Airmails (1988-91)	
C117	44¢ New Sweden	3.00
C118	45¢ S.P. Langley	3.00
C119	36¢ Sikorsky	4.00
C120	45¢ French Rev	4.50
C122-25	45¢ Future Mail	8.00
C126	$1.80 Future Mail S/S	8.00
C128	50¢ Harriet Quimby	4.00
C129	40¢ William Piper	4.00
C130	50¢ Antarctic Treaty	5.00
C131	50¢ America	4.00
	1983-93 Official Issues	
O127-29,30-35	1¢/$5 (5 pgs)	25.00
O129A,136	14¢&22¢ Issues	5.00
O138-39	(14¢&22¢) "D" Sht. & Coil	3.00
O138A,141	15¢,25¢ Coils	4.00
O138B	20¢ Coil	3.50
O140	(25¢) "E" Coil	3.50
O143	1¢ Offset	4.50
O144	(29¢) "F" Coil	5.00
O145,47-48	19¢,23¢,29¢ Sgls. & Coil	5.00
O146	4¢ Make-up rate	4.00
O146A	10¢ Official	4.00

AMERICAN COMMEMORATIVE PANELS

1474

The U.S. Postal Service has provided panels for commemorative and Christmas issues since Scott #1464-67 (Sept. 20, 1972). Each panel features mint stamps along with appropriate steel engravings and interesting stories about the subject. **Prices are for panels sealed in original sleeves. Panels without sleeves sell at about 80% of these prices.**

Scott No.	Subject	Price
	1972 Commemoratives	
1464-67	Wildlife	10.00
1468	Mail Order	9.00
1469	Osteopathic Medicine	9.00
1470	Tom Sawyer	7.50
1471	Christmas 1972	12.50
1472	'Twas Night...Xmas	12.50
1473	Pharmacy	10.00
1474	Stamp Collecting	9.00
	1973 Commemoratives	
1475	Love	12.50
1476	Pamphleteers	10.00
1477	Posting Broadside	10.00
1478	Post Rider	11.00
1479	Drummer	15.00
1480-83	Boston Tea Party	32.50
1484	George Gershwin	10.00
1485	Robinson Jeffers	10.00
1486	Henry O. Tanner	10.00
1487	Willa Cather	10.00
1488	Copernicus	10.00
1489-98	Postal People	9.00
1499	Harry S. Truman	12.50
1500-02,C86	Electronics	10.00
1503	Lyndon B. Johnson	12.50
1504	Angus Cattle	10.00
1505	Chautauqua	10.00
1506	Kansas Wheat	10.00
1507	Christmas 1973	15.00
1508	Xmas Needlepoint	15.00
	1974 Commemoratives	
1525	Vet. of Foreign Wars	10.00
1526	Robert Frost	10.00
1527	Expo '74	11.00
1528	Horse Racing	12.50
1529	Skylab	15.00
1530-37	Univ. Postal Union	12.50
1538-41	Mineral Heritage	12.50
1542	Fort Harrod	10.00
1543-46	Cont. Congress	12.50
1547	Energy Conserv	10.00
1548	Sleepy Hollow	10.00
1549	Retarded Children	10.00
1550	Xmas Angel Altarpc.	15.00
1551	Xmas "Rd-Winter"	15.00
	1975 Commemoratives	
1553	Benjamin West	10.00
1554	Paul L. Dunbar	12.50
1555	D.W. Griffith	10.00
1556	Pioneer	15.00
1557	Mariner	15.00
1558	Coll Bargaining	10.00

Scott No.	Subject	Price
1559-62	Contrib. to Cause	10.00
1563	Lexing. & Concord	11.00
1564	Bunker Hill	11.00
1565-68	Military Services	11.00
1569-70	Apollo Soyuz	15.00
1571	Int'l Women's Year	10.00
1572-75	Postal Bicentennial	12.50
1576	Wld. Peace thru Law	10.00
1577-78	Bank & Commerce	12.50
1579	Christmas Madonna	12.50
1580	Christmas Card	12.50
	1976 Commemoratives	
1629-31	Spirit of '76	17.50
1632	INTERPHIL '76	17.00
1646-7,51-2	State Flags	37.50
1683	Telephone Cent.	12.50
1684	Commer. Aviation	17.50
1685	Chemistry	14.00
1690	Benjamin Franklin	14.00
1691-94	Dec. of Indepen	12.50
1695-98	Olympics	17.00
1699	Clara Maass	14.00
1700	Adolph S. Ochs	14.50
1701	Copley Nativity	17.50
1702	Currier Winter Past.	25.00
	1977 Commemoratives	
1704	Wash. at Princeton	17.50
1705	Sound Recording	37.50
1706-09	Pueblo Art	125.00
1710	Lindbergh Flight	125.00
1711	CO Centennial	25.00
1712-15	Butterflies	25.00
1716	Lafayette	25.00
1717-20	Skilled Hands	25.00
1721	Peace Bridge	25.00
1722	Herkimer/Oriskany	25.00
1723-24	Energy Conserv	30.00
1725	Alta, CA	25.00
1726	Art. of Confed.	25.00
1727	Talking Pictures	40.00
1728	Surrender/Saratoga	25.00
1729	Xmas/Wash./V. For	30.00
1730	Xmas/Rural Mailbox	50.00
	1978 Issues	
1731	Carl Sandburg	15.00
1732-33	Captain Cook	25.00
1744	Harriet Tubman	20.00
1745-48	American Quilts	27.50
1749-52	American Dance	18.00
1753	French Alliance	18.00
1754	Dr. Papanicolaou	15.00
1755	Jimmie Rodgers	20.00
1756	George M. Cohan	27.50

Scott No.	Subject	Price
1758	Photography	15.00
1759	Viking Missions	60.00
1760-63	American Owls	45.00
1764-67	American Trees	45.00
1768	Madonna & Child	22.50
1769	Xmas Hobby Horse	22.50
	1979-80 Commemoratives	
1770	Robert F. Kennedy	15.00
1771	Martin L. King, Jr.	15.00
1772	Year of the Child	12.00
1773	John Steinbeck	12.00
1774	Albert Einstein	15.00
1775-78	PA Toleware	15.00
1779-82	Amer. Architecture	12.50
1783-86	Endangered Flora	15.00
1787	Seeing Eye Dogs	15.00
1788	Special Olympics	17.50
1789	John Paul Jones	15.00
1790/C97	Olympic Games	18.00
1791-94	15¢ Summer Olym	17.50
1795-98	15¢ Winter Olym	20.00
1799	Virgin & Child	18.00
1800	Santa Claus	18.00
1801	Will Rogers	17.50
1802	Vietnam Vets	18.00
	1980 Commemoratives	
1803	W.C. Fields	12.50
1804	Benjamin Banneker	20.00
1821	Frances Perkins	12.50
1823	Emily Bissell	12.50
1824	H. Keller/A. Sullivan	12.50
1825	Vet. Administration	12.50
1826	Gen. B. de Galvez	12.50
1827-30	Coral Reefs	15.00
1831	Organized Labor	12.00
1832	Edith Wharton	12.00
1833	Amer. Education	12.00
1834-37	NW Indian Masks	15.00
1838-41	Amer. Architecture.	12.50
1842	Xmas St. Glass Win.	18.00
1843	Xmas Antique Toys	18.00
	1981 Commemoratives	
1874	Everett Dirksen	15.00
1875	Whitney M. Young	20.00
1876-79	American Flowers	15.00
1910	Amer. Red Cross	13.00
1911	Savings & Loan	12.50
1912-19	Space Achievement	17.50
1920	Prof. Management	12.50
1921-24	Wildlife Habitats	18.00
1925	Int'l Yr. Disable Per.	11.00
1926	E. St. Vincent Millay	11.00
1928-31	Amer. Architecture.	12.50
1932-33	Jones/Zaharias	42.50
1934	Frederic Remington	12.50
1935-36	18¢ & 20¢ J. Hoban	12.50
1937-38	Yorktown/V Capes.	12.50
1939	Xmas Madonna/Ch.	17.50
1940	Xmas "Teddy Bear"	17.50
1941	John Hanson	11.00
1942-45	U.S. Desert Plants.	17.00
	1982 Commemoratives	
1950	Roosevelt	15.00
1951	Love	18.00
1952	G. Washington	15.00
1955-56,65-66	State Birds/Fl	42.50
2003	Netherlands	15.00
2004	Library of Congress	16.00
2006-09	World's Fair	17.50
2010	Horatio Alger	15.00
2011	Aging	20.00
2012	Barrymores	22.50
2013	Dr. Mary Walker	17.50
2014	Int'l Peace Garden	20.00
2015	America's Libraries	20.00
2016	Jackie Robinson	60.00
2017	Touro Synagogue	20.00
2018	Wolf Trap	22.50
2019-22	Amer. Architecture.	22.50
2023	Francis of Assisi	22.50
2024	Ponce de Leon	22.50
2025	Kitten & Puppy	30.00
2026	Xmas Tiepolo Art	30.00
2027-30	Xmas Snow Scene	30.00
	1983 Commemoratives	
2031	Science & Industry	10.00
2032-35	Balloons	12.50
2036	Sweden/US Treaty	10.00
2037	Civ.Conserv.Corps	10.00
2038	Joseph Priestley	10.00
2039	Voluntarism	9.00
2040	German Immigr.	10.00
2041	Brooklyn Bridge	11.00
2042	Tenn. Valley Auth	10.00
2043	Physical Fitness	9.00

Scott No.	Subject	Price
2044	Scott Joplin	15.00
2045	Medal of Honor	12.50
2046	Babe Ruth	40.00
2047	Nath. Hawthorne	10.00
2048-51	13¢ Olympics	17.50
2052	Treaty of Paris	12.50
2053	Civil Service	12.50
2054	Metropolitan Opera	12.50
2055-58	American Inventors	12.50
2059-62	Streetcars	15.00
2063	Xmas Traditional	17.50
2064	Xmas Contemp	17.50
2065	Martin Luther	15.00
	1984 Commemoratives	
2066	Alaska Statehood	9.00
2067-70	Winter Olympics	12.50
2071	FDIC	9.00
2072	Love	10.00
2073	Carter G. Woodson	12.50
2074	Soil/Water Conserv.	9.00
2075	Credit Un.Act/1934	9.00
2076-79	Orchids	12.50
2080	Hawaii Statehood	11.00
2081	Nat'l. Archives	9.00
2082-85	Summer Olympics	12.50
2086	Louisiana World Expo	11.00
2087	Health Research	9.00
2088	Douglas Fairbanks	9.00
2089	Jim Thorpe	15.00
2090	John McCormack	9.00
2091	St. Lawren. Seaway	11.00
2092	Mig. Bird Stamp Act	15.00
2093	Roanoke Voyages	9.00
2094	Herman Melville	9.00
2095	Horace Moses	10.00
2096	Smokey the Bear	12.50
2097	Roberto Clemente	60.00
2098-2101	Dogs	13.00
2102	Crime Prevention	10.00
2103	Hispanic Americans	10.00
2104	Family Unity	10.00
2105	Eleanor Roosevelt	10.00
2106	Nation of Readers	10.00
2107	Xmas Traditional	12.50
2108	Xmas Santa Claus	12.50
2109	Vietnam Vets Mem.	15.00
	1985 Issues	
2110	Jerome Kern	10.00
2137	Mary M. Bethune	12.00
2138-41	Duck Decoys	12.50
2142	Winter Spec. Olymp.	10.00
2143	Love	12.50
2144	Rural Electrification	9.00
2145	AMERIPEX '86	12.50
2146	Abigail Adams	9.00
2147	Auguste Bartholdi	15.00
2152	Korean War Vets	11.00
2153	Social Security Act	9.00
2154	World War I Vets	10.00
2155-58	American Horses	15.00
2159	Public Education	9.00
2160-63	Int'l. Youth Year	12.50
2164	Help End Hunger	9.00
2165	Xmas Traditional	15.00
2166	Xmas Contemp	15.00
	1986 Issues	
2167	Arkansas Statehood	9.00
2201a	Stamp Col. bk./4	12.00
2202	Love	11.00
2203	Sojourner Truth	12.00
2204	Republic of Texas	10.00
2209a	Fish booklet	11.00
2210	Public Hospitals	8.00
2211	Duke Ellington	12.50
2216-19	US Presid., 4 panels	40.00
2220-23	Polar Explorers	11.00
2224	Statue of Liberty	12.50
2235-38	Navajo Art	11.00
2239	T.S. Elliot	10.00
2240-43	Woodcarved Figs	11.00
2244	Xmas Traditional	10.00
2245	Xmas Contemp	10.00
	1987 Issues	
2246	22¢ MI Statehood	10.00
2247	22¢P-Am. Games	9.00
2248	22¢Love	10.00
2249	22¢ J.Bap. Sable	10.00
2250	22¢Enrico Caruso	11.00
2251	22¢Girls Scouts	10.00
2267-74a	22¢ Sp. Occ. Bk	10.00
2275	22¢ United Way	8.00
2286-2335	22¢ Am.Wildlife(5)	50.00

2381-85

cott No.	Subject	Price
1987-90 Bicentennial Issues		
336	22¢ Delaware	15.00
337	22¢ Penn	10.00
338	22¢ New Jersey	10.00
239	22¢ Georgia	10.00
340	22¢ Conn	10.00
341	22¢ Mass	10.00
342	22¢ Maryland	10.00
343	25¢ S. Carolina	9.00
344	25¢ New Hamp	10.00
345	25¢ Virginia	10.00
346	25¢ New York	10.00
347	25¢ North Carolina	12.50
348	25¢ Rhode Island	12.50
1987 (continued)		
349	22¢ U.S.-Moroc. Rel.	9.00
350	22¢ Faulkner	10.00
351-54	22¢ Lacemaking	10.00
359a	22¢ Const. Bklt.	10.00
360	22¢ Const. Signing	10.00
361	22¢ CPA	50.00
366a	22¢ Locom. Bklt.	12.50
367	22¢ Xmas Madon	10.00
'368	22¢ Xmas Orn	10.00
1988 Issues		
'369	22¢ '88 Wint. Olym.	10.00
370	22¢ Australia Bicent.	9.00
371	22¢ J.W. Johnson	10.00
372-75	22¢ Cats	13.00
'376	22¢ K. Rockne	15.00

Scott No.	Subject	Price
2377	25¢ F. Ouimet	35.00
2378-79	25¢-45¢ Love	10.00
2380	25¢ Sum. Olym	10.00
2385a	25¢ Classic Cars bk	10.00
2386-89	25¢ Ant. Expl	10.00
2390-93	25¢ Carousel	12.00
2395-98	25¢ Occasions bk	10.00
2399-2400	25¢ Christmas	10.00
1989-90 Issues		
2401	25¢ Montana	10.00
2402	25¢ Randolph	12.50
2403	25¢ N.Dakota	10.00
2404	25¢ Wash. Sthd.	10.00
2409a	25¢ Steamboats bklt	15.00
2410	25¢ Wld. Stamp Expo	10.00
2411	25¢ Arturo Toscanini	10.00
2412	25¢ House of Reps	12.50
2413	25¢ U.S. Senate	12.50
2414	25¢ Exec./GW Inaug.	12.50
2415	25¢U.S.Supreme Court	12.50
2416	25¢ S.Dakota Sthd.	10.00
2417	25¢ Lou Gehrig	45.00
2418	25¢ E. Hemingway	12.50
2420	25¢ Letter Carriers	12.50
2421	25¢ Bill of Rights	12.50
2422-25	25¢ Prehis. Animals	30.00
2426/C21	25¢/45¢ Pre-Columbian Customs	12.50
2427-28	25¢ Christmas	15.00
2434-37	25¢ Classic Mail	12.50

Scott No.	Subject	Price
1990 Issues		
2439	25¢ Idaho Sthd	12.50
2440,41a	25¢ Love	12.50
2442	25¢ Ida B. Wells	30.00
2444	25¢ Wyoming Sthd	10.00
2445-48	25¢ Classic Films	25.00
2449	25¢ Marianne Moore	10.00
2474a	25¢ Lighthouse bklt	22.50
2496-2500	25¢ Olympians	15.00
2505a	25¢ Headress Bklt.	15.00
2506-07	25¢ Marsh Is. & Micro. Joint Issue	12.50
2508-11	25¢ Sea Creatures	22.50
2512/C127	25¢,45¢ America	15.00
2513	25¢ D.D. Eisenhower	15.00
2514,14a	25¢ Christmas	15.00
1991 Issues		
2532	50¢ Switzerland	12.50
2533	29¢ Vermont	12.50
2534	29¢ Savings Bonds	10.00
2535-36	29¢ Love.	12.50
2538	29¢ William Saroyan	12.50
2549a	29¢ Fishing Flies bk	15.00
2550	29¢ Cole Porter	12.50
2551	29¢ Desert Shield	52.50
2553-57	29¢ Summer Olymp	15.00
2558	29¢ Numismatics	12.50
2559	29¢ WW II	20.00
2560	29¢ Basketball	20.00
2561	29¢ Dist.of Columbia	12.50
2566a	29¢ Comedians bklt.	17.50
2567	29¢ Jan Matzeliger	15.00
2577a	29¢ Space bklt	17.50
2578-79	29¢ Christmas	15.00
1992 Issues		
2611-15	29¢ Winter Olympics	15.00
2616	29¢ World Columbian	15.00
2617	29¢ W.E.B. DuBois	20.00
2618	29¢ Love	15.00
2619	29¢ Olympic Baseball	50.00
2620-23	29¢ Columb.Voyages	15.00
2624-29	1¢/$5 Columbus S/S Set of 3 Panels	110.00
2630	29¢ Stock Exchg	20.00
2631-34	29¢ Space Accomp.	20.00
2635	29¢ Alaska Highway	12.50
2636	29¢ Kentucky Sthd.	12.50
2637-41	29¢ Summer Olymp.	15.00
2646a	29¢ Humming. B. Pn.	17.00
2647-96	29¢ Wildflowers (5)	75.00
2697	29¢ WW II S/S	20.00
2698	29¢ Dorothy Parker.	12.50
2699	29¢ Dr. von Karman	15.00
2700-03	29¢ Minerals	20.00
2704	29¢ Juan Cabrillo	15.00
2709a	29¢ Wild Animals Pn.	20.00
2710,14a	29¢ Christmas	20.00
2720	29¢ Chinese New Yr	20.00
1993 Issues		
2721	29¢ Elvis	30.00
2722	29¢ Oklahoma	17.50
2723	29¢ Hank Williams	20.00

Scott No.	Subject	Price
2737b	29¢ Rock 'n Roll	30.00
2745a	29¢ Space Fantasy.	17.50
2746	29¢ Percy L. Julian.	20.00
2747	29¢ Oregon Trail	15.00
2748	29¢ World Games	15.00
2749	29¢ Grace Kelly	25.00
2750-3	29¢ Circus	17.50
2754	29¢ Cherokee Strip.	12.50
2755	29¢ Dean Acheson.	15.00
2756-9	29¢ Sports Horses	20.00
2764a	29¢ Garden Flowers	20.00
2765	29¢ WW II S/S	20.00
2766	29¢ Joe Louis	25.00
2770a	29¢ Broadway Musicals, Booklet Pane	22.50
2775-8	29¢ Country-West	25.00
2779-82	29¢ Postal Museum	17.50
2783-4	29¢ Deaf Commun.	17.50
2785-8	29¢ Youth Classics.	25.00
2789,91-4	29¢ Christmas	20.00
2804	29¢ Nthn.Marianas.	17.50
2805	29¢ Columbus Lands in Puerto Rico	15.00
2806	29¢ AIDS	17.50
1994 Issues		
2807-11	29¢ Winter Olympics	15.00
2812	29¢ Edward R.Murrow	12.50
2814a	29¢ Love, Bklt Pane	15.00
2816	29¢ Allison Davis	17.50
2817	29¢ Chinese New Year	15.00
2818	29¢ Buffalo Soldiers	20.00
2819-28	29¢ Silent Screen Stars	17.50
2833a	29¢ Garden Flowers, Pane of 5	15.00
2837	29¢,40¢,50¢ World Cup Soccer, S/S of 3	15.00
2838	29¢ WWII S/S	20.00
2839	29¢ Norman Rockwell	15.00
2841	29¢ Moon Landing	17.50
2847a	29¢ Locomotives, Pane of 5	15.00
2848	29¢ George Meany.	12.50
Airmails		
C101-04	28¢ Olympics	12.50
C105-08	40¢ Olympics	12.50
C109-12	35¢ Olympics	17.50
C117	44¢ New Sweden	9.00
C120	45¢ French Rev	11.00
C122-25	45¢ Future Mail	15.00
C130	50¢ Antarctic Treaty	12.50
C131	50¢ America	12.50

We Are Always Interested In Purchasing Your Collections of Souvenir Cards, Pages, Panels, Mint Sets and Ceremony Programs

FIRST DAY CEREMONY PROGRAMS

1246

First Day Ceremony Programs are made available at ceremonies dedicating a new stamp issue. Although programs may vary in shape, size, and content, they usually contain the words "First Day Ceremony Program."

Unless noted otherwise, prices for the years 1940-57 are for programs without stamps or cancels. **Programs with stamps and cancels (1940-57) sell for about twice the listed price.** Program prices for the years 1958-Date are for programs with stamps and cancels. **Programs without stamps and cancels (1958-Date) sell for about 50% of the listed prices.**

Anyone interested in more information regarding ceremony programs should consider joining the American Ceremony Program Society which publishes a journal, The Ceremonial, 8 times a year. Membership information is available from: Mr. David Rosenthal, 48 Hilliary Lane, Westbury, NY 11590-1647.

Scott No.	Subject	Price
	1940-47	
863	10¢ Samuel Clemens	200.00
873	10¢ B.T. Washington	150.00
882	5¢ E. MacDowell	90.00
890	2¢ Samuel F.B. Morse	125.00
936	3¢ Coast Guard	100.00
937	3¢ Alfred E. Smith	90.00
942	3¢ Iowa	90.00
944	3¢ Santa Fe	90.00
945	3¢ Thomas A. Edison	90.00
946	3¢ Joseph Pulitzer	90.00
950	3¢ Utah	90.00
951	3¢ U.S.F. Constitution	100.00
	1948	
952	3¢ Everglades Park	90.00
953	3¢ G.W. Carver	85.00
957	3¢ Wisconsin Cent	85.00
958	5¢ Swedish Pioneers	85.00
961	3¢ U.S.-Canada	85.00
962	3¢ Francis Scott Key	75.00
964	3¢ Oregon Terr	75.00
966	3¢ Palomar Observ	75.00
967	3¢ Clara Barton	75.00
968	3¢ Poultry Industry	70.00
971	3¢ Volunteer Firemen	70.00
970	3¢ Fort Kearny	70.00
976	3¢ Fort Bliss	75.00
979	3¢ American Turners	70.00
	1949-51	
981	3¢ Minnesota Terr	60.00
982	3¢ Washington & Lee	70.00
984	3¢ Annapolis	60.00
985	3¢ G.A.R.	70.00
986	3¢ Edgar Allen Poe	70.00
990	3¢ Nat'l. Capitol Sesq.	70.00
993	3¢ Railroad Engineers	70.00
994	3¢ Kansas City Cent.	75.00
995	3¢ Boy Scouts	75.00
996	3¢ Indiana Terr. Sesqui.	70.00
998	3¢ United Confed. Vets	70.00
999	3¢ Nevada Cent	50.00
1000	3¢ Landing of Cadillac	50.00
1001	3¢ Colorado Sthd	50.00
1002	3¢ Amer. Chemical Soc.	50.00
1003	3¢ Battle of Brooklyn	50.00

Scott No.	Subject	Price
	1952	
1004	3¢ Betsy Ross	50.00
1005	3¢ 4-H Clubs	50.00
1006	3¢ B & O Railroad	75.00
1007	3¢ Am. Auto Assn	50.00
1009	3¢ Grand Coulee Dam	50.00
1010	3¢ Lafayette	50.00
1011	3¢ Mt. Rushmore	75.00
1012	3¢ Civil Engineers	50.00
1014	3¢ Gutenberg Bible	60.00
1015	3¢ Newspaper Boys	50.00
	1952-54	
1017	3¢ National Guard	50.00
1018	3¢ Ohio Sesqui	50.00
1019	3¢ Washington Terr	50.00
1020	3¢ Louisiana Purchase	50.00
1021	5¢ Opening of Japan	90.00
1022	3¢ American Bar Assn.	50.00
1023	3¢ Sagamore Hill	50.00
1024	3¢ Future Farmers	50.00
1025	3¢ Trucking Industry	50.00
1026	3¢ General Patton	80.00
1027	3¢ New York City	60.00
1028	3¢ Gadsden Purchase	50.00
1029	3¢ Columbia Univ	50.00
	1954-61 Liberty Series	
	(Sc#1030/1056 are priced with stamps)	
1030	½¢ Franklin	37.50
1031	1¢ Washington	40.00
1031A	1¼¢ Palace of Govs	15.00
1033	2¢ Jefferson	50.00
1034	2½¢ Bunker Hill	45.00
1035	3¢ Statue of Liberty	50.00
1036	4¢ Lincoln	75.00
1037	4½¢ Hermitage	50.00
1038	5¢ James Monroe	60.00
1039	6¢ Teddy Roosevelt	50.00
1040	7¢ Woodrow Wilson	75.00
1041	8¢ Statue of Liberty	25.00
1042	8¢ Liberty, Giori Press	20.00
1042A	8¢ Pershing	35.00
1043	9¢ The Alamo	60.00
1044	10¢ Independence Hall	60.00
1044A	11¢ Statue of Liberty	50.00

Scott No.	Subject	Price
1045	12¢ Harrison	25.00
1047	20¢ Monticello	30.00
1048	25¢ Paul Revere	100.00
1049	30¢ Robert E. Lee	75.00
1050	40¢ John Marshall	125.00
1051	50¢ Susan B. Anthony	100.00
1052	$1 Patrick Henry	135.00
	Liberty Series Coils	
1054	1¢ Washington	40.00
1054A	1¼¢ Palace of Govs	25.00
1055	2¢ Jefferson	45.00
1056	2½¢ Bunker Hill	50.00
	1954-55	
1060	3¢ Nebraska	45.00
1061	3¢ Kansas Terr	45.00
1062	3¢ George Eastman	50.00
1063	3¢ Lewis & Clark Exp.	45.00
1064	3¢ PA Fine Arts Acad	50.00
1065	3¢ Land Grant Colleges	45.00
1066	8¢ Rotary International	50.00
1067	3¢ Armed Forces Res	45.00
1068	3¢ New Hampshire	45.00
1069	3¢ Soo Locks	45.00
1071	3¢ Fort Ticonderoga	50.00
1072	3¢ Andrew Mellon	45.00
	1956	
1073	3¢ Ben Franklin	40.00
1074	3¢ B.T. Washington	30.00
1075	11¢ FIPEX S/S	25.00
1076	3¢ FIPEX	20.00
1077	3¢ Wildlife, Turkey	60.00
1078	3¢ Wildlife, Antelope	60.00
1079	3¢ Wildlife, Salmon	60.00
1080	3¢ Pure Food & Drugs	40.00
1081	3¢ Wheatland	50.00
1082	3¢ Labor Day	50.00
1083	3¢ Nassau Hall	25.00
1084	3¢ Devil's Tower	20.00
1085	3¢ Children	35.00
	1957	
1087	3¢ Polio	35.00
1088	3¢ Coast & Geo Survey	20.00
1089	3¢ Architects	30.00
1090	3¢ Steel Industry	40.00
1091	3¢ Naval Review	15.00
1092	3¢ Oklahoma Sthd	25.00
1093	3¢ School Teachers	50.00
1095	3¢ Shipbuilding	20.00
1096	8¢ Ramon Magsaysay	30.00
1097	3¢ Lafayette	50.00
1098	3¢ Whooping Cranes	20.00
1099	3¢ Religious Freedom	20.00
	1958-59	
1100	3¢ Gardening-Horticul	60.00
1104	3¢ Brussels Fair	35.00
1105	3¢ James Monroe	30.00
1106	3¢ Minnesota Sthd	25.00
1107	3¢ Int'l Geophysical Yr	15.00
1109	3¢ Mackinac Bridge	20.00
1110-11	4¢-8¢ Simon Bolivar	40.00
1112	4¢ Atlantic Cable	50.00
1113	1¢ Lincoln Sesqui	45.00
1114	3¢ Lincoln Sesqui	40.00
1115	4¢ Lincoln-Douglas	30.00
1116	4¢ Lincoln Sesqui	25.00
1117-18	4¢-8¢ Lajos Kossuth	40.00
1119	4¢ Freedom of Press	30.00
1120	4¢ Overland Mail	40.00
1121	4¢ Noah Webster	35.00
1122	4¢ Forest Conservation	35.00
1123	4¢ Fort Duquesne	60.00
1124	4¢ Oregon Sthd	50.00
1125-26	4¢-8¢ San Martin	30.00
1127	4¢ NATO	60.00
1128	4¢ Arctic Exploration	40.00
1130	4¢ Silver Centennial	40.00
1131	4¢ St. Lawrence Swy	40.00
1133	4¢ Soil Conservation	45.00
1134	4¢ Petroleum Industry	40.00
1135	4¢ Dental Health	40.00
1136-37	4¢-8¢ Ernest Reuter	30.00
1138	4¢ Ephraim McDowell	50.00
	1960	
1139	4¢ Washington "Credo"	25.00
1140	4¢ Franklin "Credo"	25.00
1141	4¢ Jefferson "Credo"	15.00
1142	4¢ F.Scott Key "Credo"	20.00
1143	4¢ Lincoln "Credo"	12.00
1144	4¢ Patrick Henry "Credo"	40.00

Scott No.	Subject	Price
1145	4¢ Boy Scouts	90.00
1147-48	4¢-8¢ Masaryk	15.00
1149	4¢ World Refugee Yr	40.00
1150	4¢ Water Conservation	30.00
1151	4¢ SEATO	30.00
1152	4¢ American Woman	35.00
1153	4¢ 50-Star Flag	30.00
1154	4¢ Pony Express	45.00
1155	4¢ Handicapped Empl.	25.00
1156	4¢ World Forestry Cong	60.00
1157	4¢ Mexican Indep	50.00
1158	4¢ U.S.-Japan Treaty	15.00
1159-60	4¢-8¢ Paderewski	12.00
1161	4¢ Robert A. Taft	40.00
1162	4¢ Wheels of Freedom	25.00
1163	4¢ Boy's Clubs	30.00
1164	4¢ Automated P.O.	10.00
1165-66	4¢-8¢ Mannerheim	35.00
1167	4¢ Camp Fire Girls	50.00
1168-69	4¢-8¢ Garibaldi	15.00
1170	4¢ Senator George	20.00
1171	4¢ Andrew Carnegie	50.00
1172	4¢ John Foster Dulles	15.00
1173	4¢ Echo I	30.00
	1961	
1174-75	4¢-8¢ Gandhi	15.00
1176	4¢ Range Conservation	50.00
1177	4¢ Horace Greeley	30.00
1178	4¢ Fort Sumter	40.00
1179	4¢ Battle of Shiloh	25.00
1180	5¢ Battle of Gettysburg	35.00
1181	5¢ Battle of Wilderness	25.00
1182	5¢ Appomattox	40.00
1183	4¢ Kansas Sthd	20.00
1184	4¢ Senator Norris	20.00
1185	4¢ Naval Aviation	50.00
1186	4¢ Workmen's Comp	12.00
1187	4¢ Frederick Remington	20.00
1188	4¢ China Republic	30.00
1189	4¢ Basketball	25.00
1190	4¢ Nursing	15.00
	1962	
1191	4¢ New Mexico Sthd	25.00
1192	4¢ Arizona Sthd	25.00
1194	4¢ Malaria Eradication	15.00
1195	4¢ Charles Ev. Hughes	25.00
1196	4¢ Seattle World's Fair	25.00
1197	4¢ Louisiana Sthd	30.00
1198	4¢ Homestead Act	17.50
1199	4¢ Girl Scouts	60.00
1200	4¢ Brien McMahon	20.00
1201	4¢ Apprenticeship	12.50
1202	4¢ Sam Rayburn	30.00
1203	4¢ Dag Hammarskjold.	30.00
1205	4¢ Christmas	16.00
1206	4¢ Higher Education	15.00
1207	4¢ Winslow Homer	30.00
	1963	
1208	5¢ Flag	15.00
1209	1¢ Jackson	12.50
1213	5¢ Washington	25.00
1225	1¢ Jackson Coil	12.00
1230	5¢ Carolina Charter	20.00
1231	5¢ Food for Peace	15.00
1232	5¢ West Virginia Sthd	25.00
1233	5¢ Emancipation Procl	15.00
1234	5¢ Alliance for Progress	25.00
1235	5¢ Cordell Hull	15.00
1236	5¢ Eleanor Roosevelt	30.00
1237	5¢ Science	30.00
1238	5¢ City Mail Delivery	30.00
1239	5¢ Red Cross	15.00
1240	5¢ Christmas	35.00
1241	5¢ Audubon	22.50
	1964	
1242	5¢ Sam Houston	30.00
1243	5¢ Charles M. Russell	35.00
1244/U546	5¢ NY World's Fair	18.00
1245	5¢ John Muir	20.00
1246	5¢ John F. Kennedy	22.50
1247	5¢ NJ Tercentenary	25.00
1248	5¢ Nevada Sthd	25.00
1249	5¢ Register & Vote	15.00
1250	5¢ Shakespeare	60.00
1251	5¢ Mayo Brothers	30.00
1252	5¢ Music	13.00
1253	5¢ Homemakers	15.00
1254-57	5¢ Christmas, 1964	125.00
1258	5¢ Verazzano Bridge	20.00
1259	5¢ Modern Art	15.00
1560	5¢ Radio	60.00

FIRST DAY CEREMONY PROGRAMS

1421-22

cott No.	Subject	Price
	1965 Commemoratives	
261	5¢ Battle/New Orleans	35.00
262	5¢ Sokol Society	10.00
263	5¢ Cancer	20.00
264	5¢ Churchill	10.00
265	5¢ Magna Carta	50.00
266	5¢ Int'l Cooperation Yr	25.00
267	5¢ Salvation Army	25.00
268	5¢ Dante	15.00
269	5¢ Herbert Hoover	15.00
270	5¢ Robert Fulton	15.00
271	5¢ St. Augustine, FL	25.00
272	5¢ Traffic Safety	15.00
273	5¢ Copley	20.00
274	11¢ ITU	30.00
275	5¢ Adlai Stevenson	25.00
276	5¢ Christmas 1965	30.00
	1965-81 Prominent Americans	
278	1¢ Jefferson	30.00
278a	Pane of 8	35.00
279	1¼¢ Gallatin	15.00
280	2¢ Wright	25.00
280a	Bk. pane of 5	30.00
280c	Bk. pane of 6	50.00
281	3¢ Parkman	20.00
282	4¢ Lincoln	20.00
283	5¢ Washington	47.50
283B	5¢ Wash. re-engr	13.00
284	6¢ F.D. Roosevelt	15.00
285	8¢ Einstein	35.00
286	10¢ Jackson	30.00
286A	12¢ Henry Ford	35.00
287	13¢ J.F. Kennedy	40.00
288	15¢ Holmes	30.00
289	20¢ Marshall	35.00
290	25¢ Douglass	35.00
291	30¢ Dewey	45.00
292	40¢ Paine	50.00
293	50¢ Lucy Stone	65.00
294	$1 O'Neill	85.00
295	$5 Moore	125.00
297	3¢ Parkman coil	20.00
299	1¢ Jefferson coil	35.00
303	4¢ Lincoln coil	35.00
304	5¢ Wash. coil	20.00
305C	$1 O'Neill	65.00
	1966 Commemoratives	
306	5¢ Migrat. Bird Treaty	25.00
307	5¢ Hum. Treat./Animal	19.00
308	5¢ Indiana Statehood	10.00
309	5¢ Circus	15.00
310	5¢ SIPEX	20.00
311	5¢ SIPEX Souv. Sht	20.00
312	5¢ Bill of Rights	35.00
313	5¢ Polish Millenium	12.50
314	5¢ Nat'l. Parks Service	15.00

Scott No.	Subject	Price
1315	5¢ Marine Reserves	25.00
1316	5¢ Women's Clubs	25.00
1317	5¢ Johnny Appleseed	30.00
1318	5¢ Beautif./America	35.00
1319	5¢ Great River Road	15.00
1320	5¢ Sav. Bond/Srvcmen	12.50
1321	5¢ Christmas 1966	30.00
1322	5¢ Mary Cassatt	30.00
	1967 Commemoratives	
1323	5¢ Nat'l. Grange	25.00
1324	5¢ Canada Centenary	17.50
1325	5¢ Erie Canal	17.50
1326	5¢ Peace/Lions	12.50
1327	5¢ Thoreau	12.50
1328	5¢ NE Statehood	12.50
1329	5¢ Voice of America	30.00
1330	5¢ Davy Crockett	30.00
1331-32	5¢ Space Twins	35.00
1333	5¢ Urban Planning	25.00
1334	5¢ Finnish Independ	20.00
1335	5¢ Thomas Eakins	20.00
1336	5¢ Christmas 1967	17.50
1337	5¢ MS Statehood	20.00
	1968-69 Issues	
1338	6¢ Flag	12.50
1338A	6¢ Flag coil	10.00
1339	6¢ IL Statehood	25.00
1340	6¢ Hemisfair	25.00
1341	$1 Airlift	75.00
1342	6¢ Youth/Elks	15.00
1343	6¢ Law & Order	25.00
1344	6¢ Register and Vote	20.00
1345-54	6¢ Historic Flags	40.00
1355	6¢ Walt Disney	90.00
1356	6¢ Marquette	12.50
1357	6¢ Daniel Boone	15.00
1358	6¢ AK River Navigation	30.00
1359	6¢ Leif Erikson	30.00
1360	6¢ Cherokee Strip	17.50
1361	6¢ Trumbull Painting	30.00
1362	6¢ Waterfowl Conserv.	30.00
1363	6¢ Christmas 1968	37.50
1364	6¢ Chief Joseph	30.00
	1969 Commemoratives	
1365-68	6¢ Beautification	30.00
1369	6¢ American Legion	15.00
1370	6¢ Grandma Moses	25.00
1371	6¢ Apollo 8	30.00
1372	6¢ W.C. Handy	15.00
1373	6¢ CA Settlement	20.00
1374	6¢ John Wesley Powell	25.00
1375	6¢ AL Statehood	30.00
1376-79	6¢ Botanical Congr	30.00
1380	6¢ Daniel Webster	25.00
1381	6¢ Baseball	95.00

Scott No.	Subject	Price
1382	6¢ Football	75.00
1383	6¢ Eisenhower Memor.	15.00
1384	6¢ Christmas 1969	30.00
1385	6¢ Hope/Crip. Child	15.00
1386	6¢ Harnett Painting	25.00
	1970 Commemoratives	
1387-90	6¢ Natural History	30.00
1391	6¢ Maine Statehood	25.00
1392	6¢ Wildlife Conserv.	20.00
	1970-74 Regular Issues	
1393	6¢ Eisenhower	25.00
1393D	7¢ Franklin	30.00
1395c	8¢ Eisenhower bklt./4	50.00
1395d	8¢ Eisenhower bklt./7	55.00
1396	8¢ Postal Service	10.00
1397	14¢ LaGuardia	25.00
1398	16¢ Ernie Pyle	35.00
1399	18¢ Elizabeth Blackwell	15.00
1400	21¢ Amadeo Giannini	20.00
	1970 Commems. (cont.)	
1405	6¢ Edgar Lee Masters	25.00
1406	6¢ Women's Suffrage	30.00
1407	6¢ SC Founding	20.00
1408	6¢ Stone Mountain	20.00
1409	6¢ Fort Snelling	15.00
1410-13	6¢ Anti-Pollution	40.00
1414-18	6¢ Christmas 1970	40.00
1414a-18a	6¢ Christmas Prec	125.00
1419	6¢ U.N. 25th Anniv	15.00
1420	6¢ Mayflower	20.00
1421	6¢ D.A.V	18.00
1422	6¢ Servicemen	18.00
	1971-72 Commemoratives	
1423	6¢ American Wool Ind.	20.00
1424	6¢ Douglas MacArthur.	20.00
1425	6¢ Blood Donors	20.00
1426	8¢ MO Sesquicent	30.00
1427-30	8¢ Wildlife Conserv	40.00
1431	8¢ Antarctic Treaty	20.00
1433	8¢ John Sloan	20.00
1434-35	8¢ Space Achiev	25.00
1436	8¢ Emily Dickinson	17.50
1437	8¢ San Juan	30.00
1438	8¢ Drug Abuse	30.00
1439	8¢ CARE	35.00
1440-43	8¢ Historic Preserv	50.00
1444-45	8¢ Christmas	15.00
1446	8¢ Sidney Lanier	25.00
1447	8¢ Peace Corps	12.50
1452	6¢ Wolf Trap	30.00
1453	8¢ Yellowstone Park	30.00
1454	15¢ Mt. McKinley	40.00
1455	8¢ Family Planning	25.00
1456-59	8¢ Colonial Craftsmen	25.00
1460-62,C85	Olympics	25.00
1463	8¢ PTA	20.00
1464-67	8¢ Wildlife	20.00
1468	8¢ Mail Order	35.00
1469	8¢ Osteopathic Medicine	15.00
1470	8¢ Tom Sawyer	15.00
1471-72	8¢ Christmas 1972	40.00
1473	8¢ Pharmacy	15.00
1474	8¢ Stamp Collecting	20.00
	1973-74 Commemoratives	
1475	8¢ Love	20.00
1476	8¢ Pamphleteers	15.00
1477	8¢ Posting Broadside	15.00
1478	8¢ Post Rider	15.00
1479	8¢ Colonial Drummer	15.00
1480-83	8¢ Boston Tea Party	25.00
1484	8¢ George Gershwin	80.00
1485	8¢ Robinson Jeffers	20.00
1486	8¢ Henry O. Tanner	30.00
1487	8¢ Willa Cather	7.50
1488	8¢ Copernicus	15.00
1489-98	8¢ Postal People	12.50
1499	8¢ Harry S. Truman	20.00
1500-02,C86	8¢ Electronics	35.00
1503	8¢ Lyndon B. Johnson.	20.00
1504	8¢ Angus Cattle	20.00
1505	10¢ Chautauqua	35.00
1506	10¢ Kansas Wheat	15.00
1507-08	8¢ Christmas 1973	25.00
	1973-74 Regular Issues	
1509	10¢ Crossed Flags	25.00
1510d	10¢ Jeff. Mem,bk/6	25.00
1518	6.3¢ Bulk Rate coil	15.00

Scott No.	Subject	Price
	1974 Commemoratives	
1525	10¢ VFW	30.00
1526	10¢ Robert Frost	20.00
1527	10¢ Expo '74	20.00
1528	10¢ Horse Racing	35.00
1529	10¢ Skylab	20.00
1530-37	10¢ Univ. Postal Union	20.00
1538-41	10¢ Mineral Heritage	40.00
1542	10¢ Fort Harrod	12.50
1543-46	10¢ Cont. Congress	30.00
1547	10¢ Energy Conserv	10.00
1548	10¢ Sleepy Hollow	30.00
1549	10¢ Retarded Children	30.00
1550-51	10¢ Christmas 1974.	50.00
1550-52	10¢ Christmas 1974.	70.00
	1975 Commemoratives	
1553	10¢ Benjamin West	30.00
1554	10¢ Paul L. Dunbar	25.00
1555	10¢ D.W. Griffith	25.00
1556	10¢ Pioneer	30.00
1557	10¢ Mariner	20.00
1558	10¢ Coll Bargaining	20.00
1559	10¢ Sybil Ludington	15.00
1560	10¢ Salem Poor	20.00
1561	10¢ Haym Salomon	20.00
1562	10¢ Peter Francisco	20.00
1563	10¢ Lexing. & Concord	25.00
1564	10¢ Bunker Hill	20.00
1565-68	10¢ Military Services	20.00
1571	10¢ Int'l Women's Year	20.00
1572-75	10¢ Postal Bicent	25.00
1577-78	10¢ Bank & Comm	15.00
1579-80	10¢ Christmas 1975.	30.00
	1975-81 Americana Issues	
1581-82,84-85	1¢-4¢ Issues	15.00
1592	10¢ Petit./Redress	12.50
1593	11¢ Free./Press	20.00
1594,1816	12¢ Conscience	20.00
1595a-c	13¢ Lib.Bell bk 6,7,8	15.00
1595d	Bklt. pn. of 5	25.00
1596	13¢ Eagle/Shield	20.00
1597	15¢ Ft. McHenry	15.00
1597/98a/1618C	Reg. Issue, B. Pn. & Coil	80.00
1603	24¢ Old No. Church	20.00
1604	28¢ Rem. Outpost	15.00
1605	29¢ Lighthouse	15.00
1606	30¢ Am. Schools	20.00
1608	50¢ "Betty" Lamp	30.00
1611	$2 Kero. Lamp	20.00
1612	$5 R.R. Lantern	30.00
1614	7.7¢ Bulk Rate coil	15.00
1615	7.9¢ Bulk Rate coil	15.00
1615C	8.4¢ Bulk Rate coil	30.00
1616	9¢ Assembly coil	25.00
1617	10¢ Redress coil	20.00
1618	13¢ Libty. Bell coil	20.00
1622	13¢ Flag/Ind. Hall	15.00
1623a	$1 Flag/Capitol, Vend Bklt. pf. 10½x11	100.00
1623c	Same, perf. 10	30.00
1625	13¢ Flag/Indep. Coil	75.00
	1976 Commemoratives	
1632	13¢ INTERPHIL '76	20.00
1633-82	13¢ State Flags	70.00
1683	13¢ Telephone Cent	20.00
1684	13¢ Commer. Aviation.	15.00
1685	13¢ Chemistry	15.00
1686-89	13¢ Bicentennial S/S	40.00
1690	13¢ Benjamin Franklin	20.00
1691-94	13¢ Dec. of Indepen	50.00
1695-98	13¢ Olympics	25.00
1699	13¢ Clara Maass	15.00
1701-03	13¢ Christmas 1976.	25.00
	1977 Commemoratives	
1704	13¢ Wash. at Princeton	25.00
1705	13¢ Sound Recording.	20.00
1706-09	13¢ Pueblo Art	17.50
1710	13¢ Lindbergh Flight	30.00
1711	13¢ CO Centennial	20.00
1712-15	13¢ Butterflies	20.00
1716	13¢ Lafayette	25.00
1717-20	13¢ Skilled Hands	15.00
1721	13¢ Peace Bridge	25.00
1722	13¢ Herkimer/Oriskany	30.00
1725	13¢ Alta, CA	12.50
1726	13¢ Art. of Confederation	25.00
1727	13¢ Talking Pictures	40.00
1728	13¢ Surrender/Saratoga	25.00
1729	13¢ Valley Forge	30.00
1730	13¢ Christmas Mailbox	15.00

FIRST DAY CEREMONY PROGRAMS

1862

Scott No.	Subject	Price
1978 Issues		
1731	13¢ Carl Sandburg....	15.00
1732-33	13¢ Cpt. Cook.........	25.00
1734	13¢ Ind. Hd. Penny ...	20.00
1737a	15¢ Rose bklt...........	30.00
1742a	15¢ Windmills bklt.....	60.00
1744	13¢ Harriet Tubman ..	40.00
1745-48	13¢ American Quilts.	30.00
1749-52	13¢ American Dance	25.00
1753	13¢ French Alliance ..	20.00
1754	13¢ Dr. Papanicolaou	30.00
1755	13¢ Jimmie Rodgers.	30.00
1756	15¢ George M. Cohan	25.00
1758	15¢ Photography.......	25.00
1759	15¢ Viking Missions ..	25.00
1760-63	15¢ American Owls..	30.00
1764-67	15¢ American Trees.	30.00
1768	15¢ Madonna & Child	10.00
1769	15¢ Xmas Horse	25.00
1979 Commemoratives		
1770	15¢ Robert F. Kennedy	50.00
1771	15¢ Martin L. King, Jr.	40.00
1772	15¢ Year of the Child	30.00
1773	15¢ John Steinbeck ..	30.00
1774	15¢ Albert Einstein....	30.00
1775-78	15¢ PA Toleware	25.00
1779-82	15¢ Amer. Architec. .	10.00
1783-86	15¢ Endang'd Flora..	30.00
1787	15¢ Seeing Eye Dogs	40.00
1788	15¢ Special Olympics	40.00
1789	15¢ John Paul Jones	25.00
1790	10¢ Olym. Games.....	20.00
1791-94	15¢ Summer Olym ...	30.00
1795-98	15¢ Winter Olym	25.00
1799	15¢ Virgin & Child.....	15.00
1800	15¢ Santa Claus	25.00
1801	15¢ Will Rogers.........	15.00
1802	15¢ Vietnam Vets......	17.50
1980 Issues		
1803	15¢ W.C. Fields	30.00
1804	15¢ Benjamin Banneker	30.00
1805-10	15¢ Letter Writing......	20.00
1821	15¢ Frances Perkins.	10.00
1822	15¢ Dolly Madison	20.00
1823	15¢ Emily Bissell........	15.00
1824	15¢ H.Keller/A.Sullivan	30.00
1825	15¢ Vet. Administration	15.00
1826	15¢ Gen. B. de Galvez	25.00
1827-30	15¢ Coral Reefs	35.00
1832	15¢ Edith Wharton	20.00
1833	15¢ Amer. Education	15.00
1834-37	15¢ NW Indian Masks	25.00
1838-41	15¢ Amer. Architecture	20.00
1842	15¢ Xmas St. Glass..	15.00
1843	15¢ Xmas Antique Toys	35.00
1980-85 Great Americans		
1844	1¢ Dorothea Dix........	12.50
1845	2¢ I. Stravinsky	10.00

Scott No.	Subject	Price
1846	3¢ Henry Clay...........	10.00
1847	4¢ Carl Shurz............	10.00
1848	5¢ Pearl S. Buck.......	30.00
1849	6¢ W. Lippmann........	10.00
1850	7¢ A. Baldwin............	8.00
1851	8¢ Henry Knox..........	10.00
1852	9¢ S. Thayer	7.50
1853	10¢ R. Russell	10.00
1854	11¢ A. Partridge........	8.00
1855	13¢ Crazy Horse.......	35.00
1856	14¢ S. Lewis	10.00
1857	17¢ R. Carson...........	20.00
1858	18¢ G. Mason	10.00
1859	19¢ Sequoyah...........	10.00
1860	20¢ Ralph Bunche	12.50
1861	20¢ T. Gallaudet	20.00
1862	20¢ Truman	12.50
1863	22¢ Audubon	8.00
1864	30¢ Dr. Laubach	15.00
1865	35¢ Dr. C. Drew.........	20.00
1866	37¢ R. Millikan	10.00
1867	39¢ G. Clark..............	10.00
1868	40¢ L. Gilbreth	12.00
1869	50¢ C. Nimitz	20.00
1981-83 Issues		
1874	15¢ Everett Dirksen ..	30.00
1875	15¢ Whitney M. Young	15.00
1876-79	15¢ Amer. Flowers...	25.00
1889a	18¢ Animals bk/10	30.00
1890-93a	18¢,6¢ Flag & Stars	22.50
1896b	20¢ Flag bklt. pn./10 .	10.00
1981-84 Transportation Coils		
1897	1¢ Omnibus	12.50
1897A	2¢ Locomotive	20.00
1898	3¢ Handcar...............	20.00
1898A	4¢ Stagecoach..........	25.00
1899	5¢ Motorcycle	30.00
1904	10.9¢ Hansom Cab...	25.00
1907	18¢ Surrey	50.00
1981 Commemoratives		
1910	18¢ Amer. Red Cross	17.00
1911	18¢ Savings & Loan .	16.00
1912-19	18¢ Space Achiev....	40.00
1920	18¢ Prof. Management	12.50
1921-24	18¢ Wildlife Habitats	12.50
1925	18¢ Int'l Yr. Disab Per.	14.00
1926	18¢ E.St.Vincent Millay	20.00
1927	18¢ Alcoholism	15.00
1928-31	18¢ Amer. Architec ..	12.50
1932,33	18¢ Zaharias/Jones ..	27.50
1934	Frederic Remington ..	20.00
1935-36	18¢ & 20¢ J. Hoban.	40.00
1937-38	18¢ Btl.Yrktn/V Capes	20.00
1939	20¢ Xmas Madon/Ch.	17.50
1940	20¢ Xmas "Teddy"....	25.00
1941	20¢ John Hanson......	15.00
1942-45	20¢ Desert Plants	30.00

Scott No.	Subject	Price
1982 Issues		
1949a	20¢ Sheep bk pn/10 ..	30.00
1950	20¢ F.D. Roosevelt....	20.00
1951	20¢ Love....................	17.50
1952	20¢ G. Washington....	12.50
1953-2002	20¢ Birds & Flowers	20.00
2003	20¢ Netherlands	30.00
2004	20¢ Library of Cong...	12.50
2005	20¢ Consumer Coil....	15.00
2006-09	20¢ World's Fair	15.00
2010	20¢ Horatio Alger	10.00
2011	20¢ Aging	15.00
2012	20¢ Barrymores.........	8.00
2013	20¢ Dr. Mary Walker .	12.50
2014	20¢ Int'l Peace Garden	15.00
2015	20¢ America's Libraries	12.50
2016	20¢ Jackie Robinson.	100.00
2017	20¢ Touro Synagogue	20.00
2018	20¢ Wolf Trap............	10.00
2019-22	20¢ Amer. Architec...	10.00
2023	20¢ Francis of Assisi.	30.00
2024	20¢ Ponce de Leon ...	12.50
2025	20¢ Kitten & Puppy....	30.00
2026	20¢ Xmas Tiepolo Art	12.50
2027-30	20¢ Xmas Snow Scene	25.00
1983 Commemoratives		
2031	20¢ Science & Indus .	12.50
2032-35	20¢ Balloons............	30.00
2036	20¢ Sweden/US Treaty	12.50
2037	20¢ Civ.Cons.Corps ..	18.00
2038	20¢ Joseph Priestley.	14.00
2039	20¢ Volunteerism	12.50
2040	20¢ German Immig....	20.00
2041	20¢ Brooklyn Bridge ..	15.00
2042	20¢ Tenn. Valley Auth	15.00
2043	20¢ Physical Fitness .	20.00
2044	20¢ Scott Joplin.........	60.00
2045	20¢ Medal of Honor...	25.00
2046	20¢ Babe Ruth	75.00
2047	20¢ Nath. Hawthorne	15.00
2048-51	13¢ Olympics............	15.00
2052	20¢ Treaty of Paris	25.00
2053	20¢ Civil Service........	8.00
2054	20¢ Metropolitan Opera	10.00
2055-58	20¢ American Inven .	10.00
2059-62	20¢ Streetcars	17.50
2063	20¢ Xmas Traditional	8.00
2064	20¢ Xmas Contemp...	8.00
2065	20¢ Martin Luther	15.00
1984 Commemoratives		
2066	20¢ Alaska Statehood	7.50
2067-70	20¢ Winter Olympics	20.00
2071	20¢ FDIC	7.50
2072	20¢ Love....................	10.00
2073	20¢ Carter Woodson .	15.00
2074	20¢ Soil/Water Cons .	12.50
2075	20¢ Credit Un.Act......	7.50
2076-79	20¢ Orchids...............	15.00
2080	20¢ Hawaii Statehood	10.00
2081	20¢ Nat'l. Archives.....	10.00
2082-85	20¢ Summer Olympics	12.50
2086	20¢ LA World Expo ...	10.00
2087	20¢ Health Research.	7.50
2088	20¢ Douglas Fairbanks	8.00
2089	20¢ Jim Thorpe.........	30.00
2090	20¢ John McCormack	27.50
2091	20¢ St. Lawrn. Seaw'y	10.00
2092	20¢ Mig. Bird Act.......	8.00
2093	20¢ Roanoke Voyages	20.00
2094	20¢ Herman Melville..	17.50
2095	20¢ Horace Moses	10.00
2096	20¢ Smokey the Bear	20.00
2097	20¢ Rob. Clemente ...	100.00
2098-2101	20¢ Dogs	12.50
2102	20¢ Crime Prevention	10.00
2103	20¢ Hispanic Amer. ...	10.00
2104	20¢ Family Unity........	12.50
2105	20¢ Eleanor Roosevelt	10.00
2106	20¢ Nation of Readers	10.00
2107	20¢ Xmas Traditional	10.00
2108	20¢ Xmas Santa Claus	15.00
2109	20¢ Vietnam Vets Mem	12.50
1985 Issues		
2110	Jerome Kern.............	10.00
2114-15	22¢ Flag...................	10.00
2115b	22¢ Test coil	10.00
2116a	22¢ Flag bklt. bk./5	12.50
2121a	22¢ Seashells bk/10 ..	15.00
2122	$10.75 Eagle bklt.sgl.	100.00

Scott No.	Subject	Price
1985-89 Transportation Coils		
2123	3.4¢ School Bus........	10.00
2124,28	4.9¢,8.3¢ Issues........	15.00
2125	5.5¢ Star Rt. Truck....	15.00
2127	7.1¢ Tractor..............	15.00
2127a	7.1¢ Tractor Zip+4.....	10.00
2129	8.5¢ Tow Truck	10.00
2131	11¢ Stutz Bearcat......	15.00
2132	12¢ Stanley Stmr.......	12.00
2134	14¢ Iceboat	12.50
2135	17¢ Dog Sled	15.00
2136	25¢ Bread Wagon	10.00
1985 Issues (cont.)		
2137	22¢ Mary M. Bethune	10.00
2138-41	22¢ Duck Decoys.....	12.50
2142	22¢ Winter Spec.Olym	10.00
2143	22¢ Love	10.00
2144	22¢ Rural Electrif.......	7.50
2145	22¢ AMERIPEX '86...	12.50
2146	22¢ Abigail Adams	10.00
2147	22¢ Frederick Bartholdi	15.00
2149	18¢ G. Wash. coil......	15.00
2150	21.1¢ Zip+4 coil.........	15.00
2152	22¢ Korean War Vets	12.50
2153	22¢ Social Security Act	20.00
2154	22¢ World War I Vets	12.50
2155-58	22¢ American Horses	15.00
2159	22¢ Public Education	7.50
2160-63	22¢ Int'l. Youth Year.	15.00
2164	22¢ Help End Hunger	7.50
2165	22¢ Xmas Traditional	12.50
2166	22¢ Xmas Contemp ..	10.00
1986 Issues		
2167	22¢ Arkansas Statehood	10.00
1986-93 Great Americans		
2168	1¢ M. Mitchell	10.00
2169	2¢ Mary Lyon	15.00
2170	3¢ Dr. P.D. White	10.00
2171	4¢ Fr. Flanagan.........	8.00
2172	5¢ Hugo Black...........	12.00
2173	5¢ Munoz Marin	7.50
2176	10¢ Red Cloud	12.00
2177	14¢ Julia W. Howe	10.00
2178	15¢ Buffalo Bill	17.50
2179	17¢ B. Lockwood.......	10.00
2180	21¢ C. Carlson	30.00
2182	23¢ M. Cassatt..........	10.00
2183	25¢ Jack London.......	15.00
2184	28¢ Sitting Bull	7.50
2184A	29¢ Earl Warren	8.00
2184B	29¢ Jefferson	7.50
2185	35¢ Dennis Chavez...	7.50
2186	40¢ C.L. Chennault ...	10.00
2188	45¢ Cushing..............	10.00
2190	52¢ H. Humphrey	10.00
2191	56¢ John Harvard......	7.50
2192	65¢ H. Arnold	10.00
2193	75¢ Wendell Wilkie....	10.00
2194	$1 Dr. B. Revel..........	10.00
2194A	$1 Johns Hopkins......	20.00
2195	$2 W.J. Bryan............	20.00
2196	$5 B. Harte	30.00
1986 (cont.)		
2201a	Stamp Col. bk./4........	20.00
2202	Love	7.50
2203	Sojourner Truth	12.50
2204	Republic of Texas	25.00
2209a	Fish bklt. pane/5........	15.00
2210	Public Hospitals.........	7.50
2211	Duke Ellington	17.50
2216-19	US Pres. shts., 4 pgs.	30.00
2220-23	Polar Explorers..........	15.00
2224	Statue of Liberty	90.00
2226	2¢ Locom. re-engr.....	15.00
2235-38	Navajo Art	10.00
2239	T.S. Elliot..................	9.00
2240-43	Woodcarved Figs	9.00
2244	Xmas Traditional	9.00
2245	Xmas Contemp	10.00
1987 Issues		
2246	MI Statehood.............	10.00
2247	Pan-Amer. Games	7.50
2248	Love	10.00
2249	J. Bap. Pnt. du Sable	25.00
2250	Enrico Caruso	9.00
2251	Girls Scouts...............	15.00

FIRST DAY CEREMONY PROGRAMS

2410

cott No.	Subject	Price
1987-88 Transportation Coils		
252	3¢ Con. Wag	10.00
253,62	5¢,17.5¢ Coils	15.00
254	5.3¢ Elevator, Prec.	10.00
255	7.6¢ Carretta, Prec.	12.50
256	8.4¢ Wheelchair, Prec.	10.00
257	10¢ Canal Boat	12.50
258	13¢ Police Wag,Prec.	10.00
259	13.2¢ RR Car, Prec	10.00
260	15¢ Tugboat	10.00
261	16.7¢ Pop.Wag,Prec.	15.00
263	20¢ Cbl. Car	10.00
264	20.5¢ Fire Eng, Prec.	15.00
265	21¢ RR Mail Car,Prec	12.00
266	24.1¢ Tandem Bike,Pre	10.00
1987-88 Issues		
267-74a	22¢ Sp. Occ. Bk	20.00
275	22¢ United Way	10.00
276	22¢ Flag/Fireworks	10.00
278	25¢ Flag/Clouds	10.00
280	25¢ Flag/Yosem. coil.	7.50
281	25¢ Honeybee coil	25.00
283a	25¢ Pheasant Bk/10	15.00
284-85b	25¢ Owl/Grosbk. Bk	10.00
286-2335	Am. Wildlife (10)	10.00
1987-90 Bicentennial Issues		
336	22¢ Delaware	10.00
337	22¢ Penn	10.00
338	22¢ New Jersey	10.00
239	22¢ Georgia	10.00
340	22¢ Conn	12.50
341	22¢ Mass	10.00
342	22¢ Maryland	8.00
343	25¢ S. Carolina	10.00
344	25¢ New Hamp	10.00
345	25¢ Virginia	8.00
346	25¢ New York	10.00
347	25¢ North Carolina	7.50
348	25¢ Rhode Island	7.50
1987 Issues (cont.)		
349	22¢ U.S.-Moroc. Rel.	12.50
350	22¢ Faulkner	15.00
351-54	22¢ Lacemaking	13.00
359a	22¢ Const. Bklt.	15.00
361	22¢ CPA	30.00
366a	22¢ Loco. Bklt.	20.00
367	22¢ Xmas Madon	10.00
368	22¢ Xmas Orn	25.00
1988 Issues		
369	22¢ '88 Wnt. Olym	7.50
370	22¢ Australia Bicent.	15.00
371	22¢ J.W. Johnson	15.00
372-75	22¢ Cats	15.00
376	22¢ Knute Rockne	25.00
377	25¢ F. Ouimet	20.00

Scott No.	Subject	Price
2378	25¢ Love	15.00
2379	45¢ Love	10.00
2380	25¢ Sum. Olym	12.50
2385a	25¢ Classic Cars bk.	12.50
2386-89	25¢ Ant. Expl	13.00
2390-93	25¢ Carousel Anim	25.00
2394	$8.75 Express Mail	35.00
2395-98a	25¢ Spec. Occas.bk.	15.00
2399	25¢ Xmas Tradn'l	12.50
2400	25¢ Xmas Contemp	15.00
1989 Issues		
2401	25¢ Montana Sthd	7.50
2402	25¢ A.P. Randolph	7.50
2403	25¢ N.Dakota Sthd	7.50
2404	25¢ Washington sthd.	7.50
2409a	25¢ Steamboats bklt.	10.00
2410	25¢ Wld. Stamp Expo	7.50
2411	25¢ A. Toscanini	8.00
2412	25¢ House of Reps	7.50
2413	25¢ U.S. Senate	100.00
2414	25¢ Exec.Branch/GW	7.50
2415	25¢U.S.Sup.Ct.('90)	10.00
2416	25¢ S.Dakota sthd	7.50
2417	25¢ Lou Gehrig	20.00
2418	25¢ E. Hemingway	7.50
2419	$2.40 Moon Landing	20.00
2420	25¢ Letter Carriers	7.50
2421,UX135	25¢ Bill of Rights/ 15¢ Cityscape	10.00
2422-25	25¢ Dinosaurs	25.00
2427,27a	25¢ Christmas Art	10.00
2428,29a	25¢ Christmas Sleigh	10.00
2431	25¢ Eagle, self-adh	7.50
2433/UX144	Set of 3 Subscriber Programs	75.00
2433	90¢ WSE Lincoln S/S	15.00
2434-37	25¢ Traditional Mail	15.00
2438	25¢ Tradit'l.Mail S/S	15.00
1990-93 Issues		
2439	25¢ Idaho Sthd	7.50
2440,41a	25¢ Love, sht. & bklt.	10.00
2442	25¢ Ida B. Wells	10.00
2443a	15¢ Bch. Umbr., bklt.	7.50
2444	25¢ Wyoming Sthd	7.50
2445-48	25¢ Classic Films	15.00
2449	25¢ Marianne Moore	7.50
2452	5¢ Circus Wagon	7.50
2453/57	5¢/10¢ Canoe/Trailer	7.50
2464,93,94	23¢ Wagon/ 29¢ Ducks (2)	15.00
2468	$1.00 Seaplane coil	10.00
2474a	25¢ Lighthouse bklt.	10.00
2475	25¢ ATM Plastic Flag	10.00
2476	$2 Bobcat	10.00
2478	29¢ Red Squirrel	7.50
2479	29¢ Rose	7.50
2491	45¢ Pumpkinseed	7.50

Scott No.	Subject	Price
2495a	29¢ African Violet, Bklt	10.00
2496-2500	25¢ Olympics	10.00
2505a	25¢ Indian Headdress	10.00
2506-07	25¢ Marsh Is. & Micro. Joint Issue	10.00
2508-11	25¢ Sea Creatures	15.00
2512/C127	25¢,45¢ America	10.00
2513	25¢ D.D. Eisenhower	7.50
2514	Sht. stamps only	7.50
2514,14a	25¢ Xmas & B. Pane	7.50
2515	Sht. stamps only	7.50
2515-16	25¢ Xmas & B. Pane	15.00
1991-93 Issues		
2523	29¢ Flag/Mt. Rush	9.00
2531	29¢ Flag/Mem'l. Day	9.00
2532	50¢ Switzerland	7.50
2533	29¢ Vermont Sthd	7.50
2534	29¢ Savings Bonds	7.50
2535-36,U621	Love Issues	10.00
2538	29¢ Saroyan	10.00
2539	$1.00 USPS Logo & Olympic Rings	10.00
2540	$2.90 Priority Mail	20.00
2541	$9.95 Express Mail	35.00
2543	$2.90 Space Vehicle	12.50
2549a	29¢ Fishing Flies bk.	12.50
2550	29¢ Cole Porter	12.50
2551	29¢ Des'rt Shld/St'm	35.00
2553-57	29¢ Summer Olymp	15.00
2558	29¢ Numismatics	7.50
2559	29¢ WW II shtlt./10	15.00
2560	29¢ Basketball	15.00
2561	29¢ Dist. of Columbia	7.50
2566a	29¢ Comedians bklt.	15.00
2567	29¢ Jan Matzeliger	7.50
2577a	29¢ Space bklt	12.50
2578	(29¢)Christmas/Tradit	7.50
2579/85	Christmas Santa 5 stamps	12.50
2593a	29¢ Pledge bklt.	12.50
2595-97	29¢ Eagle	25.00
2603-04	(10¢) Eagle	10.00
1992 Issues		
2616	29¢ World Columbian	7.50
2617	29¢ W.E.B. DuBois	10.00
2618	29¢ Love	12.50
2620-23	29¢ Columb. Voyages	10.00
2624	1¢/$1 Columb's S/S	10.00
2625	2¢/$4 Columb's S/S	17.50
2626	5¢/50¢ Columb's S/S	10.00
2627	6¢/$3 Columb's S/S	15.00
2628	10¢/$2 Columb's S/S	12.50
2629	$5.00 Columb's S/S	20.00
2630	29¢ NY Stock Exch	7.50
2631-34	29¢ Space Accomp	15.00
2635	29¢ Alaska Hwy	7.50
2636	29¢ Kentucky Sthd	7.50
2647-96	29¢ Wildflowers (2)	15.00
2697	29¢ WW II S/S	18.00
2698	29¢ Dorothy Parker	7.50
2699	29¢ Dr. von Karman	20.00
2700-03	29¢ Minerals	12.50
2704	29¢ J.R. Cabrillo	7.50
2709a	29¢ Wild Animals bk.	10.00
2710a	29¢ Christmas Trad. Sheet & Bklt. Pn.	12.50
2711-14	29¢ Christmas Trains	12.50
2719	29¢ Same. ATM sgl	10.00
2720	29¢ Chinese New Yr.	12.50
1993 Issues		
2721	29¢ Elvis Presley Record format	20.00
2724-30	29¢ Rock 'n Roll	15.00
2745a	29¢ Space Fant. bk	12.50
2746	29¢ Percy L. Julian	12.50
2747	29¢ Oregon Trail	10.00
2748	29¢ World Games	10.00
2749	29¢ Grace Kelly	15.00
2750-53	29¢ Circus	12.50
2754	29¢ Cherokee Strip	7.50
2755	29¢ Dean Acheson	7.50
2756-59	29¢ Sports Horses	12.50
2764a	29¢ Garden Flwrs bk	10.00
2765	29¢ WW II Sheetlet	15.00
2766	29¢ Joe Louis	15.00
2779-82	29¢ Postal Museum	12.50
2783-84	29¢ Deaf Commun	12.50
2785-88	29¢ Youth Classics	10.00
2789	29¢ Xmas Madonna	10.00
2799-2803	29¢ Self-adhesive Christmas	10.00

Scott No.	Subject	Price
2804	29¢ Nthn. Marianas	10.00
2805	29¢ Columbus Lands in Puerto Rico	10.00
2806	29¢ AIDS	15.00
1994 Issues		
2807-11	29¢ Winter Olympics	10.00
2812	29¢ Edward R. Murrow	7.50
2813	29¢ Sunrise S/A	7.50
2814-15	29¢, 50¢ Love	10.00
2816	29¢ Dr. Allison Davis	10.00
2817	29¢ Chinese New Year	10.00
2818	29¢ Buffalo soldiers	10.00
2819-28	29¢ Silent Screen	12.50
2833a	29¢ G. Flowers, bklt	7.50
2834-37	29¢-50¢ Soccer, Singles and S/S	12.50
2838	29¢ WWII Sheetlet	15.00
2839-40	29¢-50¢ Norman Rockwell, single & S/S	12.50
2841	29¢ Moon Landing, Sheet of 12	15.00
2847a	29¢ Locomotives, bklt	10.00
Airmails		
#C32-48/Programs w/o stamps		
C32	5¢ Skymaster	70.00
C34	10¢ Pan Am Bldg	45.00
C35	15¢ NY Skyline	50.00
C40	6¢ Alexandria	75.00
C43	15¢ UPU	45.00
C44	25¢ UPU	45.00
C45	6¢ Wright Bros	60.00
C46	80¢ Hawaii	75.00
C47	6¢ Powered Flight	50.00
C48	4¢ Eagle	40.00
#C51 to date/Programs w/stamps		
C51	7¢ Blue Jet	40.00
C52	7¢ Blue Jet coil	30.00
C53	7¢ Alaska	30.00
C54	7¢ Balloon	50.00
C55	7¢ Hawaii Sthd	40.00
C56	10¢ Pan Am Games	20.00
C57	10¢ Liberty Bell	30.00
C58	15¢ Statue of Liberty	35.00
C59	25¢ Lincoln	35.00
C60	7¢ Red Jet	30.00
C60a	Booklet Pane	40.00
C61	7¢ Red Jet coil	35.00
C62	13¢ Liberty Bell	20.00
C63	15¢ Liberty, re-drawn.	40.00
C64	8¢ Capitol	35.00
C66	15¢ Mont. Blair	15.00
C67	6¢ Bald Eagle	17.50
C68	8¢ Amelia Earhart	17.50
C69	8¢ Goddard	10.00
C70	8¢ Alaska	17.50
C71	20¢ Audubon	20.00
C72	10¢ 50 Star Runway	20.00
C74	10¢ Jenny	12.50
C75	20¢ USA	12.00
C76	10¢ Moonlanding	20.00
C77/UXC10	9¢ Delta Plane	20.00
C78	11¢ Jet	30.00
C78a	Booklet Pane	45.00
C79	13¢ Winged Env	10.00
C79a/83	Bklt. pane, coil	30.00
C80	17¢ Statue of Liberty	35.00
C81	21¢ USA	12.50
C82	11¢ Jet coil	30.00
C84	11¢ City of Refuge	35.00
C87	18¢ Stat. of Liberty	15.00
C89-90	25¢ & 31¢ Airmails	35.00
C91-92	31¢ Wright Brothers	15.00
C93-94	21¢ Octave Chanute	15.00
C95-96	25¢ Wiley Post	20.00
C97	31¢ Olym. Games	25.00
C98	40¢ P. Mazzei	15.00
C99-100	28¢,35¢ Scott,Curtiss	25.00
C101-04	28¢ Olympics	20.00
C105-08	40¢ Olympics	25.00
C109-12	35¢ Olympics	27.50
C113-14	33¢,39¢ Verv,Sperry	15.00
C115/UXC22	Transpacific Flt.	15.00
C116	44¢ Fr. J. Serra	10.00
C117	44¢ New Sweden	15.00
C118/UXC24	Langley/DC-3	12.50
C119	36¢ Sikorsky	15.00
C120	45¢ French Rev	12.50
C122-25	45¢ Future Mail	15.00
C126	$1.80 Future Mail S/S	15.00
C128	50¢ Harriet Quimby	10.00
C130	50¢ Antarctic Treaty	17.50
C131	50¢ America	10.00

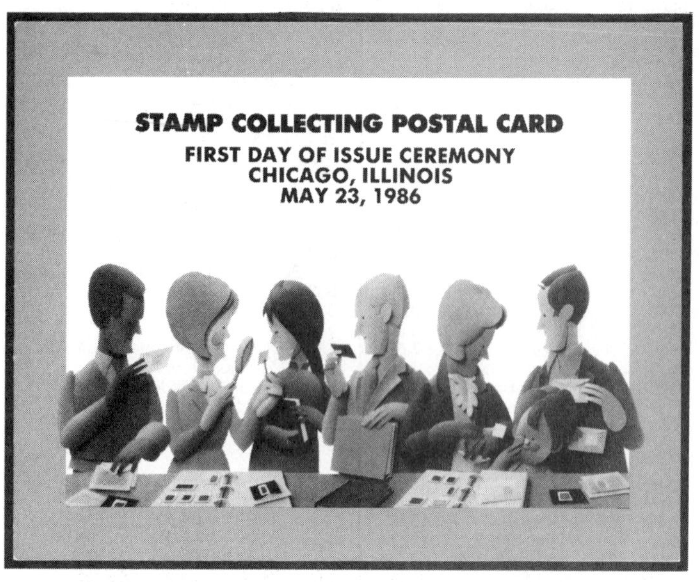

UX110

Scott No.	Subject	Price
Special Delivery		
E21	30¢ Letter	35.00
E22	45¢ Arrows	30.00
E23	60¢ Arrows	25.00
Postage Dues		
J89-101	1¢-$5 Postg. Dues (w/o stamps)	95.00
1988-93 Official Coils		
O138A,141	15¢,25¢ Issues	12.50
O146A	10¢ Official	15.00
1988-92 Duck Stamps		
RW55	$10.00 Snow Goose	45.00
RW56	$12.50 Lesser Scaup	35.00
RW57	$12.50 Whist. Duck	40.00
RW58	$15.00 King Elders	40.00
RW59	$15.00 Spec. Elder	40.00
Postal Stationery 1960-69 Issues		
U541	1¼¢ Franklin	40.00
U542	2½¢ Washington	40.00
U543	4¢ Pony Express	40.00
U544/UX48	5¢/4¢ Lincoln	25.00
U547,49	1¼¢ Bell,Ironsides	20.00
U548	1.4¢ Liberty Bell	20.00
U550	5¢ Eagle	25.00
U551	6¢ Liberty Head	15.00
1970-76 Issues		
U554	6¢ Moby Dick	20.00
U555	6¢ Brotherhood	30.00
U557/UC43	8¢ Eagle	30.00
U563	8¢ Bowling	25.00
U564	8¢ Aging	25.00
U565	8¢ Transpo '72	30.00
U567	10¢ Liberty Bell	30.00
U568	1.8¢ Volunteer	15.00
U571	10¢ Seafaring	30.00
U572	13¢ Homemaker	15.00
U573	13¢ Farmer	20.00
U574	13¢ Doctor	20.00
U575	13¢ Craftsman	20.00
U576	13¢ Liberty Tree	20.00
1976-80 Issues		
U577	2¢ Star & Pinwheel	10.00
U578	2.1¢ Hexagon	17.50
U582	13¢ Bicentennial	12.50
U587	15¢ Auto Racing	20.00
U589	3.1¢ Non-Profit	15.00
U595	15¢ Veterinary	25.00
U597	15¢ Bicycle	25.00
U598	15¢ America's Cup	20.00
U599	15¢ Honeybee	25.00
Postal Stationery 1981-89		
U600	18¢ Blinded Veteran	15.00
U602	20¢ Great Seal	15.00

Scott No.	Subject	Price
U603	20¢ Purple Heart	15.00
Postal Stationery 1981-89 (cont.)		
U605	20¢ Paralyzed Vets	7.50
U606	20¢ Small Business	10.00
U609	6¢ Old Ironsides	10.00
U614	25¢ Philatelic Env	6.00
U616	25¢ Love	6.00
U617	25¢ Space Hologram	10.00
U620	11.1¢ Non-Profit	10.00
U622	29¢ Magazine Industry	7.50
U623	29¢ Geese	7.50
U629	29¢ Disabled Americans	7.50
Air Postal Stationery		
UC18	6¢ Skymaster	50.00
UC33	7¢ Jet, Blue	50.00
UC34	7¢ Jet, Carmine	60.00
UC35	11¢ Jetliner & Globe	60.00
UC37	8¢ Jet, Triangle	25.00
UC38	11¢ Kennedy Airletter	20.00
UC39	13¢ Kennedy Airletter	15.00
UC40	10¢ Jet, Triangle	20.00
UC42	13¢ Human Rts	20.00
UC44	15¢ Birds in Flight	20.00
UC46	15¢ Ballooning	25.00
UC47	13¢ Birds in Flight	20.00
UC50	22¢ "USA"	20.00
UC51	22¢ "USA"	15.00
UC53	30¢ "USA", Blue, Red & Brown	20.00
UC54	30¢ "USA", Yellow, Blue & Black	20.00
UC55	30¢ World Trade	12.50
UC56	30¢ Comm. Year	17.50
UC57	30¢ Olympics	20.00
UC58	36¢ Land Sat. Satellite	12.00
UC60	36¢ Mark Twain, Halley's Comet	12.50
UC62	39¢ Montgomery Blair	15.00
Official Postal Stationery 1989		
UO81-82	45¢ & 65¢ Envelopes	10.00
Postal Cards 1956-78		
UX45/UY16	4¢ Liberty	60.00
UX49	7¢ "USA"	45.00
UX50	4¢ Customs	42.50
UX51	4¢ Social Security	30.00
UX52	4¢ Coast Guard	30.00
UX53	4¢ Census	50.00
UX54	8¢ "USA"	25.00
UX55	5¢ Lincoln	25.00
UX56	5¢ Women Marines	35.00
UX57	5¢ Weather Service	25.00
UX58	6¢ Paul Revere	20.00
UX59/UXC11	10¢ "USA"	20.00
UX60	6¢ Hospitals	30.00
UX64	6¢ John Hanson	15.00

Scott No.	Subject	Price
UX65	6¢ Liberty	20.00
UX66	8¢ Samuel Adams	20.00
UX67/UXC15	12¢ Visit USA	20.00
UX68	7¢ Chris Thomson	17.50
UX69	9¢ Witherspoon	15.00
UX70	9¢ Caeser Rodney	10.00
UX71	9¢ Court House	25.00
UX72	9¢ Nathan Hale	17.50
UX73	10¢ Music Hall	20.00
UX74	(10¢) John Hancock	15.00
UX75	10¢ John Hancock	15.00
UX76	14¢ Cutter "Eagle"	12.50
UX77	10¢ Molly Pitcher	15.00
Postal Cards 1979-88		
UX78	10¢ G.R. Clark	15.00
UX79	10¢ Pulaski	20.00
UX80	10¢ Olympics	20.00
UX81	10¢ Iolani Palace	25.00
UX82	14¢ Winter Olympics	20.00
UX83	10¢ Salt Lake Temple	17.50
UX84	10¢ Rochambeau	30.00
UX85	10¢ King's Mt	25.00
UX86	19¢ Golden Hinde	20.00
UX87	10¢ Cowpens	20.00
UX89	12¢ Isaiah Thomas	20.00
UX90	12¢ N. Greene	17.50
UX91	12¢ Lewis & Clark	25.00
UX93	13¢ Morris	20.00
UX94	13¢ F. Marion	15.00
UX95	13¢ LaSalle	15.00
UX96	13¢ Music Academy	20.00
UX97	13¢ St. Louis P.O	20.00
UX98	13¢ Georgia	20.00
UX99	13¢ Old P. Office	15.00
UX100	13¢ Yachting	15.00
UX101	13¢ Maryland	10.00
UX102	13¢ Olympics	10.00
UX103	13¢ Baraga	14.00
UX104	13¢ Rancho S.P	10.00
UX105	(14¢) Charles Carroll	15.00
UX106	14¢ Charles Carroll	8.00
UX107	25¢ Flying Cloud	10.00
UX108	14¢ George Wythe	8.00
UX109	14¢ Conn. Anniv	10.00
UX110	14¢ Stamp Coll	8.00
UX111	14¢ Francis Vigo	12.50
UX112	14¢ Rhode Island	10.00
UX113	14¢ Wisconsin Ty	9.00
UX114	14¢ Nat'l. Guard	7.50
UX115	14¢ Steel Plow	10.00
UX116	14¢ Const. Conv	10.00
UX117	14¢ U.S. Flag	10.00
UX118	14¢ Pride in Am	10.00
UX119	14¢ Timberline Ldg	10.00
UX120	15¢ Am. the Beaut	10.00
UX121	15¢ Blair House	8.00
UX122	28¢ Yorkshire	8.00
UX123	15¢ Iowa Terr	10.00
UX124	15¢ NW/Ohio Terr	8.00
UX125	15¢ Hearst Castle	8.00
UX126	15¢ Fed. Papers	10.00

Scott No.	Subject	Price
Postal Cards 1989-94		
UX127	15¢ The Desert	6.00
UX128	15¢ Healy Hall	6.00
UX129	15¢ Wetlands	6.00
UX130	15¢ Okla. Land Run	9.00
UX131	21¢ The Mountains	6.00
UX132	15¢ The Seashore	6.00
UX133	15¢ The Woodlands	6.00
UX134	15¢ Hull House	6.00
UX135	15¢ Independ. Hall	8.00
UX136	15¢ Balt. Harbor	8.00
UX137	15¢ Manhattan Skyline	8.00
UX138	15¢ Capitol Bldg	12.00
UX139-42	15¢ Cityscapes Rouletted sheet of 4	15.00
UX143	15¢ White House	12.00
UX144	15¢ Jefferson Mem	12.00
UX145	15¢ Am. Papermaking	15.00
UX146	15¢ Literacy	9.00
UX147	(15¢) Geo. Bingham	7.50
UX148	15¢ Isaac Royall House	7.50
UX150	15¢ Stanford Univ	6.00
UX151	15¢ Constit. Hall, DC	6.00
UX152	15¢ Chicago Orch. Hall	7.50
UX154	19¢ Carnegie Hall	7.50
UX155	19¢ Old Red	7.50
UX156	19¢ Bill of Rights	10.00
UX157	19¢ Notre Dame	10.00
UX159	19¢ Old Mill	7.50
UX160	19¢ Wadsworth Ath'nm	7.50
UX161	19¢ Cobb Hall	8.00
UX162	19¢ Walter Hall	7.50
UX164	19¢ Columb.Rvr.Gorge	7.50
UX165	19¢ Ellis Island	9.00
UX166	19¢ Wash.Nat'l.Cath'drl	7.50
UX167	19¢ Wren Building	7.50
UX168	19¢ Holocaust	9.00
UX169	19¢ Fort Recovery	7.50
UX170	19¢ Playmakers	7.50
UX172	19¢ Beecher Hall	7.50
UX173	19¢ Mass. Hall	7.50
UX174	19¢ Lincoln Home	7.50
UX175	19¢ Wittenberg	7.50
UX176	19¢ Canyon de Chelly	7.50
Air Post Cards 1958-88		
UXC2	5¢ Eagle	50.00
UXC3	5¢ Eagle, redrawn	50.00
UXC4	6¢ Bald Eagle	50.00
UXC5	11¢ SIPEX, Travel	20.00
UXC6	6¢ Virgin Islands	25.00
UXC7	6¢ Boy Scouts	30.00
UXC8	13¢ Travel USA	15.00
UXC9	8¢ Eagle, Precan	15.00
UXC14	11¢ Mail Early	15.00
UXC16	21¢ Visit USA	20.00
UXC17	21¢ Curtiss Jenny	15.00
UXC18	21¢ Olympics	25.00
UXC19	28¢ Trans-Pacific	20.00
UXC20	28¢ Soaring	12.50
UXC21	28¢ Speedskating	12.50
UXC23	33¢ Ameripex	7.50

CONFEDERATE STATES OF AMERICA

1,4 2,5 6,7 8

11 12 13 14

1861-62 (OG + 40%) (C)

ott's No.		Unused Fine	Unused Ave.	Used Fine	Used Ave.
	5¢ Jefferson Davis, Green	135.00	85.00	95.00	55.00
	10¢ T. Jefferson, Blue	175.00	105.00	135.00	85.00
	2¢ Andrew Jackson, Green	350.00	225.00	500.00	350.00
	5¢ Jefferson, Rose	95.00	55.00	75.00	45.00
	10¢ T. Jefferson, Rose	650.00	400.00	375.00	225.00
	5¢ J. Davis, London Print, Clear	9.00	5.50	20.00	12.50
	5¢ J. Davis, Local Print, Coarse	10.00	6.00	11.50	7.50

1862-63 (OG + 40%) (C)

	2¢ A. Jackson, Brown Red	38.50	22.50	225.00	150.00
	10¢ J. Davis, Blue "TEN CENTS"	550.00	325.00	425.00	250.00
	10¢ Blue "TEN CENTS", Frame Line	1950.00	1350.00	1050.00	625.00
	10¢ Blue, No Frame Line, Die A	8.50	5.50	12.50	7.50
2	10¢ Same, Filled in Corners, Die B	9.50	6.00	12.50	7.50
3	20¢ Washington, Green	27.50	18.50	250.00	165.00
4	1¢ J.C. Calhoun, Orange (unissued)	70.00	40.00	...	...

CANAL ZONE

5 73 84/101 96

1904 U.S. 1902-03 Issue Ovptd. "CANAL ZONE" "PANAMA" VF Used + 50% (C)

ott's No.		Very Fine NH	Very Fine Unused	F-VF NH	F-VF Unused	F-VF Used
	1¢ Frank., Bl. Grn. (#300)	52.50	33.75	35.00	22.50	19.50
	2¢ Wash., Carmine (#319)	45.00	28.50	28.50	20.00	18.00
	5¢ Lincoln, Blue (#304)	185.00	120.00	115.00	80.00	52.50
	8¢ M. Wash., V. Blk. (#306)	290.00	190.00	185.00	125.00	72.50
	10¢ Webster,Red Brn.(#307)	290.00	180.00	175.00	120.00	75.00

1924-25 U.S. Stamps of 1923-25 Overprinted "CANAL ZONE" (Flat Top "A") Flat Press, Perf. 11 VF Used + 30% (B)

0	½¢ N. Hale (#551)	1.50	1.10	1.10	.75.	.65
1	1¢ Franklin (#552)	2.40	1.60	1.70	1.20	.70
1e	1¢ Bklt. Pane of 6 (#552a)	300.00	215.00	210.00	150.00	...
2	1½¢ Harding (#553)	3.00	2.25	2.25	1.65	1.25
3	2¢ Washington (#554)	13.75	9.50	10.00	7.00	1.50
3a	2¢ Bklt. Pane of 6 (#554c)	365.00	275.00	265.00	200.00	...
4	5¢ T. Roosevelt (#557)	33.50	24.00	25.00	18.00	8.00
5	10¢ Monroe (#562)	70.00	48.50	53.50	36.50	17.50
6	12¢ Cleveland (#564)	57.50	35.50	42.50	27.50	25.00
7	14¢ Indian (#565)	47.50	32.50	33.50	22.50	16.50
8	15¢ Liberty (#566)	75.00	56.50	55.00	37.50	30.00
9	30¢ Buffalo (#569)	50.00	32.50	37.50	25.00	23.50
0	50¢ Amphitheater (#570)	97.50	72.50	70.00	50.00	38.50
1	$1 Lincoln Mem. (#571)	380.00	270.00	285.00	195.00	110.00

1925-28 Same as Preceding but with Pointed "A", VF Used + 30% (B)

4	2¢ Washington (#554)	47.50	31.50	35.00	23.50	9.00
4d	2¢ Bklt. Pane of 6 (#554c)	395.00	285.00	275.00	195.00	...
5	3¢ Lincoln (#555)	6.50	4.50	4.75	3.50	2.50
6	5¢ T. Roosevelt (#557)	6.00	4.25	4.50	3.25	2.25
7	10¢ Monroe (#562)	55.00	36.50	40.00	27.50	9.50
8	12¢ Cleveland (#564)	37.50	24.00	27.50	18.50	12.00
9	14¢ Indian (#565)	33.50	22.50	23.50	17.50	16.50
0	15¢ Liberty (#566)	11.50	7.75	8.25	6.00	3.50
1	17¢ Wilson (#623)	7.00	4.85	5.00	3.65	2.75

1925-28 Pointed "A" (cont.)

Scott's No.		Very Fine NH	Very Fine Unused	F-VF NH	F-VF Unused	F-VF Used
92	20¢ Golden Gate (#567)	10.50	7.00	7.50	5.50	3.50
93	30¢ Buffalo (#569)	10.50	7.00	7.50	5.50	3.75
94	50¢ Amphitheater (#570)	400.00	260.00	285.00	200.00	140.00
95	$1 Lincoln Mem (#571)	190.00	135.00	135.00	100.00	50.00

1926 Sesquicentennial Issue Overprinted "CANAL ZONE"

96	2¢ Liberty Bell (#627)	6.75	4.50	4.75	3.75	3.50

1926-27 Rotary Press, Perf. 10, Overprinted "CANAL ZONE" VF Used + 75% (B)

97	2¢ Washington (#583)	85.00	57.50	49.50	33.50	9.75
98	3¢ Lincoln (#584)	17.50	11.50	10.00	6.75	4.50
99	10¢ Monroe (#591)	28.50	20.00	16.50	11.50	6.00

1927-31 Rotary Press, Perf. 11x10½, Overprinted "CANAL ZONE" VF Used + 30% (B)

100	1¢ Franklin (#632)	3.00	2.25	2.25	1.65	1.20
101	2¢ Washington (#634)	3.65	2.75	2.50	1.80	.80
101a	2¢ Bklt. Pane of 6 (#634d)	415.00	300.00	290.00	210.00	...
102	3¢ Lincoln (#635) (1931)	7.00	4.50	5.00	3.50	3.00
103	5¢ T. Roosevelt (#637)	33.50	21.50	23.50	16.50	10.50
104	10¢ Monroe (#642) (1930)	26.50	18.50	19.50	14.00	10.00

105 107 110 112

1928-40 Flat Plate Printing VF Used + 20% (B)

105-14	**Set of 10**	**12.50**	**9.00**	**9.50**	**7.25**	**4.95**
105	1¢ General Gorgas	.30	.25	.25	.21	.18
106	2¢ General Goethels	.30	.25	.25	.21	.18
106a	2¢ Booklet Pane of 6	30.00	22.75	23.75	17.50	...
107	5¢ Gaillard Cut (1929)	1.85	1.45	1.50	1.20	.60
108	10¢ General Hodges (1932)	.45	.35	.37	.28	.20
109	12¢ Colonel Gaillard (1929)	1.50	1.15	1.25	.95	.75
110	14¢ Gen. W.L. Sibert (1937)	1.60	1.20	1.30	1.00	1.00
111	15¢ Jackson Smith (1932)	.75	.60	.60	.45	.45
112	20¢ Adm. Rousseau (1932)	1.00	.85	.85	.65	.25
113	30¢ Col. Williamson (1940)	1.50	1.10	1.20	.90	.85
114	50¢ J. Blackburn (1929)	2.75	2.10	2.30	1.75	.75

PLATE BLOCKS

	NH VF	NH F-VF	Unused F-VF		NH VF	NH F-VF	Unused F-VF
105 (6)	1.25	1.00	.70	110 (6)	18.50	15.00	11.50
106 (6)	3.50	2.75	2.00	111 (6)	11.50	9.00	6.00
107 (6)	18.50	15.00	9.00	112 (6)	12.50	9.75	7.00
108 (6)	8.50	7.00	5.25	113 (6)	16.50	12.75	9.00
109 (6)	16.50	13.00	10.00	114 (6)	25.00	20.00	15.00

115 117 118 120

1933 Rotary Press, Perf. 11x10½ VF Used + 30% (B)

115	3¢ Washington (#720)	4.65	3.15	3.35	2.35	.32
116	14¢ Indian (#695)	8.75	6.00	6.25	4.50	3.00

1934-39 Issues VF Used + 30% (B)

117	3¢ General Goethals	.30	.25	.25	.21	.18
117a	3¢ Booklet Pane of 6	87.50	62.50	62.50	47.50	...
118	½¢ Franklin (#803) (1939)	.30	.25	.25	.21	.18
119	1½¢ M. Wash. (#805) (1939)	.30	.25	.25	.21	.18

PLATE BLOCKS

	NH VF	NH F-VF	Unused F-VF		NH VF	NH F-VF	Unused F-VF
115	52.50	40.00	30.00	118	3.25	2.50	2.00
116	100.00	75.00	50.00	119	3.25	2.50	2.00
117 (6)	2.35	1.80	1.40				

CANAL ZONE

1939 25th Anniversary Series VF + 20%

Scott's No.		Plate Blocks F-VF NH	F-VF Unus.	F-VF NH	Unus.	F-VF Used
120-35	**Set of 16**	**1475.00**	**1175.00**	**115.00**	**83.50**	**56.50**
120	1¢ Balboa, before (6)	11.00	9.00	.45	.35	.35
121	2¢ Balboa, after (6)	12.00	10.00	.60	.50	.50
122	3¢ Gaillard Cut, before (6)	11.00	9.00	.55	.45	.25
123	5¢ Gaillard Cut, after (6)	18.00	15.00	1.40	1.00	.85
124	6¢ Bas Obispo, before (6)	38.50	32.50	2.95	2.15	1.95
125	7¢ Bas Obispo, after (6)	38.50	32.50	2.75	2.00	1.95
126	8¢ Gatun Locks, before (6)	52.50	42.50	4.50	3.25	2.75
127	10¢ Gatun Locks, after (6)	52.50	42.50	3.85	2.75	2.50
128	11¢ Canal Channel, before (6)	120.00	100.00	9.25	6.75	6.75
129	12¢ Canal Channel, after (6)	100.00	80.00	7.75	5.75	5.50
130	14¢ Gamboa, before (6)	110.00	90.00	8.25	6.00	5.75
131	15¢ Gamboa, after (6)	135.00	110.00	11.75	8.00	4.25
132	18¢ P. Miguel Locks, before (6)	130.00	105.00	11.75	8.00	7.25
133	20¢ P. Miguel Locks, after (6)	170.00	135.00	12.50	9.50	5.25
134	25¢ Gatun Spillway, before (6)	275.00	215.00	20.00	14.50	11.50
135	50¢ Gatun Spillway, after (6)	275.00	225.00	23.50	17.50	4.25

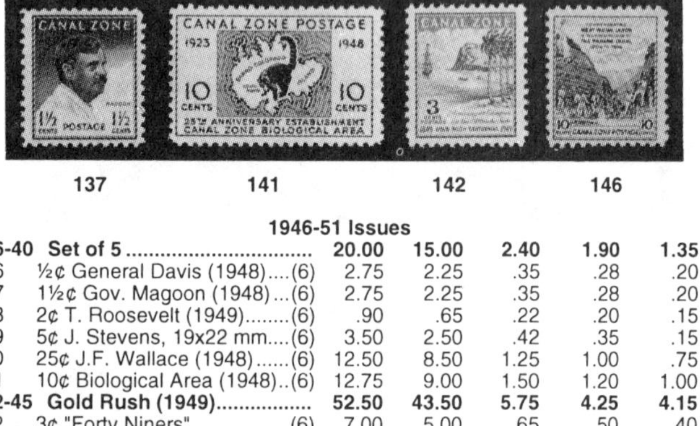

137 141 142 146

1946-51 Issues

Scott's No.		Plate Blocks F-VF NH	F-VF Unus.	F-VF NH	Unus.	F-VF Used
136-40	**Set of 5**	**20.00**	**15.00**	**2.40**	**1.90**	**1.35**
136	½¢ General Davis (1948) (6)	2.75	2.25	.35	.28	.20
137	1½¢ Gov. Magoon (1948) (6)	2.75	2.25	.35	.28	.20
138	2¢ T. Roosevelt (1949) (6)	.90	.65	.22	.20	.15
139	5¢ J. Stevens, 19x22 mm (6)	3.50	2.50	.42	.35	.15
140	25¢ J.F. Wallace (1948) (6)	12.50	8.50	1.25	1.00	.75
141	10¢ Biological Area (1948) (6)	12.75	9.00	1.50	1.20	1.00
142-45	**Gold Rush (1949)**	**52.50**	**43.50**	**5.75**	**4.25**	**4.15**
142	3¢ "Forty Niners" (6)	7.00	5.00	.65	.50	.40
143	6¢ Journey to Las Cruces (6)	7.50	5.50	.75	.60	.55
144	12¢ Las Cruces Trail (6)	19.50	16.50	1.75	1.25	1.25
145	18¢ To San Francisco (6)	22.50	18.50	2.75	2.00	2.00
146	10¢ W. Indian Labor (1951) (6)	30.00	22.50	3.25	2.50	1.75

1955-58 Commemoratives

148 149 150

Scott's No.		Plate Blocks NH	F-VF NH	F-VF Used
147	3¢ Panama Railroad (6)	8.00	.80	.60
148	3¢ Gorgas Hospital (1957)	4.35	.55	.40
149	4¢ S.S. Ancon (1958)	3.50	.50	.35
150	4¢ T. Roosevelt (1958)	3.75	.55	.40

1960-62 Issues

151 152 153 157

Scott's No.		Plate Blocks NH	F-VF NH	F-VF Used
151	4¢ Boy Scouts	4.50	.55	.45
152	4¢ Administration Bldg	1.00	.25	.17
		Line Pairs		
153	3¢ Goethals, Coil	1.00	.22	.15
154	4¢ Admin. Bldg., Coil	1.25	.22	.15
155	5¢ Stevens, Coil (1962)	1.50	.35	.25

CANAL ZONE
1960-62 Issues (cont.)

Scott's No.		Plate Blocks NH	F-VF NH	F-VF Used
156	4¢ Girl Scouts (1962)	2.75	.45	.35
157	4¢ Thatcher Ferry Bridge ('62)	3.35	.35	.28

1968-78 Issues

158 159 163 165

Scott's No.		Plate Blocks NH	F-VF NH	F-VF Used
158	6¢ Goethals Monument Balboa	2.25	.35	.22
159	8¢ Fort San Lorenzo (1971)	2.75	.45	.20
160	1¢ Gorgas,Coil,Pf.10 Vert.(1975)...Line Pair	.95	.20	.20
161	10¢ Hodges,Coil,Pf.10 Vert.(1975) Line Pair	5.25	.75	.40
162	25¢ Wallace,Coil,Pf.10 Vert.(1975) Line Pair	19.50	2.50	2.40
163	13¢ Dredge Cascadas (1976)	2.35	.40	.35
163a	13¢ Booklet Pane of 4	...	3.00	...
164	5¢ Stevens, Rotary, 19x22½mm (1977)	4.50	.75	.50
165	15¢ Towing Locomotive (1978)	2.25	.40	.40

AIR MAIL STAMPS

C3 C5 C6 C17

Scott's No.		Very Fine NH	Very Fine Unused	F-VF NH	F-VF Unused	F-VF Used
	1929-31 Surcharges on Issues of 1928-29 VF Used + 30% (B)					
C1	15¢ on 1¢ Gorgas T.I (#105)	13.50	8.25	12.00	6.25	5.75
C2	15¢ on 1¢ Gorgas T.II (1931)	160.00	115.00	140.00	87.50	87.50
Type I: Flag "5" points up. Type II: Flag of "5" is curved up.						
C3	25¢ on 2¢ Goethals (#106)	6.00	4.00	4.50	3.00	2.10
C4	10¢ on 50¢ Blackburn (#114)	14.00	9.00	10.50	7.50	7.25
C5	20¢ on 2¢ Goethals (#106)	9.00	6.00	6.75	4.50	1.85
	1931-49 Series Showing "Gaillard Cut" VF Used + 20% (B)					
C6-14	**Set of 9**	**31.75**	**22.50**	**25.50**	**18.75**	**6.75**
C6	4¢ Red Yellow (1949)	1.20	.90	1.00	.75	.75
C7	5¢ Yellow Green	.80	.60	.65	.50	.35
C8	6¢ Yellow Brown (1946)	1.20	.90	1.00	.75	.35
C9	10¢ Orange	1.45	1.10	1.20	.90	.35
C10	15¢ Blue	1.80	1.35	1.50	1.10	.27
C11	20¢ Red Violet	3.25	2.40	2.65	2.00	.27
C12	30¢ Rose Lake (1941)	5.25	3.50	4.25	2.95	1.10
C13	40¢ Yellow	5.25	3.75	4.25	3.15	1.10
C14	$1 Black	13.25	9.75	11.00	8.00	2.50

PLATE BLOCKS

	NH VF	NH F-VF	Unused F-VF		NH VF	NH F-VF	Unused F-VF
C6 (6)	8.00	6.50	4.50	C11 (6)	26.50	21.50	16.50
C7 (6)	6.00	5.00	4.00	C12 (6)	44.00	36.50	27.50
C8 (6)	8.50	7.00	5.00	C13 (6)	44.00	36.50	27.50
C9 (6)	13.75	11.50	8.50	C14 (6)	117.50	97.50	75.00
C10 (6)	15.00	12.75	9.50				

1939 25th Anniversary of Canal Opening VF + 20%

Scott's No.		Plate Blocks NH	Plate Blocks Unused	F-VF NH	F-VF Unused	F-VF Used
C15-20	**Set of 6**	**850.00**	**650.00**	**72.50**	**53.75**	**38.50**
C15	5¢ Plane over Sosa Hill (6)	40.00	30.00	4.25	3.25	2.95
C16	10¢ Map of Central America (6)	43.50	32.50	3.75	2.75	2.75
C17	15¢ Fort Amador (6)	49.50	37.50	4.50	3.50	1.20
C18	25¢ Cristobal Harbor (6)	185.00	135.00	12.50	9.50	7.50
C19	30¢ Gaillaird Cut (6)	135.00	110.00	11.50	8.00	6.50
C20	$1 Clipper Landing (6)	450.00	350.00	39.50	29.50	19.50

NOTE: PRICES THROUGHOUT THIS LIST ARE SUBJECT TO CHANGE WITHOUT NOTICE IF MARKET CONDITIONS REQUIRE. MINIMUM ORDER MUST TOTAL AT LEAST $20.00

C21 C32 C33

1951 "Globe and Wing" Issue

cott's No.		Plate Blocks NH	Unus.	F-VF NH	Unus.	F-VF Used
21-26	**Set of 6**	**220.00**	**180.00**	**25.00**	**20.00**	**11.50**
21	4¢ Red Violet (6)	7.00	5.50	.85	.70	.40
22	6¢ Brown (6)	5.50	4.00	.65	.50	.32
23	10¢ Red Orange (6)	9.50	7.50	1.15	.90	.50
24	21¢ Blue (6)	80.00	67.50	8.75	7.00	4.50
25	31¢ Cerise (6)	85.00	67.50	8.50	6.75	4.25
26	80¢ Gray Black (6)	45.00	35.00	6.25	5.00	1.75

1958 "Globe and Wing" Issue

cott's No.		Plate Blocks F-VF NH	F-VF NH	F-VF Used
27-31	**Set of 5**	**180.00**	**26.50**	**9.00**
27	5¢ Yellow Green	7.00	1.25	.75
28	7¢ Olive	6.50	1.15	.60
29	15¢ Brown	31.50	5.00	2.25
30	25¢ Orange Yellow	90.00	11.00	2.95
31	35¢ Dark Blue	52.50	9.00	2.75
	1961-63 Issues			
32	15¢ U.S. Army Carib. School	15.00	1.75	1.10
33	7¢ Anti-Malaria (1962)	4.00	.70	.50
34	8¢ Globe & Wing (1963)	5.50	.75	.35
35	15¢ Alliance for Progress (1963)	14.00	1.50	1.00
	1964 50th Anniversary of Canal Opening			
36-41	**Set of 6**	**67.50**	**12.50**	**8.75**
36	6¢ Jet over Cristobal	3.00	.55	.50
37	8¢ Gatun Locks	3.50	.65	.45
38	15¢ Madden Dam	8.75	1.50	.75
39	20¢ Gaillard Cut	11.50	2.25	1.10
40	30¢ Miraflores Lock	16.50	3.00	2.75
41	80¢ Balboa	27.50	5.25	3.50
	1965 Seal & Jet Plane			
42-47	**Set of 6**	**32.50**	**6.00**	**3.25**
42	6¢ Green & Black	2.50	.40	.35
43	8¢ Rose Red & Black	2.75	.45	.18
44	15¢ Blue & Black	3.00	.45	.35
45	20¢ Lilac & Black	3.50	.80	.50
46	30¢ Reddish Brown & Black	5.50	1.10	.55
47	80¢ Bistre & Black	16.50	3.00	1.50
	1968-76 Seal & Jet Plane			
48-53	**Set of 6**	**25.00**	**5.00**	**2.75**
48	10¢ Dull Orange & Black	2.10	.40	.20
48a	10¢ Booklet Pane of 4 (1970)	...	4.15	...
49	11¢ Olive & Black (1971)	2.50	.50	.25
49a	11¢ Booklet Pane of 4	...	3.35	...
50	13¢ Emerald & Black (1974)	5.50	1.10	.40
50a	13¢ Booklet Pane of 4	...	5.50	...
51	22¢ Violet & Black (1976)	6.00	1.20	.65
52	25¢ Pale Yellow Green & Black	4.00	.85	.65
53	35¢ Salmon & Black (1976)	6.50	1.25	.75

1941-47 OFFICIAL AIRMAIL STAMPS VF Used + 20%
Issue of 1931-46 Overprinted OFFICIAL PANAMA CANAL "PANAMA CANAL" 19-20 mm long

cott's No.		Very Fine NH	Unused	F-VF NH	Unused	F-VF Used
O1-7,14	**Set of 8**	**165.00**	**125.00**	**140.00**	**100.00**	**50.00**
O 1	5¢ Yellow Green (#C7)	7.50	5.50	6.00	4.50	2.25
O 2	10¢ Orange (#C9)	14.50	10.50	11.50	8.75	2.85
O 3	15¢ Blue (#C10)	17.50	13.50	14.50	10.00	4.00
O 4	20¢ Rose Violet (#C11)	21.00	15.50	17.00	13.00	6.00
O 5	30¢ Rose Lake (#C12) (1942)	25.50	20.00	21.50	16.50	6.50
O 6	40¢ Yellow (#C13)	30.00	22.50	25.00	18.50	10.00
O 7	$1 Black (#C14)	42.50	27.50	35.00	22.50	15.00
O 14	6¢ Yel. Brown (#C8) (1947)	16.50	12.50	13.50	10.00	5.00

1941 OFFICIAL AIRMAIL STAMPS
Issue of 1931-46 Overprinted OFFICIAL PANAMA CANAL "PANAMA CANAL" 17 mm long

					Used VF	F-VF
O 8	5¢ Yellow Green (#C7)	...	...	...	200.00	155.00
O 9	10¢ Orange (#C9)	...	...	...	290.00	225.00
O 10	20¢ Red Violet (#C11)	...	...	...	215.00	165.00
O 11	30¢ Rose Lake (#C12)	...	...	...	70.00	55.00
O 12	40¢ Yellow (#C13)	...	...	...	225.00	175.00

POSTAGE DUE STAMPS
1914 U.S. Dues Ovptd. "CANAL ZONE", Perf. 12 VF Used + 50% (C)

Scott's No.		Very Fine NH	Unused	F-VF NH	Unused	F-VF Used
J1	1¢ Rose Carmine (#J45a)	140.00	95.00	95.00	65.00	16.00
J2	2¢ Rose Carmine (#J46a)	375.00	250.00	250.00	170.00	50.00
J3	10¢ Rose Carmine (#J49a)	...	...	825.00	600.00	50.00
	1924 U.S. Dues Ovptd. "CANAL ZONE", Flat "A" VF Used + 40% (B)					
J12	1¢ Carmine Rose (#J61)	230.00	150.00	160.00	110.00	27.50
J13	2¢ Claret (#J62b)	140.00	85.00	100.00	60.00	12.00
J14	10¢ Claret (#J65b)	525.00	350.00	375.00	250.00	45.00
	1925 U.S. Ovptd. "CANAL ZONE POSTAGE DUE" VF Used + 40% (B)					
J15	1¢ Franklin (#552)	185.00	130.00	130.00	90.00	16.00
J16	2¢ Washington (#554)	45.00	31.50	32.50	22.50	6.75
J17	10¢ Monroe (#562)	87.50	58.50	62.50	42.50	10.50
	1925 U.S. Dues Ovptd. "CANAL ZONE", Sharp "A" VF Used + 40% (B)					
J18	1¢ Carmine Rose (#J61)	18.50	12.00	13.00	8.50	2.75
J19	2¢ Carmine Rose (#J62)	29.50	19.50	21.00	14.00	4.50
J20	10¢ Carmine Rose (#J65)	225.00	150.00	160.00	110.00	18.50
	1929-30 Issue of 1928 Surcharged "POSTAGE DUE" VF Used + 30% (B)					
J21	1¢ on 5¢ Gaillard Cut (#107)	6.50	4.50	5.00	3.50	2.10
J22	2¢ on 5¢ Blue	11.75	7.75	9.00	6.00	3.00
J23	5¢ on 5¢ Blue	11.75	7.75	9.00	6.00	3.50
J24	10¢ on 5¢ Blue	11.75	7.75	9.00	6.00	3.50
	1932-41 Canal Zone Seal VF + 25% (B) VF Used + 30%					
J25-29	**Set of 5**	**5.95**	**4.75**	**4.65**	**3.75**	**3.25**
J25	1¢ Claret	.30	.25	.25	.21	.18
J26	2¢ Claret	.30	.25	.25	.21	.18
J27	5¢ Claret	.70	.55	.55	.45	.30
J28	10¢ Claret	2.75	2.25	2.25	1.75	1.65
J29	15¢ Claret (1941)	2.15	1.75	1.70	1.35	1.20
	1941-47 OFFICIAL STAMPS VF Used + 30% (B) Issues of 1928-46 Overprinted "OFFICIAL PANAMA CANAL"					
O1	1¢ Gorgas, Type 1 (#105)	2.60	2.10	2.00	1.50	.45
O2	3¢ Goethals, T. 1 (#117)	5.35	4.00	4.25	3.00	.80
O3	5¢ Gaillard Cut, T. 2 (#107)	...	...	...	...	32.50
O4	10¢ Hodges, Type 1 (#108)	9.00	6.75	6.50	5.00	2.00
O5	15¢ Smith, Type 1 (#111)	16.00	12.00	11.50	9.00	2.50
O6	20¢ Rousseau, T. 1 (#112)	21.50	16.00	15.00	11.00	3.00
O7	50¢ Blackburn, T. 1 (#114)	60.00	40.00	39.50	29.50	6.00
O8	50¢ Blackburn, T. 1A (#114)	...	...	...	...	625.00
O9	5¢ Stevens, T. 1 (#139) ('47)	13.00	9.75	9.50	7.00	3.50

Type 1: Ovptd. "10mm", Type 1A: Ovptd. "9mm", Type 2: Ovptd. "19½mm".

CUBA VF + 50% (C)

223 228 E2 J4

1899 U.S. Stamps of 1895-98 Surcharged for Use in Cuba

Scott's No.		NH Fine	Unused Fine	Ave.	Used Fine	Ave.
221	1¢ on 1¢ Franklin (#279)	6.00	4.25	2.75	.60	.35
222	2¢ on 2¢ Wash. (#267)	6.75	4.75	2.50	.50	.30
222a	2¢ on 2¢ Wash. (#279B)	7.50	5.25	3.00	.50	.30
223	2½¢ on 2¢ Wash. (#279B)	4.75	3.25	2.10	.60	.35
223a	2½¢ on 2¢ Wash. (#267)	4.35	3.00	1.85	2.40	1.45
224	3¢ on 3¢ Jackson (#268)	11.00	8.00	5.00	1.50	.90
225	5¢ on 5¢ Grant (#281a)	11.00	8.00	5.00	1.50	.90
226	10¢ on 10¢ Webster (#282C)	25.00	17.50	11.50	7.50	4.50
	1899 Issues of Republic under U.S. Military Rule					
227	1¢ Statue of Columbus	4.65	3.25	1.95	.22	.15
228	2¢ Royal Palms	4.65	3.25	1.95	.22	.15
229	3¢ Allegory "Cuba"	4.65	3.25	1.95	.30	.18
230	5¢ Ocean Liner	5.50	3.75	2.50	.35	.22
231	10¢ Cane Field	14.00	10.00	6.25	.75	.45
	1899 SPECIAL DELIVERY					
E1	10¢ on 10¢ Blue (#E5)	140.00	100.00	65.00	75.00	45.00
E2	10¢ Messenger, Orange	55.00	40.00	25.00	12.50	7.50
	1899 POSTAGE DUE					
J1	1¢ on 1¢ Claret (#J38)	40.00	27.50	18.50	3.75	2.25
J2	2¢ on 2¢ Claret (#J39)	40.00	27.50	18.50	3.75	2.25
J3	5¢ on 5¢ Claret (#J41)	40.00	27.50	18.50	3.75	2.25
J4	10¢ on 10¢ Claret (#J42)	37.50	25.00	16.50	1.65	1.00

GUAM VF + 60% (C)

1 4 12 E1

1899 U.S. Stamps of 1895-98 Overprinted "GUAM"

Scott's No.		NH Fine	Unused Fine	Unused Ave.	Used Fine	Used Ave.
1	1¢ Franklin (#279)	27.50	18.50	12.00	27.50	16.00
2	2¢ Wash. (#267)	25.00	17.50	10.50	26.50	16.00
2a	2¢ Wash. (#279c)	28.50	20.00	13.50	30.00	20.00
3	3¢ Jackson (#268)	150.00	100.00	60.00	135.00	80.00
4	4¢ Lincoln (#280a)	150.00	100.00	60.00	135.00	80.00
5	5¢ Grant (#281a)	35.00	23.50	16.50	35.00	20.00
6	6¢ Garfield (#282)	150.00	100.00	60.00	125.00	75.00
7	8¢ Sherman (#272)	150.00	100.00	60.00	130.00	80.00
8	10¢ Webster (#282C)	55.00	35.00	22.50	55.00	35.00
10	15¢ Clay (#284)	165.00	110.00	65.00	150.00	90.00
11	50¢ Jefferson (#275)	325.00	225.00	135.00	275.00	175.00
12	$1 Perry (#276)	465.00	315.00	190.00	425.00	240.00
	1899 SPECIAL DELIVERY					
E1	10¢ Blue (on U.S. #E5)	185.00	120.00	72.50	160.00	100.00

HAWAII

11 15,23 21 25

1857-68 Issues (OG + 30%) (C)

Scott's No.		Unused Fine	Unused Ave.	Used Fine	Used Ave.
8	5¢ Kamehameha III, Blue	325.00	185.00	315.00	185.00
9	5¢ Blue, Bluish Paper	140.00	85.00	100.00	60.00
10	5¢ Blue, Reissue	22.50	13.75	...	...
11	13¢ Dull Rose, Reissue	200.00	125.00	...	...
15	1¢ Numeral, Black, Grayish	325.00	200.00	...	...
16	2¢ Black	450.00	285.00	400.00	250.00
19	1¢ Black	325.00	200.00	...	...
20	2¢ Black	375.00	230.00	...	...
21	5¢ Blue, Bluish Paper	425.00	260.00	325.00	195.00
22	5¢ Blue, Interisland	325.00	200.00	400.00	250.00
23	1¢ Black	175.00	100.00	...	...
24	2¢ Black	175.00	100.00	...	...
25	1¢ Dark Blue	160.00	95.00	...	...
26	2¢ Dark Blue	150.00	90.00	...	...

1861-86 Issues (OG + 20%, NH + 100) (C)

27-29 30 32,39,52C 35,38,43 36,46

Scott's No.		Unused Fine	Unused Ave.	Used Fine	Used Ave.
27	2¢ Kamehameha IV, Pale Rose	165.00	100.00	110.00	65.00
28	2¢ Pale Rose, Vert. Laid Paper	165.00	100.00	110.00	65.00
29	2¢ Red, Thin Wove Paper	40.00	25.00	...	...
30	1¢ Victoria Kamamalu, Purple	7.50	4.50	5.75	3.50
31	2¢ Kamehameha IV, Vermilion	10.50	6.25	6.50	4.00
32	5¢ Kamehameha V, Blue	80.00	50.00	18.00	11.50
33	6¢ Kamehameha V, Green	16.50	10.00	5.75	3.50
34	18¢ Kekuanaoa, Dull Rose	75.00	42.50	32.50	18.75
35	2¢ Kalakaua, Brown	5.75	3.50	2.00	1.25
36	12¢ Leleiohoku, Black	35.00	22.50	17.50	11.50

HAWAII

1882-91 Issues (OG + 20%) (C)

37,42 40,44-45 41 47 52

Scott's No.		NH Fine	Unused Fine	Unused Ave.	Used Fine	Used Ave.
37	1¢ Likelike, Blue	5.50	3.50	2.25	6.50	4.2
38	2¢ Kalakaua, Lilac Rose	135.00	82.50	52.50	26.50	16.5
39	5¢ Kamehameha V, Ultra	17.00	10.50	6.50	2.25	1.4
40	10¢ Kalakaua, Black	30.00	20.00	13.50	13.50	8.5
41	15¢ Kapiolani, Red Brown	70.00	42.50	27.50	20.00	12.0
42	1¢ Likelike, Green	3.00	1.90	1.25	1.25	.7
43	2¢ Kalakaua, Rose	4.85	3.00	1.90	.75	.4
44	10¢ Kalakaua, Red Brown	28.00	18.50	11.00	6.00	3.9
45	10¢ Kalakaua, Vermilion	35.00	23.50	14.00	10.50	7.0
46	12¢ Leleiohoku, Red Lilac	95.00	60.00	37.50	26.50	17.5
47	25¢ Kamehameha I, Dk. Viol.	140.00	90.00	55.00	45.00	28.5
48	50¢ Lunalilo, Red	195.00	120.00	75.00	65.00	40.0
49	$1 Kaleleonalani, Rose Red	280.00	175.00	110.00	115.00	70.0
50	2¢ Orange Verm., Imperf	...	130.00	85.00	...	...
51	2¢ Carmine, Imperf	...	22.50	13.50	...	...
52	2¢ Liliuokalani, Dull Violet	7.50	4.00	2.25	1.10	.7
52C	5¢ Kamehameha, V.D. Ind.	150.00	90.00	55.00	85.00	50.0

1893 Issues of 1864-91 Overprinted "Provisional Government 1893" VF + 40% (C)

Scott's No.		NH Fine	Unused Fine	Unused Ave.	Used Fine	Used Ave.
	Red Overprints					
53	1¢ Purple (#30)	7.00	4.50	2.75	6.00	3.5
54	1¢ Purple (#37)	5.75	3.75	2.25	5.75	3.2
55	1¢ Green (#42)	2.15	1.35	.75	2.50	1.5
56	2¢ Brown (#35)	8.00	5.50	3.25	12.50	8.0
57	2¢ Dull Violet (#52)	2.10	1.35	.80	1.20	.7
58	5¢ Deep Indigo (#52C)	12.50	8.00	4.75	17.50	11.0
59	5¢ Ultramarine (#39)	7.00	4.25	2.50	3.00	1.7
60	6¢ Green (#33)	13.50	8.50	5.00	16.00	10.0
61	10¢ Black (#40)	10.00	6.00	3.50	8.75	5.2
62	12¢ Black (#36)	10.75	6.75	4.15	11.00	6.7
63	12¢ Red Lilac (#46)	175.00	110.00	65.50	140.00	85.0
64	25¢ Dark Violet (#47)	30.00	18.00	11.00	30.00	18.5
	Black Overprint					
65	2¢ Rose Vermilion (#31)	70.00	42.50	27.50	45.00	30.0
66	2¢ Rose (#43)	1.85	1.10	.70	2.25	1.3
67	10¢ Vermilion (#45)	16.50	10.50	6.50	23.50	15.7
68	10¢ Red Brown (#44)	8.50	5.50	3.35	9.00	5.5
69	12¢ Red Lilac (#46)	335.00	210.00	135.00	335.00	200.0
70	15¢ Red Brown (#41)	24.00	15.00	9.50	27.50	16.5
71	18¢ Dull Rose (#34)	30.00	19.00	11.00	31.00	18.7
72	50¢ Red (#48)	75.00	47.50	28.50	75.00	45.0
73	$1 Rose Red	140.00	90.00	55.00	130.00	75.0

74,80 76 79 O1

1894-99 Issues VF + 40% (B)

Scott's No.		NH Fine	Unused Fine	Unused Ave.	Used Fine	Used Ave.
74	1¢ Coat of Arms, Yellow	2.70	1.80	1.10	1.25	.7
75	2¢ Honolulu, Brown	2.95	1.95	1.15	.70	.4
76	5¢ Kameha I, Rose Lake	5.50	3.65	2.20	1.75	1.1
77	10¢ Star & Palms, Yel. Grn.	6.75	4.50	2.75	4.50	2.7
78	12¢ S.S. "Arawa", Blue	15.00	9.00	5.50	13.00	7.7
79	25¢ Dole, Deep Blue	15.00	9.00	5.50	13.00	7.7
80	1¢ Arms, Green (1899)	2.25	1.50	.90	1.20	.7
81	2¢ Honolulu, Rose (1899)	2.25	1.50	.90	1.20	.7
82	5¢ Kameha I, Blue (1899)	6.75	4.50	2.75	3.00	1.8

1896 OFFICIALS VF + 40% (B)

Scott's No.		NH Fine	Unused Fine	Unused Ave.	Used Fine	Used Ave.
O1	2¢ Thurston, Green	50.00	32.50	20.00	16.50	10.0
O2	5¢ Black Brown	50.00	32.50	20.00	16.50	10.0
O3	6¢ Deep Ultramarine	50.00	32.00	20.00	16.50	10.0
O4	10¢ Bright Rose	50.00	32.50	20.00	16.50	10.0
O5	12¢ Orange	80.00	50.00	30.00	16.50	10.0
O6	25¢ Gray Violet	100.00	60.00	40.00	20.00	12.5

PHILIPPINE ISLANDS VF + 50% (C)

213 226 E1 J1

cott's No.	1899 U.S. Stamps of 1894-98 Overprinted "PHILIPPINES"	NH Fine	Unused Fine	Unused Ave.	Used Fine	Used Ave.
12	50¢ Jefferson (#260)	...	350.00	225.00	175.00	115.00
13	1¢ Franklin (#279)	4.50	3.25	1.85	1.00	.60
14	2¢ Wash. (#279d)	2.00	1.25	.80	.75	.45
14a	2¢ Wash. (#267)	2.75	1.75	1.20	1.00	.60
15	3¢ Jackson (#268)	8.00	5.50	3.25	1.95	1.15
16	5¢ Grant (#281)	7.75	5.35	3.15	1.50	.90
17	10¢ Webster Ty. I (#282C)	25.00	16.00	11.50	4.25	2.75
17A	10¢ Webster, Ty. II (#283)	275.00	185.00	115.00	40.00	25.00
18	15¢ Clay (#284)	45.00	32.50	22.50	8.25	4.95
19	50¢ Jefferson (#275)	160.00	110.00	70.00	40.00	25.00
	1901 U.S. Stamps of 1895-98 Overprinted "PHILIPPINES"					
20	4¢ Lincoln (#280b)	30.00	20.00	13.50	5.50	3.35
21	6¢ Garfield (#282)	37.50	25.00	17.50	7.00	4.25
22	8¢ Sherman (#272)	42.50	28.50	19.50	7.50	4.50
23	$1 Perry, Ty. I (#276)	525.00	350.00	235.00	225.00	140.00
23A	$1 Perry, Ty. II (#276A)	3000.00	2000.00	1375.00	1050.00	650.00
24	$2 Madison (#277a)	700.00	450.00	325.00	300.00	185.00
25	$5 Marshall (#278)	1500.00	950.00	625.00	650.00	425.00
	1903-04 U.S. Stamps of 1902-03 Overprinted "PHILIPPINES"					
26	1¢ Franklin (#300)	6.00	4.00	2.75	.45	.27
27	2¢ Wash. (#301)	10.50	7.00	4.25	1.95	1.15
28	3¢ Jackson (#302)	95.00	65.00	42.50	17.00	10.50
29	4¢ Grant (#303)	100.00	70.00	47.50	24.00	14.50
30	5¢ Lincoln (#304)	16.00	11.00	6.65	1.40	.85
31	6¢ Garfield (#305)	110.00	75.00	50.00	23.50	13.75
32	8¢ M. Wash. (#306)	52.50	35.00	23.50	13.50	8.00
33	10¢ Webster (#307)	27.50	18.50	12.00	3.25	1.95
34	13¢ Harrison (#308)	45.00	30.00	20.00	16.50	9.75
35	15¢ Clay (#309)	82.50	55.00	32.50	12.50	7.50
36	50¢ Jefferson (#310)	185.00	125.00	85.00	40.00	27.50
37	$1 Farragut (#311)	650.00	400.00	275.00	255.00	150.00
38	$2 Madison (#312)	...	1050.00	700.00	825.00	500.00
39	$5 Marshall (#313)	...	1250.00	850.00	950.00	550.00
40	2¢ Wash. (#319)	7.50	5.00	3.00	2.50	1.50
	1901 SPECIAL DELIVERY U.S. #E5 Ovptd. "PHILIPPINES"					
1	10¢ Messenger, Dark Blue	135.00	90.00	60.00	110.00	65.00
	1899-1901 POSTAGE DUES U.S. Dues Ovptd. "PHILIPPINES"					
1	1¢ Deep Claret (#J38)	7.00	4.50	2.75	1.80	1.10
2	2¢ Deep Claret (#J39)	6.85	4.35	2.60	1.80	1.10
3	5¢ Deep Claret (#J41)	16.00	10.00	6.00	3.25	1.95
4	10¢ Deep Claret (#J42)	21.00	13.50	8.15	6.50	4.00
5	50¢ Deep Claret (#J44)	200.00	135.00	90.00	90.00	60.00
6	3¢ Deep Claret (#J40)	21.50	13.75	8.25	9.50	5.65
7	30¢ Deep Claret (#J43)	225.00	150.00	100.00	90.00	60.00

PUERTO RICO VF + 50% (C)

210a 211 212 215 J2

	1899 U.S. Stamps of 1895-98 Overprinted "PORTO RICO"					
10	1¢ Franklin (36 Angle)	9.00	6.00	3.65	1.65	1.00
10a	1¢ (#279) (25 Angle)	12.00	8.00	4.85	2.25	1.35
11	2¢ Wash. (36 Angle)	8.00	5.50	3.35	1.50	.90
11a	2¢ (#267) (25 Angle)	10.50	7.50	4.50	1.50	.90
12	5¢ Grant, Blue (#281a)	12.00	8.00	4.85	2.35	1.45
13	8¢ Sherman (36 Angle)	42.50	26.50	15.00	16.00	12.50
13a	8¢ (#272) (25 Angle)	50.00	32.50	18.50	18.50	13.50
14	10¢ Webster (#282C)	28.50	18.50	10.50	5.75	3.50
	1900 U.S. Stamps of 1895-98 Overprinted "PUERTO RICO"					
15	1¢ Franklin (#279)	8.00	5.75	3.50	1.75	1.05
16	2¢ Wash. (#267)	7.50	5.25	3.25	1.40	.85
16a	2¢ Orange Red (#279d)	9.00	6.00	3.65	1.40	.85
	1899 Postage Dues; U.S. Dues Overprinted "PORTO RICO"					
1	1¢ (#J38) (36 Angle)	30.00	20.00	11.00	7.50	4.50
1a	1¢ Claret (25 Angle)	35.00	23.00	12.00	9.00	5.50
2	2¢ (#J39) (36 Angle)	20.00	13.50	8.25	6.75	4.00
2a	2¢ Claret (25 Angle)	26.00	17.50	10.50	7.50	4.50
3	10¢ (#J42) (36 Angle)	200.00	135.00	80.00	55.00	32.50
3a	10¢ Claret (25 Angle)	235.00	165.00	90.00	60.00	35.00

U.S. TRUST TERRITORIES OF THE PACIFIC

THE MARSHALL ISLANDS, MICRONESIA, AND PALAU ARE U.S. TRUST TERRITORIES WITH SEPARATE AUTONOMOUS GOVERNMENTS

MARSHALL ISLANDS

31

Scott's No.	1984 Commemoratives	Plate Block	F-VF NH
31-34	20¢ Postal Service Inaugural, attd	6.00	2.50
35-49A	1¢-$1 Definitives	60.00	12.50
39a	13¢ Booklet Pane of 10	...	12.50
40a	14¢ Booklet Pane of 10	...	11.50
41a	20¢ Booklet Pane of 10	...	12.50
41b	13¢/20¢ Bklt. Pane of 10 (5 #39, 5 #41)	...	14.00
42a	22¢ Booklet Pane of 10	...	11.50
42b	14¢/22¢ Bklt. Pane of 10 (5 #40, 5 #42)	...	12.50
50-53	40¢ U.P.U. Congress, attd	6.00	3.00
54-57	20¢ Ausipex Dolphins, attd	3.25	2.25
58	20¢ Xmas, 3 Kings, Strip of 4, attd	7.50	3.25
58	Christmas with tabs, attd.	...	4.95
58	Christmas Sheetlet of 16	...	12.50
59-62	20¢ Marshalls Constitution, attd	3.50	2.25

63-64

	1984-85		
63-64	22¢ Audubon, attd	3.85	1.65
65-69	22¢ Sea Shells, attd	6.50	2.75
70-73	22¢ Decade for Women, attd	3.50	2.25
74-77	22¢ Reef and Lagoon Fish, attd	3.50	2.35
78-81	22¢ International Youth Year, attd	3.75	2.50
82-85	14¢,22¢,33¢,44¢ Christmas	13.50	2.75
86-90	22¢ Halley's Comet, attd	17.50	6.75
86-90	Halley's Comet with tabs, attd	...	35.00
91-94	22¢ Medicinal Plants, attd	3.50	2.25
	1986-87		
107	$2 Wotje & Erikub, 1871 Terrestrial Globe	24.75	5.50
108	$5 Bikini, Stick Chart	57.50	12.75
109	$10 Stick Chart (1987)	87.50	19.95
110-13	14¢ Marine Invertebrates, attd	3.00	1.95
114	$1 Ameripex S/S (C-54 Globemaster)	...	3.95
115-18	22¢ Operation Crossroads, attd	3.50	2.65
119-23	22¢ Seashells, attd	7.00	3.25
124-27	22¢ Game Fish, attd	3.25	2.75
128-31	22¢ Christmas / Year of Peace, attd	4.25	3.50

136-137 163

	1987		
132-35	22¢ Whaling Ships, attd	3.25	2.75
136-41	33¢,39¢,44¢ Pilots	14.50	6.50
142	$1.00 Amelia Earhart / CAPEX S/S	...	3.00
143-51	14¢,22¢,44¢ U.S. Const. Bicent	...	7.00
152-56	22¢ Seashells, attd	7.50	3.50
157-59	44¢ Copra Industry, attd	6.50	2.95
160-63	14¢,22¢,33¢,44¢ Christmas	13.50	2.75

Scott's No.		Plate Block	F-VF NH
	1988-89		
164-67	44¢ Marine Birds, attd	5.25	4.50
168-83	1¢-$5 Fish Definitives (16)	135.00	29.50
184	$10 Fish Definitive ('89)	90.00	20.00
170a	14¢ Booklet Pane of 10	...	6.00
171a	15¢ Booklet Pane of 10	...	8.00
173a	22¢ Booklet Pane of 10	...	7.00
173b	14¢ & 22¢ Bklt. Pane of 10 (5 ea.)	...	6.25
174a	25¢ Booklet Pane of 10	...	9.50
174b	15¢ & 25¢ Booklet Pane of 10	...	8.50
188	15¢ Olympics, Javelin, Strip of 5 (10)	4.75	2.25
189	25¢ Olympics, Runner, Strip of 5 (10)	6.50	3.00
190	25¢ Robt. Louis Stevenson S/S of 9	...	8.75
191-94	25¢ Colonial Ships and Flags, attd	3.35	2.85
195-99	25¢ Christmas, strip of 5 (10)	6.95	3.25
200-04	25¢ John F. Kennedy, Strip of 5	...	3.75
205-08	25¢ Space Shuttle, Strip of 4 (8)	7.25	2.95
205-08	Tab Strip	...	4.25
	1989		
209-12	45¢ Links to Japan, attd	5.00	4.50
213-15	45¢ Alaska State 30th Anniv., Strip of 3	...	3.50
216-20	25¢ Seashells, Strip of 5 (10)	7.50	3.65
221	$1.00 Hirohito Memorial S/S	...	2.65
222-25	45¢ Migrant Birds, attd	5.95	4.75
226-29	45¢ Postal History, attd	6.25	5.25
230	25¢ Postal History, S/S of 6	...	12.75
231	$1.00 PHILEXFRANCE, S/S	...	12.50
232-38	25¢/$1 Moon Landing, 20th Anniv., Bklt. sgls	...	18.50
238a	$2.50 Booklet Pane of 7 (6x25¢,$1)	...	19.00

239 298

Scott's No.		Plate Block	F-VF NH
	*** WW II Anniversaries 1939-1989**		
239	25¢ Invasion of Poland	3.00	.70
240	45¢ Sinking of HMS Royal Oak	5.00	1.00
241	45¢ Invasion of Finland	5.00	1.00
242-45	45¢ Battle of River Platte, attd	5.00	4.00
	*** WW II Anniversaries 1940-1990**		
246-47	25¢ Invas. of Norway & Denmark, attd	2.75	1.20
248	25¢ Katyn Forest Massacre	3.00	.70
249-50	25¢ Invasion of Belgium, attd	3.00	1.35
251	45¢ Churchill Becomes Prime Minister	5.00	1.00
252-53	45¢ Evacuation at Dunkirk	5.00	2.00
254	45¢ Occupation of Paris	5.00	1.00
255	25¢ Mers-el-Kebir & Burma Rd	2.75	.60
256	25¢ Burma Road	2.75	.60
257-60	45¢ U.S. Destroyers for G.B., atd	5.00	4.00
261-64	45¢ Battle of Britain, attd	5.00	4.00
265	45¢ Tripartite Pact, 1940	5.00	1.00
266	25¢ FDR Elected to Third Term	2.75	.60
267-70	25¢ Battle of Taranto, attd	2.75	2.40
	*** WW II Anniversaries 1941-1991**		
271-74	30¢ Four Freedoms, attd	3.25	2.80
275	30¢ Battle of Beda Fomm	3.25	.70
276-77	29¢ German Invasion of Greece & Yugoslavia, attd	3.25	1.40
278-81	50¢ Sinking of the Bismarck, attd	5.50	4.50
282	30¢ Germany Invades Russia	3.25	.70
283-84	29¢ Atlantic Charter, attd. pair	3.25	1.40
285	29¢ Siege of Moscow	3.25	.70
286-87	30¢ Sinking of the USS Reuben James, attd	3.25	1.40
288-91	50¢ Japanese Attack Pearl Harbor, attd. block of 4	5.50	4.50
292	29¢ Japanese Capture Guam	3.25	.70
293	29¢ Fall of Singapore	3.25	.70
294-95	50¢ Flying Tigers, attd	5.50	2.25
296	29¢ Fall of Wake Island	3.25	.70
	*** WW II Anniversaries 1942-1992**		
297	29¢ FDR & Churchill at Arcadia Conference	3.25	.70
298	50¢ Japanese enter Manila	5.25	1.10
299	29¢ Japanese take Rabaul	3.25	.70
300	29¢ Battle of Java Sea	3.25	.70
301	50¢ Fall of Rangoon	5.25	1.10
302	29¢ Battle for New Guinea	3.25	.70
303	29¢ MacArthur Leaves Corregidor	3.25	.70
304	29¢ Raid on Saint-Nazaire	3.25	.70
305	29¢ Surrender of Bataan	3.25	.70
306	50¢ Doolittle Raid on Tokyo	5.25	1.10

THE MARSHALL ISLANDS (continued)

327-28

Scott's No.		Plate Block	F-VF NH
	*** WW II Anniversaries 1942-1992 (cont.)**		
307	29¢ Fall of Corregidor	3.25	.7
308-11	50¢ Battle of the Coral Sea, attd	5.25	4.4
312-15	50¢ Battle of Midway, attd	5.25	4.4
316	29¢ Village of Lidice Destroyed	3.25	.7
317	29¢ Fall of Sevastopol	3.25	.7
318-19	29¢ Convoy, attd	3.25	1.4
320	29¢ Marines Land on Guadalcanal	3.25	.7
321	29¢ Battle of Savo Island	3.25	.7
322	29¢ Dieppe Raid	3.25	.7
323	50¢ Battle of Stalingrad	5.25	1.1
324	29¢ Battle of Eastern Solomons	3.25	.7
325	50¢ Battle of Cape Esperance	5.25	1.1
326	29¢ Battle of El Alamein	3.25	.7
327-28	29¢ Battle of Barents Sea, attd. pair	3.25	1.4
	*** WW II Anniversaries 1943-1993**		
329	29¢ Casablanca Conference	3.25	.7
330	29¢ Liberation of Kharkov	3.25	.7
331-34	50¢ Battle of Bismarck Sea, attd. block of 4	5.25	4.4
335	50¢ Interception of Yamamoto	5.25	1.1
336-37	29¢ Battle of Kursk	3.25	1.4

346-65A 399 412

Scott's No.		Plate Block	F-VF NH
	1989-92		
341-44	25¢ Christmas 1989, attd	5.50	4.3
345	45¢ Milestones in Space, Sheet of 25 diff. designs	...	43.5
346-65A	1¢/$2 Birds (21) (1990-92)	110.00	25.0
361a	95¢ Essen '90 Min. Sht. of 4 (#347,350,353,361)	...	5.5
	1990		
366-69	25¢ Children's Games, attd	6.50	4.5
370-76	25¢,$1 Penny Black, 150th Anniv., bklt. sgls	...	17.0
376a	Booklet Pane of 7 (6x25¢,$1)	...	17.5
377-80	25¢ Endangered Sea Turtles, attd	6.50	5.5
381	25¢ Joint Issue with Micronesia & U.S.	9.95	1.2
382	45¢ German Reunification	6.75	1.5
383-86	25¢ Christmas, attd	4.75	4.0
387-90	25¢ Breadfruit, attd	4.75	4.0
	1991		
391-94	50¢ US Space Shuttle Flights, 10th Anniv., attd	6.50	5.5
395-98	52¢ Flowers, attd	7.75	6.3
398a	52¢ Phila Nippon, min. sht. of 4	...	6.5
399	29¢ Operation Desert Storm	7.75	1.3
400-06	29¢,$1 Birds, set of 7 booklet singles	...	18.7
406a	Booklet Pane of 7 (6x29¢,$1)	...	19.0
407-10	12¢,29¢,50¢ (2) Air Marshall Island Aircraft	19.00	4.5
411	29¢ Admission to United Nations	12.50	.9
412	30¢ Christmas, Peace Dove	5.75	1.2
413	29¢ Peace Corps in Marshall Islands	5.50	1.1
	1992		
414-17	29¢ Ships, Strip of 4 (8)	11.00	4.6
418-24	50¢,$1 Voyages of Discovery, set of 7 booklet sgls.	...	14.7
424a	Booklet Pane of 7 (6x50¢ + $1)	...	15.0
425-28	29¢ Traditional Handcrafts, attd (8)	8.75	3.7
429	29¢ Christmas	4.75	1.0
430-33	9¢,22¢,28¢,45¢ Birds	13.00	2.7

443-63A　　474

ott's o.		Plate Block	F-VF NH

1993-95

-40	50¢,$1 Reef Life, 7 booklet sgls	...	16.50
a	Booklet Pane of 7 (6x50¢,$1)	...	12.00
-63A	10¢-$10 Sailing Ships, Set of 20	235.00	49.50
A/462B	32¢-$3 Ships Definitives, set of 4 (1995)	36.50	7.75
	15¢-75¢ Sailing Vessels, Souv. Sheet of 4 (1994)	...	3.35

* WW II Anniversaries 1943-1993 (continued)

-70	52¢ Invasion of Sicily, attd. blk. of 4	5.25	4.40
	50¢ Bombing Raids on Schweinfurt	5.25	1.10
	50¢ Liberation of Smolensk	5.25	1.10
	29¢ Landing at Bougainville	3.25	.70
	50¢ US Invasion of Tarawa	5.25	1.10
	52¢ Tehran Conference	5.25	1.10
-77	29¢ Battle of North Cape, attd. pair	3.00	1.25

* WW II Anniversaries 1944-1994

	29¢ Eisenhower Commands SHAEF	3.00	.60
	50¢ Invasion of Anzio	5.00	1.00
	52¢ Siege of Leningrad Ends	5.00	1.00
	29¢ U.S. Frees Marshall Islands	3.00	.60
	29¢ Japanese Defeat at Truk	3.00	.60
	52¢ Bombing of Germany	5.00	1.00
	50¢ Rome Falls to Allies	5.00	1.00
-88	75¢ D-Day Landings, attd	7.75	6.25
	50¢ V-1 Bombs Strike England	5.00	1.00
	29¢ Landing on Saipan	3.00	.60
	50¢ Battle of Philippine Sea	5.00	1.00
	29¢ U.S. Liberates Guam	3.00	.60
	50¢ Warsaw Uprising	5.00	1.00
	50¢ Liberation of Paris	5.00	1.00
	50¢ Marines Land on Peliliu	5.00	1.00
	52¢ MacArthur Returns to Philippines	5.00	1.00
	52¢ Battle of Leyte Gulf	5.00	2.00
-99	50¢ German Battleship "Tirpitz" Sunk, attd	5.00	2.00
-3	50¢ Battle of the Bulge	5.00	4.00
	50¢ MacArthur Returns to Philippines, Souvenir Sheet of 2	...	2.00

WWII Anniversaries 1945-1995

	32¢ Yalta Conference	3.25	.65
	55¢ Bombing of Dresden	5.50	1.10
	$1 Iwo Jima Invaded	9.95	2.00
	32¢ Remagen Bridge Taken	3.25	.65
	55¢ Marines Invade Okinawa	5.50	1.10
	50¢ Death of F.D. Roosevelt	5.00	1.00
	32¢ US/USSR Troops Link	3.25	.65
	60¢ Soviet Troops Conquer Berlin, Georgi Zhukov	6.00	1.25
	55¢ Allies liberate concentration camps	5.50	1.15
-16	75¢ V.E. Day, Block of 4	7.50	6.25
	32¢ United Nations Charter	3.25	.65
	$1 U.N. Charter Souvenir Sheet	...	2.00
	55¢ Postdam Conference	5.50	1.15

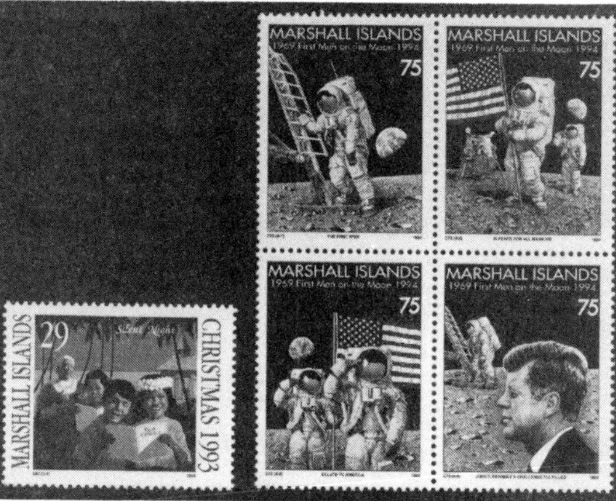

576　　583-86

THE MARSHALL ISLANDS (continued)

Scott's No.		Plate Block	F-VF NH

WWII Anniversaries 1945-1995 (continued)

...	60¢ Churchill's Resignation	6.00	1.25
...	$1 Atomic Bomb dropped on Hiroshima	9.95	2.00
...	75¢ V.J. Day, Block of 4	7.50	6.25

*** WW II Anniversary Issues are are available in Tab singles, Tab pairs and Tab blocks for an additional 25%.**

1993-94

567-70	29¢ Capitol Complex	12.50	2.40
571	50¢ Mobil Oil Tanker, Eagle Souv. Sheet	...	1.00
572-75	29¢ Life in 1800's, attd	2.95	2.40
576	29¢ Christmas	2.95	.60
577	$2.90 15th Anniv. Constitution Souv. Sht. (1994)	...	5.95
578	29¢ 10th Anniv. Postal Service Souv. Sht. (1994)	...	.60
579-80	50¢ Soccer Cup, attd	5.00	2.00
582	50¢ Solar System, sheet of 12	...	11.95
583-86	75¢ Moon Landing, 25th Anniv. attd	7.50	5.95
586b	75¢ Moon Landing, Souv. Sheet of 4	...	5.95
587	29¢, 52¢, $1 Butterflies, Souv. Sheet of 3	...	3.65
588	29¢ Christmas	2.95	.60

1995

589	50¢ Year of the Boar, Souv. Sheet	...	1.00
590	55¢ Underseas Glory, Block of 4	5.50	4.50
...	55¢ John F. Kennedy, Strip of 6	...	6.75
...	75¢ Marilyn Monroe, Block of 4	...	5.95
...	Same, Miniature Sheet of 12	...	17.85
...	32¢ Cats, Block of 4	...	2.65

C1-2

1985-89 Airmails

C1-2	44¢ Audubon, attd	6.75	3.25
C3-6	44¢ Ameripex - Planes, attd (1986)	5.95	5.25
C7	44¢ Operation Crossroads, S/S (1986)	...	5.75
C8	44¢ Statue of Liberty/Peace Year (1986)	6.00	1.35
C9-12	44¢ Girl Scouts, attd (1986)	4.50	4.00
C13-16	44¢ Marine Birds, attd (1987)	4.85	4.25
C17-20	44¢ Amelia Earhart/CAPEX attd (1987)	5.50	4.50
C21	45¢ Astronaut and Space Shuttle (1988)	5.50	1.20
C22-25	12¢,36¢,39¢,45¢ Aircraft (1989)	21.75	4.75
C22a	12¢ Bklt. Pane of 10	...	4.50
C23a	36¢ Bklt. Pane of 10	...	11.75
C24a	39¢ Bklt. Pane of 10	...	12.50
C25a	45¢ Bklt. Pane of 10	...	14.50
C25b	36¢-45¢ Bklt. Pane of 10 (5 each)	...	13.50

MICRONESIA

1984-88 Definitives & Commemoratives

Scott's No.		Plate Block	F-VF NH
1-4	20¢ Postal Service Inaugural, attd	3.50	2.50
5-20	1¢/$5 Definitives	85.00	19.50

21 22

Scott's No.		Plate Block	F-VF NH
21,C4-6	20¢,28¢,35¢,40¢ AUSIPEX	21.50	4.50
22,C7-9	20¢,28¢,35¢,40¢ Christmas	47.50	9.75
23,C10-12	22¢,33¢,39¢,44¢ Ships (1985)	24.50	4.50
24,C13-14	22¢,33¢,44¢ Christmas (1985)	23.50	3.95
25-28,C15	22¢,44¢ Audubon (1985)	11.00	5.00
31-39,C34-36	3¢-$10 Definitives & Airs (12) (1985-88)	140.00	27.50
33a	15¢ Booklet Pane of 10	...	5.50
36a	25¢ Booklet Pane of 10	...	8.25
36b	15¢ & 25¢ Booklet Pane of 10 (5 ea.)	...	7.00
45,C16-18	22¢,33¢,39¢,44¢ Ruins (1985)	24.50	4.95
46,C19-20	22¢ Int'l Peace Year (1986)	26.50	5.50
48-51	22¢ on 20¢ (surcharges on #1-4), attd (1986)	3.95	2.40
52,C21-24	22¢,33¢,39¢,44¢ AMERIPEX (1986)	27.50	5.75
53	22¢ Passport (1986)	4.25	.90
54-5,C26-7	5¢,22¢,33¢,44¢ Christmas (1986)	22.95	4.75

1987-88 Commemoratives

Scott's No.		Plate Block	F-VF NH
56,C28-30	22¢,33¢,39¢,44¢ Homeless, Events	22.50	4.95
57	$1.00 CAPEX S/S	...	4.50
58,C31-33	22¢,33¢,39¢,44¢ Christmas	21.50	4.50
59-62,C37-8	22¢,44¢ Colonial Flags, attd (1988)	10.75	6.50
63-66	25¢ Olympics, attd., two pair (1988)	9.50	3.65
67-70	25¢ Christmas, attd (1988)	3.25	2.75
71	25¢ Truk Lagoon S/S of 18 (1988)	...	11.50

82 83/102 142

1989 Definitives & Commemoratives

Scott's No.		Plate Block	F-VF NH
72-75	45¢ Flowers, attd	4.75	4.00
76	$1.00 Hirohito Memorial S/S	...	2.25
77-80	25¢-45¢ Sharks, attd. two pair	7.50	3.25
81	25¢ Moon Landing, 20th Anniv., S/S of 9	...	5.25
82	$2.40 Moon Landing, 20th Anniv	23.75	5.50
83/102	1¢/$5 Seashell definitives (12)	110.00	23.75
85a	15¢ Booklet Pane of 10	...	4.50
88a	25¢ Booklet Pane of 10	...	6.50
88b	15¢ & 25¢ Booklet Pane of 10 (5 ea.)	...	6.50
103	25¢ WSE, Fruits & Flowers, Sht. of 18	...	11.75
104-05	25¢,45¢ Christmas	9.00	1.95

1990 Commemoratives

Scott's No.		Plate Block	F-VF NH
106-09	10¢,15¢,20¢,25¢ World Wildlife Fund	9.00	2.25
110-113	45¢ Stamp World London '90, attd	5.00	4.00
114	$1.00 S.W. London '90, Whalers at kill, S/S	...	2.50
115	$1.00 Penny Black, 150th Anniv., S/S	...	2.50
116-20	25¢ Pohnpei Agric. & Trade School, Strip of 5 (10)	8.50	3.50
121	$1.00 Int'l. Garden Expo, Osaka, Japan S/S	...	2.25
122-23	25¢,45¢ Loading Mail, Airport & Truk Lagoon	9.50	2.25
124-26	25¢ Joint issue w/Marsh. Isl. & U.S., strip of 3 . (6)	5.25	2.35
127-30	45¢ Moths, attd	5.00	4.25
131	25¢ Christmas, S/S of 9	...	5.75

1991 Commemoratives

Scott's No.		Plate Block	F-VF NH
132	25¢,45¢ New Capital of Micronesia, S/S	...	2.00
133	$1 New Capital, S/S	...	2.50

FEDERATED STATES OF MICRONESIA (continued)

Scott's No.		Plate Block	F-VF NH
134-37	29¢-50¢ Turtles, attd. two pairs	19.95	8.7
138-41	29¢ Operation Desert Storm, strip of 4	3.75	3.0
142	$2.90 Frigatebird, Flag	...	5.5
142a	$2.90 Frigatebird, S/S	...	5.7
143	29¢ Phila Nippon '91, min. sht. of 3	...	1.9
144	50¢ Phila Nippon '91, min. sht. of 3	...	2.9
145	$1 Phila Nippon S/S	...	1.9
146-48	29¢,40¢,50¢ Christmas	...	2.7
149	29¢ Pohnpei Rain Forest, min. sht. of 18	...	12.5

1992 Commemoratives

Scott's No.		Plate Block	F-VF NH
150	29¢ Peace Corps, strip of 5	...	3.5
151	29¢ Discovery of America, strip of 3	...	5.7
152-53	29¢,50¢ U.N. Membership Anniv	...	2.0
153a	Same, S/S of 2	...	2.2
154	29¢ Christmas	...	.8

157-66 172 194

1993-94 Definitives & Commemoratives

Scott's No.		Plate Block	F-VF NH
155	29¢ Pioneers of Flight, se-ten. blk. of 8	...	5.9
157-166	10¢-$2.90 Fish, Set of 16	99.50	20.9
168	29¢ Golden Age of Sail, min. sht. of 12	...	12.5
172	29¢ Thomas Jefferson	...	.9
173-76	29¢ Pacific Canoes, attd	...	3.5
177	29¢ Local Leaders, strip of 4	...	2.9
178	50¢ Pioneers of Flight, block of 8	...	8.5
179-80	29¢-50¢ Pohnpei	...	2.3
181	$1 Pohnpei Souvenir Sheet	...	2.4
182-83	29¢-50¢ Butterflies, two pairs	...	4.0
184-85	29¢-50¢ Christmas	...	2.2
186	29¢ Yap Culture, sheet of 18	...	11.5

1994 Commemoratives

Scott's No.		Plate Block	F-VF NH
187-89	29¢,40¢,50¢ Kosrae	12.00	2.5
190	29¢-50¢ Butterflies, sheet of 4	...	3.9
191	29¢ Pioneers of Flight, block of 8	...	6.9
192	29¢ Micronesian Games, block of 4	...	2.5
193	29¢ Native Costumes, block of 4	...	2.5
194	29¢ Anniversary of Constitution	...	.7
195	29¢ Flowers, Strip of 4	5.95	2.4
196-97	50¢ World Cup Soccer, attd	5.00	2.0
198	29¢ Postal Service, 10th Anniv., Block of 4	2.95	2.4
199	29¢, 52¢, $1 Philakorea Dinosaurs, Souvenir Sheet of 3	...	3.6
200	50¢ Pioneers of Flight, Block of 8	...	7.9
201	29¢ Migratory Birds, Block of 4	2.95	2.4
202-3	29¢-50¢ Christmas	7.95	1.6
204-7	32¢ Local Leaders	12.95	2.6

1995

Scott's No.		Plate Block	F-VF NH
208	50¢ Year of the Boar Souv. Sheet	...	1.0
209	32¢ Chuuk Lagoon, underwater scenes, Blk of 4	3.25	2.6
210	32¢ Pioneers of Flight, block of 8	...	5.2
211	32¢ Dogs of the World, block of 4	3.25	2.6
...	32¢-$3 Fish Definitives, set of 4	45.00	9.5
...	32¢ Hibiscus, Strip of 4	...	2.6
...	$1 United Nations 50th Anniv. Souv. Sheet	...	2.0

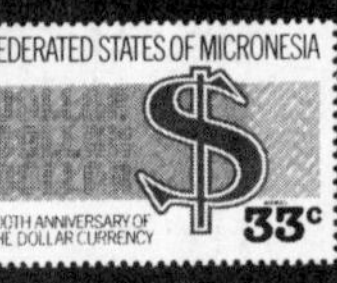

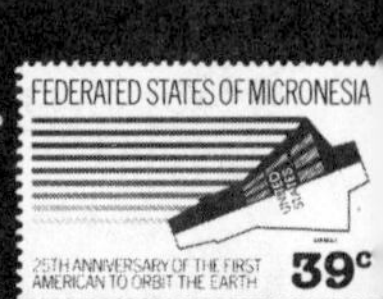

C15 C28 C29

Airmails & Postal Stationery

Scott's No.		Plate Block	F-VF NH
C1-3	28¢,35¢,40¢ Aircraft (1984)	14.75	3.3
C25	$1.00 Ameripex S/S (1986)	...	4.5
C39-42	45¢ Federated State Flags, attd (1989)	4.85	4.2
C43-46	22¢,36¢,39¢,45¢ Aircraft Serving Micronesia ('90)	16.95	3.7
C47-48	40¢,50¢ Aircraft (1992)	10.00	2.1
C49	$2.90 Moon Landing Souvenir Sheet (1994)	...	5.9
U1	20¢ National Flag (1984)	...	18.5
U2	22¢ Tall Ship Senyavin (1986)	...	9.7
U3	29¢ on 30¢ New Capital (1991)	...	1.3

REPUBLIC OF PALAU

1 5 9 21

1983 Commemoratives

ott's o.		Plate Block	F-VF NH
4	20¢ Postal Service Inaugural, attd	5.95	3.75
3	20¢ Birds, attd	5.50	2.25

1983 Marine Definitives

21	1¢/$5 Definitives, Set of 13	130.00	26.50
a	13¢ Booklet Pane of 10	...	11.75
b	13¢/20¢ Bklt. Pane of 10 (5 #13, 5 #14)	...	13.75
b	20¢ Booklet Pane of 10	...	12.75

28 38

1983-84 Commemoratives

-27	20¢ Whales, attd	3.75	2.25
-32	20¢ Christmas, Strip of 5 (10)	8.50	3.75
-40	20¢ Henry Wilson, Block of 8	9.50	5.00
-50	20¢ Seashells, Block of 10, attd (1984) (10)	6.50	5.50
-54	40¢ 19th UPU Congress (1984)	5.50	4.25
-58	20¢ Ausipex, attd (1984)	4.25	2.40
-62	20¢ Christmas, attd (1984)	4.25	2.40

1985 Commemoratives & Definitives

-66	22¢ Audubon, attd	4.00	3.00
-70	22¢ Shipbuilding, attd	3.50	2.25
'85	14¢/$10 Marine Life (7)	135.00	27.50
a	14¢ Booklet Pane of 10	...	10.00
a	22¢ Booklet Pane of 10	...	12.50
b	14¢/22¢ Bklt. Pane of 10 (5 #75, 5 #76)	...	13.75
89	44¢ International Youth Yr., attd	5.00	4.00
-93	14¢,22¢,33¢,44¢ Christmas	17.50	3.35
	$1.00 Trans-Pacific Air Anniv. S/S	...	3.65
-98	44¢ Halley's Comet, attd	5.00	4.25

1986 Commemoratives

-102	44¢ Songbirds, attd	5.25	4.25
3	14¢ AMERIPEX Sea & Reef, Sheet of 40	...	50.00
4-08	22¢ Seashells, attd (10)	8.00	3.65
9-12,C17	22¢ Int'l. Peace Year, attd	9.50	4.50
3-16	22¢ Reptiles, attd	3.50	3.00
7-21	22¢ Christmas, attd (10)	5.50	2.50

122-123 145

1987-88 Commemoratives & Definitives

B-E	44¢ Butterflies, attd	5.50	4.85
2-25	44¢ Fruit Bats, attd	5.50	4.75
3/41	1¢/$5 Flowers (16) (1987-88)	110.00	22.50
2	$10 Flower Bouquet (1988)	100.00	21.75
9a	14¢ Bklt. Pane of 10	...	4.25
1a	15¢ Bklt. Pane of 10 (1988)	...	3.50
2a	22¢ Bklt. Pane of 10	...	6.50
2b	14¢/22¢ Bklt. Pane of 10 (5 ea.)	...	6.50
3a	25¢ Bklt. Pane of 10 (1988)	...	6.00
3b	15¢/25¢ Bklt. Pane of 10 (5 ea.) (1988)	...	5.50

1987 Commemoratives

Scott's No.		Plate Block	F-VF NH
146-49	22¢ CAPEX, attd	3.25	2.50
150-54	22¢ Seashells, attd (10)	7.25	3.25
155-63	14¢,22¢,44¢ U.S. Constitution Bicent., attd. (3 pair)	...	5.85
164-67	14¢,22¢,33¢,44¢ Japanese Links	13.50	2.85
168	$1 S/S Japanese Links to Palau	...	2.65
173-77	22¢ Christmas, attd (10)	8.50	3.35
178-82	22¢ "Silent Spring" Symb. Species, attd (10)	8.50	3.35

191-95

1988 Commemoratives

183-86	44¢ Butterflies & Flowers, attd	5.00	4.35
187-90	44¢ Ground Dwelling Birds, attd	5.25	4.50
191-95	25¢ Seashells (5), attd (10)	7.00	3.25
196	25¢ Postal Indep. S/S of 6 (FINLANDIA)	...	3.75
197	45¢ USPPS S/S of 6 (PRAGA '88)	...	6.00
198-202	25¢ Christmas, strip of 5	...	3.25
203	25¢ Palauan Nautilus, S/S of 5	...	3.75

1989 Commemoratives

204-07	45¢ Endangered Birds, attd	5.25	4.50
208-11	45¢ Exotic Mushrooms, attd	5.25	4.50
212-16	25¢ Seashells, strip of 5 (10)	7.75	3.65
217	$1 Hirohito Memorial S/S	...	2.85
218	25¢ Moon Landing, 20 Anniv., S/S of 25	...	13.95
219	$2.40 Moon Landing, 20th Anniv	25.75	5.65
220	25¢ Literacy, block of 10	6.95	5.95
221	25¢ World Stamp Expo, Fauna, Min. sheet of 25	...	11.50
222-26	25¢ Christmas, attd (10)	7.50	3.25

258

1990 Commemoratives

227-30	25¢ Soft Coral, attd	3.00	2.65
231-34	45¢ Forest Birds, attd	4.85	4.25
235	25¢ Stamp World London '90, S/S of 9	...	4.95
236	$1.00 Penny Black, 150th Anniv. S/S	...	2.65
237-41	45¢ Orchids, strip of 5 (10)	10.75	4.95
242-45	45¢ Butterflies & Flowers, attd	4.75	3.95
246	25¢ Lagoon Life, Sheetlet of 25	...	15.00
247-48	45¢ Pacifica/Mail Delivery, attd	6.50	2.95
249-53	25¢ Christmas, attd	...	2.85
254-57	45¢ U.S. Forces in Palau, 1944, attd	4.75	4.25
258	$1 U.S. Forces in Palau, 1944, S/S	...	2.50

1991-92 Commemoratives & Definitives

259-62	30¢ Coral, attd	3.50	3.00
263	30¢ Angaur, The Phospate Island, Sheet of 16	...	11.00
264/85	1¢/$2 Bird Definitives (16) (1991-92)	95.00	19.50
286	$5 Bird Definitive ('92)	47.50	9.50
287	$10 Bush Warbler ('92)	95.00	19.00
270a	19¢ Palau Fantail, Bklt. Pane of 10	...	4.00
272a	29¢ Fruit Dove, Bklt. Pane of 10	...	6.25
272b	19¢ Fantail & 29¢ Fruit Dove,Bklt. Pane of 10(5 ea)	...	5.50
288	29¢ Cent. of Christianity in Palau, Sheet of 6	...	3.85
289	29¢ Marine Life, Sheet of 20	...	17.50
290	20¢ Desert Shield/Desert Storm, min. sheet of 9	...	5.00
291	$2.90 Fairy tern, Yellow/Ribbon	...	5.50
292	$2.90 Same, S/S	...	5.75
293	29¢ Women's Conf. & Palau,10th Anniv,min sht of 8	...	5.75
294	50¢ Giant Clam Cultivation, S/S of 5	...	5.25
295	29¢ Pearl Harbor/Pacific Theater Anniv,Shtlt of 6	...	3.75
296	$1.00 Phila Nippon S/S	...	2.35
297	29¢ Peace Corps in Palau, min. sht. of 6	...	3.85

Scott's No.		Plate Block	F-VF NH
	1991-92 (Cont'd)		
298	29¢ Christmas, strip of 5, attd (10)	7.50	3.50
299	29¢ WWII in the Pacific, min. sht. of 10	...	7.25

300

1992 Commemoratives

Scott's No.		Plate Block	F-VF NH
300	50¢ Butterflies, attd	5.00	4.25
301	29¢ Shells, strip of 5 (10)	7.50	3.50
302	29¢ Columbus & Age of Discovery, min. sht of 20...	...	12.75
303	29¢ Biblical Creation/Earth Summit, min sht of 24...	...	15.95
304-09	50¢ Summer Olympics, S/S	...	7.50
310	29¢ Elvis Presley, min. sht. of 9	...	6.95
311	50¢ WWII, Aircraft of the Pacific Theater, min sht of 10	...	10.75
312	29¢ Christmas, strip of 5	...	3.35

1993 Commemoratives

Scott's No.		Plate Block	F-VF NH
313	50¢ Animal Families, block of 4	4.75	4.00
314	29¢ Seafood, block of 4	...	2.85
315	50¢ Sharks, block of 4	4.75	4.00
316	29¢ WWII, Pacific Theater, min. sheet of 10	...	5.95
317	29¢ Christmas, strip of 5	...	3.35
318	29¢ Prehistoric & Legendary Sea Creatures, sht.of 25	...	14.95
319	29¢ Indigenous People, sheet of 4	...	2.50
320	$2.90 Indigenous People, Souvenir Sheet	...	5.75
321	29¢ Jonah and the Whale, sheet of 25	...	14.95

323

1994 Commemoratives

Scott's No.		Plate Block	F-VF NH
322	40¢ Palau Rays, block of 4	...	3.25
323	20¢ Crocodiles, block of 4	...	1.65
324	50¢ Seabirds, block of 4	4.75	4.00
325	29¢ WWII, Pacific Theater, min. sheet of 10	...	5.95
326	50¢ WWII, D-Day, min. sheet of 10	...	9.95
327	29¢ Baron Pierre de Coubertin	...	.60
328-33	50¢, $1, $2 Coubertin and Winter Olympics Stars, Set of 6 Souv. Sheets	...	11.95

REPUBLIC OF PALAU (continued)

Scott's No.		Plate Block	F-VF NH
334-36	29¢, 40¢, 50¢ Philakorea '94 Philatelic Fantasies, Wildlife, 3 Souv. Sheets of 8	...	19.5
337	29¢ Apollo XI Moon Landing 25th Anniv., Miniature Sheet of 2	...	11.9
338	29¢ Independence Day Strip of 5	...	2.
338	Same, Sheetlet of 15	...	8.8
339	$1 Invasion of Peleliu Souvenir Sheet	...	2.0
340	29¢ Disney Tourism Sheetlet of 9	...	5.5
341-43	$1, $2.90 Disney Tourism, 3 Souv. Sheets	...	9.
344	20¢ Year of the Family, Min. Sheet of 12	...	4.
345	29¢ Christmas '94 Strip of 15	...	2.9
345	Same, Sheetlet of 15	...	8.8
346-48	29¢, 50¢ World Cup of Soccer, Set of 3 Sheetlets of 12	...	14
	1995		
350	32¢ Elvis Presley, Sheetlet of 9	...	5.
351-64	1¢-$5 Fish Definitives (14)	125.00	25.9
357a	20¢ Fish, Booklet Pane of 10	...	4.
358a	32¢ Fish, Booklet Pane of 10	...	6.
358b	20¢, 32¢ Fish, Bklt. Pane of 10 (5 each)	...	5.5
365	$10 Fish Definitive	95.00	20.0
366	32¢ Tourism, Lost Fleet, Sheetlet of 18	...	11.9
...	32¢ Earth Day '95, Sheetlet of 18	...	11.9
...	50¢ Jet Aircraft, Sheetlet of 12	...	12.5
...	$2 Jet Aircraft, Souvenir Sheet	...	4.
...	32¢ Underwater Ships, Sheetlet of 18	...	11.9

1988 Semi-Postals

Scott's No.		Plate Block	F-VF NH
B1-4	25¢ + 5¢,45¢ + 5¢ Olympic Sports, 2 pairs	10.00	4.

C5 C10

Airmails

Scott's No.		Plate Block	F-VF NH
C1-4	40¢ Birds, attd (1984)	6.00	3.
C5	44¢ Audubon (1985)	7.50	1.
C6-9	44¢ Palau-Germany Exchange Cent., attd	6.00	4.
C10-13	44¢ Trans-Pacific Anniv., attd	6.50	4.
C14-16	44¢ Remelik Memorial, strip of 3 (1986)	9.00	4.
C14-16	Remelik Mem., with tabs, attd	12.00	5.
C17	44¢ Peace Year, St. of Liberty	6.00	1.
C18-20	36¢,39¢,45¢ Aircraft (1989)	12.75	2.
C18a	36¢ Bklt. Pane of 10	...	8.7
C19a	39¢ Bklt. Pane of 10	...	9.
C20a	45¢ Bklt. Pane of 10	...	10.
C20b	36¢/45¢ Bklt. Pane of 10 (5 each)	...	9.
C21	50¢ Palauan Bai (#293a), self adh (1991)	5.95	1.
C22	50¢ Birds, Block of 4 (1995)	...	4.
C22	Same, Sheetlet of 16	...	16.

Postal Stationery

Scott's No.		Plate Block	F-VF NH
U1	22¢ Parrotfish (1989)	...	4.
U2	22¢ Spearfishing	...	7.
U3	25¢ Chambered Nautilus (1991)	...	1.
UC1	36¢ Birds (1985)	...	6.
UX1	14¢ Giant Clam (1985)	...	3.

FREE!

Stamps of the Marshall Islands.

Return this card for your

FREE GIFT!

$7.53 Face Value.
Nothing to buy.
Absolutely no obligation.

The *Stamps and Philatelic Center of the Republic of the Marshall Islands* has a FREE GIFT for you — a colorful selection of Mint Stamps issued by the Marshall Islands.

These beautiful stamps — a *$7.53 face value* — are yours to keep with absolutely no obligation!

Why are we offering you this FREE GIFT?

Because we know you'll more fully appreciate the significance, desirability and beauty of these Marshall Islands stamps if you can actually see them for yourself ... *free and without any obligation.*

With your free gift, we'll include information on how you can collect the beautiful *Stamps of the Marshall Islands* — conveniently, systematically and at *Face Value* prices — the very same prices you'd pay at any post office in the Marshall Islands!

So don't wait.

To receive your **FREE GIFT**, simply return the attached reply card. Offer valid by mail only.

No obligation.

Nothing to buy.

But supplies of these beautiful stamps are limited, so please respond *today.*

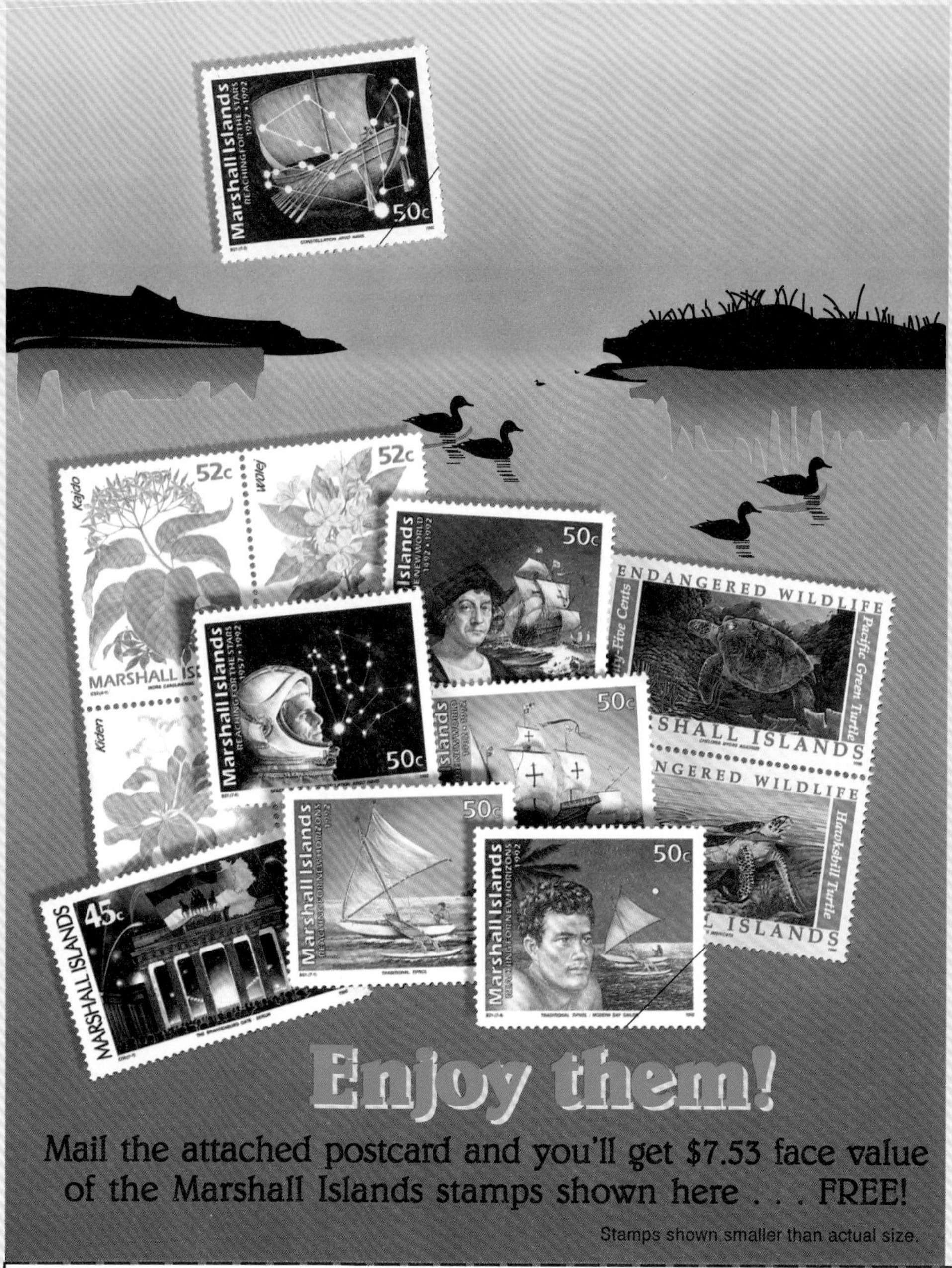

BGWL-9901

Return this card to receive your FREE Marshall Islands postage stamps.

YES! **Please send me my *FREE* Marshall Islands postage stamps — *$7.53 Face Value* — along with complete information about how I can collect the Stamps of the Marshall Islands conveniently and systematically, at *Face Value* prices. I understand my *FREE* stamps are mine to keep and I'm under no obligation whatsoever! (Limit: One Free Gift per address.)**

Mr./Mrs./Ms.______________________________

PLEASE PRINT

Address______________________________

City____________________ State________ Zip____________

Original cards only. Photocopies and facsimiles not valid.

59-62

All Trust Territory FDC's have official cancels and cachets except as noted.
(Marshall Islands #31-57, 107-08 have commercial cachets.)

Scott #	Description	One Cover	Separate Covers
	MARSHALL ISLANDS		
	1984		
1-34	20¢ Postal Service Inaugural attd. 5/2/84	10.00	20.00
5-49A	1¢-$1 Defin. 6/12,12/19/84,6/5/85 (3 FDC's)	15.00	40.00
9a	13¢ Booklet Pane of 10	18.50	...
0a	14¢ Booklet Pane of 10	12.00	...
1a	20¢ Booklet Pane of 10	18.50	...
1b	13¢,20¢ Booklet Pane of 10 (5 #39, 5 #41)	23.50	...
2a	22¢ Booklet Pane of 10	12.00	...
2b	14¢,22¢ Booklet Pane of 10 (5 #40, 5 #42)	15.00	...
0-53	40¢ 19th UPU Congress, attd. 6/19/84	5.00	15.00
0-53	Hamburg FD Cancel	6.00	17.50
4-57	20¢ AUSIPEX Dolphins, attd. 9/5/84	6.00	14.00
4-57	AUSIPEX FD Cancel	8.00	17.50
8	20¢ Christmas, 3 Kings, Strip of 4 11/7/84	7.00	...
9-62	20¢ Marshalls Constitution, attd. 12/19/84	5.00	14.00
	1985		
3-64/C1-2	22¢/44¢ Audubon, attd. 2/15/85	8.50	15.00
5-69	22¢ Seashells, attd. 4/17/85	6.00	14.00
0-73	22¢ Decade for Women, attd. 6/5/85	6.00	14.00
4-77	22¢ Reef and Lagoon Fish, attd. /15/85	6.00	14.00
8-81	22¢ International Youth Year, attd. 8/31/85	6.00	14.00
2-85	14¢,22¢,33¢,44¢ Xmas, 4 Sgls. 10/21/85	6.00	14.00
6-90	22¢ Halley's Comet, attd. 1/21/85	12.50	20.00
6-90	22¢ Halley's Comet with Tabs, attd.	27.50	37.50
1-94	22¢ Medicinal Plants, attd. 12/31/85	5.00	12.50
	1986-87		
07-08	$2,$5 Definitives 3/7/86	19.50	21.75
09	$10 Definitive 3/31/87	21.50	...
10-13	14¢ Marine Invertebrates, attd. 3/31/86	2.75	12.50
14	$1 AMERIPEX S/S (C-54 Globemstr.) 5/22/86	5.00	...
14	AMERIPEX FD Cancel	6.00	...
14,C3-6	AMERIPEX, Set of 5	10.00	...
15-18	22¢ Operation Crossroads, attd. 7/1/86	4.75	12.50
15-18	Bikini FD Cancel	7.50	15.00
19-23	22¢ Seashells, attd. 8/1/86	4.50	12.50
24-27	22¢ Game Fish, attd. 9/10/86	4.00	12.50
28-31	22¢ Christmas/Year of Peace, attd. 10/28/86	4.00	12.50
	1987		
32-35	22¢ Whaling Ships 2/20/87	4.00	12.50
36-41	33¢,39¢,44¢ Pilots 3/12/87 (3 Pairs)	9.50	17.50
36-41	INTERPEX FD Cancel	14.50	22.50
42	$1 Amelia Earhart / CAPEX S/S 6/15/87	5.00	...
42	CAPEX FD Cancel	12.75	...
43-51	14¢,22¢,44¢ U.S. Const. 7/16/87 (3 Strips of 3)	9.50	19.50
52-56	22¢ Seashells, attd. 9/1/87	4.50	9.50
57-59	44¢ Copra Industry, attd. 12/10/87	4.35	8.50
60-63	14¢,22¢.33¢,44¢ Xmas 12/10/87	4.35	8.50
	1988-89		
64-67	44¢ Marine Birds, attd. 1/27/88	4.35	8.50
68-83	1¢/$5 Fish Def. (16) 3/17,7/19/88 (3 FDC's)	23.50	35.00
84	$10 Blue Jack Definitive 3/31/89	25.00	...
70a	14¢ Bklt. Pane of 10 3/31/88	11.00	...
71a	15¢ Bklt. Pane of 10 12/15/88	10.00	...
73a	22¢ Bklt. Pane of 10 3/31/88	11.00	...
73b	14¢,22¢ Bklt. Pane of 10 (5 ea.) 3/31/88	12.00	...
74a	25¢ Bklt. Pane of 10 12/15/88	10.00	...
74b	15¢,25¢ Bklt. Pane of 10 (5 each) 12/15/88	11.00	...
88-89	15¢,25¢ Summer Olympics, strips of 5 6/30/88	13.75	21.50
90	25¢ Robert Louis Stevenson S/S of 9 7/19/88	11.95	...
91-94	25¢ Colonial Ships & Flags, attd. 9/2/88	3.75	8.50
95-99	25¢ Christmas, strip of 5 11/7/88	4.25	8.25
00-04	25¢ John F. Kennedy, strip of 5 11/22/88	4.25	9.00
05-08,C21	25¢ (4),45¢ Space Shuttle 12/23/88 (2 FDC's)	6.50	9.50
09-12	45¢ Links to Japan, attd. 1/19/89	4.50	8.75
13-15	45¢ Links to Alaska, attd. 3/31/89	4.50	8.50
16-20	25¢ Seashells, attd. 5/15/89	4.25	9.00
21	$1 Hirohito Memorial S/S 5/15/89	3.75	...

Scott #	Description	One Cover	Separate Covers
	MARSHALL ISLANDS		
222-25	45¢ Migrant Birds, attd. 6/27/89	4.25	8.00
226-29	45¢ PHILEXFRANCE, attd. 7/7/89	5.75	9.50
230	25¢ PHILEXFRANCE S/S of 6 7/7/89	7.25	...
231	$1 PHILEXFRANCE S/S 7/7/89	7.95	...
232-38	25¢,$1 Moon Landing 20th Anniv., set of 7 bklt. sgls. 8/1/89	...	32.50
238a	Bklt. Pane of 7	26.50	...
	WW II Anniversaries 1939-1989		
239	25¢ Invasion of Poland 9/1/89	3.25	...
240	45¢ HMS Royal Oak Sinking 10/13/89	3.75	...
241	45¢ Invasion of Finland 11/30/89	3.75	...
242-45	45¢ Battle of the River Plate 12/13/89	...	11.50
	WW II Anniversaries 1940-1990		
246-47	25¢ Invasion of Denmark & Norway 4/9/90	...	7.50
248	25¢ Katyn Forest Massacre 4/16/90	2.50	...
249-50	25¢ Invasion of Belgium 5/10/90	...	5.00
251	45¢ Winston Churchill, Prime Minister 5/10/90	3.00	...
252-53	45¢ Evacuation at Dunkirk 6/4/90	...	5.50
254	45¢ Occupation of Paris 6/14/90	3.00	...
255	25¢ Battle of Mars-el-Kebir 7/3/90	2.50	...
256	25¢ Burma Road 7/18/90	2.50	...
257-60	45¢ U.S. Destroyers for Brit. Bases 9/9/90	...	12.00
261-64	45¢ Battle of Britain 9/15/90	...	12.00
265	45¢ Tripartite Pact 9/27/90	3.00	...
266	25¢ FDR Elected to Third Term 11/5/90	2.50	...
267-70	25¢ Battle of Taranto 11/11/90	...	13.75
	WW II Anniversaries 1941-1991		
271-74	30¢ Four Freedoms 1/6/91	...	11.50
275	30¢ Battle of Beda Fomm 2/5/91	2.75	...
276-77	29¢ Greek & Yugoslav Invasions 4/6/91	...	5.50
278-81	50¢ Sinking of the Bismarck 5/27/91	...	12.50
282	30¢ German Invasion of Russia 6/22/91	2.75	...
283-84	29¢ Atlantic Charter 8/14/91	...	5.50
285	29¢ Siege of Moscow 10/2/91	3.75	...
286-87	30¢ Sinking of the USS Reuben James 10/31/91	...	5.50
288-91	50¢ Japanese Attack Pearl Harbor 12/7/91	...	12.50
292	29¢ Japanese Capture Guam 12/10/91	2.75	...
293	29¢ Fall of Singapore 12/10/91	2.75	...
294-95	50¢ Flying Tigers 12/20/91	...	6.00
296	29¢ Fall of Wake Island 12/23/91	2.75	...
	WW II Anniversaries 1942-1992		
297	29¢ Arcadia Conf., 50th Anniv. 1/1/92	2.75	...
298	50¢ Fall of Manila 1/2/92	3.00	...
299	29¢ Japanese Take Rabaul 1/23/92	2.75	...
300	29¢ Battle of Java Sea 2/15/92	2.75	...
301	50¢ Fall of Rangoon 3/8/92	3.00	...
302	29¢ Battle for New Guinea 3/8/92	2.75	...
303	29¢ MacArthur Leaves Corregidor 3/11/92	2.75	...
304	29¢ Raid on Saint-Nazaire 3/27/92	2.75	...
305	29¢ Surrender of Bataan 4/9/92	2.75	...
306	50¢ Doolittle Raid on Tokyo 4/18/92	3.00	...
307	29¢ Fall of Corregidor 5/6/92	2.75	...
308-11	50¢ Battle of Coral Sea 5/8/92	...	12.00
312-15	50¢ Battle of Midway 6/4/92	...	12.00
316	29¢ Village of Lidice Destroyed 6/10/92	2.75	...
317	29¢ Fall of Sevastopol 7/3/92	2.75	...
318-19	29¢ Convoy PQ17 Destroyed 7/5/92	...	5.50
320	29¢ Marines Land on Guadalcanal 8/7/92	2.75	...
321	29¢ Battle of Savo Island 8/9/92	2.75	...
322	29¢ Dieppe Raid 8/19/92	2.75	...
323	50¢ Battle of Stalingrad 8/19/92	3.00	...
324	29¢ Battle of Eastern Solomons 8/24/92	2.75	...
325	50¢ Battle of Cape Esperance 10/11/92	3.00	...
326	29¢ Battle of El Alamein 10/23/92	2.75	...
327-28	29¢ Battle of Barents Sea 12/31/92	...	5.50

236

399

MARSHALL ISLANDS

Scott #	Description	One Cover	Separate Covers
	WW II Anniversaries 1943-1993		
329	29¢ Casablanca Conference 1/14/93	2.75	...
330	29¢ Liberation of Kharkov 2/16/93	2.75	...
331-34	50¢ Battle of Bismarck Sea 3/3/93	...	12.50
335	50¢ Interception of Yamamoto 4/18/93	3.25	...
336-37	29¢ Battle of Kursk 7/5/93	...	5.25
	1989-92 Regulars & Commemoratives		
341-44	25¢ Christmas, attd.10/25/89	...	21.75
345	45¢ Milestones in Space S/S of 25 10/24/89	35.00	...
345/65A	1¢/$2 Birds (21) 3/8/90, 10/11/90, 2/22/91, 3/8/91 11/6/91, 2/3/92, 4/24/92	...	77.50
361a	95¢ ESSEN '90, Min. Sheet of 4 4/19/90	20.00	...
366-69	25¢ Children's Games, attd. 3/15/90	...	21.50
370-76	25¢, $1 Penny Black, 150th Anniv., Bklt. pane of 7 (6x25¢, $1) 4/6/90	...	32.50
377-80	25¢ Sea Turtles, attd. 5/3/90	...	22.50
381	25¢ Joint Issue w/Micronesia & U.S. 9/28/90	4.50	...
382	45¢ German Reunification 10/3/90	6.25	...
383-86	25¢ Christmas, attd., 10/25/90	...	19.75
387-90	25¢ Breadfruit, attd., 12/15/90	...	14.75
	1991-92		
391-94	50¢ U.S. Space Shuttle, attd., 4/12/91	...	19.95
395-98	52¢ Flowers, 6/10/91	...	19.95
399	29¢ Operation Desert Storm 7/4/91	3.50	...
400-406	29¢,$1 Birds, Bklt. pane of 7 (6x29¢,$1) 7/16/91	...	25.00
407-10	12¢,29¢,50¢ (2) Air Marshall Isl. Aircraft 9/10/91	...	16.50
411	29¢ Admission to U.N. 9/24/91	5.00	...
412	30¢ Christmas 10/25/91	3.35	...
413	29¢ Peace Corps in Marshall Isl. 11/26/91	3.95	...
414-17	29¢ Ships, strip of 4 2/15/92	15.00	15.75
418-24	50¢,$1 Voyages of Discovery, Bklt. Pane of 7 (6x50¢,$1) 5/23/92	...	25.00
425-28	29¢ Traditional Handicrafts, strip of 4 9/9/92	4.50	13.50
429	29¢ Christmas 10/29/92	2.75	...
430-33	19¢/45¢ Birds 11/10/92	3.75	10.50
	1993-95		
434-40	50¢,$1 Reef Life (6x50¢,$1) 5/26/93	...	22.50
443/58	10¢-75¢ Ships, set of 8 6/24/93,10/14/93	...	23.75
446/62A	19¢-$2.90 Ships, Set of 4 4/19/94	...	16.50
455/57A	20¢-55¢ Ships, Set of 4 9/23/94	...	11.95
453A/462B	32¢-$3 Ships Definitives, set of 4 5/5/95	...	18.00
460	$1 Sailing Vessel 5/29/93	4.25	...
462	$2 Sailing Vessel 8/26/93	6.25	...
463	$5 Sailing Vessel 3/15/94	12.50	...
463A	$10 Sailing Vessel 8/18/94	22.50	...
464	15¢-75¢ Sailing, Souvenir Sheet of 4 2/18/94	10.75	...
	WW II Anniversaries 1943-1993		
467-70	52¢ Invasion of Sicily 7/10/93	...	12.50
471	50¢ Bombing Raids on Schweinfurt 8/17/93	3.25	...
472	29¢ Liberation of Smolensk 9/25/93	2.75	...
473	29¢ Landing at Bougainville 11/1/93	2.75	...
474	50¢ US Invasion of Tarawa 11/20/93	3.25	...
475	52¢ Tehran Conference 12/1/93	3.25	...
476-77	29¢ Battle of North Cape 12/26/93	...	5.25
	WW II Anniversaries 1944-1994		
478	29¢ Eisenhower - SHAEF 1/16/94	2.65	...
479	50¢Invasion of Anzio 1/22/94	3.25	...
480	52¢ Siege of Leningrad Ends 1/27/94	3.25	...
481	29¢ U.S. Frees Marshall Islands 2/4/94	2.65	...
482	29¢ Japanese Defeat at Truk 2/17/94	2.65	...
483	52¢ Bombing of Germany 2/20/94	3.25	...
484	50¢ Rome Falls to Allies 6/4/94	3.25	...

C8

MARSHALL ISLANDS

Scott #	Description	One Cover	Separate Covers
	WW II Anniversaries 1944-1994 (continued)		
485-88	75¢ D-Day Landings 6/6/94	...	14.00
489	50¢ V-1 Bombs Strike England 6/13/94	3.25	...
490	29¢ Landing on Saipan 6/15/94	2.65	...
491	50¢ Battle of Philippine Sea 6/19/94	3.25	...
492	29¢ U.S. Liberates Guam 7/21/94	2.65	...
493	50¢ Warsaw Uprising 8/1/94	3.25	...
494	50¢ Liberation of Paris 8/25/94	3.25	...
495	50¢ Marines Land on Peliliu 9/15/94	2.65	...
496	52¢ MacArthur Returns to Philippines 10/20/94	3.25	...
497	52¢ Battle of Leyte Gulf 10/24/94	3.25	...
498-99	50¢ German Battleship "Tirpitz" Sunk 11/12/94	...	6.50
500-3	50¢ Battle of the Bulge 12/16/94	...	12.50
562	50¢ MacArthur Returns to Philippines, Souvenir Sheet of 2 10/20/94	4.25	...
	WWII Anniversaries 1945-1995		
504	32¢ Yalta Conference 2/4/95	2.75	...
505	55¢ Bombing of Dresden 2/13/95	3.50	...
506	$1 Iwo Jima Invaded 2/19/95	4.50	...
507	32¢ Remagen Bridge Taken 3/7/95	2.75	...
508	55¢ Marines Invade Okinawa 4/1/95	3.50	...
509	50¢ Death of F.D. Roosevelt 4/12/95	3.25	...
510	32¢ US/USSR Troops Link 4/25/95	2.75	...
511	60¢ Soviet Troops in Berlin 5/2/95	3.35	...
512	55¢ Allies Liberate Concentration Camps 5/4/95	3.25	...
513-16	75¢ V-E Day, Set of 4 5/8/95	...	14.50
...	32¢ United Nations Charter 6/26/95	2.75	...
...	$1 United Nations Souv. Sheet 6/26/95	4.50	...
...	55¢ Potsdam Conference 7/17/95	4.00	...
...	60¢ Churchill's Resignation 7/26/95	4.15	...
...	$1 Atomic Bomb dropped on Hiroshima 8/6/95	4.50	...
...	75¢ V.J. Day, Set of 4 9/2/95	...	14.50
	1993-94		
567-70	29¢ Capitol Complex 8/11/93	...	10.75
571	50¢ Mobil Oil Tanker 8/25/93	3.65	...
572-75	29¢ Life in 1800's 9/15/93	...	10.75
576	29¢ Christmas 10/25/93	2.65	...
577	$2.90 Constitution Souvenir Sheet 5/1/94	7.95	...
578	29¢ Postal Service Souvenir Sheet 5/2/94	2.65	...
579-80	50¢ World Soccer Cup	...	6.25
582	50¢ Solar System, Set of 12 7/20/94	...	36.50
583-86	75¢ Moon Landing, 25th Anniv. 7/20/94	...	14.50
587	29¢, 52¢, $1 Butterflies Souv. Sht. 8/16/94 (2)	11.50	...
588	29¢ Christmas 10/28/94	2.65	...
	1995		
589	50¢ Year of the Boar Souvenir Sheet 1/2/95	3.25	...
590	55¢ Underseas Glory (4 designs) 3/20/95	...	13.00
...	55¢ J.F. Kennedy, set of 6 5/29/95	...	18.75
...	75¢ Marilyn Monroe, set of 4 6/1/95	...	14.50
...	32¢ Cats, set of 4 7/5/95	...	10.75
	Airmails		
C1-2	44¢ Audubon, attd. 2/15/86	4.50	7.50
C3-6	44¢ AMERIPEX Planes, attd. 5/22/86	5.75	11.50
C7	44¢ Operation Crossroads S/S 7/1/86	3.95	...
C7	Bikini FD Cancel	5.95	...
C8	44¢ Statue of Liberty/Peace Year 10/28/86	3.00	...
C9-12	44¢ Girl Scouts, attd. 12/8/86	4.50	11.00
C13-16	44¢ Marine Birds, attd. 1/12/87	4.50	11.00
C17-20	44¢ Amelia Earhart/CAPEX, attd. 6/15/87	5.00	9.00
C17-20	CAPEX FD Cancel	6.75	12.50
C22-25	12¢,36¢,39¢,45¢ Aircraft 4/24/89	4.00	7.75
C22a/25b	12¢/45¢ Booklet Panes of 10 (5) 6/10/89	...	42.50

77-80

Scott #	Description	One Cover	Separate Covers
	MICRONESIA		
	1984-1988		
-4	20¢ Postal Service Inaugural, attd. 7/12/84	7.50	15.00
-20	1¢/$5 Definitives 7/12/84 (4 FDC's)	...	30.00
1,C4-6	20¢,28¢,35¢,40¢ AUSIPEX 9/21/84	10.00	16.50*
2,C7-9	20¢,28¢,35¢,40¢ Christmas 12/20/84	10.00	16.00*
3,C10-12	22¢,33¢,39¢,44¢ Ships 8/19/85	9.50	17.50*
4,C13-14	22¢,33¢,44¢ Christmas 10/15/85	9.50	18.50*
5-28	22¢ Audubon, attd. 10/30/85	9.00	17.50*
1-39,C34-36	3¢-$10 Bird Definitives and Airs (6 FDC's) #31-32,35,C34-36 (8/1/88), #34 (4/14/86), #33,36-38 (9/1/88), #39 (10/15/85)	...	40.00
3a	15¢ Bklt. Pane of 10 11/30/88	5.25	...
6a	25¢ Bklt. Pane of 10 11/30/88	7.25	...
6b	15¢,25¢ Bklt. Pane of 10 (5 ea.) 11/30/88	6.75	...
5,C16-18	22¢,33¢,39¢,44¢ Nan Madol Ruins	9.50	22.50*
6,C19-20	22¢,44¢ Peace Year,Comet,Nauruans 5/16/86	10.50	22.50*
8-51	22¢ on 20¢ (Surcharges on #1-4), attd. 5/19/86	...	38.50*
2,C21-24	22¢,33¢,39¢,44¢,75¢ AMERIPEX 5/22/86	9.00	17.50*
2,C21-24	AMERIPEX FD Cancel	16.50	25.00*
3	22¢ Passport 11/4/86	5.75	...
4-55,C26-27	5¢,22¢,33¢,44¢ Xmas 10/15/86 (2)	12.50	17.50
6,C28-30	22¢,33¢,39¢,44¢ Homeless, Events 6/13/87	12.75	17.50*
7	$1 CAPEX S/S 6/13/87	13.00	...
8,C31-33	22¢,33¢,39¢,44¢ Xmas 11/16/87	13.00	17.50*
9-62,C37-38	22¢,44¢ Colonial Eras 7/20/88 (2)	11.00	18.50
3-66	25¢,45¢ Summer Olympics, 2 pairs 9/1/88	6.75	12.00
7-70	25¢ Christmas, attd. 10/28/88	5.00	7.95
1	25¢ Truk Lagoon Monument S/S of 18 12/19/88 (3)	19.95	33.50
	1989-1990		
2-75	45¢ Mwarmwarms, attd. 3/31/89	5.75	8.50
6	$1 Emperor Hirohito Memorial S/S 5/15/89	4.00	...
7-80	25¢,45¢ Sharks (2 pairs) 7/7/89	5.75	9.50
1	25¢ 1st Moon Landing, 20th Anniv., S/S of 9 7/20/89 (3)	10.75	10.50
2	$2.40 1st Moon Landing, 20th Anniv. 7/20/89	6.95	...
3/102	1¢/$5 Seashells (12) 9/26/89 (2)	27.50	35.00
5a	15¢ Booklet Pane of 10 9/14/90	6.00	...
8a	25¢ Booklet Pane of 10 9/14/90	8.00	...
8b	15¢,25¢ Booklet Pane of 10 (5 ea.) 9/14/90	7.00	...

First Day of Use, No Official Cachet

Scott #	Description	One Cover	Separate Covers
	1989-1991		
03	25¢ Kosrae Fruits & Flowers S/S of 18 11/18/89	22.50	35.00
03	Same, World Stamp Expo, DC cancel	25.00	38.50
04-05	25¢,45¢ Christmas 12/14/89	3.95	5.75
06-09	10¢/25¢ Wildlife 2/19/90	3.95	5.75
10-13	45¢ Stamp World London, attd. 5/3/90	5.75	8.50
14	$1 Stamp World London S/S 5/3/90	4.00	...
15	$1 Penny Black, 150th Anniv. 5/6/90	4.00	...
16-20	25¢ Pohnpei Agric. & Trade School, attd. 7/31/90	4.50	9.00
21	$1 Int'l. Garden & Greenery Expo S/S 7/31/90	4.00	...
22-23	25¢,45¢ Mail Plane & Boat 8/24/90	3.50	5.00
24-26	25¢ Jt. Issue Marsh. Isl. & U.S., strip of 3 9/28/90	3.50	5.50
27-30	45¢ Moths, attd. 11/10/90	5.75	8.00
31	25¢ Christmas S/S of 9 11/19/90	6.50	...
32	25¢,45¢ New Capitol of Micronesia S/S 1/15/91	3.50	...
33	$1 New Capitol S/S 1/15/91	4.00	...
34-35	29¢ Turtles, attd. 3/14/91	3.00	6.00
36-37	50¢ Turtles, attd. 3/14/91	5.00	6.50
38-41	29¢ Desert Shield/Desert Storm, strip of 4 7/30/91	4.50	7.00
42	$2.90 Frigatebird, flag 7/30/91	7.95	...
42a	$2.90 Same, S/S 7/30/91	7.95	...
43	29¢ Phila Nippon '91, min. sheet of 3 9/1/91	3.75	...
43a-c	Set of 3 singles	...	5.50
44	50¢ Phila Nippon '91, min. sheet of 3 9/1/91	5.00	...
44a-c	Set of 3 singles	...	6.50
45	$1 Phila Nippon S/S 9/1/91	4.00	...
46-48	29¢,40¢,50¢ Christmas 10/30/91	4.50	6.50
49	29¢ Rain Forest, min. sht. of 18 11/18/91 (3)	17.50	...

C43-46

Scott #	Description	One Cover	Separate Covers
	MICRONESIA		
	1992-1994		
150	29¢ Peace Corps, strip of 5 4/10/92	13.50	...
151	29¢ Discovery of America, Strip of 3 5/23/92	7.95	...
152-53	29¢,50¢ Anniv. of UN Membership 9/24/92	3.85	5.50
153a	Same, S/S of 2	5.25	...
154	29¢ Christmas 12/4/92	3.25	...
155	29¢ Pioneers of Flight, block of 8 4/12/93	7.50	21.00
157/166	10¢-$2.90 Fish, Set of 4 5/20/94	9.50	...
159/65	19¢-$1 Fish, Set of 8 5/14/93,8/26/93 (2)	10.75	...
160A/165A	25¢-$2 Fish, Set of 4 8/5/94	9.25	...
168	29¢ Golden Age of Sail, min. sht. of 12 5/21/93	10.75	27.50
172	29¢ Thomas Jefferson 7/4/93	2.75	...
173-76	29¢ Pacific Canoes, attd. 7/21/93	4.50	...
177	29¢ Local Leaders, strip of 4 9/16/93	4.50	...
178	50¢ Pioneers of Flight, block of 8 9/25/93	10.50	24.75
179-80	29¢-50¢ Pohnpei 10/5/93	3.75	...
181	$1 Pohnpei Souvenir Sheet 10/5/93	4.25	...
182-83	29¢-50¢ Butterflies, two pairs 10/20/93	5.75	...
184-85	29¢-50¢ Christmas 11/11/93	3.95	...
186	29¢ Yap Culture, sheet of 18 12/15/93 (3)	16.75	...
	1994		
187-89	29¢,40¢,50¢ Kosrae 2/11/94	4.50	...
190	29¢-50¢ Butterflies, sheet of 4 2/18/94	10.75	...
191	29¢ Pioneers of Flight, block of 8 3/4/94	6.75	20.75
192	29¢ Micronesian Games, block of 4 3/26/94	4.50	...
193	29¢ Native Costumes, block of 4 3/31/94	4.50	...
194	29¢ Anniversary of Constitution 5/10/94	2.65	...
195	29¢ Flowers, Strip of 4 6/6/94	4.50	...
196-97	50¢ World Cup Soccer 6/17/94	4.25	...
198	29¢ Postal Service, 10th Anniv. 7/12/94	4.50	...
199	29¢, 52¢, $1 Philakorea, Dinosaurs, Souvenir Sheet of 3 8/16/95 (2)	11.50	...
200	50¢ Pioneers of Flight, Set of 8 9/20/94	...	25.00
201	29¢ Migratory Birds 10/20/94	4.50	...
202-3	29¢-50¢ Christmas 11/2/94	3.75	...
204-7	32¢ Local leaders, 4 designs 12/27/94	4.75	...
	1995		
208	50¢ Year of the Boar Souvenir Sheet 1/2/95	3.25	...
209	32¢ Chuuk Lagoon, block of 4 2/6/95	4.75	...
210	32¢ Pioneers of Flight, set of 8 3/4/95	...	21.75
211	32¢ Dogs of the World, block of 4 4/5/95	4.75	...
...	32¢-$3 Fish Definitives 5/15/95	11.75	...
...	32¢ Hibiscus, Strip of 4 6/1/95	4.75	...
...	$1 United Nations Souv. Sheet 6/26/95	4.50	...
	Airmails - Stationery		
C1-3	28¢,35¢,40¢ Airpost 7/12/84	5.50	10.00
C25	$1 AMERIPEX S/S 5/22/86	8.75	...
C39-42	45¢ Micronesia Flags, attd. 1/19/89	5.75	8.00
C43-46	22¢/45¢ Aircraft Serving Micronesia 7/16/90	5.00	7.50
C47-48	40¢,50¢ Aircraft 3/27/92	4.00	6.00
C49	$2.90 Moon Landing Souvenir Sheet 7/20/94	7.95	...
U1	20¢ National Flag 7/12/84	10.75	...
U3	29¢ on 30¢ 3/3/91	8.25	...

51-54

PALAU

Palau FDC's (#1-58, 75-81, C1-4) have Commercial Cachets.

1983

Scott #	Description	One Cover	Separate Covers
1-4	20¢ Postal Service Inaugural 3/10/83	5.95	17.50
1-4	INTERPEX FD Cancel	11.75	25.00
5-8	20¢ Birds 3/16/83	5.00	15.00
9-21	1¢/$5 Definitives (3 covers)	32.50	57.50
13a	13¢ Booklet Pane of 10	18.50	...
13b	13¢/20¢ Booklet Pane of 10 (5 #13, 5 #14)	27.50	...
14b	20¢ Booklet Pane of 10	18.50	...
24-27	20¢ Whales, attd. 9/21/83	4.00	12.50
28-32	20¢ Christmas, attd. 11/18/83	4.50	13.50
33-40	20¢ Capt. Wilson's Voyage, attd. 12/14/83	5.50	22.50
33-40	London FD Cancel	11.50	25.00

1984-86

Scott #	Description	One Cover	Separate Covers
41-50	20¢ Seashells, attd. 3/15/84	8.75	19.95
41-50	INTERPEX FD Cancel	16.75	25.00
51-54	40¢ 19th UPU Congress 6/19/84	5.75	12.50
51-54	Hamburg FD Cancel	9.25	16.50
55-58	20¢ Traditional Fishing attd. 9/6/84	5.00	12.50
55-58	AUSIPEX FD Cancel	7.50	15.00
59-62	20¢ Christmas, attd. 12/5/84	5.00	12.50
63-66/C5	22¢/44¢ Audubon, attd. 2/6/85	6.00	12.50
67-70	22¢ Shipbuilding, attd. 3/27/85	4.00	12.50
75/81	14¢/44¢ Marine Life, Set of 6 6/11/85	6.50	12.50
75a	14¢ Booklet Pane of 10	15.00	...
76a	22¢ Booklet Pane of 10	15.00	...
76b	14¢/22¢ Booklet Pane of 10 (5 #75, 5 #76)	17.50	...
85	$10 Spinner Dolphins 3/31/86	25.00	...
86-89	44¢ International Youth Year, attd. 7/15/85	5.50	12.50
90-93	14¢,22¢,33¢,44¢ Christmas 10/21/85	5.00	12.50
94	$1 Trans-Pacific Air Anniv. S/S 1/21/85	4.00	...
95-98	44¢ Halley's Comet, attd. 12/21/85	5.50	12.50

1986-88

Scott #	Description	One Cover	Separate Covers
99-102	44¢ Songbirds, attd. 2/24/86	5.75	12.50
103	14¢ AMERIPEX Sea & Reef, Sht. of 40 5/22/86	47.50	67.50
104-08	22¢ Seashells, attd. 8/1/86	5.00	12.50
109-12,C17	22¢ International Peace Year 9/19/86	6.00	12.50
113-16	22¢ Reptiles, attd. 10/28/86	4.00	12.50
117-21	22¢ Christmas, attd. 11/26/86	4.00	12.50
121B-E	44¢ Butterflies, attd. 1/5/87	5.00	12.50
122-25	22¢ Fruit Bats, attd. 2/23/87	4.75	12.50
126/45	1¢-$5 Flowers (16) 3/12/87,7/1/88 (2 FDC's)	22.50	30.00
126/45	INTERPEX FD Cancel (12) 3/12/88	26.50	32.50
130a	14¢ Bklt. Pane of 10 3/31/87	7.50	...
131a	15¢ Bklt. Pane of 10 7/5/88	7.00	...
132a	22¢ Bklt. Pane of 10 3/31/87	8.50	...
132b	14¢,22¢ Bklt. Pane of 10 (5 ea.) 3/31/87	8.50	...
133a	25¢ Bklt. Pane of 10 7/5/88	7.50	...
133b	15¢,25¢ Bklt. Pane of 10 (5 ea.) 7/5/88	8.50	...
145A	$10 Flower Bouquet 3/17/88	25.00	...

1987-88

Scott #	Description	One Cover	Separate Covers
146-49	22¢ CAPEX attd. 6/15/87	3.25	10.00
146-49	CAPEX FD Cancel	4.50	12.50
150-54	22¢ Seashells attd. 8/25/87	4.00	12.50
155-63	14¢,22¢,44¢ U.S. Const. Bicent. (3 Strips of 3) 9/17/87 (3 FDC's)	7.50	17.50
164-67	14¢,22¢,33¢,44¢ Japanese Links 10/16/87	4.50	9.50
168	$1 S/S Japanese Links to Palau 10/16/87	5.00	...
173-77	22¢ Christmas attd. 11/24/87	3.75	8.00
178-82	22¢ "Silent Spring" Symb. Spec. atd. 12/15/87	3.75	7.50

PALAU

1988-90

Scott #	Description	One Cover	Separate Covers
183-86	44¢ Butterflies & Flowers, attd. 1/25/88	3.95	7.50
187-90	44¢ Ground Dwelling Birds, attd. 2/29/88	3.95	7.50
191-95	25¢ Seashells (5), attd. 5/11/88	3.75	9.50
196	25¢ Postal Indep. S/S of 6 (FINLANDIA) 6/2/88	5.50	...
197	45¢ U.S. Posses. Phil. Soc. S/S of 6 8/26/88	7.50	...
198-202	25¢ Christmas, attd. 11/7/88	3.75	7.50
203	25¢ Chambered Nautilus S/S of 5 12/23/88	3.95	...
204-07	45¢ Endangered Birds, attd. 2/9/89	4.75	7.75
208-11	45¢ Exotic Mushrooms, attd. 3/16/89	4.75	7.75
212-16	25¢ Seashells, attd. 4/12/89	3.95	7.50
217	$1 Emperor Hirohito Memorial S/S 5/17/89	5.50	...
218	25¢ 1st Moon Landing, 20th Anniv. S/S 7/20/89	15.75	...
219	$2.40 Moon Landing, 20th Anniv. 7/20/89	5.95	...
220	25¢ Literacy, block of 10 10/13/89	6.00	10.50
220	With Tabs	8.75	...
221	25¢ World Stamp Expo., Sht. of 20 11/20/89	13.75 (4)	...
221	Washington, D.C. cancel	16.75 (4)	...
222-26	25¢ Christmas, attd. 12/18/89	3.75	7.50
227-30	25¢ Soft Coral, attd. 1/3/90	3.00	6.00
231-34	45¢ Forest Birds 3/16/90	4.50	7.00
235	25¢ Prince Lee Boo Visits Engl., S/S of 9 5/6/90	6.00	...
235	London FD Cancel	7.75	...
236	$1 Penny Black, 150th Anniv. S/S 5/6/90	3.00	...
236	London FD Cancel	4.00	...
237-41	45¢ Orchids, attd. 6/4/90	5.00	9.50
242-45	45¢ Butterflies & Flowers, attd. 7/6/90	4.50	8.95
246	25¢ Lagoon Life, Sheetlet of 25 8/10/90	16.50	...
247-48	45¢ Pacifica/Mail Delivery, attd. 8/24/90	3.00	5.50
249-53	25¢ Christmas, attd. 11/28/90	3.25	7.50
254-57	45¢ U.S. Forces in Palau, 1994 attd. 12/7/90	4.50	7.00
258	$1 U.S. Forces in Palau, 1994 S/S 12/7/90	3.00	...

1991-92

Scott #	Description	One Cover	Separate Covers
259-62	30¢ Coral, attd. 3/4/91	3.75	6.50
263	30¢ Angaur, min. sht. of 16 3/14/91	10.50	...
264-286	1¢/$2 Bird Definitives (17) 4/18/91, 1992	...	39.50
287	$10 Bird Definitive 9/10/92	21.00	...
270a	19¢ Palau Fantail, bklt. pane of 10 8/23/91	14.00	...
272a	29¢ Palau, fruit dove, bklt. pane of 10 8/23/91	15.00	...
272b	19¢,29¢ bklt. pane of 10 (5x19¢, 5x29¢) 8/23/91	15.00	...
288	29¢ Christianity in Palau, min. sht. of 6 4/28/91	5.50	...
289	29¢ Marine Life, min. sht. of 20 5/24/91	15.75	...
290	20¢ Desert Shield/Desert Storm, min.sht.of 9 7/2/91	6.75	...
291	$2.90 Desert Shield/Storm 7/2/91	6.50	...
292	$2.90 Desert Shield/Storm S/S 7/2/91	7.25	...
293	29¢ Republic of Palau, 10th Anniv., min. sht. of 8 7/9/91	5.50	...
294	50¢ Giant Clams, min. sht. of 5 9/17/91	5.50	...
295	29¢ Japanese Heritage, min. sht. of 6 11/19/91	4.75	...
296	$1 Phila Nippon S/S 11/19/91	3.50	...
297	29¢ Peace Corps in Palau, min. sht. of 6 12/6/91	4.50	...
298	29¢ Christmas, strip of 5, attd. 11/14/91	4.50	...
299	29¢ WWII in the Pacific, min. sht. of 10 12/6/91	10.00	...
300	50¢ Butterflies, blk. of 4 1/20/92	5.50	7.50
301	29¢ Shells, strip of 5 3/11/92	4.50	7.50
302	29¢ Age of Discovery, min. sheet of 20 5/25/92	13.50	...
303	29¢ Biblical Creation, min. sht. of 24 6/5/92	15.00	...
304-09	50¢ Summer Olympics S/S 7/10/92	... (3)	15.00
310	29¢ Elvis Presley, min. sht. of 9 8/17/92	8.75	...
311	50¢ WWII in the Pacific, min. sht. of 10 9/10/92	12.50	...
312	50¢ Christmas, strip of 5 10/1/92	4.50	7.50

cott #	Description	One Cover	Separate Covers
	PALAU		
	1993-94		
3	50¢ Animal Families, block of 4 7/9/93	5.50	...
4	29¢ Seafood, block of 4 7/22/93	3.50	...
5	50¢ Sharks, block of 4 8/11/93	5.50	...
6	29¢ WW II, Pacific Theater, min.sht.of 10 9/23/93	10.95	...
7	29¢ Christmas, strip of 5 10/22/93	4.50	...
8	29¢ Prehistoric and Legendary Sea Creatures, sheet of 25 11/26/93	16.50	...
9	29¢ Indigenous People, sheet of 4 12/8/93	3.50	...
0	$2.90 Indigenous People, Souv. Sheet 12/8/93	7.50	...
1	29¢ Jonah and the Whale, sheet of 25 12/28/93	16.50	...
2	40¢ Palau Rays, block of 4 1/28/94	4.50	...
3	20¢ Crocodiles, block of 4	3.00	...
4	50¢ Seabirds, block of 4 4/12/94	5.50	...
5	29¢ WW II, Pacific Theater, min.sht. of 10 4/12/94	10.95	...
6	50¢ WW II, D-Day, min.sht.of 10 4/12/94	15.95	...
7	29¢ Baron Pierrede Coubertin 6/15/94	1.75	...
8-33	50¢, $1, $2 Coubertin and Winter Olympics Stars, Set of 6 Souv. Sheets 6/15/94	16.50	...
4-36	29¢, 40¢, 50¢ Philakorea '94 Philatelic Fantasies, Wildlife, 3 Souv. Sheets of 8 8/15-25/94	22.50	...
7	29¢ Apollo XI Moon Landing 25th Anniv. Miniature Sheet of 2 7/7/94	13.50	...
8	29¢ Independence Day Strip of 5 10/1/94	4.50	...
9	$1 Invasion of Peleliu Souv. Sht 9/15/94	3.00	...
0	29¢ Disney Tourism Sheetlet of 9 9/1/94	6.50	...
1-43	$1, $2.90 Disney Tourism, 3 Souv. Sheets 9/1/94	12.75	...
4	20¢ Year of the Family, Min. Sheet of 12	5.95	...
5	29¢ Christmas '94 Strip of 5 11/1/94	3.95	...
6-48	29¢, 50¢ World Cup of Soccer, Set of 3 Sheetlets of 12 12/1/94	29.50	...
	1995		
0	32¢ Elvis Presley, Sheetlets of 9 1/26/95	6.95	...
1-64	1¢-$5 Fish Definitives (14) 1/2/95 (3)	28.50	...
5	$10 Fish Definitive 3/1/95	21.00	...
6	32¢ Earth Day '95, Sheetlet of 18 3/1/95	12.95	...
	32¢ Tourism, Lost Fleet, Sheetlet of 18 3/1/95	12.95	...
	50¢ Jet Aircraft, Sheetlet of 12 4/5/95	12.95	...
	$2 Jet Airliner, Souv. Sheet 4/5/95	4.95	...
	32¢ Underwater Ships, Sheetlet of 18 5/27/95	12.95	...

Scott #	Description	One Cover	Separate Covers
	PALAU		
	Semi-Postals		
B1-4	25¢,45¢ Olympic Sports, 2 pairs 8/8/88	6.50	9.75
	Airmails		
C1-4	40¢ Birds, attd. 6/12/84	5.75	12.50
C1-4	Expo '84 FD Cancel	9.50	16.00
C6-9	44¢ Palau-Germany Exch. Cent. attd. 9/1/85	5.00	12.50
C10-13	44¢ Trans-Pacific Anniv., attd. 11/21/85	5.00	12.50
C14-16	44¢ Remeliik Memorial, attd. 6/30/86	5.50	12.50
C17	44¢ Peace Yr., Statue of Liberty 9/19/86	2.50	...
C17	Stamp Festival FD Cancel	3.25	...
C18-20	36¢,39¢,45¢ Aircraft 5/17/89	3.75	7.00
C18a/20b	36¢/45¢ Booklet Pane of 10 (4)	...	33.50
C21	50¢ Palauan Bai, self adh. (#293a) 7/9/91	2.50	...
C22	50¢ Birds, block of 4 1/26/95	5.50	...
	Postal Stationery		
U1	22¢ Parrotfish 2/14/85	2.95	...
U2	22¢ Spearfishing 2/14/85	4.25	...
U3	25¢ Nautilus 1991	6.95	...
UC1	36¢ Birds 2/14/85	4.25	...
UX1	14¢ Giant Clam 2/14/85	2.95	...

UNITED NATIONS

1 2 8 11

ott's .		MI Block of 4	F-VF NH	F-VF Used
1	1¢-$1 Regular Issue	39.50	7.95	6.50
	1¢ Peoples, Magenta	.60	.20	.15
	1½¢ U.N. Hdqtrs. Blue Green	.60	.20	.15
	1½¢ Precancelled	...	...	30.00
	2¢ Peace, Justice, Sec. Purple	.60	.20	.15
	3¢ Flag, Magenta & Blue	.60	.20	.15
	5¢ UNICEF, Blue	.60	.20	.15
	10¢ Peoples, Chocolate	1.25	.25	.20
	15¢ Flag, Violet & Blue	1.35	.30	.20
	20¢ World Unity, Dark Brown	3.50	.75	.50
	25¢ Flag, Olive Gray & Blue	2.75	.60	.50
	50¢ U.N. Hdqtrs., Indigo	22.50	5.00	3.75
	$1 Peace, Justice Sec., Red	9.00	2.00	1.25

13 17 21

	1952			
	5¢ War Memorial Building	1.25	.25	.20
14	3¢-5¢ Human Rights, Flame	2.25	.50	.40
	1953			
16	3¢-5¢ Refugee Family	3.75	.80	.75
18	3¢-5¢ Univ. Postal Union	6.25	1.35	.75
20	3¢-5¢ Technical Assistance	4.50	.90	.75
22	3¢-5¢ Human Rights, Hands	9.00	1.85	.75

23 25 27 30

	1954			
24	3¢-8¢ Food & Agriculture Org	6.75	1.50	.85
26	3¢-8¢ Int'l. Labor Organ	11.50	2.50	1.25
28	3¢-8¢ U.N. European Office	17.00	3.75	2.00
30	3¢-8¢ Human Rights, Mother	55.00	11.50	3.50

31 35 47

	1955			
32	3¢-8¢ Int'l Civil Aviation	20.00	4.00	2.00
34	3¢-8¢ UNESCO Emblem	3.50	.70	.65
37	3¢-8¢ 10th Anniversary	14.75	3.25	1.25
	3¢-8¢ 10th Anniv. Souv. Sheet	...	145.00	50.00
	3¢-8¢ Second Print, Retouched	...	155.00	60.00
40	3¢-8¢ Human Rights	3.50	.75	.75

Scott's No.		MI Block of 4	F-VF NH	F-VF Used
41-42	3¢-8¢ Telecommunications	3.85	.85	.75
43-44	3¢-8¢ World Health Organ	3.50	.75	.75
45-46	3¢-8¢ General Assembly	1.00	.30	.20
47-48	3¢-8¢ Human Rights	.90	.30	.20

53 55 63 67

	1957			
49-50	3¢-8¢ Meteorological Org	.90	.30	.20
51-52	3¢-8¢ U.N. Emergency Force	.90	.30	.20
53-54	3¢-8¢ Same, re-engraved	1.00	.30	.20
#53-54	**The area around the circles is shaded, giving a halo effect.**			
55-56	3¢-8¢ Security Council	.90	.30	.20
57-58	3¢-8¢ Human Rights	.90	.30	.20
	1958			
59-60	3¢-8¢ Atomic Ener. Agency	.90	.30	.20
61-62	3¢-8¢ Central Hall London	.90	.30	.20
63-64	4¢-8¢ Reg. U.N. Seal	.90	.30	.20
65-66	4¢-8¢ Economic & Social C.	.90	.30	.20
67-68	4¢-8¢ Human Rights	.90	.30	.20

69 73 77 86

	1959			
69-70	4¢-8¢ Flushing Meadows	1.10	.30	.22
71-72	4¢-8¢ Economic Comm. - Europe	2.25	.50	.35
73-74	4¢-8¢ Trusteeship Council	1.10	.30	.22
75-76	4¢-8¢ World Refugee Year	1.15	.30	.20
	1960			
77-78	4¢-8¢ Chailot Palace Paris	1.00	.30	.20
79-80	4¢-8¢ Econ. C. - Asia & Far East	1.00	.30	.20
81-82	4¢-8¢ World Forestry Congress	1.00	.30	.20
83-84	4¢-8¢ 15th Anniversary	1.25	.30	.20
85	4¢-8¢ 15th Anniv. Souvenir Sheet	...	1.75	1.70
85v	Same broken "v" Variety	...	67.50	65.00
86-87	4¢-8¢ International Bank	1.25	.30	.20

88 97 108 112

	1961			
88-89	4¢-8¢ Court of Justice	1.25	.30	.20
90-91	4¢-7¢ Monetary Fund	1.25	.30	.20
92	30¢ Regular Flags	2.25	.50	.40
93-94	4¢-11¢ Econ. C. - Latin America	2.25	.50	.35
95-96	4¢-11¢ Econ. Comm. - Africa	2.25	.40	.20
97-99	3¢-13¢ Children's Fund	2.35	.45	.35
	1962			
100-01	4¢-7¢ House & Urban Dev.	1.75	.30	.22
102-03	4¢-11¢ World Health Organ	1.90	.40	.27
104-07	1¢-11¢ Regulars	3.50	.75	.30
108-09	5¢-15¢ Hammarskjold	3.00	.60	.45
110-11	4¢-11¢ Operations in Congo	2.50	.50	.45
112-13	4¢-11¢ Peaceful Outer Space	1.60	.30	.25

NOTE: PRICES THROUGHOUT THIS LIST ARE SUBJECT TO CHANGE WITHOUT NOTICE IF MARKET CONDITIONS REQUIRE. MINIMUM MAIL ORDER MUST TOTAL AT LEAST $20.00.

114 119 133 134

Scott's No.		MI Block of 4	F-VF NH	F-VF Used
114-15	5¢-11¢ Science & Technology	1.65	.35	.27
116-17	5¢-11¢ Freedom from Hunger	1.65	.35	.27
118	25¢ UN in West New Guinea	2.50	.55	.30
119-20	5¢-11¢ General Assembly Bldg.	1.65	.35	.27
121-22	5¢-11¢ Human Rights	1.90	.40	.27
	1964			
123-24	5¢-11¢ Maritime Consultative Org.	1.65	.35	.27
125-28	2¢-50¢ Regulars	5.95	1.15	.60
129-30	5¢-11¢ Trade & Development	1.65	.35	.30
131-32	5¢-11¢ Control Narcotics	1.65	.35	.30
133	5¢ Ending Nuclear Tests	.60	.20	.15
134-36	4¢-11¢ Education Progress	1.65	.35	.32

137 139 154 161

Scott's No.		MI Block of 4	F-VF NH	F-VF Used
	1965			
137-38	5¢-11¢ Development Fund	1.25	.30	.25
139-40	5¢-11¢ Peace Force - Cyprus	1.25	.30	.25
141-42	5¢-11¢ Telecommunications Union	1.25	.30	.25
143-44	5¢-15¢ 20th Anniv. I. Coop. Yr.	1.60	.35	.30
145	5¢-12¢ 20th Anniv. Souvenir Sht.	...	.50	.45
146-50	1¢-$1 Regulars	15.00	3.15	2.35
151-53	4¢-11¢ Population Trends	1.65	.35	.35
	1966			
154-55	5¢-15¢ Fed. of U.N. Assoc.	1.40	.30	.27
156-57	5¢-11¢ W.H.O. Headqtrs. Geneva	1.75	.35	.27
158-59	5¢-11¢ Coffee Agreement	1.40	.30	.27
160	15¢ Peacekeeping - Observers	1.25	.30	.25
161-63	4¢-11¢ UNICEF 20th Anniv.	1.50	.32	.28

164 170 185 190

Scott's No.		MI Block of 4	F-VF NH	F-VF Used
	1967			
164-65	5¢-11¢ Development Program	1.25	.30	.25
166-67	1½¢-5¢ Regulars	.90	.30	.20
168-69	5¢-11¢ Independent Nations	1.25	.30	.25
170-74	4¢-15¢ Expo '67, Montreal	3.15	.65	.65
175-76	5¢-15¢ Tourist Year	1.40	.30	.27
177-78	6¢-13¢ Disarmament	1.65	.35	.30
179	6¢ Chagall Souvenir Sheet	...	.55	.50
180	6¢ Chagall Window Stamp	.75	.20	.15
	1968			
181-82	6¢-13¢ Secretariat	1.65	.35	.30
183-84	6¢-75¢ Art, Starcke Statue	8.50	1.75	1.60
185-86	6¢-13¢ Industrial Development	1.40	.30	.25
187	6¢ Regular, U.N. Development	.60	.20	.15
188-89	6¢-20¢ World Weather Watch	1.95	.42	.37
190-91	6¢-13¢ Human Rights	1.95	.42	.37

192 197 203 209

Scott's No.		MI Block of 4	F-VF NH	F-V Use
192-93	6¢-13¢ Train. & Research Inst.	1.65	.35	.3
194-95	6¢-15¢ U.N. Building, Santiago	1.90	.40	.3
196	13¢ Regular "U.N." & Emblem	1.15	.25	.2
197-98	6¢-13¢ Peace Through Law	1.65	.35	.3
199-200	6¢-20¢ Labor & Development	2.10	.45	.4
201-02	6¢-13¢ Art, Tunisian Mosaic	1.65	.35	.3
	1970			
203-04	6¢-25¢ Art, Peace Bell	2.25	.50	.4
205-06	6¢-13¢ Mekong Basin Dev.	1.40	.30	.3
207-08	6¢-13¢ Fight Against Cancer	1.40	.30	.3
209-11	6¢-25¢ 25th Anniversary	3.85	.85	.7
212	6¢-25¢ 25th Anniv. Souv. Sheet	...	.80	.7
213-14	6¢-13¢ Peace, Justice & Progress	1.95	.40	.3

215 216 220 224

Scott's No.		MI Block of 4	F-VF NH	F-V Use
	1971			
215	6¢ Peaceful Uses of the Sea	.60	.20	.1
216-17	6¢-13¢ Support for Refugees	1.65	.35	.3
218	13¢ World Food Program	1.10	.23	.2
219	20¢ U.P.U. Headquarters	1.40	.30	.2
220-21	8¢-13¢ Racial Discrimination	1.85	.35	.3
222-23	8¢-60¢ Regulars	5.25	1.15	1.0
224-25	8¢-21¢ U.N. Int'l. School	2.50	.55	.5

228 232 236 242

Scott's No.		MI Block of 4	F-VF NH	F-V Use
	1972			
226	95¢ Regular, Letter	8.00	1.75	1.5
227	8¢ No Nuclear Weapons	.85	.20	.1
228	15¢ World Health Day, Man.	1.25	.27	.2
229-30	8¢-15¢ Human Environment	2.35	.45	.3
231	21¢ Economic Comm. - Europe	2.25	.40	.3
232-33	8¢-15¢ Maria Sert. Mural	2.25	.42	.3
	1973			
234-35	8¢-15¢ Disarmament Decade	2.65	.50	.3
236-37	8¢-15¢ Against Drug Abuse	2.65	.50	.4
238-39	8¢-21¢ Volunteer Program	2.85	.55	.5
240-41	8¢-15¢ Namibia	2.85	.55	.5
242-43	8¢-21¢ Human Rights	2.85	.55	.5

NOTE: PRICES ARE FOR SETS OR SINGLES AS LISTED.

UNITED NATIONS 1974

244 252 256 260

cott's No.		MI Block of 4	F-VF NH	F-VF Used
44-45	10¢-21¢ ILO Headquarters	3.00	.65	.60
46	10¢ U.P.U. Centenary	1.15	.25	.15
47-48	10¢-18¢ Art, Brazil Mural	3.00	.55	.50
19-51	2¢-18¢ Regulars	2.50	.55	.50
52-53	10¢-18¢ Population Year	3.00	.60	.55
54-55	10¢-25¢ Law of the Sea	3.00	.65	.60
	1975			
56-57	10¢-26¢ Peaceful-Outer Space	3.00	.65	.60
58-59	10¢-18¢ Women's Year	3.50	.75	.45
30-61	10¢-26¢ 30th Anniversary	3.50	.75	.55
32	10¢-26¢ 30th Anniv. Souv. Sht	...	.90	.80
33-64	10¢-18¢ Namibia	2.75	.50	.45
65-66	13¢-26¢ Peacekeeping Force	3.00	.65	.60

272 278 283 289

	1976			
67-71	3¢-50¢ Regulars	8.75	1.75	1.50
72-73	13¢-26¢ U.N. Associations	3.00	.65	.60
74-75	13¢-31¢ Trade & Development	3.75	.80	.70
76-77	13¢-25¢ Human Settlement	3.75	.80	.75
78-79	13¢-31¢ 25th Postal Anniversary	17.50	3.75	2.25
78-79	Same, Sheetlets of 20	...	75.00	...
30	13¢ World Food Council	1.75	.30	.22
	1977			
31-82	13¢-31¢ Intellectual Property	3.75	.80	.70
33-84	13¢-25¢ Water Conference	3.50	.75	.65
35-86	13¢-31¢ Security Council	3.75	.75	.70
37-88	13¢-25¢ Racial Discrimination	3.50	.75	.75
39-90	13¢-18¢ Peaceful - Atomic Energy	3.00	.65	.60

296 298 310 312

299 301 302

UNITED NATIONS 1978

Scott's No.		MI Block of 4	F-VF NH	F-VF Used
291-93	1¢-$1 Regulars	11.00	2.25	1.75
294-95	13¢-31¢ Smallpox-Erad	3.95	.85	.75
296-97	13¢-18¢ Namibia	3.00	.60	.50
298-99	13¢-25¢ Civil Aviation Organ	3.75	.80	.75
300-01	13¢-18¢ General Assembly	3.50	.65	.60
302-03	13¢-31¢ Technical Coop.	5.50	1.10	.85
	1979			
304-07	5¢-20¢ Regulars	5.00	1.10	.85
308-09	15¢-20¢ Disaster Relief	4.25	.75	.60
310-11	15¢-31¢ Year of the Child	4.75	1.00	.85
310-11	Same, Sheetlets of 20	...	19.50	...
312-13	15¢-31¢ Namibia	3.75	.80	.70
314-15	15¢-20¢ Court of Justice	3.75	.80	.65

316 325 344 346

	1980			
316-17	15¢-31¢ New Economic Order	4.50	.90	.70
318-19	15¢-20¢ Decade for Women	3.75	.80	.65
320-21	15¢-31¢ Peacekeeping Oper.	4.25	.90	.90
322-23	15¢-31¢ 35th Anniversary	3.75	.80	.70
324	15¢-31¢ 35th Anniv. - Souv. Sht	...	.75	.75
*325-40	15¢ World Flag Series of 16	14.00	3.25	3.00

325	Turkey	329	Guinea	333	Jugoslavia	337	Madagascar
326	Luxembourg	330	Surinam	334	France	338	Cameroun
327	Fiji	331	Bangladesh	335	Venezuela	339	Rwanda
328	Vietnam	332	Mali	336	El Salvador	340	Hungary

341-42	15¢-20¢ Econ. & Social Council	3.75	.80	.70
	1981			
343	15¢ Palestinian People	1.60	.35	.30
344-45	20¢-35¢ Disabled Persons	5.25	1.15	.95
346-47	20¢-31¢ Bulgarian Mural	5.00	1.10	.80
348-49	20¢-40¢ Energy Conference	5.75	1.25	1.10
*350-65	20¢ World Flag Series of 16	22.50	5.25	5.00

350	Djibouti	354	Malta	358	Ukraine	362	U.S.
351	Sri Lanka	355	Czech.	359	Kuwait	363	Singapore
352	Bolivia	356	Thailand	360	Sudan	364	Panama
353	Eq. Guinea	357	Trinidad & T.	361	Egypt	365	Costa Rica

366-67	18¢-28¢ Volunteers	6.00	1.35	.70

371 390 394 397

	1982			
368-70	17¢-40¢ Definitives	9.75	2.10	1.35
371-72	20¢-40¢ Human Environment	8.00	1.50	1.15
373	20¢ Peaceful Use of Space	4.00	.80	.40
*374-89	20¢ World Flag Series of 16	28.50	6.00	5.50

374	Austria	378	Mozambique	382	Philippines	386	Cape Verde
375	Malaysia	379	Albania	383	Swaziland	387	Guyana
376	Seychelles	380	Dominica	384	Nicaragua	388	Belgium
377	Ireland	381	Solomon Isl.	385	Burma	389	Nigeria

390-91	20¢-28¢ Nature Conservation	6.50	1.35	.90
	1983			
392-93	20¢-40¢ Communications Year	6.75	1.40	1.00
394-95	20¢-37¢ Safety at Sea	7.25	1.50	1.25
396	20¢ World Food Program	3.50	.75	.40
397-98	20¢-28¢ Trade & Development	6.50	1.50	1.00
*399-414	20¢ World Flag Series of 16	28.50	6.50	5.75

399	U. Kingdom	403	Malawi	407	China	411	Somalia
400	Barbados	404	Byelorussia	408	Peru	412	Senegal
401	Nepal	405	Jamaica	409	Bulgaria	413	Brazil
402	Israel	406	Kenya	410	Canada	414	Sweden

415-16	20¢-40¢ Human Rights	7.50	1.60	1.35
415-16	Same, Sheetlets of 16	...	29.50	...

* Sheets of 16 will be supplied at MI 4 price.

NOTE: WORLD FLAGS ARE ISSUED IN SHEETS OF 16, EACH WITH 4 DIFFERENT BLOCKS.

417 419 421

Scott's No.		MI Block of 4	F-VF NH	F-VF Used
417-18	20¢-40¢ Population Conf.	7.00	1.50	1.00
419-20	20¢-40¢ FAO Food Day	7.50	1.65	1.10
421-22	20¢-50¢ UNESCO	9.50	1.95	1.40
423-24	20¢-50¢ Refugee Futures	8.00	1.75	1.10
*425-40	20¢ World Flag Series of 16	55.00	13.00	11.50

425	Burundi	429	Tanzania	433	Poland	437	Paraguay
426	Pakistan	430	United Arab Emirates	434	Papua New Guinea	438	Bhutan
427	Benin					439	Central Afric. Republic
428	Italy	431	Ecuador	435	Uruguay		
		432	Bahamas	436	Chile	440	Australia

441-42	20¢-35¢ Youth Year	8.00	1.75	1.10

466 468 473

1985

443	23¢ ILO-Turin Centre	3.25	.75	.50
444	50¢ U.N. Univ. in Japan	6.00	1.25	1.10
445-46	22¢-$3 Definitives	26.50	5.75	5.00
447-48	22¢-45¢ 40th Anniversary	7.50	1.50	1.35
449	22¢-45¢ 40th Anniv. Souvenir Sht.	...	2.75	1.50
*450-65	22¢ World Flag Series of 16	57.50	14.50	12.50

450	Grenada	454	Uganda	458	Liberia	462	Sultanate of Oman
451	Federal Rep. of Germ.	455	St. Thomas & Prince	459	Mauritius		
				460	Chad	463	Ghana
452	Saudi Arabia	456	USSR	461	Dominican Republic	464	Sierra Leone
453	Mexico	457	India			465	Finland

466-67	22¢-33¢ UNICEF	6.75	1.50	1.10

1986

468	22¢ Africa in Crisis	3.50	.75	.45
469-72	22¢ UN Development Program, attd.	10.75	9.75	4.50
473-74	22¢-44¢ Philately	7.50	1.65	1.10
475-76	22¢-33¢ International Peace Year	8.75	1.90	1.20
*477-92	22¢ World Flag Series of 16	56.50	13.50	8.50

477	New Zealand	481	Maldives	485	Iceland	489	Romania
478	Lao PDR	482	Ethiopia	486	Antigua & Barbuda	490	Togo
479	Burkina Faso	483	Jordan			491	Mauritania
480	Gambia	484	Zambia	487	Angola	492	Colombia
				488	Botswana		

493	22¢,33¢,39¢,44¢ WFUNA S/S	...	6.25	4.75

516 517 518

1987

494	22¢ Trygve Lie	5.50	1.20	.35
495-96	22¢-44¢ Shelter for the Homeless	9.50	1.85	.90
497-98	22¢-33¢ Life Yes/Drugs No	8.75	1.85	.90
*499-514	22¢ 1987 World Flag Series of 16	57.50	13.50	6.50

499	Comoros	503	Japan	507	Argentina	511	Bahrain
500	DPR Yemen	504	Gabon	508	Congo	512	Haiti
501	Mongolia	505	Zimbabwe	509	Niger	513	Afghanistan
502	Vanuatu	506	Iraq	510	St. Lucia	514	Greece

UNITED NATIONS 1987 (Cont.)

Scott's No.		MI Block of 4	F-VF NH	F-VF Used
515-16	22¢-39¢ U.N. Day	6.75	1.50	.90
515-16	Miniature Sheets of 12	...	23.50	...
517-18	22¢-44¢ Child Immunization	10.75	1.95	1.00

519 524 544

1988

519-20	22¢-33¢ World Without Hunger	11.00	2.25	1.00
521	3¢ UN For a Better World	1.00	.20	.15
522-23	25¢-44¢ Forestry, pair	23.75	10.75	...
522-23	Miniature Sheet of 12	...	55.00	...
524-25	25¢-50¢ Int'l. Volunteers Day	11.00	2.25	1.25
526-27	25¢-38¢ Health in Sports	12.50	2.75	1.50
*528-43	25¢ World Flag Series of 16	55.00	12.75	8.00

528	Spain	532	Yemen Arab Rep.	536	Qatar	540	Iran
529	St. Vincent & Gren.			537	Zaire	541	Tunisia
		533	Cuba	538	Norway	542	Samoa
530	Ivory Coast	534	Denmark	539	German Dem. Rep.	543	Belize
531	Lebanon	535	Libya				

544	25¢ Human Rights Anniv.	4.25	.75	.35
545	$1 Human Rights Anniv. S/S	...	2.50	1.50

1989

546-47	25¢-45¢ World Bank	13.50	3.00	1.00
548	25¢ UN Peace Keeping, Nobel Prize	7.00	1.50	.35
549	45¢ UN Headquarters	5.50	1.20	.55
550-51	25¢-36¢ World Weather Watch	13.75	3.15	.90
552-53	25¢-90¢ UN Offices Vienna, 10th Anniv.	25.00	5.75	1.15

554	Indonesia	558	South Africa	562	Honduras	566	Algeria
555	Lesotho	559	Portugal	563	Kampucea	567	Brunei
556	Guatemala	560	Morocco	564	Guinea-Bissau	568	St.Kitts-Nevis
557	Netherlands	561	Syrian Arab Republic	565	Cyprus	569	United Nations

*554-69	25¢ World Flags Series of 16	62.50	14.50	7.50
570-71	25¢-45¢ Declaration of Human Rights	...	1.80	.90
570-71	Strips of 3 with Tabs at Bottom	...	5.25	...
570-71	Miniature Sheets of 12	...	22.50	...

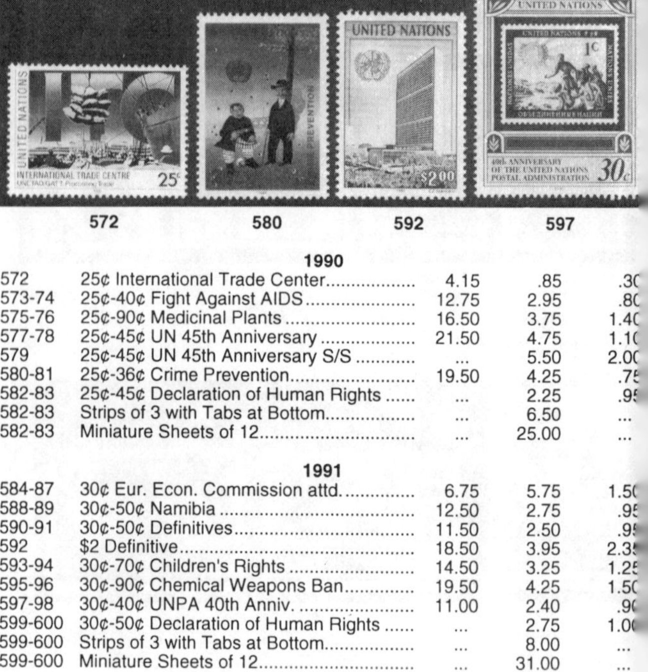

572 580 592 597

1990

572	25¢ International Trade Center	4.15	.85	.30
573-74	25¢-40¢ Fight Against AIDS	12.75	2.95	.80
575-76	25¢-90¢ Medicinal Plants	16.50	3.75	1.40
577-78	25¢-45¢ UN 45th Anniversary	21.50	4.75	1.10
579	25¢-45¢ UN 45th Anniversary S/S	...	5.50	2.00
580-81	25¢-36¢ Crime Prevention	19.50	4.25	.75
582-83	25¢-45¢ Declaration of Human Rights	...	2.25	.95
582-83	Strips of 3 with Tabs at Bottom	...	6.50	...
582-83	Miniature Sheets of 12	...	25.00	...

1991

584-87	30¢ Eur. Econ. Commission attd.	6.75	5.75	1.50
588-89	30¢-50¢ Namibia	12.50	2.75	.95
590-91	30¢-50¢ Definitives	11.50	2.50	.95
592	$2 Definitive	18.50	3.95	2.35
593-94	30¢-70¢ Children's Rights	14.50	3.25	1.25
595-96	30¢-90¢ Chemical Weapons Ban	19.50	4.25	1.50
597-98	30¢-40¢ UNPA 40th Anniv.	11.00	2.40	.90
599-600	30¢-50¢ Declaration of Human Rights	...	2.75	1.00
599-600	Strips of 3 with Tabs at Bottom	...	8.00	...
599-600	Miniature Sheets of 12	...	31.00	...

UNITED NATIONS 1992

601

611

624

ott's o.		MI Block of 4	F-VF NH	F-VF Used
	1992			
1-02	30¢-50¢ World Heritage	12.50	2.75	.95
3-04	29¢ Clean Oceans attd	4.75	1.65	.70
3-04	Miniature Sheet of 12	...	13.75	...
5-08	29¢ UNICED: Earth Summit attd.	3.50	2.85	1.50
9-10	29¢ Mission to Planet Earth attd.	18.50	7.00	3.50
9-10	Miniature Sheet of 10	...	35.00	...
1-12	29¢-50¢ Science & Technology	9.00	2.10	.95
3-15	4¢,29¢,40¢ Definitives	8.50	1.95	1.00
6-17	29¢-50¢ Declaration of Human Rights	...	2.25	.95
6-17	Strips of 3 with Tabs at Bottom	...	6.50	...
6-17	Miniature Sheet of 12	...	25.00	...
	1993			
8-19	29¢-52¢ Aging	8.50	1.95	.95
0-23	29¢ Endangered Species attd	3.25	2.75	1.75
0-23	Miniature sheet of 16	...	11.00	...
4-25	29¢-50¢ Healthy Environments	11.00	2.40	.95
6	5¢ Definitive	.95	.20	.15
7-28	29¢-35¢ Human Rights	...	1.80	.75
7-28	Strips of 3 with Tabs at Bottom	...	5.25	...
7-28	Miniature Sheets of 12	...	19.75	...
9-32	29¢ Peace attd.	3.25	2.75	1.50
3-36	29¢ Environment - Climate (8)	6.75	2.75	1.50
3-36	Miniature Sheet of 24	...	17.50	...

647-50 651

	1994			
7-38	29¢-45¢ Year of the Family	8.00	1.65	.75
9-42	29¢ Endangered Species	3.35	2.75	1.40
9-42	Miniature Sheets of 16	...	11.50	...
3	50¢ Refugees	5.50	1.10	.65
4-46	10¢,19¢,$1 Definitives	12.75	2.65	1.50
7-50	29¢ Natural Disaster, block of 4	3.50	2.85	1.95
1-52	29¢-52¢ Population Development	8.00	1.65	.95
3-54	29¢-50¢ Development Partnership	8.00	1.65	.95
	1995			
5	32¢ U.N. 50th Anniversary	3.15	.65	...
6	50¢ Social Summit	4.75	1.00	...
7-60	32¢ Endangered Species	3.25	2.65	...
1-62	32¢-55¢ Youth: Our Future	8.75	1.80	...
3-64	32¢-50¢ 50th Anniv. of U.N.	8.35	1.70	...
5	82¢ 50th Anniversary Souv. Sheet	...	1.70	...
6-67	32¢-40¢ Conference on Women	7.25	1.50	...

UNITED NATIONS AIRMAILS

C1 C5 C7

Scott's No.		MI Block of 4	F-VF NH	F-VF Used
	1951 First Airmail Issue			
C1-4	6¢-25¢ Airmail Issue	8.75	1.75	1.50
	1957-59			
C5-7	4¢,5¢,7¢ Airmails	1.75	.50	.45
	1963-69			
C8-10	6¢-13¢ Airmails	2.15	.55	.45
C11-12	15¢ & 25¢ Airmails (1964)	5.50	1.20	.75
C13	20¢ Jet Plane (1968)	1.95	.40	.30
C14	10¢ Wings & Envelopes (1969)	1.50	.30	.25
	1972-77			
C15-18	9¢-21¢	5.00	1.10	.90
C19-21	13¢-26¢ Airmails (1974)	4.50	.95	.85
C22-23	25¢ & 31¢ Airmails (1977)	5.25	1.10	.95
	U.N. IN NEW YORK 1951-94			
1-654,C1-23	Complete	...	530.00	...
1/654,C1-23	Without Souvenir Sheet #38	...	360.00	...

FOR VERY FINE, ADD 20% TO PRICE LISTED.

UNITED NATIONS - GENEVA, SWITZERLAND
DENOMINATIONS ARE GIVEN IN SWISS CURRENCY
MOST DESIGNS ARE SIMILAR TO U.N. NEW YORK ISSUES

1 4 8 14

1969-70

Scott's No.		MI Block of 4	F-VF NH	F-VF Used
1-14	5¢-10 fr. Regular Issue	47.50	10.75	9.75

16 18 22

Scott's No.		MI Block of 4	F-VF NH	F-VF Used
	1971			
15	30¢ Peaceful Use of Sea	1.15	.25	.25
16	50¢ Support for Refugees	1.75	.40	.35
17	50¢ World Food Program	1.75	.40	.40
18	75¢ U.P.U. Headquarters	2.35	.50	.60
19-20	30¢-50¢ Racial Discrimination	3.50	.75	.75
21	1.10 fr. U.N. Int'l. School	3.85	.80	.90
	1972			
22	40¢ Palace of Nations	1.65	.35	.35
23	40¢ No Nuclear Weapons	2.35	.50	.60
24	80¢ World Health Day, Man	3.00	.65	.75
25-26	40¢-80¢ Human Environment	5.75	1.25	1.25
27	1.10 fr. Econ. Comm. - Europe	5.25	1.10	1.25
28-29	40¢-60¢ Art, Maria Set Mural	5.75	1.25	1.50

36 37 43 45

Scott's No.		MI Block of 4	F-VF NH	F-VF Used
	1973			
30-31	60¢-1.10 fr. Disarmament Decade	6.50	1.40	1.50
32	60¢ Against Drug Abuse	2.50	.55	.55
33	80¢ Volunteer Program	3.00	.65	.70
34	60¢ Namibia	2.95	.65	.65
35-36	40¢-80¢ Human Rights	5.25	1.10	.85
	1974			
37-38	60¢-80¢ ILO Headquarters	5.75	1.25	1.10
39-40	30¢-60¢ U.P.U. Centenary	3.75	.80	.70
41-42	60¢-1 fr. Art, Brazil Mural	5.75	1.25	1.35
43-44	60¢-80¢ Population Year	6.25	1.35	1.10
45	1.30 fr. Law of the Sea	5.75	1.25	1.00

50 55 59 61

1975

Scott's No.		MI Block of 4	F-VF NH	F-VF Used
46-47	60¢-90¢ Peaceful - Outer Space	5.75	1.25	1.1
48-49	60¢-90¢ Women's Year	6.75	1.40	1.3
50-51	60¢-90¢ 30th Anniversary	5.75	1.25	1.1
52	60¢-90¢ 30th Anniv. - Souv. Sheet	...	1.10	1.1
53-54	50¢-1.30 fr. Namibia	7.00	1.50	1.3
55-56	60¢-70¢ Peacekeeping Force	5.75	1.25	1.0
	1976			
57	90¢ U.N. Association	5.25	1.10	.8
58	1.10 fr. Trade & Development	4.95	1.00	1.0
59-60	40¢-1.50 fr. Human Settlements	6.75	1.50	1.3
61-62	80¢-1.10 fr. 25th Postal Anniv	20.00	4.25	4.0
61-62	Same, Sheetlets of 20	...	85.00	...
63	70¢ World Food Council	3.50	.65	.5

65 71 73 77

Scott's No.		MI Block of 4	F-VF NH	F-VF Used
	1977			
64	80¢ Intellectual Property	3.50	.70	.7
65-66	80¢-1.10 fr. Water Conference	7.75	1.65	1.5
67-68	80¢-1.10 fr. Security Council	7.00	1.50	1.3
69-70	40¢-1.10 fr. Racial Discrimination	6.50	1.35	1.2
71-72	80¢-1.10 fr. Peaceful - Atomic Energy	7.00	1.50	1.3
	1978			
73	35¢ Regular, Tree of Doves	1.70	.35	.3
74-75	80¢-1.10 fr. Smallpox Eradication	7.00	1.50	1.3
76	80¢ Namibia	5.75	1.25	.6
77-78	70¢-80¢ Civil Aviation Organ	7.00	1.50	1.1
79-80	70¢-1.10 fr. General Assembly	9.00	1.75	1.2
81	80¢ Technical Cooperation	3.00	.65	.6

82 93 96

Scott's No.		MI Block of 4	F-VF NH	F-VF Used
	1979			
82-83	80¢-1.50 fr. Disaster Relief	9.00	2.00	1.7
84-85	80¢-1.10 fr. Year of the Child	6.25	1.30	1.2
84-85	Same, Sheetlets of 20	...	27.50	...
86	1.10 fr. Namibia	4.50	.95	.8
87-88	80¢-1.10 fr. Court of Justice	7.75	1.65	1.5
	1980			
89	80¢ New Economic Order	3.75	.80	.7
90-91	40¢-70¢ Decade for Women	6.50	1.35	1.1
92	1.10 fr. Peacekeeping Forces	5.00	1.00	.9
93-94	40¢-70¢ 35th Anniversary	5.75	1.20	1.1
95	40¢-70¢ 35th Anniv. - Souv. Sheet	...	1.25	1.1
96-97	40¢-70¢ Econ. & Social Council	5.25	1.00	.9

99 103 105 107

Scott's No.		MI Block of 4	F-VF NH	F-VF Used
	1981			
98	80¢ Palestinian People	4.50	.80	.6
99-100	40¢-1.50 fr. Disabled Persons	8.50	1.75	1.5
101	80¢ Art, Bulgarian Mural	4.25	.85	.6
102	1.10 fr. Energy Conference	6.00	1.25	1.2
103-04	40¢-70¢ Volunteers	6.00	1.25	1.2

1982

Scott's No.		MI Block of 4	F-VF NH	F-VF Used
105-06	30¢-1 fr. Definitives	6.25	1.35	1.20
107-08	40¢--1.20 fr. Human Environment	8.75	1.75	1.50
109-10	80¢-1 fr. Peaceful Use of Space	8.50	1.85	1.70
111-12	40¢-1.50 fr. Nature Conservation	10.75	2.40	1.95

113 114 116

1983

Scott's No.		MI Block of 4	F-VF NH	F-VF Used
113	1.20 fr. Communications Year	5.00	1.65	1.40
114-15	40¢-80¢ Safety at Sea	7.50	1.40	1.15
116	1.50 fr. World Food Program	9.00	1.85	1.85
117-18	80¢-1.10 fr. Trade & Development	10.00	2.10	2.10
119-20	40¢-1.20 fr. Human Rights	10.00	2.00	1.85
119-20	Same, Sheetlets of 16	...	35.00	...

121 131 140

1984

Scott's No.		MI Block of 4	F-VF NH	F-VF Used
121	1.20 fr. Population Conference	6.75	1.35	1.25
122-23	50¢-80¢ FAO Food Day	7.75	1.50	1.35
124-25	50¢-70¢ UNESCO	10.00	2.25	1.75
126-27	35¢-1.50 fr. Refugee Futures	9.50	2.00	1.75
128	1.20 fr. Youth Year	8.00	1.65	1.40

1985

Scott's No.		MI Block of 4	F-VF NH	F-VF Used
129-30	80¢-1.20 fr. ILO - Turin Centre	14.75	2.85	1.50
131-32	50¢-80¢ U.N. Univ. in Japan	9.00	1.95	1.00
133-34	20¢-1.20 fr. Definitives	11.00	2.40	1.00
135-36	50¢-70¢ 40th Anniversary	9.00	2.00	.80
137	50¢-70¢ 40th Anniv. Souvenir Sheet	...	2.75	1.50
138-39	50¢-1.20 fr. UNICEF	17.50	3.85	1.50

140 145 154 160

1986

Scott's No.		MI Block of 4	F-VF NH	F-VF Used
140	1.40 fr. Africa in Crisis	11.50	2.50	1.00
141-44	35¢ UN Development Program, attd	13.50	11.75	6.75
145	5¢ Definitive	.80	.20	.15
146-47	50¢-80¢ Philately	11.00	2.50	.95
148-49	45¢-1.40 fr. Int'l. Peace Year	14.50	3.25	1.40
150	35¢,45¢,50¢,70¢ WFUNA S/S	...	6.00	2.50

1987

Scott's No.		MI Block of 4	F-VF NH	F-VF Used
151	1.40 fr. Trygve Lie	9.00	2.00	1.25
152-53	90¢-1.40 fr. Bands/Sphere Definitives	12.50	2.75	2.00
154-55	50¢-90¢ Shelter for the Homeless	10.00	2.25	1.25
156-57	80¢-1.20 fr. Life Yes/Drugs No	13.50	2.75	1.75
158-59	35¢-50¢ U.N. Day	9.50	1.95	.80
158-59	Miniature Sheets of 12	...	24.50	...
160-61	90¢-1.70 fr. Child Immunization	22.50	4.50	2.25

UNITED NATIONS - GENEVA, SWITZERLAND

164 171 173 178

1988

Scott's No.		MI Block of 4	F-VF NH	F-VF Used
162-63	35¢-1.40 fr. World Without Hunger	14.00	2.85	1.65
164	50¢ UN for a Better World	4.75	.95	.50
165-66	50¢-1.10 fr. Forest Conservation, pair	25.00	11.50	...
165-66	Miniature Sheet of 12	...	57.50	...
167-68	80¢-90¢ Int'l. Volunteers Day	13.50	2.75	1.60
169-70	50¢-1.40 fr. Health in Sports	16.00	3.00	1.70
171	90¢ Human Rights 40th Anniv.	7.50	1.65	.75
172	2 fr. Human Rights 40th Anniv. S/S	...	3.85	2.50

1989

Scott's No.		MI Block of 4	F-VF NH	F-VF Used
173-74	80¢-1.40 fr. World Bank	19.50	4.15	2.00
175	90¢ Peace Keeping, Nobel Prize	8.50	1.75	.75
176-77	90¢-1.10 fr. World Weather Watch	20.00	4.25	1.65
178-79	50¢-2 fr. UN Offices in Vienna,10th Anniv	20.00	4.75	1.50
180-81	35¢-80¢ Declaration of Human Rights	...	2.25	.75
180-81	Strips of 3 with Tabs at Bottom	...	6.50	...
180-81	Miniature Sheets of 12	...	26.50	...

182 184 199

1990

Scott's No.		MI Block of 4	F-VF NH	F-VF Used
182	1.50 fr. International Trade Center	16.50	3.50	1.00
183	5 fr. Definitive	36.50	7.50	4.00
184-85	50¢-80¢ Fight Against AIDS	16.00	3.50	1.00
186-87	90¢-1.40 fr. Medicinal Plants	19.75	4.35	1.85
188-89	90¢-1.10 fr. UN 45th Anniversary	21.50	4.50	1.75
190	90¢-1.10 fr. UN 45th Anniversary S/S	...	4.75	3.25
191-92	50¢-2 fr. Crime Prevention	21.50	4.75	2.25
193-94	35¢-90¢ Declaration of Human Rights	...	2.50	1.15
193-94	Strips of 3 with Tabs at Bottom	...	7.00	...
193-94	Miniature Sheets of 12	...	27.50	...

1991

Scott's No.		MI Block of 4	F-VF NH	F-VF Used
195-98	90¢ Eur. Econ. Commission, attd	8.75	7.50	3.00
199-200	70¢-90¢ Namibia	18.00	3.75	1.40
201-02	80¢-1.50 fr. Definitives	20.75	4.35	1.95
203-04	80¢-1.10 fr. Children's Rights	19.50	3.95	1.65
205-06	80¢-1.40 fr. Chemical Weapons Ban	21.00	4.25	1.80
207-08	50¢-1.60 fr. UNPA 40th Anniv	21.50	4.50	1.75
209-10	50¢-90¢ Human Rights	...	3.00	1.25
209-10	Strips of 3 with Tabs at Bottom	...	8.75	...
209-10	Miniature Sheets of 12	...	33.75	...

211 222 232

1992

Scott's No.		MI Block of 4	F-VF NH	F-VF Used
211-12	50¢-1.10 fr. World Heritage	19.75	4.25	1.50
213	3 fr. Definitive	24.50	5.00	2.75
214-15	80¢ Clean Oceans, attd	8.00	3.50	1.40
214-15	Miniature Sheet of 12	...	21.00	...
216-19	75¢ UNICED: Earth Summit, attd	6.00	5.00	2.50
220-21	1.10 fr. Mission to Planet Earth, attd	10.75	5.00	2.15
220-21	Miniature Sheet of 10	...	25.00	...
222-23	90¢-1.60 fr. Science & Technology	19.50	4.35	2.25
224-25	50¢-90¢ Human Rights	...	3.00	1.20
224-25	Strips of 3 with Tabs at Bottom	...	8.75	...
224-25	Miniature Sheets of 12	...	33.75	...

UNITED NATIONS - GENEVA, SWITZERLAND

Scott's No.		MI Block of 4	F-VF NH	F-VF Used
	1993			
226-27	50¢-1.60 fr. Aging	17.50	3.75	1.50
228-31	80¢ Endangered Species, attd	6.75	5.95	2.50
228-31	Miniature Sheet of 16	...	23.75	...
232-33	60¢-1 fr. Healthy Environments	13.50	2.85	1.25
234-35	50¢-90¢ Declaration of Human Rights	...	3.00	1.20
234-35	Strips of 3 with Tabs at Bottom	...	8.75	...
234-35	Miniature Sheets of 12	...	33.75	...
236-39	60¢ Peace, attd	4.50	3.50	1.75
240-43	1.10 fr. Environment - Climate (8)	14.50	6.50	3.00
240-43	Miniature Sheet of 24	...	37.50	...

244 255 258

Scott's No.		MI Block of 4	F-VF NH	F-VF Used
	1994			
244-45	80¢-1 fr. Year of the Family	12.50	2.65	1.25
246-49	80¢ Endangered Species	5.50	4.75	2.50
246-49	Miniature Sheet of 16	...	19.75	...
250	1.20 fr. Refugees	9.00	1.85	.80
251-54	60¢ Natural Disaster, Block of 4	4.75	3.85	1.85
255-57	60¢,80¢,1.80 fr. Definitives	24.50	4.95	3.00
258-59	60¢-80¢ Population Development	9.95	2.10	1.35
260-61	80¢-1 fr. Development Partnership	13.95	2.80	1.50
1-261	**U.N. in Geneva, 1969-94**	**...**	**310.00**	**...**
	1995			
262	80¢ U.N. 50th Anniversary	6.00	1.25	...
263	1 fr Social Summit	7.50	1.55	...
264-67	80¢ Endangered Species	5.95	4.95	...
268-69	80¢ 1 fr Youth: Our Future	13.75	2.80	...
270-71	60¢-180 fr 50th Anniv. of U.N.	16.50	3.35	...
272	2.40 fr 50th Anniv. Souv. Sheet	...	3.35	...
273	60¢-1 fr Conference on Women	12.00	2.50	...

UNITED NATIONS - VIENNA, AUSTRIA
DENOMINATIONS ARE GIVEN IN AUSTRIAN CURRENCY

5 8 9 12

Scott's No.		MI Block of 4	F-VF NH	F-VF Used
	1979 Regular Issue			
1-6	50¢-10¢ Regulars	9.00	2.00	2.00
	1980			
7	4s New Economic Order 27.50 (T)	12.50 (B)	1.00	1.10
8	2.50s Regular, Dove	1.85	.40	.30
9-10	4s-6s Decade for Women	5.50	1.10	1.10
11	6s Peacekeeping Forces	4.75	1.00	1.00
12-13	4s-6s 35th Anniversary	5.50	1.20	1.25
14	4s-6s 35th Anniv. - Souv. Sheet	...	1.00	1.00
15-16	4s-6s Econ. & Social Council	5.75	1.25	1.20

21 22 27

Scott's No.		MI Block of 4	F-VF NH	F-VF Used
	1981			
17	4s Palestinian People	3.50	.75	.65
18-19	4s-6s Disabled Persons	4.50	1.00	1.00
20	6s Art, Bulgarian Mural	4.00	.80	.75
21	7.50s Energy Conference	4.50	.95	.95
22-23	5s-7s Volunteers	8.00	1.60	1.60

UNITED NATIONS - VIENNA, AUSTRIA

Scott's No.		MI Block of 4	F-VF NH	F-VF Used
	1982			
24	3s Definitive	2.25	.50	.35
25-26	5s-7s Human Environment	10.50	2.00	1.50
27	5s Peaceful Use of Space	4.50	1.00	.60
28-29	5s-7s Nature Conservation	8.25	1.75	1.25

30 31 33

Scott's No.		MI Block of 4	F-VF NH	F-VF Used
	1983			
30	4s Communications Year	4.00	.80	.50
31-32	4s-6s Safety at Sea	6.00	1.35	1.10
33-34	5s-7s World Food Program	5.50	1.20	1.10
35-36	4s-8.50s Trade & Development	5.50	1.20	1.10
37-38	5s-7s Human Rights	9.75	2.10	1.50
37-38	Same, Sheetlets of 16	...	32.50	...
	1984			
39	7s Population Conference	4.75	1.00	.85
40-41	4.50-6s FAO Food Day	8.35	1.70	1.50
42-43	3.50-15s UNESCO	10.75	2.25	2.00
44-45	4.50-8.50s Refugee Futures	9.00	2.00	1.50
46-47	3.50-6.50s Youth Year	8.00	1.75	1.50

48 49 57

Scott's No.		MI Block of 4	F-VF NH	F-VF Used
	1985			
48	7.50s ILO - Turin Centre	5.75	1.25	.85
49	8.50s U.N. Univ. in Japan	7.00	1.50	.85
50-51	4.50-15s Definitives	15.75	3.35	2.00
52-53	6.50-8.50s 40th Anniversary	9.50	2.00	1.75
54	6.50-8.50 40th Anniv. Souvenir Sht	...	3.50	3.25
55-56	4s-6s UNICEF	14.50	2.95	1.50
	1986			
57	8s Africa in Crisis	9.50	1.95	.75
58-61	4.50s UN Dev. Program, attd	15.00	13.50	2.00
62-63	3.5s-6.5s Philately	12.00	2.50	1.00
64-65	5s-6s Int'l. Peace Year	13.00	2.75	1.75
66	4s-7s WFUNA S/S	...	6.75	5.00

67 70 84

Scott's No.		MI Block of 4	F-VF NH	F-VF Used
	1987			
67	8s Trygve Lie	8.00	1.65	.90
68-69	4s-9.50s Shelter for Homeless	12.00	2.50	1.75
70-71	5s-8s Life Yes/Drugs No	10.50	2.35	2.00
72-73	2s-17s Definitives	13.50	3.00	2.00
74-75	5s-6s U.N. Day	12.50	2.75	1.50
74-75	Miniature Sheet of 12	...	17.50	...
76-77	4s-9.50s Child Immunization	15.00	3.25	1.75
	1988			
78-79	4s-6s World Without Hunger	10.50	2.25	1.25
80-81	4s-5s Forest Conservation, pair	24.50	10.75	...
80-81	Miniature Sheet of 12	...	62.50	...
82-83	6s-7s Int'l. Volunteers Day	15.75	3.25	1.50
84-85	6s-8s Health in Sports	15.75	3.25	2.00
86	5s Human Rights 40th Anniv	6.75	1.30	.65
87	11s Human Rights 40th Anniv. S/S	...	2.75	2.35

UNITED NATIONS - VIENNA, AUSTRIA

90 93 101 121

Scott's No.		MI Block of 4	F-VF NH	F-VF Used
	1989			
88-89	5.50s-8s World Bank	17.00	3.50	1.75
90	6s Peace Keeping, Nobel Prize	7.25	1.50	.80
91-92	4s-9.50s World Weather Watch	21.00	4.65	1.70
93-94	5s-7.50s UN Offices in Vienna, 10th Anniv.	25.00	5.75	1.50
95-96	4s-6s Human Rights 40th Anniv	...	2.50	1.20
95-96	Strips of 3 with Tabs at Bottom	...	7.50	...
95-96	Miniature Sheets of 12	...	29.50	...
	1990			
97	12s International Trade Center	12.00	2.50	1.50
98	1.50s Definitive	2.00	.45	.20
99-100	5s-11s Fight Against AIDS	19.00	4.00	2.10
101-02	4.5s-9.5s Medicinal Plants	19.00	4.00	1.95
103-04	7s-9s UN 45th Anniversary	19.00	4.00	2.10
105	7s-9s UN 45th Anniversary S/S	...	5.00	3.00
106-07	6s-8s Crime Prevention	20.00	4.25	1.85
108-09	4.5s-7s Human Rights	...	3.00	1.20
108-09	Strips of 3 with Tabs at Bottom	...	8.95	...
108-09	Miniature Sheets of 12	...	35.00	...
	1991			
110-13	5s Eur. Econ. Commission, attd	7.00	5.85	2.50
114-15	6s-9.50s Namibia	21.75	4.50	1.50
116	20s Definitives	18.75	4.00	1.95
117-18	7s-9s Children's Rights	16.75	3.75	1.60
119-20	5s-10s Chemical Weapons Ban	17.75	4.00	1.50
121-22	5s-8s UNPA 40th Anniv	17.75	4.00	1.20
123-24	4.50s-7s Human Rights	...	3.00	1.20
123-24	Strips of 3 with Tabs at Bottom	...	8.95	...
123-24	Miniature Sheets of 12	...	35.00	...
	1992			
125-26	5s-9s World Heritage	18.50	4.00	1.50
127-28	7s Clean Oceans, attd	8.00	3.50	1.50
127-28	Miniature Sheet of 12	...	24.50	...
129-32	5.5s UNICED: Earth Summit, attd	7.50	6.50	2.50
133-34	10s Mission to Planet Earth, attd	14.75	6.75	2.50
133-34	Miniature Sheet of 10	...	32.50	...
135-36	5.5s-7s Science & Technology	15.00	3.25	1.35
137-38	5.5s-7s Definitives	15.00	3.25	1.35
139-40	6s-10s Human Rights	...	3.50	1.65
139-40	Strips of 3 with Tabs at Bottom	...	9.75	...
139-40	Miniature Sheets of 12	...	38.50	...
	1993			
141-42	5.5s-7s Aging	14.50	3.00	1.25
143-46	7s Endangered Species, attd	8.00	6.50	2.75
143-46	Miniature Sheet of 16	...	25.00	...
147-48	6s-10s Healthy Environments	15.00	3.35	1.50
149	13s Definitive	11.50	2.50	1.25
150-51	5s-6s Human Rights	...	2.75	1.25
150-51	Strips of 3 with Tabs at Bottom	...	8.00	...
150-51	Miniature Sheets of 12	...	31.50	...
152-55	5.5s Peace, attd	5.75	4.65	2.50
156-59	7s Environment - Climate (8)	14.00	6.50	3.00
156-59	Miniature Sheet of 24	...	37.50	...

162-65 166

UNITED NATIONS - VIENNA, AUSTRIA

Scott's No.		MI Block of 4	F-VF NH	F-VF Used
	1994			
160-61	5.5s-8s Year of the Family	11.50	2.50	1.50
162-65	7s Endangered Species	6.25	5.00	2.75
162-65	Miniature Sheet of 16	...	21.00	...
166	12s Refugees	10.95	2.25	1.25
167-69	50g,4s,30s Definitives	29.75	6.25	2.50
170-73	6s Natural Disaster, Block of 4	5.35	4.35	2.40
174-75	5.50s-7s Population Development	11.50	2.30	1.25
176-77	6s-7s Development Partnership	11.75	2.35	1.35
1-177	**U.N. in Vienna, 1979-94**	...	**245.00**	...
	1995			
178	7s U.N. 50th Anniversary	6.50	1.35	...
179	14s Social Summit	13.00	2.65	...
180-83	7s Endangered Species	6.50	5.35	...
184-85	6s-7s Youth: Our Future	12.00	2.45	...
186-87	7s-10s 50th Anniv. of U.N.	16.50	3.40	...
188	17s 50th Anniv. Souv. Sheet	...	3.40	...
189-90	5-50s-6s Conference on Women	11.00	2.30	...

UNITED NATIONS POSTAL STATIONERY

Scott's No.		Mint Entire
	ENVELOPE ENTIRES	
U1	3¢ Emblem (1953)	.90
U2	4¢ Emblem (1953)	.75
U3	5¢ Wthr. Vane (1963)	.30
U4	6¢ Wthr. Vane (1969)	.30
U5	8¢ Hdqtrs (1973)	.50
U6	10¢ Hdqtrs (1975)	.50
U7	22¢ Bouquet (1985)	7.00
U8	25¢ NY Headqtrs ('89)	3.00
U9	25¢+4¢ Schg on U8 (91)	2.25
	AIRMAIL ENVELOPE ENTIRES	
UC3	7¢ Flag (1959)	2.75
UC6	8¢ Emblem (1963)	.75
UC8	10¢ Emblem (1969)	.50
UC10	11¢ Birds (1973)	.60
UC11	13¢ Globe (1975)	.55
	AIRLETTER SHEETS	
UC1	10¢ Air Letter (1952)	31.50
UC2	10¢ "Air Letter/Aero..." White Border (1954)	10.00
UC2a	10¢ Same, No White Border (1958)	7.50
UC4	10¢ Flag (1960)	.90
UC5	11¢ Gull, blue (1961)	1.50
UC5a	11¢ Greenish (1965)	2.75
UC7	13¢ Plane (1968)	.55
UC9	15¢ Globe (1972)	.90
UC12	18¢ Hdqtrs (1975)	.75
UC13	22¢ Birds (1977)	.90
UC14	30¢ Paper Airplane (82)	2.25
UC15	30¢+6¢ Surcharge (87)	17.50
UC16	39¢ NY Headqrtrs (89)	2.95
UC17	39¢+6¢ Surcharge on UC16 (1991)	2.25
UC18	45¢ Winged Hand ('92)	1.50
	GENEVA AIRLETTER SHEET	
UC1	65¢ Plane (1969)	2.25
	VIENNA ENVELOPE ENTIRES	
U1	6s Vienna Centre (95)	1.95
U2	7s Landscape (1995)	2.10
	VIENNA AIRLETTER SHEET	
UC1	9s Bird (1982)	3.95
UC2	9s + 2s Surchrg (86)	35.00
UC3	11s Birds in Flight (87)	3.75
UC4	11s + 1s Surchrg (92)	13.50
UC5	12s Vienna Offices (92)	3.00

Scott's No.		Mint Entire
	POSTAL CARDS	
UX1	2¢ Hdqtrs (1952)	.20
UX2	3¢ Hdqtrs (1958)	.65
UX3	4¢ Map (1963)	.20
UX4	5¢ Post Horn (1969)	.25
UX5	6¢ "UN" (1973)	.28
UX6	6¢ "UN" (1975)	.40
UX7	9¢ Emblem (1977)	.50
UX8	13¢ Letters (1982)	.45
UX9-13	15¢ NY HQ Views(89)	4.50
UX14-18	36¢ NY HQ Views (1989)	6.75
UX19	40¢ UN HQ (1992)	1.50
	AIRMAIL POSTAL CARDS	
UXC1	4¢ Wing (1957)	.25
UXC2	4¢ + 1¢ Surch (1959)	.60
UXC3	5¢ Wing (1959)	1.35
UXC4	6¢ Space (1963)	.55
UXC5	11¢ Earth (1966)	.50
UXC6	13¢ Earth (1968)	.55
UXC7	8¢ Planes (1969)	.35
UXC8	9¢ Wings (1972)	.40
UXC9	15¢ Planes (1972)	.60
UXC10	11¢ Clouds (1975)	.50
UXC11	18¢ Pathways ('75)	.55
UXC12	28¢ Flying Mailman(82)	.70
	GENEVA POSTAL CARDS	
UX1	20¢ Post Horn (1969)	1.00
UX2	30¢ Earth (1969)	1.50
UX3	40¢ Emblem (1977)	.70
UX4	70¢ Ribbons (1977)	1.15
UX5	50¢ "UN" Emblm (85)	4.00
UX6	70¢ Peace Dove(85)	6.00
UX7	70¢ + 10¢ Surch (86)	2.65
UX8	90¢ Gen Offices (92)	1.50
UX9	50¢+10¢ Surch (93)	1.75
UX10	80¢ Palais des Nations (1993)	2.50
	VIENNA POSTAL CARDS	
UX1	3s Branch (1982)	2.00
UX2	5s Glove (1982)	1.75
UX3	4s Emblem (1985)	4.00
UX4	5s + 1s Surch (1992)	5.50
UX5	6s Regschek Paint(92)	3.00
UX6	5s Peoples (1993)	1.95
UX7	6s Donaupark (1993)	1.50
UX8	5s + 50g (1994)	1.25

12

Scott #	Description	Separate Covers	One Cover
	NEW YORK		
	1951		
1-11	1¢-$1 Regular Issue 10/24+11/16	75.00	60.00
	1952		
12	5¢ Charter 10/24/52	...	1.10
13-14	3¢-5¢ Human Rights 12/10/52	1.65	1.40
	1953		
15-16	3¢-5¢ Refugee Family 4/24/53	2.25	1.75
17-18	3¢-5¢ Univ. Postal Union 6/12/53	2.50	2.00
19-20	3¢-5¢ Tech. Assistance 10/24/53	1.60	1.20
21-22	3¢-5¢ Human Rights 12/10/54	6.95	5.75
	1954		
23-24	3¢-8¢ F.A.O. 2/11/54	1.85	1.50
25-26	3¢-8¢ Int'l. Labor Organ. 5/10/54	2.50	2.00
27-28	3¢-8¢ U.N. Euro. Office 10/25/54	3.50	3.00
29-30	3¢-8¢ Human Rights 12/10/54	6.95	5.75
	1955		
31-32	3¢-8¢ Int'l. Civil Aviat. 2/9/55	3.50	3.00
33-34	3¢-8¢ UNESCO Emblem 5/11/55	1.80	1.50
35-37	3¢-8¢ 10th Anniv. 10/24/55	2.50	2.00
38	3¢-8¢ 10th Anniversary S/S 10/24/55	...	75.00
39-40	3¢-8¢ Human Rights 12/9/55	1.80	1.60
	1956		
41-42	3¢-8¢ I.T.U 2/17/56	1.80	1.60
43-44	3¢-8¢ W.H.O. 4/6/56	1.80	1.60
45-46	3¢-8¢ General Assembly 10/24/56	1.00	.60
47-48	3¢-8¢ Human Rights 12/10/56	1.00	.60
	1957		
49-50	3¢-8¢ Meteor Org. 1/28/57	1.00	.60
51-52	3¢-8¢ U.N. Emerg. Force 4/8/57	1.00	.60
55-56	3¢-8¢ Security Council 10/24/57	1.00	.60
57-58	3¢-8¢ Human Rights 12/10/57	1.00	.60
	1958		
59-60	3¢-8¢ Atomic Ener. Agency 2/10/58	1.00	.60
61-62	3¢-8¢ Central Hall London 4/14/58	1.00	.60
63-64	4¢-8¢ Reg. U.N. Seal 6/2 & 10/24	1.00	.60
65-66	4¢-8¢ Economic & Social C. 10/24	1.00	.60
67-68	4¢-8¢ Human Rights 12/10/58	1.00	.60
	1959		
69-70	4¢-8¢ Flushing Meadows 3/30/59	1.00	.60
71-72	4¢-8¢ Econ. Comm. Europe 5/18/59	1.00	.60
73-74	4¢-8¢ Trusteeship Coun. 10/23/59	1.00	.60
75-76	4¢-8¢ World Refugee Year 12/10/59	1.00	.60
	1960		
77-78	4¢-8¢ Chalot Palace Paris 2/29/60	1.00	.60
79-80	4¢-8¢ ECAFE 4/11/90	1.00	.60
81-82	4¢-8¢ World Forestry Cong. 8/29/60	1.00	.60
83-84	4¢-8¢ 15th Anniversary 10/24/60	1.00	.60
85	4¢-8¢ 15th Anniv. S/S 10/24/60	...	3.75
85v	Same broken "v" 10/24	...	120.00
86-87	4¢-8¢ International Bank 12/9/60	1.00	.60
	1961		
88-89	4¢-8¢ Court of Justice 2/13/61	1.00	.60
90-91	4¢-7¢ Monetary Fund 4/17/61	1.00	.60
92	30¢ Regular Flags 6/5/61	...	1.00
93-94	4¢-11¢ Econ. C. Lat. Am. 9/18/61	1.00	.60
95-96	4¢-11¢ Econ. Comm. Africa 10/24/61	1.00	.60
97-99	3¢-13¢ Children's Fund 12/14/61	1.50	.80

Scott #	Description	Separate Covers	One Cover
	NEW YORK		
	1962		
100-01	4¢-7¢ House & Urban Dev. 2/28/62	1.00	.60
102-03	4¢-11¢ Wld. Health Organ. 3/30/62	1.00	.60
104-07	1¢-4¢ Regulars 5/25/62	2.00	1.20
108-09	5¢-15¢ Hammarskjold 9/17/62	1.00	.60
110-11	4¢-11¢ Oper. in Congo 10/24/62	1.00	.60
112-13	4¢-11¢ Outer Space 12/3/62	1.00	.60
	1963		
114-15	5¢-11¢ Science & Tech. 2/4/63	1.00	.60
116-17	5¢-11¢ Freedom from Hung. 3/22/63	1.00	.60
118	25¢ UNTEA 10/1/63	...	.85
119-20	5¢-11¢ General Assembly 11/4/63	1.00	.60
121-22	5¢-11¢ Human Rights 12/10/63	1.00	.60
	1964		
123-24	5¢-11¢ Maritime Organ. 1/13/64	1.00	.60
125-27	2¢-10¢ Regulars 5/29/64	1.50	.90
128	50¢ Reg. Weather Vane 3/6/64	...	1.35
129-30	5¢-11¢ Trade & Develop. 6/15/64	1.00	.60
131-32	5¢-11¢ Control Narcotics 9/21/64	1.00	.60
133	5¢ End Nuclear Tests 10/23/64	...	.50
134-36	4¢-11¢ Education Prog. 12/7/64	1.10	.85
	1965		
137-38	5¢-11¢ Development Fund 1/25/65	1.00	.60
139-40	5¢-11¢ Peace Force Cyprus 3/4/65	1.00	.60
141-42	5¢-11¢ Telecomm. Union 5/17/65	1.00	.60
143-44	5¢-15¢ 20th Anniv. ICY 5/26/65	1.00	.60
145	5¢-12¢ 20th Anniv. S/S 5/26/65	...	1.50
146-49	1¢-25¢ Regulars 9/20 & 10/25/65	3.00	2.25
150	$1 Regular Emblem 3/25/65	...	2.95
151-53	4¢-11¢ Population 11/29/65	1.50	.90
	1966		
154-55	5¢-15¢ Fed. U.N. Assoc. 1/31/66	1.00	.60
156-57	5¢-11¢ W.H.O. Headqtrs. 5/26/66	1.00	.60
158-59	5¢-11¢ Coffee Agreement 9/19/66	1.00	.60
160	15¢ Peacekpg. Obsrv. 10/24/66	...	.50
161-63	4¢-11¢ UNICEF 11/28/66	1.50	.90
	1967		
164-65	5¢-11¢ Develop. Program 1/23/67	1.00	.60
166-67	1½¢-5¢ Regulars 3/17 & 1/23/67	1.00	.60
168-69	5¢-11¢ Independ. Nations 3/17/67	1.00	.60
170-74	4¢-15¢ Expo '67 Montreal 4/28/67	2.65	2.00
175-76	5¢-15¢ Tourist Year 6/19/67	1.00	.60
177-78	6¢-13¢ Disarmament 10/24/67	1.00	.60
179	6¢ Chagall S/S 11/17/67	...	1.00
180	6¢ Chagall Window 11/17/67	...	.50
	1968		
181-82	6¢-13¢ Secretariat 1/16/68	1.00	.60
183-84	6¢-75¢ Art, Starcke Stat. 3/1/68	5.75	5.00
185-86	6¢-13¢ Industrial Dev. 4/18/68	1.00	.60
187	6¢ Regular, U.N. Hdqtrs. 5/31/68	...	.50
188-89	6¢-20¢ Wld. Weather Watch 9/19/68	1.00	.60
190-91	6¢-13¢ Human Rights 11/22/68	1.00	.65
	1969		
192-93	6¢-13¢ Train. & Res. Inst. 2/10/69	1.00	.60
194-95	6¢-15¢ U.N. Bldg., Chile 3/14/69	1.00	.60
196	13¢ Regular U.N. & Emblem 3/14/69	...	.50
197-98	6¢-13¢ Peace Through Law 4/21/69	1.00	.60
199-200	6¢-20¢ Labor & Dev. 6/5/69	1.00	.65
201-02	6¢-13¢ Tunisian Mosaic 11/21/69	1.00	.60

175-76

UNITED NATIONS FIRST DAY COVERS

254-55

cott #	Description NEW YORK	Separate Covers	One Cover
	1970		
03-04	6¢-25¢ Art, Peace Bell 3/13/70	1.00	.70
05-06	6¢-13¢ Mekong Basin Dev. 3/13/70	1.00	.60
07-08	6¢-13¢ Fight Cancer 5/22/70	1.00	.60
09-11	6¢-25¢ 25th Anniversary 6/26/70	1.50	1.20
12	6¢-25¢ 25th Anniv. S/S 6/26/70	...	1.25
13-14	6¢-13¢ Peace, Just. & Pro. 5/20/70	1.00	.60
	1971		
15	6¢ Peaceful Uses of the Sea 1/25/71	...	.50
16-17	6¢-13¢ Support Refugees 3/2/71	1.00	.60
18	13¢ World Food Program 4/13/71	...	.50
19	20¢ U.P.U. Headquarters 5/28/71	...	.60
20-21	8¢-13¢ Racial Discrim. 9/21/71	1.00	.60
22-23	8¢-60¢ Regulars 10/22/71	2.25	1.85
24-25	8¢-21¢ U.N. Int'l. School 11/19/71	1.00	.75
	1972		
26	95¢ Regular, Letter 1/5/72	...	2.50
27	8¢ No Nuclear Weapons 2/14/72	...	.50
28	15¢ World Health Day, Man. 4/7/72	...	.50
29-30	8¢-15¢ Human Environment 6/5/72	1.00	.60
31	21¢ Economic Comm. Europe 9/11/72	...	.65
32-33	8¢-15¢ Maria Sert. Mural 11/17/72	1.00	.60
	1973		
34-35	8¢-15¢ Disarmament Decade 3/9/73	1.00	.60
36-37	8¢-15¢ Against Drug Abuse 4/13/73	1.00	.60
38-39	8¢-21¢ Volunteer Program 5/25/73	1.00	.70
40-41	8¢-15¢ Namibia 10/1/73	1.00	.60
42-43	8¢-21¢ Human Rights 11/16/73	1.00	.70
	1974		
44-45	10¢-21¢ ILO Headquarters 1/11/74	1.05	.85
46	10¢ U.P.U. Centenary 3/22/74	...	.50
47-48	10¢-18¢ Art, Brazil Mural 5/6/74	1.00	.70
49-51	2¢-18¢ Regualrs 6/10/74	1.50	.90
52-53	10¢-18¢ Population Year 10/18/74	1.10	.85
54-55	10¢-25¢ Law of the Sea 11/22/74	1.10	.95
	1975		
56-57	10¢-26¢ Peaceful-O. Space 3/14/75	1.15	1.00
58-59	10¢-18¢ Women's Year 5/9/75	1.00	.80
60-61	10¢-26¢ 30th Anniversary 6/26/75	1.05	.90
62	10¢-26¢ 30th Anniv. S/S 6/26/75	...	1.40
63-64	10¢-18¢ Namibia 9/22/75	1.00	.80
65-66	13¢-26¢ Peacekpg. Force 11/21/75	1.15	.95
	1976		
267-71	3¢-50¢ Regulars 1/6 & 11/19/76	2.75	2.25
272-73	13¢-26¢ U.N. Assoc. 3/12/76	1.35	1.15
274-75	13¢-31¢ Trade & Dev. 4/23/76	1.30	1.10
276-77	13¢-25¢ Human Settlement 5/28/76	1.15	1.00
278-79	13¢-31¢ 25th Postal Ann. 10/8/76	8.75	7.75
280	13¢ World Food Council 11/18/76	...	.50
	1977		
281-82	13¢-31¢ Intellect Prop. 3/11/77	1.30	1.00
283-84	13¢-25¢ Water Conference 4/22/77	1.25	1.00
285-86	13¢-31¢ Security Council 5/27/77	1.35	1.10
287-88	13¢-25¢ Racial Discrim. 9/19/77	1.25	1.00
289-90	13¢-18¢ Atomic Energy 11/18/77	1.00	.85
	1978		
291-93	1¢-$1 Regulars 1/27/78	3.50	3.00
294-95	13¢-31¢ Smallpox-Erad. 3/31/78	1.30	1.10
296-97	13¢-18¢ Namibia 5/5/78	1.00	.80
298-99	25¢ ICAO 6/12/78	1.20	1.00
300-01	13¢-18¢ General Assembly 9/15/78	1.00	.85
302-03	13¢-31¢ Technical Coop. 11/17/78	1.40	1.10

Scott #	Description NEW YORK	Separate Covers	One Cover
	1979		
304-07	5¢-20¢ Regulars 1/19/79	1.85	1.40
308-09	15¢-20¢ Disaster Relief 3/9/79	1.25	1.00
310-11	15¢-31¢ Yr. of the Child 5/4/79	3.50	2.85
312-13	15¢-31¢ Namibia 10/5/79	1.40	1.15
314-15	15¢-20¢ Court of Justice 11/9/79	1.25	1.00
	1980		
316-17	15¢-31¢ New Econ. Order 1/11/80	1.50	1.25
318-19	15¢-20¢ Decade for Women 3/7/80	1.20	1.00
320-21	15¢-31¢ Peacekpg. Oper. 5/16/80	1.50	1.25
322-23	15¢-31¢ 35th Anniversary 6/26/80	1.45	1.25
324	15¢-31¢ 35th Anniv. S/S 6/26/80	...	1.30
325-40	15¢ 1980 Flag Series 9/26/80	8.50	...
341-42	15¢-20¢ Econ. & Soc. 11/21/80	1.15	1.00
	1981		
343	15¢ Palestinian People 1/30/81	...	.70
344-45	20¢-35¢ Disabled Persons 3/6/81	1.60	1.35
346-47	20¢-31¢ Bulgarian Mural 4/15/81	1.50	1.25
348-49	20¢-40¢ Energy Conf. 5/29/81	1.75	1.50
350-65	20¢ 1981 Flag Series 9/25/81	12.00	...
366-67	18¢-28¢ Volunteers 11/13/81	1.40	1.15
	1982		
368-70	17¢-40¢ Definitives 1/22/82	2.35	2.10
371-72	20¢-40¢ Human Environ. 3/19/82	1.80	1.50
373	20¢ Peaceful, Use of Space 6/11/82	...	.80
374-89	20¢ 1982 Wld. Flag Series 9/24/82	11.50	...
390-91	20¢-28¢ Nature Conserv. 11/19/82	1.65	1.40
	1983		
392-93	20¢-40¢ Commun. Year 1/28/83	1.95	1.60
394-95	20¢-37¢ Safety at Sea 3/18/83	2.00	1.75
396	20¢ World Food Program 4/22/83	...	.75
397-98	20¢-28¢ Trade & Develop. 6/6/83	1.50	1.30
399-414	20¢ 1983 Flag Series 9/23/83	11.50	...
415-16	20¢-40¢ Human Rights 12/9/83	2.35	2.00
	1984		
417-18	20¢-40¢ Population Conf. 2/3/84	2.00	1.75
419-20	20¢-40¢ FAO Food Day 3/15/84	2.00	1.75
421-22	20¢-50¢ UNESCO 4/18/84	2.35	2.00
423-24	20¢-50¢ Refugee Futures 5/29/84	2.15	1.85
425-40	20¢ 1984 Flag Series 9/20/84	13.50	...
441-42	20¢-35¢ Youth Year 11/15/84	2.00	1.75
	1985		
443	23¢ ILO-Turin Centre 2/1/85	...	.95
444	50¢ U.N. Univ. in Japan 3/15/85	...	1.50
445-46	22¢-$3 Definitives 5/10/85	7.00	6.00
447-48	22¢-45¢ 40th Anniv. 6/26/85	2.15	1.85
449	22¢-45¢ 40th Anniv. S/S 6/26/85	...	2.00
450-65	22¢ 1985 Flag Series 9/20/85	14.50	...
466-67	22¢-33¢ UNICEF 11/22/85	2.00	1.75
	1986		
468	22¢ Africa in Crisis 1/31/86	...	.95
469-72	22¢ UN Dev. & Prog. attd. 3/14/86	...	5.00
469-72	UN Dev. & Prog., set of 4 singles	6.00	...
473-74	22¢-44¢ Philately 5/22/86	2.15	1.85
475-76	22¢-33¢ Int'l. Year of Peace 6/20/86	2.00	1.75
477-92	22¢ 1986 World Flag Series 9-19-86	12.50	...
493	22¢,33¢,39¢,44¢ WFUNA S/S 11/14/86	...	5.50
	1987		
494	22¢ Trygve Lie 1/30/87	...	.95
495-96	22¢-44¢ Shelter for the Homeless 3/13/87	2.15	1.85
497-98	22¢-33¢ Life Yes/Drugs No 6/12/87	2.00	1.75
499-514	22¢ 1987 World Flag Series 9/18/87	12.50	...
515-16	22¢-39¢ U.N. Day 10/23/87	2.10	1.80
517-18	22¢-44¢ Child Immunization 11/20/87	2.15	1.85

493

UNITED NATIONS FIRST DAY COVERS

C19-21

Scott #	Description	Separate Covers	One Cover
	NEW YORK		
	1988		
519-20	22¢-33¢ World Without Hunger 1/29/88	2.00	1.75
521	3¢ UN For a Better World 1/29/88	...	.75
522-23	25¢-50¢ Forest Conservation 3/18/88	8.50	7.50
524-25	25¢-50¢ Int'l. Volunteers Day 5/6/88	2.25	1.95
526-27	25¢-38¢ Health in Sports 6/17/88	2.50	2.15
528-43	25¢ World Flag Series of 16 9/19/88	13.50	...
544-45	25¢,$1 S/S Human Rights Anniv. 12/9/88	3.75	2.75
	1989		
546-47	25¢-45¢ World Bank 1/27/89	2.25	1.85
548	25¢ UN Peace Force, Nobel Prize 3/17/89	...	.95
549	45¢ UN Headquarters 3/17/89	...	1.25
550-51	25¢-36¢ World Weather Watch 4/21/89	2.15	1.85
552-53	25¢-90¢ UN Of. in Vienna Anniv. 8/23/89	3.50	2.50
554-69	25¢ World Flags Series of 16 9/22/89	13.50	...
570-71	25¢-45¢ Human Rights 11/17/89	2.25	1.85
	1990		
572	25¢ International Trade Center 2/2/90	...	2.00
573-74	25¢-40¢ Fight Against AIDS 3/16/90	2.25	1.85
575-76	25¢-90¢ Medicinal Plants 5/4/90	3.50	2.50
577-78	25¢-45¢ UN 45th Anniversary 6/26/90	2.25	1.85
579	25¢-45¢ UN 45th Anniversary S/S	...	2.50
580-81	25¢-36¢ Crime Prevention 9/13/90	2.15	1.85
582-83	25¢-45¢ Human Rights 11/16/90	2.25	1.85
	1991		
584-87	30¢ Eur. Econ. Commission attd. 3/15/91	6.00	3.50
588-89	30¢-50¢ Namibia 5/10/91	3.00	2.35
590-91	30¢-50¢ Definitives 9/11/91	3.00	2.35
592	$2 UN Headquarters Definitive 5/10/91	...	5.00
593-94	30¢-70¢ Children's Rights 6/14/91	3.50	2.75
595-96	30¢-90¢ Chemical Weapons Ban 9/11/91	4.00	3.25
597-98	30¢-40¢ UNPA 40th Anniv. 10/24/91	3.00	2.25
599-600	30¢-50¢ Human Rights 11/20/91	3.00	2.35
	1992		
601-02	30¢-50¢ World Heritage 1/24/92	3.00	2.35
603-04	29¢ Clean Oceans attd. 3/13/92	3.00	2.25
605-08	29¢ UNICED: Earth Summit attd. 5/22/92	6.00	3.50
609-10	29¢ Mission to Planet Earth attd. 9/4/92	4.50	3.75
611-12	29¢-50¢ Science & Technology 10/2/92	3.00	2.35
613-15	4¢,29¢,40¢ Definitives 10/2/92	4.50	2.00
616-17	29¢-50¢ Human Rights S/S 12/10/92	3.00	2.35
	1993		
618-19	29¢-52¢ Aging 2/5/93	3.00	2.35
620-23	29¢ Endangered Species attd. 3/3/93	3.00	2.25
624-25	29¢-50¢ Healthy Environments 5/7/93	3.00	2.35
626	5¢ Definitive 5/7/93	...	.95
627-28	29¢-35¢ Human Rights 6/11/93	3.00	2.35
629-32	29¢ Peace attd. 9/21/93	3.00	2.25
633-36	29¢ Environment - Climate 10/29/93	3.00	2.25
	1994		
637-38	29¢-45¢ Year of the Family 2/4/94	3.00	2.35
639-42	29¢ Endangered Species 3/18/94	3.00	2.25
643	50¢ Refugees 4/29/94	...	1.50
644-46	10¢,19¢,$1 Definitives 4/29/94	3.50	2.65
647-50	29¢ Natural Disaster 5/27/94	3.00	2.25
651-52	29¢-52¢ Population-Development 9/1/94	3.00	2.35
653-54	29¢-50¢ Development Partnership 10/28/94	3.00	2.35
	1995		
655	32¢ U.N. 50th Anniversary 1/195	...	1.20
656	50¢ Social Summit 2/3/95	...	1.50
657-60	32¢ Endangered Species 3/24/95	3.20	2.50
661-62	32¢-55¢ Youth: Our Future 5/26/95	3.15	2.50
663-64	32¢-50¢ 50th Anniv. of U.N. 6/26/95	3.10	2.40
665	82¢ 50th Anniv. Souv. Sheet 6/26/95	...	2.40
666-67	32¢-40¢ Conference on Women 9/5/95	3.00	2.25

Scott #	Description	Separate Covers	One Cover
	NEW YORK		
	Airmail Issues		
	1951-59		
C1-4	6¢-25¢ 1st Airmail Issue 12/14/51	21.50	17.5
C5-7	4¢-7¢ Airmail 5/27/57 & 2/9/59	1.50	...
	1963-69		
C8-10	6¢-13¢ Airmail 6/17/63	1.50	.9
C11-12	15¢ & 25¢ Airmail 5/1/64	1.30	1.
C13	20¢ Jet Plane 4/18/68	...	1.0
C14	10¢ Wings & Envelopes 4/21/69	...	.6
	1972-77		
C15-18	9¢-21¢ Airmail 5/1/72	2.25	1.75
C19-21	13¢-26¢ Airmail 9/16/74	2.50	2.00
C22-23	25¢ & 31¢ Airmail 6/27/77	2.25	1.90
	U.N. Postal Stationery		
	Stamped Envelopes		
U1	3¢ Emblem 9/15/53	...	4.25
U2	4¢ Emblem 9/22/58	...	.80
U3	5¢ Weather Vane 4/26/63	...	.85
U4	6¢ Weather Vane 4/26/63	...	.75
U5	8¢ Headquarters 1/12/73	...	.75
U6	10¢ Headquarters 1/10/75	...	.85
U7	22¢ Bouquet 5/10/85	...	2.00
U8	25¢ UN Headquarters 3/17/89	...	2.25
U9	25¢ + 4¢ Surcharge on U8 4/15/91	...	2.00
UC3	7¢ Flag and Plane 9/21/59	...	1.50
UC6	8¢ Emblem 4/26/63	...	.90
UC8	10¢ Emblem 1/8/69	...	.85
UC10	11¢ Birds 1/12/73	...	.85
UC11	13¢ Globe 1/10/75	...	.90
	Airletter Sheets		
UC1	10¢ Air Letter 8/29/52	...	6.75
UC2	10¢ Air Letter / Aerogramme 9/14/54	...	60.00
UC4	10¢ Flag 1/18/60	...	1.00
UC5	11¢ Gull, Blue 6/26/61	...	1.00
UC7	13¢ Plane 5/31/68	...	.85
UC9	15¢ Globe 10/16/72	...	.85
UC12	18¢ Headquarters 1/10/75	...	1.25
UC13	22¢ Birds 6/27/77	...	1.10
UC14	30¢ Airplane 4/28/82	...	3.25
UC15	30¢ + 6¢ Surcharge on UC14 7/7/87	...	12.50
UC16	39¢ UN Headquarters 3/17/89	...	2.50
UC17	39¢ + 6¢ Surcharge on UC16 2/12/91	...	2.50
UC18	45¢ Winged Hand 9/4/92	...	2.00
	Postal Cards		
UX1	2¢ Headquarters 7/18/52	...	1.50
UX2	3¢ Headquarters 9/22/58	...	.90
UX3	4¢ Map 4/26/63	...	.85
UX4	5¢ Post Hom 1/8/69	...	.75
UX5	6¢ "UN" 1/12/73	...	.85
UX6	8¢ "UN" 1/10/75	...	.85
UX7	9¢ Emblem 6/27/77	...	.85
UX8	13¢ Letters 4/28/82	...	.95
UX9-13	15¢ UN Headquarters, 5 Diff. Views 3/17/89	...	1.25 ea
UX14-18	36¢ UN Headquarters, 5 Diff. Views 3/17/89	...	1.60 ea
UX19	40¢ U.N. Headquarters 9/4/92	...	1.50
	Airmail Postal Cards		
UXC1	4¢ Wing 5/27/57	...	.60
UXC2	4¢ + 1¢ 6/8/59 (first day of public use)	...	40.00
UXC3	5¢ Wing 5/21/59	...	.60
UXC4	6¢ Space 4/26/63	...	.75
UXC5	11¢ Earth 6/9/66	...	.90
UXC6	13¢ Earth 5/31/68	...	.85
UXC7	8¢ Plane 1/8/69	...	.85
UXC8	9¢ Wing 10/16/72	...	.90
UXC9	15¢ Planes 10/16/72	...	.90
UXC10	11¢ Clouds 1/10/75	...	1.00
UXC11	18¢ Pathways 1/10/75	...	1.10
UXC12	28¢ Mailmen 4/28/82	...	1.25

UC12

1

cott #	Description GENEVA	Separate Covers	One Cover
	1969-70		
-14	5¢-10¢ fr. Regular 10/4 + 9/22	40.00	...
	1971		
5	30¢ Peaceful Use of Sea 1/25/71	...	.85
6	50¢ Support for Refugees 3/12/71	...	1.00
7	50¢ World Food Program 4/13/71	...	1.25
8	75¢ U.P.O. Headquarters 5/28/71	...	2.65
9-20	30¢-50¢ Racial Discrim. 9/21/71	2.15	1.90
1	1.10 fr. Int'l. School 11/19/71	...	3.35
	1972		
2	40¢ Palace of Nations 1/15/72	...	1.00
3	40¢ No Nuclear Weapons 2/14/72	...	2.00
4	80¢ World Health Day 4/7/72	...	2.00
5-26	40¢-80¢ Human Environment 6/5/72	3.50	3.00
7	1.10 fr. Econ. Comm. Europe 9/11/72	...	3.00
8-29	40¢-80¢ Sert Mural 11/17/72	3.35	3.00
	1973		
0-31	60¢-1.10 Disarm. Decade 3/9/73	3.35	3.00
2	60¢ Against Drug Abuse 4/13/73	...	1.75
3	80¢ Volunteer Program 5/25/73	...	1.85
4	60¢ Namibia 10/1/73	...	1.75
5-36	40¢-80¢ Human Rights 11/16/73	2.50	2.00
	1974		
7-38	60¢-80¢ ILO Headqtrs. 1/11/74	2.65	2.15
9-40	30¢-60¢ UPU Centenary 3/22/74	2.10	1.85
1-42	60¢-1 fr. Brazil Mural 5/6/74	2.75	2.40
3-44	60¢-80¢ Population Year 10/18/74	2.40	2.15
5	1.30 fr. Law of the Sea 11/22/74	...	2.15
	1975		
6-47	60¢-90¢ Peace - Out. Space 3/14/75	2.25	2.00
8-49	60¢-90¢ Women's Year 5/9/75	2.65	2.40
0-51	60¢-90¢ 30th Anniv. 6/26/75	2.15	1.90
2	30¢ Anniv. S/S 6/26/75	...	2.40
3-54	50¢-1.30 fr. Namibia 9/22/75	2.40	2.15
5-56	60¢-70¢ Peacekpg. Force 11/21/75	1.90	1.65
	1976		
7	90¢ U.N. Association 3/12/76	...	1.70
8	1.10 fr. Trade & Develop. 4/23/76	...	1.90
9-60	40¢-1.50 fr. Human Settle. 5/28/76	2.75	2.40
1-62	80¢-1.10 fr. 25th Post Ann. 10/8/76	11.00	10.00
3	70¢ World Food Council 11/19/76	...	1.35
	1977		
4	80¢ Intellect Prop. 3/11/77	...	1.30
5-66	80¢-1.10 fr. Water Conf. 4/22/77	2.75	2.40
7-68	80¢-1.10 fr. Sec. Count. 5/29/77	2.75	2.40
9-70	40¢-1.10 fr. Racial Disc. 9/19/77	2.35	2.10
1-72	80¢-1.10 fr. Atom. Energy 11/18/77	2.80	2.45
	1978		
73	35¢ Regular 1/27/78	...	.80
74-75	80¢-1.10 fr. Smallpox 3/31/78	2.75	2.40
76	80¢ Namibia 5/5/78	...	1.30
77-78	70¢-80¢ Civil Aviat. Org. 6/12/78	2.15	1.90
79-80	70¢-1.10 fr. Gen. Assem 9/15/78	2.85	2.50
81	80¢ Technical Coop. 11/19/78	...	1.30
	1979		
82-83	80¢-1.50 fr. Disaster Relief 3/9/79	2.95	2.60
84-85	80¢--1.10 fr. Year of Child 5/4/79	4.50	3.75
86	1.10 fr. Namibia 10/5/79	...	1.75
87-88	80¢-1.10 fr. Court of Just. 11/9/79	2.85	2.50

Scott #	Description GENEVA	Separate Covers	One Cover
	1980		
89	80¢ New Econ. Organ. 1/11/80	...	1.35
90-91	40¢-70¢ Dec. for Women 3/7/80	1.85	1.60
92	1.10 fr. Peacekpg. Force 5/16/80	...	1.70
93-94	40¢-70¢ 35th Anniv. 6/26/80	1.85	1.60
95	40¢-70¢ 35th Anniv. S/S 6/26/80	...	2.50
96-97	40¢-70¢ Econ. & Social Co. 11/21/80	1.70	1.50
	1981		
98	80¢ Palestinian People 1/30/81	...	1.50
99-100	40¢-1.50 fr. Disabled Persons 3/6/81	2.50	2.25
101	80¢ Bulgarian Mural 4/15/81	...	1.35
102	1.10 fr. Energy Conf. 5/29/81	...	1.50
103-04	40¢-70¢ Volunteers 11/13/81	1.85	1.60
	1982		
105-06	30¢-1 fr. Definitives 1/22/82	1.95	1.70
107-08	40¢-1.20 fr. Human Environ. 3/19	2.25	2.00
109-10	80¢-1 fr. Peac. Use of Space 6/11	2.50	2.25
111-12	40¢-1.50 fr. Nat. Cons. 11/19/82	2.85	2.50
	1983		
113	1.20 fr. Commun. Year 1/28/33	...	1.85
114-15	40¢-80¢ Safety at Sea 3/28/83	1.60	1.40
116	1.50 fr. World Food Prog. 4/22/83	...	2.50
117-18	80¢-1.10 fr. Trade & Dev. 6/6/83	3.00	2.75
119-20	40¢-1.20 fr. Human Rights 12/9	3.25	2.90
	1984		
121	1.20 fr. Population Conf. 2/3/84	...	1.65
122-23	50¢-80¢ FAO Food Day 3/15/84	2.00	1.75
124-25	50¢-70¢ UNESCO 4/18/84	2.35	2.10
126-27	35¢-1.50 fr. Refugee 5/29/84	2.75	2.40
128	1.20 fr. Youth Year 11/15/84	...	1.75
	1985		
129-30	80¢-1.20 fr. ILO-Turin Centre 2/1	2.50	2.25
131-32	50¢-80¢ UN Univ. of Japan 3/15/85	1.75	1.50
133-34	20¢-1.20 fr. Definitives 5/10/85	1.95	1.75
135-36	50¢-70¢ 40th Anniversary 6/26/85	1.75	1.60
137	50¢-70¢ 40th Anniv. S/S 6/26/85	...	2.50
138-39	50¢-4 fr. UNICEF 11/22/85	4.00	3.00
	1986		
140	1.40 fr. Africa in Crisis 1/31	...	1.75
141-44	35¢ UN Dev. attd. 3/14/86	...	7.50
141-44	UN Dev. set of 4 singles	8.50	...
145	5¢ Definitive 3/14/86	...	.95
146-47	50¢-80¢ Philately 5/22/86	1.65	1.45
148-49	45¢-1.40 fr. Int. Peace 6/20/86	2.35	2.10
150	35¢,45¢,50¢,70¢ WFUNA S/S 11/14/86	...	2.75
	1987		
151	1.40 fr. Trygve Lie 1/30/87	...	1.75
152-53	90¢-1.40 fr. Bands/Sphere Definitives 1/30/87	3.00	2.75
154-55	50¢-90¢ Shelter for the Homeless 3/13/87	2.00	1.75
156-57	80¢-1.20 fr. Life Yes/Drugs No 6/12/87	2.50	2.25
158-59	50¢-1.70 fr. U.N. Day 10/23/87	3.00	2.75
160-61	35¢-90¢ Child Immunization 11/20/87	3.00	2.75
	1988		
162-63	35¢-1.40 fr. World Without Hunger 1/29/88	2.50	2.25
164	50¢ UN For a Better World 1/29/88	...	1.00
165-66	50¢-1.40 fr. Forest Conservation 3/18/88	10.50	9.50
167-68	80¢-90¢ Int'l. Volunteers Day 5/6/88	2.50	2.25
169-70	50¢-1.40 fr. Health in Sports 6/17/88	2.50	2.25
171-72	90¢,2 fr. S/S Human Rts. Decl. Anniv. 12/9/88	4.25	3.75
	1989		
173-74	80¢-1.40 fr. World Bank 1/27/89	2.75	2.50
175	90¢ UN Peace Force, Nobel Prize 3/17/89	...	1.25
176-77	90¢-1.10 fr. World Weather Watch 4/21/89	2.50	2.25
178-79	50¢-2 fr. UN Offices in Vienna Anniv. 8/23/89	3.50	3.00
180-181	35¢-80¢ Human Rights 11/17/89	1.65	1.40

119-20

182

Scott #	Description	Separate Covers	One Cover
	GENEVA		
	1990		
182	1.50 fr. International Trade Center 2/2/90	...	1.95
183	5 fr. Definitive 2/2/90	...	6.95
184-85	50¢-80¢ Fight Against AIDS 3/16/90	1.95	1.75
186-87	90¢-1.40 fr. Medicinal Plants 5/4/90	3.25	3.00
188-89	90¢-1.10 fr. UN 45th Anniversary 6/26/90	2.75	2.50
190	90¢-1.10 fr. UN 45th Anniversary S/S 6/26/90	...	3.50
191-92	50¢-2 fr. Crime Prevention 9/13/90	3.75	3.25
193-94	35¢-90¢ Human Rights 11/16/90	1.75	1.50
	1991		
195-98	90¢ Eur. Econ. Commission attd. 3/15/91	6.00	5.00
199-200	70¢-90¢ Namibia 5/10/91	3.50	2.75
201-02	80¢-1.50 fr. Definitives 5/10/91	4.50	3.75
203-04	80¢-1.10 fr. Children's Rights 6/14/91	4.00	3.25
205-06	80¢-1.40 fr. Chemical Weapons Ban 9/11/91	4.50	3.75
207-08	50¢-1.60 fr. UNPA 40th Anniv. 10/24/91	4.25	3.50
209-10	50¢-90¢ Human Rights 11/20/91	3.00	2.50
	1992		
211-12	50¢-1.10 fr. World Heritage 1/24/92	3.50	2.75
213	3 fr. Definitive 1/24/92	...	4.95
214-15	80¢ Clean Oceans attd. 3/13/92	3.50	2.75
216-19	75¢ UNICED: Earth Summit attd. 5/22/92	6.00	4.95
220-21	1.10 fr. Mission to Planet Earth attd. 9/4/92	4.25	3.75
222-23	90¢-1.60 fr. Science & Technology 10/2/92	4.50	4.25
224-25	50¢-90¢ Human Rights 12/10/92	3.00	2.50
	1993		
226-27	50¢-1.60 fr. Aging 2/5/93	4.25	3.50
228-31	80¢ Endangered Species, block of 4 3/3/93	7.00	3.75
232-33	60¢-1 fr. Healthy Environments 5/7/93	3.50	2.75
234-35	50¢-90¢ Human Rights 6/11/93	3.00	2.50
236-39	60¢ Peace, block of 4, attd. 9/21/93	5.50	3.75
240-43	1.10 fr. Environment - Climate 10/29/93	6.50	4.50
	1994		
244-45	80¢-1 fr. Year of the Family 2/4/94	4.00	3.00

UC 1

Scott #	Description	Separate Covers	One Cover
	GENEVA		
	1994		
246-49	80¢ Endangered Species 3/18/94	7.25	5.50
250	1.20 fr. Refugees 4/29/94	...	2.50
251-54	60¢ Natural Disaster 5/24/94 (4)	6.00	4.50
255-57	60¢,80¢,1.80 fr. Definitives 9/1/94	8.00	6.25
258-59	60¢-80¢ Population Development 9/1/94	3.50	2.75
260-61	80¢-1 fr. Development Partnership 10/28/94	4.00	3.25
	1995		
262	80¢ U.N. 50th Anniversary 1/1/95	...	1.70
263	1 fr Social Summit 2/3/95	...	2.00
264-67	80¢ Endangered Species 3/24/95	7.25	5.50
268-69	80¢-1 fr Youth: Our Future 5/26/95	4.00	3.25
270-71	60¢-1.80 fr 50th Anniv. of U.N. 6/26/95	5.25	4.25
272	2.40 fr 50th Anniv. Souv. Sheet 6/26/95	...	4.25
273-74	60¢-1 fr Conference on Women 9/5/95	3.75	3.00
	GENEVA AIRLETTER SHEETS		
UC1	65¢ Plane 10/4/69	...	4.75
	GENEVA POSTAL CARDS		
UX1	20¢ Post Horn 10/4/69	...	1.85
UX2	30¢ Earth 10/4/69	...	2.00
UX3	40¢ Emblem 6/27/77	...	1.90
UX4	70¢ Ribbons 6/27/77	...	2.00
UX5	50¢ "UN" 5/10/	...	1.95
UX6	70¢ Bird 5/10/85	...	2.25
UX7	70¢ + 10¢ Surcharge on UX6 1/2/86	...	8.75
UX8	90¢ Letters 9/4/92	...	2.25
UX9	50¢ + 10¢ Surcharge on UX5 5/7/93	...	2.25
UX10	80¢ Palais des Nations 5/7/93	...	2.00

11

Scott #	Description	Separate Covers	One Cover
	VIENNA		
1-6	50g-10s Regular Issue 8/24/79	6.00	5.00
	1980		
7	4s Economic Order 1/11/80	...	3.35
8	2.50s Regular, Dove 1/11/80	...	.75
9-10	4s-6s Decade for Women 3/7/80	2.75	2.50
11	6s Peacekeeping Forces 5/16/80	...	1.75
12-13	4s-6s 35th Anniversary 6/26/80	2.85	2.60
14	4s-6s 35th Anniv. S/S 6/26/80	...	3.50
15-16	4s-6s Econ. & Soc. Coun. 11/21/80	2.10	1.85
	1981		
17	4s Palestinian People 1/30/81	...	1.40
18-19	4s-6s Disabled Persons 3/6/81	2.15	1.90
20	6s Art, Bulgarian Mural 4/15/81	...	1.30
21	7.50s Energy Conference 5/29/81	...	1.75
22-23	5s-7s Volunteers 11/13/81	2.75	2.50
	1982		
24	3s Definitive 1/22/81	...	.75
25-26	5s-7s Human Environment 3/19/82	2.25	2.00
27	5s Peaceful Use of Space 6/11/82	...	1.10
28-29	5s-7s Nature Conserv. 11/16/82	2.25	2.00
	1983		
30	4s Communications Yr. 1/28/83	...	.75
31-32	4s-6s Safety at Sea 3/18/83	1.95	1.75
33-34	5s-7s World Food Prog. 4/22/83	2.35	2.10
35-36	4s-8.50s Trade & Dev. 6/6/83	2.50	2.25
37-38	5s-7s Human Rights 12/9/83	2.85	2.50
	1984		
39	7s Population Conf. 2/3/84	...	1.25
40-41	4.50s-6s FAO Food Day 3/15/84	1.95	1.75
42-43	4.50s-8.50s UNESCO 3/15/84	3.00	2.75
44-45	4.50s-8.50s Refugee 3/29/84	2.00	1.75
46-47	3.50s-6.50s Youth Year 11/15/84	2.00	1.75
	1985		
48	7.50s ILO-Turin Centre 2/1/85	...	1.10
49	8.50s UN Univ. of Japan 3/15/85	...	1.20
50-51	4.50s-15s Definitives 5/10/85	2.85	2.50
52-53	6.50s-8.50s 40th Anniv. 6/26/85	2.50	2.25
54	6.50s-8.50s 40th Anniv. S/S 6/26/85	...	3.50
55-56	4s-6s UNICEF 11/22/85	2.25	2.00
	1986		
57	8s African Crisis 1/31/86	...	1.20
58-61	4.50s UN Dev. attd. 3/14/86	...	2.75
58-61	UN Dev. set of 4 singles	4.40	...
62-63	3.50s-6.50s Philately 5/22	1.75	1.50
64-65	6s-7s Int. Year 6/20/86	2.50	2.25
66	3.50s,4s,5s,6s WFUNA S/S 11/14/86	...	5.75
	1987		
67	8s Trygve Lie 1/30/87	...	1.20
68-69	4s-9.50s Shelter for Homeless 3/13/87	2.50	2.25
70-71	5s-8s Life Yes/Drugs No 6/12/87	2.75	2.50
72-73	2s-17s Definitives 6/12/87	3.10	2.85
74-75	5s-6s U.N. Day 10/23/87	2.25	2.00
76-77	4s-9.50s Child Immunization 11/20/87	2.50	2.25
	1988		
78-79	4s-6s World Without Hunger 1/29/88	2.00	1.75
80-81	4s-5s Forest Conservation 3/18/88	9.50	8.00
82-83	6s-7.50s Int'l Volunteers Day 5/6/88	2.10	1.85
84-85	6s-8s Health in Sports 6/17/88	2.50	2.25
86-87	5s-11s Human Rts. Decl. Anniv. 12/9/88	4.00	3.50

Scott #	Description	Separate Covers	One Cover
	VIENNA		
	1989		
88-89	5.5s-8s World Bank 1/27/89	2.50	2.25
90	6s UN Peace Force, Nobel Prize 3/17/89	...	1.10
91-92	4s-9.5s World Weather Watch 4/21/89	2.50	2.25
93-94	5s-7.5s UN Offices in Vienna Anniv. 8/23/89	2.25	2.00
95-96	4s-6s Human Rights 11/17/89	2.00	1.75
	1990		
97	12s International Trade Center 2/2/90	...	1.95
98	1.5s Definitive 2/2/90	...	.75
99-100	5s-11s Fight Against AIDS 3/16/90	2.75	2.50
101-02	4.5s-9.5s Medicinal Plants 5/4/90	2.60	2.35
103-04	7s-9s UN 45th Anniversary 6/26/90	2.75	2.50
105	7s-9s UN 45th Anniversary S/S	...	3.50
106-07	6s-8s Crime Prevention 9/13/90	2.50	2.25
108-09	4.5s-7s Human Rights 11/16/90	2.10	1.85
	1991		
110-13	5s Eur. Econ. Commission attd. 3/15/91	5.00	4.00
114-15	6s-9.50s Namibia 5/10/91	4.00	3.25
116	20s Definitive 5/10/91	...	4.25
117-18	7s-9s Children's Rights 6/14/91	4.00	3.25
119-20	5s-10s Chemical Weapons Ban 9/11/91	4.25	3.50
121-22	5s-8s UNPA 40th Anniv. 10/24/91	3.75	3.00
123-24	4.50s-7s Human Rights 11/20/91	3.50	2.75
	1992		
125-26	5s-9s World Heritage 1/24/92	3.75	3.25
127-28	7s Clean Oceans attd. 3/13/92	3.75	3.25
129-32	5.5s UNICED: Earth Summit attd. 5/22/92	6.00	4.95
133-34	10s Mission to Planet Earth attd. 9/4/92	4.95	4.50
135-36	5.5s-7s Science & Technology 10/2/92	3.40	3.00
137-38	5.5s-7s Definitives 10/2/92	3.40	3.00
139-40	6s-10s Human Rights 12/10/92	4.50	3.75
	1993		
141-42	5.5s-7s Aging 2/5/93	3.40	3.00
143-46	7s Endangered Species, block of 4 3/3/93	7.00	5.75
147-48	6s-10s Healthy Environments 5/7/93	4.00	3.75
149	13s Definitive 5/7/93	...	2.25
150-51	5s-6s Human Rights 6/11/93	3.25	2.50
152-55	5.5s Peace, block of 4, attd. 9/21/93	6.00	4.95
156-59	7s Environment - Climate 10/29/93	7.50	6.50
	1994		
160-61	5.5s-8s Year of the Family 2/4/94	4.25	3.50
162-65	7s Endangered Species 3/18/94	6.50	5.50
166	12s Refugees 4/29/94	...	2.75
167-69	50g,4s,30s Definitives 4/29/94	8.25	6.75
170-73	6s Natural Disaster 5/24/94 (4)	6.50	4.95
174-75	5.50s-7s Population Development 9/1/94	3.65	2.85
176-77	6s-7s Development Partnership 10/28/94	3.75	2.95
1995			
178	7s U.N. 50th Anniversary 1/195	...	1.65
179	14s Social Summit 2/3/95	...	3.00
180-83	7s Endangered Species 3/24/95	6.50	5.50
184-85	6s-7s Youth: Our Future 5/26/95	3.75	2.95
186-87	7s-10s 50th Anniv. of U.N. 6/26/95	5.00	3.95
188	17s 50th Anniv. Souv. Sheet 6/2/65	...	3.95
189-90	5•50s-6s Conference on Women 9/5/95	3.50	2.75
	VIENNA AIRLETTER SHEETS		
UC1	9s Bird 4/28/82	...	3.95
UC2	9s + 2s Surcharge on UC1 2/3/86	...	17.50
UC3	11s Birds in Flight 1/30/87	...	3.00
UC5	12s Donaupark 9/4/92	...	3.75
	VIENNA POSTAL CARDS		
UX1	3s Branch 4/28/82	...	2.50
UX2	5s Glove 4/28/82	...	2.50
UX3	4s Emblem 5/10/85	...	2.35
UX4	5s + 1s Surcharge on UX2 1/1/92	...	5.95
UX5	6s Regschek Painting 9/4/92	...	2.50
UX6	5s Peoples 5/7/93	...	1.85
UX7	6s Donaupark 5/7/93	...	2.00

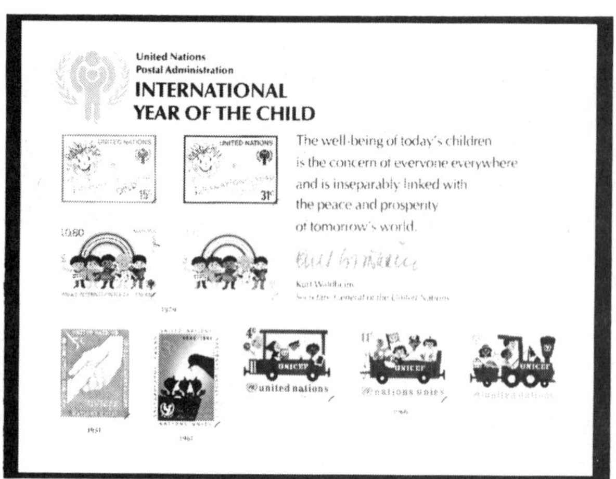

15

		Mint Card	First Day of Issue N.Y.	Geneva	Vienna
1	World Health Day 1st Print........4/7/72	1.50	16.50	150.00	...
1A	World Health Day 2nd Print.......4/7/72	5.75	20.00	160.00	...
2	UN Art 11/17/72	1.25	1.10	1.10	...
3	Disarmament............................3/9/73	1.25	1.10	1.10	...
4	Human Rights 11/16/73	1.50	1.25	1.25	...
5	Univ. Postal Union..................3/22/74	1.50	1.25	1.25	...
6	Population Year.....................10/18/74	12.50	2.50	2.50	...
7	Outer Space 3/14/75	4.50	2.00	2.00	...
8	Peacekeeping.........................11/21/75	3.25	2.00	2.00	...
9	WFUNA 3/12/76	7.50	2.50	2.50	...
10	Food Council 11/19/76	3.50	2.50	2.00	...
11	WIPO......................................3/11/77	2.25	1.50	1.50	...
12	Combat Racism.......................9/19/77	2.50	1.95	1.95	...
13	Namibia 5/5/78	1.50	1.50	1.50	...
14	Civil Aviation...........................6/12/78	1.75	1.75	1.75	...
15	Year of the Child.......................5/4/79	1.25	1.25	1.25	...
16	Court of Justice 11/9/79	2.50	2.50	2.50	...
17	Decade for Women 3/7/80	17.50	9.50	8.50	8.50
18	Econ. & Social Council............11/7/80	1.50	1.25	1.25	1.50
19	Disabled Persons 3/6/81	1.25	1.25	1.25	1.50
20	Energy Sources.......................5/29/81	1.50	1.50	1.50	1.50
21	Environment 3/19/82	2.00	1.85	1.85	2.00
22	Outer Space 6/11/82	2.00	1.85	1.85	2.00
23	Safety at Sea..........................3/18/83	2.00	1.85	1.85	2.00
24	Trade & Development 6/6/83	3.50	3.50	3.50	4.00
25	Population 2/3/84	3.50	3.50	3.50	4.00
26	Youth Year 11/15/84	5.00	4.00	4.50	5.00
27	ILO - Turin Centre 2/1/85	5.00	6.00	5.50	5.50
28	UNICEF 11/22/85	5.75	4.25	4.75	4.75
29	Stamp Collecting 5/22/86	15.00	8.00	8.00	8.00
30	Int'l. Peace Year.....................6/20/86	6.00	5.00	5.00	5.00
31	Shelter for Homeless..............3/13/87	5.75	4.25	4.25	4.50
32	Child Immunization...............11/20/87	5.50	5.00	5.00	5.00
33	Int'l. Volunteers Day 5/6/88	7.50	5.00	5.00	5.00
34	WHO/Sports Health................6/17/88	7.50	5.50	5.50	5.50
35	World Bank.............................1/27/89	7.50	5.50	5.50	6.00
36	World Weather Watch 4/21/89	7.50	5.00	5.00	5.00
37	Fight Against AIDS.................3/16/90	11.50	5.00	5.00	5.50
38	Crime Prevention....................9/13/90	7.50	5.00	5.00	5.50
39	European Econ. Commiss.......3/15/91	7.50	7.50	7.50	7.50
40	Children's Rights 6/14/91	6.50	5.00	5.00	5.50
41	Mission to Planet Earth 9/4/92	6.50	5.00	5.00	5.50
42	Science and Technology.........10/2/92	6.00	4.00	4.00	4.50
43	Healthy Environments 5/7/93	5.25	4.25	4.25	4.50
44	Peace 9/21/93	6.50	6.00	7.50	7.50
44A	Peace-Gold Hong Kong overprint	10.95	...	...	...
45	Year of the Family 2/4/94	6.00	6.00	6.00	6.00
46	Population-Development...........9/1/94	6.00	6.00	6.00	6.00
47	Social Summit 2/3/95	5.50	6.00	6.50	7.00
48	Youth: Our Future..................5/26/95	5.50	6.00	6.50	6.50

CANADA

1,4   2,5,10   7   8   9

PROVINCE OF CANADA
1851 Laid Paper, Imperforate

cott's No.		Unused Fine	Unused Ave.	Used Fine	Used Ave.
	3p Beaver, Red	...	...	600.00	300.00
	6p Albert, Grayish Purple	...	...	750.00	375.00

1852-1857 Wove Paper, Imperforate (OG + 50%) (C)

cott's No.		Unused Fine	Unused Ave.	Used Fine	Used Ave.
	3p Beaver, Red, Thick Paper	...	600.00	110.00	75.00
d	3p Thin Paper	...	700.00	150.00	100.00
	6p Albert, Slate Gray	...	...	600.00	375.00
	10p Cartier, Blue	...	...	800.00	400.00
	½p Victoria, Rose	475.00	275.00	350.00	220.00
	7½p Victoria, Green	...	...	1500.00	650.00
0	6p Albert, Reddish Purple, Thick	...	...	...	1200.00

1858-59 Wove Paper, Perforated 12 (OG + 50%) (C)

cott's No.		Unused Fine	Unused Ave.	Used Fine	Used Ave.
1	½p Victoria, Rose	...	750.00	575.00	325.00
2	3p Beaver, Red	...	1100.00	375.00	200.00
3	6p Albert, Brown Violet	...	...	...	1450.00

14   15   16,17   18   19   20

1859 (OG + 50%) (C)

cott's No.		Unused Fine	Unused Ave.	Used Fine	Used Ave.
4	1¢ Victoria, Rose	165.00	100.00	27.50	15.00
5	5¢ Beaver, Vermilion	175.00	100.00	12.00	7.00
6	10¢ Albert, Black Brown	...	...	...	825.00
7	10¢ Red Lilac	375.00	235.00	45.00	25.00
8	12½¢ Victoria, Yellow Green	250.00	150.00	39.50	20.00
9	17¢ Cartier, Blue	450.00	270.00	65.00	35.00

CANADA
1864 (OG + 50%) (C)

Scott's No.		Unused Fine	Unused Ave.	Used Fine	Used Ave.
20	2¢ Victoria, Rose	275.00	185.00	130.00	85.00

DOMINION OF CANADA

1868-1876 Large "Cents" Issue, Perf. 12 (OG + 30%) (C)

21   22-23,31   25,33   26   29-30

Scott's No.		Unused Fine	Unused Ave.	Used Fine	Used Ave.
21	½¢ Victoria, Black	32.50	21.50	27.50	16.50
21a	½¢ Perf. 11½ x 12	32.50	21.50	27.50	16.50
21c	½¢ Thin Paper	35.00	22.50	32.50	21.50
22	1¢ Brown Red	250.00	160.00	37.50	25.00
22a	1¢ Watermarked	...	...	160.00	105.00
22b	1¢ Thin Paper	275.00	175.00	37.50	25.00
23	1¢ Yellow Orange	475.00	300.00	70.00	40.00
24	2¢ Green	250.00	150.00	30.00	15.00
24a	2¢ Watermarked	...	725.00	165.00	110.00
24b	2¢ Thin Paper	300.00	190.00	35.00	19.50
25	3¢ Red	500.00	280.00	11.50	6.00
25a	3¢ Watermarked	1650.00	850.00	150.00	95.00
25b	3¢ Thin Paper	550.00	325.00	15.00	9.50
26	5¢ Olive Green, Perf. 11½ x 12	575.00	325.00	65.00	35.00
27	6¢ Dark Brown	500.00	315.00	35.00	22.50
27b	6¢ Watermarked	...	1250.00	750.00	400.00
27c	6¢ Thin Paper	650.00	375.00	55.00	32.50
28	12½¢ Blue	300.00	165.00	37.50	22.50
28a	12½¢ Watermarked	1125.00	600.00	150.00	95.00
28b	12½¢ Thin Paper	325.00	195.00	52.50	35.00
29	15¢ Gray Violet	37.50	22.50	18.50	11.50
29a	15¢ Perf. 11½ x 12	575.00	275.00	110.00	62.50
29b	15¢ Red Lilac	450.00	300.00	50.00	25.00
29c	15¢ Gray Violet Wmkd	...	1400.00	375.00	210.00
29e	15¢ Gray Violet, Thin Paper	375.00	235.00	65.00	40.00
30	15¢ Gray	35.00	21.00	17.50	11.50
30a	15¢ Perf. 11½ x 12	475.00	275.00	110.00	60.00

1868 Laid Paper, Perf. 12 (OG + 30%) (C)

Scott's No.		NH Fine	Unused Fine	Unused Ave.	Used Fine	Used Ave.
31	1¢ Brown Red	...	...	...	2150.00	950.00
33	3¢ Bright Red	...	...	...	450.00	200.00

34 35 37,41 44 46

1870-1889 Small "Cents" Issue, Perf. 12 (OG + 20%) VF + 60% (C)

34	½¢ Victoria Black	8.50	4.50	2.40	4.50	2.40
35	1¢ Yellow	28.50	15.00	7.50	.60	.30
35a	1¢ Orange	110.00	57.50	35.00	5.75	3.15
35d	1¢ Orange, Pf. 11½ x 12	190.00	100.00	60.00	8.50	5.50
36	2¢ Green	37.50	20.00	13.00	.80	.45
36d	2¢ Blue Green	67.50	35.00	19.50	2.25	1.35
36e	2¢ Green, Pf. 11½ x 12	225.00	125.00	75.00	12.50	8.00
37	3¢ Dull Red	80.00	42.50	22.50	1.50	.80
37a	3¢ Rose	425.00	225.00	135.00	6.50	3.65
37b	3¢ Copper Red	...	675.00	375.00	25.00	15.00
37c	3¢ Orange Red	75.00	40.00	22.50	1.15	.65
37d	3¢ Cop. Red 12½ x 12	...	...	...	450.00	300.00
37e	3¢ Red, Perf. 11½ x 12	250.00	135.00	75.00	5.75	3.50
38	5¢ Slate Green	375.00	200.00	110.00	11.00	7.50
38a	5¢ Ol. Gr., Pf. 11½ x 12	575.00	295.00	180.00	20.00	13.50
39	6¢ Yellow Brown	350.00	190.00	100.00	11.00	7.50
39b	6¢ Brown, 11½ x 12	600.00	300.00	185.00	20.00	13.50
40	10¢ Dull Rose Lilac	500.00	275.00	165.00	30.00	20.00
40c	10¢ Rose Ll., 11½ x 12	1200.00	500.00	265.00	165.00	95.00

1888-1893 Small "Cents" Issue, Perf. 12 VF + 60% (C)

41	3¢ Bright Vermilion	24.00	13.50	7.00	.25	.15
41a	3¢ Rose Carmine	425.00	225.00	120.00	5.50	3.65
42	5¢ Gray	60.00	32.50	16.00	2.75	1.50
43	6¢ Red Brown	60.00	32.50	15.75	7.50	4.15
43a	6¢ Chocolate	95.00	50.00	25.00	10.75	6.00
44	8¢ Gray	60.00	32.50	18.50	3.00	1.65
45	10¢ Brown Red	165.00	90.00	50.00	22.50	12.50
46	20¢ Vermilion	250.00	150.00	85.00	37.50	22.50
47	50¢ Deep Blue	300.00	165.00	110.00	27.50	13.75

1897 Jubilee Issue VF Used + 60% (B)

50 55 60

Scott's No.		NH VF	NH F-VF	Unused VF	Unused F-VF	Used F-VF
50	½¢ Victoria, Black	140.00	85.00	75.00	45.00	60.00
51	1¢ Orange	13.00	7.50	6.75	4.00	3.50
52	2¢ Green	17.00	10.00	10.75	6.25	6.25
53	3¢ Bright Rose	13.00	7.50	7.00	4.00	1.35
54	5¢ Deep Blue	45.00	26.50	27.50	16.50	13.50
55	6¢ Yellow Brown	225.00	140.00	135.00	80.00	95.00
56	8¢ Dark Violet	57.50	35.00	25.00	15.00	15.00
57	10¢ Brown Violet	135.00	85.00	75.00	45.00	45.00
58	15¢ Steel Blue	240.00	150.00	140.00	87.50	80.00
59	20¢ Vermillion	250.00	160.00	145.00	90.00	90.00
60	50¢ Ultramarine	275.00	170.00	165.00	100.00	100.00
61	$1 Lake	1100.00	675.00	650.00	400.00	425.00
62	$2 Dark Purple	1725.00	1150.00	1000.00	675.00	325.00
63	$3 Yellow Bistre	1900.00	1275.00	1200.00	800.00	625.00
64	$4 Purple	1900.00	1275.00	1200.00	800.00	625.00
65	$5 Olive Green	1950.00	1300.00	1275.00	850.00	600.00

66 74 85-86 87

CANADA

1897-1898 Issue, Maple Leaves in Four Corners, VF Used + 50% (B)

Scott's No.		NH VF	NH F-VF	Unused VF	Unused F-VF	Used F-VF
66	½¢ Victoria, Black	8.75	6.00	5.75	3.75	3.50
67	1¢ Blue Green	17.50	11.00	11.00	7.00	.55
68	2¢ Purple	24.50	14.50	14.00	8.50	1.00
69	3¢ Carmine (1898)	24.50	14.50	14.00	8.50	.25
70	5¢ Dark Blue	110.00	70.00	57.50	35.00	3.50
71	6¢ Brown	97.50	60.00	53.50	32.50	12.50
72	8¢ Orange	165.00	100.00	85.00	50.00	5.50
73	10¢ Brown Violet (1898)	275.00	170.00	150.00	90.00	40.00

1898-1902 Issue, Numerals in Lower Corners VF Used + 60% (B)

74	½¢ Victoria, Black	3.25	1.90	1.90	1.15	1.00
75	1¢ Gray Green	18.00	11.00	11.50	7.00	.18
76	2¢ Purple	20.00	12.50	12.50	7.50	.18
77	2¢ Carmine, Die I (1898)	25.00	15.00	15.75	9.50	.18
77a	2¢ Carmine, Die II	27.50	16.50	16.50	10.00	.25
78	3¢ Carmine	32.50	20.00	20.00	12.50	.30
79	5¢ Blue	120.00	75.00	72.50	45.00	.70
80	6¢ Brown	165.00	100.00	95.00	57.50	23.50
81	7¢ Olive Yellow (1902)	115.00	67.50	65.00	40.00	10.00
82	8¢ Orange	250.00	150.00	120.00	75.00	11.00
83	10¢ Brown Violet	290.00	180.00	135.00	85.00	10.00
84	20¢ Olive Green (1900)	600.00	375.00	275.00	175.00	50.00

1898 Imperial Penny Post VF Used + 50% (B)

85	2¢ Map, Blk. Lav. Carm	30.00	20.00	18.75	12.50	4.50
86	2¢ Black, Blue, Carmine	30.00	20.00	18.75	12.50	4.50

1899 Surcharges VF Used + 60% (B)

87	2¢ on 3¢ Carmine (on #69)	18.50	11.50	8.25	5.00	3.00
88	2¢ on 3¢ Carmine (on #78)	20.00	13.50	11.50	6.75	2.50

89 96 100

1903-1908 King Edward VII VF Used + 60% (B)

89	1¢ Edward VII, Green	20.00	12.50	12.00	7.50	.18
90	2¢ Carmine	20.00	12.50	12.00	7.50	.18
90a	2¢ Imperforate Pair	52.50	33.75	35.00	22.50	...
91	5¢ Blue	100.00	60.00	60.00	35.00	2.00
92	7¢ Olive Bistre	72.50	45.00	40.00	25.00	2.00
93	10¢ Brown Lilac	200.00	115.00	110.00	65.00	4.00
94	20¢ Olive Green	475.00	295.00	295.00	185.00	16.50
95	50¢ Purple (1908)	750.00	475.00	440.00	275.00	45.00

1908 Quebec Tercentenary VF + 75% (B)

96-103	**Set of 8**	**775.00**	**450.00**	**395.00**	**230.00**	**190.00**
96	½¢ Prince & Princess	7.00	4.00	3.95	2.25	2.25
97	1¢ Cartier & Champlain	17.50	10.00	8.75	5.00	2.75
98	2¢ Alexandria & Edward	21.00	12.00	10.50	6.00	.75
99	5¢ Champlain's Home	70.00	45.00	35.00	22.50	20.00
100	7¢ Montcalm & Wolfe	115.00	75.00	60.00	40.00	25.00
101	10¢ 1700 View of Quebec	160.00	90.00	75.00	45.00	45.00
102	15¢ Champlain Heads West	195.00	110.00	95.00	55.00	52.50
103	20¢ Cartier Arrival	275.00	160.00	140.00	80.00	75.00

104-105 116-118 135 140

1912-1925 "Admiral Issue" Perf. 12 VF Used + 50% (B)

104	1¢ George V. Green	9.50	6.25	5.50	3.50	.18
104a	1¢ Booklet Pane of 6	37.50	25.00	25.00	16.50	...
105	1¢ Yellow (1922)	8.00	5.25	4.50	3.00	.18
105a	1¢ Booklet Pane of 4	75.00	52.50	52.50	35.00	...
105b	1¢ Booklet Pane of 6	45.00	32.50	35.00	22.50	...
106	2¢ Carmine	7.50	5.00	4.50	3.00	.18
106a	2¢ Booklet Pane of 6	38.50	25.50	26.50	17.50	...
107	2¢ Yellow Green (1922)	7.50	5.00	4.00	2.75	.18
107a	2¢ Thin Paper	7.50	5.00	4.00	2.75	.25
107b	2¢ Booklet Pane of 4	63.50	41.50	41.50	27.50	...
107c	2¢ Booklet Pane of 6	440.00	295.00	315.00	210.00	...
108	3¢ Brown (1918)	9.00	6.00	5.25	3.50	.18
108a	3¢ Booklet Pane of 4	120.00	82.50	82.50	55.00	...
109	3¢ Carmine (1923)	8.00	5.25	4.50	3.00	.18
109a	3¢ Booklet Pane of 4	60.00	40.00	37.50	25.00	...
110	4¢ Olive Bistre (1922)	30.00	20.00	18.50	12.50	1.50
111	5¢ Dark Blue	97.50	65.00	55.00	37.50	.30

1912-1925 "Admiral Issue" Perf. 12, VF Used + 50% (B)

Scott's No.		NH VF	NH F-VF	Unused VF	Unused F-VF	Used F-VF
12	5¢ Violet (1922)	15.50	10.50	9.00	6.00	.30
12a	5¢ Thin Paper	25.00	16.50	15.50	10.50	6.50
13	7¢ Yellow Ochre	35.00	23.50	20.00	13.50	1.25
13a	7¢ Olive Bistre	35.00	23.50	20.00	13.50	1.50
14	7¢ Red Brown (1924)	20.00	13.50	11.50	7.50	5.25
15	8¢ Blue (1925)	30.00	20.00	18.50	12.50	6.00
16	10¢ Plum	165.00	110.00	85.00	57.50	.85
17	10¢ Blue (1922)	45.00	30.00	26.50	17.50	.95
18	10¢ Bister Brown (1925)	37.50	25.00	20.00	13.50	.80
19	20¢ Olive Green	72.50	48.50	40.00	27.50	.65
20	50¢ Black Brown (1925)	75.00	50.00	45.00	30.00	1.60
20a	50¢ Black	135.00	90.00	75.00	50.00	3.00
22	$1 Orange (1923)	127.50	85.00	75.00	55.00	5.75

1912 Coil Stamps, Perf. 8 Horizontally VF Used + 50% (B)

23	1¢ Dark Green	80.00	52.50	49.50	32.50	27.50
24	2¢ Carmine	80.00	52.50	49.50	32.50	27.50

1912-1924 Coil Stamps, Perf. 8 Vertically VF Used + 50% (B)

25	1¢ Green	16.50	11.00	9.75	6.50	.50
26	1¢ Yellow (1923)	12.50	8.25	7.50	5.00	4.75
26a	1¢ Block of four	62.50	40.00	38.50	25.00	...
27	2¢ Carmine	26.50	17.50	15.00	10.00	.40
28	2¢ Green (1922)	14.00	9.75	9.00	6.00	.40
28a	2¢ Block of four	62.50	40.00	38.50	25.00	...
29	3¢ Brown (1918)	11.50	7.75	6.75	4.50	.40
30	3¢ Carmine (1924)	67.50	45.00	45.00	30.00	5.00
30a	3¢ Block of four	935.00	625.00	635.00	425.00	...

*126a,128a,130a are from Part.-Perf. Sheets - Pairs are at half block prices.

1915-1924 Coil Stamps, Perf. 12 Horizontally VF Used + 50% (B)

31	1¢ Dark Green	9.00	6.00	5.25	3.50	4.25
32	2¢ Carmine	22.50	15.00	15.00	10.00	9.00
33	2¢ Yellow Green (1924)	115.00	75.00	67.50	45.00	40.00
34	3¢ Brown (1921)	9.00	6.00	5.25	3.50	4.00

1917 Confederation VF Used + 100% (B)

35	3¢ "Fathers of Confed."	45.00	22.50	30.00	15.00	.35

1924 Imperforate VF Used + 20% (B)

36	1¢ Yellow	52.50	42.50	35.00	28.50	28.50
37	2¢ Green	52.50	42.50	35.00	28.50	28.50
38	3¢ Carmine	27.50	22.50	18.50	15.00	15.00

1926 Surcharges VF Used + 30% (B)

39	2¢ on 3¢ - One Line	65.00	50.00	49.50	32.50	35.00
40	2¢ on 3¢ - Two Lines	26.50	20.00	20.00	13.50	15.00

141 145 146 148

1927 Confederation Issue VF Used + 30% (B)

41-45	**Set of 5**	**35.00**	**27.50**	**23.50**	**18.00**	**7.25**
41	1¢ John A. MacDonald	3.00	2.25	1.95	1.50	.35
42	2¢ "Fathers of Confed."	1.95	1.50	1.30	1.00	.18
43	3¢ Parliament Building	9.00	7.00	6.25	4.75	3.25
44	5¢ Sir Wilfrid Laurier	5.50	4.25	3.50	2.75	1.50
45	12¢ Map of Canada	17.50	13.50	11.75	9.00	2.85

1927 Historical Issue VF Used + 30% (B)

46-48	**Set of 3**	**31.50**	**24.50**	**21.00**	**16.00**	**6.85**
46	5¢ Thomas d'Arcy McGee	4.00	3.00	2.60	2.00	1.40
47	12¢ Laurier & MacDonald	10.00	7.50	6.50	5.00	2.50
48	20¢ Baldwin & Lafontaine	19.50	15.00	13.50	10.00	3.25

1928-29 Scroll Series VF Used + 40% (B)

149 154 155 156

49-59	**Set of 11**	**735.00**	**485.00**	**415.00**	**295.00**	**90.00**
49	1¢ George V. Orange	2.75	2.00	1.75	1.25	.20
49a	1¢ Booklet Pane of 6	19.00	13.50	12.50	9.00	...
50	2¢ Green	1.30	.90	.85	.60	.18
50a	2¢ Booklet Pane of 6	28.50	20.00	18.00	13.00	...
51	3¢ Dark Carmine	19.00	13.50	10.50	7.50	7.50

1928-29 Scroll Series (cont.)

Scott's No.		NH VF	NH F-VF	Unused VF	Unused F-VF	Used F-VF
152	4¢ Bistre (1929)	15.00	10.50	10.00	7.00	3.25
153	5¢ Deep Violet	8.50	6.00	4.25	3.00	1.50
153a	5¢ Booklet Pane of 6	125.00	90.00	77.50	55.00	...
154	8¢ Blue	11.75	8.50	7.00	5.00	3.50
155	10¢ Mt. Hurd	12.00	8.50	6.25	4.50	.70
156	12¢ Quebec Bridge (1929)	15.50	11.00	10.50	7.50	4.00
157	20¢ Harvest Wheat (1929)	31.50	22.50	19.00	13.50	6.00
158	50¢ "Bluenose" (1929)	300.00	195.00	175.00	125.00	30.00
159	$1 Parliament (1929)	365.00	235.00	210.00	150.00	35.00

1929 Coil Stamps, Perf. 8 Vertically VF Used + 40% (B)

160	1¢ Orange	25.00	17.50	17.50	12.50	12.50
161	2¢ Green	18.75	13.85	13.95	10.00	1.75

1930-31 King George V & Pictorials VF Used + 40% (B)

162-63 173 174 175

162-77	**Set of 16**	**550.00**	**375.00**	**350.00**	**250.00**	**45.00**
162	1¢ George V. Orange	1.10	.75	.70	.50	.33
163	1¢ Deep Green	1.65	1.20	1.10	.80	.18
163a	1¢ Booklet Pane of 4	125.00	90.00	85.00	60.00	...
163c	1¢ Booklet Pane of 6	21.00	15.00	14.00	10.00	...
164	2¢ Dull Green	1.40	1.00	.90	.65	.18
164a	2¢ Booklet Pane of 6	33.50	24.00	21.00	15.00	...
165	2¢ Deep Red, Die II	2.30	1.65	1.60	1.15	.18
165a	2¢ Deep Red, Die I	1.75	1.25	1.20	.85	.20
165b	2¢ B. Pane of 6, Die I	28.00	20.00	19.00	13.50	...
166	2¢ Dark Br., Die II (1931)	1.75	1.25	1.00	.75	.18
166a	2¢ B. Pane of 4, Die II	130.00	90.00	95.00	67.50	...
166b	2¢ Dark Brown, Die I	6.25	4.50	4.25	3.00	2.50
166c	2¢ B. Pane of 6, Die I	35.00	25.00	25.00	17.50	...
167	3¢ Deep Red (1931)	2.50	1.75	1.60	1.15	.18
167a	3¢ Booklet Pane of 4	35.00	25.00	25.00	17.50	...
168	4¢ Yellow Bistre	12.50	9.00	8.50	6.00	3.00
169	5¢ Dull Violet, Flat Plate	7.00	5.00	4.25	3.00	2.25
169a	5¢ Dull Violet, Rotary	7.00	5.00	4.25	3.00	2.25
170	5¢ Dull Blue	4.00	2.80	2.65	1.90	.18
171	8¢ Dark Blue	21.00	15.00	14.00	10.00	4.50
172	8¢ Red Orange	7.25	5.50	5.00	3.50	2.25
173	10¢ Library of Parliament	9.00	6.50	6.25	4.50	.70
174	12¢ Citadel at Quebec	17.50	12.50	12.00	8.50	3.75
175	20¢ Harvesting Wheat	31.50	22.50	21.00	15.00	.30
176	50¢ Museum-Grand Pre	225.00	150.00	140.00	100.00	9.50
177	$1 Mt. Edith Cavell	250.00	165.00	150.00	110.00	18.50

Die I: Dot of Color in "P" of Postage. Die II: Large Dot in "P".

1930-31 Coil Stamps, Perf. 8½ Vertically VF Used + 40% (B)

178-83	**Set of 6**	**77.50**	**55.00**	**46.50**	**33.50**	**12.75**
178	1¢ Orange	14.00	10.00	9.00	6.50	5.50
179	1¢ Green	8.50	6.00	5.25	3.75	3.00
180	2¢ Dull Green	7.00	5.00	4.50	3.25	2.50
181	2¢ Carmine	17.50	12.50	11.25	8.00	1.50
182	2¢ Dark Brown (1931)	12.50	9.00	7.75	5.50	.40
183	3¢ Deep Red (1931)	21.00	15.00	12.00	8.50	.30

1931 Design of 1912, Perf. 12 x 8 VF Used + 30% (B)

184	3¢ George V Carmine	4.00	3.00	2.50	2.00	1.85

190 192 194 195

1931 Cartier Issue VF + 30% (B)

190	10¢ Sir Georges Cartier	9.75	7.50	6.50	5.00	.18

1932 Surcharges VF + 30% (B)

191	3¢ on 2¢ Deep Red, Die II	1.30	1.00	.85	.65	.18
191a	3¢ on 2¢ Deep Red, Die I	2.60	2.00	1.95	1.50	1.00

1932 Imperial Conference VF + 30% (B)

192-94	**Set of 3**	**14.50**	**11.00**	**10.50**	**8.00**	**5.25**
192	3¢ George V	1.00	.75	.65	.50	.18
193	5¢ Prince of Wales	6.50	5.00	4.50	3.50	1.50
194	13¢ Allegory	8.00	6.00	5.75	4.50	3.75

1932 George V. Medallion, VF Used + 30% (B)

Scott's No.		VF	NH F-VF	Unused VF	Unused F-VF	Used F-VF
195-201	**Set of 7**	**105.00**	**77.50**	**72.50**	**56.50**	**7.95**
195	1¢ George V. Dark Green	1.00	.75	.70	.55	.18
195a	1¢ Booklet Pane of 4	110.00	82.50	80.00	60.00	...
195b	1¢ Booklet Pane of 6	30.00	23.50	23.50	18.00	...
196	2¢ Black Brown	1.10	.85	.80	.60	.18
196a	2¢ Booklet Pane of 4	110.00	82.50	80.00	60.00	...
196b	2¢ Booklet Pane of 6	26.50	20.00	19.50	15.00	...
197	3¢ Deep Red	1.30	1.00	1.00	.75	.18
197a	3¢ Booklet Pane of 4	30.00	22.50	21.50	16.50	...
198	4¢ Ocher	38.75	30.00	29.00	22.50	3.50
199	5¢ Dark Blue	7.85	5.85	5.35	4.00	.18
200	8¢ Red Orange	23.50	18.00	16.50	12.50	2.65
201	13¢ Citadel at Quebec	40.00	30.00	26.50	20.00	1.75

202 208 209

1933 Pictorials VF + 30%

Scott's No.		VF	NH F-VF	Unused VF	Unused F-VF	Used F-VF
202	5¢ U.P.U. Meeting	8.50	6.50	5.50	4.25	2.00
203	20¢ Grain Exhib. (on #175)	36.50	27.50	24.00	18.00	9.00
204	5¢ "Royal William"	10.00	7.50	6.50	5.00	2.00

1933 Coil Stamps, Perf. Vertically VF + 30% (B)

Scott's No.		VF	NH F-VF	Unused VF	Unused F-VF	Used F-VF
205	1¢ George V. Dark Green	18.00	13.50	12.50	9.50	1.50
206	2¢ Black Brown	19.50	15.00	13.00	10.00	.45
207	3¢ Deep Red	14.50	10.50	9.75	7.50	.25

1934 Commemoratives VF + 30%

Scott's No.		VF	NH F-VF	Unused VF	Unused F-VF	Used F-VF
208	3¢ Cartier at Quebec	3.50	2.75	2.60	2.00	.85
209	10¢ Loyalists Monument	21.50	16.50	14.25	11.00	5.25
210	2¢ Seal of New Brunswick	2.40	1.85	1.65	1.25	1.35

1935 Silver Jubilee VF + 20%

211 213 214 216

Scott's No.		Plate Blocks NH	Plate Blocks Unused	F-VF NH	F-VF Unused	F-VF Used
211-16	**Set of 6**	**...**	**...**	**16.00**	**12.00**	**7.25**
211	1¢ Princess Elizabeth (6)	3.50	2.75	.35	.28	.18
212	2¢ Duke of York (6)	7.50	6.25	.65	.55	.15
213	3¢ George V and Mary (6)	15.00	11.50	1.70	1.25	.15
214	5¢ Prince of Wales (6)	35.00	23.50	4.00	2.75	2.00
215	10¢ Windsor Castle (6)	50.00	30.00	5.00	3.75	1.75
216	13¢ Royal Yacht "Brittania" (6)	70.00	35.00	6.00	4.25	3.50

1935 George V & Pictorials VF + 20%

217 222 223 227

Scott's No.		Plate Blocks NH	Plate Blocks Unused	F-VF NH	F-VF Unused	F-VF Used
217-27	**Set of 11**	**...**	**...**	**130.00**	**85.00**	**13.00**
217	1¢ George V Green (8)	2.50	2.00	.25	.20	.15
217a	1¢ Booklet Pane of 4	...	...	50.00	35.00	...
217b	1¢ Booklet Pane of 6	...	...	20.00	13.50	...
218	2¢ Brown (8)	3.50	2.75	.35	.28	.15
218a	2¢ Booklet Pane of 4	...	...	50.00	35.00	...
218b	2¢ Booklet Pane of 6	...	...	14.00	9.50	...
219	3¢ Dark Carmine (8)	5.00	4.00	.50	.40	.15
219a	3¢ Booklet Pane of 4	...	...	14.50	10.00	...

1935 George V & Pictorials (cont.)

Scott's No.		Plate Blocks NH	Plate Blocks Unused	F-VF NH	F-VF Unused	F-VF Used
220	4¢ Yellow (6)	21.00	16.00	2.65	2.00	.35
221	5¢ Blue (6)	18.00	14.00	2.25	1.75	.15
222	8¢ Deep Orange (6)	20.00	15.00	2.65	2.00	1.30
223	10¢ Mounted Police (6)	48.00	34.00	6.50	4.75	.15
224	13¢ Confederation Conf (6)	50.00	35.00	6.50	4.75	.50
225	20¢ Niagara Falls (6)	175.00	130.00	22.50	15.00	.35
226	50¢ Parliament, Victoria (6)	235.00	160.00	30.00	20.00	3.25
227	$1 Champlain Monument (6)	485.00	325.00	70.00	45.00	7.00

1935 Coil Stamps, Perf. 8 Vertically VF + 20% (B)

Scott's No.		Plate Blocks NH	Plate Blocks Unused	F-VF NH	F-VF Unused	F-VF Used
228	1¢ George V, Green	...	...	11.00	7.75	1.60
229	2¢ Brown	...	...	9.00	6.50	.55
230	3¢ Dark Carmine	...	...	9.00	6.50	.25

231 237 241 242

1937 George VI VF + 20% (B)

Scott's No.		Plate Blocks NH	Plate Blocks Unused	F-VF NH	F-VF Unused	F-VF Used
231-36	**Set of 6**	**...**	**...**	**7.50**	**5.95**	**.80**
231	1¢ George VI, Green	2.25	1.85	.35	.30	.15
231a	1¢ Booklet Pane of 4	...	...	10.50	7.50	...
231b	1¢ Booklet Pane of 6	...	...	1.50	1.00	...
232	2¢ Brown	2.75	2.25	.45	.35	.15
232a	2¢ Booklet Pane of 4	...	...	9.00	6.00	...
232b	2¢ Booklet Pane of 6	...	...	4.50	3.00	...
233	3¢ Carmine	2.50	2.00	.50	.40	.15
233a	3¢ Booklet Pane of 6	...	...	2.00	1.50	...
234	4¢ Yellow	12.50	10.00	2.25	1.75	.15
235	5¢ Blue	11.75	9.50	2.25	1.75	.15
236	8¢ Orange	11.75	9.50	2.25	1.75	.30

1937 Coronation Issue VF + 20% (B)

Scott's No.		Plate Blocks NH	Plate Blocks Unused	F-VF NH	F-VF Unused	F-VF Used
237	3¢ George VI and Elizabeth	1.70	1.40	.22	.20	.15

1937 Coil Stamps, Perf. 8 Vertically VF + 20% (B)

Scott's No.		Plate Blocks NH	Plate Blocks Unused	F-VF NH	F-VF Unused	F-VF Used
238	1¢ George VI, Green	...	...	1.40	.90	.65
239	2¢ Brown	...	...	2.00	1.40	.25
240	3¢ Carmine	...	...	4.00	2.75	.15

1938 Pictorials VF + 20%

Scott's No.		Plate Blocks NH	Plate Blocks Unused	F-VF NH	F-VF Unused	F-VF Used
241-45	**Set of 5**	**...**	**...**	**110.00**	**67.50**	**7.50**
241	10¢ Memorial Hall	21.50	15.00	4.50	3.25	.15
242	13¢ Halifax Harbor	37.50	25.00	7.50	5.00	.30
243	20¢ Ft. Garry Gate, Winnipeg	75.00	47.50	15.00	10.00	.20
244	50¢ Vancouver Harbor	115.00	70.00	20.00	12.50	3.00
245	$1 Chateau de Ramezay	320.00	210.00	67.50	42.50	4.50

246 247 248

Scott's No.		Plate Blocks NH	Plate Blocks Unused	F-VF NH	F-VF Unused	F-VF Used
246-48	**Set of 3**	**3.65**	**2.90**	**.55**	**.50**	**.35**
246	1¢ Elizabeth & Margaret Rose	1.25	1.00	.22	.20	.15
247	2¢ War Memorial, Ottawa	1.25	1.00	.22	.20	.15
248	3¢ George VI and Elizabeth	1.25	1.00	.22	.20	.15

1942-43 War Set

249 250 253 262

1942-43 War Set

Scott's No.		Plate Blocks NH	Plate Blocks Unused	F-VF NH	F-VF Unused	Used
249-62	**Set of 14**	...	...	**110.00**	**75.00**	**11.50**
249	1¢ George VI, Green	.85	.70	.22	.20	.15
249a	1¢ Booklet Pane of 4	...	...	4.00	2.75	...
249b	1¢ Booklet Pane of 6	...	...	1.50	1.25	...
249c	1¢ Booklet Pane of 3	...	...	1.50	1.00	...
250	2¢ Brown	1.75	1.25	.35	.25	.15
250a	2¢ Booklet Pane of 4	...	...	4.00	2.75	...
250b	2¢ Booklet Pane of 6	...	...	4.00	2.75	...
251	3¢ Dark Carmine	2.15	1.65	.35	.25	.15
251a	3¢ Booklet Pane of 4	...	...	1.75	1.25	...
252	3¢ Rose Violet (1943)	1.75	1.25	.35	.25	.15
252a	3¢ Booklet Pane of 4	...	...	1.50	1.00	...
252b	3¢ Booklet Pane of 3	...	...	2.00	1.65	...
252c	3¢ Booklet Pane of 6	...	...	4.00	2.75	...
253	4¢ Grain Elevators	10.00	7.25	1.25	.80	.50
254	4¢ George VI. Carm.(1943)	1.85	1.40	.35	.25	.15
254a	4¢ Booklet Pane of 6	...	...	1.75	1.25	...
254b	4¢ Booklet Pane of 3	...	...	1.75	1.25	...
255	5¢ George VI, Deep Blue	4.50	3.00	.90	.60	.15
256	8¢ Farm Scene	9.50	6.50	1.75	1.25	.30
257	10¢ Parliament Buildings	20.00	12.00	3.50	2.50	.15
258	13¢ "Ram" Tank	27.50	16.50	4.50	3.25	2.75
259	14¢ "Ram" Tank (1943)	32.50	24.50	7.00	5.00	.20
260	20¢ Corvette	35.00	26.00	7.50	5.25	.20
261	50¢ Munitions Factory	137.50	90.00	26.50	19.00	1.50
262	$1 Destroyer	315.00	215.00	65.00	42.50	6.75

1942-43 Coil Stamps, Perf. 8 Vertically

Scott's No.		Plate Blocks NH	Plate Blocks Unused	F-VF NH	F-VF Unused	Used
263-67	**Set of 5**	...	...	**8.75**	**5.95**	**1.80**
263	1¢ George VI, Green	...	...	.80	.60	.30
264	2¢ Brown	...	...	1.35	.95	.65
265	3¢ Dark Carmine	...	...	1.35	.95	.65
266	3¢ Rose Violet (1943)	...	...	2.25	1.50	.20
267	4¢ Dark Carmine (1943)	...	...	3.35	2.25	.15

1946 Reconversion "Peace" Issue

268 271 273

Scott's No.		Plate Blocks NH	Plate Blocks Unused	F-VF NH	F-VF Unused	Used
268-73	**Set of 6**	...	...	**55.00**	**37.50**	**4.65**
268	8¢ Farm Scene	5.25	4.50	1.10	.95	.50
269	10¢ Great Bear Lake	5.75	5.00	1.10	.95	.15
270	14¢ Hydroelectric Station	12.50	10.00	2.50	2.00	.18
271	20¢ Combine	16.00	12.50	3.00	2.50	.15
272	50¢ Logging	90.00	56.00	15.00	11.00	1.50
273	$1 Train Ferry	180.00	117.50	35.00	25.00	2.50

274 275 276 283

1947-48 Commemoratives

Scott's No.		Plate Blocks NH	F-VF NH	F-VF Used
274	4¢ Alexander Graham Bell	.85	.20	.15
275	4¢ Citizenship	.85	.20	.15
276	4¢ Royal Wedding (1948)	.85	.20	.15
277	4¢ Parliament (1948)	.75	.20	.15

1948 Coils, Perf. 9½ Vertically

Scott's No.		Plate Blocks NH	F-VF NH	F-VF Used
278	1¢ George VI, Green	...	2.75	1.50
279	2¢ George VI, Brown	...	9.50	5.50
280	3¢ George VI, Rose Violet	...	6.00	1.75
281	4¢ George VI, Dark Carm	...	9.00	2.25

1949 Commemoratives

Scott's No.		Plate Blocks NH	F-VF NH	F-VF Used
282	4¢ Founding of Newfoundland	.75	.20	.15
283	4¢ Halifax Anniversary	.75	.20	.15

CANADA

1949 George VI with "Postes-Postage" In Design

284 289 294 302

Scott's No.		Plate Blocks NH	F-VF NH	F-VF Used
284-88	**Set of 5**	...	**1.95**	**.60**
284	1¢ George VI, Green	.85	.20	.15
284a	1¢ Book. Pane of 3 (1951)	...	.65	...
285	2¢ Sepia	1.00	.20	.15
286	3¢ Rose Violet	1.10	.25	.15
286a	3¢ Book. Pane of 3 (1950)	...	1.15	...
286b	3¢ Book. Pane of 4	...	1.25	...
287	4¢ Dark Carmine	1.75	.40	.15
287a	4¢ Book. Pane of 3 (1951)	...	8.00	...
287b	4¢ Book. Pane of 6 (1951)	...	10.50	...
288	5¢ Deep Blue	4.50	1.00	.15

1950 George VI without "Postes-Postage" In Design

Scott's No.		Plate Blocks NH	F-VF NH	F-VF Used
289-93	**Set of 5**	...	**1.90**	**1.15**
289	1¢ George VI, Green	.85	.20	.15
290	2¢ Sepia	2.00	.30	.15
291	3¢ Rose Violet	.95	.20	.15
292	4¢ Dark Carmine	1.25	.25	.15
293	5¢ Deep Blue	6.00	1.10	.75

1950 Regular Issue

Scott's No.		Plate Blocks NH	F-VF NH	F-VF Used
294	50¢ Oil Wells, Alberta	55.00	11.50	1.30

1950 Coil Stamps, Perf. 9½ Vertically (without "Postes-Postage")

Scott's No.		Plate Blocks NH	F-VF NH	F-VF Used
295	1¢ George VI, Green	...	.30	.25
296	3¢ Rose Violet	...	.60	.50

(with "Postes-Postage")

Scott's No.		Plate Blocks NH	F-VF NH	F-VF Used
297	1¢ George VI, Green	...	.30	.22
298	2¢ Sepia	...	2.00	1.40
299	3¢ Rose Violet	...	1.50	.20
300	4¢ Dark Carmine	...	11.50	.65

1950-1951 Regular Issue

Scott's No.		Plate Blocks NH	F-VF NH	F-VF Used
301	10¢ Fur Resources	4.50	.85	.15
302	$1 Fishing (1951)	300.00	60.00	11.00

303 311 314 315

1951 Commemoratives

Scott's No.		Plate Blocks NH	F-VF NH	F-VF Used
303	3¢ Robert L. Borden	1.10	.22	.15
304	4¢ William L. King	1.10	1.25	.15

1951 Color Changes (with "Postes-Postage")

Scott's No.		Plate Blocks NH	F-VF NH	F-VF Used
305	2¢ George VI, Olive Green	.70	.20	.15
306	4¢ Orange Vermillion	1.00	.22	.15
306a	4¢ Booklet Pane of 3	...	1.50	...
306b	4¢ Booklet Pane of 6	...	2.25	...
309	2¢ Ol. Gr., Coil Pf. 9½ Vert.	...	1.25	.60
310	4¢ Or. Verm., Coil Pf. 9½ Vert.	...	2.35	.70

1951 Int'l. Philatelic Exhibition "CAPEX"

Scott's No.		Plate Blocks NH	F-VF NH	F-VF Used
311-14	**Set of 4**	...	**4.00**	**1.90**
311	4¢ Trains of 1851 & 1951	2.25	.50	.15
312	5¢ Steamships	7.50	1.50	1.20
313	7¢ Plane & Stagecoach	4.50	.90	.30
314	15¢ 1st Canada Stamp	4.50	.90	.27

1951 Commemoratives

Scott's No.		Plate Blocks NH	F-VF NH	F-VF Used
315	4¢ Royal Visit	.85	.20	.15

316 317 320

1952 Regular Issue

Scott's No.		Plate Blocks NH	F-VF NH	F-VF Used
316	20¢ Paper Industry	7.00	1.35	.15

1952 Commemoratives

Scott's No.		Plate Blocks NH	F-VF NH	F-VF Used
317	4¢ Red Cross Conference	1.00	.20	.15
318	3¢ John J.C. Abbott	1.00	.20	.15
319	4¢ Alexander Mackenzie	1.00	.20	.15

1952-53 Regular Issues

Scott's No.		Plate Blocks NH	F-VF NH	F-VF Used
320	7¢ Canada Goose	1.75	.35	.15
321	$1 Totem Pole (1953)	60.00	12.50	.70

322 325 330 334

1953 Wildlife Commemoratives

Scott's No.		Plate Blocks NH	F-VF NH	F-VF Used
322	2¢ Polar Bear	1.00	.20	.15
323	3¢ Moose	1.00	.20	.15
324	4¢ Bighorn Sheep	1.10	.23	.15

1953 Queen Elizabeth II Issue

Scott's No.		Plate Blocks NH	F-VF NH	F-VF Used
325-29	**Set of 5**	**...**	**.95**	**.60**
325	1¢ Elizabeth II, Brown	.60	.20	.15
325a	1¢ Booklet Pane of 3	...	.65	...
326	2¢ Green	.60	.20	.15
327	3¢ Carmine Rose	.75	.20	.15
327a	3¢ Booklet Pane of 3	...	1.25	...
327b	3¢ Booklet Pane of 4	...	1.25	...
328	4¢ Violet	1.15	.24	.15
328a	4¢ Booklet Pane of 3	...	1.50	...
328b	4¢ Booklet Pane of 6	...	1.75	...
329	5¢ Ultramarine	1.40	.30	.15

1953 Coronation Issue

Scott's No.		Plate Blocks NH	F-VF NH	F-VF Used
330	4¢ Elizabeth II	.85	.20	.15

1953 Queen Elizabeth II Coils, Perf. 9½ Vertically

Scott's No.		Plate Blocks NH	F-VF NH	F-VF Used
331	2¢ Elizabeth II, Green	...	1.10	.90
332	3¢ Carmine Rose	...	1.10	.90
333	4¢ Violet	...	2.50	1.50

1953 Regular Issue

Scott's No.		Plate Blocks NH	F-VF NH	F-VF Used
334	50¢ Textile Industry	19.00	4.25	.20

336 337 349 351

1954 Wildlife Commemoratives

Scott's No.		Plate Blocks NH	F-VF NH	F-VF Used
335	4¢ Walrus	1.50	.28	.15
336	5¢ Beaver	1.50	.30	.15
336a	5¢ Booklet Pane of 5	...	1.90	...

1954 Queen Elizabeth II Issue

Scott's No.		Plate Blocks NH	F-VF NH	F-VF Used
337-43	**Set of 7**	**...**	**2.25**	**.85**
337	1¢ Elizabeth II, V. Brown	.60	.20	.15
337a	1¢ Booklet Pane of 5	...	.75	...
338	2¢ Green	.60	.20	.15
338a	2¢ Min. Pane of 25 (1961)	...	4.50	...
338a	Pack of 2	...	9.00	...
339	3¢ Carmine Rose	.75	.20	.15
340	4¢ Violet	.90	.22	.15
340a	4¢ Booklet Pane of 5	...	1.50	...
340b	4¢ Booklet Pane of 6	...	5.00	...
341	5¢ Bright Blue	1.20	.22	.15
341a	5¢ Booklet Pane of 5	...	1.50	...
341b	5¢ Min. Pane of 25 (1961)	...	7.50	...

CANADA

1954 Queen Elizabeth II Issue (cont.)

Scott's No.		Plate Blocks NH	F-VF NH	F-VF Used
342	6¢ Orange	1.70	.35	.15
343	15¢ Gannet, Gray	5.00	1.10	.15

1954 Elizabeth II Coil Stamps, Perf. 9½ Vertically

Scott's No.		Plate Blocks NH	F-VF NH	F-VF Used
345	2¢ Elizabeth II, Green	...	.40	.20
347	4¢ Violet	...	1.25	.22
348	5¢ Bright Blue	...	2.10	.18

1954 Commemoratives

Scott's No.		Plate Blocks NH	F-VF NH	F-VF Used
349	4¢ J.S.D. Thompson	1.30	.25	.15
350	5¢ M. Bowell	1.30	.25	.15

1955 Regular Issue

Scott's No.		Plate Blocks NH	F-VF NH	F-VF Used
351	10¢ Eskimo in Kayak	1.50	.30	.15

352 356 359 360

1955 Commemoratives

Scott's No.		Plate Blocks NH	F-VF NH	F-VF Used
352-58	**Set of 7**	**...**	**1.80**	**.85**
352	4¢ Wildlife - Musk Ox	1.25	.25	.15
353	5¢ Whooping Cranes	1.40	.30	.15
354	5¢ Civil Aviation Org	1.40	.30	.15
355	5¢ Alberta - Saskatchewan	1.40	.30	.15
356	5¢ Boy Scout Jamboree	1.40	.30	.15
357	4¢ Richard B. Bennett	1.25	.25	.15
358	5¢ Charles Tupper	1.25	.25	.15

1956 Commemoratives

Scott's No.		Plate Blocks NH	F-VF NH	F-VF Used
359-61,364	**Set of 4**	**...**	**1.05**	**.50**
359	5¢ Ice Hockey	1.25	.25	.15
360	4¢ Wildlife - Caribou	1.35	.30	.15
361	5¢ Mountain Goat	1.35	.30	.15

362 364 365 369

1956 Regular Issues

Scott's No.		Plate Blocks NH	F-VF NH	F-VF Used
362	20¢ Paper Industry	6.00	1.25	.15
363	25¢ Chemistry Industry	7.50	1.50	.15

1956 Commemoratives

Scott's No.		Plate Blocks NH	F-VF NH	F-VF Used
364	5¢ Fire Prevention	1.15	.25	.15

1957 Commemoratives

Scott's No.		Plate Blocks NH	F-VF NH	F-VF Used
365-74	**Set of 10**	**...**	**4.35**	**2.85**
365-68	5¢ Outdoor Recreation, attd	1.85	1.40	1.35
365-68	Set of 4 Singles	...	1.25	.80
369	5¢ Wildlife - Loon	1.35	.28	.15
370	5¢ David Thompson	1.10	.25	.15
371	5¢ U.P.U. - Parliament	1.10	.25	.15
372	15¢ U.P.U. - Post Horn	10.00	2.00	1.60
373	5¢ Mining Industry	1.10	.24	.15
374	5¢ Royal Visit	1.10	.24	.15

1958 Commemoratives

376 378 380 381

Scott's No.		Plate Blocks NH	F-VF NH	F-VF Used
375-82	**Set of 8**	**...**	**1.80**	**1.00**
375	5¢ Newspaper Industry (Blank)	2.25	.30	.18
376	5¢ Int'l. Geophysical Year (Blank)	2.25	.25	.15
377	5¢ British Columbia Cent	2.25	.25	.15
378	5¢ Explorer La Verendrye	1.50	.25	.15
379	5¢ Quebec Anniversary	3.50	.25	.15
380	5¢ National Health	1.35	.25	.15
381	5¢ Petroleum Industry	1.35	.25	.15
382	5¢ 1st Elected Assembly	1.35	.25	.15

1959 Commemoratives

383 385 387

Scott's No.		Plate Block	F-VF NH	F-VF Used
3-88	**Set of 6**	**...**	**1.35**	**.75**
3	5¢ Golden Anniv. of Flight	1.50	.25	.15
4	5¢ 10th Anniv. of N.A.T.O.	1.35	.25	.15
5	5¢ Country Women of the World	1.25	.25	.15
6	5¢ Royal Tour	1.25	.25	.15
7	5¢ St. Lawrence Seaway	3.25	.25	.15
8	5¢ Plains of Abraham	1.25	.25	.15

1960-1961 Commemoratives

390 391 393 395

9-95	**Set of 7**	**...**	**1.60**	**.85**
9	5¢ Girl Guides Association	1.20	.25	.15
0	5¢ Battle of Long Sault	1.20	.25	.15
1	5¢ Northland Devel. (1961)	1.20	.25	.15
2	5¢ E. Pauline Johnson (1961)	1.20	.25	.15
3	5¢ P. Minister A. Meighen (1961)	1.20	.25	.15
4	5¢ Colombo Plan (1961)	1.20	.25	.15
5	5¢ Resources for Tomorrow (1961)	1.20	.25	.15

396 398 400 401

1962 Commemoratives

6-400	**Set of 5**	**...**	**1.10**	**.65**
6	5¢ Education	1.20	.25	.15
7	5¢ Red River Settlement	1.20	.25	.15
8	5¢ Jean Talon	1.20	.25	.15
9	5¢ Victoria B.C. Centenary	1.20	.25	.15
0	5¢ Trans-Canadian Highway	1.20	.25	.15

1962-63 Queen Elizabeth Issue

1-05	**Set of 5**	**...**	**.85**	**.60**
1	1¢ Deep Brown (1963)	.40	.20	.15
1a	1¢ Booklet Pane of 5	...	3.00	...
2	2¢ Green (1963)	3.25	.20	.15
2a	2¢ Miniature Pane of 25 (pack of 2)	13.50	6.50	...
3	3¢ Purple (1963)	.70	.20	.15
4	4¢ Carmine (1963)	.90	.20	.15
4a	4¢ Booklet Pane of 5	...	3.00	...
4b	4¢ Miniature Pane of 25	...	9.75	...
5	5¢ Violet Blue	1.10	.20	.15
5a	5¢ Booklet Pane of 5 (1963)	...	3.75	...
5b	5¢ Miniature Pane of 20 (1963)	...	10.75	...

1963-64 Coil Stamps, Perf. 9½ Horiz.

6	2¢ Elizabeth, Green	...	3.00	1.40
7	3¢ Purple (1964)	...	2.10	.95
8	4¢ Carmine	...	3.00	1.25
9	5¢ Violet Blue	...	3.00	.45

411 413 417

1963 Commemoratives

Scott's No.		Plate Block	F-VF NH	F-VF Used
410,412-13	**Set of 3**	**...**	**.65**	**.35**
410	5¢ Sir Casimir S. Gzowski	1.15	.24	.15
	1963 Regular Issues			
411	$1 Export Trade, Crate & Map	77.50	15.00	2.25
	1963 Commemoratives			
412	5¢ Explorer M. Frobisher	1.15	.24	.15
413	5¢ First Post Route	1.15	.24	.15
	1963-1964 Regular Issues			
414	7¢ Jet at Ottawa Airport (1964)	1.85	.45	.45
415	15¢ Canada Geese (1963)	12.00	2.50	.20
	1964 Commemoratives			
416,431-35	**Set of 6**	**...**	**1.15**	**.75**
416	5¢ "Peace on Earth"	1.15	.24	.15

418 431 434

1964-1966 Coat of Arms & Flowers

417-29A	**Set of 14**	**14.75**	**2.75**	**1.90**
417	5¢ Canadian Unity, Maple Leaf	1.00	.20	.15
418	5¢ Ontario, White Trillium	1.00	.20	.18
419	5¢ Quebec, White Garden Lily	1.00	.20	.15
420	5¢ Nova Scotia, Mayflower/1965	1.00	.20	.15
421	5¢ New Brunswick, Purple Violet ('65)	1.00	.20	.15
422	5¢ Manitoba, Prairie Crocus ('65)	1.75	.20	.15
423	5¢ British Columbia, Dogwood ('65)	1.00	.20	.15
424	5¢ Pr. Edward I., Lady's Slipper ('65)	1.00	.20	.15
425	5¢ Saskatchewan, Prairie Lily ('66)	1.00	.20	.18
426	5¢ Alberta, Wild Rose ('66)	1.00	.20	.15
427	5¢ Newfoundland, Pitcher Plant ('66)	1.75	.20	.15
428	5¢ Yukon, Firewood ('66)	1.00	.20	.18
429	5¢ Northwest Terr., Mountain Avens ('66)	1.00	.20	.15
429A	5¢ Canada, Maple Leaf ('66)	1.00	.20	.15
	1964 Regular Issue			
430	8¢ on 7¢ Jet Aircraft (on #414) (Blank)	1.50	.30	.30
	1964 Commemoratives			
431	5¢ Charlottestown Conference	1.15	.24	.15
432	5¢ Quebec Conference	1.00	.20	.15
433	5¢ Queen Elizabeth Visit	1.00	.20	.15
434	3¢ Christmas, Family & Star	.75	.20	.15
434a	3¢ Minature Pane of 25 (pack of 2)	14.00	7.00	...
435	5¢ Christmas, Family & Star	1.15	.20	.15
	1964 Regular Issue			
436	8¢ Jet at Ottawa Airport	1.75	.35	.20

1965 Commemoratives

437 440 441 443

437-44	**Set of 8**	**...**	**1.50**	**1.00**
437	5¢ International Cooperation Year	.90	.20	.15
438	5¢ Sir Wilfred Grenfell	.90	.20	.15
439	5¢ National Flag	.90	.20	.15
440	5¢ Sir Winston Churchill	1.15	.24	.15
441	5¢ Interparliamentary Union	.90	.20	.15
442	5¢ Ottawa Centennial	.90	.20	.15
443	3¢ Christmas, Gifts of Wise Men	.70	.20	.15
443a	3¢ Miniature Pane of 25 (pack of 2)	10.50	5.25	...
444	5¢ Christmas, Gifts of Wise Men	1.25	.20	.15

1966 Commemoratives

445 448 450 451

Scott's No.		Plate Block	F-VF NH	F-VF Used
445-52	**Set of 8**	...	**1.50**	**1.00**
445	5¢ Satellite Alouette II	1.00	.20	.15
446	5¢ LaSalle Arrival Tercentary	1.00	.20	.15
447	5¢ Highway Safety	1.00	.20	.15
448	5¢ London Conf. Centenary	1.00	.20.	.15
449	5¢ Atomic Energy	1.00	.20	.15
450	5¢ Parliamentary Association	1.00	.20	.15
451	3¢ Christmas, Praying Hands	.70	.20	.15
451a	3¢ Minature Pane of 25 (pack of 2)	7.00	3.50	...
452	5¢ Christmas, Praying Hands	1.00	.20	.15

1967 Commemoratives

453,469-77	**Set of 10**	...	**1.90**	**1.30**
453	5¢ Canadian Centenary	1.00	.20	.15

1967-72 Definitive Issue, Perf. 12

454 459,460 461 465B

454-65B	**Set of 14**	...	**15.75**	**2.35**
454	1¢ Elizabeth & Dog Team, Brown	.80	.20	.15
454a	1¢ Booklet Pane of 5	...	.75	...
454b	B. Pane of 5 (1 #454 & 4 #459), Perf. 10(1968)	...	2.25	...
454c	B. Pane of 10 (5 #454 & 5 #457) Perf.10(1968)	...	3.50	...
454d	1¢ Booklet Single, Perf. 10 (1968)	...	.25	.18
454e	1¢ Booklet Single, Perf. 12½ x 12 (1969)	...	.40	.18
455	2¢ Elizabeth & Totem Pole, Green	.95	.20	.15
455a	B. Pane of 8 (4 #455, 4 #456)	...	2.00	...
456	3¢ Elizabeth & Combine, Purple	1.50	.20	.15
456a	3¢ Booklet Single, Perf. 12½ x 12 (1971)	...	.75	.40
457	4¢ Elizabeth & Seaway Lock, Carmine	1.50	.20	.15
457a	4¢ Booklet Pane of 5	...	1.50	...
457b	4¢ Miniature Pane of 25	...	18.50	...
457c	4¢ B. Pane of 25, Perf. 10 (1968)	...	8.00	...
457d	4¢ Booklet Single, Perf. 10	...	.70	.25
458	5¢ Elizabeth & Fishing Port, Blue	1.25	.20	.15
458a	5¢ Booklet Pane of 5	...	6.00	...
458b	5¢ Miniature Pane of 20	...	25.00	...
458c	5¢ B. Pane of 20, Perf. 10 (1968)	...	7.50	...
458d	5¢ Booklet Single, Perf. 10	...	.70	.25
459	6¢ Elizabeth & Trans, Orange, Perf. 10 (1968)	3.50	.32	.15
459a	6¢ Booklet Pane of 25, Perf. 10 (1969)	...	8.00	...
459b	6¢ Orange, Perf. 12½ x 12 (1969)	3.00	.30	.15
460	6¢ Black, Die I, Perf. 12½ x 12 (1970)	1.75	.20	.15
460a	6¢ Die I, B. Pane of 25, Perf. 10 (1970)	...	15.00	...
460g	6¢ Die I, Booklet Single, Perf. 10	...	1.50	.45
460b	6¢ Die I, B.Pane of 25, Perf. 12½x12 (1970)	...	16.50	...
460c	6¢ Black, Die II. Perf. 12½ x 12 (1970)	2.00	.25	.15
460d	6¢ Die II, B. Pane of 4, Perf. 12½ x 12 (1970)	...	5.00	...
460e	6¢ Die II, B. Pane of 4, Perf. 10 (1970)	...	7.00	...
460h	6¢ Die II, Booklet Single, Perf. 10	...	1.75	.85
460f	6¢ Die II, Perf. 12 (1973)	2.25	.40	.18
461	8¢ "Alaska Highway"	1.80	.30	.15
462	10¢ "The Jack Pine"	1.60	.30	.15
463	15¢ "Bylot Island"	3.50	.60	.15
464	20¢ "The Ferry, Quebec"	3.75	.70	.15
465	25¢ "The Solemn Land"	6.95	1.35	.15
465A	50¢ "Summer's Stores"	20.00	4.00	.20
465B	$1 "Oilfield, Edmonton"	42.50	8.50	.70

#460 has weak shading lines around "6"; #460c has lines strengthened.

1967-70 Coil Stamps, Perf. 9½ or 10 Horiz.

466	3¢ Elizabeth & Oil Rig	...	1.60	1.00
467	4¢ Elizabeth & Canal Lock	...	.80	.65
468	5¢ Elizabeth & Fishing Port	...	1.65	.80
468A	6¢ Elizabeth, Orange (1969)	...	.33	.15
466B	6¢ Elizabeth, Black (1970)	...	.33	.15

CANADA

1967 Commemoratives (See also #453)

469 473 476

Scott's No.		Plate Block	F-VF NH	F-V Use
469	5¢ Expo '67, Montreal	1.00	.20	.1
470	5¢ Women's Franchise	1.00	.20	.1
471	5¢ Royal Visit, Elizabeth II	1.00	.20	.1
472	5¢ Pan American Games	1.00	.20	.1
473	5¢ Canadian Press	1.00	.20	.1
474	5¢ Georges P. Vanier	1.15	.24	.1
475	5¢ Toronto Centennial	1.00	.20	.1
476	3¢ Christmas, Singing Children	.80	.20	.1
476a	3¢ Miniature Pane of 25	5.50	2.75	..
477	5¢ Christmas, Singing Children	.85	.20	.1

1968 Commemoratives

479 485 486 488

478-89	**Set of 12**	...	**3.85**	**2.5**
478	5¢ Wildlife - Gray Jays	3.75	.40	.1
479	5¢ Meteorological Readings	1.00	.20	.1
480	5¢ Wildlife - Narwhal	1.00	.20	.1
481	5¢ Int'l. Hydrological Decade	1.00	.20	.1
482	5¢ Voyage of "Nonsuch"	1.15	.20	.1
483	5¢ Lacrosse Players	1.15	.20	.1
484	5¢ George Brown and "Globe"	1.15	.20	.1
485	5¢ Henry Bourassa - Journalist	1.15	.20	.1
486	15¢ World War I Armistice	8.00	1.65	1.2
487	5¢ John McCrae - Poet	1.15	.20	.1
488	5¢ Christmas - Eskimo Carving	.75	.20	.1
488a	5¢ Booklet Pane of 10	...	2.75	..
489	6¢ Christmas - Mother & Infant	1.10	.22	.1

1969 Commemoratives

491 496 500 502

490-504	**Set of 15**	...	**9.50**	**6.**
490	6¢ Sports - Curling	1.00	.20	.
491	6¢ Vincent Massey	1.00	.20	.
492	50¢ Aurele de Fey Suzor-Cote	15.00	3.00	2.
493	6¢ Int'l. Labor Organization	1.00	.20	.
494	15¢ Non-Stop Atlantic Flight	8.00	1.75	1.
495	6¢ Sir William Osler	1.00	.20	.
496	6¢ White-Throated Sparrow	1.85	.40	.
497	10¢ Ipswich Sparrow	3.75	.80	.
498	25¢ Hermit Thrush	9.75	2.00	1.
499	6¢ Charlottetown Bicentennial	1.00	.20	.
500	6¢ Canada Summer Games	1.00	.20	.
501	6¢ Sir Isaac Brock	1.00	.20	.
502	5¢ Christmas, Children	.75	.20	.
502a	5¢ Booklet Pane of 10	...	3.00	..
503	6¢ Christmas, Children	.75	.20	.
504	6¢ Stephen Leacock	1.10	.20	.

NOTE: STARTING IN 1967, MANY PLATE BLOCKS HAVE IMPRINTS WITHOUT PLATE NUMBERS.

1970 Commemoratives

505 508 513

ott's o.		Plate Block	F-VF NH	F-VF Used
5-18,531	**Set of 15**	...	**11.50**	**9.75**
5	6¢ Manitoba Centenary	.95	.20	.15
6	6¢ Northwest Territory	.90	.20	.15
7	6¢ Biological Program	.90	.20	.15
8-11	25¢ Expo '70, Tokyo, attd	9.50	8.50	8.50
8-11	Set of 4 Singles	...	7.75	7.75
2	6¢ Henry Kelsey - Explorer	.90	.20	.15
3	10¢ 25th Anniv. of United Nations	3.50	.70	.50
4	15¢ 25th Anniv. of United Nations	5.00	1.00	.90
5	6¢ Louis Riel, Metis Leader	.90	.20	.15
6	6¢ Sir A. Mackenzie - Explorer	.90	.20	.15
7	6¢ Sir Oliver Mowat	.95	.20	.15
8	6¢ Group of Seven	.95	.20	.15

1970 Christmas - Children's Designs

519 524 530

		Plate Block	F-VF NH	F-VF Used
9-30	**Set of 12 Singles**	...	**4.50**	**2.35**
9-23	5¢ Christmas, attached	(10) 5.75	2.50	...
9-23	Set of 5 Singles	...	1.60	.75
4-28	6¢ Christmas, attached	(10) 6.75	3.00	...
4-28	Set of 5 Singles	...	1.65	.75
9	10¢ Christ Child in Manger	2.25	.45	.30
0	15¢ Snowmobile & Trees	4.35	.85	.85

532 533 535 543

1970 Commemoratives (continued)

		Plate Block	F-VF NH	F-VF Used
1	6¢ Donald Alexander Smith	.90	.20	.15

532 533 535 543

1971 Commemoratives

		Plate Block	F-VF NH	F-VF Used
2-42,552-58	**Set of 18**	...	**5.35**	**3.95**
2	6¢ Emily Carr - Painter	.85	.20	.15
3	6¢ Discovery of Insulin	.85	.20	.15
4	6¢ Sir Ernest Rutheford	.85	.20	.15
5	6¢ Maple Leaf - Spring	1.15	.24	.15
6	6¢ Maple Leaf - Summer	1.15	.24	.15
7	7¢ Maple Leaf - Autumn	1.15	.24	.15
8	7¢ Maple Leaf - Winter	1.15	.24	.15
9	6¢ Louis Papineau	.85	.20	.15
0	6¢ Samuel Hearne	.85	.20	.15
1	15¢ Radio Canada Int'l	7.00	1.50	1.25
2	6¢ Census Centennial	.85	.20	.15

1971-72 Definitive Issue

		Plate Block	F-VF NH	F-VF Used
3	7¢ Elizabeth & Transportation, Green	3.00	.25	.15
3a	B. Pane of 5 (1 #454,1 #456,3 #543)	...	3.00	...
3b	B. Pane of 20 (4 #454,4 #456,12 #543)	...	7.75	...
4	8¢ Elizabeth & Parliament, Slate	3.00	.25	.15
4a	B. Pane of 6 (3 #454,1 #460c,2 #544)	...	1.75	...
4b	B. Pane of 18 (6 #454,1 #460c,11 #544)	...	6.00	...
4c	B. Pane of 10 (4 #454,1 #460c,5 #544) (1972)	...	2.25	...
9	7¢ Green, Coil, Perf. 10 Horiz	...	.40	.15
0	8¢ Slate, Coil, Perf. 10 Horiz	...	.30	.15

CANADA

1971 Commemoratives (continued)

554 556 561

Scott's No.		Plate Block	F-VF NH	F-VF Used
552	7¢ British Columbia Centenary	.85	.20	.15
553	7¢ Paul Kane - Painter	2.50	.35	.15
554	6¢ Christmas, Snowflake	.85	.20	.15
555	7¢ Christmas, Snowflake	1.00	.20	.15
556	10¢ Christmas, Snowflake	2.00	.40	.35
557	15¢ Christmas, Snowflake	3.65	.75	.75
558	7¢ Pierre Laporte	2.40	.20	.15

1972 Commemoratives

		Plate Block	F-VF NH	F-VF Used
559-61,606-10	**Set of 8**	...	**2.25**	**1.75**
559	8¢ Figure Skating	1.00	.20	.15
560	8¢ World Health Day	1.40	.30	.18
561	8¢ Frontenac Anniversary	1.00	.20	.15

1972-76 Canadian Indians

562 564 568 570

1972 Indians of the Plains

		Plate Block	F-VF NH	F-VF Used
562-63	8¢ Plains Indians, attached	1.70	.70	.55
562-63	Set of 2 Singles	...	.65	.30
564-65	8¢ Plains Indians, attached	1.70	.70	.55
564-65	Set of 2 Singles	...	.65	.30

1973 Algonkian Indians

		Plate Block	F-VF NH	F-VF Used
566-67	8¢ Algonkians, attached	1.50	.60	.55
566-67	Set of 2 Singles	...	.55	.30
568-69	8¢ Algonkians, attached	1.50	.60	.55
568-69	Set of 2 Singles	...	.55	.30

1974 Pacific Coast Indians

		Plate Block	F-VF NH	F-VF Used
570-71	8¢ Pacific Indians, attached	1.50	.60	.55
570-71	Set of 2 Singles	...	.55	.30
572-73	8¢ Pacific Indians, attached	1.50	.60	.55
572-73	Set of 2 Singles	...	.55	.30

576 578 580 582

1975 Subarctic Indians

		Plate Block	F-VF NH	F-VF Used
574-75	8¢ Subarctic, attached	1.20	.50	.45
574-75	Set of 2 Singles	...	.45	.30
576-77	8¢ Subarctic, attached	1.20	.50	.45
576-77	Set of 2 Singles	...	.45	.20

1976 Iroquois Indians

		Plate Block	F-VF NH	F-VF Used
578-79	10¢ Iroquois, attached	1.20	.50	.45
578-79	Set of 2 Singles	...	.45	.30
580-81	10¢ Iroquois, attached	1.20	.50	.45
580-81	Set of 2 Singles	...	.45	.30
562-81	**Canadian Indians, set of 20**	...	**5.25**	**2.65**

1972 Earth Sciences

		Plate Block	F-VF NH	F-VF Used
582-85	15¢ Sciences, attached	(16) 35.00	7.00	7.00
582-85	Set of 4 Singles	...	6.50	5.50

1972-1977 Definitive Issue, Perf. 12 x 12½ or 12½ x 12

586 593 594 599

Scott's No.		Plate Block	F-VF NH	F-VF Used
586-601	**Set of 17**	...	**14.50**	**5.85**
586	1¢ Sir John A. MacDonald	.60	.20	.15
586a	B. Pane of 6 (3 #586,1 #591,2 #593) ('74)	...	.50	...
586b	B. Pane of 18 (6 #586,1 #591,11 #593)('75)	...	1.75	...
586c	B. Pane of 10 (2 #586,4 #587,4 #593c)('76)	...	1.25	...
587	2¢ Sir Wilfred Laurier ('73)	.60	.20	.15
588	3¢ Sir Robert L. Borden ('73)	.60	.20	.15
589	4¢ W.L. Mackenzie King ('73)	.60	.20	.15
590	5¢ Richard B. Bennett ('73)	.80	.20	.15
591	6¢ Lester B. Pearson ('73)	.80	.20	.15
592	7¢ Louis St. Laurent ('74)	.90	.20	.15
593	8¢ Queen Elizabeth II, Perf. 12 x 12½ ('73)	1.00	.20	.15
593b	8¢ Queen Elizabeth II, Perf. 13 x 13½ ('76)	3.75	.70	.30
593A	10¢ Queen Elizabeth II, Perf. 13 x 13½ ('76)	1.00	.20	.15
593c	10¢ Booklet Single, Perf. 12 x 12½ ('76).	...	.25	.15
594	10¢ Forests, Tagged, Narrow Side Bars .	1.00	.20	.15
594a	10¢ Redrawn, Perf. 13½ ('76)	1.25	.25	.15
595	15¢ Mountain Sheep, Tagged Narrow Bars	1.40	.30	.15
595a	15¢ Redrawn, Perf. 13½ ('76)	1.65	.35	.20
596	20¢ Prairie Mosaic, Tagged Narrow Bars	2.10	.45	.15
596a	20¢ Redrawn, Perf. 13½ ('76)	2.40	.50	.15
597	25¢ Polar Bears, Tagged Narrow Bars....	2.50	.50	.15
597a	25¢ Redrawn, Perf. 13½ ('76)	3.00	.65	.15
598	50¢ Seashore	4.75	1.00	.15
598a	50¢ Redrawn, Perf. 13½ ('76)	8.25	1.70	.18
599	$1 Vancouver, Revised ('73)	12.50	2.25	.50
599a	$1 Redrawn, Perf. 13½ ('77)	11.00	2.25	.40
600	$1 Vancouver, Original, Perf. 11	20.00	4.50	1.75
601	$2 Quebec Buildings, Perf. 11	18.00	3.75	2.25
604	8¢ Elizabeth II, Coil, Perf. 10 Vert	...	.20	.15
605	10¢ Elizabeth II, Coil, Perf. 10 Vert	...	.25	.15

1972 Commemoratives (continued)

606 608 610

Scott's No.		Plate Block	F-VF NH	F-VF Used
606	6¢ Christmas, Candles	.90	.20	.15
607	8¢ Christmas, Candles	1.00	.20	.15
608	10¢ Christmas, Candles & Fruit	1.95	.40	.35
609	15¢ Christmas, Candles & Prayer Book..	3.25	.70	.70
610	8¢ C. Krieghoff, Painter	1.80	.25	.15

1973 Commemoratives

620 623 625

Scott's No.		Plate Block	F-VF NH	F-VF Used
611-28	**Set of 18**	...	**5.50**	**4.50**
611	8¢ Monsignor de Laval	.90	.20	.15
612	8¢ Mounties - G.A. French	1.20	.25	.15
613	10¢ Mounties - Spectograph	1.65	.35	.30
614	15¢ Mounties - Municipal Rider	3.15	.70	.60
615	8¢ Jeanne Mance - Nurse	.90	.20	.15
616	8¢ Joseph Howe - Journalist	.90	.20	.15
617	15¢ J.E.H. MacDonald - Painter	2.50	.50	.45

NOTE: STARTING IN 1973, ALL CANADIAN STAMPS ARE TAGGED.

1973 Commemoratives (cont.)

Scott's No.		Plate Block	F-VF NH	F-VF Used
618	8¢ Prince Edward I Centenary	.90	.20	.1
619	8¢ Scottish Settlers Bicentenary	.90	.20	.1
620	8¢ Royal Visit, Elizabeth II	.90	.20	.1
621	15¢ Royal Visit, Elizabeth II	3.25	.70	.6
622	8¢ Nellie McClung, Suffragette	.90	.20	.1
623	8¢ 21st Olympics Publicity	.90	.20	.1
624	15¢ 21st Olympics Publicity	2.50	.55	.5
625	6¢ Christmas - Ice Skate	.70	.20	.1
626	8¢ Christmas - Dove	.90	.20	.1
627	10¢ Christmas - Santa Claus	1.25	.25	.2
628	15¢ Christmas - Shepherd and Star	2.50	.55	.5

1974 Commemoratives

629 634 644

648 650 655

Scott's No.		Plate Block	F-VF NH	F-VF Used
629-55	**Set of 27**	...	**8.95**	**5.5**
629-32	8¢ Summer Olympics, attd	1.50	1.25	1.[illegible]
629-32	Set of 4 Singles	...	1.20	[illegible]
633	8¢ Winnipeg Centenary	1.00	.22	[illegible]
634-39	8¢ Letter Carriers, attached (6)	4.00	3.25	3.[illegible]
634-39	Set of 6 Singles	...	3.00	1.[illegible]
640	8¢ Agriculture Education	1.00	.22	[illegible]
641	8¢ Telephone Centenary	1.00	.22	[illegible]
642	8¢ World Cycling Champs	1.00	.22	[illegible]
643	8¢ Mennonite Settlement	1.00	.22	[illegible]
644-47	8¢ Winter Olympics, attached	1.50	1.25	1.[illegible]
644-47	Set of 4 Singles	...	1.20	[illegible]
648	8¢ Universal Postal Union	.90	.20	[illegible]
649	15¢ Universal Postal Union	3.50	.75	[illegible]
650	6¢ Christmas "Nativity"	.70	.20	[illegible]
651	8¢ Christmas "Skaters in Hull"	.85	.20	[illegible]
652	10¢ Christmas "The Ice Cone"	1.45	.30	[illegible]
653	15¢ Christmas "Village"	2.75	.55	[illegible]
654	8¢ Marconi Centenary	.90	.20	[illegible]
655	8¢ William H. Merritt, Welland Canal.....	.90	.20	[illegible]

1975 Commemoratives

657 662 664 669

658 670 674

1975 Commemoratives

Scott's No.		Plate Block	F-VF NH	F-VF Used
56-80	**Set of 25**	**...**	**15.25**	**11.50**
56	$1 Olympics "The Sprinter"	12.00	2.50	1.95
57	$2 Olympics "The Plunger"	23.50	5.25	4.50
58-59	8¢ Writers, attached	.95	.40	.35
58-59	Set of 2 Singles	...	.35	.30
60	8¢ Marguerite Bourgeoys	.90	.20	.15
61	8¢ Alphonse Desjardins	.90	.20	.15
62-63	8¢ Religious Leaders, attached	1.10	.45	.40
62-63	Set of 2 Singles	...	.40	.35
64	20¢ Olympics - Pole Vaulting	3.00	.65	.50
65	25¢ Olympics - Marathon Running	3.50	.75	.55
66	50¢ Olympics - Hurdling	6.00	1.35	1.00
67	8¢ Calgary Centennial	1.00	.20	.15
68	8¢ Women's Year	1.00	.20	.15
69	8¢ Supreme Court Centenary	1.00	.20	.15
70-73	8¢ Canadian Ships, attached	2.50	2.00	1.85
70-73	Set of 4 Singles	...	1.95	1.40
74-75	6¢ Christmas, attached	.85	.45	.35
74-75	Set of 2 Singles	...	.40	.30
76-77	8¢ Christmas, attached	1.00	.45	.35
76-77	Set of 2 Singles	...	.40	.30
78	10¢ Christmas, Gift Box	1.00	.20	.20
79	15¢ Christmas, Tree	1.85	.40	.40
80	8¢ Royal Canadian Legion	1.00	.20	.15

1976 Commemoratives

684 692 697 704

687 700

Scott's No.		Plate Block	F-VF NH	F-VF Used
81-703	**Set of 23**	**...**	**17.50**	**12.75**
81	8¢ Olympic Ceremonies	.95	.20	.15
82	20¢ Olympic Ceremonies	2.75	.60	.50
83	25¢ Olympic Ceremonies	3.50	.75	.70
84	20¢ Olympics - Communication Arts	4.75	1.00	.65
85	25¢ Olympics - Handcraft Tools	5.50	1.20	.70
86	50¢ Olympics - Performing Arts	9.00	1.95	1.25
87	$1 Olympic Site - Tower and Church	12.00	2.50	1.90
88	$2 Olympic Site - Olympic Stadium	25.00	5.25	4.00
89	20¢ Winter Olympic Games	3.50	.80	.65
90	20¢ HABITAT - U.N. Conference	2.00	.45	.45
91	10¢ U.S. Bicentennial - B. Franklin	1.20	.25	.20
92-93	8¢ Royal Military College, attd.	1.00	.45	.40
92-93	Set of 2 Singles	...	.40	.30
94	20¢ Olympiad for Physically Disabled	2.85	.60	.55
95-96	8¢ Authors, attached	1.00	.45	.35
95-96	Set of 2 Singles	...	.40	.30
97	8¢ Xmas - Stained Glass Window	.75	.20	.15
98	10¢ Xmas - Stained Glass Window	.95	.20	.15
99	20¢ Xmas - Stained Glass Window	1.95	.40	.40
00-03	10¢ Canadian Ships, attached	1.60	1.25	1.25
00-03	Set of 4 Singles	...	1.20	1.10

1977 Commemoratives

Scott's No.		Plate Block	F-VF NH	F-VF Used
04,732-51	**Set of 21**	**...**	**5.50**	**3.95**
04	25¢ Queen Elizabeth II Silver Jubilee	3.00	.65	.50

1977-1979 Definitive Issues, Perf. 12 x 12½

707 723 726

1977-1979 Definitive Issues, Perf. 12 x 12½

Scott's No.		Plate Block	F-VF NH	F-VF Used
705-27	**Set of 22**	**...**	**13.75**	**4.95**
705	1¢ Wildflower - Bottle Gentian	.60	.20	.15
707	2¢ Wildflower - W. Columbine	.60	.20	.15
708	3¢ Wildflower - Canada Lily	.60	.20	.15
709	4¢ Wildflower - Hepatica	.60	.20	.15
710	5¢ Wildflower - Shooting Star	.60	.20	.15
711	10¢ Wildflower - Lady's Slipper	.80	.20	.15
711a	10¢ Same (1978, Perf. 13)	1.00	.20	.15
712	12¢ Wildflower - Jewelweed, Pf. 13 x 13½ (1978)	1.75	.35	.20
713	12¢ Elizabeth II, Perf. 13 x 13½	1.15	.25	.15
713a	12¢ Booklet Sngl., Perf. 12 x 12½	...	.30	.15
714	12¢ Houses of Parliament, Perf. 13 ('78)	1.10	.22	.15
715	14¢ Houses of Parliament, Perf. 13 ('78)	1.20	.25	.15
716	14¢ Eliz. II, 13 x 13½ ('78)	1.20	.25	.15
716a	14¢ Bklt. Sgl., Perf. 12 x 12½ ('78)	...	.30	.15
716b	14¢ B. Pane of 25, Perf. 12 x 12½ ('78)	...	5.75	...
717	15¢ Tree - Trembling Aspen, Perf. 13½	1.85	.40	.15
718	20¢ Tree - Doug. Fir, Perf. 13½	1.60	.35	.15
719	25¢ Trees - Sugar Maple, Perf. 13½	2.00	.45	.15
720	30¢ Trees - Red Oak, Perf. 13½ ('78)	2.25	.50	.20
721	35¢ Trees - Winter Pine, Perf. 13½ ('79)	2.70	.60	.30
723	50¢ Streets-Prairie Town, Perf.13½ ('78)	4.35	.95	.25
723A	50¢ Same, "1978" on Lic. Plate	4.25	.90	.20
724	75¢ Streets-Row Houses, Perf.13½ ('78)	5.75	1.25	.35
725	80¢ Streets-Maritime, Perf. 13½ ('79)	6.50	1.35	.40
726	$1 Bay of Fundy, Perf. 13½ ('79)	8.00	1.75	.50
726a	$1 Untagged	8.50	1.85	.60
727	$2 Kluane National Park, Perf.13½ ('79)	16.00	3.50	1.15
729	12¢ Parliament, Coil, Perf. 10 Vert	...	.22	.15
730	14¢ Parliament, Coil, Perf. 10 Vert. ('78)	...	.25	.15

1977 Commemoratives (continued)

733 736 738

741 744 748

Scott's No.		Plate Block	F-VF NH	F-VF Used
732	12¢ Wildlife - Eastern Cougar	1.10	.22	.15
733-34	12¢ Thomson Paintings, attd	1.10	.45	.40
733-34	Set of 2 Singles	...	.44	.30
735	12¢ Canadian-born Gov. Generals	1.10	.22	.15
736	12¢ Order of Canada 10th Anniv	1.10	.22	.15
737	12¢ Peace Bridge - 50th Anniv	1.10	.22	.15
738-39	12¢ Pioneers, attached	1.10	.45	.40
738-39	Set of 2 Singles	...	.44	.30
740	25¢ Parliamentary Conference	3.00	.65	.65
741	10¢ Christmas - Christmas Star	.95	.20	.15
742	12¢ Christmas - Angelic Choir	1.10	.22	.15
743	25¢ Christmas - Christ Child	2.20	.45	.45
744-47	12¢ Sailing Ships, attached	1.15	.90	.90
744-47	Set of 4 Singles	...	.85	.75
748-49	12¢ Inuit Hunting, attached	1.10	.45	.40
748-49	Set of 2 Singles	...	.44	.30
750-51	12¢ Inuit Hunting, attached	1.10	.45	.40
750-51	Set of 2 Singles	...	.44	.30

1978 Commemoratives

Scott's No.		Plate Block	F-VF NH	F-VF Used
752-56,757-79	**Set of 28**	**...**	**9.35**	**6.25**
752	12¢ Peregrine Falcon	1.10	.24	.15
753	12¢ CAPEX, 12p Queen Victoria	1.00	.22	.15
754	14¢ CAPEX, 10p Cartier	1.20	.25	.15
755	30¢ CAPEX, ½p Queen Victoria	2.40	.50	.50
756	$1.25 CAPEX, 6p Prince Albert	8.00	1.75	1.25
756a	$1.69 CAPEX Souvenir Sheet	...	2.85	2.75
757	14¢ Commonwealth Games, Symbol	1.15	.24	.15
758	30¢ Commonwealth Games, Badminton	2.25	.50	.40

1978 Commemoratives (continued)

759 765 776

753 763 768

Scott's No.		Plate Block	F-VF NH	F-VF Used
759-60	14¢ Commonwealth Games, attd	1.20	.50	.40
759-60	Set of 2 Singles	...	.48	.30
761-62	30¢ Commonwealth Games, attd	2.50	1.10	1.10
761-62	Set of 2 Singles	...	1.00	.90
763-64	14¢ Captain Cook, attached	1.20	.50	.40
763-64	Set of 2 Singles	...	.48	.30
765-66	14¢ Resource Develop., attd	1.20	.50	.40
765-66	Set of 2 Singles	...	.48	.30
767	14¢ Canadian National Exhibition	1.20	.24	.15
768	14¢ Mere d'Youville	1.20	.24	.15
769-70	14¢ Travels of Inuit, attached	1.20	.50	.40
769-70	Set of 2 Singles	...	.48	.30
771-72	14¢ Travels of Inuit, attached	1.20	.50	.40
771-72	Set of 2 Singles	...	.48	.30
773	12¢ Christmas, Madonna	.95	.20	.15
774	14¢ Christmas, Virgin & Child	1.15	.24	.15
775	30¢ Christmas, Virgin & Child	2.25	.50	.45
776-79	14¢ Ice Vessels, attd	1.25	1.10	1.00
776-79	Set of 4 Singles	...	1.00	.75

1979 Commemoratives

780,813-46	**Set of 35**	**...**	**11.25**	**6.50**
780	14¢ Quebec Winter Carnival	1.15	.24	.15

1977-1983 Definitives, Perf. 13 x 13½
Designs of #705-730 plus new designs

781-792	**Set of 11**	**...**	**2.90**	**1.45**
781	1¢ Wildflower, Bot. Gentian ('79)	.60	.20	.15
781a	1¢ Bklt. Sgl., Perf. 12 x 12½	...	.20	.15
781b	B. Pane of 6 (2 #781a & 4 #713a)	...	1.00	...
782	2¢ Wildflower, W. Colum	.60	.20	.15
782a	B. Pane of 7 (4 #782b, 3 #716a) ('78)	...	.80	...
782b	2¢ B. Sgl. Perf. 12 x 12½ ('78)	...	.20	.15
783	3¢ Wildflower-Canada Lily ('79)	.60	.20	.15
784	4¢ Wildflower-Hepatica ('79)	.60	.20	.15
785	5¢ Wildflower-Shooting Star ('79)	.60	.20	.15
786	10¢ Wildflower-Lady's Slipper	.80	.20	.15
787	15¢ Wildflower-Canada Violet ('79)	1.20	.25	.15
789	17¢ Elizabeth II ('79)	1.35	.28	.15
789a	B. Sgl. Perf. 12 x 12½ ('79)	...	.30	.15
789b	B. Pane of 25, Perf. 12 x 12½ ('79)	...	6.75	...
790	17¢ Houses of Parliament / 1979	1.35	.28	.15
791	30¢ Elizabeth II (1982)	2.25	.50	.15
792	32¢ Elizabeth II (1983)	2.50	.55	.15
797	1¢ Parl. B. Sgl. Perf. 12 x 12½ ('79)	...	.60	.25
797a	B. Pane/6 (1 #797,3 #800,2 #789a)	...	1.00	...
800	5¢ Parl. B. Sgl. Perf. 12 x 12½ ('79)	...	.20	.15
806	17¢ Parl. Coil, Perf. 10 Vert	...	.35	.15

1979 Commemoratives (continued)

813 815 817

CANADA

1979 Commemoratives (continued)

821 839 843

Scott's No.		Plate Block	F-VF NH	F-VF Used
813	17¢ Wildlife, Turtle	1.35	.28	.1
814	35¢ Wildlife, Whale	3.25	.70	.4
815-16	17¢ Postal Code, attached	1.50	.60	.5
815-16	Set of 2 Singles	...	.55	.3
817-18	17¢ Writer & Poet, attached	1.50	.60	.5
817-18	Set of 2 Singles	...	.55	.3
819-20	17¢ Colonels, attached	1.50	.60	.5
819-20	Set of 2 Singles	...	.55	.4
821-32	17¢ Flags, Set of 12 Singles	...	3.60	2.4
832a	Sheetlet of Twelve Flags	...	3.75	3.7
833	17¢ Canoe-Kayak Meet	1.35	.28	.1
834	17¢ Women's Field Hockey	1.35	.28	.1
835-36	17¢ Inuit, attached	1.45	.60	.5
835-36	Set of 2 Singles	...	.55	.3
837-38	17¢ Inuit, attached	1.45	.60	.5
837-38	Set of 2 Singles	...	.55	.3
839	15¢ Christmas - Antique Toy Train	1.15	.25	.1
840	17¢ Christmas - Antique Toy Horse	1.40	.30	.1
841	35¢ Christmas - Antique Knitted Doll	2.70	.60	.4
842	17¢ Int'l. Year of the Child	1.35	.28	.1
843-44	17¢ Flying Boats, attached	1.45	.60	.5
843-44	Set of 2 Singles	...	.55	.3
845-46	35¢ Flying Boats, attached	3.20	1.35	1.2
845-46	Set of 2 Singles	...	1.30	1.0

1980 Commemoratives

849 856 860 870

847-77	**Set of 31**	**...**	**11.50**	**6.9**
847	17¢ Arctic Islands	1.35	.28	.1
848	35¢ Winter Olympics, Skier	2.85	.60	.5
849-50	17¢ Artists, attached	1.45	.60	.5
849-50	Set of 2 Singles	...	.55	.3
851-52	35¢ Artists, attached	2.95	1.30	1.2
851-52	Set of 2 Singles	...	1.20	.9
853	17¢ Atlantic Whitefish	1.40	.30	.1
854	17¢ Greater Prairie Chicken	1.40	.30	.1
855	17¢ Montreal Flower Show	1.35	.28	.1
856	17¢ Rehabilitation Congress	1.35	.28	.1

857 865 873

857-58	17¢ "O Canada" Centenary, attd	1.45	.60	.5
857-58	Set of 2 Singles	...	.55	.3
859	17¢ John George Diefenbaker	1.35	.28	.
860-61	17¢ Musicians, attached	1.45	.60	.5
860-61	Set of 2 Singles	...	.55	.
862	17¢ Ned Hanlan, Oarsman	1.35	.28	.
863	17¢ Saskatchewan, Wheat Field	1.35	.28	.
864	17¢ Alberta, Strip Mining	1.35	.28	.
865	35¢ Uranium Resources	2.85	.60	.
866-67	17¢ Inuit Spirits, attached	1.45	.60	.
866-67	Set of 2 Singles	...	.55	.
868-69	35¢ Inuit Spirits, attached	2.95	1.30	1.
868-69	Set of 2 Singles	...	1.20	1.
870	15¢ Christmas, "Christmas Morning"	1.20	.25	.
871	17¢ Christmas, "Sleigh Ride"	1.35	.28	.
872	35¢ Christmas, "McGill Cab Stand"	2.90	.60	.
873-74	17¢ Military Aircraft, attached	1.50	.65	.
873-74	Set of 2 Singles	...	.60	.
875-76	35¢ Military Aircraft, attached	2.95	1.30	1.
875-76	Set of 2 Singles	...	1.20	1.
877	17¢ E.P. Lachapelle, Physician	1.35	.28	.

1981 Commemoratives

879-82 889

cott's No.		Plate Block	F-VF NH	F-VF Used
78-906	**Set of 29**	**...**	**9.35**	**5.50**
78	17¢ 18th Century Mandora	1.35	.28	.15
79-82	17¢ Feminists, attached	1.50	1.25	1.20
79-82	Set of 4 Singles	...	1.20	.70
83	17¢ Endangered Wildlife, Marmot	1.35	.28	.15
34	35¢ Endangered Wildlife, Wood Bison	3.00	.65	.60
35-86	17¢ Beatified Woman, attached	1.45	.60	.55
35-86	Set of 2 Singles	...	.55	.30
37	17¢ Marc-Aurele Fortin, Painter	1.35	.28	.15
38	17¢ Frederic H. Varley, Painter	1.35	.28	.15
39	35¢ Paul-Emile Borduas, Painter	2.95	.60	.55
30-93	17¢ Historic Maps, attached	(8) 3.00	1.25	1.20
30-93	Set of 4 Singles	...	1.20	.80
34-95	17¢ Botanists, attached	1.45	.60	.55
34-95	Set of 2 Singles	...	.55	.30
36	17¢ Montreal Rose	1.35	.28	.15
37	17¢ Niagara-on-the-Lake	1.35	.28	.15
38	17¢ Acadian Congress Centenary	1.35	.28	.15
39	17¢ Aaron Mosher Labor	1.35	.28	.15
30	15¢ 1781 Christmas Tree	1.15	.25	.15
31	15¢ 1881 Christmas Tree	1.15	.25	.15
32	15¢ 1981 Christmas Tree	1.15	.25	.15
33-04	17¢ Aircraft, attached	1.50	.65	.55
33-04	Set of 2 Singles	...	.60	.30
35-06	35¢ Aircraft, attached	2.95	1.25	1.20
35-06	Set of 2 Singles	...	1.20	1.00

907 909 914

1981 "A" Interim Definitives

7	(30¢) "A" and Maple Leaf, Perf. 13 x 13½	2.35	.50	.15
8	(30¢) "A" and Maple Leaf, Coil	...	.80	.18

1982 Commemoratives

9-16,954-75	**Set of 30**	**...**	**18.50**	**10.65**
9	30¢ Youth Exhibit, 1851 3d Beaver	2.40	.50	.18
0	30¢ 1908 15¢ Champlain	2.40	.50	.18
1	35¢ 1935 10¢ Mountie	2.85	.60	.55
2	35¢ 1928 10¢ Mt. Hurd	2.85	.60	.55
3	60¢ 1929 50¢ Bluenose	5.75	1.15	.90
3a	Exhibition Souvenir Sheet	...	3.25	3.25
4	30¢ Jules Leger, Governor-Gen'l	2.40	.50	.15
5	30¢ Marathon of Hope - Terry Fox	2.40	.50	.15
6	30¢ New Consitution	2.40	.50	.15

1982-89 Artifacts and Definitives

917 923 927 931

Scott's No.		Plate Block	F-VF NH	F-VF Used
917-37	**Set of 23**	**...**	**29.50**	**10.65**
917	1¢ Decoy, Perf. 14 x 13½	.60	.20	.15
917a	1¢ Perf. 13 x 13½ (1985)	.60	.20	.15
918	2¢ Fishing Spear, Perf. 14 x 13½	.60	.20	.15
918a	2¢ Perf. 13 x 13½ (1985)	.60	.20	.15
919	3¢ Stable Lantern, Perf. 14 x 13½	.60	.20	.15
919a	3¢ Perf. 13 x 13½ (1985)	.60	.20	.15
920	5¢ Bucket, Perf. 14 x 13½	.60	.20	.15
920a	5¢ Perf. 13 x 13½ (1985)	.60	.20	.15
921	10¢ Weathercock, Perf. 14 x 13½	.90	.22	.15
921a	10¢ Perf. 13 x 13½ (1985)	1.10	.28	.15
922	20¢ Ice Skates	1.90	.42	.15
923	30¢ Maple Leaf, Red & Blue Pf.13x13½	2.30	.50	.15
923a	Bklt. Pane of 20, Pf. 12 x 12½	...	9.75	...
923b	Bklt. Sgl., Pf. 12 x 12½	...	.70	.30
924	32¢ Maple Leaf, Red & Brown on Beige, Pf. 13 x 13½ ('83)	2.30	.55	.15
924a	Bklt. Pane of 25, Pf. 12 x 12½ ('83)	...	12.50	...
924b	Bklt. Sgl., Pf. 12 x 12½ ('83)	...	.60	.15
925	34¢ Parliament Library ('85)	2.50	.60	.15
925a	Parl. Bklt. Pane of 25 ('85)	...	12.50	...
925b	Bluer sky, Pf. 13½ x 14, bklt. sgl	...	.60	.15
925c	Same, Bklt. Pane of 25	...	12.95	...
926	34¢ Queen Elizabeth II ('85)	2.50	.60	.15
926A	36¢ Queen Elizabeth II ('87)	25.00	4.00	2.50
926B	36¢ Parliamentary Library ('87)	2.75	.60	.15
926Bc	Booklet Pane of 10 ('87)	...	5.50	...
926Bd	Booklet Pane of 25 ('87)	...	13.50	...
926Be	Bklt. Sgl., Perf. 13½ x 14 ('87)	...	.95	.45
927	37¢ Wooden Plow ('83)	2.85	.60	.25
928	39¢ Artifacts, Settle Bed ('85)	3.00	.65	.20
929	48¢ Hand Hewn Cradle ('83)	3.75	.80	.30
930	50¢ Artifacts, Sleigh ('85)	4.00	.85	.25
931	60¢ Ontario Street Scene	4.50	1.00	.30
932	64¢ Wood Burning Stove ('83)	5.25	1.10	.40
933	68¢ Artifacts, Spinning Wheel ('85)	5.25	1.15	.35
934	$1.00 Glacier National Park ('84)	8.00	1.75	.50
935	$1.50 Waterton Lakes Nat'l. Park	11.50	2.50	.70
936	$2.00 Banff National Park ('85)	16.00	3.50	1.25
937	$5.00 Point Pelee Nat'l. Park ('83)	37.50	8.50	2.50

Booklet Stamps

938-48	**Set of 11**	**...**	**3.85**	**1.65**
938	1¢ Parl. East, Bklt. Sgl. ('87)	...	.20	.15
939	2¢ West Parl. Bldg., Booklet Sgl. ('85)	...	.20	.15
939a	Slate Green, bklt. sgl. ('89)	...	.20	.15
940	5¢ Maple Leaf, Booklet Single	...	.20	.15
941	5¢ East Parl. Bldg., Booklet Sgl. ('85)	...	.20	.15
942	6¢ Parl., West B. Sgl. ('87)	...	.20	.15
943	8¢ Maple Leaf, Bklt. Single ('83)	...	.20	.15
944	10¢ Maple Leaf, Booklet Single	...	.25	.20
945	30¢ Maple Leaf, Red, Bklt. Sgl	...	.70	.20
945a	Bklt. Pane of 4 (2 #940,#944,#945) Pf. 12 x 12½	...	1.10	...
946	32¢ Maple Leaf, Brown, Bklt. Sgl. ('83)	...	.60	.15
946b	Bklt. Pane of 4 (2 #941, #943, #946, Pf. 12 x 12½)	...	1.00	...
947	34¢ Center Parl. Bldg., Bklt. Sgl. ('85)	...	.60	.15
947a	B. Pane of 6 (3 #939,2 #941, #947)	...	1.25	...
948	36¢ Parl. Library, Bklt. Sgl. ('87)	...	.60	.20
948a	Vend Bklt. of 5 (2 #938,2 #942, #948)	...	.90	...

Coil Stamps

950-53	**Set of 4**	**...**	**2.50**	**.60**
950	30¢ Maple Leaf, Red	...	.90	.20
951	32¢ Maple Leaf, Brown ('83)	...	.55	.15
952	34¢ Parliament ('85)	...	.60	.15
953	36¢ Parliament ('87)	...	.60	.15

1982 Commemoratives (continued)

955 969 973

954	30¢ Salvation Army	2.40	.50	.15

1982 Canada Day Paintings

955-66	30¢ Canada Day Paintings, Set of 12 Sgls	...	8.00	5.50
966a	Sheetlet of 12 Paintings	...	8.00	8.00

1982 Commemoratives (continued)

Scott's No.		Plate Block	F-VF NH	F-VF Used
967	30¢ Regina Centennial	2.40	.50	.15
968	30¢ Henley Rowing Regatta	2.40	.50	.15
969-70	30¢ Bush Aircraft, attached	2.40	1.10	.90
969-70	Set of 2 Singles	...	1.00	.30
971-72	60¢ Bush Aircraft, attached	5.00	2.00	1.90
971-72	Set of 2 Singles	...	1.95	1.40
973	30¢ Christmas, Nativity	2.40	.50	.15
974	35¢ Christmas, Shepherds	2.75	.60	.45
975	60¢ Christmas, Wise Men	4.75	1.00	.70

1983 Commemoratives

Scott's No.		Plate Block	F-VF NH	F-VF Used
976-1008	**Set of 33**	...	**23.75**	**11.50**
976	32¢ Communications Year	2.60	.55	.18
977	$2 Commonwealth Day	22.50	5.00	3.00
978-79	32¢ Poet & Author, attached	2.60	1.15	1.00
978-79	Set of 2 Singles	...	1.10	.35

980

981

983

Scott's No.		Plate Block	F-VF NH	F-VF Used
980	32¢ St. John Ambulance	2.80	.55	.18
981	32¢ World University Games	2.80	.55	.18
982	64¢ World University Games	5.50	1.10	.75

1983 Historic Forts Commemorative Booklet

Scott's No.		Plate Block	F-VF NH	F-VF Used
983-92	32¢ Historic Forts, Set of 10 Bklt. Sgls	...	6.00	3.25
992a	Booklet Pane of 10	...	6.50	6.50

993 995 996

1983 Commemoratives (continued)

Scott's No.		Plate Block	F-VF NH	F-VF Used
993	32¢ Boy Scout Jamboree	2.50	.55	.18
994	32¢ World Council of Churches	2.50	.55	.18
995	32¢ Sir Humphrey Gilbert	2.50	.55	.18
996	32¢ Discovery of Nickel	2.50	.55	.18
997	32¢ Josiah Henson	2.50	.55	.18
998	32¢ Antoine Labelle	2.50	.55	.18

999 1003 1004

Scott's No.		Plate Block	F-VF NH	F-VF Used
999-1000	32¢ Steam Trains, attd	2.50	1.15	1.10
999-1000	Set of 2 Singles	...	1.10	.50
1001	37¢ Samson 0-6-0, 1838	2.80	.60	.50
1002	64¢ Adam Brown 4-4-0, 1860	5.50	1.10	.85
1003	32¢ Dalhousie Law School	2.50	.55	.18
1004	32¢ Christmas, Urban Church	2.50	.55	.18
1005	37¢ Christmas, Family	2.75	.60	.45
1006	64¢ Christmas, Rural Church	5.50	1.10	.75
1007-08	32¢ Army Regiment, attd	2.50	1.15	1.00
1007-08	Set of 2 Singles	...	1.10	.35

FROM 1941 TO PRESENT, ADD 20% FOR VERY FINE QUALITY
Minimum of 10¢ Per Stamp

CANADA

1013 1038

Scott's No.		Plate Block	F-VF NH	F-VF Used
1009-44	**Set of 36**	...	**20.50**	**8.50**
1009	32¢ Yellowknife	2.50	.55	.18
1010	32¢ Montreal Symphony	2.50	.55	.18
1011	32¢ Cartier Landing	2.50	.55	.18
1012	32¢ Voyage of Tall Ships	2.50	.55	.18
1013	32¢ Red Cross Society	2.50	.55	.18
1014	32¢ New Brunswick	2.50	.55	.18
1015	32¢ St. Lawrence Seaway	2.50	.55	.18

1984 Canada Day Paintings

Scott's No.		Plate Block	F-VF NH	F-VF Used
1016-27	32¢ Canada Day Paintings, Set of 12 Sgls.	...	6.50	2.75
1027a	Sheetlet of Twelve Paintings	...	6.75	6.75

1984 Commemoratives (continued)

Scott's No.		Plate Block	F-VF NH	F-VF Used
1028	32¢ United Empire Loyalists	2.50	.55	.18
1029	32¢ Catholic Church in Newfoundland	2.50	.55	.2
1030	32¢ Papal Visit	2.50	.55	.2
1031	64¢ Papal Visit	5.25	1.10	.45
1032-35	32¢ Lighthouses, attd	2.50	2.25	1.8
1032-35	Set of 4 Singles	...	2.10	.8
1036-37	32¢ Locomotives, attd	2.50	1.20	1.0
1036-37	Set of 2 Singles	...	1.10	.4
1038	37¢ Grand Trunk 2-6-0, 1886	2.85	.60	.5
1039	64¢ Canadian Pacific 4-6-0, 1905	5.25	1.10	.9
1039a	Locomotive Souvenir Sheet	...	2.75	2.7
1040	32¢ Christmas, Annunciation	2.50	.55	.2
1041	37¢ Christmas, Three Kings	2.85	.60	.5
1042	64¢ Christmas, Snow in Bethlehem	5.25	1.10	.7
1043	32¢ Royal Canadian Air Force	2.50	.55	.2
1044	32¢ Newspaper, La Presse	2.50	.55	.2

1985 Commemoratives

1046 1062 1075 1076

Scott's No.		Plate Block	F-VF NH	F-VF Used
1045-76	**Set of 32**	...	**19.75**	**7.9**
1045	32¢ Int'l. Youth Year	2.50	.55	.2
1046	32¢ Canadian Astronaut	2.50	.55	.2
1047-48	32¢ Decade of Women, attd	2.50	1.20	1.0
1047-48	Set of 2 Singles	...	1.10	.4
1049	32¢ Gabriel Dumont	2.50	.55	.1
1050-59	34¢ Historic Forts, Set/10 Bklt Sgls	...	6.50	2.5
1059a	Historic Forts, Bklt. Pane/10	...	7.00	7.0
1060	34¢ Louis Hebert	2.75	.60	.2
1061	34¢ Interparliamentary Union	2.75	.60	.2
1062	34¢ Girl Guides 7th Anniv	2.75	.60	.2
1063-66	34¢ Lighthouse, attd	2.75	2.40	2.1
1063-66	Set of 4 Singles	...	2.30	.8
1066b	$1.36 Souvenir Sheet of 4	...	2.75	2.5
1067	34¢ Christmas	2.75	.60	.2
1068	39¢ Christmas	3.25	.65	.4
1069	68¢ Christmas	5.50	1.15	.7
1070	32¢ Christmas, Bklt. Sgl	...	.75	.2
1070a	Christmas Bklt. Pane/10	...	7.00	7.0
1071-72	34¢ Trains, attd	2.75	1.20	.5
1071-72	Set of 2 Singles	...	1.15	.4
1073	39¢ Trains	3.00	.65	.5
1074	68¢ Trains	5.50	1.15	.9
1075	34¢ Royal Canadian Navy	2.75	.60	.2
1076	34¢ Montreal Fine Arts Museum	2.75	.60	.2

1986 Commemoratives

1078

1084

1117

:ott's Io.		Plate Block	F-VF NH	F-VF Used
77-79,1090-1121	**Set of 35**	...	**21.95**	**8.75**
77	34¢ 1988 Calgary Winter Olympics	2.75	.60	.20
78	34¢ EXPO '86	2.75	.60	.20
79	39¢ EXPO '86	3.00	.65	.50
	1986-87 Regular Issues			
80-84	**Set of 5**	...	**11.50**	**3.50**
80	25¢ Butter Stamp (1987)	1.75	.40	.15
81	42¢ Linen Chest (1987)	3.25	.70	.20
82	55¢ Iron Kettle (1987)	4.50	.95	.30
83	72¢ Cart (1987)	5.75	1.25	.35
84	$5 La Maurice Nat'l. Park	37.50	8.50	2.75
	1986 Commemoratives (continued)			
90	34¢ Philippe Aubert de Gaspe	2.75	.60	.20
91	34¢ Molly Brant	2.75	.60	.20
92	34¢ EXPO '86	2.75	.60	.20
93	68¢ EXPO '86	5.50	1.15	.55
94	34¢ Canadian Forces Post. Serv	2.75	.60	.20
95-98	34¢ Birds, attd	3.75	3.00	2.00
95-98	Set of 4 Singles	...	2.90	.90
99-1102	34¢ Canada Day, attd	2.75	2.40	2.00
99-1102	Set of 4 Singles	...	2.30	.80
03	34¢ Canadian Broadcasting Corp	2.75	.60	.20
04-07	34¢ Canada Exploration, attd	2.75	2.40	2.00
04-07	Set of 4 Singles	...	2.30	.80
07b	34¢ CAPEX '87 Souv. Sheet	...	2.30	2.10
08-09	34¢ Frontier Peacemakers, attd	2.75	1.20	1.00
08-09	Set of 2 Singles	...	1.15	.40
10	34¢ International Peace Year	2.75	.60	.20
11-12	34¢ Calgary Winter Olympics, attd	2.75	1.20	.90
11-12	Set of 2 Singles	...	1.15	.40
13	34¢ Christmas	2.75	.60	.20
14	39¢ Christmas	3.00	.65	.50
15	68¢ Christmas	5.50	1.15	.75
16	29¢ Christmas, Bklt. Sgl. Perf. 13½	...	.60	.20
16a	Bklt. Pane of 10, Perf. 13½	...	5.50	...
16b	Bklt. Sgl., Perf. 12½	...	8.50	...
16c	Bklt. Pane of 10, Perf. 12½	...	75.00	...
17	34¢ John Molson	2.75	.60	.20
18-19	34¢ Locomotives, attd	2.75	1.20	.90
18-19	Set of 2 Singles	...	1.15	.40
20	39¢ Locomotive	3.00	.65	.55
21	68¢ Locomotive	4.75	1.00	.90

1122

1130

1134

1987 Commemoratives

		Plate Block	F-VF NH	F-VF Used
22-54,1125A	**Set of 34**	...	**23.50**	**11.50**
22	34¢ CAPEX '87	2.75	.60	.20
23	36¢ CAPEX	2.85	.60	.22
24	42¢ CAPEX	3.25	.70	.55
25	72¢ CAPEX	5.65	1.20	.90
25A	$1.84 CAPEX S/S	...	3.15	2.95
26-29	34¢ Exploration of Canada, attd	2.75	2.40	2.00
26-29	Set of 4 Singles	...	2.30	.80
30	36¢ '88 Calgary Wnt. Olym. Skating	2.75	.60	.20
31	42¢ '88 Calgary Wnt. Olympic Bobsledding	3.25	.70	.55
32	36¢ Volunteer Week	3.75	.80	.20
33	36¢ Law Day	2.85	.60	.20
34	36¢ Engineering Institute	2.85	.60	.20
35-38	36¢ Canada Day, attd	2.85	2.40	2.25
35-38	Set of 4 Singles	...	2.30	.95
39-40	36¢ Steamships, attd	2.85	1.20	1.00
39-40	Set of 2 Singles	...	1.15	.48
41-44	36¢ Underwater Archaeology, attd	2.85	2.40	2.25
41-44	Set of 4 Singles	...	2.30	.95

CANADA

1987 Commemoratives (cont.)

1145

1148

1152-53

Scott's No.		Plate Block	F-VF NH	F-VF Used
1145	36¢ Air Canada 50th Anniv	2.85	.60	.22
1146	36¢ Francophone Int'l. Summit	2.85	.60	.22
1147	36¢ Commonwealth Heads of Gov't	2.85	.60	.22
1148	36¢ Christmas	2.85	.60	.20
1149	42¢ Christmas	3.25	.70	.60
1150	72¢ Christmas	5.75	1.25	.90
1151	31¢ Christmas Bklt. Sgl	...	.55	.25
1151a	Christmas Bklt. Pane of 10	...	5.25	...
1152-53	36¢ Calgary Wnt. Olympics, attd	2.85	1.20	1.00
1152-53	Set of 2 Singles	...	1.15	.50
1154	36¢ Grey Cup 75th Anniv	2.85	.60	.20

1987-91 Regular Issues

1162 1165 1166 1173

		Plate Block	F-VF NH	F-VF Used
1155-83	**Set of 30**	...	**31.95**	**10.95**
1155	1¢ Flying Squirrel, Pf. 13 x 13½ (1988).	.60	.20	.15
1155a	1¢ Perf 13 x 12½ (1991)	11.50	2.50	.20
1156	2¢ Porcupine (1988)	.60	.20	.15
1157	3¢ Muskrat (1988)	.60	.20	.15
1158	5¢ Hare (1988)	.60	.20	.15
1159	6¢ Red Fox (1988)	.70	.20	.15
1160	10¢ Skunk, Pf. 13 x 13½ (1988)	.85	.20	.15
1160a	10¢ Perf. 13 12½ (1991)	7.00	1.35	.20
1161	25¢ Beaver (1988)	1.90	.40	.15
1162	37¢ Elizabeth II	2.75	.60	.15
1163	37¢ Parliament Perf. 13½ x 13	2.75	.60	.15
1163a	Booklet Pane of 10 (1163c) ('88)	...	5.75	...
1163b	Booklet Pane of 25 (1163c) ('88)	...	14.00	...
1163c	Bklt. sgl., Pf. 13½ x 14 ('88)	...	.65	.15
1164	38¢ QE II pf. 13 x 12½ ('88)	3.00	.65	.15
1164a	Bklt. sgl., pf. 13 x 13½ ('88)	...	.70	.15
1164b	Bklt. Pane of 10 + 2 labels	...	6.50	...
1165	38¢ Parliament Clock Tower ('88)	3.00	.65	.15
1165a	Bklt. Pane of 10 + 2 labels	...	6.50	...
1165b	Bklt. Pane of 25 + 2 labels	...	16.00	...
1166	39¢ Flag & Clouds ('89)	3.00	.65	.15
1166a	Bklt. Pane of 10	...	6.50	...
1166b	Bklt. Pane of 25	...	16.00	...
1166c	Perf. 12½ x 13 ('90) (Blank)	33.50	6.50	.25
1167	39¢ Elizabeth II, Perf. 13 x 13½ ('90)	3.00	.65	.15
1167a	Bklt. Pane of 10	...	6.50	...
1167b	Perf. 13 ('90) (Blank)	10.00	2.00	.15
1168	40¢ Elizabeth II ('90)	3.25	.70	.15
1168a	Bklt. Pane of 10 + 2 labels	...	6.75	...
1169	40¢ Flag & Mountains ('90)	3.25	.70	.15
1169a	Bklt. Pane of 25 + 2 labels	...	16.50	...
1169b	Bklt. Pane of 10 + 2 labels	...	6.50	...
1170	43¢ Lynx ('88)	3.50	.75	.20
1171	44¢ Walrus ('89), Perf. 14½ x 14	3.75	.80	.25
1171a	Perf. 12½ x 13	...	.95	.25
1171b	Perf. 12½ x 13, Bklt. Pane of 5+label	...	4.50	...
1171c	Perf. 13½ x 13 ('89) (Blank)	...	100.00	8.50
1172	45¢ Pronghorn ('90) Perf. 14½ x 14 ('90)	3.50	.75	.30
1172f	Perf. 12½ x 13 ('90)	...	.85	.30
1172b	Bklt. Pane of 5 + label, Perf. 12½ x 13..	...	3.75	...
1172d	Perf. 13 ('90) (Blank)	6.00	1.25	.30
1172A	46¢ Wolverine, Perf. 13 ('90)	3.75	.80	.30
1172Ac	Wolverine, Perf. 12½ x 13 ('90)	...	.80	.30
1172Ae	Bklt. pn. of 5 + label, Perf. 12½x13 ('91)	...	3.95	...
1172Ag	Wolverine, Perf. 14½ x 14 ('90)	3.75	.80	.30
1173	57¢ Killer Whale ('88)	4.50	.95	.30
1174	59¢ Musk-ox ('89)	4.50	1.00	.40
1174a	Perf. 13 ('89) (Blank)	29.50	5.75	.50

1987-91 Regular Issues (cont.)

1175 1183 1185

Scott's No.		Plate Block	F-VF NH	F-VF Used
1175	61¢ Timber Wolf ('90) Perf. 14½ x 14 ('90)	4.50	1.00	.40
1175a	Perf. 13 ('90)............................(Blank)	42.50	8.00	.50
1176	63¢ Harbor Porpoise ('90)	4.75	1.05	.40
1176a	Perf. 13 ('91)............................(Blank)	4.95	1.10	.40
1177	74¢ Wapiti ('88)	5.85	1.25	.40
1178	76¢ Grizzly Bear, Perf. 14½ x 14 ('89)..	5.75	1.25	.40
1178a	Bklt sgl. perf. 12½ x 13	...	1.50	.55
1178b	Bklt. pane of 5 + label, Perf. 12½x13....	...	7.00	...
1178c	Perf. 13....................................(Blank)	135.00	27.50	2.50
1179	78¢ Beluga ('90) Perf. 14½ x 14 ('90) ...	6.00	1.35	.50
1179a	Bklt. Pane of 5, Perf. 12½ x 13	...	7.00	...
1179b	Perf. 13 ('90)............................(Blank)	10.00	2.00	.50
1179c	Perf. 12½ x 13......................................	...	1.50	.50
1180	80¢ Peary Caribou, Perf. 13 ('90).........	6.25	1.40	.60
1180a	Perf 12½ x 13 ('90)............................	...	1.50	.60
1180b	Bklt. Pane of 5+label, Perf. 12½x13 ('91)	...	6.95	...
1180c	Perf. 14½ x 14 ('91)............................	6.25	1.40	.60
1181	$1 Runnymede Library ('89)................	7.75	1.75	.60
1182	$2 McAdam Train Station ('89)............	15.50	3.50	1.25
1183	$5 Bonsecours Market ('90)	38.50	8.50	3.00

1988-90 Booklet Stamps

Scott's No.		F-VF NH	F-VF Used
1184-90	**Set of 7**	**3.15**	**.95**
1184	1¢ Flag, Perf. 13½ x 14 (1990)	.20	.15
1184a	1¢ Perf. 12½ x 13 (1990)	2.75	1.00
1185	5¢ Flag, Perf. 13½ x 14 (1990)	.20	.15
1185v	5¢ Perf. 12½ x 13..	1.50	.80
1186	6¢ Parliament (1988)......................................	.22	.15
1187	37¢ Parl. Library Bklt. Sgl. ('88)....................	.60	.15
1187a	Bklt. Pane of 4 (#938,2 #942,#1187)	.90	...
1188	38¢ Parliament Center, bklt. sgl. ('89)	.65	.15
1188a	Bklt. pane of 5 (3 #939a, 1186, 1188)...........	.95	...
1189	39¢ Canadian Flag, bklt. sgl. ('90)..................	.65	.15
1189a	Bklt. pn. of 4 (#1184,2 #1185,#1189)..............	.95	...
1189v	Perf. 12½ x 13, bklt. sgl	4.50	.25
1189v	Same, Bklt. pn. of 4 (#1184a,2 #1185v,#1189v).......	10.00	...
1190	40¢ Canadian Flag, bklt. sgl. ('90)..................	.75	.15
1190a	Bklt. pane of 4 (2 #1184,1185,1190).................	.95	...

1193 1203 1204

1989-91 Self-Adhesive Stamps

Scott's No.		F-VF NH	F-VF Used
1191	38¢ National Flag, bklt. sgl. ('89)....................	.80	.40
1191a	Bklt. pane of 12	9.00	...
1192	39¢ Flag & Landscape, bklt. sgl. ('90)..............	.80	.40
1192a	Bklt. pane of 12	9.00	...
1193	40¢ Flag & Seacoast, bklt. sgl. ('91)................	.80	.40
1193a	Bklt. pane of 12	9.00	...

1988-90 Coil Stamps, Perf. 10 Horizontal

Scott's No.		F-VF NH	F-VF Used
1194-94c	**Set of 4**	**2.50**	**.60**
1194	37¢ Parl. Library ('88)......................................	.60	.15
1194A	38¢ Parl. Library ('89)......................................	.65	.15
1194B	39¢ Canadian Flag ('90)...................................	.65	.20
1194C	40¢ Canadian Flag ('90)...................................	.70	.20

1988 Commemoratives

Scott's No.		Plate Block	F-VF NH	F-VF Used
1195-1228	**Set of 34**..	**...**	**24.00**	**9.25**
1195-96	37¢ Winter Olympics, attd	2.95	1.30	1.00
1195-96	Set of 2 Singles...	...	1.25	.50
1197	43¢ Winter Olympics..................................	3.50	.75	.60
1198	74¢ Winter Olympics..................................	5.25	1.25	.75
1199-1202	37¢ Explorers, attd	3.35	3.00	2.00
1199-1202	Set of 4 Singles	...	2.95	1.00
1203	50¢ Canadian Art..	3.95	.85	.80
1204-05	37¢ Wildlife Conservation., attd	2.95	1.30	1.00
1204-05	Set of 2 Singles...	...	1.25	.50

1988 Commemoratives (continued)

1214 1215 1216

Scott's No.		Plate Block	F-VF NH	F-VF Used
1206-09	37¢ Science & Technology, attd	3.35	3.00	2.0
1206-09	Set of 4 Singles....................................	...	2.90	1.0
1210-13	37¢ Butterflies, attd	3.35	3.00	2.0
1210-13	Set of 4 Singles....................................	...	2.90	1.0
1214	37¢ St. John's City Cent.......................	2.75	.60	.2
1215	37¢ 4-H Clubs Anniv	2.75	.60	.2
1216	37¢ Les Forges du Saint-Maurice.........	2.75	.60	.2
1217-20	37¢ Kennel Club Cent. (Dogs) attd	3.35	3.00	2.0
1217-20	Set of 4 Singles....................................	...	2.90	1.0

1221 1223 1226 1228

Scott's No.		Plate Block	F-VF NH	F-VF Used
1221	37¢ Canadian Baseball Sesqui	3.75	.80	.2
1222	37¢ Christmas	2.75	.60	.2
1223	43¢ Christmas	3.50	.75	.6
1224	74¢ Christmas	5.25	1.25	.7
1225	32¢ Christmas, bklt. single	...	.55	.2
1225a	Bklt. Pane of 10....................................	...	5.50	...
1226	37¢ Bishop Inglis...................................	2.75	.60	.2
1227	37¢ Frances Anne Hopkins..................	2.75	.60	.2
1228	37¢ Angus Walters................................	2.75	.60	.2

1989 Commemoratives

1229 1241 1249

Scott's No.		Plate Block	F-VF NH	F-VF Used
1229-63	**Set of 34**	**...**	**24.00**	**8.5**
1229-32	38¢ Small Craft Series, attd	3.25	3.00	1.5
1229-32	Set of 4 Singles....................................	...	2.90	1.0
1233-36	38¢ Explorers/Canadian North, attd......	3.25	3.00	1.5
1233-36	Set of 4 Singles....................................	...	2.90	1.0
1237-40	38¢ Canada Day, attd	3.25	3.00	1.5
1237-40	Set of 4 Singles....................................	...	2.90	1.0
1241	50¢ Canadian Art	4.35	.95	.7
1243-44	38¢ Poets, attd	3.25	1.35	.7
1243-44	Set of 2 Singles....................................	...	1.30	.5
1245-48	38¢ Mushrooms, attd.............................	3.25	3.00	1.5
1245-48	Set of 4 Singles....................................	...	2.90	1.6
1249-50	38¢ Canadian Infantry Regiments, attd.	*200.00	1.35	.7
1249-50	Set of 2 Singles....................................	...	1.30	.6

*** Printing difficulties caused a severe shortage of inscription blocks.**

1989 Commemoratives (cont.)

1251 1252 1260

;cott's No.		Plate Block	F-VF NH	F-VF Used
251	38¢ International Trade	3.00	.65	.20
252-55	38¢ Performing Arts	3.25	3.00	1.25
252-55	Set of 4 Singles	...	2.90	1.00
256	38¢ Christmas Landscape, pf. 13 x 13½	3.00	.65	.20
256a	Bklt. pane of 10, perf. 13 x 12½	...	17.50	...
256b	Bklt. sgl., perf. 13 x 12½	...	1.75	.20
257	44¢ Christmas Landscape	3.50	.75	.60
257a	Bklt. pane of 5 + label	...	12.00	...
258	76¢ Christmas Landscape	6.00	1.30	.85
258a	Bklt. pane of 5 + label	...	16.00	...
259	33¢ Christmas bklt. sgl	...	.70	.30
259a	Bklt. Pane of 10	...	7.00	...
260-63	38¢ WWII Outbreak, 50th Anniv., attd	3.25	3.00	1.25
260-63	Set of 4 Singles	...	2.90	1.00

1990 Commemoratives

1264 1270 1271

264-71,1274-1301	**Set of 36**	...	**25.65**	**9.35**
264-65	39¢ Norman Bethune, attd	3.25	1.40	.75
264-65	Set of 2 Singles	...	1.35	.50
266-69	39¢ Small Crafts, attd	3.25	3.00	1.60
266-69	Set of 4 Singles	...	2.90	1.00
270	39¢ Multicultural Heritage of Canada	3.00	.65	.20
271	50¢ Canadian Art, The West Wind	4.00	.85	.75

1990 Regular Issues

272-73	39¢ Postal Truck bklt. singles	...	1.35	.40
273a	Bk. pn. of 8 (4 Eng. + 4 Fr. Inscriptions)	...	5.25	...
273b	Bk. pn. of 9 (4 Eng. + 5 Fr. Inscriptions)	...	7.50	...

1990 Commemoratives (continued)

274-77	39¢ Dolls, attd	3.25	3.00	1.60
274-77	Set of 4 Singles	...	2.90	1.00
278	39¢ Canada Day, 25 Anniv. of Flag	3.00	.65	.20
279-82	39¢ Prehistoric Life, attd	3.25	3.00	1.60
279-82	Set of 4 Singles	...	2.90	1.00
283-86	39¢ Forests, World Congress, attd	3.25	3.00	2.25
283-86	Set of 4 Singles	...	2.90	1.00
283a-86b	Min. sheets of 4 (Set of 4)	...	19.50	...

1287 1288 1293 1294

287	39¢ Climate Observations Sesqui	3.00	.65	.20
288	39¢ International Literacy Year	3.00	.65	.20
289-92	39¢ Canadian Lore and Legend, attd	3.25	3.00	1.35
289-92	Set of 4 Singles, Perf. 12½ x 13	...	2.90	1.00
289v-92v	39¢ Lore, Perf. 12½ x 12, attd	...	22.50	12.00
293	39¢ Agnes Macphail, 1st Woman MP	3.00	.65	.20
294	39¢ Christmas, National Art	3.00	.65	.20
294a	Booklet Pane of 10	...	6.50	...
295	45¢ Christmas, National Art	3.50	.75	.55
295a	Booklet Pane of 5 + label	...	4.00	...

CANADA

1990 Issues (cont.)

Scott's No.		Plate Block	F-VF NH	F-VF Used
1296	78¢ Christmas, National Art	6.00	1.35	.75
1296a	Booklet Pane of 5 + label	...	6.75	...
1297	34¢ Christmas, National Art, bklt. sgl	...	.60	.20
1297a	Bklt. Pane of 10	...	6.00	...
1298-1301	39¢ WWII, Canada Mobilizes, attd	3.25	3.00	1.40
1298-1301	Set of 4 Singles	...	2.90	1.40

1991 Commemoratives

1302-05 1310 1316

1302-48	**Set of 46**	...	**34.75**	**13.95**
1302-05	40¢ Physicians, attd	3.25	2.80	1.60
1302-05	Set of 4 Singles	...	2.75	1.00
1306-09	40¢ Prehistoric Life in Canada, attd	3.25	2.80	1.60
1306-09	Set of 4 Singles	...	2.75	1.00
1310	50¢ Canadian Art, Emily Carr	4.25	.90	.75
1311-15	40¢ Public Gardens, bklt. sgls, strip of 5	...	3.75	1.75
1311-15	Set of 5 Singles	...	3.65	1.25
1315a	Booklet Pane of 10	...	6.95	...
1316	40¢ Canada Day	3.25	.70	.20
1317-20	40¢ Small Craft, attd	3.25	2.80	1.60
1317-20	Set of 4 Singles	...	2.75	1.00
1321-25	40¢ River Heritage, bklt. sgls., strip of 5	...	3.75	1.75
1321-25	Set of 5 Singles	...	3.65	1.25
1325a	Booklet Pane of 10	...	6.95	...
1326-29	40¢ Ukrainian Migration to Canada, attd	3.25	2.80	1.60
1326-29	Set of 4 Singles	...	2.75	1.00
1330-33	40¢ Salute to Dangerous Pub. Serv.orgs,attd	3.25	2.80	1.60
1330-33	Set of 4 Singles	...	2.75	1.00
1334-37	40¢ Canadian Folktales, attd	3.25	2.80	1.60
1334-37	Set of 4 Singles	...	2.75	1.00

1339 1349 1358 1359

1338	40¢ Queen's University, bklt. single	...	.75	.20
1338a	Booklet Pane of 10	...	6.95	...
1339	40¢ Santa at Fireplace	3.25	.70	.20
1339a	Booklet Pane of 10	...	6.95	...
1340	46¢ Santa with Tree	3.75	.80	.55
1340a	Booklet Pane of 5	...	3.95	...
1341	80¢ Sinterklass & Girl	6.50	1.40	.75
1341a	Booklet Pane of 5	...	6.95	...
1342	35¢ Greet More, Santa Claus, bklt. sgl.	...	.60	.20
1342a	Bklt. Pane of 10	...	5.95	...
1343	40¢ Basketball Centennial	3.25	.70	.20
1344	40¢,46¢,80¢ Basketball S/S of 3	...	2.95	2.95
1345-48	40¢ World War II Anniv., block or strip	3.25	2.80	1.60
1345-48	Set of 4 Singles	...	2.75	1.00

1991-94 Regular Issues

1349-76	**Set of 22**	...	**20.95**	**6.40**
1349	1¢ Blueberry (1992)	.60	.20	.15
1350	2¢ Strawberry (1992)	.60	.20	.15
1351	3¢ Crowberry (1992)	.60	.20	.15
1352	5¢ Rose Hip (1992)	.60	.20	.15
1353	6¢ Black Raspberry (1992)	.60	.20	.15
1354	10¢ Kinnikinnik (1992)	.80	.20	.15
1355	25¢ Saskatoon Berry (1992)	1.80	.45	.15
1358	42¢ Canadian Flag & Rolling Hills	3.50	.75	.20
1358a	Booklet Pane of 10	...	7.50	...
1358b	Booklet Pane of 50	...	37.50	...
1358c	Booklet Pane of 25	...	18.95	...
1359	42¢ QE II, Karsh Portrait	3.50	.75	.20
1359a	Booklet Pane of 10	...	7.50	...
1360	43¢ QE II, Karsh Portrait (1992)	3.50	.75	.20
1360a	Booklet Pane of 10	...	7.50	...
1360B	43¢ Flag & Prairie (1992)	3.50	.75	.20
1360Bc	Booklet Pane of 10	...	7.50	...
1360Bd	Booklet Pane of 25	...	18.95	...

1991-94 Regular Issues (continued)

1361 1371 1388 1395

Scott's No.		Plate Block	F-VF NH	F-VF Used
1361	48¢ McIntosh Apple Tree, Perf. 13	3.75	.80	.20
1361a	Bklt. single, Perf. 14½x14 on 3 sides	...	.80	.25
1361b	Booklet Pane of 5	...	3.95	...
1362	49¢ Delicious Apple, Perf. 13 (1992)	3.85	.80	.20
1362a	Perf. 14½ x 14	...	.85	.25
1362b	Booklet Pane of 5, Perf. 14½ x 14	...	3.95	...
1362v	Booklet Pane of 5, Perf. 13	...	7.95	...
1363	50¢ Snow Apple (1994)	3.95	.85	.20
1363a	Booklet Pane of 5	...	4.25	...
1366	65¢ Black Walnut Tree	4.95	1.10	.35
1367	67¢ Beaked Hazlenut (1992)	5.25	1.10	.35
1368	69¢ Shagbark Hickory (1994)	5.50	1.15	.35
1371	84¢ Stanley Plum Tree, Perf. 13	6.50	1.40	.40
1371a	Bklt. single, Perf. 14½x14 on 3 sides	...	1.50	.50
1371b	Booklet Pane of 5	...	7.50	...
1372	86¢ Bartlett Pear, Perf. 13 (1992)	7.25	1.50	.50
1372	Perf. 14½ x 14	...	1.50	.50
1372b	Booklet Pane of 5, Perf. 14½ x 14	...	7.50	...
1372v	Booklet Pane of 5, Perf. 13	...	14.95	...
1373	88¢ Westcot Apricot 4 Sides Tagged(1994)	7.00	1.45	.50
1373a	Booklet Pane of 5, 4 Sides Tagged	...	7.25	...
1373p	88¢ 2 Sides and Center Tagged	...	2.95	...
1373ap	Booklet Pane of 5, 2 Sides/Center Tagged	...	14.50	...
1375	$1 Yorkton Court House (1994)	7.75	1.70	.60
1376	$2 Truro Normal School (1994)	15.00	3.35	1.25
1388	42¢ Flag/Mountains,Self adhes.bklt.sgl.('92)	...	.80	.35
1388a	Bklt. Pane of 12	...	9.50	...
1389	43¢ Flag/Seashore,Self adhes.bklt.sgl.('92)	...	.80	.35
1389a	Bklt. Pane of 12	...	9.50	...
1394	42¢ Canadian Flag & Rolling Hills Coil	...	.75	.20
1395	43¢ Canadian Flag, Coil (1992)	...	.75	.20

1992 Commemoratives

1407 1413 1419

Scott's No.		Plate Block	F-VF NH	F-VF Used
1399-1455	**Set of 57**		**41.95**	**14.95**
1399-1403	42¢ Winter Olympics, strip of 5 bklt. stamps	...	3.75	1.60
1399-1403	Set of 5 Singles	...	3.65	1.25
1403b	Bklt. Pane of 10	...	7.50	...
1404-05	42¢ 350th Anniv. of Montreal, attd. pair	3.50	1.50	.80
1404-05	Set of 2 Singles	...	1.45	.50
1406	48¢ Jacques Cartier	3.75	.80	.45
1407	84¢ Christopher Columbus	6.95	1.50	.60
1407a	$2.16 Explorers S/S of 4, regular edition	...	3.95	1.95
1407a var	Same, special ed., w/Maisonneuve sig.	...	160.00	...
1408-12	42¢ Rivers, strip of 5 bklt. stamps	...	3.75	1.60
1408-12	Set of 5 Singles	...	3.65	1.25
1412b	Bklt. Pane of 10	...	7.50	...
1413	42¢ Alaska Highway	3.50	.75	.20
1414-18	42¢ Summer Olympics,strip of 5 bklt.stamps	...	3.75	1.60
1414-18	Set of 5 Singles	...	3.65	1.25
1418b	Bklt. Pane of 10	...	7.50	...
1419	50¢ Canadian Art	4.00	.85	.75
1431a	42¢ Canada Day, min.sht.of 12 paintings	...	8.95	5.95
1420-31	Set of 12 Singles	...	8.75	4.75
1432-35	42¢ Canadian Folklore, attd	3.50	3.00	1.50
1432-35	Set of 4 Singles	...	2.95	1.00
1436-40	42¢ Minerals, strip of 5 bklt. stamps	...	3.75	1.60
1436-40	Set of 5 Singles	...	3.65	1.25
1440b	Bklt. Pane of 10	...	7.50	...
1441-42	42¢ Space Exploration, Pair	3.50	1.60	.65
1441-42	Set of 2 Singles	...	1.50	.50

1992 Commemoratives (continued)

1445 1446-47 1453

Scott's No.		Plate Block	F-VF NH	F-VF Used
1443	42¢ Hockey, Early Years	...	.75	.2
1443a	Skates, sticks, bklt. pane of 8	...	5.95	...
1444	42¢ Hockey, Six-Team Years	...	.75	.2
1444a	Team emblems, bklt. pane of 8	...	5.95	...
1445	42¢ Hockey, Expansion Years	...	.75	.2
1445a	Goalie's mask, bklt. pane of 9	...	6.65	...
1446-47	42¢ Order of Canada & R. Michener, pair	3.95	1.65	.8
1446	42¢ Order of Canada	...	.75	.2
1447	42¢ Roland Michener	...	.90	.3
1448-51	42¢ WWII, Dark Days Indeed, attd	3.50	3.00	1.5
1448-51	Set of 4 Singles	...	2.95	1.0
1452	42¢ Christmas, Jouluvana, perf. 12½	3.50	.75	.2
1452a	Perf. 13½	3.50	.75	.2
1452b	Booklet Pane of 10	...	6.95	...
1453	48¢ Christmas, La Befana	3.75	.80	.4
1453a	Booklet Pane of 5	...	3.95	...
1454	84¢ Christmas, Wehlnachsmann	6.75	1.40	.4
1454a	Booklet Pane of 5	...	6.95	...
1455	37¢ Christmas, Special Rate, Bklt. Sgl.	...	.60	.2
1455a	Booklet Pane of 10	...	5.95	...

1460 1466 1484

1993 Commemoratives

Scott's No.		Plate Block	F-VF NH	F-VF Used
1456-1506	**Set of 51**	...	**42.95**	**19.5**
1456-59	43¢ Canadian Woman, attd	3.50	3.00	1.5
1456-59	Set of 4 Singles	...	2.95	1.0
1460	43¢ Stanley Cup Centennial	3.50	.75	.2
1461-65	43¢ Hand-crafted textiles, strip of 5	...	3.75	1.6
1461-65	Set of 5 Singles	...	3.65	1.2
1465b	Booklet Pane of 10	...	7.50	...
1466	86¢ Canadian Art	7.00	1.50	1.0
1467-71	43¢ Historic Hotels, Strip of 5 bklt. sgls	...	3.75	1.6
1467-71	Set of 5 Singles	...	3.65	1.2
1471b	Booklet Pane of 10	...	7.50	...
1483a	43¢ Canada Day, Provincial & Territorial Parks, miniature sheet of 12	...	8.95	5.9
1472-83	Set of 12 Singles	...	8.75	4.9

1485.89 1491-94 1495-98

Scott's No.		Plate Block	F-VF NH	F-VF Used
1484	43¢ Founding of Toronto	3.50	.75	.2
1485-89	43¢ Rivers, Strip of 5 bklt. sgls.	...	3.75	1.6
1485-89	Set of 5 Singles	...	3.65	1.2
1489b	Booklet Pane of 10	...	7.50	...
1490	$3.56 Motor Vehicles, Souv. Sheet of 6	...	6.25	6.2
1490a-f	Set of 6 Singles	...	...	5.9
1491-94	43¢ Folk Songs, attd	3.50	3.00	1.6
1491-94	Set of 4 Singles	...	2.95	1.0

1993 Commemoratives (continued)

cott's No.		Plate Block	F-VF NH	F-VF Used
495-98	43¢ Dinosaurs, attd	3.50	3.00	1.60
495-98	Set of 4 Singles	...	2.95	1.00
499	43¢ Christmas, Swiety Mikolaj	3.50	.75	.20
499a	Booklet Pane of 10	...	7.50	...
500	49¢ Christmas, Ded Moroz	3.95	.85	.40
500a	Booklet Pane of 5	...	4.25	...
501	86¢ Christmas, Father Christmas	7.00	1.50	.50
501a	Booklet Pane of 5	...	7.35	...
502	38¢ Christmas, Santa Claus, bklt. sgl	...	.65	.20
502a	Booklet Pane of 10	...	6.35	...
503-06	43¢ World War II, attd	3.50	3.00	1.60
503-06	Set of 4 Singles	...	2.95	1.00

1509 1510 1511-15

1994 Regular Issues

507-08	43¢ Greetings	...	1.50	.50
508a	Booklet Pane of 10 (5 each)	...	6.95	...
510	43¢ T. Eaton Co.	...	.75	.25
510a	Prestige Booklet of 10	...	6.95	...

1994 Commemoratives

509, 1511-1540 Set of 42		**...**	**40.75**	**21.75**
509	43¢ Jeanne Sauve with Tab	...	.75	.35
509	Block of 4 w/4 different tabs	3.50	3.00	...
511-15	43¢ Rivers, Strip of 5 bklt. sgls	...	3.75	1.60
511-15	Set of 5 Singles	...	3.65	1.25
515b	Booklet Pane of 10	...	7.50	...
516	88¢ Canadian Art, Vera	7.00	1.50	1.00
517-18	43¢ Commonwealth Games, Lawn Bowls and Lacrosse Pair	3.50	1.50	.80
517-18	Set of 2 Singles	...	1.45	.50
519-20	43¢ Commonwealth Games, High Jump and Wheelchair Marathon, Pair	7.00	1.50	.80
519-20	Set of 2 Singles	...	1.45	.50

1522 1529-32

521	50¢ Commonwealth Games	4.25	.85	.40
522	88¢ Commonwealth Games	7.00	1.50	1.00
523	43¢ Year of the Family, Souv. Sht. of 5	...	3.75	3.75
524	43¢ Canada Day, Maple Trees, Miniature Sheet of 12	...	8.95	5.95
524a-1	Same, Set of 12 Singles	...	8.75	4.95
525-26	43¢ Billy Bishop and Mary Travers, Pair	3.50	1.50	.80
525-26	Set of 2 Singles	...	1.45	.50
527	43¢, 50¢, 88¢ Public Service Vehicles, Souvenir Sheet of 6	...	5.95	4.95
528	43¢ Civil Aviation	3.50	.75	.25
529-32	43¢ Prehistoric Life, attd.	3.50	3.00	1.60
529-32	Set of 4 Singles	...	2.95	1.00
533	43¢ Christmas, Singing Carols	3.50	.75	.20
533a	Booklet Pane of 10	...	7.50	...

CANADA

1534 1537-40

Scott's No.		Plate Block	F-VF NH	F-VF Used
1534	50¢ Christmas, Choir	3.95	.85	.40
1534a	Booklet Pane of 5	...	4.25	...
1535	88¢ Christmas, Caroling	7.00	1.50	.50
1535a	Booklet Pane of 5	...	7.35	...
1536	38¢ Christmas, Soloist, bklt. sgl.	...	.65	.20
1536a	Booklet Pane of 10	...	6.35	...
1537-40	43¢ World War II, attd.	3.50	3.00	1.60
1537-40	Set of 4 Singles	...	2.95	1.00
	1995 Commemoratives			
1541-44	43¢ World War II, attd.	3.50	3.00	1.60
1541-44	Set of 4 Singles	...	2.95	1.00
1545	88¢ Art, "Floraison"	7.00	1.50	1.00
...	(43¢) Canada Flag 30th Anniv.	3.50	.75	.25
...	(43¢) Fortress of Louisbourg, Strip of 5 Bklt. Singles	...	3.75	1.60
...	Same, Set of 5 singles	...	3.65	1.25
...	Same, Booklet Pane of 10	...	7.50	...
...	43¢, 50¢, 88¢ Farm and Frontier Vehicles, Souvenir Sheet of 6	...	5.95	4.95
...	43¢ Golf, Strip of 5 Bklt. Sgls.	...	3.75	1.60
...	Same, Set of 5 Singles	...	3.65	1.25
...	Same, Booklet Pane of 10	...	7.50	...
...	43¢ Canada Day, Set of 3 Souvenir Sheets bearing 10 different stamps	...	7.50	...
...	43¢ Lunenburg Academy	3.50	.75	.25
...	43¢ Manitoba	3.50	.75	.25
...	43¢ Migratory Wildlife, Block of 4	3.50	3.00	1.60
...	Same, Set of 4 singles	...	2.95	1.00

CANADA
SEMI-POSTALS

B1 B4 B7 B10

Scott's No.		Plate Block	F-VF NH	F-VF Used
B1-12	Set of 12	...	5.50	5.50
	1974 Olympic Games			
B1	8¢+2¢ Olympic Emblem, Bronze	1.55	.32	.32
B2	10¢+5¢ Olympic Emblem, Silver	2.40	.50	.50
B3	15¢+5¢ Olympic Emblem, Gold	3.10	.65	.65
	1975 Olympic Games - Water Sports			
B4	8¢+2¢ Swimming	1.55	.32	.32
B5	10¢+5¢ Rowing	2.40	.50	.50
B6	15¢+5¢ Sailing	3.10	.65	.65
	1975 Olympic Games - Combat Sports			
B7	8¢+2¢ Fencing	1.55	.32	.32
B8	10¢+5¢ Boxing	2.40	.50	.50
B9	15¢+5¢ Judo	3.10	.65	.65
	1976 Olympic Games - Team Sports			
B10	8¢+2¢ Basketball	1.55	.32	.32
B11	10¢+5¢ Vaulting	2.40	.50	.50
B12	20¢+5¢ Soccer	3.50	.75	.75

AIR MAIL STAMPS

C1 C2 C5

1928-1932 Airmail Issues VF + 30% (B)

Scott's No.		NH VF	NH F-VF	Unused VF	Unused F-VF	Used F-VF
C1	5¢ Allegory (1928)	11.00	8.00	7.25	5.35	2.00
C2	5¢ Globe, Brown (1930)	55.00	41.50	36.50	27.50	16.50
C3	6¢ on 5¢ Allegory (1932)	8.00	6.00	5.00	3.75	1.90
C4	6¢ on 5¢ Ottawa (1932)	17.50	13.50	11.50	8.50	7.00

C6 C7 C9

1935-46 Airmail Issues VF + 20%

Scott's No.		Plate Blocks NH	Plate Blocks Unused	F-VF NH	F-VF Unused	F-VF Used
C5	6¢ Daedalus, Red Brown	11.50	8.50	1.95	1.50	.75
C6	6¢ Steamer (1938)	13.00	9.75	2.50	1.85	.20
C7	6¢ Student Flyers (1942)	16.50	12.50	3.25	2.40	.65
C8	7¢ Student Flyers (1943)	3.75	2.75	.60	.45	.15
C9	7¢ Canada Geese (1946)	3.00	2.25	.60	.45	.15
C9a	7¢ Booklet Pane of 4	...	...	2.35	1.85	...

CANADA

AIRMAIL SPECIAL DELIVERY 1942-1947

CE1 E1

Scott's No.		Plate Blocks NH	Plate Blocks Unused	F-VF NH	F-VF Unused	F-VF Used
CE1	16¢ Aerial View	11.50	9.00	2.00	1.50	1.35
CE2	17¢ Aerial Veiw (1943)	14.00	11.00	2.75	2.10	1.95
CE3	17¢ Plane, Original Die (1946)	23.00	18.00	5.00	3.75	3.65
CE4	17¢ Corrected Die (1947)	23.00	18.00	5.00	3.75	3.65

CE3 has circumflex (e) over second "E" of "EXPRESS". CE4 has an accent (e).

AIRMAIL OFFICIAL STAMPS 1949-1950

Scott's No.		Plate Blocks NH	Plate Blocks Unused	F-VF NH	F-VF Unused	F-VF Used
CO1	7¢ Ovptd. "O.H.M.S." (C9)	45.00	35.00	9.50	7.50	3.50
CO2	7¢ Ovptd. "G" (#C9) (1950)	82.50	65.00	16.50	12.50	12.50

SPECIAL DELIVERY STAMPS 1898-1933
E1 VF Used + 40% (B) E2-5 VF Used + 30% (B)

E2 E3 E4

Scott's No.		NH VF	NH F-VF	Unused VF	Unused F-VF	Used F-VF
E1	10¢ Blue Green (1898)	87.50	57.50	42.50	27.50	5.50
E2	20¢ Carmine (1922)	72.50	55.00	40.00	30.00	6.00
E3	20¢ Mail Transport (1927)	13.50	9.00	8.50	5.75	6.50
E4	20¢ "TWENTY" (1930)	58.50	42.50	35.00	25.00	11.00
E5	20¢ "20 CENTS" (1933)	50.00	37.50	30.00	22.50	14.00

E6 E7

E10 E11

SPECIAL DELIVERY 1935-1946 VF + 20%

Scott's No.		Plate Blocks NH	Plate Blocks Unused	F-VF NH	F-VF Unused	F-VF Used
E6	20¢ Progress (6)	65.00	42.50	9.00	5.50	4.00
E7	10¢ Arms, Green (1939)	22.50	17.50	4.50	3.50	2.50
E8	20¢ Arms, Carm. (1938)	195.00	140.00	25.00	17.50	20.00
E9	10¢ on 20¢ (#E8) (1939)	33.50	24.00	5.00	3.50	3.50
E10	10¢ Arms & Flags (1942)	10.50	8.00	2.25	1.75	1.00
E11	10¢ Arms (1946)	7.25	6.00	1.50	1.25	.65

SPECIAL DELIVERY OFFICIAL STAMPS 1949-1950

Scott's No.		Plate Blocks NH	Plate Blocks Unused	F-VF NH	F-VF Unused	F-VF Used
EO1	10¢ Ovptd. "O.H.M.S." (#E11)	75.00	55.00	15.00	11.00	11.00
EO2	10¢ Ovptd. "G" (#E11) (1950)	120.00	90.00	28.50	22.50	22.50

NOTE: PRICES THROUGHOUT THIS LIST ARE SUBJECT TO CHANGE WITHOUT NOTICE IF MARKET CONDITIONS REQUIRE. MINIMUM ORDER MUST TOTAL AT LEAST $20.00.

REGISTRATION STAMPS 1875-1888 (OG + 20%) VF + 50% (C)

F1 J1 J6 J11

cott's No.		NH Fine	Unused Fine	Unused Ave.	Used Fine	Used Ave.
1	2¢ Orange, Perf. 12	75.00	42.50	26.00	2.50	1.40
1a	2¢ Vermillion, Perf. 12	95.00	50.00	30.00	5.75	3.10
1b	2¢ Rose Carmine, Perf. 12	210.00	125.00	75.00	65.00	36.50
1d	5¢ Orange, Perf. 12 x 11½	...	215.00	130.00	65.00	36.50
2	5¢ Dark Green, Perf. 12	110.00	60.00	36.50	2.50	1.40
2a	5¢ Blue Green, Perf. 12	115.00	65.00	40.00	2.75	1.55
2b	5¢ Yellow Green, Perf. 12	150.00	90.00	55.00	3.75	2.25
2d	5¢ Green, Perf. 12 x 11½	...	500.00	300.00	140.00	85.00
3	8¢ Blue (1876)	...	275.00	185.00	250.00	135.00

POSTAGE DUE STAMPS
1906-1928 VF Used + 40% (B)

cott's No.		NH VF	NH F-VF	Unused VF	Unused F-VF	Used F-VF
1	1¢ Violet	10.50	7.50	6.50	4.50	1.95
1a	1¢ Thin Paper	14.00	10.00	8.50	6.00	4.50
2	2¢ Violet	10.75	7.50	6.25	4.50	.50
2a	2¢ Thin Paper	14.00	10.00	8.50	6.00	5.00
3	4¢ Violet (1928)	62.50	45.00	40.00	28.50	9.00
4	5¢ Violet	11.50	8.00	7.00	5.00	.75
4a	5¢ Thin Paper	10.75	7.50	6.25	4.50	3.75
5	10¢ Violet (1928)	42.50	30.00	25.50	17.50	6.00
	1930-1932 VF Used + 30% (B)					
6	1¢ Dark Violet	9.50	7.50	5.75	4.50	2.00
7	2¢ Dark Violet	6.50	5.00	4.00	3.00	.50
8	4¢ Dark Violet	12.75	10.00	7.75	6.00	1.75
9	5¢ Dark Violet (1931)	12.75	10.00	7.75	6.00	3.00
10	10¢ Dark Violet (1932)	80.00	62.50	48.75	37.50	5.00
	1933-1934 VF Used + 30% (B)					
11	1¢ Dark Violet (1934)	9.50	7.50	5.75	4.50	3.50
12	2¢ Dark Violet	4.25	3.25	2.60	2.00	.65
13	4¢ Dark Violet	11.75	9.00	7.00	5.50	3.75
14	10¢ Dark Violet	17.50	13.50	11.50	8.75	3.00

J15 J23 J28 MR1 MR3

POSTAGE DUE STAMPS
1935-1965 VF + 20%

cott's No.		Plate Block	F-VF NH	F-VF Used
15	1¢ Dark Violet	1.50	.20	.15
16	2¢ Dark Violet	1.50	.20	.15
16B	3¢ Dark Violet ('65)	12.50	2.00	.95
17	4¢ Dark Violet	1.85	.30	.15
18	5¢ Dark Violet ('48)	2.75	.40	.25
19	6¢ Dark Violet ('57)	12.50	2.00	1.25
20	10¢ Dark Violet	2.10	.30	.15
	1967 Regular Size 20 x 17 mm., Perf. 12			
21	1¢ Carmine Rose	5.75	.22	.22
22	2¢ Carmine Rose	1.25	.22	.22
23	3¢ Carmine Rose	1.25	.22	.22
24	4¢ Carmine Rose	2.50	.40	.40
25	5¢ Carmine Rose	8.75	1.50	1.40
26	6¢ Carmine Rose	2.25	.35	.35
27	10¢ Carmine Rose	2.25	.40	.40
	1969-1978 Modular Size 20 x 15¾ mm., Perf. 12			
28	1¢ Dextrose (Yellow Gum) ('70)	2.50	.50	.35
28a	1¢ Perf. 12½ x 12 ('77)	.60	.20	.15
28v	1¢ Carmine Rose, White Gum ('74)	1.65	.35	.25
29	2¢ Carmine Rose ('73)	1.25	.20	.15
30	3¢ Carmine Rose ('74)	1.50	.30	.15
31	4¢ Dextrose (Yellow Gum) ('69)	1.80	.30	.25
31a	4¢ Perf. 12½ x 12 ('77)	.60	.20	.15
31v	4¢ Carmine Rose, White Gum ('74)	.85	.20	.15
32	5¢ Carmine Rose, Pf. 12½ x 12 ('77)	.60	.20	.15
32a	5¢ Perf. 12 ('69)	110.00	22.50	22.50
33	6¢ Carmine Rose ('73)	.80	.20	.15

CANADA

1969-1978 Modular Size 20 x 15¾ mm., Perf. 12 (Cont'd)

Scott's No.		Plate Block	F-VF NH	F-VF Used
J34	8¢ Dextrose (Yellow Gum)	1.85	.30	.25
J34a	8¢ Perf. 12½ x 12 ('78)	2.00	.35	.20
J34v	8¢ Carmine Rose, White Gum ('74)	1.10	.20	.15
J35	10¢ Dextrose (Yellow Gum) ('69)	2.25	.50	.15
J35a	10¢ Perf. 12½ x 12 ('77)	1.00	.20	.15
J35v	10¢ Carmine Rose, White Gum ('73)	1.10	.20	.20
J36	12¢ Dextrose (Yellow Gum) ('69)	3.75	.65	.50
J36a	12¢ Perf. 12½ x 12 ('77)	10.00	2.00	1.25
J36v	12¢ Carmine Rose, White Gum ('73)	1.30	.25	.25
J37	16¢ Carmine Rose ('74)	1.75	.30	.30
J38	20¢ Carmine Rose, Perf. 12½ x 12 ('77)	2.10	.40	.35
J39	24¢ Carmine Rose, Perf. 12½ x 12 ('77)	2.30	.45	.40
J40	50¢ Carmine Rose, Perf. 12½ x 12 ('77)	4.50	.90	.85

WAR TAX STAMPS 1915-1916 VF Used + 50% (B)

Scott's No.		NH VF	NH F-VF	Unused VF	Unused F-VF	Used F-VF
MR1	1¢ George V, Green	11.50	7.50	6.00	4.00	.15
MR2	2¢ Carmine	11.50	7.50	6.00	4.00	.15
MR3	2¢ + 1¢ Carm., T.1 ('16)	18.50	12.00	10.00	6.50	.15
MR3a	2¢ + 1¢ Carm., Type II	165.00	110.00	95.00	62.50	2.15
MR4	2¢ + 1¢ Brown, Type II	15.00	10.00	7.75	5.25	.15
MR4a	2¢ + 1¢ Brown, Type I	...	...	240.00	160.00	6.00
MR5	2¢ + 1¢ Carm., Perf. 12 x 8	50.00	32.50	26.50	17.50	15.00
MR6	2¢ + 1¢ Carm., P.8 Vert. Coil.	145.00	95.00	82.50	55.00	3.00
MR7	2¢ + 1¢ Br.,T.II P.8 Vt. Coil	18.00	12.00	10.50	7.25	.50
MR7a	2¢ + 1¢ Br.,T.I P.8 Vt. Coil	150.00	100.00	97.50	65.00	3.75

OFFICIAL STAMPS (VF + 30%)
1949-50 Issues of 1942-46 Overprinted O.H.M.S.

Scott's No.		Plate Blocks NH	Plate Blocks Unused	F-VF NH	F-VF Unused	F-VF Used
O1	1¢ George VI, Green (249)	9.50	7.25	1.95	1.50	.50
O2	2¢ George VI, Brown (250)	100.00	80.00	12.50	8.50	8.50
O3	3¢ George VI, Violet (252)	9.75	7.25	2.00	1.50	1.00
O4	4¢ George VI, Carmine (254)	16.00	11.50	3.00	2.10	.55
O6	10¢ Great Bear Lake (269)	17.00	13.75	3.50	2.75	.50
O7	14¢ Hydroelectric Sta. (270)	26.75	21.75	5.00	3.50	1.65
O8	20¢ Reaper (271)	72.50	60.00	13.50	10.00	2.50
O9	50¢ Lumbering (272)	950.00	700.00	175.00	125.00	125.00
O10	$1 Train Ferry (273)	285.00	200.00	42.50	30.00	30.00
	1950 Issues of 1949-50 Overprinted O.H.M.S.					
O11	50¢ Development (294)	135.00	95.00	27.50	18.50	15.00
O12	1¢ George VI, Green (284)	3.65	3.00	.35	.30	.30
O13	2¢ George VI, Sepia (285)	3.75	3.00	.95	.75	.75
O14	3¢ G. VI, Rose Violet (286)	5.00	4.00	1.15	.90	.45
O15	4¢ G. VI, Carmine (287)	5.00	4.00	1.15	.90	.15
O15A	5¢ G. VI, Deep Blue (288)	10.75	9.00	1.95	1.65	1.30
	1950 Issues of 1948-50 Overprinted G					
O16	1¢ George VI, Green (284)	1.70	1.40	.27	.22	.15
O17	2¢ George VI, Sepia (285)	5.50	4.50	1.10	.90	.70
O18	3¢ G. VI, Rose Violet (286)	5.50	4.50	1.10	.90	.20
O19	4¢ G. VI, Carmine (287)	5.50	4.50	1.10	.90	.15
O20	5¢ G. VI, Deep Blue (288)	13.00	10.75	1.35	1.10	.75
O21	10¢ Great Bear Lake (269)	11.00	9.50	2.25	1.85	.40
O22	14¢ Hydroelectric Sta. (270)	28.50	25.00	6.00	5.00	1.50
O23	10¢ Reaper (271)	70.00	55.00	13.50	10.75	.90
O24	50¢ Oil Development (294)	45.00	36.50	9.00	7.00	4.25
O25	$1 Train Ferry (273)	375.00	300.00	75.00	60.00	60.00
O26	10¢ Fur Trading (301)	6.25	5.25	1.40	1.15	.20
	1951-53 Issues of 1951-53 Overprinted G					
O27	$1 Fisheries (302)	375.00	300.00	75.00	60.00	60.00
O28	2¢ G. VI, Olive Green (305)	2.00	1.65	.42	.35	.15
O29	4¢ George VI, Orange (306)	4.25	3.50	.75	.60	.15
O30	20¢ Forestry Products (316)	10.00	8.50	2.25	1.80	.18
O31	7¢ Canada Goose (320)	13.75	11.00	3.65	3.00	.80
O32	$1 Totem Pole (321)	70.00	57.50	15.00	12.50	7.75
	1953-55 Issues of 1953-55 Overprinted G					
O33	1¢ Queen Elizabeth (325)	1.40	1.25	.30	.27	.15
O34	2¢ Queen Elizabeth (326)	1.50	1.35	.30	.27	.15
O35	3¢ Queen Elizabeth (327)	1.50	1.35	.35	.30	.15
O36	4¢ Queen Elizabeth (328)	2.25	1.95	.50	.45	.15
O37	5¢ Queen Elizabeth (329)	2.25	1.95	.50	.45	.15
O38	50¢ Textile (334)	26.00	22.50	5.50	4.75	1.00
O38a	50¢ Textile, Flying G (1961)	23.50	18.75	5.00	4.00	2.00
O39	10¢ Eskimo (351)	4.00	3.50	.85	.75	.15
O39a	10¢ Eskimo, Flying G (1962)	10.75	9.00	1.75	1.50	.85
	1955-56 Issues of 1955-56 Overprinted G					
O40	1¢ Queen Elizabeth (337)	1.30	1.15	.28	.25	.25
O41	2¢ Queen Elizabeth (337)	1.85	1.60	.40	.35	.15
O43	4¢ Queen Elizabeth (340)	5.25	4.50	1.10	.95	.15
O44	5¢ Queen Elizabeth (341)	1.85	1.60	.40	.35	.15
O45	20¢ Paper Industry (362)	8.00	6.75	1.75	1.50	.18
O45a	20¢ Paper, Flying G (1962)	32.50	27.50	4.75	4.00	.45

1963 Issue of 1962-63 Overprinted G

Scott's No.		Plate Block	F-VF NH	F-VF Used
O46	1¢ Queen Elizabeth (401) (Blank)	3.00	.65	.65
O47	2¢ Queen Elizabeth (402) (Blank)	3.00	.65	.65
O48	4¢ Queen Elizabeth (404) (Blank)	7.50	.75	.75
O49	5¢ Queen Elizabeth (405) (Blank)	2.75	.45	.45

CANADA "TAGGED" ISSUES

(A) = Wide Side Bars
(B) = Wide Bar in Middle
(C) = Bar at Left or Right
(D) = Narrow Bar in Middle
(E) = Narrow Side Bars - General

Scott's No.		F-VF NH
	1962-63 Elizabeth II	
337-41p	1¢-5¢, Set of 5	9.50
337p	1¢ Violet Brown (A)	1.20
338p	2¢ Green (A)	1.20
339p	3¢ Carmine Rose (A)	1.20
340p	4¢ Violet (B)	3.25
341p	5¢ Blue (A)	3.50
401-5p	1¢-5¢, Set of 5	1.60
401p	1¢ Brown (A)	.20
402p	2¢ Green (A)	.20
403p	3¢ Purple (A)	.25
404p	4¢ Carmine (C)	.70
404pa	4¢ Carmine (D)	.90
404pb	4¢ Carmine (B)	3.50
405p	5¢ Violet Blue (A)	.45
405q	5¢ Min. Pane of 20	37.50
	1964-67	
434p	3¢ Brown (A)	.75
434q	3¢ Min. Pane of 25	11.00
435p	5¢ 1964 Xmas (A)	1.00
443p	3¢ 1965 Xmas (A)	.25
443q	3¢ Min. Pane of 25	8.00
444p	5¢ 1965 Xmas (A)	.30
451p	3¢ 1966 Xmas (A)	.25
451q	3¢ Min. Pane of 25	4.65
452p	5¢ 1966 Xmas (A)	.45
453p	5¢ Flag over Globe (A)	.40

Scott's No.		F-VF NH
	1967-72 Definitives, Pf. 12	
454p	1¢ Brown (A)	.25
454pa	1¢ Brown (B)	.25
454pb	1¢ Brown (E)	.20
454ep	1¢ Booklet single, Perf. 12½ x 12 (E)	.45
455p	2¢ Green (A)	.25
455pa	2¢ Green (B)	.20
455pb	2¢ Green (E)	.20
456p	3¢ Purple (A)	.20
456pa	3¢ Purple (E) precan	.35
457p	4¢ Carmine (C)	.55
457pa	4¢ Carmine (B)	.40
457pb	4¢ Carmine (E)	.55
458p	5¢ Blue (A)	.55
458bp	5¢ Min. Pane of 20	45.00
458pa	5¢ Blue (B)	.35
459p	6¢ Orange, Pf. 10 (A)	.50
459bp	6¢ Orange, Perf. 12½ x 12 (A)	.60
460p	6¢ Black, Die I, Perf. 12½ x 12 (A)	.35
460cp	6¢ Black, Die II, Perf. 12½ x 12 (B)	.50
460cpa	6¢ Black, Bklt. Sgl., Die II (E)	.45
460fp	6¢ Black, Die I (B)	.40
460fpa	6¢ Black, Die I (B)	.75
462p	10¢ Jack Pine (A)	1.00
462pa	10¢ Jack Pine (E)	.90
463p	15¢ Bylot Island (A)	1.00
463pa	15¢ Bylot Island (E)	1.00
464p	20¢ Ferry (A)	1.50

Scott's No.		F-VF NH
465p	25¢ Solemn Land (A)	2.75
	1967-69	
476p	3¢ 1967 Xmas (A)	.25
476q	3¢ Min. Pane of 25	4.00
477p	5¢ 1967 Xmas (A)	.30
488p	5¢ 1968 Xmas (B)	.25
488q	5¢ B. Pane of 10	4.50
489p	6¢ 1968 Xmas (A)	.30
502p	5¢ 1969 Xmas (B)	.20
502q	5¢ B. Pane of 10	3.50
503p	6¢ 1969 Xmas (A)	.25
	1970	
505p	6¢ Manitoba (A)	.40
508-11p	25¢ Expo '70 (A)	13.00
513p	10¢ UN (A)	.90
514p	15¢ UN (A)	1.40
519-30p	5¢-15¢ Set of 12	7.50
519-23p	5¢ Strip of 5 (B)	2.75
524-28p	6¢ Strip of 5 (B)	3.50
529p	10¢ Manager (B)	.55
530p	15¢ Snowmobile (B)	1.00
	1971-72	
541p	15¢ Radio Canada (A)	2.75
543p	7¢ Green (A)	.50
544p	8¢ Slate (A)	.35
544pa	8¢ Slate (E)	.30
544q	B.Pn.of 6 [#454pb (3), 460cpa (1),544pa (2)]	2.00
544r	B.Pn.of 18 [#454pb (6), 460cpa (1),544pa (11)]	5.50

Scott's No.		F-VF NH
544s	B.Pn.of 10 [#454pb (4), 460cpa (1),544pa (5)]	2.5
550p	8¢ Coil, Slate (E)	.4
554p	6¢ Snowflake (B)	.2
555p	7¢ Snowflake (A)	.5
557p	15¢ Snowflake (A)	.9
560p	8¢ World Health (E)	.6
561p	8¢ Fronterac (E)	.7
562-63p	8¢ Indians (E)	1.1
564-65p	8¢ Indians (E)	1.1
582-85p	15¢ Sciences (E)	12.0
	1972 Pictorials	
594	10¢ Forests (E)	.2
594p	10¢ Forests (A)	.9
595	15¢ Mountain Sheep (E)	.3
595p	15¢ Mountain Sheep (A)	1.1
596	20¢ Prairie Mosaic (E)	.4
596p	20¢ Prairie Mosaic (A)	1.4
597	25¢ Polar Bears (E)	.5
597p	25¢ Polar Bears (A)	1.8
	1972 Commemoratives	
606p	6¢ Christmas (E)	.2
606pa	6¢ Christmas (A)	.3
607p	8¢ Christmas (E)	.3
607pa	8¢ Christmas (A)	.3
608p	10¢ Christmas (E)	.6
608pa	10¢ Christmas (A)	.7
609p	15¢ Christmas (E)	1.0
609pa	15¢ Christmas (A)	1.2
610p	8¢ Krieghoff (E)	.3

MINT CANADA COMMEMORATIVE YEAR SETS
All Fine To Very Fine, Never Hinged

Year	Scott Nos.	Qty.	F-VF NH
1947-49	274-77,82-83	6	1.10
1951-52	303-04,11-15,17-19	10	4.50
1953-54	322-24,35-36,49-50	7	1.55
1955	352-58	7	1.80
1956	359-61,64	4	1.05
1957	365-74	10	4.35
1958	375-82	8	1.80
1959	383-88	6	1.35
1960-61	389-95	7	1.60
1962	396-400	5	1.10
1963	410,12-13	3	.65
1964	416,431-35	6	1.15
1964-66	417-29A (Coats of Arms & Flowers)	14	2.75
1965	437-44	8	1.50
1966	445-52	8	1.50
1967	453,469-77	10	1.90
1968	478-89	12	3.85
1969	490-504	15	9.50
1970	505-18,531	15	11.50
1970	519-30 (Christmas)	12	4.50
1971	532-42,552-58	18	5.35
1972	559-61,606-10	8	2.25

Year	Scott Nos.	Qty.	F-VF NH
1972-76	562-81 (Indians)	20	5.2
1973	611-28	18	5.5
1974	629-55	27	8.9
1975	656-80	25	15.2
1976	681-703	23	17.5
1977	704,732-51	21	5.5
1978	752-56,757-79	28	9.3
1979	780,813-46	35	11.2
1980	847-77	31	11.5
1981	878-906	29	9.3
1982	909-16,954-75	30	18.5
1983	976-1008	33	23.7
1984	1009-44	36	20.5
1985	1045-76	32	19.7
1986	1077-79,1090-1121	35	21.9
1987	1122-54,1125A	34	23.5
1988	1195-1228	34	24.0
1989	1229-63	34	24.0
1990	1264-71,1274-1301	36	25.6
1991	1302-48	46	34.7
1992	1399-1455	57	41.9
1993	1456-1506	51	42.9
1994	1509, 1511-40	42	40.7

CANADA DUCK STAMPS

AB 1

NS 2

CANADA

No.	Description	F-VF NH
N 1	'85 $4 Mallards Bklt	18.00
N 2	'86 $4 Canvasbks Bklt	15.00
N 2B	'86 Min. Sheet of 16	275.00
N 3	'87 $6.50 Can. G'se Bklt	11.00
N 3B	'87 Min. Sheet of 16	275.00
N 4	'88 $6.50 Pintails Bklt	14.00
N 4B	'88 Min. Sheet of 16	275.00
N 5	'89 $7.50 Snow G'se Bklt	14.50
N 5B	'89 Min. Sheet of 16	275.00
N 6	'90 $7.50 Wood Duck Bklt	13.00
N 6B	'90 Min. Sheet of 16	220.00
N 7	'91 $8.50 Blk. Duck Bklt	13.00
N 7B	'91 Min. Sheet of 16	220.00
N 7J	'91 Joint Issue w/US	31.50
N 7JI	'91 J'nt Issue w/US, Impf.	72.50
N 8	'92 $8.50 Cmn Elders Bklt	13.00
N 8B	'92 Min. Sheet of 16	220.00
N 9	'93 $8.50 Hd'd Mergans'r	13.00
N 9B	'93 Min. Sheet of 16	220.00
N 10	'94 $8.50 Ross' Geese	13.00
N 11	'95 $8.50 Redheads	13.00

anada Set 1985-94 (10) 125.00

ALBERTA

No.	Description	F-VF NH
B 1	'89 $6 Canada Geese	23.00
B 2	'90 $7 Mallards	20.00
B 3	'91 $7.71 Pintails	18.00
B 4	'92 $7.90 Snow Geese	17.00
B 5	'93 $7.90 Canvasbacks	15.00
B 6	'94 $7.90 Redheads	13.00

lberta Set 1989-94 (6) 95.00

BRITISH COLUMBIA

No.	Desscription	F-VF NH
BC 1	'95 $6 Bighorn Sheep	8.00
BC 1B	'95 Same, Booklet	10.00
BC 1M	'95 Same, Mini Sheet	30.00

MANITOBA

No.	Desscription	F-VF NH
	Winnipeg Duck Stamp	11.00
	Winnipeg Duck, Flourescent Paper	11.00
MAN 1	'94 $6 Polar Bear	8.00
MAN 1B	'94 Same, Booklet	9.50
MAN 1M	'94 Same, Mini Sheet 4	34.00

NEW BRUNSWICK

No.	Desscription	F-VF NH
NB 1	'94 $6 White Tail Deer	8.00
NB 1B	'94 Same, Booklet	10.00
NB 1M	'94 Same, Mini Sheet of 4	34.00
NB 2	'95 $6 Cougar	8.00
NB 2B	Same, Booklet	10.00
NB 2M	Same, Mini Sheet of 4	30.00

NEWFOUNDLAND

No.	Desscription	F-VF NH
NEWF 1	'94 $6 Woodland Caribou	8.00
NEWF 1B	'94 Same, Booklet	8.50
NEWF 1M	'94 Same, Mini Sht. 4	34.00

NOVA SCOTIA

No.	Description	F-VF NH
NS 1	'92 $6 Whitetail Deer	12.00
NS 1B	'92 $6 Wh'tail Deer Bklt	15.00
NS 1M	'92 $6 Mini Sheet of 4	45.00
NS 2	'93 $6 Summer Pheasant	9.00
NS 2B	'93 $6 Pheasant Bklt	12.50
NS 2M	'93 $6 Mini Sheet of 4	34.00
NS 3	'94 $6 Wood Duck	8.00
NS 3B	'94 Same, Booklet	10.00
NS 3M	'94 Same, Mini Sheet of 4	27.00
NS 4	'95 $6 Coyote	8.00
NS 4B	Same, Booklet	10.00
NS 4M	Same, Mini Sheet of 4	30.00

ONTARIO

No.	Description	F-VF NH
ON 1	'93 $6 Ruffled Grouse	11.00
ON 1B	'93 $6 Grouse Bklt	9.00
ON 1M	'93 $6 Mini Sheet of 4	34.00
ON 2	'94 $6 Deer	8.00
ON 2B	'94 Same, Booklet	9.00
ON 2M	'94 Same, Mini Sheet of 4	34.00
ON 3	'95 $6 Fish	8.00
ON 3B	Same, Booklet	10.00
ON 3M	Same, Mini Sheet of 4	30.00

PRINCE EDWARD ISLAND

No.	Description	F-VF NH
PEI 1	'94 $6 Geese	8.00
PEI 1B	'94 Same, Booklet	9.00
PEI 1M	'94 Same, Mini Sheet of 4	34.00
PEI 2	'95 $6 Canada Geese	8.00
PEI 2B	Same, Booklet	9.00
PEI 2M	Same, Mini Sheet of 4	30.00

QUEBEC

No.	Description	F-VF NH
QU 1	'88 $6 Ruffled Grouse	120.00
QU 1M	'88 $6 Mini Sheet of 4	225.00
QU 1MI	'88 Imperf. Sheet of 4	1100.00
QU 2	'89 $6 Black Ducks	37.50
QU 2M	'89 $6 Mini Sheet of 4	140.00
QU 2MI	'89 Imperf. Sheet of 4	350.00
QU 3	'90 $6 Common Loons	22.00
QU 3M	'90 $6 Mini Sheet of 4	135.00
QU 3MI	'90 Imperf. Sheet of 4	350.00
QU 4	'91 $6 Cmn Gldneyes	16.00
QU 4M	'91 $6 Mini Sheet of 4	83.40
QU 4MI	'91 Imperf. Sheet of 4	350.00
QU 5	'92 $6.50 Lynx	12.50
QU 5M	'92 $6 Mini Sheet of 4	90.00
QU 5MI	'92 Imperf. Sheet of 4	280.00
QU 6	'93 $6.50 Pergrn Falcon	12.50
QU 6M	'93 $6.50 Mini Sheet of 4	60.00
QU 6MI	'93 $6.50 Impf Sht. of 4	225.00
QU 7	'94 $7 Beluga Whale	13.00
QU 7M	'94 Same, Mini Sheet of 4	45.00
QU 7MI	'94 Same, Imperf. Sht. 4	225.00
QU 8	'95 $7 Moose	12.00
QU 8M	'95 Same, Mini Sht of 4	45.00
QU 8MI	'95 Same, Imperf. Sheet of 4	225.00

Quebec Set 1988-93 (7) 225.00

SASKATCHEWAN

No.	Description	F-VF NH
SK 1	'88 $5 American Widg'n	50.00
SK 2	'89 $5 Bull Moose	50.00
SK 3	'90 $5 Shp Tail'd Grouse	50.00
SK 4	'93 $6 Mallards	8.00
SK 4B	'93 $6 Mallards Bklt	10.00
SK 4M	'93 $6 Mini Sht. of 4	34.00
SK 5	'94 $6	8.00
SK 5B	Same, Booklet	8.00
SK 5M	Same, Mini Sheet of 4	34.00
SK 6	'95 $6 Antelope	8.00
SK 6B	Same, Booklet	9.00
SK 6M	Same, Mini Sheet of 4	30.00

BRITISH COLUMBIA AND VANCOUVER ISLAND

Scott's No.		Unused Fine	Unused Ave.	Used Fine	Used Ave.
2	2½p Victoria, Dull Rose	190.00	90.00	125.00	60.00
	1865 Vancouver Island (OG + 50%) (C)				
4	10¢ Victoria, Blue, Imperf	1250.00	850.00	850.00	550.00
5	5¢ Victoria, Rose, Perf. 14	250.00	150.00	140.00	75.00
6	10¢ Victoria, Blue, Perf. 14	275.00	150.00	140.00	75.00
	1865 British Columbia (OG + 50%) (C)				
7	3p Seal, Blue, Perf. 14	70.00	45.00	70.00	45.00
	1867-1869 Surcharges on #7 Design, Perf. 14 (OG + 40%) (C)				
8	2¢ on 3p Brown (Black Surch)	75.00	47.50	75.00	47.50
9	5¢ on 3p Bright Red (Black)	125.00	75.00	125.00	75.00
10	10¢ on 3p Lilac Rose (Blue)	850.00	500.00	...	...
11	25¢ on 3p Orange (Violet)	125.00	75.00	125.00	75.00
12	50¢ on 3p Violet (Red)	425.00	285.00	...	...
13	$1 on 3p Green (Green)	750.00	450.00	...	...
	1869 Surcharges on #7 Design, Perf. 12½ (OG + 40%) (C)				
14	5¢ on 3p Bright Red (Black)	750.00	425.00	750.00	425.00
15	10¢ on 3p Lilac Rose (Blue)	600.00	375.00	575.00	350.00
16	25¢ on 3p Orange (Violet)	425.00	240.00	425.00	240.00
17	50¢ on 3p Green (Green)	500.00	300.00	550.00	350.00
18	$1 on 3p Green (Green)	900.00	550.00	900.00	550.00

NEW BRUNSWICK

Scott's No.		Unused Fine	Unused Ave.	Used Fine	Used Ave.
	1851 Imperforate - Blue Paper - Unwatermarked (OG + 50%) (C)				
1	3p Crown & Flowers, Red	950.00	525.00	200.00	125.00
2	6p Olive Yellow	...	1250.00	500.00	250.00
3	1sh Bright Red Violet	...	...	...	1100.00
4	1sh Dull Violet	...	...	...	1450.00

1860-1863 - Perf. 12 - White Paper (OG + 30%, NH + 80%) (C)

6 7 8 9 10

Scott's No.		Unused Fine	Unused Ave.	Used Fine	Used Ave.
6	1¢ Locomotive, Red Lilac	12.50	7.50	12.50	7.50
6a	1¢ Brown Violet	18.50	11.50	20.00	10.00
7	2¢ Victoria, Orange (1863)	5.50	3.25	5.50	3.25
8	5¢ Victoria, Green	5.50	3.25	4.50	3.00
8b	5¢ Olive Green	60.00	40.00	12.50	8.00
9	10¢ Victoria, Vermillion	18.50	12.00	18.50	10.00
10	12½¢ Steam & Sailing Ship, Blue	30.00	17.50	27.50	15.00
11	17¢ Prince of Wales, Black	22.50	13.50	22.50	13.50

NEWFOUNDLAND

1,15A-16 3,11A 13,20 23

1857 Imperf. Thick Wove Paper, Mesh (OG + 50%) (C)

Scott's No.		Unused Fine	Unused Ave.	Used Fine	Used Ave.
	1p Crown & Flowers, Brn. Violet	60.00	35.00	100.00	65.00
	3p Triangle, Green	250.00	160.00	300.00	200.00
	5p Crown & Flowers, Vlt. Brown	200.00	120.00	250.00	165.00
	8p Flowers, Scarlet Vermillion	200.00	120.00	225.00	150.00

1860 Imperf. Thin Wove Paper, No Mesh (OG + 50%) (C)

Scott's No.		Unused Fine	Unused Ave.	Used Fine	Used Ave.
1	2p Flowers, Orange	200.00	135.00	225.00	150.00
1A	3p Triangle, Green	37.50	24.00	75.00	50.00
2	4p Flowers, Orange	...	...	600.00	400.00
2A	5p Crown & Flowers, Vlt. Brown	60.00	30.00	125.00	80.00
3	6p Flowers, Orange	...	...	500.00	350.00

1861-62 Imperforate Thin Wove Paper (OG + 50%) (C)

Scott's No.		Unused Fine	Unused Ave.	Used Fine	Used Ave.
5A	1p Crown & Flowers, Vlt. Brown	100.00	60.00	140.00	95.00
7	2p Flowers, Rose	80.00	50.00	150.00	100.00
8	4p Flowers, Rose	27.50	15.50	55.00	30.00
9	5p Crown & Flowers, Red Brown	35.00	20.00	50.00	31.50
0	6p Flowers, Rose	15.00	8.00	48.50	32.50
1	6½ Flowers, Rose	50.00	24.00	100.00	57.50
2	8p Flowers, Rose	45.00	20.00	175.00	110.00
3	1sh Flowers, Rose	30.00	15.00	100.00	65.00

24 28-29 32-32A 35-36

1865-1894 Perf. 12 (OG + 30%, NH + 80%) (C)

Scott's No.		Unused Fine	Unused Ave.	Used Fine	Used Ave.
4	2¢ Codfish, Green, Yellow Paper	40.00	27.50	22.50	12.50
4a	2¢ Green, White Paper	30.00	18.50	16.00	9.00
5	5¢ Harp Seal, Brown	275.00	185.00	200.00	135.00
6	5¢ Harp Seal, Black (1868)	150.00	100.00	85.00	55.00
7	10¢ Prince Albert, Black, Yel. Paper	150.00	100.00	50.00	35.00
7a	10¢ Black, White Paper	70.00	45.00	30.00	16.50
8	12¢ Victoria, Red Brown, Yel.Paper.	185.00	125.00	115.00	75.00
8a	12¢ Red Brown, White Paper	24.50	13.00	24.50	13.00
9	12¢ Brown, White Paper (1894)	24.50	13.00	22.50	12.00
0	13¢ Fishing Ship, Orange	60.00	40.00	40.00	27.50
1	24¢ Victoria, Blue	20.00	14.00	18.50	12.50

1868-1894 Perf. 12 (OG + 30%, NH + 80%) (C)

Scott's No.		Unused Fine	Unused Ave.	Used Fine	Used Ave.
2	1¢ Prince of Wales, Violet	22.50	15.00	20.00	10.00
2A	1¢ Brown Lilac (1871)	30.00	16.00	30.00	16.00
3	3¢ Victoria, Vermillion (1870)	150.00	100.00	115.00	65.00
4	3¢ Blue (1873)	150.00	100.00	16.00	9.00
5	6¢ Victoria, Dull Rose (1870)	8.50	5.00	8.50	5.00
6	6¢ Carmine Lake (1894)	10.00	7.00	10.00	7.00

1876-1879 Rouletted (OG + 30%, NH + 80%) (C)

Scott's No.		Unused Fine	Unused Ave.	Used Fine	Used Ave.
7	1¢ Prince of Wales, Brn. Lilac (1877)	40.00	27.50	15.00	10.00
8	2¢ Codfish, Green (1879)	50.00	34.00	25.00	16.00
9	3¢ Victoria, Blue (1877)	135.00	90.00	7.00	4.75
0	5¢ Harp Seal, Blue	100.00	60.00	7.00	4.75

1880-1896 Perf. 12 (OG + 20%) VF + 50% (C)

41-45 46-48 56-58 59

NEWFOUNDLAND

1880-1896 Perf. 12 (OG + 20%) VF + 50% (C)

Scott's No.		NH Fine	Unused Fine	Unused Ave.	Used Fine	Used Ave.
41	1¢ Prince, Vlt. Brown	16.00	8.00	4.25	6.50	3.25
42	1¢ Gray Brown	16.00	8.00	4.25	6.50	3.25
43	1¢ Brown (1896)	45.00	22.50	12.50	16.50	9.25
44	1¢ Deep Green (1887)	9.00	5.00	3.00	2.50	1.50
45	1¢ Green (1897)	10.00	5.50	3.50	4.50	2.50
46	2¢ Codfish, Yellow Green	20.00	10.00	6.00	9.50	5.00
47	2¢ Green (1896)	35.00	20.00	12.00	12.50	7.50
48	2¢ Red Orange (1887)	15.00	8.50	4.50	5.25	3.00
49	3¢ Victoria, Blue	25.00	12.50	7.50	3.00	1.65
51	3¢ Umber Brown (1887)	20.00	10.00	6.50	3.00	1.65
52	3¢ Violet Brown (1896)	55.00	30.00	16.50	27.50	15.00
53	5¢ Harp Seal, Pale Blue	250.00	150.00	90.00	8.00	4.50
54	5¢ Dark Blue (1887)	100.00	60.00	35.00	6.00	3.25
55	5¢ Bright Blue (1894)	25.00	12.50	7.50	4.50	2.25

1887-1896 (OG + 20%) VF + 50% (C)

Scott's No.		NH Fine	Unused Fine	Unused Ave.	Used Fine	Used Ave.
56	½¢ Dog, Rose Red	8.50	4.25	2.50	4.00	2.25
57	½¢ Orange Red (1896)	37.50	22.50	12.00	24.00	14.00
58	½¢ Black (1894)	8.00	4.00	2.25	3.50	1.85
59	10¢ Schooner, Black	57.50	32.50	20.00	30.00	16.00

60 61 63 69 74

1890 Issue (OG + 20%) VF + 40% (C)

Scott's No.		NH Fine	Unused Fine	Unused Ave.	Used Fine	Used Ave.
60	3¢ Victoria, Slate	9.50	5.50	3.00	.60	.35

1897 Cabot Issue VF Used + 30% (B)

Scott's No.		NH VF	NH F-VF	Unused VF	Unused F-VF	Used F-VF
61-74	**Set of 14**	**360.00**	**265.00**	**190.00**	**137.50**	**105.00**
61	1¢ Victoria	2.60	2.00	1.45	1.10	1.10
62	2¢ Cabot	3.25	2.50	1.75	1.35	1.10
63	3¢ Cape Bonavista	5.00	3.75	2.60	2.00	1.00
64	4¢ Caribou Hunting	6.50	5.00	4.50	3.25	2.50
65	5¢ Mining	8.50	6.50	5.25	4.00	2.50
66	6¢ Logging	7.50	5.75	4.00	3.00	3.00
67	8¢ Fishing	15.00	11.50	8.50	6.50	4.50
68	10¢ Ship "Matthew"	21.50	16.50	11.75	9.00	4.25
69	12¢ Willow Ptarmigan	22.50	17.50	12.50	9.50	5.25
70	15¢ Seals	22.50	17.50	12.50	9.50	5.75
71	24¢ Salmon Fishing	22.50	17.50	12.50	9.50	6.00
72	30¢ Colony Seal	65.00	50.00	35.00	27.50	25.00
73	35¢ Iceberg	165.00	105.00	80.00	52.50	45.00
74	60¢ King Henry VII	15.00	11.50	8.50	6.50	6.00

1897 Surcharges VF Used + 50% (C)

Scott's No.		NH VF	NH F-VF	Unused VF	Unused F-VF	Used F-VF
75	1¢ on 3¢ Type a (#60)	31.50	21.00	18.75	12.50	10.00
76	1¢ on 3¢ Type b (#60)	150.00	100.00	90.00	60.00	70.00
77	1¢ on 3¢ Type c (#60)	675.00	450.00	450.00	300.00	335.00

78 79-80 81-82 85 86

1897-1901 Royal Family Issue VF Used + 30% (B)

Scott's No.		NH VF	NH F-VF	Unused VF	Unused F-VF	Used F-VF
78	½¢ Edward VII as Child	3.50	2.75	1.95	1.50	1.85
79	1¢ Victoria, Carm. Rose	5.25	4.00	2.75	2.10	2.50
80	1¢ Yellow Green (1898)	2.60	2.00	1.65	1.25	.18
81	2¢ Prince, Orange	5.75	4.50	3.25	2.50	3.00
82	2¢ Vermillion (1898)	11.00	8.50	5.75	4.50	.50
83	3¢ Princess (1898)	19.50	15.00	10.50	8.00	.50
84	4¢ Duchess (1901)	23.50	18.00	13.50	10.50	3.00
85	5¢ Duke of York (1899)	26.50	20.00	16.50	12.50	2.00

1908 Map Stamp VF Used + 30% (B)

Scott's No.		NH VF	NH F-VF	Unused VF	Unused F-VF	Used F-VF
86	12¢ Map of Newfoundland	30.00	22.50	16.50	12.50	1.00

NOTE: PRICES THROUGHOUT THIS LIST ARE SUBJECT TO CHANGE WITHOUT NOTICE IF MARKET CONDITIONS REQUIRE. MINIMUM ORDER MUST TOTAL AT LEAST $20.00.

1910 Guy Issue (Lithographed) Perf. 12 except as noted VF Used + 30% (B)

87 88 91 92-92A,98 96,102

Scott's No.		NH VF	NH F-VF	Unused VF	Unused F-VF	Used F-VF
87-97	**Normal Set of 12**	**500.00**	**385.00**	**260.00**	**185.00**	**175.00**
87	1¢ James I, 12 x 11	2.60	2.00	1.30	1.00	.90
87a	1¢ Perf. 12	4.50	3.50	2.95	2.25	1.80
87b	1¢ Perf. 12 x 14	4.00	3.00	2.25	1.75	1.25
88	2¢ Co. Arms	9.00	7.00	5.25	4.00	.75
88a	2¢ Perf. 12 x 14	7.75	5.75	4.25	3.25	.75
88c	2¢ Perf. 12 x 11½	...	...	300.00	225.00	225.00
89	3¢ John Guy	14.50	11.00	8.00	6.00	6.00
90	4¢ The "Endeavor"	24.00	18.50	17.50	12.50	7.50
91	5¢ Cupids, Perf. 14 x 12	15.00	11.50	8.50	6.50	3.00
91a	5¢ Perf. 12	20.00	15.00	11.75	9.00	3.75
92	6¢ Claret (Z Reversed)	125.00	95.00	60.00	45.00	45.00
92A	6¢ Claret (Z Normal)	45.00	35.00	22.50	16.50	16.50
93	8¢ Mosquito, Pale Brown	80.00	60.00	40.00	28.50	28.50
94	9¢ Logging, Ol. Green	80.00	60.00	40.00	28.50	28.50
95	10¢ Paper Mills, Black	80.00	60.00	40.00	28.50	27.50
96	12¢ Edward VII, L. Brown	80.00	60.00	40.00	28.50	28.50
97	15¢ George V, Gray Black	100.00	75.00	50.00	35.00	35.00

1911 Guy Issue (Engraved) Perf. 14 VF Used + 30% (B)

Scott's No.		NH VF	NH F-VF	Unused VF	Unused F-VF	Used F-VF
98-103	**Set of 6**	**575.00**	**435.00**	**255.00**	**195.00**	**195.00**
98	6¢ Brown Violet	32.50	25.00	16.50	12.50	12.50
99	8¢ Mosquito, Bistre Brn	100.00	75.00	39.50	30.00	30.00
100	9¢ Logging, Ol. Grn	92.50	70.00	32.50	25.00	25.00
101	10¢ Paper Mills, Vi. Black	145.00	110.00	65.00	50.00	50.00
102	12¢ Edward VII, Red Brn	120.00	90.00	58.50	45.00	45.00
103	15¢ George V, Slate Gr	120.00	90.00	58.50	45.00	45.00

104 105 107 115

1911 Royal Family Coronation Issue VF Used + 30% (B)

Scott's No.		NH VF	NH F-VF	Unused VF	Unused F-VF	Used F-VF
104-14	**Set of 11**	**375.00**	**285.00**	**170.00**	**130.00**	**120.00**
104	1¢ Queen Mary	3.00	2.25	1.50	1.15	.18
105	2¢ George V	3.25	2.50	1.65	1.25	.18
106	3¢ Prince of Wales	30.00	22.75	16.00	12.00	12.00
107	4¢ Prince Albert	28.50	21.50	14.50	10.75	9.00
108	5¢ Princess Mary	13.00	10.50	6.50	5.00	1.25
109	6¢ Prince Henry	25.00	19.50	13.00	10.00	10.00
110	8¢ George (color paper)	120.00	90.00	43.50	33.50	33.50
110a	8¢ White Paper	120.00	90.00	45.00	35.00	35.00
111	9¢ Prince John	32.50	25.00	16.50	12.50	12.50
112	10¢ Queen Alexandra	52.50	40.00	21.50	16.50	16.50
113	12¢ Duke of Connaught	45.00	35.00	21.50	16.50	16.50
114	15¢ Seal of Colony	50.00	37.50	21.50	16.50	16.50

1919 Trail of the Caribou Issue VF Used + 30% (B)

Scott's No.		NH VF	NH F-VF	Unused VF	Unused F-VF	Used F-VF
115-26	**Set of 12**	**335.00**	**250.00**	**165.00**	**125.00**	**105.00**
115	1¢ Suvla Bay	2.25	1.65	1.20	.90	.25
116	2¢ Ubigue	3.50	2.50	1.75	1.25	.35
117	3¢ Gueudecourt	4.00	3.00	2.00	1.50	.20
118	4¢ Beaumont Hamel	6.50	5.00	3.50	2.75	1.00
119	5¢ Ubigue	8.50	6.50	4.25	3.25	1.00
120	6¢ Monchy	32.50	25.00	16.50	12.50	12.50
121	8¢ Ubigue	32.50	25.00	16.50	12.50	10.00
122	10¢ Steenbeck	20.00	15.00	8.50	6.50	2.50
123	12¢ Ubigue	70.00	50.00	32.50	25.00	20.00
124	15¢ Langemarck	52.50	40.00	26.50	20.00	20.00
125	24¢ Cambral	70.00	50.00	32.50	25.00	25.00
126	36¢ Combles	52.50	40.00	26.50	20.00	20.00

1920 Stamps of 1897 Surcharged VF Used + 30% (B)

Scott's No.		NH VF	NH F-VF	Unused VF	Unused F-VF	Used F-VF
127	2¢ on 30¢ Seal (#72)	8.50	6.50	5.75	4.50	4.50
128	3¢ on 15¢ Bars 10½ mm	295.00	225.00	195.00	150.00	165.00
129	3¢ on 15¢ Bars 13½ mm	16.50	12.50	9.00	7.50	7.50
130	3¢ on 35¢ Iceberg (#73)	14.00	10.50	9.00	7.50	7.50

NEWFOUNDLAND

1923-1924 Pictorial Issue VF Used + 30% (B)

131 132 133 139

Scott's No.		NH VF	NH F-VF	Unused VF	Unused F-VF	Used F-VF
131-44	**Set of 14**	**180.00**	**135.00**	**112.50**	**87.50**	**80.00**
131	1¢ Twin Hills	3.25	2.40	2.25	1.75	.20
132	2¢ South West Arm	2.10	1.60	1.50	1.15	.18
133	3¢ War Memorial	3.25	2.40	2.25	1.75	.18
134	4¢ Humber River	3.00	2.25	1.95	1.50	1.40
135	5¢ Coast of Trinity	5.00	3.75	3.25	2.50	1.60
136	6¢ Upper Steadies	6.00	4.50	4.00	3.00	3.00
137	8¢ Quidi Vidi	5.00	3.75	3.25	2.50	2.35
138	9¢ Caribou Crossing	42.50	32.00	23.50	18.00	18.00
139	10¢ Humber River Canyon	5.50	4.25	3.50	2.75	1.60
140	11¢ Shell Bird Island	9.00	7.00	6.50	5.00	5.00
141	12¢ Mt. Moriah	9.50	7.25	6.75	5.25	5.25
142	15¢ Humber River	12.00	9.00	7.75	6.00	5.75
143	20¢ Placentia (1924)	14.00	10.00	8.75	6.75	4.50
144	24¢ Topsail Falls (1924)	72.50	55.00	45.00	35.00	35.00

145,163,172 146,164,173 148,166,175 155

1928 Publicity Issue - Unwatermarked - Thin Paper VF Used + 30% (B)

Scott's No.		NH VF	NH F-VF	Unused VF	Unused F-VF	Used F-VF
145-59	**Set of 15**	**107.50**	**87.50**	**78.50**	**60.00**	**46.50**
145	1¢ Map, Deep Green	1.95	1.50	1.25	.95	.50
146	2¢ "Caribou", Deep Carm	2.50	1.95	1.75	1.35	.50
147	3¢ Mary & George V, Br	3.25	2.50	2.15	1.65	.30
148	4¢ Prince, Lilac Rose	4.00	3.00	2.50	1.90	1.50
149	5¢ Train, Slate Green	7.50	5.75	5.25	4.00	2.75
150	6¢ Newfld. Hotel Ultra	5.50	4.25	4.00	3.00	2.50
151	8¢ Lt. Red Brn	7.50	5.75	5.25	4.00	3.25
152	9¢ Myrtle Green	8.75	6.75	6.50	5.00	4.00
153	10¢ War Mem., Dark Violet	8.75	6.75	6.50	5.00	3.50
154	12¢ P.O. Brown Carmine	6.50	5.00	4.50	3.50	2.75
155	14¢ Cabot Tower, Red Br	8.75	6.75	6.50	5.00	2.75
156	15¢ Nonstop, Dark Blue	9.50	7.25	7.00	5.50	4.50
157	20¢ Colonial, Gray Blk	8.75	6.75	6.50	5.00	3.00
158	28¢ P.O. Gray Green	30.00	22.50	17.00	13.50	12.50
159	30¢ Grand Falls	9.00	7.00	6.50	5.00	4.50

1929 Stamp of 1923 Surcharged VF Used + 30% (B)

Scott's No.		NH VF	NH F-VF	Unused VF	Unused F-VF	Used F-VF
160	3¢ on 6¢ Upper Steadies	4.50	3.25	3.50	2.65	2.65

1929-31 Publicity Issue Re-engraved - Like Preceding but Thicker Paper VF Used + 30% (B) (See your favorite Specialized catalog for details)

Scott's No.		NH VF	NH F-VF	Unused VF	Unused F-VF	Used F-VF
163-71	**Set of 9**	**165.00**	**122.50**	**95.00**	**75.00**	**45.00**
163	1¢ Green	2.10	1.60	1.50	1.15	.40
164	2¢ Deep Carmine	2.10	1.60	1.50	1.15	.18
165	3¢ Deep Red Brown	2.35	1.80	1.70	1.30	.18
166	4¢ Magenta	3.50	2.65	2.50	1.90	.90
167	5¢ Slate Green	5.25	4.00	3.75	2.85	.90
168	6¢ Ultramarine	14.00	10.50	9.75	7.50	6.00
169	10¢ Dark Violet	8.50	6.50	5.25	4.00	1.50
170	15¢ Deep Blue (1930)	55.00	40.00	32.50	25.00	21.00
171	20¢ Gray Black (1931)	80.00	60.00	42.50	32.50	17.00

1931 Publicity Issue - Re-engraved - Wmk. Arms VF Used + 30% (B)

Scott's No.		NH VF	NH F-VF	Unused VF	Unused F-VF	Used F-VF
172-81	**Set of 11**	**250.00**	**190.00**	**170.00**	**127.50**	**83.50**
172	1¢ Green	3.25	2.50	1.95	1.50	.80
173	2¢ Red	5.00	3.75	2.95	2.25	1.10
174	3¢ Red Brown	4.50	3.50	2.95	2.25	.80
175	4¢ Rose	6.00	4.50	4.25	3.00	1.20
176	5¢ Greenish Gray	12.50	9.50	8.50	6.50	5.50
177	6¢ Ultramarine	21.50	16.50	14.50	11.00	12.00
178	8¢ Red Brown	23.50	18.00	15.50	12.00	12.00
179	10¢ Dark Violet	15.00	12.00	11.00	8.50	5.50
180	15¢ Deep Blue	50.00	37.50	32.50	25.00	22.50
181	20¢ Gray Black	67.50	55.00	50.00	37.50	7.50
182	30¢ Olive Brown	52.50	40.00	35.00	26.50	19.00

1932-1937 Industrial Set, Perf. 13½ or 14 VF Used + 20%

183-84,253 190-91,257 199,266 210,264

Scott's No.		NH VF	NH F-VF	Unused VF	Unused F-VF	Used F-VF
83-99	**Set of 17**	**95.00**	**76.50**	**62.50**	**51.75**	**35.00**
83	1¢ Codfish, Green	1.65	1.35	1.15	.95	.30
83a	1¢ Booklet Pane of 4	110.00	90.00	72.50	60.00	...
84	1¢ Gray Black	.40	.30	.27	.22	.18
84a	1¢ Bk. Pane of 4, Pf. 13½	80.00	65.00	52.50	43.50	...
84b	1¢ Bk. Pane of 4, Pf. 14	90.00	75.00	62.50	52.50	...
85	2¢ George V, Rose	1.65	1.35	1.15	.95	.18
85a	2¢ Bk. Pane of 4	60.00	50.00	39.50	32.50	...
86	2¢ Green	1.65	1.35	1.10	.90	.18
86a	2¢ Bk. Pane of 4, Pf. 13½	33.50	27.50	22.00	18.50	...
86b	2¢ Bk. Pane of 4, Pf. 14	45.00	37.50	30.00	25.00	...
87	3¢ Queen Mary	1.35	1.10	.90	.75	.18
87a	3¢ Bk. Pane of 4, Pf. 13½	80.00	65.00	52.50	43.50	...
87b	3¢ Bk. Pane of 4, Pf. 14	90.00	75.00	62.50	52.50	...
87c	3¢ Bk. Pane of 4, Pf. 13	110.00	90.00	72.50	60.00	...
88	4¢ Prince, Deep Violet	5.50	4.50	3.95	3.25	1.25
89	4¢ Rose Lake	.75	.60	.50	.40	.18
90	5¢ Caribou V. Brown (I)	7.50	6.00	4.75	4.00	.80
91	5¢ Deep Violet (II)	1.10	.90	.75	.60	.18
91a	5¢ Deep Violet (I)	14.00	11.50	7.50	6.35	.75
92	6¢ Elizabeth, Dull Blue	12.00	10.00	7.75	6.50	6.50
93	10¢ Salmon, Olive Black	1.50	1.25	1.00	.85	.55
94	14¢ Dog, Intense Black	3.00	2.50	2.10	1.75	1.50
95	15¢ Seal Pup, Magenta	3.00	2.50	2.10	1.75	1.50
96	20¢ Cape Race, Gray Green	3.00	2.50	2.10	1.75	.75
97	25¢ Sealing Fleet, Gray	3.75	2.75	2.25	1.90	1.60
98	30¢ Fishing Fleet, Ultra	35.00	28.50	22.00	18.50	16.50
99	48¢ Red Brown (1937)	16.50	13.50	11.50	9.50	3.85

190,191a Antler under "T" higher, #191 Antlers are even height.

1932 New Values VF Used + 20%

Scott's No.		NH VF	NH F-VF	Unused VF	Unused F-VF	Used F-VF
08	7¢ Duchess, Red Brown	1.75	1.40	1.20	1.00	1.00
09	8¢ Corner Brook, Or. Red	1.75	1.40	1.20	1.00	.90
10	24¢ Bell Island, Light Blue	4.25	3.50	3.00	2.50	2.40

1933 "L & S Post" Overprinted on C9 VF + 20%

Scott's No.		NH VF	NH F-VF	Unused VF	Unused F-VF	Used F-VF
11	15¢ Dog Sled & Plane	11.00	9.00	7.75	6.50	6.00

1933 Sir Humphrey Gilbert Issue VF + 20%

212 213 216 222

Scott's No.		NH VF	NH F-VF	Unused VF	Unused F-VF	Used F-VF
12-25	**Set of 14**	**185.00**	**150.00**	**110.00**	**90.00**	**87.50**
212	1¢ Sir Humphrey Gilbert	1.00	.85	.80	.65	.50
213	2¢ Compton Castle	1.35	1.10	1.00	.85	.50
214	3¢ Gilbert Coat of Arms	2.10	1.75	1.40	1.15	.60
215	4¢ Eton College	2.10	1.75	1.40	1.15	.35
216	5¢ Token	2.75	2.25	1.80	1.50	.85
217	7¢ Royal Patents	21.50	17.50	11.50	9.50	11.50
218	8¢ Leaving Plymouth	10.00	8.00	6.25	5.25	5.25
219	9¢ Arriving St. John's	11.00	9.00	7.00	5.75	5.75
220	10¢ Annexation	12.00	10.00	7.00	5.75	4.50
221	14¢ Coat of Arms	24.50	20.00	14.00	11.50	10.50
222	15¢ Deck of "Squirrel"	26.00	21.00	15.00	12.50	11.00
223	20¢ 1626 Map of Nwfld	15.00	12.50	9.00	7.50	7.00
224	24¢ Queen Elizabeth I	33.50	27.50	20.00	16.50	16.50
225	32¢ Gilbert Statue at Truro	33.50	27.50	20.00	16.50	16.50

NEWFOUNDLAND

1935 Silver Jubilee Issue VF + 20%

226 230 233

Scott's No.		F-VF NH	F-VF Unused	F-VF Used
226-29	**Set of 4**	**12.00**	**7.50**	**6.50**
226	4¢ Bright Rose	1.25	.75	.45
227	5¢ Violet	1.25	.75	.65
228	7¢ Dark Blue	3.00	2.00	2.00
229	24¢ Olive Green	7.00	4.50	4.50

1937 Coronation Issue VF + 20%

Scott's No.		F-VF NH	F-VF Unused	F-VF Used
230-32	**Set of 3**	**2.85**	**1.90**	**1.25**
230	2¢ Deep Green	.75	.50	.35
231	4¢ Carmine Rose	.75	.50	.30
232	5¢ Dark Violet	1.50	1.00	.65

1937 Coronation Issue (Long Set) VF + 20%

Scott's No.		F-VF NH	F-VF Unused	F-VF Used
233-43	**Set of 11**	**27.00**	**18.50**	**16.00**
233	1¢ Codfish	.45	.30	.20
234	3¢ Map (I), Fine	1.85	1.25	.80
234a	3¢ Map (II), Coarse	1.65	1.10	.60
235	7¢ Caribou	2.00	1.40	1.20
236	8¢ Corner Brook Paper Mills	2.00	1.40	1.20
237	10¢ Salmon	3.75	2.50	2.25
238	14¢ Newfoundland Dog	3.00	2.10	1.85
239	15¢ Harp Seal Pup	3.60	2.40	2.00
240	20¢ Cape Race	2.50	1.75	1.50
241	24¢ Loading Iron Ore	3.25	2.30	2.10
242	25¢ Sealing Fleet	3.25	2.30	2.00
243	48¢ Fishing Fleet	3.75	2.50	2.25

245 249 252

1938 Royal Family, Perf. 13½ VF + 20%

Scott's No.		F-VF NH	F-VF Unused	F-VF Used
245	2¢ George VI, Green	1.50	1.00	.15
246	3¢ Elizabeth, Dark Carmine	1.50	1.00	.15
247	4¢ Elizabeth, Light Blue	1.75	1.25	.15
248	7¢ Queen Mother, Ultra marine	1.50	1.00	1.10

1939 Royal Visit VF + 20%

Scott's No.		Plate Blocks NH	Plate Blocks Unused	F-VF NH	F-VF Unused	F-VF Used
249	5¢ George VI - Elizabeth	8.00	6.50	.80	.65	.65

1939 Royal Visit Surcharge VF + 20%

Scott's No.		Plate Blocks NH	Plate Blocks Unused	F-VF NH	F-VF Unused	F-VF Used
250	2¢ on 5¢ (#249)	11.75	9.50	1.15	.85	.85
251	4¢ on 5¢ (#249)	10.50	8.50	.90	.65	.65

1941 Grenfell Issue VF + 20%

Scott's No.		Plate Blocks NH	Plate Blocks Unused	F-VF NH	F-VF Unused	F-VF Used
252	5¢ Grenfell	2.75	2.25	.40	.30	.30

1941-1944 Industrial Set, Perf. 12½ VF + 20%

Scott's No.		Plate Blocks NH	Plate Blocks Unused	F-VF NH	F-VF Unused	F-VF Used
253-66	**Set of 14**	...	...	**14.50**	**11.50**	**9.00**
253	1¢ Codfish, Dark Gray	1.50	1.25	.25	.20	.15
254	2¢ George VI, Deep Green	1.50	1.25	.25	.20	.15
255	3¢ Elizabeth, Rose Carm	2.25	1.85	.30	.25	.15
256	4¢ Princess Elizabeth, Blue	3.25	2.50	.60	.45	.15
257	5¢ Caribou, Violet (I)	3.25	2.50	.60	.45	.15
258	7¢ Queen Mother (1942)	...	...	.90	.70	.75
259	8¢ Corner Brook, Red	5.75	4.50	.75	.55	.55
260	10¢ Salmon, Brown Black	5.75	4.50	.75	.55	.50
261	14¢ Dog, Black	8.00	6.50	1.50	1.15	1.10
262	15¢ Seal Pup, Rose Violet	8.00	6.50	1.50	1.15	1.10
263	20¢ Cape Race, Green	9.75	7.50	1.50	1.15	1.10
264	24¢ Bell Island, Deep Blue	10.75	8.50	1.75	1.35	1.40
265	25¢ Sealing Fleet, Slate	10.75	8.50	1.75	1.55	1.40
266	48¢ Fishing, Red Br. (1944)	16.00	12.00	3.00	2.25	1.40

267 269 270

1943 University Issue VF + 20%

Scott's No.		Plate Blocks NH	Plate Blocks Unused	F-VF NH	F-VF Unused	F-VF Used
267	30¢ Memorial Univ.	10.00	8.00	1.30	1.10	.85

1946 Two Cent Provisional VF + 20%

268	2¢ on 30¢ (#267)	3.50	3.00	.30	.25	.25

1947 Issues VF + 20%

269	4¢ Princess Elizabeth	2.35	2.00	.30	.25	.15
270	5¢ Cabot	2.75	2.25	.30	.25	.20

AIRMAIL STAMPS

1919-21 Overprint Issues VF Used + 20% (B)

Scott's No.		NH VF	NH F-VF	Unused VF	Unused F-VF	Used F-VF
C2	$1 on 15¢ "Trans-Atlantic"	295.00	225.00	195.00	150.00	150.00
C2a	$1 on 15¢ No Comma	385.00	295.00	235.00	180.00	180.00
C3	35¢ "Halifax", No Period	240.00	185.00	155.00	120.00	120.00
C3a	35¢ Period after "1921"	260.00	200.00	175.00	135.00	135.00

C7,C10 C6,C9 C8,C11

1931 Airs, Unwatermarked VF Used + 30% (B)

C6	15¢ Dog Sled & Airplane	12.00	9.00	8.00	6.00	6.00
C7	50¢ Trans-Atlantic Plane	30.00	23.50	19.50	15.00	15.00
C8	$1 Flight Routes	85.00	65.00	52.50	40.00	40.00

1931 Airs, Watermarked VF Used + 30% (B)

C9	15¢ Dog Sled & Airplane	9.50	7.00	6.50	5.00	5.00
C10	50¢ Trans-Atlantic Plane	45.00	35.00	29.50	22.50	21.50
C11	$1 Flight Routes	140.00	105.00	80.00	60.00	52.50

C13 C19 J3

1932 DO-X Trans-Atlantic Surcharge VF Used + 30% (B)

Scott's No.		NH VF	NH F-VF	Unused VF	Unused F-VF	Used F-VF
C12	$1.50 on $1 Routes (#C11)	400.00	300.00	275.00	210.00	250.00

1933 Labrador Issue VF Used + 20%

C13-17	**Set of 8**	**200.00**	**160.00**	**125.00**	**102.50**	**110.00**
C13	5¢ "Put to Flight"	15.00	12.00	9.00	7.50	7.50
C14	10¢ "Land of Heart's Delight"	21.50	18.00	12.50	10.50	10.50
C15	30¢ "Spotting the Herd"	37.50	30.00	24.00	20.00	22.50
C16	60¢ "News from Home"	67.50	55.00	42.50	35.00	40.00
C17	75¢ "Labrador, Land of Gold"	67.50	55.00	42.50	35.00	40.00

1933 Balbo Flight VF Used + 20%

C18	$4.50 on 75¢ (#C17)	475.00	395.00	325.00	275.00	275.00

1943 St. John's VF + 20%

Scott's No.		Plate Blocks NH	Plate Blocks Unused	F-VF NH	F-VF Unused	F-VF Used
C19	7¢ View of St. John's	3.00	2.50	.40	.35	.25

POSTAGE DUE STAMPS 1939-1949 VF + 20%
Unwatermarked, Perf. 10½ x 10 Unless Otherwise Noted

Scott's No.		F-VF NH	F-VF Unused	F-VF Used
J1	1¢ Yellow Green	3.75	2.50	2.50
J1a	1¢ Perf. 11 (1949)	2.75	2.00	2.75
J2	2¢ Vermillion	3.75	2.50	2.50
J2a	2¢ Perf. 11 x 9 (1946)	4.50	3.00	3.00
J3	3¢ Ultramarine	5.25	3.50	3.00
J3a	3¢ Perf. 11 x 9 (1949)	5.25	3.50	3.50
J4	4¢ Yellow Orange	6.75	4.50	3.75
J4a	4¢ Perf. 11 x 9 (1949)	6.50	4.50	4.50
J5	5¢ Pale Brown	3.75	2.50	2.50
J6	10¢ Dark Violet	3.50	2.40	2.40
J7	10¢ Watermarked, Perf. II	8.50	5.75	7.50

NOTE: PRICES THROUGHOUT THIS LIST ARE SUBJECT TO CHANGE WITHOUT NOTICE IF MARKET CONDITIONS REQUIRE. MINIMUM ORDER MUST TOTAL AT LEAST $20.00.

NOVA SCOTIA

1851-1853 - Imperforate - Blue Paper (OG + 50%) (C)

2,3

Scott's No.		Unused Fine	Unused Ave.	Used Fine	Used Ave.
1	1p Victoria, Red Brown	1200.00	700.00	250.00	175.00
2	3p Crown & Flowers, Blue	415.00	220.00	75.00	50.00
3	3p Dark Blue	600.00	330.00	85.00	55.00
4	6p Yellow Green	...	1250.00	300.00	200.00
5	6p Dark Green	...	2750.00	525.00	350.00
6	1sh Reddish Violet	...	...	...	1500.00
7	1sh Dull Violet	...	...	...	1500.00

1860-1863 - Perf. 12 - White or Yellowish Paper (VF + 50%, NH + 25%, #10, 10a NH + 75%) (C)

8 9 11 12 13

Scott's No.		Unused Fine	Unused Ave.	Used Fine	Used Ave.
8	1¢ Victoria, Black	3.25	2.00	3.00	2.00
9	2¢ Lilac	4.50	3.00	4.50	3.00
10	5¢ Blue	230.00	115.00	7.00	3.85
11	8½¢ Green	3.50	2.25	12.00	7.50
12	10¢ Vermillion	4.50	3.00	4.50	3.00
13	12½¢ Black	19.00	11.50	15.00	10.50

PRINCE EDWARD ISLAND

1,5 2,6 9 10

1861 - Perf. 9 - Typographed (OG + 50%)

Scott's No.		Unused Fine	Unused Ave.	Used Fine	Used Ave.
1	2p Victoria, Dull Rose	250.00	160.00	100.00	70.00
2	3p Blue	465.00	300.00	225.00	150.00
3	6p Yellow Green	750.00	500.00	325.00	225.00
	1862-1865 - Perf. 11,11½,12 and Compound - Typographed (OG + 30%, NH + 80%)				
4	1p Victoria, Yellow Orange	13.50	9.50	13.50	9.50
5	2p Rose	4.00	2.50	4.00	2.50
6	3p Blue, White Paper	5.50	3.00	5.00	3.00
6a	3p Yellowish Paper	7.50	4.15	5.00	3.00
7	6p Yellow Green	45.00	25.00	45.00	25.00
8	9p Violet	35.00	16.50	35.00	16.50
	1868-1870 Issues (OG + 30%, NH + 80%)				
9	4p Victoria, Black	5.50	3.75	13.50	8.50
9a	4p Yellowish Paper	10.50	7.50	15.00	10.00
10	4½p Brown (1870)	25.00	17.50	30.00	20.00

1872 Issue, Perf. 12,12½ (OG + 20%, NH + 60%)

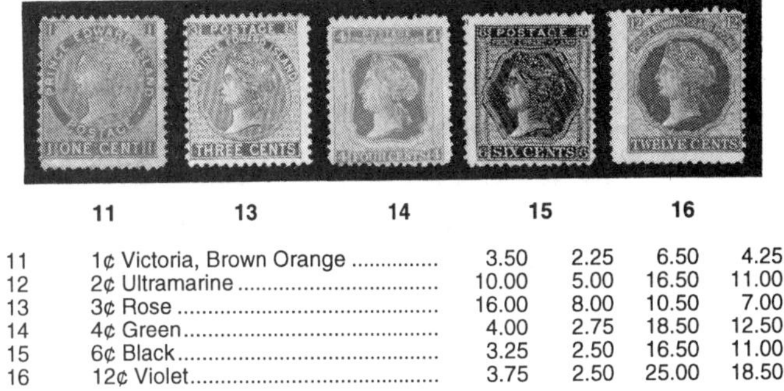

11 13 14 15 16

Scott's No.		Unused Fine	Unused Ave.	Used Fine	Used Ave.
11	1¢ Victoria, Brown Orange	3.50	2.25	6.50	4.25
12	2¢ Ultramarine	10.00	5.00	16.50	11.00
13	3¢ Rose	16.00	8.00	10.50	7.00
14	4¢ Green	4.00	2.75	18.50	12.50
15	6¢ Black	3.25	2.50	16.50	11.00
16	12¢ Violet	3.75	2.50	25.00	18.50

★ U.S. TOPICAL ALBUMS ★SPACE ★ CHRISTMAS ★ BLACK HERITAGE

THE BROOKMAN HERITAGE SERIES

All 3 Albums are fully illustrated on heavy, art-stock pages - printed on one side only, showing spaces for singles, plate blocks and first day covers. The 3-ring Album binders are elegant, luxuriously padded and lettered in gold. In addition, periodic supplements will keep your albums up to date.

BROOKMAN HONORS "AMERICA IN SPACE"

Brookman's America in Space Stamp Album pays tribute to America's contribution to the exploration of space.

COMPLETE ALBUM (through 1993) ONLY $29.95

NEW 1994 SUPPLEMENT ONLY $3.95

BROOKMAN'S BRAND NEW "CHRISTMAS IN AMERICA"

Brookman's popular 2-volume Christmas Album features U.S. stamps issued for the Yuletide Season.

VOLUME I 1962-1979 ONLY $39.95

VOLUME II 1980-1993 ONLY $45.95

2-VOLUME ALBUM (through 1993) ONLY $85.90

NEW 1994 SUPPLEMENT ONLY $5.95

HONORING AMERICA'S BLACK HERITAGE

Brookman's Black Heritage Stamp Album Honors The Contributions Of Black Americans To The Development Of The Nation

COMPLETE ALBUM THROUGH 1993 ONLY $35.95

NEW 1994 SUPPLEMENT ONLY $5.95

AVAILABLE FROM YOUR FAVORITE DEALER OR DIRECT FROM BROOKMAN

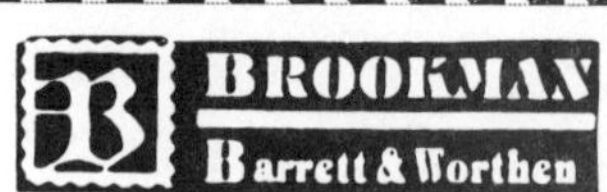

10 Chestnut Dr.
Bedford, NH 03110

$5 THIS COUPON IS WORTH $5.00 $5

Subtract $5.00 from orders over $55.00

ONE COUPON PER ORDER

Available from:

Or Brookman, Bedford, NH 03110

$5 $5

$10 THIS COUPON IS WORTH $10.00 $10

Subtract $10.00 from orders over $110.00

ONE COUPON PER ORDER

Available from:

Or Brookman, Bedford, NH 03110

$10 $10

$10 THIS COUPON IS WORTH $10.00 $10

Subtract $10.00 from orders over $110.00

ONE COUPON PER ORDER

Available from:

Or Brookman, Bedford, NH 03110

$10 $10

$10 THIS COUPON IS WORTH $10.00 $10

Subtract $10.00 from orders over $110.00

ONE COUPON PER ORDER

Available from:

Or Brookman, Bedford, NH 03110

$10 $10

$25 THIS COUPON IS WORTH $25.00 $25

Subtract $25.00 from orders over $275.00

ONE COUPON PER ORDER

Available from:

Or Brookman, Bedford, NH 03110

$25 $25

$40 THIS COUPON IS WORTH $40.00 $40

Subtract $40.00 from orders over $450.00

ONE COUPON PER ORDER

Available from:

Or Brookman, Bedford, NH 03110

$40 $40

HOW TO WRITE YOUR ORDER—PLEASE USE THE ORDER BLANK

1. Fill out date, phone #
2. Print name and address, information including ZIP CODE
3. Note Minimum order of $20.00
4. If ordering by Visa or Master Card, please indicate charge # and expiration date
5. If paying by check, please make payments in U.S. Funds
6. Example of how to write up your orders below

From page no.	Qty Want-ed	Country and Items ordered: Specify Scott Numbers plus first day cover, souvenir card, plate block, mint sheet or other description	Quality Wanted	Un-used	used	Price Each	Leave Blank
6	1	U.S. 294	F-VF		✓	3.50	
27	1	U.S. 1156 Mint Sheet	F-VFNH	✓		6.25	
103	1	Alabama AL1	"			10.00	
202	1	Canada 321 Plate Block	"			60.00	
137	1	U.S. C72b First Day Cover				3.00	
198	1	U.S. PS58 Souvenir Card		✓		4.50	
145	1	U.S. UX178-97		✓		35.00	

PAY SHIPPING/ INSURANCE AS FOLLOWS:

All stamp orders & other orders from:
$20.00 to $49.99 - $3.50
Orders other than stamps:
$50.00 to $199.99 - $5.50
$200.00 & over - $8.00

Total this page	122.25	
Total from reverse		
Total of all items ordered	122.25	
Shipping/Insurance (see chart at left)	5.50	
SUBTOTAL	127.75	
Sales Tax (if any)		
Less any discounts, refund checks, coupons, etc.	-10.00	
TOTAL ENCLOSED	$117.75	

SATISFACTION GUARANTEED
MINIMUM ORDER MUST TOTAL AT LEAST $20.00
On orders outside the U.S., additional postage will be billed if necessary

EASY ORDER FORM--1996 EDITION

Please send the items listed below for which I enclose $____________ Date:____________

Name:______________________________________Street:____

City:__________________________________State/Zip:______________________Phone:____________________

Minimum order must total $20.00. Be sure to include shipping charges.

Payment by: Check [ ] Visa [ ] Mastercard [ ] #________________________________Exp. Date:________

From page no.	Qty Want-ed	Country and Items ordered: Specify Scott Numbers plus first day cover, souvenir card, plate block, mint sheet or other description	Quality Wanted	Un-used	used	Price Each	Leave Blank

PAY SHIPPING/ INSURANCE AS FOLLOWS:			
All stamp orders & other orders from:	Total this page	________	________
$20.00 to $49.99 - $3.50	Total from reverse	________	________
Orders other than stamps:	Total of all items ordered	________	________
$50.00 to $199.99 - $5.50	Shipping/Insurance (see chart at left)	________	________
$200.00 & over - $8.00	**SUBTOTAL**	________	________
	Sales Tax (if any)	________	________
	Less any discounts, refund checks, coupons, etc.		
	TOTAL ENCLOSED		

SATISFACTION GUARANTEED

MINIMUM ORDER MUST TOTAL AT LEAST $20.00

On orders outside the U.S., additional postage will be billed if necessary

Easy Order Form (continued)

From page no.	Qty Want-ed	Country and Items ordered: Specify Scott Numbers plus first day cover, souvenir card, plate block, mint sheet or other description	Quality Wanted	Un-used	used	Price Each	Leave Blank
		Total This Page					

EASY ORDER FORM--1996 EDITION

Please send the items listed below for which I enclose $____________ Date:____________

Name:______________________________________Street:____

City:________________________________State/Zip:______________________Phone:____________________

Minimum order must total $20.00. Be sure to include shipping charges.

Payment by: Check [ ] Visa [ ] Mastercard [ ] #________________________________Exp. Date:________

From page no.	Qty Wanted	Country and Items ordered: Specify Scott Numbers plus first day cover, souvenir card, plate block, mint sheet or other description	Quality Wanted	Unused	used	Price Each	Leave Blank

PAY SHIPPING/ INSURANCE AS FOLLOWS:

All stamp orders & other orders from:

$20.00 to $49.99 - $3.50

Orders other than stamps:

$50.00 to $199.99 - $5.50

$200.00 & over - $8.00

Total this page		
Total from reverse		
Total of all items ordered		
Shipping/Insurance (see chart at left)		
SUBTOTAL		
Sales Tax (if any)		
Less any discounts, refund checks, coupons, etc.		
TOTAL ENCLOSED		

SATISFACTION GUARANTEED

MINIMUM ORDER MUST TOTAL AT LEAST $20.00

On orders outside the U.S., additional postage will be billed if necessary

Easy Order Form (continued)

From page no.	Qty Want-ed	Country and Items ordered: Specify Scott Numbers plus first day cover, souvenir card, plate block, mint sheet or other description	Quality Wanted	Un-used	used	Price Each	Leave Blank
		Total This Page					